CURRENT LAW YEAR BOOK 1979

AUSTRALIA
The Law Book Company Ltd.
Sydney : Melbourne : Brisbane

CANADA AND U.S.A.
The Carswell Company Ltd.
Agincourt, Ontario

INDIA
N. M. Tripathi Private Ltd.
Bombay

ISRAEL
Steimatzky's Agency Ltd.
Jerusalem : Tel Aviv : Haifa

MALAYSIA : SINGAPORE : BRUNEI
Malayan Law Journal (Pte.) Ltd.
Singapore

NEW ZEALAND
Sweet & Maxwell (N.Z.) Ltd.
Wellington

PAKISTAN
Pakistan Law House
Karachi

CURRENT LAW YEAR BOOK
1979

Being a Comprehensive Statement of
the Law of 1979

General Editor
PETER ALLSOP, M.A.
Barrister

Assistant General Editor
KATHRYN FITZHENRY, B.A., LL.B.
Solicitor

Administration
GAIL WIGHTMAN

Editors

English Cases :
G. R. BRETTEN, M.A., LL.B., *Barrister*
JONATHAN BROCK, M.A., *Barrister*
C. M. BUTLER, LL.B., *Barrister*
J. ELVIDGE, *Barrister*
I. F. GOLDSWORTHY, *Barrister*
J. GROVE HULL, M.A., LL.B., *Barrister*
JERVIS KAY, LL.B., *Barrister*
EDMUND LAWSON, M.A., *Barrister*
SIMON LEVENE, M.A., *Barrister*
ANTHONY PITTS, *Barrister*
JOHN PUGH-SMITH, B.A., *Barrister*
CLARE RENTON, *Barrister*
ROBERT WEBB, LL.B., *Barrister*

Scots, Irish and Dominion Cases :
DAVID E. B. GRANT, B.A., LL.B., *Barrister*

European Communities :
V. E. HARTLEY BOOTH, LL.B., *Barrister*

Delegated Legislation :
W. J. TATE, LL.B., *Barrister*

Northern Ireland :
S. F. R. MARTIN, LL.B., *Barrister*

Damages Awards :
DAVID KEMP, B.A., *Barrister*
DERRICK TURRIFF, *Barrister*

Articles :
P. C. T. STEWART, *Barrister*

LONDON
SWEET & MAXWELL LTD.   STEVENS & SONS LTD.

The Mode of Citation

of the CURRENT LAW YEAR BOOK

is *e.g.*:

[1979] C.L.Y. 1270

SBN O 421 26910 3

Published in 1980 by
Sweet & Maxwell Limited of
11 New Fetter Lane, London,
and printed in Great Britain
by The Eastern Press Limited
of London and Reading

PREFACE

THIS volume completes thirty-three years of Current Law publishing. It supersedes the monthly issues of *Current Law* for 1979 and covers the law from January 1 to December 31 of that year.

Citators

The Case Citator and the Statute Citator are contained in a separate volume, issued with this volume.

The *Current Law Citator* covers cases during the years 1977, 1978 and 1979 and statutes during the period 1972–79. There are permanent bound volumes covering cases during the period 1947–76 and statutes during 1947–71.

The present volume contains a table of cases digested and reported in 1979 and the usual tables covering 1979 Statutory Instruments and their effect on the orders of earlier years and a table of Northern Ireland Statutory Rules and Orders.

Articles

In continuation of the consolidated Index of Articles 1947–56 published in the *Current Law Year Book 1956* there is an alphabetical index of articles published during 1979 in the present volume. This index includes the full title and reference of an article and the name of its author.

Index

The Subject-matter Index in this volume has been compiled by Claire Booth, LL.B., Solicitor. Due to the ever-increasing size of the index it was decided to include in 1977 references from 1972 onwards only. This provides an overlap of five years in the index which covers in great detail the whole of the law decided, enacted, issued or published during the years 1972–79. In addition this index includes all statutes enacted since 1947. The full thirty-year Index from 1947–76 may be found in the 1976 *Year Book*.

Statutes and Orders

Sixty Acts received the Royal Assent during the year. A complete list of Statutes appears under the title STATUTES AND ORDERS.

The number of Statutory Instruments during 1979 was 1,770. Of these, 955 are general and 815 are local and, although numbered, only 1,238 of these were printed. The effect on the orders of 1947 to 1979 is shown in a table following the list for 1979.

Cases

The number of cases digested herein is 1,777. This figure does not include the short reports showing what damages have been awarded in cases of injury

5

or death. Sixty-three of these decisions have been collected and edited by Mr. David Kemp and Mr. Derrick Turriff, and an alphabetical table of these decisions will be found on page 39 together with a list of sub-headings under which they are digested.

The *Year Book* again includes a selection of cases of persuasive force from the Scottish courts and the courts of the British Dominions and from the English county courts. It also includes a section on the law of the European Communities.

Court of Appeal

As a service to the profession *Current Law* this year continues the publication of brief notes of decisions of the Court of Appeal (Civil Division) which have not hitherto been reported but whose transcripts are available in the Supreme Court Library at the Royal Courts of Justice. *Current Law* is indebted to Mr. Avtar S. Virdi, Barrister, who has prepared the notes of the details of the cases. Transcripts of these cases were previously available in the Bar Library.

Northern Ireland

All Northern Irish Acts and Orders and the cases reported from the courts of Northern Ireland have been digested together with a selection of the cases reported from the courts of Eire. This work has been carried out by our editor in Northern Ireland, Mr. S. F. R. Martin.

How to Use Current Law

Those who want to get the full benefit of the service offered are reminded that they should study " How to Use Current Law " which is always available from the publishers.

The General Editor thanks those who have pointed out errors and have sent in notes of interesting cases.

March 1980.   P. A.

CONTENTS

THE LAW OF 1979 DIGESTED UNDER TITLES:

CONTENTS

TABLE OF CASES

9

TABLE OF CASES

TABLE OF CASES

11

TABLE OF CASES

TABLE OF CASES

TABLE OF CASES

TABLE OF CASES

TABLE OF CASES

TABLE OF CASES

TABLE OF CASES

TABLE OF CASES

TABLE OF CASES

31

TABLE OF CASES

COURT OF APPEAL

(Civil Division)

SUPREME COURT LIBRARY TRANSCRIPTS

Decisions of the Court of Appeal (Civil Division) during the period April 1978–March 1979, of which transcripts have been lodged in the Supreme Court Library and which have not been reported elsewhere in this Yearbook. These transcripts were formerly lodged in the Bar Library.

DAMAGES FOR PERSONAL INJURIES OR DEATH

The cases listed below are digested under the following headings in descending order of the amount of damages awarded:

Injuries of Maximum Severity
Multiple Injuries
Brain and Skull
Face
Jaw and Teeth
Burns and Scars
Sight
Hearing
Neck
Spine
Respiratory Organs
Reproductive and Excretory Organs

Sacrum, Pelvis and Hip
Wrist
Hand
Fingers and Thumb
Leg
Knee
Ankle
Foot
Miscellaneous Injuries
Minor Injuries
Osteo-arthritis

DAMAGES FOR PERSONAL INJURIES OR DEATH

TABLE OF STATUTORY INSTRUMENTS 1979

TABLE OF STATUTORY INSTRUMENTS

1979	C.L.Y.	1979	C.L.Y.
199	2792	292	1263
200 (C. 6)	2656	293	2475
201 (C. 7)	2656	294 (N.I. 1)	1996
202	2657	296 (N.I. 3)	1978
203	2657	297 (N.I. 4)	1984
204	2630	299	507
207	647	300	1460
208	647	301	1460
209	281	302	1460
210	2062	303	1460
211	1771	304	111
213 (S. 21)	3406	305	2468
214 (S. 22)	3406	306	2499
215	122	310 (S. 29)	2843
218	1748	313	2667
219	824	314	623
220	824	315	1758
221	77	317	2222
222	75	318	1770
223	2509	319 (S. 30)	3092
224	2759	320 (S. 31)	2862
226 (S. 24)	3302	321	2273
227 (S. 25)	3202	322	1927
228	2789	323	67
229	2392	324 (S. 32)	3322
232 (S. 23)	2921	325 (S. 33)	3322
233	2295	326	1748
234	1393	327	1377
235 (S. 26)	3510	328	2615
236	2355	329 (C. 8)	2656
237	141	333	814
238	2578	334	906
239 (S. 27)	3216	335	2792
240	78	336	1377
241	616	337	2234
242	2761	338	824
243	2747	339	812
244	2761	341	2475
245	2761	342	860
246	2761	343	2792
248	2792	344	2792
249	1334	345	2509
251	2667	346	1467
253 (S. 28)	3134	347 (S. 34)	3064
255	241	348 (S. 36)	3057
256	1317	349 (S. 36)	3039
257	65	350	2155
258	2405	351	2155
259	2405	352	531
260	814	353	83
263	2155	356 (S. 37)	3188
264	2522	357	64
265	2522	358	2515
266	1558	359	2509
267	141	360	2155
268	1323	361	2285
269	2674	364	2393
270	2076	365	1763
276	626	366	74
277	2580	367 (C. 9)	2545
280	2155	368	824
281	2155	369 (C. 10)	2544
284	245	370	2578
285	1793	374	1769
289	1755	375	2504
290	2537	378 (S. 39)	3135
291	1895	379 (S. 38)	2828

TABLE OF STATUTORY INSTRUMENTS

1979		C.L.Y.	1979		C.L.Y.
380	(S. 40)	3097	471		2789
381		218	472		2789
382		1758	473		2789
383	(S. 41)	3084	474		2789
384		1325	478		802
385		1769	479		2792
386		2667	489		1515
387		2667	490		1515
388		1377	491		2463
393		71	492		623
394	(C. 11)	2545	495		181
395		2202	496	(S. 49)	3006
396	(N.I. 5)	1993	497		1297
397		1377	500		2792
398		1323	502		2792
399		751	503		1323
400		779	504		1317
401		2359	505		2792
402	(L. 5)	2176	508	(S. 50)	3238
406		2071	510		623
407		2061	511		1557
408		1515	512		2792
409	(S. 42)	3322	513		2792
410	(S. 43)	3322	514		141
411	(S. 44)	3078	516	(S. 51)	3300
412	(S. 45)	3018	520		1373
413	(C. 12)	1535	521		823
414		141	522		2176
415		1534	526		1377
416		1534	536		2792
417		2233	537		2792
419		1686	541	(S. 52)	3132
420		1686	542		814
421		1323	543		823
422	(C. 13)	1956	544		2667
423		90	545		2667
427		2078	546		2667
428		812	547		135
429		828	550	(S. 53)	3289
430		828	551		2405
431		1927	552		2405
432		2601	553		2405
433		69	554		628
434		824	555		637
437		90	556		1377
438		90	557		2792
439		2369	558		2667
445	(S. 46)	3509	561		2792
446	(S. 47)	3361	562		2792
451	(S. 48)	3006	563		2586
452		177	564		639
453		1296	565		643
454		1536	566		623
455	(C. 14)	1538	567		623
456		1296	568		2269
457		1541	569		9
458		1541	570	(L. 5)	1731
459		1312	571		2724
460		1291	572		115
461		2583	573		1537
462		2456	574		1537
463		2509	575		1537
466		2789	576		233
467		2789	577		361
468		2789	578		2670
469		2789	579		1557
470		2789	586		58

TABLE OF STATUTORY INSTRUMENTS

1979	C.L.Y.	1979	C.L.Y.
587	81	704 (S. 63)	3246
588	828	705 (S. 64)	3247
589	1927	706	2730
591	2515	710	1685
592	2063	711	1602
593	2792	712	2475
595 (S. 54)	3076	719	187
596	2792	720	187
597	2509	721	2482
599	2475	722	2730
600	1944	723 (S. 65)	3301
601	214	727	2534
604	1333	729	2794
606	1360	730	4
607	63	731 (C. 15)	1720
609	1377	737	641
610	1377	738	1837
611	135	739	1836
612 (S. 55)	2921	740	2273
613 (S. 56)	3302	741	1323
614 (S. 57)	2825	742	1323
615	294	743	1323
616	294	744	1323
623	2667	745	533
626	1377	746	1973
627	623	747	1465
628	2514	748	2665
631	2464	749	2398
632	2522	750 (C. 16)	96
633	2393	751	85
634	1377	752	1337
635	1377	754	113
636	1377	756 (C. 17)	2162
637	1377	757 (L. 6)	1719
638	73	758 (L. 7)	1719
639	73	759 (S. 66)	3132
640	1373	760 (S. 67)	3006
641	2407	761 (S. 68)	3231
642	2509	762	2070
643	2509	763	1349
647	2273	764	1377
648	2273	765	137
650	1377	766 (S. 69)	3008
654	2357	767 (S. 70)	3287
655	638	768 (S. 71)	3089
656 (S. 58)	3016	770	859
657	2761	771	2070
659	24	773	85
660	2670	774	74
661	2373	775 (S. 72)	3188
667	2373	776 (S. 73)	3198
668	2062	778	2667
669 (S. 59)	3135	779	288
670 (S. 60)	3300	780	163
671 (S. 61)	3188	781	2514
672 (S. 62)	3186	782	60
676	2515	783 (S. 74)	3280
677	1834	784 (S. 75)	3280
679	2792	785 (S. 76)	3276
680	2059	786 (C. 18)	2606
681	1834	789 (S. 77)	2824
684	2792	790	2475
693	1328	791	1341
694	2090	792	1341
695	809	793	2667
696	1559	794	2265
700	1333	795	2392

TABLE OF STATUTORY INSTRUMENTS

TABLE OF STATUTORY INSTRUMENTS

1979	C.L.Y.	1979	C.L.Y.
960 (S. 90)	3018	1066	1324
961	2495	1067	2509
962	1377	1071	1685
966 (L. 10)	759	1072	2262
967 (L. 11)	381	1073 (S. 96)	3094
968 (L. 12)	2133	1078	2792
969	1696	1079	2792
972 (C. 27)	377	1082	1377
973 (S. 91)	3509	1083	2407
975	2665	1084 (S. 97)	3245
976	2475	1085	2215
977	1542	1086	1672
978 (L. 13)	1784	1087	1324
986	1377	1088	2351
987	1377	1089	2351
991	2094	1091	2222
992	2522	1092	2351
993	2509	1094	62
994	2792	1095	69
995	2792	1099	2373
996	2534	1100 (S. 98)	3132
997	2547	1101 (S. 99)	3386
998	1305	1107	1685
1003	74	1108	1685
1004	74	1109	1685
1005	74	1110	1685
1007	90	1111	1685
1008	1765	1112	1685
1011	1773	1113	1685
1012	1773	1114	1758
1013	85	1116 (S. 100)	3132
1014	1394	1121	1377
1015	1685	1122	1675
1016	1685	1123	1690
1019	1563	1124	2393
1020	2792	1125	2375
1021	824	1126	1377
1022	2011	1127 (S. 101)	3373
1023	2409	1131	1685
1024	2667	1135 (S. 102)	3132
1026 (S. 92)	3342	1136	2407
1027	1685	1137	1324
1028	1685	1138	227
1029	1377	1142	622
1030 (C. 28)	2545	1145	2361
1031 (C. 29)	2544	1146	616
1033 (S. 93)	3059	1148	623
1034 (S. 94)	3065	1149 (L. 15)	381
1035	1377	1155 (S. 103)	2920
1038	2225	1156	1377
1040	1758	1160	1539
1041 (S. 95)	3136	1163	2514
1042	2657	1164	2155
1043 (C. 30)	2656	1165	294
1045 (L. 14)	380	1166	294
1046	1377	1167	2358
1047	2070	1168	2792
1049	2667	1175	1326
1050	1377	1176	1323
1051	1377	1181	1758
1054	86	1182	623
1058	2407	1183	2405
1059	1377	1184	135
1060	1377	1185 (S. 104)	3007
1061	1377	1186 (S. 105)	3012
1062	2291	1187 (C. 31)	2656
1065	2792	1188	1377
		1189	2657

TABLE OF STATUTORY INSTRUMENTS

1979		C.L.Y.	1979		C.L.Y.
1190		2522	1298		832
1193		812	1299		2509
1194		2273	1300		1377
1195	(S. 106)	3188	1301		223
1196		2789	1302		1377
1198		2351	1303		2233
1199		2514	1307	(S. 109)	3359
1203		1772	1308	(S. 110)	3136
1204		151	1309		2723
1205		1323	1310		177
1206		2075	1311		1291
1207		2667	1312		2057
1214	(C. 32)	1389	1314		775
1215		2369	1315		2207
1216		2091	1316		2218
1218		616	1317		775
1220	(L. 16)	1722	1318		141
1221	(L. 17)	1740	1319		1394
1222	(L. 18)	1784	1320		1685
1223		1378	1321		1685
1224		1350	1322		1685
1225		146	1323		1685
1226		1266	1324		1685
1227	(S. 107)	3006	1327		1685
1228	(C. 33)	2803	1328		1685
1229		1377	1329		2792
1230		246	1330		2792
1231		1444	1331		2273
1232		2076	1332		2273
1240		616	1333		2273
1243		1557	1334		2273
1245		1377	1335		2273
1246		1373	1336		2273
1247		1373	1337		2273
1248		1377	1338		2273
1249		80	1339		2273
1254		1332	1340		2485
1255		1377	1341		1685
1257		2798	1342		2796
1258		228	1346		1685
1259		2071	1347		1685
1260		1360	1348		1685
1263	(S. 108)	3287	1349		1685
1264		1685	1358		1753
1265		1685	1359		2796
1266		1685	1360		2061
1267		2469	1361		2792
1270		2222	1365		85
1271		2667	1366	(S. 111)	3079
1272		1377	1367	(S. 112)	3079
1273		2409	1368		1685
1274		135	1369		2792
1275		2059	1370		1377
1276		2060	1373		2231
1277		2067	1374		200
1278		2509	1375		2079
1280		2723	1376		77
1281		85	1377		1373
1284		1738	1378		1288
1285		1739	1379		2730
1286		2061	1380		1377
1287		2071	1381		1377
1288		85	1382	(L. 19)	2151
1289		1333	1383		2079
1290		1333	1385		2708
1294		2502	1386		1377
1295		1685	1388		2287

1979	C.L.Y.	1979	C.L.Y.
1390 (S. 113)	3322	1489	644
1391 (S. 114)	3188	1490	2587
1393	629	1492	2667
1394	2155	1494	1685
1395	2155	1495	1685
1403	880	1496	1685
1404	1553	1497	1377
1405 (S. 118)	3427	1498	2792
1406	2071	1499	2789
1407	1975	1503	1377
1408 (S. 115)	3355	1504	1308
1409 (S. 116)	3355	1505	1308
1410 (S. 117)	3068	1506	2076
1411	1685	1513 (S. 123)	3509
1412	2336	1514	2234
1416	2064	1515	1391
1417	141	1516	2228
1421	2222	1519	2475
1422	1323	1520 (S. 124)	3418
1426	1329	1521 (S. 125)	3322
1427	1944	1522 (S. 126)	3322
1428	2074	1523	1685
1429	2509	1524	1685
1430	1308	1525	1685
1431	2509	1527	2792
1432	2067	1528	2792
1433	1377	1531 (S. 127)	3509
1434	2207	1533	2287
1435	2218	1534	2063
1436	2797	1535	1749
1437	626	1537 (S. 128)	3086
1438 (S. 119)	3057	1539	1758
1441	2601	1540	2060
1442 (L. 20)	2424	1541	1089
1443 (S. 120)	3273	1542	2176
1445	200	1543	2088
1446	1263	1544 (C. 36)	256
1447	2407	1545	266
1448	2475	1546	266
1449	2475	1548	2667
1450	2482	1549	1497
1451	322	1550	224
1452	2482	1551	638
1453	2482	1552	806
1454	1460	1553	882
1455	1317	1554	2751
1456	123	1555	1346a
1457	2792	1556	1496a
1459	2798	1557	2060a
1461 (S. 121)	3489	1558	1496a
1469	1377	1559	70
1470	2091	1560	2792
1471 (S. 122)	3509	1561 (L. 22)	775
1472	1685	1562 (S. 129)	3215
1473	1685	1563 (S. 130)	3090
1474	1685	1564 (S. 131)	3188
1475 (C. 34)	2406	1565	1675
1476	1542	1567	1333
1479	1377	1568	1339
1480	1377	1569	2522
1481	1377	1570	1331
1482	1377	1571	200
1483	2515	1572 (N.I. 11)	1978
1484	2675	1573 (N.I. 12)	1994
1485 (C. 35)	2656	1574 (N.I. 13)	1953
1486	2657	1575 (N.I. 14)	1936
1488 (L. 21)	380	1576	1987

TABLE OF STATUTORY INSTRUMENTS

1979		C.L.Y.	1979		C.L.Y.
1577		2475	1685	(C. 42)	2374
1578	(C. 37)	2479	1686		809
1585		1758	1687		1462
1586		1390a	1688		230
1587		2902	1689		1924
1588		81	1690		742
1589		163	1691		1323
1590		168a	1692		1318
1592		281	1693	(S. 141)	3087
1593		2482	1694		2515
1595		2667	1695		1685
1596	(S. 132)	2824	1697		1373
1597	(S. 133)	3202	1698	(S. 142)	3285
1598	(S. 134)	3510	1699	(S. 143)	3132
1599		141	1701		87
1600		208	1702		90
1601		200	1703		85
1602		1333	1704		1134a
1603		207a	1705		23
1604		1761	1706		2475
1605		2798	1707		2475
1612		2798	1710	(N.I. 17)	1983
1613		2800	1711		1279
1614		2756a	1712		1291
1615		1685	1713	(N.I. 18)	1967
1616		1685	1714	(N.I. 19)	1908
1617		66a	1715		361
1618		254	1716	(L. 23)	2176
1619		382	1717		622
1630	(S. 135)	3339	1718		622
1631	(S. 136)	3057	1719		2795
1632	(S. 137)	2923	1720		2798
1633	(S. 138)	3064	1722		867
1635		4	1723		959
1638		1762a	1724		2058
1639		226a	1725		2176
1641	(S. 139)	3088	1726		2534
1642		906	1727		2088
1649		622	1732		2339
1653		200	1733		1373
1654		200	1734		1377
1655		200	1735		1373
1656		2466	1736		2515
1657		1927	1737		1711
1659		2456	1738		2655
1660		2273	1739		1377
1661		2273	1740		2667
1662		2273	1741		859
1663		1685	1742		294
1664		1360	1743		294
1665		1377	1744		2069
1666		1377	1745		1758
1667		2013	1746		2363
1668		84	1747		622
1669		88	1748		68
1670		1685	1750		2202
1671		626	1751		2202
1672		2	1752		2799
1673		2	1753		2801
1674		1360	1754		2791
1675		1360	1755	(S. 144)	3158
1676		1444	1756	(S. 145)	3013
1677		2282	1759		1758
1678		2282	1760		1758
1679		826	1761		2404
1682	(S. 140)	3010	1762		1377
1683		1974	1763		1377
1684		2504	1767		2785

TABLE OF S.R. & O. AND S.I. 1894–1979

AFFECTED BY

STATUTORY INSTRUMENTS OF 1979

1894
840 revoked No. 134 § 2215

1907
740 revoked No. 341 § 2475

1912
1750 revoked No. 379 (S. 38) § 2828

1915
1948 revoked No. 719 § 187

1920
1250 amended No. 1442 (L. 20) § 2424

1921
827 amended No. 1442 (L. 20) § 2424

1922
729 revoked No. 341 § 2375
806 revoked No. 1365 § 85

1926
848 revoked No. 1230 § 246

1927
642 amended No. 1455 § 1317
715 amended No. 1449 § 2475
1266 revoked No. 1085 § 2215

1928
628 amended No. 864 § 1070

1929
952 amended No. 427 § 2078

1930
41 amended No. 533 § 2405
106 amended No. 552 § 2405
1016 amended No. 1138 § 227

1931
679 amended No. 427 § 2078

1933
37 amended No. 865 § 1070
309 amended No. 319 (S. 30) § 3092
479 amended No. 319 (S. 30) § 3092
789 amended No. 249 § 1334

1934
190 amended No. 1085 § 2215
703 amended No. 319 (S. 30) § 3092
1346 amended No. 706 § 2730

1935
488 amended No. 347 (S. 34) § 3064
488 amended No. 1034 (S. 94) § 3065

1936
390 revoked No. 341 § 2475
626 amended No. 1045 (L. 14) § 380
626 amended No. 1488 (L. 21) § 380

1937
271 amended No. 1294 § 2502
783 revoked No. 72 § 1706

1938
110 revoked No. 72 § 1706
653 revoked No. 637 § 1377
668 revoked No. 72 § 1706
844 revoked No. 1085 § 2215
1441 revoked No. 134 § 2215

1939
445 revoked No. 1302 § 1377

1940
2009 amended No. 427 § 2078

1943
107 revoked No. 72 § 1706

1947
2034 amended No. 1660 § 2273
2037 revoked No. 1331 § 2273
2049 revoked No. 1331 § 2273
2051 revoked No. 1333 § 2273

1948
604 amended No. 1286 § 2061
1888 amended No. 1087 § 1324
2817 amended No. 799 (S. 78) § 2822

1949
330 amended No. 209 § 281
330 amended No. 1592 § 281
382 revoked No. 1545 § 266
1816 amended No. 1254 § 1332
1816 amended No. 1641 (S. 139) § 3088

1950
1386 amended No. 1085 § 2215
1725 amended No. 973 (S. 91) § 3509

1951
1196 revoked No. 1254 § 1332
1725 revoked No. 792 § 1341
1726 revoked No. 791 § 1341

1952
565 amended No. 1630 (S. 135) § 3339
944 amended No. 1286 § 2061
1906 amended No. 1409 (S. 116) § 3355
2113 amended No. 1590 § 168a
2229 amended No. 1146 § 616
2230 amended No. 1146 § 616
2231 amended No. 1146 § 616
2274 amended No. 1168 § 2792

S.R. & O. AND S.I. 1894–1979 AFFECTED IN 1979

1953
197 revoked No. 291 § 1895
592 amended No. 1707 § 2475
593 amended No. 1707 § 2475
640 revoked No. 564 § 639
1492 revoked No. 712 § 2475
1551 amended No. 1457 § 2792
1702 amended No. 711 § 1602

1954
1611 revoked No. 1146 § 616
1711 amended No. 952 (L. 8) § 1733

1955
926 amended No. 1457 § 2792

1956
1022 amended No. 1286 § 2061
1166 revoked No. 1254 § 1332
1355 revoked No. 1641 (S. 139) § 3088
1770 revoked No. 318 § 1770
1778 amended No. 318 § 1770
1914 revoked No. 1456 § 123

1957
191 amended No. 427 § 2078
496 amended No. 1457 § 2792
606 revoked No. 1545 § 266
1315 revoked No. 72 § 1706

1958
313 amended No. 427 § 2078
685 revoked No. 1050 § 1377
1208 amended No. 794 § 2265

1959
29 revoked No. 72 § 1706
277 amended No. 1567 § 1333
477 amended No. 1185 (S. 104) § 3007

1960
543 amended No. 543 § 823
1337 amended No. 800 (S. 79) § 2817
1395 amended No. 324 (S. 32) § 3322
1471 amended No. 280 § 2155

1961
243 amended No. 1563 (S. 130) § 3090
437 revoked No. 1035 § 1377
856 revoked No. 950 (S. 88) § 3132
946 revoked No. 1703 § 85
1931 revoked No. 1254 § 1332
1942 revoked No. 1641 (S. 139) § 3088
2251 revoked No. 1095 § 69
2395 revoked No. 1456 § 123

1962
800 amended No. 508 (S. 50) § 3238
1287 amended No. 1254 § 1332
1289 amended No. 1091 § 2222
1302 revoked No. 1545 § 266
1312 revoked No. 1456 § 123
1765 amended No. 365 § 1763
2045 amended No. 1550 § 224
2387 revoked No. 1456 § 123

1963
231 revoked No. 72 § 1706
685 revoked No. 1230 § 246

1963—*cont.*
935 revoked No. 1678 § 2282
1707 amended No. 1605 § 2798
1710 amended No. 1612 § 2798

1964
39 revoked No. 729 § 2794
696 revoked No. 116 § 775
1148 amended No. 1286 § 2061
1202 revoked No. 114 § 2582
1291 amended No. 1457 § 2792
1410 amended No. 95 (S. 8) § 2923
1410 amended No. 1632 (S. 137) § 2923

1965
321 amended No. 348 (S. 35) § 3057
321 amended No. 516 (S. 51) § 3300
321 amended No. 670 (S. 60) § 3300
321 amended No. 1033 (S. 93) § 3059
321 amended No. 1410 (S. 117) § 3068
321 amended No. 1438 (S. 119) § 3057
321 amended No. 1631 (S. 136) § 3057
1026 revoked No. 680 § 2059
1289 revoked No. 1678 § 2282
1500 amended No. 105 (L. 2) § 382
1500 amended No. 1619 § 382
1776 amended No. 35 (L. 1) § 2176
1776 amended No. 402 (L. 5) § 2176
1776 amended No. 522 § 2176
1776 amended No. 1542 § 2176
1776 amended No. 1716 (L. 23) § 2176
1776 amended No. 1725 § 2176
1815 amended No. 41 § 2798
1939 revoked No. 1661 § 2273
1952 amended No. 1571 § 200
1993 amended No. 565 § 643
1995 amended No. 1558 § 1496a
2011 amended No. 1707 § 2475
2039 revoked No. 1662 § 2273
2079 revoked No. 72 § 1706

1966
100 revoked No. 1662 § 2273
164 amended No. 996 § 2534
165 amended No. 1190 § 2522
237 revoked No. 1752 § 2799
238 amended No. 955 § 2801
813 revoked No. 883 § 1375
905 revoked No. 72 § 1706
1032 revoked No. 837 § 2665
1045 amended No. 1286 § 2061
1351 revoked No. 1333 § 2273

1967
172 amended No. 1519 § 2475
480 amended No. 931 § 137
556 revoked No. 1331 § 2273
971 revoked No. 1316 § 2218
972 revoked No. 1315 § 2207
1062 amended No. 1595 § 2667
1189 amended No. 1331 § 2273
1189 amended No. 1335 § 2273
1199 amended No. 1186 (S. 105) § 3012
1442 revoked No. 1546 § 266
1527 revoked No. 1456 § 123
1692 revoked No. 563 § 2586
1821 amended No. 192 § 127
1873 amended No. 1668 § 84

1968

25 amended No. 1543 § 2088
97 amended No. 1426 § 1329
98 amended No. 1427 § 1944
182 amended No. 452 § 177
182 amended No. 1310 § 177
207 amended No. 882 § 74
208 amended No. 1698 (S. 142) § 3285
655 amended No. 1457 § 2792
656 amended No. 569 § 9
736 revoked No. 72 § 1706
1053 amended No. 1267 § 2469
1074 revoked No. 991 § 2094
1077 amended No. 1751 § 2202
1094 revoked No. 1655 § 200
1181 amended No. 1537 (S. 128) § 3086
1230 amended No. 360 § 2155
1232 revoked No. 1333 § 2273
1233 revoked No. 1331 § 2273
1381 revoked No. 1393 § 629
1541 revoked No. 1605 § 2798
1558 amended No. 1551 § 638
1618 revoked No. 741 § 1323
1919 amended No. 1220 (L. 16) § 1722
1920 amended No. 1221 (L. 17) § 1740

1969

67 revoked No. 41 § 2798
483 amended No. 695 § 809
483 amended No. 1689 § 1924
487 amended No. 213 (S. 21) § 3406
860 revoked No. 1655 § 200
861 revoked No. 1655 § 200
882 amended No. 1740 § 2667
888 amended No. 401 § 2359
905 amended No. 322 § 1927
905 amended No. 1657 § 1927
1325 revoked No. 1678 § 2282
1370 revoked No. 114 § 2582
1500 revoked No. 916 § 199
1675 amended No. 49 § 1761

1970

57 revoked No. 1456 § 123
179 revoked No. 1605 § 2798
308 revoked No. 837 § 2665
400 amended No. 1570 § 1331
545 revoked No. 1007 § 90
548 amended No. 841 § 2581
548 amended No. 1490 § 2587
789 revoked No. 1331 § 2273
823 revoked No. 930 § 135
1021 amended No. 668 § 2062
1127 amended No. 383 (S. 41) § 3084
1127 amended No. 1693 (S. 141) § 3087
1146 amended No. 1750 § 2202
1284 revoked No. 383 (S. 41) § 3084
1490 revoked No. 1227 (S. 107) § 3006
1714 amended No. 1719 § 2795
1880 amended No. 1315 § 2207
1880 revoked No. 1434 § 2207
1881 amended No. 1316 § 2218
1881 revoked No. 1435 § 2218
1946 revoked No. 1316 § 2218
2038 revoked No. 1333 § 2273

1971

62 amended No. 263 § 2155
90 amended No. 1633 (S. 138) § 3064

1971—*cont.*

145 amended No. 1286 § 2061
156 amended No. 694 § 2090
156 amended No. 1216 § 2091
156 amended No. 1470 § 2091
157 revoked No. 991 § 2094
226 amended No. 160 § 1308
226 amended No. 1504 § 1308
227 amended No. 1505 § 1308
232 amended No. 1287 § 2071
232 amended No. 1406 § 2071
249 amended No. 320 (S. 31) § 2862
253 amended No. 748 § 2665
329 revoked No. 837 § 2665
618 amended No. 427 § 2078
659 revoked No. 1470 § 2091
694 amended No. 803 § 2348
720 revoked No. 305 § 2468
769 amended No. 1744 § 2069
969 revoked No. 72 § 1706
973 amended No. 1760 § 1758
1060 revoked No. 1553 § 882
1061 amended No. 427 § 2078
1062 amended No. 427 § 2078
1141 revoked No. 1470 § 2091
1450 amended No. 1585 § 1758
1469 amended No. 1407 § 1975
1537 amended No. 824 (S. 81) § 3010
1537 amended No. 1682 (S. 140) § 3010
1632 revoked No. 1331 § 2273
1685 revoked No. 1188 § 1377
1861 amended No. 1226 § 1266
1901 revoked No. 1470 § 2091
2044 revoked No. 1618 § 254
2052 amended No. 310 (S. 29) § 2843
2089 amended No. 1408 (S. 115) § 3355
2124 amended No. 94 (S. 7) § 3279
2161 revoked No. 72 § 1706

1972

74 revoked No. 1470 § 2091
87 revoked No. 594 (S. 54) § 3076
91 revoked No. 792 § 1341
178 amended No. 514 § 141
223 amended No. 5 § 141
339 revoked No. 1470 § 2091
421 amended No. 837 § 2665
454 revoked No. 929 § 135
455 revoked No. 930 § 135
457 revoked No. 253 (S. 28) § 3134
583 amended No. 259 § 2405
585 revoked No. 837 § 2665
640 amended No. 1585 § 1758
641 amended No. 1388 § 2287
641 amended No. 1533 § 2287
673 amended No. 577 § 361
673 revoked No. 1715 § 361
820 revoked No. 1038 § 2225
904 amended No. 838 § 2614
918 amended No. 1519 § 2475
919 amended No. 1519 § 2475
971 amended No. 1309 § 2723
990 amended No. 1276 § 2060
1148 amended No. 224 § 2759
1195 revoked No. 1470 § 2091
1200 amended No. 1585 § 1738
1203 amended No. 1319 § 1394
1234 revoked No. 837 § 2665
1277 revoked No. 668 § 2062

53

1972—*cont.*

1294 amended No. 1519 § 2475
1295 amended No. 1519 § 2475
1523 revoked No. 1577 § 2475
1584 revoked No. 1655 § 200
1585 revoked No. 1655 § 200
1610 amended No. 730 § 4
1636 revoked No. 1545 § 266
1653 amended No. 762 § 2070
1668 amended No. 1635 § 4
1697 amended No. 1519 § 2475
1724 amended No. 910 § 352
1805 revoked No. 97 § 2475
1843 revoked No. 1254 § 1332
1873 amended No. 1519 § 2475
1874 amended No. 1519 § 2475
1906 revoked No. 1641 (S. 139) § 3088
2025 revoked No. 1702 § 90
2076 amended No. 1760 § 1758

1973

33 revoked No. 1470 § 2091
72 revoked No. 1715 § 361
74 revoked No. 1553 § 882
120 revoked No. 883 § 1375
149 revoked No. 838 § 2614
288 amended No. 1541 § 1089
349 amended No. 281 § 2155
356 revoked No. 1470 § 2091
390 amended No. 325 (S. 33) § 3322
428 amended No. 406 § 2071
428 amended No. 1287 § 2071
430 amended No. 75 § 2071
431 amended No. 76 § 2071
433 amended No. 784 (S. 75) § 3280
434 amended No. 783 (S. 74) § 3280
497 amended No. 1527 § 2792
687 revoked No. 1188 § 1377
702 revoked No. 1393 § 629
728 revoked No. 1751 § 2202
740 amended No. 1573 (N.I. 12) § 1994
772 revoked No. 1715 § 361
797 amended No. 326 § 1748
806 amended No. 654 § 2356
963 revoked No. 1715 § 361
966 amended No. 407 § 2061
966 amended No. 855 § 1311
966 amended No. 1286 § 2061
994 revoked No. 133 § 2057
1040 revoked No. 1641 (S. 139) § 3088
1053 revoked No. 1254 § 1332
1087 revoked No. 114 § 2582
1089 revoked No. 1715 § 361
1101 revoked No. 1198 § 2351
1121 amended No. 214 (S. 22) § 3406
1199 amended No. 1089 § 2351
1268 amended No. 385 § 1769
1287 amended No. 468 § 2789
1288 amended No. 467 § 2789
1289 amended No. 474 § 2789
1306 amended No. 473 § 2789
1307 amended No. 471 § 2789
1310 amended No. 107 (S. 12) § 3085
1310 amended No. 1641 (S. 139) § 3088
1340 amended No. 1254 § 1332
1359 amended No. 466 § 2789
1360 amended No. 472 § 2789
1361 amended No. 470 § 2789
1368 revoked No. 1470 § 2091

1973—*cont.*

1396 revoked No. 72 § 1706
1437 amended No. 469 § 2789
1521 amended No. 1617 § 66a
1583 revoked No. 1470 § 2091
1654 amended No. 771 § 2070
1751 revoked No. 1715 § 361
1964 revoked No. 1702 § 90
2012 revoked No. 739 § 1836
2038 revoked No. 1393 § 629
2114 amended No. 1255 § 1377
2163 amended No. 1573 (N.I. 12) § 1994
2221 amended No. 427 § 2078

1974

44 amended No. 210 § 2062
82 amended No. 656 (S. 58) § 3016
179 revoked No. 429 § 828
180 revoked No. 430 § 828
181 revoked No. 431 § 1927
268 revoked No. 1434 § 2207
269 revoked No. 1435 § 2218
285 amended No. 681 § 1834
447 amended No. 1565 § 1675
458 revoked No. 6 § 2500
505 amended No. 705 (S. 64) § 3247
508 amended No. 704 (S. 63) § 3246
520 amended No. 2 § 2063
520 amended No. 592 § 2063
520 amended No. 1534 § 2063
522 amended No. 704 (S. 63) § 3246
522 amended No. 705 (S. 64) § 3246
529 amended No. 1285 § 1739
600 amended No. 1307 (S. 109) § 3359
648 amended No. 338 § 824
648 amended No. 1679 § 826
649 revoked No. 1470 § 2091
668 amended No. 170 (L. 4) § 1735
702 revoked No. 1456 § 123
706 amended No. 953 (L. 9) § 1777
745 revoked No. 883 § 1375
908 revoked No. 954 § 1144
942 revoked No. 218 § 1748
991 amended No. 1656 § 2466
1183 revoked No. 1702 § 90
1217 revoked No. 1470 § 2091
1276 revoked No. 1715 § 361
1365 revoked No. 1470 § 2091
1372 amended No. 837 § 2665
1486 amended No. 1738 § 2655
1497 revoked No. 429 § 828
1497 revoked No. 430 § 828
1497 revoked No. 431 § 1927
1595 revoked No. 186 (S. 18) § 3079
1757 amended No. 345 § 2509
1757 revoked No. 643 § 2509
1779 revoked No. 1198 § 2351
1817 revoked No. 792 § 1341
1910 amended No. 705 (S. 64) § 3247
1973 revoked No. 1470 § 2091
2005 amended No. 1724 § 2048
2010 amended No. 345 § 2509
2059 amended No. 345 § 2509
2059 revoked No. 642 § 814
2060 revoked No. 1732 § 2339
2079 amended No. 1067 § 2509
2136 amended No. 1072 § 2262
2143 amended No. 124 (C. 3) § 1956

54

1975

116 amended No. 1519 § 2475
159 revoked No. 912 § 1533
183 revoked No. 991 § 2094
205 amended No. 1555 § 1346a
211 revoked No. 1470 § 2091
225 amended No. 240 § 78
369 revoked No. 1333 § 2792
431 revoked No. 1715 § 361
468 revoked No. 676 § 2515
488 amended No. 1561 (L. 22) § 775
492 amended No. 9 § 2515
492 amended No. 358 § 2515
492 revoked No. 591 § 2515
536 amended No. 1385 § 2708
539 amended No. 1405 (S. 118) § 3427
554 amended No. 359 § 2509
554 revoked No. 597 § 2509
555 amended No. 223 § 2509
558 amended No. 1163 § 2514
559 amended No. 1278 § 2509
560 revoked No. 628 § 2514
563 amended No. 463 § 2509
563 amended No. 1278 § 2509
563 amended No. 1432 § 2067
564 amended No. 934 § 2509
564 amended No. 940 § 2509
564 amended No. 1299 § 2509
566 amended No. 642 § 2509
566 amended No. 643 § 2509
598 amended No. 375 § 2504
598 amended No. 1684 § 2504
609 revoked No. 648 § 2273
650 amended No. 235 (S. 26) § 3510
650 amended No. 1597 (S. 133) § 3202
652 amended No. 227 (S. 25) § 3202
652 amended No. 1597 (S. 133) § 3202
686 amended No. 1562 (S. 129) § 3215
714 amended No. 1388 § 2287
850 amended No. 338 § 824
915 revoked No. 1470 § 2091
967 amended No. 1457 § 2792
1024 amended No. 1013 § 85
1036 amended No. 1450 § 2482
1058 amended No. 359 § 2509
1058 amended No. 597 § 2509
1058 amended No. 628 § 2514
1058 amended No. 642 § 2509
1058 amended No. 1278 § 2509
1086 revoked No. 1456 § 123
1121 amended No. 1248 § 1377
1132 amended No. 655 § 638
1166 amended No. 628 § 2514
1166 amended No. 642 § 2509
1173 amended No. 80 § 2798
1173 amended No. 847 § 2798
1173 amended No. 1342 § 2796
1173 amended No. 1459 § 2798
1198 amended No. 1552 § 806
1205 revoked No. 1639 § 226a
1309 revoked No. 294 (N.I. 1) § 1996
1322 amended No. 1041 (S. 95) § 3136
1324 revoked No. 1470 § 2091
1326 amended No. 1760 § 1758
1329 amended No. 434 § 824
1343 amended No. 968 (L. 12) § 2133
1346 amended No. 966 (L. 10) § 759
1350 amended No. 780 § 163
1350 amended No. 1589 § 163

1975—cont.

1351 amended No. 779 § 288
1394 revoked No. 318 § 1770
1473 amended No. 1535 § 1749
1475 revoked No. 221 § 77
1486 amended No. 1254 § 1332
1487 revoked No. 752 § 1337
1503 amended No. 396 (N.I. 5) § 1993
1513 revoked No. 720 § 187
1526 revoked No. 186 (S. 18) 3079
1537 amended No. 264 § 2522
1537 amended No. 265 § 2522
1537 amended No. 632 § 2522
1537 amended No. 992, § 2522
1537 amended No. 1569 § 2522
1573 amended No. 172 § 2529
1573 amended No. 597 § 2509
1597 amended No. 1641 (S. 139) § 3088
1598 amended No. 383 (S. 41) § 3084
1598 revoked No. 1073 (S. 96) § 3094
1694 revoked No. 774 § 74
1709 revoked No. 304 § 111
1789 revoked No. 207 § 647
1790 revoked No. 1240 § 616
1803 amended No. 106 (L. 3) § 2136
1829 revoked No. 1694 § 2515
1837 revoked No. 1715 § 361
1844 revoked No. 1470 § 2091
1855 revoked No. 591 § 2515
1873 amended No. 1224 § 1350
1874 amended No. 1257 § 2798
1884 revoked No. 395 § 2202
1885 amended No. 1751 § 2202
1987 revoked No. 705 (S. 64) § 3247
2124 amended No. 796 § 2373
2193 revoked No. 1715 § 361
2210 revoked No. 1748 § 68
2223 amended No. 1669 § 88
2233 amended No. 1597 (S. 133) § 3202

1976

1 revoked No. 591 § 2515
59 amended No. 1574 (N.I. 13) § 1953
88 revoked No. 591 § 2515
189 revoked No. 1702 § 90
202 amended No. 749 § 2398
227 revoked No. 1715 § 361
304 amended No. 1692 § 1318
323 revoked No. 1198 § 2351
334 revoked No. 739 § 1836
341 revoked No. 1549 § 1497
354 revoked No. 1557 § 2060a
391 amended No. 1373 § 2231
409 amended No. 359 § 2509
409 amended No. 597 § 2509
409 amended No. 628 § 2514
409 amended No. 642 § 2509
428 amended No. 1711 § 1279
460 revoked No. 1732 § 2339
465 amended No. 169 § 531
466 amended No. 168 § 531
475 amended No. 766 (S. 69) § 3008
490 amended No. 1516 § 2228
507 revoked No. 591 § 2515
533 amended No. 643 § 2509
538 revoked No. 1470 § 2091
565 revoked No. 839 § 2614
582 amended No. 1573 (N.I. 12) § 1994
582 amended No. 1575 (N.I. 14) § 1956

1976—*cont.*

585 amended No. 270 § 2076
585 amended No. 1232 § 2076
612 revoked No. 1121 § 1377
615 amended No. 628 § 2514
684 revoked No. 655 § 638
738 amended No. 258 § 2405
738 amended No. 1761 § 2404
794 revoked No. 1752 § 2799
838 revoked No. 555 § 637
901 revoked No. 555 § 637
937 revoked No. 1092 § 2351
940 amended No. 1519 § 2475
1035 amended No. 607 § 63
1041 amended No. 1574 (N.I. 13) § 1953
1043 amended No. 396 (N.I. 5) § 1993
1068 amended No. 1004 § 74
1073 amended No. 767 (S. 70) § 3287
1073 amended No. 1263 (S. 108) § 3287
1076 amended No. 1412 § 2336
1081 amended No. 614 (S. 57) § 2825
1112 amended No. 194 § 800
1133 amended No. 1003 § 74
1135 amended No. 1223 § 1378
1156 amended No. 919 § 207
1203 revoked No. 1748 § 68
1204 revoked No. 797 § 2079
1204 revoked No. 1383 § 2079
1206 amended No. 1218 § 616
1207 amended No. 1146 § 616
1209 amended No. 693 § 1328
1221 amended No. 768 (S. 71) § 3089
1242 amended No. 1014 § 1394
1265 revoked No. 954 § 1144
1267 amended No. 998 § 1305
1274 revoked No. 1470 § 2091
1284 revoked No. 1005 § 74
1330 revoked No. 1605 § 2798
1595 revoked No. 1727 § 2088
1644 amended No. 978 (L. 13) § 1784
1701 revoked No. 1376 § 77
1736 amended No. 597 § 2509
1736 amended No. 628 2514
1736 amended No. 642 § 2509
1768 amended No. 1222 (L. 18) § 1784
1783 amended No. 1318 § 141
1784 revoked No. 1715 § 361
1807 revoked No. 1359 § 2796
1840 revoked No. 797 § 2079
1840 revoked No. 1383 § 2079
1866 amended No. 1 § 2211
1939 amended No. 337 § 2234
1977 amended No. 439 § 2369
1977 amended No. 1215 § 2369
1982 amended No. 1184 § 135
1983 amended No. 1417 § 141
1987 amended No. 47 § 817
1987 amended No. 1206 § 2075
2012 amended No. 1677 § 2282
2019 amended No. 1101 (S. 99) § 3386
2056 revoked No. 1203 § 1772
2062 amended No. 42 § 2339
2094 amended No. 398 § 1323
2111 revoked No. 1388 § 2287
2128 amended No. 384 § 1325
2145 amended No. 1603 § 207a
2153 revoked No. 1715 § 361
2156 amended No. 396 (N.I. 5) § 1993
2163 revoked No. 221 § 77
2226 revoked No. 1088 § 2351

1977

2 revoked No. 797 § 2079
2 revoked No. 1383 § 2079
25 amended No. 1568 § 1339
38 revoked No. 1203 § 1772
56 revoked No. 1715 § 361
85 amended No. 1593 § 2482
90 revoked No. 1456 § 123
91 revoked No. 1456 § 123
113 amended No. 1694 § 2515
113 revoked No. 1694 § 2515
114 revoked No. 591 § 2515
166 revoked No. 1545 § 266
176 amended No. 1638 § 1762a
314 amended No. 237 § 141
320 amended No. 1277 § 2067
326 amended No. 1099 § 2373
328 amended No. 661 § 2373
328 amended No. 667 § 2373
342 amended No. 597 § 2509
342 amended No. 628 § 2514
342 amended No. 642 § 2509
344 amended No. 400 § 779
345 revoked No. 399 § 751
402 amended No. 347 (S. 34) § 3064
420 revoked No. 125 § 1792
440 amended No. 744 § 1323
471 amended No. 705 (S. 64) § 3247
484 revoked No. 1203 § 1772
486 amended No. 1023 § 2409
508 amended No. 189 § 2419
530 revoked No. 1545 § 266
531 revoked No. 1545 § 266
543 revoked No. 591 § 2515
544 revoked No. 591 § 2515
545 amended No. 1388 § 2287
582 revoked No. 1470 § 2091
587 revoked No. 218 § 1748
610 amended No. 396 (N.I. 5) § 1993
610 amended No. 396 (N.I. 11) § 1993
633 revoked No. 380 (S. 40) § 3097
638 revoked No. 591 § 2515
682 revoked No. 838 § 2614
683 revoked No. 837 § 2665
705 revoked No. 838 § 2614
706 revoked No. 837 § 2665
716 amended No. 1182 § 2405
777 revoked No. 1746 § 2363
799 amended No. 801 § 2792
826 revoked No. 1450 § 2482
827 amended No. 289 § 1755
830 revoked No. 1715 § 361
879 revoked No. 1203 § 1772
880 revoked No. 1203 § 1772
920 revoked No. 1331 § 2273
927 amended No. 1254 § 1332
942 revoked No. 503 § 1323
967 revoked No. 1203 § 1772
968 revoked No. 1203 § 1772
976 revoked No. 804 (S. 80) § 3373
982 amended No. 462 § 2456
982 amended No. 1659 § 2456
985 amended No. 1404 § 1553
1005 revoked No. 1727 § 2088
1006 revoked No. 1470 § 2091
1026 amended No. 1641 (S. 139) § 3088
1074 amended No. 638 § 73
1075 amended No. 639 § 73
1083 revoked No. 503 § 1323

1084 revoked No. 504 § 1317
1097 amended No. 215 § 122
1103 revoked No. 738 § 1837
1134 revoked No. 104 § 623
1195 revoked No. 1203 § 1772
1250 amended No. 924 (N.I. 8) § 2001
1256 revoked No. 1715 § 361
1282 revoked No. 229 § 2392
1288 amended No. 628 § 2514
1289 revoked No. 781 § 2514
1292 revoked No. 504 § 1317
1301 amended No. 1659 § 2456
1319 amended No. 414 § 141
1330 revoked No. 1751 § 2202
1361 amended No. 628 § 2514
1361 amended No. 1684 § 2504
1367 revoked No. 1545 § 266
1368 amended No. 54 § 254
1369 revoked No. 1545 § 266
1400 amended No. 1088 § 2351
1437 amended No. 267 § 141
1437 amended No. 1274 § 135
1438 revoked No. 1092 § 2351
1443 amended No. 260 § 814
1443 amended No. 542 § 814
1444 amended No. 628 § 2514
1509 amended No. 628 § 2514
1509 amended No. 642 § 2509
1517 revoked No. 1135 (S. 102) § 3132
1568 revoked No. 504 § 1317
1622 amended No. 1520 (S. 124) § 3418
1632 revoked No. 1715 § 361
1637 revoked No. 504 § 1317
1638 revoked No. 503 § 1323
1638 revoked No. 504 § 1323
1662 revoked No. 1203 § 1772
1706 amended No. 676 § 2515
1707 amended No. 676 § 2515
1707 revoked No. 676 § 2515
1734 revoked No. 1333 § 2273
1734 revoked No. 1334 § 2273
1754 revoked No. 1342 § 2796
1755 revoked No. 591 § 2515
1759 amended No. 1614 § 2756a
1779 revoked No. 904 § 644
1795 amended No. 819 § 2792
1892 revoked No. 143 (S. 14) § 3375
1917 revoked No. 1092 § 2351
1953 revoked No. 591 § 2515
1953 revoked No. 591 § 2575
1954 revoked No. 792 § 1341
1960 revoked No. 1748 § 68
1987 revoked No. 591 § 2515
1988 revoked No. 1470 § 2091
1989 revoked No. 1727 § 2088
2021 revoked No. 648 § 2273
2025 amended No. 1301 § 223
2030 revoked No. 706 § 2730
2039 amended No. 1724 § 2058
2052 amended No. 1301 § 223
2054 amended No. 604 § 1333
2054 amended No. 700 § 1333
2054 amended No. 1290 § 1333
2055 amended No. 600 § 1944
2055 amended No. 1289 § 1333
2056 amended No. 1649 § 622
2072 amended No. 599 § 2475
2086 revoked No. 503 § 1323

2087 revoked No. 504 § 1317
2127 amended No. 36 § 1764
2127 amended No. 1040 § 1758
2129 amended No. 315 § 1758
2156 amended No. 1572 (N.I. 11) § 1978
2157 amended No. 297 (N.I. 4) § 1984
2167 revoked No. 45 § 1765
2171 amended No. 318 § 1770
2180 amended No. 1694 § 2515
2186 revoked No. 495 § 181

1978

26 revoked No. 1342 § 2796
30 amended No. 61 § 494
32 amended No. 37 § 85
32 amended No. 773 § 85
62 revoked No. 1376 § 77
70 revoked No. 591 § 2515
97 amended No. 34 § 1326
113 revoked No. 348 (S. 35) § 3057
196 revoked No. 211 § 1771
199 amended No. 56 § 2486
214 revoked No. 586 § 58
228 revoked No. 738 § 1837
267 revoked No. 86 § 1312
286 revoked No. 1434 § 2207
287 revoked No. 1435 § 2218
293 revoked No. 1092 § 2351
327 revoked No. 839 § 2614
345 amended No. 642 § 2509
345 amended No. 643 § 2509
360 revoked No. 91 (S. 4) § 3078
390 revoked No. 770 § 859
392 revoked No. 642 § 2509
409 amended No. 345 § 2509
411 revoked No. 318 § 1770
415 amended No. 385 § 1769
423 revoked No. 591 § 2515
428 revoked No. 366 § 74
433 amended No. 597 § 2509
433 amended No. 628 § 2514
462 amended No. 1659 § 2456
483 amended No. 1280 § 2723
507 revoked No. 591 § 2515
524 revoked No. 597 § 2509
545 revoked No. 384 § 1325
553 revoked No. 1223 § 1378
554 amended No. 1599 § 141
600 revoked No. 798 § 2464
641 amended No. 155 § 623
692 revoked No. 875 § 1528
693 amended No. 154 § 141
698 amended No. 155 § 623
708 revoked No. 751 § 85
756 revoked No. 1331 § 2273
764 amended No. 56 § 2486
772 revoked No. 504 § 1317
788 revoked No. 1388 § 2287
795 amended No. 491 § 2463
796 amended No. 164 § 626
796 amended No. 276 § 626
796 amended No. 1671 § 626
821 revoked No. 591 § 2515
835 revoked No. 34 § 1326
861 revoked No. 1094 § 62
922 revoked No. 399 § 751
893 amended No. 1146 § 616

1978—*cont.*

931 revoked No. 1023 § 2409
939 amended No. 1258 § 228
950 revoked No. 677 § 1834
960 revoked No. 586 § 58
998 amended No. 840 (S. 84) § 3008
1000 revoked No. 781 § 2514
1001 revoked No. 45 § 1765
1010 revoked No. 888 § 74
1011 revoked No. 1041 (S. 95) § 3136
1014 amended No. 660 § 2670
1017 amended No. 843 § 2291
1017 amended No. 1062 § 2291
1045 amended No. 924 (N.I. 8) § 2001
1045 amended No. 1573 (N.I. 12) § 1994
1059 revoked No. 1659 § 2456
1060 revoked No. 1715 § 361
1073 revoked No. 823 § 2512
1083 amended No. 60 § 2269
1083 amended No. 178 § 2269
1083 revoked No. 568 § 2269
1086 amended No. 1559 § 70
1092 revoked No. 1751 § 2202
1096 amended No. 333 § 814
1097 revoked No. 889 § 805
1098 revoked No. 900 § 805
1102 revoked No. 905 § 2015
1111 revoked No. 1088 § 2351
1121 amended No. 899 § 1751
1122 amended No. 954 § 1144
1127 amended No. 881 § 2495
1128 revoked No. 1278 § 2509
1137 revoked No. 939 § 1308
1141 revoked No. 837 § 2665
1159 amended No. 346 § 1467
1159 amended No. 1576 § 1987
1162 revoked No. 1019 § 1563
1169 revoked No. 1470 § 2091
1188 revoked No. 1281 § 85
1190 revoked No. 1084 (S. 97) § 3245
1191 amended No. 898 § 2495
1243 amended No. 967 (L. 11) § 381
1243 amended No. 1149 (L. 15) § 381
1260 amended No. 1145 (L. 15) § 381
1266 revoked No. 1226 § 1266
1295 amended No. 1724 § 2058
1307 amended No. 129 § 2392
1318 revoked No. 1092 § 2351
1329 revoked No. 1385 § 2708
1334 revoked No. 1388 § 2287
1389 amended No. 4 § 2080
1395 amended No. 490 § 1515
1399 revoked No. 1307 (S. 109) § 3359
1425 revoked No. 1155 (S. 103) § 2920
1468 revoked No. 790 § 2475
1480 amended No. 1288 § 85
1491 revoked No. 600 § 1944
1498 revoked No. 604 § 1333
1504 amended No. 417 § 2233
1504 amended No. 1303 § 2233
1511 revoked No. 597 § 2509
1525 amended No. 113 § 2057
1525 amended No. 1312 § 2057
1543 amended No. 976 § 2475
1592 revoked No. 586 § 58
1599 amended No. 321 § 2273
1599 amended No. 740 § 2273
1599 amended No. 1194 § 2273
1599 amended No. 1338 § 2273

1978—*cont.*

1651 revoked No. 504 § 1317
1652 revoked No. 503 § 1323
1669 revoked No. 591 § 2515
1683 revoked No. 1331 § 2273
1686 revoked No. 1632 (S. 137) § 2923
1698 amended No. 359 § 2509
1699 revoked No. 894 § 1391
1703 revoked No. 591 § 2515
1716 amended No. 364 § 2393
1717 revoked No. 1555 § 1346a
1741 revoked No. 616 § 294
1742 revoked No. 615 § 294
1747 amended No. 1756 (S. 145) § 3013
1752 revoked No. 1550 § 224
1764 amended No. 1416 § 2064
1778 amended No. 1723 § 959
1786 amended No. 1146 § 616
1790 revoked No. 384 § 1325
1795 revoked No. 1565 § 1675
1802 revoked No. 942 § 1774
1811 revoked No. 1092 § 2351
1817 amended No. 409 (S. 42) § 3322
1840 revoked No. 1694 § 2515
1842 amended No. 1349 § 1685
1855 revoked No. 1388 § 2287
1866 amended No. 1718 § 622
1870 revoked No. 1088 § 2351
1875 revoked No. 1596 (S. 132) § 2824
1877 revoked No. 591 § 2515
1933 amended No. 153 § 631
1933 amended No. 1142 § 622

1979

9 revoked No. 591 § 2515
12 revoked No. 48 § 2792
45 amended No. 1008 § 1765
60 revoked No. 178 § 2269
86 revoked No. 459 § 1312
91 revoked No. 411 (S. 44) § 3078
97 amended No. 1519 § 2475
156 amended No. 1390 (S. 113) § 3322
178 revoked No. 568 § 2269
181 amended No. 510 § 623
191 amended No. 492 § 623
193 revoked No. 797 § 2079
193 revoked No. 1383 § 2079
226 revoked No. 613 (S. 56) § 3302
231 amended No. 510 § 623
232 revoked No. 612 (S. 55) § 2921
269 revoked No. 837 § 2665
314 revoked No. 1148 § 623
358 revoked No. 591 § 2515
359 amended No. 597 § 2509
364 amended No. 633 § 2393
364 amended No. 1124 § 2393
367 revoked No. 394 (C. 11) § 2545
378 revoked No. 669 (S. 59) § 3135
409 amended No. 1521 (S. 125) § 3322
432 amended No. 1441 § 2601
462 revoked No. 1659 § 2456
551 revoked No. 1183 § 2405
571 amended No. 1167 § 2358
577 revoked No. 1715, § 361
586 amended No. 1175 § 1326
587 amended No. 1588 § 81
591 amended No. 1483 § 2515
600 amended No. 1289 § 1333
604 amended No. 700 § 1333

1979—*cont.*
604 amended No. 1290 § 1333
615 revoked No. 1165 § 294
616 revoked No. 1166 § 294
628 amended No. 781 § 2514
628 amended No. 1199 § 2514
631 revoked No. 798 § 2464
641 amended No. 1273 § 2409
647 revoked No. 1333 § 2273
648 revoked No. 1331 § 2273
680 revoked No. 1275 § 2059
694 revoked No. 1470 § 2091
738 amended No. 897 § 1837
789 revoked No. 1596 (S. 132) § 2824
796 amended No. 1437 § 626
797 revoked No. 1375 § 2079
837 amended No. 1642 § 906
937 amended No. 1556 § 1496a

1979—*cont.*
939 revoked No. 1430 § 1308
941 revoked No. 1748 § 68
949 amended No. 1428 § 2074
993 amended No. 1429 § 2509
1136 amended No. 1273 § 2409
1165 revoked No. 1742 § 294
1166 revoked No. 1743 § 294
1216 revoked No. 1470 § 2091
1331 revoked No. 1660 § 2293
1332 revoked No. 1660 § 2273
1333 revoked No. 1660 § 2273
1334 revoked No. 1660 § 2273
1335 revoked No. 1660 § 2273
1336 revoked No. 1660 § 2273
1337 revoked No. 1660 § 2273
1438 amended No. 1631 (S. 136) § 3057
1585 amended No. 1745 § 1758

NORTHERN IRELAND

TABLE OF STATUTORY RULES AND ORDERS 1978–79

1978	C.L.Y.	1979	C.L.Y.
328	1988	10	1929
348 (C. 17)	1983	11	1929
350	1983	12	1894
351	1926	13	1893
352	1983	14	1993
353	1904	15	1988
354	1969	18	1906
355	1988	19	1942
356	1978	20	1942
357	1926	21	1983
358	1977	22	1893
359	1977	23	1963
360	1894	24	1942
361	1931	25	1963
362 (C. 18)	1931	26	1984
363	1978	28 (C. 1)	1995
365 (C. 19)	1902	29	1934
366	1893	30	1964
367	1978	31	1907
368	1894	32	1992
369	1993	33	1904
370	1907	34	1983
371	1993	35	1934
372	1993	36	1941
373	1987	38	1988
374	1964	41	1893
375	1964	42	1893
376	1964	43	1942
377 (C. 20)	2001	44	1926
378	1907	45	1939
379	1935	47	1993
380	1907	48	1986
384 (C. 21)	1931	49	1944
385	1993	50	1891
386	1963	51	1944
387	1993	52	1952
393	1988	53	1952
394	1988	54 (C. 2)	1993
395	1963	55	1988
396 (C. 22)	1925	56	1963
397	1942	57	1966
398	1975	58	1978
399	1970	59	1978
400	1993	60 (C. 3)	1908
401	1993	61	1988
403	1934	62	1988
404	1942	64	1894
405	1942	65	1988
406 (C. 23)	1931	66	1995
407	1907	67	1975
		68	1993
1979	**C.L.Y.**	69	1988
1	1929	70	1988
3	1988	71	1988
4	1963	72	1947
5	1939	73	1899
6	1931	74	1948
7	1931	75	1988
8	1963	76	1995
9	1929	77	1993

1979	C.L.Y.	1979	C.L.Y.
78	1993	158	1978
79	1897	159	1964
80	1942	160	1978
82	1906	161	1978
83	1988	162	1988
84	1988	163	1988
85	1949	164	1988
86	1978	166	1893
87	1978	167	1940
88	1975	168	1988
89	1925	169	1988
90	1978	171	1931
91	1941	172	1933
92	1993	173	1949
93	1934	174	1975
94	1934	175	1978
95	1934	176	1978
96	1893	177	1978
97	1993	178	1942
98	1993	179	1927
99 (C. 4)	1925	180	1988
100	1893	182	1933
101	1893	183	1933
102	1993	184	1894
103	1978	185	1938
104	1978	186	1993
105	1978	187	1938
106	1907	188	1978
107	1907	189	1978
108	1907	191 (C. 8)	1903
109	1907	193	1993
110	1907	194 (C. 9)	1908
111	1907	195	1908
112	1907	196	1988
113	1907	197	2000
114	1907	199	1988
115	1907	202	1988
116	1907	203	1933
117	1907	204	1933
118	1907	205	1978
119 (C. 5)	1978	206	1978
120	1951	207	1934
121	1997	208	1993
122	1991	209	1977
125	1934	210	1903
126	1894	211	1993
127	1893	212	2000
128	1893	213	1987
129	1893	214	1963
130	1893	215	1970
131	1993	216	1970
132	1964	217	1893
133	1964	218	1893
134	1964	219	1926
135 (C. 6)	1993	220	1891
136 (C. 7)	1993	221	1891
137	1988	226	1903
138	1893	227	1903
143	1933	228	1903
144	1933	229	1903
145	1945	231	1903
146	1988	232	1903
147	1988	233	1988
149 (C. 8)	1908	235	1942
150	1945	236	1988
154	1907	238	1938
155	1908	239	1932
156	1984	240	1934

1979		C.L.Y.	1979		C.L.Y.
241		1969	324		1931
242		1993	325	(C. 14)	1903
243		1993	326		1894
244		1993	327	(C. 15)	1897
245		1926	330		1988
246		1938	331		1977
247		1934	332		1992
248		1978	333		1996
249		1926	334		1976
250		1949	335		1959
251		1948	338		1975
256		1993	339		1975
258		1966	341		1988
259		1993	342		1988
260		1894	343		1988
261		1894	344		1988
262		1978	345		1988
264		1957	346		2003
265		1939	347		1934
266		1988	348		1988
267		1894	349		1988
268		1988	350		1988
270	(C. 10)	1993	351		1988
271		1993	352		1988
272		1993	353		1988
273		1993	354		1993
274		1993	355		1903
275		1993	356		1988
276		1941	357		1893
277		1941	358		1984
281		1894	359		1934
283		1926	360		1934
284		1932	361		1939
285		1893	362		1988
286		1993	364	(C. 16)	1902
287		1904	365		1988
288		1983	371		1993
289		1894	372		1978
290		1937	373		1978
291		1926	374		1894
292	(C. 11)	1990	376		1893
293		1944	377		1993
294		1976	378		1931
297		1926	379		1951
298		1893	380		1975
299		1958	381		1988
301	(C. 12)	1993	382		1931
302	(C. 13)	1993	384		2000
303		1993	385		1988
304		1934	386		1988
305		1931	387		1975
306		1931	388		1988
307		1931	389		1988
308		1942	390		1988
310		1940	391		1993
311		1934	392		1993
312		1934	393		1939
313		1993	394		1993
314		1993	395		1894
315		1926	396		1988
316		1988	397		1975
317		1988	399		1975
318		1988	400		1988
319		1988	401		1998
320		1988	402		1942
321		1988	404		1988
322		1988	406		1977
323		1990	411		1977

UNREPORTED CASES

COURT OF APPEAL (CIVIL DIVISION)

1. Administrative Law—habeas corpus—illegal immigrant

Applicant fraudulently entered U.K. in 1975 using a "rogue U.K. passport" obtained by fraud—in June 1977 he was arrested and had been in prison now for 17 months waiting deportation—deportation delayed because High Commissioner for India claimed that he was English and ought to stay in England —application for *habeas corpus* refused—appeal dismissed—delay long and unfortunate but applicant had "brought it all on himself." December 21, 1978. *Re* GILL.

2. —— immigration—appeal against deportation order

Applicant, a citizen of Mauritius, arrived in U.K. in June 1971 as a visitor on condition that she did not remain longer than June 15, 1971—in July 1975 the Secretary of State for Home Affairs decided to make deportation order in respect of applicant who was apparently still in the U.K.—notification of order sent to applicant at only known address but alleged by applicant not to have been received by her until June or July 1976, she having moved to another address—in June 1976 applicant applied for permanent stay— the Divisional Court *held*, *inter alia*, that delay in making application after notification by Secretary of State in July 1975 was such that no relief should be granted to applicant—applicant's appeal dismissed—right to consider first question of delay and then (if necessary) substance of application: Appeal from Divisional Court. January 31, 1979. *Re* APPLICATION BY TARACHRANE.

3. —— —— illegal entrant

Applicant came to England in June 1976 on a Nigerian passport which falsely gave his place and date of birth as England, January 3, 1957—applicant admitted without leave as a patrial—applicant later detained as illegal immigrant awaiting removal to Nigeria—Divisional Court dismissed appeal on basis that applicant had not discharged onus of proof that he was born in England in accordance with the Immigration Act 1971, s. 3 (8)—whether applicant an illegal entrant within s. 33 (1) of the 1971 Act—appeal dismissed—observation that it was unnecessary to decide honesty of appellant for the purposes of the 1971 Act. July 4, 1978. R. *v.* SECRETARY OF STATE FOR THE HOME DEPARTMENT, *ex p.* UKUEKU.

4. —— —— —— evidence

On August 7, 1978, applicant, a young Sikh woman, entered U.K. pursuant to Immigration Rules H.C. 80, No. 23, saying that she was coming to U.K. intending to marry a man called JS—marriage apparently arranged for September 4 but on August 29 applicant was arrested on ground that she was an illegal entrant in that she obtained leave to enter by deception because her true object in arriving in U.K. was to associate with a man called CS with whom she had gone through a form of marriage in India—CS was already lawfully married and his estranged wife and three children lived in England—whether reasonable grounds for Secretary of State to believe that leave to enter obtained by deception—evidence—applicant's appeal dismissed. November 16, 1978. KAUR *v.* HOME OFFICE.

5. On August 4, 1973, applicant presented a passport saying that he was a Mr. Frank Miah and was given indefinite leave to enter U.K. as a young son (16 or 17) of parents already settled in U.K.—applicant went into business in Horsham and business was doing well—in 1978 police obtained information that applicant was not Frank Miah but in truth a Mr. Gous Miah and after investigation arrested applicant as an illegal entrant—applicant's appeal dismissed—" very considerable evidence " necessary and in fact present to show that applicant was an illegal entrant. Appeal from Wien J. November 17, 1978. MIAH v. SECRETARY OF STATE FOR THE HOME OFFICE.

6. Inquiries in the applicant's case were " triggered off " by information received from certain informers that applicant was not person he claimed to be—Secretary of State concluded after investigation that applicant was an illegal entrant—whether Secretary of State acted wrongly in taking into account evidence from informers and whether that evidence ought wholly to have been excluded from his adjudication as inadmissible in law—whether Secretary of State ought to file evidence that in his opinion informer was a reliable witness—applicant's appeal dismissed. December 21, 1978. EJAZ v. SECRETARY OF STATE FOR HOME AFFAIRS.

7. —— —— —— " indefinite leave to enter "

Applicant came to England illegally in 1970—in September 1976 he went to Pakistan, married, and returned to England in December 1976—the immigration officer, after some questions, stamped the applicant's passport with " indefinite leave to enter "—in January 1978 applicant was discovered to be an illegal entrant and ordered to be deported—no authority on part of immigration officer to give " indefinite leave to enter " when man not lawfully settled here—application for habeas corpus dismissed—appeal dismissed—leave to appeal to the House of Lords refused. July 12, 1978. R. v. SECRETARY OF STATE FOR THE HOME DEPARTMENT, ex p. NASIR ALI.

8. —— —— limited leave to enter

Applicant, a non-patrial Commonwealth citizen from Australia, entered U.K. in February 1976 and was given leave to enter as a visitor for six months only with no conditions restricting employment—applicant had no work permit—in April 1976 she took employment with Law Society as private secretary to Society's catering manager—Law Society applied to Department of Employment (Overseas Labour Section) for permission to employ applicant as an overseas worker—Department of Employment refused application and Secretary of State at Home Office accordingly refused to extend applicant's stay in U.K. —whether, inter alia, Secretary of State at Home Office failed to exercise his discretion in law—Latiff v. Secretary of State [1972] C.L.Y. 22—Immigration Act 1971, ss. 14, 19—Immigration Rules H.C. 80, 5—application for certiorari dismissed. December 14, 1978. PEARSON v. THE IMMIGRATION APPEAL TRIBUNAL.

9. —— —— —— appeal

In August 1974 applicant was granted leave to enter U.K. as a visitor for a month—stay extended—in October 1975 applicant applied for leave to stay as a student—application refused by letter which also stated, wrongly, that applicant was entitled to appeal against decision within 14 days under s. 14 (1) of Immigration Act 1971—whether estoppel giving rise to jurisdiction in appeal tribunal to hear appeal—applicant's appeal dismissed. November 17, 1978. MITTU v. SECRETARY OF STATE FOR THE HOME OFFICE.

10. —— —— **non-patrial—deportation**

Appellant, a young woman born in Tanzania on October 23, 1956, was admitted into England in September 1969 as a student—in July 1970 she returned to Tanzania for her school holidays and in September 1970 returned to England—in February 1971 she returned to Tanzania for mid-term holidays but was unable to come back because funds could no longer be remitted to England for her education—in August 1971 she returned as a visitor and then was given leave to remain as a student until October 1973—from October 1973 to January 1978 she remained without permission—in January 1978 the Home Secretary served a deportation order under s. 3 (5) (*a*) of the Immigration Act 1971 (c. 77) and she was taken into custody under para. 2 (3) of Sched. 3 to the 1971 Act—whether applicant exempt from deportation as being " ordinarily resident " in the U.K. under s. 7 (1) (*b*) of the 1971 Act—application for leave to issue a writ of habeas corpus dismissed by the Divisional Court—applicant's appeal dismissed. Appeal from Divisional Court of Q.B.D. April 12, 1978. *Re* K.

11. —— —— **unlawful entry**

The applicant obtained by deception from the British High Commission in Ghana permission to enter England and thereby entered England in July 1972—in 1977 she returned to Ghana and came back in February 1978, whereupon the immigration officer refused her entry because he was not satisfied that she was " settled in the U.K. when [she] left "—statement of Immigration Rules 1973, paras. 1, 51—application refused. July 13, 1978. *Re* AN APPLICATION BY MONICA OPONG.

12. —— **nationality—marriage to U.K. citizen**

Applicant, who was born in Germany in May 1947, came to England and claimed to be entitled to British nationality on the ground that she married a British national here on January 22, 1975—British Nationality Act 1948, s. 6 (2) —marriage showed name of woman as S. G. Sauerbier and applicant claimed that she was that woman and she had used a false name—whether applicant the woman who married on date shown—evidence—only one out of three of applicant's witnesses coming forward to swear affidavit—Secretary of State not satisfied that applicant was person who married on January 22, 1975, and refused certificate of British nationality—applicant's appeal dismissed—proper machinery when validity of a marriage is debated was under the Matrimonial Causes Act 1973, s. 45. December 18, 1978. PUTTICK (ORSE. PROLL) *v.* SECRETARY OF STATE FOR THE HOME DEPARTMENT.

13. —— **natural justice**

Plaintiff, airport director of Leeds-Bradford Airport for some 20 years, was suspended from work awaiting the hearing of disciplinary proceedings against him—defendants were local authorities of area and controlled workings of airport—elaborate code of procedure involving three tribunals to govern investigation—first tribunal, special sub-committee of airport committee, held inquiry and decided to send matter to disciplinary sub-committee for hearing— plaintiff applied for injunction alleging breach of natural justice in that, *inter alia*, he had been refused representation by counsel at hearing—judge refused injunction—plaintiff's appeal dismissed—observation on *Stevenson* v. *United Road Transport Union* [1977] C.L.Y. 3072; *Pett* v. *Greyhound Racing Association* [1968] C.L.Y. 22 inapplicable in circumstances where employer was deciding whether or not there were grounds upon which he could properly dismiss employee. Appeal from Blackett-Ord V.-C. October 3, 1978. SELLER *v.* WEST YORKSHIRE METROPOLITAN COUNTY COUNCIL.

14. Agency—authority ostensible authority

Defendant gave instructions to a Mr. L to buy certain property for her, using her maiden name, and that certificate of title when obtained should be handed over to her—L purchased the property for defendant but later, still having land certificate with him, he fraudulently created a charge (in January 1976) on property to secure a loan of £7,000 from the plaintiff moneylenders—only two instalments paid under charge and therefore plaintiffs started proceedings for possession against defendant—judgment for possession obtained in default of appearance—defendant (in Nigeria) applied through solicitors to set aside judgment swearing that she had no knowledge whatever of proceedings—judgment set aside—whether, *inter alia*, L had ostensible authority (or whether defendant estopped from denying that L had authority) to bind defendant by charge created by L's dealing with land certificate—*Rimmer* v. *Webster* [1902] 2 Ch. 153—plaintiffs' appeal dismissed. October 13, 1978. LEWIN FINANCE CO. v. JAGEDE.

15. —— evidence

Under R.S.C. (1979), Ord. 113, judge granted plaintiff landlords possession of a flat as against defendant—defendant's application to stay order for possession so that she may have opportunity of putting forward evidence to show that tenancy was granted to her by agent (ground floor tenant) of owners—evidence not supporting defendant's case—application dismissed. Appeal from Browne-Wilkinson J. July 24, 1978. LYONS v. HADDADEEN.

16. ——undisclosed principal—evidence

Plaintiffs entered into a contract whereby "the Fajara Hotel" agreed to provide them with certain rooms in an hotel—contract was signed "on behalf of Hotel Fajara Ltd." and not on behalf of defendants (alleged to be managing agents of the Fajara Hotel)—whether contract entered into on behalf of defendants—evidence—judge granted plaintiffs injunction restraining defendants from "re-allocating rooms allocated to plaintiffs pursuant to the agreement"—defendants' appeal allowed—plain on face of contractual document that contract was between plaintiffs and Hotel Fajara Ltd. and not between plaintiffs and defendants. Appeal from Park J. December 21, 1978. KUONI TRAVEL v. HOTEL MANAGEMENT INTERNATIONAL.

17. Agriculture—agricultural holding—lease—agreement

First defendant (ex-husband of second defendant) owned three farms and in 1966 took from plaintiff a lease of an adjoining farm, subject of dispute—from 1966 to 1974 defendants farmed three freehold farms and rented one as one farming enterprise—in 1974 matrimonial troubles arose between defendants, husband departed temporarily abroad and his interest in rented farm was terminated by notice to quit in March 1976—negotiations between parties for a new lease but plaintiff in end was not willing to grant new lease as future dealings were uncertain because of defendants' pending matrimonial litigation and plaintiff sued for possession—correspondence between parties from April 1976 onwards—whether firm agreement with regard to granting of a fresh lease—*Von Hatzfeldt-Wildenburg* v. *Alexander* [1912] 1 Ch. 284—whether wife had acquired licence from landlord to be in occupation of rented farm—judge dismissed plaintiff's claim for possession and declared, on second defendant's counterclaim that she was plaintiff's tenant from year to year on terms agreed in correspondence—plaintiff's appeal allowed—order for possession in 28 days. November 30, 1978. BROWN v. REEP.

18. Arbitration—effect on proceedings—tripartite submissions

Plaintiff had a contract with defendants to construct part of the M5 motorway and subcontracted part of that work to other contractors, R— disputes arose between plaintiffs and R on the one hand and between plaintiffs and defendants on the other—parties agreed to enter into a tripartite submission to single arbitrator—R and plaintiffs came to terms and tripartite arbitration became in effect one between two parties only—whether plaintiffs bound by matters pleaded by them in defence to R's claim and/or precluded from leading evidence or making submissions in the arbitration against defendants which sought to establish that those matters of defence were wrong— consultative case under s. 21 (1) (a) of the Arbitration Act 1950—judge held against defendants—defendants' appeal dismissed—*Stott* v. *West Yorkshire Road Car Co.* [1971] C.L.Y. 9541 followed. Appeal from Willis J. November 6, 1978. A. MONK & CO. v. DEVON COUNTY COUNCIL.

19. —— special case—appeal

Dispute between claimants in the arbitration, the sellers under three contracts of sale, and the respondents, buyers under the contracts—judgment on an award in the form of a special case stated by the Board of Appeal of the Grain and Free Trade Association given by Kerr J. in July 1977—point sought to be raised before Kerr J. which admittedly had not been taken before Board of Appeal—judge allowed point to be argued before him but took view that he should not decide point without giving Board of Appeal opportunity of expressing their view on it and accordingly was prepared to remit award to Board on certain conditions and allowed stay of six weeks by reference to possibility of appeal—conditions not satisfied and in view of lapse of time court not to allow point to be argued before it—buyers not given option again of going back to Board—buyers' appeal dismissed—observation on an abuse of the special case procedure. Appeal from Kerr J. December 19, 1978. WILLIAM H. PIM JNR. & CO. v. PHOEBUS D. KYPRIANOU CO.

20. Banking—account

Up to June 1969 the plaintiff had an account with a branch of the defendant bank—on May 1 he instructed the bank to transfer £250 to another bank where he opened an account on Monday, May 5—on Saturday, May 3, he drew £200 cash from the previous branch—credit transfer in his new account showed only £50 but bank unable to explain until a very late stage why only £50 had been transferred and not £250—plaintiff's claim in 1976 for £200 plus interest dismissed—plaintiff's (in person) appeal dismissed. June 6, 1978. ARORA v. BARCLAYS BANK.

21. —— duty of care

In 1976 plaintiff and his wife opened a joint account with defendant bank for the purpose of investment of £20,000—after a number of cheques were drawn and signed only by plaintiff, bank found from mandate that only plaintiff and wife jointly or survivor of them if one died could operate account and wrote to plaintiff that until clarification (or new mandate) bank would undertake transactions on the instructions of both plaintiff and his wife only—no clarification forthcoming but much correspondence—judge dismissed plaintiff's action for damages for breach of duty and breach of contract after three days' hearing—plaintiff's (in person) appeal dismissed—bank acted with " perfect propriety " throughout—" futile litigation; whole dispute a storm in a teacup." Appeal from May J. December 20, 1978. PARIKH v. MIDLAND BANK.

22. Bankruptcy—garnishee proceedings—ranking with other creditors

Plaintiffs, suppliers of beer, obtained judgment for £1,913 against first defendant, whose property had been taken over by mortgagees and sold leaving, after expenses, £7,159 in the hands of first defendant's solicitors, second defendants—plaintiffs granted a garnishee order absolute against second defendants—whether in circumstances plaintiffs ought to rank *pari passu* with other creditors—matter for discretion of court—garnishee's appeal allowed, not a case where garnishee order ought to be made absolute—plaintiffs to rank *pari passu* with other creditors in equity and fairness. May 17, 1978. WHITBREAD FLOWERS v. THURSTON.

23. Bills of Exchange—cheque—dishonoured cheque—R.S.C., Ord. 14, proceedings

Plaintiffs brought an action upon a dishonoured cheque, both defendants having notice of dishonour—particulars alleged that first defendant acted either on his own behalf or alternatively on behalf of second defendants, Ringwell Shoes Ltd. (a one-man company of which first defendant was director) in drawing the cheque, plaintiffs presented it for payment and it was dishonoured—form of cheque a printed form in which first defendant's signature appeared under words " Ringwell Shoes "—first defendant alleged that he was induced to give cheque by a false assurance but did not allege knowledge on part of plaintiffs—whether valid answer to plaintiffs' claim—master gave summary judgment to plaintiffs against first defendant but gave leave to second defendants to defend—judge upheld order on appeal—defendants' appeal dismissed—observations on ss. 108 (4), 33 of the Companies Act 1948. Appeal from Caulfield J. July 28, 1978. CALZATURIFICIO FIORELLA S.P.A. v. WALTON.

24. Boundaries and Fences—boundary dispute—boundary line between two gardens

Dispute concerned, *inter alia*, a strip of land 4 ft. 4 in. wide at its widest, lying between defendant's garden and land belonging to the plaintiffs—judge inspected site before he started case and then inspected it again after he had heard all the evidence and read the documents—similar number of witnesses on each side—judge held that strip of land was part of the plaintiffs' land—defendant's appeal dismissed. June 13, 1978. SCUDDER v. WADE.

25. Clubs and Associations—sex discrimination—recreation facilities—football

Plaintiff, a girl now aged 12 years, played football at school with boys and applied to be registered as a member of the Muskham United football team which eventually was a member of the Football Association—application refused because defendants said that under their rules mixed teams and matches between men's and women's teams were not permissible—whether discrimination on grounds of sex—Sex Discrimination Act 1975, ss. 29 (1), 44—judge granted declaration in favour of plaintiff and awarded her damages—defendants' appeal allowed—" football " not within Sex Discrimination Act 1975. July 28, 1978. BENNETT v. THE FOOTBALL ASSOCIATION.

26. Company Law—articles of association—board resolution

Plaintiff company brought an action making claims against defendants in consequence of alleged arrangement between defendants to set up a competing business in same line as business of plaintiff company—first defendant was shareholder and a director of plaintiff company—board resolution passed at meeting when four directors were present (including first defendant), against first defendant's opposition, authorising institution of proceedings against defendants—whether resolution ineffective because as alleged only two directors were competent to vote—articles of association—master took view that point should be determined as a preliminary point but judge (on appeal) took view that it should be litigated instead—Companies Act, 1948, Table A—defendants' appeal bound to fail—defendants' application for leave to appeal refused. Appeal from Graham J. January 11, 1979. FIONA ROSE v. HEALY.

27. —— director—loan to director

Defendant, employed by plaintiff company since 1939 and managing director at relevant time, wished to buy certain property—a scheme was entered into whereby (in 1966) plaintiff bought house and thereafter contracted to sell it to defendant—plaintiff paid deposit and defendant went into possession on basis that he would pay whole purchase price (£14,000) to plaintiff by instalments over period of time—in 1973 plaintiff, having been taken over in 1971, issued writ, *inter alia*, to have agreement for sale of house by it to defendant set aside —whether, *inter alia*, true nature of the scheme was that plaintiff lent £14,000 to defendant so that transaction was in breach of s. 90 of Companies Act 1948 —defendant's appeal allowed—plaintiff's cross-appeal dismissed. July 13, 1978. J. CROWTHER & SONS (MILNSBRIDGE) v. CROWTHER.

28. —— winding up—creditor's petition

On a petition presented by the company's accountants, the judge ordered, *inter alia*, that a provisional liquidator be appointed—the appellant applied for leave to appeal out of time against the orders contending (i) that he paid the debt in question of the hearing, and (ii) that the judge was wrong to find that the company was insolvent—merits of appeal considered—payment after presentation of petition void under s. 227 of the Companies Act 1948 (c. 38)— appellant failed to discharge onus that company was not insolvent—applications for leave to appeal out of time dismissed. April 19, 1978. *Re* DIAPEC TOOLS.

29. —— —— cross-claim against petitioner creditor

Petitioner company was an importer into U.K. of electrical goods and C Ltd. carried on business of exporting electrical goods from U.K. to Republic of Ireland—in 1977 parties agreed that C Ltd. would have an exclusive franchise for a three-year period for the export of petitioner's goods to Republic of Ireland—C Ltd. fell into " considerable indebtedness " to petitioner and after various negotiations petitioner wrote letter (on June 29, 1978) that no stock would be supplied unless and until certain conditions were met—in August 1978 petitioner presented petition alleging debt of £128,383 under contract —genuine dispute about £85,409 of that sum—judge concluded that C Ltd. had a cross-claim against petitioner in a sufficient sum to cover sum in petition and dismissed petition on that basis—whether C Ltd. had a genuine and arguable cross-claim—whether petitioner's letter of June 29 repudiated franchise agreement—petitioner's appeal allowed. Appeal from Brightman J. December 18, 1978. *Re* CAPAX.

30. Compulsory Purchase—compensation—freeholder without good title

In June 1971 appellant council entered into possession of about an acre of land in respect of which claimant leaseholders had obtained outline planning permission in 1965 for five detached bungalows—possible freeholder uncertain of good title to freehold—compensation payable for compulsory acquisition by council—lands tribunal awarded £10,900 after various deductions from a starting figure of £14,250, net value of freehold in possession— whether lands tribunal failed to find whether or not reputed freeholder would have been in market as a purchaser—whether any evidence to support that finding—whether reasons given by lands tribunal inadequate—Council's appeal by way of case stated dismissed. July 3, 1978. HONISETT v. ROTHER DISTRICT COUNCIL.

31. Contract—agreement—evidence

Plaintiff, plumber, bought a piece of land in 1973 to build himself a house on "do-it-yourself" basis and entered into an arrangement with a Mr. Moulds, now managing director of defendant company, who had known plaintiff's parents when plaintiff was a little boy—building of house went seriously wrong structurally—plaintiff brought action alleging an oral agreement whereby defendants would build him the "shell" of the house, including roof, and supply all materials therefor, for sum of £2,000—defence denied such agreement—judge concluded that on the evidence there was no contract in the legal sense but only an informal arrangement and that defendants had not been shown to have caused the structural damage—plaintiff's appeal dismissed. June 20, 1978. JARMAN v. SAWTRY BUILDING SUPPLIES.

32. —— —— negotiation stage

Judge ordered that plaintiff recover forthwith possession of certain land against defendant—defendant's case that plaintiff company had orally agreed to sell him land (on which he wanted to park his car) but pleadings showed that matter never went beyond the stage of negotiation—no binding contract—defendant's (in person) appeal dismissed. March 1, 1979. GREYWILL (CONSTRUCTION) v. JERVIS.

33. —— breach—evidence

Plaintiff, having seen a brochure, entered into a contract with defendant for the letting of defendant's house in France for a two-week holiday with family from April 5–19, 1975, at a total rent of £90—house found to be cold, damp and unusable and not in accordance with details in brochure or what plaintiff had been led to expect—plaintiff and his family stayed in hotels and cut holiday short by one week—after six-day hearing, with many witnesses being called on behalf of defence, judge accepted plaintiff and his wife as completely reliable witnesses and decided case in plaintiff's favour and awarded £250 special damages and £250 general damages—defendant's appeal dismissed. June 15, 1978. DOWNING v. ROSS.

34. —— —— negligence—exemption clause

On March 19, 1969, a television mast (property of plaintiffs), over 1,250 feet high and constructed between 1964 and 1966 to a "comparatively novel design" oscillated dangerously and suddenly collapsed—first defendants were main contractors for design construction and erection of mast and second defendants were sub-contractors employed by first defendants at insistence of plaintiffs—no privity of contract between plaintiffs and second defendants; privity of contract between plaintiffs and first defendants and between first defendants and second defendants—plaintiffs alleged breach of contract and negligence against first defendants and in second action negligence, breach of warranty and negligent misstatement against second defendants—first defendants, in consequence, in event of being liable to plaintiffs, sought to recover against second defendants—second defendants denied all liability and further claimed that even if first defendants were liable to plaintiffs, second defendants were protected by exemption clause in sub-contract between it and first defendants—judge *held*, (1) first defendants were liable to plaintiffs for breach of contract; (2) first defendants were entitled to recover over from second defendants in respect of that breach on view that

exemption clause in sub-contract afforded no protection to second defendants;
(3) second defendants were directly liable to plaintiffs for negligence, breach
of warranty and negligent misstatement—evidence—primary cause of accident
—negligence issue—*Hughes* v. *Lord Advocate* [1963] C.L.Y. 970—construction of contracts—what (if any) respective contractual obligations of parties—
Young & Marten v. *McManus Childs* [1968] C.L.Y. 324—*Samuel* v. *Davis*
[1943] K.B. 526—exemption clause—whether second defendants gave a direct
contractual promise or warranty to plaintiffs in relation to alleged freedom
of certain masts (including mast in question) from danger from oscillation
—whether gratuitous promise unsupported by consideration—whether negligent misstatement—second defendants' appeal dismissed. Appeal from
O'Connor J. November 10, 1978. INDEPENDENT BROADCASTING AUTHORITY v.
E.M.I. ELECTRONICS.

35. —— implied term

Plaintiff main contractors employed defendant sub-contractors on basis of
the printed ICE sub-contract form and the letter accompanying the quotation
for the sub-contract—clause in contract provided "The above quotations
(*i.e.* fixed amount quotation of some £434,000) will remain Fixed Price until
June 3, 1975; any work carried out after this date to be negotiated "—work
not completed by June 3, 1975—question, *inter alia*, of rates to be paid after
June 3, 1975—sub-contract subject to implied terms that the rates for the work
to be carried out after June 3, 1975, would be reasonable rates—plaintiffs'
appeal by way of case stated dismissed. June 26, 1978. PETER LIND & CO.
v. CONSTABLE HART & CO.

35a. Plaintiff sub-contractors claimed moneys for work done from the defendant
main contractors—main contract in RIBA form—payment provisions in main
contract for sub-contractors—express term of sub-contract requiring monthly
valuations to take place in conjunction with main contract valuations and to be
certified at same time and paid within 14 days—necessary implication from
express terms that main contractors to take all appropriate steps to secure
monthly valuations and issuing of certificate—main contractors unable to rely
on absence of valuation by architect to refuse to pay reasonable sum for work
done by sub-contractors—defendants' appeal dismissed. Appeal from Stocker J.
June 28, 1978. DUKES BLANCHARD v. CERAF.

36. —— inducement of breach—injunction

Plaintiffs acquired by agreement the exclusive right to exploit by publication
the life story of Joyce McKinney and Keith May, who had broken their bail
pending trial for certain offences and had gone to the United States—the
defendant newspaper published articles about the couple pursuant to an
agreement covering recent events since their departure and the reasons for their
departure from England—plaintiffs applied to restrain the defendants from
doing so, the injunction being framed widely—judge granted injunction—
whether agreement with plaintiffs tainted with illegality—whether defendants
committing any tort—difficulty of framing injunction exactly—defendants'
appeal allowed. Appeal from Browne-Wilkinson J. May 19, 1978. GUCCIONE v.
EXPRESS PAPERS.

37. —— misrepresentation—evidence

Plaintiff brought an action alleging, on advice, simple misrepresentation
alleging that he bought a business and leasehold premises in Chislehurst on
strength and in reliance of three misrepresentations made by first defendant
on behalf of all three defendants in three documents—judge concluded that
plaintiff had not proved on balance of probability that there were misrepre-

sentations as alleged—plaintiff's (in person) appeal dismissed—observations on allowing application to amend pleadings to allege fraud. Appeal from Talbot J. November 22, 1978. MEYER v. MACGREGOR.

38. —— —— rescission

Plaintiff landlords granted to defendant tenants a 125-year lease of plot of land on November 15, 1973, with view to development by erecting an office building—by terms of lease tenants undertook to obtain appropriate planning permission and to erect office building—applications for planning permisssion unsuccessful—in 1977 tenants discovered that there was no planning permission for adjoining plot of land contrary to alleged representations made to them at time their lease was being negotiated and they brought an action claiming, *inter alia*, rescission of lease—landlords denied having made representations and in alternative claimed that tenants had affirmed lease (and agreement relating thereto) by payment of two instalments of rent in June/September 1977—in February 1978 landlords issued writ claiming £6,250 arrears of rent due on December 25, 1977, plus interest, and tenants put in defence repeating allegations set out in their statement of claim—whether tenants affirmed lease —whether tenants debarred from rescinding by reason of delay—whether lease could be set aside—judge gave landlords summary judgment for arrears of rent—tenants' appeal allowed—observations on *Leaf* v. *International Galleries* (1950) C.L.C. 9247; *Angel* v. *Jay* [1911] 1 K.B. 666. Appeal from Megarry V.-C. October 5, 1978. HEARTLAND PROPERTY INVESTMENTS v. RENOWN INVESTMENTS.

39. —— terms—express warranty

In March 1971 plaintiffs bought a house on an estate of the defendants, who were house builders and developers, and found central heating system leaking because steel pipes in it had corroded—plaintiffs spent £282 in replacing steel pipes with copper ones and brought action against defendants—defendants served third party notice contending that third party, plumber and heating engineer employed by them and who had provided the steel pipes for central heating system on terms that pipes would comply with N.H.B.R.C.'s requirements, was liable—whether defendants entitled to look to third party for compliance with N.H.B.R.C.'s requirements—whether express warranty that third party would supply piping suitable for purpose required—judge held that defendants should succeed against third party for the sum of £282 plus costs—third party's appeal dismissed. October 31, 1978. PERROTT v. HILLS STRUCTURES AND FOUNDATIONS AND B. MOUNTFORD (THIRD PARTY).

40. —— —— implied term

Plaintiffs, an engineering company desirous of taking advantage of investment grants in development areas, entered into complicated financial and other arrangements with defendants whereby, *inter alia*, defendants' goods (bought by plaintiffs for £500,000 as agents for defendants) were leased out to plaintiffs for certain terms of years—Department of the Environment "sticky" with investment grants—basing agreements "ran on and time came" when plaintiffs, under terms of agreement, claimed that they were entitled to return of certain bills of exchange given by them to defendants—judge gave summary judgment to plaintiffs for a sum of between £200,000 to £300,000—whether implied agreement or duty on plaintiffs to use their best endeavours and do all that was reasonable and practical to get investment grants in—whether triable issue— defendants' appeal allowed—unconditional leave to defend. Appeal from Donaldson J. July 7, 1978. GLACIER METAL CO. v. INDUSTRIAL LEASING & FINANCE.

UNREPORTED CASES

41. County Court Practice—action—striking out for want of prosecution

Plaintiff's action for damages for personal injuries arising out of an accident was struck out for want of prosecution—whether judge wrong in holding that inordinate and inexcusable delay was attributable to or caused by default on plaintiff's part—whether resultant prejudice not shown—*Birkett* v. *James* [1977] C.L.Y. 2410—whether registrar's decision dismissing plaintiff's application that defendant ought not to be allowed to strike out plaintiff's action because defendant himself was in breach of court order receivable or wrong—whether registrar accepted jurisdiction to hear defendant's application to strike out without notice being given to the plaintiff—plaintiff's appeal dismissed. April 27, 1978. McFauld v. A. C. Flynn (trading as Wallspan).

42. —— consent order—costs—discretion

Plaintiff brought an action against defendants for wrongful dismissal and defendants claimed that they were entitled to dismiss plaintiff for breaches of his written employment agreement and they counterclaimed for an account, damages and an injunction—parties compromised and consent order made which stated, *inter alia*, that costs of action " be taxed on Scale IV and paid by defendants to plaintiff "—County Court Rules (1936), Ord. 47, r. 21 (5)—whether discretion of registrar under above rule excluded by consent order—construction of consent order—judge held that discretion of registrar had been excluded—plaintiff's appeal allowed—only possible meaning was relevant provisions of County Court Rules relating to taxation under Scale IV must apply. December 20, 1978. Allsuch v. Kaye.

43. —— costs—discretion

Plaintiff's car collided with defendant's dog who had strayed onto the highway—plaintiff brought an action in negligence claiming damages not exceeding £200 including special damage of repairs to car of £77·02 and alleged that he had suffered " shock, general shaking up "—defendant, a member of the National Farmers Union, denied negligence—judge found defendant liable and awarded plaintiff damages of £77·02 plus costs to be taxed on Scale 1 on basis that defendant's insurers' conduct was unreasonable—defendant's appeal on costs only allowed—no material on which judge could come to conclusion that defendant's insurers' conduct was unreasonable—County Court Rules 1936, Ord. 47, r. 5 (4) (iii), June 29, 1978. Taylor (trading as H. Taylor & Son) v. Ashworth.

44.

Plaintiffs, suing on behalf of committee members of a certain hospital committee, formed for purpose of building a hospital in Punjab, brought proceedings in county court against defendants, office holders of the hospital committee, on basis that there was a reasonable belief that trust fund might be unimplied—Attorney-General became interested in matter and started proceedings in High Court in respect of same trust raising some wider issues—in circumstances plaintiffs withdrew their claim in county court—defendants ready with defence—judge ordered plaintiffs' action to be discontinued and that defendants should pay one-half of plaintiff's costs—defendants' appeal allowed—defendants not at fault to justify order for costs—order for no costs on either side—observation on combined effect of C.C.R. (1936), Ord. 18, and *Lambton* v. *Parkinson* (1886) 35 W.R. 545. January 15, 1979. Khan v. Amin.

45. —— —— taxation

Defendant (in person) applied for taxation of the successful plaintiff's bill of costs to be transferred from the Newbury County Court, where taxation would in the ordinary way have taken place, to the Winchester County Court on the basis that he would not have a proper taxation in the Newbury County Court— application dismissed—defendant's appeal, misconceived and impudent, dismissed—no basis for allegations made by defendant. May 20, 1978. SUTTON v. TINGEY.

46. —— declaration—jurisdiction—boundary dispute

Plaintiff was owner of house at No. 182 Barrier Bank and defendants were owners of adjacent house No. 180—plaintiff brought action in county court that boundary line between the two properties went in such a way that the whole of an outdoor toilet (which plaintiff wished to demolish) was on his property and that none of it was on property of defendants—judge inspected properties in question and after full hearing held that plaintiff had not made out his case and made a declaration that "water closet is situated half on Mr. Jones' property and half on Mr. Tyrell's property and boundary runs through centre of it and there are mutual rights of user"—defendants had called no evidence and had not asked for any declaration—whether, *inter alia*, judge had jurisdiction to make declaration—plaintiff's (in person) appeal dismissed— judge had jurisdiction in circumstances of case, plaintiff himself in effect having asked court to make a declaration or other similar order as to where boundary line lay. November 13, 1978. JONES v. TYRELL.

47. —— discovery—" fair and convenient disposal of proceedings "

Plaintiffs claimed possession and other relief in respect of property mortgaged to them by defendants stating that a substantial sum including interest was owed to them by defendants—defence was that the sum claimed was excessive, that plaintiffs had charged an excessive interest rate because of " political manipulations of economy "—first defendants required discovery of items including certain accounts related to " political manipulations " alleged —judge ordered, *inter alia*, limited discovery on basis of conclusions that might be reached at trial as to whether rate of interest was to be a reasonable rate or a normal rate in ordinary banking practice or a normal rate in accordance with plaintiffs' and defendants' normal banking practice—first defendants' appeal dismissed. February 5, 1979. NATIONAL WESTMINSTER BANK v. DOWNEY.

48. —— jurisdiction—application to enlarge claim after payment into court of original claim

Plaintiff claimed £200 as moneys due to him by reason of his employment with defendant, an estate agent, including sums due by way of commission earned—defence alleged that all commission due had been paid—in December 1975 judge gave defendant " in principle for plaintiff for commission due " and ordered that an account be taken—matter came before registrar on April 14, 1976, by which date defendant had accepted judgment and had paid £200 into court—registrar gave judgment for plaintiff for £200—whether plaintiff entitled to increase amount of his claim to £1,000—County Court Rules (1936), Ord. 11, r. 8; Ord. 15, r. 7—plaintiff's appeal dismissed—plaintiff's action was now complete and *res judicata*. December 12, 1978. SOMERVILLE v. LEDGER (TRADING AS MORRIS & LEDGER).

49. —— new trial—defendant not given opportunity to meet new matter arising at trial

Plaintiff freeholder of a house brought proceedings to recover possession of house from defendant for non-payment of rent, particulars of claim alleging that there had been a tenancy, protected under the Rent Act, from the plaintiff as landlord to the defendant as tenant—defendant admitted the tenancy but alleged in the defence that all due rents were paid up to a fortnight after the date of the particulars of claim—at the trial plaintiff while giving evidence contradicted his pleadings and denied that there was a tenancy—judge took view that, *inter alia*, defendant was no more than a mere licensee of the plaintiff and held the plaintiff entitled to possession on the ground that there was no tenancy—defendant's appeal allowed—defendant given no opportunity of meeting case raised by evidence—new trial ordered. May 2, 1978. LOOKER *v.* SMITH-FERRY.

50. —— particulars of claim—amendment

Plaintiff, aged 69 at time of accident in May 1974, brought an action for damages for personal injuries suffered when she tripped over a broken piece of paving stone in road—particulars served in 1976 and limited to upper limit of county court jurisdiction, *i.e.* £1,000—jurisdiction increased to £2,000 in April 1977—at outset of hearing in August 1977 plaintiff applied to amend her particulars of claim by increasing damages claimed to £2,000—judge refused amendment on basis that it would seriously "embarass" defendants and proceeded to decide issues in favour of plaintiff—medical reports—plaintiff's appeal on amendment point allowed—County Court Rules 1936, Ord. 15, rr. 3, 4. June 27, 1978. PLATT *v.* REDBRIDGE BOROUGH COUNCIL.

51. —— procedural irregularities—objection at trial

Plaintiff started summary proceedings in High Court under R.S.C., Ord. 113, for possession of flat occupied by defendant—originating application made without any name being put in for defendant on ground that defendant was in occupation without licence or consent—proceedings adjourned to county court by consent—affidavits under R.S.C., Ord. 113, and order of county court said not to be served in time and no particulars of claim filed—defendant's case that plaintiff had orally agreed that she should have a tenancy—at end of all evidence, defence counsel made final submissions and submitted that procedural irregularities had prejudiced defendant in her case—judge ordered defendant to give possession to plaintiff—whether any prejudice to defendant as a result of irregularities—whether irregularities waived—defendant's appeal dismissed—if there were irregularities which went to jurisdiction of court or propriety of proceedings they should be taken at beginning; if not taken at beginning and case is conducted on its merits as this case was, then irregularities are waived. July 26, 1978: SASH *v.* SPRING.

52. Criminal Law—contempt of court—committal

Golton pleaded guilty to charge of aiding and abetting three other men by lending them a gun and was sentenced to three years' imprisonment—one of the other men pleaded guilty to attempted murder but remaining two pleaded not guilty—pleas pre-arranged by four men—at the trial of the two who pleaded not guilty Golton was brought to give evidence for prosecution but refused to take oath and was ordered to be punished for contempt of court by three months' imprisonment—Golton's appeal under s. 13 of the Administration of Justice Act 1960 that by giving evidence he would have broken one of the codes prevailing amongst "the criminal classes" and, *inter alia*, would have been "sentencing (himself) to solitary confinement" dismissed. July 14, 1978. *Re* GOLTON.

53. Damages—detinue—substituted fur coat

In 1973 plaintiff handed over a black seal fur coat and paid £45 to defendant, a furrier, for certain work to be done on it but was handed back a substituted fur coat (sealskin and coney and some fur from her old coat) less valuable than her old coat—judge gave judgment for plaintiff and awarded her £70 damages, *i.e.* £100 1973 value of old coat less £30 value of substituted coat—whether plaintiff's claim was for breach of contract or detinue—plaintiff's appeal allowed —plaintiff awarded £100 damages for detinue, £50 damages for detention of article, and £45 damages for breach of contract in that there was a total failure of consideration on defendant's part. November 2, 1978. RIDGEWELL *v.* CLAYTON.

54. —— fatal accident—assessment

Plaintiff, whose husband was killed at age 39 from an accident in August 1974, and who had two children aged 13 and seven years, remarried in November 1975—deceased earned about £50 a week just before the accident—judge arrived at a dependency of £30 a week for the wife, from which he deducted an agreed amount of £8 for the children, and awarded a total sum of £15,000 using a multiplier of 13—plaintiff's appeal, that, *inter alia*, taking dependency of £30 a week was too low, dismissed—sum meant for children should properly be awarded to children separately from award to their mother; order of judge varied accordingly. Appeal from Faulks J. April 24, 1978. DEVLIN *v.* MATTHEW HALL MECHANICAL SERVICES.

55. —— —— broad application

Three dependent daughters, M, S and L, were aged 19, 16, and 14 years at time of the motor accident in August 1973 in which parents were killed— parents earned £2,900 per annum at time of accident and would have earned £5,100 at date of trial—eldest girl married with one child but lived at home for time being to save enough money to be able to buy a house with husband— judge took multiplier and dependency per week to girls as follows: M two and a half years at £13, S four years at £7·50, and L two years total dependency at £12·50 and another four years of partial dependency at £7·50, and awarded a total sum of £7,810 including £7,718 under the Fatal Accidents Act—defendants' appeal that multiplier and dependency too high, dismissed—broad approach required—no valid criticism of total figure awarded. Appeal from Lawson J. June 30, 1978. GEE *v.* BROWNSWORD AND F.M.C. MEAT.

56. —— —— quantum

Plaintiff, widow of Mr. Nightingale, who was killed in a road accident, was awarded a total of £9,610 damages against defendant under Fatal Accidents Acts—deceased aged 63 at time of accident—award of damages arrived at by dividing period after deceased's death into three—for last period judge took a dependancy of £1,400 taking into account a pension of the deceased and a multiplier of 5½—whether wrong—defendant's appeal on liability and quantum dismissed—impossible to say that total figure of £9,610 wrong. Appeal from Milmo J. November 16, 1978. NIGHTINGALE *v.* MURFITT.

57. —— landlord and tenant—breach of covenant of quiet enjoyment and nuisance

The plaintiffs were the protected tenants of flats later purchased by the defendant who moved into the "middle flat" with his common law wife and her children and began a campaign ("of a familiar kind") to get the plaintiffs out of the premises—the plaintiffs sued for damages and injunctions for breaches of covenant of quiet enjoyment and, in the alternative, nuisance—no defence served—judge made usual order for assessment of damages against the defendant whereby registrar assessed following damages: first plaintiff: £1,000 aggravated damages plus £500 exemplary damages; second plaintiff: £750 aggravated damages plus £1,500 exemplary damages—£1,500 fines already paid by defen-

dant—whether exemplary damages payable having regard to award for aggravated damages—defendant's appeal allowed—aggravated damages increased to
£1,250 and £1,000 respectively—no award for exemplary damages in this particular case. Appeal from Jupp J. April 28, 1978. DEVONSHIRE v. JENKINS.

58. —— personal injuries—quantum

Plaintiff suffered serious injury to his left leg from an accident at work when
he was aged 52½—defendants admitted liability—plaintiff already suffered from
extensive osteo-arthritic changes in left leg and was over-weight—injuries were
a comminuted fracture of the upper end of the tibia, the main fracture being
transverse but a vertical component going into the knee joint—judge awarded,
inter alia, £5,000 damages for pain and suffering and loss of amenity—defendant's appeal allowed—£5,000 damages reduced to £4,000. Appeal from
Cantley J. May 9, 1978. MAIDEN v. NATIONAL COAL BOARD.

59. Plaintiff, aged 17 at time of accident, was knocked from his motor bicycle
in a road accident for which he was found 20 per cent. to blame—injuries,
unpleasant but "not in any way severe," were cuts, bruises, fracture of right
leg, fracture of left wrist, and injury to left knee—right leg wholly recovered
—left knee and wrist still causing trouble—real possibility of arthritis in
left knee—judge awarded £4,500 general damages—defendants' appeal dismissed.
Appeal from Talbot J. June 9, 1978. MORLEY v. TORRINGTON.

60. Plaintiff, aged 32 at time of accident in September 1972, competent secretary
typist, was unmarried with a six-year-old daughter who was attending school—
plaintiff knocked down by car driven by defendant—liability agreed on a 50–50
basis—injuries were a closed head injury, concussion, contusion of brain,
lacerations, cominuted fracture of right femur and fracture of right fibula
with minimal displacement—considerable time spent in hospital—she re-started
work in November 1973—judge awarded, *inter alia*, £12,000 general damages
for pain and suffering and loss of amenities, £1,037 loss of earnings up to
November 1973, £1,910 for earnings at £10 a week up to date of trial and
£3,000 for future loss of earnings—defendant's appeal dismissed—plaintiff's
cross-appeal allowed whereby £3,000 damages for future loss of earnings
increased to £4,900 (*i.e.* £700 a year net for seven years). July 6, 1978.
CUNNINGHAM v. HUTCHINS.

61. Plaintiff, aged 25 at time of accident in October 1975, was knocked
unconscious in road accident involving her car and taken to hospital, examined
and allowed to go home—no issue as to liability—plaintiff suffered from
persistent headaches, was kept in hospital for two days for observation, and
discharged to care of her family doctor—medical report indicated minor
symptoms after four weeks from time of accident—persistent headaches present
three to four months after accident—judge awarded, *inter alia*, £100 general
damages for pain and suffering and loss of amenities—plaintiff's appeal allowed
—£100 damages increased to £200. July 7, 1978. BYRNE v. OXFORD.

62. Plaintiff, aged 31 years at time of motor accident in March 1975, suffered
two minor lacerations of the head, a slight injury to right hand and wrist,
and a seriously comminuted double fracture of left clavicle—plaintiff off work
(which involved lifting heavy TV sets) for eight weeks, returned to light work
for three weeks but after that resumed his full work—two later periods away
from work, four weeks in July 1975 and a week in January 1976, because of
injuries—judge awarded £650 for the fracture, £300 for disfigurement, and £700
for future trouble—whether execessive—defendants' appeal dismissed. October
10, 1978. RECKLESS v. P. G. ALLDAY & Co.

63. Plaintiff, a lady aged 69 at time of road accident in August 1976, suffered fracture of base of left femoral neck necessitating hospital visits and operative treatment but in October 1976 she had a pulmonary embolism due to deep venous thrombosis from both legs resulting in anti-coagulation and further hospitalisation—active life by plaintiff before accident—agreed medical report—judge awarded plaintiff £6,000 damages for pain, suffering and loss of amenities—whether award inconsistent with conventional bracket of damages for similar disability—defendant's appeal on damages dismissed—plaintiff's appeal that judge was wrong to find parties 50/50 to blame for the accident and should have found defendant more to blame than 50 per cent. dismissed. October 20, 1978. HAMMOND v. HUGHES.

64. Plaintiff, who suffered a " whiplash " injury to her neck in a road accident, she being a passenger in a car being driven by her husband and she having her inertia seat-belt on, was awarded damages which included £600 general damages for pain, suffering and loss of amenity—minor road accident—expert witnesses—evidence from parties themselves in witness box—judge found defendant liable and gave judgment in favour of plaintiff—defendant's (in person) appeal dismissed. November 8, 1978. CARRIER v. HARWOOD-BEE.

65. Plaintiff, aged 28 at time of accident at work, was employed by defendants as an electrical fitter—heavy object, a transformer box, fell over when something supporting it collapsed and trapped and injured plaintiff's left arm—plaintiff was left-handed—permanent disability and the whole of the dexterity and movement and function of both the forearm and hand was seriously diminished—radius and ulna fractured; and there had to be a bone graft, the bone being taken from plaintiff's hip—plaintiff back at work with defendants as Grade 2 clerk—defendants admitted liability and judge awarded, *inter alia*, £9,500 for future loss of earnings (including £3,000 for lost promotion prospects) and £1,500 for reduced employability—whether excessive—whether the £1,500 should have been awarded at all—defendants' appeal allowed—total figure of damages awarded (£19,084) reduced by £1,500, that being a reduction in the head of damage relating to promotion opportunities only (*i.e.* the £3,000 reduced to £1,500). November 14, 1978. WREN v. N.E. ELECTRICITY BOARD.

66. Plaintiff, employed as a maintenance fitter by defendants for some seven years, suffered a nasty injury at work to his left forearm—plaintiff a right handed man was aged 28 at time of injury—injury was a permanently damaged wrist, a permanently weakened thumb, a pain in the left shoulder and loss of movement in left shoulder which was likely to stay for some years—liability agreed on 50/50 basis—judge awarded plaintiff, *inter alia*, £3,000 damages for unemployability and £5,400 damages for loss of future earnings—whether the £3,000 should not have been awarded—whether the £5,400 too high—defendants' appeal dismissed. November 21, 1978. DRUMMOND v. J. HEWITT & SON (FENTON).

67. Plaintiff, a factory worker, aged 57 at time of accident in November 1975, was thrown against partition separating passengers from bus driver when he got up to ask bus driver to stop bus and bus driver braked violently—plaintiff's injuries were a broken right scapula and fractures of two ribs—plaintiff treated in casualty department of hospital and sent home under care of general practitioner and off work for some seven weeks—no restrictions in arms but intermittent pain which was worse under pressure—judge awarded plaintiff, *inter alia*, £400 general damages—plaintiff's appeal that the £400 was much too low dismissed—fairly common type injury—*Lindley* v. *Hickson & Welsh* [1978] C.L.Y. 782 and *Walker* v. *Hickson & Welsh* [1978] C.L.Y.

783—observation that it would be wrong to have any figure as a minimum sum for general damages. February 15, 1979. MOORE v. MAIDSTONE & DISTRICT MOTOR SERVICES.

68. Both cases arising out of motor accident for which defendants liable— Price, aged 13 at time of accident, suffered a "localised bruising and abrasion" of left ankle, off school for a fortnight, but no suffering of general health, and went back to active school life playing games, etc., after four weeks of accident—awarded £100 general damages—Miss Savage, aged 49, "a very heavy woman indeed," suffered shock after being knocked down by car and complained of "little aching in lower back and painful twinges in right ankle"—off work for some time—injuries recovered completely— awarded £200 general damages—plaintiffs' appeals that awards too low on evidence dismissed—observation, that as a matter of practice there was no "minimum" sums for general damages, in *Moore* v. *Maidstone & District Motor Services* [1979] C.L.Y. (Unreported Cases § 67) reiterated. March 5, 1979. PRICE v. QUINN; SAVAGE v. CALVERT.

69. ⸺ ⸺ ⸺ arms, hands and legs

In May 1970 plaintiff suffered injuries in an accident for which the defendants were held to be two-thirds to blame and the plaintiff one-third—very serious injuries suffered by plaintiff who before the accident ran full-time a village shop with his wife—bone fractures to arms, hands and legs—fractures fully united in March 1977—right arm all right, substantial function in left arm, arthritis in left knee causing considerable pain with 50 per cent. chance for operation either to fuse joint or put in a replacement joint in 10 years' time— plaintiff able to walk with stick but knee painful—plaintiff awarded £23,615 overall which included, *inter alia*, £4,500 general damages, £10,920 for loss of future earnings and £6,364 which contained award for work done by plaintiff's wife—plaintiff's appeal dismissed—overall award of damages proper—general damages increased to £7,000 but other damages reduced accordingly. Appeal from Bristow J. May 17, 1978. TERRY v. SOUTHERN ELECTRICITY BOARD.

70. ⸺ ⸺ ⸺ brain and skull

In September 1973 plaintiff, a girl of $16\frac{1}{4}$ years, suffered injuries because of defendant's negligence—defendant admitted liability—her injuries included a head injury which severely disturbed her mental and cerebral capacity and she went through a considerable personality change—she had been of very modest scholastic standard but of bright personality and had enjoyed an outdoor life—she left school at the age of 14 and in June 1975 she was pregnant and married a young man whom she had known for some time and was managing to cope reasonably with motherhood and her domestic life with her husband—no physical incapacity or disfigurement—prospects of survival of marriage—subsequent report that, *inter alia*, quantum of plaintiff's cerebral trauma was severe and that she had become "more juvenile" with no prospect of improvement with age—plaintiff awarded £25,000 damages—whether excessive—defendant's appeal dismissed. Appeal from Payne J. May 12, 1978. EVANS v. GRIFFITHS.

71. ⸺ ⸺ ⸺ earlier injuries

As a young man in the Services the plaintiff met with an accident resulting in both his legs having to be amputated below the knee—plaintiff coped well and maintained a family and had an established position in the civil service, in the administrative grade—in October 1972, when plaintiff was aged 54, plaintiff suffered a "whiplash injury" when another vehicle rammed the back of his car—positive character of plaintiff—medical reports—judge awarded £6,000 for pain and suffering and loss of amenity and £750 for premature retirement brought about as a result of the injuries—whether damages excessive —first defendants' appeal allowed—£6,750 to be looked at as one figure as compensation for pain and suffering and loss of amenity—£6,750 reduced to £4,500. June 18, 1978. BOXSHALL v. GREATER LONDON COUNCIL.

72. —— —— —— **fractures**

Plaintiff, 22 years old, suffered injuries when her moped collided with a van, being driven by defendant's servant, emerging from a side road—injuries were a Colles fracture of right wrist of unusual severity, laceration and fracture of terminal phalanx of right index finger and fractures of both pubic rami— plaintiff recovered satisfactorily from injuries except the Colles fracture of wrist which was to affect her for rest of her life—extent of disability—medical reports—judge awarded plaintiff £2,000 general damages—plaintiff's appeal allowed—award increased to £3,500 with interest. Appeal from Griffiths J. January 15, 1979. HENSHALL v. WARD.

73. —— —— —— **hip**

Plaintiff, aged 38 at time of road accident in January 1976, suffered a very serious hip injury (his main injury) and was not able to get back to full weight bearing walking until May 1976—in August he returned to his pre-accident job at a salary of £3,000 per annum net—defendants admitted liability and judge awarded a total of £9,000 damages without splitting up the award into individual items in view of the Court of Appeal decision in *Cookson* v. *Knowles* [1977] C.L.Y. 7350—plaintiff's appeal allowed—plaintiff awarded £7,000 for pain, suffering and loss of amenities and £5,000 for loss of promotion at work, risk in labour market and for time off if hip operation became necessary, treating all those items together. Appeal from O'Connor J. November 17, 1978. MADDEN v. PERSONAL REPRESENTATIVES OF HUGHES (DECD.)

74. —— —— —— **leg**

Plaintiff, a successful jockey aged 37 at time of accident in November 1970, was injured whilst riding his motorscooter in a road accident for which the defendant was found wholly to blame—injuries were to plaintiff's left leg resulting in removal of knee-cap—judge awarded £1,100 for pain and suffering and loss of amenity and £250 loss of earnings—plaintiff's appeal allowed— £1,100 damages increased to £1,600 but impossible to increase the £250 award. July 10, 1978. MULLANE v. BODMAN.

75. —— —— —— **thigh**

Plaintiff, who suffered from rheumatoid arthritis in her knees and hands, was seriously injured when she fell during the course of her work with the defendants, she then being 44 years old—major injury was a fracture of the right femur—judge awarded her £14,007 damages (for injuries and loss and interest) having found the defendants negligent—whether findings of fact upon which judge founded his judgment, and inferences drawn from those findings, untenable on the evidence—whether £4,500 general damages too low—whether any contributory negligence on plaintiff's part—defendants' appeal dismissed—plaintiff's cross appeal allowed—proper figure for plaintiff's pain and suffering and loss of amenity was £6,000. Appeal from Slynn J. May 24, 1978. WHYATT v. METAL BOX CO.

76. —— professional negligence—breach of contract

Plaintiff employed defendant, an architect, on terms of RIBA conditions of employment in respect of conversion of her property into two maisonettes and a flat—defendant made drawings, made applications for planning permission and for various grants and invited a builder known to defendant to tender—in plaintiff's action for negligence judge found that defendant was negligent: (1) in failing to put work of converting house out to competitive tender, and (2) in passing defective work, in failing to supervise work and in certifying payment—plaintiff awarded £1,365 total damages and defendant awarded, on her counterclaim, £800 being the balance of defendant's fees—whether judge wrong in law in holding that defendant was entitled to recover whole of her fees despite her negligent performance of her duties; whether fees ought to have been abated—*Mondel* v. *Steel*, 8 M. & W. 300—whether abatement could be applied to a claim for professional services—whether judge wrong in law in failing to award plaintiff damages for distress and frustration—whether, *inter alia*, judge wrong not to award plaintiff as damages cost of surveyors' reports— plaintiff's duty to mitigate loss—plaintiff's appeal dismissed. June 9, 1978. HUTCHINSON v. HARRIS.

77. —— sale of goods—breach of warranty

Plaintiff bought an outboard motor engine for his boat from defendant who warranted, *inter alia*, that engine had been regularly serviced and had recently been serviced—defendant in breach of warranties and judge awarded plaintiff £250 for labour and parts necessary to effect repairs to engine—plaintiff had used engine on holiday when, after one day's use, it completely seized up and plaintiff's two-week family holiday alleged to be completely spoilt—whether ultimate condition of engine caused by breach of warranty, namely defective condition in which engine was delivered to plaintiff—plaintiff's duty to mitigate damages—evidence—whether damages in respect of loss of and enjoyment in contemplation of parties at time of contract—plaintiff's appeal allowed—Sale of Goods Act 1893, s. 53—plaintiff awarded £550 (full value of engine) plus £150, a broad assessment of fair compensation. January 25, 1979. POW v. HAGGER.

78. Divorce and Matrimonial Causes—breakdown of marriage—evidence

Parties, who were of the Sikh religion, married in India in July 1960— husband came to England in 1964 and wife followed in 1973—three children now aged 17, 16 and 14 years—in July 1976 wife left with children after violence by husband—husband applied for divorce and wife cross-petitioned for judicial separation—eight-day hearing and a long judgment by judge who preferred evidence on behalf of wife where it conflicted with that given on behalf of husband—husband's petition for divorce dismissed and wife granted a decree of judicial separation on her cross-prayer—husband's appeal dismissed. November 6, 1978. SINGH v. KAUR.

79. Wife presented petition for divorce on ground of behaviour—husband resisted petition but sought no matrimonial relief himself—judge delivered long and careful judgment dealing with every single allegation in petition in detail and concluded that wife's version of incidents (which included violence on part of husband) was to be preferred in general to the husband's and judge accepted wife's version where it was in conflict with the husband's and held that wife had established her case—husband's (in person) appeal dismissed. December 20, 1978. NEWTON v. NEWTON.

80. —— decree nisi—appeal

Parties married in Tel Aviv in April 1945 and came to England in 1961 with their four children—in November 1976 wife presented petition on ground of five years' separation—husband, after counsel's advice, indicated that he would not enter any answer but later changed his mind and sought to appeal against decree nisi already pronounced—no error of court alleged—proper remedy for husband was to apply to set aside decree under the Matrimonial Causes Rules (1977), r. 54 (9)—husband's appeal accordingly dismissed. February 16, 1979. FINN v. FINN.

81. —— —— rescission of decree

Wife filed petition for divorce on ground of unreasonable behaviour while husband was in prison for contempt of order not to interfere with matrimonial home—husband indicated intention to defend immediately after release from custody through solicitors but unable to get legal aid to defend so unable to instruct solicitors further—no answer filed by husband—decree nisi granted as on an undefended case—judge refused husband's application to rescind decree nisi, being of view that marriage had broken down and husband had had ample time for case to be defended with or without solicitors —husband's appeal dismissed. October 13, 1978. MISHRA v. MISHRA.

82. —— financial provision—equal division of assets

Husband and wife, now aged 34 and 33 respectively, married in July 1968— no children—wife finally left in January 1974 and in 1976 the marriage was dissolved on wife's petition alleging unreasonable conduct—parties lived in caravans and eventually lived in a caravan on a two-acre piece of land bought by the parties for £500, provided by the wife, from the wife's sister and sold produce from the land from stalls—wife worked on land before marriage and came from a smallholding stock and husband also came from a family engaged in road-side stalls—judge decided that the joint property of the parties, valued at £4,100, ought to be shared equally and that wife ought to have the land business and accordingly ordered the husband to transfer his legal and beneficial interest in it to the wife—husband's appeal dismissed. May 8, 1978. COOPER v. COOPER.

83. —— —— periodical payments

Husband continued to live in the matrimonial home in presence of wife and three sons, aged 14, 12 and nine years, for long time after divorce and left in January 1978—husband's 1977 gross earnings including overtime were £5,000 odd—registrar ordered husband to continue to discharge wife's mortgage repayments and general and water rate, and that he should give £4 a week to wife and £7 a week for each child—on appeal judge reduced wife's £4 a week to £1 a week leaving rest of the order unchanged—husband's appeal that unreasonable to expect him to work substantial overtime hours dismissed—wife's cross appeal dismissed—observations made on unapproved respondent solicitor's note of judgment sent to judge for approval at very last moment before appeal. May 9, 1978. PUTTNAM v. PUTTNAM.

84. —— irretrievable breakdown of marriage—evidence

Parties (both now over 50) married in 1949 when they were in their early 20s—several children all of whom now grown up—wife finally left in July 1977 and in October she petitioned for divorce—judge found that husband had behaved in such a way that wife could not reasonably be expected to live with him but found that marriage had not irretrievably broken down and dismissed wife's petition—whether husband had discharged onus of showing that marriage had not irretrievably broken down—Matrimonial Causes Act 1973, s. 1 (4)—wife's appeal allowed and decree granted. October 6, 1978. SMITH v. SMITH.

85. —— jurisdiction—domicile

Wife, now aged 21 years and born in Tanganyika in July 1957 and holding British Protectorate passport, married husband in 1974 and lived in Belgian Congo and later in Zaïre—in 1976 she left and came to England intending to live here with her parents—after seven months she went back to Zaïre for reconciliation which failed—she came back to England on October 15, 1977, on visitor's permit—in March 1978 she applied to stay in England permanently but application refused—appeal against refusal pending—in November 1977 she filed divorce petition (which was undefended) asserting that she had acquired domicile of choice—judge dismissed petition for want of jurisdiction taking point of law that it was not possible for petitioner to establish domicile of choice because she was under order to leave country subject to right of appeal and accordingly judge heard no more evidence—wife's appeal allowed—judge did not have all available evidence on issue of domicile—rehearing ordered—assistance of Queen's Proctor invoked. Appeal from Mrs. Lane J. October 3, 1978. SADRUDIN v. SADRUDIN.

86. —— nullity—wilful refusal to consummate marriage

The wife petitioned for nullity of marriage on the ground that the marriage had never been consummated because of the respondent's wilful refusal to consummate it in that he persistently refused to go through with the Sikh religious ceremony, the parties being of the Sikh religion—county court judge dismissed petition because he found no evidence to support it—wife's appeal dismissed. May 8, 1978. KAUR v. LALRIA.

87. —— —— —— evidence

Husband and wife (wife previously married) went through a form of marriage in August 1976 and in October 1976 wife presented a petition for judicial separation alleging conduct dating back to the date of the marriage—husband denied allegations and cross-petitioned for a decree on the ground of wilful refusal to consummate by wife—wife's petition stayed and case to proceed on husband's cross-petition—judge having seen and heard husband give evidence was not satisfied that husband had used appropriate tact, persuasion and encouragement, nor that there had been wilful refusal, but judge adjourned matter for corroborative evidence to be adduced by husband—when matter came back before judge husband sought to place before court affidavit by him—judge refused to see affidavit evidence on previous view formed of husband and held that there were no satisfactory grounds for adducing affidavit evidence on issue—husband's appeal dismissed. February 1, 1979. R. v. R.

88. —— practice—delay in filing answer

Marriage broke down in February 1976—negotiations took place between parties' solicitors with view to avoiding contest in court—in November 1977 wife filed petition—no indication of intention to defend given by husband—in May 1978 wife's petition set down in Special Procedure list—negotiations finally broke down and husband's solicitors applied for leave to file answer out of time—judge granted leave—wife's appeal allowed—leave to file answer out of time a tactical move by husband—interests of justice not served by giving leave—sooner marriage dissolved the better. October 4, 1978. DAVIES v. DAVIES.

89. —— —— setting aside decree—special procedure

Parties married in Pakistan in May 1960—four children now aged 15, 12, 11 and eight years—in August 1978 wife presented petition for judicial separation on ground of husband's conduct alleging violence and claimed custody—no answer filed by husband—case proceeded under the special procedure and came before judge on November 17, 1978—later husband decided to file answer and cross petition for divorce explaining that he thought that wife's petition was for divorce and that he himself wanted a divorce—owing to oversight husband's applications not signed and accordingly on November 21 husband applied to set aside decree and for leave to file answer out of time and to cross-petition for divorce—on January 5, 1979, judge granted husband's applications—wife appealed contending that judge not entitled to grant leave and could only stand matter over with a view to an application being made to registrar—*Day* v. *Day* [1979] C.L.Y. 792—Matrimonial Causes Rules 1977, r. 54 (1) (9). February 12, 1979. KHWAJA v. KHWAJA.

90. —— special procedure—rescission of decree nisi

In April 1978 wife (a solicitor) petitioned for divorce alleging unreasonable behaviour and on May 12 petition was served on husband's solicitors who acknowledged service (on July 31) indicating intention to defend—no answer filed—much bitterness between parties—on June 4 husband arrested by police on complaints by wife against him of burglary and assault and husband remanded in custody pending trial—husband in custody for four months but on October 4 acquitted by jury of both charges against him—formal notice received by husband that decree nisi under special procedure was to be pronounced on October 3, same day as husband's trial—judge refused to allow husband (by counsel) leave to file answer to petition out of time—parties unaware of *Day* v. *Day* [1979] C.L.Y. 792 as case not reported at time—husband's appeal allowed—husband given leave to file answer out of time upon conditions—*Day* v. *Day* applied. January 12, 1979. STEMP v. STEMP.

91. Easements and Prescription—easement—acquisition

Plaintiffs claimed that third defendant had no title to certain land claimed by her and alternatively that they had rights over certain space acquired by prescription or lost modern grant, and that they were entitled to a right of way at all times and for all purposes over a lane which extended 15 feet in width—defence alleged, *inter alia*, that no part of lane and no easement which may be established was on or over land which was or had been in third defendant's ownership or her predecessors' in title—construction of award in 1806—evidence —judge found in favour of defendants—plaintiffs' appeal dismissed—evidence did not show a right being asserted but merely drivers using area as and when they had to—right alleged one of an essentially casual nature. Appeal from Foster J. December 19, 1978. IRONSIDE v. COOK.

92. —— evidence of prescriptive title

Defendant carried on business of a haulage contractor and parked his vehicles on certain land near his house pursuant to a licence granted to him in 1972 by plaintiff council for a consideration of £100 to use land—in December 1975 council determined licence by notice—defendant continued to park his vehicles on land and council claimed, *inter alia*, damages for trespass—defendant claimed to be owner of land under a prescriptive title—historical evidence—judge found in favour of the council—defendant's (in person) appeal dismissed. October 6, 1978. EPSOM & EWELL BOROUGH COUNCIL v. HOLLEY.

93. Education—merger of colleges—governing body

In 1969 two institutions, the College of Technology and the Oastler College of Education, merged together under an instrument of government and articles of government created by order of the Huddersfield County Borough Council acting as the local education authority pursuant to s. 1 (2) of the Education (No. 2) Act 1968 (c. 37)—in September 1974 a new tripartite polytechnic came into existence when the Huddersfield College of Education (Technical) joined and certain amendments were made to the instrument of government—whether plaintiffs, full-time staff members of the College of Education and continuing to be full-time staff members of the new polytechnic, entitled to be appointed to governing body—construction of instrument of government (which was not a standard form document)—judge refused to make declarations asked by plaintiffs—plaintiffs' appeal dismissed. Appeal from Cantley J. April 21, 1978. DIXON v. CHAIRMAN OF THE GOVERNORS AND THE GOVERNORS OF THE HUDDERSFIELD POLYTECHNIC.

94. Employment—confidential information—injunction

First defendant was employed by plaintiffs (engaged in the business of printing) as a sales representative—no restrictive covenant in employment preventing first defendant from engaging in business in competition with plaintiffs after termination of employment—employment ended on April 10 pursuant to first defendant's notice to terminate employment given on April 3—on April 5 second defendants, carrying on business as printers, agreed to employ first defendant as a freelance sales representative canvassing printing work on their behalf—on April 17 plaintiffs discovered that first defendant was soliciting and obtaining work from their former customers for second defendants and on May 10 issued writ claiming, inter alia, injunction to restrain both defendants "from communicating with, approaching or contracting by way of trade, or disclosing or making use of any confidential information in relation to customers of plaintiffs with whom first defendant had dealt with in last 12 months" and names of those customers (46 in all) were set out—plaintiffs' case that both prior to and after departure from employment first defendant was actively engaged in a conspiracy with second defendants to filch plaintiffs' customers from them by giving out confidential information —whether continued dealings between second defendants and plaintiffs' customers amounted to a continuing infringement of any legal rights of plaintiffs—whether information used by first defendant to obtain from second defendants custom of former customers of plaintiffs was confidential to him— whether both defendants were acting in conspiracy—judge granted interlocutory injunctions on basis that there was a serious question to be tried between parties and that balance of convenience lay in granting injunctions— defendants' appeal allowed on undertaking by second defendants to keep a record of all their dealings with plaintiffs' customers as listed. Appeal from Boreham J. October 17, 1978. FIDELITY LITHOGRAPHIC CO. v. LYNCH.

95. —— identity of employer

F was employed in Nigeria as chief accountant of a Nigerian company which was parent company of an English subsidiary, Nigerline (U.K.), the appellants—in February 1975 Nigerian company made arrangements for sending F to England to be managing director of company—appellant company applied for work permit giving its own name as employers of F and in due course gave details of salary, etc., to English tax authorities—F arrived in England in April 1975 to start work on basis of a three-year contract—in November 1975 Nigerian company determined F's agreement—F claimed for unfair dismissal— whether F employed by appellant company or by Nigerian company—whether question of law—Employment Appeal Tribunal held F was employed by appellant company—appellant company's appeal dismissed. October 16, 1978. NIGERLINE (U.K.) v. FOLAMI.

96. —— unfair dismissal—claim—time bar

Claimant was dismissed from her 11-year-old work with the respondent company on February 7, 1977—on February 8 she, assisted by her son, filled in a form at the employment exchange to claim compensation for unfair dismissal and had it posted (to the Central Office of the Industrial Tribunals)—in March she went back to the employment exchange because she had received no acknowledgment of her claim—claimant aware that time limit for her claim would expire on May 6 under the Trade Union and Labour Relations Act 1974, Sched. 1, para. 21 (4)—on April 29 she received a letter from the conciliation body ACAS that she should complete an(other) application form—on May 2 she showed that letter to her son, on May 6 she collected a new form, on May 9 she signed it and on May 10 her son posted it—Industrial Tribunal and the Employment Appeal Tribunal (by a majority) held her claim time barred—claimant's appeal dismissed—words " reasonably practicable " in para. 21 (4) to be construed ordinarily, without too much analysis. July 17, 1978. SACH v. D. B. COURT.

97. —— —— compensation—amount

Applicant was held to have been unfairly dismissed when his employers, the respondent company, dispensed with his services in April 1975 after he became very ill and was off work for many weeks—industrial tribunal assessed what would have happened if he had not been unfairly dismissed, and calculated his loss at £2,840 on basis that his services would have been dispensed with in autumn 1975—E.A.T. upheld decision of industrial tribunal—applicant's appeal dismissed. Appeal from Bristow J. June 16, 1978. BUSHELL v. STANDARD TELEPHONE & CABLES.

98. Executors and Administrators—injunction—sale of chattels

Plaintiff was a beneficiary under the will of the deceased made in August 1976 and the first three defendants were the executors of the will—a large part of the deceased's estate consisted of jewellery, furniture and pictures—atmosphere of suspicion and recrimination throughout history of administration of estate—beneficiaries unable to agree distribution in specie of testatrix's chattels and pursuant to directions in the will decided that chattels should be sold—Messrs. Christie, Manson and Wood instructed to sell chattels on executors' behalf—s. 23 (1) of the Trustee Act 1925—plaintiff granted injunction to restrain executors from selling chattels without reserve prices save where reserve prices undesirable or unnecessary and executors personally ordered to pay plaintiff's costs of the motion—executors' appeal allowed—evidence as a whole not justifying plaintiff's fears that sales might in any way result in sale at an undervalue or otherwise constitute a maladministration of any part of the estate—relief sought by plaintiff not shown to be just and necessary—no ground for making an order for costs against executors personally. Appeal from Foster J. May 18, 1978. TAYLOR v. KULICK.

99. Gifts—extension on mother's house for use of wife

Mr. JG married Mrs. VG in England in November 1956 and had two children, boy and girl now aged 18 and 17 years—in 1963 they went to California and husband went into a successful motor business—children sent back to school in England and Mrs. VG came with them—extension built at considerable cost (£18,000) to Mr. JG's mother's bungalow for somewhere for Mrs. VG and children to stay—marriage dissolved in 1977, Mr. JG remarried and children went to live with him in California—status of Mrs. VG in relation to the extension—possession action by mother—judge found on evidence that extension was an unequivocal gift by son to his mother and that Mrs. VG had no interest in extension at all and no right to stay there —Mrs. VG's appeal dismissed—mother's cross-appeal dismissed. July 5, 1978. GAMBLE v. GAMBLE.

100. —— undue influence—evidence

During the spring and summer of 1975 and onwards property, including over 1,900 gold sovereigns, was physically handed over in differing amounts by plaintiff to his nephew, defendant, on different occasions—plaintiff's case that property handed over for safe custody only so that defendant was no more than a gratuitous bailee under obligation to return it on demand—defendant's case that property was an outright gift—judge disbelieved plaintiff's story and accepted defendant's story and reached conclusion that this was not a case where in equity the gifts should be set aside on the ground of presumed undue influence—plaintiff's appeal dismissed. Appeal from Slade J. July 26, 1978. DENT v. RADCLYFFE.

101. Guarantee and Indemnity—guarantee—enforceability—sufficient memorandum

In July 1967 plaintiff became a wholly owned subsidiary of Wilson Lovatt group and in October 1968 Mr. R, financial director of Wilson Lovatt, saw regional director of first defendant bank about arranging to fit plaintiff account " for interest purposes with other group companies banking in Wolverhampton "—in May 1969 defendant bank wrote to Mr. R that as they were allowing set-off against plaintiff's credit balanced at Norwich, plaintiff should join in " interlocking guarantee " held for group and Mr. R replied that he was agreeable and that he was sure that board of Wilson Lovatt would also be agreeable —interlocking guarantee signed (after resolution passed by plaintiff) by then chairman and director of plaintiff—indorsement not required by defendant bank to be signed again on behalf of Wilson Lovatt and of other subsidiaries— proceedings instituted by liquidator of plaintiff claiming, inter alia, declarations that plaintiff not liable to defendant bank as guarantor of Wilson Lovatt and its other subsidiary companies—whether, inter alia, Wilson Lovatt and subsidiary companies agreed to guarantee plaintiff and if so whether guarantee enforceable—whether, inter alia, Mr. R had actual or ostensible authority to guarantee indebtedness of plaintiff—Statute of Frauds, 1677, s. 4—failure of persons to sign again not sufficient to make indorsement an insufficient memorandum—defendant bank's appeal allowed. Appeal from Whitford J. June 22, 1978. FORD & CARTER v. MIDLAND BANK.

102. Hire-purchase—contract—fundamental breach

Plaintiff, a car-hire operator, bought a new Vauxhall on hire-purchase from first defendant, a finance company, and through second defendant, a garage— manufacturing defects of serious kinds found in car which eventually broke down completely—expert evidence for plaintiff that car broke down owing to manufacturing defects not challenged by defendants—judge was not satisfied that there was fundamental breach and held that the contract continued and hire-purchase instalments continued in favour of finance company—plaintiff's appeal allowed—judge wrong in not accepting expert's evidence—clear fundamental breaches of contract—plaintiff given £1,106 damages including £800 for loss of being able to have any employment for three months when car was rendered unusable—counterclaim for hire-purchase instalments dismissed. May 5, 1978. ROTHMAN v. V.M.C. FINANCE.

103. Husband and Wife—ancillary relief—considerations for refusal

Parties married in March 1964 and had two children now aged 13 and 10 years—matrimonial home bought freehold in 1970 in husband's name—in August 1973 wife left, formed an association with a Mr. B, had a child by him in October 1977 and in December 1977 purchased a house in her and B's joint names—husband lived in the matrimonial home and was on social security because he had to look after children—negotiations for divorce started in 1976 and in September 1977 a decree nisi was granted on the basis of the husband's consent—wife later applied for ancillary relief under Matrimonial Causes Rules 1977, r. 68—registrar granted application and judge upheld it —factors to be considered: (1) whether there was an agreement which influenced husband in giving consent; (2) if leave granted wife's prospects of obtaining an order; (3) general merit of case—husband's appeal allowed. November 2, 1978. HUMPHREY v. HUMPHREY.

104. —— —— costs

Parties married in 1957—two children, girl and boy now aged 19 and 17—in 1975 wife left taking children and in June 1975 she petitioned for divorce on ground of husband's behaviour—on December 1, 1977, judge pronounced decree nisi and ordered that matrimonial home should be sold and one-half of proceeds of sale paid to wife and that husband should pay wife's costs of the hearing—agreement was reached between parties on December 1, 1977, that proceeds of sale of matrimonial home should be divided equally— husband's (in person) appeal contending that he should not be required to pay wife's costs dismissed—judge exercised discretion correctly. December 8, 1978. BRITTAIN v. BRITTAIN.

105. —— —— financial provision—lump sum

Husband and wife, now aged 42 and 40, married in September 1970—both parties previously married and husband had a daughter, J, now aged 16, by his previous marriage—parties separated in June 1976 and in 1977 husband obtained decree, on an undefended suit, on ground of wife's adultery and obtained custody of J—husband lived in former matrimonial home with another woman (who earned £35 per week) and her son aged 12 and J who had left school but was retarded and had had difficulty in retaining employment—a business and flat belonging to wife's father and uncle was transferred to wife as a result of the break-up of her marriage and wife lived in flat and earned some £1,000 a year from the business—wife owed her father £4,000 on an interest-free IOU and £5,000 to bank—judge allowed an appeal by husband against part of order by registrar which provided that husband should pay wife a lump sum of £2,499—*Trippas* v. *Trippas* [1973] C.L.Y. 925d—wife's appeal dismissed. January 12, 1979. CHAPPLE v. CHAPPLE.

106. —— —— matrimonial home

Husband and wife now aged 50 and 47 respectively married in 1955—two children, girls now aged 20 and 14—in 1974 parties separated and in February 1978 decree nisi obtained by husband on ground of two years' separation with consent was made absolute—matrimonial home bought in 1968 and now valued at £9,000 with an equity of £7,000—no other capital assets—husband worked as a foreman car body repairer earning £68 per week gross and lived with younger daughter in a house which was damp and in need of modernisation and of which tenant was a Mrs. G whom husband proposed to marry as soon as possible—wife continued to live in matrimonial home and had a boyfriend, a Mr. D, a divorced man with two children aged 10 and seven, and there was a reasonable prospect of wife marrying and making her home with him—elder daughter had been living with her aunt for some time—registrar ordered, *inter alia*, that matrimonial home be sold within three months and net proceeds of sale be divided equally between parties and judge (on appeal) affirmed that decision—wife's appeal dismissed. November 21, 1978. STREET v. STREET.

107. Parties married in July 1961 when husband was 23 and wife 22 years old —two children, girl and boy now aged 11 and nine years—marriage came under strain from 1974 onwards and in summer 1977 wife began divorce proceedings —in December 1977 husband left and now lived in temporary accommodation which he was permitted to use by his employers—wife continued to live in matrimonial home (their fourth house) which was bought in 1975 for £11,250 with a £9,000 building society interest only mortgage linked to an endowment policy—house now valued at £18,000 with an equity therefore of £9,000, and surrender value of endowment policy was £1,200—judge ordered, *inter alia*, that husband should hold house on trust for himself and wife in equal shares as tenants in common with no sale taking place until further order or agreement by parties and that husband should continue to pay the premiums on the endowment policy and that wife should pay mortgage instalments and that order for periodical payments of £55 per month to wife, £26·43 per month to girl and £21·45 per month to boy ordered by registrar should stand —husband's appeal allowed—observations on principle in *Re H's Settlement* [1939] W.N. 318 and *Re Hooker's Settlement* [1954] C.L.Y. 3041. November 28, 1978. HALE v. HALE.

108. Husband and wife now 45 and 44 years married in August 1963—four children, one girl aged 14 and three boys aged 13, eight and seven years— matrimonial home bought on mortgage in joint names in 1968 now worth £22,000 with equity of some £19,000—wife worked during marriage and paid various outgoings—husband financially irresponsible during marriage—in 1977 wife obtained decree nisi of divorce now made absolute on ground of husband's conduct and in July 1978 was granted custody of children—husband lived with brother in unsatisfactory circumstances and earned £95 per week as a bus driver and wife earned £75 as a mental nurse—judge ordered that matrimonial home should be transferred to wife and in return she should pay husband a lump sum of £6,000 within three months and that in default of payment house should be sold and net proceeds divided two-thirds to wife and one-third to husband and ordered husband to pay periodical payments of £5 per week to each child—on appeal new evidence showed that impossible for wife to raise £6,000 to pay husband—wife's appeal allowed—house transferred to wife absolutely—husband's periodical payments reduced to £1 per week per child. December 13, 1978. BELGRAVE v. BELGRAVE.

109. Parties married in June 1971 when husband was 32 and wife 19 years of age—two children, boy and girl, now aged six and three years—in October 1977 wife left with children and went to live with her mother and her mother's mother in a little three-bedroomed house—custody given to mother—matrimonial home bought in husband's name three months before marriage and now valued at £5,000—both parties worked during marriage—husband, " an unmitigated liar, whose evidence was completely unreliable," had made away with family savings of over £4,000—there were arrears of £600 in respect of interim maintenance payments of £12 per week for wife and £5 per week for each child—on wife's application for a lump sum and transfer of property judge ordered that husband transfer an interest of three-tenths in the matrimonial home to wife and same interest to children—wife's appeal allowed—ordered, *inter alia*, that house to be transferred absolutely to wife, husband to pay costs of the conveyance. February 5, 1979. VENEZIALE v. VENEZIALE.

110. Parties married in October 1972 having cohabited since 1964—three children, a boy now aged 17 (child of wife by previous marriage) and a girl and a boy now aged 14 and three—decree absolute in July 1977 on wife's petition on ground of conduct including allegations of violence—matrimonial home bought on mortgage in 1968 and now valued at £6,000 with equity of some £5,500—wife left with children and husband continued to live in matrimonial home—registrar found that parties were beneficially entitled to equal shares in matrimonial home and ordered husband to transfer his interest to wife subject to mortgage liability outstanding—judge upheld registrar's order recognising that it was likely to involve husband going into lodgings—later inquiries by court showed that wife and children had a completely safe and secure home with local authority—husband's appeal allowed—wife's interest not to be enforced until husband's death or earlier sale—typical *Brown* v. *Pritchard* type of case ("think in terms of homes, not money"). February 12, 1979. WALLBANK *v.* WALLBANK.

111. —— —— property adjustment

Parties married in February 1971 when husband was 31 and wife 25 years old—one child, a girl now aged 12 years, adopted by parties in 1972—matrimonial home bought on mortgage in November 1972 in joint names and was now valued at £17,500 with equity of £10,000—in December 1976 husband left and wife presented divorce petition based on husband's conduct and in January 1977 wife applied for ancillary relief—husband now lived in his flat with his parents and earned about £6,500 per annum from his business as an amusement caterer and as a taxi operator and had business assets valued at £17,000, a car valued £500, and his share in the equity of matrimonial home was £5,000—wife had an income of about £1,800 per annum and her only capital was her share in matrimonial home—registrar ordered that husband should (1) transfer to wife all his interest in matrimonial home; (2) procure transfer to wife of a taxi plate; (3) pay wife lump sum of £1,000 within 21 days; (4) pay wife maintenance pending suit of £7 per week (decree not having been made absolute); (5) pay child £15 per week—on appeal judge set aside order and ordered, *inter alia*, that husband should convey matrimonial home on trust for sale on certain terms—wife's appeal allowed—registrar's order reinstated except that £1,000 not to be paid and child's periodical payments reduced to £10 per week—case dealt with primarily on a capital transfer basis—observations on *Re H's Settlement* [1939] W.N. 318 and *Re Hooker's Settlement* [1954] C.L.Y. 3041. November 7, 1978. GOODRICH *v.* GOODRICH.

112. —— contempt of court—committal

Husband was in serious breach of undertakings given by him in September 1977 not to molest his wife and judge committed him to prison for six weeks for breach of those undertakings—successful application for bail made by husband day after order for committal so that he spent only 24 hours in prison—whether he should be sent back to prison to serve remainder of six weeks—interests of wife and children—attempts at reconciliation between parties in early 1978 failed—shortly before order for committal husband obtained new work at very substantial salary and alleged that job likely to be affected—subsisting orders against husband not only against molestation but also against going anywhere near where wife lived—husband's appeal allowed (but not "easily") and remainder of term set aside. November 2, 1978. SUDBURY *v.* SUDBURY.

113. Comparatively young parties who had been close to each other until a short time ago—wife pregnant by husband and due to have baby on May 5,

1979—on November 12, 1978, husband breached undertaking given on October 30 (when parties were living together under same roof with their children) not to molest petitioner wife by knocking wife about and stamping on her feet— on receiving notice to commit husband again assaulted wife and kicked her leg —on November 28 judge committed husband to prison for six months to protect wife and as yet unborn child—husband's appeal allowed—imprisonment reduced to 23 days, time which husband had already spent in prison—contempt purged by period already spent in prison. January 12, 1979. WALKER v. WALKER.

114. —— domestic violence—injunction

As divorce case was to be heard on December 4, the sensible way of dealing with case was to discharge the so-called "ouster injunction" but to leave the "molestation injunction" standing—appropriate directions given, court being very concerned about the welfare of the children of the marriage— husband's appeal allowed to extent indicated. November 10, 1978. MOYO v. MOYO.

115. —— financial provision—consent order

In December 1974 a consent order was made whereby husband, *inter alia,* agreed to pay wife £150,000 lump sum to be inclusive of wife's claim for a lump sum and of all her costs of proceedings—whether a lump sum order within s. 23 of the Matrimonial Causes Act 1973—interest on £150,000— ss. 17, 18 of the Judgments Act 1838—not necessary in this case to decide whether or not a lump sum order was a judgment debt within meaning of the 1838 Act—*K.* v. *K.* [1977] C.L.Y. 837, *Caudery* v. *Finnerty* (1892) 61 L.J. Q.B. 496—judge declared that wife was entitled to interest at the rate of $7\frac{1}{2}$ per cent. per annum on £150,000—husband's appeal allowed—(an apparently valid order of the court purported to be made in July 1974 was a nullity and was formally set aside). Appeal from Reeve J. November 9, 1978. MEADOWS v. MEADOWS.

116. —— —— lump-sum payment

Husband now aged 66 and wife 53 years met in 1954 and married in 1960— trouble with the marriage started in 1974 and the husband paid the wife £5,000 to provide for her future security—in June 1977 the wife left and in December 1977 the marriage was dissolved—husband had been originally in the police but now ran a successful business from the matrimonial home, which was valued at £40,000, and where he lived with the two children of the marriage, aged 20 and 16 years—wife worked as a receptionist earning a small amount—judge ordered, *inter alia,* that wife, agreed to be entitled to half share in matrimonial home, should transfer her share to husband in payment by husband of £20,000 —wife's appeal that £20,000 too low dismissed—judge wrong not to deduct from husband's capital ascertained income tax liability of £20,851—wife had done extremely well. May 2, 1978. WALTON v. WALTON.

117. Parties both now aged 31 married in June 1966—four children now aged 12, 10, six and one—husband left for another woman at time of wife's last pregnancy but association lasted only three months—wife left with children when last child was born and went to live with her parents and now lived in a council house and was wholly maintained by social security—husband lived in matrimonial home and earned £45 per week gross as a semi-skilled motor mechanic—house valued at £11,000 with equity of £5,000 and wife had one-third interest in it—judge ordered husband to pay wife lump sum of £2,000 within six months and made a nominal order for periodical payments for wife and £6 per week in all for four children—husband's appeal allowed—

husband to hold property subject to charge of one-third of net proceeds of sale, charge free of interest and unenforceable until husband either sold property or died. October 24, 1978. CHINNOCK v. CHINNOCK.

118. —— —— **periodical payments**

Parties married in 1955 when husband was 21 and wife 20 years of age—three children, the younger two (subject-matter of the appeal) being twin girls now aged 17—marriage broke down in 1971 and was dissolved in 1973—terms of settlement that wife to get matrimonial home proceeds and husband to pay £208 per annum for each child of family until they attain 17 or further order —both parties remarried—husband earned £5,000 for annum gross and after expenses had little money left and found it extremely difficult without the extra income of his wife who was now unemployed—wife earned £45 per week gross, £38 net, and lived with children in a semi-detached three-bedroomed house with a small mortgage—some £6,500 net to be received by wife's family—wife comparatively comfortably placed while husband unable to meet all his commitments—judge ordered husband to pay £10 a week for each child until completion of their full-time education or further order—father's appeal allowed— wrong for husband to provide for children after they were 18; and wife to maintain them until they were 18. June 28, 1978. EGLEY v. JACOBS.

119. Husband and wife now aged 29 and 26 years married in August 1970—two children, boy and girl now aged seven and two years—parties lived in council flat—they separated in November 1977 and in February 1978 decree nisi granted on wife's petition based on husband's adultery—husband earned £3,744 per annum gross and paid £267·50 tax, £130 per annum other expenses and £15 per week rent for his present accommodation—registrar ordered husband to pay wife £21 per week and children £9·15 per week—wife in receipt of £6 per week child benefit—judge upheld order—husband's appeal allowed—total amount payable by husband reduced to £24 per week, change to be retrospective. October 27, 1978. TAYLOR v. TAYLOR.

120. —— —— **profits out of use of matrimonial home**

Husband and two children of marriage (of whom husband had custody) lived in former matrimonial home, a seven-bedroomed property with usual living accommodation—judge gave wife a one-third interest in the house and ordered that she " shall be entitled to one-third of all net future rents in respect " of house—whether " net future rents " limited to sums of money received under tenancies in true sense—whether profit made on lettings to lodgers excluded —construction of order—intention was that until house sold, wife should get one-third of any profit which husband made out of his use of house—husband's appeal dismissed. October 17, 1978. CURTIS v. CURTIS.

121. —— —— **property adjustment**

Parties now in late forties married in July 1960, it being W's second marriage —four children, two from W's former marriage and two from present marriage, all grown up and self-supporting—marriage broke up in 1972—divorce in May 1977—W lived with three of children in matrimonial home, a three-bedroomed house, valued at £24,000 with equity of some £22,000—beneficial interest in house agreed to be held by parties in equal shares—H lived with his mother in an old people's flat since 1972 but his mother died recently and he said that he would have to move—W lived on social security but had earning capacity of £30 per week as a typist—H not working but received £50 per week from a family business and claimed that he was unable to work because of " some kind of illness " to his hands—judge ordered (on appeal from registrar) that trust for sale on house be postponed until W chose to exercise it on footing that she would be responsible for mortgage repayments—H's appeal dismissed —observation that reasonably firm evidence necessary about accommodation position of parties. January 23, 1979: HORROD v. HORROD.

122. —— —— successful farming enterprise

Parties both now aged 44 married in 1958—three children, two boys aged 20 (university undergraduate) and 17, and a girl—both younger children attending school—decree absolute in May 1978 marriage having broken down in 1975—children with mother—family situation based on a successful farming enterprise with a good standard of living—farm originally some 400 acres but 171 acres sold for £167,000 and wife provided with £32,000 cash with which she bought a house and a car—husband lived on farm and earned some £5,000 per annum —farm valued at some £200,000 net after tax—judge ordered husband to pay wife lump sum of £6,000 together with proceeds of insurance policy at £10,000 in 1992 and periodical payments at the rate of £1,600 to wife, £200 to elder boy, £400 to younger boy and £400 to girl, mother undertaking to pay school fees—wife's appeal allowed—wife given 20 per cent. charge on farm—wife's periodical payments increased to £3,000—observation on making no order for costs in situation where party with no capital is legally aided—observation on *P. v. P.* [1978] C.L.Y. 813. January 16, 1979. HAYTER v. HAYTER.

123. —— injunction—domestic violence—interests of child

Only child of marriage, now aged 12—mother finally left matrimonial home, a small cottage, where lived her husband, child of the marriage, husband's former wife and her mother, and went to live with parents who lived nearby—child hostile to her mother but had a close relationship with father and got on well with father's former wife—mother alleged that father was violent and father alleged that mother neglected child—former wife's evidence that she and her mother had arrived temporarily because they were asked to help in divorce proceedings between parties—judge refused mother's application that she be allowed back into matrimonial home and ordered a welfare report and gave urgency to case and stated that welfare officer takes steps to reconcile child with mother—since judge's order welfare officer had been unable to act because of industrial action and secondly father and his former wife had decided to remarry—mother's appeal allowed—father ordered to allow mother back into cottage—former wife and her mother ordered to leave. Appeal from Bush J. February 13, 1979. HAYES v. HAYES.

124. —— —— protection of wife's claim to financial relief

Husband and wife now aged 44 and 43 married in March 1954—four children, three of whom grown up and youngest 15—wife worked from 1966 onwards earning and contributing to family funds—in March 1975 wife left alleging unreasonable behaviour and youngest child later joined her—in 1975 husband obtained loan of £600 from Barclays Bank and charged matrimonial home with it—husband later left matrimonial home and " disappeared " having taken his belongings with him—wife unable to serve petition for divorce praying for, *inter alia*, financial relief on husband and service dispensed with—in July 1978 bank entered into possession of matrimonial home and arranged a sale of house to realise amount of their unpaid loan—matrimonial home only real asset of parties—whether wife ought to be granted injunction protecting her claim for financial provision—Matrimonial Causes Act 1973, s. 37 (2)—wife's appeal allowed—interlocutory injunction granted restraining husband (but not bank) from disposing of or dealing with proceeds of sale of house (which may be credited to his account with bank). February 7, 1978. LEEMAN v. LEEMAN.

125. —— matrimonial home

Parties, now in their 70s, married in 1924—three children, two sons and a daughter—matrimonial home, bought in 1949, consisted of a bungalow and land later converted into a " caravan site "—husband left in 1964 and wife obtained divorce in 1969 on the ground of desertion—in 1975 husband applied for property adjustment order—wife received some £4,300 per annum in rent from caravans while husband's income was his old age pension and supplementary benefit—wife's offer of £15,000 in settlement of husband's claims not accepted—judge ordered property to be sold (by auction, with reserve price of £45,000) and proceeds to be divided as to two-thirds to wife and one-third to husband—property situation such that only possible buyers of property were wife and her son who was not on good terms with wife and who had a " stranglehold " on the property—effect of order to make wife homeless or force her to buy another house—Matrimonial Causes Act 1973, s. 25—delay in husband's application to be taken into account to do justice—wife's appeal allowed—periodical payments case—husband's application dismissed. July 21, 1978. LAMB v. LAMB.

126. Judge found that matrimonial home was bought as a joint venture, on mortgage, by parties as " two young people " when they got married and held that it was owned equally and that, in interests of wife and children of marriage, right course was to transfer husband's interest to wife—husband's (in person) appeal dismissed. October 9, 1978. FOWLER v. FOWLER.

127. Husband and wife now aged 41 and 33 respectively married in July 1965—two children a girl of eight and a boy of four and a half years—parties separated in 1976 and decree made in early 1977—husband earned £70 per week and now lived in rented accommodation as a protected tenant—wife lived at matrimonial home with children and had a considerable earning capacity but was not working at the moment—house valued at £14,000 with equity of £9,500 and there was an insurance policy for husband for £4,500 (to cover the mortgage on the house) present surrender value of which was £1,000—registrar ordered £15 per week for the wife and £6 per week for each child and ordered that house be sold but not until youngest child attained 18 or the wife remarried or started cohabiting with another man—judge varied order and ordered that parties should hold property as trustees for sale on trust for themselves and their children as tenants in common, power of sale (unless otherwise agreed) not to be exercised until youngest child attained 18 or wife remarried or started to cohabit with another man—wife's appeal and husband's cross-appeal allowed—wife to have house subject to mortgage and subject to a charge of £4,500 not to be exercised until certain usual events. October 24, 1978. HOMES v. HOMES.

128. Husband and wife, now aged 51 and 54 respectively, married in August 1950—two children, boy aged 16, who had left school and was in employment, and girl now aged 14 years—in June 1975 husband left and in July 1977 wife obtained a decree nisi on the ground of husband's adultery with co-respondent, M, who was aged 38 with two children, boy of 13 and girl of 11 (partially maintained by their father) by a former marriage, and whom the husband married in February 1978—matrimonial home bought in joint names for £11,500 and now valued at between £52,000 to £55,000 with equity of £48,000 at least— husband bought new house with M in joint names for £20,500 and equity in new house was £5,000, half of which belonged to husband—husband also had investment of £1,000 in a building society and an insurance policy with a surrender value of £1,700—wife earned £40 per week as part-time secretary and M earned £10 per week doing similar work—husband capable

of earning some £8,000 per annum—judge ordered that matrimonial home be sold immediately and a lump sum of £32,500 be paid out of proceeds of sale to wife—*Goodfield* v. *Goodfield* (June 19, 1975; unreported); *Martin* v. *Martin* [1978] C.L.Y. 2343—wife's appeal allowed—house to be sold in January 1983 (after youngest child had attained 18) and husband to have charge of two-fifths of net proceeds of sale. November 15, 1978. BLEZARD *v.* BLEZARD.

129. —— —— exclusion of husband

Parties met in 1975 and married in August 1977 when husband was 55 and wife 35 years old—husband had several children from before but only one boy, 15 years old, was being looked after by him—wife had two children from before, a girl and a boy aged 11 and five years respectively—they lived in council accommodation but in December 1977 purchased a new house together —trouble in the family caused by jealousy of a Miss Murray, who was the mother of a child by the husband—husband's boy taken into care and mother started proceedings for judicial separation and refused to allow husband into the new house—allegations of violence not decided on by judge who, *inter alia*, dismissed the wife's cross-application to exclude husband from the matrimonial home—wife's appeal dismissed. June 7, 1978. WILLIAMSON *v.* WILLIAMSON.

130. Parties married in 1960—two children, both boys aged 16 and 15, with whom the wife continued to live in the matrimonial home paying the mortgage repayments and outgoings on the house which was in parties' joint names— marriage dissolved in 1977 on wife's petition alleging unreasonable behaviour —in September 1976 husband undertook, *inter alia*, not to molest wife and children and to restrict himself in the use of the house—husband seldom used house but wife applied to exclude him altogether alleging bad behaviour which upset her and the children when he did visit—wife's previous application to commit husband for breach of undertaking had been dismissed—wife's present application dismissed—wife's appeal dismissed—judge properly of view that incidents alleged insufficient to justify excluding husband from house altogether. June 12, 1978. GOODRIDGE *v.* GOODRIDGE.

131. Parties married in 1952—four children, a girl and two boys, all aged over 18 and away from home, and younger boy, D, now aged 12 years—in March 1978 wife left taking D and went to live with her sister—she petitioned for divorce on the ground of the husband's behaviour and applied to exclude him from the matrimonial home which belonged to him—various allegations of violence against husband—judge concluded, *inter alia*, that there was no real danger of violence to the wife and refused to continue an injunction obtained *ex parte* by the wife against molestation and which restrained the husband from entering the matrimonial home—wife's appeal dismissed—observation that wrong for a boy of 12 to be called to give evidence against his father in a case of this character. June 15, 1978, H. *v.* H.

132. Parties married in November 1959—four children, two girls aged 18 and 16, and two boys aged 12 and 9 years—matrimonial home a maisonette council accommodation, comprising three bedrooms—in May 1978 wife left and petitioned for divorce alleging unreasonable conduct, including serious violence throughout the marriage—five specific allegations of violence since December 1977—husband in bad health suffering from high blood pressure and had had at least three heart attacks—judge refused to order husband out of matrimonial house—wife's appeal allowed—situation of wife and children with husband ought not to be allowed to continue. June 19, 1978. FOLEY *v.* FOLEY.

133. Parties married in June 1974—two children, girl and boy now aged two and just one year—in June 1977 wife petitioned for divorce on ground of unreasonable behaviour and applied for an order, *inter alia*, excluding husband from matrimonial home—judge made order excluding husband till hearing of action in July 1977—two reconciliations between the parties—in October 1977 undertakings given by husband to court—in June 1978 wife applied to commit husband for contempt of court for being in breach of his undertakings—judge decided that wife had not made out a case for committal but had made out a case for excluding husband from matrimonial home and of his own motion ordered husband to leave matrimonial home within two days—husband's appeal allowed—order discharged—no motion before judge to exclude husband from matrimonial home. June 22, 1978. WATKINS *v.* WATKINS.

134. Parties married in 1949 and had three children, all now over 18—marriage dissolved in February 1978 on wife's petition alleging unreasonable behaviour—matrimonial home bought by husband in his sole name and mortgage instalments paid off by him—wife in good job but husband's work position uncertain—wife alleged having difficult time living with husband—no alternative accommodation available for wife—life for parties together intolerable or " impossible "—judge ordered husband to leave matrimonial home within six weeks of order—husband's appeal dismissed. June 30, 1978. BHAMRA *v.* BHAMRA.

135. Parties married in 1959 and had been living in England since 1962—husband was a professional psychologist with a private clinic at the matrimonial home—three children, the two younger children aged 16 and 14 lived in matrimonial home and attended day schools—in September 1977 wife filed petition for divorce—in May 1978 a consent order was made whereby the parties undertook not to molest or abuse each other—in June 1978 wife applied to court alleging breaches by husband of his undertakings—judge found that there was an impossible situation of antagonism and strain between the parties but found no violence and ordered the husband, *inter alia,* to leave the matrimonial home—husband's appeal that result of order would be to detriment of whole family because he was unable to work because of emotional turmoil resulting from situation dismissed. July 18, 1978. GILL *v.* GILL.

136. Parties, in their early middle ages, married in 1975—three children, all grown up and living away—wife applied for injunction excluding husband from matrimonial home alleging violence and constant drunkenness resulting in bad behaviour—husband denied allegations—judge found no violence on part of husband but found that there was much tension between parties and accordingly continued on certain undertakings an injunction requiring husband to leave matrimonial home within 28 days—wife's appeal that husband should leave forthwith dismissed. September 1, 1978. MCKINNON *v.* MCKINNON.

137. In 1973 matrimonial home was transferred into the parties' joint names from husband's sole name—in April 1975 wife left and parties thereafter lived apart—in June 1978 wife obtained an *ex parte* order from judge that husband admit her back into matrimonial home, wife having nowhere to live—matrimonial home let off in flats and rooms and husband retained only two rooms for his own occupation—proceedings for judicial separation long pending—impossible " highly provocative, highly explosive " situation between parties and wife got hurt in a quarrel—judge ordered wife to leave—wife's application for leave to appeal out of time dismissed—only practical solution was to dissolve marriage as soon as possible and for a property adjustment order to be made. October 3, 1978. RUDOWSKI *v.* RUDOWSKA.

138. Parties married in September 1962—four children, boy aged 18 (not living with parents) and two girls aged 16 and seven and a boy aged eight—in November 1977 wife petitioned for divorce on ground of conduct alleging, *inter alia*, violence and drinking to excess—husband had had drinking problem and wife since 1975 had had intermittent depressions and an anxiety state—husband carried on business as a self-employed builder and painter from matrimonial home—judge made order excluding husband from matrimonial home but made certain arrangements with regard to husband being able to carry on business from matrimonial home—husband's appeal that order made was wrong in all the circumstances dismissed. December 13, 1978. RELPH *v*. RELPH.

139. Parties married in March 1968—two children, boys, N born in February 1962 (of whom husband denied being father but was accepted as a member of family) and T born in March 1970—husband self-employed as a taxi-driver and wife worked as a clerical officer in civil service earning some £200 per month—matrimonial home a three-bedroomed house jointly owned—in June 1978 wife presented petition for divorce on ground of husband's conduct alleging certain acts of violence on her and N and sought custody and financial relief—negotiations between parties—judge granted wife injunction restraining husband from molesting or interfering with her but refused to make order that husband should vacate matrimonial home, judge having found that husband's presence in house constituted no danger to wife nor was it harmful to children—evidence—wife's appeal dismissed—inevitable strain on children by reason of breakdown of marriage but situation in matrimonial home not unbearable. December 18, 1978. LEWIS *v*. LEWIS.

140. Parties married in October 1953—two sons aged 23 and 20 still living at home but self-supporting—matrimonial home the usual three-bedroomed house —marriage broke up in 1977 and divorce proceedings pending—husband was associating with a lady who lived in a small flat with her children where it was said husband could not live—wife applied for order that husband (who occupied one bedroom) should leave house alleging various matters including that she was having to sleep in a double bed with her son of 20—whether fair, just and reasonable to exclude husband from house—husband's appeal allowed—situation one of mere inconvenience which could be ameliorated by a little goodwill within the family—intervention of court not really necessary. January 11, 1979. YOUNG *v*. YOUNG.

141. Parties married in October 1965—two children, girl and boy now aged 10 and eight—on November 26, 1978, wife left with children after two incidents of violence by husband when he kicked her out of bed and struck her after she had refused him sexual intercourse and had said that she had no feelings for him—wife lived at various addresses with friends in difficult circumstances—on November 28 wife petitioned on ground of unreasonable behaviour alleging violence (including two incidents above) and very same day applied for order that husband be excluded from matrimonial home (a three-bedroomed house owned by parties jointly and in which they had lived for over 10 years)—no previous approach or request to husband that he should leave matrimonial home—judge refused to order husband to vacate matrimonial home but made order, *inter alia*, against non-molestation—wife's appeal dismissed—observation on wife's making application on same day as petition presented and on material on which it was made. January 15, 1979. LACEY *v*. LACEY.

142. Long history of matrimonial difficulties and discord and of reconciliations —wife filed petition in 1973 on ground of unreasonable behaviour—withdrew it on a reconciliation—filed petition again in November 1978—shortly afterwards

judge restrained husband from, *inter alia*, assaulting or molesting wife or child of marriage, girl under 18, and from entering matrimonial home—power of arrest attached which came to an end after December 29—agreement by parties' solicitors purported to extend injunctions and power of arrest from December 1978 to February 1979—husband arrested by police as being in breach of injunctions because of presence in matrimonial home on December 29, 1978—in January 1979 judge discharged injunctions—wife's appeal allowed—new injunctions ordered—observation that injunctions should be drawn in clear terms both as to actions which are enjoined and as to dates between which injunction is to run. January 24, 1979. HEATON v. HEATON.

143. —— —— —— **welfare of children**

Parties married in March 1955 when husband was 22 and wife 20 years of age—three children, boy aged 16 and two girls aged 12 and nine years—marriage dissolved by decree nisi in September 1978 on wife's petition which included allegations of violence and which was undefended—matrimonial home, a three-bedroomed house, bought in 1963, mortgage on which had been paid off—in October 1978 wife applied for injunctions against molestation and for husband's eviction from house and also applied for interim custody of children—whether wife suitable to have custody—judge declined to hear oral evidence because he thought that issues of custody and ouster were inextricably linked in this case and adjourned application pending an expedited welfare report with reference to the children—wife's appeal dismissed. December 19, 1978. SMITH v. SMITH.

144. —— —— **exclusion of wife**

Parties (both from West Indies) married in England in July 1961—10 children of whom five were grown up and other five ranged from 10½ to 16 years—matrimonial home a big house bought in 1965—trouble in marriage in 1976 and in February 1977 wife petitioned for divorce on the ground of husband's conduct—decree nisi in November 1977—in February 1978 custody application heard (after " a long, much too long an adjournment ") and judge gave custody of five children to father and made a local authority supervision order—both parties continued to live in matrimonial home—father found situation in matrimonial home intolerable and applied, *inter alia*, for an order that wife vacate matrimonial home—judge refused order sought by father—father's appeal allowed—mother's interest in matrimonial home protected by father undertaking not to dispose of house pending making of a property adjustment order. December 7, 1978. FOSTER v. FOSTER.

145. —— —— —— **interests of children**

Parties (both Nigerian) married in Nigeria in March 1973—husband was previously married and had lived in England for many years—two children, boy aged three years and girl aged nine months—matrimonial home comprising three floors bought by husband in his own name—in November 1977 wife left after a quarrel and returned in October 1978 and started living in top floor flat of matrimonial home—on January 23, 1979, judge ordered that wife, who had told an untruth about not being served with process, should leave matrimonial home by February 6 and should not molest husband—judge not informed of existence and situation of children, in particular that they were living with mother in top floor flat—mother's appeal allowed—new trial ordered. February 8, 1979. LATUNJI v. LATUNJI.

146. —— —— **respective shares**

Husband, an Italian doctor, and wife, English, married in October 1972—two children, boy and girl, now aged five and three years—in June 1975 parties finally separated—shortly afterwards wife presented petition for divorce on ground of unreasonable behaviour which was contested and was dismissed —matrimonial home bought in February 1975 and conveyed into parties' joint names as " beneficial joint tenants "—husband alleged in s. 17 proceedings that he was induced to convey the house into joint names by fraud in that marriage was, unknown to him, on verge of breakdown and that wife knew this but pretended that marriage was not unhappy and not on verge of breakdown— judge found against husband and held that parties had an equal share in property—husband's appeal dismissed. Appeal from Wood J. October 5, 1978. IRANI v. IRANI.

147. Parties married in August 1970—one child now just over three years old— by December 1976 marriage broke down and husband finally left under a court order in June 1977—wife (now aged 28 years) granted decree nisi in October 1977 and also given custody—only capital asset was matrimonial home (owned equally) bought in 1970 in husband's name on a 100 per cent. G.L.C. mortgage for £5,150 and now valued at £20,000; £782 of loan paid off—wife earned £50 per week gross from her full-time job and paid child-minder to look after child—husband earned £5,800 per annum gross as a car salesman and now lived in a flat bought on mortgage for £14,500—judge ordered that husband should transfer house to wife subject to a £3,000 charge and pay £700 lump sum in instalments of £5 per week—£6·50 per week paid to child under existing order—husband's appeal dismissed—wife's cross-appeal allowed—whole of husband's interest transferred to wife with no other claims by wife being made (wife to pay half of outstanding £980 loan owed by husband to bank). October 13, 1978. PAGE v. PAGE.

148. Parties, Sicilian by origin, married in Sicily in April 1968—two children, boy and girl, now aged nine and six years—matrimonial home bought in joint names in 1975 for £12,750 on a mortgage of £9,750, balance of £3,000 being paid out of joint savings—trouble in marriage—marriage eventually dissolved in March 1977 and care and control of children given to mother—house valued today at £14,750 with equity of £5,000—registrar transferred husband's interest in house to wife and ordered him to pay her £20 per week for herself and children—judge upheld order—realities of situation—husband's prospects of " ever touching a penny " of capital represented by house extremely remote —husband's fears that wife would sell house upon transfer to her and would leave for Sicily could be covered safely by immediate lump sum application by husband—husband's appeal dismissed. Appeal from Baker P. October 16, 1978. SCALA v. SCALA.

149. Parties married in 1964—two children, boys, now aged 14 and 10½ years— wife left with children in March 1977 and now lived with her quite old parents who helped, as best as they could, look after children—matrimonial home, bought on mortgage with a deposit of £1,000 provided by wife's parents, was now worth £28,000 with an equity of some £22,000—wife now unemployed but at time of registrar's order earned about £33 per week and got 50p per week for herself and £5 per week for each child from husband—husband was a painter and decorator and now lived at matrimonial home and his total earnings, including income of woman he was now living with, were quite substantial—registrar made a *Mesher* v. *Mesher* type of order—judge, however, ordered house to be sold and one half of proceeds of sale plus £1,000 to be paid to wife and rest to husband—wife's appeal allowed—*Mesher* v. *Mesher* type of order appropriate in present case. October 17, 1978. NICHOLSON v. NICHOLSON.

150. Husband and wife, now aged 41 and 34 years, married in September 1963 —two children, boys, now aged 11 and eight years parties separated and husband left in July 1976 and now lived in a one-room council flat—husband who suffered from multiple sclerosis was unemployed and was unlikely to be able to do any work in the future and lived on disability benefit and a mobility allowance—wife did part-time work but was partially dependent on the Supplementary Benefits Commission who paid her an allowance and also paid mortgage interest on matrimonial home—house bought in husband's sole name was now worth £14,500—registrar ordered husband to transfer house to wife absolutely, dismissed wife's claim for periodical payments and made a nominal order for maintenance of the children—judge (on appeal) ordered house to be transferred to wife subject to a charge of 20 per cent. of net proceeds of sale— wife's appeal allowed and, on basis of wife's offer, house transferred to wife absolutely on her paying to husband a sum of £1,000—husband's cross-appeal dismissed. October 19, 1978. HYLAND v. HYLAND.

151. Husband and wife now aged 50 and 48 years married in May 1960 having lived together for some time before marriage—six children, four over 18 and the other two, boy and girl, now aged 15 and 11 years—second eldest child still lived at home and contributed to the family budget from his £2,300 per annum earnings—trouble in marriage in March 1974 and husband left under court order in June 1976 and decree nisi granted in June 1977 but not yet made absolute—only capital asset was matrimonial home which was now valued at £15,500 with a " protected tenant " in it but £19,000 without—exact status of tenant not yet clear—net equity in house £9,500—both parties worked and contributed to family budget during marriage—husband earned £56 per week gross and wife £31 per week gross (£26 net) and she also received £2·50 per week child benefit and £3·50 per week family income supplement and £12 per week maintenance by husband for two youngest children—tenant paid her £8 per week—judge ordered, inter alia, that house be held on trust for sale (sale postponed) and upon sale proceeds to be divided as to one-third to wife and two-thirds to husband—wife's appeal allowed—division to be 50/50 and order of judge varied in other respects also (judge having been misled by s. 17 approach). Appeal from Reeve J. October 19, 1978. RICHMOND v. RICHMOND.

152. Parties married in July 1961—three children now aged 16, 15 and 11 years —in July 1976 wife committed adultery with co-respondent and husband was granted decree absolute on ground of adultery in September 1976—wife continued association with co-respondent but likelihood of her marriage to him was remote at moment because co-respondent's wife was not willing to divorce him—husband remarried a woman who had available a substantial sum of money following her own divorce to be able to buy a house with comparatively small mortgage—matrimonial home was bought in 1955 for £14,000 and now had an equity of about £10,000—wife earned £3,400 per annum gross and there was an interim order for £7·50 per week for each child against the husband—registrar ordered house to be sold immediately and proceeds divided equally but judge (on appeal) ordered, inter alia, that proceeds should be held on trust for wife to be used for purchase of a house for wife and children— husband's appeal dismissed. October 23, 1978. JENKIN v. JENKIN.

153. Parties married in June 1963—two children, girl and boy now aged 14 and 11 years—in June 1976 husband started association with another woman which still continued—decree nisi on ground of adultery granted to wife in November 1977—matrimonial home now worth £7,000—husband, now aged 38 years, earned some £51 per week and wife, now aged 33 years, earned some £16 per week—£6 per week for wife and £7 per week for each child interim main-

tenance order against husband—judge under misapprehension that application before him was for an injunction ousting husband from matrimonial home (instead of for a property adjustment order) and ordered, *inter alia*, that house be held on trust for parties as tenants in common and that it be available for use by them both—wife's appeal allowed—house to be transferred to wife absolutely but her periodical payments order of £6 per week reduced to a nominal sum. October 25, 1978. MERCER *v.* MERCER.

154. Landlord and Tenant—agreement—whether tenancy or licence

Plaintiff, parish priest of St. Michael's Roman Catholic Church, sought possession of parish hall against first defendant, secretary of St. Michael's Catholic Church Social Club, and second defendant, Social Club itself—" considerable confusion as to who are the parties "—agreement in question in common landlord and tenant terms—parish hall under day-to-day administration of parish priest and defendants' occupation was a " few days during a few hours of the week "—whether agreement really created an enforceable tenancy agreement between parties—*Clore and Theatrical Properties Ltd.* v. *Westby & Co.* [1936] 3 All E.R. 483—judge concluded that only a licence had been created and granted plaintiff possession—defendants' appeal dismissed—" plainly a licence " created between parties. January 16, 1979. AYLWARD *v.* GALLAGHER.

155. —— business tenancy—possession

In October 1975 plaintiffs granted a lease to first defendants for a period of 20 years at a rent of £11,500 per annum payable quarterly in advance on usual quarter days—defendants fell into arrears with one-quarter's rent due in June 1977 (£2,875) and plaintiffs obtained judgment for that rent but judgment never satisfied—following two quarters' rent not paid and on December 29, 1977, plaintiffs issued writ claiming possession and £5,750 arrears of rent plus interest —in R.S.C., Ord. 14, proceedings master gave defendants unconditional leave to defend in respect of possession claim but gave plaintiffs summary judgment for money claimed—whether plaintiffs had waived right of forfeiture of lease by claiming rent in respect of period part of which had still to run—judge (on appeal) held that plaintiffs were entitled to summary judgment which included an order for possession—defendants' appeal dismissed. January 19, 1979. JOPATE ESTATES *v.* BLM ADVERTISING.

156. —— covenant—implied covenant

Defendant left premises, a warehouse, let to him by plaintiff at a rent of £50 per month, without informing plaintiff that he was leaving—plaintiff visited premises two months later and found that premises had been damaged and left in a dirty condition—judge gave judgment for plaintiff for £374 damages for breach of implied covenant to yield up premises in good and tenantable repair and dismissed defendant's counterclaim for work claimed to be done to premises —defendant's (in person) appeal dismissed; no note of judge's judgment present. December 19, 1978. ELLEY *v.* LEADEHAM.

157. —— licence—contractual licence—termination

Plaintiff brought an action for damages alleging that she had been wrongfully turned out of a hostel, owned by the third defendants, the London Hostels Association, on June 18, 1977, she having peacefully lived in hostels owned by the third defendants for six years—defendants pleaded that the provision of board and lodging for the plaintiff was subject to the conditions of admission of the third defendants and that plaintiff's contract was validly terminated by one week's written notice in accordance with the conditions—plaintiff's case that defendants gave no notice or had failed to prove that they gave notice—registrar and judge found in favour of defendants—plaintiff's (in person) appeal dismissed. December 18, 1978. BOTELHO v. GROVE.

158. —— possession—breach of covenant

On June 22, 1977, plaintiff landlords served on defendant tenant notice under s. 146 of Law of Property Act 1925 alleging breaches of two covenants of defendant's 21-year lease (from September 1971) of business premises—second breach alleged was that covenant not to assign, etc., premises had been broken in that defendant " had underlet and/or parted with and/or shared possession and/or occupation " of premises with P Ltd. —on August 5 plaintiffs issued writ—judge (allowing appeal from master) held that plaintiffs were entitled to summary judgment for possession under R.S.C., Ord. 14, and refused defendant relief from forfeiture under R.S.C., Ord. 14, r. 10—whether, *inter alia*, s. 146, notice gave insufficient time to remedy breaches—whether waiver by plaintiffs of right to obtain order for possession because of their " without prejudice " letter in March 1978 asserting wish to have rent review carried out under lease—whether judge wrong in failing to consider nature of occupancy of P Ltd.—defendant's appeal dismissed. November 9, 1978. ROYAL EXCHANGE ASSURANCE v. BELL.

159. —— —— calculation of mesne profits

Plaintiffs let premises to first defendant (second and third defendants being guarantors) for 20 years from March 25, 1975—rent payable quarterly in advance and on a rising basis—lease forfeited on May 21, 1977, for non-payment of rent payable on March 25, 1977, namely, £5,000 in advance, down to June 24, 1977—plaintiffs given judgment for possession and for £5,000 due in March and unpaid, and for mesne profits to be assessed—first defendants vacated premises on September 13, 1977—whether mesne profits should be calculated (i) at contractual rate of £20,000 per annum or at market rate current at time of forfeiture; (ii) from May 21 (date of forfeiture) or from June 24 (end of quarterly period)—master assessed mesne profits on basis of contractual rate as from June 24—*Ellis* v. *Rowbotham* [1900] 1 Q.B. 740—appeal dismissed. January 11, 1979. M. BLOOM (KOSHER) & SON v. HARBAX METROPOLITAN PROPERTIES.

160. —— —— signature on document

Judge ordered, *inter alia,* that plaintiffs should recover from the defendants possession of certain premises occupied by them, having found that a certain document, upon which the case turned, was indeed signed by the defendant and his wife and that the document had not been altered after their signatures had been appended thereto (contrary to the allegations by defendants)—first defendant's (in person) appeal dismissed. November 8, 1978. FIRST NATIONAL SECURITIES v. MICHAEL.

161. —— —— suspension of possession order

Defendant had a service tenancy of premises, of which the plaintiff company was landlord, since 1955—in 1969 his employment ended but he continued to occupy premises but was not a " very good payer of rent "—notices to quit for non-payment of rent served on defendant in 1972, 1973, 1974, 1975, 1977 and 1978 plus numerous demands for payment—order for possession made in 1976 which led to issue of warrants in 1976 and 1977 but defendant paid up day before execution was due—in April 1978 judge made an order, *inter alia,* for possession, suspended for 28 days and for so long thereafter as the defendant punctually paid the arrears of rent and costs in addition to the current rent and "judgment shall cease to be enforceable when the arrears of rent, mesne profits and costs are satisfied"—Rent Act 1977, ss. 98, 100—plaintiff landlord's appeal dismissed. November 13, 1978. R. DURTNELL & SONS v. SMITH.

162. —— —— trespasser

Plaintiff, acting on behalf of the President of the Family Division (in whom the property of a Mrs. Figg vested in March 1976 when she died intestate, with no heirs and no next-of-kin), was granted possession of the property against the defendant who had no status in relation to the property—defendant's (in person) appeal, on ground, *inter alia*, that he was in possession before the plaintiff's title had been established in law, dismissed. July 5, 1978. SOLICITOR FOR THE AFFAIRS OF H.M. TREASURY v. HAYDEN.

163. —— rent—review

Question in issue was in respect of a review clause in lease which gave plaintiff landlords (defendant being tenant) right to have a review of rent after first seven years of lease—not found necessary by appeal court to set out facts—whether a document dated March 17, 1976, constituted a notice to tenant for purposes of putting into operation machinery laid down in lease with regard to rent review—whether defendant's solicitors by their conduct had put themselves in a position where they could not deny that there remained here a right on part of plaintiffs to have a review carried out by independent arbitration—master decided in favour of defendant—plaintiffs' appeal dismissed. November 3, 1978. FRANKLIN v. SCHWARTZ.

164. —— —— unpaid rent—rent restrictions

On June 13, 1958, defendants granted lease of business premises to plaintiff company for a term of 14 years commencing on June 24, 1958, and expiring on June 23, 1972, at yearly rent of £2,500 payable quarterly in arrear—in December 1971 plaintiffs served notice requesting new tenancy commencing from June 24, 1972, at increased rent of £11,000 a year—negotiations for new tenancy terms of which were eventually agreed on December 19, 1972—new lease executed on March 23, 1973, whereby defendants leased premises to plaintiffs for a term of 17 years from June 24, 1972, at yearly rent of £17,500 payable quarterly in arrear—defendants claimed for some £33,411 unpaid rent in certain proceedings started by plaintiffs—Counter Inflation (Temporary Provisions) Act 1972 and Counter Inflation (Business Rents) Order 1972, regs. 2 (2), 3—effect of regulations in respect of period from December 1, 1972, to March 19, 1975—"standard rate" of rent—rate or rent payable under tenancy on November 5, 1972—*Secretary of State for Social Services* v. *Rosetti Lodge Investment Co.* [1975] C.L.Y. 1851 and *Tavistock Developments* v. *Bankes Woods & Partners* [1974] C.L.Y. 2056 distinguished—defendants' appeal dismissed. Appeal from Walton J. December 8, 1978. PIRO SHOES v. BENNETT.

165. —— tenancy agreement—construction

In 1961 plaintiff became the tenant of the ground floor flat of a semi-detached house signing a printed form, meant really to be used in relation to a conventional block of flats and not in relation to flats in a semi-detached house—in 1969 the defendant obtained a lease of the upper flat—whether words "and premises" in the parcels of the plaintiff's tenancy agreement meant to include, *inter alia*, the back garden and the front garden of the house—judge regarded words, upon the facts of this case, as pure surplusage—plaintiff's appeal dismissed. June 15, 1978. MODY v. GOGARTY.

166. —— unlawful eviction

Plaintiff claimed damages for unlawful eviction and for the return of personal effects said to have been seized by the defendant—judgment given in favour of defendant in December 1976—plaintiff's (in person) " two-year old " appeal dismissed—explanation of why appeal had taken so long to come on to be heard was that documents required for hearing of appeal not produced by plaintiff. December 18, 1978. BAIDEN v. CHABRA.

167. —— wrongful eviction—evidence

Plaintiff brought an action against defendants for damages for, *inter alia*, wrongful eviction claiming he was a tenant of defendants—defendants denied (but later conceded) wrongful eviction and alleged, *inter alia*, that plaintiff was not a tenant—judge accepted plaintiff's evidence and found in his favour and awarded damages of £1,000 in all—defendants' (in person) appeal that judgment was against weight of evidence dismissed. June 30, 1978. DECKER v. OLAJIDE.

168. Loans—nature of loan—whether moneylending transaction

Plaintiffs claimed possession of a house against the defendant and moneys said to be due under a legal charge said to be assigned to the plaintiffs— legal charge was in respect of a loan of £5,800 alleged to be made by another company to enable the defendant to buy the freehold of the house, where she was already a tenant—defendant claimed that a moneylending transaction was made, that in truth the money was lent by the plaintiffs, and that the plaintiffs not being registered moneylenders, the charge was void or unenforceable because of the Moneylenders Acts—judge found in favour of the defendant and granted, on defendant's counterclaim, a declaration that the charge was unenforceable and should be delivered up for cancellation—plaintiffs' appeal dismissed. May 26, 1978. LINVALIAN v. MITCHELL.

169. Minors—access

Parties married in January 1972 having met in 1969 but mother having been then married but divorced in 1971 shortly after birth of their elder child—two children, a boy and a girl now eight and three years old respectively—mother suffered bad health, with treatment in hospital as an out-patient, because of excessive drinking and taking of drugs—in June 1975 father left but returned in December for an attempted reconciliation which was unsuccessful—in April 1976 mother attempted suicide and was taken into hospital for psychiatric treatment—she was discharged in February 1977, had had no relapse and was capable of caring for the children—marriage dissolved in March 1978 on mother's cross-petition on grounds of cruelty and adultery and custody was given to father with certain regular access to mother—mother's appeal that access should be more frequent dismissed—judge came to entirely right con- clusion—bringing of appeals against access orders in these circumstances deprecated. April 26, 1978. WINFIELD v. WINFIELD.

170. Parties married in September 1973 and separated in March 1976—one child, a boy, now two and a half years old—mother granted a decree nisi on ground of father's behaviour in July 1977—decree absolute in August 1977— custody given to mother living at her parents' home—visiting access by father did not go smoothly; father behaved badly and convicted of assault and given conditional discharge—in May 1978 judge gave father staying access on alternate weekends with conditions attached—mother's appeal that it was premature at this stage to grant staying access now, having regard to the history, dismissed. May 11, 1978. KETTLE v. KETTLE.

171. Mother, who had been separated from father for a long time, obtained injunction preventing father having any contact with children—younger child, a boy, run over and was lying unconscious in hospital since May 24—on June 28 judge granted father access—mother's appeal dismissed—extraordinary appeal, a most blatant waste of public money. July 19, 1978. GEORGE v. GEORGE.

172. Parents married in December 1969—two children, boy and girl now aged six and seven years—in November 1975 wife petitioned on the ground of husband's adultery and marriage was dissolved in December 1976—mother should have care and control and father access once a week—in July 1976 there was a snatching episode by the father, and children, in particular the girl, refused to see him—supervised access given to father in December 1976 proved unsuccessful—father, now married, had not seen children for some two years and applied for access—judge directed that children be committed to care of local council and that requirements of the Matrimonial Causes Rules 1977, r. 93 (1), be dispensed with and gave father substantial staying access—mother's appeal allowed—care order discharged and no suggestion that children not being cared for in way they should—access orders discharged— Official Solicitor appointed as guardian *ad litem* of children. August 10, 1978. R. v. R.

173. Father and mother married in February 1964 when they were aged 32 and 24 years respectively—one child, a boy, now aged just nine years—father a bookmaker and mother a fashion model who had been previously married—mother petitioned for divorce in November 1970 and obtained decree nisi in March 1971 and custody was given to her—she remarried a rich and successful man soon afterwards and had two girls now aged six and four years by third marriage—father saw boy frequently—in May 1977 mother stopped access alleging bad behaviour by father—no welfare report yet available—father had a long and serious record of criminal activities, convictions and sentences of imprisonment and had been living a dishonest life for at least 25 years—possibility of father being sent to prison early in New Year—boy in boarding preparatory school and had no knowledge of father's real way of life—judge ordered limited and qualified access to father—mother's appeal allowed—Official Solicitor appointed as guardian *ad litem* and matter transferred to High Court. October 18, 1978. B. v. G.

174. Parents married in June 1970—one child a girl born in December 1970 and now aged eight years—in December 1973 mother left with child alleging violence by father—father had access in 1974 but from September 1975 child had not seen father—mother had remarried and had another child by second marriage—settled family unit of mother, her second husband and two children —whether in best interests of child to re-start access by father after lapse of more than three and a half years—little or no effort by father to see child— child had very hazy recollection of father and had come to regard mother's second husband her father—judge ordered that there should be no access by father and discharged earlier order made at time of decree nisi—father's appeal dismissed—order varied to read there should be no access by father until further order. December 20, 1978. BLACKWELL v. BROWN.

175. —— —— **appeal out of time against access order**

Mother applied for leave to appeal out of time against an order for access made in November 1977—mother adopted a policy of non-co-operation with the court and had succeeded in defeating order of court made in November 1977 and father finally issued summons for contempt of court—mother's application unmeritorious and dismissed—however, essential to hear evidence relating to what had happened to children over year and therefore welfare report ordered with appropriate steps to be taken thereafter. October 9, 1978. WILSON v. LONG.

176. —— —— " artificial insemination " baby

Mother, now aged 21, agreed with father, in return for a substantial sum of money, to be artificially impregnated with father's semen to produce a baby which would then be handed over to father and the lady with whom he was living (and whom he later married) and who could have no more children of her own—mother changed her mind about handing over baby during pregnancy—child born in July 1977—wide gulf socially and culturally between mother and father—judge took view that it was almost inconceivable that child should ever be handed over to care of father, given character of parties —judge gave care and control to mother and gave father access and made a supervision order in favour of the local authority—mother's appeal against giving father access allowed—*J*. v. *C.* [1969] C.L.Y. 1802—no good keeping wholly artificial and painful tie going—only possible solution that there be no access by father henceforward. Appeal from Comyn J. July 18, 1978. *Re* A MINOR; A. *v.* C.

177. —— —— attracting penal notices to access orders

Father and mother now aged 39 and 37 married in July 1961—four children, all boys, now aged 15, 12½, nine and five—in October 1976 mother left to live with a Mr. P to whom she was now married—home of four children always with father who gave up his employment to look after them—difficulties with access which proved unsuccessful because of attitude of two elder boys— matter of custody never raised—judge made order providing both visiting and staying access by all four children and attached penal notices to it—father's appeal that wrong to order access in respect of the two elder boys allowed— penal notice to be omitted from order—observations on attaching penal notices to access orders. January 26, 1979. LOW *v.* PORTER.

178. —— —— hearing

Parents married in December 1961—two children, boys now aged 12 and nine years—in August 1975 mother left taking boys and now lived in a council house with boys—father had regular access until December 1975 when father petitioned for divorce on the ground of adultery and applied for custody— in February 1976 father was given defined access on undertaking not to bring boys into contact with family of Mrs. M, whom he had now married, and custody matter was stood over for welfare officer's report—report favourable of mother and recommended regular access by father—father failed to follow recommendation and last saw children in December 1976 when there was trouble because of Mrs. M—in June 1978 the judge varied previous order without hearing mother or anyone on her behalf—mother's appeal allowed— mother ought to have been given an adjournment and opportunity of appearing —new trial ordered. July 13, 1978. MURRELLS *v.* MURRELLS.

179. —— —— interim custody

Two children, boy and girl, now aged nine and four-and-a-half-years— parents married in May 1969—mother had two children by previous marriages, girls now aged 17 and 13—younger girl T accepted into family as a member but father and T at loggerheads for many years—mother's petition for divorce filed in February 1978 on ground of unreasonable behaviour, a large proportion

of the allegations centring upon difficulties between father and T—" appalling "
effect upon children of bickering and upleasantness between father and mother
—judge awarded interim custody to mother and ordered father to vacate
matrimonial home and made complicated order giving father staying access—
mother's appeal on access only allowed—father to have no access at least
until Christmas—father's cross-appeal dismissed—hearing of suit as soon as
possible highly desirable. July 25, 1978. GUTH v. GUTH.

180. Parents married in May 1971—father, Jugoslav, had lived in England for
many years, while mother, French, had lived in England since marriage—one
child now aged six years—in November 1977 parents separated when mother
took child and went to live in France—difficulties in access—in May 1978
mother filed petition for divorce—petition to be defended by father—in
August 1978 judge ordered that child be returned to England and placed in
interim custody of father—no evidence of arrangements for child—mother's
appeal allowed—child not to be removed from mother's custody without
further order. August 17, 1978. M v. M.

181. —— —— transvestite father

Parents married in 1961—three children, girls now aged 12, 10 and eight years
—marriage reasonably happy until February 1977 when father told mother by
letter that he had been a transvestite for a long time—in May 1977 father left
and in June mother obtained a decree nisi of divorce, petition being undefended,
on the ground of behaviour alleging that father was a transexual and intended
to dress and live as a woman—custody granted to mother and mother agreed
to keep father informed of children's progress—father had not seen children to
speak to since he left—father intended when he left to have genital surgery and
live and function as a female but said he would not do so in order to see
children—guarded prognosis by doctor that father made a stupendous effort to
overcome his transexual compulsion—welfare reports present—father's application for access refused—father's appeal dismissed. Appeal from Dunn J. June 16,
1978. M. v. M.

182. —— adoption—consent of natural parent to adoption

Boy, A, born in December 1971 and now seven years—natural father and
mother, now aged 33 and 30, married in 1967 and A was their only child—
adoptive parents, Mr. and Mrs. W, now aged 58 and 47, married in 1969 and
lived with their own son aged 15, two teenage sons of Mrs. W's previous
marriage, and daughter aged 17 of Mr. W's previous marriage—in November
1972 A was admitted to hospital—doctor reported that A had " been subject of
severe and repeated assaults over a period of some three weeks prior to admission "—place of safety order made in December 1972 and A was placed in
interim care of Mr. and Mrs. W (who were approved foster parents)—in
February 1973 a full care order made—natural parents had fortnightly access
—visits became less frequent and eventually stopped because of bad effect on
A—report of social worker—in October 1977 Mr. and Mrs. W gave notice of
intention to adopt A—judge concluded that there had been "persistent ill
treatment " of A by natural parents and made adoption order in favour of
Mr. and Mrs. W—Children Act 1975, s. 12 (2)—natural parents' appeal
dismissed. January 22, 1979. Re A. (A MINOR).

183. —— —— future security of children—consent of natural parent

Two children, girl and boy, born June 1973 and June 1974 respectively—
natural mother, now aged 25, lived with father from 1972 onwards—unfortunate
and mistaken association as father gave very little help to children and mother

and in 1975 abandoned mother leaving her penniless and in debt—mother left children with neighbour to follow father who was later imprisoned within weeks neighbour put children into care of local authority (and care order made in due course under s. 1 of Children and Young Persons Act 1969) and children placed with foster parents, adoptive parents, with whom children had now been for nearly four years—in 1976 mother returned and moved to father's parents' house, formed association with father's father (aged in advanced 60's), moved out with him, gave birth to his child in April 1977 and in September 1977 married him—adoption applications by foster parents—mother failed to get care orders discharged and recognised (on appeal) that children should spend childhood years with adoptive parents—judge held that mother was unreasonably withholding consent to adoption and made adoption orders dispensing with mother's consent stating that no other course would give sufficient security to children and adoptive parents—whether interim custody order more suitable—Children Act 1975, s. 19—mother's appeal dismissed. February 14, 1979. *Re S.* (MINORS).

184. —— **custody**

Parents married in September 1970 when father was 20 and mother 19 years old—three children, two boys aged six and five, and a girl aged two years—marriage soon became unhappy and parents separated in April 1977, wife having formed an association with another man—neither party remarried but mother contemplating marrying man with whom she was now associating—each parent agreed that other perfectly able to look after children but mother unable to get on with the two boys—judge awarded joint custody with care and control to father and reasonable access to mother—mother's appeal that she should have care and control of girl only dismissed. April 14, 1978. JOHNSON *v.* JOHNSON.

185. Parties married in September 1960 when father was 34 and wife 23 years old—three children, two boys aged 15 and 10 years and a girl 13 years old—father finally left in October 1976—various allegations by parties against each other including drunkenness and adultery but husband refused to accede to cross-decrees in divorce—access worked well until about July 1977 when children refused to go and see father because they said he had been dictatorial towards them—no access between December 1977 and March 1978 when judge gave custody to father with access to mother—matters giving rise to dislike of father by children—mother's appeal allowed—wrong and an act of gratuitous cruelty to order children to be under the care (at any rate at present) of their father—children wanted to be with mother—judge fell into trap of concentrating on the question of who was responsible for the breakdown of access—custody care and control to mother with access to father with supervision order. April 20, 1978. HARRIS *v.* HARRIS.

186. Mother and father, now 31 and 51 years old respectively, married in April 1967—two children, twin girls, now eight years old—father previously married (previous wife died in 1965) and had four children by that marriage, all boys aged 27, 24, 18 and 14, the two eldest being married—mother previously married and had a 13-year-old boy by that marriage—all children living with parties—in December 1975 mother left taking her 13-year-old boy with her and went to live with a married man, aged 38, separated from his wife, and in October 1976 had a boy by him—marriage dissolved in 1977—no allegations by parties against each other as to children—although children had been living with father, very generous access was given to mother—children equally happy at either parent's home—judge gave custody to mother on basis that children

of this age should as a general rule be with mother—father's appeal dismissed. April 24, 1978. ALDER v. ALDER.

187. Parties married in July 1956—three children, a boy and two girls, the youngest girl being six years old now and the subject-matter of the appeal—in December 1973 mother left taking girl with her and went to live with the co-respondent to whom she was now married—shortly afterwards she returned the girl to the father—in March 1974 the marriage was dissolved on father's petition and joint custody of boy and girl was granted with care and control to the father—in March 1975 father remarried a widow with three children aged seven, six and four years—in December 1975 boy went to stay with mother and in May 1977 a consent order was made committing his custody to mother—favourable reports on respective households, mother's household being a public-house run together with her husband's parents—judge gave custody to mother and refused stay of execution—unpleasant scene created during child's handing over—traumatic experience for child—course taken by judge open to criticism but best interests of child served by her remaining now with mother—father's appeal dismissed. April 26, 1978. BEAUCHAMP v. PENHALLOW.

188. Parents married in May 1956—only child, a girl, born in January 1966—baby unwelcome as parents were not expecting to have the baby and mother particularly felt " tied down "—relationship between parties deteriorated and in 1973 divorce by consent was granted, parties having lived apart for two years—custody, care and control given to mother by consent—no relationship between father (who remarried in December 1973) and child for many years but in 1975 they had a successful holiday for three weeks—in 1975 social workers observed that mother and child " did not get on " and recommended specialised thera-peutic care for child in an environment away from the mother—child sent to establishment run by Dr. Barnardo's Homes and mother went to Persia for two years with a man with whom she had started going out—in May 1977 father discovered fully the situation and applied for a variation of the custody order—court welfare and other reports present—long county court hearing—educa-tional psychologist report presented to court at a late juncture making it imprac-ticable for father's legal advisers to test validity of views expressed therein—judge refused to vary the order—father's appeal allowed—child to go to live with father at earliest convenient date in the ordinary home environment with an affectionate and responsible father and step-mother anxious to play her part. May 12, 1978. W. v. W.

189. Father and mother, now 32 and 40 years old respectively, married in January 1971—one child, a girl, now nearly seven years old—in October 1975 mother left to live with a divorced man leaving girl behind—girl put in charge of father's parents and lived with them happily until Christmas 1977 when she went to live with father and a woman, C, whom he intended to marry and her eight-year-old boy from her former marriage and another boy now aged five months born to father and C—in February 1976 the magistrates gave custody to father with care and control to his parents—on May 2, 1978, after a hearing lasting no longer than an hour and a half, with interruptions, the judge gave custody to mother—father's appeal allowed—no real reasons given by judge—serious doubts about mother's position—new trial ordered before judge of Family Division. May 24, 1978. YOXALL v. YOXALL.

190. Parties married in September 1969 when both were aged 22—two children, boys aged seven and three years—the husband committed adultery with a Mrs. B and the wife left finally in October 1977 to live with her mother and pre-

sented a petition for judicial separation—council house available to wife if custody granted to her—husband's house included Mrs. B and her two children, boys aged 10 and seven—mother remained in constant contact with the children —parties granted joint custody with care and control to mother—father's appeal dismissed. June 7, 1978. MACE v. MACE.

191. Parties married in June 1967—five children, three girls and two boys aged four to 10 years—boys, subject of the appeal, aged seven and six—youngest girl a spastic unable to look after herself at all—mother now lived in council accommodation with the girls, the two boys having been taken by father when mother, under stress, took an overdose of drugs in May 1977 and spent a fortnight in hospital—heavy burden of looking after five children—welfare reports present—judge gave custody to mother being satisfied that the mother was right when she said she was able to look after children notwithstanding the burden—father's appeal dismissed. June 8, 1978. BICKFORD v. BICKFORD.

192. Parties married in November 1963, the father and mother now being 41 and 35 years of age respectively—three children, all girls aged 14, 13 and eight years —in May 1972 mother left and in August 1972 father obtained custody in the magistrates' court—in June 1977 father obtained decree nisi of divorce on the ground of a separation of more than five years—mother had regular access to the children including staying access at Christmas 1977—father's mother aged 60 gave some help to father with the children—father and children lived in three-bedroomed house bought by father on mortgage—in early 1978 father became engaged to marry a Mrs. Thompson, who had a daughter aged 13 and a son aged nine, but children were unhappy about it—mother lived in a flat in a " deprived area," but hoped to get council accommodation—welfare reports present—judge gave custody to mother with a supervision order hoping that parties would arrange wide and generous access—judge refused to grant a certificate of satisfaction with the arrangements—father's appeal dismissed. June 8, 1978. HEWITSON v. HEWITSON.

193. Parties married in October 1971 after having lived together for 11 years— two children, girls now aged 13 and 10 years—mother had two children from an association with another man, both girls now aged 20 and 18 years—in June 1973 magistrates found proved wife's complaint that husband guilty of persistent cruelty and granted custody to her—in June 1974 wife obtained council accommodation and moved to live there together with the four children—in March 1975 she presented a petition for divorce on the ground of unreasonable behaviour—in July 1975 the children of the marriage returned to live with father—wife's eldest girl had had two illegitimate children before she was 17— judge held that although both parents able adequately to look after children, the permissiveness in the wife's home was not suitable for children and gave custody to father—mother's appeal that not sufficient weight attached to children's wishes to be with her dismissed. June 13, 1978. WILSON v. WILSON.

194. Parents, now in their early fifties, married in February 1956—four children, youngest a girl, now nearly 14 years old—in December 1977 marriage was dissolved on the basis of two years' separation and custody matter was adjourned for a welfare officer's report—parties continued to live under the same roof— youngest child better off emotionally with father—judge having seen and heard various people give evidence decided that custody should be with father but mother to have reasonable access at all times—mother's appeal dismissed. June 19, 1978. SHIRLEY v. SHIRLEY.

195. Parents married in September 1965—two children, boy nearly 12 and girl now six years of age—marriage became difficult by 1976 and in February 1977 mother left and went to live with a Mr. S (co-respondent), a married man with two children, boys aged six and two, who had separated from his wife— father, an architect, looked after children well with help from neighbours— in May 1977 magistrate awarded custody to father—divorce proceedings started in October 1977—welfare officer made no recommendation as to custody but recommended liberal access to whichever parent did not obtain it—judge gave custody to father but care and control to mother—father's appeal that judge did not pay sufficient regard to, *inter alia,* the status quo dismissed. June 20, 1978. HURST *v.* HURST.

196. Parents married in September 1962—two children, a boy and a girl now nearly 15 and eight years old respectively—on Christmas Eve 1974 mother left and went at first to live at her mother's house and then with the mother of the man, Mr. S, to whom she was now married—father obtained decree nisi on basis of mother's adultery with a Mr. R—father, a fishmonger, able to give some four days a week of his time to the children and doing " extremely well " in bringing them up since mother's departure as appeared from two school reports—welfare officer concluded after " very careful investigation " that children were somewhat tense with father and were completely happy and relaxed with mother—judge dismissed mother's application for custody leaving children with father—mother's appeal allowed—in true interests of children that custody should be awarded to mother, as emerged from welfare officer's report—children not to be separated and very strong case for transferring custody of girl to mother. June 20, 1978. WESTON *v.* WESTON.

197. Father and mother, now 33 and 29 years of age respectively, married in June 1971—two children, a boy and a girl, now aged five and a half and three and a half years respectively—in April 1975 father left leaving children with mother and went to live with a Miss V whom he had known since 1974— regular access by father plus two long weekends of staying access—in 1976 an attempted reconciliation broke down and in October 1977 father presented a petition for divorce founded on mother's adultery with a Mr. S, previously married, whom she had first met in 1964—strange relationship of mother with Mr. S who in 1970 was sentenced to 18 months' imprisonment for assault occasioning actual bodily harm and had since been convicted for dishonesty and a large number of offences of petty crime—judge formed bad opinion of Mr. S and took the view, *inter alia,* that mother's and his marriage would be interspersed in future with violence and nothing could be worse for the children than life in that sort of home—custody given to father with reasonable access to mother—mother's appeal dismissed. June 21, 1978. ROBINSON *v.* ROBINSON.

198. Father and mother married in June 1972 when father was 23 and mother 24 years of age—one child, a boy now aged five years—mother diagnosed as manic depressive but found by judge to be well from May 1977 and that risk of recurrence of her illness was not serious—father formed an attachment with co-respondent who was divorced from her husband and had custody of her two children—finely balanced case—judge gave custody to father with care and control to mother—father's appeal that he should have care and control as well as custody dismissed. June 23, 1978. GIBSON *v.* GIBSON.

199. Parties married in October 1966 when father was 24 and mother 26 years of age—two children, both boys, 10 and 9 years of age—in 1972/1973 relations between the parties deteriorated and mother finally left in 1975 having petitioned

for divorce in October 1974—marriage dissolved in 1977 and judge expressed limited satisfaction as regards the children—father lived with and intended to marry a Mrs. W, who had two children of a previous marriage, and who in March 1978 gave birth to a boy by the father—mother had been living with a Mr. J, who was aged 32, and previously married with four children who were living with their mother—welfare reports present—judge described case as being a very difficult and finely balanced one but was satisfied, *inter alia*, that mother would make a good job as a mother and devote herself to the children and gave custody to mother contrary to conclusion expressed by welfare officer—father's appeal dismissed. Appeal from Bush J. June 29, 1978. OATHAM *v.* OATHAM.

200. Parents married in 1968—one child, a girl, now aged eight years—mother was a manic depressive and suffered post-natal depression—marriage broke down after mother and child went to Spain in 1975 for a holiday—mother suffered bad health and had frequently to go into hospital and she never returned to the matrimonial home after she first went into hospital in August 1975—judge found the mother an unreliable witness but found that she was physically and mentally perfectly fit to look after children—medical evidence was that mother would remain susceptible to stress—mother presently living with a Mr. HW in accommodation which was unsuitable and impermanent—father lived in a small flat with a Miss S and had a child by her born in November 1977 and planned to have further children but no marriage—welfare reports present—judge gave custody to father—mother's appeal dismissed with view taken that if mother could stabilise situation and obtain proper accommodation and continue to be well she would be well advised to make further application but that at this stage it would be premature to order a new trial. July 3, 1978. MARTIN *v.* MARTIN.

201. Parties married in 1967 when father was 18 and mother 16 years of age—three children, two girls now aged 10 and nine and boy aged five and a half years—older girl suffered from cystic fibrosis—in January 1976 mother left and went to live with a Mr. M whom she married in February 1978—marriage dissolved in 1977 on father's petition based on adultery—father looked after children with help from maternal grandmother but in October 1976 put children in care of local authority—in December 1976 two younger children released into father's care and control—judge ordered, *inter alia*, that mother should have custody of children, that care order should continue as regards eldest child but should be discharged as regards two younger children who should remain in care and control of the county council until further order —long term custody not anticipated by local authority social worker— mother's accommodation difficulty—father's appeal allowed—new trial ordered to give local authority opportunity of putting forward view as to what in long term would be in the best interest of children. July 3, 1978. MOREY *v.* SHERWOOD.

202. Father and mother now aged 29 and 25 respectively, married in June 1971 —one child, a boy now aged four years—in August 1977 parties separated and mother went to live with another man, J, aged 43, and who had been twice previously married and twice divorced and had families by previous wives— no plan of mother and J to get married—father and child now lived with parents and father's two brothers and sister aged 25, 18 and 11 respectively, in a four-bedroomed house—marriage dissolved in 1978—welfare officer concluded that though far from ideal best arrangement for child was to leave child in *de facto* care and control of paternal grandparents and to give custody to father—judge followed recommendation of welfare officer—mother's appeal dismissed. July 4, 1978. PRATT *v.* PRATT.

203. Parties married in March 1970 when father was 17 and mother 16 years of age—three children, a girl now aged eight years and two boys now aged two and a half years and nine months—in July 1977 mother left taking children with her, she then being pregnant with youngest child—mother returned girl to father shortly afterwards—mother lived in three-bedroomed council house while father lived with his parents—both parties devoted to the children—judge awarded custody of girl to father and of boys to mother— mother's appeal that she should have custody of girl also allowed. July 4, 1978. STANNERS v. STANNERS.

204. Parents married in August 1969 when mother (English) was 26 and father (a Yugoslavian) 22 years of age—two children, boy and girl now aged seven and a half and four years—in August 1977 mother left taking boy with her—girl was and remained in *de facto* care and control of paternal grandparents, aged 65 and 64, who were living in Yugoslavia but now lived with father in matrimonial home—in February 1978 mother was granted a decree nisi on undefended petition alleging behaviour—mother now lived with her sister and brother-in-law and did not go out to work—no problem concerning material welfare of children—common ground that children ought to be brought up together—clash of cultures in background—various allegations made against mother by father—judge gave custody to mother—father's appeal dismissed. Appeal from Comyn J. July 11, 1978. KOSANOVIC v. KOSANOVIC.

205. Following breakdown of marriage in March 1977 mother left taking four children of marriage, all boys aged seven, four and twins aged three and went to live with her parents who were aged in their mid-fifties—a few days later father took older boys away and now lived with his parents who were in their mid-sixties—father doing a good job in looking after two children—serious criticism of mother by father—in June 1978 judge, who found case a difficult one, gave custody of all children to mother—father's appeal dismissed. Appeal from Baker P. July 13, 1978. HUXLEY v. HUXLEY.

206. Boy aged five—father and mother now aged 31 and 25 years respectively —marriage broke down in 1976 when mother had affair and father started divorce proceedings because of that—mother left and was now living with a married man G (whose wife had left him) with his 10-year-old son and they intended to get married—mother had miscarriage of child by G in 1977 and was now expecting twins by him—father took active interest in looking after boy from beginning of troubles and looked after him " very successfully "—boy isolated at father's home, a cottage " in very attractive environment "—judge gave custody to mother—father's appeal dismissed. July 25, 1978. DAVIES v. DAVIES.

207 Father and mother, now aged 37 and 38 years, married in May 1961— three children, two girls now aged 14 and seven and boy aged 17 years—last seven years of marriage unhappy and stressful—mother became depressed and from time to time left home for short periods—in December 1977 father left home and moved into a two-roomed flat near his shop and started living with co-defendant, D, a young woman aged 19 who worked in his shop and whom he had known for a short time only—boy and elder girl later went to live with father and D—in February 1978 mother petitioned for divorce and decree nisi granted in April—mother a good mother and D capable of looking after children—welfare officer concluded that it was advantageous to keep children together and with father—judge gave custody of girls to father—mother's appeal relating to custody of younger girl only allowed. July 25, 1978. JELLY v. JELLY.

208. Parents married in August 1969—four children, three girls now aged eight, seven, and five, and a boy aged two years—in October 1976 father committed adultery and mother left taking eldest child to live with her mother—father moved to his own step-mother's home with three youngest children—shortly afterwards mother took away two youngest girls but because of accommodation difficulties brought children back to father, who was living with his step-sister, in January 1977—in October 1977 mother found suitable accommodation and applied for custody—judge impressed by mother and found that no fault lay with her at time of parting in October 1976 and granted her care and control of all children—father's appeal dismissed. Appeal from Comyn J. July 26, 1978. *Re* A MINOR.

209. Girl, born in May 1968, now aged 10 years—Chinese parents, industrious and very prosperous, lived in Northern Ireland with large family of girl's six brothers and sisters—father, a conscientious gentleman, confided baby girl to care of foster mother with intention of bringing her into his own family when she was about nine or 10—girl " bonded totally " to foster mother who had brought her up for whole of her life and did not know her own family at all—judge ordered that girl should remain with foster mother—father's appeal dismissed. Appeal from Baker P. July 27, 1978. *Re* A MINOR.

210. Parents married in May 1972 in Denmark, wife being Danish—two children, girls aged five and three years—in February 1977 mother left and a week later took younger girl with her—decree nisi granted to father in June 1978 on his cross-petition alleging adultery—mother worked as part-time hairdresser and lived in flat with younger girl going to school—father was area representative for S.W. England for firm which made venetian blinds and lived in rented bungalow in village with elder girl going to school—welfare report—judge gave custody to mother—father's appeal dismissed. October 4, 1978. BATTEN *v.* BATTEN.

211. Child, a boy, now aged a little under five years—in August 1977 mother left taking boy and went to live with a Mr. B with whom she had been associating for some time—no divorce proceedings—father (who had his 16-year-old daughter by a previous marriage living with him) had frequent access to boy—judge gave custody to father largely because mother had got boy into the habit of addressing Mr. B as " daddy "—mother's appeal allowed—exaggerated weight attached to boy addressing B as " daddy "—no evidence that boy emotionally insecure with mother—custody to mother. October 4, 1978. *Re* A MINOR.

212. Parents married in November 1971—two children, girls, now aged five and three years—in 1976 parties moved to a farm, father (a farmer) was then farming—in December 1977 mother left alleging a depressive breakdown on her part and in January 1978 petitioned for divorce on ground of unreasonable behaviour and in July 1978 obtained decree nisi—children looked after by father with help from his parents and later father's mother moved to farm to look after children—access to mother was given reluctantly—welfare report —custody given to mother—father's appeal dismissed. October 6, 1978. ARMETT *v.* ARMETT.

213. Two children, girls now aged 11½ and 10 years—older girl born in April 1967 when parents were not married—parents married in May 1968 and younger girl born in September 1968—trouble in marriage in 1970 and magistrates' court gave custody of both children to father but care and control to mother—reconciliation in December 1971—in June 1976 father left and

went to live about 50 miles away—matrimonial home sold and mother and children moved to her parents' home nearby—grandmother looked after children while mother was out at work as a ground hostess at Humberside Airport—welfare reports—in January 1977 magistrates gave joint custody to parents with care and control to mother and a few days later mother presented divorce petition on ground of husband's adultery—father had considerable access to younger girl and in October 1971 he took younger girl on holiday and failed to return her and in May 1978 applied for her custody—in June 1978 mother and children moved to live with a Mr. W and his daughter—judge found case difficult and awarded custody of younger girl to father and elder girl to mother—mother's appeal dismissed. October 6, 1978. KEIGHTLEY v. KEIGHTLEY.

214. Father and mother, now aged 34 and 32 years respectively, married in August 1967—three children, girls now aged 10¾, nine and a half and eight years —in June 1976 mother started an association with a Mr. L and in August she left to live with Mr. L and was now married to him—in February 1977 father met Mrs. L (wife of person whom mother married) and in August 1978 he married her—husband's divorce petition presented in March 1977 and decree nisi granted in September 1977—access proceedings in county court by mother—welfare reports—judge took view that if father had custody there would be "the most appalling" pressure on the children and they would be shut out from their mother altogether and gave custody to mother contrary to welfare report recommendations—father's appeal dismissed. October 11, 1978. BROOKS v. BROOKS.

215. Parents married in December 1973—two children, girl and boy, now aged four and a half and one and a half years—boy suffered from serious disability and required "special hospital" visits three times a week—in July 1978 father finally left—difficulties over access—in August 1978 father took girl out but never brought her back taking her instead to live at his parents' home about 10 miles away from matrimonial home—judge ordered, as interim measures pending welfare officer's report, that custody of girl be with father with supervised access and custody of boy with mother with supervised access—welfare report not available until November 1978—mother's appeal allowed—order varied by giving interim custody of girl also to mother with same supervised access as boy—matter to be reheard before November 11 in view of Guardianship Act 1973, s. 2 (4). October 17, 1978. Re N. D. (A MINOR).

216. Father and mother began to live together in 1964 and married in March 1966—four children, boys, now aged 14, 11, nine-and-a-half (named S, subject-matter of appeal) and six-and-a-half years— in 1975 mother began association with a Mr. A and in May 1976 she finally left taking youngest child with her to live with A and in November 1976 had a girl by him aged now two years —second eldest boy later went to live with her—decree nisi on father's petition in September 1977—father in difficult position as he worked as an accountant in London but lived in matrimonial home which was in Chelmsford but coped with difficult position "exceptionally well"—in April 1976 a "criminal care order" made in respect of eldest boy—in July 1978 a Mrs. F (whom father had met in January 1977) moved in to live with father together with her two children, a girl of five and a boy of eight years of age, from a previous marriage —on mother's application judge gave custody of S to mother—father's appeal dismissed. October 20, 1978. MORDECAI v. MORDECAI.

217. Father and mother, now aged 45 and 38 years respectively, married in March 1956—three children, a boy, now aged over 18 (and living with mother),

and two girls now aged 14 and 13 years both now at a secondary modern school—mother formed association with another man, W, who was much older than herself, and in January 1977 she left, presented a divorce petition in May 1977 and was granted a decree nisi in October 1977—in July 1977 mother went to live with W in his flat—father began to live with a Mrs. G who had been twice married and twice divorced and had five children, three of whom moved in with her into former matrimonial home (from where father ran a plant hire firm)—exceptional difficulties in case because girls extremely disturbed by parents' separation and continuing conflict between parents had a bad effect on them—" most careful " welfare report but welfare officer unable to recommend that " custody to either parent is in interests of these girls "—mother handicapped by feelings of guilt and father weak and insensitive—judge gave custody to mother—father's appeal dismissed. October 20, 1978. MORRELL v. MORRELL.

218. Parents married in August 1968 when they were both very young and wife was pregnant—two children, girl and boy, now aged nine and a half and six and a half years—in January 1972 mother left leaving children behind and chidren were put into care of mother's parents—in 1973 children came into care of father and from then until January 1978 father and his present wife looked after them—mother flirted about, had affairs and then had a short-lived marriage to a Mr. Stubbs—she had psychiatric treatment from time to time—she eventually settled down and in September 1977 applied for access and was granted a very limited order for access—in January 1978 an incident happened and father handed over girl to mother who was then living with her father and step-mother with their two young children—in September judge gave custody of girl to mother—father's appeal dismissed. October 24, 1978. STUBBS v. WOOD.

219. Father and mother now aged 48 and 42 years married in October 1953—first child, boy (over 18), born two months after marriage—second child, boy (over 18), born in March 1955 and third child, boy D, born in February 1972 and now aged six-and-a-half years—marriage unhappy in 1976 and in February 1977 mother petitioned for divorce on the ground of behaviour—in August 1977 mother left, taking D, and lived in a rented house getting about £30 per week from the DHSS—decree nisi granted in August 1977—no access by father for many months—welfare report—difficult case—judge concerned about mother " over-mothering " D and found that mother induced D's antagonistic attitude towards father but granted her custody contrary to recommendation of probation officer—father's appeal dismissed. October 27, 1978. BUDGIE v. BUDGIE.

220. Parents married in December 1970 when mother was 18 and father 25 years old—two children, boy and girl, now aged seven and just five years—marriage broke down in December 1977 and mother left taking children and set up house with the co-respondent, Mr. W—father, who was employed by the local authority, continued to live in the former matrimonial home, which was a council house, and applied for judicial separation and had his 64-year-old mother to help look after children—judge gave custody to father—mother's appeal allowed—rehearing ordered. November 1, 1978. GOSS v. GOSS.

221. Two children, girls, now aged nine and six years—parents married in 1965 —mother formed an association with a Mr. V who lived close by and in September 1977 she left taking children and now lived with V—father snatched children back soon afterwards but returned them shortly thereafter under a court order—shortly afterwards he took them away again in breach of

order taking a great dislike to V—mother reacted slowly to this incident but judge gave custody to her having heard evidence and seen all parties—father's appeal dismissed. Appeal from Sir George Baker P. November 1, 1978. MEAKINS v. MEAKINS.

222. On October 20, 1978, judge, against the views of welfare officers, transferred care of little girl to mother who was still very young and who had been in great difficulty—child had been living with father since parties separated in July 1977—not clear from judgment why judge felt so strongly about the case —solution was to leave child with mother on an interim basis with a view to having whole matter looked at again in " not too distant future " (January or February 1979)—appropriate directions given—father's appeal allowed. November 6, 1978. PEERS v. PEERS.

223. Parents married in October 1965—two children, boy and girl now aged 10 and seven years—in February 1974 mother left taking children but in Summer 1974 returned children to father because of accommodation difficulties—in December 1974 father obtained custody on an unopposed application under Guardianship of Infants Acts—in mid 1975 mother went to live and work in Holland but continued to return at three-monthly intervals and had access— in December 1977 she married a Mr. J, a Norwegian national, having obtained in September 1976 a decree of divorce on ground of two years' separation plus consent and in January 1978 she gave birth to J's son—mother returned to England with J and son and they now lived in a three-bedroomed council house and J worked as a milkman—father lived with a married woman B, who was separated from her husband and had custody of their two children—B worked flexible hours as a shorthand typist—in October 1978 judge gave custody to mother—borderline case—father's appeal dismissed. November 13, 1978. JOHANSEN v. SMITH.

224. Parents married in March 1963—two children, boys P now aged 15 and M 11 years—marriage broke up in late 1969 and in November 1970 mother obtained decree nisi on ground of father's conduct—decree made absolute in March 1971, and custody granted to mother because father, having remarried in 1971, lived only 300 yards away—P spent much time with father and in September 1971, in accordance with his wishes, his care and control was transferred to father—in October 1973 custody of both boys was given to father by consent because of strong recommendation by welfare officer that M ought to go and stay with father and brother—unsatisfactory access and antagonistic attitude taken by father and P towards mother—M expressed wish to stay with mother—little to choose between two households as far as material benefits concerned—judge gave custody of M to mother against view expressed in new welfare report—father's appeal dismissed. Appeal from Bush J. November 17, 1978. WEST v. WEST.

225. Child, girl aged four-and-a-half years—mother and father after a short marriage now lived separately—father lived in difficult circumstances in that lady with whom he was living had one child who was subject to a hereditary illness and was having another baby in January—mother had never had a really settled life—" a lot to be said " in favour of both parties—judge, after six days' hearing, granted custody to mother—father's appeal dismissed. December 14, 1978. Re F. (A MINOR).

226. Parties married in June 1971 and went to live with father's father in his house together with his grown-up daughter by an earlier marriage—one child boy now aged six and a half years—in August 1977 mother left without child because she had nowhere to take him—father worked from early morning

until early afternoon and was available when child was free from school—since March 1978 mother had been able to find, equip and furnish a suitable accommodation adequate for child—nothing said against either household—*status quo* argument—evidence and welfare reports—judge gave custody to mother with generous access to father and grandfather—whether child unwilling to go to mother—father's appeal dismissed. December 20, 1978. LEWIS *v.* LEWIS.

227. Parents married in June 1965—two children, boys, aged 12 and nine years—in April 1968 mother left taking children and went to live with a Mr. E, a married man who had living with him his 10-year-old son of his marriage—three weeks later elder boy returned to father with mother's consent because he was unhappy and had formed a dislike for Mr. E—younger boy snatched by father but snatched back by mother—uncontested decree on ground of adultery obtained by father—decent parents reasonable in outlook save when concerned with custody—welfare report—judge saw boys privately during hearing—judge convinced that boys should be together in same place and gave custody of both to father—mother's appeal dismissed. Appeal from Comyn J. December 20, 1978. PAGET *v.* PAGET.

228. Only child of marriage girl aged six years—parents married in 1972 having lived together since March 1971—mother brought with her a son (of whom she had care and control) by a previous marriage, dissolved because of her adultery with a Mr. K—in July 1977 mother left leaving children behind and went to live with a Mr. F who lived only a few minutes away from matrimonial home—father continued to live in matrimonial home, which was a two-bedroomed house let to father by mother's mother—much bitterness between parties—boy did not want to see mother—welfare reports—judge concluded that best course was that care and control of girl should be transferred to mother but that of boy should remain with father having in mind nearness of two households—father's appeal allowed—care and control of both children given to father—judge gave insufficient weight to desirability of children being brought up together in situation. December 20, 1978. *Re* C. AND D. (MINORS).

229. Parents married in January 1970—two children, girls aged five and three years—in February 1978 mother left without children and went to live with another man, C, and presented petition for divorce alleging violence and sought custody of children—interim order for custody made in mother's favour but in June 1978 she agreed to children going back into care of father—father lived with another woman and her small daughter and his parents—uncertainty about mother's future in relation to C—judge ordered that custody should remain with father but subject to an existing supervision order—necessary for children to have a period of stability which was more likely to be available in father's home—mother's appeal dismissed. December 21, 1978. POLKINGHORNE *v.* POLKINGHORNE.

230. Parents married in 1972—two children girls aged five and four years—in 1976 and 1977 there was trouble between parties over money matters and mother was convicted of forging cheques and banker's orders belonging to her husband—mother left and petitioned for divorce and applied for custody, care and control—mother now back in matrimonial home and living with another man and they were considering marriage—father lived with a Mrs. K, a teacher with a child of her own—judge gave custody to father—mother's appeal allowed—custody given to mother—judge placed too much emphasis on the moral and financial difficulties of the mother and not enough on the position she " undoubtedly occupied " in relation to the children's lives. December 21, 1978. SAMMELLS *v.* SAMMELLS.

231. Parents (West Indians) married in November 1965—three children, boy A nearly 10, and two girls M and J aged now 12 and eight years—marriage started to break down in 1970—allegations by parties against each other of adultery—petition on ground of unreasonable behaviour by father in March 1978—both parties worked—father an enterprising man who worked on night shift and studied during daytime and obtained considerable promotion at work and was offered an " excellent post " in Barbados at substantial salary—mother worked 7.30 a.m. to 2.30 p.m. and neighbours saw children off to school— welfare reports—judge granted custody of A to father and gave father leave to take A to Barbados with him; custody of J given to mother; with regard to M judge granted interim custody to mother on basis that M would visit father at Easter in Barbados and a final decision would be made thereafter—mother's appeal dismissed. January 11, 1979. Lewis v. Lewis.

232. Parents married in March 1953 when father aged 21 and mother 18 years old—five children, four girls and one boy—two eldest girls in full-time employ-ment—boy aged 16 and two younger girls aged 14 and 12 all at school—in 1968 mother started association with co-respondent, a married man with two children, and in November 1976 (after father discovered relationship) she left home to live with him—father had major responsibility thereafter for children —in 1977 father met another woman, a divorcee with three children, girl aged 14 and two boys aged 13 and five, and they intended to get married—early 1978 father petitioned on ground of adultery and decree nisi granted in March 1978—mother applied for custody of three younger children—in November 1978 judge, who had a " substantial body of evidence " before him, granted custody to mother—difficult case—father's appeal dismissed. January 12, 1979. Pearsall v. Pearsall.

233. Boys aged 12 and seven—judge dismissed mother's application for custody and ordered that children should remain in custody of father—trouble over access because of father's intransigent attitude towards mother's adultery— mother lived with co-respondent who slept in separate bed when children went to mother for staying access—no reason supplied by judge for his decision— differences between legal representatives as to what had been happening about access—mother's appeal allowed—order of judge to be treated as interim order —rehearing ordered before judge of Family Division—up-to-date welfare report ordered. January 17, 1979. Worley v. Worley.

234. Child girl now aged six years—allegations by mother against father of sexual behaviour with neighbour denied by father—mother's petition on ground of behaviour dismissed—immediately after divorce suit judge gave custody to mother who lived with a Mr. T whom she hoped to marry as soon as free to do so—psychiatric evidence—welfare reports—negative attitude by father against divorcing mother—ordinary case to be dealt with on ordinary basis with " no psychiatric stuff " as alleged by father—father's (in person) appeal dismissed. Appeal from Reeve J. January 18, 1979. T. v. R.

235. Father and mother, now aged 26 and 27, married in August 1971—one child girl now aged two years—pregnancy difficult and after birth child had several illnesses and mother complained that father gave her little support during this time—in March 1975 father left his service in R.A.F. in favour of civilian employment and period of unsettled behaviour by father followed—in August 1977 father told brother that he had another woman, a Mrs. Hall, 27 years old, whose husband had recently left her and who had a nine-year-old daughter— in consequence mother left (without child) and went to live with her parents in Scotland—parents' house a four-bedroomed house in which lived, apart from

mother, her parents, three other children of parents (two boys aged 21 and 20, both engaged to be married, and girl aged 19) and paternal grandfather aged 87 —mother alleged she was frightened as to whether she could support child herself and after assurance from Mrs. Hall that she would care for child, she left child behind—in January 1978 mother petitioned on ground of husband's adultery and applied for custody—decree nisi in April 1978—welfare report—evidence— judge rejected suggestion that mother had in any way abandoned her claim to have custody of child and gave custody to mother—difficult case—father's appeal dismissed. January 19, 1979. BATES v. BATES.

236. Father and mother now aged 55 and 45 married in September 1967—one child, boy aged 10—mother previously married with two children, boy and girl, who lived with her—marriage began to break down in 1973 and 1974— in August 1978 mother presented petition for divorce on ground of unreasonable behaviour and shortly afterwards moved out to live in a cottage about five miles away but, because of father's presence, was unable to take boy with her although she wished to do so—in October father filed answer and cross-petition on ground of mother's unreasonable behaviour—welfare report—evidence— in December 1978 judge, who formed adverse view of mother, gave custody to father attaching importance to maintenance of status quo and against recom- mendation of welfare officer—mother's appeal allowed—" entirely fortuitous status quo " which had lasted only a short time—strong case for mother— case to be heard before judge of Family Division. February 2, 1979. CELER v. CELER.

237. Mother and father aged 47 and 45 married in 1968—three children, two boys and girl aged 10, eight and seven years—father had a son (now over 18) by earlier marriage and mother had a daughter (now over 18) by earlier of two marriages (one of which ended by her being widowed)—in 1976 mother started cohabiting with manager of establishment where she worked as a bar- maid and was now married to him—decree absolute in 1978 and father awarded custody—father lived in council flat with children and was helped by his family in looking after them—mother and her new husband (who had a daughter aged over eight years and who came from Sicily) decided to go and live in a village in Sicily where husband had some property on which he was building a house and where he intended to establish himself as a restauranteur—girl (aged eight) expressed wish to be with mother and her husband rather than with her father and brothers—welfare report—problem of education—difficult case—judge granted custody of girl to mother—father's appeal dismissed. Appeal from Payne J. February 8, 1979. CONTI v. BOARDMAN.

238. —— —— agreement

Two children, boy and girl, aged seven and five years—special procedure divorce between parents—agreement between parents that there should be joint custody—neither of parties legally represented when matter came before judge —judge took view that case not appropriate for a joint custody order and ordered that children should remain in custody of mother with reasonable access to father—father's appeal allowed—parties in difficulty because not legally represented at hearing and taken by surprise—matter to be reconsidered by judge in due course with parties properly represented. January 30, 1979. WOOD v. WOOD.

239. —— —— care and control to paternal grandmother

Parties married in December 1972 when mother was already pregnant with child—child, a boy, now aged five years—mother suffered bouts of depression requiring her to go into hospital and in September 1975 a "place of safety order" was made whereby the child was placed in the care of father's mother (who had remarried) and in October a care order was made in favour of the local authority who boarded the child out to father's mother—in March 1978 a decree nisi of divorce was pronounced on the basis of mother's association with the co-respondent and made absolute in June—mother lived with co-respondent, who was previously married and had obtained a decree nisi in 1972 which had not yet been made absolute, together with his son from that marriage—mother had staying access to children and applied for care of the children, her case being that she had made a complete recovery—medical evidence plus evidence from four social workers—judge granted mother custody but ordered that children should not be removed (without further order) from care and control of father's mother—mother's appeal dismissed—application to adduce fresh evidence of psychiatrist who had, since hearing, visited children during access in mother's home with mother's approval, dismissed. June 22, 1978. SPAIN v. SPAIN.

240. —— —— change of name

Parties married in July 1969 when father was 22 and mother 18 years of age—one child, boy, aged six years—parties separated in 1974 when mother left taking child and went to live with G to whom she was now married and by whom she had another boy in August 1977—first marriage dissolved in December 1975—father now lived with another woman and had a child by her—since separation father had been moving around to and from Australia, where his parents lived, and played only a remote role in child's life—G fulfilled role of father since boy was two-and-a-half years old and boy was called with surname of G—upon father's objection mother changed surname at school from G back to Malkin—judge ordered, *inter alia*, that boy shall retain his father's surname of Malkin—wife's appeal allowed—no order made but it was made plain that court relied on parents to be sensible in situation. December 19, 1978. MALKIN v. MALKIN (NOW GULLIFORD).

241. —— —— conditions attached to custody order

Two children of parties, girl and boy now eight and six years old—welfare report disclosed that before mother had met father in late 1969 she had formed a number of associations with other men and in September 1966 had given birth to a boy who was in her care—at custody hearing father agreed mother should have custody—judge had "grave doubts" whether mother was right person to have custody and considered making a care order but in result gave custody to mother subject to a supervision order and to undertaking by mother (and corresponding undertaking by father) not to have living in her home or sleeping in her room any man to whom she was not married—view by probation officer that no need for undertaking and that welfare services would monitor situation—judge refused mother's subsequent application to be released from undertaking—mother's appeal dismissed. March 9, 1979. *Re* G. (MINORS).

242. —— —— custody issue tied up with property issue

Father, a Ukranian, and mother, Polish, now aged 50 and 29 years respectively, married in January 1969—two children, a boy and a girl, now aged eight and four years—marriage broke down in 1974–75 by which time mother had had serious nervous breakdown and had developed intense relationship with another woman which had now ended—father, a machinist, was hardworking and lived in the matrimonial home and looked after children with assistance from housekeepers—marriage dissolved in May 1976 and an order for joint custody made with care and control to father—mother, a State

Enrolled Nurse, now worked four nights a week and occasional week-ends; she at first shared a flat with another woman but in January 1978 moved into a house bought by them together on mortgage—mother's application for variation of previous order in that she be given care and control dismissed—difficult and finely balanced case—not possible to resolve problem of the children independently of the issue relating to the former matrimonial home—good access by mother indicating " inevitable drift " by children toward her—subject to father's security in matrimonial home great deal to be said for acceding to mother's application—property application not before Court of Appeal—mother invited to make concession over the matrimonial home—no order made on appeal but indication given that if " driven to it " court would allow the appeal and order a new trial. July 20, 1978. KOWAL v. KOWAL.

243. —— —— custody to father

Parents married in 1970—two children, boys now aged five and four years —trouble early in marriage when father had a brief adulterous association with another woman—financial difficulties—in 1976 father started associating with A, with whom he now lived in a comfortable four-bedroomed house in a West Country village with a school nearby and elder boy well settled at that school—marriage broke down in July 1977 when father admitted to mother that he had another woman and incidents of violence followed—in August 1977 mother presented petition for divorce but did not claim custody—in October 1977 father obtained secure employment with the Post Office and A gave up employment and father and A intended to marry as soon as possible—judge granted custody to father in October 1978—mother's appeal dismissed. November 17, 1978. HARRIS v. HARRIS.

244.

Parents married in March 1966—two children girl and boy now aged nine and seven years—reasonably happy marriage with father hardworking and fond of home, wife and children and mother a conscientious person who contributed to family budget by working—when she was 32 years old (father then aged 33), mother fell in love with a Mr. W aged 24 years and started associating with him and they proposed to marry provided a successful relationship was established between W and the children—W saw himself as a " friend and not a father " to children—decree nisi of divorce pronounced—father had strong objection to W meeting children and planned to look after children (if given custody) with help of a Mrs. E who was herself " caught up in matrimonial proceedings "—judge found that mother was an affectionate, caring and successful mother and that father was a hardworking and devoted father—having seen and heard all adults involved and having seen welfare report, judge granted custody to father—mother's appeal dismissed. November 24, 1978. CARRINGTON v. CARRINGTON.

245. —— —— enforcement of order

Parents (Sri Lankans) were married in Sri Lanka in 1963 and had two children boy and girl now aged 14 and 11 years—in 1971 father came to England and was joined by mother in August 1972—they bought a home—friction between parties and petition by father seeking divorce on ground of desertion—answer and cross-petition on ground of father's conduct by mother—welfare reports— three successive judgments by judge—in January 1978 when matter came before judge for the first time he ordered that boy should be in care of mother and girl in care of father—strong unwillingness by girl to see mother and by boy to see father—on second occasion, when mother was about to be rehoused in more suitable local authority accommodation, judge ordered that both children should be in care of mother—impossible to persuade girl to go to mother (except by physical force)—judge finally ordered that girl should remain in care and custody of father—mother's appeal that more persuasion should be applied by local authority to try and induce girl to go to mother dismissed—impossible to order child to be transferred by force. Appeal from Hollings J. February 12, 1979. *Re* S. (A MINOR).

246. —— —— **interim care and control**

On October 20, 1978, judge ordered that pending hearing of wife's petition for dissolution of marriage, wife should be allowed to stay in matrimonial home and should have care and control of two children of marriage, a girl aged 12 and a boy aged 11—wife had formed a liaison with another man and left matrimonial home on September 15, 1978, and shortly afterwards went to live with that man in a one-bedroom flat—welfare report (ordered on November 7) indicated that children had marked antipathy to wife—care and control given to father who lived in matrimonial home pending hearing of wife's petition—father's appeal allowed. November 21, 1978. CAZALET-SMITH v. CAZALET-SMITH.

247. Parents married in January 1974—one child a girl now aged two years—in June 1978 mother left taking child to live with her mother and her husband in a two-bedroomed flat—in July mother petitioned for divorce on ground of father's behaviour—in his acknowledgment of service father said that he did not intend to defend suit nor to apply for custody but wished to have access—on September 16 mother, who had had psychiatric treatment before, was admitted to hospital under Mental Health Act 1959, s. 25, and child was taken to foster parents, it being alleged that mother's mother (because of her age and state of health) was unable to look after child—father removed child from foster parents with approval of local authority's welfare representative and took child back to matrimonial home and looked after her with aid of a child minder—recently, on advice of local family doctor, father put child with foster parents to get her out of reach of mother—in October on mother's application for interim care and control judge adjourned matter for a welfare report which he ordered—mother's appeal dismissed—no access to mother for time being. November 24, 1978. KENT v. KENT.

248. Parents married in 1966—three children girl and two boys now aged 12, 11 and seven—decree absolute in September 1977 on father's petition—in July 1977 judge gave interim custody to mother with defined access to father—father now stated he had met a widow with two children boys aged 13 and 11, and was living with them in four-bedroomed house where there was sufficient accommodation for his children and applied for custody—mother had had a problem in relation to elder boy, G—judge saw G in his room before any oral evidence was heard and granted interim care and control of eldest and youngest children to mother and interim care and control of G to father—mother's appeal dismissed—impossible to fault unusual course of seeing G taken by judge in this particular case. January 30, 1979. STARR v. STARR.

249. —— —— **interim custody**

Parties, both previously married, married in September 1969—two children, twins, a boy and a girl, aged seven years—marriage was satisfactory until 1975 when things deteriorated and mother suffered mental illness and was admitted to hospital—in February 1978 father petitioned for divorce on the ground of wife's behaviour and applied for interim custody—mother's case that father a violent man but father denied that and alleged mother unsuitable to have custody because of her mental illness and bad relationship with boy—welfare report concluded that children needed to be together and suggested that father and his mother had provided children with security in the past and were more likely to provide them with a balanced upbringing and consistent handling necessary for those children—judge held, *inter alia*, that father should have interim custody with reasonable access to mother—mother's appeal dismissed. June 16, 1978. H. *v.* H.

250. Parents married in March 1965—two children, boy and girl now aged 11 and nine years—great deal of unhappiness in marriage with violence by father towards mother—marriage started to break up in 1977 and eventually broke up in April 1978 when father left—father visited mother afterwards and made a nuisance of himself and there were assaults on mother—on June 5, 1978, mother presented a petition for divorce based on father's conduct—on June 9, after a further incident by father, mother left matrimonial home and went to live with relations in Portsmouth—on June 23 she applied for an injunction against molestation by father but no order made on father giving undertaking not to repeat his conduct—mother returned to matrimonial home but left for Portsmouth for second time after father " invaded " home in middle of night on August 9—father had access to children and on October 1, after having access, instead of returning girl, he kept her and took her to her grandmother where she was now living—judge adjourned generally mother's application for interim custody and for an order that girl should be returned to her pending an investigation and report by a court welfare officer—mother's appeal allowed —girl to be returned forthwith and mother to have interim custody of both children. October 26, 1978. JENKINS *v.* JENKINS.

251. Parties married in June 1971 and had a boy now seven years old—father consented to another man having intercourse with mother in order to give her a child, father himself being unable to do so, and another child born to mother, a girl now seven months old, of whom respondent was not the father—father worked away temporarily (because of job transfer) and came home at weekends—in December 1978 father left taking boy with him alleging that boy had asked him to take him away—medical evidence that boy suffered from suppressed anxiety and that (in this particular case) custody of boy should be with father—medical evidence that mother highly strung and had had severe emotional strains to go through—suitable living arrangements provided for father and boy by father's superiors at work (in Post Office)—judge dismissed mother's application and instead granted interim custody of boy to father—mother's appeal dismissed. February 5, 1979. *Re* B. (A MINOR).

252. —— —— jurisdiction

Father brought over his two children from Rhodesia so as to necessitate their being taken into care by local authority and in November 1976 a juvenile court made care orders under Children and Young Persons Act 1969, s. 1, committing children to care of local authority—in March 1977 father filed petition for divorce which included prayer for custody of two children— whether jurisdiction to entertain custody application whilst there were care orders—judge held that he had no jurisdiction—*H.* v. *H.* [1973] C.L.Y. 2189 —father's appeal allowed. October 11, 1978. ELLARD *v.* ELLARD AND CHESHIRE COUNTY COUNCIL.

253. —— —— lesbian mother

Two children, girl and a boy now aged seven and six years old respectively— parents, father now 39 and mother 30 years of age, met in 1967—girl born in October 1970—parents married in January 1971—boy born in August 1972—

in March 1977 a lesbian relationship started between mother and a Mrs. D who lived with her husband and two children—in August 1977 mother left to live with the Ds—in December mother returned to attend to the care of the children—judge gave custody to father on basis that although there was no danger in this case of children being turned into homosexuals, there was a real danger of social embarrassment and hurt to the children in the circumstances—mother's appeal dismissed. June 21, 1978. SMITH v. SMITH.

254. —— —— new circumstances

Judge ordered that custody of one of seven children of the family, a girl T now aged 14 years, be transferred to mother, all other children (except a boy D, with respect to whom custody proceedings were adjourned for Social Services to be informed, the judge considering making a care order) being already in mother's care—father appealed—appeal papers in a most unsatisfactory state so that court literally knew nothing about matter—mother did not appear on appeal—T had not gone to mother and refused to go—further investigation required—appeal allowed not necessarily because judge wrong but because in new circumstances problem of T, as well as D, should be looked at again—rehearing ordered in relation to T and D together. October 11, 1978. McCANN v. McCANN.

255. —— —— religious education

Parents, mother Roman Catholic, married in February 1972 and agreed that children should be educated in non-denominational schools, mother then being pregnant with the older boy—two children, boys now aged six and two years—father formed association with another woman with whom he was now living—decree nisi based on father's adultery granted in March 1978—both parents school teachers—father educated in Roman Catholic school but ceased to be a practising Roman Catholic by time of marriage—mother more active in church-going since separation than before, and during separation younger child was baptised into Roman Catholic Church without father's knowledge—judge gave custody to mother provided that children should be " educated at whatever non-denominational schools the parents jointly choose or failing agreement " at a given school—mother's appeal against part of order giving directions regarding children's schools dismissed. July 11, 1978. HANLEY v. HANLEY.

256. —— —— retrial

Judge granted custody of only child of parties, boy now aged six and a half years, from father to mother with supervision by social services and access to father—unopposed affidavit by father to adduce fresh evidence that despite repeated efforts to effect transfer boy had shown strong determination not to live with mother—new trial ordered of custody issue before judge of Family Division—fresh welfare report ordered—father's appeal allowed. January 31, 1979. MORGAN v. MORGAN.

257. —— —— variation of order

Children, two girls, now aged seven and two years, were in custody, care and control of mother—father aware of mother's association with a Mr. B, whom mother intended to marry, but mother concealed association from welfare officer, her solicitors and from court—father said nothing of association in his evidence-in-chief but mother " caught " in cross-examination—judge refused to vary existing custody order on father's application—father's appeal dismissed. October 12, 1978. WINDMILL v. WINDMILL.

258. —— education

Parents married in 1955—two children, girls, now aged 11 and 10 years—in 1975 father left, marriage was dissolved and in July 1975 custody was given to mother—regular access by father every week—elder girl now in a comprehensive school—father wished younger girl to go to grammar school and judge ordered that father be at liberty to choose school to be attended by her by obtaining her a place at a certain school within a month or so—mother objected because child well settled at existing school and happy—mother's appeal allowed. October 26, 1978. BENSON v. BENSON.

259. —— wardship—care and control

Wards of court, boy and girl, now aged nine and five years—father, English, now aged 37, and mother, Israeli, now aged 38 years, married in England in November 1967—marriage unhappy from 1970 onwards because of sexual problems and financial difficulties arising from father being unemployed for substantial periods of time—three separate suicide attempts by mother in 1970 and 1971 because of stresses in marriage—father now in good job—in March 1977 mother flew to Israel with children but without telling father—father started wardship proceedings and mother ordered to return children forthwith and a " consent order " made and children handed over to father in July 1977—father and children went to live with and later opposite his parents—mother allowed some access by consent on undertakings given by her and in August she issued summons for care and control of children—court welfare officer's evidence—four day hearing—judge in a " long and careful judgment " gave care and control to mother—father's appeal dismissed. Appeal from Balcombe J. October 26, 1978. *Re* H. (MINORS).

260. —— —— jurisdiction

Child in question born in November 1977—father and mother, who were not married, were now aged 20 and 21 respectively—father out of touch with child from second day of its life because he was in custody—mother and child lived in various places like hostels and bed and breakfast accommodation—in July 1978 local authority obtained a place of safety order and child had been in care since then—series of interim care orders and in November 1978 matter came before juvenile court for full hearing—justices refused to make a care order stating that provisions of s. 1 (2) (*a*) of the Children and Young Persons Act 1969 had not been satisfied—on same day, immediately after the juvenile court proceedings, local authority issued originating summons making child a ward of court—whether court should assume wardship jurisdiction—whether conflict of jurisdiction—*Re* D. [1977] C.L.Y. 1930—parents' appeal dismissed. Appeal from Purchas J. February 2, 1979. *Re* C. (A MINOR).

261. —— —— mother in Ireland

Two children, girls now aged four and a half and three and a half years—mother married M in Ireland (both were citizens of the Republic of Ireland) in 1966 and in 1968 had a son—mother left because of M's drinking, gambling and bad temper, and came to London in May 1977 and started relationship with father of the two girls—unsatisfactory life in London—in May 1976 mother had an accident (probably due to her intoxication) and was admitted to hospital and children were taken into care and had been in and out of care ever since—in July 1977 mother decided to go back to Ireland and to be reconciled with M and left children with father—children taken into care and made wards of court by father who feared their being removed to Ireland by mother—welfare reports showing disturbing picture—mother reconciled with her husband since July 1977 and alleged to be in a stable household, she and her husband having mended their ways—judge ordered that children should remain wards of court and that they should be placed in the care and control of Hammersmith London Borough—mother's appeal dismissed. Appeal from Purchas J. November 16, 1978. M. *v.* M. AND HAMMERSMITH LONDON BOROUGH.

262. —— —— removal of child from jurisdiction—holiday overseas

Parents married in India in June 1965 and three weeks later came to live in England—one child, a boy, now aged 12 years—in 1972 the parents separated, mother alleging that father had deserted her—in 1977 mother started proceedings for judicial separation and in January 1978 was granted custody by the magistrates—father's appeal against that order pending—in May 1978 father learnt that mother intended to take boy to India for a six-week holiday on May 20 and issued a wardship summons—whether court had jurisdiction to hear wardship application—whether right at present time to allow boy of 12 to be away from school for six weeks—weather in India a relevant factor—father's appeal allowed—wardship restored. June 15, 1978. *Re* A MINOR.

263. Moneylenders—loan—money or silver

Defendants were administrators of estate of SB, Israeli citizen living in Israel, who was related by marriage to DL (who died in 1971), one of two directors of the plaintiff company, a small family company—in September/October 1961, while SB was on visit to England, plaintiff company entered into legal charge on certain freehold property owned by them as security for due performance by them of their obligation to deliver to SB sixty bars of pure silver which SB was then selling to plaintiff company for plaintiff company to sell and use the proceeds—whether security given as part of or in connection with moneylending transaction in which SB was lender—whether separate legally binding oral agreement made in 1965 between SB and DL whereby plaintiff company entitled to have security discharged on payment of £25,000—judge prepared to " look behind the recital in the legal charge," concluded that plaintiff company had not proved that SB made them " a loan of money as distinct from silver bars " and found in favour of the defendants on issues involved—plaintiffs appeal dismissed—defendants' cross appeal as to amount of their entitlement on their counterclaim dismissed. Appeal from Mocatta J. June 9, 1978. LAZARUS ESTATES *v.* BIDERMAN.

264. Mortgages—equitable interest—priority—evidence

In February 1967 Mr. CW purchased a home on mortgage and shortly after house became matrimonial home of Mr. and Mrs. CW (now Mrs. S)—in September 1973 Mr. CW obtained from the appellant a loan on the security of a legal charge by way of second mortgage on house—in December 1975 in proceedings under the Married Women's Property Act 1893 a consent order was made in county court providing, *inter alia,* that Mrs. CW was entitled to one-half share in equity of house before the second charge valued at £1,580—other half (to appellants) to be accounted for—no evidence called to support claim that Mrs. CW had an equitable interest which took priority over that of appellants in relation to funds in court after house sold and first mortgagee satisfied—appeal allowed—case sent back for rehearing. January 12, 1979. *Re* WILKINSON.

265. —— 'equitable mortgage—release

In the course of a meeting to settle actions brought by the defendants, a bank manager and a bank, against the plaintiff for considerable sums of money, the title deeds and land certificate of plaintiff's registered land were handed over to the defendants with the intention of creating an equitable mortgage—legal charge in substitution of equitable charge drafted, drawn up and engrossed and signed in two parts but parts never exchanged—title deeds later handed back—whether triable issue that equitable charge subsequently released or not—defendants' motion to vacate a caution by the plaintiff dismissed—appeal dismissed. Appeal from Brightman J. June 29, 1978. IGHOFOSE v. NASR.

266. —— mortgagee's power of sale—promissory estoppel

In January 1969 the plaintiff and her husband entered into a mortgage by way of legal charge in favour of the first defendants for securing the sum of £20,000 upon a flat—the mortgagors fell into arrears in respect of the interest payable under the mortgage and in March 1976 the first defendant went into possession—in August 1976 the plaintiff learned from solicitors for the first defendants that the first defendants were proposing to sell the property—on October 27, 1976, the plaintiff (as alleged in the statement of claim) telephoned the solicitors and informed them that the husband was prepared to pay off all sums due under the charge and solicitors accepted that the moneys would be forthcoming but " said that there was no immediate urgency as nothing was happening anyway for two weeks "—on November 1, 1976, the first defendants entered into a contract of sale with the second defendants—whether statement by defendants' solicitors giving rise to promissory estoppel—whether promissory estoppel could have rendered the statutory power of sale unexercisable—plaintiff's statement of claim struck out (on a preliminary issue) as not disclosing any cause of action—plaintiff's appeal dismissed. Appeal from Oliver J. April 21, 1978. KNIGHTLY v. SUN LIFE ASSURANCE SOCIETY.

267. —— possession of mortgaged property—arrears of mortgage payments

In December 1975 an order for possession was made in plaintiff's favour for non-payment of mortgage repayments by defendants (husband and wife)—order suspended for such period as defendants should punctually pay instalments due in addition to arrears to be paid by January 16, 1976—payments were not made as ordered and in May 1977 a warrant for possession was issued for defendants to be finally evicted on (after various applications by the defendants) June 21—on June 20 defendants paid by giro to plaintiff's bank money owing—notification of payment received by plaintiffs on June 22—warrant duly executed and defendants put out of possession—whether, *inter alia*, execution of warrant valid after payment by defendants—County Court Rules, Ords. 25 and 71 (1)—defendants' appeal dismissed. July 20, 1978. GREATER LONDON COUNCIL v. MAKALWALA.

268. —— —— interest of wife

In March 1978 judge ordered that plaintiffs should have possession of premises mortgaged to defendant but judgment not to be enforced for 28 days or so long thereafter as defendant paid moneys currently falling due under mortgage and £108 per month towards arrears—defendant appealed seeking further time and alternatively claiming that his wife had rights in respect of premises charged, she having registered a caution in November 1978—defendant's (in person) appeal dismissed. November 29, 1978. NATIONAL WESTMINSTER BANK v. DURLING.

269. Negligence—breach of duty

M was employed by defendants as a ganger and was engaged on excavation of a trench—pipeline to be laid in trench—two power lines carrying 20,000 volts running at right angles over trench—M electrocuted and killed, while trying, with another person, to erect a system of poles to alert jib drivers of danger overhead—whether defendants negligent at common law—whether defendants in breach of, *inter alia*, reg. 44 (1) of the Construction and General Provisions Regulations—whether all "practicable steps" taken to prevent danger to persons employed from any live electric cable which was liable to be a source of danger—judge found defendants not liable—Mrs. M's appeal allowed—M 80 per cent. responsible for cause of accident, his employers 20 per cent. July 27, 1978. *Re* MOLLEY, DECD.

270. —— breach of duty of care—evidence

Plaintiff, widow and administratrix of N. C. Smyth, deceased, brought an action against defendant under Fatal Accidents Acts—deceased was killed by being knocked down by defendant's van in a "commonplace road accident" while trying to cross Soho Road, Birmingham, a busy main road, at about 9 p.m. when there was a fair amount of traffic and when traffic lights were green for traffic on Soho Road—deceased had been drinking and had come out of a public-house on one side of road and intended to go to another one on other side—evidence of witnesses—judge dismissed plaintiff's claim and entered judgment for defendant—plaintiff's appeal allowed—both deceased and defendant equally to blame for accident—defendant thus liable to extent of one-half of such damages as may be assessed. November 30, 1978. SMYTH *v.* YOUNAS.

271. —— cattle—straying onto highway—party liable

Plaintiff was driver of car which was damaged when it collided with defendant's cow (which was killed) on a road in neighbourhood of third party's railway line which ran under road—defendant's case that cattle had escaped through defective fence on southern boundary of his land, the part of fence for which third party was responsible—third-party proceedings against British Railways Board taken by defendant but no such proceedings taken by plaintiff —judge found against defendant on balance of probabilities and gave judgment for plaintiff for £1,038 and dismissed counterclaim by defendant with costs and gave judgment for third party against defendant with costs—defendant's appeal against judge's refusal of indemnity against third party dismissed—appeal misconceived. January 11, 1979. JONES DEWEY & TURNER *v.* PEARSON AND BRITISH RAILWAYS BOARD (THIRD PARTY).

272. —— causation—apportionment of blame

Accident between motor cars at cross-roads controlled by traffic lights just after 2 a.m.—judge found defendant approached traffic lights at an excessive speed and "jumped" traffic lights just as they were changing from amber to red although defendant could have pulled up, and the plaintiff started onto junction when traffic lights were showing red and amber—judge held both to blame for the collision apportioning blame 80 per cent. to plaintiff and 20 per cent. to defendant—plaintiff's appeal against apportionment dismissed— plaintiff's appeal against £75 general damages (plaintiff aged 20 and off work for a week because of scrape on right side of forehead and pain in back) allowed—general damages increased to £150 that being right kind of figure for comparatively minor injuries. January 26, 1979. ROSSITER *v.* LUNT.

273. —— —— evidence

First defendant whilst driving a cattle truck in course of his employment with second defendant decided to make a U-turn to head back along direction that he was supposed to be going—plaintiff's car collided with off-side rear of cattle truck whilst attempting to pass truck—plaintiff's and first defendant's versions of accident and evidence of independent witness—judge found in favour of plaintiff—defendants' appeal dismissed. Appeal from O'Connor J. October 11, 1978. HENDERSON v. POPLE.

274. —— —— —— quantum of damages

Defendants were highway authority for length of highway where plaintiff's husband met with his fatal accident on March 25, 1969, at 6.40 p.m. at a cross-roads—evidence of eye witness, plus, *inter alia*, detailed history of accidents occurring at cross-roads over a period of a number of years prior to above fatal accident—cross-roads a notorious accident "black spot"—judge found defendants liable in that accident was the result of pending road works which, *inter alia*, detracted one's attention from road signs, and also found contributory negligence against deceased—whether conclusions of judge supported by evidence—defendants' appeal dismissed—proper apportionment 50/50 basis—plaintiffs' appeal on apportionment and on question of quantum of damages allowed. Appeal from Thesiger J. December 18, 1978. JACOEL v. WEST RIDING COUNTY COUNCIL.

275. —— duty of care—breach—evidence

At three o'clock on a fine afternoon in August T, an experienced lorry driver aged 42, holding a HGV licence with a clean record, died when a tractor unit that he was driving went through the rails at left-hand side of a narrow bridge and into silt at bottom of dock there—different versions of how accident happened—judge gave judgment for defendants in a claim by plaintiff, T's wife, under the Fatal Accidents Act—evidence before the judge—whether sufficient evidence to establish that there was a danger of using bridge of which defendants ought to have given warning or more warning than they did—plaintiff's appeal dismissed—defendants not in breach of their duty to deceased—narrow bridge with projections easy to be seen would show any reasonably careful driver the need to approach bridge with care. Appeal from Park J. January 22, 1979. EDESON v. BRITISH TRANSPORT DOCKS BOARD.

276. At 9.30 a.m. on October 8, 1974, the plaintiff was driving his motor car along a road when three horses ran out of a farm road entrance on right through an open gate—car hit middle horse causing his death and damage to plaintiff's car—plaintiff's case that there was or must have been negligence on defendant's part in failing to keep animals in unless defendant could explain accident away—judge drew inference from facts found that defendant failed to exercise reasonable care in preventing horses escaping—border line case—defendant's appeal dismissed. February 12, 1979. KEEL v. ANTROBUS.

277. —— —— children

Plaintiff, eight years old at time of accident in May 1975, was playing football with other boys in a school playing field adjoining a bus depot—perimeter wall consisting of concrete posts and slabs put up by defendants round the playing field—plaintiff injured while climbing back over wall having retrieved ball kicked over fence—top slab of wall came away—no evidence that balls frequently kicked over fence—children not known to come over wall—judge found for defendants—plaintiff's appeal dismissed. July 22, 1978. COMBER v. MERSEYSIDE PASSENGER TRANSPORT EXECUTIVE.

278. —— —— school authority

Just before a Christmas party at school in 1974, the plaintiff, a girl, then aged 13 years, fell down some stairs while carrying two plates with cakes and sandwiches—plaintiff's right hand badly cut—she brought an action against the defendant school authority alleging negligence, her case being that she was told to hurry up as they were late by a part-time teacher—perfectly safe staircase—judge found against the plaintiff and held that there was no negligence on the part of the defendants—plaintiff's appeal dismissed. Appeal from Goff J. July 14, 1978. ADLINGTON *v.* LEICESTERSHIRE COUNTY COUNCIL.

279. —— —— whether foreseeable accident

Plaintiff was employed by defendants (for about 20 years) as a fitter's mate—in February 1973 he was working with a fitter in the overhaul of a piece of machinery and injured his left eye, making him effectively blind in that eye, when a piece of metal flew up and stuck in the eye as he was hammering to loosen the door of the machinery on which he was working—whether employers negligent at common law—whether accident reasonably foreseeable and ought to have been foreseen by the defendant employers—judge decided against the plaintiff—plaintiff's appeal dismissed. Appeal from Crichton J. May 8, 1978. GRIFFITHS *v.* CENTRAL ELECTRICITY GENERATING BOARD.

280. —— evidence—behaviour of defendant

Plaintiff brought an action against the defendant alleging that he had run into a lamp-post while driving his car because of the conduct of the defendant and suffered personal injury and damage—defendant admitted that there was a collision between the plaintiff's motor-car and a lamp-post but made no admission as to the cause of the accident and the nature and extent of the damage and denied every allegation contained in the particulars of the statement of claim—judge believed plaintiff's evidence and gave judgment finding defendant liable and awarded damages—defendant's appeal dismissed—defendant's application for leave to adduce fresh evidence dismissed because of background of conduct of litigation on the defendant's part. May 3, 1978. DENNISON *v.* JERVIS.

281. —— liability—apportionment—evidence—damages

In August 1971 there was a collision between offside front wing of defendant's car and offside rear wheel arch of plaintiff's van—judge apportioned blame as to 85 per cent. on defendant and 15 per cent. on plaintiff and awarded plaintiff, in a claim for damages for personal injuries, £12,455 special damage, £16,000 for loss of future earnings, and £2,500 general damages for pain, suffering and loss of amenity—defendant appealed contending, *inter alia,* that judge was wrong in his apportionment of liability—action tried six and a half years after accident—evidence available—judge accepted evidence for plaintiff and rejected that for defendant—defendant's appeal allowed—plaintiff one-third to blame and defendant two-thirds—plaintiff aged 54 and able to carry on his job as taxi driver—special damage reduced to £4,033, and loss of future earnings to £4,050—general damages for pain, suffering and loss of amenity increased to £5,000. November 28, 1978. COATES *v.* FARNHILL.

282. —— master and servant—safe system of work

Plaintiff, a heavy goods vehicle driver employed by defendants, wanted to secure his lorry load but found his usual ropes gone—usual ropes were kept by drivers after they obtained them from yard foreman, under whose control they were kept but drivers were known to take ropes from each other's cabs—plaintiff went to yard foreman but he had no ropes left so he asked plaintiff to look around for some—plaintiff found some ropes lying in the yard and while he was tying his lorry load one of the ropes snapped when plaintiff pulled hard on it and plaintiff fell and injured his ankle—drivers' job to examine ropes that they used and to discard ropes which were unsuitable for use—whether defendants negligent in failing to provide and maintain a safe system for inspection and issue of ropes for use by drivers—whether burden upon defendants to explain accident—Employers' Liability (Defective Equipment) Act 1969—judgment given in favour of defendants—plaintiff's appeal dismissed. November 2, 1978. GLEAVE v. NORTH WESTERN BRITISH ROAD SERVICES.

283. —— medical diagnosis—evidence

Plaintiff, pursuing a career in the RAF, brought an action against the defendant, an Air Force Marshal in the RAF, claiming that defendant was negligent in diagnosing that plaintiff was suffering from epilepsy and paranoia— effect of diagnosis was to put an end to plaintiff's career in the RAF—judge found evidence did not prove the case of negligence against the defendant and dismissed action—evidence before judge—plaintiff's (in person) appeal dismissed. Appeal from Mars-Jones J. November 20, 1978. MCCORMICK v. O'CONNOR.

284. —— post office—breach of duty

On a counterclaim by the defendant, an ex-employee of the plaintiff P.O., for damages for injuries resulting from breach of statutory duty and negligence, the judge found that there was no negligence by the P.O. but that there was a technical breach of s. 14 of the Offices and Shops Act 1963 and awarded the defendant nominal damages of £5—defendant's (in person) appeal dismissed—judgment below justified on evidence which was heard. July 13, 1978. POST OFFICE v. JOHNSTON.

285. —— professional negligence

Plaintiff claimed in respect of a contract made between himself and the defendants in respect of the spraying of his car alleging shoddy workmanship— judge gave judgment in favour of the defendants—plaintiff's (in person) appeal that judge came to wrong conclusion on the evidence dismissed—plaintiff's application to adduce fresh evidence dismissed. May 18, 1978. LONG v. BROOK SHAW.

286. —— —— architect

Plaintiff, an architect, brought an action against the defendant, a solicitor, experienced in property matters, for fees due for her professional services in respect of conversion work to be carried out at the defendant's property— defendant denied indebtedness to plaintiff and counterclaimed for money paid upon a consideration which had wholly failed and alleged " breach of contract and/or negligence "—conversion work abandoned because estimated cost too high—plaintiff's terms of appointment—defendant's amended particulars of professional negligence disallowed by judge who found in favour of the plaintiff on the evidence—defendant's appeal dismissed. June 23, 1978. ALEXANDER v. RENDALL.

287. —— —— evidence

In October 1969, plaintiff, then aged 19, was admitted into hospital and operated on for triple arthrodesis of his left foot—on November 1 gas gangrene was observed at the operation scar and on November 6 plaintiff's left leg was amputated through the calf followed by a second necessary amputation on November 10—plaintiff discharged from hospital on December 20, but twice readmitted in the following year following accidents and injury to left leg—writ issued by plaintiff in May 1972 and case heard in March 1977 —damages agreed subject to liability—plaintiff's case that infection and resultant condition the direct result of negligence of the defendants plus that the defendants negligently failed to treat plaintiff's said condition resulting in loss of leg—defendants denied negligence—judge found that plaintiff failed to prove any negligence on the part of the defendants—appeal that the judge ought to have found negligence and that his judgment was against the weight of the evidence—appeal allowed—judgment for plaintiff in the agreed sum of damages of £8,500. Appeal from Michael Davies J. June 30, 1978. THOMPSON v. WEST MIDLANDS REGIONAL HEALTH AUTHORITY.

288. —— road traffic—collision

Accident at 8 a.m. on a day in December between plaintiff's car being driven on main road (with a 30 m.p.h. speed limit) and defendant's car coming out of side road—main road wet and surface slightly greasy or muddy—plaintiff's speed put at 40 to 45 m.p.h. by police officer, calculation being based on positions of cars after accident—evidence—judge came to conclusion that cause of accident was plaintiff's " grossly excessive " speed and dismissed plaintiff's action—plaintiff's appeal dismissed—no general principle in case. November 15, 1978. CHRISTIE v. YOUNG.

289. —— statutory duty—breach

Plaintiff was injured as he was getting off a ladder onto a deck situated 12 feet high on a movable scaffolding being used in building of a telephone exchange—scaffolding toppled over and landed on plaintiff—whether defendants liable for breach of statutory duty for negligence—Construction (Working Places) Regulations, reg. 15—plaintiff, weighing 17 stones, yanked himself by rail onto scaffolding—whether ordinary user—plaintiff's appeal allowed—clear evidence that scaffolding toppled over in ordinary user—no contributory negligence on plaintiff's part—judgment for plaintiff with damages to be assessed. Appeal from Payne J. May 12, 1978. JACKSON v. MILLER BUCKLEY CONSTRUCTION CO.

290. —— vehicles—skid

Plaintiff's husband was killed when he was thrown from the first defendants' eight-ton tipper lorry being driven by the second defendant while going to work on a contract for the first defendants—the lorry skidded and overturned while negotiating a gentle right curve on a wet and slippery road—plaintiff alleged negligence in that the braking system of the lorry was defective or that the skid was caused by driving too fast and braking too hard—the judge found that although the skid had not been caused initially by the second defendant's negligence, the second defendant was negligent in not preventing the slide to develop to the extent it did and accordingly gave judgment for the plaintiff—whether judge's conclusions justified by evidence—defendant's appeal dismissed. Appeal from May J. May 4, 1978. MCGOVERN v. QUINNS CONTRACTORS.

291. Partnership—breach of partnership rules—injunction

Parties, who were married, but divorced in 1974, together set up and ran an equestrian centre in partnership—planning permission given in 1972 for use of land as equestrian centre but not for " any public event without the prior consent in writing of the local planning authority "—in 1974 parties entered into a deed dissolving partnership, land was to be vested freehold in husband, and wife, " the mainstay of the business," was to carry on riding school for a time until she could find alternative premises for business and she was given until May 1, 1979, to find alternative premises—wife proposed to hold horse hunter trials at premises and judge, on husband's application, granted an injunction restraining her from doing so—wife's appeal dismissed—*inter alia*, strong prima facie case that there would be a breach of the partnership deed. Appeal from Jupp J. September 15, 1978. CADBURY v. CADBURY.

292. —— existence of partnership—evidence

Plaintiffs, property developers, and defendants, builders, were involved in land being developed and houses being built for sale—agreement dated July 17, 1974—agreement contained no reference to sharing of losses but contained provision for sharing of profits—whether nature of parties' involvement one of partnership—plaintiffs claimed that defendants were partners and defendants claimed that plaintiffs were building owners and defendants were builders employed as such—analysis of agreement—evidence and admissible surrounding circumstances—Partnership Act 1890, ss. 1 (1), 24 (1)—judge held that relationship was one of partnership—defendants' appeal dismissed. Appeal from Fox J. November 24, 1978. WALKER WEST DEVELOPMENTS v. F. J. EMMETT.

293. Plaintiff brought action against defendants for price of goods sold—whether defendants had represented to plaintiff at time goods were bought that they were partners—judge heard evidence from plaintiff and first defendant and gave judgment for plaintiff having accepted plaintiff's evidence in its entirety—no note of judge's reasons—first defendant's appeal that judge was wrong to find a partnership dismissed—grounds of appeal without substance. January 18, 1979. ISLAM v. HUSSAIN.

294. Patents and Designs—infringement—interlocutory injunction—balance of convenience

Plaintiffs sought by injunction to restrain the defendants, a small young company, from counselling and procuring the infringement of their patents—defendants relied upon prior user and obviousness of alleged invention—judge refused injunction—whether judge exercised discretion wrongly—plaintiffs' appeal dismissed. Appeal from Whitford J. July 10, 1978. CONDOR INTERNATIONAL v. HIBBING.

295. —— patents—specifications—obviousness

Patent in suit related to printing inks and process of printing using a water soluble dye in conjunction with a polyethyleneimine for fixing and making the ink impervious—judge, on appeal from hearing at patent office, reversed decision of hearing officer and decided against applicants on the ground that alleged invention was obvious having regard to what was known in the art—whether judge misdirected himself—applicants' application for leave to appeal out of time allowed with qualification. Appeal from Whitford J. July 24, 1978. Re AN APPLICATION BY USHER WALKER.

296. Pensions and Superannuation—contributory pension scheme—construction of rules

A contributory pension scheme was established by plaintiff company in February 1975 by a declaration of trust—B, an employee of the company, died an undischarged bankrupt in August 1975 aged 62 years which was under pensionable age under scheme—£59 contributions paid by company to B's personal representatives and £7,059 benefit payment to be paid to defendants in certain proportions pursuant to a resolution passed by company four days before expiration of 12 months from date of B's death—personal representatives argued that as actual payment of sums decided to be distributed had not been made within 12 months after B's death, power to make such payments was no longer exercisable (and accordingly £7,059 was payable to them) under rules of pension scheme—construction of rules—judge decided in favour of personal representatives—fourth defendant's (who lived with B at time of his death and was engaged to be married to him) appeal allowed. Appeal from Walton J. October 16, 1978. RAMAC HOLDINGS v. CHAPMAN.

297. Practice—action—dismissal for want of prosecution

A road built by first defendants pursuant to a contract entered into in January 1968 started to break down in 1970–1971 and remedial works costing some £74,000 had to be carried out from April 1975 to May 1976—writ issued by plaintiffs in January 1974 and served in January 1975—pleadings closed in July 1975—action transferred to official referee in August 1976—summons for directions issued in December 1977—whether inordinate and inexcusable delay and whether causing prejudice—judge dismissed defendants' application to dismiss plaintiff's action for want of prosecution—defendants' appeal dismissed. July 20, 1978. MURRAYFIELD REAL ESTATE CO. v. C. BRYANT & SON.

298. Plaintiff, a young man in his thirties, badly injured his back by being blown off a trestle ladder while working for defendants on construction of a protective fence at a Borstal institution—statement of claim served with writ in October 1974 alleged simply negligence and made no allegation that there was a failure to provide a scaffolding despite repeated requests and no allegation of breach of statutory duty—defence denied, *inter alia*, negligence and in April 1975 defendants made a request for particulars of statement of claim —nothing happened thereafter until January 1978 when certain correspondence started by plaintiff's solicitors—master and judge (on appeal) dismissed plaintiff's claim for want of prosecution—plaintiff's appeal dismissed. Appeal from Jones J. October 18, 1978. WORROW v. BINNS FENCING.

299. —— —— —— waiver of delay

Plaintiffs' claim for some £152,000 originated in January 1968 as an account stated and was settled, there being a course of dealing between parties—sum (said to arise from accounts and contra accounts getting out of balance) admitted as being owed by defendants, who claimed, however, that that sum could be set off against certain sums due to defendants from plaintiffs— events giving rise to applications to strike out plaintiffs' claim ran from April 1972 to May 1977, when summons to strike out issued—in January 1977 further request for further and better particulars of defence was filed, a summons thereon issued and on April 6 defendants appeared on summons and had it adjourned to May 16—judge found inexcusable and inordinate delay on plaintiffs' part but found that defendants, by their conduct towards the end period, had waived or acquiesced in delay and therefore dismissed summons for dismissal for want of prosecution—defendants' appeal dismissed. Appeal from Mocatta J. October 5, 1978. PEDTRAX v. SHELL-MEX AND B.P.

300. —— —— summary judgment

Plaintiff brought action for £3,000 given to defendant to buy grocery business in contemplation of marriage which did not take place—defendant signed document agreeing to pay back money " which I recognise I owe her "— " shadowy " counterclaim by defendant—plaintiff applied for summary judgment under R.S.C. Ord. 14 and judge gave defendant leave to defend conditionally on payment of £3,000 into court—defendant's appeal that he should have unconditional leave to defend because finding £3,000 now would ruin him dismissed. June 16, 1978. METCALF v. LANSING.

301. —— —— trial—adjournment for filing evidence in reply

Plaintiffs brought an action for return of large number of articles seized by police on June 2, 1978—affidavits sworn by plaintiffs on June 21 and 22 received by defendant on June 23—on defendant's application judge adjourned matter for 14 days to give defendant opportunity of filing evidence in reply to plaintiffs' affidavits—plaintiffs' " over-hasty " appeal dismissed—no " desperate urgency " shown for plaintiffs to have articles back—clearly right for court to know defendant's case. Appeal from Kenneth Jones J. June 27, 1978. ALI *v.* METROPOLITAN POLICE COMMISSIONER.

302. —— amendment of defendant's name—appeal

Plaintiffs sued defendant in respect of a contract which had involved loan of money in connection with the purchase of a car—defendant's name spelt as " Mahoney " in contract and proceedings instituted with defendant's name as " Mahoney "—at hearing plaintiffs were given leave to amend name to " Mahony "—defendant's (in person) appeal dismissed—appeal misconceived. November 29, 1978. UNITED DOMINIONS TRUST *v.* MAHONY.

303. —— appeal—appeal out of time

In April 1974 Templeman J. sanctioned a scheme of arrangement relating to applicant company and in February 1976 Blackett-Ord V.-C. made winding-up order for the compulsory liquidation of the company—applicant shareholder applied for leave to appeal out of time contending that scheme had proved disastrous—application refused. Appeals from Templeman J. and Blackett-Ord V.-C. October 3, 1978. *Re* EDWARD WOOD CO.

304. —— —— case stated—question of law

Whether error of law when lands tribunal says, *e.g.* that it " prefers " the evidence of certain comparables and goes on to say " I have rejected the second as an acceptable comparable "—whether lands tribunal has refused to *admit* such evidence—nonsense—misunderstanding of English language—appellant's (in person) appeal dismissed. June 28, 1978. COLLINS *v.* HOBBS.

305. —— —— documents for appeal

Plaintiff (in person) applied for leave to appeal against an order of master that judgment (relating to a large sum of money) entered for plaintiff against defendants under R.S.C., Ord. 14, r. 3, be set aside—judge upheld order of master—various grounds of appeal—no papers produced to show evidence relied on by defendants before master and judge—application refused. Appeal from Wien J. August 31, 1978. H.R.H. THE PRINCESS ALEXANDRIA DINIZULU *v.* ROSE.

306. —— —— non-compliance with rules

Judgment entered for the defendants on January 21, 1977—notice of appeal by plaintiffs (in person) given on March 14, 1977—appeal set down on March 17, 1977—notice of setting down not given by appellants to respondents—no documents provided as required by the rules—no response by appellants to communications sent by court officials—plaintiff appellants not present at hearing of appeal—appeal dismissed with costs. Appeal from Kerr J. July 27, 1978. BERKELEY TRADING CO. (A FIRM) *v.* FOURDALE EXPORT SERVICES.

307. —— —— relevant documents

Plaintiff solicitors claimed balance of fees said to be due to them for professional services rendered—defendant claimed in defence that plaintiffs had failed properly to carry out her instructions—registrar and judge found in favour of plaintiffs—defendant's (in person) appeal dismissed because on material before court no possible basis for saying that order of judge below was wrong—up to defendant appellant to put forward such documents as were relevant on the hearing of the appeal. December 18, 1978. SPEECHLY, BIRCHAM *v.* MARSHALL.

308. —— —— setting aside default judgment—misconceived appeal

In July 1977 judgment was signed against the defendant in default of defence—defendant appealed (in person) alleging that writ in proceedings was never served on him nor application to sign judgment in default against him— appeal misconceived and dismissed—appropriate procedure, if what defendant says was true, was to go back to judge and ask him to set aside default judgment. Appeal from Caulfield J. June 26, 1978. HULKS *v.* BEE.

309. —— contempt—committal

On July 7, an order committing husband to prison was made and a warrant of attachment for his arrest issued on basis that husband had been guilty of contempt by refusing to disclose the whereabouts of one of two children of marriage—later husband appeared in court and judge confirmed committal order not accepting husband's purge of his contempt—whether on face of orders contempt shown to commit husband to prison—official solicitor's appeal allowed—impossible to read implied terms into an order of the court in committal for contempt involving liberty of the subject. June 9, 1978. DEODAT *v.* DEODAT.

310. The husband had been kept in imprisonment for 11 months on the basis of a committal which Court of Appeal held on June 9 to be invalid—later on June 9 judge committed husband to further two months' imprisonment, starting on June 9, for breach of injunction prohibiting the husband from molesting his then wife (see § 309 above)—whether further imprisonment excessive for the particular act of contempt in view of imprisonment already served— husband's appeal allowed. June 13, 1978. DEODAT *v.* DEODAT.

311. Husband was in breach of his undertaking to court by driving to a cul-de-sac near matrimonial home, by failing to remove his car from garage as ordered, and by going to matrimonial home to prevent his greenhouse being pulled down and sold—parties married in 1962 and had three children— marriage broken down in 1977 when wife left with children—judge made a suspended committal order on husband—husband's appeal allowed—situation did not require custodial sentence. July 20, 1978. WITHERS *v.* WITHERS.

312. Defendant aimed a blow (which missed) at complainant, a bailiff of court, when complainant called at defendant's house to serve a default summons on him—on complaint, on August 11, judge committed, *inter alia*, defendant to prison for 14 days but suspended committal warrant until August 29 and suspension was to continue pending hearing of an appeal (if any)—committal order made under s. 30 (1) of County Courts Act 1959—whether prison sentence too severe—one of defendant's grounds of appeal that he had been on bail and it had been a period of very acute anxiety for him—defendant's appeal dismissed —observation that maximum financial penalty of £50 under the 1959 Act unnecessarily low nowadays. November 2, 1978. PEARSON *v.* MARTIN.

313. Plaintiff, who had recently broken off her relationship with the defendant, started an action against him for assault and was granted an interlocutory injunction restraining the defendant from assaulting her or coming near her house— in July 1978 plaintiff's application to commit defendant for breach of that in-

junction was adjourned with liberty to restore, defendant being given a severe warning that repetition of his behaviour would lead to imprisonment—plaintiff alleged further breaches of injunction and applied for her July 1978 application to be restored—notice of application sent by registrar of court to defendant's solicitors but no notice sent to defendant personally—defendant had gone away to North of England and did not receive letter from his solicitors of adjourned hearing until day after hearing had taken place—County Court Rules (1936), Ord. 25, r. 68 (2)—defendant committed to prison for 28 days—defendant's appeal allowed. November 29, 1978. ALDOUS v. WHETTON.

314. —— costs—discretion—conduct of defendants

Defendants, manufacturers and dealers in clothing, including jeans, were in breach of their undertaking to remove certain advertisements (appearing on buses), which used a name associated with plaintiffs' jeans, within stated time—advertisements removed four days after end of time stated in under-taking—judge did not regard defendants' contempt as a serious one because of efforts made by defendants, " albeit belatedly," and on plaintiffs' motion for contempt made no order leaving parties to bear their own respective costs—plaintiffs' appeal that defendant should have been ordered to pay their costs of motion dismissed—observation on *Re Witten* (1887) 4 T.L.R. 36. Appeal from Oliver J. February 2, 1979. BLUE BELL INC. v. FALMER INTERNATIONAL.

315. —— —— reality of situation

Plaintiffs, steel stockholders, supplied a small amount of steel to the defen-dants, a small firm of furniture makers, for making corner pieces for tables—defendants cut the steel up into the required patterns at which stage it was noticed that the wrong quality of steel had been supplied—correspondence between parties—amount of defective steel supplied by plaintiffs—plaintiffs' claim of £413·94 for goods sold and delivered—defendants claimed some £5,000 for, *inter alia*, loss of profits but unable to prove their case on loss of profits—three-day hearing before judge—defendants' loss quantified by judge on guesswork because evidence inadequate—judgment for plaintiffs for £413·94 with costs, counsel for the defendants having conceded plaintiffs' claim, and for the defendants for £500 with costs—plaintiffs' appeal allowed with costs—no order as to costs in court below on either the claim or the counter-claim—reality of situation that substantial time taken up by plaintiffs' abortive attempt to establish a custom of the trade and similarly substantial time taken up by defendants in abortive exercise in attempt to prove loss of profit and fictitious case. May 23, 1978. SERIC STEEL SUPPLY v. POLLARD FURNITURE.

316. —— —— security of costs

Plaintiff brought an action in nuisance against first defendant and her brother, a minor—various interlocutory matters—hearing of action started but adjourned upon certain allegations being made against defendants' legal representatives—defendants separately represented by counsel and counsel present for Official Solicitor's Department because of allegations against minor, the second defen-dant—plaintiff, appearing in person, failed to turn up at adjourned hearing and produced a doctor's certificate excusing him from going to work—judge adjourned case further on terms that plaintiff pay into court £200 for costs thrown away—plaintiff's (in person) appeal dismissed. November 29, 1978. OBINWE v. ABOOD.

317. —— discovery—documents at police station

Plaintiff in an action against defendants, police officers, for malicious prose-cution, false imprisonment and assault, sought further discovery of " all documents which state the names and/or addresses of all persons other than police officers who were present " at a certain police station at certain times and the reasons why such persons were there—master refused order and judge dismissed appeal from master—plaintiff's appeal dismissed—order sought by plaintiff too wide. Appeal from Kenneth Jones J. July 19, 1978. DONNELY *v.* DAVIES.

318. —— —— review of order

In April 1977 the Court of Appeal dismissed for want of prosecution plaintiff's action in negligence (started in March 1970) against defendants, a firm of solicitors, which alleged mishandling of her case against a hospital which had detained plaintiff as being a person of unsound mind—plaintiff now applied to Court of Appeal for a review of its decision in April 1977 under R.S.C., Ord. 24, r. 17, producing " fresh evidence "—application dismissed—evidence produced by plaintiff not fresh as it was previously available and in any event it was unlikely to influence result of case—Ord. 24, r. 17, to be narrowly applied—court not to reverse its previous decision or vary it except in circumstances where it would grant a new trial—principles stated in *Ladd* v. *Marshall* [1954] C.L.Y. 2507 applicable. Appeal from O'Connor J. November 23, 1978. DHARGHALKAR *v.* COLES & STEVENSON.

319. —— discovery of documents—relevance of documents

HY Ltd. were head contractors for certain building work and defendants were sub-contractors for part of that work and plaintiffs were sub-sub-contractors —no direct contractual relationship between plaintiffs and HY Ltd.—in their contracts with defendants plaintiffs undertook to provide and fit " acoustic chambers " by August 1973—various disputes between plaintiffs and defendants —whether a term of contracts that plaintiffs would be entitled to adjustment of the price if contractual work not completed by August 1973—plaintiffs' allegation that delays took work beyond August 1973 through no fault of their own—most of matters put into issue by defendants—plaintiffs applied for further discovery against defendants of certain documents passing between defendants and HY Ltd.—relevance of documents—plaintiffs' appeal allowed. December 1, 1978. HOTCHKISS DUCTWORK *v.* INDUSTRIAL ACOUSTICS CO.

320. —— dismissal of action—want of prosecution—whether equitable to allow action to proceed

In 1953 plaintiff employed by defendants, was injured in accident at work and in August 1976 he issued writ claiming damages for those injuries—writ served on defendants in July 1977 and within time permitted the statement of claim was served—defendants applied to dismiss action for want of prosecution —Limitation Act 1975—*Biss* v. *Lambeth, Southwark and Lewisham Area Health Authority* [1978] C.L.Y. 2425, *Walkley* v. *Precision Forgings* [1978] C.L.Y. 1845—fair trial of case not possible after 25 years—not equitable to allow action to proceed any further—circumstances to which court is to have regard in considering whether it is equitable to allow action to proceed or not to be generally investigated on a summons and not at trial—defendants' appeal allowed. October 27, 1978. HATTAM *v.* NATIONAL COAL BOARD.

321.—— enforcement of security

Plaintiff company obtained summary judgment to recover amount of loan paid to defendants pursuant to agreement to make a film—defence and counterclaim struck out because defendants failed to provide certain particulars thereof—judge made order in favour of plaintiff ordering sale of assets charged by charging agreement by way of enforcement of plaintiff's security—plaintiff alleged to have taken obstructive course calculated to prevent film agreement ever being implemented—construction of film agreement between plaintiff and defendants—defendants' appeal dismissed—plaintiff entitled to behave as it did under the terms of the film agreement. Appeal from Goulding J. October 20, 1978. PERBEN v. THE MARIO GHIO PRODUCTION GROUP.

322. —— hearing date—postponement

Defendants had been deprived of all their counsel except one who was very junior and judge considered that in those circumstances right course, in interests of justice to both parties, and in spite of the wishes and interests of plaintiff himself, was to vacate date which he himself had fixed in June (with approval of the Court of Appeal) and to vary order by postponing (for the second time) date of hearing of action until October 2—Practice Direction of the Lord Chief Justice [1958] C.L.Y. 2746—plaintiff's appeal dismissed. Appeal from Thompson J. October 23, 1978. MAXWELL v. PAGE.

323. —— injunction

Plaintiffs, a Sicilian company, agreed to sell some 29,000 tons of gas oil free on board at a port in Sicily at a price of $3,500,000—" string of sellers and buyers," last two being a Panamanian company, the seventh defendants, who sold to a German company, first defendants—cargo loaded, bills of lading issued, but " hitch in transfer of shipping documents down line of buyers "—oil arrived at Bremen in Germany and ship handed over cargo to first defendants without requiring bill of lading to be produced—first defendants sold cargo on to further buyers (who paid for it) and paid its own sellers, seventh defendants, $3,500,000—indemnity given by a group in England to seventh defendants in respect of cargo—plaintiffs brought proceedings to follow moneys and were granted injunction against any disposal or usage of moneys and certain orders for discovery and filing of affidavits by defendants by certain dates—second, fourth, fifth and sixth defendants' application for stay of execution refused but time limit for filing of affidavits extended. Appeal from Mocatta J. December 1, 1978. MEDITERRANEAN REFFINERIA SICILLIANA PETROLI S.P.A. v. MABANAFT GMBH.

324. —— —— interlocutory—balance of convenience

Plaintiffs were a company specialising in the extermination of pests in the food industry and premises connected with the storage and sale of food—first defendant had been employed by the plaintiffs since 1959 and in December 1977, when he was a director and national manager of the plaintiffs, he resigned together with some other directors and joined the second defendants, a company in exactly the same line of business as the plaintiffs—no service agreement between plaintiffs and first defendants—plaintiffs applied for injunctions to, inter alia, restrain the defendants from competing and continuing to compete with the plaintiffs by the unfair use of confidential information obtained by first defendant in the course of his employment with the plaintiffs in relation to the plaintiffs' customers and employees—ex parte injunctions obtained by plaintiffs discharged by judge—plaintiffs' appeal with further uncontradicted evidence before court allowed—judge wrong to conclude that plaintiffs could be adequately compensated in damages and did not need the protection of any injunction. Appeal from Kilner-Brown J. May 25, 1978. PRESTOXIN v. BOARDMAN.

325. —— —— —— restrictive covenant

Property known as Coral Wood had been let by council as lessors to second defendants—lease contained provision that lessee should not engage in gaming of any kind—plaintiffs, councillors on Torbay Borough Council, sought through Attorney-General to bring a relator action to stop an amendment of lease which would permit second defendants to use property for purposes of gaming —main question was construction of Gaming Act 1968, s. 44 (1)—judge refused injunction sought by plaintiffs—plaintiffs' appeal dismissed. November 3, 1978. KIDD v. TORBAY BOROUGH COUNCIL.

326. —— —— " Mareva " type injunction

" Mareva " type injunction granted to plaintiffs on July 29 was discharged on August 2 on the ground that it related mainly to funds which were not presently within jurisdiction but which would or might become assets of defendants within the jurisdiction in future and that it was inappropriate on the balance of convenience—plaintiffs' appeal dismissed. Appeal from Wien J. August 4, 1978. CYBEL INC. OF PANAMA v. TIMPUSHIP.

327. —— —— restraint of trade—balance of convenience

Plaintiff, a dental surgeon, worked at defendant's dental surgery in Sheffield as an associate from November 1976 to June 1977 when her employment was terminated by defendant—clauses in employment agreement provided, *inter alia*, that plaintiff would not work as dental surgeon within a radius of five miles from defendant's surgery—reasonableness of clauses to be decided at trial—plaintiff proposed to start work within the five-mile radius with another dental surgery and defendant applied for injunction—judge granted injunction —plaintiff's appeal allowed—damages not an adequate remedy because if injunction granted plaintiff would be unable to take up appointment and may be required to leave home to take employment elsewhere, even if she could find any at all—balance of convenience in circumstances was in favour of plaintiff —*Fellowes & Son* v. *Fisher* [1975] C.L.Y. 2642 referred to. Appeal from Smith J. August 17, 1978. KENNETH v. MYERSCOUGH.

328. —— judgment—enforcement—charging order against partnership property

Plaintiff, a man of 68, badly injured and in ill health, obtained judgment against defendant for damages for personal injuries (received in a road accident in March 1971) for the sum of £8,950—judgment stayed on payment of £30 per month—payments not kept up and plaintiff applied for a charging order against a freehold estate known as Castle Hotel (run by defendant and his wife) under the Administration of Justice Act 1956, s. 35, and R.S.C., Ord. 50, r. 1—hotel was partnership property, defendant and his wife being the partners, and accordingly application was required to be made under the Partnership Act 1890, s. 23 (2), and R.S.C., Ord. 81, r. 10—Partnership Act 1890, s. 33 (2)—no jurisdiction to make charging order on plaintiff's original application—defendant's appeal allowed. November 14, 1978. ALLISON v. CLARK.

329. —— —— execution—stay of execution

Applicant defaulted in meeting rating demands made by respondent council and justices made an order for execution thereof—later council agreed to allow payment by " very modest monthly " instalments but applicant still failed to pay—application for leave for an order of judicial review refused by Divisional Court and appeal pending to Court of Appeal—" tenuous " grounds of appeal—applicant's application for stay of execution of orders made by justices refused. August 31, 1978. GARLAND v. KENSINGTON AND CHELSEA ROYAL BOROUGH.

330. —— —— **judgment on admissions of fact**

Plaintiff, personal representative of estate of her deceased husband, brought an action in September 1974 by a specially indorsed writ claiming a loan of £22,500 plus agreed interest—defendants made admissions by letter written in 1973 of fact of a loan of £21,800 plus interest being due shortly after death of plaintiff's husband but events had occurred since then giving rise to their pleaded defence by way of set off—whether plaintiff entitled to judgment under R.S.C., Ord. 27, r. 3—plaintiff's appeal dismissed. Appeal from Caulfield J. October 5, 1978. ENGELSMAN v. LONDON AND BERKSHIRE PROPERTIES.

331. —— —— **setting aside judgment**

On February 16, 1978, plaintiff obtained judgments for £5,290 plus interest, a direction for an account, and costs against defendants in an action in which on January 25, 1978, defendants' solicitors gave notice withdrawing defendants' defence in action—judge refused application under R.S.C., Ord. 35, r. 2, to set aside judgments—first defendant's (in person) appeal dismissed. November 3, 1978. STOCKS v. HUMAN.

332. —— —— **stay of execution**

Plaintiff obtained judgment against defendants in default of appearance on October 19—defendants failed to appear at the trial because their solicitors apparently had forgotten the case was in the list for trial—on October 25, defendants obtained stay of execution of the judgment on terms that they bring into court the sum of £8,660 within 14 days—defendants' appeal dismissed—judge fully acquainted with history of proceedings and his order was not one that could be interferred with on appeal. Appeal from Thompson J. November 10, 1978. ANAND v. NANDA.

333. —— **leave to defend—costs**

Plaintiffs obtained judgment in default of appearance against defendant—defendant (with new solicitors) applied to have judgment set aside on ground that it was entered by mistake and that she had a defence on merits—judge ordered that judgment should be set aside and that defendant should have leave to defend on condition that she pay into court costs thrown away (some £260) at once—defendant legally aided with nil contribution and unable to pay costs thrown away—arguable defence on merits—defendant's appeal allowed—unconditional leave to defend with order simply that defendant pay costs thrown away by reason of having judgment set aside—order not a condition. Appeal from Parker J. December 4, 1978. CUMMINGS v. JARITZ-WILSON.

334. —— **legal aid—means of assisted party**

Judgment for £566·21 damages with costs to be taxed on a common fund basis was given against the defendant, who was unemployed, and legally aided with a nil contribution—whether judge took into account the means of the defendant in making order as to costs having regard to s. 8 of the Legal Aid Act 1974 (c. 4)—defendant's appeal as to costs allowed—case sent back to judge for exercise of powers under reg. 20 of the Legal Aid (General) Regulations 1971. June 6, 1978. BROWN v. TAYLOR.

335. —— **new trial—real issue never canvassed in evidence**

Plaintiff company, agricultural merchants, claimed damages for breach of contract for sale of straw and hay not delivered—defendant's case that he was not seller—judge found that defendant was sole principal seller—on second day of hearing defendant gave notice that he was going to take a new point based on ss. 18, 20 of the Sale of Goods Act 1893—new point dismissed by judge on ground that defendant did not provide anywhere near amount of contract goods he had contracted to provide—new point not canvassed in evidence because judge did not think much of it—whether evidence on which judge could find that contract goods were complete when contract was signed by defendant—new trial ordered because issue in case never properly tried—judge's decision that defendant was seller to be *res judicata*. January 12, 1979. CURTIS & CO. (OUNDLE) v. WILLIAMS.

336. —— order—final order

In November 1976, plaintiff builders claimed a certain sum of money for work and labour done and materials supplied—in April 1972 defendants served a defence, counterclaim and set-off alleging various matters including bad workmanship—in July plaintiffs delivered a reply and defence to counter-claim and requested further and better particulars—as the particulars were not forthcoming the plaintiff obtained in November 1977 an order of the judge for the particulars to be served within 14 days and on December 20, 1977, obtained a final order for the particulars to be served within 14 days—particulars delivered on January 27, 1978—in February 1978 the deputy official referee ordered that the defence, counter-claim and set-off be struck out and that judgment be entered for the plaintiffs—whether judge wrong to treat the "final order" as final—defendants' appeal dismissed—*obiter* observations on *Whistler* v. *Hancock* (1878) 3 Q.B.D. 83. May 18, 1978. J. M. BROWN v. DENNIS PRICE.

337. —— originating application—dismissed for want of prosecution—delay

Parties married in July 1957 and in 1958 bought a house in which they lived until 1968 when marriage broke up and wife left—in October 1970 she obtained decree nisi (now absolute) on ground of husband's adultery and in December 1970 she issued originating application (which contained insufficient particularisation) under the Married Women's Property Act 1882 claiming, *inter alia,* a half share in matrimonial home or proceeds of sale thereof—in February 1971 registrar ordered husband to file, *inter alia,* answer within 28 days but husband failed to do so—negotiations between parties—documentation by husband complete—matter next came before court in June 1976 because of delay on wife's side—delay both inordinate and inexcusable—whether delay prejudicial—registrar granted husband's application to discuss wife's application for want of prosecution but judge reversed his decision—*Birkett* v. *James* [1977] C.L.Y. 2410—husband's appeal allowed—material factor was wife's failure to plead any material matter in her originating application to show existence of a claim to house or proceeds of sale of house in equal shares or in any shares. December 12, 1978. BROWN v. BROWN.

338. —— pleadings—amendment

Judge granted plaintiffs leave to amend their statement of claim, and thereby to increase the amount of claim against defendants "very drastically"—defendants' appeal expedited because action listed for hearing next day on issues as to liability—defendants' appeal allowed—granting of leave to amend made conditional with regard to cost. July 11, 1978. GARROD & LOFTHOUSE v. TIME-LIFE INTERNATIONAL (NEDERLAND) B.V.

339. —— —— different case presented at trial

Plaintiffs were farmers and defendants were suppliers of oil fuel—oil leaked from a tank at the plaintiffs' farm and caused damage to materials there—judge found that leakage caused when defendants' driver delivered oil at the plaintiffs' farm and accidentally dislodged a gauge in the oil tank which amounted to breach of duty and negligence—accident pleaded in specific way but shown to have happened differently at trial—whether radical departure from the way claim pleaded—defendants' appeal on various grounds dismissed—decision of judge on inference from the facts—no fundamentally different case from pleadings put forward and no injustice resulted. Appeal from Stocker J. May 12, 1978. SHELDRICK (HINXWORTH) v. ARNDALE FUELS.

340. —— —— **further particulars**

Plaintiffs instituted three actions (two were later consolidated) to recover proceeds (£500,000) of their cheques collected by banks without authority as damages for conversion or money had and received—paras. 6 and 7 of the Statement of Claim were as follows: " (6) In drawing signing delivering or causing to be delivered the said cheque as aforesaid Wade [a director of plaintiff company and a customer of defendants] acted wrongfully, in breach of his duties as a director of the plaintiffs and in fraud of the plaintiffs. (7) In the premises the defendants have converted the said cheque to their own use and wrongfully deprived the plaintiffs of the same whereby the plaintiffs have suffered damage "—defence contained allegation of unlawful conspiracy making sum sued for irrecoverable—judge refused to order certain further particulars of paras. 6 and 7—R.S.C., Ord. 18, r. 12—*Morison* v. *London County and Westminster Bank* [1914] 3 K.B. 356—defendants' appeal allowed in part. Appeal from Foster J. November 30, 1978. BRIMAN PROPERTIES v. BARCLAYS BANK.

341. —— —— **issue at trial—new issue**

Plaintiff employee of defendants was injured whilst manoeuvring an abnormally heavy refuse container at a school together with two other employees, one of whom was driver of dust cart used for removing refuse and was alleged to be in charge of operation—writ for personal injury alleging negligence on part of defendants was served very shortly before expiry of three year limitation period—plaintiff's case as pleaded alleged that defendants failed to provide a dust cart fitted with a hydraulic hoist suitable for lifting a heavy weight and that they required plaintiff to manhandle a container of excessive weight—judge thought that duty was not a reasonably foreseeable one and dismissed plaintiff's action—whether defendant council vicariously liable for negligence of driver of dust cart—matter not put to driver in witness box at trial and not pleaded on that basis—unfair to defendants to allow issue to be raised at this late stage—plaintiff's appeal dismissed. November 22, 1978. BRADY v. BLACKPOOL BOROUGH COUNCIL.

342. —— —— **striking out as disclosing no reasonable cause of action**

Agreement was made between Mr. and Mrs. Hyde and Wiggins Teape Ltd. whereby Mr. and Mrs. Hyde paid £10,000 to Wiggins Teape Ltd. to pay off or compromise bills of £13,467 incurred by Mr. and Mrs. Hyde at plaintiff hotel on behalf of Wiggins Teape Ltd.—plaintiff hotel sued Mr. and Mrs. Hyde for bills of £3,467 not paid off and they served third party notice on Wiggins Teape Ltd. claiming to be indemnified—master dismissed third party proceedings on basis that it disclosed no reasonable cause of action and judge affirmed matter—Mr. and Mrs. Hyde's appeal allowed—triable issue showed—matter remitted to master to give third party directions. Appeal from Willis J. June 16, 1978. TRUST HOUSE FORTE HOTELS v. HYDE AND WIGGINS TEAPE.

343. —— —— **successive amendment of pleadings**

In November 1970 a contract was made between plaintiffs and defendants, specialists in design and manufacture of drying towers, under which defendants were to design, manufacture and instal a drying tower at plaintiffs' factory—certain machinery for use in tower supplied by a company, D Ltd., under a direct contract with plaintiffs—defendants completed installation of tower in May 1971—tower unsatisfactory and in January 1973 plaintiffs served statement of claim against defendants alleging that defendants were in breach of contract in supplying a tower which was incapable of performing certain specified drying operations and in consequence plaintiffs suffered heavy financial loss—amended defence and counterclaim served in June 1974 alleging various things but no suggestion that tower defective because of faults or inadequacies in machinery supplied by D Ltd.—expert reports and negotiations—in July 1977 an independent expert of defendants produced report blaming defective operation of tower on faults or deficiencies in machinery supplied by D Ltd.—limitation period for action against D Ltd. had expired—defendants applied to amend further their defence to say that D Ltd. was responsible for defects in tower and not defendants—whether need for amendment arose from fault of defendants—whether plaintiffs themselves in fault in not making an alternative claim against D Ltd. before limitation period expired—registrar and judge allowed defendants' application—plaintiffs' appeal allowed—defendants at fault in not obtaining expert report earlier than July 1977—plaintiffs not at fault. Appeal from Neill J. December 14, 1978. SHANNONVALE PLASTICS v. GREENBANK ENGINEERING CO.

344. —— service out of the jurisdiction

Plaintiffs, a Stockport firm which manufactured and sold tiles in Stockport, entered into a contract whereby defendants, a firm of tile making machinery manufacturers in Florence, were to supply machinery designed to produce tricolour tiles—machinery to be bought by plaintiffs and sold by defendants f.o.b. an Italian port with a f.o.b. price—parties had had contractual relations over a long period since 1960s—" considerable " doubt as to when, where and how contract made and what its exact terms were—alleged breaches by defendants committed in Italy—judge (on appeal from registrar) refused leave to plaintiffs to issue and serve notice of writ on defendants outside jurisdiction under R.S.C., Ord. 11—plaintiffs' appeal dismissed. Appeal from Chapman J. October 4, 1978. A. QUINLIOTTI & CO. v. LONGINOTTI S.P.A.

345. —— setting aside judgment in default of defence—fault of solicitors

Plaintiffs brought an action claiming some £18,580 as hire charges on a " very uncertain statement of claim "—owing to fault of defendants' then solicitor judgment was signed in default of defence and plaintiffs' solicitor got a charging order on first defendant's house (matrimonial home and only asset, first defendant being only partner of any substance in third defendants, a firm)—judge gave defendants leave to defend on condition that £6,000 be paid into court—defendants' appeal allowed—good defence shown—right course in circumstances was to set aside judgment in default and charging order with no conditions at all. Appeal from Balcombe J. July 19, 1978. LINDSEY SCAFFOLDING v. CUMMINGS.

346. —— stay of proceedings—actions in two jurisdictions

Plaintiffs, a United States of America corporation, claimed against the defendants, an English company, in respect of alleged infringement of two U.K. letters patent—defendants denied validity of patents and denied infringement—issues to be decided by U.K. court—proceedings currently taking place in U.S.A. Federal Court consisting of an action by Western Electric (plaintiffs) against a Florida corporation, Milgo Electronics (which jointly with Racal Ltd., an English company, owned defendant company) alleging infringement of 10 U.S. patents said to belong to Western Electric (plaintiffs)

—defendants applied for stay of U.K. proceedings on basis that defendants in U.S. proceedings had raised defences which, if established, would result in plaintiffs in U.K. action being restrained by order of U.S. court (under U.S. law) from proceeding with their U.K. action—U.S. proceedings unlikely to reach judgment stage for a number of years—U.K. action expected to reach judgment stage in 1980—" balancing operation "—defendants' appeal against refusal of stay and against striking out of paragraph six of their defence dismissed. Appeal from Whitford J. October 25, 1978. WESTERN ELECTRIC CO. INC. v. RACAL-MILGO.

347. —— —— arbitration

Plaintiff brought an action by writ for final balance of an account said to be due to him from defendants under terms of a building contract—contract contained agreement to refer to arbitration disputes arising under contract—judge granted defendants a stay of action pursuant to s. 4 of the Arbitration Act 1950—plaintiff was impecunious and could not afford to arbitrate and had been granted a legal aid certificate to bring action at public expense—whether plaintiff's impecuniosity arising from breaches of the contract—*Fakes* v. *Taylor Woodrow* [1973] C.L.Y. 97—plaintiff's appeal dismissed. Appeal from Bristow J. October 19, 1978. SMART v. CLARKE.

348. —— summary judgment—arguable defence

Plaintiffs claimed some £37,500 under a " labour only " contract made with defendants—defendants contended that plaintiffs did bad work for which they were paid and that the bad work had not been remedied—contract contained on invoice—certain allegations in plaintiffs' affidavit not sought to be answered by defendants—master gave plaintiffs judgment for £7,500 and gave leave to defend as to remaining £30,000—judge upheld order—defendants' appeal dismissed—up to defendants to show arguable defence. Appeal from Milmo J. October 3, 1978. McKENNA'S BUILDING CONTRACTORS v. TERRAPIN BUILDING & CIVIL ENGINEERING.

349.

Defendants entered into a contract of guarantee with plaintiffs to guarantee a sum of money which had been lent (under a defective deed and which deed had not been registered) by the plaintiffs to a company of which defendants were directors—cl. 8 of guarantee stated that guarantee shall not be discharged nor the guarantor's liability affected by reason of " any failure of any security "—question of construction requiring an examination of authorities—case not within type of case envisaged by Russell L.J. in *Bigg* v. *Boyd Gibbins* [1971] C.L.Y. 1860—not proper case for summary judgment under R.S.C., Ord. 14—defendants' appeal allowed. Appeal from Donaldson J. October 30, 1978. ROYAL TRUST CO. OF CANADA v. BEADLE.

350. —— —— bill of exchange

Judge gave summary judgment for £10,000 in favour of plaintiffs on a bill of exchange with conditional leave to defend the plaintiffs' claim in respect of three other bills of exchange—on October 9 defendant applied for a stay of execution and on October the judge gave summary judgment for whole sum claimed by plaintiffs—unsatisfactory affidavit by defendant—impossible to make out from defence what transaction involved was—defendant given leave to defend on condition that he bring into court whole amount of judgment plus pay into court £1,000 as security for plaintiff's costs of action and deliver an intelligible and comprehensive defence (not demurrable) within 14 days. Appeal from Mocatta J. November 27, 1978. MERCHANTS SWISS (IN LIQUIDATION) v. THAKORE (SUING AS SUNIL CREDIT FINANCE).

351. —— —— **conditional leave to defend**

Plaintiff issued writ against defendant, a solicitor's managing clerk, claiming repayment of a loan of £2,000 together with compensation for devaluation and capital erosion of principal at rate of £800 per annum—defence denied defendant was indebted to plaintiff as alleged or at all—plaintiff issued proceedings for summary judgment supported by affidavit exhibiting a letter from defendant acknowledging loan—master gave defendant leave to defend conditional on his payment into court of £2,000 and judge affirmed that order—defendant's (in person) appeal dismissed. Appeal from Donaldson J. December 1, 1978. Ross *v.* LISSNER.

352. —— —— **defence by way of set-off arising after judgment by master**

In 1974, plaintiff building contractors agreed with the defendant local authority to build for them a sports complex on the basis of the " Standard Form of Building Contract Local Authorities Edition With Quantities 1963 Edition "—in December 1977 plaintiffs brought a claim for £107,707 on basis of unpaid interim certificates issued by defendants' architect—defendants entered appearance but nothing more happened until spring 1978 when on April 5, 1978, master gave plaintiffs summary judgment, there being no affidavit by defendants setting out any defence they might have—defendants appealed to judge within time limited by the rules and on May 8, 1978, obtained certain certificate from their architect which gave rise to a defence by way of set-off of some £30,000 against the plaintiffs' claim owing to certain delay in the building works by the plaintiffs—judge considered affidavits and evidence of both sides and dismissed defendants' appeal—defendants' appeal therefrom dismissed. Appeal from Talbot J. October 27, 1978. HARRY NEAL *v.* THE MAYOR, ALDERMEN AND BURGESSES OF THE LONDON BOROUGH OF WALTHAM FOREST.

353. —— —— **unconditional leave to defend**

Plaintiff claimed some £7,334 (including interest) in respect of work done and services rendered and materials supplied in respect of conversion of a property owned by defendant, a man of means—£1,750 paid by defendant in October 1977 in addition to earlier payments of £5,000 and £3,000 in June 1977 and counterclaim raised by defendant of £2,000 in respect of specified work not completed—master gave plaintiff judgment for whole amount of claim—judge (on appeal) gave plaintiff judgment for some £2,330 and ordered defendant to bring that sum into court as a condition of stay—defendant's appeal allowed—defendant given unconditional leave to defend. Appeal from Talbot J. October 20, 1978. EDWARDS *v.* AKERELE.

354. —— **trial—adjournment**

Plaintiff purchaser brought an action for specific performance of a contract for the sale of land against defendant vendor—dispute of fact between parties as to whether or not plaintiff had paid amount of deposit stipulated in contract —defendant, a Bangladeshi who spoke no English, had obtained legal aid for all steps in the action up to but not including the trial and wanted to call witnesses, two of whom were out of the country at present—judge took view that defendant had had long enough to prepare his case and that justice could be done on material available and refused adjournment of trial to first convenient date in Hilary Term 1980—defendant's appeal dismissed—open to defendant to renew application before judge on " Tuesday next " when matter would come on for trial. Appeal from Blackett-Ord V.-C. November 10, 1978. ALI *v.* ULLAH.

355. —— —— fresh trial

Plaintiff's husband, employed by defendants as a room blaster from 1951 to 1963, died of pneumoconiosis in October 1971, having been found under disability by the Pneumoconiosis Panel in April 1964—in June 1972 plaintiff consulted solicitors and in September 1974, when further information was obtained, first writ against defendants was issued—in November defendants denied liability—in March 1975 legal aid certificate was extended and in July 1975 a second writ was issued with leave and two writs were served together in August 1975—whether claims statute-barred—Limitation Act 1975, s. 2—judge found, *inter alia*, that deceased had had other employments, apart from G.E.C. in the course of which he had been exposed to dusty conditions and that it would be impossible to investigate the true cause of the disease and that the documents of the Pneumoconiosis Panel had been destroyed as a matter of routine and refused to exercise his discretion in the plaintiff's favour—plaintiff appealed seeking to adduce fresh evidence from a doctor who treated plaintiff and plaintiff's fellow employees and seeking a new trial—*Ladd* v. *Marshall* [1954] C.L.Y. 2507 considerations ought to be applied strictly in circumstances—appeal dismissed. Appeal from Boreham J. July 18, 1978. COTTON v. G.E.C. Co.

356. —— —— limiting issues at trial

Plaintiff shipowners brought a claim for U.S.$7 million for unpaid hire outstanding and for damages arising out of repudiation of the charter of their ship to the defendant charterers, an Australian company—defendants put in a defence and counterclaim alleging, *inter alia*, fraud and misrepresentation and claiming some U.S.$20 million—"mammoth case" which had already lasted 55 days and said by judge to be costing £5,000 a day—judge, having listened to case for over 50 days, made an order limiting the issues that were to be dealt with in a certain way—R.S.C., Ord. 33, r. 4 (2)—defendants' appeal dismissed. Appeal from Goff J. July 12, 1978. ASSOCIATED BULK CARRIERS v. BROKEN HILL PROPRIETARY CO.

357. —— —— litigant in person—alleged bias of arbitrator

Defendant conducted her own case in an arbitration on a claim by plaintiff for £30 for work done on a gas boiler at defendant's residence—defence was that there was an "exchange agreement" so that no payments were due—defendant's cross-examination was frequently interrupted by arbitrator's rulings on relevance of her questions and refused defendant's request for adjournment and defendant became upset and "stormed out, stating that she wished to have no further part in the case" and arbitrator proceeded to award plaintiff £30 plus plaint fee—two and a half day hearing—defendant applied to judge to set aside award on grounds that arbitrator was biased and conducted trial unfairly—judge refused application—defendant's (in person) appeal dismissed. December 1, 1978. WARREN'S HEATING SERVICE CO. v. NEWMAN.

358. Real Property and Conveyancing—adverse possession—fencing

Plaintiff brought an action in trespass claiming to be in possession of land more than 15 feet to the south of defendant's land alleging that he (plaintiff) erected a chain-link fence in November 1973 and that defendants unlawfully entered property in 1976—defence admitted that plaintiff had put up fence but denied that he was in possession—proper title of land in a Mr. Davis—judge found for plaintiff and concluded that plaintiff had established 12 years' adverse possession—first defendant's appeal dismissed—putting up fence was "plainest possible" evidence of taking possession, even if plaintiff had not got it before. June 30, 1978. SARGENT v. HENDERSON.

359. —— beneficial ownership—evidence

Plaintiff claimed posession of property on ground that he and his wife were the owners of the property, a house in which the defendant (plaintiff's elder brother) and his wife lived as plaintiff's guests—defendant denied plaintiff's claim and claimed that he and his wife occupied the property as beneficial owners and not as guests as alleged—judge found in favour of plaintiff—defendant's appeal dismissed—defendant bound to fail on basis of findings of fact. January 31, 1979. BAHBRA v. BAHBRA.

360. —— boundary dispute

Plan annexed to conveyances of various sites showed boundary between site now owned by plaintiffs and that now owned by defendants as being different from that apparent on ground—judge, after seven days of hearing, accepted plaintiffs' evidence and rejected defendant's evidence and found in favour of plaintiffs on basis that what mattered in circumstances was that which would have been obvious on ground at time of sales—defendant's (in person) appeal dismissed—no possible ground of appeal shown. June 26, 1978. NEWBLE v. MARSH.

361. —— contract—inquiries before contract—misrepresentation

Plaintiff made a claim relating to the contribution which he had to pay under cl. 2 (4) of a lease dated April 14, 1964, towards painting of the ironwork supporting raft on which rested his hairdresser's shop—lease purchased from defendant in December 1974—claim based on various misrepresentations including misrepresentation alleged to be contained in answer given by defendant to the third inquiry before contract in Law Society's standard form requiring particulars of all notices relating to the property—whether two letters addressed to all relevant lessees from lessors advising of work and cost relating to supporting ironwork and raft amounted to " notices relating to the property " within words of inquiry—judge found against plaintiff—plaintiff's appeal allowed—letters amounted to " notices relating to property," words being construed in their plain grammatical meaning. December 21, 1978. DJAN v. DALORTO.

362. —— covenant—breach of covenant

Defendant company had been developing and letting houses built on a building estate owned by it—in 1971 defendant sold a house to D—instrument of transfer contained covenant by purchaser that, *inter alia*, he would not erect on land any new or additional buildings, walls, fences, etc., unless transferors' consent had first been obtained, such consent not to be unreasonably withheld—plaintiff company acquired part of the back garden of D's house and adjoining house and obtained planning permission to erect a dwelling-house on it and applied to defendant for permission to build in accordance with covenant—defendant refused permission and judge dismissed plaintiff's action for a declaration on grounds that: (1) proposed development would necessarily involve breach of fencing covenant and that if defendant gave consent it would by implication waive any rights against D under fencing covenant; (2) defendant was justified in refusing consent on ground that it considered that proposed development would adversely affect the amenities and value of other parts of estate—plaintiff's appeal dismissed. Appeal from Megarry V.-C. October 18, 1978. LATTIMERGRANGE v. ARTAGEN PROPERTIES.

363. —— —— —— injunction

Plaintiffs, builders and vendors, sold a house on a comparatively new housing estate to defendants, Mr. and Mrs. B—conveyance stated that house was not to be used "otherwise than as a private dwelling-house only and purchaser shall not carry on any trade or business whatever" thereon—Mrs. B was a registered child-minder and looked after children at house, providing service on a regular basis for payment for a maximum of four children on every weekday —whether a business—*Thorn* v. *Madden* [1925] Ch. 847, *Tendler* v. *Sproule* (1947) C.L.C. 8469—judge granted injunction to restrain defendants from carrying on child-minding concern—defendants' appeal dismissed. Appeal from Blackett-Ord V.-C. October 6, 1978. HAMBLETON HOMES (YORKSHIRE) v. BURTON.

364. —— ownership of property—whether property acquired jointly

In January 1971 plaintiff, a widow, and defendant, a married man, both then aged about 50, by arrangement between them purchased a bungalow in Canvey Island for £2,650 (plus extras), £800 of it being provided by plaintiff in cash and rest, about £2,000, being left on mortgage—conveyance taken in defendant's name because local council would not grant a mortgage to a woman alone—parties lived in bungalow until 1974 when defendant left—plaintiff continued to live in bungalow paying all mortgage instalments herself ever since—judge found that parties intended that bungalow would be plaintiff's and that defendant would contribute a weekly sum for his keep—defendant's appeal dismissed—question essentially for the judge below. November 15, 1978. POULSON v. WHEELER.

365. —— possession—whether occupants licensees or tenants

By a document called a licence and dated August 4, 1976, the plaintiffs, owners of the premises in question, a one-roomed flat, granted to "the licensees [defendants] the right to use and occupy" the premises for certain purposes for a period of two months—the agreement required the defendants to pay "an acknowledgment" of £28 a month and stated, *inter alia*, that the occupation of the property "shall not create any tenarcy . . . nor give the licensees any estate or interest"—the "licence" was extended twice for a period of, first, three months and, secondly, six months—whether parties entered into a licence agreement or a tenancy agreement or lease-negotiations leading up to the grant of the licence—judge held agreement to be a licence and granted plaintiffs possession of the premises—defendants' appeal dismissed. April 6, 1976. MANCHESTER CITY COUNCIL v. THE HULME PEOPLE'S RIGHTS CENTRE.

366. —— sale of land—memorandum in writing

Plaintiff wished to sell his premises for £9,500 but defendant (plaintiff's tenant) unable to obtain loan of more than £9,000—oral agreement therefore that contracts would be exchanged and there would be conveyance and completion which would show purchase price of property as £9,000 and further sum of £500 would be paid by defendant thereafter at some date not later than two years—conveyance duly executed and defendant entered into possession— in July 1973 plaintiff got defendant to sign a document relating to £500—defendant failed to pay £500 as agreed and plaintiff brought action for £500—Law of Property Act 1925, s. 40—judge held that there was a collateral contract in respect of £500 and accordingly gave judgment for plaintiff—defendant's appeal allowed—no collateral contract—no sufficient memorandum under s. 40 because July 1973 document was inconsistent with contract and conveyance—case governed by *Daulia* v. *Four Millbank Nominees* [1978] C.L.Y. 2051. November 1, 1978. CROSS v. HETENYI.

367. Rent Restriction—furnished letting—possession—tenant not in personal occupation

Plaintiff was granted possession of a flat let to the first defendant in 1971, the judge having found that the first defendant, for all practical purposes, had changed her home and moved out of the flat when she went to live with another man in 1976 together with children bearing his name—Rent Act 1977 (c. 42), s. 2 (1) (3)—first defendant's appeal dismissed. May 5, 1978. HUMPHRIES v. ALVAREZ.

368. —— possession—resident, landlord

Plaintiff applied for possession of premises let by him to defendant claiming that he was a resident landlord although, as he alleged, his work as an electronics engineer employed by Marconi Ltd. took him away frequently to other parts of country—defendant's evidence that plaintiff stayed at premises only occasionally—Rent Act 1977, s. 12 (1)—*Beck* v. *Scholz* [1953] C.L.Y. 3148—judge concluded that plaintiff used premises as a convenience (and not as a home) and dismissed plaintiff's action—finely balanced facts—right test applied by judge—impossible to say that judge came to wrong conclusion—plaintiff's appeal dismissed. December 20, 1978. LALONDE v. KEMP.

369. —— statutory tenancy—surrender by operation of law

In May 1976 the defendants (husband and wife) were granted a Case 10 letting of the plaintiffs' (husband and wife) house for three months—in August letting was extended by oral arrangement—plaintiffs returned from abroad and asked for defendants to vacate premises within seven days—on September 22 plaintiffs started proceedings for possession and hearing was fixed for November 3—on October 8 plaintiff husband " lost his patience " and used his key to enter premises and took up occupation—whether action unlawful—judge found in favour of plaintiffs on main claim—defendants' appeal dismissed—on the fact there was a surrender by defendants of their statutory tenancy by operation of law—*Foster* v. *Robinson* (1951) C.L.C. 5626 considered. July 5, 1978. PONSFORD v. SWINSTEAD.

370. Road Traffic—insurance—limitation of liability

Plaintiff was sitting in front passenger seat of S's Jaguar motor car when car (being driven by S at a very fast speed) went off road and into an adjoining restaurant, no other car being concerned—plaintiff was only survivor of accident; S and three other passengers were killed—condition 6 of S's car insurance policy limited liability of insurance company and was as follows: " The insured shall take all reasonable steps to safeguard from loss or damage and maintain in efficient condition the insured vehicle "—accident caused by failure of steering gear—whether S had not taken proper steps to maintain vehicle in an efficient condition—evidence—insurance underwriters' appeal dismissed. December 12, 1978. WICKINGS v. THE OFFICIAL SOLICITOR AND PILCHER.

371. Sale of Goods—acceptance—act inconsistent with ownership of seller

Defendants purchased from the plaintiff a crusher plant which was in Northern Ireland but was to be delivered to defendants at appointed place in Birmingham—toggle plates found to be damaged at time of delivery in breach of condition that crusher should be fit for purpose required—defendants effected repairs costing some £450 not to toggle plates but to the electrical machinery of the crusher—whether unequivocal act by defendant buyers that they were not going to exercise right to reject goods—Sale of Goods Act 1893,

s. 35—plaintiff's claim for price of goods sold and delivered dismissed by judge on ground that defendants had not accepted crusher but rejected it—plaintiff's appeal allowed—plaintiff awarded purchase price less abatement in respect of damaged toggle plates. July 6, 1978. SHERIDAN *v.* J. R. CALVERT (QUARRY PLANT).

372. —— breach of contract—repudiation

C, managing director of defendant company, agreed with plaintiff company (through salesman) that he would buy a 1971 Rolls Royce (price £7,250) from them and by way of payment would transfer to plaintiffs his Jaguar motor car with a cash balance of £4,750—C later discovered that he could get £3,100 for his Jaguar instead of £2,500 given by plaintiffs and refused to hand over Jaguar and offered to buy Rolls Royce for £7,250 cash—plaintiffs refused and thereafter sold Rolls Royce for £6,000 at auction, it being alleged that true market price of Rolls Royce was above £7,250—an agreement between plaintiffs and defendants partly evidenced in writing and extrinsic evidence admissible to cast light upon document—whether agreement that C should have option either of trading in Jaguar or of paying the full price in cash for Rolls Royce or whether his obligation was to pay £4,750 by way of cash and also hand over Jaguar—whether breach entitled plaintiffs to refuse to hand over Rolls Royce—amount of plaintiffs' loss—plaintiffs' duty to mitigate loss—plaintiffs not justified in refusing C's offer of £7,250—damages in respect of Jaguar agreed—plaintiffs' appeal allowed. January 18, 1979. SAVOY MOTOR CO. *v.* ALGIN AIR.

373. —— delivery—evidence

Plaintiffs' servant took goods ordered by defendants to building where they were to be delivered, off-loaded the goods with help of three men he supposed were sent by site foreman at building, and was given by one of three men a receipt (with a 50p tip) which was wrong colour and was not signed but which servant failed to notice—goods disappeared—plaintiffs sued for price of goods sold and delivered and judge found in their favour—whether judge misdirected himself (1) in failing to consider whether or not plaintiffs had taken all reasonable care to deliver goods to defendants and (2) in finding that site agent was agent of defendants and in finding that delivery to him was delivery to defendants—defendants' appeal dismissed. October 10, 1978. TANKARD CARPETS *v.* DODSON-BULL INTERIORS.

374. —— sale by sample

Plaintiffs brought action in the High Court by specially indorsed writ claiming £659·33 as the price of goods sold and delivered (in May 1974) without stating the nature of the goods—defence was, *inter alia*, that the contract was the sale of goods by sample and that the bulk delivered by plaintiffs did not correspond with relevant sample—witnesses on both sides were of the utmost integrity—judge dismissed plaintiffs' claim—plaintiffs' appeal allowed—new trial ordered in county court—judge failed to decide real issue between parties in which there was an acute conflict of evidence—mistake made in negotiations between parties as to the sample, fault for which to be carefully investigated in greater detail at new trial. May 10, 1978. BOWATER PACKAGING *v.* JAMES SOUTHERTON MARTINEAU & SMITH.

375. Tort—assault—evidence

Plaintiff claimed damages limited to £1,000 against defendant for assaulting him with a golf club and defendant counterclaimed £25 damages against plaintiff for assaulting her—conflict of fact—judge heard case for four days and found that plaintiff was assailant and defendant was not and dismissed plaintiff's action and gave judgment for defendant on her counterclaim—plaintiff's (in person) appeal dismissed. December 19, 1978. ROSE v. ROE.

376. —— conversion—evidence

In February 1975 plaintiff let a furnished flat to D—after moving in D disposed of plaintiff's furniture by dumping it on a skip left in the road—in January 1976 the local authority made a compulsory purchase order on the premises—plaintiff claimed value of the furniture alleging conversion by the defendant—defendant's case was that he had disposed of the furniture, which was of a very poor quality and quite valueless, with the plaintiff's agreement, so that defendant could bring in and use his own furniture—judge dismissed plaintiff's claim—plaintiff's (in person) appeal dismissed—issue of fact not decided wrongly by judge. May 17, 1978. NEALE v. NEALE.

377. Town and Country Planning—compensation—jurisdiction to make consent award

At the hearing of the claimant's claim for compensation under ss. 165 and 170 of the Town and Country Planning Act 1971 (c. 78), the lands tribunal made a consent award on the basis of an agreement between the parties—whether lands tribunal had jurisdiction to make consent award—appeal by way of case stated dismissed—unique and unprecedented facts including the form of the case stated—decision of Court of Appeal no authority for any proposition of law and dependent upon its own special facts. May 16, 1978. GAY v. WEST WILTSHIRE DISTRICT COUNCIL.

378. Trade Unions—election to office of district delegate—rules for election—construction of rules

Plaintiff, a member of the defendant trade union, was one of two candidates in the second ballot for election to the office of district delegate for the Kent and South Eastern District—plaintiff was elected but protests alleging irregularities in the ballot were received and the defendants informed the plaintiff that the protests had been upheld and accordingly that the other candidate had higher rates—single issue agreed to be tried before court—whether plaintiff not validly elected on the ground that certain votes should be considered void because list of out-of-benefit members not duly read contrary to r. 11 (13) (h) of the defendants' Rule Book—construction of rule—whether view taken by union relevant to construction—judge found in favour of plaintiff—defendants' appeal dismissed—defendants' application for leave to adduce further evidence dismissed because matter had been decided on agreed issue. Appeal from Whitford J. April 24, 1978. WRIGHT v. AMALGAMATED SOCIETY OF BOILERMAKERS, ETC.

379. Trespass—assault and battery—evidence

Plaintiff was awarded some £3,454 damages in respect of injury to his leg, a spiral fracture of right fibula, suffered when a scuffle took place between him and first defendant, a police constable, when first defendant tried to arrest plaintiff after refusal by him to take a breathalyser test—different versions of how fracture occurred—judge found in favour of plaintiff's version and thereby found first defendant liable—defendants' appeal dismissed. Appeal from Rees J. November 15, 1978. SCOTT v. PHILLIPS AND NORTHUMBRIA POLICE AUTHORITY.

380. —— possession—trespass to land—gypsies

Appellants, named persons and others (coming within statutory description of " gypsies " within s. 6 of the Caravan Sites Act 1968), moved as trespassers into land owned by respondent council—council applied for possession under summary procedure provided by County Court Rules 1936, Ord. 26, as amended by County Court (Amendment No. 3) Rules 1977—six of named appellants found by judge to be not present on site on day original application was served —whether there was proper service of notice of application under Ord. 26— judge granted possession to council—appeal dismissed. May 9, 1978. SWANSEA CITY COUNCIL v. RAFFERTY.

381. Vendor and Purchaser—sale of land—breach of contract—rescission

By contract dated February 21, 1973, defendants agreed to purchase from plaintiffs for £850,000 14·41 acres of waste land with a view to developing site as a residential building estate—contract contained special conditions which included, inter alia, the conditions that (1) purchaser could rescind contract if prior to date of completion compulsory acquisition of the property or any part thereof shall have been commenced by any authority having statutory power thereafter, (2) power to rescind shall be exercisable by service of a notice in writing—in 1970 a draft C.P.O. was published and in November 1973 Secretary of State for Environment made a C.P.O. providing for, inter alia, compulsory acquisition of 2·3 acres of land in question —on March 20, 1974, defendants served written notice on plaintiffs purporting to rescind contract pursuant to above mentioned special conditions—plaintiffs issued writ claiming, inter alia, declaration that contract did not give power to rescind on ground of compulsory purchase procedures announced before date of contract, i.e. February 21, 1973, and that defendants' notice did not effectively rescind contract—in second action plaintiffs claimed damages for breach of contract—actions consolidated—whether, on true construction of conditions, defendants entitled to rescind—whether notice of rescission valid —whether by wrongly insisting on right to rescind defendants had repudiated contract—defendants' appeal dismissed (Buckley L.J. dissenting). Appeal from Fox J. October 26, 1978. WOODAR INVESTMENT DEVELOPMENT v. GEORGE WIMPEY & CO.

382. Wills—family provision—reasonable provision

Appellant child of deceased was born in May 1972 two months after mother had left deceased—mother married deceased in November 1971 when they were aged 23 and 47 years, respectively, after a seven-month courtship— deceased made some voluntary payments of £5 per week for maintenance of child but never saw child and never knew her name—net estate of deceased came to £17,000—deceased left one-quarter share for child not to be paid until she attained 18 and if she failed to attain 18 her share was to go to certain charities (like the other three-quarters share)—judge, inter alia, increased child's share to one-half under Inheritance (Provision for Family and Dependants) Act 1975—appeal for an increased share and that age limitation be removed dismissed. Appeal from Reeve J. November 1, 1978. CHATTERTON v. EXECUTORS OF THE WILL OF CHATTERTON, DECD.

383. Plaintiff, daughter of testator, had no disability and was aged 54 years—she was married with a grown-up family of three children and her husband had his own business which was not particularly prosperous—deceased's estate was valued at £23,000 (about half of that being represented by house in which he lived) and he left £2,000 to plaintiff, one or two other small legacies, and residue to Miss H, his unmarried daughter, who was aged a few years younger than

plaintiff and was one of executors (defendants) of deceased's will—Miss H had gone to work throughout her adult life and earned now about £3,000 per annum and she had capital amounting to £17,000—whether provision made for plaintiff in her father's will adequate—Inheritance (Provision for Family and Dependants) Act 1975, ss. 1, 2, 3—judge dismissed plaintiff's application under 1975 Act for further provision—plaintiff's appeal dismissed. November 6, 1978. RANN v. JACKSON.

DATES OF COMMENCEMENT

Statutes

(in alphabetical order)

ADMINISTRATION OF JUSTICE ACT 1977—September 3, 1979: [1979] C.L.Y. 377. S. 20.

ADMINISTRATION OF JUSTICE (EMERGENCY PROVISIONS) (SCOTLAND) ACT 1979— March 22, 1979; [1979] C.L.Y. 2101.

AGRICULTURAL STATISTICS ACT 1979—April 22, 1979: [1979] C.L.Y. 55.

ALCOHOLIC LIQUOR DUTIES ACT 1979—April 1, 1979: [1979] C.L.Y. 615.

ANCIENT MONUMENTS AND ARCHAEOLOGICAL AREAS ACT 1979—July 16, 1979: [1979] C.L.Y. 2606. Ss. 48, 49.

APPROPRIATION ACT 1979—April 4, 1979: [1979] C.L.Y. 2263.

APPROPRIATION (No. 2) ACT 1979—July 27, 1979: [1979] C.L.Y. 2264.

ARBITRATION ACT 1979—August 1, 1979: [1979] C.L.Y. 96.

BANKING ACT 1979—October 1, 1979: [1979] C.L.Y. 150. Pts. I, III, ss. 38, 40–45, 47, 48 (1)–(6), 49, 50, 52, Scheds. 1–4.

CAPITAL GAINS TAX ACT 1979—April 6, 1979: [1979] C.L.Y. 1456.

CHRONICALLY SICK AND DISABLED PERSONS (NORTHERN IRELAND) ACT 1978— December 28, 1978: [1979] C.L.Y. 1902. All except for s. 14.
October 31, 1979: [1979] C.L.Y. 1902. S. 14.

COMPANIES ACT 1976—November 28, 1979: [1979] C.L.Y. 256. S. 34 (1) (part), Sched. 1 (part).

CONSOLIDATED FUND ACT 1979—March 22, 1979: [1979] C.L.Y. 2267.

CONSOLIDATED FUND (No. 2) ACT 1979—December 20, 1979: [1979] C.L.Y. 2268.

CONSUMER CREDIT ACT 1974—January 27, 1980: [1979] C.L.Y. 2374. Certain repeals in Sched. 5.

CREDIT UNIONS ACT 1979—April 4, 1979: [1979] C.L.Y. 1495. Ss. 32, 33. August 20, 1979: [1979] C.L.Y. 1496.

CRIMINAL EVIDENCE ACT 1979—April 22, 1979: [1979] C.L.Y. 429.

CROWN AGENTS ACT 1979—April 4, 1979: [1979] C.L.Y. 30.

CUSTOMS AND EXCISE DUTIES (GENERAL RELIEFS) ACT 1979—April 1, 1979: [1979] C.L.Y. 618.

CUSTOMS AND EXCISE MANAGEMENT ACT 1979—April 1, 1979: [1979] C.L.Y. 619.

DOMESTIC PROCEEDINGS AND MAGISTRATES' COURTS ACT 1978—September 17, 1979: [1979] C.L.Y. 1720. S. 40 and Sched. 2, paras. 30, 31.
November 1, 1979: [1979] C.L.Y. 1720. Ss. 16–18, 28, 29 (1) (2) (5), 30, 75–85, 88 (1)–(4), Sched. 2, paras. 10, 12, 21, 25, 38–40, 45 (c) and Sched. 3 (certain repeals).

EDUCATION ACT 1979—July 26, 1979: [1979] C.L.Y. 807.

ELECTRICITY (SCOTLAND) ACT 1979—April 22, 1979: [1979] C.L.Y. 829.

EUROPEAN ASSEMBLY (PAY AND PENSIONS) ACT 1979—July 26, 1979: [1979] C.L.Y. 1151.

EUROPEAN COMMUNITIES (GREEK ACCESSION) ACT 1979—December 20, 1979: [1979] C.L.Y. 1152.

EXCHANGE EQUALISATION ACCOUNT ACT 1979—May 4, 1979: [1979] C.L.Y. 2276.

EXCISE DUTIES (SURCHARGE OR REBATES) ACT 1979—April 1, 1979: [1979] C.L.Y. 625.

FILMS ACT 1979—February 22, 1979: [1979] C.L.Y. 2203.

DATES OF COMMENCEMENT

FINANCE ACT 1979—April 4, 1979: [1979] C.L.Y. 2277.

FINANCE (NO. 2) ACT 1979—July 26, 1979: [1979] C.L.Y. 2278. Except for ss. 2, 3.
June 12, 1979: [1979] C.L.Y. 2278. s. 2.
August 13, 1979: [1979] C.L.Y. 2278. s. 3.

FORESTRY ACT 1979—May 29, 1979; [1979] C.L.Y. 1342.

HOUSE OF COMMONS (REDISTRIBUTION OF SEATS) ACT 1979—March 22, 1979: [1979] C.L.Y. 2014.

HOUSING ACT 1974—October 9, 1979: [1979] C.L.Y. 1389. S. 130, Scheds. 13, 15.

HYDROCARBON OIL DUTIES ACT 1979—April 1, 1979: [1979] C.L.Y. 630.

INDEPENDENT BROADCASTING AUTHORITY ACT 1979—April 4, 1979: [1979] C.L.Y. 2584.

INDUSTRY ACT 1979—April 4, 1979: [1979] C.L.Y. 2668.

INTERNATIONAL CARRIAGE OF PERISHABLE FOODSTUFFS ACT 1976—October 1, 1979: [1979] C.L.Y. 1535.

INTERNATIONAL MONETARY FUND ACT 1979—May 4, 1979: [1979] C.L.Y. 2280.

INTERNATIONALLY PROTECTED PERSONS ACT 1978—May 24, 1979: [1979] C.L.Y. 1538.

ISLE OF MAN ACT 1979—December 20, 1979: [1979] C.L.Y. 635. Ss. 6, 7, 10, 11.
April 1, 1980: [1979] C.L.Y. 635. Remaining provisions.

JUDICATURE (NORTHERN IRELAND) ACT 1978—February 21, 1979: [1979] C.L.Y. 1956. S. 122 (1), Sched. 5, Pt. II (part).
April 18, 1979: [1979] C.L.Y. 1956. All provisions of the Act not yet in force.
September 1, 1979: [1979] C.L.Y. 1956. S. 122 (1). Sched. 5, Pt. II (part).

JUSTICES OF THE PEACE ACT 1979—March 6, 1980: [1979] C.L.Y. 1732.

KIRIBATI ACT 1979—June 19, 1979: [1979] C.L.Y. 188.

LAND REGISTRATION (SCOTLAND) ACT 1979—April 4, 1979: [1979] C.L.Y. 1564. Ss. 1, 16–23, 30.

LEASEHOLD REFORM ACT 1979—April 4, 1979: [1979] C.L.Y. 1611.

LEGAL AID ACT 1979—July 20, 1979: [1979] C.L.Y. 2162. Ss. 4, 13 (1) (2).

MATCHES AND MECHANICAL LIGHTERS DUTIES ACT 1979—April 1, 1979: [1979] C.L.Y. 636.

MEDICAL ACT 1978—September 27, 1979: [1979] C.L.Y. 1754. Ss. 1 (13) (14), 3, 5, 15, 16, 31 (1) (3), Scheds. 1; 6, paras. 1–3, 5–12, 14, 19, 37, 48 (a), 49, 56, 59; 7.

MERCHANT SHIPPING ACT 1970—August 1, 1979: [1979] C.L.Y. 2476. Ss. 15, 19, 95 (2), 100 (3) (part), Sched. 5 (part).

MERCHANT SHIPPING ACT 1974—August 1, 1979: [1979] C.L.Y. 2477. Ss. 14, 15, Sched. 4.

MERCHANT SHIPPING ACT 1979—August 1, 1979: [1979] C.L.Y. 2479. Ss. 1–6, 12, 13 (1) (part), 16, 20–22, 26, 32 (1), 33, 34, 35 (1), 36 (1) (3), 37 (1)–(3) (5) (7) (8), 39–41, 47 (1) (2) (part) (3), 48, 49, 50 (1) (2) (4) (part), 51 (1) (3), 52, Sched. 1, 2 (part), 7 (part).
October 1, 1979: [1979] C.L.Y. 2479. Ss. 27, 28, 46 (part), 47 (2) (part), 50 (4) (part), Sched. 7 (part).
December 17, 1979: [1979] C.L.Y. 2479. Ss. 15 (1) (2), 19 (2) (3), 38 (5), 47 (1) (2).
January 1, 1980: [1979] C.L.Y. 2479. Ss. 13 (1) (part) (2)–(4), 29, 30, 42–45, 47 (2) (part), 50 (4) (part), Scheds. 2 (part), 6, 7 (part).

NURSES, MIDWIVES AND HEALTH VISITORS ACT 1979—April 4, 1979: [1979] C.L.Y. 1762. Ss. 21 (2), 24.

DATES OF COMMENCEMENT

PENSIONERS' PAYMENTS AND SOCIAL SECURITY ACT 1979—July 26, 1979: [1979] C.L.Y. 2068.

PNEUMOCONIOSIS, ETC. (WORKERS' COMPENSATION) ACT 1979—July 4, 1979: [1979] C.L.Y. 2535.

PRICE COMMISSION AMENDMENT ACT 1979—February 12, 1979: [1979] C.L.Y. 2284.

PROSECUTION OF OFFENCES ACT 1979—May 4, 1979: [1979] C.L.Y. 539.

PUBLIC HEALTH LABORATORY SERVICE ACT 1979—March 29, 1979: [1979] C.L.Y. 2216.

REPRESENTATION OF THE PEOPLE ACT 1979—April 4, 1979: [1979] C.L.Y. 827.

SALE OF GOODS ACT 1979—January 1, 1980: [1979] C.L.Y. 2396.

SHIPBUILDING ACT 1979—December 20, 1979: [1979] C.L.Y. 2498.

SOCIAL SECURITY ACT 1979—March 22, 1979: [1979] C.L.Y. 2543. All except for ss. 11 and 12, Sched. 1, paras. 2–22 and Sched. 3, paras. 5–7, 11, 14–20, 22, 23, 29 (a) (b).

March 29, 1979: [1979] C.L.Y. 2544. S. 3 (3) (mobility allowance).

April 6, 1979: [1979] C.L.Y. 2543. Ss. 11 and 12, Sched. 1, paras. 2–22 and Sched. 3, paras. 5–7, 11, 14–20, 22, 23, 29 (a) (b).

June 6, 1979: [1979] C.L.Y. 2544. S. 3 (3) (for all purposes not already in force).

September 5, 1979: [1979] C.L.Y. 2544. S. 3 (3) (mobility allowance).

November 28, 1979: [1979] C.L.Y. 2544. S. 3 (3) (purposes other than mobility allowance).

SOCIAL SECURITY PENSIONS ACT 1975—March 7, 1979: [1979] C.L.Y. 2545. Ss. 22, 65 (1), Sched. 4, paras. 47, 49, 51–53 (limited operation).

March 29, 1979: [1979] C.L.Y. 2545. S. 65 (1), Sched. 4, paras. 47, 49, 51–53 (mobility allowance).

March 31, 1979: [1979] C.L.Y. 2545. S. 65 (1) (limited operation).

June 6, 1979: [1979] C.L.Y. 2545. S. 65 (1), Sched. 4, paras. 47, 49, 51–53 (for all other purposes not yet in force).

June 7, 1979: [1979] C.L.Y. 2545. Ss. 22, 65 (1) (limited operation).

September 5, 1979: [1979] C.L.Y. 2545. Ss. 22, 65 (1) (limited operation).

SOUTHERN RHODESIA ACT 1979—November 14, 1979: [1979] C.L.Y. 202.

STOCK EXCHANGE (COMPLETION OF BARGAINS) ACT 1976—February 12, 1979; [1979] C.L.Y. 2579.

TOBACCO PRODUCTS DUTY ACT 1979—April 1, 1979: [1979] C.L.Y. 645.

TOWN AND COUNTRY PLANNING ACT 1971—April 2, 1979: [1979] C.L.Y. 2656. S. 20, Sched. 23, Pt. I (Berkshire and Oxfordshire).

April 16, 1979: [1979] C.L.Y. 2656. S. 20, Sched. 23, Pt.I (Humberside).

August 13, 1979: [1979] C.L.Y. 2656. S. 20, Sched. 23, Pt. I (Cheshire).

September 10, 1979: [1979] C.L.Y. 2656. S. 20, Sched. 23, Pt. I (Suffolk).

October 15, 1979: [1979] C.L.Y. 2656. S. 20, Sched. 23, Pt. I (Hertfordshire).

December 10, 1979: [1979] C.L.Y. 2656. S. 20, Sched. 23, Pt. I (Lancashire).

TRUSTEE SAVINGS BANKS ACT 1976—November 21, 1979: [1979] C.L.Y. 2406. S. 36 (1) (2), Scheds. 5, paras. 8 (1) (a), 15 (a); 6 (part).

VACCINE DAMAGE PAYMENTS ACT 1979—March 22, 1979: [1979] C.L.Y. 2602.

WAGES COUNCILS ACT 1979—April 22, 1979: [1979] C.L.Y. 1071.

WEIGHTS AND MEASURES ACT 1979—April 4, 1979: [1979] C.L.Y. 2802. Ss. 14, 16–18, 21, 22, 24.

October 2, 1979: [1979] C.L.Y. 2803. Ss. 6, 7, Sched. 3.

October 4, 1979: [1979] C.L.Y. 2802. S. 20 (part) and Sched. 5, para. 1.

January 1, 1980: [1979] C.L.Y. 2802. Ss. 1–5, 8–13, 15, 20 (part), 23 (part) and Scheds. 1 and 2, Sched. 5, para. 16 and Sched. 7.

ZIMBABWE ACT 1979—December 20, 1979: [1979] C.L.Y. 209.

TABLE OF ABBREVIATIONS

A.B.L.R. = Australian Business Law Review.
A.C. = Appeal Cases (Law Reports).
A.J.I.L. = American Journal of International Law.
A.L.J. = Australian Law Journal.
A.L.J.R. = Australian Law Journal Reports.
A.L.R. = Argus Law Reports.
A.T.C. = Annotated Tax Cases.
ATLA L.Rep. = Association of Trial Lawyers of America Reporter.
A.T.R. = Australian Tax Review.
Acct. = Accountant.
Acct.Rec. = Accountants Record.
Accty. = Accountancy.
Air Law = Air Law.
All E.R. = All England Reports.
Anglo-Am. = Anglo-American Law Review.
Art. = Article.
Aus. = Australia.

B.J.A.L. = British Journal of Administrative Law.
B.T.R. = British Tax Review.
Brit.J.Criminol. = British Journal of Criminology
Build.L.R. = Building Law Reports.
Business L.R. = Business Law Review.

c. = Chapter (of Act of Parliament).
C.A. = Court of Appeal.
C.C.A. = Court of Criminal Appeal.
C.I.L.J.S.A. = Comparative and International Law Journal of Southern Africa.
C.L. = Current Law.
C.L.B. = Commonwealth Law Bulletin.
C.L.C. = Current Law Consolidation.
C.L.J. = Cambridge Law Journal.
C.L.L.R. = City of London Law Review.
C.L.P. = Current Legal Problems.
C.L.R. = Commonwealth Law Reports.
C.L.Y. = Current Law Year Book.
C.M.L.R. = Common Market Law Reports.
C.M.L.Rev. = Common Market Law Review.
C.P.L. = Current Property Law.
Can. = Canada.
Can.Bar J. = Canadian Bar Journal.
Can.B.R. or Canadian B.R. = Canadian Bar Review
Can.C.L. = Canadian Current Law.
Ch. = Chancery (Law Reports).
Chart.Sec. = Chartered Secretary.
Chart.Surv. = Chartered Surveyor.
Chart.Surv.R.Q. = Chartered Surveyor Rural Quarterly.
Chart.Surv.U.Q.=Chartered Surveyor Urban Quarterly.
Com.Cas. = Commercial Cases.
Commercial Acct. = Commercial Accountant.
Conv.(N.S.) (or Conv. or Conveyancer) = Conveyancer and Property Lawyer (New Series).

Court = Court.
Cox C.C. = Cox's Criminal Cases.
Cr.App.R. = Criminal Appeal Reports.
Crim.L.J. = Criminal Law Journal.
Crim.L.R. = Criminal Law Review.
Crim.R. = Criminal Reports.
Cts.-Martial App.Ct. = Courts-Martial Appeal Court.
Cty.Ct. = County Court.

D.C. = Divisional Court
D.L.R. = Dominion Law Reports.

E. = England.
E.A.T. = Employment Appeal Tribunal.
E.C.R. = European Court Reports.
E.C.S.C. = European Coal and Steel Community.
E.E.C. = European Economic Community.
E.G. = Estates Gazette.
E.I.P.R. = European Intellectual Property Review.
E.H.H.R. = European Human Rights Reports.
E.L.Rev. = European Law Review.
E.P.L. Leaflet = Excess Profits Levy Leaflet.
E.P.T. Leaflet = Excess Profits Tax Leaflet.

F.L.R. = Federal Law Reports.
F.S.R. = Fleet Street Law Reports.
Fam. = Family Division (Law Reports).
Fam.Law = Family Law.

H.L. = House of Lords.
Harv.L.R. or Harvard L.R. = Harvard Law Review.

I.C.L.Q. = International and Comparative Law Quarterly.
I.C.R. = Industrial Court Reports.
I.L.J. = Industrial Law Journal.
I.L.T. or Ir.L.T. = Irish Law Times.
I.L.T.R. = Irish Law Times Reports.
Imm.A.R. = Immigration Appeal Reports.
I.R. or Ir.R. = Irish Reports (Eire).
I.R.L.R.=Industrial Relations Law Reports.
Ir.Jur. = Irish Jurist.
Ir.Jur.(N.S.) = Irish Jurist (New Series).
Ir.Jur.Rep. = Irish Jurist Reports.
I.T.R. = Industrial Tribunal Reports.

J. and JJ. = Justice, Justices.
J.A.L. = Journal of African Law.
J.B.L. = Journal of Business Law.
J.C. = Justiciary Cases.
J.C.L. = Journal of Criminal Law.
J.C.L. & Crim. = Journal of Criminal Law and Criminology.
J.Crim.L., C. & P.S. = Journal of Criminal Law, Criminology and Police Science.

163

TABLE OF ABBREVIATIONS

J.I.B. = Journal of the Institute of Bankers.
J.L.A. = Jewish Law Annual.
J.L.S = Journal of the Law Society of Scotland.
J.P. = Justice of the Peace Reports.
J.P.L. = Journal of Planning and Environmental Law.
J.P.N. = Justice of the Peace Journal.
J.R. = Juridical Review.
J.S.P.T.L. = Journal of the Society of Public Teachers of Law.
Jam. = Jamaica.

K.B. = King's Bench (Law Reports).
K.I.R. = Knight's Industrial Reports.

L.A.G.Bul. = Legal Action Group Bulletin
L.C. = Lord Chancellor.
L.C.J. or C.J. = Lord Chief Justice.
L.Exec. = Legal Executive.
L.G.C. = Local Government Chronicle.
L.G.R. = Local Government Reports.
L.G.Rev. = Local Government Review.
L.J. = Law Journal Newspaper.
L.J. and L.JJ. = Lord Justice, Lords Justices
L.J.A.C.R. = Law Journal Annual Charities Review.
L.J.N.C.C.R. = Law Journal Newspaper County Court Reports.
L.J.R. = Law Journal Reports.
L.P. = Reference to denote Lands Tribunal decisions (transcripts available from the Lands Tribunal).
L.Q.R. = Law Quarterly Review.
L.R. = Law Reports.
L.R.R.P. = Reports of Restrictive Practices Cases.
L.S.Gaz. = Law Society Gazette.
L.T. = Law Times.
L.Teach. = Law Teacher.
L.T.J. = Law Times Journal.
L.V.App.Ct. = Lands Valuation Appeal Court (Scotland).
L.V.C. = Reference to denote Lands Tribunal decisions (transcripts available from the Lands Tribunal).
Ll.L.Rep. = Lloyd's List Reports (before 1951).
Ll.P.C. = Lloyd's Prize Cases.
Lloyd's M.C.L.Q. = Lloyd's Maritime and Commercial Law Quarterly.
Lloyd's Rep. = Lloyd's List Reports (1951 onwards).

M.L.J. = Malayan Law Journal.
M.L.R. = Modern Law Review.
M.P.R. = Maritime Provinces Reports.
M.R. = Master of the Rolls.
McGill L.J. = McGill Law Journal.
Mag.Ct. = Magistrates' Court.
Mal. = Malaya.
Mal.L.R. = Malaya Law Reveiw.
Man.Law = Managerial Law.
Med.Sci. & Law = Medicine, Science and the Law.
Melbourne Univ.L.R. = Melbourne University Law Review.
Mel.L.J. = Melanesian Law Journal.

NATO R. = NATO Reveiw.
N.I. = Northern Ireland; Northern Ireland Reports.
N.I.L.Q. = Northern Ireland Legal Quarterly.
N.I.L.R. = Northern Ireland Law Reports.
N.Z.L.R. = New Zealand Law Reports.
N.Z.U.L.R. = New Zealand Universities Law Review.
New L.J. = New Law Journal.
New L.R. = New Law Reports, Ceylon.
Nig.L.J. = Nigerian Law Journal.

Oklahoma L.R. = Oklahoma Law Review.
Ord. = Order.
Osgoode Hall L.J. = Osgoode Hall Law Journal.

P. = Probate, Divorce and Admiralty (Law Reports).
P. & C.R. = Property and Compensation Reports.
P.C. = Privy Council.
P.L. = Public Law.
P.Q. = Political Quarterly.
P.S. = Petty Sessions.
P.T. = Profits Tax Leaflet.
Pr.A.S.I.L. = Proceedings of the American Society of International Law.
Prof.Admin. = Professional Administration.

Q.B. = Queen's Bench (Law Reports).
Q.J.P.R. = Queensland Justice of the Peace Reports.
Q.L.R. = Queensland Law Reporter.
Q.S. = Quarter Sessions.
Q.S.R. = Queensland State Reports.

r. = Rule.
R.A. = Rating Appeals.
R. & I.T. = Rating and Income Tax.
R. & V = Rating and Valuation.
R.C.N. = Rating Case Notes.
R.F.L.=Reports of Family Law (Canadian).
R.I.C.S. = Royal Institution of Chartered Surveyors, Scottish Lands Valuation Appeal Reports.
R.P.C. = Reports of Patent, Design and Trade Mark Cases.
R.P.Ct. = Restrictive Practices Court.
R.R.C. = Ryde's Rating Cases.
R.T.R. = Road Traffic Reports.
R.V.R. = Rating and Valuation Reporter
reg. = Regulation.
Reg.Acct. = Registered Accountant.

s. = Section (of Act of Parliament).
S. or Scot. = Scotland.
S.A. = South Africa.
S.A.L.J. = South African Law Journal.
S.A.L.R. = South African Law Reports.
S.A.S.R. = South Australian State Reports.
S.C. = Session Cases.
S.C.(H.L.) = Session Cases (House of Lords).

TABLE OF ABBREVIATIONS

S.C.(J.) = Session Cases (High Court of Justiciary).
S.I. = Statutory Instruments.
S.J. = Solicitors' Journal.
S.J.Suppl. = Supplement to the Solicitors' Journal.
S.L.C.R. = Scottish Land Court Reports.
S.L.C.R.App. = Scottish Land Court Reports (appendix).
S.L.G. = Scottish Law Gazette.
S.L.R. = Statutes Law Reform Act (Statute Citator only).
S.L.R. = Scottish Law Reporter (Reports 1865–1925).
S.L.R. = Scottish Law Review (Articles 1912–63).
S.L.T. = Scots Law Times.
S.L.T.(Land Ct.) = Scots Law Times Land Court Reports.
S.L.T.(Lyon Ct.) = Scots Law Times Lyon Court Reports.
S.L.T.(Notes) = Scots Law Times Notes of Recent Decisions.
S.L.T.(Sh.Ct.) = Scots Law Times Sheriff Court Reports.
S.N. = Session Notes.
S.R. & O. = Statutory Rules and Orders.
S.T.C. = Simon's Tax Cases.
Sc.Jur. = Scottish Jurist.
Sec. = Secretary.
Sec.Chron. = Secretaries' Chronicle.
Sec.J. = Secretaries' Journal.
Sh.Ct.Rep. = Sheriff Court Reports (Scottish Law Review) (1885–1963).
Sol. = Solicitor.
Sydney L.R. = Sydney Law Review.

T.C. or Tax Cas. = Tax Cases.
T.C. Leaflet = Tax Case Leaflet.
T.L.R. = Times Law Reports.
I.R. = Taxation Reports.
Tas.S.R. = Tasmanian State Reports.
Tax. = Taxation.
Traff.Cas. = Railway, Canal and Road Traffic Cases.
Trial = Trial.
Trib. = Tribunal.
Tulane L.R. = Tulane Law Review.

U.G.L.J. = University of Ghana Law Journal.
U.T.L.J. = University of Toronto Law Journal.

V.A.T.T.R. = Value Added Tax Tribunal Reports.
V.L.R. = Victorian Law Reports.

W.A.L.R. = West Australian Law Reports
W.I.A.S. = West Indies Associated States.
W.I.R. = West Indian Reports.
W.L.R. = Weekly Law Reports.
W.N. = Weekly Notes (Law Reports).
W.W.R. = Western Weekly Reports.
Washington L.Q. = Washington Law Quarterly.

Yale L.J. = Yale Law Journal

CURRENT LAW YEAR BOOK

1979

ADMINISTRATIVE LAW

1. British Nationality. See ALIENS.

2. Crown agents

CROWN AGENTS ACT 1979 (APPOINTED DAY) ORDER 1979 (No. 1672) [10p], made under the Crown Agents Act 1979 (c. 43), s. 1 (1) and S.I. 1979 No. 1451 art. 2 (1); appoints January 1, 1980, as the day on which there shall come into being as a body corporate named the Crown Agents for Oversea Governments and Administrations and a body corporate named the Crown Agents Holding and Realisation Board to function under and in accordance with the 1979 Act.

CROWN AGENTS (FIRST ACCOUNTING YEAR) ORDER 1979 (No. 1673) [10p], made under the Crown Agents Act 1979, s. 31 (2) and S.I. 1979 No. 1451, art. 2 (1); prescribes January 1, 1980, as the date on which the first accounting year shall begin for the purposes of the 1979 Act.

3. Human rights—telephone tapping. See MALONE *v.* METROPOLITAN POLICE COMMISSIONER, § 2098.

4. Immigration

IMMIGRATION (CONTROL OF ENTRY THROUGH REPUBLIC OF IRELAND) (AMENDMENT) ORDER 1979 (No. 730) [10p], made under the Immigration Act 1971 (c. 77), ss. 9 (6) and 32 (1); operative on August 1, 1979; excludes from the operation of s. 1 (3) of the 1971 Act persons who entered the Republic from the U.K. after overstaying their leave.

IMMIGRATION (PORTS OF ENTRY) (AMENDMENT) ORDER 1979 (No. 1635) [10p], made under the Immigration Act 1971, s. 33 (3); operative on January 1, 1980; amends the list of seaports and hoverports specified in the Schedule to the Immigration (Ports of Entry) Order 1979 as ports of entry.

5. —— application to Divisional Court

The following Practice Direction was issued by the Queen's Bench Division on June 7, 1979:

In order to simplify the presentation of applications to the Divisional Court against decisions reached under the Immigration Act 1971, three forms have been prepared. Form 1 is for use in connection with applications in respect of a refusal of leave to enter; form 2 is for applications in respect of refusal to vary leave or an appeal against a variation of leave; form 3 is for applications made where the applicant has been detained after entry and where no application to remain or for variation of leave to remain has been made.

Copies of the forms may be obtained from the chief clerk of the Crown Office and should be used in all appropriate cases, and will be, we hope, of assistance both to the court and to litigants on this subject.

[1979] 2 All E.R. 880.

6. —— court's power to order release

[Immigration Act 1971 (c. 77), s. 24 (1) (*b*), para. 2 (1), Sched. 3; Courts Act 1971 (c. 23), s. 9 (2) (*c*).]

Magistrates can release someone, if they think fit, after making a recommendation for deportation pending the making of the order, and the Crown Court has exactly the same powers.

O appealed against the magistrates' recommendation for deportation after conviction for an Immigration Act offence. His appeal was dismissed and the judge refused to consider an application for his release on the ground that there was no jurisdiction to hear the application. On application for mandamus, *held,* granting the application, that the Crown Court had power to do anything the magistrates could do, which included releasing him if considered proper.

R. *v.* INNER LONDON CROWN COURT, *ex p.* OBAJUWANA (1979) 69 Cr.App.R. 125, D.C.

7. —— entry—indefinite leave—authority of officer
[Immigration Act 1971 (c. 77), s. 4 (1), Sched. 2, para. 16 (2).]
Where an immigration officer mistakenly and without being induced by misrepresentation stamps an immigrant's passport with leave to enter indefinitely, the immigrant cannot thereafter be alleged to be an unlawful immigrant.

The applicant, an Indian, was on two occasions in 1974 and 1977, upon entering the United Kingdom, mistakenly given indefinite leave to enter by the immigration officer; there was no fraud or misrepresentation by the applicant. His passport was stamped accordingly. After the second entry the applicant considered himself lawfully entitled to remain here, and set up a business which he ran until arrested and detained in custody as an illegal immigrant. *Held,* allowing his application for habeas corpus, that the immigration officer had authority under s. 4 (1) of the 1971 Act to grant leave to enter indefinitely; the fact that he had done so mistakenly did not make the applicant's remaining in this country illegal. (Dictum of Geoffrey Lane L.J. in *R.* v. *Secretary of State for the Home Department, ex p. Hussain* [1978] C.L.Y. 13 applied; *R.* v. *Secretary of State for the Home Department, ex p. Choudhary* [1978] C.L.Y. 12 distinguished.)

R. *v.* SECRETARY OF STATE FOR THE HOME DEPARTMENT, *ex p.* RAM [1979] 1 W.L.R. 148, D.C.

8. —— registration of minor as citizen—person entitled to apply
[British Nationality Act 1948 (c. 56), s. 7.] The Secretary of State for Home Affairs can only order the registration of a minor as a citizen of the United Kingdom where the application is made by a parent or guardian of the minor: R. *v.* SECRETARY OF STATE FOR HOME AFFAIRS, *ex p.* AKHTAR, *The Times,* December 27, 1979, D.C.

9. Inquiries
FEES FOR INQUIRIES (VARIATION) (AMENDMENT) ORDER 1979 (No. 569) [10p], made under the Public Expenditure and Receipts Act 1968 (c. 14), s. 5, Sched. 3, para. 6; operative on July 21, 1979; amends S.I. 1968 No. 656 and increases the maximum fee payable per day which a Minister may determine under s. 250 (4) of the Local Government Act 1972 for the services of an officer engaged in an inquiry held under that section.

10. Judicial review—board of prison visitors—disciplinary proceedings. See R. *v.* BOARD OF VISITORS OF HULL PRISON, *ex p.* ST. GERMAIN, § 2195.

11. —— domestic tribunals—tribunal revising rules
[Can.] A teachers' association entered into an agreement with the Department of Education to create a teachers' salary qualification board. The board was empowered to set rules, and to serve as a tribunal for the final resolution of disputes. On an application, the board held that P had a four-year equivalent educational qualification. Some three years later, P, having completed further post-graduate work, applied to the board for re-assessment. During the same three years the board revised its rules. She was again assessed as having a four-year equivalent educational qualification. P brought an action for a declaration that the board's assessment was a nullity. *Held,* the board could not, having reached a decision on a set of facts under the rules, reconsider the matter at a later date under revised rules and reach a different decision, because its first decision is final under the rules. Here, where the board changed the rules, and P after further education applied to have her qualification upgraded, the board could not decide that under the changed rules she still had only a four-year equivalent university education. (*Lee* v. *Showmen's Guild of Great Britain* [1952] C.L.Y. 3505 applied): LAMBERT v. ALBERTA TEACHERS' ASSOC. (1978) 90 D.L.R. (3d) 498, Alta.Sup.Ct.

12. —— duty to act fairly—directors of housing corporation determining tenant's lease

[Can.] Directors of a housing corporation met to decide to terminate the lease of a tenant. The tenant applied for judicial review of the decision. *Held,* the directors were not acting in a quasi-judicial or judicial fashion. Nor were they governed by any rule or principle of procedural fairness when they granted a lease to an applicant. But once an applicant became a tenant the situation altered, and at that juncture the directors were governed by the principle of procedural fairness, even when they were acting in an administrative fashion. On the facts, they were acting fairly when they made the tenant aware of the complaints which gave rise to the proposed termination, and gave the tenant the opportunity to remedy the complaints. (*Selvarajan* v. *Race Relations Board* [1976] C.L.Y. 26 considered): *Re* WEBB AND ONTARIO HOUSING CORP. (1978) 93 D.L.R. (3d) 187, Ont.Ct. Appeal.

13. Lands Tribunal. See RATING AND VALUATION.

14. Natural justice—application—principles

A failure of natural justice, at first instance, in domestic proceedings may be put right at the appellate stage, for example where the inquiry stage can be said to have merged in the appellate proceedings.

P's horse failed to win a race in Australia having run unexpectedly poorly. Charges were brought against P and the jockey. On an inquiry under the Australian Jockey Club Rules of Racing, the stewards interviewed the jockey, the trainer, the trainer's foreman and P, watched film of the race and inquired into the betting. P claimed that he had wanted the horse to win, and had bet on it. The stewards found that the jockey was guilty of an offence, and P was party to it, and disqualified him for one year. P appealed to the committee of the Australian Jockey Club, where he was represented by counsel. There was a complete rehearing and review of the evidence and the opportunity to cross-examine witnesses. P's appeal was dismissed. P applied to the court for a declaration that the disqualification was void, on the ground that there was a lack of natural justice at the stewards' inquiry stage, that their decision was invalid, and that therefore the committee had no jurisdiction to hear the appeal. The application was refused. On P's appeal to the judicial committee, *held,* dismissing the appeal, that (1) if there had been a lack of natural justice at the inquiry, the committee still had jurisdiction to hear an appeal; (2) the test was whether after both original and appellate stages P had had a fair deal of the kind he had bargained for when joining the organisation. Since the committee had given P's case a full and fair consideration at the appeal stage, a failure of natural justice at the inquiry stage was irrelevant. (*Pillai* v. *Singapore City Council* [1968] C.L.Y. 297 applied; *Australian Workers' Union* v. *Bowen (No. 2)* (1948) 77 C.L.R. 601, *Meyers* v. *Case* (1913) 17 C.L.R. 90, *Reid* v. *Rowley* [1977] 2 N.Z.L.R. 472 and *Twist* v. *Randwick Municipal Council* (1976) 51 A.L.J.R. 193 approved; *Annamunthodo* v. *Oilfields Workers' Trade Union* [1961] C.L.Y. 8923, *Re Cardinal and Board of Commissioners of Police of City of Cornwall* (1974) 42 D.L.R. (3d) 323 and *Leary* v. *National Union of Vehicle Builders* [1970] C.L.Y. 8 distinguished; *Hall* v. *New South Wales Trotting Club* [1976] 1 N.S.W.L.R. 323, *Ethell* v. *Whalan* [1971] 1 N.S.W.L.R. 416, and *Denton* v. *Auckland City* [1969] N.Z.L.R. 256 doubted; *White* v. *Kuzych* (1951) C.L.C. 10396 considered.)

CALVIN v. CARR [1979] 2 W.L.R. 755, P.C.

15. —— application for licence—bias of local authority—judicial review

[N.Z.] A operated a stud pig farm for many years without an effective trades licence. B was a dairy company and built a milk powder factory next door. B then objected to the presence of A's farm and to its unlicensed operation. The Medical Officer of Health recommended that A be granted a licence subject to conditions with which A was willing to comply. A then applied to the local county council for the necessary licence: both A and B were represented before the council committee. At the hearing A objected to the fact that five of the 12 councillors who sat on the committee were shareholders in B. One of these five was a director of B: he had in fact insisted on A making the application. The objection was overruled. The Council then granted A a licence, but made the grant subject to conditions which had the effect of making the grant ineffective. There was a right of appeal only against a refusal to grant a licence. A applied to the court for a review of the council's decision. *Held*, the council should have excluded from the decision-making process the five members who were shareholders of A. Although it is often not possible in local body affairs to exclude members who have an interest in the matters under decision, if it is possible it should be ensured that such decisions are made by disinterested persons (*John* v. *Rees* [1969] C.L.Y. 353, *Re Pergamon Press* [1970] C.L.Y. 286, *Wiseman* v. *Borneman* [1969] C.L.Y. 1748 referred to): MEADOWVALE STUD FARM *v*. STRATFORD COUNTY COUNCIL [1979] 1 N.Z.L.R. 342, N.Z.Sup.Ct.

16. —— **board of prison visitors—disciplinary procedure.** See R. *v*. HULL PRISON BOARD OF VISITORS, *ex p*. ST. GERMAIN (No. 2), § 2196.

17. —— **conviction by magistrates—opportunity to state case before appeal judge**
    A appealed to the Crown Court against a conviction by magistrates. As he was cross-examining a witness for the respondents he paused, whereupon the judge rose, saying " appeal dismissed," and left the court. *Held*, allowing A's appeal, that there had been a breach of the rules of natural justice. It was not possible to say the result would have been the same if A had had a proper opportunity to present his case: R. *v*. CARLISLE CROWN COURT, *ex p*. ARMSTRONG [1979] Crim.L.R. 253, D.C.

18. —— **disciplinary proceedings—fire service—whether superior involved in considering sentence.** See R. *v*. LEICESTERSHIRE FIRE AUTHORITY, *ex p*. THOMPSON, § 1310.

19. —— **infringement of human rights—failure to observe statutory procedure**
    [Trinidad and Tobago (Constitution) Order in Council 1962, ss. 1 (*a*) (*b*), 6 (1), 102 (4).]
    Where a party chooses deliberately not to apply for the appropriate judicial remedy given him by the law, but makes an application to the High Court for breach of fundamental rights under the Constitution, complaining of unlawful administrative action where no such issues are at stake, his application is an abuse of process and misconceived.
    The Teaching Service Commission in Trinidad transferred a teacher to another school without giving him the required three months' notice. The teacher considered the transfer a punishment, but instead of availing himself of the ordinary review procedure, he applied to the High Court for a declaration that the fundamental human rights guaranteed him by the Constitution had been violated. *Held*, dismissing the teacher's appeal, that it was an abuse of the process of the court to make such an application as a means of avoiding the necessity of applying for the appropriate judicial remedy for unlawful administrative action.
    HARRIKISSOON *v*. ATT.-GEN. OF TRINIDAD AND TOBAGO [1979] 3 W.L.R. 62, P.C.

20. —— **inquiry—applicants' failure to appear through mistake**
    A compulsory purchase order was made under the Housing Act 1969, s. 32 (1). The premises were subject to protected tenancies. An inquiry was postponed pending agreement between the owners and the local authority as to the rehousing of the tenants and the acceptance of new tenants. The owners did not appear at the inquiry because they were under the mistaken impression the order was to be withdrawn. They applied for the confirmation of the order to be withdrawn on the ground that there had been a breach of the rules of natural justice. *Held*, the applicants had only themselves to blame for their absence. Their impression that the inquiry would not proceed on May 3 was not reasonable in the circumstances: ACKERMAN *v*. SECRETARY OF STATE FOR THE ENVIRONMENT AND CAMDEN LONDON BOROUGH [1979] J.P.L. 616, Willis J.

21. —— **public inquiry—objections not heard at second inquiry.** See LOVELOCK *v*. SECRETARY OF STATE FOR TRANSPORT, § 1371.

22. —— **unfair dismissal proceedings—complaint of indiscipline—officer making complaint also assisting tribunal.** See HADDOW *v.* INNER LONDON EDUCATION AUTHORITY, § 981.

23. **Parliamentary Commissioner**

PARLIAMENTARY COMMISSIONER ORDER 1979 (No. 915) [10p], made under the Parliamentary Commissioner Act 1967 (c. 13), s. 5 (4); operative on August 25, 1979; narrows the exception to the jurisdiction of the Paliamentary Commissioner for Administration which is made by Sched. 3, para. 2 to the 1967 Act by excluding from it action taken by career consular officers in relation to U.K. citizens who have the right of abode in the U.K.

PARLIAMENTARY COMMISSIONER (No. 2) ORDER 1979 (No. 1705) [10p], made under the Parliamentary Commissioner Act 1967, s. 4 (2); operative on January 24, 1980; provides for the Northern Ireland Court Service to be subject to investigation by the Parliamentary Commissioner for Administration.

24. **Tribunals**

TRIBUNALS AND INQUIRIES (VACCINE DAMAGE TRIBUNALS) ORDER 1979 (No. 659) [10p], made under the Tribunals and Inquiries Act 1971 (c. 62), s. 15 (1) and (2); operative on July 12, 1979; brings under the supervision of the Council on Tribunals, tribunals constituted under s. 4 of the Vaccine Damage Payments Act 1979.

25. —— **discretion to fix costs**

[Can.] It has been held, that when a court is reviewing a decision of an inferior tribunal which fixed the costs of the parties to a proceeding—when the tribunal had a statutory discretion to fix them—the court may not concern itself with the amounts, but can only determine whether the tribunal erred in law. Where the amounts of such costs are fixed on the basis of guidelines promulgated by the tribunal, the use of such guidelines is not erroneous if they do not have the effect of pre-determining the exercise of the tribunal's discretion (*Padfield* v. *Minister of Agriculture* [1968] C.L.Y. 1667 referred to; *Re Poyser & Mills Arbitration* [1963] C.L.Y. 43 applied): *Re* GREEN, MICHAELS & ASSOCIATES AND PUBLIC UTILITIES BOARD (1979) 94 D.L.R. (3d) 641, Alta.Sup.Ct.

BOOKS AND ARTICLES, See *post,* pp. [1], [13].

AGENCY

26. **Advertising agency—money had and received—whether principal or agent**

P, an advertising agency, sought to recover from D its fees for inserting certain advertisements in the national and local Press on D's behalf. D admitted P's claim, but pleaded a set-off in respect of various sums it had previously paid to P so that P in turn could pay the newspaper in which D's business had been advertised. P, which was in receivership, conceded that it had failed to pay these sums over to the newspapers concerned, but contended that it acted as principal not agent in its dealings with both advertisers and publishers and was therefore under no liability to account to the advertiser for any money received from it. Representatives of the Newspapers Proprietors Association, the Institute of Practitioners in Advertising and the International Publishing Corporation gave evidence as to the custom of the trade. *Held*, P had established, as a matter of trade custom, that an advertising agency is a principal in its relations with advertisers and publishers, and there is no privity of contract between publisher and advertiser when the latter engages the services of an advertising agency. Only the agency is liable to the publisher, whom the agency must pay whether or not it has itself been paid by the advertiser. The agency cannot be required to repay to the advertiser any moneys which the advertiser may have paid to it but which it has not paid to the publisher. There was no implied term that such moneys should be repaid to the advertiser, nor could it be recovered by the advertiser as money had and received. (*Emmett* v. *De Witt* (1957), unreported, Gorman J., followed): PRESS AND GENERAL PUBLICITY SERVICES *v.* PERCY BILTON, November 3, 1978; Westminster County Ct., Judge Ruttle. (*Ex rel. Gordon Bennett, Esq., Barrister.*)

27. **Capacity—call options—whether broker acting as principal or agent**

D were overseas members of the London Cocoa Terminal Market Association (" the association ") and members of the International Commodities Clearing House (" the clearing house "), with branches in Amsterdam (DA) and London (DL). In early 1973, P, who were also overseas members of the association, instructed DA to grant call options in 64 lots of July cocoa. The order was passed to DL, who, in accordance with the market procedure, instructed a trading member of the association to conclude the contracts for the options. The concluded contracts were registered with the clearing house in D's name. DA informed P that the options had been sold " for your account." All the options were exercised by the dates stipulated in the contracts, and the declarations pursuant to the clearing house regulations were made to the clearing house, which in turn notified DL of the exercise of the options. DA informed P that declarations had been made in the case of 20 call options only, and on July 12 P instructed DA to " liquidate this long position." Later, DA confirmed that 44 lots had been sold for P's account. D then advised DA that the 44 options had been declared. DA advised P that they were 44 lots short, which P denied. On July 23, without P's authority, D purported to purchase 44 lots of July cocoa for P's account. P stated that the contract was not authorised and returned the contract note sent to them by D. D contended that they acted as P's agents procuring the conclusion of the options, and when the options were exercised, P were bound whether or not they were informed. P argued that their relationship with D was principal to principal and since D had failed to give notice in relation to 44 options, the options were deemed to be abandoned and P were 44 lots long on July 12 when they instructed D to liquidate their position. On a special case stated, *held*, dismissing D's appeal, that (1) by putting the option on the market, D's agency with P ceased and D were free to " buy " the option from themselves, and in so doing were principals taking the option from P, and free to deal with the resulting rights and liabilities as their own; (2) the fact that D were entitled to commission from P did not mean that the transaction was throughout one of agency; (3) D were under a contractual duty, by implication, to give notice to P of the exercise of the option; (4) once it was realised that D were entitled, at their own sole choice, to deal as they wished with the rights and liabilities comprised in P's option, they were required at their peril to declare to P their decision to exercise them; (5) the argument that in deciding against D P obtained a windfall whereas if D were right fairness would result was not of much assistance: LIMAKO B.V. *v.* H. HENTZ & CO. INC. [1979] 2 Lloyd's Rep. 23, C.A.

28. **Contract—appropriation of principal's goodwill—passing off.** See INTERNATIONAL SCIENTIFIC COMMUNICATIONS INC. *v.* PATTISON, § 1354.

29. —— **proper law—whether governed by English law.** See ATLANTIC UNDERWRITING AGENCIES AND DAVID GALE (UNDERWRITING) *v.* COMPAGNIA DI ASSICURAZIONE DI MILANO S.P.A., § 313.

30. **Crown Agents Act 1979 (c. 43)**

This Act reconstitutes as a body corporate, and makes other provision with respect to, the Crown Agents for Oversea Governments and administrations.

S. 1 reconstitutes the Crown Agents as a body corporate; s. 2 vests property, rights and liabilities in the Crown Agents; s. 3 outlines the general functions of the Crown Agents; s. 4 concerns authorised agency activities; s. 5 deals with authorised non-agency activities; s. 6 specifies ancillary powers of the Crown Agents; s. 7 imposes a duty to act as agents of certain governments on request; s. 8 relates to pre-funding of agency activities; s. 9 outlines the duties of the Crown Agents with respect to management of activities; s. 10 empowers the Minister to obtain information from the Crown Agents; s. 11 provides for annual reports; s. 12 regulates control by the Crown Agents of subsidiaries; s. 13 sets out the general financial duties of the Crown Agents; s. 14 relates to directions by the Minister as to reserves of the Crown Agents and their wholly-owned subsidiaries; s. 15 deals with management of liquid assets of the Crown Agents and their wholly-owned subsidiaries; s. 16 provides for payments to the Minister; s. 17 relates to the Crown Agents' commencing capital debt; s. 18 outlines the borrowing powers of the Crown Agents and their wholly-owned subsidiaries; s. 19 places a limit on certain liabilities of the Crown Agents and their subsidiaries; s. 20 allows the Minister to make grants and loans to the Agents; s. 21 provides for Treasury guarantees; s. 22 relates to accounts and audit; s. 23 empowers the Minister to give directions with respect to financial matters; s. 24 imposes a duty on the Crown Agents to insure against insurable financial risks; s. 25 establishes the Crown Agents Holding and Realisation Board; s. 26 concerns the position with respect to recoverable grants paid to unincorporated Agents; s. 27 exempts the Crown Agents from certain revenue provisions; s. 28 makes provisions as to revenues of, and alienations by, former Agents; s. 29 deals with administrative expenses incurred by the Minister; s. 30 provides for orders, regulations and consents under the Act; s. 31 is the interpretation section; s. 32 contains consequential amendments, transitional provisions and repeals; s. 33 deals with citation and extent. The Act extends to Northern Ireland.

The Act received the Royal Assent on April 4, 1979, and came into force on that date.

31. Estate agents—agency contract—" sold by " notice—whether breach of contract
The plaintiff estate agents were instructed to sell the defendant's house. The defendant asked that no " For Sale " board be erected outside the property. A few days after exchange of contracts, the plaintiffs, without reference to the defendants, erected a " Sold By " board. The defendant telephoned the plaintiffs to express his annoyance and said that either the board must be removed immediately or he would charge the plaintiffs an advertising charge of 10 per cent. of their bill. The board was not removed and on completion of the sale the defendant moved out of the property and wrote confirming his intention to deduct the 10 per cent. The plaintiffs duly sent their account and when it was paid 10 per cent. (£106·92) had been deducted. In an action to recover the balance the plaintiffs contended that (1) it was the custom among estate agents to erect boards outside properties they were instructed to sell and there was a distinction between " For Sale " and " Sold By " boards; (2) even if it had been a term of the contract that no board should be erected, the defendant had suffered no loss and was entitled to no more than nominal damages; (3) the defendant had failed to mitigate any loss by taking down the sign himself; and (4) as there had been no variation of the original contract to provide for the deduction, there was no basis in law for that deduction. *Held,* (1) it was a custom of estate agents to erect such boards and in the absence of any agreement to the contrary it was within an agent's authority to erect such a sign; (2) in this particular case, it was a term of the agency contract that no sign should be erected and the plaintiffs were therefore in breach; and (3) the defendant had suffered no damage at all and was merely annoyed. In the absence of any agreement or variation between the parties there was no basis in law for the 10 per cent. deduction. Nominal damages of £5 would be awarded and the plaintiffs were therefore entitled to judgment in the sum of £101·92: BENHAM AND REEVES v. CHRISTENSEN, July 24, 1979; Mayor's and City of London Court, Mr. Registrar Myers. (*Ex rel. Charles Douthwaite, Esq., Barrister.*)

32. —— commission—effective introduction
[Aust.] D owned land; he appointed P, an estate agent, to sell it. P introduced company A to D; A made several unsuccessful offers to purchase the land for the price asked by D. Meanwhile, D entered into negotiations with company B which had not been introduced by P, and which was also prepared to meet D's price. While D was negotiating separately with the two companies, they came to know of each other; in order to avoid bidding up the price they agreed that whichever of them bought the land, they would complete the purchase and subsequent development " jointly on a basis of equality." Without knowing of this agreement, D sold the land to a company formed by company B; company A and company B held an equal number of shares in the purchaser company. *Held,* by majority, the agent P had not introduced the purchaser to the owner D or to the land, nor was he an effective cause of the sale. He was not entitled to commission. (*Burchell* v. *Gowrie & Blockhouse Collieries* [1910] A.C. 614 distinguished.) *Per* Jacobs and Murphy JJ.: The agent P was the effective cause of a purchase by com-

pany A of a half interest in the land. He was therefore entitled to half the usual commission on the sale of the whole of the land: HOOKER *v.* ADAMS ESTATES PTY. (1977) 138 C.L.R. 52, Aust. High Ct.

33.　The plaintiff firm sued the defendant for £27,500 commission on R.I.C.S. Scale 19 for introducing a tenant for commercial premises in North London. The defendant was co-ordinating the development of which the premises formed part and alleged that (1) it was acting as agent for the developers who were responsible for the commission; and (2) the tenant had in fact been introduced by another party at an earlier date. *Held*, the plaintiff had effectively introduced the tenant even though the defendant knew of the identity of the tenant before. On the facts, the defendant had retained the plaintiff. The scale had been agreed and a *quantum meruit* could not lie, however attractive that might be. Judgment for plaintiff with costs. There was no basis for the third party proceedings, dismissed with costs: HAMPTON AND SONS *v.* TRADE AND GENERAL SECURITIES (1979) 250 E.G. 451, Peter Pain J.

34.　—— —— **payable on introduction of lessees to suitable premises**
The plaintiff estate agents claimed commission on introducing defendant lessees to property at Leicester Square W.C.1 which they subsequently occupied. The defendants first inspected that property some 10 months before the plaintiffs, who were neither the lessors' agents nor retained by them, introduced them to it. *Held*, as the defendants had lost interest in the property after their initial inspection, the plaintiffs' introduction was the effective cause of the transaction and they were entitled to commission on a *quantum meruit* basis: REIFF DINER & CO. *v.* CATALYTIC INTERNATIONAL INC. (1978) 246 E.G. 743, Judge Laughton-Scott.

35.　—— —— **quantum meruit**
D asked P to find them offices to rent in London. P told D that if P introduced D to a property, and P were not already retained to act for the lessors, P would look to D for their fees, which were to be in accordance with para. 24 of the R.I.C.S. scale. This provided " for negotiating a tenancy or lease when acting on behalf of the tenant or lessee: (a) for seeking or negotiating the tenancy or lease or property on the instructions of a client . . . for abortive work under this part of this scale, a fee on a quantum meruit basis." If the negotiations were not abortive, the fee was to be 10 per cent. of the first year's rent. P found a property for D, but D negotiated with a third party for the lease. P claimed £4,646, being 10 per cent. of the rental. *Held*, P did not relate the work which para. 24 requires to the earning of the commission. Merely finding a property was not enough, because if that was a part of the agreement they had to seek and negotiate the lease. Any negotiating they may have done did not in fact result in the tenancy. However, as D had gone behind P's back in negotiating with third parties, and never gave P a chance to go on, the work which they had in fact done was, as far as they were concerned, abortive under para. 24 (a) and therefore they were entitled to a fee on quantum meruit basis. £1500, to be inclusive of VAT, was awarded to the plaintiffs (*Reiff Diner & Co. v. Catalytic International Inc.* [1979] C.L.Y. 34 followed): SINCLAIR GOLDSMITH *v.* MINERO PERU COMERCIAL (1978) 248 E.G. 1015, O'Connor J.

36.　—— —— **reasonable figure**
The vendor appellant instructed the respondent estate agent to sell a house. There was no agreement as to the rate of commission but the respondent said he was " the cheapest in town." The house was sold for £13,500 and he claimed £286·20 commission on the old sliding scale. The appellant offered not more than £100. The respondent admitted in evidence that £60 would be a fair figure as a *quantum meruit*. The county court judge awarded the full claim, less an agreed discount of £10. *Held*, dismissing the appeal, there was and had been before the judge no evidence to show that £276·20 was unreasonable. The figure of £60 was irrelevant because the remuneration had been agreed on a commission rather than *quantum meruit* basis: LEWIS & GRAVES *v.* HARPER (1979) 250 E.G. 1287, C.A.

37. —— **sale of house—two agents instructed—which agent operative cause of sale—costs of action**

In August 1975 the defendant wished to sell his house. Both plaintiffs, being estate agents, received instructions and in both cases they were to be entitled to commission in the event of their introducing a purchaser who exchanged contracts. On October 3, 1975, as a result of an appointment made by the first plaintiff, the eventual purchasers viewed the property, and expressed interest. On October 10 they made an offer for the property. For unexplained reasons the purchasers made their offer through the second plaintiff who until then had done nothing to interest them in the property but who thereafter conducted all negotiations. Contracts were exchanged in December 1975. *Held,* that the first plaintiff was the operative cause of the sale and judgment was entered for them. Judgment for the defendant was entered against the second plaintiff. The question then arose as to costs. The second plaintiff submitted its account in December 1975 and the first plaintiff in February 1976. The defendant was unable to tell who was entitled to the commission. He contacted the purchasers who were unable to assist him. The defendant placed the disputed sum with his solicitors who told both agents that their client accepted his liability to pay one or other of the agents (or a proportion to both agents). Both plaintiffs then commenced proceedings and the actions were consolidated. The judge found that the defendant wished to discharge his financial obligations but was prevented from doing so by the competing claims of the two agents. On the authority of *Greatorex* v. *Shackle* [1895] 2 Q.B. 249 he could not institute interpleader proceedings. He could not make a payment into court to protect his position on costs and had done the only sensible thing he could do. The judge distinguished *The Bosworth (No.* 2) [1960] C.L.Y. 2485 because in that case the defendant could protect himself by payment into court. The judge's expressed intention was to ensure that the defendant should not be penalised in the action. An order was made that the first plaintiff recover all the costs of the action and consolidated action against the defendant. The defendant could recover all his costs of the actions and consolidated actions against the second plaintiff to include all costs that the defendant had to pay to the first plaintiff: MOSS KAYE & ROY FRANK & CO. *v.* JONES; ALAN SADICK & CO. *v.* JONES, July 26, 1979, Judge Pickering, Willesden County Ct. (*Ex rel. Daniel Pearce-Higgins, Esq., Barrister.*)

38. Estate Agents Act 1979 (c. 38)

This Act makes provision with respect to the carrying on of certain activities in connection with the disposal and acquisition of property used for residential purposes.

S. 1 applies the Act to estate agency work; s. 2 defines interests in land; s. 3 relates to orders prohibiting unfit persons from doing estate agency work; s. 4 provides for the making of orders warning against continuing certain practices; s. 5 contains supplementary provisions as to orders under ss. 3 and 4; s. 6 deals with revocation and variation of orders under ss. 3 and 4; s. 7 provides for appeals against such orders; s. 8 establishes a register of orders; s. 9 gives the Director of Fair Trading power to require information; s. 10 restricts the disclosure of information; s. 11 gives powers of entry and inspection; s. 12 defines " clients' money," " contract deposit," " pre-contract deposit " and " connected contract "; s. 13 deals with clients' money held on trust or as agent; s. 14 relates to the keeping of client accounts; s. 15 makes provisions as to the interest on clients' money; s. 16 concerns insurance cover for clients' money; s. 17 makes certain exemptions from s. 16; s. 18 provides for information to clients of prospective liabilities; s. 19 regulates pre-contract deposits outside Scotland; s. 20 prohibits pre-contract deposits in Scotland; s. 21 deals with transactions in which an estate agent has a personal interest; s. 22 empowers the Secretary of State to make regulations as to standards of competence; s. 23 prohibits bankrupts from engaging in estate agency work; s. 24 provides for supervision by Council on Tribunals; s. 25 specifies the general duties of the Director of Fair Trading; s. 26 defines the enforcement authorities under the Act; s. 27 makes obstruction and personation of authorised officers an offence; s. 28 contains general provisions as to offences; s. 29 provides for services of notices; s. 30 relates to orders and regulations under the Act; s. 31 defines

" business associate " and " controller "; s. 32 defines " associate "; s. 33 is the general interpretation section; s. 34 makes financial provisions; s. 35 relates to Scotland; s. 36 contains the short title, commencement and extent. The Act extends to Northern Ireland.

The Act received the Royal Assent on April 4, 1979, and comes into force on a day to be appointed.

39. Insurance agent—implied authority—interim insurance arranged—whether insurer bound

In non-marine insurance a broker has implied authority to enter into a contract of interim insurance as agent for the insurer.

When the owner of a Ford car bought in its place an MG, he wished to transfer his comprehensive " any driver " insurance cover to the new car. His wife was told by brokers that the same would be done, she supplying all the necessary information. Thereafter the insured's son was involved in an accident whilst driving the MG with his father's consent. After the accident, the father received notice from the brokers indicating that insurance cover was restricted to himself. In proceedings brought against the son in connection with the accident, the son joined the brokers and insurers as third parties. Arnold J. gave judgment against the brokers for negligently failing to inform the wife of the insurance to be arranged. *Held*, allowing the appeal, that the brokers were clearly acting as authorised agents of the insurers in issuing temporary cover; and that accordingly the insurers were liable to indemnify the son.

STOCKTON *v.* MASON; VEHICLE AND GENERAL INSURANCE CO. (IN LIQUIDATION) AND ARTHUR EDWARDS (INSURANCE) (THIRD PARTIES) [1979] R.T.R. 130, C.A.

40. —— theft—moneys received on account of another—agent using insurance premiums for own purposes. See R. *v.* BREWSTER, § 596.

41. Non-existent principal—individual's liability—measure of damages

[Can.] It has been *held* that where an individual purports to contract with a third party on behalf of a corporation not yet formed there is no contract with either the individual or the corporation. The individual is liable to the third party for breach of warranty of authority. The measure of damages is based upon what the third party would have recovered from the company had it existed, and where the company has subsequently been formed and become insolvent, the third party is entitled only to nominal damages (*Newborne* v. *Sensolid* (*Great Britain*) [1953] C.L.Y. 498, *Starkey* v. *Bank of England* [1903] A.C. 114 referred to): DELTA CONSTRUCTION CO. *v.* LIDSTONE (1979) 96 D.L.R. (3d) 457, Newfld.Sup.Ct.

42. —— whether person signing contract in non-existent company's name liable

[Can.] It has been *held,* that where a person signs a contract in the name of a corporation, adding his own name after the word " per," and it subsequently turns out that the corporation has never existed, the contract is a nullity and the signer is not personally bound in the absence of breach of warranty of authority or fraud (*Kelner* v. *Baxter* (1866) L.R. 2 C.P. 174 distinguished; *Newborne* v. *Sensolid* (*Great Britain*) [1953] C.L.Y. 498 applied): GENERAL MOTORS ACCEPTANCE *v.* WEISMAN (1979) 96 D.L.R. (3d) 159, Middlesex County Ct.

43. Sale of goods—seller's agent—motorcar—authority to demonstrate car controls. See NELSON *v.* RAPHAEL, § 2371.

44. Undisclosed principal—judgment against agent—merger of liability of principal —Statute of Frauds—guarantee

[Aus.] Four persons formed a syndicate to speculate in shares on the Stock Exchange. They traded through the medium of a private company whose only members were one of the syndicate (M) and his wife. The company (C) became indebted to stockbrokers (S). S threatened to sell certain shares they held against C's orders and to apply the proceeds of sale against C's debt. The proposed sale was postponed upon M's undertaking that he would either pay the sum owed by C or put C in funds so that it could pay it. M did neither. S sold the shares and sued C for the balance of the debt. As C had no substantial assets, S then sued M on his undertaking. It was pleaded in defence that there had not been a note or memorandum in writing to satisfy the Statute of Frauds. The statement of claim alleged that M was C's agent. The trial judge refused the application of S to amend to plead that C had acted as agent for M and the other members of the syndicate. The judge found that C had acted as agent for the syndicate; accordingly the contract alleged against M was not to answer for the debt, default or miscarriages of another person within the meaning of the Statute of Frauds. *Held*, that (1) the finding that C acted as agent for the syndicate was not contrary to the pleadings; (2) M's promise to answer for the debt or default of C was not within the scope of the Statute of Frauds: a contract is not within the Statute by which the defendant promises to discharge a liability for which he or his property is already subject. (*Fitzgerald* v. *Dressler* (1859) 141 E.R. 861 applied; *Harbing India Rubber* v. *Martin* [1902] 1 K.B. 778 and *Davys* v. *Buswell* [1913] 2 K.B. 47 distinguished): MARGINSON v. IAN POTTER & Co. (1976) 136 C.L.R. 161, High Ct. of Aus.

BOOKS AND ARTICLES, See *post*, pp. [1], [13].

AGRICULTURE

45. Agricultural holdings—compensation on surrender to authority—value of licence to remain
[Land Compensation Act 1973 (c. 26), s. 48.] The appellants, W and others, were entitled to compensation under the Act on their surrender of a yearly agricultural tenancy. Surrender took place in July 1973 but the appellants were granted a gratuitous licence by the acquiring authority to occupy and farm part of the surrendered land for a further three years and three months therefrom. In 1977 the Lands Tribunal assessed the amount of compensation at £14,525, including a deduction for profits made by the appellants by virtue of their occupation by licence since the surrender. The appellants appealed, arguing that the profits were not deductible, and contended for a figure of £24,005. *Held*, allowing the appeal, that the grant of the licence should not be construed so as to confer a benefit on the respondent acquiring authority. Accordingly the post-surrender/acquisition profits should not be deducted from the compensation and the appellants were entitled to the higher figure: WAKERLEY v. ST. EDMUNDSBURY BOROUGH COUNCIL (1979) 249 E.G. 639, C.A.

46. —— death of tenant—survivors—when eligible
[Agriculture (Miscellaneous Provisions) Act 1976 (c. 55), s. 18 (2).] When a tenant of an agricultural holding dies leaving survivors eligible to apply for the tenancy, the date on which eligibility is determined is the date of the tenant's death: JACKSON v. HALL; WILLIAMSON v. THOMPSON, *The Times*, December 20, 1979, H.L.

47. —— " grass keeps "—definition
[Agricultural Holdings Act 1948 (c. 63), s. 2 (1).] A " grass keep " agreement is a particular kind of holding which has an established and accepted definition amongst the farming community. It grants a licence to the licensee to pasture his beasts on the licensor's land, and to mow the grass if he wishes, and take away the mown grass or hay. Apart from that, the licensee has no other rights in the land by virtue of the licence. It is an essential feature of a " grass keep " agreement that it is for less than one year. Consequently, such an agreement is not within the proviso of s. 2 (1) of the Agricultural Holdings Act 1948, being " a licence to occupy land . . . in contemplation of the use of the land only for grazing or mowing during some specified period of the year ": LUTON v. TINSEY (1978) 249 E.G. 239, C.A.

48. —— notice to quit—consent—whether good husbandry relevant
[Agricultural Holdings Act 1948 (c. 63), s. 25 (1).] The applicant tenant applied for certiorari to quash the agricultural land tribunal's decision to consent to the operation of a notice to quit on the grounds of greater hardship. An earlier application on another ground had been successful and the matter had been remitted to the tribunal. The tribunal had then considered the poor state of the land in question and the fact that another prospective

tenant had offered a higher rent than the applicant had at first been prepared
to offer. The applicant had, at a late stage in the original proceedings, offered
the same rent: the tribunal had then considered evidence of his poor performance as a farmer. *Held*, the tribunal had been entitled to look into the
behaviour of the applicant and to find in favour of the landlord. Application
dismissed: R. *v.* AGRICULTURAL LAND TRIBUNAL FOR THE SOUTH EASTERN
AREA, *ex p.* PARSLOW (1979) 251 E.G. 667, D.C.

49. —— **rent of farm land and caravan site—whether site was improvement—rate
relief**

[Agricultural Holdings Act 1948 (c. 63), s. 8.] Upon an arbitration to determine the rent of 300 acres of land in Cornwall the arbitrator stated a special
case to the court for a number of questions. The tenant had built and paid for
a caravan site for 190 caravans on nine and a quarter acres: 202 acres were
farmed and the remainder was buildings or waste. *Held*, the land was an
agricultural holding but, in view of the much greater income from the caravan
site, should be valued as part farm and part caravan site. The works of
building the site were tenant's improvements within s. 8 (2) (*a*). Some account
must be taken in the rent of the latent value released or to be released by the
improvements. The arbitrator must ensure to the tenant the benefit of rate
relief, however difficult that might be. The arbitrator was required to hear
evidence rather than rely on his professional experience. Rate relief must be
full relief, quantified if necessary (*Guthe* v. *Broach* [1956] C.L.Y. 98 considered): TUMMON *v.* BARCLAYS BANK TRUST Co. (1979) 250 E.G. 980, Judge
Goodall, Bodmin County Ct.

50. —— **rents—payment by post**

[Agricultural Holdings Act 1948 (c. 63) (as amended by Agriculture Act 1958
(c. 71), s. 8 (1) and Sched. 1, para. 8), s. 24 (1) (2) (*d*).]

Where the sending of a cheque by post is the accepted mode of payment,
the rent is paid when the cheque is put in the post, subject only to its being
honoured.

M was the tenant of an agricultural holding from year to year for which
the rent was payable by equal payments on April 6 and October 11 each
year. The rent was normally paid by cheque sent through the post. In March
1975 the landlords' agent requested M to send the rent to him at Goole
rather than to the landlords direct thereafter. On October 21, 1975, the rent
being overdue, a notice was sent to M under s. 24 of the 1948 Act requiring
M to pay the rent due within two months from the service of notice on him.
M received the notice on October 22. One of the landlords received by post
at her home a cheque for the rent on December 24. The cheque and covering
letter were dated December 20. The envelope had a first-class stamp and was
posted December 22, 1975. The landlords served 12 months' notice on M for
failing to comply with the s. 24 notice. The arbitrator stated a case of law
for the county court whether the tenant had failed to pay the rent due within
two months. The judge held that M had failed to do so. M appealed. *Held*,
allowing the appeal, that the accepted mode of payment direct to the agent
did no more than provide an alternative destination for the cheque and when
the cheque had been put in the post, subject only to its being honoured, the
rent had been paid. Since this had not been later than December 22 the
rent had been paid in time. (*Norman* v. *Ricketts* (1886) 3 T.L.R. 182 and
Tankexpress A/S v. *Compagnie Financière Belge des Petroles S.A.* (1949)
C.L.C. 9486 applied; *Pennington* v. *Crossley & Sons* (1897) 13 T.L.R. 513
distinguished.)

BEEVERS *v.* MASON (1978) 37 P. & C.R. 452, C.A.

51. —— **tenancy from year to year—surrender**

[Agricultural Holdings Act 1948 (c. 63), s. 2 (1).] L and T met in November
1963 to discuss T's use of L's land. It was orally agreed that T would be granted
a succession of written six-month agreements allowing him to graze L's land,
and that these agreements would continue " for several years." T subsequently
signed such an agreement, in reliance on the assurance that he would be able
to occupy the land for several years. For thirteen years T grazed L's land, and
the last agreement was signed on June 1, 1977. On September 15, 1977, L gave

T notice to vacate the land on November 30, 1977. T claimed to be protected by s. 2 (1) of the Agricultural Holdings Act 1948. The county court judge found that (1) there was a collateral agreement made between L and T before the first agreement was signed; (2) T signed the agreement in reliance on that agreement; (3) the written agreement was not a genuine one as far as the specified period of six months was concerned, and (4) on the footing that grazing rights were granted for a period exceeding one year, the effect of s. 2 was to create a letting from year to year. He then found that a time came, on or before June 1, 1977, when the collateral agreement was discharged, and that in signing the agreement of that date T surrendered the letting from year to year, and as a result of that had only a six month right to graze the land: consequently he was not entitled to the protection of the 1948 Act. T appealed. *Held,* allowing the appeal, the effect of the agreement to give T "several" years gave him a tenancy of three years certain and thereafter for six months at a time until he was given reasonable notice. This series of transactions took effect as a letting from year to year under the Act. The written agreements were all subject to the same vice, in that they provided for the grazing rights to continue for six months only. As the agreement of June 1, 1977, was not genuine, the signing of it could not operate as a surrender by T. The original agreement, creating a letting from year to year, continued and was protected by the Act. (*Scene Estates* v. *Amos* [1957] C.L.Y. 46 applied; *Johnson* v. *Moreton* [1977] C.L.Y. 55 considered): SHORT BROS. (PLANT) *v.* EDWARDS (1978) 249 E.G. 539, C.A.

52. —— widow of farmworker occupying cottage—whether a statutory tenant—transitional provisions of 1976 Act
[Rent (Agriculture) Act 1976 (c. 80), ss. 2 (1), 4 (3), Sched. 9, para. 3.]
On a true construction, the words "at all material times" in para. 3 of Sched. 9 to the 1976 Act mean at all times in the past at which any fact existed or event occurred which, if the Act had been in force, would have been relevant for the decision of the question with which the paragraph was concerned.

C, a full-time agricultural worker, was provided with a cottage by his employer. In 1968 C fell ill and his employment was terminated, but he and his wife continued to live in the cottage without payment. In 1972 the cottage was sold, but the new owners (the plaintiffs) allowed C and his wife to stay on. In 1973 C died, but his widow stayed in the cottage still without payment. In 1977 the plaintiffs began an action for possession; C's widow claimed the protection of the 1976 Act which had come into force on January 1, 1977. At first instance it was held that the transitional provisions did not avail her. On appeal, *held,* allowing the appeal, that the Act was deemed to have been in force in 1968 when C was a "qualifying" worker, and the fresh licence granted to him when his employment was terminated was a "relevant" licence, so C continued as a protected occupier becoming a statutory tenant. (*Lauri* v. *Renad* [1892] 3 Ch. 402 considered.)
SKINNER *v.* COOPER [1979] 1 W.L.R. 666, C.A.

53. Agricultural land—report
The Northfield Committee has published its "Report of the Committee of Inquiry into the Acquisition and Occupancy of Agricultural Land." The Report covers agricultural structure, occupancy, ownership and acquisition, taxation, land prices, rents and tenure legislation and is available from HMSO (Cmnd. 7599) [£6·00].

54. —— valuation—capital gains tax purposes. See HALLEY *v.* WEIGHTMAN, § 1455.

55. Agricultural Statistics Act 1979 (c. 13)
This Act consolidates certain enactments relating to agricultural statistics.
S. 1 gives power to obtain agricultural statistics; s. 2 provides for the furnishing of information as to dealings in land used for agriculture; s. 3 restricts the disclosure of information; s. 4 gives penalties for failing to furnish information; s. 5 deals with service of notices; s. 6 is the interpretation section; s. 7 contains amendments and repeals; s. 8 deals with citation, commencement and extent. This Act does not extend to Scotland or Northern Ireland.

The Act received the Royal Assent on March 22, 1979, and came into force on April 22, 1979.

56. Agriculture (Miscellaneous Provisions) Act 1968—amendment

AGRICULTURE (MISCELLANEOUS PROVISIONS) ACT 1968 (AMENDMENT) REGULATIONS 1979 (No. 25) [10p], made under the Agriculture (Miscellaneous Provisions) Act 1976 (c. 55), s. 7; operative on February 9, 1979; amend the 1968 Act by substituting references to " area " for reference to " acreage " in s. 40 (3) (c) of that Act.

57. Animals. See ANIMALS.

58. Butter subsidies

BUTTER SUBSIDY (PROTECTION OF COMMUNITY ARRANGEMENTS) REGULATIONS 1979 (No. 586) [20p], made under the European Communities Act 1972 (c. 68), s. 2 (2), operative on May 25, 1979; consolidate previous amendments made enabling subsidy paid on butter under certain Council Regulations to be recovered where the butter has been exported from the U.K., or has, without the authority of the Intervention Board for Agricultural Produce, been used for manufacture; prohibiting the use of subsidised butter for manufacture unless the Board has authorised such use, and requiring records to be kept about the exports.

59. Cattle. See ANIMALS.

60. Cereals

HOME-GROWN CEREALS AUTHORITY (RATE OF LEVY) ORDER 1979 (No. 782) [20p], made under the Cereals Marketing Act 1965 (c. 14), s. 1; operative on August 1, 1979; specifies in respect of home-grown wheat, barley and oats the rate of levy to be raised in respect of the year beginning with August 1, 1979, to meet the amounts apportioned by the Ministers to these kinds of home-grown cereals to finance the Home-Grown Cereals Authority in the performance of their non-trading functions under Part 1 of the 1965 Act.

61. Cereals Marketing Act 1965—amendment

CEREALS MARKETING ACT 1965 (AMENDMENT) REGULATIONS 1979 (No. 26) [10p], made under the Agriculture (Miscellaneous Provisions) Act 1976 (c. 55), s. 7; operative on February 9, 1979; amends the 1965 Act by substituting references to " area " for references to " acreage " in ss. 13 (4), 15 (1), 16 (6) (a).

62. Common agricultural policy

COMMON AGRICULTURAL POLICY (WINE) REGULATIONS 1979 (No. 1094) [50p], made under the European Communities Act 1972 (c. 68), s. 2 (2); operative on October 1, 1979; provide for the enforcement of EEC Regulations concerned with the production and marketing of wine and related products.

63. Corn returns

CORN RETURNS (AMENDMENT) REGULATIONS 1979 (No. 607) [20p], made under the Corn Returns Act 1882 (c. 37), ss. 4, 5, 14; operative on August 1, 1979; amend S.I. 1976 No. 1035 by substituting a new form of return for the previous form.

64. Corn Sales Act 1921—amendment

CORN SALES ACT 1921 (AMENDMENT) REGULATIONS 1979 (No. 357) [10p], made under the Agriculture (Miscellaneous Provisions) Act 1976 (c. 55), s. 7; operative on May 1, 1979; substitute references in the 1921 Act to imperial pounds for references to kilograms.

65. Eggs

EGGS AUTHORITY (RATES OF LEVY) ORDER 1979 (No. 257) [20p], made under the Agriculture Act 1970 (c. 40), s. 13 (2) (b), (6); operative on April 1, 1979; specifies the rate of levy for the accounting period beginning April 1, 1979, and ending March 31, 1980.

66. European Communities. See EUROPEAN COMMUNITIES.

66a. Feeding stuffs

FERTILISERS AND FEEDING STUFFS (AMENDMENT) REGULATIONS 1979 (No. 1617) [50p], made under the Agriculture Act 1970 (c. 40), ss. 66 (1), 68 (1), 74A and 84; operative on January 4, 1980; restrict the use of certain substances, delete a colourant and a substance from lists of those permitted and extend or restrict the use of some preservatives.

67. Grants

GRANTS FOR GUARANTEES OF BANK LOANS (EXTENSION OF PERIOD) ORDER 1979 (No. 323) [10p], made under the Agriculture Act 1967 (c. 22), s. 64 (7); operative on April 1, 1979; extends for a further five years the period during which a grant may be made by the Minister of Agriculture in respect of a guarantee given as security for a loan given to a person carrying on an agriculture or horticultural business.

68. Hill farming

HILL LIVESTOCK (COMPENSATORY ALLOWANCES) (AMENDMENT) REGULATIONS 1979 (No. 941) [10p], made under the European Communities Act 1972 (c. 68), s. 2 (2); operative on July 27, 1979; amend S.I. 1975 No. 2210 by raising the overall limit on payments to 53·70 units of account per hectare of eligible land and by amending the references to the maximum permitted headage payments in respect of cattle and sheep in accordance with Reg. 1054/78/EEC.

HILL LIVESTOCK (COMPENSATORY ALLOWANCES) REGULATIONS 1979 (No. 1748) [40p], made under the European Communities Act 1972, s. 2 (2); operative on January 1, 1980; consolidate the Hill Livestock (Compensatory Allowances) Regulations 1975 (No. 2210) and amendments to the same, increase the compensatory allowance payable in respect of certain livestock and increase the overall limit on payments for each hectare of eligible land.

69. Hops

INTERVENTION FUNCTIONS (DELEGATION) (HOPS) REGULATIONS 1979 (No. 433) [10p], made under the European Communities Act 1972 (c. 68), s. 6 (2) (*a*), (8); operative on April 27, 1979; empower the Hops Marketing Board to act for the Intervention Board for Agricultural Produce by carrying out in England functions which the Intervention Board may delegate to it with respect to hops.

HOPS CERTIFICATION REGULATIONS 1979 (No. 1095) [40p], made under the European Communities Act 1972, s. 2 (2); operative on October 1, 1979; provide for the implementation in the U.K. of the Community hop certification system set up under the Community provisions referred to in reg. 1 (2); for certification to be carried out by certifying officers authorised by the Minister of Agriculture, Fisheries and Food or the Secretary of State; and provide for inspection of certification centres and premises where hops are to be found.

70. Horticulture

FRUITING PLUM TREES (PLANTING GRANTS) SCHEME 1979 (No. 876) [20p], made under the Agriculture Act 1970 (c. 40), s. 29; operative on August 1, 1979; authorises the payment of a grant towards expenditure incurred for the purposes of or in connection with, a plum production business.

PLUM MATERIAL AND CLEARANCE GRANTS SCHEME 1979 (No. 877) [20p], made under the Agriculture Act 1970, s. 29; operative on August 1, 1979; authorises the payment of a grant towards capital expenditure for the purposes of, or in connection with, a plum material business. Grant payable under the Scheme is limited to 25 per cent. of the total approved expenditure.

FARM AND HORTICULTURE DEVELOPMENT (AMENDMENT) REGULATIONS 1979 (No. 1559) [10p], made under the European Communities Act 1972 (c. 68), s. 2 (2); operative on December 31, 1979; amend S.I. 1978 No. 1086 in order to express the guidance premium in sterling terms, to take account of the provisions of Council Directive 78/1017/EEC.

71. Levies

MEAT AND LIVESTOCK COMMISSION LEVY SCHEME (CONFIRMATION) ORDER 1979 (No. 393) [25p], made under the Agriculture Act 1967 (c. 22), s. 13; operative on March 30, 1979; revokes and replaces S.I. 1968 No. 1224 and provides for the imposition of charges for enabling the Commission to meet their expenses.

72. Northern Ireland. See NORTHERN IRELAND.

73. Plant health

DUTCH ELM DISEASE (LOCAL AUTHORITIES) (AMENDMENT) ORDER 1979 (No. 638) [10p], made under the Plant Health Act 1967 (c. 8), ss. 3 (1)

(2) (4), 5 (1) as read with the Agriculture (Miscellaneous Provisions) Act 1972 (c. 62), s. 20; operative on July 11, 1979; amends S.I. 1977 No. 1074.

DUTCH ELM DISEASE (RESTRICTION ON MOVEMENT OF ELMS) (AMENDMENT) ORDER 1979 (No. 639) [25p], made under the Plant Health Act 1967, s. 3 (1) (2) (4) as read with the Agriculture (Miscellaneous Provisions) Act 1972, s. 20; operative on July 11, 1979; amends S.I. 1977 No. 1075 by adding to restricted areas and by adding provisions relating to notices.

74. Plant varieties and seeds

SEEDS (NATIONAL LISTS OF VARIETIES) REGULATIONS 1979 (No. 133) [40p], made under the Plant Varieties and Seeds Act 1964 (c. 14), s. 16 (1), (1A) and (8), as amended by the European Communities Act 1972 (c. 68), s. 4 (1), Sched. 4, para. 5 (1)–(3); operative on March 12, 1979; require the Minister of Agriculture, Fisheries and Food and the Secretaries of State for Scotland, Wales and Northern Ireland jointly to prepare and publish national lists of varieties of specified kinds of agricultural and vegetable crops.

SEED POTATOES (FEES) REGULATIONS 1979 (No. 366) [10p], made under the Plant Varieties and Seeds Act 1964, s. 16 (1), (1A) (e), (5) (a), (8), as amended by the European Communities Act 1972, s. 4 (1), Sched. 4, para. 5 (1)–(3); operative on April 24, 1979; prescribe fees in respect of matters arising under S.I. 1978 No. 215.

VEGETABLE SEEDS REGULATIONS 1979 (No. 774) [90p], made under the Plant Varieties and Seeds Act 1964, ss. 16 (1)–(5) (8), 17 (1)–(4), 24 (5), 26 (2) (3), 36; operative on August 1, 1979; re-enact with modifications S.I. 1975 No. 1694. The Regulations restrict the marketing of vegetable seeds to specified grades, as defined, and require them to be sold in sealed packages which are to be labelled or marked with prescribed particulars.

PROTECTION OF SEED CROPS (NORTH ESSEX) ORDER 1968 (VARIATION) ORDER 1979 (No. 882) [10p], made under the Plant Varieties and Seeds Act 1964 s. 33 (3) (a) (b) and S.I. 1978 No. 207; operative on September 3, 1979; varies part of the boundary of an area in Essex which has been specified as an area in which s. 33 of the 1964 Act has been brought into force for the protection of certain specified seed crops from injurious cross-pollination.

SEEDS (FEES) REGULATIONS 1979 (No. 888) [50p], made under the Plant Varieties and Seeds Act 1964, s. 16 (1), (1A) (e), (5) (a), (8); operative on August 1, 1979; supersede S.I. 1978 No. 1010 and prescribe new fees in respect of matters arising out of S.I. 1976 Nos. 1133, 1283, 1068, 1284, S.I. 1979 No. 774 and S.I. 1974 No. 760.

CEREAL SEEDS (AMENDMENT) REGULATIONS 1979 (No. 1003) [30p], made under the Plant Varieties and Seeds Act 1964, ss. 16 (1)–(5) (8), 26 (3), 36; operative on September 10, 1979; amend the 1976 (No. 1133) Regulations and give effect to EEC Directives requiring certain alterations in labelling requirements.

BEET SEEDS (AMENDMENT) REGULATIONS 1979 (No. 1004) [30p], made under the Plant Varieties and Seeds Act 1964, ss. 16 (1)–(5) (8), 17 (1)–(4), 24 (5), 26 (2) (3), 36; operative on September 10, 1979; amend the 1976 (No. 1068) Regulations and give effect to Directive 78/692/EEC requiring certain alterations in labelling requirements.

OIL AND FIBRE PLANT SEEDS REGULATIONS 1979 (No. 1005) [90p], made under the Plant Varieties and Seeds Act 1964, ss. 16 (1)–(5) (8), 17 (1)–(4), 24 (5), 26 (2) (3), 36; operative on September 10, 1979; supersede the 1976 (No. 1284) Regulations which regulate the marketing in Great Britain of seeds of oil and fibre plants. The Regulations also give effect to Directive 66/402/EEC on the marketing of the seeds.

75. Sugar

SUGAR BEET (RESEARCH AND EDUCATION) ORDER 1979 (No. 222) [20p], made under the Sugar Act 1956 (c. 48), s. 18 (1) and (2); operative on April 1, 1979; provides for the assessment and collection of contributions for the year beginning April 1, 1979, from the British Sugar Corporation and from growers of home-grown beet, towards the programme of research and education set out in the Schedule to the Order.

**76. Tenancy—qualifying worker—meaning of " engaged whole time in agriculture "
—pheasants for sport**

[Rent (Agriculture) Act 1976 (c. 80) s. 1.] A gamekeeper employed to rear pheasants for sport is not employed in agriculture within the meaning of the 1976 Act, and therefore not entitled to the security of tenure provisions given to agricultural workers housed by their employers in that Act. Not every rural activity is included within the definition of agriculture (*Lord Glendyne* v. *Rapley* [1978] C.L.Y. 72 followed): EARL OF NORMANTON v. GILES, *The Times,* December 18, 1979, H.L.

77. Tractors

AGRICULTURAL OR FORESTRY TRACTORS AND TRACTOR COMPONENTS (TYPE APPROVAL) REGULATIONS 1979 (No. 221) [50p], made under the European Communities Act 1972 (c. 68), s. 2 (2); operative on April 3, 1979; provide for the type approval of certain agricultural or forestry tractors which conform to Council directives with respect to design, construction, equipment and marking.

AGRICULTURAL OR FORESTRY TRACTORS AND TRACTOR COMPONENTS (TYPE APPROVAL) (FEES) REGULATIONS 1979 (No. 1376) [40p], made under the Finance Act 1973 (c. 51), s. 56 (1) and (2); operative on November 28, 1979; prescribe the fees payable for the testing of tractors and the issue of documents in connection with the type approval of such tractors for the purposes of the specified Community Directives.

BOOKS AND ARTICLES. See *post,* pp. [1], [13].

ALIENS

78. British nationality

BRITISH NATIONALITY (AMENDMENT) REGULATIONS 1979 (No. 240) [20p], made under the British Nationality Act 1948 (c. 56), s. 29 (1), as extended and amended by the Cyprus Act 1960 (c. 52), s. 4 (7), the British Nationality Act 1964 (c. 22), s. 3 (2), the British Nationality (No. 2) Act 1964 (c. 54), s. 6 (2), and the British Nationality Act 1965 (c. 34), s. 5 (2); operative on April 4, 1979; increase certain fees payable under S.I. 1975 No. 225 in respect of the conferment on adults of citizenship of the U.K. and Colonies or British subject status.

79. Immigration. See ADMINISTRATIVE LAW.

ANIMALS

80. Badgers

BADGERS (AREA OF SPECIAL PROTECTION) ORDER 1979 (No. 1249) [10p], made under the Badgers Act 1973 (c. 57), s. 6; operative on December 1, 1979; declares the county of West Yorkshire to be an area of special protection for badgers for the purposes of the 1973 Act.

81. Bees

IMPORTATION OF BEES (PROHIBITION) ORDER 1979 (No. 587) [10p], made under the Agriculture (Miscellaneous Provisions) Act 1954 (c. 39), s. 10 (1) (*a*) (*c*); operative on May 25, 1979; prohibits the importation of bees into Great Britain from any of the specified countries.

IMPORTATION OF BEES (PROHIBITION) (AMENDMENT) ORDER 1979 (No. 1588) [10p], made under the Agriculture (Miscellaneous Provisions) Act 1954, 10 (1) (*a*) (*c*) (8); operative on December 31, 1979; amends S.I. 1979 No. 587 by continuing it in operation until June 30, 1980, and adding Hungary, Malaysia and Thailand to the list of countries from which the importation of bees into Great Britain is prohibited.

82. Carriage of live birds—causing injury or unnecessary suffering—extension of jurisdiction

The defendants, foreign nationals, were convicted of causing injury or unnecessary suffering to some live birds carried by air to London via Kuwait. The court *held*, that the order under which charges were made gave the court extra-territorial jurisdiction since the order applied to the carriage of animals " to or from " Great Britain: AIR INDIA v. WIGGINS (1979) 123 S.J. 718, D.C.

83. Conservation

CONSERVATION OF WILD CREATURES AND WILD PLANTS (ESSEX EMERALD MOTH) ORDER 1979 (No. 353) [10p], made under the Conservation of Wild Creatures and Wild Plants Act 1975 (c. 48), Sched. 1; operative on March 26, 1979; adds the Essex Emerald Moth to the wild creatures which are protected under the 1975 Act.

84. Coypus

COYPUS (KEEPING) (AMENDMENT) REGULATIONS 1979 (No. 1668) [10p], made under the Destructive Imported Animals Act 1932 (c. 12), s. 2 (c) as applied by S.I. 1977 No. 1993; operative on January 1, 1980; further amend S.I. 1967 No. 1873 by increasing the fee for a licence to keep coypus from £24·50 to £29.

85. Diseases

DISEASES OF ANIMALS (APPROVED DISINFECTANTS) (AMENDMENT) ORDER 1979 (No. 37) [25p], made under the Diseases of Animals Act 1950 (c. 36), ss. 1 (1), 11 (vi) (vii) (ix), 50 (1), 85 (1); operative on January 31, 1979; amends S.I. 1978 No. 32 by adding to the list of approved disinfectants and by deleting from the approved list certain other disinfectants.

DISEASES OF ANIMALS (FEES FOR THE TESTING OF DISINFECTANTS) ORDER 1979 (No. 751) [20p], made under the Agriculture (Miscellaneous Provisions) Act 1963 (c. 11), s. 16 (1) (5); operative on July 27, 1979; prescribes revised fees payable for the testing of disinfectants for the purpose of determining their suitabilty for listing as approved disinfectants in the Schedule to S.I. 1978 No. 32.

DISEASES OF ANIMALS (APPROVED DISINFECTANTS) (AMENDMENT) (No. 2) ORDER 1979 (No. 773) [70p], made under the Diseases of Animals Act 1950, ss. 1 (1), 11 (vi) (vii), 20 (viii) (ix), 50 (1), 85 (1); operative on July 17, 1979; amends S.I. 1978 No. 32 by substituting new schedules for Scheds. 1 and 2 to that Order.

AUJESZKY'S DISEASE OF SWINE ORDER 1979 (No. 815) [20p], made under the Diseases of Animals Act 1950, ss. 1, 8 (3), 10, 11, 84 (3) (a); operative on August 1, 1979; extends the meaning of the expression " disease " in the 1950 Act to cover Aujeszky's disease of swine.

TRANSIT OF ANIMALS (ROAD AND RAIL) (AMENDMENT) ORDER 1979 (No. 1013) [20p], made under the Diseases of Animals Act 1950, ss. 1 (1), (2) (a), 20 (ix) (x), 85 (1); operative on September 1, 1979; amends S.I. 1975 No. 1024 which regulates the carriage by road and rail of farm animals and horses.

DISEASES OF ANIMALS (MISCELLANEOUS FEES) (REVOCATION) ORDER 1979 (No. 1281) [10p], made under the Agriculture (Miscellaneous Provisions) Act 1963, s. 16 (1) (5); operative on November 8, 1979; revokes S.I. 1978 No. 1188.

BRUCELLOSIS (ENGLAND AND WALES) (AMENDMENT) ORDER 1979 (No. 1288) [20p], made under the Diseases of Animals Act 1950, ss. 5, 85 (1) as read with S.I. 1971 No. 531; operative on November 1, 1979; amends S.I. 1978 No. 1480 by adding Kidderminster and Market Drayton livestock markets to the first eradication area described in Sched. 1 to that Order, and by adding certain specified areas of England and Wales to the attested areas described in Sched. 2 to that Order.

EPIZOOTIC ABORTION (REVOCATION) ORDER 1979 (No. 1365) [10p], made under the Diseases of Animals Act 1950, s. 85 (1); operative on November 1, 1979; revokes S.R. & O. 1922 No. 806. Epizootic Abortion is the disease now referred to as brucellosis in cattle. The disease is provided for in S.I. 1978 Nos. 1480 and 1875.

IMPORTATION OF HAY AND STRAW ORDER 1979 (No. 1703) [20p], made under the Diseases of Animals Act 1950, ss. 1, 24, 85 (1); operative on February 1, 1980; prohibits the landing in Great Britain, without licence, of any hay or straw from a place outside Great Britain with certain exceptions.

86. Endangered species

ENDANGERED SPECIES (IMPORT AND EXPORT) ACT 1976 (MODIFICATION) ORDER 1979 (No. 1054) [20p], made under the Endangered Species (Import and Export) Act 1976 (c. 72), ss. 3, 11; operative on September 19, 1979;

modifies the Schedules to the 1976 Act by controlling the importation and exportation of certain products from animals.

87. Horses

IMPORTATION OF EQUINE ANIMALS ORDER 1979 (No. 1701) [40p], made under the Diseases of Animals Act 1950 (c. 36), ss. 1, 24, 84 (3) (*a*) and 85 (1); operative on February 1, 1980; prohibits the landing in Great Britain of equine animals from a place outside Great Britain unless under the authority of a licence.

88. Mink

MINK (KEEPING) (AMENDMENT) REGULATIONS 1979 (No. 1669) [10p], made under the Destructive Imported Animals Act 1932 (c. 12), s. 2 (*c*) as applied by S.I. 1977 No. 1994; operative on January 1, 1980; further amend S.I. 1975 No. 2223 by increasing the fee for keeping mink from £28·50 to £35.

89. Northern Ireland. See NORTHERN IRELAND.

90. Protection of birds

WILD BIRDS (SPECIAL PROTECTION IN SEVERE WEATHER) ORDER 1979 (No. 70) [10p], made under the Protection of Birds Act 1954 (c. 30), s. 13, and the Protection of Birds Act 1967 (c. 46), s. 7; operative on January 26, 1979; creates periods of special protection for all wild birds listed in Sched. 3 to the 1954 Act during which they are protected in the same manner as they are during the close season.

WILD BIRDS (LAPLAND BUNTING) ORDER 1979 (No. 423) [10p], made under the Protection of Birds Act 1954, ss. 9 (1), 13 (1); operative on March 30, 1979; adds the Lapland Bunting to Sched. 1, Pt. I to the 1954 Act.

WILD BIRDS (DUNSFOLD AERODROME) ORDER 1979 (No. 437) [10p], made under the Protection of Birds Act 1954, ss. 9, 13; operative on April 5, 1979; makes it legal for lapwings to be killed or taken, or their nests or eggs to be destroyed or taken by authorised persons within the area of Dunsfold Aerodrome, Godalming, Surrey.

WILDS BIRDS (VARIOUS SPECIES) ORDER 1979 (No. 438) [10p], made under the Protection of Birds Act 1954, ss. 9 (1), 13 (1); operative on April 5, 1979; adds specified wild birds to Sched. 4 to the 1954 Act which provides that such birds may not be sold alive unless close-ringed and bred in captivity.

WILD BIRDS (IMPORTATION) ORDER 1979 (No. 1007) [10p], made under the Protection of Birds Act 1954, s. 7 (2) (b), as amended by the Endangered Species (Import and Export) Act 1976 (c. 72), s. 13 (6); operative on August 13, 1979; prohibits the importation of birds of prey except by licence under s. 10 of the 1954 Act; revokes S.I. 1970 No. 545.

IMPORTATION OF BIRDS, POULTRY AND HATCHING EGGS ORDER 1979 (No. 1702) [40p], made under the Diseases of Animals Act 1950 (c. 36), ss. 1, 24, 45, 84 (2) (3), 85 (1); operative on February 1, 1980; prohibits the landing in Great Britain, without licence, of any live poultry or other birds or hatching eggs from any place outside Great Britain and sets out other supplementary provisions. The Order also creates a criminal offence for the intentional contravention of certain provisions of the Order.

91. Veterinary surgeons. See MEDICINE.

BOOKS AND ARTICLES. See *post*, pp. [1], [13].

ANNUITIES AND RENTCHARGES

ARTICLES. See *post*, p. [13].

ARBITRATION

92. Agricultural holdings. See AGRICULTURE.

93. Appeal—Board of Appeal—order to state special case

V sold to P barley for delivery c.i.f. one safe port west coast Italy by a contract incorporating G.A.F.T.A. 61, cl. 13, which set out the provisions for payment against shipping documents. When the vessel arrived at La Spezia, V gave notice of appropriation to P, who rejected the cargo because it was infested by insects. Three weeks later, the shipping documents were tendered, but P rejected them. P appealed against the umpire's finding in favour of V, and invited the Board of Appeal to state their award in the form of a special case. The Board declined to do so, and P applied for an order directing them to do so under s. 21 (1) of the Arbitration Act 1950. *Held*, that (1) P's argument on the construction of cl. 13 raised a clear-cut and substantial question of law of the sort covered by the decision of the Court of Appeal in *The Lysland* [1973] C.L.Y. 105; (2) even if, as V argued, the question of whether P were estopped from or had waived their right to put forward their argument by not complaining of the absence or late tender of the shipping documents at the time was primarily a question of fact rather than of law, it could not be said that the answer to that question of fact was so clear that the question of law, on the construction of cl. 13, would not arise; (3) the Board would be directed to state their award in the form of a special case: CEREALMANGIMI S.P.A. *v.* TOEPFER; THE EUROMETAL [1979] 2 Lloyd's Rep. 72, Lloyd J.

94. —— **new appeals procedure—case stated appeals superseded**
[Arbitration Act 1979 (c. 42), s. 1.] There was no jurisdiction to hear this appeal since no point of law was involved in the issue of whether the delay after a port strike was sufficient to frustrate a charterparty: PIONEER SHIPPING AND ARMADA MARINE S.A. *v.* B.T.P. TIOXIDE, *The Times*, November 16, 1979, C.A.

95. **Arbitration Act 1979 (c. 42)**
This Act amends the law relating to arbitrations.
S. 1 imposes restrictions on judicial review of arbitration awards; s. 2 relates to determination of preliminary point of law by the court; s. 3 concerns exclusion agreements affecting rights under ss. 1 and 2; s. 4 states that exclusion agreements are not to apply in certain cases unless entered into after commencement of arbitration; s. 5 deals with interlocutory orders; s. 6 makes minor amendments relating to awards and appointment of arbitrators and umpires; s. 7 contains provisions as to the application of certain provisions of Pt. I of the Arbitration Act 1950; s. 8 contains the short title, commencement, repeals and extent. The Act does not apply to Scotland or Northern Ireland.
The Act received the Royal Assent on April 4, 1979, and comes into force on a day to be appointed.

96. —— **commencement**
ARBITRATION ACT 1979 (COMMENCEMENT) ORDER 1979 (No. 750 (C. 16)) [10p], made under the Arbitration Act 1979 (c. 42), s. 8 (2); operative on August 1, 1979; brings the 1979 Act into operation.

97. **Arbitration clause—breach of confidential information—whether governed by clause**
[Arbitration Act 1950 (c. 27), ss. 4, 24; Arbitration Act 1975 (c. 3), s. 1.] In 1974 the plaintiff disclosed information regarding machines for making air gun pellets, in return for royalties upon sales. It was agreed that confidentiality would continue after the agreement expired. Any dispute arising out of or in connection with the contract was to be referred to arbitration. A dispute occurred. The defendants continued to use the information but ceased to pay royalties. The plaintiff sought damages and an injunction to restrain use of the confidential information. The plaintiffs alleged that the claim for breach of confidence was not governed by the arbitration clause. *Held*, (1) the proceedings should be stayed; (2) the contract dealt with confidentiality after the expiry of the contract, and therefore the arbitration clause governed the issue; (3) where there is a non-domestic arbitration agreement the court has no discretion to set it aside even if fraud is alleged: PACZY *v.* HAENDLER & NATERMANN GmbH [1979] F.S.R. 420, Whitford J.

98. **Arbitrator—agreement providing for three arbitrators—only two appointed—whether jurisdiction to make award**
[Arbitration Act 1950 (c. 27), ss. 8 (1) (2), 9 (1).]
Where two arbitrators are in agreement they have jurisdiction to make an award without calling in an umpire; their failure to appoint an umpire where

one ought to have been appointed is at most a procedural mishap not affecting the award.

The owners of a vessel were in dispute with the charterers. The charterparty provided that a dispute should go to a board of three arbitrators, each side appointing one, and the two themselves appointing the third. The owners appointed their man and the charterers' representative (they had refused to make an appointment). The two arbitrators made an award without ever appointing an umpire. A judge gave leave to enforce the award and the charterers took out a summons seeking to set aside the order. *Held,* that s. 9 (1) of the Act applied as if the third arbitrator were an umpire, but as both arbitrators were in agreement, their failure to appoint an umpire was a procedural slip without any effect on the award. (*Re Arbitration between British Metal Corp. and Ludlow Brothers* [1938] 1 All E.R. 135 distinguished; *GKN Centrax Gears* v. *Matbro* [1976] C.L.Y 95 applied.)

TARMAREA S.R.L. *v.* REDERIAKTIEBOLAGET SALLY [1979] 2 All E.R. 989, Mocatta J.

99. —— **appointment—whether appointed within time limit.** See ETS SOULES & CIE *v.* INTERNATIONAL TRADE DEVELOPMENT CO., § 2379.

100. —— **special case—whether arbitrator should state special case**

Two disputes arising out of a contract between P, main contractors, and D, sub-contractors, were referred to arbitration. The first concerned the construction of a clause in the contract which prescribed the amount which D were to be paid, and the arbitrator stated his award in the form of a consultative case. The second concerned an allegation that P had by their words or conduct repudiated the contract so as to justify D in ceasing work, but on this issue the arbitrator had declined to state a special case. P applied for an order pursuant to s. 21 (1) of the Arbitration Act 1950 that the arbitrator should state his award in the form of a special case. *Held,* that (1) it could not be said that because the court always had a power to order a special case on the question of frustration, a dispute as to repudiation also always fell within s. 21 (1), since repudiation embraced several disparate grounds for the discharge of the contract which bore little resemblance to discharge by commercial frustration; (2) here, since the essential issue of whether P's conduct went to the root of the contract so closely resembled the issue raised by a dispute as to commercial frustration that it would be artificial to draw a distinction between the two for the purposes of s. 21 (1); and since there was room for doubt how far a party could push an honest if mistaken view of his contractual rights and duties before he found himself in repudiation, this was the kind of legal issue appropriate for a decision of the High Court (*Federal Commerce and Navigation Co.* v. *Molena Alpha Inc.* [1979] C.L.Y. 2452 considered); (3) accordingly the arbitrator would be ordered to state a case: PETER LIND & CO. *v.* CONSTABLE HART & CO. [1979] 2 Lloyd's Rep. 248, Mustill J.

101. —— **validity of appointment**

P, disponent owners, chartered the L and the S to D. Laytime disputes arose under both charters, and on September 9, 1975, P's agents wrote to the arbitrator, A, stating " we are pleased to confirm your appointment as owners' arbitrator in respect of laytime disputes arising under [charters]." On September 10, 1975, P's agents wrote to D's agents stating " please notify charterers that owners have already appointed their arbitrator," and inviting them to appoint their own. In February 1977, D received a letter from solicitors, who stated that they were acting on behalf of the registered owners of the L. D replied alleging that A had been appointed on behalf of the registered owners of the L and the S, who were not parties to the charter; and that the appointment should have been made on behalf of P, who were now out of time as 12 months had passed since final discharge. *Held,* dismissing D's appeal, that (1) where there was a charterparty made by disponent owner on their own behalf and not as agents for the registered owners, the meaning of the word " Owners " in any document relating to the charterparty depended on the context in which it was used; (2) when the word " Owner " was used in connection with the appointment of an arbitrator in disputes under a charterparty, the only sensible meaning to give the word was " those who in the capacity of owners are making a claim under the charterparty," in this instance, P: CARRAS SHIPPING CO. *v.* THE FOOD CORP. OF INDIA; THE DELIAN LETO AND THE DELIAN SPIRIT [1979] 2 Lloyd's Rep. 179, C.A.

102. Award—application to remit award—evidence available at time of hearing

C, time charterers, claimed to be entitled to redeliver the vessel at an earlier date because of the poor performance of the vessel, which amounted to repudiatory conduct by O, owners. The dispute was referred to arbitration, at which C's expert was present. No adjournment was asked for, and the award was duly published. C applied to have the award remitted on the grounds that (a) they had been taken by surprise by O's suggestion that the engine failure had been caused by a fatigue fracture and not by bad maintenance; (b) they had been taken by surprise by O's evidence as to the market rate for the vessel at the time of her unexpected redelivery; (c) the charterparty was ambiguous in not stating to whom the discount on hire was payable; and (d) C's expert had had further thoughts concerning the contaminated cargo, which C alleged was due to bad tank cleaning, and O alleged was due to C's choice of successive cargoes. *Held*, that (1) with regard to (a) the fact that C's expert had thought of further rebutting evidence which was available at the time of the hearing was not a ground for reopening the arbitration; (2) with regard to (b), the evidence was available to C at the time of the hearing, and if they were taken by surprise by O's case, they still had the six weeks between the hearing and the publication of the award in which to ask the arbitrators to receive further evidence; (3) with regard to (c), the ambiguity of the charterparty ought to have been argued at the hearing; (4) with regard to (d), the evidence could have been available to C at the hearing, and if the matter had been crucial, C had the six weeks in which to ask the arbitrators to admit further evidence. Application dismissed: WHITEHALL SHIPPING CO. *v.* KOMPASS SCHIFFAHRTSKONTOR GMBH; THE STAINLESS PATRIOT [1979] 1 Lloyd's Rep. 589, Donaldson J.

103. —— conditions imposed by arbitrators—whether in excess of jurisdiction

[Arbitration Act 1950 (c. 27).] Owners of a ship chartered it by three consecutive charterparties to charterers. There were cross-claims which went to arbitration. The arbitrator made an interim award in respect of the third charterparty to the charterer's of $81,000, on condition that the charterers gave security in that sum in respect of the owners' claim in the two other arbitrations. The judge held that this award was in excess of the arbitrators' jurisdiction. It was *held,* on appeal, that s. 14 of the Arbitration Act 1950 gave a discretion to arbitrators, and they had discretion to impose conditions. As this was an interim award it was only fair and just that there should be a set-off when the matters arose out of the same transactions. The appeal was allowed: JAPAN LINE *v.* AGGELIKI CHARIS COMPANIA MARITIMA S.A. (1979) 123 S.J. 487, C.A.

104. —— misconduct of arbitrators—rules of evidence

Disputes arose between V and P. Without prejudice correspondence took place, but the negotiations came to nothing and the dispute was referred to arbitration subject to, *inter alia,* the B.A.S.M. rules for the conduct of arbitrations, which provided, by r. 15, " the Arbitrators are at liberty to act upon evidence and/or information as they may think fit and to call for such documents in the possession of the parties to the dispute as they deem necessary." Arbitrators who were not lawyers were appointed, and P sent to the arbitrator appointed by them the without prejudice correspondence. The arbitrators found for P, and V applied for the award to be set aside on the ground of technical misconduct in that the arbitrators had regard to the without prejudice correspondence. *Held*, that (1) r. 15 was not so wide as to entitle arbitrators in the absence of consent to have regard to evidence of without prejudice negotiations; (2) it was highly undesirable as a matter of public policy that, save by consent, without prejudice correspondence should be put to arbitration, particularly where they were lay arbitrators and not lawyers; (3) the correspondence was given by P to their own arbitrator, and, if there was prejudice, it had resulted from P's own act and this was a proper case for the award to be set aside: FINNEY LOCK SEEDS *v.* GEORGE MITCHELL (CHESTERHALL) [1979] 2 Loyd's Rep. 301, Sir Douglas Frank, Q.C.

105. —— —— whether award should be remitted

Disputes arising between V and P were referred to arbitration; and the Board of Appeal of GAFTA awarded P $10,000 on the issue of damages. On the issue of carrying charges it was accepted that V were entitled to $31,000, and the Board awarded interest on part only of the claim. The Board further awarded, in substance, that on the question of costs V should pay the whole of the original arbitration costs and the whole of the appeal award. V sought the remission of the award on the ground that the Board was guilty of technical misconduct in failing to award interest on part of the award and in failing to award V the costs of the arbitration proceedings as opposed to the parties' costs. *Held,* that (1) since the award was unusual on its face, there was a rebuttable presumption that the arbitrators were wrong, and if P wished to hold the award, they had to indicate factors which the arbitration could have relied upon as justifying their award (*Iramountana Armadora S.A.* v. *Atlantic Shipping Co. S.A.* [1978] C.L.Y. 99 considered); (2) the court was not concerned with what in fact moved the arbitrators to reach their conclusion as to costs, but solely with whether there was material upon which they could have justified their order; here the Board could have justified its order and the court was not entitled to interfere with it (*Dincen* v. *Walpole* [1969] C.L.Y. 104 applied); (3) there was no justification for the Board denying V's interest on part of the carrying charges claim, and interest had to go on until the date of payment; and the award would be remitted to the Board to reconsider the question of interest: WARINCO A.G. *v.* ANDRE & CIE S.A. [1979] 2 Lloyd's Rep. 298, Donaldson J.

106. —— motion to set aside or remit—whether extension of time should be granted

O let their vessels to C under two charterparties, cl. 18 of which made provisions for the calculation of laytime; and cl. 19 of which provided, *inter alia,* " dispatch money to be paid by [O] at half the demurrage rate for all laytime saved at loading and for discharging ports." A dispute in respect of the calculation of dispatch money was referred to arbitration; and the awards, which were made on written submissions, were dated December 1, 1975. On the same day, the arbitrator sent notice that the awards were available for collection, which O's solicitors in London received on December 4, and C's solicitors in Haifa received on December 8. O's solicitors collected the awards on December 12 and on the same day the arbitrator sent the awards to C's solicitors, who received them on December 19. On January 23, C issued two notices of motion to set aside or remit the awards for alleged errors of law. O contended that the motions were out of time, since under R.S.C., Ord. 73, r. 5, such motion might be made at any time within six weeks after the award has been " made and published to the parties," and time was to be calculated from the date of receipt of notice of availability of the awards. C contended that time ran from the date of receipt of a copy of the award; and, alternatively, applied for an extension of time. *Held,* that (1) publication to the parties was completed on notice of availability (*Brooke* v. *Mitchell* (1840) 9 L.J. (N.S.) Ex. 269 applied); (2) since the delay was only four days, C's solicitors were abroad and the Christmas period had intervened, the court would exercise its discretion and extend the time; (3) it would be proper to extend the time to enable the motion to proceed, since the arbitrator had not begun with the prima facie presumption that time saved under the dispatch clause was to be calculated in the same way as demurrage, and then gone on to consider whether the wording of the clause rebutted that presumption (*Mawson Shipping Co. v. Beyer* [1914] 1 K.B. 304 applied); (4) it was clear that the parties were using the word " laytime " as being " laytime used for or required to be used for, in the sense of availability for, loading "; and cl. 19 specified that what was to be saved or regarded as saved were only the days or the aggregate of the days which under cl. 18 were to be regarded as laytime; and, although the arbitrator should have approached the matter slightly differently, had he done so his conclusion would have been no different, and his conclusion was entirely right. Motion dismissed. Summonses to extend time allowed: THE ARCHIPELAGOS AND DELFI [1979] 2 Lloyd's Rep. 289, Parker J.

107. —— nomination—delay in receiving papers—whether injustice

V contracted to sell beans to P under contracts which incorporated the terms of G.A.F.T.A. 30 and provided for arbitration in London under the rules of G.A.F.T.A. The contracts also provided: " the export licence is guaranteed by [V]." V were unable to obtain export licences for the contractual shipment period, and on September 2, 1977, P, who needed immediate delivery, declared V in default, nominated an arbitrator and called upon V to nominate theirs: V failed to do this, and on October 14 G.A.F.T.A. informed them that it had appointed the arbitrator. V's paper did not arrive in London until November 2, and their solicitors asked for a postponement of the hearing date, November 8. However, the award was considered on November 8, V being told that if they were dissatisfied with it they would have to go to the G.A.F.T.A. Board of Appeal. The agreed awards ordered V to pay P $105,750. On V's application to have the awards set aside, *held*, that (1) the necessity for speed in first-tier arbitrations could not justify departing from the principle that each party must know the nature of the case against him and be given a chance to deal with it; arbitrators ought not to make awards in default of defence unless sure that the defaulting party did not wish to present its case; (2) only where a party had had no opportunity to put forward a case or where such opportunity was not reasonably known to exist did the arbitrator have to satisfy himself that there was no wish to put forward a case or give further time for this to be done, and this was not the case here; (3) V could not complain that the arbitrators had not disclosed the evidence on market values before them to V as V could have tendered their own evidence on this; (4) the right to appeal to the G.A.F.T.A. Board of Appeal, though not decisive, could be taken into account when considering whether to exercise the discretion of relieving V of the consequences of their own wholly unjustified inactivity; (5) there was no injustice in refusing to allow V to go back to first-tier arbitration and leaving them to exercise their right of appeal. Application dismissed: THOS. P. GONZALEZ CORP. *v.* MULLER'S MUHLE, MULLER GMBH & CO. K.G. [1978] 2 Lloyd's Rep. 541, Donaldson J.

108. —— payment subject to condition—validity

[Arbitration Act 1950 (c. 27), ss. 21 (1) (*b*), 28.]

Arbitrators may impose conditions, such as payment, on the stating of a special case.

A dispute between owners and charterers went to arbitration on the issue of damages only. The arbitrators held that the bulk of the sum, $475,000, was payable to the owners whichever side prevailed. The charterers asked for the award to be stated in the form of a special case. The arbitrators agreed to do so on condition that the sum was paid into a joint account. On the charterers' summons, the judge upheld the arbitrators. On appeal by the charterers, *held*, dismissing the appeal, that the condition was properly imposed. (*Halfdan Grieg & Co. A/S* v. *Sterling Coal & Navigation Corpn.*; *The Lysland* [1973] C.L.Y. 105 distinguished.)

ANTCO SHIPPING *v.* SEABRIDGE SHIPPING [1979] 1 W.L.R. 1103, C.A.

109. —— remission

C sold cargoes of steel strip to L, an associated company of C, the sale contract providing that the price was to be calculated on a c.i.f. basis and for payment to be made 30 days after shipment. The cargoes were carried on O's vessel, the G, no bills of lading being issued. A dispute arose between C as time charterer and O concerning damage to the cargoes, one of the issues being whether C had a right to sue, or at least to be awarded substantial damages. The umpire found that because of the terms of payment and the non-existent bills of lading he could not decide whether property in the goods passed before, during or after delivery, but that in any event the loss fell on C's group of companies and that C who were acting as *pater familias* for their associated companies had the right to sue. On C's application to remit the award in order to call further evidence in the hope of proving that property was to pass on delivery to L, *held*, that the need to do justice based on full facts far outweighed the need to treat the facts found as sacrosanct, since neither party had gone out of its way to assist the umpire by giving him all relevant information in its possession or power, and the award would be remitted for the umpire to consider any evidence relevant to the right to sue which either party might wish to adduce: BJORN-JENSEN & CO. *v.* LYSAGHT (AUSTRALIA); THE GAMMA [1979] 1 Lloyd's Rep. 494, Donaldson J.

110. —— whether arbitrator misconducted himself

A contracted to construct for B an oil transhipment terminal designed by E, engineers. A redesigned a part of the terminal, and it was agreed that a " complete design " would be submitted to E, who would then approve or disapprove it within 14 days. It was further agreed that E could order A to change the character, quality and kind of work included in the contract, no such variation to be made without an order in writing of E. Disputes arose, and the arbitrator found in favour of B. On A's application by notice of motion contending that the award was bad in point of law and/or that the arbitrator had misconducted himself, *held,* dismissing the application, that (1) there was a patent contradiction between the drawings and calculations submitted for the amended design, and until E was provided with a reconciling explanation, there was no " complete design " submitted in accordance with the contract; (2) the fact that E's order to vary part of the structure, with which A had unambiguously complied, was oral did not bring it outside the contract; and in the absence of waiver, A had to comply with the contractual requirement as to giving notice of intention to claim extra payment; (3) that contractual requirement was to be construed as meaning that the notice was to be given as soon after the date of the order as practicable, and this A had failed to do: HERSENT OFFSHORE S.A. AND AMSTERDAMSE BALLAST BETON- EN WATERBOUW B.V. *v.* BURMAH OIL TANKERS [1978] 2 Lloyd's Rep. 565, Thompson J.

111. Awards

ARBITRATION (FOREIGN AWARDS) ORDER 1979 (No. 304) [20p], made under the Arbitration Act 1950 (c. 27), s. 35 (1), and the Arbitration Act 1975 (c. 3), s. 7 (2); operative on April 12, 1979; specifies Grenada as a state which is party to the 1927 Geneva Convention on the Execution of Foreign Arbitral Awards. Also specifies states which are parties to the 1958 New York Convention on the Recognition and Enforcement of Foreign Arbitral Awards.

112. Central Arbitration Committee—reference by Secretary of State—alleged noncompliance with fair wages resolution

[Arbitration Act 1950 (c. 27), ss. 21 (1) (*b*), 32.]

Where the parties to a reference are not parties to the contract there is no submission of a dispute to arbitration within the meaning of s. 32 of the Arbitration Act 1950.

A company entered into a contract with the Ministry of Defence and its terms incorporated the Fair Wages Resolution of the House of Commons. The union complained that the terms of the Resolution were not being complied with and the complaint was referred to the Central Arbitration Committee. The company requested the Committee to state their case in the form of a special case. They refused. The company applied to the court for such an order. The court refused. On appeal, *held,* that the reference had been made by the union which was not a party to the contract and so there was not a submission of a dispute by the parties under an arbitration agreement. A reference to the Central Arbitration Committee by the Secretary of State under the terms of the Fair Wages Resolution was not a reference to private arbitration. (*R.* v. *Industrial Court, ex p. A.S.S.E.T.* [1964] C.L.Y. 1290 disapproved.)

IMPERIAL METAL INDUSTRIES (KYNOCH) *v.* AMALGAMATED UNION OF ENGINEERING WORKERS (TECHNICAL ADMINISTRATIVE AND SUPERVISORY SECTION) [1979] I.C.R. 23, C.A.

113. Commodity contracts

ARBITRATION (COMMODITY CONTRACTS) ORDER 1979 (No. 754) [20p], made under the Arbitration Act 1979 (c. 42), s. 4 (2); operative on August 1, 1979; specifies commodity markets or exchanges in England and Wales and descriptions of contracts for the purpose of s. 4 of the 1979 Act which defines

" commodity contract " for the purposes of agreements excluding the right of appeal under s. 1 of the Act or determinations of questions of law under s. 2.

114. Costs—whether arbitrator guilty of technical misconduct

O's vessel, the A, arrived at Valparaiso, where there were two berthings, on each of which the A suffered damage by ranging due to bad weather. O claimed damages on the basis that the charterers, C, were in breach of the requirement in the charterparty that C provide a safe berth in a safe port. The umpire found that the port was unsafe; that at the first berthing the master was not at fault and O entitled to recover; and that at the second berthing the master was at fault and O were not entitled to recover. The items of damage pleaded were not attributed to the respective berthings, and the umpire, who was only asked to determine liability, ultimately decided that each party should bear its own costs, and that each should pay half of the costs of the award. On an application to set aside the award as to costs on the ground of technical misconduct, *held,* that (1) the umpire's award was made on the basis that partial success resulted automatically in apportionment of costs, but that he did not have the material before him to make such an award; (2) although the umpire had approached costs in a sensible way, he had not done so in accordance with the principles laid down clearly by the courts, that costs follow the event; and the matter would be remitted to the umpire for further consideration: BLUE HORIZON SHIPPING CO. S.A. *v.* E. D. & F. MAN; THE AGHIOS NICOLAOS [1979] 1 Lloyd's Rep. 475, Parker J.

115. International disputes

ARBITRATION (INTERNATIONAL INVESTMENT DISPUTES) (JERSEY) ORDER 1979 (No. 572) [10p], made under the Arbitration (International Investment Disputes) Act 1966 (c. 41), s. 6; operative on July 1, 1979; extends to Jersey the provisions of the 1966 Act.

116. Notice to arbitrate—telex message—when notice served

Under English law, notice to arbitrate sent abroad by telex is served when the telex message arrives at the office of the recipient, even if the office is for some reason closed at the time of receipt: N.V. STOOMV MAATS " DE MAAS " *v.* NIPPON YUSEN KAISHA, *The Times,* December 8, 1979, Parker J.

117. Practice—extension of time—amount of award

[Arbitration Act 1950 (c. 27), s. 27.] S. 27 of the Arbitration Act 1950, which gives the court power to extend time for commencing arbitration proceedings, is not confined to claims in respect of causes of action; it extends to an arbitration to fix the amount of a salvage award under Lloyd's standard salvage agreement, cl. 6: SIOUX INC. *v.* CHINA SALVAGE CO., KWANGCHOW BRANCH, *The Times,* December 13, 1979, C.A.

118. —— limitation of time—appointment of arbitrator

In November, 1977, C's application for an extension of time under s. 27 of the Arbitration Act 1950 for the appointment of an arbitrator under a charterparty was dismissed, the issues in dispute relating to events that happened in July 1975 at a port on the St. Lawrence River. C appealed on the grounds that the amount of the claim was very large; that the substantial delay beyond the contractual time in the appointing of an arbitrator was, in the circumstances of the case, excusable; that the fault, in so much as there was fault, was excused by a substantial number of factors; and that the delay had caused no real prejudice to the other party. *Held,* that whether or not the court would have exercised its discretion in the same way at first instance, it was not satisfied that the way in which the judge had exercised his discretion or the material before him was wrong. Appeal dismissed: CAST SHIPPING *v.* TRADAX EXPORT S.A.; THE HELLAS IN ETERNITY [1979] 2 Lloyd's Rep. 280, C.A.

119. —— —— exercise of discretion

By a contract of affreightment with D, P agreed to provide vessels to carry cargoes of grain. The contract gave P freedom to nominate vessels, and further contained an arbitration clause which provided a nine-month time limit from final discharge. One of the vessels nominated by P and accepted by D was time chartered from C, but there was no similar arbitration clause in the charter between P and C. The vessel was ordered by D to Houston, where, while loading, she grounded in the mud. However, she was refloated and loading completed, and on April 21, 1976, she delivered her cargo. No arbitration proceedings had been started by the end of the nine-month time limit on January 21, 1977. However, in March 1978, C amended their complaint in the U.S. in respect of claims against P to include a claim for damages for unsafe berth damage to the vessel. In July P communicated with D to amend the claim made against them and asked for an indemnity should they be found liable to C. D contended that P were time barred, and P applied for an extension of time under s. 27 of the Arbitration Act, 1950. *Held,* dismissing P's appeal, that the judge was justified in refusing the application on the grounds that C's case against P was apparently without foundation; that P had failed to get a matching arbitration clause from C; and that there was an unexplained delay by P between March and July, and no undue hardship would be caused to P if the application was refused; and there were no grounds on which the Court would be justified in interfering with the judge's decision: SANKO STEAMSHIP CO. *v.* TRADAX EXPORT S.A. [1979] 2 Lloyd's Rep. 273, C.A.

120. **Submission—contract for shipment of goods—whether arbitration clause included in contract**

P requested from D an estimate for the shipment of her goods to New Zealand. D sent a written estimate on a standard form and subject to their standard conditions of business. The goods were destroyed by fire while in D's possession, and P brought an action against D for the value of the goods. D applied for a stay under the Arbitration Act 1975, s. 1 (1), on the ground that there had been a valid submission by reason of the arbitration clause contained in the standard form. P contended that any contract never included the pointed condition and therefore never included the arbitration clause. *Held,* on appeal, that (1) only the court, and not the arbitrator, could decide whether or not there had been a submission to arbitration; (2) s. 1 (1) only applied where there was an agreement in writing to submit to arbitration and on the evidence it was an open question whether or not there was such an agreement; (3) as long as there was a dispute as to whether or not there was an arbitration agreement, it could not be said that there was an agreement, and accordingly s. 1 (1) was not complied with; (4) even if there was an arbitration agreement, it was highly likely to be a domestic arbitration agreement and s. 1 (1) would not apply in any event: WILLCOCK *v.* PICKFORDS REMOVALS [1979] 1 Lloyd's Rep. 244, C.A.

121. **Want of prosecution—inordinate delay—power of arbitrator**

When parties submit their differences to arbitration they are under an obligation to pursue that method of proceeding. The claimants must proceed with reasonable dispatch so that the respondents are not prejudiced by delay. If the claimants are guilty of inordinate delay, then the respondents may accept that conduct as repudiating the arbitration agreement, and may apply to the court for an injunction to restrain the claimants from proceeding with the arbitration. (Decision of Donaldson J. affirmed): BREMER VULCAN SCHIFFBAU UND MASCHINENFABRIK *v.* SOUTH INDIA SHIPPING CORP.; GREGG *v.* RAYTHEON, *The Times,* November 28, 1979, C.A.

BOOKS AND ARTICLES. See *post,* pp. [1], [13].

ARMED FORCES

122. **Air Force**

ROYAL AIR FORCE TERMS OF SERVICE (AMENDMENT) REGULATIONS 1979 (No. 215) [10p], made under the Armed Forces Act 1966 (c. 45), s. 2 and the Armed Forces Act 1976 (c. 52), s. 2; operative on April 5, 1979; amend S.I. 1977 No. 1097 by revoking reg. 9 (2) (3) thereof. The effect is to remove the requirement that a person shall have completed four years' service before giving notice under reg. 9 (1) to extend his term of service to one exceeding 15 years.

123. Army

IMPRISONMENT AND DETENTION (ARMY) RULES 1979 (No. 1456) [£2], made under the Army Act 1955 (c. 18), ss. 119, 122–124, 126, 127 and 129, The Courts-Martial (Appeals) Act 1968 (c. 20), s. 52, and the Armed Forces Act 1976 (c. 52), Sched. 3, para. 12, operative on January 1, 1980; provide, *inter alia*, for the control of military establishments, for their inspection, for their classification and for the remission of sentences. The Rules also provide for military corrective training, its aims and stages, including parole, and for the treatment, employment and control of soldiers under sentence.

124. Continuation of Acts

ARMY, AIR FORCE AND NAVAL DISCIPLINE ACTS (CONTINUATION) ORDER 1979 (No. 906) [10p], made under the Armed Forces Act 1976 (c. 52), s. 1 (2); continues in force for a further 12 months the Army Act 1955, the Air Force Act 1955 and the Naval Discipline Act 1957.

125. Exemption from estate duty—wound inflicted on active service—whether cause of death. See BARTY-KING *v.* MINISTRY OF DEFENCE, § 743.

126. National insurance. See NATIONAL INSURANCE.

127. Navy

ROYAL NAVY TERMS OF SERVICE (AMENDMENT) REGULATIONS 1979 (No. 192) [10p], made under the Armed Forces Act 1966 (c. 45), s. 2; operative on May 1, 1979; further amend S.I. 1967 No. 1821 by extending the maximum period by which a person entered into naval service may extend his service from five years to 10 years.

128. Offences—power to condone

[Army Act 1955 (c. 18), s. 134.] Under s. 134 of the Army Act 1955 the commanding officer of a soldier can condone an offence if, and only if, " he has knowledge of all the relevant circumstances." The power is unusual because it dispenses with the ordinary law of the land. The court *held*, that it could seldom be used under peacetime conditions and was not meant to be used out of a desire to keep a good soldier in the services or to protect the good name of a regiment. A major who purported to condone an alleged offence was not the defendant's commanding officer and so the defendant's plea in bar to his trial failed: R. *v.* BISSET (1979) 123 S.J. 718, Court Martial Appeal Ct.

ARREST

129. Obstruction—power of police. See WERSHOF *v.* METROPOLITAN POLICE COMMISSIONER, § 2093.

130. Validity—breach of peace—reasonable suspicion that defendant may commit breach

P was charged with assault occasioning actual bodily harm to a police officer in resisting arrest. The police officer had wrongly thought P to be subject to a court order excluding him from the house where his estranged wife and daughter lived. P refused to leave the house and was allegedly in a violent temper as a result of which the police arrested him for " conduct likely to cause a breach of the peace." *Held*, upholding a submission of no case to answer, that the common law power to arrest was confined to cases in which the breach of the peace was committed in the presence of the arrestor, or where one had been committed and its renewal was now threatened. (R. *v.* *Lockley* (1864) 4 F. & F. 155 and R. *v.* *Light* (1857) 27 L.J.M.C. 1, *inter alia*, considered; *Piddington* v. *Bates* [1960] C.L.Y. 752 distinguished): R. *v.* PODGER [1979] Crim.L.R. 524, Bristol Crown Ct.

131. —— breath test—failure to state suspicion of excess alcohol. See SIDDIQUI *v.* SWAIN, § 2318.

132. —— —— requirement by one officer—arrest by another. See KNIGHT *v.* TAYLOR, § 2324.

133. —— non-criminal matter—warrant not in actual possession of constable

[Magistrates' Courts Act 1952 (c. 55), s. 102 (4).]

S. 102 (4) of the Magistrates' Courts Act 1952 does not apply in a non-criminal case, and a constable not in actual possession of the warrant in such a case cannot make a lawful arrest.

A constable purported to arrest D for non-payment of fines, which was a civil matter. The warrant at the time was half a mile away at the police station. D resisted arrest and was convicted of assaulting a constable in the execution of his duty. On appeal by D, *held*, allowing the appeal, that in a civil matter the constable had to be in actual possession of the warrant, so that the person assessed could obtain his release by paying the sum stated on the warrant. The conviction for assault would therefore be quashed. (*R. v. Purdy* [1974] C.L.Y. 2860 applied.)

DE COSTA SMALL *v.* KIRKPATRICK (1978) 68 Cr.App.R. 186, D.C.

AUCTIONEERS AND VALUERS

134. Auction—vanishing purchaser—negligence—failure to secure name and address of purchaser

The defendants, a well-known firm of auctioneers, offered the plaintiff's house for sale at an auction in a London hotel. The house was knocked down to a third party at £9,800. The auctioneers attempted to procure his name and address but he vanished. The house was later resold for £9,000. The plaintiff claimed the difference of £800 with consequential damages by reason of the alleged negligence of the defendants. *Held*, dismissing the claim, the defendants were not negligent in failing to secure the name and address of the purchaser. The evidence showed that a purchaser had never vanished before in the defendants' auctions and that grave difficulties would have ensued from a resale at that time. Furthermore the auctioneer had no power to coerce the purchaser. The remedy lay against the purchaser. General remarks about auctioneers and consequential damage: HARDIAL SINGH *v.* HILLYER AND HILLYER (1979) 251 E.G. 951, Forbes J.

AVIATION

135. Air navigation

AIR NAVIGATION (RESTRICTION OF FLYING) (GREENHAM COMMON) REGULA-TIONS 1979 (No. 547) [10p], made under S.I. 1976 No. 1783, art. 64; operative on June 20, 1979; prohibits flying on June 20, 1979, in the area of Greenham Common.

AIR NAVIGATION (RESTRICTION OF FLYING) (EXHIBITION OF FLYING) REGU-LATIONS 1979 (No. 611) [10p], made under S.I. 1976 No. 1783, art. 64; operative on July 26, 1979; prohibits flying in specified areas on specified dates.

AIR NAVIGATION (ISLE OF MAN) ORDER 1979 (No. 929) [40p], made under the Civil Aviation Act 1949 (c. 67), ss. 8, 41, 57, 58; operative on September 1, 1979; revokes S.I. 1972 No. 454 and provides that S.I. 1976 No. 1783, as amended, shall apply to the Isle of Man.

AIR NAVIGATION (NOISE CERTIFICATION) ORDER 1979 (No. 930) [70p], made under the Civil Aviation Act 1949, ss. 8, 57, 58, 59, 61 and the Civil Aviation Act 1968 (c. 61), s. 19 (2); operative on August 1, 1979; revokes and replaces with modifications S.I. 1970 No. 823.

AIR NAVIGATION (GENERAL) (ISLE OF MAN) REGULATIONS 1979 (No. 1184) [10p], made under S.I. 1976 No. 1783, arts. 9 (4), 11 (2) (5), 14, 27 (1) (*c*), 28 (4), 29 (1), 35A, 79 and S.I. 1979 No. 929; operative on October 12, 1979; provide that S.I. 1976 No. 1982 shall have effect in the Isle of Man.

CIVIL AVIATION (NAVIGATION SERVICES CHARGES) (THIRD AMENDMENT) REGULATIONS 1979 (No. 1274) [10p], made under the Civil Aviation (Euro-control) Act 1962 (c. 8), ss. 4, 7 and the Civil Aviation Act 1968, s. 15; operative on November 1, 1979; amend S.I. 1977 No. 1437 by increasing certain specified fees.

136. Airport authority—ban on minicab drivers—validity of banning notices

[Airports Authority Act 1975 (c. 78), ss. 1 (1), 2 (1) (3), 9 (1); Heathrow Airport–London By-laws 1972, by-law 5 (55) (59).]

The airports authority has both a common law and a statutory power to exclude members of the public from its property.

P were minicab drivers who had a large number of convictions for
touting at Heathrow airport. The airports authority without warning notified
them that thenceforth they were prohibited from entering Heathrow except
as bona fide airline passengers. P claimed a declaration that the authority
had no power to ban them, that the banning notices were invalid and had
been made in breach of the rules of natural justice. *Held,* dismissing the claim,
that (1) the airports authority had a common law power to exclude members
of the public from its property, though it must exercise such power reasonably
(dictum of Diplock L.J. in *Mixnam's Properties* v. *Chertsey Urban District
Council* [1964] C.L.Y. 3556 applied); (2) such a power also existed by virtue
of the statutory duty to provide services and facilities for passengers; (3)
banning entry to the airport was within the ambit of regulating the conduct
of persons within the aerodrome; and (4) since P's only expectation was to
flout the by-laws natural justice did not apply. (*Schmidt* v. *Secretary of State
for Home Affairs* [1969] C.L.Y. 81 considered.)
  CINNAMOND v. BRITISH AIRPORTS AUTHORITY [1979] R.T.R. 331, Forbes J.

137. Carriage by air
  CARRIAGE BY AIR (STERLING EQUIVALENTS) ORDER 1979 (No. 765) [10p],
made under the Carriage by Air Act 1961 (c. 27), s. 4 (4); operative on August
1, 1979; specifies the sterling equivalents of amounts, expressed in gold
francs, as the limit of the air carrier's liability under the Warsaw Convention
of 1929 as amended by the Hague Protocol of 1955.
  CARRIAGE BY AIR ACTS (APPLICATION OF PROVISIONS) (SECOND AMENDMENT)
Order 1979 (No. 931) [20p], made under the Carriage by Air Act 1961, s. 10
as applied by the Carriage by Air (Supplementary Provisions) Act 1962 (c. 43),
s. 5 (2); operative on August 1, 1979; amends S.I. 1967 No. 480 by substituting
special drawing rights for gold francs as the unit in which the limits of the
air carrier's liability are expressed for the purposes of non-international
carriage.

138. —— exclusions of liability for death and loss of baggage
  [Can.] P claimed damages from D resulting from the death of her husband
and the loss of his baggage in the crash of an aircraft owned and operated
by D in Tokyo on March 4, 1966. D admitted liability, but claimed to be
able to limit their liability under arts. 3 and 4 of the Warsaw Convention 1924.
Held, on appeal, that (1) the words of art. 3 (2) were plain and unambiguous,
in that the absence, irregularity or loss of a ticket would not affect the existence
or validity of a contract of carriage, and only where no ticket was delivered
would the benefit of limitation be lost; here, D delivered a ticket, thus
preserving their right to limit; (2) the type and arrangement of the print on the
ticket was legible by the ordinary person using ordinary diligence, and the
content met the requirements of the Convention; and D were entitled to
limit in respect of the loss of baggage as well as of the loss of life (*Canadian
Pacific Airlines* v. *Montreal Trust Co. and Stampleman* [1977] C.L.Y. 2033
distinguished): LUDECKE v. CANADIAN PACIFIC AIRLINES [1979] 2 Lloyd's
Rep. 260, Can.Sup.Ct.

139. —— limitation of liability—Warsaw Convention
  P owned two boxes of platinum which had been flown from South Africa to
Heathrow by D1 and were to be flown to Philadelphia by D2. On September 8,
1970, the boxes, which had been stored in D2's warehouse were conveyed to
D2's aircraft, where they were put into the care of D2's loaders. At Philadelphia
one of the boxes was found to be missing, it being accepted that it had been
stolen after it had been loaded but before the aircraft took off. P claimed
$102,000, the value of the platinum. D2 authorised D1 to settle the claim, and
advised that the limit of liability under art. 22 of the Warsaw Convention was
$369.23. D1 sent a cheque for that sum to P who receipted the cheque and
banked it. Thereafter P returned the cheque, stating that it was not acceptable
and claiming the full sum. P denied that by receipting the cheque there was an
agreement to discharge D2 from liability, and further relied on art. 25 of the
Convention, which provided, *inter alia,* that the carrier shall not be entitled to
avail himself of the provisions of the Convention which limit this liability if
the damage is caused by the wilful misconduct of any servant or agent of the

carrier acting within the scope of his employment. *Held*, that (1) mere payment of a sum which was received was not in itself an accord and satisfaction in the absence of sufficient material in the document to show that it was paid and accepted in full and final settlement, and such was not the case here; (2) the act of the loader entrusted with carefully loading the box stealing or combining to steal it was wilful misconduct within the scope of his employment. Judgment for P: RUSTENBURG PLATINUM MINES, JOHNSON MATTHEY (PTY.) AND MATTHEY BISHOP INC. *v.* SOUTH AFRICAN AIRWAYS AND PAN AMERICAN WORLD AIRWAYS INC. [1979] 1 Lloyd's Rep. 19, C.A.

140. —— **loss of contents of baggage—whether " damage "**
[Carriage by Air Act 1961 (c. 27), Sched. 1, art. 26 (2); Carriage by Air and Road Act 1979 (c. 28), s. 2 (1), (2).]
In actions prior to the Carriage by Air and Road Act 1979, " damage " which must be complained of within seven days of receipt of baggage under art. 26 (2) of Sched. 1 to the Carriage by Air Act 1961, is confined to physical injury to the baggage, and does not include loss of contents.
In 1975 P returned from holiday in Italy in D Co.'s aircraft. On arrival he found that his luggage was badly torn, and reported the matter to the airlines representative forthwith. When he got home, he found that some of the contents were missing. He notified his insurers who did not claim from D Co. for four weeks. D Co. accepted liability for the damage to the baggage, but repudiated liability for the loss of contents, on the ground that it was damage which had not been notified within seven days under art. 26 (2) of Sched. 1 to the Carriage by Air Act 1961. The judge at first instance gave P a declaration that no complaint was required in respect of partial loss of contents. On appeal by D Co., *held*, dismissing the appeal, that " damage " did not include partial loss. The *travaux préparatoires* to art. 26 (2) of the Warsaw Convention could not be used as an aid to construction, and since the loss had occurred in 1975, s. 2 (1) of the Carriage by Air and Road Act 1979 which provides that " damage " in art. 26 (2) shall include partial loss of baggage, did not apply. (Dicta of Lord Reid and Lord Simon of Glaisdale in *Black-Clawson International* v. *Papierwerke Waldhof-Aschaffenburg Aktiengesellschaft A.G.* [1975] C.L.Y. 361, of Lord Wilberforce, Viscount Dilhorne and Lord Salmon in *James Buchanan & Co.* v. *Babco Forwarding and Shipping (U.K.)* [1976] C.L.Y. 231 and of Judge Shapiro in *Schwimmer* v. *Air France* (1976) 14 Avi. 17, 466 applied.)
FOTHERGILL *v.* MONARCH AIRLINES [1979] 3 W.L.R. 491, C.A.

141. **Civil aviation**
CIVIL AVIATION (AIR TRAVEL ORGANISERS' LICENSING) (THIRD AMENDMENT) REGULATIONS 1979 (No. 5) [10p], made under the Civil Aviation Act 1971 (c. 75), s. 26, and the Tribunals and Inquiries Act 1971 (c. 62), s. 10 operative on April 1, 1979; further amends S.I. 1972 No. 223 and provides that an application for a new licence by an existing licence-holder will no longer keep the original licence in force unless accompanied by the appropriate fee and the requisite particulars.
CIVIL AVIATION (ROUTE CHARGES FOR NAVIGATION SERVICES) (SECOND AMENDMENT) REGULATIONS 1979 (No. 154) [20p], made under the Civil Aviation (Eurocontrol) Act 1962 (c. 8), ss. 4 and 7 (1), the Civil Aviation Act 1968 (c. 61), s. 15 (3); and the Civil Aviation Act 1971, Sched. 10, para. 6; operative on April 1, 1979; give effect to a new tariff in relation to flights which enter the airspace defined in reg. 6 where the U.K. provides air navigation services. The new tariff reflects the 1977 costs of providing the service and a higher rate of cost recovery and has been agreed internationally under the Eurocontrol Convention and the Multilateral Agreement relating to the collection of route charges.
CIVIL AVIATION (CANADIAN NAVIGATION SERVICES) (SECOND AMENDMENT) REGULATIONS 1979 (No. 237) [10p], made under the Civil Aviation (Eurocontrol) Act 1962, ss. 4, 7, and the Civil Aviation Act 1968, s. 15; s. 15, and by the Civil Aviation Act 1971, Sched. 10, paras. 6 and 7; operative on April 1, 1979; amend S.I. 1977 No. 314.
CIVIL AVIATION (NAVIGATION SERVICES CHARGES) (SECOND AMENDMENT)

REGULATIONS 1979 (No. 267) [10p], made under the Civil Aviation (Euro-control) Act 1962, ss. 4, 7, and the Civil Aviation Act 1968, s. 15; operative on April 1, 1979; further amend S.I. 1977 No. 1437 in relation to specified charges.

HEATHROW AIRPORT—LONDON NOISE INSULATION GRANTS (SCHOOLS) (AMENDMENT) SCHEME 1979 (No. 414) [10p], made under the Civil Aviation Act 1971, s. 29; operative on May 1, 1979; varies S.I. 1977 No. 1319 by increasing the total maximum grant payable from £220,000 to £230,000.

CIVIL AVIATION AUTHORITY (FIFTH AMENDMENT) REGULATIONS 1979 (No. 514) [25p], made under the Civil Aviation Act 1971, ss. 5 (2), 24 (3) (6) and the Tribunals and Inquiries Act 1971 (c. 62), s. 10; operative on May 30, 1979; further amends S.I. 1972 No. 178 in relation to the grant, revocation, suspension or variation of an air transport licence.

AIR NAVIGATION (FIFTH AMENDMENT) ORDER 1979 (No. 1318) [20p], made under the Civil Aviation Act 1949 (c. 67), ss. 8 and 57 operative on November 19, 1979, except for arts. 2 (6) (a) (ii) and (iii) and (b), which come into operation on January 1, 1981; amends S.I. 1976 No. 1783.

RULES OF THE AIR AND AIR TRAFFIC CONTROL (FIFTH AMENDMENT) REGULATIONS 1979 (No. 1417) [10p], made under S.I. 1976 No. 1783, art. 60 (1); operative on December 1, 1979; amend S.I. 1976 No. 1983 by applying Special Rules in certain specified circumstances.

CIVIL AVIATION (JOINT FINANCING) (SECOND AMENDMENT) REGULATIONS 1979 (No. 1599) [10p], made under the Civil Aviation (Eurocontrol) Act 1962, ss. 4, 7; operative on January 1, 1980; amend S.I. 1978 No. 554 as amended by altering the charge payable by operators of aircraft to the Civil Aviation Authority in respect of crossings between Europe and North America.

142. Northern Ireland. See NORTHERN IRELAND.

ARTICLES. See *post*, p. [13].

BAILMENTS

143. Bailee—negligence—duty—vehicle immobilised—theft

A bailee of a motor car is not negligent in leaving it suitably immobilised on a public highway or on premises open to public access.

The defendants, garage proprietors, repaired cars but had limited lock-up accommodation for the vehicles. The plaintiffs, with knowledge of this, brought a car to be repaired which involved the removal of the cylinder head. Thereafter, the car could not be driven away under its own power and was left locked on the forecourt. The car was stolen and had components removed. The trial judge found that the car was probably towed away and that, although it was not foreseeable that the car would be towed away, it was foreseeable that the components could be removed while the car was on the forecourt and, therefore, the defendants had failed in their duty as bailees. *Held*, allowing the appeal, that (1) there was no absolute duty on bailees of motor cars to keep them in lock-up accommodation; (2) it was not negligent to leave suitably immobilised cars on public highways or premises with public access; (3) it was wrong to condemn the defendant as negligent where the practical difficulties of the defendant which were known to the plaintiff outweighed the likelihood of the components being stolen.

IDNANI v. ELISHA (TRADING AS GRAFTON SERVICE STATION) [1979] R.T.R. 488, C.A.

144. Warehouseman—lien—whether general lien effective against non-contracting goods-owners

D, warehousemen, did business with A, freight forwarders, on the terms of the General Conditions of Contract of the National Association of Warehouse-keepers, which provided, *inter alia*, by cl. 8, " the warehouse keeper shall have a lien on all goods for all money due to him for storage or carriage of and other charges or expenses in connection with such goods and shall also have a general lien on all goods for any money due to him from the customer or the owners of such goods upon any account whatsoever. . . ." P sent goods to A for shipment to West Africa, and A sent them to D to be containerised. Before paying D's charges, A went into liquidation, and D accordingly claimed a general lien in respect of P's goods. P paid £1494·61 into court to obtain their release and brought an action to recover this sum, claiming that the lien was invalid. *Held*, allowing P's appeal, that (1) cl. 8 on its true construction gave D the right to refuse to deliver up to P possession of their goods until D had been paid the whole debt owing to them by A (not merely by P); the word " or " in the phrase " the customer or the owners " in cl. 8 must be read conjunctively; (2) however, here, on the evidence, P did not know that A did not containerise the goods themselves, but had this work carried out on their behalf by D; (3) P had no " contemplation and intention " that A would give out the work to D, and this was the minimum requisite if D were to hold P bound by the general lien as asserted; (4) no general lien was available to D which they were entitled to exercise to defeat P's claims. (*Cassils & Co. and Sassoon & Co.* v. *Holder Wood Bleaching Co.* (1915) 84 L.J.K.B. 834 applied): CHELLARAM & SONS (LONDON) v. BUTLERS WAREHOUSING & DISTRIBUTION [1978] 2 Lloyd's Rep. 412, C.A.

145. —— whether bound to warn of absence of fire insurance
[Can.] A warehouseman received goods for storage. *Held*, he was not obliged to inform the owner of the absence of insurance against loss by fire. Where the warehouseman exercises reasonable care in storing the goods, he is not liable for their destruction by an act of arson that could not reasonably have been prevented: MASON v. MORROW'S MOVING & STORAGE (1978) 87 D.L.R. (3d) 234, Bt.Col.C.A.

BOOKS AND ARTICLES. See *post*, pp. [1], [13].

BANKING

146. Asian Development Bank
ASIAN DEVELOPMENT BANK (SECOND REPLENISHMENT OF THE ASIAN DEVELOPMENT FUND) ORDER 1979 (No. 1225) [10p], made under the Overseas Aid Act 1968 (c. 57), s. 2 (1); operative on October 10, 1979; provides for the payment to the Development Fund of a sum of £55,172,379 as a contribution by way of the second replenishment of the Fund and of a sum of £4,158,987 as a supplementary contribution.

147. Bank—duty to customer—nature of documents not understood
[Can.] Where a widow, shortly after her husband's death, is asked by a bank to sign documents that amount to her taking over her husband's debts to the bank, and she signs the documents appreciating neither the nature and effect of the documents nor her own legal position, the documents are not enforceable. In such a situation the bank has an obligation to ensure that its customer is fully appraised of the hazardous course she is taking, and ought to satisfy itself that she is independently advised. (*Lloyds Bank* v. *Bundy* [1974] C.L.Y. 1691 applied): ROYAL BANK OF CANADA v. HINDS (1978) 88 D.L.R. (3d) 428, Ont.H.C.J.

148. —— status—whether department of state. See HISPANO AMERICANA MERCANTIL S.A. v. CENTRAL BANK OF NIGERIA, § 318.

149. Banking Act 1979 (c. 37)
This Act regulates the acceptance of deposits in the course of a business, confers functions on the Bank of England with respect to the control of institutions carrying on deposit-taking businesses, makes provision with respect to advertisements inviting the making of deposits, prohibits fraudulent inducement to make a deposit and repeals certain enactments relating to banks and banking.

Pt. I (ss. 1–20) relates to the control of deposit-taking: s. 1 concerns control of deposit-taking and defines " deposit "; s. 2 makes certain exceptions from the prohibition in s. 1 (1); s. 3 relates to recognition as a bank and licences; s. 4 deals with the annual report and list of recognised and licensed institutions; s. 5 contains provisions with respect to the procedure on applications for recognition or a full licence; s. 6 sets out the grounds for revocation of recognition or licence; s. 7 outlines the powers and procedure of the Bank of

England with regard to revocation; s. 8 empowers the Bank of England to give directions in connection with termination of deposit-taking authority; s. 9 specifies the duration of directions and direction-making power; s. 10 deals with conditional licences; s. 11 allows for appeals from decisions of the Bank of England; s. 12 concerns regulations with respect to appeals; s. 13 contains provisions as to further appeals on points of law; s. 14 imposes a duty to notify changes of directors, etc.; s. 15 states that audited accounts of licensed institutions shall be open to inspection; s. 16 gives the Bank of England powers to obtain information and require production of documents; s. 17 allows for investigations on behalf of the Bank of England; s. 18 provides for winding up on a petition from the Bank of England; s. 19 concerns confidentiality of information obtained by the Bank; s. 20 relates to information disclosed to the Bank from other sources.

Pt. II (ss. 21–33) provides for a deposit protection scheme: s. 21 establishes the Deposit Protection Board; s. 22 sets up the Deposit Protection Fund; s. 23 specifies contributory institutions and makes general provisions as to contributions; s. 24 deals with initial contributions; s. 25 provides for further contributions; s. 26 relates to special contributions and power to borrow; s. 27 specifies the maximum and minimum contributions; s. 28 allows for payments to depositors when an institution becomes insolvent; s. 29 relates to protected deposits; s. 30 deals with trustee deposits and joint deposits; s. 31 states the liability of insolvent institutions in respect of payments made by the Deposit Protection Board; s. 32 allows for repayments in respect of contributions; s. 33 outlines the tax treatment of contributions and repayments.

Pt. III (ss. 34–37) concerns advertisements and banking names: s. 34 provides for control of advertisements for deposits; s. 35 contains specific prohibitions directed at licensed institutions; s. 36 restricts the use of certain names and descriptions; s. 37 provides for transitory exceptions from s. 36 (1).

Pt. IV (ss. 38–52) contains miscellaneous and general provisions: s. 38 makes miscellaneous amendments to the Consumer Credit Act 1974; s. 39 sets out the offence of fraudulent inducement to make a deposit; s. 40 concerns representative offices of overseas deposit-taking institutions; s. 41 contains general provisions relating to offences; s. 42 deals with offences committed by unincorporated institutions; s. 43 excludes certain provisions relating to the rehabilitation of offenders; s. 44 relates to evidence taken in proceedings under the Act; s. 45 provides for the service of notices; s. 46 repeals certain enactments relating to banks and banking; s. 47 concerns the defence of contributory negligence; s. 48 deals with municipal banks; s. 49 defines " director," " controller " and " manager "; s. 50 is the general interpretation section; s. 51 makes consequential amendments and repeals; s. 52 deals with the short title, commencement and extent. The Act extends to Northern Ireland.

The Act received the Royal Assent on April 4, 1979, and comes into force on a day to be appointed.

150. —— commencement
BANKING ACT 1979 (COMMENCEMENT NO. 1) ORDER 1979 (No. 938 (C. 26))
[10p], made under the Banking Act 1979 (c. 37), s. 52 (3); operative on October 1, 1979; brings into force Pts. I and III, ss. 38, 40–45, 47, 48 (1)–(6), 49, 50, 52 and Scheds. 1–4 of the Act.

151. —— exempt transactions
BANKING ACT 1979 (EXEMPT TRANSACTIONS) REGULATIONS 1979 (No. 1204)
[20p], made under the Banking Act 1979 (c. 37), s. 2 (1) (5); operative on October 1, 1979; prescribe certain transactions to which the prohibition on deposit-taking imposed by s. 1 of the 1979 Act does not apply.

152. Cheques. See BILLS OF EXCHANGE.

153. Exchange control—breach of conditions—priority of security
[Exchange Control Act 1947 (c. 14), ss. 16, 17 (2).]
Where there is a contractual obligation to a bank to service and repay a loan out of certain securities and those securities are later charged to another bank, the first bank has an equitable interest in those securities which takes priority over the second bank's equitable charge.

SBC made a loan to IFT to enable it to purchase securities in FIBA, an

Israeli company. IFT covenanted with SBC to observe the exchange control conditions imposed by the Bank of England. Triumph, the parent company of IFT, got into serious financial difficulties and was advanced large sums of money by Lloyds. The security for this loan included a charge granted by IFT over the investments in FIBA purchased with the loan from SBC. Triumph went into liquidation. SBC claimed a right to require its loan to be repaid out of the proceeds of sale of the investments in FIBA acquired with its loan (in accordance with the exchange control conditions imposed by the Bank of England) and priority over Lloyds' rights under the charge, and that the grant by IFT of a charge over the FIBA securities was in breach of the Exchange Control Act 1947. *Held,* that (1) SBC had the right to insist on the loan to IFT being repaid out of the proceeds of sale of FIBA securities and that right prevailed over Lloyds' charge. It was not necessary for SBC to have to establish that the parties to the loan had intended to create an equitable charge in the proceeds of sale (*Palmer* v. *Carey* [1926] A.C. 703 and *Barclays Bank* v. *Quistclose Investments* [1968] C.L.Y. 459 considered); (2) Lloyds' charge was void for infringing the 1947 Act, therefore an injunction would be granted against Lloyds. Had the charge been valid an injunction could not have been granted if Lloyds did not have actual notice of SBC's rights (*De Mattos* v. *Gibson* (1858) 4 De G. & J. 276, *Manchester Ship Canal Co.* v. *Manchester Racecourse Co.* [1901] 2 Ch. 37 and *Lord Strathcona Steamship Co.* v. *Dominion Coal Co.* [1926] A.C. 108 considered); (3) Lloyds were liable in damages for knowingly interfering with SBC's contractual right to have the proceeds of sale applied in repayment of the loan (*Smith* v. *Morrison*; *Smith* v. *Chief Land Registrar* [1974] C.L.Y. 2044 and *Pritchard* v. *Briggs* [1978] C.L.Y. 2497 distinguished).

SWISS BANK CORP. v. LLOYDS BANK [1979] 2 All E.R. 853, Browne-Wilkinson J.

154. Guarantee—construction of letter of lien

In December 1970, P deposited with the London branch of the D bank, a company incorporated in Pakistan, £25,000 on the terms of a letter of lien, which provided, *inter alia,* by cl. 1, " In consideration of your granting a loan to T we guarantee to you repayment of the said loan "; by cl. 2, " By way of security we are hereby giving to you a lien and/or right of set off against the balance in our account "; by cl. 4, " We confirm that your rights shall not be prejudiced by [T's] release from liability by operation of law or otherwise "; and by cl. 5, " Our liabilities hereunder shall be as that of principal debtors." D accordingly made loans to T, which in March 1972 was taken over by the Bangladesh Jute Board. In the same month, D's undertaking in Bangladesh, including their right to be repaid the loans made to T, was transferred to and vested in the Janata Bank. P claimed the return of the deposit since there was no sum due from T to D, the debts having been validly transferred from D to the Janata Bank. D contended that they had never in fact been repaid, and were entitled to retain the deposit until they had. *Held,* that (1) the word " repayment " in cl. 1 clearly meant " repayment to you," so that what was guaranteed was performance of T's obligation to repay D; (2) the words " release from liability " in cl. 4 meant " release from liability to repay you," so that D's rights under cl. 1 still existed in that T's release from liability to repay D was brought about " by operation of law or otherwise," which was expressly provided in cl. 4 should not prejudice D's rights; (3) when T's liability was released, P's liability as guarantor continued, by virtue of cl. 5, as that of principal debtor; (4) since the rights and obligation under cl. 1 were still continuing, and D's rights under cl. 2 were ancillary to cl. 1 in that the deposit was security for performance of D's obligations under cl. 1, D were entitled to maintain their lien or right of set off against the deposit account. Judgment for D: GENERAL PRODUCE CO. v. UNITED BANK [1979] 2 Lloyd's Rep. 255, Lloyd J.

155. Letter of credit—delay in payment—whether plaintiff could claim loss in sterling

In March 1977, P, an English export company carrying on business in the U.K., sold certain equipment to a Nigerian company for U.S. $125,939.22

c. & f. Apapa/Lagos, shipment on or before September 15, 1977. Payment was to be by irrevocable letter of credit, which the buyers arranged to be issued by D, a Nigerian bank with a branch in London. Under the U.K. exchange control regulations, P were authorised to have a U.S. $ hold account to which all U.S. $ received for exports had to be credited, and their excess sold to an authorised bank in exchange for sterling by the end of each month. The documents were presented through P's bank, and were in order when the letter of credit was due to expire. Payment ought to have been made by October 5, but was in fact made on December 12, despite efforts made on behalf of P urging D to meet their obligations, and with no explanation being given for the inexcusable default. P claimed £2,987·17, being the loss resulting from a change in the dollar-sterling rate between October 5 and December 12; interest on the sterling equivalent of $125,939.22 during the same period; and £190 paid for services in seeking to obtain payment. *Held*, that (1) since D knew or ought to have known the terms on which P held dollars, and that they were merchants and not dealers in foreign currency, they ought to have foreseen that P would sell the dollars either on receipt or at the end of the month; (2) P's claim was properly made on the basis of national sales on October 5 and December 5, even if they may have delayed selling until the end of the month; (3) it was foreseeable that P would incur reasonable expense in seeking to obtain payment in the event of default; (4) D's obligation was a foreign money obligation within the rule laid down in *Miliangos* v. *George Frank (Textiles)* [1975] C.L.Y. 2657; (5) it was for P to choose the currency in which to claim and to prove that a judgment in that currency would most truly express their loss and compensate them for that loss (*The Despina R* [1978] C.L.Y. 710 applied); (6) although the price was agreed to be paid in U.S. $, P's loss was incurred in sterling, and this was foreseeable by D; (7) any payment made in a currency other than sterling fell to be credited against any sterling loss at the rate of exchange ruling at the date of payment and P were entitled to the sums claimed: OZALID GROUP (EXPORT) v. AFRICAN CONTINENTAL BANK [1979] 2 Lloyd's Rep. 231, Donaldson J.

156. —— Mareva injunction—security for costs

P contracted to supply 240,000 tonnes of cement c.i.f. Lagos, payment to be by irrevocable, transferable and divisible letters of credit against documents, including, *inter alia*, bills of lading. After the bank, D had paid large sums of money in respect of 94,000 tonnes supposed to have been shipped on eight vessels, there arose strong evidence that the bills of lading were forged, and a doubt as to whether the eight vessels had ever existed, and D refused to pay any more money due in respect of demurrage. P claimed against D and obtained a *Mareva* injunction. D counterclaimed in respect of monies over-paid, and sought security for costs. *Held,* on appeal, that if forged documents were presented in respect of any one parcel of the whole 240,000 tonnes which were covered by the letter of credit, D had a defence against being liable for that parcel, and a counterclaim for money paid on false documents (*Edward Owen Engineering* v. *Barclays Bank International* [1977] C.L.Y. 162 considered); (2) the claim for demurrage was so closely connected with the cross-claim in respect of the forged documents that it might well be a case for an equitable set-off (*Federal Commerce & Navigation Co.* v. *Molera Alpha Inc.* [1978] C.L.Y. 2731 considered); (3) since P did not have a good arguable case, and since there was no danger of D's assets going outside the jurisdiction or of D dishonouring their obligation if found liable, it would not be right to grant a *Mareva* injunction; (4) P, being a Liechtenstein company which was in liquidation, should provide security for costs in the sum of £20,000: ETABLISSEMENT ESEFKA INTERNATIONAL ANSTALT v. CENTRAL BANK OF NIGERIA [1979] 1 Lloyd's Rep. 445, C.A.

157. Liability to customer—mistake of fact—bank acting without mandate

[Bills of Exchange Act 1882 (c. 61), s. 50 (2) (c).]

A bank, which overlooks its customer's instructions to stop payment of a cheque and in consequence pays the cheque on presentation, can, in certain circumstances, recover the money from the payee as having been paid under a mistake of fact.

A customer of Barclays Bank drew a cheque for £24,000 in favour of a building company. A receiver of the company was appointed the next day, and on hearing this the customer instructed Barclays to stop payment of the cheque. The receiver presented the cheque and through an oversight Barclays paid it. Barclays, their demand for return of the moneys having been refused, brought an action claiming repayment as money paid under a mistake of fact. *Held,* that if a person pays money to another under a mistake of fact he is prima facie entitled to recover it as money paid under a mistake of fact and Barclays were entitled to succeed in their claim (1) because their mistake in overlooking the stop instruction had caused them to pay the cheque; (2) they had acted without mandate since the drawer had countermanded payment and the payee had therefore given no consideration for the payment; and (3) there was no evidence of a change in the defendant's position and no notice of dishonour was required in the circumstances.

BARCLAYS BANK *v.* W. J. SIMMS SON AND COOKE (SOUTHERN) [1979] 3 All E.R. 522, Robert Goff J.

BOOKS AND ARTICLES. See *post,* pp. [1], [13].

BANKRUPTCY

158. Annual report—1978

The Department of Trade has published the Annual Report on Bankruptcy and Deeds of Arrangement which shows a continued decline in the numbers of personal and business failures resulting in bankruptcy and execution of deeds of arrangement in 1978. The report is available from HMSO [£1·50].

159. Conditional discharge—review of order in light of Insolvency Act 1976.

[Bankruptcy Act 1914 (c. 59), s. 108 (1); Insolvency Act 1976 (c. 60), s. 7 (4) (5).]

On the true construction of s. 7 (5) of the Insolvency Act 1976, a conditional order is an order where conditions are imposed precedent, not subsequent, to discharge.

D was adjudicated bankrupt in 1964. On his application for discharge in 1968, the registrar granted discharge suspended for six months subject to the condition of payment of £20,000 in six-monthly instalments of £1,000 to the Official Receiver. Regular payments were made. In 1977 the Insolvency Act 1976 came into force, providing by s. 7 (4) that a person adjudicated bankrupt more than five years before should be discharged absolutely, including, by s. 7 (5), on a conditional order. D stopped payment, and the Official Receiver sought a review. The county court judge held that D was absolutely discharged by s. 7 (4) and that the order was no longer open to review. On appeal by the Official Receiver, *held,* allowing the appeal, that a conditional order under s. 7 (5) did not include an order where conditions subsequent were imposed. Since the conditions in the present case were conditions subsequent, D had been discharged in 1968 on the expiration of the six months' period of suspension. As he had not been discharged by virtue of s. 7 (4), the order was still open to review. (*Re a Debtor (No. 946 of 1926)* [1939] 1 All E.R. 735 and *Re Tabrisky, ex p. Board of Trade* (1947) C.L.C. 664 applied.)

Re A DEBTOR (No. 13 OF 1964), *ex p.* OFFICIAL RECEIVER *v.* THE DEBTOR [1979] 3 All E.R. 15, D.C.

160. Debts due to Crown—set-off

[Bankruptcy Act 1914 (c. 59), s. 31.]

When proving in a bankruptcy, one Crown department may set off against a debt owed by it debts owed by the bankrupt to other Crown departments.

X Co. was wound up. The Commissioners of Customs and Excise owed the company £4,055 in respect of VAT input tax. X Co. owed the Inland Revenue £4,726, and the Department of Health and Social Security £951. The Customs and Excise mistakenly settled most of their indebtedness. X Co.'s debts were over £80,000. *Held,* the Commissioners were entitled to recover the money paid under s. 31 of the Bankruptcy Act 1914 by way of set-off against the debts owed to the other departments, and as moneys paid under a mistake. (Dictum of Lord Wright in *Norwich Union Fire Insurance Society* v. *Price* [1934] A.C.

462 and *National Westminster Bank* v. *Halesowen Presswork and Assemblies* [1972] C.L.Y. 193 applied.)
Re CUSHLA [1979] 3 All E.R. 415, Vinelott J.

161. Discharge—automatic—discretion of court to order
[Insolvency Act 1976 (c. 60), s. 7 (1) (2).]
The court was intended by Parliament to make an order for automatic discharge of a bankrupt only after serious consideration of all the circumstances and not as a mere formality.
R was adjudicated bankrupt. At his public examination the Official Receiver indicated that this was not a suitable case for an automatic discharge. The registrar agreed but heard R's submissions on the matter. The registrar then directed that an automatic discharge would not apply. R appealed contending that the registrar had failed to give him an open-minded hearing and had failed to give sufficient weight to the submissions made. *Held*, automatic discharge orders were not intended by Parliament to be mere formalities. They should only be granted after serious consideration of all the circumstances of the case and no attempt should be made to define precisely what circumstances would justify making or withholding such orders. An appellate court could only interfere where the court below had applied a wrong principle, or taken into account matters irrelevant in law, or excluded matters which ought properly to have been taken into account, or reached a conclusion no court properly instructing itself on the law could have reached. The appeal would be dismissed.
Re REED (A DEBTOR) [1979] 2 All E.R. 22, D.C.

162. EEC Draft Convention
The Department of Trade has published the text of the EEC Draft Bankruptcy Convention which provides rules for dealing with bankruptcies and company liquidations across national frontiers in the EEC. A copy of the Convention is available from Insolvency Service, Department of Trade, Room 116, 2/14 Bunhill Row, London EC1.

163. Fees
BANKRUPTCY FEES (AMENDMENT) ORDER 1979 (No. 780) [10p], made under the Bankruptcy Act 1914 (c. 59), s. 133, and the Public Offices Fees Act 1879 (c. 58), ss. 2, 3; operative on July 23, 1979; increases to £5·75 the fee payable for insertion in the *London Gazette* of notices in bankruptcy proceedings.
BANKRUPTCY FEES (AMENDMENT No. 2) ORDER 1979 (No. 1589) [10p], made under the Bankruptcy Act 1914, s. 133 and the Public Offices Fees Act 1879 (c. 58), ss. 2, 3; operative on January 1, 1980; abolishes the use of adhesive stamps and the separate fee payable for the insertion in the *London Gazette* of notices authorised by the Act or Bankruptcy Rules.

164. Offences—undischarged bankrupt—obtaining credit—time limit for proceedings —" first discovery " of offence
[Bankruptcy Act 1914 (c. 59), ss. 155 (*a*), 164 (2).] On December 4, 1975, the official receiver prepared a statement which D signed on December 30, 1975. The statement contained an admission of an offence of obtaining credit without disclosing that D was an undischarged bankrupt, contrary to s. 155 (*a*) of the 1914 Act. An information was preferred on December 6, 1976. *Held*, dismissing D's appeal, that the information was in time, having been preferred within one year from the first discovery of the offences required by s. 164 (2). The date of first discovery was that upon which the official receiver had sufficient evidence to prosecute, namely December 30, 1975: BROWNE v. PHILLIPS [1979] Crim.L.R. 381, D.C.

165. Payment into court—attached earnings—protected transaction
[Bankruptcy Act 1914 (c. 59), s. 45; Attachment of Earnings Act 1971 (c. 32), s. 13 (1).]
An order made under the Attachment of Earnings Act 1971 does not effect an assignment of those moneys to a judgment creditor, but any payments made to the creditors without notice of any act of bankruptcy are protected transactions by s. 45 of the Bankruptcy Act 1914.
On June 21, 1977, a consolidated attachment of earning order was made

in favour of four judgment creditors. The county court accumulated payments made on July 1, August 5, September 5 and October 3, without making a distribution. On October 3 a receiving order was made against the debtor based on an act of bankruptcy committed on July 1. On October 17 the debtor was declared bankrupt and the Official Receiver applied for a declaration that the payments belonged to the debtor's estate, while the creditors contended that there had been an assignment of the money deducted under the order. *Held*, that the order did not effect an assignment, but that since, on the facts, the creditors had no notice of any act of bankruptcy the first three payments were protected by s. 45 of the 1914 Act, but the October 3 payment was not protected as not having been made before the date of the receiving order.

Re GREEN (A BANKRUPT), *ex p.* OFFICIAL RECEIVER *v.* CUTTING [1979] 1 All E.R. 832, Walton J.

166. Practice—cross-examination—non-attendance—affidavit evidence. See *Re* A DEBTOR (No. 2283 OF 1976), § 1265.

167. Receiving order—application to set aside—registrar's decision
  [Bankruptcy Rules 1952 (S.I. 1952 No. 2113), r. 179.]
  Where a registrar has completed the hearing of an application to set aside a bankruptcy notice, the application has been " heard " for the purposes of the Bankruptcy Rules even though an appeal is pending.

  Petitioning creditors obtained judgment against a debtor for non-payment of a debt, and then, the judgment debt unsatisfied, served a bankruptcy notice. The debtor applied to set the notice aside; the application was heard and dismissed. The debtor then lodged notice of appeal against the dismissal but failed to set down the appeal despite several extensions of time. While the appeal was still outstanding the registrar made a receiving order against him. The debtor appealed against the receiving order on the ground that the registrar had failed to take account of the pending appeal. *Held*, dismissing the appeal, that where the registrar had completed the hearing of an application to set aside notice of bankruptcy, the application was " heard " even though an appeal was pending. (*Re a Debtor (No. 10 of 1953), ex p. the Debtor* v. *Ampthill Rural District Council* [1953] C.L.Y. 265 applied; *Re Marendez* (unreported), February 2, 1979, distinguished.)

  Re A DEBTOR (No. 44 OF 1978), *ex p.* THE DEBTOR *v.* CHANTRY MOUNT AND HAWTHORNS [1979] 3 All E.R. 265, D.C.

168. —— payment to sheriff—whether payment to creditor
  [Bankruptcy Act 1914 (c. 59), ss. 4 (1) (*a*), 41.]
  Payment of money to a sheriff only constitutes payment to the judgment creditor when the creditor is in a position to maintain an action against the sheriff for money had and received, *i.e.* after 14 days following payment to the sheriff without notice by him of a bankruptcy notice or the making of a receiving order.

  C obtained judgment against D, and in due course filed a bankruptcy petition. Eight days before the receiving order was made, C levied execution and the sheriff received a sum on C's account which reduced the debt to a sum less than the minimum of £200 required for the presentation of a petition under s. 4 (1) (*a*) of the Bankruptcy Act 1914, as amended. D appealed against the registrar's refusal to rescind the receiving order, on the ground that the court had no jurisdiction to make the order. *Held*, dismissing the appeal, that the claim could only be satisfied when C was in a position to maintain an action against the sheriff for money had and received, *i.e.* only when all the conditions precedent necessary to constitute his right to the money had been fulfilled. (*Re William Hockley* [1962] C.L.Y. 380 distinguished.)

  Re A DEBTOR (No. 2 OF 1977), *ex p.* THE DEBTOR *v.* GOACHER [1979] 1 All E.R. 870, D.C.

168a. Rules
  BANKRUPTCY (AMENDMENT) RULES 1979 (No. 1590) [10p], made under the Bankruptcy Act 1914 (c. 59), s. 132; operative on January 1, 1980; amend the Bankruptcy Rules 1952 as necessary to take account of S.I. 1979 No.

1589 which abolishes the use of adhesive stamps for the payment of fees and the separate fee for the insertion of notices in the *London Gazette.*

BOOKS. See *post,* p. [1].

BASTARDY AND LEGITIMATION

ARTICLES. See *post,* p. [13].

BILLS OF EXCHANGE

169. Assignment—priority of bank over proceeds

In January 1971 D1 executed in favour of D2, a bank, a debenture, cl. 3 of which provided, *inter alia,* " [D1] as beneficial owner hereby charges with payment or discharge of all monies and liabilities hereby covenanted to be paid or discharged by [D1] by way of first fixed charge all book debts and other debts now and from time to time due or owing to [D1] "; and cl. 5 of which provided, *inter alia,* " During the continuance of this security [D1] shall pay into [D1's] account with [D2] all monies which it may receive in respect of the book debts and other debts hereby charged and shall not without the prior consent of [D2] in writing purport to charge or assign the same in favour of any other person and shall if called upon to do so by [D2] execute a legal assignment of such book debts and other debts to [D2]." By March 1972 D1 had a substantial overdraft with D2, and also owed £8,707·64 to P. As a result of a meeting on March 24, 1972, between D1, D2 and P, it was agreed that D1 would assign to P certain bills of exchange held by D2, and whose total value was nearly £8,500. At the meeting, D2 did not produce a copy of the debenture, but pointed out that the assignment could only be executed subject to D2's charge on the bills, and indicated that once the overdraft was eliminated there was no reason why D2 should not release their charge on the bills. On the same day, a deed of assignment of the bills from D1 to P was executed, and notice of it given to D2. On April 18, 1972, when D1's overdraft stood at £49·51, the proceeds of one of the bills was paid into D1's account, and between then and July the proceeds of other of the bills were collected by D2 and paid into D1's account. P claimed the proceeds received by D2 upon collection of the bills. *Held,* that (1) on the facts, by March 24, 1972, P had notice of the existence of the debenture, and the provisions of cl. 3, but had no notice of the provisions of cl. 5 until June 30, 1972; (2) the bills were book debts within ordinary legal terminology and within the meaning of the debenture; (3) the debenture conferred on D2 a specific charge in equity on all future debts to D1, and D2; rights attached in equity to the proceeds of the bills as soon as they were paid, subject to P's rights as assignees of the bills; (4) the provisions of cl. 5 amounted to a restriction on D1's right to deal with their equity of redemption under a specific charge of book debts; and although valid as between D1 and D2, they were special provisions which P would not neces- sarily have expected to find in a mortgage creating a specific charge on future book debts, and of which they had no notice on the date when they took their assignment of the bills; (5) since the deed of assignment effected an outright assignment, and was not intended to reserve to D1 an equity of redemption, the assignment was not registrable as a charge on the book debts under s. 95 of the Companies Act 1948; (6) since P were entitled to assume that D1 had an equity of redemption in the bills which they could dispose of in the ordinary way and D2 had failed to ensure that P had full knowledge of cl. 5 before they took their assignment, they were also entitled to assume, having taken the assignment and given D2 notice of it, that D2 could no longer enlarge the scope of the debenture by making the bills stand as cover for fresh advantages made by them to D1 (*Deeley* v. *Lloyds Bank* [1912] A.C. 756; *Clayton's Case* (1816) 1 Mer. 572 applied); (7) D2 could not apply the proceeds of the bills in reduction of D1's indebtedness arising exclusively from credit given by D2 to D1 after receipt of the notice of assignment; and P were entitled to priority over D2 in respect of the proceeds of the bills save as to a sum of £49·51 being the balance of D1's indebtedness at the date when

D2 received notice of the assignment: SIEBE GORMAN & CO. *v.* BARCLAYS BANK; SAME *v.* R. H. MCDONALD AND BARCLAYS BANK [1979] 2 Lloyd's Rep. 142, Slade J.

170. **Cheques—theft—chose in action—rights over cheques appropriated.** See R. v. KOHN, § 591.

171. **Construction—intention of parties—whether loan transactions**
[N.Z.] M, a member of the S group, had provided clients with finance for development and other commercial ventures. Finance was arranged by bills of exchange drawn on the client, which were accepted by M for an acceptance fee, and then discounted to a discount house. After August 1975 client bills were usually discounted to C, also a member of the S group. Clients were required to cover all acceptances of bills by handing to M a promissory note or post-dated cheque for an amount covering the value of the bill and pay default interest if M was not reimbursed at maturity. If a client needed long-term finance, bills would be "rolled over" as they matured. That meant that new bills would be drawn, accepted and discounted on the same day as the old bills matured. The face value of the new bill would include the face value of the old bill, an amount to cover the discount on the new bill, and more acceptance fees. At trial the judge held the documents were a half-way house between a sham and an unassailable transaction, and further were moneylending transactions. On appeal, *held,* there was no half-way house between a sham and an unassailable transaction covering a situation where the documents recorded the intentions of the parties, but which were held not to express the pith and sub-stance of the transaction. Accordingly, the transactions involving client bills of exchange did not constitute loan transactions, nor were they contravening the Moneylenders Act 1908. (*Chow Yoong Hong* v. *Choong Fah Rubber Manu-factory* [1962] C.L.Y. 1931; *I.R.C.* v. *Duke of Westminster* [1936] A.C. 1 applied: *Re* SECURITIBANK (No. 2) [1978] 2 N.Z.L.R. 136, N.Z.Ct. of Appeal.

172. —— **no date fixed for payment**
P claimed from D $223,536, the balance of moneys said to be due on a bill of exchange dated September 28, 1974, Seoul, Korea, which provided "for U.S. $298,048·00 at 90 days D/A of this Bill of Exchange. Pay to Korea Exchange Bank or order," with the printed word "sight" crossed out between the words "D/A" and "of." D contended that the instrument did not indicate a fixed or determinable future time for payment, and so was not within the definition of a bill of exchange contained in s. 3 of the Bills of Exchange Act 1882. P contended that it came within s. 11 (1) of the Act, being an instrument expressed to be payable at a fixed period after sight. *Held,* allowing D's appeal, that (1) the instrument lacked the clarity to make the "acceptance" part of the symbol "D/A" part of the order to the drawee to pay, since this was not ordinarily the case; (2) to achieve the required certainty as to the date of maturity in the event of non-acceptance as well as in the event of acceptance, the bill had to be "expressed to be payable after sight," as required by s. 11 (1), and not after acceptance, since although acceptance included sight, there could be sight without acceptance; (3) the instrument was not expressed to be payable at a fixed or determinable future time, and therefore not a bill of exchange within the meaning of the Act: KOREA EXCHANGE BANK *v.* DEBENHAMS (CENTRAL BUYING) [1979] 1 Lloyd's Rep. 538, C.A.

173. **Dishonour—sale of goods—whether failure of consideration**
P and D had had dealings with each other for eight or nine years, and by the end of 1977 the account between them had reached a state of some con-fusion. In January 1978, D agreed to accept a bill of exchange in the sum of 1,000,000 Austrian schillings payable on October 15, 1978, and to pay P £3,000 per month commencing in February 1978 on account of their indebtedness to P. Payments were made in February and March, but thereafter were stopped because of defective goods supplied by P in respect of which D claimed to be entitled to a refund of £11,000. P presented the bill of exchange in due course, and the bill was dishonoured. P issued a writ and applied for summary judgment. *Held,* on appeal that (1) on the information available to the court, there was an arguable case that there was no consideration for the bill except

to the extent of 400,897 schillings (*Forman* v. *Wright*, 11 C.B. 481 applied); (2) accordingly there would be judgment in the sum of 400,897 schillings, and leave to defend on the balance of 599,103 schillings on condition that D brought that sum into court: THONI GMBH & CO. K.G. *v.* R.T.P. EQUIPMENT [1979] 2 Lloyd's Rep. 382, C.A.

174. Indorsement—by company director—liability
[Bills of Exchange Act 1882 (c. 61), s. 26 (1).]

If a dispute arises as to whether an indorsement on a bill of exchange is signed in a personal or representative capacity, evidence is admissible to show that the indorser signed in his personal capacity despite the words " for and on behalf of the company " appearing later on the bill.

A company which had become an unsatisfactory payer needed goods for its business which the plaintiffs agreed to supply on the oral condition that two officers of the company personally indorsed bills of exchange. The defendant indorsed the bill but with the words " for and on behalf of the company " added and signed in the space for " Director." The bills were subsequently dishonoured. The plaintiffs contended that notwithstanding the added words evidence was admissible to show the defendant has signed in his personal capacity. *Held*, evidence was admissible to resolve an issue as to capacity as here, and since there was clear evidence to show the agreement to sign in a personal capacity, the defendant was personally liable on the bills.

ROLFE, LUBELL & CO. *v.* KEITH [1979] 1 All E.R. 860, Kilner Brown J.

175. Mareva injunction—principles applicable. See MONTECCHI *v.* SHIMCO (U.K.); NAVONE *v.* SAME, § 2143.

BOOKS AND ARTICLES. See *post*, pp. [1], [14].

BOUNDARIES AND FENCES

ARTICLES. See *post*, p. [14].

BRITISH COMMONWEALTH

176. Bahamas—constitution—application for citizenship—executive discretion

The respondent applied for Bahamanian citizenship. Under the constitution such applications were subject to any exceptions or qualifications " provided by or under an Act of Parliament." The Minister under the proviso to s. 7 of the Nationality Act 1973 could refuse an application if he was satisfied the applicant fell within one of five groups of undesirable persons or that it would be against the public interest. The respondent's application was rejected without stating any reasons. On appeal the respondent succeeded and a declaration that he was entitled to be registered was granted. On appeal by the Attorney-General, *held*, the words " provided by or under an Act of Parliament " meant that such circumstances had to be precisely defined by Parliament and not left to executive discretion. The proviso purporting to give such a discretion was therefore *ultra vires* the constitution and void. The matter was remitted to the Minister for determination according to law: ATT.-GEN. *v.* RYAN (1979) 123 S.J. 621, P.C.

177. Bermuda

BERMUDA CONSTITUTION (AMENDMENT) ORDER 1979 (No. 452) [10p], made under the Bermuda Constitution Act 1967 (c. 63), s. 1; operative on May 28, 1979; gives effect to the recommendations related to the composition of the Constituency Boundaries Commission decided upon at a Constitutional Conference held in Bermuda in February 1979.

BERMUDA CONSTITUTION (AMENDMENT) (No. 2) ORDER 1979 (No. 1310) [40p], made under the Bermuda Constitution Act 1967, s. 1; operative on December 1, 1979; gives effect to recommendations of the Constitutional Conference that was held in Bermuda in February and July 1979 for amending the Constitution of Bermuda.

178. —— status of children under Constitution
[Bermuda Constitution Order 1968 (S.I. 1968 No. 182), Sched. 2, s. 11 (5).]

A "child" who is deemed to belong to Bermuda by s. 11 (5) of the Bermuda Constitution Order 1968 includes an illegitimate child.

M, the Jamaican mother of four illegitimate children all born in Jamaica, married F, a Bermudian. The family took up residence in Bermuda. The children were under 18. The Minister ordered the children to leave Bermuda. The Supreme Court refused a declaration that the children were deemed to belong to Bermuda. The Court of Appeal upheld this appeal. On appeal by the Minister to the Judicial Committee, *held*, dismissing the appeal, that s. 11 of the Constitution dealt with an individual's rights and freedoms, subs. 5 (*d*) clearly recognised the unity of the family as a group, and the word "child" included also illegitimate children.

MINISTER OF HOME AFFAIRS *v.* FISHER [1979] 2 W.L.R. 889, P.C.

179. British nationality. See ALIENS.

180. Colonial courts—precedent—House of Lords decision—whether binding. See DE LASALA *v.* DE LASALA, § 2200.

181. Commonwealth Development Corporation

COMMONWEALTH DEVELOPMENT CORPORATION REGULATIONS 1979 (No. 495) [10p], made under the Commonwealth Development Corporation Act 1978 (c. 2), Sched. 1, para. 1; operative on June 1, 1979; deal with the terms of appointment and conditions of tenure of members of the Development Corporation and with the proceedings of the Corporation. They revoke S.I. 1977 No. 2186.

182. Fiji—sale of land and chattels—contract referring to land only

[Indemnity, Guarantee and Bailment Ordinance (Laws of Fiji, 1967 rev., s. 208), s. 59 (*d*); Law of Property Act 1925 (c. 20), s. 40 (1).]

Where a contract is for the sale of both land and chattels, a memorandum of agreement that refers only to the land and not the chattels is an insufficient memorandum.

The vendors agreed to sell their interest in two parcels of land together with some chattels to the purchaser. The contract and the purchase price were treated as indivisible between the land and the chattels. The written memorandum referred to the land and not to the chattels. When the vendors refused to complete, the purchaser obtained an order for specific performance and damages. On the vendors' appeal the Fiji Court of Appeal treated the terms of the agreement relating to the chattels as collateral and the purchase price as apportionable between the land and the chattels. Therefore, the memorandum was sufficient for the purposes of s. 59 (*d*) of the Ordinance. On the vendors' appeal to the Judicial Committee, *held*, allowing the appeal that where the contract was for the sale of both land and chattels, a memorandum that referred to the land and not to the chattels was an insufficient memorandum and, where the purchaser asserted an indivisible contract for an indivisible price, the court could not treat the terms of the agreement relating to the chattels as collateral and so apportion the purchase price between the land and the chattels so as to make the memorandum within s. 59 (*d*).

RAM NARAYAN S/O SHANKAR *v.* RISHAD HUSSAIN SHAH S/O TASADUQ HUSSAIN SHAH [1979] 1 W.L.R. 1349, P.C.

183. Fugitive offenders. See EXTRADITION.

184. Hong Kong—bribery offence—order for payment by defendant—duplicity.

[Prevention of Bribery Ordinance, s. 10 (1) (*b*).] D was charged with being in control of "pecuniary resources or property" disproportionate to his official emoluments, contrary to s. 10 (1) (*b*) of Hong Kong's Prevention of Bribery Ordinance. The trial judge found D to be in control of both unexplained pecuniary resources and property. *Held*, dismissing D's appeal against conviction, that " or " in s. 10 (1) (*b*) should be read conjunctively and the section created only one offence which could be committed in one or both of two ways. Accordingly, the charge was not bad for duplicity: CHEUNG CHEE-KWONG *v.* THE QUEEN; ATT.-GEN. *v.* CHEUNG CHEE-KWONG [1979] Crim.L.R. 788, P.C.

185. —— power to order new trial

[Criminal Procedure Ordinance (Laws of Hong Kong 1972, rev. c. 221).]

The Court of Appeal of Hong Kong need not regard the probability of conviction as a condition precedent or of paramount importance when exercising its discretion to order a new trial after upholding an appeal against conviction under s. 83E (1) of the Criminal Procedure Ordinance 1972.

D's conviction for murder was quashed by the Court of Appeal of Hong Kong on the ground that the judge had misdirected the jury on the law of self-defence. The court ordered a new trial under s. 83E (1) of the Criminal Procedure Ordinance 1972. D appealed to the Judicial Committee against that order, contending that before making it the Court of Appeal had to be satisfied that a reasonable jury properly directed would probably convict. *Held*, dismissing the appeal, that although the court would not order a retrial where a conviction was improbable, in any other case the strength of the evidence was just one of the factors to be considered in determining what was in the interests of justice. (Dictum of the Court of Appeal of Hong Kong in *Aplin* v. *The Queen* [1976] H.K.L.R. 1028, 1039, disapproved.)

AU PUI-KUEN *v.* ATT.-GEN. OF HONG KONG [1979] 2 W.L.R. 274, P.C.

186. Immigration. See ADMINISTRATIVE LAW.

187. Kiribati

KIRIBATI INDEPENDENCE ORDER 1979 (No. 719) [£2·00], made under the Kiribati Act 1979 (c. 27), ss. 2, 6; operative on July 12, 1979; provides for the Constitution of the Gilbert Islands as an independent Republic under the name of Kiribati.

KIRIBATI APPEALS TO JUDICIAL COMMITTEE ORDER 1979 (No. 720) [40p], made under the Judicial Committee Act 1833 (c. 41), s. 24 and the Kiribati Act 1979, s. 6; operative on July 12, 1979; makes provision in respect of appeals from the High Court of Kiribati to the Judicial Committee of the Privy Council.

188. Kiribati Act 1979 (c. 27)

This Act provides for the attainment by the Gilbert Islands of fully responsible status as the Republic of Kiribati.

S. 1 proclaims independence for Kiribati; s. 2 provides for the constitution of Kiribati as a republic; s. 3 deals with the operation of existing law; s. 4 makes consequential modifications to British Nationality Acts; s. 5 provides for retention of U.K. citizenship in certain cases; s. 6 relates to appeals to the Privy Council from the courts of Kiribati; s. 7 is the interpretation section; s. 8 gives the short title.

The Act received the Royal Assent on June 19, 1979, and came into force on that date.

189. Malaysia—appeal against sentence—no right of appeal

D petitioned for special leave to appeal from a decision of the Federal Court of Malaysia to His Majesty the Yang di Pertuan Agong. *Held*, that the Judicial Committee had no jurisdiction to entertain an appeal since the right of appeal to the Yang di Pertuan Agong in criminal matters in all cases except those where an appeal or application for leave was pending on January 1, 1978, was abolished by the Courts of Judicature (Amendment) Act 1976, s. 13 (4): LEE CHOW MENG *v.* PUBLIC PROSECUTOR, MALAYSIA [1979] Crim.L.R. 465, P.C.

190. —— constitution—retrospective amendment.

[Federal Constitution of Malaysia, art. 135 (1), proviso.]

For pending actions to be affected by retrospective legislation the language of the statute must be such that the only possible conclusion is that the legislature intends it so to apply.

The appellant, H, a police officer in Malaysia, was convicted of an offence and dismissed. Under the constitution he could only be dismissed by an authority of sufficient rank as had power to make a similar appointment. The chief police officer who dismissed him had power to dismiss but not to appoint. H brought an action claiming his dismissal was void and succeeded. After judgment amending legislation was passed that validated the dismissal, and the government then appealed to the Federal Court, which allowed the appeal. H appealed to the Privy Council. *Held*, dismissing the appeal, that as a result of the amendment H was deprived of his right to maintain his dismissal was invalid.

ZAINAL BIN HASHIM v. GOVERNMENT OF MALAYSIA [1979] 3 All E.R. 241, P.C.

191. —— income tax—loss—double taxation agreement. See HOCK HENG CO. SDN. BHD. v. DIRECTOR-GENERAL OF INLAND REVENUE, § 1463.

192. —— —— trade—isolated transactions. See INTERNATIONAL INVESTMENT v. THE COMPTROLLER-GENERAL OF INLAND REVENUE, § 1491.

193. —— security area proclamation—validity
[Constitution of Malaysia, arts. 8 (1), 150 (2); Emergency (Essential Powers) Act 1964 (No. 30 of 1964), s. 2; Emergency (Essential Powers) Ordinance 1969 (No. 1 of 1969), s. 2; Essential (Security Cases) (Amendment) Regulations 1975; Internal Security Act 1960 (Laws of Malaysia Act 82), ss. 47 (1) (2), 57 (1); Arms Act 1960 (No. 21 of 1960), s. 9; Firearms (Increased Penalties) Act 1971 (Laws of Malaysia Act 37), s. 8.]
In Malaysia, the ruler's emergency powers to legislate were not self-extendible once Parliament was sitting. The Attorney-General's decision to prefer charges was valid.
Per curiam: If the ruler abused his discretion by failing to revoke the 1969 Proclamation the cabinet could be compelled by mandamus to require him to revoke it.
D was found in possession of a revolver and ammunition in a security area and was charged with offences for which the mandatory penalty was death. The area had been designated a security area in 1969 by an emergency proclamation of the ruler made when Parliament was not sitting as he was empowered to do by the Constitution. If this proclamation was still effective in 1976 the offences committed by D were " security offences " and by Regulations made in 1975 were to be tried by a special procedure. D was tried by this special procedure and found guilty. He appealed on the grounds that the Regulations were invalid; that the 1969 proclamation had lapsed; and that the Attorney-General's decision to prosecute him was unconstitutional. *Held*, the Regulations were *ultra vires* the Constitution and void. Once Parliament was sitting again the ruler had no power to make Regulations having the force of law. The 1969 proclamation could not lapse without being revoked. The Attorney-General had correctly charged D although the trial upon that charge was a nullity. (Decision of the Federal Court of Malaysia reversed; *Public Prosecutor* v. *Khong Teng Khen* [1976] 2 M.L.J. 166 overruled.)
TEH CHENG POH ALIAS CHAR MEH v. PUBLIC PROSECUTOR, MALAYSIA [1979] 2 W.L.R. 623, P.C.

194. New Zealand—appeal to Privy Council—jurisdiction. See THOMAS v. THE QUEEN, § 2198.

195. —— bills of exchange—intention of parties—whether loan transactions. See *Re* SECURITIBANK (No. 2), § 171.

196. Northern Ireland. See NORTHERN IRELAND.

197. Recognition and enforcement of judgments and orders—service of process
The Commonwealth Secretariat has published a report of the Second Working Meeting entitled "Recognition and Enforcement of Judgments and Orders and the Service of Process within the Commonwealth." The report is available from the Commonwealth Secretariat, Marlborough House, Pall Mall, London SW1Y 5HX.

198. St. Christopher, Nevis and Anguilla—emergency powers—no evidence against detainee—compensation
[Constitution of St. Christopher, Nevis and Anguilla (S.I. 1967 No. 228, Sched. 2), ss. 3 (6), 103; Leeward Islands (Emergency Powers) Order in Council 1959 (S.I. No. 2206), s. 3 (1); Emergency Powers Regulations 1967 (St. Christopher, Nevis and Anguilla), reg. 3 (1).]
Emergency powers exercised by the Governor are to be construed so as to conform with the Constitution of St. Christopher, Nevis and Anguilla.
Under the Constitution coming into force in February 1967 all existing laws were to be construed so as to bring them into conformity with the Constitution. The 1959 order conferred on the Leewards Islands Governor the power in an

emergency to make such laws as appeared to him necessary or expedient for the maintenance of public order; under the Constitution such order was to cease to have legal affect in September 1967. In May 1967 the Governor declared a state of emergency and made the 1967 Regulations empowering him to detain a person without trial if satisfied that such detention was necessary. The plaintiff, a man of good character and an opposition politician, was detained under such regulations in distressing conditions for some two months until August 1967, when at a tribunal hearing the Crown conceded that they had no evidence against him. The plaintiff was at first instance awarded $5,000 damages for false imprisonment, no evidence to justify his detention being proffered by the state. The Court of Appeal increased the award to $18,000, including an unspecified amount of exemplary damages. *Held,* dismissing the state's appeal, that notwithstanding that the 1959 order continued in force until September 1967, the powers exercisable thereunder were to conform with the Constitution; that the 1967 Regulations were valid if they were construed so as to be in conformity with the Constitution; accordingly detention could be ordered only if the Governor had reasonable grounds for considering it to be necessary or expedient; that, since there was no evidence as to the existence of such grounds, the plaintiff was entitled to damages; and that it was not incumbent upon the court to specify the extent to which the damages were exemplary. (*Secretary of State for Education and Science* v. *Tameside Metropolitan Borough* [1976] C.L.Y. 829, considered; dictum of Lord Devlin in *Rookes* v. *Barnard* [1964] C.L.Y. 3703, explained.)

ATT.-GEN. OF ST. CHRISTOPHER, NEVIS AND ANGUILLA v. REYNOLDS [1979] 3 All E.R. 129, P.C.

199. St. Vincent

SAINT VINCENT CONSTITUTION ORDER 1979 (No. 916) [£2·50], made under the West Indies Act 1967 (c. 4), s. 5 (4); operative on October 27, 1979; provides a new constitution for St. Vincent.

SAINT VINCENT MODIFICATION OF ENACTMENTS ORDER 1979 (No. 917) [30p], made under the West Indies Act 1967, ss. 13 (2) (3), 14; operative on October 27, 1979; amends and modifies certain enactments as a consequence of the termination of the status of association of St. Vincent with the U.K.

SAINT VINCENT TERMINATION OF ASSOCIATION ORDER 1979 (No. 918) [10p], made under the West Indies Act 1967, ss. 10 (2), 17 (2); operative on October 27, 1979; terminates the status of association of St. Vincent with the U.K.

200. Southern Rhodesia

SOUTHERN RHODESIA (IMMUNITY FOR PERSONS ATTENDING MEETINGS AND CONSULTATIONS) ORDER 1979 (No. 820) [10p], made under the Southern Rhodesia Act 1965 (c. 76) s. 2; operative on July 13, 1979; confers immunity from suit and legal process and personal inviolability on certain persons present in the U.K. with the agreement of the Secretary of State, in connection with their attendance at meetings and consultations to achieve a constitutional settlement in Southern Rhodesia.

SOUTHERN RHODESIA (IMMUNITY FOR PERSONS ATTENDING MEETINGS AND CONSULTATIONS) (NO. 2) ORDER 1979 (No. 1374) [20p], made under the Southern Rhodesia Act 1965, s. 2; operative on October 31, 1979; confers immunity from suit and legal process and personal immunity on certain persons present in the U.K. in connection with their attendance at meetings and consultations to achieve a constitutional settlement in Southern Rhodesia.

SOUTHERN RHODESIA (EXPIRING ORDERS) (CONSEQUENTIAL PROVISIONS) ORDER 1979 (No. 1445) [20p], made under the Southern Rhodesia Act 1979 (c. 52), s. 3; operative on the expiration of s. 2 of the Southern Rhodesia Act 1965; makes provision consequential on the lapse of a number of Orders made under s. 2 of the Southern Rhodesia Act 1965. When that section expires a number of Orders relating to sanctions and other economic measures lapse with it.

SOUTHERN RHODESIA CONSTITUTION (INTERIM PROVISIONS) ORDER 1979 (No. 1571) [20p], made under the Southern Rhodesia Act 1979, s. 3; ss. 1 and 3, operative on December 4, 1979, the remainder on December 12, 1979.

SOUTHERN RHODESIA (LEGAL PROCEEDINGS AND PUBLIC LIABILITIES) ORDER

1979 (No. 1601) [20p], made under the Southern Rhodesia Act 1979, s. 3; operative on December 7, 1979; replaces S.I. 1979 No. 1445. It is designed to make provision consequential upon the lapse of certain Orders made under s. 2 of the Southern Rhodesia Act 1965 and to ameliorate, and provide for certain consequences of unconstitutional action in Southern Rhodesia. It also contains provisions relating to S.I. 1965 No. 2049 and S.I. 1967 No. 478 affecting the Reserve Bank of Rhodesia.

SOUTHERN RHODESIA (COMMONWEALTH FORCES) (JURISDICTION) ORDER 1979 (No. 1653) [20p], made under S.I. 1965 No. 1952, s. 3 (1) (c); operative on December 13, 1979; makes provision in relation to Commonwealth forces stationed in Southern Rhodesia.

SOUTHERN RHODESIA (CONSTITUTION OF ZIMBABWE) (ELECTIONS AND APPOINTMENTS) ORDER 1979 (No. 1654) [40p], made under the Southern Rhodesia Act 1979, s. 2; operative on December 13, 1979, save for s. 3 (2), 4, 5, 6 (2), 7 which are operative on a day to be appointed; makes provision for the holding of elections and the making of certain appointments in Rhodesia for the purpose of enabling the Independence Constitution of Zimbabwe to function from Independence Day.

SOUTHERN RHODESIA (UNITED NATIONS SANCTIONS: ISLANDS AND OVERSEAS TERRITORIES) (REVOCATIONS) ORDER 1979 (No. 1655) [10p], made under the United Nations Act 1946 (c. 45), s. 1; operative on December 13, 1979; revokes five specified Orders which were made under s. 1 of the 1946 Act in order to give effect to resolutions of the Security Council of the UN in relation to economic sanctions against Southern Rhodesia.

201. —— **duty of Crown to protect from unlawful arrest.** See MUTASA v. ATT.-GEN., § 611.

202. Southern Rhodesia Act 1979 (c. 52)
This Act provides for the grant of a constitution for Zimbabwe and related matters.

S. 1 empowers the Crown to provide a constitution for Zimbabwe; s. 2 gives power to bring particular provisions of new constitution into force before appointed day; s. 3 contains miscellaneous provisions with respect to Southern Rhodesia; s. 4 contains short title and extent.

The Act received the Royal Assent on November 14, 1979, and came into force on that date.

203. Trinidad and Tobago—Constitution—unemployment levy—validity
[Trinidad and Tobago (Constitution) Order in Council 1962 (S.I. 1962 No. 1875), Sched. 2, ss. 1 (a), 6, 85 (3); Unemployment Levy Act 1970 (No. 16 of 1970), ss. 2, 7, 14, 17, 19.]

Where the purposes of an unemployment levy as defined in the Act are undoubtedly public purposes, a levy is not an unauthorised exaction but a legitimate exercise of the power to tax.

Parliament passed the Unemployment Levy Act 1970 to relieve the social unrest created by massive unemployment. The Act imposed a levy on incomes and profits for the purpose of the relief of unemployment and the training of the unemployed, which were paid into the " unemployment fund." Under s. 19, the Governor-General has the power to make regulations prescribing, *inter alia,* the projects for which advances from the fund could be made, and the rate of the levy. By s. 14, the Minister for finance had the power to make advances for any purpose provided for under the Act or by the regulations made under it. The High Court declared that the Act was *ultra vires* the Constitution and void. The Court of Appeal set aside the declaration and, on appeal to the Judicial Committee on the grounds that (1) the Act provided no impost for public purposes to make the levy a tax; (2) the scheme of expenditure was unconstitutional; (3) the levy infringed the rights guaranteed by s. 1 (a) of the Constitution, *held,* dismissing the appeal, that (1) since the purposes defined in the Act were public purposes and the advances from the fund were made for those purposes the levy was a legitimate exercise of the power to tax; (2) the court could not declare the Act unconstitutional by reason of any conflict between s. 85 (3) of the Constitution and s. 19 (c) of the Act where the application was based upon the deprivation of property contrary to s. 1 (*a*); (3) " due process of law " includes both procedural and substantive law, but the operation of the Act was not so uncertain or unpredictable in the hands of the executive so as to render the exaction without due process of law.

MOOTOO *v.* ATT.-GEN. OF TRINIDAD AND TOBAGO [1979] 1 W.L.R. 1334, P.C.

204. —— delay in execution of murderer—contravention of rights under Constitution
[Constitution of the Republic of Trinidad and Tobago Act 1976 (No. 4 of 1976), Sched., ss. 4 (*a*), 14, 87, 88, 89.]

Delay between the passing of sentence and the notice of execution may be so prolonged as to raise a reasonable belief in the defendant that his sentence had been commuted to life imprisonment, but such delay does not amount to an infringement of the defendant's right to life under the Constitution unless the delay can be shown to be itself unreasonable.

Per curiam: Where the delay was due to a failure by the appropriate body to advise the President, the aggrieved person should apply for the appropriate remedy in public law, namely, an order of mandamus requiring the Minister to refer the case for consideration.

The applicant was convicted of murder and was sentenced to death. When his appeals to the Court of Appeal and the Privy Council were dismissed, he petitioned the Governor-General for mercy and accordingly, the sentence was respited pending the Governor-General's decision. During this period, a republican Constitution came into force and the Governor-General became the President but the power of pardon remained unaffected. With the new Constitution there was a General Election, after which the President received from the Minister the advice of the newly constituted advisory committee rejecting the petition and, accordingly, the warrant for execution was issued. The High Court and the Court of Appeal dismissed his application for redress on the ground that the delay of seven and a half months before the warrant for execution was issued contravened his right to life guaranteed by the Constitution. On his appeal to the Judicial Committee *held,* dismissing the appeal, that in the present case it was not unreasonable for the executive to wait until after the elections before constituting the appropriate body to consider the case and to advise the President; accordingly the delay did not amount to an infringement of the applicant's right to life under s. 4 (*a*) of the Constitution.

ABBOTT *v.* ATT.-GEN. OF TRINIDAD AND TOBAGO [1979] 1 W.L.R. 1342, P.C.

205. —— land registration—priority—registration of settlement
[Trinidad.] [Registration of Deeds Ordinance (Revised Ordinance 1950, c. 28, No. 2), s. 16 (2).]

The effect of s. 16 (2) of the Registration of Deeds Ordinance is that a purchaser for value of land without notice of a previous unregistered deed relating to the land has a right which crystallises at the time of purchase to have the previous deed adjudged void as against him accordingly, that right cannot be abrogated by a subsequent registration.

O, the owner of land, settled land on herself for life, remainder to A, the appellant, and another. O then sold the land without notice of the trust to R, the respondent. The settlement deed was then registered pursuant to the Registration of Deeds Ordinance. Subsequently, the conveyance to R was registered. A obtained a declaration in the High Court that he was entitled to the freehold under the settlement. That decision was reversed by the Court of Appeal of Trinidad and Tobago. On appeal by A to the Judicial Committee, *held,* dismissing the appeal, that since R was a purchaser for value without notice, then by s. 16 (2) of the Ordinance he was entitled to the freehold.

MAHABIR *v.* PAYNE [1979] 1 W.L.R. 507, P.C.

206. —— tenancy—order for possession—procedure to be followed
[Summary Ejectment Ordinance, ss. 3, 4, 5.] The tenant, M, died intestate and an order for possession of the land was granted. The occupier of the land successfully appealed on the ground, *inter alia,* that the Administrator General, on whom the property developed on the intestacy, should have been a party to the complaint. *Held,* the Order contemplated that the complaint should be

against the persons actually in occupation; the tenant did not need to be a party: Isaac v. Francis (1979) 123 S.J. 859, P.C.

207. Turks and Caicos Islands

Turks and Caicos Islands (Constitution) (Amendment) Order 1979 (No. 919) [10p], made under the West Indies Act 1962 (c. 19), s. 5; operative on August 24, 1979; amends S.I. 1976 No. 1156 so as to provide for the appointment of not more than two Parliamentary Secretaries.

207a. Virgin Islands

Virgin Islands (Constitution) (Amendment) Order 1979 (No. 1603) [10p], made under the West Indies Act 1962 (c. 19), ss. 5 and 7; operative on a day to be appointed; provides for the possibility of the appointment of a third Minister to the Executive Council for the Virgin Islands.

208. Zimbabwe

Zimbabwe Constitution Order 1979 (No. 1600) [£2·50], made under the Southern Rhodesia Act 1979 (c. 52), s. 1; operative on the day that Southern Rhodesia becomes independent under the name of the Republic of Zimbabwe; provides for the constitution of the Republic of Zimbabwe.

209. Zimbabwe Act 1979 (c. 60)

This Act provides for Zimbabwe to attain a fully responsible status as a Republic.

S. 1 grants independence to Southern Rhodesia (from thence to be known as Zimbabwe) on such day as appointed by Order in Council; s. 2 deals with nationality; s. 3 gives amnesty in respect of certain acts done before the date on which the Governor of Southern Rhodesia took up office; s. 4 concerns supplementary provisions relating to independence; s. 5 sets out provisions for Zimbabwe should she wish to become a member of the Commonwealth at any time; s. 6 makes provisions as to existing laws; s. 7 contains the short title and miscellaneous provisions.

The Act received the Royal Assent on December 20, 1979, and came into force on that day.

Books and Articles. See *post*, pp. [1], [14].

BUILDING AND ENGINEERING, ARCHITECTS AND SURVEYORS

210. Advice—negligence—architects' failure to advise clients. See B. L. Holdings v. Robert J. Wood and Partners, § 1850.

211. Building contract—implied term—fitness and quality of materials

[Eire.] N engaged a contractor S to build a factory specifying that the roof was to be supplied and erected under sub-contract by H which manufactured and supplied superstructures. Under the sub-contract H agreed to indemnify S against any liability which might arise under the main contract as a result of H's breach of the sub-contract. Over a year after completion of the building the roof began to leak and became unsuitable for its purpose. An arbitrator found that it was largely due to the defective design of roof lights. On a case stated by the arbitrator McMahon J. held that as S was precluded from exercising any skill or judgment as to fitness for purpose of the roof it would not be reasonable to require S to undertake responsibility for the adequacy of the roof's design. On appeal, *held*, disallowing the appeal, that there is normally implied in a building contract a term making the contractor liable to the employer for any loss or damage suffered by him as a result of the sub-contractor's goods, materials or installations not being fit for the purpose but that such an implied term cannot be held to exist unless it comes within the presumed intention of the parties and should not be read into the contract unless it would be reasonable to do so. No such term could be implied in relation to the fitness of the roof's design (*Young & Marten* v. *McManus Childs* [1968] C.L.Y. 324; *Gloucestershire County Council* v. *Richardson* [1968] C.L.Y. 325 considered): Norta Wallpapers (Ireland) v. Sisk and Sons (Dublin) [1978] I.R. 114, Sup.Ct. of Ireland.

212. ⸺ standard form RIBA—architect's certificates—ownership of unfixed materials

[Sale of Goods Act 1893 (c. 71), s. 25 (2).] The plaintiffs entered into a standard form RIBA sub-contract, known as a " blue form," with T & C Ltd. as non-nominated sub-contractors to supply and fix a quantity of roofing slates. The main contract, being the Standard Form of Building Contract Local Authorities Edition, was between T & C Ltd. and the defendants. Although the main contract was delayed, work continued and the defendants' architect issued three interim certificates to T & C Ltd., which included references to the slates brought onto site by the plaintiffs. T & C Ltd. were paid in full for the slates by the defendants. T & C Ltd went into receivership; the main and sub-contracts automatically determined. The slates were never fixed and the plaintiffs sought the return of the slates or their value and damages for their detention. *Held*, that (1) there was no privity of contract between the plaintiffs and the defendants. Neither the main contract, nor the sub-contracts, nor the certificates operated so as to pass title to the defendants; (2) s. 25 (2) of the Sale of Goods Act 1893 did not apply because, (a) the contract was not for the sale of goods; (b) the slates were on site as this was the usual practice and custom of the building industry, and T & C Ltd. did not thereby become buyers in possession; (c) the defendants had some knowledge that the plaintiffs might have taken their materials onto site notwithstanding that the plaintiffs were non-nominated sub-contractors without any contractual relationship with the defendants. Judgment for the plaintiff for the value of the slates at the time of detention and damages for detinue: DAWBER WILLIAMSON ROOFING *v.* HUMBERSIDE COUNTY COUNCIL, October 22, 1979, Mais J. (*Ex rel. P. J. M. Heppel, Esq., Barrister and Graham & Rosen, Solicitors.*)

213. ⸺ whether builder has duty of care in giving estimate

[N.Z.] P, who were builders, estimated the construction of two residential units at $30,500 when requested so to do by D. Some months later, P received specifications supplied by D's architect, which showed P that the units contemplated by D were of a more extensive type than those upon which they had based their estimate. Thereafter building works began; P encountered problems with the foundations and costs escalated. Both before and after work commenced D continuously enquired about the final price but received no indication of any significant attention. P then told D the final price would be $57,500. D said in evidence that he expected the final price to exceed the estimate, but nothing like $57,500; he would have continued to a total price of $40,000. D decided to complete the units. P declined to complete for a total sum of $40,000. D accepted the lowest tender at $38,750. *Held*, P was under a duty of care to D when giving its original estimate. A reasonable builder would have told D of its misgivings shortly after the substantial work began. D established a breach of duty by P before D become finally committed to the uneconomic completion of the units. (*Hedley Byrne* v. *Heller* [1963] C.L.Y. 2416 and *Anns* v. *Merton London Borough* [1977] C.L.Y. 2030 applied): ABRAMS *v.* ANCLIFFE [1978] 2 N.Z.L.R. 420, N.Z.Sup.Ct.

214. Building regulations

BUILDING (REPEALS AND AMENDMENTS) REGULATIONS 1979 (No. 601) [10p], made under the Public Health Act 1936 (c. 49), s. 61 (1); the Public Health Act 1961 (c. 64), s. 4 (2) (5); the Health and Safety at Work etc. Act 1974 (c. 37), s. 62 (5); operative on June 27, 1979; make redundant, in relation to factories, regulations made under the Thermal Insulation (Industrial Buildings) Act 1957.

215. Channel tunnel. See HIGHWAYS AND BRIDGES.

216. Dangerous premises. See NEGLIGENCE.

217. Factories. See FACTORIES.

218. House-building standards

HOUSE-BUILDING STANDARDS (APPROVED SCHEME ETC.) ORDER 1979 (No. 381) [20p], made under the Defective Premises Act 1972 (c. 35), s. 2 (3) (4) (6); operative on April 18, 1979; approves the Scheme to be operated by the

National House-Building Council and the forms of Notice of Insurance Cover issued by the Council in relation to dwellings erected pursuant to the scheme.

219. Housing. See HOUSING.

220. Mortgages. See MORTGAGES.

221. Negligence—duty of care—builders—third parties or purchasers. See THOMAS *v.* WHITEHOUSE, § 1862.

222. Northern Ireland. See NORTHERN IRELAND.

BOOKS AND ARTICLES. See *post*, pp. [2], [14].

BUILDING SOCIETIES

223. Authorised investments

BUILDING SOCIETIES (AUTHORISED INVESTMENTS) (AMENDMENT) ORDER 1979 (No. 1301) [10p], made under the Building Societies Act 1962 (c. 37), s. 58; operative on December 3, 1979; amends S.I. 1977 No. 2052 by adding sterling certificates of deposit issued by certain banks and Passenger Transport Executives to the classes of investments in which building societies may place funds not immediately required for their purposes.

224. Fees

BUILDING SOCIETIES (FEES) REGULATIONS 1979 (No. 1550) [20p], made under the Building Societies Act 1962 (c. 37), s. 123 (1); operative on January 1, 1980; increases fees payable in connection with the exercise by the Central Office and the Chief Registrar of their functions under the 1962 Act.

225. Mortgages. See MORTGAGES.

226. —— prior finance company loan—illegal transaction

[Building Societies Act 1962 (c. 37), s. 32 (1).]

S. 32 (1) of the Building Societies Act 1962 is designed to protect the society's property for the benefit of all members, and the society has rights even in relation to a mortgage registered in breach of s. 32 (1) which is in consequence an illegal act.

The plaintiff purchased a house with the assistance of a bridging loan from a finance company, on the solicitor's undertaking to hold the title deeds until repayment. Subsequently a sum was advanced on mortgage by a building society and a land charge duly registered. The society had intended to comply with s. 32 (1) of the Act but had overlooked the prior equitable charge. On the plaintiff's motion to vacate the register, *held*, refusing the motion, that although the transaction was illegal, the society was entitled to recover the money advanced and to enforce the security for its repayment. (Dictum of Clauson J. in *Hayes Bridge Estate* v. *Portman Building Society* [1936] 2 All E.R. 1400 applied.)

NASH *v.* HALIFAX BUILDING SOCIETY [1979] 2 W.L.R. 184, Browne-Wilkinson J.

226a. Special advances

BUILDING SOCIETIES (SPECIAL ADVANCES) ORDER 1979 (No. 1639) [10p], made under the Building Societies Act 1962 (c. 37), s. 21 (6); operative on December 6, 1979; increases from £20,000 to £25,000 the limit beyond which an advance made by a building society to an individual is to be treated as a special advance for the purposes of the Building Societies Act 1962.

BOOKS. See *post*, p. [2].

BURIAL AND CREMATION

227. Cremation

CREMATION REGULATIONS 1979 (No. 1138) [20p], made under the Cremation Act 1902 (c. 8), s. 7, as amended by the Cremation Act 1952 (c. 31), s. 2, and as extended by the Births and Deaths Registration Act 1926 (c. 48), s. 10; operative on November 1, 1979; make new provision for the documents which may be accepted by the medical referee of a cremation authority to enable him to authorise the cremation of the remains of a person who has died outside England and Wales.

228. Fees

HUMAN REMAINS REMOVAL LICENCE (PRESCRIBED FEE) ORDER 1979 (No. 1258) [10p], made under the Fees (Increase) Act 1923 (c. 4), s. 7 (1); operative on November 1, 1979; increases to £6 the prescribed fee for a licence issued under s. 25 of the Burial Act 1857 for the removal of human remains interred in a place of burial.

CAPITAL TAXATION

229. Capital gains tax. See INCOME TAX.

230. Capital transfer tax

CAPITAL TRANSFER TAX (INTEREST ON UNPAID TAX) ORDER 1979 (No. 1688) [10p], made under the Finance Act 1975 (c. 7), Sched. 4, para 19; operative on January 1, 1980; increases the annual rates of interest on unpaid and on repayments of capital transfer tax, so that the rate of interest if the chargeable transfer was made on death is now 9 per cent. and in any other case the rate is 12 per cent.

231. —— settlement—government securities—excluded property

[Finance Act 1975 (c. 7), Sched. 7, para. 3.] In 1976 non-resident trustees of a discretionary settlement purchased " exempt " gilt-edged securities. The trustees then appointed that the income from the securities should be held on trust for non-resident children of the settlor. The trustees claimed that liability for capital transfer tax on the appointment was avoided by the exemption in F.A. 1975, Sched. 7, para. 3. *Held,* allowing the trustees' appeal, that assuming that for the exemption to apply the conditions in para. 3 of Sched. 7 had to be satisfied immediately before the appointment, in this case the requirement was satisfied, as at that time the only objects of the trust were the non-resident children and a charity, and the latter was not a person for whose benefit the settled property might be applied or who might become beneficially entitled to the property: VON ERNST & CIE v. I.R.C., *The Times,* December 6. 1979, C.A.

232. —— —— interest in possession

[Finance Act 1975 (c. 7), Sched. 5, para. 6 (2).]

Where a beneficiary's entitlement to income is able to be defeated by the exercise of trustees of a power to accumulate, he nevertheless has an " interest in possession " for capital transfer tax purposes.

Property was settled upon trust for such of the settlor's children and their issue as the trustees should appoint during the trust period. Subject to any such appointment the trustees had power to accumulate so much of the income as they thought fit during 21 years from the date of the settlement. Subject to the foregoing, the trustees were to hold the trust fund and the income for such of the settlor's children as attained the age of 21 years or married under that age, and if more than one in equal shares. The settlor had three daughters, including F. By February 1974 all three had attained 21 years of age. In March 1976 the trustees made an appointment in favour of F. The Inland Revenue claimed that the appointment created an interest in possession in favour of F, and that, no such interest having previously existed in the settled property, a charge to capital transfer tax arose under F.A. 1975, Sched. 5, para. 6 (2). *Held,* affirming the decision of Fox J., that the interests of the daughters in the trust fund prior to the appointment were interests in possession, so that no liability for capital transfer tax arose. (*Att.-Gen.* v. *Power* [1906] 2 I.R. 272, and *Gartside* v. *I.R.C.* [1968] C.L.Y. 1207 distinguished.)

PEARSON v. I.R.C. [1979] 3 W.L.R. 112, C.A.

233. Double taxation

DOUBLE TAXATION RELIEF (TAXES ON ESTATES OF DECEASED PERSONS AND ON GIFTS) (REPUBLIC OF SOUTH AFRICA) ORDER 1979 (No. 576) [30p], made under the Finance Act 1975 (c. 7), Sched. 7, para. 7; the Double Taxation Convention with the Republic of South Africa which forms the Schedule to the Order applies to death duties and gift taxes. The taxes covered by the Convention are the U.K. capital transfer tax and the South African estate duty and donations tax.

BOOKS AND ARTICLES. See *post,* pp. [2], [14].

CARRIERS

234. Carriage by Air and Road Act 1979 (c. 28)

This Act enables effect to be given to provisions of protocols signed at Montreal on September 25, 1975, and modifies art. 26 (2) of the Warsaw Convention; it also amends certain Acts relating to carriage by air or road.

S. 1 substitutes a new Sched. 1 to the Carriage by Air Act 1961 so as to give effect to protocols Nos. 3 and 4; s. 2 modifies art. 26 (2) of the Warsaw Convention; s. 3 amends certain Acts in consequence of the revision of conventions relating to carriage by air or road; s. 4 replaces gold francs by special drawing rights for the purposes of certain relevant enactments; s. 5 relates to the conversion of special drawing rights into sterling; s. 6 contains supplemental provisions; s. 7 gives the short title.

The Act received the Royal Assent on April 4, 1979, and will come into force on a day to be appointed by Her Majesty in Council.

235. Carriage by road—C.M.R. conditions—limitation of time—jurisdiction

H agreed to manufacture two lathes for P, the contracts being negotiated between H and E, P's agents in Spain. Arrangements for the carriage of the lathes from Birmingham to Madrid were made between E and D, who had dealt together before, the contracts being made informally by telephone without D knowing whether E or ned the lathes or was acting as agents. E also entered into a floating policy with the S Insurance Co., the first declaration being the carriage of the lathes from Birmingham to Madrid by T.I.R. truck. When nearing Madrid, there was an accident to the trailer carrying the lathes, which were badly damaged, but were transferred to another vehicle. On arrival in Madrid, the lathes were rejected by P and sent back to Barcelona without being unloaded. They were then returned to Birmingham, where two new lathes were made and sent out to Spain. It was common ground that the Carriage by Road Act 1965 and the C.M.R. Convention applied. On P's claim for damages, *held*, that (1) in arranging for the carriage of the lathes, E was acting as an ordinary forwarding agent, and the fact that he did not disclose P's name did not prevent P from suing as undisclosed principals; (2) the waybill showed the name and address of P in Madrid as consignee, and the final destination as Madrid; and although the lathes remained in Barcelona for a few hours while D arranged a sub-contract for the carriage on to Madrid, there was only one contract between P and D from Birmingham to Madrid, and the C.M.R. Convention applied to the part of the journey from Barcelona to Madrid; (3) the fact that the lathes were rejected and sent back to Barcelona without being unloaded was one of the circumstances preventing the delivery of the goods at their destination as envisaged by art. 15 of the Convention; accordingly there was no delivery as in art. 32 (1) (*a*) of the Convention, and therefore no relevant period of limitation as provided for by the Convention; (4) alternatively to (3), D knew of the accident; the letters to D from P and S constituted ample evidence of written claims within art. 32 (2) to suspend the Convention limitation period; and since D had not rejected the claims, they failed on the time bar issue; (5) the fact that D had sub-contracted the first stage of the journey from Birmingham did not prevent them from being the carriers from the beginning of the journey, and no problem as to jurisdiction arose. (*Jones* v. *European and General Express Co.* (1920) 4 Ll.L.Rep. 127; *Ulster-Swift and Pigs Marketing Board (Northern Ireland)* v. *Taunton Meat Haulage and Fransen Transport N.V.* [1977] C.L.Y. 2553a applied): Moto Vespa S.A. *v.* MAT (Britannia Express) and Mateu & Mateu S.A. and Vincente Belloch Galvez; Same *v.* Mateu & Mateu S.A. and Vincente Belloch Galvez [1979] 1 Lloyd's Rep. 175, Mocatta J.

236. Carriage by sea. See Shipping and Marine Insurance.

237. Limitation of action—expiry of time—second plaintiff added—Hague Rules. See Balfour Guthrie (Canada) v. Victoria Shipping, § 1667.

Articles. See *post*, p. [14].

CHARITIES

238. Charitable purposes—recreation—promotion of a specific game

[Charities Act 1960 (c. 58), s. 4; Recreational Charities Act 1958 (c. 17), s. 1.]

A trust to encourage association football and other sports is not a trust for charitable purposes.

One of the purposes of the Football Association Youth Trust is to organise or to provide facilities which will enable or encourage pupils of schools or universities in the United Kingdom to play association football, or other games or sports, and thereby to assist in ensuring that due attention is given to the physical education and development of such pupils as well as to the development and occupation of their minds. The Inland Revenue applied for a declaration that the trust was not entitled to be registered as a charity under s. 4 of the Charities Act 1960 on the grounds that this object was not exclusively charitable. *Held* (Bridge L.J. dissenting, dismissing the appeal from the decision of Walton J., that (1) the trust was not for the promotion of " education " in the sense in which that word was used in the law of charities; (2) as the fund could be used to promote certain forms of sport which were not beneficial to the community, the trust could not be classed as charitable under that head; (3) as the fund could be used for promoting forms of sport which were not in the interests of social welfare, it could not be charitable under the Recreational Charities Act 1958, s. 1.

I.R.C. *v.* McMULLEN [1979] 1 W.L.R. 130, C.A.

239. Charity Commissioners' Report

The Charity Commissioners have published their annual report for 1978, commenting that 3,506 charities were registered during the year bringing the total number registered to 129,212. The Report is available from HMSO (H.C. 94) [£1·35].

240. Church school—closure of school—reverter

[School Sites Act 1841 (c. 38), s. 2.]

Where a reverter occurs under s. 2 of the School Sites Act 1841, an equitable interest arises in favour of the original estate interest and the legal estate remains with the successors in title of the persons to whom the original conveyance was made.

H owned part of a piece of land in fee simple and C had a life interest in another part. They both conveyed the land pursuant to the provisions of the School Sites Act 1841 to the rector and churchwardens and their successors on trust. In 1973 the land ceased to be used for such purposes. The representatives of the persons entitled under the reverter provisions of the Act sought the court's determination whether the legal estate reverted automatically to the persons entitled or remained vested in the rector and churchwardens on trust for the persons entitled or on some other and, if so, what trusts. *Held*, as soon as a s. 2 reverter occurred, an equitable interest arose in favour of the original estate interest and the legal estate remained with the successors in title of the persons to whom the original conveyance was made. The legal estate was held in trust for the persons entitled under the reverter provisions who were entitled to a conveyance of the legal estate under s. 3 (3) of the Law of Property Act 1925. (*Att.-Gen.* v. *Shadwell* [1910] 1 Ch. 92; *Att.-Gen.* v. *Price* [1912] 1 Ch. 667; *Re Cawston's Conveyance; Hassard-Short* v. *Cawston* [1940] 1 Ch. 27; and *Re Ingleton Charity, Croft* v. *Att.-Gen.* [1956] C.L.Y. 1049 considered.)

Re CLAYTON'S DEED POLL [1979] 2 All E.R. 1133, Whitford J.

241. Commissioners' scheme

CHARITIES (ARUNDELL STREET FUND, THE CITY OF WESTMINSTER) ORDER 1979 (No. 255) [20p], made under the Charities Act 1960 (c. 58), s. 19 (1); operative on March 21, 1979; gives effect to a scheme relating to a charity consisting of a fund for the widening of Whitcourt Street, Wardour Street or Argyll Place in the City of Westminster.

242. Northern Ireland. See NORTHERN IRELAND.

243. Rating. See RATING AND VALUATION.

244. Rating relief—licensee occupying house owned by charity
[General Rate Act 1967 (c. 9), s. 40 (1).]
In determining for the purpose of rating who is in paramount occupation as between the owner and persons resident in premises, it is necessary to take into account both the degree of control exercised by the owner over the premises and the purpose for which the owner allowed the residence in the premises.

A registered charity, one of whose objects was the giving of assistance to ex-servicemen, allowed a disabled ex-serviceman to occupy one of their houses rent free under the terms of a licence. The licensee was responsible for rates and other charges and undertook to conform to the charity's regulations in respect of occupation. The charity applied for rating relief for the premises but their application was refused. On the charity seeking declarations by originating summons, *held*, granting the declarations, that the charity was in paramount occupation and such occupation was for the purposes of charity. (*Westminster City Council* v. *Southern Railway Co.* [1936] A.C. 511, and *Soldiers, Sailors and Airmen's Families Association* v. *Merton London Borough Council* [1966] C.L.Y. 10256 applied.)

FORCES HELP SOCIETY AND LORD ROBERTS WORKSHOPS *v.* CANTERBURY CITY COUNCIL (1978) 77 L.G.R. 541, Slade J.

245. Scheme for administration
CHARITIES (SACKVILLE COLLEGE EAST GRINSTEAD) ORDER 1979 (No. 284) [30p], made under the Charities Act 1960 (c. 58), s. 19 (1) (2); operative on March 24, 1979; gives effect to a Scheme of the Charity Commissioners for the regulation of Sackville College at East Grinstead, an almshouse charity, together with certain subsidiary charities associated therewith.

246. Street collectors
STREET COLLECTIONS (METROPOLITAN POLICE DISTRICT) REGULATIONS 1979 (No. 1230) [40p], made under the Police, Factories, etc. (Miscellaneous Provisions) Act 1916 (c. 31), s. 5; operative on January 1, 1980; revoke and replace S.R. & O. 1926 No. 848 and S.I. 1963 No. 685; the principal changes relate to the relaxing of certain provisions concerning collections held in connection with a procession, the opening of collecting boxes, the certification of accounts and the publication of details of the collection.

247. Value added tax. See VALUE ADDED TAX.

BOOKS AND ARTICLES. See *post*, pp. [2], [14].

CLUBS AND ASSOCIATIONS

248. Membership—international federation—meaning of "country"—estoppel by representation as to fact
Taiwan is a "country" for the purposes of membership of the International Amateur Athletic Federation.

The International Amateur Athletic Federation, an unincorporated association controlling international amateur athletics, had as it members national associations controlling athletics in their respective countries. Under the association's rules, only one member for each country could be affiliated. The Chinese mainland association was made a member, and later the Taiwan association was also elected to membership. Mainland China protested that Taiwan was not a country, but one of China's provinces, and eventually resigned in protest. The Federation later resolved that the Mainland China association should be recognised as the sole representative for China and Taiwan, with the result that Taiwan was no longer considered a member. The Taiwan association sought declarations that it was and remained a member of the Federation. *Held*, granting the declaration sought, that (1) "country" in the context of the rule was not a political division but a division for the purpose of the control of amateur athletics, and Taiwan was a country within the meaning of the rule; (2) in the alternative, the Federation has elected Taiwan a member, and was estopped from denying the representation of fact that Taiwan was a "country" within the meaning of the rule. (*Harington* v.

Sendall [1903] 1 Ch. 921 and *Re Tobacco Trade Benevolent Association Charitable Trusts* [1958] C.L.Y. 386 considered.)

REEL *v.* HOLDER [1979] 1 W.L.R. 1252, Forbes J.

249. Receiver—husband's interest in club—whether extending to capital or income— receiver's fees as manager

In 1973 a receiver was appointed of a club owned by a husband whose wife was seeking as maintenance the " rents, profits and moneys receivable " in respect of her husband's interest in the club. In 1974 the receiver was also ordered to act as manager of the club. After the club had made a loss, Balcombe J. made a charging order nisi on the premises in respect of the maintenance arrears and held that the 1973 order applied to income only and as there was no profit the receiver's fees could not be paid. On appeal, *held*, allowing the appeal, that the 1973 order did create a receivership over corpus but as this did not extend to the business, the receiver could only claim his receivership fees out of the capital and not his fees as manager: SMITH *v.* SMITH (1979) 123 S.J. 584, C.A.

BOOKS. See *post*, p. [2].

COMMONS

250. Customary rights—quarrying

M granted a lease of seven acres of land to C, who covenanted to con- struct a caravan site there; this C did. S contended that the land was subject to rights of common, and claimed to have rights of grazing, estovers, turbary and pannage. M said that any rights of common had been extinguished by quarrying which had taken place on the land prior to 1926. *Held*, dismissing S's claim, that quarrying, which had taken place on the land for some 200 years up to about 1896, would have extinguished any previously existing prescriptive rights. For the court to hold that such rights existed now, it would have to be shown that such rights had existed not later than 1905; on the evidence, the judge was satisfied that the land was not common land prior to 1926: SYMONDS *v.* MALVERN HILLS DISTRICT COUNCIL (1978) 248 E.G. 238, Great Malvern County Ct., Judge Heron.

251. Open spaces. See OPEN SPACES AND RECREATION GROUNDS.

252. Registration—decisions of the Commons Commissioner

Re BEAFORD MOOR, TORRIDGE, DEVON, Ref. 209/D/149 (the Commissioner *held*, that he could not presume that rights of common—which were the subject of the present dispute—were for the inhabitants of the parish as individuals because as a general rule a right of common exercisable by the inhabitants of a locality or of any other fluctuating and indefinite body of persons is not recognised by law (see *Gateward's Case* (1607) 6 Co.Rep. 59.) But, exceptionally, a right of common may be held on a charitable trust; a trust for the benefit of the inhabitants of a locality is charitable (see *Goodman* v. *Saltash* (1882) 7 A.C. 633).

Re LOWER COW PASTURE, SHUTHONGER COMMON, AND COWHAM, TWYNING, GLOUCESTERSHIRE (No. 2) Ref. 213/D/175–184 (the land comprised in the Register Unit consisted of three acres known as (a) Lower Cow Pasture, (b) Shuthonger Common, and (c) a number of contiguous areas together described as Cowham. The whole of the land was subject to 123 rights known as cow pastures, now owned in varying numbers by second persons, who were held to be entitled to the exclusive right of pasture over the land. A number of applications for registration were made: P applied for registration at Entry No. 2, for 76 cow pastures exercisable over Lower Cow Pasture and most of Cowham, and 36 cow pastures over another part of Cowham called M; B applied for registration at Entry No. 10, to graze 76 cattle or 304 sheep, etc., over Shuthonger Common. Until a few months before the registration at Entry No. 2 was made, P were the owners of 76 cow pastures exercisable over Lower Cow Pasture, Shuthonger Common and Cowham. B then agreed to buy these cow pastures in so far as they were exercisable over Shuthonger Common. The parties executed a conveyance on July 12, 1967, which stated there were conveyed to B 76 rights of pasture over Shuthonger Common. The question to be decided was what, if anything, B acquired by the conveyance, and what remained with P. *Held*, although the 1967 conveyance is worded as a transfer to B of the right to graze 76 cattle over Shuthonger Common, its effect in law was to extinguish the right by merger. A man cannot have a right to take a profit out of his own land as a separate right apart from the ordinary incidents of ownership. The decision in *Johnson* v. *Barnes* (1873) L.R. 8 C.P. 527, would have applied to this case if the owners of the whole of the 123 cow pastures had agreed to release their rights over Shuthonger Common).

Re MILL GREEN, WARGRAVE, BERKSHIRE, Ref. No. 202/D/95–96 (the Commissioner considered whether the land was a " town or village green " within s. 22 (1) of the Commons Registration Act 1965, applying the three limbs of the definition: (1) whether the land is allotted for exercise or recreation; (2) whether it is land subject to a customary right of local inhabitants to indulge in lawful sports or pastimes; and (3) whether such inhabitants have indulged in such sports and pastimes as of right for less than 20 years. *Held*, that (1) there was no evidence of such user; (2) the fact that the land is subject to a tithe is not enough to show it was not a village green, but as the tithe here was at the same rate as other land in the parish, it indicated that the land was not subject to inhabitants' right to use it for sports or pastimes; (3) such sports or pastimes as took place did so through the indulgence of landowners and not as of right).

Re RUSH GREEN, HARLESTON, SUFFOLK Ref. 234/D/84 (it was necessary to consider whether Rush Green was still waste land as defined by Watson B. in *Att.-Gen.* v. *Hanmer* (1858) 27 L.J. Ch. 837, *i.e.* open, uncultivated and unoccupied. Part of the land, referred to as B, was not hedged or fenced in any way. Since 1932 the objectors and their predecessors cut and burnt the grass and trimmed the hedgerows therearound. They used the land to store sugar beet and manure, and also agricultural machinery. In 1968 they grubbed out and filled in the hedge and ditch separating B from an adjoining field and partly drained B. In 1969 they ploughed B and left it fallow for two years, and in 1973 it was again ploughed and subsequently drilled and cropped. Since then B has been left rough and uncultivated. *Held,* what the commissioner had to decide was whether the land is waste land of a manor at the date of the hearing, and not just the state of affairs at the date of registration: see *Central Electricity Generating Board* v. *Clwyd County Council* [1976] C.L.Y. 250. As B was in the occupation of the objectors before 1969, it ceased to be waste land as defined by Watson B. at that time. But more difficult to determine was the legal effect of allowing the land to revert to its present uncultivated condition. The effect of ploughing and cropping B was to convert it from waste land into demesne land of the manor; however, there is no authority stating whether or not demesne land can become waste land. As land which has ceased to be parcel of a manor by severance does not become parcel of the manor again on a subsequent purchase by the Lord of the manor, it follows that waste land of a manor is land which has been waste from time immemorial and does not include land which has gone out of cultivation at a known time. Even if, contrary to the above view, waste land of a manor can re-acquire its status as such, it can only do so if the Lord of the manor abandons his rights over it as demesne land which he acquired by the approvement. Abandonment of a right is necessarily a question of fact; here there is no such evidence of abandonment, which would usually have to be for a period of 20 years).

Re THE GREEN, TITCHMARSH, NORTHAMPTONSHIRE. Ref. 226/D/29–34 (the Commissioner *held* that he had no jurisdiction in these proceedings to determine whether a part of the lands in question were owned by the county council who were the objectors, or by the parish council by whose application the relevant registrations were made, or by anyone else. Nor could he determine whether the land was wholly or partly highway, as was contended by the county council. However, he accepted that on the question whether the land was subject to a customary recreational right, evidence as to highway and as to ownership is relevant to the existence of such a customary right, because as a general rule recreational use is incompatible with highway use, and land owned or reputed to be owned by a parish council is more likely than other land to be subject to a customary recreational right).

Re THE POND BY LITTLE MOSELEY LODGE, HUGHENDEN, BUCKS. Ref. No. 203/D/33 (the Commissioner *held*, that the mere fact that land was allotted in 1862 as a public pond or watering place was not evidence that it was within the s. 22 definition (that common land is " waste land of a manor not subject to rights of common ") of the 1965 Act as at the date of registration, which was in 1969).

253. —— waste land of manor—severance from manor before registration
[Commons Registration Act 1965 (c. 64), ss. 1 (1) (*a*), 22 (1) (*b*).]
Land which has ceased to be connected with a manor before the date of registration does not come within the statutory definition of " waste land of a manor."

Certain land known as Box Hill Common was formerly land of the manor of Box. A local authority provisionally registered the land under the 1965 Act, to which the owner objected. The Commons Commissioner found that the land was severed in 1878, was " open, uncultivated and unoccupied " and refused to confirm the registration. He was overturned on appeal by Foster J., and on the owner's appeal, *held*, allowing the appeal, that on a true construction of ss. 1 (1) (*a*) and 22 (1) " waste land of a manor " could not comprehend land which had ceased to be connected with the manor before the date of registration. (*Re Chewton Common* [1977] C.L.Y. 273 disapproved.)

Re Box HILL COMMON [1979] 2 W.L.R. 177, C.A.

ARTICLES. See *post*, p. [15].

COMPANY LAW

254. Accounts and returns
COMPANIES (ANNUAL RETURN) (AMENDMENT) REGULATIONS 1979 (No. 54) [10p], made under the Companies Act 1948 (c. 38), s. 454 (2) (*b*); operative on February 12, 1979; amend the form of annual return to be made under the 1948 Act by a company having a share capital.

COMPANIES (ACCOUNTS) REGULATIONS 1979 (No. 1618) [10p], made under the Companies Act 1948, s. 454 (1) (4), and the Companies Act 1967 (c. 81), s. 56 (6); operative on December 31, 1979; change certain requirements of the Companies Act as to matters to be stated in a company's accounts, with regard to (1) a company which is neither holding company nor a subsidiary, and (2) any company in connection with employee emoluments.

255. Annual report—1978
The Department of Trade has published its annual report " Companies in 1978," giving details of the administration of the Companies Acts 1948–1976 and of company law reform and harmonisation of EEC company law. The report is available from HMSO [£2·50].

256. Companies Act 1976—commencement
COMPANIES ACT 1976 (COMMENCEMENT No. 6) ORDER 1979 (No. 1544 (C. 36)) [10p], made under the Companies Act 1976 (c. 69), s. 45 (3); brings s. 34 (1) of and Sched. 1 of the 1979 Act, so far as they are not already in operation, into force on November 28, 1979.

257. Companies Court—postal facilities
The following Practice Direction was issued by the Companies Court in October 1979:

1. These directions apply to proceedings in chambers in the High Court in London under the Companies (Winding-up) Rules 1949 and under R.S.C. Ord. 102. They are made with a view to enabling certain formal business in the chambers of the Companies Court Registrar in London to be transacted by post when this is more expeditious, economical or convenient. They will be reviewed from time to time and, in the light of practical experience, may be varied, extended or withdrawn as seen fit. Parties may nevertheless continue to transact such business by personal attendance if they so wish.

2. Definitions:—

" Ord 102 "	—	Ord. 102 of the Rules of the Supreme Court
" The Winding-up Rules "	—	The Companies (Winding-up) Rules 1949
" The Registrar "	—	the Registrar and the companies court registrar as defined in the Winding-up Rules and Ord. 102 respectively.

3. The classes of business which may be transacted by post subject to the general and specific provisions of this Practice Direction are set out in the Schedule hereto.

4. *General Directions*

(1) The use of postal facilities is at the risk of the solicitor or party concerned who should have regard to any material time limits prescribed and should enclose all necessary papers.

(2) Applications for the conduct of business by post must be made by a letter signed by or on behalf of the solicitor for a party or by the party if he is acting in person:

(a) Specifying precisely what the Court is being asked to do.

(b) Enclosing any requisite documents, and

(c) Enclosing an adequately stamped envelope of adequate size properly addressed to the sender for the return of any relevant documents to him.

(3) The letter of application together with any requisite documents must be posted in a prepaid envelope properly addressed to:

> The High Court of Justice,
> Companies Court,
> Registrar's Chambers: Room No. 312,
> Thomas More Building,
> Royal Courts of Justice,
> Strand,
> London WC2A 2LL

If any deficiency is found in or among the necessary documents, a note marked " Please Call " will be sent to the solicitors or litigant in person but the deficiency will not be specified. It will not be possible to enter into correspondence concerning deficiencies.

(4) Applications will be treated as having been made at the date and time of the actual receipt of the requisite documents in the Registrar's Chambers and for this purpose the date and time of despatch will be disregarded.

(5) If an acknowledgment of the receipt of papers is required they must be accompanied by a list setting out the papers in question, sent with a stamped and addressed envelope. The Court will not accept responsibility for papers which are alleged to have been sent to it unless an acknowledgment is produced.

(6) The documents required for the conduct of any business by post will include all those documents which would have been required had the business been conducted by personal attendance.

(7) Any application by post which does not comply with the relevant rules or with this direction will be rejected and, in any other case, the Court may exercise its power to decline to deal with a postal application. If any application is rejected the party making the application will be notified by post and he should then conduct the business in question by personal attendance in the ordinary way.

(8) It is emphasised that any party applying for the issue of proceedings by post will be responsible for the service of all documents requiring to be served under the Rules in the same way as if the proceedings had been issued on personal attendance and that the costs of any adjournment occasioned by non-service of any necessary documents are likely to be awarded against the party responsible.

(9) On making any application by post the proper amount of any Court

fees payable must be enclosed together with a stamped addressed envelope. Any cheque or other draft should be made payable to H.M. Paymaster-General.

   5. *Particular classes of business*
      (1) *The presentation of petitions*
         (a) *Winding-up petitions and petitions under s.* 210 *of the Act*
            A typed copy and at least two additional copies (not carbons) certified by the petitioner or his solicitor to be true copies of the typed copy of the petition should be sent to the Court. To facilitate the verification of petitions within the time limit imposed by the Winding-up Rules the Court will generally accept and file affidavits sworn within seven days before receipt of the petition at the Registrar's Chambers and sent with the petition.
         (b) *Petitions to confirm reduction of capital or to sanction schemes of arrangement*
            A typed copy of the petition and one other copy (not a carbon) certified by the petitioner's solicitor to be a true copy of the typed copy should be sent to the Court together with the appropriate fee and a stamped addressed envelope.
      (2) *The issue of summonses and applications for the restoration or adjournment of summonses*
   In dealing with any postal application for the issue of a summons not being an originating summons requiring an appearance, the proper officer of the Court will allocate an appropriate time and date for the first hearing and will seal and return one copy of the summons for service, if necessary. Any specific requests for a particular date will be considered by the proper officer but there can be no guarantee that they can be met. Generally speaking the first available appointment will be allotted having regard to any time needed for service of the summons, for swearing and filing evidence and for completion of any other necessary formalities. Counsels' appointments at 12 o'clock will not be allotted unless specifically requested.

   Applications for the restoration or adjournment of summonses will be dealt with in similar manner.

   An originating summons requiring an appearance will be sealed and returned to the sender for service.

      (3) *The issue of notices of motion*
   A typed copy and two additional copies of the notice of motion should be sent to the Court together with the appropriate fee payable (if any) and a stamped addressed envelope. The typed copy *must* be signed by the applicant personally or by his solicitors. The proper officer will appoint the date for hearing the motion allowing sufficient time for service if necessary and will seal and return one copy of the notice to the sender.

   6. *Drawing up of orders*
   In future, subject to the exception mentioned below, all orders, whether made by the Judge or Registrar, and whether made in court or in chambers, will, unless otherwise directed, be drafted in the Chambers of the Registrar. It is therefore of the utmost importance that solicitors should ensure that all documents required to enable such orders to be drawn expeditiously (*e.g.* briefs, copy charges, etc.,) are lodged in Chambers as soon as possible after the matter has been heard, particularly in cases where limitations as to time are involved. In the case of any order other than a winding-up order, a copy of the draft order will be sent to the solicitors for the parties, together with an appointment to settle the same. Should the parties be in agreement with the form of the order as drafted they may return the same marked " approved " and the order will be engrossed in that form and the appointment to settle vacated. If any variation in the form of order is desired by any party he must notify all other parties of the variation desired and thereafter all parties must attend on the appointment to settle and discuss the matter with the appropriate official.

   The exceptions referred to above are:—

(a) Orders by the Registrar on the application of the Official Receiver or for which the Treasury Solicitor is responsible under the existing practice.

(b) Orders of the Registrar or the Judge in relation to reductions of capital, share premium account or capital redemption reserve fund or in relation to schemes of arrangement under ss. 206–208 of the Act.

7. This Practice Direction will come into effect on October 15, 1979.

THE SCHEDULE

(1) The presentation of petitions under Ord. 102 and the Winding-up Rules.

(2) The issue of summonses under Ord. 102 and the Winding-up Rules.

(3) The issue of notices of motion under Ord. 102 and the Winding-up Rules.

(4) The issue of third party notices (where leave to issue such notice has been granted) and notices under Winding-up Rule 68.

(5) The filing and lodging of affidavits, exhibits and other documents required to be filed or lodged.

(6) Entry of appearances.

(7) The issue of notices of appointments for the hearing of originating summonses to which an appearance is required.

(8) Fixing appointments for the restoration of adjourned summonses.

(9) Drawing up orders.

(10) The issue of certificates of taxation.

(11) The adjournment of summonses by consent.

(12) Notification that proceedings have been disposed of.

[1979] 1 W.L.R. 1416.

258. —— procedure—functions of chief clerk

The following practice direction was issued by the Companies Court in October 1979:

1. It has been decided that the Chief Clerk of the Companies Court may assist the Registrar in the hearing of the following applications and making orders thereon:

(a) applications by the Official Receiver to consider reports of first meetings of creditors and contributories, to dispense with the submission of statements of affairs and to extend the time for holding first meetings of creditors and contributories;

(b) applications to extend the time for filing affidavits verifying winding-up petitions;

(c) applications to extend the date of hearing of winding-up petitions;

(d) applications for leave to amend proceedings; and

(e) applications for substituted service within the jurisdiction by post only.

2. The evidence (if any) in support of any such application must be lodged in Room 312, Thomas More Building, and will be considered by the Chief Clerk who will deal provisionally with the application. The Registrar will initial the note of any order made before the order takes effect.

3. The Chief Clerk may also without reference to the Registrar—

(a) give leave to file affidavits notwithstanding any irregularity in their form, and

(b) sign certificates of attendances in chambers for the purpose of taxation of costs.

4. Any party may require the application to be heard by the Registrar instead of the Chief Clerk; and when an application has been heard by the Chief Clerk any party dissatisfied with the Chief Clerk's decision may thereupon require the matter to be adjourned to the Registrar who will consider it afresh.

5. Nothing in this Practice Direction will prevent the Registrar from dealing with any of the matters listed above if it is appropriate or convenient for him to do so.

[1979] 1 W.L.R. 1413.

259. Company accounting—Green Paper

In a Green Paper " Company Accounting and Disclosure " the Government has announced new proposals for easing the burden of small firms. This will be done by reducing the amount of financial and accounting information which small companies must disclose under the Companies Acts. The paper is available from HMSO (Cmnd. 7654) [£2·50].

260. **Contracts—non-existent company—whether persons signing contract liable.** See GENERAL MOTORS ACCEPTANCE *v.* WEISMAN, § 42.

261. **Corporation tax.** See CORPORATION TAX.

262. **Directors—breach of statutory duty—liability for cheque**
    [Companies Act 1948 (c. 38). W Ltd., of which the defendant was managing director, owed the plaintiff money. A cheque drawn on the company's account signed by the defendant omitted the " Ltd.," contrary to s. 108 (1) of the Companies Act 1948. The cheque was not met, but the plaintiffs later accepted instalments from W Ltd. till that company defaulted and went into liquidation. The plaintiffs brought an action against the defendant personally relying on s. 108 (4) of the Act and succeeded. The defendant was not, however, a surety for the debt, but liable for breach of statutory duty: BRITISH AIRWAYS BOARD *v.* PARISH (1979) 123 S.J. 319, C.A.

263. —— **complaint of unfair dismissal—whether an employee—jurisdiction of tribunal.** See PARSONS *v.* ALBERT J. PARSONS AND SONS, § 965.

264. —— **indorsement of bills of exchange—liability.** See ROLFE, LUBELL & CO. *v.* KEITH, § 174.

265. **Factoring agreement—payments made to company—conversion by director**
    If a defendant pays into his own bank account cheques which are subject to a trust to hand over to the plaintiff under a factoring agreement, the defendant is liable to the plaintiff for conversion, the damages being measured by the cheques' face value.
    P Co. purchased the book debts of X Co. under a standard factoring agreement. Under the agreement if any payment was made direct to X Co. it was to be held in trust for, and immediately handed to P Co. D, a director, paid four such cheques into X Co.'s bank account. P Co. obtained judgment against D in conversion for the face value of the cheques. On appeal by D, *held*, dismissing the appeal, that the trust gave P Co. the right to sue in conversion, and the face value of the cheques was the measure of damage regardless of whether there was any right to recover the amount from the original debtor. (*Healey* v. *Healey* [1915] 1 K.B. 938 and *Marquess of Bute* v. *Barclays Bank* [1954] C.L.Y. 3422 approved; *Jarvis* v. *Williams* [1955] C.L.Y. 2841 distinguished.)
    INTERNATIONAL FACTORS *v.* RODRIGUEZ [1978] 3 W.L.R. 877, C.A.

266. **Forms**
    COMPANIES (FORMS) (REVOCATION) ORDER 1979 (No. 1545) [10p], made under the Companies Acts 1948 to 1976; operative on December 17, 1979; revokes S.I. 1949 No. 382 as amended.
    COMPANIES (FORMS) (REVOCATION) REGULATIONS 1979 (No. 1546) [10p], made under the Companies Act 1967 (c. 81), ss. 43 (1), 44 (1), 56 (1) (*b*); operative on December 17, 1979; revokes S.I. 1967 No. 1442 which prescribed forms for the purposes of ss. 43, 44 of the 1967 Act.

267. **Insider dealing—consultative document**
    The Government has published a consultative document containing draft clauses as possible amendments to the present Companies Bill. These clauses make insider dealing a criminal offence. The document is available from the Department of Trade (Victoria Street) Library, Room LG37, 1 Victoria Street, London SW1 [60p].

268. **Insolvency—winding up by receiver—power under debenture**
    [Companies Act 1948 (c. 38), Sched. 1, Table A, Pt. 1, art. 80.]
    A receiver has no power to present a petition for winding up as the company's agent, unless the articles confer such a power on the directors; he may, however, have such power under a debenture.
    Per curiam: The practice of directors presenting petitions to wind up insolvent companies in the name of the company but without reference to the shareholders or any specific power in the articles should be discontinued.

A debenture over all the company's assets and undertakings provided that a receiver appointed under the debenture should be the company's agent with power to take possession of the property charged, and to do all other acts and things " incidental or conducive " to any power conferred by the debenture. The company's articles incorporated art. 80 of Table A which provides that the business of the company should be managed by the directors. The company became insolvent and a receiver was appointed under the debenture. The company owned a lease of premises which were unoccupied and in respect of which rates were payable unless the company could claim exemption on the ground that it was subject to a winding-up order. Accordingly, the receiver, as the company's agent, presented a petition for the compulsory winding up of the company on the ground that it was just and equitable to do so. The directors did not oppose the petition, but the shareholders had not approved the winding up in general meeting. *Held,* the receiver had no power to present the petition as the company's agent, since the powers conferred on the directors to manage the company by art. 80 of Table A did not include the power to wind it up; however, the receiver did have such a power under the debenture, since the order would protect the company's assets from depletion through the payment of rates, and protection of assets was " incidental to the power to take possession." Accordingly, an order would be made. (*Smith* v. *Duke of Manchester* (1883) 24 Ch.D. 611 and *Re Galway and Salthill Tramway Co.* [1918] 1 I.R. 62 applied; dictum of Shaw L.J. in *Newhart Developments* v. *Co-operative Commercial Bank* [1978] C.L.Y. 233 explained.)

Re EMMADART [1979] 1 All E.R. 599, Brightman J.

269. Insurance companies. See INSURANCE.

270. Memorandum and articles—objects—whether carrying on a business—tax
[Mal.] [Income Tax Act 1967 (No. 47 of 1967), ss. 4 (a) (d), 43 (1) (a).]
Where a company is incorporated for the purpose of making a profit, any gainful use to which its assets are put prima facie amounts to carrying on a business.

Per curiam: In the case of a private individual the mere receipt of rents from property may well not raise the presumption that he is carrying on a business.
In 1964 a company abandoned the tobacco business after incurring losses, and let a warehouse which had been part of its business premises. In 1967 the remainder of the premises had been let. By 1968 five successive lettings had been made. The company, on being assessed for income tax in respect of the rents, claimed to set off accumulated losses as their rents were derived from a business source. Their claim was disallowed, later upheld by the High Court, and then that decision was reversed by the federal court. On appeal, *held*, allowing the appeal, that (1) rents could constitute income from a business source notwithstanding they were also classified as " rents "; and (2) where a company was incorporated for the purpose of making profits any gainful use of its assets prima facie amounted to the carrying on of a business. (*Commissioner of Income Tax* v. *Hanover Agencies* [1967] C.L.Y. 284 applied.)

AMERICAN LEAF BLENDING CO. SDN. BHD. v. DIRECTOR-GENERAL OF INLAND REVENUE [1978] 3 W.L.R. 985, P.C.

271. Northern Ireland. See NORTHERN IRELAND.

272. Offences—company officer—order for production of books—right of appeal
[Companies Act 1948 (c. 81), s. 441.] The D.P.P. applied for an order under s. 441 of the 1948 Act for production and inspection of books, records, correspondence and papers of a company. The affidavit in support of the application indicated that the company had sent out fraudulent statements making exaggerated monetary claims. *Held,* allowing an appeal against refusal of the order, that (1) a person exercising a function central to the company's administration was an " officer " within s. 441 and the judge had erred in declining jurisdiction on the ground that s. 441 only applied to failure to comply with positive requirements as to management of the company. An appeal therefore lay despite s. 441 (3) which provided that the decision of a judge on an application under s. 441 shall not be appealable: *Re* A COMPANY [1979] Crim.L.R. 650, C.A.

273. Receivers—right of set-off—taxes and " drawbacks "

[Can.] It has been *held*, that where a company owes taxes to the Revenue and also has a right to " drawbacks," namely repayment by the Government of customs duty and excise taxes paid in unrelated transactions, the Government may set off the one debt against the other even where the claim to the drawbacks is made by a receiver appointed to manage the company's affairs by a creditor. A debenture operates as an assignment by way of charge and is therefore ineffective to vest an independent right to the drawbacks in the creditor (*Robbie* v. *Witney Warehouse* [1963] C.L.Y. 390 and *Rother Iron Works* v. *Canterbury Precision Engineers* [1973] C.L.Y. 338 referred to): CLARKSON v. THE QUEEN (1978) 94 D.L.R. (3d) 348, Fed.C.A.

274. —— sale of lands—use of seal

[Eire] [Conveyancing Act 1881 (c. 41), s. 46.] A bank appointed a receiver of a company's assets under a power in a debenture issued by the company to secure payment of moneys advanced by the bank. The conditions of the debenture provided that the receiver would have power to sell the assets and to effect any such sale by deed in the name and on behalf of the company, the receiver to be the attorney of the company to execute, seal and deliver the deed. Under its articles of association the company's seal could be used only by the authority of the directors. A deed of transfer of the company's lands was executed by the company's seal being affixed without the authority of the directors and by the receiver's signature. On an application by the Registrar of Titles the High Court held that the deed of transfer was ineffective. On appeal, *held*, allowing the appeal, that (1) the receiver had no power to use the seal of the company as its articles of association continued in force and bound him; and (2) by reason of the receiver's powers under the debenture and s. 46 of the Conveyancing Act 1881 the execution of the deed by the receiver in his own name was effective to vest the lands in the purchaser: INDUSTRIAL DEVELOPMENT AUTHORITY v. MORAN [1978] I.R. 159, Sup.Ct. of Ireland.

275. Reduction of share account premium—notices of extraordinary general meeting—validity

[Companies Act 1948 (c. 38), s. 141 (2).] An amended resolution, relating to the reduction of a company's share account premium, was passed without opposition. *Held*, the resolution passed differed from that specified in the notices communicated to shareholders, in form and substance. The notices were therefore invalid. The *de minimis* principle is not applicable: *Re* MOORGATE MERCANTILE HOLDINGS (1979) 123 S.J. 551, Slade J.

276. Register

COMPANIES (REGISTERS AND OTHER RECORDS) REGULATIONS 1979 (No. 53) [40p], made under the Stock Exchange (Completion of Bargains) Act 1976 (c. 47), s. 3 (4); operative on February 12, 1979; make provision in respect of registers and other records provided for under the Companies Act 1948–76.

277. —— rectification—breach of exchange control

[Exchange Control Act 1947 (c. 14), s. 8 (1); Companies Act 1948 (c. 38), s. 116 (1) (a) (2).]

An issue of shares in breach of exchange control legislation is wholly void and any registration made pursuant thereto is accordingly invalid.

The applicant company which was wholly owned by a foreign company resident outside the scheduled territories in 1974 issued 200,000 £1 shares to the foreign company in consideration of the transfer to it of sterling investments valued at £200,000 and the foreign company was entered in the register as the holder of those shares. It was not realised until 1977 that exchange control permission should have been obtained for such transaction, whereafter the company applied for rectification of the register by striking out the foreign company's name as holder of the shares. The company obtained exchange control permission for the issue of 50,000 £1 shares to the foreign company and sought that the order for rectification should include approval for its proposal to issue those shares to the foreign company, repaying £150,000 of the original consideration. *Held*, making the order sought, that the register entry was invalid and would be rectified, the foreign company having obtained no title or interest in the 200,000 shares by reason of the breach of s. 8 (1) of the 1947 Act; and that the further order relating to the 50,000 shares was properly ancillary to the rectification and was not approving a disguised reduction of capital, since in law the company's capital had not been increased by the 1974 share issue.

Re TRANSATLANTIC LIFE ASSURANCE CO. [1979] 3 All E.R. 352, Slade J.

278. Shareholders—suit by minority shareholder on behalf of itself and others—action in tort—jurisdiction. See PRUDENTIAL ASSURANCE CO. v. NEWMAN INDUSTRIES, § 2175.

279. Stamp duty. See STAMP DUTIES.

280. Stock Exchange. See STOCK EXCHANGE.

281. Winding up

COMPANIES (WINDING-UP) (AMENDMENT) RULES 1979 (No. 209) [25p], made under the Companies Act 1948 (c. 38), s. 365 (1) and the Insolvency Act 1976 (c. 60), s. 10; operative on April 1, 1979; amend S.I. 1949 No. 330 by removing the requirement that applications in the High Court under s. 343 of the 1948 Act may be heard only by a judge, enabling advertisements of petitions to be confined to the *London Gazette*, by affording guidance as to who may verify the petition by affidavit on behalf of the petitioner, by extending the time for filing affidavits verifying the petition, extending the time for service of notice of applications, by removing the requirement that directions of the court dispensing with proofs of debt may be given only by the judge.

COMPANIES (WINDING-UP) (AMENDMENT No. 2) RULES 1979 (No. 1592) [10p], made under the Companies Act 1948, s. 365 (1); operative on January 1, 1980; amend the Companies (Winding-up) Rules 1949 as necessary to take account of S.I. 1979 No. 1591 which abolishes the use of adhesive stamps for the payment of fees and the separate fee the insertion of notices in the London *Gazette*.

282. —— compulsory liquidation—examination of bank officers—in advance of pending litigation

[Companies Act 1948 (c. 81), s. 268.]

The court will not be predisposed to refuse an order made under s. 268 where the liquidator's object is not to obtain an unfair advantage in proceedings, an advantage unavailable to an ordinary litigant, but to elicit information to assist him in deciding whether to institute proceedings against a third party.

A company, in business as estate developers, belonged to a group of companies depending principally on the parent company for finance. The parent company was in financial difficulties, and the company in January and May 1974 executed legal charges in favour of its bankers (the banks) to secure payment of all future moneys owed by the parent company to the banks. These charges were far in excess of the company's indebtedness to the parent company. The company was wound up and the liquidator began inquiries into the circumstances of the January and May charges, making it clear that he considered the charges possibly fraudulent and taking counsel's opinion on litigation. The banks refused to answer his inquiries and he applied for an order under s. 268 requiring the attendance of bank officials for oral examination. The banks, by notice of motion, asked that the order be discharged as the liquidator had previously decided to issue proceedings and was attempting unfairly to improve his position in those proceedings. *Held,* dismissing the motion, that where the court was satisfied that the liquidator's application was to elicit further information for the purpose of deciding whether to institute proceedings, it would not be predisposed to refuse it as oppressive, for the purpose of s. 268 was to enable the liquidator to complete his function as expeditiously as possible. (*Re North Australian Territory Co.* (1890) 45 Ch.D. 87 and *Re Rolls Razor* [1968] C.L.Y. 463 applied; *Re Bletchley Boat Co.* [1974] C.L.Y. 353 distinguished.)

Re CASTLE NEW HOMES [1979] 2 All E.R. 775, Slade J.

283. —— —— examination of company auditor—in advance of pending litigation

[Companies Act 1948 (c. 81), s. 268.]

Where the court is satisfied that an order made under s. 268 will not be

used in an unfair or oppressive way, but is fairly required to assist a
liquidator in the discharge of his duties, which include deciding whether to
bring an action against anyone, the court will be slow to refuse to grant the
order.

A company collapsed, was compulsorily wound up and a liquidator
appointed. X had commenced proceedings concerning the company when
the liquidator applied under s. 268 to examine B, a partner of the company's
auditors. B moved to discharge the order, on the grounds, *inter alia,* that it
would provide X with information he would not otherwise have, and would
be oppressive where the liquidator was contemplating an action against B.
Held, refusing to discharge the order, that the court would be slow to refuse
an order where no writ had yet been issued and the order was fairly required
to assist the liquidator in the proper discharge of his duties. (*Re Metropolitan
Bank, Heiron's Case* (1880) 15 Ch.D. 139, *Re North Australian Territory Co.*
(1890) 45 Ch.D. 87, and *Re Bletchley Boat Co.* [1974] C.L.Y. 353 distinguished.)
Re SPIRAFLITE (1974) [1979] 2 All E.R. 766, Megarry J.

284. —— corporation tax—sale by liquidator. See *Re* MESCO PROPERTIES, § 372.

285. —— creditor—whether secured—action in rem against ship
[Companies Act 1948 (c. 38), s. 231.] A creditor issued a writ against a
ship owned by a company prior to its going into liquidation and entered a
caveat in proceedings *in rem* commenced by another creditor, neither serving
the writ, nor arresting the ship. Oliver J. held that the creditor did not become
a secured creditor on issue of its writ *in rem.* On appeal, counsel for the
creditors argued not only that the creditors were secured but also that (1) the
court's discretion under s. 231 being unfettered, it should allow a maritime
claimant to continue an action *in rem* after the commencement of a winding
up so as to ensure the priority of maritime claimants; and (2) a claimant who
had issued the writ and entered a caveat before commencement of a winding
up should be allowed to continue his action because he should be treated as
being in the same position as if he had arrested. *Held,* that (1) there was no
reason for equating the date of the creation of the status of a secured creditor
with the date when the Admiralty jurisdiction was " invoked "; the test should
be, whether immediately before presentation of the winding-up petition the
creditor could properly assert as against all the world that the ship was security
against its claim; (2) the discretion given to the court by s. 231 gave the court
freedom to do what was right and fair in the circumstances; (3) an object of
the citation *in rem* was to avoid the need for recurrent arrests. Relief under
s, 231 should not be confined to a claimant who had served a writ on the
ship as distinct from a claimant who had issued a writ but not served it.
Leave to proceed in the action ought to be granted to the creditor under
s. 231 even if the creditor could not be regarded as a secured creditor at the
commencement of the winding up. Appeals allowed: *Re* ARO Co., *The Times,*
November 30, 1979, C.A.

**286. —— disposition of property with intent to defraud creditors—jurisdiction of
Companies Court**
[Law of Property Act 1925 (c. 20), s. 172 (1); R.S.C., Ord. 5, r. 2 (*b*).]
The Companies Court has jurisdiction to grant relief under s. 172 of the
Law of Property Act 1925 on a summons in a liquidation.
Per curiam: The decision will not affect existing practice that third party
proceedings are not normally available in the Companies Court in relation to
a claim against a stranger which does not arise in consequence of the winding-
up.

S Ltd., although trading at a loss, agreed to pay £88,000 to X Ltd. for the
cancellation of an agency contract. One month later S Ltd. was deemed unable
to pay its debts. S Ltd. then agreed to sell Y Ltd. the factory premises at
less than market price. In the winding-up the liquidator sought a declaration
that the two agreements were void, being made with intent to defraud creditors.
The preliminary point was taken that R.S.C., Ord. 5, r. 2 (*b*) required such
actions to be started by writ and the Companies Court had no jurisdiction.
Held, the Companies Court was part of the High Court and so had jurisdiction
to grant relief under s. 172. The provisions of R.S.C., Ord. 5 go not to juris-

diction but to procedure. The court would exercise its discretion and hear the
summonses. (Dicta of Jessel M.R. in *Re Union Bank of Kingston-upon-Hull*
(1880) 13 Ch.D. 808 and of Salter J. in *Re F. & E. Stanton* [1927] All E.R.Rep.
496 applied; *Re Centrifugal Butter Co.* [1913] 1 Ch. 188 distinguished.)
Re SHILENA HOSIERY CO. [1979] 2 All E.R. 6, Brightman J.

287. —— distribution of assets—possible law suit
The court would not order distribution of the company's assets, following
a voluntary liquidation, because it would be unjust on the facts to shut out
possible claimants in a dispute over liability for an air crash where the plane
was powered by the company's engines. Distribution could go ahead provided
the liquidators could obtain insurance cover for the dividend which would
protect the company should it be held liable to pay compensation to the
dependants of those involved. The order dismissing the appeal would not
therefore be drawn up for three weeks to allow time to negotiate insurance:
Re R.-R. REALISATIONS, *The Times*, November 27, 1979, Sir Robert Megarry
V.-C.

288. —— fees
COMPANIES (DEPARTMENT OF TRADE) FEES (AMENDMENT) ORDER 1979
(No. 779) [10p], made under the Companies Act 1948 (c. 38), s. 365 (3)
and the Public Offices Fees Act 1879 (c. 58), ss. 2, 3; operative on July 23,
1979; increases to £5·75 the fee payable for insertion in the *London Gazette*
of notices relating to companies in compulsory winding-up.

289. —— fraudulent trading—foreign company's pending claim—cessation of trading
followed by assets distribution to other creditors
[Companies Act 1948 (c. 38), s. 332 (1).]
Where the only allegation is the bare fact of preferring one creditor to
another it cannot be said that this is *per se* fraudulent within the meaning of
s. 332 of the Companies Act.
The company entered into a contract in 1966 with an Italian company. A
dispute arose between the parties and proceedings were taken out in the Italian
courts and judgment entered against the company in 1973. In 1971 the company had ceased to trade, but being a wholly owned subsidiary of F Ltd.
to which it was heavily indebted, all its assets were sold to F and set off
against its debt. Over the next two years the company's assets were got in and
applied in discharging established debts without taking account of the pending
Italian claim. After voluntary winding up the liquidator received the judgment
of the Italian court and admitted proof of the debt in liquidation. On a
summons by the liquidator seeking a declaration and on the respondent's
summons to strike out the liquidator's summons, *held*, that " carrying on any
business " could include the collection and distribution of assets, but that the
mere preference of one creditor to another did not *per se* constitute fraud.
(*Re Bird, ex p. The Debtor* v. *I.R.C.* [1962] C.L.Y. 169; *Re Lloyd's Furniture
Palace* [1925] Ch. 853 and *Tomkins* v. *Saffery* (1877) 3 App.Cas. 213 applied.)
Re SARFLAX [1979] 2 W.L.R. 202, Oliver J.

290.—— moneys paid under mistake—tracing. See CHASE MANHATTAN BANK *v.*
ISRAEL-BRITISH BANK (LONDON), § 1077.

291. —— petition—opposition by contributory—considerations
[Companies Act 1948 (c. 38), ss. 225 (1), 346 (1).]
Although the court has discretion under ss. 225 (1) and 346 (1) of the Companies Act 1948 to consider the wishes of a contributory on a winding-up
petition, it will normally attach little weight to such considerations in comparison with the wishes of an unpaid creditor.
A creditor of X Co. in the sum of £300,000 petitioned the court to wind up
the company, as X Co. was unable to pay its debts. One contributor, who was a
director, opposed the petition on the grounds that the company's position was
substantially due to the fault of another director, and that without him, X Co.
could recover. He therefore sought an adjournment of the petition, which the
creditor opposed. *Held*, the creditor did not need to concern himself with
internal disputes in the company; the contributory's wishes carried little weight
in comparison with the creditor, and the application would be refused. (Dictum

of Lord Cranworth in *Bowes* v. *Hope Life Insurance and Guarantee Co.* (1865)
11 H.L.Cas. 402 applied; *Re Brighton Hotel Co.* (1868) 6 Eq. 339 distinguished.)
Re CAMBURN PETROLEUM PRODUCTS [1979] 3 All E.R. 297, Slade J.

292. —— **possession order—property in possession of third party**
  [R.S.C., Ord. 45, r. 3 (*a*).]
  Where a company in liquidation has no defence to a landlord's claim for
possession of premises, the court may make an order for possession in the
winding-up proceedings even though third parties are in possession of the
premises.
  L, the landlord, applied for an order for possession of premises leased to
a company in liquidation against the liquidator in winding-up proceedings.
The company had no defence to the claim, but the premises had been let to
third parties. The registrar refused the order on the ground that the third
parties, who had no *locus standi* in the winding-up proceedings might be
prejudiced. On L's motion to vary the order, *held*, allowing the motion, that
the third parties' rights were protected by R.S.C., Ord. 45, r. 3, whereby the
registrar could not give L leave to issue a writ of possession enforcing the order
until notice had been given enabling them to apply for relief against forfeiture.
The order for possession would accordingly be made. (*General Share and Trust
Co.* v. *Wetley Brick and Pottery Co.* (1882) 20 Ch.D. 260 applied.)
  Re BLUE JEANS SALES [1979] 1 All E.R. 641, Oliver J.

293. —— **views of creditors—whether unfettered discretion**
  [Companies Act 1948 (c. 38), ss. 222, 346 (1).]
  A judge's discretion whether to grant a winding-up order or not is unfettered,
and although the views of the majority creditors in value should be considered,
they cannot be the decisive factor.
  The petitioning creditor company placed its wholly owned subsidiary in a
creditors' voluntary liquidation. It then presented a winding-up petition for
compulsory liquidation, on the grounds that the company's assets could thereby
be more expeditiously and economically realised. The petition was supported
by another company from the same group. The petition was opposed by seven
independent creditors who were together the minority creditors in value, who
wished to continue with the voluntary liquidation. The judge at first instance
dismissed the petition in the exercise of his discretion. On appeal by the
petitioning creditor, *held*, dismissing the appeal, that the judge's discretion was
unfettered under ss. 222 and 346 (1) of the Companies Act 1948 whether to
grant a compulsory winding-up order or not. Although the views of the
majority creditors in value was a factor to be considered, this could not be
the decisive factor, otherwise that would constitute a fetter on the judge's
discretion. (Decision of Brightman J. affirmed.)
  Re SOUTHARD & Co. [1979] 1 W.L.R. 1198, C.A.

  BOOKS AND ARTICLES. See *post*, pp. [2], [15].

COMPULSORY PURCHASE

294. Acquisition of land
  ACQUISITION OF LAND (RATE OF INTEREST AFTER ENTRY) (SCOTLAND) REGU-
LATIONS 1979 (No. 615) [10p], made under the Land Compensation (Scotland)
Act 1963 (c. 51), s. 40 (1); operative on July 5, 1979; decrease from 14 per cent.
to 13 per cent. per annum the rate of interest payable where entry is made,
before payment of compensation, on land in Scotland which is being purchased
compulsorily.
  ACQUISITION OF LAND (RATE OF INTEREST AFTER ENTRY) REGULATIONS 1979
(No. 616) [10p], made under the Land Compensation Act 1961 (c. 33), s. 32 (1);
operative on July 5, 1979; decrease from 14 per cent. to 13 per cent. per annum
the rate of interest payable where entry is made, before the payment of compensation, on land in England and Wales which is being purchased compulsorily.
  ACQUISITION OF LAND (RATE OF INTEREST AFTER ENTRY) (SCOTLAND) (NO. 2)
REGULATIONS 1979 (No. 1165) [10p], made under the Land Compensation
(Scotland) Act 1963, s. 40 (1); operative on October 16, 1979; increase
from 13 to 14 per cent. per annum, the rate of interest payable where entry

is made, before payment of compensation, on land in Scotland which is being compulsorily purchased.

ACQUISITION OF LAND (RATE OF INTEREST AFTER ENTRY) (No. 2) REGULATIONS 1979 (No. 1166) [10p], made under the Land Compensation Act 1961, s. 32 (1); operative on October 16, 1979; increase from 13 to 14 per cent. per annum, in respect of any period after the coming into operation of these Regulations, the rate of interest payable where entry is made, before payment of compensation, on land being compulsorily purchased.

ACQUISITION OF LAND (RATE OF INTEREST AFTER ENTRY) (SCOTLAND) (No. 3) REGULATIONS 1979 (No. 1742) [10p], made under the Land Compensation (Scotland) Act 1963, s. 40 (1); operative on January 25, 1980; increase to 17 per cent. the rate of interest payable where entry is made, before payment of compensation on land in Scotland which is being purchased compulsorily.

ACQUISITION OF LAND (RATE OF INTEREST AFTER ENTRY) (No. 3) REGULA-TIONS 1979 (No. 1743) [10p], made under the Land Compensation Act 1961, s. 32 (1); operative on January 25, 1980; increase to 17 per cent. the rate of interest payable where entry is made, before payment of compensation, on land in England and Wales which is being purchased compulsorily.

295. —— " any house or other building "—churchyard and outbuildings
[Land Clauses Consolidation Act 1845 (c. 18), s. 92.]
A substantial place of worship is within the expression " any house or other building " as used in the Land Clauses Consolidation Act.

D owned land on which stood a large church, a hall, two small outbuildings and a car park. This land adjoined P's bus depot. The church land was held on charitable trusts and managed as a single unit. P wished to enlarge its bus garage and served a notice for the compulsory purchase of the hall, two small outbuildings and car park on D's land. D wanted P to take the whole property and not just the parts included in the order. P sought a declaration that the church was not a " house or other building " and that D was not entitled to require P to take more land than was comprised in the order. *Held*, a substantial place of worship was within the expression " any house or other building " and even assuming that the church was not a house but was another building the remaining land was an integral part of the whole of D's property. P was not entitled to the declaration sought. (*Richards* v. *Swansea Improvement and Tramways Co.* (1878) 9 Ch.D. 425 applied; *Barnes* v. *Southsea Rly. Co.* (1884) 27 Ch.D. 536 distinguished.)

LONDON TRANSPORT EXECUTIVE *v.* CONGREGATIONAL UNION OF ENGLAND AND WALES (INC.) (1979) 37 P. & C.R. 155, Goulding J.

296. Coal mines. See MINING LAW.

297. Compensation—certificate of appropriate alternative development—date of certificate
[Land Compensation Act 1961 (c. 33), ss. 17 (4), 18, 22 (2).]
In assessing compensation for compulsory purchase, the application of the relevant planning policies should as nearly as possible coincide with the date of the assessment of compensation.

Per curiam: Browne J. and Lord Denning M.R. are in error in *Jelson* v. *Minister of Housing and Local Government* [1969] C.L.Y. 3480. The first circumstance amounting to a proposal to acquire is not the service of a notice to treat but notice of the making of a compulsory purchase order.

The respondent local authority offered to purchase a site owned by the applicants. When applying for a certificate of appropriate alternative develop-ment, the applicants specified residential development as being the expected development of the existing site, but the local authority issued a certificate specifying only an open form of development. An appeal by the applicants was dismissed. In the decision letter it was stated that the date of the written offer to purchase was the relevant date and that publications or matters arising after that date would be disregarded. A second case raised a similar point and they were argued together. In the first case it was also argued that the Minister's decision was obscure and contradictory. *Held*, allowing the applica-tions, that (1) in assessing compensation for compulsory purchase the application of the relevant planning policies should as nearly as possible coincide with the date of the assessment. The Minister should have had regard to the planning policies at the time of his decision and had misdirected himself in holding that he should not do so; (2) there had been no obscurity or contradiction in the reasons given by the Minister in his decision in the first case. (Dictum of Lord Macnaghten in *Bwllfa and Merthyr Dare Steam Collieries* (1891) v. *Pontypridd Waterworks Co.* [1903] A.C. 426 and *Birmingham Corporation* v. *West Midland Baptist (Trust) Association (Inc.)* [1969] C.L.Y. 433 applied; *Jelson* v. *Minister of Housing and Local Government* [1969] C.L.Y. 3480 distinguished.)

ROBERT HITCHINS BUILDERS *v.* SECRETARY OF STATE FOR THE ENVIRONMENT; WAKELEY BROTHERS (RAINHAM, KENT) *v.* SECRETARY OF STATE FOR THE ENVIRONMENT (1979) 37 P. & C.R. 140, Sir Douglas Frank Q.C.

298. —— **disturbance—bank interest and charges—whether allowable**
Bank charges and interest incurred in producing new premises are part of the purchase price. They cannot therefore be claimed as a separate head of compensation.

P Co. agreed to sell their factory to the D council under a notional compulsory acquisition. P Co. could not find ready-built new premises so they built a new factory themselves. The enterprise was financed by P Co.'s bank. Building took nearly a year. P Co. claimed £4,285 compensation for bank interest and charges incurred in financing the capital progressively laid out. The lands tribunal found for P Co. On appeal, *held*, allowing the appeal that there was a rebuttable presumption that the purchase price paid for new premises was something for which a claimant had received value for money. Bank charges and interest were part of that price, and P Co. must be presumed to have received value for money. The lands tribunal should not have regarded it as a separate item for compensation.

SERVICE WELDING *v.* TYNE AND WEAR COUNTY COUNCIL (1979) 38 P. & C.R. 352, C.A.

299. —— —— **cost of resettlement**
JB's head office was moved, upon acquisition, to new premises and JB claimed, *inter alia*, £375,000 compensation for increased costs of operating the new premises. The Lands Tribunal rejected this head of claim. *Held*, dismissing JB's appeal, three questions are to be asked: (1) can it ever be right to award a sum for increased operating costs? (2) if so, in what circumstances? (3) do those circumstances exist here? The answer to (1) was yes. The answer to (2) was yes if it could be shown that the applicant had no option but to incur the increased costs and had received no benefit as a result of them. As to (3), in the present case, although JB had had no alternative but to incur the extra expenses it had benefited from the expenditure and was thus not entitled to compensation: J. BIBBY AND SONS *v.* MERSEYSIDE COUNTY COUNCIL (1979) 251 E.G. 757, C.A.

300. —— **loss of profits—road closure**
[Public Health Act 1936 (c. 49), s. 278; Arbitration Act 1950 (c. 27), s. 26.]
The plaintiff claimed £2,500 by specially indorsed writ for compensation awarded to him by an arbitrator appointed under the 1936 Act for loss of profits occasioned by the closure of roads around his motor repair garage in Brixton, London S.W.9 in 1975–76. The defendants argued that the plaintiff could or should have proceeded to apply for leave to enforce the award under the 1950 Act and R.S.C., Ord. 73. It was further argued that a claim for loss of profits in the absence of total closure of the business was not a competent award in the circumstances. *Held*, the method of enforcement was valid (general remarks on arbitration as to liability and quantum: *Lingke* v. *Christchurch Corporation* [1912] 3 K.B. 595 applied). Loss of profits was an appropriate claim. The claim would have been good against a private individual according to the test in *Lingke* at p. 604 and in *Harper* v. *G. N. Hayden & Sons* [1933] 1 Ch. 298. £2,500 awarded: LEONIDIS *v.* THAMES WATER AUTHORITY (1979) 251 E.G. 669, Parker J.

301. —— —— **whether compensation to be reduced by amount of possible tax**
[Land Compensation Act 1961 (c. 33), s. 5 (6); Finance Act 1969 (c. 32), Sched. 19, para. 11.]
Where the capital and income elements of compensation for compulsory acquisition are apportioned so that the Crown is entitled to levy tax on that

part of the sum apportioned as loss of profits, the company is entitled to the gross sum in compensation without deduction for tax.

A council, in pursuit of a compulsory purchase order, made an agreement with the company to pay certain compensation. A gross figure was agreed reflecting a small apportionment for capital compensation, and a much larger figure in respect of loss of profits. The council contended that the sum should be paid less tax. No assurance had been given by the Crown that corporation tax would not be levied. *Held*, the effect of the 1969 Finance Act was to allow compensation for loss of profits to be treated as a trading receipt and liable to tax. The company was therefore entitled to receive the gross sum in compensation. (*West Suffolk County Council* v. *W. Rought* [1956] C.L.Y. 1275 distinguished.)

STOKE-ON-TRENT CITY COUNCIL v. WOOD MITCHELL & Co. [1979] 2 All E.R. 65, C.A.

302. —— notice of claim—quantification of claim—authority's right to withdraw notice to treat

[Land Compensation Act 1961 (c. 33), ss. 4, 5 (5), 31.] The plaintiff trustees took out a construction summons to determine whether their notice of claim under the Compulsory Purchase Act 1965 in answer to the acquiring authority's notice to treat was valid in view of the requirements of s. 4 of the 1961 Act. If the notice of claim was ineffective the authority now wished to withdraw the notice to treat under s. 31. The notice of claim did not quantify in figures the amount of the claim. Since the claim was based on the cost of equivalent reinstatement under s. 5 (5) the assessment would be on the basis of actual future rebuilding cost: the plaintiffs therefore argued that Parliament could not have intended to demand the inclusion of a notional figure. *Held*, dismissing the summons, the notice of claim was bad and the authority was entitled to withdraw the notice to treat. S. 4 required, *inter alia*, the amount claimed to be inserted in the notice of claim. Such a demand was not so manifestly anomalous as to allow of avoidance. Other statutory rights, such as claims on disturbance, required similar provisional assessment and, in any event, a figure in the notice of claim could be amended later so long as one appeared in the original form. (*Birmingham Corporation* v. *West Midland Baptist* (*Trust*) *Association Inc.* [1969] C.L.Y. 433 and *Stock* v. *Frank Jones* (*Tipton*) [1978] C.L.Y. 1167 considered): TRUSTEES FOR METHODIST CHURCH PURPOSES v. NORTH TYNESIDE METROPOLITAN BOROUGH COUNCIL (1979) 250 E.G. 647, Browne-Wilkinson J.

303. —— Pointe Gourde—scheme underlying acquisition—whether acquiring authority's own scheme

In 1965, the respondent embarked on a campaign to develop land next to B's for industrial purposes. In 1966 they began talks with the County Council. In 1968 the County Council produced its own plans, which involved the acquisition of B's land, and also resolved to discuss with the respondents the extent of the latter's involvement in this. Meanwhile, the respondents decided to acquire B's land and annex it to the adjoining area; they made a compulsory purchase order in July 1969. In August 1969 the County Council published a list of sites, including B's land (or " Scheme 3 "), where it would support development. B claimed that his land was being acquired under the respondents' scheme alone, and that Scheme 3 was a scheme by an authority other than the acquiring authority; accordingly, he was entitled to benefit from the increase in value of his property attributable to the County Council's scheme. *Held*, dismissing his appeal, although Scheme 3 had originally in form been a scheme by an authority other than the acquiring authority, which had had a scheme of its own, Scheme 3 had by merger become one to which the acquiring authority was a party, and this merger, having happened before the date of the compulsory purchase order was valid (decision of Lands Tribunal [1977] C.L.Y. 326, upheld; *Wilson* v. *Liverpool Corporation* [1971] C.L.Y. 8984 applied): BIRD v. WAKEFIELD METROPOLITAN DISTRICT COUNCIL (1978) 248 E.G. 499, C.A.

304. —— provision in deed relating to land—whether compensation payable for effect on other land

BR owned a plot of land (" the red land ") lying along the north side of a plot of land of BI's (" the blue land "). In March 1973, BG approved the draft of a deed that would grant BG the right to use a strip of land along the south side of the red land, for laying gas pipes. In April, BI contracted to buy the red land from BR. In May, the deed of grant was executed, giving BG an easement over the red land. In June the red land was conveyed to BI. Because of the lie of the land, it was essential to have access over the blue land to make full use of the red land. In November 1973 BI got planning permission to erect warehouses and offices partly on the red and partly on the blue land. BI were prevented from putting up the buildings by the terms of the May 1973 deed. Cl. 6 (1) of the deed provided for compensation in such an event, but in that clause there was no reference to the blue land. BI claimed to be entitled to compensation for damage to their interest in both the red and the blue land. The Court of Appeal found that BI were not entitled to compensation for damage to their interest in the blue land. BI appealed. *Held*, allowing the appeal, it was not possible to construe cl. 6 as conferring on BR or BI a right to compensation for injurious affection of the blue land; compensation was therefore to be assessed on the basis of the effect on the red land. This land had, however, " a quality " which made it specially suitable for the purpose of a particular purchaser, *i.e.* for the purpose of a joint development with the blue land. The value of the red land to BI as owners of the blue land should be taken into account although they were the only purchaser of it able to realise its full potentiality. R. 3 in s. 5 of the Land Compensation Act 1961 did not apply as it could not be said on the evidence that there was no market apart from the special needs of the particular purchaser: BLANDRENT INVESTMENT DEVELOPMENTS *v.* BRITISH GAS CORP. (1979) 252 E.G. 269, H.L.

305. Inquiry—failure to consider alternative scheme—whether decision should be quashed

A public inquiry was held into objections to a compulsory purchase order under the Housing Act 1957. The Secretary of State in confirming the order failed to deal with one of the objector's alternative schemes for the houses. The question arose on application to quash the decision whether any reasonable Secretary of State could have regarded the point as insubstantial. *Held*, the matter had been put forward seriously by the applicant and had been dealt with in the closing submissions of the council. Decision quashed: LONDON WELSH ASSOCIATION *v.* SECRETARY OF STATE FOR THE ENVIRONMENT AND CAMDEN LONDON BOROUGH [1979] J.P.L. 464, Forbes J.

306. Lands Tribunal decisions

APPLEBY & IRELAND *v.* HAMPSHIRE COUNTY COUNCIL (Ref./273/1976) (1978) 247 E.G. 1183 (in 1973 A & I's premises in Basingstoke were required for redevelopment, and in 1974 the company moved to Alton, some 12 miles away, on a reduced scale. The company claimed that the measure of compensation was the loss sustained on the actual move to Alton, and the authority that it was limited to the loss that would have been sustained if the company had instead relocated itself within Basingstoke in 1973. The latter would have resulted in a much smaller loss; the two questions to be asked in determining whether the company's action was reasonable were (1) when the company agreed to give up possession, was it able to find within Basingstoke alternative accommodation that (a) could be made suitable for its special needs; (b) would be available in time for the company's agreed date of leaving its former premises; (c) was available on reasonable terms; (2) did the company have sufficient finance readily at hand to enable such a move to be made? *Held*, (1) yes: inaction by the company had resulted in its having to move to Alton rather than elsewhere in Basingstoke; (2) yes. If in March 1973 a realistic claim on a removals basis had been submitted, the company would have been provided with enough money. The company was awarded £131,000 as against its claim for £159,450, the difference of £28,450 being attributed to the unnecessary removal to Alton).

BASTED *v.* SUFFOLK COUNTY COUNCIL (Ref./170/1978) (1979) 251 E.G. 1289 (claim for value of terraced house in Lowestoft divided into two self-contained flats. Claimant bought in 1968 for £2,000 and spent £500 on decorations. He claimed two and a half times increase in property values 1968–1979. The authority produced local comparables. Claimant asked £6,250, the authority £2,750. *Held*, there was no support for claimant's figures. There was an albeit limited market for tenanted like properties within r. (2) of s. 5 of the Land Compensation Act 1961. Authority's figure upheld).

BISHOP (TRADING AS GUTTERIDGE SHOE REPAIRERS) *v.* ROYAL BOROUGH OF KINGSTON-UPON-THAMES (Ref. 167/1977) (1979) 3 P. & C.R. 308 (the sole point at issue was the compensation for loss of goodwill. The valuation was agreed to be £1,000 but B claimed this figure had been depreciated by the scheme underlying the acquisition. The authority maintained it was B's own actions which had depreciated the goodwill. *Held*, compensation of £1,000 should be awarded since it was B's decision to buy another business elsewhere and not the scheme underlying the development which had caused the drop in profits).

COURAGE *v.* KINGSWOOD DISTRICT COUNCIL (Ref./108/1977) (1978) 247 E.G. 307 (compulsory purchase order made in 1970, confirmed 1971. A notice to treat was served on April 28, 1972, together with a notice of entry, giving notice to enter and take possession within 14 days. C had padlocked the gate to the property to keep out the public. In July 1972 K's workmen entered the property, cleared a large area of it, erected a shed, and dug five trial bores. In February 1973, C sent K the key to the padlock. K said compensation should be assessed as at July 1972, when they took possession. C said that K had not taken possession until C had sent them the key. *Held*, "take possession" means or includes the doing of acts only consistent with ownership or the right to ownership; what K did in July 1972 was, having served notice of entry, to enter and carry out works preparatory to building of houses. This was only consistent with having taken possession, not with mere entry. Compensation was therefore assessed as at July 1972).

DICCONSON HOLDINGS *v.* ST. HELENS METROPOLITAN BOROUGH (Ref. 129/1977) (1979) 249 E.G. 1075 and 1178 (the claimant company served a purchase notice on the acquiring authority as to an area of 0·488 acre behind which was a considerable area of agricultural land. The claimant argued that the reference land was a golden strip or key to the farmland if planning permission were granted for its development. A number of planning applications had been refused as to the farmland and the authority argued that permission was unlikely to be granted and that the reference land was not suitable as access for prospective development. *Held*, on reference, that the compensation payable would be £25,000, allowing £7,000 as the price a speculator would pay for the chance of development. The reference land would provide a suitable access and a reasonably-minded speculator would expect planning permission to be granted as to the locked farmland in seven or eight years).

EASTON *v.* NEWCASTLE-UPON-TYNE METROPOLITAN BOROUGH COUNCIL (Ref. 21/1978) (1979) 250 E.G. 165 (on reference as to the amount of compensation payable on compulsory purchase of a lock-up shop in Newcastle-upon-Tyne in 1972, *held*, that (1) the compensation for the extinguishment of the business would be the claimant's figure of net profits of £1,698 with the authority's suggested multiplier of two years' purchase, the claimant having contended for three and a half; (2) £15 accounting fees should be payable to the claimant; (3) the new scale 5 surveyors' charges of the R.I.C.S., estimated at £160, should be awarded to the claimant rather than the suggested figure of £511·30).

EBADAT ALI *v.* NOTTINGHAM CITY COUNCIL (Ref. No. 65/1978) (1979) 38 P. & C.R. 229 (notice to treat was served on a house unfit for human habitation. The question arose whether the owner-occupier's supplement was payable under Sched. 5 to the Housing Act 1969. The council contended that the tribunal lacked jurisdiction. *Held*, the court could not substitute its own opinion for that of the authority unless the authority had acted unreasonably. In this case there was evidence that the owner had not made all reasonable inquiries, that the council had therefore not acted unreasonably and the tribunal had no jurisdiction).

FREDERICK POWELL & SON *v.* DEVON COUNTY COUNCIL (Ref./293/1977) (1979) 250 E.G. 659 (the acquiring authority required 1·6 acres of a six-acre plot on which the claimant planned to built 105 dwellings. As a result of acquisition only 76 houses could be built. Claim for injurious affection to the remaining land on basis of increased proportionate cost of overheads. *Held*, although the acquisition denied the claimant the development of the subject land at lower costs than the retained land the inability to continue to average costs over the whole six acres did not depreciate the retained land. No injurious affection).

HEARTS OF OAK BENEFIT SOCIETY v. LEWISHAM BOROUGH COUNCIL (Ref. 116/1977) (1979) 249 E.G. 967 (a society owned the freehold interest in eight houses, the compensation payable on compulsory purchase being agreed at £500 in one instance and at large as to the rest. The society claimant sought a figure of £8,100 for all eight houses and the acquiring authority £4,350. The agreed date of valuation was May 21, 1973. The value of the ground rents as to the seven houses in dispute was agreed to be £3,850. The claimant sought to add to that figure some £3,750 being half the estimated marriage value to the head leaseholders on a hypothetical purchase by them. *Held*, there was a " very large " marriage value in this instance but there was no reason for concluding that the head leaseholders would always be interested in purchasing. A special allowance should be made for the marriage value and a figure of £5,500 compensation be ordered for all eight houses).

HOVERINGHAM GRAVELS v. CHILTERN DISTRICT COUNCIL (Ref./7/1974) (1979) 252 E.G. 815 (HG owned two and a half acres in Chesham, Bucks. This was acquired in two parts (" front " and " back ") by different authorities. The Court of Appeal remitted the matter to the Tribunal for quantification of the amount which HG had suffered as owner of the front land by severance of the back land. HG claimed that compensation should be assessed as at the date of the present appeal. *Held*, it was wrong to extend the appropriate date merely because of an appeal; this could affect decisions as to whether or not to appeal and could lead to anomalies. £21,265 would be awarded. If the Tribunal had erred in law as to the date of assessment it would have fixed additional loss on severance at £36,605).

LAING HOMES v. EASTLEIGH BOROUGH COUNCIL (Ref. 176/1977) (1979) 250 E.G. 350 and 459 (the claimant LH Ltd. bought 3·4 acres (the reference land in 1972 as the apparent key to some 85 acres (the development land). The acquiring authority wished a spine road to run through both areas. Having failed to acquire the development land, LH transferred that part of the reference land required for the road to the authority on March 4, 1977, the valuation date. LH claimed £1m. compensation: the authority offered £1. *Held*, rejecting both valuations, compensation of £12,750 to be awarded. By the valuation date there was no realistic permanent alternative to building the spine road across the reference land. But by reason of three agreements between the authority and the developer of the development land the potential development value thereof had already been released: the reference land was not an access key. Insofar as it had special suitability value that too should be disregarded under s. 5 (3). However there was no evidence that the reference land could not be developed in the absence of the spine road and accordingly no betterment under s. 7. The reference land would have had some development value and there was no inference that LH would have had to build its share of the spine road. Therefore there had to be more than nominal compensation. Accepting the authority's figure of £25,000 per acre development value, compensation would show a 25 per cent. deduction for the ransom value cost of the access (*Lambe* v. *Secretary of State for War* [1955] C.L.Y. 382 followed; *Pointe Gourde Quarrying and Transport Co.* v. *Sub-Intendent of Crown Lands* (1947) C.L.C. 1433 considered).

MIT SINGH v. DERBY CITY COUNCIL (Ref. No. 161/1977) (1978) 37 P. & C.R. 527 (reference was to determine the compensation payable upon the compulsory purchase of the claimant's freehold interest in a house in Derby. The parties had agreed the values of the freehold, disturbance, and the owner-occupier supplement, if payable. The question arose of jurisdiction of the tribunal, and the authority contended that the owner-occupier supplement was not payable. *Held*, (1) the tribunal had jurisdiction because the agreement was conditional; (2) the owner-occupier supplement was not payable because the tenant had real control during the qualifying period as he had a tenancy of the whole house. The claimant had not occupied the house although his son had slept in the back bedroom).

NOLAN v. SHEFFIELD METROPOLITAN DISTRICT COUNCIL (Ref./256/1977) (1979) 251 E.G. 1179 (claim for disturbance compensation by tenant rehoused by council after acquisition of house in housing action area: Land Compensation Act 1973, s. 38 (1) (*a*). Meaning of "reasonable expenses in removing." No English authority: Tribunal considered *Glasgow Corporation* v. *Anderson* [1976] C.L.Y. 295. Compensation of £219 awarded. Items allowed: materials for minor repairs to and redecoration of new home, loss (by theft) of rose bushes and kitchen table, loss of wages. Items disallowed: new wall cupboards and fireplace surrounds to provide comparable facilities, loss of fishpond, claimant's time in removing, new carpets and fitting, rent during repair period. Test is whether payment is in a true sense a " disturbance payment " and not mere cost of removal operation).

PANCHAL v. PRESTON BOROUGH COUNCIL (Ref. 53/1978) (1978) 247 E.G. 817 (the claimant purchased and went to live at 8, Salmon Street, Preston in 1965. On March 1, 1972, the Council's clearing programme was published, and showed the premises as scheduled for clearance in 1974. In January 1974 the claimant was advised by one of the Council's officers that he should remain in occupation of the premises in order to qualify for the owner-occupier supplement. Consequently, when he and his family bought another property on February 5, 1974, and moved there, he left some items of furniture behind, and up until the expiry of the two-year period ending April 5, 1974, he slept there for a few nights at a time, although there was a three-week period when he did not, through illness. *Held,* he was in occupation during the relevant period, and during the three-week absence he continued to occupy it, as if he were in hospital, or on holiday. Accordingly, to the site value of £180 would be added an owner-occupier's supplement of £1,799·89).

RAKUSEN PROPERTIES; RAKUSEN GROUP; LLOYD RAKUSEN AND SON v. LEEDS CITY COUNCIL (Ref. 289/1977) [1979] J.P.L. 36 (a property company which was part of a group conducted as a single unit, served a purchase notice on the ground that the premises had become incapable of reasonably beneficial use in their existing state. A trading company, part of the group, carried on business there. The purchase notice was confirmed. A fire occurred and insurance moneys were received. The claimants did not expend these on reinstating the factory on account of the purchase notice. The question arose whether the claimants were entitled to compensation for disturbance. *Held,* the company was not entitled to compensation for disturbance because (1) the trading loss since the fire was not the result of the confirmation of the purchase note. The acquiring authority was not in possession and the trading company had freely decided not to rebuild; (2) the claimants would not have resumed profitable production after the fire since it was the refusal of planning permission rendering the premises incapable of reasonably beneficial use which had resulted in service of the purchase notice).

RATHGAR PROPERTY CO. v. HARINGEY LONDON BOROUGH; MERRIDALE MOTORS v. SAME (Ref. 180–181/1976) (1977) 248 E.G. 693 (amount of compensation payable for 0·02 acres of land in Haringey, North London, acquired as access to a three-acre site developed by the acquiring authority. This was not the only possible access, though it was the most desirable, to the site. As the claimants did not have monopoly of access to the site, their claim for 50 per cent. of the increase in the three-acre site's value was dismissed. Under r. (3) of s. 5 of the Land Compensation Act 1961 the subject land has special suitability as an access to the three-acre site for development purposes, but that purpose was not one to which the subject land could only be applied in pursuance of statutory powers, since it was a purpose to which the land could be put irrespective of the ownership for the time being of the three-acre site. *Held,* compensation of £19,000 between the two claimants, being the cost of each alternative access).

SADIK AND SADIK v. LONDON BOROUGH OF HARINGEY (Ref. 51/1977) (1978) 37 P. & C.R. 120 (claimants used the services of an interpreter and translator during negotiations for compulsory purchase. The tribunal *held,* that in this case it was proper to award £254 towards the cost of interpreting services, as compensation).

SHARIF v. BIRMINGHAM CITY COUNCIL (Ref./164/1977) 249 E.G. 147 (under-leasehold interest in three-storey terraced house in Birmingham, with six months and three weeks left to run. It had the benefit of a valid notice to en-franchise under the Leasehold Reform Act. The freehold value and the cost of enfranchisement were agreed at £2,500 and £625 respectively, but the acquiring authority claimed to be able to deduct from the resulting £1,875 (1) surveyors' and legal fees of £125, (2) contingency allowances of £187, and (3) £250 for the time and trouble of enfranchisement. Held, (1) should be deducted, since S would not have to incur these expenses on enfranchisement, but (2) and (3) would not be allowed, as there was no evidence that this would have been any-thing but a very straightforward enfranchisement. £1,750 would be awarded, plus £94 and £75 for disturbance to the two claimants).

SMITH v. LEWISHAM LONDON BOROUGH (Ref. 122/1978) (1979) 250 E.G. 1090 (in a claim for disturbance arising from the acquisition of a house in Deptford, the tribunal allowed the actual cost of removal and of abortive journeys to view alternative premises. The claimants—each nearly 80 years of age—and their son had great difficulty in finding a house that they could afford. After strenuous efforts the son found a house in Spalding, Lincolnshire, as it was reasonable so to have done. The proper basis for compensation for fixtures such as carpets is their value to an incoming tenant or purchaser).

TAYLOR v. CHELTENHAM BOROUGH COUNCIL (Ref./3/1977) (1978) 246 E.G. 923 (the property was a listed building in need of extensive repairs. Its condition was so poor that it had a minus value as far as the council (who were obliged by statute to purchase it) were concerned. Any purchase of the property would have been a speculation; a householder would be unlikely to buy it for his own use, and possibly a builder might buy it to keep his men employed. Whoever bought it, the only temptation would be a knockdown price. A sale at more than £2,000 was unthinkable, and accordingly this figure was awarded).

WATERWORTH v. BOLTON METROPOLITAN BOROUGH COUNCIL (Ref. 102/1977) (1978) 37 P. & C.R. 104 (the authority acquired 30 acres in 1972. The claimants ultimately sold their remaining 8·5 acres to a company which obtained planning permission because it could provide satisfactory access via other land which it owned. Reference was to determine the compensation payable for severance of 8·5 acres measured by depreciation in market value at the date of severance. Held, (1) the question was what damage, if any, had been sustained by the owner; (2) the subject land should not be regarded as completely land-locked as the evidence in 1972 when the 30 acres were acquired was that the access problem would be overcome by the building of a road. Accordingly, development of land was deferred, not extinct. One should regard planning per-mission as deferred for seven years for the purposes of the claim although in fact planning permission was granted three years later. £63,648 awarded, although it exceeded the dead ripe value of the land in 1972).

WATSON v. WARRINGTON BOROUGH COUNCIL (Ref. No. 207/1978) (1979) 250 E.G. 977 (warehouse in centre of Warrington, held on 999-year lease, used by family hardware business. DV argued for end-multiplier of three years' purchase. Held, he had wrongly allowed the market value to colour his valuation of the goodwill. The proper test was the value of the goodwill to the claimant. £5,000 would be allowed for goodwill; a total of £12,881 com-pensation was awarded (Remnant v. London County Council (1952) C.L.C. 525 and Shulman (Tailors) v. Greater London Council [1967] C.L.Y. 538 applied).

WILKINSON v. MIDDLESBROUGH BOROUGH COUNCIL (Ref./63/1978) (1979) 250 E.G. 867 (on a preliminary point of law as to the basis of compensation the claimant veterinary surgeons,. having served a blight notice, argued for the reinstatement basis under s. 5, r. (5), of the Land Compensation Act 1961. The acquiring authority contended for the r. (2) basis. Held, compensation on r. (2) basis. Considering the requirements set out in Sparks v. Leeds City Council [1977] C.L.Y. 332, the subject land would continue to be devoted to the purpose of the veterinary practice but there could be a market for the land, even with a multi-partner practice. Accordingly r. (5) was inappropriate).

307. Notice—service on one of joint owners—substantial prejudice
[Acquisition of Land (Authorisation Procedure) Act 1946 (c. 49), Sched. 1.]
The respondent was joint owner of a house with her husband. They filled it
with tenants and failed to keep it in repair. The appellant local authority
found it to be a "massive housing problem" and resolved to acquire it.
Due to misleading information given by the respondent's husband to the
authority, no notice was served on her. A purchase order was made and confirmed on inquiry. The respondent applied under the 1946 Act to quash it on
affidavit evidence setting out her lack of notice as substantial prejudice to her
interests. The deputy judge allowed her to be cross-examined *de bene esse*,
then ruled that she should not have been and finally found in her favour on
the affidavits. The Secretary of State and the authority appealed and she
cross-appealed alleging breach of natural justice by the failure to serve the
notice. *Held*, allowing the appeal and dismissing the cross-appeal, that cross-
examination on affidavits in proceedings for prerogative writ, judicial review
or in applications of this kind should not be allowed except where it is really
necessary. In any event, the respondent was not seriously prejudiced by reason
of her not being served with the order: her husband had told her of it. There
is no such thing as a "technical" breach of natural justice and no breach had
here occurred. The onus of proof under para. 15 of Sched. 1 to the Act is on
the person opposing the order (*Performance Cars* v. *Secretary of State for the
Environment* [1977] C.L.Y. 2986 considered): GEORGE v. SECRETARY OF STATE
FOR THE ENVIRONMENT (1979) 259 E.G. 339, C.A.

ARTICLES. See *post*, p. [16].

CONFLICT OF LAWS

**308. Contract—foreign jurisdiction clause—whether court different from that in
contemplation**
A foreign jurisdiction clause will no longer apply if the court to which it
refers is operating in a different state by whose constitution the law may be
changed at any time.
In 1973, P, an Angolan resident, agreed to sell shares in a group of companies to D Co., an English company established in Angola with no assets in
the U.K. Payment was to be by four instalments. The contract provided
that if a dispute arose, the District Court of Luanda was to be considered the
sole competent court to adjudicate. In 1975 the regime in Portugal was over-
thrown, and Angola was promised independence. P left Angola and his property
there was confiscated. Angola became a sovereign independent state. The
fourth instalment was not paid and P issued a writ in London. D Co. applied
to stay the proceedings on the ground, *inter alia*, that the dispute should be
tried in Luanda. Donaldson J. found that the court when the contract was
made was not now the same court as the parties had contemplated and refused
the stay. On appeal by D Co., *held*, dismissing the appeal, that even though
the named court continued to exist physically and administer substantially
the same law, it was now a court administering the law of a sovereign inde-
pendant state without the final right of appeal to Lisbon, with differently
selected judges, and under a new constitution whereby the law might be
changed at any time. Accordingly, the court referred to in the foreign jurisdiction clause was not the same court. (Dicta of Brandon J. in *The Eleftheria*
[1969] C.L.Y. 3293 and Wilmer J. in *The Fehmarn* [1958] C.L.Y. 3122
considered.)
CARVALHO v. HULL, BLYTH (ANGOLA) [1979] 1 W.L.R. 1228, C.A.

309. —— proper law—title to goods
Paintings were stolen in England from their plaintiff owner, taken to Italy
and sold to D under a contract made in Italy; Italian law governing the
contractual rights of the parties. When D sent the paintings back to England
for sale by auction, the plaintiff came to an agreement with the auctioneers
that the paintings should be sold but that the proceeds of sale should not be
distributed pending the determination of the question of title. *Held*, on a
preliminary point, that the local law should be applied, *i.e.* Italian domestic

law, to determine title to the paintings (*Cammell* v. *Sewell* (1858) 3 H. & N. 617 applied): WINKWORTH v. CHRISTIE MANSON AND WOODS, *The Times*, November 20, 1979, Slade J.

310. **Divorce and matrimonial causes—foreign decree—whether obtained by judicial or other proceedings.** See QUAZI v. QUAZI, § 772.

311. **Jurisdiction—damage to cargo—whether action should be stayed**
    P shipped goods on D's ship at Calcutta for Rotterdam under bills of lading which provided by cl. 4, *inter alia*, that disputes should be decided in the place where D had their principal place of business, *i.e.* Bombay. On arrival at Rotterdam, the goods were found to have been contaminated by fuel oil which had passed from a wing tank into No. 6 lower hold through a hole in the after bulkhead about five feet above the bottom of the hold which could have been seen quite easily on any normal inspection of the hold. P contended that the hole must have been there before the goods were loaded and that D accordingly had no defence to their claim. D applied for a stay of proceedings on the grounds that P had agreed that disputes between the parties should be decided in Bombay. *Held*, that (1) on the facts, the hole must have been present before the goods were loaded, D had suggested no defence to that part of the claim, and accordingly there was no dispute on the question of liability, which ought to be submitted to the court in India; (2) the stay would be refused, in that there was no multiplicity of proceedings in respect of the two matters which might still be in dispute, namely title to sue and quantum, as they related only to this action; that, since the Hague Rules applied, there was no difference in the relevant law whether the proceedings were heard in Bombay or in London; that all the relevant evidence was documentary evidence and in Europe; and that if a stay were granted, the proceedings in India would be time barred (*The Eleftheria* [1969] C.L.Y. 3293 considered): THE VISHVA PRABHA [1979] 2 Lloyd's Rep. 286, Sheen J.

312. **Northern Ireland.** See NORTHERN IRELAND.

313. **Proper law—alleged agency agreement—whether agreement governed by English law**
    P1, a company incorporated in the British Virgin Islands, and D an insurance company incorporated in Italy, entered into a purported agreement by which P1 were to act as D's underwriting agents. The agreement provided for arbitration under the rules of the International Chamber of Commerce in Geneva, and was executed by P1 in Luxembourg and by D in Italy. P1 then entered into a sub-delegation agreement with P2, by which P2 were to carry out the day-to-day management of the business, and which provided that the law governing the agreement would be that governing the head agreement. This agreement was executed by P1 in Luxembourg and by P2 in England. On March 13, 1978, D's solicitors notified P1's solicitors in London that in D's view there was no concluded agreement between the parties. As a result of a meeting in London on March 14, D's solicitors wrote a letter on March 15 setting out that it had been agreed, *inter alia*, to hold a meeting in Milan. On April 20 the meeting took place, as a result of which D telexed P1's solicitors in the Channel Islands, terminating the agency. On June 16, leave was obtained to serve on D out of the jurisdiction notice of a writ by which P1 claimed damages for breach of the underwriting agreement, and P2 claimed damages for the tort of inducing breach of contract. On D's application to set aside the service under R.S.C., Ord. 11, *held*, that (1) since D were resident in Italy, and that where the agreement was negotiated and signed, the agreement was governed by Italian, and not English law; alternatively, the proper law was that of the Canton of Geneva, since, although the law of the place of arbitration was no longer conclusive, it was still a strong factor, and the parties would not have chosen arbitration under the I.C.C. rules unless they intended Swiss law to apply to the substance as well as to the procedure; (2) P1 had to show that the case came within the spirit as well as the letter of one of the heads of Ord. 11, and not merely show that they had a good arguable case that the contract was governed by English law (*Vitkovice Horni A. Hutni Tezirstvo* v. *Korner* [1951] C.L.Y. 7855 applied); (3) D's repudiation of March 13 did not operate automatically to terminate the contract since there

was no justification, in the case of principal and agent, for departing from the rule that an innocent party had an option whether or not to accept a repudiation (*Thomas Marshall (Exports)* v. *Guinle* [1978] C.L.Y. 916 considered); (4) if the repudiation of March 13 was accepted as such, such acceptance would terminate the contract, but if not, it was difficult to see how it could sound in damages; (5) even if D's conduct was a breach, the same conduct which showed refusal to accept the repudiation equally acted to waive the breach, and the letter of March 15 was merely an agreement to postpone the date of breach; (6) P1 failed to establish that their case came within Ord. 11; but even if it had, this was not a proper case for service out of the jurisdiction since the parties had specifically provided for disputes to be resolved by arbitration in Geneva; (7) the tort alleged by P2 would be regarded as having been committed in Italy and not within the jurisdiction: ATLANTIC UNDERWRITING AGENCIES AND DAVID GALE (UNDERWRITING) v. COMPAGNIA DI ASSICURAZIONE DI MILANO S.P.A. [1979] 2 Lloyd's Rep. 240, Lloyd J.

314. —— whether domestic policy superseded substantive law. See THE STEELTON (No. 2), § 2462.

315. Public international law. See INTERNATIONAL LAW.

316. Recognition—valid foreign title to sue—action to safeguard property of missing person. See KAMOUH v. ASSOCIATED ELECTRICAL INDUSTRIES INTERNATIONAL, § 1662.

317. Sovereign immunity—company acquired by Government
On May 30, 1977, P applied *ex parte* for and were granted a *Mareva* injunction to restrain D from disposing of a quantity of tea warehoused in London, and leave to issue a writ for service out of the jurisdiction and serve notice of it on D. On May 31 the writ was issued, P claiming an indemnity in respect of moneys paid by them as guarantors of D's obligations. D entered a conditional appearance, and applied for the writ and all subsequent proceedings to be set aside on the grounds that D were the government of a foreign sovereign state and did not consent to the jurisdiction of the court. *Held,* that (1) the court had to elect which of two irreconcilable Court of Appeal authorities to follow, and would follow the one which asserted the doctrine of precedent rather than the one which broke new ground by deciding that the doctrine of restrictive sovereign immunity applied to actions *in personam,* and that there was an exception to the rule of *stare decisis,* and D's application would be granted (*Thai Europe Tapioca Services* v. *Government of Pakistan Directorate of Agricultural Supplies* [1975] C.L.Y. 370 followed; *Trendtex Trading Corp.* v. *Central Bank of Nigeria* [1977] C.L.Y. 346 not followed); (2) even if *Trendtex* had applied, D's application would still have been granted, since the court would otherwise have to decide on the meaning and effect of the legislation of a foreign state in a suit to which that state was a party, and it could not be held that the restrictive doctrine of sovereign immunity extended this far: UGANDA Co. (HOLDINGS) v. GOVERNMENT OF UGANDA [1979] 1 Lloyd's Rep. 481, Donaldson J.

318. —— effect of State Immunity Act 1978
On April 22, 1975, M, an English bank, issued a letter of credit as correspondents and on the advice of D, a foreign bank, in favour of P, and were put in funds to meet the letters of credit when they fell due. P sued D on the letters of credit, and, pending the final outcome of the case, were granted an injunction restraining D from removing the funds from the jurisdiction and preventing them from being disposed of. On appeal, D contended that whatever the position at the date of *Trendtex Trading Corp.* v. *Central Bank of Nigeria* [1977] C.L.Y. 346 which in all material respects was identical to this case, the position was now different because of the coming into force of the State Immunity Act 1978 and the U.S. Foreign Sovereign Immunities Act 1976. *Held,* that (1) the 1978 Act applied only to transactions made after it came into force in November 1978, and not retrospectively, and the law applicable here was that as it stood when the contracts were made in 1975 and when the case was heard in 1976; (2) the 1976 Act did not apply since the funds were not being held by D " for its own account " as required by the Act, but

for the activities of Government departments; (3) the U.S. and U.K. statutes did not alter the international law as stated in the *Trendtex* case, and that decision had not been given *per incuriam*; (4) the court would follow *Trendtex* and hold that there was no sovereign immunity and that the injunction should be maintained pending an ultimate decision (*Trendtex Trading Corp.* v. *Central Bank of Nigeria* [1977] C.L.Y. 346 applied): HISPANO AMERICANA MERCANTIL S.A. v. CENTRAL BANK OF NIGERIA [1979] 2 Lloyd's Rep. 277, C.A.

319. —— state-owned ship—action in rem
   After the Chilean coup d'état in 1973, the Cuban Government diverted vessels containing sugar bought by the Chilean plaintiffs. Later, plaintiffs arrested a new Cuban vessel built at Sunderland and made claims in respect of the sugar cargoes. *Held,* Lord Denning M.R. dissenting as to the first holding and as to the result, that (1) the diversion of the sugar cargoes was a governmental act even if it took place in the context of a commercial transaction, and was an act of foreign policy; (2) the Cuban state was accordingly entitled to invoke state immunity: I CONGRESO DEL PARTIDO (1979) 123 S.J. 689, C.A.

   BOOKS AND ARTICLES. See *post*; pp. [3], [16].

CONSTITUTIONAL LAW

320. **British Commonwealth**. See BRITISH COMMONWEALTH.

321. **Crown—compensation—statute making illegal the carrying on of plaintiff's business**
   [Can.] P owned a profitable fish exporting business until the Fresh Water Marketing Act R.S.C. 1979 gave to a statutory corporation the exclusive right to carry on such business, except on the issue by the corporation of a licence, none of which were issued. The Act provided for compensation to owners of plant rendered redundant thereby. No compensation was paid to P, who sued for compensation for the loss of their business, including the loss of goodwill. *Held*, the loss of goodwill brought about by the Act amounted to a taking of P's property by the Crown, for which, in the absence of clear statutory language, compensation was to be presumed to be payable. (*Att.-Gen.* v. *De Keyser's Royal Hotel* [1920] A.C. 508 applied): MANITOBA FISHERIES v. THE QUEEN (1978) 88 D.L.R. (3d) 462, Can.Sup.Ct.

322. **Ministers of the Crown**
   MINISTRY OF OVERSEAS DEVELOPMENT (DISSOLUTION) ORDER 1979 (No. 1451) [20p], made under the Ministers of the Crown Act 1975 (c. 26), s. 5 (1); operative on November 21, 1979; provides for the dissolution of the Ministry of Overseas Development and for the transfer to the Secretary of State of the functions of the Minister.

323. **Northern Ireland.** See NORTHERN IRELAND.

324. **Parliament.** See PARLIAMENT.

325. **Wales Act 1978—repeal**
   WALES ACT 1978 (REPEAL) ORDER 1979 (No. 933) [10p], made under the Wales Act 1978 (c. 52), s. 80 (1)–(3); operative on July 26, 1979; repeals the Wales Act 1978.

   BOOKS AND ARTICLES. See *post*, pp. [3], [16].

CONTRACT

326. **Agency.** See AGENCY.

327. **Arbitration.** See ARBITRATION.

328. **Breach—inconvenience—measure of damages**
   [Can.] A disc jockey failed to appear at P's wedding reception. *Held*, damages could be awarded for the inconvenience caused by that failure; the appropriate measure was the reasonable cost that would have been incurred to hire a replacement at short notice. (*Bailey* v. *Bullock* (1950) C.L.C. 9801; *Stedman* v. *Swan Tours* (1951) C.L.C. 2489; *Griffiths* v. *Evans* [1953] C.L.Y.

3472 referred to): DUNN *v.* DISC JOCKEY UNLIMITED CO. (1978) 87 D.L.R. 408, Dist.Ct. of Ottawa–Carleton.

329. Carriage by air—Warsaw Convention—exclusion of liability for death and loss of baggage. See LUDECKE *v.* CANADIAN PACIFIC AIRLINES, § 138.

330. Consideration—economic duress—agreement to increased price after contract made—whether good consideration

The recovery of money paid under duress, other than to the person, is not limited to duress to goods but can include economic duress where that is constituted by a threat to break a contract, even though there is good consideration for that further contract.

By a shipbuilding contract the builders agreed to build a tanker for the owners, the price to be paid by instalments. There were no relevant provisions for subsequent adjustment of the price. The contract required the builders to open a letter of credit to provide security in the event of default. In 1973 the U.S. dollar was devalued and the builders demanded an increase in the price under a threat to break the contract, agreeing to a corresponding increase in the letter of credit. The owners agreed, reserving their rights, and paid the remaining instalments at the new level. The owners after receipt of the vessel reclaimed the excess price alleging no good consideration and economic duress. *Held,* that (1) although the rule relating to consideration in respect of performance of an existing contractual duty remained unchanged, t! builders' increase in the letter of credit provided good consideration; (2) a contract made under economic duress was voidable, even though the consideration was good. In this case however the owners had affirmed the contract. (*Silk* v. *Meyrick* (1809) 2 Camp. 31 followed. *Smith* v. *William Charlick* (1924) 34 C.L.R. 38 applied.)

NORTH OCEAN SHIPPING CO. *v.* HYUNDAI CONSTRUCTION CO. [1978] 3 All E.R. 1170, Mocatta J.

331. —— subsidiary agreements—commercial pressure

An agreement made in consideration of an act done before the making of the agreement may be enforceable where, *inter alia,* such act was done at the provisor's request.

Per curiam: Economic duress is capable of vitiating an agreement where it is such as to negative consent.

The plaintiffs agreed to sell their shares in a private company to a company of which the defendants were majority shareholders in consideration of the issue to them of shares in the purchasing company. So as not to depress the market value of such shares the plaintiffs further agreed with the defendants that they would not sell 60 per cent. of the newly issued shares until April 1974, the defendants agreeing, so that the plaintiffs might be protected against a fall in the value of the shares during such period, to purchase them at the end of that period at $2.50 each. Shortly afterwards the plaintiffs realised that the effect of such subsidiary agreement would be to deprive them of any increase in the value thereof. They therefore refused to complete the main agreement unless the defendants in substitution for the subsidiary agreement agreed to indemnify them against any reduction in value of the shares below the price of $2.50 each during the deferment period. The defendants, fearing the consequences of delay in completion of the main agreement, so agreed, the agreement being expressed to be in consideration of the plaintiffs having agreed to sell their shares in the private company. The main agreement was performed, and thereafter the value of the shares fell below $2.50 each. The plaintiffs claimed an indemnity, which was refused by the defendants on the grounds, *inter alia,* that the consideration for the indemnity agreement was past consideration and/or that any such agreement was voidable by reason of the economic duress applied by the plaintiffs. *Held,* that (1) an antecedent act could be valid consideration where it was done at the promisor's request, where the parties understood that such act was to be remunerated by the conferment of a benefit and where such benefit would have been enforceable if promised in advance; and such criteria were here satisfied; (2) a promise to perform a contractual obligation for the benefit of a third party was good consideration; and (3) the commercial pressure to which the defendants had been subjected had not been such as to negative their consent to the indemnity agreement. (*Re Casey's Patents* [1892] 1 Ch. 104 and *New Zealand Shipping Co.* v. *Satterthwaite (A. M.) & Co.* [1974] C.L.Y. 3532 applied.)

PAO ON v. LAU YIU [1979] 3 All E.R. 65, P.C.

332. **Damages—measure of damages—date from which calculated.** See WILLIAM CORY & SONS v. WINGATE INVESTMENTS (LONDON COLNEY), § 650.

333. **Exemption clause—personal injury—passenger on ship—time of contract.** See DALY v. GENERAL STEAM NAVIGATION; THE DRAGON, § 1869.

334. **Frustration—oil concession—government expropriation of one party's interest —award of " just sum "—principles applicable**
[Law Reform (Miscellaneous Provisions) Act 1934 (c. 41), s. 3; Law Reform (Frustrated Contracts) Act 1943 (c. 40), ss. 1 (3), 2 (3).]
Where a contract has been frustrated the court in deciding what, if any, sum to award will ascertain, *inter alia,* whether a valuable benefit was obtained by the defendant prior to the contract's discharge, what contractual provision for remuneration was agreed and any expenditure incurred by the defendant.
The defendant owner of an oil concession in Libya entered into an agreement with the plaintiffs whereby they would explore and develop the concession at their own expense, being entitled to recoup part of such expenditure if or when the field came on stream from the defendant's share of production. After the field came on stream the parties were to share production and further development costs. Later the parties agreed that the plaintiffs' pre-production expenses would be re-imbursed by their receiving 50 million barrels of oil. An amending agreement also provided that the plaintiffs could not recover sums paid to the defendant. The field came on stream in 1967. In 1971 the Libyan government expropriated the plaintiffs' interest and excluded them from the concession. The defendant continued to export oil from the field until his interest was expropriated in 1973. By the time of their exclusion the plaintiffs had received approximately one-third of the 50 million barrels of " reimbursement oil "; they received no further oil thereafter, but received in due course some compensation from the Libyan government, such sum being related to the value of facilities left at the field and not to the concession itself. The plaintiff claimed that the contract had been frustrated and an award of a just sum under s. 1 (3) of the 1943 Act. *Held,* that (1) the contract was frustrated in 1971; (2) as at the date of the frustration the defendant had obtained a valuable benefit (which was valued as at that date without allowance for the defendant's use thereof thereafter) in that the value of his share of the concession had been enhanced by the plaintiffs' contractual performance; half of that sum fell to be taken into account (since the other half related to the part of the concession owned by him) and it was valued at some $85 million; (3) the just sum awardable to the plaintiffs, having regard to the contractual provision as to renumeration, was $35 million taking account of the reimbursement oil already received by the plaintiffs; since the just sum was less than the benefit received by the defendant, it could properly be awarded to the plaintiffs; (4) the currency of the award should reflect the currency in which the defendant's benefit could most appropriately be valued, having regard in particular to the contractual provisions; (5) interest could be awarded under the 1934 Act upon the just sum as from the date of frustration but in its discretion the court would award interest as from the date when the plaintiffs indicated their intention to claim restitution. (*Services Europe Atlantique Sud (SEAS)* v. *Stockholm Rederiaktiebolag Svea; The Despina R.* [1978] C.L.Y. 710, applied.)

B.P. EXPLORATION CO. (LIBYA) v. HUNT (No. 2) [1979] 1 W.L.R. 783, Goff J.

335. **Mistake—compromise of void claim—duty of receivers**
[Can.] F entered into an agreement to buy a group of companies as a going concern from a receiver-manager. F subsequently repudiated the agreement and, after negotiations, paid $10,000 to the receiver-manager as a compromise in satisfaction of all claims arising out of the agreement. The court then held, on an application not involving F, that the receiver-manager had no power to offer the companies for sale. The contract with F was therefore void, and F

applied for repayment of the $10,000. *Held*, a fundamental mistake as to the validity of the claim compromised is a ground for setting aside the compromised agreement. Further, the receiver-manager as an officer of the court had a higher duty than the ordinary person not to take unfair advantage of a mistake of law. (*Magee* v. *Pennine Insurance Co.* [1969] C.L.Y. 1819 applied): TORONTO-DOMINION BANK v. FORTIN (No. 2) (1978) 88 D.L.R. (3d) 232, Brit.Col.Sup.Ct.

336. Non est factum—son mortgaging parents' home—lack of independent advice.
See AVON FINANCE CO. v. BRIDGER, § 1832.

337. Offer and acceptance—mistake—whether offer can be accepted after offeree knows of mistake
[Can.] D submitted a bid for a construction project that was, by reason of his own miscalculation, substantially lower than intended. The instructions to tenderers stated that tenders were to remain open for 60 days. D's bid was the lowest submitted; P was advised to accept it. D discovered its error, told P of it and purported to withdraw the bid. P entered into a contract with the next lowest tenderer and sued D for the difference between the two tenders. *Held*, an offeree could not accept an offer he knows to have been made under a mistake affecting a fundamental term of the contract: BELLE RIVER COMMUNITY ARENA v. W. KAUFMANN (1978) 87 D.L.R. (3d) 761, Ontario C.A.

338. —— order to be accepted on sellers' terms—acknowledgment of order on buyers' terms
[Uniform Laws on International Sales Act 1967 (c. 45), Sched. 2, art. 7.]
Where parties to a contract have made offer and counter-offer, the documents passing between the parties must be construed as a whole, but the rules set out in *Hyde* v. *Wrench* (1840) 3 Beav. 334 still apply.
The plaintiff sellers offered to deliver a machine tool on condition that orders were only to be accepted on the terms set out in the quotation. The sellers' terms included a price variation clause. The defendant buyers replied with an order containing different terms and no price variation clause. The order had a tear-off slip of acknowledgment on those terms, which acknowledgment was duly signed by the sellers. Due to the buyers' delay in accepting delivery the sellers invoked the price variation clause. The sellers were successful at first instance but on appeal, *held*, allowing the appeal, that the buyers' reply was a counter offer which the sellers had accepted by their acknowledgment (*Hyde* v. *Wrench* (1840) 3 Beav. 334 and *Trollope & Colls* v. *Atomic Power Constructions* [1963] C.L.Y. 552 applied).
BUTLER MACHINE TOOL CO. v. EX-CELL-O CORP. (ENGLAND) [1979] 1 W.L.R. 401, C.A.

339. Oral contract—confirmation by documents—whether written condition incorporated into oral contract
[Scot.] M contracted with H for the hire of a crane, by means of a telephone conversation between officials of the two companies. The same day, H delivered the crane, and during its use it overbalanced and was damaged. It was the regular practice of H when a hire was under an oral contract to post an " acknowledgment of order form " which set out the particular terms of hire, and stated: " Your order is accepted subject to the General Conditions for the hiring of plant issued by the Contractors Plant Association, a copy of which can be forwarded on request. Acceptance of the plant on site implies acceptance of all terms and conditions stated on this acknowledgment." The conditions provided, *inter alia*, for the hirer to make good to H all damage to the plant from whatever cause, fair wear and tear excepted In the previous four years M had hired such plant from H in similar circumstances. No copy of the General Conditions had been requested or sent. *Held*, H had failed to show that, as a result of the references to the conditions in written documents involved in the prior course of dealing between the parties, they had done what was reasonably necessary to bring to M's notice that the conditions would be implied in the present oral contract; and consequently the condition making M liable for loss or damage was not incorporated into the contract. (*Hardwick Game Farm* v. *S.A.P.P.A.* [1968] C.L.Y. 3526 referred to): GRAYSTON PLANT v. PLEAN PRECAST, 1976 S.C. 206, Ct.Session 2nd. Division.

340. Performance—advance payment—right to lien—urgent repairs

On June 10, 1976, P, a consulting marine engineer, flew to Nigeria, having obtained a visa without difficulty, to make a preliminary inspection of the main engine of the I, a vessel which was berthed at Port Harcourt and which belonged to D, a Nigerian company. It was agreed that the bearings should be remetalled in England and the main journals ground and honed. After his return to England on June 26, P recruited a team of eight men to execute the work, but was unable to obtain visas. On July 9, the team flew out in the hope that D would make the necessary entry arrangements, but P was unable to contact D, and the party returned to England. They obtained visas on July 16, but did not fly out until August 5, as P insisted on a substantial advance payment. After work began on August 6, it became apparent that much more work would be involved than anticipated, partly due to the shortage of materials and facilities in Port Harcourt, and the length of time it could take to hone the journals. P flew back to England on August 24 with the bearings to be remetalled, arriving back in Nigeria on September 2, whereupon the rest of the work continued. Thereafter P made several requests in respect of fees and advance payment for expenditure, culminating in a request on September 17 for payment of £40,000 by September 21, failing which the completed bearings would be withheld. Further, on September 24 P suspended work and the team returned to England. On October 27, P submitted his cost of completing repairs of £48,037, replying to D's counter-offer of £30,000 that he was ready and willing to complete the repairs, but could not reduce the estimate. When P was told that D were making alternative arrangements to complete the repairs, and asked to make the bearings available, he replied that the bearings would be available as soon as all outstanding invoices had been settled. P claimed for balance of an account, and D counterclaimed for loss incurred by additional expense and delay caused, *inter alia*, by the necessity of waiting for new bearings. *Held*, that (1) P throughout was an agent, and not a contractor, so far as D were concerned, but was personally liable on the contracts with the various sub-contractors; (2) although P was aware of the difficulties, not only was it reasonable for him to take the risk of flying out without visas in D's best interest in that the repairs were clearly urgent, it was reasonble to assume that D could be in a better position to secure admission into their own country, and P had earlier obtained a visa without difficulty, but D's London agents had specifically authorised him to do so; (3) since P was personally liable on the sub-contracts, it was essential that he be secured in advance, and a term to that effect should be implied into the contract; and P was not in breach by insisting on advance payment before flying out on August 5; (4) due to the absence of proper shore facilities, the shortage of materials and spares and the appalling working conditions on board, the repairs could not reasonably have been done any quicker; (5) P was not liable for the seven-week delay between his suspension of the contract and the arrival of a new team, since there was no reason why the new team could not have gone out the next day; (6) P was entitled to exercise a lien on a part of the vessel which was in his possession (the bearings) in respect of his work on the vessel as a whole; (7) the subsequent damage to the I's main lubricating scavenge pump was not caused by P's negligent inspection of it, but by failure properly to prime it; (8) P was not liable for the delays or the cost of obtaining new bearings, and was entitled to the whole of the amounts for which he was liable to others as well as his own fees and expenses: FRASER v. EQUITORIAL SHIPPING CO. AND EQUITORIAL LINES; THE IJAOLA [1979] 1 Lloyd's Rep. 103, Lloyd, J.

341. Privity—third party beneficiary—widow of shareholder

[Can.] An agreement among shareholders of a family-owned corporation whereby, on the death of any shareholder, those surviving undertake to cause the corporation to pay certain benefits to the widow of the deceased shareholder was *held*, to be a binding agreement. It could be enforced by the widow if she was also the personal representative of the deceased shareholder's estate. The corporation was nothing more than the instrument by which all the shareholders carried on business. (*Beswick* v. *Beswick* [1967] C.L.Y. 641, and *Dunlop Pneumatic Tyre Co.* v. *Selfridge* [1915] A.C. 847 referred to): GASPARINI *v.* GASPARINI (1978) 87 D.L.R. (3d) 282, Ont.C.A.

342. Repudiation—council contract with developer—newly elected council—ability to repudiate

[N.Z.] C, the council, initiated the project of having Ngataringa Bay reclaimed for private housing. In 1969 C and the relevant harbour board agreed (1) to promote the project and (2) that C would enter an agreement with a developer to carry it out. Thereafter C promoted the necessary special legislation, empowering C to develop the land for such purposes as C thought fit, with power to enter into any contract to carry out and execute the development. In 1971 C and D, the developer, executed a deal; cl. 6 of the deed provided that C would grant a development licence, which would provide for the ultimate transfer to D of the fee simple of the developed residential and commercial allotments of the land if (a) D gave C notice they wished to reclaim and develop the land during a stipulated period; (b) D submitted a comprehensive development scheme; and (c) C " in its discretion," taking into account the merits of the proposed development, approved the scheme. C and D cooperated for some years; in 1974 D submitted a comprehensive scheme which C approved in principle. Thereafter local elections were held; the majority of the newly elected C were opposed to this development project. In addition the Commission for the Environment considered the scheme and recommended there should be no private development in the bay. Without committing D, C thereupon revoked approval of the scheme and adopted a new policy making the scheme, in theory, more expensive. D treated C's attitude as a repudiation of the contract. *Held,* the words " in their discretion " in cl. 6 (c) meant that C had a discretion, after taking into account specified matters, to decide whether or not a submitted scheme was a satisfactory method of achieving the kind of development approved by the special legislation. It did not leave C, as newly elected, free to reject a scheme because they then believed no such development should be allowed. When C executed the deed in 1971 it fettered the discretion of its successors. C's dealings with D after the election showed that a major factor of their approach was their opinion that the bay should not be used for private housing. That was inconsistent with C's basic contractual obligations. C had repudiated the contract. (*Taupo Totara Timber* v. *Rowe* [1977] C.L.Y. 288, *Secretary of State for Employment* v. *ASLEF* (*No. 2*) [1972] C.L.Y. 1169; *Federal Commerce & Navigation Co.* v. *Molena Alpha Inc.* [1978] C.L.Y. 2731 and *Smyth* v. *Bailey* [1940] 3 All E.R. 60 applied): DEVONPORT BOROUGH COUNCIL *v.* ROBBINS [1979] 1 N.Z.L.R. 1, N.Z.C.A.

343. Restraint of trade—employment contract—restrictive covenant—wide geographical operations. See GREER *v.* SKETCHLEY, § 938.

344. Sale of goods. See SALE OF GOODS.

345. Terms—construction—whether implied term for termination—whether contract frustrated

Where a transport company has entered into an agreement with a local authority responsible for transport services that it will, for a period of 99 years, have the sole right to operate services, an implied term as to termination cannot be read into the contract merely because that local authority does not any longer have the power to operate the service even if it wished to do so.

By an agreement made in 1930, a transport company was to have the sole rights to operate transport services in two local authority areas in return for a share of the profits. The contract was for 99 years. The authorities' responsibility for operating the services was vested in a new authority in 1972. The defendants contended that as the old authorities no longer had the power to operate the services, they need no longer pay them a share of the profits. *Held,* that it was impossible to read into the contract an implied term for termination prior to the 99 years, nor did the doctrine of frustration apply. (*Staffordshire Area Health Authority* v. *South Staffordshire Waterworks Co.* [1978] C.L.Y. 337 considered.)

KIRKLEES METROPOLITAN BOROUGH COUNCIL *v.* YORKSHIRE WOOLLEN DISTRICT TRANSPORT Co. (1978) 77 L.G.R. 448, Walton J.

BOOKS AND ARTICLES. See *post,* pp. [3], [16].

COPYRIGHT

346. Broadcasting programmes—schedules—freedom of information. See DE GEILLUSTREERDE PERS N.V. *v.* THE NETHERLANDS, § 1131.

347. Compilation—information in public domain—interlocutory injunction
The patent on the herbicide Trifluralin expired. The defendants marketed it with an accompanying leaflet with detailed instructions as to use of the herbicide and information about it. Much of the information was in the public domain. The plaintiffs, original inventors, alleged that the leaflet infringed their copyright in the leaflet they provided with the tin. *Held*, on appeal, that (1) the plaintiffs had an arguable case that a breach of copyright had occurred; (2) damages were an inadequate remedy to both parties and the *status quo* should be preserved; (3) the defendants could use the information in the public domain including the plaintiffs' literature but they could not make use of the plaintiffs' skill and judgment to save themselves the trouble and cost of assembling and selecting literature. Injunction granted: ELANCO PRODUCTS *v.* MANDOPS [1979] F.S.R. 46, C.A.

348. Discovery—dominant position in EEC
The defendants applied for discovery in an action for infringement of copyright in drawings of components. They alleged that parts were bought in Italy from a company controlled by the plaintiffs and that the relief was contrary to EEC regulations because the plaintiffs occupied a dominant position within the EEC. *Held*, discovery was limited to documents relating to the way the plaintiffs had exercised claims to copyright, in drawings for components in the EEC. The plaintiffs must be protected from raising general unparticularised issues which amounted to a fishing expedition: BRITISH LEYLAND MOTOR CORP. *v.* WYATT INTERPART CO., BRITISH LEYLAND U.K., PRESSED STEEL FISHER AND BRITISH LEYLAND (AUSTIN MORRIS) [1979] 1 C.M.L.R. 395, Whitford J.

349. The plaintiffs claimed copyright in drawings of motor-car assemblies. The defendants manufactured and supplied, *inter alia*, replacement parts for the plaintiffs' cars. The plaintiffs claimed that such manufacture and sale amounted to breach of copyright. The defendants claimed that the plaintiffs were bound by arts. 3a, 30, 34 of the Treaty of Rome, and were attempting in breach to impose quantitative restrictions on the import and export of goods. They also contended that the plaintiffs were in breach of art. 85. *Held*, that (1) the plaintiffs' copyright was industrial property which they were entitled to protect; (2) the plaintiffs' action did not amount to a disguised restriction on trade. Observed " the Treaty of Rome is not a pirate's charter." Limited discovery ordered and suspended: BRITISH LEYLAND MOTOR CORP. *v.* T.I. SILENCERS [1979] F.S.R. 591, Walton J.

350. Ex parte application—unlawful interference with business
Plaintiffs made an *ex parte* application for an injunction to restrain the defendants from unlawfully interfering with their business by distributing imported records, the copyright of which was vested in the plaintiffs. *Held*, the intentional use of unlawful means to injure a person's business was an actionable wrong (*Acrow (Automation) v. Rex Chainbelt* [1971] C.L.Y. 9259 applied.) This matter fell within the three tests of *Anton Piller K.G.* v. *Manufacturing Processes* [1976] C.L.Y. 2136. The injunction would be granted: *Re* M'S APPLICATION (1978) 123 S.J. 142, C.A.

351. Film—single frame reproduced
[Copyright Act 1956 (c. 74), ss. 1, 13, 32, 48, 49; Copyright (International Conventions) Order 1972 (S.I. 1972 No. 673).] The plaintiffs produced TV films including *Starsky and Hutch*. The defendants published a pin-up poster and magazine which included photographs of Starsky and Hutch. The photograph was a reproduction of a single frame from a film and was issued by the plaintiffs and the B.B.C. as publicity material. *Held*, that (1) a copy of a single frame is not a copy of a film for the purposes of the Copyright Act; (2) a photograph of a film is not a photograph within the Act; (3) the single frame was not a substantial part of the film; (4) conversion damages would be awarded in respect of the B.B.C. photographs: SPELLING GOLDBERG PRODUCTIONS INC. *v.* B.P.C. PUBLISHING [1979] F.S.R. 494, Judge Mervyn Davies, Q.C.

352. Hong Kong

COPYRIGHT (HONG KONG) (AMENDMENT) ORDER 1979 (No. 910) [20p], made
under the Copyright Act 1956 (c. 74), s. 31 (1); operative on August 24, 1979;
amends S.I. 1972 No. 1724 so as to extend to Hong Kong those provisions
of the Act relating to the establishment and jurisdiction of the Performing
Right Tribunal.

353. Infringement—confidential information—inspection of defendant's drawings

The second and third defendants had been directors of a subsidiary of the
plaintiff company, which had accumulated drawings for manufacture of equipment for the automotive industry. The defendants contended that purchase of
the subsidiary business entitled them to use the drawings in the completion of
outstanding orders and that fresh drawings which they had since made were
not infringements or use of confidential information. The plaintiff sought
inspection of the new drawings. *Held*, (1) the new drawings were relevant to the
issue; (2) the court had power to order inspection; (3) the defendant's fear that
inspection by the plaintiffs employee would lead to use by the plaintiffs of
confidential information was unfounded: CENTRI-SPRAY CORP. *v.* CERA INTER-
NATIONAL [1979] F.S.R. 177, Whitford J.

354. —— drawings for racing cars—damages

[Copyright Act 1956 (c. 74), ss. 1, 3, 9, 17, 18, 48.] In an action for infringement of copyright the plaintiffs, N.A.V.S., alleged that the defendants, former
employees of the plaintiffs, had in breach of copyright copied drawings of the
plaintiffs' Formula One racing car, and used them to build a car known as
F.A.1. Written agreements between S, and N.A.V.S. were in force at the time
that S did the drawings. S gave the third defendant a number of drawings when
the D.N.9 was 70 per cent. completed. S left N.A.V.S. to work for another
company, to design a copy of the D.N.9, with appropriate modifications.
The F.A.1 was constructed and participated in races in 1978. *Held*, (1) the
plaintiffs were the owners of subsisting copyright in the drawings; (2) 40 per
cent. of the total number of drawings required to build the F.A.1 were
reproductions of D.N.9 drawings. The defence of s. 9 (8) was of no assistance
to the defendants. Only the third defendant could avail himself of s. 18 (2). A
flagrant and deceitful infringement had occurred and an extra award of
damages would be made: NICHOLS ADVANCED VEHICLE SYSTEM INC. *v.*
REES, OLIVER [1979] R.P.C. 128, Templeman J.

355. —— drawings of drawers

[Copyright Act 1956 (c. 74), ss. 3, 9, 48, 49.] The defendants admitted
examining drawers made by the plaintiffs and possession of drawings made by
the plaintiffs of plastic, knock-down drawers for the furniture industry. The
defendants contended that there was a commercial necessity for their drawers
to be interchangeable with the plaintiffs' or were deprived from earlier designs
of the plaintiffs. *Held,* on plaintiffs' appeal to the House of Lords, that (1)
there was a prima facie case of copying. The evidential burden had shifted;
(2) the defendants had failed to show that the similarities were not the result
of copying. They had copied many of the things which gave the plaintiffs'
product its specific individuality; (3) the Court of Appeal had erred in holding
that the trial judge's finding was based on an inference from the similarity of
the two designs; (4) the defence under s. 9 (8) related to points of resemblance
which the non-expert would fail to recognise in the three dimensional form:
L.B. (PLASTICS) *v.* SWISH PRODUCTS [1979] F.S.R. 145, H.L.

356. —— interlocutory relief—incitement of breach—proper parties

The plaintiffs sought interlocutory relief to restrain infringement of copyright
in photographs or drawings which the defendants had used in four advertisements for blank tapes. 20 of the 24 plaintiffs sought *quia timet* relief. *Held*, (1)
only the four plaintiffs who were directly involved would be granted the relief
sought; (2) the remaining 20 plaintiffs had not established that they had a
reasonable fear that the defendants would infringe their copyright and they
should cease to be parties to the action; (3) to establish incitement to breach of
copyright the plaintiffs must show a specific authorisation of an actual breach:
A & M RECORDS INC. *v.* AUDIO MAGNETICS INC. (U.K.) [1979] F.S.R. 1,
Foster J.

357. —— knowledge

[Aust.] [Copyright Act 1968 (Com.), s. 103.] The plaintiffs sought to restrain the defendants from selling infringing copies of cassette recordings which had been imported into Australia from Singapore. The defendants denied knowledge that the copies had been in infringement of copyright. *Held*, on appeal, that (1) actual and not constructive knowledge on the part of the defendant must be shown; (2) knowledge could be imputed as a matter of inference; (3) since the defendants had not called the manager to refute the inference that he knew he was dealing with copies, the court found that he knew of the infringement: R.C.A. CORP. *v.* CUSTOM CLEARED SALES PTY. [1978] F.S.R. 576, Sup.Ct. of N.S.W.

358. —— licence fees—unlawful interference

[Copyright Act 1956 (c. 74), ss. 5, 8.] The plaintiffs were two copyright owners and M.C.P.S. the organisation which acted as agents for collecting licence fees payable for mechanically reproduced musical compositions. The defendants imported and sold bootleg records. The plaintiffs sought an Anton Pillar order and M.C.P.S. alleged the tort of interference with their business by unlawful means. *Held*, on appeal by M.C.P.S., that (1) there was an unlawful interference by the defendants and M.C.P.S. were not merely seeking the payment of a debt; (2) measure of damages was the fee; (3) an Anton Piller order should be granted: CARLIN MUSIC CORP. *v.* COLLINS [1979] F.S.R. 548, C.A.

359. —— Order 14 procedure

[Copyright Act 1956 (c. 74).] The plaintiff's photographs had been taken from the plaintiff and sold to the *Daily Mail*. The plaintiff moved for relief under Ord. 14. The defendants contended that they believed that the reproduction would not infringe the plaintiff's copyright. *Held*, that (1) the defendants had not shown a plausible defence; (2) the Master could decide whether additional damages should be awarded on account of the flagrancy of the breach; (3) as to the issue of damages for conversion, the defence of innocence could not be determined as part of the Ord. 14 inquiry: LADY ANNE TENNANT *v.* ASSOCIATED NEWSPAPERS GROUP [1979] F.S.R. 298, Megarry V.-C.

360. —— practice—joinder of foreign supplier

The defendants imported and distributed in the U.K. chains made by ASK, a German company. The defendants applied for ASK to be joined on defendants in the action, alleging breach of copyright. *Held*, ASK was so bound up in the matter that they should be joined: REXNORD INC. *v.* ROLLER-CHAIN DISTRIBUTORS [1979] F.S.R. 119, Fox J.

361. International arrangements

COPYRIGHT (INTERNATIONAL CONVENTIONS) (AMENDMENT) ORDER 1979 (No. 577) [10p], made under the Copyright Act 1956 (c. 74), ss. 31, 32, 47; operative on June 21, 1979; further amends S.I. 1972 No. 673 to take account of the accession of EL Salvador to the Universal Copyright Convention.

COPYRIGHT (INTERNATIONAL CONVENTIONS) ORDER 1979 (No. 1715) [50p], made under the Copyright Act 1956, ss. 31, 32, 47; operative on January 24, 1980; supersedes (with amendments to allow for the accession of El Salvador and the Republic of Ireland to the International Convention for the Protection of performers, Producers of Phonograms and Broadcasting Organisations) certain previous Orders relating to provisions under the Copyright Act 1956 and its extension to other countries party to international copyright conventions.

362. Locus standi—person aggrieved—statue designs. See OSCAR TRADE MARK, § 2705.

363. Practice—striking out—title to copyright

[Copyright Act 1956 (c. 74), ss. 4, 20, 36; Law of Property Act 1925 (c. 20), s. 53 (1) (c).] The plaintiffs alleged infringement of copyright in three groups of drawings, S/ROB, RP and D & N. On a summons to strike out the action, it was held that independent contractors owned the copyrights. The RP drawing was made by P, when a partner of firm X. The assets of X were vested in the first plaintiffs. The judge held that the pleadings relating to the RP drawings should not be struck out as being vexatious, but those relating to S/ROB and D & N drawings should be struck out. *Held*, on appeal, S/ROB and D & N drawings were rightly struck out because of the plaintiffs lack of title. The action in respect of RP should also be struck out because there was no sufficient disposition in writing of the beneficial interest in the drawing to the plaintiffs' predecessors in title: ROBAN JIG & TOOL CO. AND ELKADART *v.* TAYLOR [1979] F.S.R. 130, C.A.

364. **Records—imports—EEC.** See POLYDOR AND RSO RECORDS INC. *v.* HARLEQUIN RECORD SHOPS AND SIMON RECORDS, § 1132.

365. —— **playing over loudspeakers in shops—whether performance " in public "**
[Copyright Act 1956 (c. 74), ss. 1 (1) (2), 2 (5).]
The playing of records over the loudspeakers in a shop where the public are permitted to enter without payment, is a performance " in public " within the meaning of the Copyright Act 1956.
The plaintiff society, the owner of performing rights in musical works protected by copyright, had not before 1976 sought licence fees from shops where records were sold. In view of the recent practice of continuous playing of music over the shops' loudspeakers for all to hear, the plaintiffs claimed that the defendants were infringing the society's rights by so doing. On the question of whether the performance was " in public," *held*, that such a performance in a shop where members of the public were encouraged to enter without payment, with a view to increasing the shop-owner's profit, was a performance " in public " within the meaning of the Act. (*Performing Right Society* v. *Hawthorns Hotel* (*Bournemouth*) [1933] Ch. 855 and *Performing Right Society* v. *Gillette Industries* [1943] Ch. 167 considered.)
PERFORMING RIGHT SOCIETY *v.* HARLEQUIN RECORD SHOPS [1979] 1 W.L.R. 851, Browne-Wilkinson J.

366. **Reversionary interests—assignments**
[Literary Copyright Act 1842 (c. 45); Copyright Act 1911 (c. 46), ss. 5, 16, 24, 35.] Under the Copyright Act 1911, interests of deceased authors reverted to the authors' legal personal representatives 25 years after death. This right did not apply to pre-1912 works. A number of points arose in relation to pre-1912 works. *Held*, that (1) the reference in the 1911 Act, s. 24 (1) (*a*), to an " express agreement " did not refer to agreements made before the passing of the 1911 Act; (2) where words were written by one person and the music by another, the proviso to s. 5 (2) of the 1911 Act did apply to the copyright; (3) a song which is a work of joint authorship is not a collective work. If it had been intended to exclude works of joint authorship from the proviso this would have been done expressly. Appeal by the plaintiffs allowed.
REDWOOD MUSIC *v.* B. FELDMAN AND CO. [1979] R.P.C. 385, C.A.

BOOKS AND ARTICLES. See *post*, pp. [3], [17].

CORONERS

367. **Juries—summoning a jury—purpose of inquest**
[Coroners (Amendment) Act 1926 (c. 59), s. 13 (2) (*e*).] Under s. 13 (2) (*e*) of the Coroners (Amendment) Act 1926 a coroner shall summon a jury if there is reason to suspect that the death occurred in circumstances the continuance or possible recurrence of which is prejudicial to the health and safety of the public. *Held*, that the sort of circumstances covered were those where, because of the type of situation, *e.g.* death by drowning, there was reason to suspect there might be further deaths. It did not cover a case of an isolated accident where a police officer may have used a weapon wrongly. Statements had been taken by the police and handed to the coroner. There was no legal obligation on the coroner to hand them over to the deceased's family. The inquest was to determine the cause of death, not to determine liability, civil or criminal: R. *v.* H.M. CORONER AT HAMMERSMITH, *ex p.* PEACH, *The Times*, November 16, 1979, D.C.

368. **Northern Ireland.** See NORTHERN IRELAND.

CORPORATION TAX

369. Assessment—appeal—absence of counsel

[Taxes Management Act 1970 (c. 9), s. 50.] The appellant company appealed against an assessment to corporation tax. On the day fixed for hearing it appointed a solicitor to represent it. Shortly after the Commissioners assembled at 10.30 a.m. the solicitor left temporarily to attend to other business. He was absent for only a few minutes, but during that time the case was called, and in the absence of representation, the assessment confirmed. The Commissioners then refused to hear submissions by the appellant company's representative. *Held*, that the Commissioners had acted unreasonably, and their determination should be quashed: R. & D. McKERRON *v.* I.R.C. [1978] T.R. 489, Ct. of Session.

370. Capital gains—group of companies—beneficial ownership

[Income and Corporation Taxes Act 1970 (c. 10), ss. 272, 273, 526 (5).]

Shares acquired for a short time by a company as part of a tax avoidance scheme may be beneficially owned by the company.

H & B Co. wished to sell its shares in OBD Co. to Seagrams without incurring liability for corporation tax on chargeable gains. To this end, the following transactions were effected: (1) V Ltd. was formed with 76 participating preference shares being allotted to H & B Co. and 24 ordinary shares being allotted to Seagrams; (2) Z Ltd. was incorporated as the wholly owned subsidiary of V Ltd.; (3) with moneys provided by Seagrams Z Ltd. purchased the shares in OBD Co. from H & B Co.; (4) V Ltd. was wound up, £76 being repaid to H & B Co. and the shares in Z Ltd. being distributed to Seagrams. The scheme depended upon I.C.T.A. 1970, s. 273 (1) applying on the sale of shares by H & B Co. to Z Ltd. The Inland Revenue contended that H & B Co. was never the beneficial owner of the 76 participating preference shares in V Ltd. so that the section could not apply. *Held*, dismissing the appeal by the Inland Revenue, (1) there was no basis on which it could be said that H & B Co. was not the beneficial owner of the 76 participating preference shares, and (2) that Z Ltd. acquired the shares in OBD Co. as principal and not as agent or nominee for Seagrams.

BURMAN *v.* HEDGES & BUTLER [1979] 1 W.L.R. 160, Walton J.

371. —— sale of subsidiary—condition of waiver of loan—whether consideration apportioned between shares and waiver

[Finance Act 1965 (c. 25), s. 19, Sched. 6, para. 8, Sched. 7, paras. 5 (3) (*b*), 11 (1).]

Where a company sells a wholly-owned subsidiary to a purchaser for more than it paid for those shares, but with a condition that the company's loan to the subsidiary be waived, then the purchaser is paying consideration for the composite obligation, and apportionment between the two obligations must be made.

AC Ltd., a company, bought the whole share capital in RF Ltd. for £114,024, and it also made RF unsecured loans totalling £500,000. AC entered into a contract with a purchaser who agreed to purchase the whole share capital for £250,000 provided AC waive the loan. AC was assessed to corporation tax on the basis of a capital gain of £135,976 on the disposal of the shares. The Court of Session upheld the assessment. On appeal, *held*, allowing the appeal on a majority, that under the contract RF was paying consideration for the composite obligation not just the shares, and an apportionment was therefore necessary; secondly, the disposal of the debt did not give rise to an allowable loss as it was not a " debt on a security " as defined by the Act.

ABERDEEN CONSTRUCTION GROUP *v.* I.R.C. [1978] A.C. 885, H.L.

372. Chargeable gain—winding up—sale by liquidator

[Companies (Winding-up) Rules 1949 (S.I. 1949 No. 330), r. 195 (1); Companies Act 1948 (c. 38), s. 267.] In the course of a compulsory winding-up, the liquidator sold properties. The company was assessed to corporation tax on chargeable gains. *Held*, that the tax was not an expense incurred in realising assets, but was a charge or expense incurred in the winding up within s. 267 of the Companies Act 1948 which the court could order should rank after the liquidator's fees (*Re Beni-Falki Mining Co.* (1933) 18 T.C. 632 applied): *Re* MESCO PROPERTIES; *Re* MESCO LABORATORIES [1979] S.T.C. 11, Brightman J.

373. Land—profit—trade

S and certain other individuals formed a group of companies to acquire properties for development and investment. Prior to October 1965 the group acquired a number of properties. In October 1965 it was decided that unfavourable economic, financial and property circumstances made it appropriate to put the group into liquidation and to realise the properties. Accordingly, between 1967 and 1969 several properties were sold, producing an aggregate profit of £912,000. The Special Commission held that three of the properties sold were held as investments and the surplus attributable to those properties was on capital account; but that the other four properties had never been held as investments of the group, and that the surplus attributable thereto was a trading profit. *Held,* reversing the decision of Goulding J., that it was for the Commissioners to determine whether properties had been acquired or held as investments, and that where this was not positively established any profit on sale was assessable as a trading profit: SIMMONS (AS LIQUIDATOR OF LIONEL SIMMONS PROPERTIES) *v.* I.R.C. [1979] S.T.C. 471, C.A.

374. Profits—capital or revenue expenditure—reduction of rent

[Income and Corporation Taxes Act 1970 (c. 10), s. 130 (*f*).]

A payment made to secure a reduction in rent payable under a lease has been held to be capital.

In 1964 the taxpayer company took a long lease of a motorway service area. The lease provided for a fixed rent plus a percentage of gross takings which included tobacco duty on tobacco sold. Increases in tobacco duty caused the rental provisions to become onerous. Accordingly, the taxpayer company negotiated a variation of the lease to exclude tobacco duty; the consideration for the variation was the sum of £122,220 paid by the company. *Held* (Lord Salmon dissenting), that the payment of £122,220 procured the improvements of a fixed asset (the lease) and was capital expenditure not deductible in computing taxable profits (*Anglo-Persian Oil Co.* v. *Dale* [1932] 1 K.B. 124 distinguished).

TUCKER *v.* GRANADA MOTORWAY SERVICES [1979] 1 W.L.R. 683, H.L.

375. Trade—profits—employers' trust

The taxpayer company formed an employees' trust under s. 54 of the Companies Act 1948, and advanced moneys to the trustees to purchase shares in the company. On termination of the trust (which could be effected by 12 months' notice given to the trustees by the company) the shares were to be sold and the proceeds repaid to the company. *Held,* that the moneys advanced by the company to the trustees were in the character of loans and were not deductible in computing the profits of the company for tax purposes: RUTTER *v.* CHARLES SHARPE & CO. (1979) 123 S.J. 522, Goulding J.

BOOKS AND ARTICLES. See *post,* pp. [3], [17].

COUNTY COURT PRACTICE

376. Action—dismissal for want of prosecution—failure to comply with order for discovery

T claimed enfranchisement of his long lease. L conceded his entitlement except that they said the property had not been his sole or main residence for the five preceding years. An order for discovery was made. This was not complied with, and an order for specific discovery of, *inter alia,* all bank statements, building society books, and documents relating to investments, was made. T submitted a palpably incomplete list of documents. and was ordered to file an affidavit of documents. The object was to find other addresses also used by T during the five-year period, and any other properties he had. The affidavit was hopelessly defective. L got an order under the Bankers' Books Evidence Act 1879, which revealed that T had been dealing in property on a large scale and had certainly been living part of the time at another address. Every document relevant to the other address should have been produced—rates, telephone and gas bills, etc. The Court of Appeal, allowing L's appeal against the county court judge's refusal to dismiss T's application for want of prosecution, *held,* that T knew quite well he had been required to produce, but such flagrant failures to comply with the orders for discovery justified the drastic effect of an order under Ord. 14, r. 9: NWOKEJI *v.* NORTHUMBERLAND COURT (STREATHAM) (1978) 247 E.G. 733, C.A.

377. Administration of Justice Act 1977—commencement

ADMINISTRATION OF JUSTICE ACT 1977—(COMMENCEMENT No. 6) ORDER 1979 (No. 972 (C. 27)) [10p], made under the Administration of Justice Act 1977 (c. 38), s. 32 (6); operative on September 3, 1979; brings s. 20 of the 1977 Act into force.

378. Adoption. See MINORS.

378a. Contempt—committal order—unamended form used

[County Court (Amendment No. 4) Rules 1978 (S.I. 1978 No. 1943), r. 4.] A committal order was made in its unamended form. *Held,* it was necessary where the liberty of the subject was concerned that the procedural requirements were complied with. In this case, the defects were in the purely formal wording and in no way invalidated the order: PALMER *v.* TOWNSEND (1979) 123 S.J. 570, C.A.

379. Costs—sum recovered under £200—discretion of court

[C.C.R., Ord. 47, r. 5 (4) (4A).] The plaintiff sued the defendant for damages of £201·62 comprising vehicle repair bills and loss of profits in a taxi business, resulting from a road traffic accident, which sum was agreed in correspondence subject to liability. The defendant, backed by an insurance company, paid the sum of £161·36 into court on the grounds of contributory negligence on the plaintiff's part of 20 per cent. or more. The plaintiff having initially rejected the payment into court, sought the court's leave to take the sum out of court late and on notice applied for costs on Scale 1, *inter alia,* pursuant to Ord. 47, r. 5 (4A). The Registrar awarded costs on Scale 1 and the defendant appealed, contending that the plaintiff was not entitled to costs, having regard to Ord. 47, r. 5 (4), the sum recovered being under £200. *Held,* (1) discretion under Ord. 47, r. 5 (4A) was not an unfettered judicial discretion. There must be some unusual salient feature of the case, touching upon " the nature of the claim and defence and the circumstances of the parties " to justify the exercise of the discretion in a party's favour; (2) where a claim on full liability was over £200 and was reduced below £200 only as a result of contributory negligence, that was capable of being a ground for the exercise of the discretion; (3) the fact that one party was assisted by an insurance company and the other was a private litigant, of itself, in the absence of further extenuating circumstances, was not a ground for the exercise of the discretion: HARGREAVES *v.* KHAN, July 20, 1979, Mr. Recorder Spafford, Manchester County Ct. (*Ex rel. B. L. Lever, Esq., Barrister.*)

380. County court rules

COUNTY COURT (AMENDMENT) RULES 1979 (No. 1045 (L. 14)) [40p], made under the County Courts Act 1959 (c. 22), s. 102, operative on September 3, 1979; make various amendments to the Rules including allowing an adoption order following divorce to be made by the relevant divorce county court and requiring summonses sent by post to go first-class.

COUNTY COURT (AMENDMENT No. 2) RULES 1979 (No. 1488 (L. 21)) [20p], made under the County Courts Act 1959 (c. 22), s. 102; operative on December 10, 1979; amend the Rules so as to: (a) bring the forms of originating application for family provision under s. 1 of the Inheritance (Provision for Family and Dependants) Act 1975 and s. 35 of the Matrimonial Causes

Act 1973 into line with the upper limit of county court jurisdiction which was raised to £15,000 by S.I. 1978 No. 176; (b) require that where the court varies or discharges an injunction to which a power of arrest has been attached under s. 2 of the Domestic Violence and Matrimonial Proceedings Act 1976 that the police shall be notified; and (c) that the police shall be notified where the court directs under s. 28 of the Domestic Proceedings and Magistrates' Courts Act 1978 that a magistrates' court order to which a power of arrest has been attached shall cease to have effect.

381. Fees

COUNTY COURT FEES (AMENDMENT) ORDER 1979 (No. 967 (L. 11)) [10p], made under the County Courts Act 1959, s. 177, the Public Offices Fees Act 1879 (c. 58), s. 2 and the Companies Act 1948 (c. 38), s. 365 (3); operative on September 3, 1979; increases specified fees.

COUNTY COURT FEES (AMENDMENT No. 2) ORDER 1979 (No. 1149 (L.15)) [10p], made under the County Courts Act 1959, s. 177; the Public Officers Fees Act 1879 (c. 58), s. 2, and the Companies Act 1948 (c. 38), s. 365 (3); operative on September 24, 1979; increases the fee payable on the commencement of proceedings for any remedy or relief other than for the recovery of a sum of money or for the delivery of goods. The increase is from £5 to £10.

382. Funds

COUNTY COURT FUNDS (AMENDMENT) RULES 1979 (No. 105 (L.2)) [10p], made under the County Courts Act 1959 (c. 22), s. 168; operative on March 1, 1979; raise the rate of interest allowed on money in a short-term investment account to 12½ per cent. per annum.

COUNTY COURT FUNDS (AMENDMENT No. 2) RULES 1979 (No. 1619) [10p], made under the County Courts Act 1959, s. 168; operative on January 1, 1980; raise the rate of interest on money placed on short term investment account under the County Court Fund Rules 1965 from 12½ per cent. to 15 per cent. per annum.

383. Jury trial—false imprisonment claim—duty of judge

[County Courts Act 1959 (c. 22), s. 94 (3).] The plaintiff brought an action in the County Court claiming damages from the L.T.E. for false imprisonment alleging he had been wrongly detained by a ticket collector. The judge refused the plaintiff's application for trial by jury on the basis that there was no genuine issue on the facts. The Court of Appeal allowed his appeal since s. 94 (3) of the County Courts Act required the judge to order a trial if the plaintiff wanted one on a claim for false imprisonment. The judge was not entitled to form a view that the claim was suspect and so not an issue: HARMSWORTH v. LONDON TRANSPORT EXECUTIVE (1979) 123 S.J. 825, C.A.

384. Northern Ireland. See NORTHERN IRELAND.

385. Parties—locus standi—unincorporated association—" tangled " litigation

[County Court Rules 1936, Ord. 5, r. 6, Ord. 13, r. 6, Ord. 15, r. 1.] Upon a claim for specific performance of a landlord's repairing obligations in a lease by an unincorporated tenants' association, the respondent landlord applied to strike out the claim for want of jurisdiction. The registrar struck it out, but the county court judge reinstated it and allowed the applicant to amend to include a tenant as representative applicant. *Held,* allowing the appeal, the claim should be struck out. The judge may have had jurisdiction to amend the parties under Ord. 15 but, in view of the " almost impossible muddle " into which the case had got, he should not have exercised his discretion as he did. The claim for specific performance had been dropped in favour of one for damages and each of the tenants would have had different claims which were unsuited to a representative action. Dicta of Lord Buckmaster in *London Association for the Protection of Trade* v. *Greenlands* [1916] A.C. 15 at p. 20 as to "tangled" litigation approved: HERMITAGE COURT OWNERS' ASSOCIATION v. CLYFTVILLE PROPERTIES (1979) 251 E.G. 261, C.A.

386. Summonses—forms—separate proceedings against many defendants

The following Practice Direction was issued by the Lord Chancellor on March 1, 1979:

1. It sometimes happens that a plaintiff needs to bring separate proceedings in one county court against a great number of defendants. One example is the recovery of water charges; another is the recovery of money due under mail order transactions. The characteristics which such proceedings have in common are that the particulars of claim do not require more than a few lines, that service can be effected by post rather than by bailiff, that the default process, rather than the ordinary process, is appropriate and that the claim in each of the proceedings concerned is substantially the same.

2. In such cases, the forms prescribed for use in default actions involve more paperwork than is necessary and this creates difficulties both for the courts and for the parties. Accordingly, variations in the forms are required to authorise the following to be included on one side of a single piece of paper: —

(a) the particulars of claim,

(b) the relevant parts of the request for the issue of a default summons,

(c) a request for service out of the district (if appropriate), supported by a statement of the grounds on which the court of issue has jurisdiction to hear the case,

(d) an application for the proceedings to be referred to arbitration in the event of a dispute (if appropriate), and

(e) a declaration that the defendant is not legally incapacitated.

3. In the Schedule to this Direction is a composite form which incorporates these variations. The composite form may be used by any plaintiff whose particulars of claim can be stated within the space provided. It will be especially useful to plaintiffs issuing proceedings in bulk. The composite form is not suitable for actions in which the particulars of claim are lengthy or complicated, and should not be used in such cases. It is important, especially in cases of bulk issue, that the forms should follow the wording and the lay-out of the Schedule and should be completed clearly; otherwise they may be rejected by the court. Also, the paper must be of a size and type suitable for the copying equipment of the court in question. Plaintiffs wishing to use the composite form as a basis for bulk issue should first make inquiries at the proposed issuing court. Not all courts yet have the necessary copying and other equipment.

4. The composite form may not be used where bailiff service is required, but only where service is to be by post. Accordingly, the plaintiff will have to complete Form 6 (Certificate for Postal Service) as required by the Rules. However, the plaintiff need not make a separate certificate for each proceeding; a single certificate may be adapted to cover as many proceedings as may be appropriate in the circumstances.

5. Where the composite form is used, the plaintiff need file only one copy of the completed form. The court will make up a summons for service by means of copying equipment. Once issued the claim will proceed in the same way as any other default action.

6. The composite form is available for use from July 1, 1979.

SCHEDULE

IMPORTANT—Before completing this Form see instructions overleaf

| | Summons Number | |
| COUNTY COURT | | |

PARTICULARS OF CLAIM

Plaintiff

Plaintiff's Solicitor

Ref. No.

Defendant

| What the claim is for | Signed | Date |

I apply for this action, if defended to be referred to arbitration (Mark box if appropriate) ☐	Amount claimed	
	Court fee	
The defendant is not a person under disability	Solicitor's costs	
	TOTAL	

JURISDICTION (*DEFENDANT OUT OF DISTRICT*)	Date of issue	
	Date of service	
The facts relied upon as showing that the cause of action arose within the district are:	By posting on the	
	Officer	

The summons in this case has not been served having been returned by the Post Office marked "Gone away" or

| Officer | Date |

Form Ex135 Combined request and particulars of claim for Default Summons **(postal service only)**

NOTES FOR GUIDANCE

Please read these notes carefully before completing the request.
IMPORTANT NOTE:
This form can only be used for issue of a default summons for postal service. It will not be accepted unless the requirements for issue are met. The form should be completed by typewriter or computer and the entries must not extend outside the boxes provided. At the discretion of the Court handwritten forms may be accepted provided the information is clearly legible and otherwise complies with the requirements.

1. *Postal Service*:
   When using this form it is necessary to sign a certificate for postal service in Form 6. When several summonses are to be used at one time only one such certificate need be prepared, suitably adapted.

2. *Plaintiff*:
   Enter the Plaintiff's name in full and residence or place of business.
   If the Plaintiff is:
   (a) A female, state whether married, single or a widow.
   (b) Suing in a representative capacity, state in what capacity.
   (c) An infant required to sue by a next friend, state that fact, and names in full, residence or place of business, and occupation of next friend.
   (d) An assignor, state that fact, and name, address and occupation of assignor.
   (e) Two or more co-partners suing in the name of their firm, add " Suing as a Firm."
   (f) An individual trading in a name other than his own, give his own name followed by the words " trading as " and the name under which he trades.
   (g) A company registered under the Companies Act 1948, state the address of the registered office, and describe it as such.

3. *Plaintiff's Solicitor*:
   If the summons is entered by a solicitor his name, address and reference number should be entered in this box.

4. *Defendant*:
   Enter the Defendant's name, and (where known) his or her initials or names in full; defendant's residence or place of business (if a proprietor of the business). State whether male or female, and if female, whether Mrs. or Miss. State occupation (where known).
   If the Defendant is:
   (a) Sued in a representative capacity, state in what capacity.
   (b) Two or more co-partners sued in the name of their firm, or a person carrying on business in a name other than his own name who is sued in such name add " (Sued as a Firm)."
   (c) A company registered under the Companies Act 1948, the address given must be the registered office of the company, and must be so described.

5. *What the claim is for*:
   Make a brief statement of the nature of your dispute: (*e.g.* goods sold and delivered, work done, money due under an agreement).

6. *Particulars of claim*:
   Give the relevant dates and sufficient other details to inform the Defendant of the nature of the claim made against him. He is entitled to ask for further particulars but there should be sufficient information in the particulars given overleaf for the Court and the Defendant to be properly aware of the basic cause of action.

7. *Signature*:
   The person completing the form should sign and date it.

8. *Person under Disability* (a person aged under 18 or a mental patient):
   A default summons cannot be issued against a defendant who is a person under disability.

9. *Arbitration*:
   If you wish you may apply for the summons, if defended, to be dealt with by arbitration by marking the box.

10. *Jurisdiction*:

Unless the Defendant or one of the Defendants resides or carries on business within the district of the Court you must show that the cause of the action (*i.e.* the circumstances or transaction giving rise to the claim) arose wholly or partly within the district of the Court. The Court has jurisdiction to entertain the action pursuant to Order 2, Rule 1 of the County Court Rules 1936, if, for instance:

(a) The claim is founded on a contract made at an address within the district (the address must be stated).

(b) The claim is founded on a contract under which payment is to be made at an address within the district (the address must be stated).

A Plaintiff seeking to use this form to pursue hire-purchase claims must provide all the information required on Form 11.

11. *Amount claimed*:

Enter the total amount you are claiming. The Court fee is based on this amount.

BOOKS AND ARTICLES. See *post*, pp. [3], [17].

CRIMINAL LAW

387. Affray—cautions—application of Judges Rules

The prosecution must put in, as part of the prosecution case, available evidence which is probative of other issues in the case, but not evidence going only to credit. It is not necessary when police are taking statements about an affray for them to check each person, see if there is evidence against that person, then caution him.

D was charged with affray. During cross-examination of the defendant, the judge allowed prosecution counsel to put in a number of uncautioned statements which had not been adduced during the prosecution case, which did not amount to admissions, and went to credit only. In doing so, the judge indicated that D's counsel would be permitted to counter them with evidence if he wished. D was convicted. On appeal, *held*, dismissing the appeal, that the prosecution need not adduce as part of its case non-probative evidence relating only to the defendant's credit. The police could not be expected to consider all persons involved and caution them under the Judges' Rules. (Dictum of Winn J. in *R.* v. *Rice* [1963] C.L.Y. 677 applied.)

R. v. HALFORD (1978) 67 Cr.App.R. 318, C.A.

388. Appeal—fresh evidence—inadmissible documents

[Criminal Appeal Act 1968 (c. 19), ss. 2, 7, 23.]

An appellant cannot put himself in a better position by appealing, on the ground that inadmissible documents make the conviction unsafe and unsatisfactory under s. 2 of the Criminal Appeal Act 1968, than he would have been in had the documents been admissible and he had appealed under s. 23 on the ground of fresh evidence.

The appellants were stopped in their car with a boot full of explosives. They claimed that they had been planted. They were convicted of possessing explosive substances contrary to s. 4 of the Explosive Substances Act 1883. After their trial, statements were obtained to the effect that two other men had confessed to planting the explosives. The statements were inadmissible as evidence. The appellants appealed under s. 2 of the Criminal Appeal Act 1968 on the ground that the statements rendered the convictions unsafe and unsatisfactory. Leave was not sought to adduce fresh evidence under s. 23, since it was accepted that the statements were inadmissible. *Held*, dismissing the appeals, that the Court of Appeal could not overturn the jury's verdicts on the basis of inadmissible documents. (*Stafford* v. *D.P.P.*; *Luvaglio* v. *D.P.P.* [1973] C.L.Y. 475 applied; dictum of Widgery L.J. in *R.* v. *Cooper* (*Sean*) [1969] C.L.Y. 818 explained.)

R. v. WALLACE; R. v. SHORT (1978) 67 Cr.App.R. 291, C.A.

389. —— —— reference by Secretary of State—whether evidence likely to be credible

[Criminal Appeal Act 1968 (c. 19), ss. 17, 23.]

Fresh evidence will not be admitted following conviction unless it is likely to be credible and would afford some defence to the charge in question.

In 1970 the appellant was convicted of a murder occurring in Luton in 1969. The appellant claimed to have been in London at the material time. In 1974 a witness, H, made a statement to the appellant's solicitors to the effect that he had seen the appellant in London on a date which he could not specify; but the effect of another witness's statement (such witness having been available, but not being called, at the trial) was that H's sightings had been on the day of the murder. The other witness, L, had previously made an inconsistent statement. The Secretary of State referred the case to the Court of Appeal under s. 17 (1) of the 1968 Act. *Held*, that the fresh evidence now available was not likely to be credible, within s. 23 (2) (*a*) of the Act and did not justify the inference that the appellant was other than at the scene of the crime, and that accordingly the evidence was inadmissible.

R. *v*. McMAHON (1978) 68 Cr.App.R. 18, C.A.

390. —— frivolous—meaning—registrar's reference
[Criminal Appeal Act 1968 (c. 19), s. 20.] T was charged with burglary under s. 9 (1) (*a*) of the Theft Act 1968. Property was stolen from the house concerned on the relevant occasion. T submitted that where the evidence showed that a theft had taken place, the prosecution were obliged to proceed under s. 9 (1) (*b*). The submission was rejected, T pleaded guilty and appealed against conviction and the Registrar of Criminal Appeals referred the case to the Court of Appeal under s. 20 of the Criminal Appeal Act 1968. *Held*, that T's point was unarguable and bound to fail. " Frivolous " in s. 20 covered such a situation and did not mean only foolish or silly. The appeal would therefore be dismissed without argument: R. *v*. TAYLOR [1979] Crim.L.R. 649, C.A.

391. —— Hong Kong—proviso—application
[Criminal Procedure Ordinance (Laws of Hong Kong 1972, c. 221), s. 83 (1); Dangerous Drugs Ordinance (Laws of Hong Kong 1974, c. 134), s. 47.]
Where the effect of a legislative provision which alters the standard and burden of proof is overlooked, the verdict of guilty cannot be other than unsafe and unsatisfactory.
Per curiam: Although the Privy Council is reluctant to interfere with a decision of the local court of criminal appeal as to the application of the proviso to s. 83 (1) of the Criminal Procedure Ordinance, it will do so where a decision is based upon an error involving some principle of general importance to the administration of criminal justice.
The appellants, who were jade merchants, were indicted jointly on one count of trafficking in a dangerous drug, namely morphine. On arrival, six parcels of jadestones, accompanied by two copies of an air waybill in which the first appellant was named as consignee, were found to contain packets of morphine, hidden in two hollowed-out jadestones. At the trial, the real issue was whether the appellants knew of the presence of morphine in the consignment. The Crown relied on the fact that the first appellant had been given the consignee's copy of the air waybill and the D.C. & I. Receipt, as giving rise to the presumptions for which s. 47 (3) and (4) of the Dangerous Drugs Ordinance provide. A common error of law was made by the Crown, in that, although not documents mentioned by name in s. 47, it was accepted that the air waybill and D.C. & I. Receipt were documents of a kind that raised the statutory presumption. The Court of Appeal held that it was not necessary to reach a final decision of whether s. 47 of the Dangerous Drugs Ordinance applied to the D.C. & I. Receipt, and applied the proviso to s. 83 (1) of the Criminal Procedure Ordinance. *Held*, allowing the appeal, that fundamental principle in the criminal law of Hong Kong is that the prosecution must prove the existence of all essential elements of the offence charged " beyond all reasonable doubt." Where, modern legislation provides that certain facts are presumed to exist, unless the contrary is proved, the effect is to allow the jury to draw an inference unless they are satisfied that on the balance of possibilities it is wrong. So they must draw it even though they think that it is equally likely to be right as to be wrong. As a result of the Court of Appeal overlooking this effect of the presumption, the jury were misdirected and believed that they were bound to convict unless on the balance of probabilities, they thought the appellants' story was true. A proper direction would have allowed them to

acquit if they thought the story was possibly true. Therefore the conviction was quashed and the case remitted to the Court of Appeal to consider whether or not to order a new trial.

KWAN PING BONG v. THE QUEEN [1979] 2 W.L.R. 433, P.C.

392. —— **joinder of informations—attempt**

S, not having objected in the juvenile court to being tried on two informations both alleging arson, appealed against conviction. In the Crown Court, S refused to consent to the two informations being tried together and submitted that there was no evidence of damage. *Held*, that (1) the Crown Court sitting in its appellate capacity and trying an appeal by way of rehearing, stands in the same position as a juvenile or magistrates' court; (2) S was not estopped from objecting to the joinder of the two informations because of his actual or implied consent thereto in the juvenile court; (3) the Crown Court in its appellate capacity could not order joinder of the two informations without the consent of the accused (*Brangwynne* v. *Evans* [1962] C.L.Y. 1852; *Aldus* v. *Watson* [1973] C.L.Y. 2085 considered); (4) on appeal, the Crown Court could only convict or acquit on the offence specified in the information: where an information charged the substantive offence only and that was not made out, the information must be dismissed, even though a prima facie case of attempted arson had been established. (*Lawrence* v. *Same* [1968] C.L.Y. 925; *Garfield* v. *Maddocks* [1973] C.L.Y. 470 considered): SEDWELL v. JAMES, September 3 and 19, 1979, Judge Picot, Q.C., Reading Crown Ct. (*Ex rel. P. J. Stage, Esq., Barrister.*)

393. —— **jurisdiction—Court of Appeal**

The applicant was awaiting trial on a criminal charge. He brought a private prosecution against an intended witness for the prosecution of his case alleging, *inter alia*, swearing a false statement. The Director of Public Prosecutions took this over and offered no evidence against the witness who was discharged. The applicant sought judicial review against the D.P.P. but the Divisional Court refused. The Court of Appeal *held*, that it had no jurisdiction to hear the appeal since it involved a criminal cause or matter by virtue of s. 31 (1) of the Supreme Court of Judicature Act 1925. Any appeal must be by way of leave to the House of Lords: R. v. D.P.P., *ex p.* RAYMOND (1979) 123 S.J. 786, C.A.

394. —— **natural justice—opportunity to state case.** See R. v. CARLISLE CROWN COURT, *ex p.* ARMSTRONG, § 17.

395. —— **petition for leave to appeal**

The following Practice Direction was issued by the House of Lords on March 6, 1979:

Criminal petitions for leave to appeal to the House of Lords in respect of which no certificate has been granted by the court below under s. 1 (2) of the Administration of Justice Act 1960 or s. 33 (2) of the Criminal Appeal Act 1968 will not be received in the Judicial Office.

This accords with the decision of this House in *Gelberg* v. *Miller* [1961] C.L.Y. 1973, which has since been held by the Appeal Committee to apply to s. 33 (2) of the Criminal Appeal Act 1968 as it applies to s. 1 (2) of the Administration of Justice Act 1960.

[1979] 1 W.L.R. 498; (1979) 123 S.J. 324.

396. —— **remission of case—justices' rejection of direction**

On a committal for sentence, but not an appeal against conviction, the Crown Court has a discretion to re-open a plea and remit the case to the magistrates; the Divisional Court will not interfere unless the court has acted in excess of jurisdiction.

N was charged with " going equipped." He had made a written confession and at the magistrates' court appeared in person and pleaded guilty. He was committed for sentence. Counsel persuaded the court to reopen the plea and remit to a named stipendiary magistrate. The magistrate refused to hear the case. On application (a) for certiorari quashing the Crown Court's order, or (b) for mandamus ordering the magistrate to hear the case, *held*, that the Crown Court was acting within its jurisdiction to remit, but mandamus would

lie directed to the justices not the named stipendiary. (*R. v. Mutford and Lothingland Justices, ex p. Harber* ⌊1971⌋ C.L.Y. 7150 applied.)
R. *v.* INNER LONDON CROWN COURT, *ex p.* SLOPER; R. *v.* CAMBERWELL GREEN MAGISTRATE, *ex p.* SLOPER (1978) 69 Cr.App.R. 1, D.C.

397. Arson—ability to foresee risk—correct test
[Criminal Damage Act 1971 (c. 48), s. 1 (1) (3).]
A person charged under s. 1 of the Criminal Damage Act 1971 must be proved actually to have foreseen the risk of some damage resulting from his actions and nevertheless to have run the risk.

S went into a large straw stack in a field and tried to go to sleep. He was cold so he lit a fire of twigs and straw in a hollow in the side of the stack. The stack caught fire and he was charged, *inter alia,* with arson. S did not give evidence at the trial but an experienced consultant psychiatrist gave evidence that S had a long history of schizophrenia and that S was capable of lighting a fire in a straw stack to keep warm without taking the danger into account. S was convicted, and appealed on the ground, *inter alia,* that the judge had failed to direct the jury that the test of whether a man was reckless or not was a subjective test. *Held,* allowing the appeal, that the conviction was unsafe because the jury had not been left to decide whether S's schizophrenia might have prevented the idea of danger entering his mind at all. (*Herrington* v. *British Railways Board* [1972] C.L.Y. 2344 applied; *R.* v. *Parker* [1977] C.L.Y. 491 explained.)
R. *v.* STEPHENSON [1979] 3 W.L.R. 193, C.A.

398. —— mens rea—intoxication
O's defence to a charge of arson contrary to s. 1 (2) of the Criminal Damage Act 1971 was that he was depressed and started a fire without thinking of the consequences, having drunk five pints of beer. The prosecution alleged recklessness as to whether people's lives would be endangered. *Held,* that self-induced intoxication was no defence to a charge under s. 1 (2) (*R.* v. *O'Driscoll* [1967] C.L.Y. 735, *D.P.P.* v. *Majewski* [1976] C.L.Y. 487 and *R.* v. *Stephenson* [1979] C.L.Y. 397 considered): R. *v.* ORPIN [1979] Crim.L.R. 722, York Crown Ct.

399. Assault—damages—exemplary—police assault on prisoner—relevance of provocation
A police sergeant was held to have struck O'C one or two unnecessary blows in attempting to restrain O'C and remove his jacket and shoes for his own protection. O'C's counsel had conceded that if there was provocation, exemplary damages were inappropriate. Severe provocation was found and very modest damages awarded. *Held,* dismissing O'C's appeal, that (1) O'C should not be bound by his counsel's concession; (2) all the circumstances were relevant in deciding whether O'C's pride and dignity had been wounded and the officer had been malicious, including provocation, so as to reduce or eliminate any aggravated damages which might otherwise be appropriate; (3) exemplary damages did not have to be awarded where a police officer had abused his authority. Everything which aggravates or mitigates the defendant's conduct is relevant. (*Rookes* v. *Barnard* [1964] C.L.Y. 3703 and *Broome* v. *Cassell & Co.* [1972] C.L.Y. 2745 applied): O'CONNOR *v.* HEWITSON [1979] Crim.L.R. 46, C.A.

400. —— on police—whether acting in execution of duty
[Police Act 1964 (c. 48), s. 51 (1).] D was one of a noisy group who refused to move on from an arcade when required to do so by X, a police constable. When X asked the group again to move D began to get up slowly. X then caught hold of D's arm and refused to let go. A struggle ensued during which D punched X several times. *Held,* allowing D's appeal against conviction of assaulting X in the execution of his duty, contrary to s. 51 (1) of the 1964 Act, that as X had not apprehended a breach of the peace, D's reaction to X's action was justified: HICKMAN *v.* O'DWYER [1979] Crim. L.R. 309, D.C.

401. —— —— —— arrest for civil matter without warrant. See DE COSTA SMALL *v.* KIRKPATRICK, § 133.

402. —— —— —— **ejecting defendant from police station**

[Police Act 1964 (c. 48), s. 5 (1).] X, Y and Z were arrested and questioned after which they were released and given an apology. A police sergeant kept Y's car keys, as Y had only a provisional licence, intending to prevent the commission of an offence. Z held a full licence. Y and Z refused to leave the police station, insisting on return of the keys. The sergeant ejected them and Z hit and kicked the sergeant. The Crown Court dismissed Z's appeal against conviction of assaulting the sergeant in the execution of his duty contrary to s. 5 (1) of the 1964 Act. *Held*, refusing an order of mandamus requiring the judge to state a case, that it was for the sergeant in charge to decide whether a person could stay at a police station. The evidence of noise and refusal to leave until the keys were returned was sufficient for the court to find that the sergeant had acted reasonably and in the execution of his duty in requiring Y and Z to leave: R. *v.* KNIGHTSBRIDGE CROWN COURT, *ex p.* UMEH [1979] Crim.L.R. 727, D.C.

403. Attempt—impossibility—obtaining free plays on fruit machine—" conditional " intent to steal

C and M used wire to obtain free plays on a fruit machine by tripping a microswitch. Each free play obtained was in the event unsuccessful. *Held*, that (1) the defendants' act was sufficiently proximate to theft to amount to attempt as it was the last act in the series which lay within their power; (2) although a man cannot attempt a crime which is impossible, this crime was possible, although success was uncertain; (3) the defendants' intention to steal was not conditional, although its fulfilment was conditional on the machine's behaviour: R. *v.* COOPER AND MILES [1979] Crim.L.R. 43, Leicester Crown Ct.

404. —— **theft—intention—loitering**

On a charge of attempted theft failure by the prosecution to prove a specific intention to steal the objects actually contained in a victim's bag is not fatal to the prosecution's case. On a charge of being a suspected person loitering with intent to commit an arrestable offence, the prosecution need not prove that at the time of loitering the defendant has formed the intent to steal a specific object.

In the first case D was charged with attempting to steal property unknown belonging to X. The facts were that D was seen at a tube station with his hand in X's bag. He took hold of an article without removing it, looked at it and put it back. D contended that there was no case and that his appropriation could only be conditional. The Crown conceded that failure to prove a specific intention to steal the objects actually contained in the bag was fatal to the prosecution and this submission was upheld. In the second case A and B were charged with loitering with intent to commit an arrestable offence, contrary to s. 4 of the Vagrancy Act 1824. A had been seen to point to a woman's shopping bag, then reach towards it. A then jostled another woman and B touched her bag. The justices allowed a submission of no case on the ground that the prosecution had to prove that at the material time A and B had formed the intent to steal specific property. On appeal by the prosecution in both cases, *held*, allowing both appeals, (1) failure to prove a specific intention to steal the objects actually contained in the bag was not fatal to the prosecution; (2) nor, in the second case, was failure to prove the intention to steal a specific object. (*R.* v. *Easom* [1971] C.L.Y. 2816 and *R.* v. *Husseyn* [1978] C.L.Y. 415 considered.)

SCUDDER *v.* BARRETT; MILES *v.* CLOVIS (NOTE) [1979] 3 W.L.R. 591, D.C.

405. Autrefois acquit—stay of indictment—court's discretion—oppressiveness

R was tried for and acquitted of. *inter alia*, theft of a hydraulic jack. In a fresh indictment he was charged with stealing an outboard motor. The outboard motor was alleged to have been stolen at the same time and from the same person as the jack. The defence to the first charge had been that the items were unwanted and the owner had said R could do what he wished with them. It was conceded that the defence of *autrefois acquit* was strictly not available to R. *Held*, that in the exercise of the court's discretion the prosecution would be stayed not to be proceeded with without the leave of the court or the Court of Appeal as the matter was stale and a conviction would not be logical in view of the earlier acquittal (*R.* v. *Humphreys* [1977] C.L.Y. 622 considered): R. *v.* ROBERTS [1979] Crim.L.R. 44, Southampton Crown Ct.

406. Bail—absconding—manner in which defendant can be sentenced
  [Bail Act 1976 (c. 63), s. 6 (5).]
  S. 6 of the Bail Act 1976 gives a judge power to deal with an absconder on the spot as though he had committed a criminal contempt of court.
  D was given bail over the weekend during his trial at the Central Criminal Court. On Sunday night he got so drunk that he failed to appear on Monday until he was brought to court at 2 p.m. At the conclusion of the trial, when the jury disagreed, D was brought before the court, where he admitted the offence of absconding. The judge sentenced him summarily to three months' imprisonment as if the offence was a criminal contempt of court under s. 6 (5) of the Bail Act 1976. On appeal, D contended that it was not a contempt in the face of the court and there was no immediate urgency which justified the judge in acting summarily. *Held*, the words " in the face of the court " had been deliberately omitted from the Act, which was designed to provide the Crown Court with the swift remedy of treating the offence as a criminal contempt without the necessity for more elaborate proceedings. The judge had the power to act as he did, but the sentence would be reduced to one month's imprisonment. (*Balogh* v. *St. Albans Crown Court* [1974] C.L.Y. 2912 distinguished.)
  R. *v.* HARBAX SINGH [1979] 2 W.L.R. 100, C.A.

407. —— pending appeal to the Court of Appeal—principles
  Bail will still only be granted on an appeal to the Court of Appeal in exceptional circumstances; those exceptional circumstances include a prima facie likelihood of success, or the risk that the sentence will have been served by the time the appeal has been heard.
  A was convicted of handling stolen goods and sentenced to 12 months' imprisonment. He appealed against sentence to the Court of Appeal. The single judge granted leave but refused bail. Application was then made to the full court. *Held*, that para. 5 of Appendix F to the pronouncement of the Advisory Council on the Penal System correctly stated that bail would only be granted by the Court of Appeal where it appeared prima facie that the appeal was likely to be successful or where there was a risk that the sentence would have been served by the time the appeal was heard. The true question was, were there exceptional circumstances which would drive the court to the conclusion that justice could only be done by the granting of bail? There was not, and bail would be refused. (*R.* v. *MacDonald* (1928) 21 Cr.App.R. 26 and *R.* v. *Howeson and Hardy* (1936) 25 Cr.App.R. 167 considered.)
  R. *v.* WATTON (1978) 68 Cr.App.R. 293, C.A.

408. Betting and gambling. See GAMING AND WAGERING.

409. Blasphemous libel—mens rea—whether intent to blaspheme necessary
  The offence of blasphemous libel is made out by proving the intentional publication of matter which is in fact blasphemous; an intent to blaspheme is not an ingredient.
  The appellants were convicted of blasphemous libel, they having published a magazine containing a poem and accompanying drawing describing in detail acts of sodomy and fellatio upon the body of Christ and describing promiscuous homosexual practices indulged in by Christ in his lifetime. The jury were directed that it was not necessary for the Crown to prove an intention by the appellants to blaspheme; such direction was upheld by the Court of Appeal. *Held*, dismissing the appellants' further appeal (Lord Diplock and Lord Edmund-Davies dissenting), that the offence was complete if the jury found that the article was blasphemous and that the appellants had intentionally published it. (Decision of C.A. [1978] C.L.Y. 420, affirmed; *R.* v. *Bradlaugh* (1883) 15 Cox C.C. 217 and *R.* v. *Ramsay and Foote* (1883) 15 Cox C.C. 231 applied.)
  R. *v.* LEMON; R. *v.* GAY NEWS [1979] 2 W.L.R. 281, H.L.

410. Breach of peace—arrest—validity. See R. *v.* PODGER, § 130.

411. Burglary—aggravated—possession of firearm—" with him "

[Theft Act 1968 (c. 60), s. 10.] If two men agree to and do enter a building as trespassers and share at the time of entry an intent that grievous bodily harm should be inflicted by one or other or both of them on a person therein, and one of them carries a firearm or weapon of offence, then the other also has the firearm or weapon " with him " and so both are guilty of aggravated burglary contrary to s. 10 of the Theft Act 1968, provided that the carrying of the firearm or weapon was in the contemplation of both before entry. The one not carrying the firearm or weapon has it " immediately available to " him within the meaning of the definition of " with him " in R. v. *Kelt* [1978] C.L.Y. 1474: R. *v.* JONES, November 30, 1979, Solomon J., Middlesex Crown Ct. (*Ex rel. James Goudie, Esq., Barrister.*)

412. —— building—freezer container

[Theft Act 1968 (c. 60), s. 9.] B and S stole goods from a freezer container in a farmyard, the container being 25 feet long by seven feet by seven feet, weighing three tons and not having been moved for over two years. *Held*, dismissing appeals against findings of guilt of burglary, that the container was " a structure of considerable size and intended to be permanent or at least to endure for a considerable time " and was therefore a building within s. 9 of the 1968 Act: B. AND S. *v.* LEATHLEY [1979] Crim.L.R. 314, Carlisle Crown Ct.

413. —— conditional intent to steal

[Theft Act 1968 (c. 60), s. 9 (1) (*a*).] G went into a house as a trespasser looking for money to steal but not knowing or believing there was any specific sum in the house. *Held*, that there was no case for G to answer on a charge of entering as a trespasser with intent to steal as his intent was conditional upon money worth stealing being found by him. (*R.* v. *Easom* [1971] C.L.Y. 2816 applied): R. *v.* GREENHOFF [1979] Crim.L.R. 108, Huddersfield Crown Ct.

414. —— intent to steal—nothing worth stealing

[Theft Act 1968 (c. 60), s. 9 (1) (*a*).]

To establish the offence of burglary with intent to steal it is not necessary to specify any particular article as being the object of the burglar's intention, nor is it a defence that the trespasser intended to steal only if he found something worth stealing.

The court considered two references by the Attorney-General concerning the necessary intention to be proved to have been had by a trespasser for the purposes of the offence under s. 9 (1) (*a*) of the 1968 Act. That offence is made out if it is proved that at the time of entry (or, in the case of an attempt, attempted entry) the defendant had an intention to steal; it matters not that the building contains nothing worth stealing. The court further indicated that in the case of theft-related offences, the indictment need not in appropriate cases specify the items to be stolen, or it may describe the items generically (such as " the contents of a handbag "), provided that the defendant thereby receives adequate details of what he is alleged to have done (Dictum of Lord Scarman in *D.P.P.* v. *Nock* [1978] C.L.Y. 430 and *R.* v. *Walkington* [1979] C.L.Y. 415 applied; *R.* v. *Easom* [1971] C.L.Y. 2816, dictum of Lord Scarman in *R.* v. *Husseyn* [1978] C.L.Y. 415 and *R.* v. *Hector* [1979] C.L.Y. 580 explained.)

Re ATT.-GEN.'S REFERENCES (NOS. 1 AND 2 OF 1979) [1979] 3 All E.R. 143, C.A.

415. —— trespasser—" part of a building "—shop counter area—whether intent to steal conditional

[Theft Act 1968 (c. 60), s. 9 (1) (*a*).]

A jury is entitled to conclude that a counter area within a shop is a part of a building from which the public are excluded.

The appellant was seen in a department store to enter into a counter area situated on the sales floor and there open the till drawer (which was empty). He then left. He was charged with entering as a trespasser " part of a building " with intent to steal. He claimed in evidence that he had not realised that he was not permitted to enter the counter area. He was convicted following the trial judge's direction to the jury in which he left to them the issues as to whether the counter area was a part of the building and whether the appellant had knowingly entered it as a trespasser. The jury were further left to decide whether at that time the appellant intended to steal. *Held*, dismissing his appeal, that (1) the jury were correctly left to consider the issue of trespass; and (2) the evidence clearly indicated the appellant's intention to steal the contents of the till; a person entering premises intending to steal is guilty of an offence notwithstanding that there is nothing in the premises worth stealing. (*R.* v. *Husseyn* [1978] C.L.Y. 415 distinguished; *R.* v. *Greenhoff* [1979] C.L.Y. 413 overruled.)

R v. WALKINGTON [1979] 2 All E.R. 716, C.A.

416. Certiorari—witness statements—prosecutor's failure to disclose

It is a denial of natural justice for a prosecutor to fail to disclose witnesses' statements favourable to the defence or call witnesses and the conviction should be quashed.

H, was convicted of driving without due care and attention contrary to Road Traffic Act 1972, s. 3. It had been in issue at the trial whether H's car had been either partly or wholly over the centre line of the road. After the trial the police notified H's solicitors of the existence of two further witnesses whose evidence might have been helpful to H. The police had not called these witnesses nor disclosed the existence of statements from these witnesses before. *Held*, although the blame fell on the prosecutor not the tribunal, there had been a clear breach of natural justice. H had not had a fair trial and certiorari should go to quash the conviction.

R. v. LEYLAND JUSTICES, *ex p.* HAWTHORN [1979] 2 W.L.R. 28, D.C.

417. Compensation order—no application—whether appropriate

In the absence of application by the loser it may be inappropriate to make a compensation order where it is not clear that the loser seeks to recover all or part of the money lost.

The defendant was convicted of obtaining by deception a number of improvement grants from the local council by falsely stating in applications therefor that the houses in question were in the occupation of various of his sons and himself. He was fined £4,000 and ordered to pay some £5,000 in compensation to the council who had not made application for compensation. *Held*, allowing his appeal and quashing the compensation order, that since it was not clear to what extent the council sought to recover the sums paid and as there was some evidence of negotiations relating thereto between the defendant and the council, this was not such an uncomplicated case that a summary order for compensation was justified.

R. v. SHAN (1979) 77 L.G.R. 600, C.A.

418. —— principles to be followed—order to be realistic

[Criminal Justice Act 1972 (c. 71), s. 1 (1).]

A compensation order must be realistic and must take account, *inter alia*, of the offender's means.

In quashing a compensation order for some £6,200 made in addition to a 15-month prison sentence imposed for offences of theft by an appellant, who at the time of his trial was apparently without substantial means, the Court of Appeal summarised the principles to be followed in respect of such orders, as follows: (1) the order is not an alternative to a sentence; (2) it should be made only where the legal position is quite clear; (3) regard must be had to the defendant's means; (4) the order must be precise and relate to offences of which the defendant has been convicted or which he seeks to have taken into consideration; (5) it must not be oppressive; (6) there may be good grounds for ordering compensation to be paid by instalments in order to remind the defendant of this crime; and (7) it must be realistic: in particular, an instalments order over a long period is undesirable.

R. v. MILLER (NOTE) (1976) 68 Cr.App.R. 56, C.A.

419. Conspiracy—burden of proof—whether crime impossible to perform—guidelines given

Where there is no evidence or information available to suggest that a conspiracy is incapable of implementation, it is not incumbent upon the Crown to prove that it was possible to carry out the agreement.

The appellants were convicted of conspiring to be concerned in the possession of cannabis. There was evidence that they were concerned in an enterprise whereby cannabis was to be acquired from a third party. During their appeals against conviction, which were dismissed, it was contended, *inter alia*, that the Crown had a duty to prove that the illegal agreement was capable of being carried out; the court gave the following guidelines, applicable to common law conspiracies: (1) if the Crown is in possession of evidence that at the time the agreement was made it would have been impossible to carry it out, it must call the evidence or make it available to the defence; (2) if there is no such evidence the Crown has no duty to prove the carrying out of the agreement to have been possible, the evidential burden of proving the contrary being initially at least upon the defence; (3) but if there is some evidence of impossibility, the probative burden rests on the Crown and the jury must be directed appropriately; and (4) if there is no evidence of impossibility, the jury need not be directed upon it. The court further distinguished an agreement which could never, if carried out, result in the commission of a crime because such a result is physically or legally impossible, from an agreement which if carried out in accordance with the conspirator's intentions would result in the commission of a crime but which cannot in fact be carried out by reason of some other person's reluctance to play a necessary role, or the conspirators' incompetence or the impregnable defences of the intended victim; in the case of the latter type of agreement, to hold that it was not a criminal conspiracy would be " to ignore the basis " of the crime. (*Haughton* v. *Smith* (1947) C.L.C. 637 considered; *D.P.P.* v. *Nock and Alsford* [1978] C.L.Y. 430 distinguished.)

R. *v.* BENNETT, WILFRED AND WEST (1979) 68 Cr.App.R. 168, C.A.

420. —— failure to implement—manufacture of controlled drug
[Misuse of Drugs Act 1971 (c. 38), s. 4 (1).]

Where persons enter into an agreement to do an unlawful act which is inherently possible of consummation, though they fail for some reason, they can properly be convicted of the conspiracy.

The appellant, H, and four others attempted to make the drug amphetamine. They had the correct formula but failed because they did not know the proper process. They were convicted of conspiracy to do an unlawful act contrary to s. 4 (1) of the 1971 Act. H appealed on the ground that the conspiracy was impossible of fulfilment. *Held*, dismissing the appeal, that H had entered into a conspiracy which was inherently possible of consummation and was rightly convicted. (*D.P.P.* v. *Nock and Alsford* [1978] C.L.Y. 430 distinguished.)

R. *v.* HARRIS (1979) 69 Cr.App.R. 122, C.A.

421. —— intention to steal—whether charge of conspiracy to defraud preferable
[Criminal Law Act 1977 (c. 45), ss. 1 (1), 5 (2).]

Where the obvious purpose of a conspiracy is to commit a specific offence such as theft, that conspiracy should be charged as conspiracy to commit the specific offence and not as conspiracy to defraud at common law.

Per curiam: It is not right to give a literal construction to s. 5 (2) when the effect of so doing would largely destroy the obvious purpose of the Act.

The five appellants visited 11 shops but stole nothing. The were charged with conspiracy to steal and at the trial were cross-examined without objection about previous convictions to show that the offences had been stealing from shops. They were convicted. They appealed on the grounds that (1) s. 5 (2) of the 1977 Act required that the charge be conspiracy to defraud contrary to common law, and (2) the cross-examination was improper. *Held*, dismissing the appeal, that (1) where the obvious purpose of the conspiracy was to commit a specific offence such as theft, the conspiracy should be charged as conspiracy to commit the specific offence contrary to s. 1 (1) of the 1977 Act and not as conspiracy to defraud at common law contrary to s. 5 (2) (dictum of Lord

Widgery C.J. in *R.* v. *Walters* [1979] C.L.Y. 492 doubted); (2) since the sole issue at the trial had been the appellants' intent, the cross-examination without objection was proper.

R. v. DUNCALF [1979] 1 W.L.R. 918, C.A.

422. —— participation—uncommunicated intention to participate

An uncommunicated intention to join in a criminal enterprise does not *per se* amount to a indictable conspiracy.

The appellant was convicted of conspiracy to supply controlled drugs. She admitted to having agreed to open a bank account in a false name for the purpose of receiving moneys for what she thought to be an illegal enterprise but asserted that it was not until a later date that she discovered the nature of the enterprise, whereafter she did no act in pursuance of the alleged conspiracy, the judge directed the jury that they might convict her upon her version of events, although she had not communicated her intention to assist in the conspiracy to her alleged co-conspirators. *Held*, allowing the appeal, that a secret and uncommunicated intention could not in these circumstances support a conspiracy count.

R. v. SCOTT (1978) 68 Cr.App.R. 164, C.A.

423. Contempt—publication of information unknown to jury

The public interest in free reporting by newspapers does not outweigh the private interest of an individual accused in ensuring his fair trial.

Border Television and the Newcastle Chronicle published the fact that X had committed other offences whilst he was on trial for theft and deception. They were charged with contempt of court. They argued that public policy required free reporting, which outweighed the private interests of the accused. *Held*, the conflict was not between public and private interests, but between two public interests, and freedom of speech must be restricted where it would prejudice the administration of justice. (Dicta of Lord Reid in *Att.-Gen.* v. *Times Newspapers* [1973] C.L.Y. 2618 applied.)

R. v. BORDER TELEVISION, *ex p.* ATT.-GEN.; R. v. NEWCASTLE CHRONICLE AND JOURNAL, *ex p.* ATT.-GEN. (1978) 68 Cr.App.R. 375, D.C.

424. Corruption—accepting a bribe—acceptor's intentions

[Prevention of Corruption Act 1906 (c. 34), s. 1; Prevention of Corruption Act 1916 (c. 64), s. 2.]

Where a gift is prima facie given corruptly, the onus is on the acceptor to show that he intended to treat it otherwise, by " double-crossing " the donor.

An engineering firm pursued the practice of suborning employees of the British Steel Corp. in order to obtain substantial construction and repairing contracts. The appellant, who was the head of new works at BSC, enjoyed the benefit of three holidays for himself and his wife at that firm's expense. At his trial for corruptly accepting the holidays, the appellant contended that he regarded them as rewards for past favours done by him as a freelance draughtsman for the firm and not as an inducement for future conduct. The only evidence given to rebut the presumption of corruption under s. 2 of the 1916 Act was that of the appellant. He was convicted after the trial judge had directed the jury that for the defence to succed it would have been necessary for the appellant to give evidence of his intention to double-cross the donor firm. *Held*, dismissing his appeal, that the appellant failed to discharge the onus upon him to show that the gifts were not corrupt. (Dictum of Lord Goddard C.J. in *R.* v. *Carr* [1957] C.L.Y. 699 applied.)

R. v. MILLS (1978) 68 Cr.App.R. 154, C.A.

425. Costs—defendant to pay—limit on amount

[Costs in Criminal Cases Act 1973 (c. 14), s. 4 (1).]

Where a convicted person is ordered to pay the costs of the prosecution, the maximum amount payable should ordinarily be set by the court making the order.

Following their convictions for theft, the appellants were fined and also ordered to pay the costs of the prosecution at the rate of £40 per month. They appealed against the order for costs. *Held*, allowing the appeals in part, that normally a limit should be placed upon the amount of costs payable;

and that such practice could here be followed, the appellants being required to pay a sum not exceeding £150 and £250 respectively. (*R.* v. *Yoxall* [1973] C.L.Y. 501 considered.)

R. v. MOUNTAIN; R. v. KILMINSTER (1978) 68 Cr.App.R. 41, C.A.

426. —— determination of sum
[Costs in Criminal Cases Act 1973 (c. 14), s. 4 (1) (*a*).]
When an unsuccessful defendant is ordered to pay costs, the order should be for payment of a fixed sum or for costs to be taxed not exceeding a fixed sum.

D pleaded guilty after some days of his trial to possession of 10,000 grammes of cannabis with intent to supply. He was sentenced to seven years' imprisonment, and the court ordered that he pay the legal aid costs of his defence and the fixed prosecution costs within six months of taxation, with 12 months' imprisonment in default. On appeal against sentence, on the question of the order for costs, *held*, allowing the appeal, that the order should have been limited to a fixed sum. A fixed payment of £1,500 would be substituted, but the sentence and the period of imprisonment in default of payment of costs would stand. (*R.* v. *Hier* [1976] C.L.Y. 419 applied.)

R. v. SMITH (1978) 67 Cr.App.R. 332, C.A.

427. Courts-martial. See ARMED FORCES.

428. Crime prevention
The Home Office has published a research paper entitled " Crime Prevention and the Police " which examines two special crime prevention exercises by the police, namely a publicity campaign aimed at reducing vehicle theft and a study of police truancy patrols. The paper is available from HMSO (Home Office Research Study No. 55) [£1·75].

429. Criminal Evidence Act 1979 (c. 16)
This Act amends s. 1 of the Criminal Evidence Act 1898 and corresponding enactments extending to Scotland and Northern Ireland.

S. 1 amends para. (*f*) (iii) of the proviso to s. 1 of the Criminal Evidence Act 1898, para. (*f*) (iii) of the proviso to ss. 141 and 346 of the Criminal Procedure (Scotland) Act 1975 and para. (*f*) (iii) of the proviso to s. 1 of the Criminal Evidence Act (Northern Ireland) 1923; s. 2 deals with the short title and commencement.

The Act received the Royal Assent on March 22, 1979, and came into force on April 22, 1979.

430. Criminal injuries compensation
The following guidelines for assessment of compensation have been published by the Criminal Injuries Compensation Board. This extract is taken from their Fourteenth Report (Cmnd. 7396):

Assessment of compensation

21. In para. 7 of our 12th Report we referred to the basis on which compensation is assessed and provided a general indication of the level of our awards for specific injuries. Para. 10 of the Scheme requires the Board to award compensation on the basis of common law damages. Therefore, we take great pains to ensure that awards are in line with awards made by the courts. All the Board Members have considerable experience in this sphere and most deal with such cases in the course of their ordinary work as lawyers. In addition, the Board's staff circulate to all Board Members reports of cases decided in the courts.

22. The Board has also initiated a procedure which is particularly helpful in ensuring that our awards are in line with awards by the courts in the types of case which arise frequently. Members of the Bench and Bar, mainly Q.C.s in England and Wales and in Scotland, are asked to participate, together with our own Board Members, in an assessment exercise. Each participant is given particulars of injuries in a number of cases and asked to state what he would award in each case. Thereafter, the figures are considered by the Board and agreement is reached as to the right figure for each case. Of course, the figures are intended only as a general guide since the severity of the injury and its effect on the victim varies widely from case to case and accordingly may justify an award appreciably higher or lower than the figures agreed upon.

23. In the last such exercise, the Board Members' assessments were broadly in line with those of the judges and members of the Bar who took part. There were two exceptions. First, we decided that our awards for damaged teeth were too low and should be increased. Second, the Board Members' "consensus" figure for rape resulting in no serious physical injuries and no more serious than usual psychological consequences was higher than that of the other participants. In this instance, since rape is not, in practice, the subject of awards of damages in the courts, we concluded that we had more experience than the other participants and we decided to adhere to our higher figure.

24. We would like to thank the members of the Bench and Bar in England and Wales and Scotland for the assistance they provided in arriving at the figures, which are set out below:

Undisplaced nasal fracture	£225
Displaced nasal fracture	£350
Fractured jaw necessitating wiring	£525
Rape (as described above)	£1,200
Laparotomy	£700
Loss of sight of eye	£6,000
Loss of two front teeth	£400

25. We deal with a large number of cases involving scarring, the severity of which differs widely. The effects of facial scarring are difficult to convey but the two cases referred to below, in which the scars were unsightly and very obvious, may give some indication of our approach to the problem:

Unmarried man, aged 20. Scar running from approximately the join of the lobe of his left ear and his face across his cheek to within an inch of the left corner of his mouth £1,750

Unmarried woman, aged 20. Scar running from left corner of her mouth backwards and downwards diagonally and ending just underneath her jaw bone £3,250

These cases were considered in the assessment exercise; the participants in the exercise were provided with photographs of the scarring.

26. One applicant, a 53-year-old housewife, employed as a nursing assistant in a mental hospital, was assaulted and injured by a patient. She sustained a fracture of the left index finger, permanently restricting movement. She told the Board at the hearing that, immediately after the injury, she was unable to do normal household tasks as a result of the injury to her finger; members of her family had to assist her, particularly in the cutting of meat because of her inability to use a fork. One day no one was available to help her and she had to cut the meat herself, holding it steady with her hand. The knife slipped, seriously cutting the web between the thumb and first finger of her left hand. In the light of *McKew* v. *Holland and Hannen and Cubitts (Scotland)* [1970] C.L.Y. 612, the Board took the cut to the web of her hand into account in assessing compensation for the injury to her left index finger. Compensation was assessed at £2,750; after deducting an excess of social security payments over loss of earnings (para. 14), £1,837 was paid to the applicant.

431. Criminal Injuries Compensation Board

The Criminal Injuries Compensation Board have published their 15th Report for the year 1978–79, which details the record increases in the number of applications and amount of compensation paid, and recommends consideration of deterrent sentences. The Report is available from HMSO (Cmnd. 7752) [£1·25].

432. Criminal Injuries Compensation Scheme

The Government has published a revised Criminal Injuries Compensation Scheme which gives effect, from October 1, 1979, to nearly all the recommendations of an interdepartmental working party which reported last year. The major changes in the Scheme are the extension to the victims of violence within the family and the increase in the amount of earnings to be taken into account when assessing compensation.

433. Criminal statistics

The Home Office has issued figures for the number of serious offences recorded by the police in England and Wales for the second quarter of 1979.

The total number of offences was 655,000, about the same number as in the second quarter of each of the previous two years. Copies are available from the Home Office, Statistical Department, Room 1617, Tolworth Tower, Surbiton, Surrey.

434. The Home Office has published figures for the number of serious offences recorded in England and Wales in the third quarter of 1979. The report entitled " Serious offences recorded by the Police—Third Quarter 1979 " is available from the Home Office, Statistical Department, Room 1617, Tolworth Tower, Surbiton, Surrey, KT6 37DS.

435. Dangerous drugs. See MEDICINE.

436. —— " occupier " of premises
[Scot.] The Dangerous Drugs Act 1965, s. 5, provides: " If a person— (a) being the occupier of premises, permits those premises to be used for the purpose of smoking . . . cannabis resin " he shall be guilty of an offence. A person convicted under this section appealed against the conviction on the ground that, as he had ceased to pay rent for the house about nine months before the date of the alleged offence and had lived in it since then as a squatter, he was not the occupier. *Held,* he was the occupier of the house within the meaning of s. 5 (a) of the 1965 Act. (*R.* v. *Mogford* [1970] C.L.Y. 1681 distinguished, and the *ratio* of Neild J. not followed): CHRISTISON v. HOGG, 1974 J.C. 55, Ct. of Justiciary.

437. Defence—not known to the law—judge's ruling—illegal immigration— " knowingly " remaining after permits' expiry
[Immigration Act 1971 (c. 77), s. 24 (1) (b).]
The circumstances in which a judge can properly rule against a defendant that his defence is not known to the law are very, very few and far between.
B, a non-patrial, was given six months limited leave to remain in the U.K. He overstayed beyond the permit's expiry and was charged with knowingly remaining in the U.K. contrary to s. 24 (1) (b) (i) of the Immigration Act 1971. He claimed that his mother's death in Nigeria had destroyed his memory, so that he had not remained " knowingly." The judge ruled that his defence was not a defence in law to the charge, and B was convicted. On appeal, *held,* dismissing the appeal, that although it was dangerous and undesirable for the judge to rule as he did, and the circumstances where a judge could properly make such a ruling were very, very few and far between, nevertheless a conviction was inevitable, and the proviso would be applied. (*MacLeay* v. *Tait* [1906] A.C. 24 considered.)
R. v. BELLO (1978) 67 Cr.App.R. 288, C.A.

438. —— self-defence—assault on retreating person
X, driving a Hillman, chased a Cortina driven by D until D stopped. Both drivers got out, D holding a metal " Krooklock." X then retreated to the Hillman and D followed and hit X with the Krooklock and broke the Hillman's windscreen. *Held,* allowing an appeal against a finding of no case to answer on charges of assault occasioning actual bodily harm and criminal damage, that D could not rely on self-defence if X, having retreated, had ceased to be a threat: PRIESTNALL v. CORNISH [1979] Crim.L.R. 310, D.C.

439. Deprivation of property—right of police to retain—use in evidence not compensation
[Theft Act 1968 (c. 60), s. 28 (1) (c); Powers of Criminal Courts Act 1973 (c. 62), ss. 35, 43.]
The police have no power to retain money or property seized from an accused person solely in anticipation of the possibility of a compensation, forfeiture or restitution order being made in due course.
M was suspected by the police of receiving stolen goods. M's house was searched and quantities of stolen goods together with English and foreign banknotes to the value of about £10,000 were seized. No charges were made in respect of the banknotes, nor were they made an exhibit at the forthcoming trial. M commenced an action in detinue claiming the notes. On an Ord. 14 summons the judge ordered the return of the money. On appeal, *held,* allowing the appeal, that because the banknotes were material evidence which it might

become necessary to adduce at the trial, the police were entitled to retain them; they were not entitled to retain them however merely in anticipation of one of the possible orders pursuant to a conviction. (*Ghani* v. *Jones* [1970] C.L.Y. 2221 distinguished.)

MALONE v. METROPOLITAN POLICE COMMISSIONER [1979] 1 All E.R. 256, C.A.

440. Evidence—accomplice—corroboration—direction
[Theft Act 1968 (c. 60), s. 22 (1).]
A judge should not confine his summing-up on corroboration to the dangers of acting on uncorroborated evidence; he should also direct the jury on what evidence is capable of amounting to corroboration.

Per curiam: On a charge of receiving stolen goods contrary to s. 22 (1) of the Theft Act 1968 the jury should be directed as to the necessary intent according to the principle laid down in *R.* v. *Griffiths* (*Leslie*) [1975] C.L.Y. 595.

D was charged with handling stolen goods. His co-defendant, the thief, pleaded guilty and gave evidence against him. When the judge dealt with corroboration in his summing-up, he warned the jury of the danger of acting on the uncorroborated evidence of an accomplice. He did not, however, identify those parts of the evidence which was capable of being corroboration. D was convicted. On appeal, *held*, allowing the appeal, that the summing-up was defective. (*R.* v. *Charles* [1976] C.L.Y. 444 applied; *R.* v. *Rance and Herron* [1976] C.L.Y. 461 considered.)

R. v. REEVES (1978) 68 Cr.App.R. 331, C.A.

441. —— accomplice's diaries—value to be attached to documents
An accomplice's diaries can only have the status of an aide-memoire; they cannot amount to corroboration of his evidence, or evidence in support.

D, head of the Obscene Publications Squad, was charged with conspiracy and accepting bribes. A pornography dealer who gave evidence at the trial for the prosecution was allowed to refresh his memory from his diaries. Copies were allowed to go to the jury, and the judge directed the jury that the diaries were powerful evidence against D, perhaps the most important documents in the case, though they did not amount to corroboration in law. D was convicted. On appeal, *held*, allowing the appeal, that the jury must have been left with the impression that if the diaries were not corroboration they were the next best thing; they were not evidence at all, and the conviction must be quashed.

R. v. VIRGO (1978) 67 Cr.App.R. 323, C.A.

442. —— admissibility—cross-examination as to truth of contents of statement— " trial-within-trial "
On a trial-within-a-trial, it is improper for the Crown to cross-examine as to the truth of the contents of a statement, the admissibility of which is being tried. The Crown may only cross-examine or lead evidence before the jury of previous inconsistent statements made during the trial-within-a-trial when the statement has been ruled admissible and the defendant gives evidence as to its reliability as opposed to its voluntariness.

A group of men killed one victim and wounded two others. D was one of those charged with wounding and murder. The only evidence against him was his own confession. D challenged its admissibility on the ground that it was not voluntary. During the trial-within-a-trial, D was cross-examined as to the truth of the contents of his statement, and he admitted having been present and involved. The statement was ruled inadmissible. The Crown, in the absence of any other evidence, then called two shorthand writers who had been present to give evidence of D's admission during the trial-within-a-trial of having been present and involved. A submission of no case was refused; D gave evidence and was cross-examined as to his admission. He was convicted of murder and malicious wounding. His appeal to the Court of Appeal of Hong Kong was dismissed. On appeal to the Judicial Committee, *held*, allowing the appeal, that the Crown should not have cross-examined as to the contents of the statement on the trial-within-a-trial, nor, since the statement had been ruled inadmissible, should there have been evidence on cross-examination later as to the previous admissions. The *voir dire* evidence was not admissible as part of the prosecution's case. It could only be raised if, the statement having

been ruled admissible, the defendant then chose to go into the witness box
and give materially inconsistent evidence. (*R.* v. *Treacy* [1944] 2 All E.R.
229, C.C.A. applied; *R.* v. *Huedish* (1958) 26 W.W.R. 685 approved; *R.* v.
Hammond [1941] 3 All E.R. 318, C.C.A. overruled.)
  WONG KAM-MING v. THE QUEEN [1979] 2 W.L.R. 81, P.C.

443. ——— ——— **previous convictions—attack on police evidence**
  [Criminal Evidence Act 1898 (c. 36), s. 1 (*f*), proviso (ii).]
  A defendant's previous convictions should not be admitted in evidence by
reason only of the defendant denying an alleged confession or that an alleged
interview with police had occured.
  The appellant was indicted for arson, the case resting upon an alleged oral
confession made to a single police officer. The appellant's counsel in cross-
examining the officer disputed that the confession had been made and suggested
further that the interview referred to by the officer had not taken place. The
trial judge permitted the Crown to cross-examine the appellant as to his
lengthy previous convictions. *Held,* allowing the appeal against conviction,
that where what is alleged amounts to no more than an emphatic denial of the
charge and there is no attempt to discredit the officer on any matter not
immediately connected with the evidence given by him (which would include
the reliability of this notebook), a defendant's bad character is not to be
admitted in evidence. (Dicta of Viscount Dilhorne in *Selvey* v. *D.P.P.* [1968]
C.L.Y. 687, applied.)
  R. v. NELSON (1978) 68 Cr.App.R. 12, C.A.

444. ——— ——— ——— **judge's discretion**
  [Criminal Evidence Act 1898 (c. 36), s. 1 (*f*) (ii).]
  Where a defendant has lost the protection of s. 1 (*f*) of the Criminal
Evidence Act 1898, previous convictions which occurred after the case in
question may be put to him.
  D was charged with stealing a bottle of whisky from a store. He claimed
that he had only taken a bottle of vodka which he had paid for, that that
bottle of vodka had been smashed by prosecution witnesses, and the whisky
planted, and that almost all the prosecution evidence was lies. At the time
of these events D was a man of good character, though subsequently he had
twice been convicted in relation to theft of and obtaining credit by a credit
card. The judge granted the Crown's application to put those matters to
him. D was convicted. On appeal, *held,* dismissing the appeal, that the
judge's exercise of his discretion had not been wrongful. (Dictum of Devlin J.
in *R.* v. *Cook* [1959] C.L.Y. 674 as approved by Viscount Dilhorne in *Selvey*
v. *D.P.P.* [1968] C.L.Y. 687 applied.)
  R. v. COLTRESS (1978) 68 Cr.App.R. 193, C.A.

445. ——— ——— **reaction when co-accused's statement read out**
  The trial judge allowed the statement of T's co-defendant, G to be admitted
in evidence against T to explain T's reaction to it. *Held,* quashing T's conviction, that even if the statement was admissible, its prejudicial value far outweighed its probative value. (*R.* v. *Christie* [1974] C.L.Y. 4587 followed; *R.* v.
Mills and Lemon (1946) C.L.C. 2062 not followed): R. v. TAYLOR [1978]
Crim.L.R. 92, C.A.

446. ——— **admissions—refusal to see solicitor—judge's discretion**
  Defendant, aged 30, was charged with burglary of a dwelling-house, contrary
to s. 9 (1) (*b*) of the Theft Act 1968. A couple, from their bedroom window,
observed his presence in the garden of the house opposite to the one in which
they lived. They saw him try the door handle, climb a pipe at the front of the
house and onto a window ledge, feel along the ledge and climb down again.
They then saw him descend feet-first toward the cellar window. Neither could
say whether or not he actually entered. Scuff marks were found on the inside
of the cellar wall and forensic tests revealed that white-wash found on the
defendant's shoes was the same sort of white-wash that was used on the cellar
walls. The defendant was interviewed by the police and made a number of
damaging admissions. He alleged that during the interviews with the police he
had persistently asked for permission to contact a solicitor. The police denied
that any such request had been made. It was sought to exclude the admissions

on the ground that they were obtained in contravention of the Judges' Rules, the police having failed to comply with any request for a solicitor to be contacted. *Held*, by the judge, that he could not be sure or satisfied beyond a reasonable doubt that what the police officers said was right as there were a number of discrepancies in their evidence. Looking at the totality of the prosecution evidence the judge could not be sure that the defendant did not ask the police for a solicitor. The police evidence was therefore inadmissible and excluded. A defence submission that the evidence as it then stood would be unsafe and unsatisfactory to go to the jury was subsequently upheld and a verdict of not guilty was entered: R. *v.* DONOHOE, February 21, 1979, Wakefield Crown Ct. (*Ex rel. G. Burrell, Esq., Barrister.*)

447. —— —— **under influence of drug**
A dose of Pethidin described by the anaesthetist as " average to large " was administered to D 10½ hours before an interview during which he was alleged to have made admissions under caution. There was no impropriety on behalf of those in authority. *Held*, that the evidence should be excluded in the exercise of the judge's discretion as the medical evidence cast some doubt on the reliability of the admissions in view of D's state of mind. (*R. v. Isequilla* [1974] C.L.Y. 602 applied): R. *v.* DAVIS [1979] Crim.L.R. 167, Snaresbrook Crown Ct.

448. —— **agent provocateur—discretion to exclude**
Save with regard to admissions and generally with regard to evidence obtained from the accused after the commission of an offence, a judge has no discretion to exclude relevant admissible evidence on the ground that it was obtained by improper or unfair means.
Two defendants were indicted on counts of conspiracy to utter forged bank notes and possession of the notes. The judge heard argument as to whether he had discretion to exclude the evidence on the assumption that the activities were induced by an *agent provocateur*. He found he had no such discretion and was upheld by the Court of Appeal. On appeal, *held*, dismissing the appeal, that the judge had no discretion to refuse to admit relevant admissible evidence on the ground that it was obtained by improper or unfair means. (*R. v. Ameer and Lucas* [1977] C.L.Y. 520 overruled; *R. v. McEvilly* [1975] C.L.Y. 552 and *R. v. Mealey; R. v. Sheridan* [1974] C.L.Y. 541 approved.)
R. *v.* SANG [1979] 3 W.L.R. 263, H.L.

449. A judge can exclude evidence which has been obtained in breach of the Judges Rules, or which has minimal probative value and much prejudicial value; but *quaere* whether he always has a discretion to disallow evidence if the strict rules of admissibility would operate unfairly against the accused.
A police officer infiltrated a drug supplying conspiracy. Having got information about the conspiracy, which was already in existence, he encouraged the conspirators to supply him with cocaine. On doing so the conspirator's were arrested. The defence sought to have the Crown's evidence excluded by the judge because it was unfairly obtained. The judge refused, and D was convicted. On appeal by D, *held*, dismissing the appeal, that the judge was bound to admit the evidence. If, which was queried, he had the discretion to exclude it, it nevertheless fell on the right side of the line drawn in *R. v. Birtles*, since the conspiracy was already in existence and the conspirators had clearly not been encouraged to commit a crime which they would not otherwise have committed. (*R. v. Birtles* [1969] C.L.Y. 2748 applied; dictum of Viscount Simon in *Harris* v. *D.P.P.* [1951] C.L.Y. 748 considered.)
R. *v.* WILLIS, WERTHEIMER, LINFORD, WILLIS AND WESTBROOK (NOTE) (1978) 68 Cr.App.R. 265, C.A.

450. —— **automatism—medical evidence.** See R. *v.* SMITH, § 509.

451. —— **committal proceedings—criminal libel—evidence of bad reputation of prosecutor—whether admissible**
Evidence of the general bad reputation of a private prosecutor alleging criminal libel is not admissible at committal proceedings.
A private prosecution was brought against the appellants, authors of a book,

charging them with criminal libel. At the committal proceedings they sought to adduce evidence of the bad reputation of the prosecutor, but the magistrate refused to admit the evidence. The appellants applied for orders of certiorari and mandamus, which were refused. On appeal, *held*, dismissing the appeal, that evidence of the general bad reputation of the prosecutor must await the trial.

R. *v*. WELLS STREET STIPENDIARY MAGISTRATE, *ex p*. DEAKIN [1979] 2 W.L.R. 665, H.L.

452. —— confession—obtained under oppressive circumstances—no impropriety on part of police

The defendant, a 24-year-old State Registered Nurse of previous good character, was jointly charged with three others on two counts of possession of cannabis and cannabis resin, and two counts of knowingly permitting the smoking of cannabis at a house jointly occupied by all four defendants (contrary to ss. 5 and 8 of the Misuse of Drugs Act 1971). She was arrested at 1.15 p.m. on February 26, 1979, by a Customs and Excise Officer, in relation to other matters, taken to the police station and detained in a cell (which the police agreed was rather cold) until 6.55 p.m., when she was interviewed by two police officers in respect of the matters charged; she then made admissions and a statement of confession. Prior to 6.55 p.m. the defendant had been alone in her cell for four and a half hours apart from two periods of rigorous questioning in relation to the other matters by Customs and Excise Officers between 2.50 p.m. and 3.30 p.m., and 5.20 p.m. and 5.50 p.m. Despite frequent requests by the defendant, the policewoman in charge of the cells refused to tell her the time (her watch having been removed from her on arrival at the police station). In addition she was offered no refreshment until about 7.15 p.m. when the police gave her a cup of tea. She gave unchallenged evidence that she was distressed by all the above factors, and also because she was not told the reason for her continued detention after the conclusion of the second interview with the Customs and Excise at 5.50 p.m. *Held*, that the judge was not satisfied that the admissions and statement were made voluntarily, although no criticism could be made of the police officers, and upholding defence submissions that (1) despite the lack of impropriety on the part of the police (*R*. v. *Isequilla* [1975] C.L.Y. 554 considered) all the above circumstances combined to sap the defendant's free will in such a way that her admissions were obtained oppressively (*R*. v. *Priestly* [1966] C.L.Y. 2294 considered); (2) the failure to provide refreshments was a breach of Judges' Rules: R. *v*. ALLERTON, August 21, 1979, Judge Skinner, Q.C., Leicester Crown Ct. (*Ex rel. Thomas Corrie, Esq., Barrister.*)

453. —— —— subnormal persons

W was of borderline subnormal intelligence. The prosecution case hinged upon alleged verbal and written statements made during an interview when only one police officer was present. She had been interviewed four times and during one interview when she was alleged to have made confessions, she was not cautioned. *Held*, that the confessions should be excluded because the safeguard provided by Home Office Circular 109/1976, para. (ii) had not been observed. The circular states that mentally handicapped adults should be interviewed only in the presence of a parent or other person having care, custody or control of him or someone who is not a police officer: R. *v*. WILLIAMS [1979] Crim.L.R. 47, Swansea Crown Ct.

454. —— —— unfairly obtained—admissibility

[Magistrates' Courts Act 1952 (c. 55), s. 38 (4).]

Police officers cannot arrest a suspect so that they make enquiries about him; but having arrested a suspect for a specific offence, they can hold him in custody whilst they make inquiries; where they have enough evidence to prefer a charge they must do so without delay, and bring him before a court.

Per curiam: An informer who has not been given any inducement to inform may always be prosecuted for crimes in which he has implicated himself in the course of implicating others.

D, as an informant, made a statement under caution to police about the theft of £2m worth of currency stolen at London Airport. The statement contained allegations, and also admissions, but the police let him go without arresting him, to lead them to the principal offenders. The offenders were arrested, then H was detained without reason being given and kept incommunicado for five days. Then D made a statement admitting handling the stolen money, and was charged. The trial judge refused to exclude the confession on the ground that although there was a breach of s. 38 (4) of the Magistrates' Courts Act 1952, and the police had acted unfairly and illegally the object of keeping D incommunicado was to find the money, not to break him, and in any event D had confessed because he thought he would gain immunity, rather than because of his unlawful detention. D was convicted. On appeal, *held*, dismissing the appeal, that the judge had exercised his discretion correctly. (*R.* v. *Gillis* (1886) 11 Cox C.C. 69, applied.)

R. v. HOUGHTON; R. v. FRANCIOSY (1978) 68 Cr.App.R. 197, C.A.

455. —— —— **voluntariness—breach of Judges' Rules and Administrative Directions**
The case against W depended upon alleged confessions to the police. W was subnormal and several breaches of the Judges' Rules were proved. *Held, inter alia*, that (1) the prosecution had failed to prove that the confessions were not obtained by oppression; (2) in deciding upon admissibility of alleged confessions a judge should ignore the weight of the evidence of the confessions, whether there were discrepancies between them and what the defendant might or might not have known, whether there was evidence outside the confession, and (except in considering Administrative Direction 4A, Appendix B of Home Office Circular No. 89/1978) the intention of the police officers during interrogations; (3) the trial judge must be careful to resist the temptation of deciding on a balance of probabilities. If he thinks it possible that the confession was obtained by inducements or oppression he must exclude it; (4) some questions, including " I will give you one more opportunity to be honest and frank as to your connection with the Michelle Booth case " seemed to have a lurking threat or inducement behind them; (5) the questions " why can't you tell the truth and get it over with? You are only making this worse by telling lies " and " why can't you be a man and admit it? These lies are not going to help you " were plain inducements; (6) if the judge is not sure there has been no breach of the Judges' Rules and Administrative Directions he has a discretion to exclude any answers or statement obtained: R. v. WESTLAKE [1979] Crim.L.R. 652, Hodgson J.

456. —— —— **young person—failure to comply with administrative direction**
D, aged 16, was arrested on suspicion of burglary. His mother would not accompany D to the police station, saying she had to see her other children to school. The officers claimed that there was reason to suppose that D would not have wished a solicitor or social worker to be present during his interview. He was asked questions in the police car and was alleged to have made admissions. *Held*, that since the officers should have refrained from questioning until D's mother, a social worker, a solicitor or some other adult other than a police officer could be present in accordance with para. 4 of the Home Office Administrative Directions on Interrogation (Home Office Circular No. 31/64) the evidence should be excluded: R. v. GLYDE [1979] Crim.L.R. 385, Kingston Crown Ct.

457. —— **exchange control offence—power of Treasury to require information.** See A. v. H.M. TREASURY; B. v. H.M. TREASURY, § 2274.

458. —— **expert witness—police accident investigation—road accident**
An experienced police officer may be permitted to give " expert " evidence as to how an accident may have occurred.
The appellant was convicted of causing death by dangerous driving. There was no eye-witness to the collision, of which the appellant claimed to have no recollection. The prosecution called a policeman for the traffic division, with considerable experience and a qualification in accident investigation, to give evidence of his findings at the scene and his conclusions as to the cause of the fatal collision. *Held*, dismissing the appeal, that provided that the evidence is kept within the sphere of the witness's expertise, there is no

objection to such " expert " evidence being admitted. (*Nickisson* v. *The Queen* [1963] W.A.R. 114, doubted.)
R. v. OAKLEY [1979] R.T.R. 417, C.A.

459. —— handling stolen goods—other goods in possession
[Theft Act 1968 (c. 60), s. 27 (3).] S. 27 (3) of the Theft Act 1968, which in certain circumstances permits the prosecution to adduce, on a charge of handling stolen goods, evidence that the defendant has had in his possession other stolen goods, is to be construed strictly; there is no power to introduce evidence of the details of the earlier transaction (*R.* v. *Smith* [1918] 2 K.B. 415 not followed): R. v. BRADLEY, *The Times*, November 20, 1979, C.A.

460. —— handwriting—admissibility of a comparison—standard of proof
[Criminal Procedure Act 1865 (c. 18), s. 8.]
The standard of proof to be applied by a judge in deciding whether it is proved to his satisfaction that writing is genuine, within s. 8 of the Criminal Procedure Act 1865, for the purposes of admitting the writing in evidence for comparison with disputed writing, is the civil standard of proof.
A was charged with assault with intent to rob. He was alleged to have knocked at an old lady's door, masquerading as a postman, and carrying a parcel and clipboard. When the door was opened he struck her, but was then driven off by her son, leaving the parcel behind. The Crown sought to compare for analysis various samples of handwriting found on A, and at his house. A disputed that this was his handwriting. The question of admissibility of the comparisons under s. 8 of the Criminal Procedure Act 1865 was raised before the judge, prior to the handwriting expert giving his evidence. The judge held that he was satisfied not beyond any reasonable doubt, but on the balance of probability that they were A's handwriting, and therefore ruled them admissible for comparison. On appeal by D, *held*, dismissing the appeal, that the judge had applied the correct test. (Dictum of Pennefather B. in *Egan* v. *Cowan* (1857) 30 L.T.O.S. 223 and *R.* v. *Silverlock* [1894] 2 Q.B. 766 distinguished.)
R. v. ANGELI [1978] 3 All E.R. 950, C.A.

461. —— identification—direction
A judge's failure to follow the guidelines given in *R.* v. *Turnbull* [1976] C.L.Y. 451 in an identification case may result in the quashing of a subsequent conviction.
The appellant was convicted, by a majority verdict, of possessing and supplying morphine, the evidence being that he had been identified by police officers as the man they had seen when posing as potential drug buyers. Prior to picking out the appellant at identification parades, some officers had seen a photograph of him. The judge failed to point out to the jury that the officers may have been relying on the photograph in identifying the appellant, nor did he warn them in general of the dangers of identification evidence. *Held*, allowing the appeal and quashing the conviction, that the failure so to warn the jury was a material misdirection. (*R.* v. *Turnbull* [1976] C.L.Y. 451, applied.)
R. v. HUNJAN (1978) 68 Cr.App.R. 99, C.A.

462. —— Judges' Rules—statement under caution—series of questions and answers
[Judges' Rules, r. 4 (*d*).]
A statement under caution which consists of a series of questions and answers may technically be a breach of the Judges' Rules, but provided no leading questions are asked and the accused's exact words are recorded, it may safely be admitted.
M was convicted of murder after stabbing another youth in a London club. A written statement under caution was taken from him in the form of a number of questions and answers. The defendant appealed against conviction on the basis that the statement was wrongly admitted. *Held*, dismissing the appeal, that there is no reason why the police should not assist an inarticulate suspect in this way, provided the questions were not leading and the answers accurately recorded in the suspect's own language.
R. v. WILLIAMS (1977) 67 Cr.App.R. 10, C.A.

463. —— policeman refreshing memory
A police officer made brief jottings of an interview with D and later

compiled notes of the interview with the aid of the jottings. *Held,* that the trial judge had wrongly ruled that the officer could only refresh his memory from the original jottings and not from his notebook. A witness may refresh his memory by reference to any writing made or verified by himself concerning and contemporaneously with the facts to which he testifies: ATT.-GEN.'s REFERENCE (No. 3 OF 1979) [1979] Crim.L.R. 786, C.A.

464. —— power to direct prosecution to proceed—function of judge

Where counsel for the Crown does not wish to proceed with a trial on indictment, the judge's approval is not merely a rubber stamp, and he may order the trial to proceed.

Four valuable mares were stolen. A pleaded guilty to theft, B to handling, and C not guilty to theft or handling. The prosecution did not wish to proceed against C, and invited Mars-Jones J. to approve that course. The judge refused to do so, and C was convicted of handling. On appeal by C, *held,* dismissing the appeal, that for prosecution counsel to seek the judge's approval of such a course was no idle formality, and the judge had the power to take the course he had taken. (*R.* v. *Soanes* (1948) C.L.C. 2260 considered; dictum of Smith L.J. in *R.* v. *Comptroller-General of Patents, Designs and Trade Marks* [1899] 1 Q.B. 909, 914 applied.)

R. v. BROAD (1978) 68 Cr.App.R. 281, C.A.

465. —— presumption of doli incapax—whether previous convictions admissible

Where the presumption of *doli incapax* is raised the prosecution can call any relevant evidence to rebut the presumption, including evidence of previous convictions.

Two youths aged 13 were charged with blackmail and tried with others including one adult, at the Crown Court. The judge ruled that as the onus of rebutting the presumption of *doli incapax* was on the Crown, the prosecution could call any relevant evidence as to background and previous convictions. The youths then formally admitted they were not incapable of criminal intent and called no evidence. They were convicted. On appeal, *held,* dismissing the appeal, that evidence of previous convictions is normally relevant to the issue of *doli incapax,* and the prosecution may therefore adduce it. (*B.* v. *R.* [1959] C.L.Y. 725, *F.* v. *Padwick* [1959] C.L.Y. 726 considered.)

R. v. B.; R. v. A. [1979] 1 W.L.R. 1185, C.A.

466. —— previous offences—cross-examination—imputation on character of prosecution witness

[Criminal Evidence Act 1898 (c. 36), s. 1 (*f*) (ii).] F1 and F2 were charged with theft from a jeweller's shop by distracting the jeweller's attention. They both attacked the character of the police and therefore gave evidence disclosing their previous convictions for dishonesty. Counsel for the prosecution put to F1 that he had been convicted of theft from a jeweller's shop and theft from a shop by distracting attention and put to F2 that she had been convicted jointly with F1 of theft from a jeweller's shop. *Held,* allowing appeals against convictions, that questions directed specifically to offences similar to the charges before the court but not admissible as " similar fact " evidence should have been excluded as being prejudicial rather than probative. The cross-examination exceeded the bounds of legitimate cross-examination as to credibility: R. v. FRANCE [1979] Crim.L.R. 48, C.A.

467. —— self-serving statements—fairness to accused

P was taxed with incriminating facts by a security officer and saw his solicitor before he was arrested. After his arrest he made two self-serving statements. The trial judge excluded the statements and about half of the interview notes, which were also self-serving. *Held,* allowing P's appeal against conviction that (1) a statement which was not an admission was admissible to show the attitude of the accused when he made it, and was not limited to the first encounter with the police; (2) admitting only statements against interest while excluding part of the same interview or series of interviews would be unfair; (3) although the prosecution might comment upon inconsistent denials, inconsistency did not make a denial an admission; (4) a statement would be excluded on rare occasions where an accused presented a carefully prepared written statement made with a view to it being made part of the prosecution's case. (*R.* v. *Storey* [1964] C.L.Y. 696 considered): R. v. PEARCE [1979] Crim.L.R. 658, C.A.

468. —— **sexual offences—cross-examination of complainant—discretion of judge**
[Sexual Offences (Amendment) Act 1976 (c. 82), s. 2 (1), (3).]
On a charge of rape, although cross-examination not permissible to blacken a complainant's character, it may be permitted if it might reasonably lead the jury, properly directed, to take a different view of her evidence.
D was charged with raping C. It was not disputed that intercourse had taken place and the sole issue was consent. Application was made to cross-examine C as to her previous sexual experience. The application was refused and D was convicted. On appeal, *held,* dismissing the appeal, that the judge had a discretion to allow cross-examination which might reasonably lead the jury properly directed in the summing-up to take a different view of the complainant's evidence than they otherwise might have. The matter was one for the judge's discretion, and the Court of Appeal would not substitute its own discretion. (*R.* v. *Lawrence* [1977] C.L.Y. 659 approved.)
R. v. MILLS (1978) 68 Cr.App.R. 327, C.A.

469. —— **similar facts—sexual offences against children**
Similar fact evidence of sexual offences against children does not fall into any special category; evidence that all the offences were against children, in their own home, and committed by their step-father does not show the necessary striking similarities.
D was charged on counts 1–3 with attempted buggery and indecent assault against his step-son who was 16; on counts 4–7 with attempting to have sexual intercourse and indecent assault upon his step-daughter who was about 9. The judge refused to sever counts 1–3 from 4–7, and directed the jury that if they thought that there had been a course of conduct of a similar pattern they could treat each complaint as corroborating the other. The allegation was that the offences had occurred in the children's home or nearby, and had something partaking of the same character. The jury convicted D on three counts only, in relation to all of which D had made admissions. On appeal by D, *held,* dismissing the appeal, that on the facts there were no striking similarities between the evidence in relation to each child, and the judge had been in error in refusing to sever the counts, and in directing the jury that the evidence in relation to each child could corroborate the evidence in relation to the other. However, as the jury had only convicted where there was an admission, the proviso would be applied. (*D.P.P.* v. *Boardman* [1974] C.L.Y. 753 and *R.* v. *Scarrott* [1977] C.L.Y. 553 applied; *Moorov* v. *Lord Advocate*, 1930 J.C. 68 considered.)
R. v. CLARKE (1978) 67 Cr.App.R. 398, C.A.

470. —— —— **shoplifting—modus operandi**
Evidence of a thief's *modus operandi* may be adduced as similar fact evidence to rebut the defence of mistake or accident.
D was charged with stealing bacon from a shop. His defence was that of mistake. At his trial, the judge allowed evidence to rebut that defence, and to establish D's *modus operandi*, that D had fallen under suspicion of stealing bacon in the same store on two previous occasions, and the way in which that suspicion had arisen. D was convicted. On appeal, *held,* dismissing the appeal, that though the case was borderline, there had been a sufficient nexus between the offence charged and the earlier offences which served to rebut the defence of accident or mistake. (*Makin* v. *Att.-Gen. for New South Wales* [1894] A.C. 57 applied; *R.* v. *Brown, Smith, Woods and Flanagan* [1963] C.L.Y. 697 considered.)
R. v. SEAMAN (1978) 67 Cr.App.R. 234, C.A.

471. —— **standard of proof—violent propensity of co-defendant**
Where each of two defendants blames the other for a crime of violence which must have been committed by one of them, evidence as to the violent propensity of one may be admissible at the instance of the other.
During the course of a burglary, the elderly occupant of the premises was

killed. B and L admitted the burglary but each alleged the other to be responsible for the killing. At trial B's counsel was refused leave to adduce in cross-examination evidence disclosed in a prosecution witness's statement that L was very violent and had assaulted the witness in the past. L in due course gave evidence as to his non-violent nature; he was convicted of manslaughter whereas the appellant was convicted of murder. *Held,* allowing his appeal and substituting a verdict of manslaughter, that the evidence as to L's violent behaviour became relevant upon L giving evidence to the contrary; and that particularly since the jury were not strongly warned as to the dangers of relying upon the account of either defendant in assessing responsibility, the court was not satisfied that the conviction for murder was safe. (Dictum of Lord Morris of Borth-y-Gest in *Lowery* v. *R.* [1973] C.L.Y. 516, applied.)

R. *v.* BRACEWELL (1978) 68 Cr.App.R. 44, C.A.

472. —— telephone tapping

The witness box during the course of a trial is not the place where defending counsel should seek to get information about suspected telephone tapping.

Per curiam: Although generally the courts would protect informers, cases might occur where the liberty of the subject should prevail. In such cases it would be for the accused to show that that was good reason.

The defendants were charged, *inter alia,* with smuggling drugs. Counsel sought to cross-examine as to whether their telephones were tapped. The questioning in each case was forbidden by the judge. On appeal, *held,* dismissing the appeal, that counsel was merely fishing for information, and the questions were irrelevant to the issue, though they might have been questions worth asking of the prosecution before trial. The witness box was not the place to seek such information.

R. *v.* HENNESSEY, SHAHEEN, ALKASSAR, SZAROWICZ AND McDERMOTT (1978) 68 Cr.App.R. 419, C.A.

473. —— unsworn statement from dock—allegation against co-accused

An incriminating statement from the dock is not evidence against a co-accused and evidence cannot be called to rebut it; therefore, the jury should be directed that it does not amount to evidence against the co-accused in any way.

A and B were on trial for murder. B, who was last on the indictment, made a statement from the dock alleging that A was behind it all, and should bear all responsibility. A's father then saw B in prison, where B indicated that he was prepared to go back on what he had said. He did not, and A sought to call his father to rebut what B had said. The trial judge refused permission. Both A and B were convicted. On appeal by A, *held,* dismissing the appeal that a statement from the dock was of the same status evidentially as a statement made in the absence of the accused, and evidence could not be called to rebut it. As the judge had directed the jury to disregard B's statement as against A, he had done all that was required.

R. *v.* GEORGE (1978) 68 Cr.App.R. 210, C.A.

474. —— —— evidence in rebuttal—statement as to good character

C was charged, *inter alia,* with fraudulent trading. He made a statement from the dock representing himself to be an honest, straightforward businessman. The Crown was allowed to call evidence in rebuttal and the official receiver testified as to companies connected with C's bankruptcy and eight companies in which he had had shareholdings or been a director which had gone into liquidation. *Held,* allowing C's appeal against conviction, that (1) the court would assume that it was proper to allow rebutting evidence after a statement from the dock where it would have been admissible had the statement been made on oath in the witness-box; (2) the court would further assume that if the statement of fact to be rebutted related only to C's character or credibility that entitled the prosecution to lead evidence of bad character; (3) however, in this case the evidence led in rebuttal was not in fact evidence of bad character: R. *v.* CAMPBELL [1979] Crim.L.R. 173, C.A.

475. —— verdict—where unanimous as to guilt but not unanimous as to which evidence to be accepted

A was charged with six counts of procuring the execution of a valuable security by deception. The prosecution led a mass of evidence. The judge refused to ask for special verdicts to find out which evidence the jury had accepted and did not direct them that they could not find any count proved unless they were all agreed that the same one of the many pieces of evidence led by the Crown proved falsity. *Held*, dismissing A's appeal, that what the jury all had to agree upon was that the prosecution had proved the charge. The jurors did not have to agree as to the details of the evidence: R. *v.* AGBIM [1979] Crim.L.R. 171, C.A.

476. **Extradition.** See EXTRADITION.

477. —— **prevention of terrorism—warrant—whether offence of political character**
[Prevention of Terrorism (Temporary Provisions) Act 1976 (c. 8), ss. 12, 14 (1); Backing of Warrants (Republic of Ireland) Act 1965 (c. 45).] C was arrested under s. 12 of the 1976 Act. S. 14 (1) defines terrorism as the use of violence for political ends. When the police received a warrant from Dublin backed for service in the U.K., charging C with offences concerning causing explosions, they re-arrested C under the Backing of Warrants (Republic of Ireland) Act 1965. *Held*, dismissing C's application for a writ of habeas corpus, that there was no evidence that the offence was of a political character within the 1965 Act, s. 2 (2), even though C had been arrested as a terrorist initially on the same information as contained in the charges in the warrant: R. *v.* GOVERNOR OF DURHAM PRISON, *ex p.* CARLISLE [1979] Crim.L.R. 175, D.C.

478. **False trade desription.** See SALE OF GOODS.

479. **Food and drugs.** See FOOD AND DRUGS.

480. **Forgery—signature authorised by another—burden of proof**
[Forgery Act 1913 (c. 27), ss. 1 (1) (2), 6 (1).]
Where it is claimed that a signature upon a document was authorised by a third party with power to do so, the burden of proof lies upon the defence.
D was a construction company area manager, in charge of five foremen. D was charged with uttering a forged tax exemption certificate, in that he knew that one of his foremen had signed it purporting to be X, a sub-contractor employee, in order to get the exemption. D was convicted. He appealed on the ground, *inter alia*, that the Crown had failed to prove that the signature was not authorised by X. *Held*, dismissing the appeal, that the onus was on D to show not only authorisation, but full authorisation which would have made X liable for the tax in due course. (*R.* v. *Vincent* [1972] C.L.Y. 578 distinguished.)
R. *v.* HISCOX (1978) 68 Cr.App.R. 411, C.A.

481. —— **signing cheque in own name—not usual signature**
[Forgery Act 1913 (c. 27), s.7.] M drew a cheque for cash using his own name but not his usual signature and presented it at his bank and was paid. He intended from the outset to and did claim repayment of the amount. *Held*, allowing M's appeal against conviction of obtaining money on a forged instrument contrary to s. 7 of the 1913 Act, that the cheque was not false within the meaning of the 1913 Act as it told no lie on its face (*R.* v. *Vincent* [1972] C.L.Y. 578 applied): R. v. MACER [1979] Crim.L.R. 659, Courts-Martial Appeal Ct.

482. **Fugitive offenders.** See EXTRADITION.

483. **Handling—stolen goods—defendant " shutting his eyes to the obvious "— direction to jury**
The appellant was convicted of dishonestly receiving stolen goods after the trial judge directed the jury upon guilty knowledge of belief as follows: " sometimes a person will suspect that goods are stolen and will deliberately shut his eyes to the circumstances, and if you come to the conclusion that was the case here, then it would be open to you, having regard to all the circumstances of the case, if you so found, to find that the defendant . . . knew or believed the van was stolen." *Held*, dismissing the appeal, that such a direction could not be said to amount to an invitation to convict if satisfied only that the appellant suspected the goods to be stolen. (Dictum of James L.J. in *R.* v. *Griffiths (Leslie George)* [1975] C.L.Y. 595 applied): R. *v.* NEALE, August 20, 1979, C.A. (*Ex rel. Edmund Lawson, Esq., Barrister.*)

484. Illegal immigration—court's power to order release. See R. v. INNER LONDON CROWN COURT, ex p. OBAJUWANA, § 6.

485. —— detention order—wrong ground given—validity

[Immigration Act 1971 (c. 77), Sched. 2, para. 16 (1) (2).]

A detention order made by an immigration officer under the Immigration Act may yet be valid even though the order is erroneous in that the wrong reason for detention is stated thereon.

An immigration officer made a detention order under the Immigration Act 1971 but stated the wrong ground for detention on the order. An application for habeas corpus was refused by the Divisional Court. On appeal, counsel for the Secretary of State sought leave to put in an affidavit exhibiting the correct reason for the detention. This was admitted, the appeal was dismissed and leave to appeal to the House of Lords on a different question refused. *Re* SHAHID IQBAL (NOTE) [1979] 1 W.L.R. 425, C.A.

486. —— entry certificate—validity—undisclosed change of circumstances

The applicant, a Pakistani, was granted a U.K. visa to join his father. Shortly after, he married in Pakistan but did not disclose the marriage to the U.K. authorities on his arrival. *Held*, dismissing the applicant's appeal, that an entry certificate may be invalidated by a failure to disclose material change in circumstances: R. v. SECRETARY OF STATE FOR THE HOME DEPARTMENT, ex p. ZAMIR, *The Times*, December 29, 1979, C.A.

487. —— leave to enter—obtained by deceit—validity

S was refused leave to enter the U.K. and this fact was stamped on her passport. She obtained a second passport in a different name and was given permission to enter the U.K. as a visitor after making certain false statements to the immigration officer. She later married a man settled in the U.K. who applied for the restrictions on S's entry to be lifted. She was later detained as an illegal immigrant. *Held*, refusing a writ of habeas corpus, that as S obtained leave to enter by deceit and was never entitled to be in the U.K. her marriage was irrelevant: R. v. SECRETARY OF STATE FOR THE HOME DEPARTMENT, ex p. SHAH [1979] Crim.L.R. 392, D.C.

488. —— prosecution out of time—certiorari following plea of guilty

[Immigration Act 1971 (c. 77), ss. 24 (1) (b) (i) (ii), 28 (1) (a); Magistrates' Courts Act 1952 (c. 55), s. 104.] B, a non-patrial, pleaded guilty before magistrates to offences under s. 24 (1) (b) (i) and (ii) of the Immigration Act 1971, namely remaining in the United Kingdom beyond the time limited by his leave and failing to observe a condition of his leave. The prosecution had in fact been brought outside the time limit imposed by s. 28 (1) (a) of the 1971 Act and s. 104 of the Magistrates' Courts Act 1952. *Held*, that certiorari would be granted to quash the convictions. (*R.* v. *Campbell, ex p. Nomikos* [1956] C.L.Y. 8302 and *R.* v. *Burnham Justices, ex p. Ansorge* [1959] C.L.Y. 1989 not followed): R. v. EASTBOURNE JUSTICES, *ex p.* BARSOUM, January 26, 1979, D.C. (*Ex rel. R. W. Spon-Smith, Esq., Barrister.*)

489. —— remaining in U.K. beyond time limit set by leave—date of offence

[Immigration Act 1971 (c. 71), ss. 14 (1), 24 (1) (b) (i), 28 (1) (a).] X, a Turkish national, had leave to remain in the U.K. for one month from December 23, 1974. On April 16, 1975, the Secretary of State refused his application for an extension of his stay but permitted him to stay until May 23, 1975, in order to make arrangements to leave. He applied again for an extension but this was refused although he was permitted to stay until July 27, 1975. On July 8, 1975, he lodged an appeal which he withdrew on August 10, 1976. He then disappeared. On December 12, 1978, an information was laid alleging that X had knowingly remained in the U.K. beyond the time limited by leave contrary to s. 24 (1) (b) (i) of the 1971 Act. *Held*, allowing an appeal against dismissal of the information, that the offence was committed not on July 28, 1975 but on August 10, 1976, since X was permitted to remain in the U.K. pending the determination of his appeal by virtue of s. 14 (1). Accordingly the information was laid within the three-year time limit: HORNE v. GAYGUSUZ [1979] Crim.L.R. 594, D.C.

490. Incitement—to arrange an assault—whether a crime

LB and DB were alleged to have paid P £50 to arrange for G to be beaten up. P did not do so. LB and DB were charged with inciting P to assault G on a day between June 1, 1977, and December 31, 1977. *Held*, allowing a submission of no case to answer, that (1) the particulars of offence in the indictment were incorrect in that they did not allege incitement of P to procure another to assault G, rather than incitement of P himself to assault G; (2) in any event it is not a crime to incite someone to be an accessory before the fact to a crime: R. *v.* BODIN AND BODIN [1979] Crim.L.R. 176, Lincoln Crown Ct.

491. Indictment—counts—joinder

[Indictment Rules 1971 (S.I. 1971 No. 1253), r. 9.] W and B were charged in one indictment with offences of affray, assault occasioning actual bodily harm and attempting to pervert the course of justice. Before the committal proceedings on the first two counts they tried to bribe the victim of the assault to modify his account. *Held,* that the third count was "founded on the same facts" as the first two counts within r. 9 of the 1971 Rules since the charges had a common factual origin: R. *v.* BARRELL AND WILSON [1979] Crim.L.R. 663, C.A.

492. —— power to amend—scheme of hiring cars with forged log-books—whether conspiracy to defraud or steal

[Indictments Act 1915 (c. 90), s. 5 (1); Administration of Justice (Miscellaneous Provisions) Act 1933 (c. 36), s. 2 (2) (*b*); Criminal Law Act 1977 (c. 45), ss. 1 (1), 5 (1) (2).]

A conspiracy to steal is properly to be regarded as something within a conspiracy to defraud, and an indictment is not invalid merely because it charges a conspiracy to defraud.

The applicants were involved in a scheme of hiring self-drive cars and selling them with forged log-books. On a voluntary bill of indictment they were charged with conspiracy to steal contrary to the 1977 Criminal Law Act. The trial judge gave leave to amend the indictment to charge conspiracy to defraud at common law. The defendants were convicted and appealed. *Held*, refusing application to appeal, that (1) the trial judge had power to amend any indictment however preferred; and (2) conspiracy to steal was something within a conspiracy to defraud, and all the elements to support a conviction were present.

R. *v.* WALTERS; R. *v.* TOVEY; R. *v.* PADFIELD [1979] R.T.R. 220, C.A.

493. Juries. See JURIES.

494. Legal aid

LEGAL AID IN CRIMINAL PROCEEDINGS (ASSESSMENT OF RESOURCES) (AMENDMENT) REGULATIONS 1979 (No. 61) [10p], made under the Legal Aid Act 1974 (c. 4), s. 34; operative on March 1, 1979; amend S.I. 1978 No. 30. They increase the figures contained in those Regs. for determining whether a person should be granted legal aid and whether a person to whom legal aid is ordered shall be required to make a contribution to his costs.

495. Magisterial law. See MAGISTERIAL LAW.

496. Malicious wounding—ability to foresee risk—correct test

[Offences against the Person Act 1861 (c. 100), s. 20.] A person may be guilty of malicious wounding, contrary to s. 20 of the Offences against the Person Act 1861, if his conduct is reckless; but he is not reckless unless he foresees the risk of causing personal injury. (*R.* v. *Stephenson* [1979] C.L.Y. 397 applied; *R.* v. *Ward* (1872) L.R. 1 C.C.R. 356 not followed): FLACK *v.* HUNT (1979) 123 S.J. 751, D.C.

497. Manslaughter—involuntary—failure to summon medical assistance for wife who did not want assistance

S's wife suffered from a medical condition giving her a marked aversion to doctors and medical treatment. Her second child was stillborn. She and S hid the body in a cupboard. Thereafter she was unwell and although S wanted to call a doctor his wife would not let him until December 31, 1977, when the doctor did not call because S had not explained the full circumstances. S called again in the afternoon and a locum called by which time S's wife had died. The judge directed the jury that in order to prove manslaughter the prosecution had to prove that S failed to get medical attention in reckless disregard of his duty to care for his wife's health. " Reckless disregard " meant that, fully appreciating that she was so ill that there was a real risk to her health if she did not get help, S did not do so, either because he was indifferent, or because he deliberately ran a wholly unjustified and unreasonable risk. The jury had to balance the weight as to whether it was right to allow S's wife's wish not to have a doctor called against her capacity to make rational decisions: R. v. SMITH [1979] Crim.L.R. 251, Birmingham Crown Ct.

498. Misuse of drugs—forfeiture of money—validity of forfeiture order

[Courts Act 1971 (c. 23), ss. 11 (2), 57; Misuse of Drugs Act 1971 (c. 38), s. 27; Powers of Criminal Courts Act 1973 (c. 62), s. 43.]

An order for forfeiture of money or goods under the Misuse of Drugs Act 1971 is a " sentence " for the purposes of s. 11 (2) of the Courts Act 1971. and it cannot be altered or imposed after the prescribed period, *i.e.* usually 28 days.

M was arrested by the Customs and Excise for smuggling cocaine. She had over £41,000 in her possession. She was sent to prison for five years. She was brought back before the judge four months later on application by the Customs and Excise, and on that occasion the judge ordered forfeiture of the money found on her under s. 27 of the Misuse of Drugs Act 1971. The Court of Appeal dismissed an appeal against that order. On appeal to the House of Lords, *held,* allowing the appeal, that the word " sentence " in s. 57 of the Courts Act 1971, and therefore under s. 11 (2), included an order for forfeiture: there was no power in the Crown Court to vary or rescind a sentence or other order after expiration of the period specified in s. 11 (2), and the order was therefore invalid. (Decision of C.A. [1978] C.L.Y. 542a reversed; *R.* v. *Jones* [1929] 1 K.B. 211 and *R.* v. *Thayne* [1969] C.L.Y. 608 considered.)

R. v. MENOCAL [1979] 2 W.L.R. 876, H.L.

499. —— forfeiture of property—conspiracy to contravene Act

Following convictions of conspiracy to contravene s. 4 of the Misuse of Drugs Act 1971 by producing or supplying a drug, the court ordered forfeiture of the appellants' property. *Held,* dismissing their appeals, that the order was valid since conspiracy to contravene a section creating an offence under the 1971 Act was also an offence under that Act and not just an offence at common law: R. v. TODD; R. v. CUTHBERTSON; R. v. McCOY [1979] Crim.L.R. 665, C.A.

500. —— offer to supply—extent of offence

[Misuse of Drugs Act 1971 (c. 38), s. 4 (3) (c).]

The offence of being "concerned in" the offer to supply controlled drugs is widely drafted so as to include persons who may be some distance away at the time of making the offer.

Police officers overheard O in the street telling others that a friend in a nearby flat could supply them with cannabis. When O arrived at B's flat, B left, pretending not to know O. Both were convicted (after neither gave evidence) of being concerned in the making of an offer to supply a controlled drug, after the jury were directed B could be convicted only if some arrangement concerning the offer had previously been made by him with O. *Held,* dismissing the appeals, that the jury were entitled to infer such arrangement from the evidence.

R. v. BLAKE; R. v. O'CONNOR (1978) 68 Cr.App.R. 1, C.A.

501. —— possession—cannabis or cannabis resin—duplicity

[Misuse of Drugs Act 1971 (c. 38), s. 5 (2).] An indictment charged B with possession of a controlled drug " being either cannabis resin or cannabis," contrary to s. 5 (2) of the 1971 Act. *Held,* that as cannabis and cannabis resin were linked in the Class B drugs list in Sched. 11, Pt. II, to the Act, the counts were not void for duplicity, the allegation being of a single act of possession of an identified substance: R. v. BEST [1979] Crim.L.R. 787, C.A.

502. —— —— **drugs posted to defendant's address at his request**
[Misuse of Drugs Act 1971 (c. 38), s. 5 (1).]
Where someone orders a drug from a supplier, and it is subsequently posted
to his address, he is in possession of the drug when it comes through the
letter box of the house, even though he is unaware of its arrival.
P lived in a bed-sit in a house comprised entirely of such accommodation.
He ordered drugs which duly arrived through the post, and were contained
in an envelope found on the hall table by the police. P was unaware of the
envelope's arrival. The appellant was convicted and appealed on the ground
that on those facts he was not " in possession " of the drug. *Held,* dismissing
the appeal, that since P had ordered the drug he was in possession when it
came through the letter box of the house in which he was living. (*R.* v.
Cavendish [1961] C.L.Y. 2006 applied; *Warner* v. *Metropolitan Police
Commissioner* [1968] C.L.Y. 2439 distinguished.)
R. *v.* Peaston (1978) 69 Cr.App.R. 203, C.A.

503. —— —— **duplicity—separate quantities charged in single count**
[Misuse of Drugs Act 1971 (c. 38).] D was charged in a single count
with possession of 26·4 mg. of cannabis resin found in various articles in his
room. The quantities found were 0·4 mg., 8 mg., 16 mg. and 2 mg. *Held,* that
(1) although the quantity of 0·4 mg. was not usable in any manner prohibited
by the 1971 Act, there was evidence on which a jury could find the larger
quantities so usable. It was not necessary to show that such quantities could
alone produce a perceptible effect provided they could contribute at least a
part of the resin needed to make up a whole cigarette; (2), the count was not
bad for duplicity (*R.* v. *Carver* [1978] C.L.Y. 546, *R.* v. *Bayliss and Oliver*
[1978] C.L.Y. 547 and *R.* v. *Peevey* [1973] C.L.Y. 514 considered): R. *v.*
Webb [1979] Crim.L.R. 462, Canterbury Crown Ct.

504. —— —— **intent to supply—intent to invite others sufficient**
[Misuse of Drugs Act 1971 (c. 38), ss. 4 (3) (*a*), 5 (3).] M persuaded two
girls to " go for a smoke " with him and began rolling a cannabis cigarette
intending to share it with the girls. He was charged with possession of
cannabis resin with intent to supply and with offering to supply the drug to
another contrary to ss. 4 (3) (*a*) and 5 (3) of the 1971 Act respectively. *Held,*
that there was a case to answer on both counts. As there was an offer of
consumption there was an offer of supply (*R.* v. *King* [1978] C.L.Y. 543 not
followed; *Holmes* v. *Chief Constable, Merseyside Police* [1975] C.L.Y. 621
and *R.* v. *Mills* [1963] C.L.Y. 615 considered): R. *v.* Moore [1979] Crim.L.R.
789, Surbiton Crown Ct.

505. —— **reports**
A recently published report by the Advisory Council on the Misuse of Drugs
recommends the reclassification of some drugs and concludes that the use of
cannabis should not be legalised. Copies of the report may be obtained from
the Library, Home Office, 50 Queen Anne's Gate, London S.W.1. [£1·75.]

506. —— **supply—distribution to co-owners by purchaser on behalf of all**
[Misuse of Drugs Act 1971 (c. 38), ss. 4 (3) (*a*), 37 (1) (3).] B and X pooled
their money and went to a supplier to buy cannabis resin. Ultimately, only B
met the supplier and paid for and received the cannabis. He then returned
and gave X his share of the cannabis. *Held,* dismissing B's appeal against conviction of supplying X with cannabis contrary to s. 4 (3) (*a*) of the 1971 Act,
that by s. 37 (1) " supplying " included " distributing " and B had certainly
distributed the drug to X (*Holmes* v. *Chief Constable of Merseyside Police*
[1975] C.L.Y. 621 applied): R. *v.* Buckley [1979] Crim.L.R. 665, C.A.

507. Misuse of Drugs Act 1971—modification
Misuse of Drugs Act 1971 (Modification) Order 1979 (No. 299) [10p],
made under the Misuse of Drugs Act 1971 (c. 38), s. 2 (2); operative on
May 14, 1979; adds to Pt. I of Sched. 2 to the 1971 Act phencyclidine.

**508. Murder—alternative verdict of manslaughter—not part of prosecution case as
opened**
Where, on a trial for murder, the evidence would support a verdict of
manslaughter, it is open to the jury to return such a verdict, and they should be

directed accordingly, notwithstanding that the prosecution have not put such an alternative as part of their case.

The defendants were indicted for murder, the prosecution allegation being that they had stoned the deceased as he ran away from them. Medical evidence suggested that death was due either to stoning or to a blow received in falling to the ground. Neither defendant gave evidence. In closing, the prosecution suggested to the jury an alternative verdict of constructive manslaughter; one defence counsel objected to such possibility being raised so late in the trial. The judge directed the jury that such a verdict was open to them and that manslaughter was the proper verdict if by violence the defendants had caused the deceased to try to escape them and that in the course of so doing he had been killed. The Court of Appeal quashed the convictions. *Held,* allowing the prosecutor's appeal and restoring the convictions, that the alternative verdict had rightly been left to the jury and that the judge's discretion as to the constituents of such offence was correct, if anything being unduly favourable to the defendants. (*Kwaku Mensah* v. *The King* [1946] A.C. 83, *R.* v. *Mackie* [1973] C.L.Y. 564 and dictum of Lord Salmon in *D.P.P.* v. *Newbury* [1976] C.L.Y. 496 applied.)

D.P.P. *v.* DALEY [1979] 2 W.L.R. 239, P.C.

509. —— **automatism—medical evidence**

Where the rules governing examination of prisoners in prison provide for the submission of reports of the prisoner's medical condition to the Director of Public Prosecutions and by him of copies to the defence, the reports cannot be regarded as confidential and, therefore, are not inadmissible.

The applicant was convicted of murder after the trial judge had allowed the cross-examination on his statements to two psychiatrists who examined him to determine his mental condition when he was in custody, and the psychiatrists to give evidence in rebuttal that the applicant's amount of automatism was not physically possible. On his application for leave to appeal on the grounds that, (1) in the absence of a plea of insanity or diminished responsibility, statements to the psychiatrists were not admissible in law as they were made in confidence in a doctor/patient relationship, or, it was unfair to admit the statements as they were given for a different purpose, *i.e.* to determine his mental condition; (2) it was for the jury to decide whether the killing was done in a state of automatism, therefore, the psychiatrists' evidence was irrelevant to that issue and should be excluded; (3) the statements were made in breach of the judges' rules and, therefore, inadmissible. *Held,* dismissing the application that (1) the rules governing the examination of prisoners in custody allowed the submission of medical reports to the Director of Public Prosecutions and by him to the defence, accordingly, they were not confidential and, therefore, admissible in law; (2) automatism was an abnormal mental condition not within the ordinary juryman's experience and a jury was entitled to expert help when the same was pleaded, therefore, the admission of that evidence was justified; (3) it was not unfair to use the reports as the applicant had known that they would be used in relation to any mental abnormality of his; (4) even if the statements had been made in breach of the judges' rules they were admissible as the jury were entitled to expert help on the plea of automatism. (Dicta of Devlin J. in *Hill* v. *Baxter* [1958] C.L.Y. 680 and of Roskill L.J. in *R.* v. *Chard* [1972] C.L.Y. 638 applied; *R.* v. *Payne* [1963] C.L.Y. 3051 distinguished.)

R. *v.* SMITH [1979] 3 All E.R. 605, C.A.

510. —— **causation**

During a fight involving 12 people in all D struck M on the head with a brick. M died from his injuries. The pathologist found that there were two principal wounds on D's head, both of which would " very probably " cause death. There was no way of ascertaining which wound was the first and there was a " reasonable and sensible " possibility that M might have recovered from the first injury, whichever it was. *Held,* that there was no case to answer on a count of murder since the prosecution had failed to prove that D was responsible for the cause of death, there being no evidence that he caused both wounds (*R.* v. *Smith* [1959] C.L.Y. 666 distinguished): *R.* v. DYOS [1979] Crim.L.R. 660, Cantley J.

511. —— **defence of alibi—direction excluding manslaughter verdict**
[West Indies Associated States Supreme Court (Grenada) Act 1971 (c. 17), s. 41 (1).]
If the West Indian Court of Appeal has applied an incorrect test when considering an appeal against conviction, the Privy Council will itself consider afresh the question as to the application of the proviso.
In the course of an armed robbery in Grenada the driver of the lorry was shot and killed. F was convicted of murder on identification evidence alone. On his appeal against conviction the Court of Appeal, accepting there had been a misdirection, went on to consider the application of the proviso. In so doing the court applied the wrong test. On appeal to the Judicial Committee, *held*, dismissing the appeal, that the court had applied the wrong test and the Judicial Committee would therefore itself consider whether to apply the proviso. In the circumstances the proviso be applied and the conviction upheld.
FERGUSON *v.* THE QUEEN [1979] 1 W.L.R. 94, P.C.

512. —— **diminished responsibility—evidence**
[Homicide Act 1957 (c. 11), s. 2 (1).]
The plea to manslaughter on the grounds of diminished responsibility should only be accepted where there is clear evidence of mental imbalance.
V became very suspicious that his wife was having an affair. He became incredibly jealous, though there was no evidence to suggest his suspicions were well founded, and stabbed his wife to death in a frenzied attack in which she suffered 34 wounds. Such medical evidence as there was as to his mental state came from the Crown. The judge accepted a plea to manslaughter and gave him life imprisonment. On appeal against sentence, on the question of acceptance of pleas, *Held*, that pleas to manslaughter on the grounds of diminished responsibility should only be accepted where there is clear evidence of mental imbalance.
R. *v.* VINAGRE (1979) 69 Cr.App.R. 104, C.A.

513. —— —— **uncontradicted medical evidence—duty of jury to consider all evidence**
[Homicide Act 1957 (c. 11), s. 2 (1).]
In considering a defence of diminished responsibility, the jury is required to have regard to all the circumstances of the case and not merely to the medical evidence adduced by one side.
The appellant denied a charge of murder on the ground of diminished responsibility. A psychiatrist called upon his behalf gave evidence that the appellant's acute anaemia coupled with drugs administered for his arrested sexual development could have produced an abnormality of mind substantially impairing his mental responsibility for his acts. The appellant had allegedly stabbed to death a young girl; after initial denials he eventually confessed to the killing, but subsequently retracted such confession. He persisted in his denial of involvement at his trial. He appealed, *inter alia,* upon the ground that no medical evidence was adduced to contradict that given upon his behalf. *Held*, dismissing the appeal, that the jury had to decide the issues upon all the evidence and not merely that of the appellant's psychiatrist: The circumstances of the killing, the appellant's conduct before and after it and his personal history were all relevant; and on the entirety of the evidence the jury's verdict was unimpeachable. (*Walton* v. R. [1977] C.L.Y. 607, followed.)
R. *v.* KISZKO (1978) 68 Cr.App.R. 62, C.A.

514. —— **provocation**
[Eire] At his trial for murder, where the accused claimed that he had been provoked, the trial judge told the jury that to justify a verdict of manslaughter the provocation had to be such that it made the accused unable to form an intention to kill or cause serious bodily harm. The accused was convicted of murder. On appeal, *held*, that an intention to kill or cause serious injury is consistent with provocation and does not prevent this defence from reducing murder to manslaughter. A new trial was ordered: THE PEOPLE *v.* MACEOIN [1978] I.R. 27, C.C.A. of Ireland.

515. Northern Ireland. See NORTHERN IRELAND.

516. Obscene publications—Committee on Obscenity and Film Censorship
The Committee on Obscenity and Film Censorship has published its
unanimous report entitled the " Report of the Committee on Obscenity and
Film Censorship." The Report, which proposes the total rewriting of the laws
on obscenity and indecency, is published by HMSO (Cmnd. 7772) [£5·25].

517. ⸺ import—EEC. See R. *v.* HENN AND DARBY, § 1180.

**518. ⸺ seizure of goods—delay in coming before magistrate—whether unlawful
interference with goods**
[Obscene Publications Act 1959 (c. 66), s. 3.] Over three weeks after the
seizure by police of a large number of allegedly obscene articles by virtue of
a warrant granted under s. 3 of the Obscene Publications Act 1959, the articles
had not been brought before a magistrate as required by subs. (3) and no
summons had been issued under that subsection. The owners of the articles
issued a writ alleging unlawful interference with goods and conversion, and
applied for an interlocutory order for the return of the articles. *Held*, that in
the circumstances the articles had not been retained by police for an unreasonable period. Interlocutory injunction refused: ROANDALE *v.* METROPOLITAN
POLICE COMMISSIONER, December 15, 1978, Park J. (*Ex rel. R. W. Spon-Smith,
Esq., Barrister.*)

519. Obtaining by deception—deceiving person other than creditor
[Vehicles (Excise) Act 1971 (c. 10), ss. 1 (1), 8 (1); Theft Act 1968 (c. 60),
s. 16 (1) (2) (*a*).]
It is not an essential ingredient of an offence under s. 16 of the Theft Act
1968 that the person deceived be a creditor or his agent, provided there is a
causal connection between the deception and the evasion of the obligation
to pay.
Because parts of the entries on K's vehicle excise licence were not visible a
police officer removed it for investigation and gave K an undated receipt on
a police memorandum form for K to display. The licence was valid but after
its expiry K continued to display the police memorandum. A police officer
saw the vehicle without a current licence but did not notify the licensing
authority because of the memorandum which the police officer was deceived
into thinking was issued in respect of a current licence. When K was charged
with dishonestly obtaining for himself a pecuniary advantage, the justices found
no case to answer because the deception was on the police to avoid prosecution
not on the licensing authorities to evade the charge for the licence. On appeal,
held, allowing the appeal, that it was an essential ingredient of an offence
under s. 16 of the 1968 Act that the person deceived be a creditor, his agent,
or some other person to whom the debt was payable provided there was a
causal connection between the deception and the evasion of the obligation
to pay.
SMITH *v.* KOUMOUROU [1979] R.T.R. 355, D.C.

**520. ⸺ false odometer reading—effect of disclaimer stating reading may not be
correct**
K altered odometer readings on motor cars for sale to give false readings
but displayed notices on them stating that the reading may not be correct. K
pleaded guilty to one count of applying a false trade description to a motor
car and one count of obtaining money by deception in relation to each motor
car: R. *v.* KING [1979] Crim.L.R. 122, Nottingham Crown Ct.

**521. ⸺ mini-cab driver—implied representation that he was an " official " cab
driver**
[Theft Act 1968 (c. 60), s. 15.]
A mini-cab driver who informs a customer that his is an " airport taxi " and
that the fare charged was " the correct fare " may thereby be guilty of obtaining
the fare by deception.
The appellant, a mini-cab driver, was approached by a foreign visitor at
Heathrow Airport and in response to the visitor's question said that his car was
" an airport taxi." The appellant drove the visitor to Ealing and there charged
him £27·50 which he claimed to be " the correct fare." He was convicted of
obtaining property by deception. *Held*, dismissing his appeal, that the judge had

rightly left it to the jury to consider whether by the use of the above words the appellant was implying that " all was official "; the fact that there was no definition of " airport taxi " therefore did not assist the appellant.

R. v. BANASTER [1979] R.T.R. 113, C.A.

522. Offensive weapon—seizure for instant use
[Prevention of Crime Act 1953 (c. 14), s. 1.]
A person seizing a weapon for immediate use in a fight is not guilty of possessing an offensive weapon.

During the course of assaulting a man in the street, the defendant was handed at his request a clasp knife which he held to the victim's head. The knife was not offensive *per se.* He appealed by case stated against his conviction by justices. *Held,* allowing the appeal, that the 1953 Act was designed to deter the carrying of offensive weapons for use if the need arose; it did not extend to the taking into possession of a weapon for immediate use. (*Ohlson* v. *Hylton* [1975] C.L.Y. 644 and *R.* v. *Humphreys* [1977] C.L.Y. 622, applied; *Harrison* v. *Thornton* [1979] C.L.Y. 523 not followed.)

BATES v. BULMAN (1978) 68 Cr.App.R. 21, D.C.

523. [Prevention of Crime Act 1953 (c. 14), ss. 1, 4.]
A stone picked up by a defendant during a fight for instant use may be an " offensive weapon " within s. 1 (1) of the Prevention of Crime Act 1953.

The defendant was convicted of possessing an offensive weapon, he having during a fight picked up a stone and thrown it at another. *Held,* dismissing the appeal, that by arming himself with, and using the stone, the appellant committed the offence charged.

HARRISON v. THORNTON (NOTE) (1966) 68 Cr.App.R. 28, D.C.

524. [Prevention of Crime Act 1953 (c. 14), s. 1.] The appellant was seen by a police officer brandishing a shovel in the direction of a group of youths who were forced to step off the footpath into the roadway to avoid being hit. *Held,* allowing the appeal and holding that there was no case for the appellant to answer, the evidence was insufficient to support a conviction because there was no evidence as to how the appellant had acquired possession of the shovel or as to his intention prior to its actual use as a weapon (*Ohlson* v. *Hylton* [1975] C.L.Y. 644 applied): R. v. AMBROSE, January 31, 1979, London Crown Ct, Judge Layton. (*Ex rel. R. J. Terry, Esq., Barrister.*)

525. Perversion of course of justice—assisting another to avoid lawful arrest
The common law offence of attempting to pervert the course of justice may be committed even where interference with police investigations is not dishonest, corrupt or threatening.

The defendants gave the registration number of unmarked police cars to another suspected of armed robbery with a view to assisting him to avoid arrest. The defendants applied for leave to appeal against conviction. *Held,* refusing the application, that police investigation of offences was part of the administration of justice and any interference with it, albeit not dishonest, corrupt or threatening was capable of amounting to an offence. (*R.* v. *Bailey* [1956] C.L.Y. 2069, and *R.* v. *Britton* [1974] C.L.Y. 3289 applied.)

R. v. THOMAS [1979] 2 W.L.R. 144, C.A.

526. Picketing. See NUISANCE; TRADE UNIONS.

527. Plea bargaining—counsel seeing judge
Both counsel for the Crown and the defence went to see the trial judge, the former for guidance as to whether a plea was acceptable, the latter for an indication as to sentence. The court said that this was a bad practice since it deprived the public of information about the reasoning behind sentences, and was to be confined to really exceptional cases: R. v. COWARD (1978) 123 S.J. 785, C.A.

528. Police officer—failing to carry out duty. See R. v. DYTHAM, § 2085.

529. Practice—allegations that voluntary statement improperly obtained—no evidence called
It is not a proper practice for the defence to make serious allegations about the honesty of the police in the taking of a statement under caution and then

to refrain from calling the defendant to give specific evidence to support the allegations.

C in his trial for s. 47 assaults on two police officers challenged the admissibility of his statement under caution. In a trial within a trial serious allegations were made against the police, and C gave evidence. In the resumed trial before the jury, the statement having been admitted, counsel for the defence called no evidence to support the allegations. C was convicted. On appeal, *held*, dismissing the appeal, that it was not a proper practice to make a major attack on the honesty of the police and then to fail to call specific evidence in support of that attack. (Dicta of Lord Goddard C.J. in *R.* v. *O'Neill*; *R.* v. *Ackers* (1950) C.L.C. 2120, applied.)

R. *v.* CALLAGHAN (1979) 69 Cr.App.R. 88, C.A.

530. —— pleas before justices—inquiry into validity in Crown Court

Unless there is prima facie evidence to show that justices wrongly exercised their discretion to refuse to accept a plea of guilty, the Crown Court should not embark upon an inquiry into the validity of such pleas.

D appealed to the Crown Court against his sentence for burglary and assault occasioning actual bodily harm. D's counsel repeated the mitigation put forward by D's solicitor in the magistrates' court that D pushed the alleged victim of the assault to shove him out of the way, and had not entered the flat which had been burgled. The deputy circuit judge inquired into the original proceedings, obtained evidence from the justices' clerk and remitted the case to the justices for pleas of not guilty to be entered on the ground that the original pleas of guilty were equivocal. The justices refused to hear the case on the ground that the original pleas of guilty were equivocal. The justices refused to hear the case on the ground that they were *functi officio*. *Held*, allowing the prosecutor's application for an order of certiorari to quash the Crown Court's decision, that the Crown Court ought not to have made such an inquiry into whether the justices should have exercised their discretion, unless there was prima facie evidence to show that they should have done so. There was no evidence that the justices should have considered exercising their discretion.

R. *v.* COVENTRY CROWN COURT, *ex p.* MANSON (1978) 67 Cr.App.R. 315, D.C.

531. Prevention of terrorism

PREVENTION OF TERRORISM (SUPPLEMENTAL TEMPORARY PROVISIONS) (NORTHERN IRELAND) (AMENDMENT) ORDER 1979 (No. 168) [10p], made under the Prevention of Terrorism (Temporary Provisions) Act 1976 (c. 8), ss. 13, 14 (5) (6) and Sched. 3, para. 1 (8); operative on April 18, 1979; amend art. 11 of S.I. 1976 No. 466 so as to reduce the maximum period for which a person who may be examined under art. 5 may be detained.

PREVENTION OF TERRORISM (SUPPLEMENTAL TEMPORARY PROVISIONS) (AMENDMENT) ORDER 1979 (No. 169) [10p], made under the Prevention of Terrorism (Temporary Provisions) Act 1976, ss. 13, 14 (5) (6), Sched. 3, para. 1 (8); operative on April 18, 1979; amends art. 10 of S.I. 1976 No. 465 so as to reduce the maximum period for which a person may be detained under the authority of an examining officer to a maximum period of 48 hours, which may be extended by the Secretary of State for a further period not exceeding five days.

PREVENTION OF TERRORISM (TEMPORARY PROVISIONS) ACT 1976 (CONTINUANCE) ORDER 1979 (No. 352) [10p], made under the Prevention of Terrorism (Temporary Provisions) Act 1976, s. 17 (2) (*a*); operation on March 25, 1979; continues in force the provisions of the 1976 Act for a twelve-month period from March 25, 1979.

532. —— statistics

The Home Office has issued figures up to the end of the first quarter of 1979 on the Prevention of Terrorism (Temporary Provisions) Acts 1974 and 1976. The figures are available from the Home Office Press Office, Queen Anne's Gate, London S.W.1.

533. Prevention of Terrorism (Temporary Provisions) Act 1976—amendment

PREVENTION OF TERRORISM (TEMPORARY PROVISIONS) ACT 1976 (AMENDMENT) ORDER 1979 (No. 745) [10p], made under the Prevention of Terrorism

(Temporary Provisions) Act 1976 (c. 8), s. 1 (3); operative on July 3, 1979; adds the Irish National Liberation Army to the list of proscribed organisations.

534. Prisons. See PRISONS.

535. —— disciplinary hearing—whether visiting justice's decision reviewable
[N.Z.] [Penal Institutions Regulations 1961.] A visiting justice hearing a charge against D of disobeying an unlawful order, refused to allow D to call witnesses (although the 1961 Regulations gave him the right to do so) and sentenced D to four days' loss of remission. *Held*, quashing the conviction and sentence, that if anyone having legal authority to determine questions affecting the rights of subjects acts in excess of that authority, certiorari will lie. As the justice had acted outside his jurisdiction, the Supreme Court had a power of review (*R.* v. *Electricity Commissioners* [1924] 1 K.B. 171 applied): DAEMAR v. HALL [1979] Crim.L.R. 317, Sup.Ct. of N.Z.

536. Private prosecutor—subsequent indictment—whether private prosecutor a litigant
Proceedings were brought by C as a private prosecutor. At the pre-trial review, C appeared in person and submitted that he was a litigant in the proceedings and was entitled to conduct the prosecution before the Crown Court. *Held*, that as the indictment had been signed C was no longer a litigant in the proceedings, which thereafter continued in the name of the sovereign. A prosecution is brought in the public interest to punish an offender, and the Crown Court is not an appropriate forum to ventilate a private grievance. Crown counsel owes a duty to the public and to the court to ensure the proceedings are fair, and this duty transcends the duty owed to the person or body that instituted the proceedings and which prosecutes the indictment. The interests of a private prosecutor will more often than not be inimical to this duty: R. v. GEORGE MAXWELL (DEVELOPMENTS), August 30, 1979, Judge David Q.C., Chester Crown Ct. (*Ex rel. T. Teague, Esq., Barrister.*)

537. Probation. See MAGISTERIAL LAW.

538. Prosecution—promises of immunity—discretion of D.P.P.
[Prosecution of Offences Act 1879 (c. 22), s. 2; Prosecution of Offences Act 1908 (c. 3), ss. 1, 2.]
The D.P.P. has a wide discretion to intervene in any private prosecution and to offer no evidence therein.
T was convicted of robbery following a trial at which S, an accomplice, was called as a Crown witness having been given an undertaking by the D.P.P. that he would not be prosecuted for his part therein. T caused to be issued a summons against S charging him with the robbery. The D.P.P. intervened in the private prosecution with a view to offering no evidence. T thereupon sought a declaration that such intervention was *ultra vires* and unlawful on the grounds, *inter alia,* that at T's trial counsel instructed by the D.P.P. had stated that S's immunity did not extend to private proceedings and that the D.P.P. was thereby estopped for offering no evidence. The D.P.P. applied to strike out the statement of claim on the ground of it disclosing no reasonable cause of action or being vexatious and/or an abuse of the process of the court. *Held*, granting the application, that the D.P.P. had a wide and unfettered discretion to intervene and offer no evidence if he considered the public interest so to require; that he was not estopped by anything said at the trial by prosecuting counsel; and that there was no substance in the allegation that the D.P.P. had acted in bad faith.
TURNER v. D.P.P. (1978) 68 Cr.App.R. 70, Mars Jones J.

539. Prosecution of Offences Act 1979 (c. 31)
This Act consolidates certain enactments relating to the prosecution of offences in England and Wales.
S. 1 provides for the appointment of the Director of Public Prosecution (the " D.P.P. ") and his assistants; s. 2 sets out the duties of the D.P.P.; s. 3 imposes a duty on the D.P.P. to appear for the Crown or prosecutor on certain appeals; s. 4 relates to private prosecutions; s. 5 relates to the furnishing of recognizances, informations, etc. by justices; s. 6 deals with consents to prosecutions; s. 7 states that consents are to be admissible in evidence; s. 8 concerns returns of crimes by chief officers of police; s. 9 empowers the

Attorney-General to make regulations bringing this Act into effect; s. 10 contains definitions; s. 11 deals with consequential amendments and repeals; s. 12 gives the short title. The Act does not extend to Scotland and Northern Ireland.

The Act received the Royal Assent on April 4, 1979, and came into force on May 4, 1979.

540. Prostitution—living on immoral earnings—escort agency—mini cab drivers

[Sexual Offences Act 1956 (c. 69), s. 30 (1) (2).]

An offence against s. 30 of the Sexual Offences Act 1956 is committed by the manager of an "escort agency" which dispatches girls to clients, and by the drivers of cabs that convey them, where the defendants must know what is going on, and do it for gain, for they are encouraging prostitution.

Prostitutes were assembling nightly at the premises of an "escort agency." They were dispatched from there to clients, and taken by mini cab drivers, who collected the agency fee plus VAT and the cab fare from the client. The girls basically were left to get what they could for their services. All this activity went on late at night or in the early hours of the morning. The manager of the agency and the drivers were convicted of "living on the earnings of prostitution." On appeal, on the grounds that the facts proved did not amount to an offence against s. 30, *held,* dismissing the appeal, that the appellants must have known what was happening, they did it for gain, and they thereby encouraged prostitution. (Dictum of Viscount Simonds in *Shaw* v. *D.P.P.* [1961] C.L.Y. 1963 approving *Calvert* v. *Mayes* [1954] C.L.Y. 726 applied.)

R. v. FARRUGIA, BORG, AGIUS AND GAUCHI (1979) 69 Cr.App.R. 108, C.A.

541. —— —— flat let to prostitute—exorbitant rental

[Sexual Offences Act 1956 (c. 69), s. 30 (1).]

A landlord taking an excessive rent from a tenant known to him to use the premises for the purposes of prostitution may be convicted of living on the earnings of prostitution.

The appellant was convicted of knowingly living wholly or in part on the earnings of prostitution, he being the landlord of flats let to prostitutes who used them for that purpose, the allegation being that the rents charged were exorbitantly in excess of normal commercial rents, he knowing that his tenants were engaged in prostitution. The appellant appealed on the grounds, *inter alia,* that such facts were insufficient to warrant conviction. *Held,* dismissing the appeal, that the jury were entitled to infer that the appellant was engaged in a joint adventure with his tenants, knowingly sharing in their immoral earnings. (Dictum of Lord Reid in *Shaw* v. *D.P.P.* [1961] C.L.Y. 1963, applied.)

R. v. CALDERHEAD; R. v. BIDNEY (1978) 68 Cr.App.R. 37, C.A.

542. Public order—conduct likely to cause breach of peace—encouraging continuance of disturbance

[Public Order Act 1936 (c. 6), s. 5.] G was charged with using threatening or abusive words or behaviour whereby a breach of the peace was likely to be occasioned. The trial judge directed the jury that it was shown that a breach of the peace was likely to be occasioned if it was shown that a fresh breach of the peace was likely to be occasioned or a prolonging of a breach of the peace that has already happened or is happening. G was one of a group of others which were throwing stones at a rival group. He was shouting insulting and provocative words at the other group. *Held,* refusing leave to appeal against conviction, that the jury had to decide whether there was the necessary likelihood of breach of the peace. There were a number of breaches of peace occurring at the same time as a result of a number of actions, namely the throwing of stones and the hurling of threatening, abusive or insulting words. Further such words might well add fuel to the flames and cause further breaches of the peace. The direction was correct: R. v. GEDGE [1979] Crim.L.R. 167, C.A.

543. —— " public place "—front garden of private house

[Public Order Act 1936 (c. 6), s. 5 (as substituted by the Race Relations Act 1965 (c. 73), s. 7), s. 9 (1) (as substituted by the Criminal Justice Act 1972 (c. 71), s. 33).]

The fact that the public can obtain access to a private house as visitors through the front garden does not make the garden a public place for the purposes of the Public Order Act 1936 as substituted; it is not sufficient that behaviour in such a place can be heard or seen by people in a public place unless it is also aimed at them.

A and B had an argument with C whilst standing at the front door of C's house, having gained access through his front garden which was about 12 feet across. The argument could be heard across the street. A and B were charged with using threatening, abusive or insulting words or behaviour in a public place with intent to provoke a breach of the peace or whereby a breach of the peace might be occasioned, contrary to s. 5 (1) of the Public Order Act 1936 as substituted. The judge directed the jury that since the public might gain access to the house via the front garden, it was a public place. A and B were convicted. On appeal, *held,* allowing the appeal, that the front garden was not a public place merely because the public could gain access through it as visitors, and therefore the conviction would be quashed. (*Wilson* v. *Skeock* (1949) C.L.C. 2267 applied; *Ward* v. *Holman* [1964] C.L.Y. 839 considered; *Robson* v. *Hallett* [1967] C.L.Y. 3993 and *Cawley* v. *Frost* [1976] C.L.Y. 557 distinguished.)

R. *v.* EDWARDS; R. *v.* ROBERTS (1978) 67 Cr.App.R. 228, C.A.

544. Recidivism—report

The Home Office has published its Research Study report entitled " Previous Convictions, Sentence and Reconviction," H.O.R.S. No. 53. It shows, *inter alia,* that of a representative sample of 5,000 offenders convicted in January 1971, about one-half were convicted again during a six-year follow up period. The report is available from HMSO [£2·25].

545. Robbery—use of force—direction to jury

[Theft Act 1968 (c. 60), s. 8 (1).]

Whether or not " force " has been used in an alleged robbery is a question for the jury; resort need not be had to old authorities where the wording of the statute is clear and simple.

The appellants were convicted of robbery. The victim gave evidence that he had been nudged and pushed off-balance and that while he was trying to keep his balance his wallet had been stolen. It was submitted on the appellants' behalf that what was alleged did not amount to " force " within the meaning of s. 8 (1) of the Act. *Held,* dismissing the appeal, that the question as to whether, on the evidence, force had been used to further theft, had properly been left to the jury.

R. *v.* DAWSON; R. *v.* JAMES (1978) 68 Cr.App.R. 170, C.A.

546. —— —— whether appropriation continuing

[Theft Act 1968 (c. 60), ss. 1 (1), 3 (1), 8 (1).]

An appropriation is a continuing act, and if force is used whilst the appropriation continues, and the other ingredients of theft are present, the offence is one of robbery.

A was charged with robbery. A and B had forced their way into Mrs. X's house; A had put his hand over her mouth while B took her jewellery. Before leaving they tied her up. A was convicted. On appeal, *held,* dismissing the appeal, that appropriation was a continuing act, and the jury were entitled to convict on the basis of A's putting his hand over Mrs. X's mouth, and also in tying her up if they were satisfied that the force was used to enable A to steal.

R. *v.* HALE (1978) 68 Cr.App.R. 415, C.A.

547. Sentence—alternative counts—sentence on both counts

Where a defendant pleads guilty to the less serious of two alternative counts, and is then convicted of the more serious count, his plea of guilty should remain recorded on the lesser count, but he should be sentenced only on the more serious one.

D pleaded guilty to possession of 225 grammes of cannabis. That count was alternative to a count of possession with intent to supply, upon which D was subsequently tried and convicted. He was sentenced to four years' imprisonment on the more serious count, and 18 months' concurrent on the other. On appeal by D, *held*, allowing the appeal, that though the plea of guilty should remain recorded, the sentence on the lesser charge amounted to a duplication, and would be set aside. The sentence of four years' imprisonment was excessive and would be reduced to 30 months.

R. *v.* BEBBINGTON (1978) 67 Cr.App.R. 285, C.A.

548. —— appeals

Accumulation of non-custodial sentences

R. *v.* DOCKER [1979] Crim.L.R. 671 (stole gramophone record—six months' imprisonment with suspended sentence of nine months activated consecutively and further three months for offence for which placed on probation during currency of the suspended sentence—varied to allow immediate release: problems of accumulation of non-custodial sentences resulting in substantial aggregate following conviction of relatively minor offence illustrated).

Aiding suicide

R. *v.* ROBEY [1979] Crim.L.R. 597 (R's wife found dead with stab wound; defence to murder count: she stabbed herself and R pushed knife right in as sure she was dying and did not wish her to suffer; convicted of aiding and abetting suicide—court bound to follow verdict but three years' imprisonment upheld).

Arson

R. *v.* JONES [1979] Crim.L.R. 190 (museum attendant set fire to empty room causing £300,000 damage—no previous convictions—no mental illness—four years' imprisonment upheld).

—— *with intent to endanger life*

R. *v.* HUTCHINSON [1979] Crim.L.R. 190 (set fire to bathroom in boarding-house; considerable damage; no injury; subsequently set fire to lavatory in hotel; no serious damage or injury—previous conviction: culpable homicide: three years' imprisonment—no mental disorder; unhappy marriage; frequently drank until unaware of actions—life imprisonment reduced to seven years' imprisonment).

Assault—alternative count

R. *v.* WORLEY, NUNN AND MARSHALL [1978] Crim.L.R. 101 (all pleaded guilty to assaulting constable, M also to common assault—plea of not guilty to alternative count of assault occasioning actual bodily harm accepted—in mitigation suggested that not guilty plea indicated appellants not accepting actual bodily harm caused—*held:* case properly opened as serious assault—trial judge did not have to accept restriction placed on plea by defence in mitigation—sentences upheld).

Bigamy

R. *v.* CROWHURST [1979] Crim.L.R. 399 (separated from wife 1960; 1973 marriage ceremony with X but marriage not consummated; 1975 marriage ceremony with Y after living with her some months and Y pregnant—had told Y he was divorced—18 months' imprisonment reduced to four; immediate sentence necessary where deception and some injury caused).

Borstal—concurrent sentences—judge's indications as to release

R. *v.* LONG [1979] Crim.L.R. 598 (June 1978: sentenced to Borstal; November 1978: sentenced to Borstal concurrent for offence in December 1977—*held*, judge had wrongly declined counsel's invitation to express hope that later sentence would not affect date of release as, if had not already been committed over later offences, could have asked for them to be taken into consideration when first sentenced).

Burglary

R. *v.* SHEEN [1979] Crim.L.R. 189 (aged 32, alcoholic—two burglaries, one criminal damage, breach of two suspended sentences and probation order for similar offence—total sentence three years' imprisonment, judge saying S a nuisance and sentence would allow treatment for alcoholism—reduced to 18 months as offences relatively trivial and fact of nuisance did not justify disproportionate sentence).

Burglary of dwellinghouse—activation of suspended sentence

R. v. MARTIN [1979] Crim.L.R. 790 (stole £240 worth of property from dwellinghouse whilst occupiers away—previous convictions: series of convictions at intervals of several years: no custodial sentences—12 months' imprisonment with six-month suspended sentence activated consecutively upheld—custodial sentence almost inevitable for burglary of dwellinghouse; statutory duty to activate suspended sentence unless unjust: no reason here to activate concurrently).

Cannabis—possession

R. v. MINOTT [1979] Crim.L.R. 673 (convicted of possessing 2·32 grammes of cannabis found at his home—previous convictions: one minor drug offence; several taking vehicles—three months' imprisonment upheld).

Child stealing

R. v. WESTELL [1979] Crim.L.R. 191 (aged 29, she took five-month-old baby from pram outside post office; found one hour later taking baby back—previous convictions: actual bodily harm to child aged 20 months, criminal damage, offences of dishonesty—unco-operative, uncommunicative, capable of violence, incapable of control over own emotions; no mental illness—two years' imprisonment upheld).

Citizen's band radio

R. v. LEVY, September 26, 1979, Snaresbrooke Crown Ct. (convicted of carrying prohibited goods, namely a citizen's band radio, knowingly and with intention to avoid the importation prohibition. Fine £250. On appeal, it appeared that fines for simple possession ranged from £50 to £150. *Held,* allowing appeal and reducing fine to £150, this was more serious than simple possession, as L had arranged for importation himself, but consistency in fines was desirable, and the fine of £250 was not in parity with the gravity of the offence). (*Ex rel. Nigel Kat, Esq., Barrister.*)

Coinage offence

R. v. LORD [1979] Crim.L.R. 730 (made 80 counterfeit 50p pieces, mostly used in gaming or vending machines—no previous convictions—unsophisticated counterfeiting on limited scale—three years' imprisonment reduced).

Community service—conviction during currency of order

R. v. WILLIAMS [1979] Crim.L.R. 535 (W committed offences during the currency of a community service order imposed on him—sentence: 15 months' imprisonment for new offences, six months concurrent for breach of community service order—concurrent sentence quashed as wrong procedure adopted: no power to sentence for breach—judge should have revoked order and sentenced for original offence by virtue of powers of Criminal Courts Act 1973, s. 17 (3), as amended by Criminal Law Act 1977, Sched. 12).

—— *failure to comply*

R. v. GARLAND [1979] Crim.L.R. 536 (Sept. 1976: 200 hours community service order for taking conveyance—March 1978: committed to Crown Court for original offence, being in breach of order, having performed only 16½ hours' community service—18 months' imprisonment upheld).

—— *power to re-sentence*

R. v. ADAIR [1979] Crim.L.R. 322 (sentenced to 12 months' imprisonment for handling and two community service orders revoked and consecutive sentences totalling four years substituted—revocation of community service orders and sentences relating to offences for which such orders passed quashed since such orders were made before May 8, 1978, when power to revoke community service order on occasion of subsequent conviction came into being by virtue of

Criminal Law Act 1977, s. 65 and Sched. 12; no power to revoke on subsequent conviction where community service order imposed before May 8, 1978).

Compensation

R. *v.* CORNWELL [1979] Crim.L.R. 399 (conspiracy to steal and theft—18 months' imprisonment and £8,600 compensation order—compensation reduced to £6,000 as only £6,000 admitted and such should only be made regarding losses admitted or proved).

—— *subsequent custodial sentence*

R. *v.* WALLIS [1979] Crim.L.R. 732 (compensation orders were made for offences on assumption W would remain on probation; he later re-offended and was sent to prison—*held*, the judge sentencing on the later occasion had no power to terminate the compensation orders but the Court of Appeal would quash them).

Conspiracy to produce L.S.D. in quantity—forfeiture of property

R. *v.* KEMP and BOTT [1979] Crim. L.R. 794 (conspiracies over seven year period to produce L.S.D. Alleged to be responsible for production of almost all L.S.D. seized in U.K. in recent years and much seized in Holland—defendants included chemist and medically qualified woman—13 years' imprisonment for main offenders concerned for long time upheld—argument that L.S.D. should be treated on different basis from heroin rejected—10 years for those involved in manufacture to lesser degree and sentences between eight and three years for those concerned in chain of distribution upheld—forfeiture order of about £250,000 representing profits of the enterprise upheld as conspiracy at common law to commit offence under Misuse of Drugs Act 1971 was an offence " under " that Act within s. 27 and power not restricted to forfeiture of articles for protection of public).

Conspiracy to supply heroin

R. *v.* FRISH AND SEN [1979] Crim.L.R. 791 (S bought 491 gm. heroin for £3,000. F contacted potential buyer who was police officer—no previous convictions—isolated transaction—nine years' imprisonment reduced to seven in each case).

Custodial sentence after adjournment to consider alternative

R. *v.* CHEW [1979] Crim.L.R. 258 (sentence for various offences postponed and bail granted for period of assessment at probation hostel—report not glowing—different sentencer sent C to prison—upheld: adjournment to see whether C suitable for hostel did not tie court's hands).

Deferred sentence

R. *v.* BENSTEAD [1979] Crim.L.R. 400 (sentence deferred four months; then good social inquiry report and no further charges but had not taken probation officer's advice to see police regarding their inquiries into other matters—six months' imprisonment quashed, although almost all served, as wrong in principle).

Defrauding revenue—long delay due to defendant's absconding

R. *v.* FRANCIS [1979] Crim.L.R. 261 (pleaded guilty to making false statements intending to defraud revenue; concealed business receipts from accountants 1962–1964—avoided payment of £1,612—when evasion discovered by Inland Revenue, F disappeared and lived under assumed name for 12 years—all money owing paid by time of court appearance—nine months' imprisonment reduced to three).

Deportation

R. *v.* SANDHU [1978] Crim.L.R. 103 (age: 25—came to U.K. 1965; parents lived in U.K. still; married; three children—sentence: 18 months' imprisonment and recommendation for deportation—recommendation quashed).

Detention of young persons

R. *v.* LLEWELLYN, BENNETT AND CRAWFORD [1978] Crim.L.R. 105 (L aged 16, B 16, C 17—pleaded guilty to various counts—members of gang terrorising women by assaulting and bag-snatching—C was ringleader—167 such offences in same area reported in two-month period—sentences: L three years' detention,

B five years' detention, C seven years' imprisonment—deterrent sentences clearly right but B's reduced to four years and C's to five).

Disparity

R. *v.* FINDING [1979] Crim.L.R. 260 (accomplice with very similar antecedents sentenced to 18 months' imprisonment suspended for two years for very similar offences by different judge—two years' imprisonment upheld as accomplice's sentence was very lenient; in such cases second judge should pass sentence appropriate for offence and leave Court of Appeal to review if thinks fit; disparity was sometimes ground of appeal where marked disparity without apparent reason or one judge sentences in ignorance of other judge's sentence on accomplice).

R. *v.* WATSON [1979] Crim.L.R. 730 (W aged 19 burgled public house with X; burgled golf club alone—no previous convictions for over three years—X, a far more sophisticated and experienced offender, sentenced to six months' imprisonment (had been to Borstal)—Borstal training upheld as being to W's own advantage).

Disputed facts

R. *v.* PRICE [1979] Crim.L.R. 468 (convicted of corruptly receiving money for showing favours as to his employer's affairs—£50 allegedly received on numerous occasions—total alleged £5,450—defence same as to each payment—judge invited jury to decide by reference to one particular payment but sentenced as to the total received—two years' imprisonment reduced to six months suspended for two years because P suffering from heart disease, hypertension, etc. which prison hospital could not cope with but judge held right to sentence on basis that single offence considered by jury was specimen offence: R. v. Huchison [1972] C.L.Y. 636, R. v. Jackson [1972] C.L.Y. 712 and D.P.P. v. Anderson [1978] C.L.Y. 628 distinguished).

Driving whilst disqualified

R. *v.* CRAVEN [1979] Crim.L.R. 324 (pleaded guilty to driving without insurance and whilst disqualified—claimed thought disqualification had expired —sentence: maximum fine (£400) and 12 months' disqualification—*held*, without mitigation, merited imprisonment; thus mitigation must have been accepted; on this basis maximum fine inappropriate; sentence reduced to £30 and nine-month disqualification).

Drug addict—serious offence

R. *v.* HEATHER [1979] Crim.L.R. 672 (threatened assistant in chemist's shop with knife and demanded drugs and syringes; given drugs including morphine and heroin—place available in hostel with experience of dealing with persons in danger of becoming addicted to drugs, as was H—five years' imprisonment correct and wrong to reduce but probation with condition of residence at hostel substituted).

Fines with suspended sentence

R. *v.* WHYBREW [1979] Crim.L.R. 599 (bank accountant dishonestly borrowed £2,000 and deprived customer of £800—no previous convictions—various mitigating circumstances—18 months' imprisonment suspended for two years upheld; £2,000 fine reduced to £1,000 as excessive in relation to W).

Gross indecency

R. *v.* MORGAN AND DOCKERTY [1979] Crim.L.R. 60 (M aged 61, D 39—met in public convenience; known resort of homosexuals; went to second convenience and committed acts of indecency witnessed by police—no previous convictions—£100 and £50 fines substituted for three-month and six-week prison sentences respectively—custodial sentence not appropriate for such offences for first offenders).

Handling—propriety of private discussions between judge and counsel

R. *v.* WINTERFLOOD [1979] Crim.L.R. 263 (indicted for robbery—denied robbery but admitted handling some of proceeds—firearm had been used and £11,000 worth of goods stolen—during trial judge sent for counsel and asked if W would plead guilty to handling if count added—this was done—sentence: three years' imprisonment—co-accused who pleaded guilty to robbery sentenced to four years'—upheld but private discussions between judge and counsel undesirable and should be avoided unless absolutely necessary).

Harassment

R. v. SPRATT, WOOD AND SMYLIE [1978] Crim.L.R. 102 (SM owned house—went with W and SP and their wives to house—SP armed with monkey wrench and cleaver—made tenant's brother, X, remove clothes so couldn't escape—when told them where thought tenant was, allowed to dress and all went there—all returned to house where X forced to clean and tidy up parts of house—£300 arrears of rent—no previous convictions—sentences: SP and W six months' imprisonment, SM, nine—upheld save SM's sentence reduced to six months as no evidence he was ringleader).

Hardship to family—whether mitigation

R. v. REGAN [1979] Crim.L.R. 261 (154 offences obtaining social security by deception over three-year period—£4,000 involved—proceedings initiated nearly 18 months after discovery of offences—four children aged eight to 17—arrangement for eldest to look after others with support of social services had not worked—youngest, diabetic, had been taken to hospital after use of unsterilised needles—18 months' imprisonment reduced to nine months suspended to allow immediate release as society's best interests served by allowing her to be free to look after children).

Heroin—fraudulent importation

R. v. JUSOH [1979] Crim.L.R. 191 (aged 21; helped primary conspirators secrete heroin with street value exceeding £1 million aboard ship, being member of crew, in return for quantity of cannabis—no previous convictions—12 years' imprisonment reduced to eight as J not one of the " big fish ").

Hospital order—restriction

R. v. HODGE [1979] Crim.L.R. 602 (age: 17—broke a window—hospital order with unlimited restriction order—restriction order quashed as no evidence to suggest she would abscond, or commit further offences if at liberty, or be a danger to others; measured risk necessary in justice and humanity).

Illegal immigrant—facilitating entry

R. v. SINGH AND SAINI [1979] Crim.L.R. 598 (arranged for mother-in-law to be driven through immigration control concealed behind rear seat—no previous convictions—sentenced on basis connected with international ring of immigrant smugglers; no profit made; both had excellent work records; evidence of connection with international ring doubtful—three years' imprisonment reduced to two and recommendation for deportation quashed; distinction to be drawn between offences committed for profit and those not committed for profit).

Incest

R v. BEDFORD [1979] Crim.L.R. 792 (left family when daughter very young. Saw her once in 20 years. Had remarried and she had married. Both unhappy. Incest followed emotional relationship. Pregnancy resulted and was terminated. Hoped to live together without sexual intercourse on B's release—two years' imprisonment upheld).

Intermediate recidivist

R. v. GREEN [1979] Crim.L.R. 600 (burglary, criminal damage—numerous previous convictions; in prison most of last eight years; out of trouble about 18 months after last release; offence after drinking—sentence of imprisonment varied to two years' probation as last chance to see if could be saved from perpetual recidivism).

R. v. RUSSELL [1979] Crim.L.R. 600 (stole from young men who had offered R hospitality but inflicted injuries on him necessitating weeks in hospital when theft discovered—very bad record; all sentences tried; out of trouble 10 months; two reports recommended probation—sentence too long but instead of reducing to length of period served, probation order with condition of residence at hostel substituted).

Life imprisonment

R. v. MOTTERSHEAD [1979] Crim.L.R. 539 (32 months after release from prison drank heavily, burgled house of 72 year-old lady, waking her up and striking her on arm with spade before running away—in 1971 had been sentenced to 10 years for burglaries and rapes of elderly ladies in their homes—no mental disorder—no evidence a danger to society or that M knew house occupied by elderly lady living alone—thus life imprisonment altered to eight years).

R. v. SAMUEL [1979] Crim.L.R. 537 (committed serious offence whilst on licence from life sentence—sentence: life imprisonment—four years' imprisonment substituted as the sentence appropriate to gravity of latest offence, since public protection could be achieved, if necessary, at end of latest sentence, by revocation of parole licence for earlier offence).

R. v. SPENCER [1979] Crim.L.R. 538 (aged 46—arson and theft—infatuated with voluntary worker at probation hostel; when advances rejected, drank, attempted to break into her house and set fire to her husband's car in car port adjoining house; car destroyed, car port badly damaged—several previous convictions, including arson—personality disorder but could not be treated in hospital; one medical witness considered him serious risk to public—life imprisonment altered to five years as S not constant danger to public and this not particularly serious case of arson).

R. v. THORNETT [1979] Crim.L.R. 538 (aged 20—three rapes, two same day, other 12 months before; threatened grave violence; two victims sexually assaulted other than intercourse, in addition—several previous convictions dishonesty and indecent exposure—on probation at time of rapes—no psychiatric disorder but unhappy childhood and marriage and emotionally unstable and immature and likely to be violent—life imprisonment upheld as fundamental consideration was protection of public).

R. v. WAIGHT [1979] Crim.L.R. 538 (aged 21—various offences of robbery, violence, possessing firearm with intent, etc.—attacked several people depositing money in night safe, shooting and injuring two; on further occasion entered bank, fired one shot and left without stealing anything; on further occasion attacked man with knife injuring hand—no psychiatric disorder; not psychopath but "immature and impulsive"; most of life in institutions—life imprisonment upheld to ensure public safety).

Manslaughter

R. v. HUDSON [1979] Crim.L.R. 601 (convicted manslaughter on indictment for murder—prosecution alleged vicious attack by H, defence alleged victim attacked H, who punched him in self-defence, knocking him to ground, where head struck pavement—seven years' imprisonment reduced to three as verdict implied that jury accepted H's version).

R. v. STUART AND WILLIAMS [1979] Crim.L.R. 793 (X caused trouble at drinking party. S and W disarmed Y who had threatened X with knife and S and W went to deal with X. During ensuing fight W pushed X down concrete staircase where he stayed all night unconscious and later died—no relevant previous convictions—four years' imprisonment reduced to two in each case—no reason to distinguish between S and W; callousness in leaving X overnight irrelevant as not charged with manslaughter by neglect).

—— *death resulting from unlawful act*

R. v. SHELTON [1979] Crim.L.R. 793 (aged 60—during family quarrel engaged in minor struggle with brother and fell on him causing accidental injury resulting in death. S had since had breakdown and been admitted to hospital—12 months' imprisonment suspended on appeal as immediate custodial sentence unnecessary).

Manslaughter of baby by depressed mother

R. v. LYNCH [1979] Crim.L.R. 117 (female aged 20—caused injuries to one-year-old daughter by, *inter alia*, violent shaking and caused death of six-week-old son by shaking—living in poor conditions; ante- and post-natal depression—two years' imprisonment upheld).

Parole—relevance in sentencing

R. v. LUKINS [1979] Crim.L.R. 325 (sentenced to 12 months' imprisonment consecutive to sentence already being served—intention that sentence would not substantially affect date on which L would be eligible for parole—sentence wrongly assumed five months in custody pending latest sentence would count towards latest sentence—reduced to seven months, being effective sentence intended; sentencer should not concern himself with prospects of parole).

Persistent offender

R. v. HARRISON [1979] Crim.L.R. 262 (burglary of elderly woman's house, leaving with nothing when challenged by neighbour—many previous convictions over many years—every method of dealing with him tried without effect—public entitled to protection from him but five years' imprisonment too long and accordingly reduced to three).

R. v. McNAMEE [1979] Crim.L.R. 602 (age: 56—obtained car from dealer by deception on hire purchase and sold it same day—41 previous appearances— five years' imprisonment and consecutive activation of six months' suspended sentence, although not necessarily wrong, varied to probation as place at hostel for persistent offenders available and M could be given yet another last chance).

Plea bargaining—discussions with judge

R. v. DAVIS [1979] Crim.L.R. 327 (conspiracy to defraud bank of £750,000 —after 10 days' trial appellant asked counsel to see judge to obtain indication of likely sentence on change of plea; judge said improper to give indication but discount would be given; later said discount would be about 20 per cent.— six years' imprisonment upheld; could not be said D deprived of complete freedom of choice of plea which was essential; was under no undue pressure— visits to judge to discuss sentence almost always wrong).

Rape

R. v. BRIGGS [1979] Crim.L.R. 467 (aged 17, raped girl aged 16; had had intercourse with her on previous and subsequent occasions but used violence on this occasion so she fled almost naked on December night—did not appreciate gravity of offence in light of other occasions when intercourse took place— several previous convictions, including violence—three years' imprisonment upheld but court said no reasons of sentencing policy why Parole Board should not recommend release on licence at whatever time it considered appropriate).

Resisting arrest with firearm

R. v. BALDWIN [1978] Crim.L.R. 104 (age: 21—pleaded guilty ten offences —drove with excess alcohol—pointed revolver at arresting officer; not loaded; disarmed after long struggle—five previous convictions; fines—three years' imprisonment upheld).

Robbery

R. v. AINSWORTH AND BLAKE [1979] Crim.L.R. 326 (two robberies; held up manager of public-house and girl friend; appeared to have gun; took money from safe; locked four people in store room and left in manager's car; A had truncheon; 10 months later held up new manager at same public-house, three staff and taxi-driver; appeared to have gun; A had cash; locked them all in storeroom; each time B telephoned police so victims could be released—five similar offences taken into consideration; amounts usually £1,000–£2,000— 10 years' imprisonment each count concurrent reduced to seven as not experienced criminals and no reason to suppose would repeat such offences).

R. v. MOSS [1979] Crim.L.R. 119 (masked with scarf, pointed unloaded air rifle at cashier at all-night service station—took £60—no previous convictions—four years' imprisonment upheld though substantial personal mitigation).

—— *disparity in age*

R. v. ARMSTRONG [1979] Crim.L.R. 61 (A and four others robbed an apparent homosexual; K, the prime mover, aged 18, was sent back to Borstal; the two others, aged 18 and 16, were placed on probation—two years' imprisonment imposed by different court upheld—age difference important; disparity, if any, minor).

Separate trial—evidence

R. *v.* DEPLEDGE [1979] Crim.L.R. 733 (conspired to rob a cashier—in sentencing D judge appeared to take into account matters which came to his attention in the course of separate trials of co-defendants—sentence upheld: where defendants convicted at separate trials of participation in same offence, unrealistic to expect judge to put out of his mind material coming to his knowledge as result of separate trials).

Shoplifting

R. *v.* WHITEHEAD [1979] Crim.L.R. 734 (stole tin of ham, tin of steak and pair of tights from self-service shop when on social security, separated, and looking after two children, one mentally handicapped and one with behavioural difficulties—no previous convictions—six weeks' imprisonment suspended for one year quashed as wrong in principle; conditional discharge substituted).

Suspended sentence—activation

R. *v.* BEACOCK [1979] Crim L.R. 797 (attempted to syphon diesel from parked lorry at night—in 1976 had been sentenced to nine months' imprisonment suspended for two years for offences in 1974 of different kind—had worked hard to build up business—nine months' imprisonment with suspended sentence activated consecutively but reduced to six months reduced to three months with suspended sentence reduced to period to allow immediate release (six months served) as offence at end of operational period of suspended sentence).

R. *v.* CLINE [1979] Crim.L.R. 469 (June 1977, sentenced to two years' imprisonment suspended for two years for five burglaries—July 1978, sentenced to one month's imprisonment for being carried in a vehicle knowing it to have been taken without authority and suspended sentence activated in full consecutively—*held*, correct to activate suspended sentence consecutively but term reduced to one year in view of relatively minor nature of most recent offence).

—— *consecutive activation*

R. *v.* MAY [1979] Crim.L.R. 603 (three burglaries of dwelling-houses—three years' imprisonment and consecutive activation of 12 months' suspended sentence imposed 12 months earlier—upheld: activated suspended sentence should be consecutive unless there were exceptional circumstances).

—— *effect on gravity of offence committed during operational period*

R. *v.* DAVIES [1979] Crim.L.R. 62 (siphoned petrol from another car when own car short of petrol. Later carrying hose and can with intent to steal petrol—sentence: 12 months' imprisonment—suspended sentences to 12 months activated consecutively—sentence for fresh offences reduced to three months since sentence should be appropriate to offences themselves and not treated as more serious because during operational period of suspended sentence).

—— *implementation*

R. *v.* BRYANT [1978] Crim.L.R. 103 (in 1976 Crown Court allowed appeal against sentence by magistrates, reduced term of imprisonment and ordered prior suspended sentence for 1974 offence to remain suspended for further year —1977: 12 months' imprisonment for further offences and suspended sentence activated consecutively—suspended sentence made concurrent as previous sentence by Crown Court against sentencing policy).

Suspended sentence plus community service

R. *v.* STARIE [1979] Crim.L.R. 731 (220 hours' community service for supplying amphetamines; 12 months' imprisonment suspended for one year for supplying L.S.D.—suspended sentence quashed as it is generally bad practice to impose a community service order and suspended sentence at same time).

Tax fraud

R. *v.* CHOWDHURY [1979] Crim.L.R. 734 (for 11 years claimed allowances in tax returns for non-existent wife and two children allegedly living in Bangladesh —when wished to marry, obtained forged death certificate in respect of non-existent wife and false documents testifying that children existed—no previous convictions—12 months' imprisonment consecutive on each count of production of false documents; three months' concurrent on other counts—reduced to 15 months' imprisonment).

Totality

R. v. McLAUGHLIN [1979] Crim.L.R. 402 (three indictments, various offences, 12 offences taken into consideration—numerous previous convictions: up to six years' imprisonment—12 months' imprisonment first indictment possession of cannabis; 18 months' second indictment going equipped for theft and attempted theft of caravan; two years on third indictment theft of two caravans and possessing controlled drug; suspended sentence 18 months' activated: theft, handling and abstracting electricity; all consecutive, total six years—had been out of trouble one year and offences related to drug dependency; had saved prisoner's life—some hope—18-month sentence reduced to 12, suspended sentence reduced to six, total reduced to four years).

Unlawful eviction

R. v. BRENNAN AND BRENNAN [1979] Crim.L.R. 603 (let house to five young men; as result of dispute over rent, came to house with large man and Alsatian dog and ordered tenants to leave, which they did—elected jury trial—no previous convictions—maximum penalty recently increased to two years—one year's imprisonment reduced to three months; imprisonment should be usual penalty where landlord uses threats or force in absence of unusual mitigation).

Violence—compensation order

R. v. WEBB [1979] Crim.L.R. 466 (during fight at party W's husband was struck across face with glass and seriously cut; W came to his assistance and hit his assailant with a glass object wounding his face—acted on spur of moment not realising gravity of using glass object—no previous convictions— 12 months' imprisonment suspended for two years reduced to six months suspended for two years: imprisonment appropriate where glass object used— £200 compensation order held wholly unrealistic in view of W's lack of means and therefore quashed).

—— *football supporters*

R. v. GLAVIN, WOODS AND JAPP [1979] Crim.L.R. 401 (football supporter attacked during match by other supporters; injuries almost caused death; W and J joined in, G aided and abetted—some provocation—previous convictions: W none, G two minor offences, J three—three years' imprisonment upheld for W and J as deterrent sentences but varied to Borstal for G).

Wounding with intent

R. v. BLAKE [1979] Crim.L.R. 735 (New Year's Eve; found wife in act of adultery; broke glass and gouged it into the man's throat—no lasting injury or scarring—nine months' imprisonment varied to six months' suspended for two years as B had been in custody and period he had served was sufficient to cancel any debt B owed to society).

Young adult—life imprisonment

R. v. SHORT [1979] Crim.L.R. 262 (aged 19—caused fires at three houses and one shop over two-year period—one elderly lady died from effects of smoke— psychiatrists agreed offences due to personal immaturity rather than mental disorder; no treatment necessary—felt great remorse, likely to mature within few years—life imprisonment reduced to eight years' imprisonment).

Young person—detention

R. v. REDMOND [1979] Crim. L.R. 192 (aged 16; attacked acquaintance with knife causing severe facial injuries and injuries to back; one ear of victim nearly severed—three previous findings of guilt: mainly criminal damage and burglary—four years' detention upheld).

549. —— —— **death by dangerous driving.** See R. v. YARNOLD, § 2300.

550. —— **bank robbery—large sums stolen**

The judgment of the Court of Appeal in *R.* v. *Turner* was not intended to lay down a ceiling of 18 years' imprisonment for robbery involving large sums of money.

After the Bank of America case, where the known proceeds were some two million pounds, the defendants were sentenced to terms of imprisonment ranging from three to 23 years. On appeal against sentence, *held,* that sentences should make it plain that those who indulged in first division crime would receive sentences which would be a warning to others and which at the same time would ensure that offenders would not be released too soon in order to batten upon the proceeds. The case of *R.* v. *Turner* [1975] C.L.Y. 559 did not lay down a ceiling of 18 years. However the sentences would be reduced from 23 to 20 years, 21 to 18 years, 18 to 15 years, 17 to 14 years, 12 to eight years and three to two years. (*R.* v. *Turner* [1975] C.L.Y. 559 considered.)

R. v. WILDE; R. v. COLSON; R. v. TAYLOR; R. v. GEAR; R. v. O'LOUGHLIN; R. v. JEFFREY (1978) 67 Cr.App.R. 339, C.A.

551. —— basis of sentencing

[Powers of Criminal Courts Act 1973 (c. 62), s. 28.] Unless a defendant qualifies for an extended sentence under s. 28 of the Powers of Criminal Courts Act 1973, he should be sentenced only on the basis of the facts proved, and not for the purpose of protecting the public: R. v. GOODEN, *The Times,* December 5, 1979, C.A.

552. —— Borstal training—imposed after sentence of detention centre for subsequent offence

It may sometimes be appropriate to sentence a young offender to Borstal training for an offence committed before an offence for which he has, in the intervening period, served a sentence at a detention centre.

In October 1976 D was involved with three others, after which he assaulted a woman police constable. In January 1977 he committed two offences of criminal damage. In March 1977 he assaulted a police officer in the execution of his duty. In May 1977 with two of the same youths, he assaulted two more constables. In July 1977 for the January and March offences he was sent to detention centre, and released in September 1977. In November he was sentenced for the October 1976 and May 1977 offences to Borstal training. His co-defendants were sent to prison. His report from detention centre had been good. *Held,* dismissing his appeal, that the October 1976 assault and the intervening assaults in May 1977 plainly called for an immediate custodial sentence, and Borstal was the appropriate way of dealing with him (*R.* v. *Binns, McEvoy, Ward* [1977] C.L.Y. 641 applied; *R.* v. *Gooding* [1956] C.L.Y. 2096 disinguished.)

R. v. FRANCIS (1978) 67 Cr.App.R. 335, C.A.

553. —— community service order—whether to be coupled with fine

[Powers of Criminal Courts Act 1973 (c. 62), ss. 14, 30.]

A court making a community service order cannot pass a further sentence at the same time in respect of one offence.

The appellant was convicted of assault and ordered to undergo community service; he was further fined £250 in respect of the same offence. *Held,* allowing his appeal, that by virtue of ss. 14 and 30 (1) of the 1973 Act a community service order can be made "instead of" any other sentence or order; and that accordingly the fine was quashed.

R. v. CARNWELL (1978) 68 Cr.App.R. 58, C.A.

554. —— compensation order—figure neither agreed nor proven

[Powers of Criminal Courts Act 1973 (c. 62), s. 35.]

A compensation order should not be made unless the sum claimed by the victim as compensation is either agreed or has been proved.

V, was convicted of taking and driving away a motorcar and of driving it recklessly. He had also crashed into and damaged another car. The owner of that car received an estimate for its repair of £209. V asserted this was excessive and in passing sentence the judge made a compensation order in the sum of £100. V, appealed against the order. *Held,* a compensation order should not be made unless the sum claimed was either agreed or had been proved. Since there had been neither agreement on nor proof of the amount claimed the order would be quashed.

R. v. VIVIAN [1979] 1 All E.R. 48, C.A.

555. —— **conditional discharge—appeal against sentence**

[Powers of Criminal Courts Act 1973 (c. 62), s. 13 (1); Criminal Appeal Act 1968 (c. 19), ss. 9, 50 (1).] D was given a conditional discharge and ordered to pay £50 costs and £10 compensation. *Held,* that (1) the " sentence " was proper; (2) the court was powerless to interfere with such a sentence in any event, even where justice requires interference, since a conditional discharge is not a conviction for the purposes of an appeal and only one who has been convicted can appeal against sentence. (*R.* v. *Tucker* [1974] C.L.Y. 743 applied): R. v. ROBINSON [1979] Crim.L.R. 785, C.A.

556. —— **death by dangerous driving—defendant ostracised by community.** See R. v. WRIGHT, § 2299.

557. —— —— **imprisonment—disqualification—disobedient learner**

[Road Traffic Act 1972 (c. 20), ss. 1 (1), 93 (1), Sched. 4, Pt. I.]

Where dangerous driving arises out of a disregard for the clear and sound instructions of the supervising driver, a sentence of £500 fine and a three years' disqualification are not too severe.

The appellant, a provisional licence holder, drove a car with two passengers under the supervision of a full licence holder. The supervising driver, who knew the route asked the appellant to slow down because of a bend ahead. Instead the appellant increased the speed and again did not slow down when told to do so. As a result of high speed at the bend, the car skidded and turned over twice, killing one of the passengers. He pleaded guilty to causing death by dangerous driving, contrary to s. 1 of the 1972 Act, and was fined £500 and disqualified for three years. On appeal against sentence, *held,* dismissing the appeal, that this was a bad case of a provisional driver disregarding the clear and sound instructions of the supervising driver, and on immediate custodial sentence might well be proper, therefore, the sentence was not too severe.

R. v. O'CONNOR [1979] R.T.R. 467, C.A.

558. —— —— —— —— **serious case**

[Road Traffic Act 1972 (c. 20), s. 93 (1), Sched. 4, Pt. I.]

Although this was unquestionably a serious case of dangerous driving it fell far short of the worst category, and a five-year disqualification was longer than called for by the circumstances of the offences.

The appellant, a doctor, drove from a minor road straight across stop lines, past a " give way " sign onto a major road into the path of an oncoming car. The ensuing collision killed the driver and passenger of the oncoming car. He pleaded guilty to causing death by dangerous driving and, was fined and disqualified for five years. He appealed on the ground that the disqualification made it impossible for him to enter private medical practice or effectively to have access to his daughter in the custody of his former wife. *Held,* allowing the appeal, that although this was a serious case, it fell far short of the " worst " category of dangerous driving cases, and the disqualification for five years was longer than called for by the circumstances of the offences, and accordingly, would be reduced to two years.

R. v. FENWICK [1979] R.T.R. 506, C.A.

559. —— —— **whether imprisonment appropriate**

In the absence of aggravating circumstances, imprisonment may be an inappropriate sentence for a first offence of causing death by dangerous driving.

Having failed to notice " slow " road markings and a bend warning sign, the appellant motorist overtook slow-moving vehicles and collided head-on with a lorry travelling in the opposite direction. He was convicted of causing the death by dangerous driving of one of his passengers and was sentenced to 28 days' imprisonment, three years' disqualification, together with an order for £200 costs. The appellant had no previous convictions; there was no evidence of any excess speed nor any suggestion of drink-driving. *Held,* quashing the prison sentence on appeal, that in the absence of aggravating circumstances an immediate prison sentence was not justified.

R. v. BRUIN [1979] R.T.R. 95, C.A.

560. —— death by reckless driving—length of disqualification

Even in a bad case, imposition of a very long period of disqualification may be counter-productive.

The appellant, aged 29, whilst driving his car and overtaking other vehicles, collided head-on with a car travelling in the opposite direction, killing a passenger in the other car. He was convicted of causing death by reckless driving. He had two convictions for driving offences, one of which was for dangerous driving. He was employed as a mini-cab driver and, due to an injury to his hand, would have difficulty in obtaining work other than as a driver. He was sentenced to six months' imprisonment and seven years' disqualification. *Held*, allowing an appeal in respect of the disqualification, that the circumstances warranted reducing the period of the disqualification to five years.

R. *v.* FARRUGIA [1979] R.T.R. 422, C.A.

561. —— deferment—whether subsequent custodial sentence appropriate

[Powers of Criminal Courts Act 1973 (c. 62), s. 1 (1).]

The principle that a substantial custodial sentence is inappropriate after a deferment where the reports on conduct are not favourable is not a rule of law, but depends on the particular facts of the case.

H was convicted of theft in November 1976 and sentence was deferred for six months. In January 1977, at the same court, he was convicted of excess alcohol and driving whilst disqualified and given an immediate 12 months' sentence. No order was made on the deferred sentence. On appeal, *held*, dismissing the appeal, that it is not a rule of law that a custodial sentence should not be imposed in these circumstances, especially where the sentence is not for the same offence as that for which sentence had been originally deferred. (*R. v. Gilby* [1975] C.L.Y. 2052 considered.)

R. *v.* HARLING (1977) 65 Cr.App.R. 320, C.A.

562. —— drunken driving—imprisonment—disqualification—costs

[Road Traffic Act 1972 (c. 20), ss. 6 (1), 93 (1).]

It is wrong for a defendant to be at risk of having to pay part of those costs which relate to offences of which he was not convicted.

The appellant pleaded guilty to driving with 222 milligrams of alcohol to 100 millilitres of blood and not guilty to two other charges, which were ordered to lie on the file so that there was no conviction on them. He was sentenced to seven days' imprisonment with a fine of £75, ordered to pay up to £100 of the prosecution's costs and to make a £50 contribution to legal aid costs and disqualified for three years. On appeal against sentence, *held*, allowing the appeal in part, that the three-year disqualification was excessive, reducing it to 18 months; it was wrong to put the appellant at risk of having to pay part of the costs related to offences of which he was not convicted and, the sentence of imprisonment would be quashed.

R. *v.* BEARDSLEY [1979] R.T.R. 472, C.A.

563. —— —— —— —— unblemished driving record

[Road Traffic Act 1972 (c. 20), ss. 6 (2), 93 (2).]

In a case where the blood alcohol concentration of a driver is very high, a sentence of imprisonment is proper not withstanding an unblemished driving record.

The appellant who was aged 59 and in continuous employment, had an unblemished driving record. He was in charge of a motor-car stationary on the hard-shoulder of a motorway with 267 milligrammes of alcohol to 100 millilitres of blood. He pleaded guilty to contravening s. 6 (2) of the 1972 Act and was sentenced to three months' imprisonment and disqualified for three years. Allowing the appeal in part, *held*, that the sentence of imprisonment was proper as the blood alcohol concentration was enormously high; but that, in view of the appellant's age and unblemished record the period of disqualification would be reduced to 18 months.

R. *v.* SALTERS [1979] R.T.R. 470, C.A.

564. —— —— —— unnecessarily long

[Road Traffic Act 1972 (c. 20), s. 93 (1), Sched. 4, Pt. I.]

In general, disqualification for a longer period is justifiable where imprisonment would delay the punitive effect of such disqualification for a considerable period.

The appellant was sentenced to five years' imprisonment in respect of various matters. He also pleaded guilty to driving with 136 milligrams of alcohol to 100 millilitres of blood, and was disqualified for three years on the basis that he should not be in a better position than a more honest and respectable citizen if he was released within the three-year period. On appeal, against sentence, *held,* allowing the appeal, that although such an approach is justifiable in many cases where the punitive effect of a disqualification is delayed for a considerable period, in the circumstances of the present case, the period of disqualification was unnecessarily long as it impeded his rehabilitation, and accordingly would be reduced to 12 months.

R. *v.* CUNNINGHAM [1979] R.T.R. 465, C.A.

565. —— duty of court to explain order

The defendant pleaded guilty to obtaining credit while an undischarged bankrupt, and was given a suspended sentence of imprisonment. *Held,* that a conditional discharge should be substituted and, since the defendant was not present at the hearing of the appeal, he should appear before one of the Q.B. judges at Leeds (sitting as a member of the C.A.) so that the court could discharge its statutory duty of explaining the effect of the order: R. *v.* QUINN, *The Times,* November 17, 1979, C.A.

566. —— imprisonment—disqualification from driving

[Theft Act 1968 (c. 60), s. 12 (1); Road Traffic Act 1972 (c. 20), s. 93 (2), Sched. 4, Pt. III, para. 2.]

There is no reason why disqualification should not be imposed in a case of robbery with a stolen vehicle, together with a sentence of imprisonment.

D, who was aged 26 and of previous good character, pleaded guilty to taking a car and to robbery of his place of work, using the car. He was sentenced to 12 months' imprisonment for the robbery, and 12 months' concurrent plus two years' disqualification for taking the vehicle. He appealed against the disqualification on the ground that he had previously been convicted of such an offence, and had not driven this car. *Held,* allowing the appeal, that although there was nothing wrong with such a sentence, especially where the sentence of imprisonment was so short, the disqualification would be cut to 15 months because of D's need to obtain employment on his release.

R. *v.* MULROY [1979] R.T.R. 214, C.A.

567. —— —— mentally disturbed offender

A sentence of imprisonment should not be disproportionate to the crime merely because the accused's mental condition makes him likely whilst at liberty to be a danger to himself and to others.

D, aged 24, was caught with a small quantity of cannabis; he was thereby in breach of probation for possession of cannabis. He was mentally disturbed due to drugs and alcohol. He was suffering from schizophrenia, and the medical reports recommended an order under s. 60 of the Mental Health Act 1959. There was no place available for him in any appropriate hospital. The prison doctor gave evidence that D had improved whilst in custody; but if he were at liberty, he might relapse and resort to anti-social behaviour. He was sentenced to two years' imprisonment. On appeal, *held,* that although the sentence of imprisonment had been nothing but beneficial so far, the punishment should fit the crime, and the penal system could not be used to make good the shortcomings of the social services and the mental health system. Accordingly, the sentence would be reduced so as to allow D to go free, since he had already served some six-and-a-half months, which was far in excess of any term that could possibly have been justified. (*R. v. Clarke (Dawn)* [1975] C.L.Y. 693 applied; *R. v. Arrowsmith* [1976] C.L.Y. 568 disapproved.)

R. *v.* TOLLEY (1978) 68 Cr.App.R. 323, C.A.

568. —— imprisonment plus fine

There is nothing wrong in principle with a sentence of imprisonment coupled with a large fine which the prisoner may not be able to pay.

D, a 29-year-old woman of previous good character, got four jobs by giving fake names and credentials and disguising herself with a wig. Having done so, in each case she disappeared within a few days taking money from the till. She obtained £5,423 all of which she spent. She pleaded guilty to four counts of theft and asked for five further offences to be taken into consideration. She was sentenced to a total of 12 months' imprisonment and fined a total of £2,000, with 12 months' imprisonment in default. On appeal against sentence, *held,* dismissing the appeal, that a total sentence of two years' imprisonment would have been by no means excessive, so the fact that D might have to serve two years was no valid ground of appeal. (*R.* v. *Savundranayagan and Walker* [1968] C.L.Y. 3070 applied.)

R. *v.* LOTT-CARTER (1978) 67 Cr.App.R. 404, C.A.

569. —— informer—discount

Public policy requires that criminals who turn informer and give substantial assistance to the police can expect substantial discounts in their sentences; but such discounts can only arise in the five years and over sentence bracket.

D pleaded guilty to 15 offences, including robberies, robberies with violence and with firearms. He asked for 33 similar offences to be taken into consideration. D had given information to the police resulting in the detection and arrest of dangerous and violent criminals in over 100 cases. He was sentenced to 10 years' imprisonment. On appeal against sentence, *held,* allowing the appeal, that where the crime was not minor, but was in the five year and over bracket, a criminal who had given substantial assistance to the police could expect and would receive a substantial discount. The sentence accordingly would be reduced to seven years. (*R.* v. *Lowe* [1978] C.L.Y. 617 applied.)

R. *v.* DAVIES AND GORMAN (1978) 68 Cr.App.R. 319, C.A.

570. —— manslaughter—father killing autistic child

On November 13, 1978, the defendant, a loving father of an autistic child aged nine, but with a mental age of between two and three, battered his child over the head with an axe and cut the boy's throat. The defendant then left the matrimonial home, telephoned the police to inform his wife, the boy's mother, and went to Wales. He was arrested, confessed and charged with murder the following day. At the trial the prosecution offered no evidence of murder and accepted a plea to manslaughter on the grounds of diminished responsibility to which course of action the judge expressed her agreement. The defendant was given a term of probation for 12 months. The judge found the case exceptional and the defendant had no convictions recorded against him. The judge was satisfied that the defendant loved his boy and that he would suffer enduring punishment in the knowledge of the event. The judge outlined several unusual features concerning the case: (1) the defendant was under treatment from a psychiatrist for a chronic condition; (2) he had looked after mentally-handicapped children as an officer in a mental institution; (3) he had suffered a nasty and painful accident not long before the offence; (4) he was loathe to part with the child to an institution; and (5) he was on a course of medication. The judge concluded that the act was quite out of character, that the defendant went through a bout of madness when it happened and that her public duty was not to add to that hell: R. *v.* TAYLOR, February 22, 1979, Heilbron J. (*Ex rel. G. Marriott, Esq., Barrister.*)

571. —— probation

The Home Office has published the "Probation and After-care Statistics, England and Wales 1978." The statistics show that the number of persons supervised by the Probation and After-care Service, excluding those subject solely to community service orders, fell in 1978 for the third consecutive year. The report is available from the Home Office, Statistical Department, Room 1806, Tolworth Tower, Surbiton, Surrey, KT6 7DS [£2·25].

572. —— suspended sentence—absconding whilst on bail—whether breach

[Powers of Criminal Courts Act 1973 (c. 62), s. 23 (1); Bail Act 1976 (c. 63), s. 6 (1) (5) (7).]

Absconding whilst on bail contrary to s. 6 (1) of the Bail Act 1976 is a breach of suspended sentence.

D was charged with rape and other offences. On the fifth day of his trial he failed to answer bail. At the time of absconding he was under a suspended sentence of six months' imprisonment. On being apprehended he was sentenced to a term of imprisonment for the offence of absconding, and the suspended sentence was implemented. On appeal, *held*, dismissing the appeal, that absconding and being sentenced for it was a "conviction," and the appeal, that the judge was bound to implement the suspended sentence unless he was of the opinion that it would be unjust to do so. (*Morris* v. *Crown Office* [1970] C.L.Y. 2254 distinguished.)

R. v. TYSON (1979) 68 Cr.App.R. 314, C.A.

573. —— —— **no order on breach—power of subsequent court**
[Powers of Criminal Courts Act 1973 (c. 62), s. 23 (1) (*d*).]
Where a court considers the breach of a suspended sentence and decides to make no order on the breach, it is not open to a subsequent court to deal again with the same breach.

F was convicted of a further offence within the period of a previous suspended sentence. He was given community service, and the court made no order on the breach of the suspended sentence. Subsequently, he was in breach of the community service order, was brought back to court and sentenced to a term of imprisonment. The judge then also sentenced him to a consecutive term for the initial suspended sentence breach. On appeal, on the question of whether the court had power to pass the consecutive sentence, *held*, allowing the appeal, that the court, having considered the breach on the earlier occasion, decided to make no order, it was not therefore open to another court to deal with the same breach.

R. v. FOLAN (1979) 69 Cr.App.R. 93, C.A.

574. Sexual offences—rape—evidence—complainant's sexual experience
[Sexual Offences (Amendment) Act 1976 (c. 82), s. 2 (1).] The defence to charges of rape and attempted rape of a 14-year-old girl was consent. *Held*, granting leave under s. 2 (1) of the 1976 Act to cross-examine the plaintiff as to conversations immediately before the alleged offences in which she spoke of previous sexual intercourse with young men, that the cross-examination was permissible at common law but prima facie forbidden by the Act. The judge had to consider whether the cross-examination was likely to have so disastrous an effect on her (as she may have attempted suicide shortly after the alleged offences) that it should be excluded irrespective of the effect on the defendants: R. v. HINDS AND BUTLER [1979] Crim.L.R. 111, Northampton Crown Ct.

575. —— **time limit for commencing proceedings—issue raised at trial**
[Sexual Offences Act 1967 (c. 60), s. 7.]
Where the issue arises at trial, the Crown's failure to prove that proceedings for a sexual offence were commenced within 12 months of the commission thereof is fatal to the prosecution case.

The appellant was tried for an offence of gross indecency. Upon the available evidence the Crown considered that the proceedings had been commenced within 12 months of the commission of the offence, but the evidence adduced at trial left the issue of the date of the offence in doubt. The trial judge rejected a defence submission that failure to prove compliance with s. 7 of the Act (which provides that "no proceedings . . . shall be commenced" after expiration of 12 months) was fatal to the Crown Case, and the appellant was convicted. *Held*, allowing his appeal, that s. 7 was not merely a procedural provision to be overlooked provided that the proceedings were brought in good faith. (*Secretary of State for Defence* v. *Warn* [1968] C.L.Y. 135 and *R.* v. *Angel* [1968] C.L.Y. 892 applied.)

R. v. LEWIS [1979] 2 All E.R. 665, C.A.

576. —— **working paper**
The Policy Advisory Committee on Sexual Offences has published its "Working Paper on the Age of Consent in relation to Sexual Offences." The principal recommendations of the Committee are that the age of consent for sexual intercourse should remain at 16 and the minimum age for homosexual relations between consenting males should be reduced from 21 to 18. The Working Paper is available from HMSO [90p].

577. Taking a conveyance—mens rea—joint enterprise
[Theft Act 1968 (c. 60), s. 12 (1); Criminal Damage Act 1971 (c. 48), s. 1 (1).]
Presence at the time of taking a car and riding in it does not necessarily evince a joint enterprise to take the car without authority.

The 11-year-old defendant was convicted of taking a car without authority and criminal damage upon the basis that he had accompanied an older boy to a car showroom where the older boy, having told the defendant that he would prove that he could drive a car, started a car and drove it forward into the showroom door, damaging the same. The defendant was sitting in the passenger seat at the time of the act of driving. The justices conceded that by accompanying the older boy knowing of his intention to drive the defendant encouraged the other's behaviour and was therefore party to a joint enterprise. *Held*, allowing the appeal, that it had to be proved that the defendant was party to the taking at the time when the car was driven; and that the proper question was whether the defendant had participated in the act of taking with the requisite mental element. (*R.* v. *Carey* (1881) 8 Q.B.D. 534 considered).
C. (A MINOR) *v.* HUME [1979] R.T.R. 424, D.C.

578. —— plea of guilty—owner subsequently stating permission would have been given
[Theft Act 1968 (c. 60), s. 12 (1) (6).]
If a defendant pleads guilty to an offence of taking a vehicle without authority, s. 12 (6) does not afford him a defence if subsequently it appears that the owner would have given him permission to take the vehicle.

The defendant, A, and several others went out in a car, owned by a friend of theirs, in the owner's absence. A pleaded guilty while his co-defendants pleaded not guilty on the basis of s. 12 (6). At the co-defendants' trial the owner gave evidence that the friends would have had his permission to take the vehicle, and the defendants were acquitted. A appealed on the basis that his plea was based on a fundamental mistake of fact. *Held*, dismissing the appeal, that as A did not have the belief required by s. 12 (6), he did not have the defence which s. 12 (6) afforded him and there was no relevant mistake.
R. *v.* AMBLER [1979] R.T.R. 217, C.A.

579. Theft—appropriation—cashier putting money in till without ringing it up
[Theft Act 1968 (c. 60), ss. 1, 3 (1).] M, a cashier, took £3·99 from a customer but did not ring it up on the till. She was arrested before she could take the money out of the till. *Held*, dismissing M's appeal against conviction of theft, that there had been a dishonest appropriation of the money by M within s. 3 (1) of the 1968 Act when, failing to ring up the till, she had put the money in it in order that it should accrue to her benefit rather than that of her employers. (*R.* v. *Meech* [1973] C.L.Y. 651 distinguished): R. *v.* MONAGHAN [1979] Crim. L.R. 673, C.A.

580. —— attempt—entering car
A person who enters a car to see whether there is anything worth stealing is not guilty of attempted theft.

A entered someone else's parked car and was seen by police examining property that was in the car. He was arrested forthwith, and charged with attempted theft. His defence was that he was looking to see if the property was worth stealing. The judge directed the jury that they had to be satisfied that A did something which had he not been interrupted would have ended in commission of the full offence, namely theft, but he did not direct the jury that absence of intention to steal the specific items was a defence. A was convicted. On appeal, *held*, allowing the appeal, that if the jury had accepted the possibility that A was merely examining the goods, he must have been acquitted. The jury had not been given the opportunity of considering A's defence and the conviction must be quashed. (*R.* v. *Easom* [1971] C.L.Y. 2816 applied.)
R. *v.* HECTOR (1978) 67 Cr.App.R. 224, C.A.

591. —— chose in action—bank account and cheque
K, a director of P Co., made out cheques on P Co.'s bank account in favour of third parties intending the payments to be for his own personal benefit.

Some of the drawings were when the account was in credit, some when it was overdrawn within an agreed facility and one when it was overdrawn beyond the facility. *Held*, dismissing K's appeal against convictions of theft of debts owed to P Co. by the bank and theft of the cheques which were P Co.'s property, that (1) the right of a customer of a bank to enforce the bank's obligation to meet cheques drawn on an account which was in credit or overdrawn within the agreed limit was a chose in action which could be stolen. The conviction relating to the drawing when the account was overdrawn beyond the facility would alone be quashed; (2) in filling in each cheque K had appropriated P Co.'s rights over the cheque. When the cheque was sent to the payee it became a bill of exchange and order to pay and the offence of theft of the cheque was at that point complete, whether or not the account was in credit and whatever happened thereafter to the cheque. The argument that there was no intention permanently to deprive P Co. of the cheque was unsustainable (*R.* v. *Duru* [1973] C.L.Y. 581 applied): R. v. KOHN [1979] Crim.L.R. 675, C.A.

592. —— duplicity of counts

Where the theft of a number of separate items from different departments of the same store is contained in one count, that count is not bad for duplicity.

W was convicted on three counts of theft, and appealed against conviction on the ground that two of the counts were bad for duplicity, in that they each included theft of various items from different departments of the same store. *Held*, applying the test laid down in *Jemmison* v. *Priddle* [1972] C.L.Y. 1599, *D.P.P.* v. *Merriman* [1972] C.L.Y. 664 and *R.* v. *Jones* (*John*) [1974] C.L.Y. 670, that the counts failed to disclose more than one offence per count. It is legitimate to charge in a single count one activity even though that activity may involve more than one act.

R. v. WILSON (1979) 69 Cr.App.R. 83, C.A.

593. —— obtaining property by deception—tendering obsolete banknotes

[Theft Act 1968 (c. 60), s. 5 (4)] W produced obsolete banknotes at a bureau de change and cashiers, believing them to be current, exchanged them for cash at the current rate of exchange, being many times their real worth. *Held*, that (1) there was no case to answer on a count of obtaining property by deception as there had been no implied representation; (2) there was a case to answer on the count of theft since W knew he was not entitled to the money (*R.* v. *Gilks* [1972] C.L.Y. 752 applied): R. v. WILLIAMS [1979] Crim.L.R. 736, Knightsbridge Crown Ct.

594. —— —— whether mutually exclusive

[Theft Act 1968 (c. 60), ss. 1 (1), 15 (1).]

A conviction is possible on both ss. 1 (1) and 15 (1) of the Theft Act 1968 in respect of the same defendant and the same property.

D obtained possession of car on hire-purchase. He gave a false name, he made no payments, and 14 days later, he sold the car. He was convicted of obtaining the car by deception contrary to s. 15 (1) of the Theft Act 1968, and theft of the car, contrary to s. 1 (1). He appealed on the ground that those sections were mutually exclusive, and a conviction was not possible on both. *Held*, dismissing the appeal, that there were two separate transactions: obtaining the car by deception from the owner by the hire-purchase agreement, and then the theft of it when it was appropriated by selling. There was a distinction to be drawn between an appropriation and an obtaining, and a permanent depriving of possession and a permanent depriving of ownership. (Dictum of Viscount Dilhorne in *Lawrence* v. *Metropolitan Police Commissioner* [1971] C.L.Y. 2418 applied.)

R. v. HIRCOCK (1978) 67 Cr.App.R. 278, C.A.

595. —— property—confidential information—examination paper

[Theft Act 1968 (c. 60), ss. 1 (1), 4 (1).]

Confidential information is not property which can be stolen.

A university student obtained a proof of his examination paper. It was accepted that he was going to put it back, and at no time intended to steal any tangible element of the paper. He was charged with theft of the intangible property, namely the confidential information. The stipendiary magistrate dismissed the charge, on the ground that confidential information could not amount to intangible property within s. 4 (1) of the Theft Act 1968. On appeal by the prosecution, *held*, dismissing the appeal, that confidential information was not property capable of being stolen.

OXFORD *v.* Moss (1978) 68 Cr.App.R. 183, D.C.

596. —— **property belonging to another—moneys received on account of another—agent using insurance premiums for own purposes**

[Theft Act 1968 (c. 60), s. 5 (3).] B, an insurance broker, acting under written agency agreements containing clauses requiring B to account for premiums not later than 20 days after receipt of the statement and providing that under further retention was sanctioned in writing any policy not taken up or renewal receipt overdue must be returned with the current accounts, otherwise B would be debited with the premiums. Over a considerable period B used premiums received on behalf of his principals for the purpose of his business as working capital. Ultimately he owed them many thousands of pounds and could not pay. In the insurance world agents were not expected to pass on to their principals the actual moneys or proceeds of cheques as received from those taking up or renewing policies. Furthermore, as a matter of general practice agents did use moneys received as premiums for the purposes of their business and ultimately accounted to their principals for equivalent amounts. Upon the trial judge's rejection of a submission that s. 5 (3) of the 1968 Act did not operate to invest the insurance companies concerned with a title to the actual moneys comprised in premiums received by B and that therefor his use of the moneys did not violate any title vested in his principals, B pleaded guilty. *Held*, dismissing B's appeal against conviction, that the terms of the contracts clearly asserted the principals' title to the actual moneys received as premiums. Whether the principals had altered or modified the contract by conduct was a matter of fact and intention for the jury: R. *v.* BREWSTER [1979] Crim.L.R. 798, C.A.

597. —— **shoplifting—property in goods—when passing**

[Theft Act 1968 (c. 60), s. 1 (1).]

As a general rule, property in goods selected by a supermarket customer does not pass until payment has been made.

Justices acceded to a submission in a shoplifting case that property in the allegedly stolen goods had passed to the defendant at the time of the goods being wrapped and handed to the defendant, who had not paid for that, the prosecution being unable to prove the defendant's dishonest state of mind at the time of such receipt. *Held,* allowing the prosecutor's appeal, that clearly property was not intended to pass until the time of payment. (*Lacis* v. *Cashmarts* [1969] C.L.Y. 689 and *Martin* v. *Puttick* [1967] C.L.Y. 822, applied; *Edwards* v. *Ddin* [1976] C.L.Y. 610, distinguished.)

DAVIES *v.* LEIGHTON (1978) 68 Cr.App.R. 4, D.C.

598. Trade descriptions—false odometer reading—taking all reasonable precautions

[Trade Descriptions Act 1968 (c. 29), ss. 1 (1) (*a*) (*b*), 2 (1) (*j*), 24.] D advertised a van for sale, intending to draw prospective purchasers' attention to the fact that the odometer reading was inaccurate. A trading standards officer who visited D was invited to look at the van. D then answered the telephone and the officer then left before D had told him of the inaccuracy. *Held,* allowing the prosecutor's appeal against D's acquittals of applying a false trade description by means of a false odometer reading contrary to ss. 1 (1) (*a*) and 2 (1) (*j*) of the 1968 Act and supplying a van to which a false trade description was applied contrary to s. 1 (1) (*b*), that (1) there was no evidence on which the justices could find D to have taken all reasonable precautions within the defence under s. 24; and (2) D's advertisement in the evening paper and his conversation with the trading standards officer amounted to an offer to supply the goods. (*Simmons* v. *Potter* [1975] C.L.Y. 3066 applied): STAINTHORPE *v.* BAILEY [1979] Crim.L.R. 677, D.C.

599. Trial—communications to jury—matters of sentence—open court

Before convicting S of causing grievous bodily harm with intent upon his wife, the jury sent a note to the judge asking whether they were allowed to make a recommendation of leniency of sentence. The judge wrote " yes " on a note to the jury, whose note was not read out in court, although its contents were communicated to counsel. The foreman, after returning the verdict, said that some members of the jury were unwilling to consider any verdict until they knew what would happen to S, because of the provocation in the case. *Held*, quashing the conviction, that (1) communications from the jury should be read in open court unless there is very strong reason to the contrary; (2) the proper course was to tell the jury in open court that matters of sentence were not for their consideration and to try the matter on the evidence: R. *v.* SAHOTA [1979] Crim.L.R. 678, C.A.

600. —— **discharge of juror—whether necessary to reswear entire jury**
A juror was discharged on his application during the prosecution opening because he thought he knew P socially. Both parties wished to continue with a full jury. *Held,* that the proper course was to discharge the whole jury and swear a new jury giving P all his challenges again: R. *v.* PAYNE [1979] Crim. L.R. 393, Middlesex Crown Ct.

601. —— **guilty plea—whether equivocal**
L pleaded guilty in the magistrates' court to obtaining property by deception. He claimed to have disclosed matters negativing dishonesty, in mitigation. The respondent claimed that he did not do so. *Held*, that in either event the plea was equivocal since a social inquiry report before the magistrate stated that L denied dishonesty and the reading of the report by the magistrate could be regarded as an event occurring before the court forming part of the case which should have raised a suspicion as to the plea's validity. *R.* v. *Durham Quarter Sessions, ex p. Virgo* [1952] C.L.Y. 2103 and *R.* v. *Marylebone Justices, ex p. Westminster City Council* [1971] C.L.Y. 2532 considered): LEAHY *v.* RAWLINSON [1978] Crim.L.R. 106, Snaresbrook Crown Ct.

602. —— **joinder of defendants—severance—discretion**
The fact that co-defendants jointly indicted have made statements incriminating another defendant does not alone justify a separate trial for that defendant.
The appellant was indicted with two others for conspiracy to burgle, it being alleged that he had supplied information to the others enabling the burglary to take place. The others, one of whom was eventually acquitted, both made statements to the police incriminating the appellant. His application for a separate trial, on the grounds of the prejudice which would result from the jury seeing such statements, was rejected. There was other evidence of the appellants' associating with one of the burglars and of his evasiveness concerning such association when seen by the police. *Held*, dismissing his appeal against conviction, that a joint offence can properly be tried jointly, although this may involve inadmissible evidence being given, provided the jury are warned that certain evidence is inadmissible against a particular defendant; that in any event the question of severance is in the discretion of the trial judge and the appellate court will not lightly interfere; and that there was admissible evidence to support the conviction which was not therefore unsafe. (*R.* v. *Smith (George)* [1967] C.L.Y. 737 distinguished.)
R. *v.* LAKE [1978] Cr.App.R. 172, C.A.

603. —— **order for new trial—principles**
[Judicature (Appellate Jurisdiction) Acts (Jamaica), s. 14 (2).]
Where an appellate court allows an appeal against conviction on the grounds that the evidence was insufficient to support conviction, it can rarely be right to order a new trial.
The defendant was convicted of murder in Jamaica, the prosecution case depending entirely upon the identification evidence of one witness. Upon allowing his appeal against conviction, the Court of Appeal ordered a new trial, against which order the defendant further appealed. *Held*, allowing the appeal and quashing the order, that since the conviction was quashed because the evidence had been insufficient to support it, it was wrong in principle and

unjust to order a retrial so as to enable the prosecution to cure any deficiencies in their case.

REID v. THE QUEEN [1979] 2 W.L.R. 221, P.C.

604. —— overt hostility by judge—material irregularity—observations on "plea bargaining"

Repeated hostile intervention by a trial judge during a defendant's evidence may amount to a material irregularity requiring a subsequent conviction to be quashed.

Per curiam: if a judge enters into a blatant plea-bargain, his fitness to sit as a judge on the criminal law Bench is called into question.

The appellant was convicted after a contested trial of an offence of failing to provide a specimen of blood or urine. He appealed on the grounds, *inter alia*, that the judge had repeatedly interrupted his evidence in a hostile manner. A further complaint of an attempt at plea-bargaining by the judge was not pursued for want of evidence. *Held*, allowing the appeal, that during the appellant's evidence in chief the judge had interrupted and/or asked more questions than asked by the appellant's own counsel; that he had further exhibited hostility to the appellant; and that accordingly justice was not seen to be done.

R. v. WISE [1979] R.T.R. 57, C.A.

605. —— power to direct prosecution to proceed. See R. v. BROAD, § 464.

606. —— release of counsel—discretion

It is within the discretion of a trial judge to permit an accused person to state reasons for wishing to dispense with the services of his counsel.

During his trial, the appellant applied to the judge to dispense with the services of his counsel. The judge declined to hear the appellant's reasons for so applying and, having ascertained that counsel was not professionally embarrassed from continuing to act, refused the application. The appellant was convicted. *Held*, dismissing his appeal, that the trial judge had a discretion whether to permit reasons to be given in support of such an application; and that although it would be normal to grant such permission it was not wrong to refuse it.

R. v. LYONS (1978) 68 Cr.App.R. 104, C.A.

607. Vagrancy. See VAGRANCY.

608. Vicarious liability—employment of child—servant acting contrary to instructions —whether principal liable

[Children and Young Persons Act 1933 (c. 12), s. 21.]

An employer is not liable for employing an under-age child, where such child is employed by his employee contrary to his instructions and without his knowledge.

The appellant employers instructed employees, who were milk roundsmen, that no unauthorised persons were to be taken on rounds. Contrary thereto and without the employers' knowledge, a roundsman employed a boy aged 10 to assist him on his rounds. The appellants were convicted by justices of unlawfully employing the boy. *Held*, allowing the employers' appeal, that the employers were not liable for the unauthorised acts of their roundsman. (*Robinson* v. *Hill* [1910] 1 K.B. 94 applied.)

PORTSEA ISLAND MUTUAL CO-OPERATIVE SOCIETY v. LEYLAND [1978] I.C.R. 1195, D.C.

609. Young offenders—summons to person over 17—offences committed when under 17—whether power to remit to juvenile court

[Children and Young Persons Act 1933 (c. 12), s. 56 (1); Children and Young Persons Act 1969 (c. 54), s. 7 (8).] J was summoned when he was aged 17 in relation to offences alleged to have been committed when he was 16. Justices remitted the case to a juvenile court. *Held*, quashing the decision, that by reason of s. 56 (1) of the 1933 Act and s. 7 (8) of the 1969 Act, the case could not be remitted to the juvenile court: R. v. BILLERICAY JUSTICES, *ex p.* JOHNSON [1979] Crim.L.R. 315, D.C.

BOOKS AND ARTICLES. See *post*, pp. [4], [17].

CROWN PRACTICE

610. Crown proceedings. See PRACTICE.

611. Declaration—duty of Crown to protect from unlawful arrest—British subject detained in Rhodesia

[Southern Rhodesia Act 1965 (c. 76), s. 1; Crown Proceedings Act 1947 (c. 44), s. 40 (2) (*b*).]

The Crown's duty to protect a subject from unlawful arrest and imprisonment is not a legal duty enforceable in a court of law, and breach of it does not give rise to a cause of action.

In 1965 Southern Rhodesia, having unilaterally declared independence, became an illegally constituted regime. The Southern Rhodesia Act of 1965 provided that the United Kingdom Government was to continue to have responsibility for the territory. M, a British subject, was arrested and detained in 1970 without trial. He was eventually released and fled to the United Kingdom where he commenced an action seeking a declaration that the government had failed in its duty to protect him and secure his release. It was contended for the Crown that the duty was not a legal duty, and that the government was protected from suit by the 1947 Act. *Held*, dismissing the claim, that the duty was not a legal duty which could be enforced in a court of law, and that in any event the government was protected by s. 40 (2) (*b*) of the 1947 Act. (Dicta in *Att.-Gen.* v. *Tomline* (1880) 14 Ch.D. 58 and *China Navigation* v. *Att.-Gen.* [1932] 2 K.B. 197 applied.)

MUTASA *v.* ATT.-GEN. [1979] 3 All E.R. 257, Boreham J.

612. Discovery—government commercial transaction—whether privileged. See BURMAH OIL CO. *v.* GOVERNOR AND COMPANY OF THE BANK OF ENGLAND, § 2129.

613. Licensing. See INTOXICATING LIQUORS.

CUSTOMS AND EXCISE

614. Agricultural products

AGRICULTURAL LEVY RELIEFS (FROZEN BEEF AND VEAL) ORDER 1979 (No. 121) [20p], made under the Import Duties Act 1958 (c. 6), s. 5 (4); operative on February 15, 1979; provides for the allocation of the U.K.'s share of a quota for the levy-free import of frozen beef and veal under the provisions of Council Regulation No. EEC/3063/78.

615. Alcoholic Liquor Duties Act 1979 (c. 4)

This Act consolidates enactments relating to the excise duties on spirits, beer, wine, made-wine and cider together with certain other enactments relating to excise.

Pt. I (ss. 1–4) contains preliminary provisions: s. 1 defines the alcoholic$_0$ liquors dutiable under the Act; s. 2 is a provision for ascertaining the strength, weight and volume of spirits and other liquors; s. 3 gives the meaning of and method of ascertaining gravity of liquids; s. 4 is the interpretation section.

Pt. II (ss. 5–35) concerns duty on spirits: s. 5 provides for the charge of excise duty on spirits; s. 6 gives power to exempt angostura bitters from duty; s. 7 gives exemption to spirits in articles used for medical purposes; s. 8 deals with repayment of duty in respect of spirits used for medical or scientific purposes; s. 9 provides for remission of duty on spirits for methylation; s. 10 concerns remission of duty on spirits for use in art or manufacture; s. 11 gives relief from duty on imported goods not for human consumption containing spirits; s. 12 deals with licences to manufacture spirits; s. 13 empowers Commissioners to make regulations as to the manufacture of spirits; s. 14 provides for an attenuation charge; s. 15 relates to a distiller's warehouse; s. 16 controls the racking of duty-paid spirits at distillery; s. 17 specifies offences in connection with removal of spirits from distillery; s. 18 concerns rectifiers' and compounders' licences; s. 19 enables Commissioners to make regulations as to rectifying and compounding; s. 20 gives a penalty for excess or deficiency in rectifier's stock; s. 21 makes restrictions relating to rectifiers; s. 22 provides for drawback on British compounds and spirits of wine; s. 23 makes an allowance for British compounds; s. 24 restricts the carrying on of other trades by distiller or rectifier; s. 25 gives the penalty for unlawful manufacture of spirits, etc.; s. 26 provides for the importation and exportation of spirits; s. 27 deals with spirits consignment and spirits advice notes; s. 28 regulates the keeping and production of spirits advice and consignment notes; s. 29 specifies offences in connection with spirits advice and consignment notes; s. 30 makes special provisions as to spirits advice and consignment notes; s. 31 restricts delivery of immature spirits for home use; s. 32 restricts transfer of British spirits in warehouse; s. 33 places restrictions on use of certain goods relieved from spirits duty; s. 34 prohibits grogging; s. 35 deals with returns as to importation, manufacture, sale or use of alcohols.

Pt. III (ss. 36–53) concerns duty on beer: s. 36 provides for a charge of excise duty on beer; s. 37 sets out the charge of duty on beer brewed in the U.K.; s. 38 deals with the duty on beer brewed in the U.K. for sale; s. 39 concerns duty on beer brewed by private brewers; s. 40 makes a charge of duty on imported beer; s. 41 exempts from duty beer brewed for private consumption; s. 42 provides for drawback on exportation, removal to warehouses and shipment as stores; s. 43 provides for warehousing of beer for exportation, etc.; s. 44 deals with remission of duty on beer used for research; s. 45 concerns repayment of duty on beer used in the production or manufacture of other beverages; s. 46 provides for remission of duty on spoilt beer; s. 47 deals with licences to brew beer; s. 48 provides for licences to use premises for adding solutions to beer; s. 49 empowers Commissioners to regulate manufacture of beer by brewers for sale; s. 50 concerns regulations as respects sugar kept by brewers for sale; s. 51 gives power to require production of books by brewers; s. 52 specifies offences by brewers for sale; s. 53 makes special provisions as to holders of limited licences to brew beer.

Pt. IV (ss. 54–61) concerns the duty on wine and made-wine: s. 54 provides for the charge of excise duty on wine; s. 55 deals with the charge of excise duty on made-wine; s. 56 regulates the making of wine and made-wine and provides for charging duty thereon; s. 57 relates to the mixing of made-wine and spirits in warehouse; s. 58 deals with the mixing of wine and spirits in warehouse; s. 59 prohibits the rendering of imported wine or made-wine sparkling in warehouse; s. 60 concerns repayment of duty on imported wine used in the production of other beverages; s. 61 provides for remission of duty on spoilt wine or made-wine.

Pt. V (ss. 62–64) deals with excise duty on cider; s. 62 imposes the duty on cider; s. 63 provides for the repayment of duty on imported cider used in the production of other beverages; s. 64 deals with remission of duty on spoilt cider.

Pt. VI (ss. 65–88) contains general control provisions: s. 65 concerns excise licences for dealing wholesale in certain alcoholic liquors; s. 66 exempts the sale of certain alcoholic liquors from licensing; s. 67 regulates the keeping of dutiable alcoholic liquors by wholesalers and retailers; s. 68 imposes a penalty for excess in stock of wholesaler or retailer of spirits; s. 69 contains miscellaneous provisions as to wholesalers and retailers of spirits; s. 70 specifies general offences in connection with sale of spirits; s. 71 imposes a penalty for mis-describing liquor as spirits; s. 72 lists offences by wholesaler or retailer of beer; s. 73 gives a penalty for mis-describing substances as beer; s. 74 deems liquor to be wine or spirits; s. 75 gives licence or authority to manufacture and deal wholesale in methylated spirits; s. 76 licenses the retailing of methylated spirits; s. 77 empowers Commissioners to make regulations relating to methylated spirits; s. 78 makes additional provisions as to methylated spirits; s. 79 provides for inspection of premises; s. 80 prohibits use of methylated spirits as a beverage or medicine; s. 81 licenses the keeping of stills otherwise than as a distiller; s. 82 gives power to make regulations with respect to stills; s. 83 gives power to enter premises of person keeping or using still; s. 84 provides for reduced duty on excise licence for sale of spirits for medical purposes; s. 85 reduces duty on part-year licences; s. 86 also deals with duty on part-year licences; s. 87 gives relief from duty on discontinuance of trade; s. 88 provides for payment of licence duty in two instalments.

Pt. VII (ss. 89–93) contains miscellaneous provisions: s. 89 is a saving provision for Cambridge University and Vintners company; s. 90 gives general power to make regulations; s. 91 concerns directions under the Act; s. 92 contains consequential amendments, repeals and saving and transitional provisions; s. 93 deals with citation and commencement.

The Act received the Royal Assent on February 22, 1979, and came into force on April 1, 1979.

616. Beers, wines and spirits

ALCOHOLIC LIQUORS (AMENDMENT OF ENACTMENTS RELATING TO STRENGTH AND TO UNITS OF MEASUREMENT) ORDER 1979 (No. 241) [25p], made under the Finance Act 1977 (c. 36), s. 7; operative on January 1, 1980; amends the Alcoholic Liquor Duties Act 1979, so as to replace the proof system of ascertaining the alcoholic strength of spirits and other liquids by the OIML system of measurement by reference to percentages of alcohol by volume.

ALCOHOLIC LIQUORS (AMENDMENT OF UNITS AND METHODS OF MEASUREMENT) REGULATIONS 1979 (No. 1146) [50p], made under the Alcoholic Liquor Duties Act 1979 (c. 4), ss. 2, 3, 8, 13, 15, 16, 19, 22, 28, 31, 33, 45, 46, 49, 56, 60, 62, 63, 77 and 82 and the Customs and Excise Management Act 1979, s. 93; operative on January 1, 1979; replace the reference in amended Regulations to the proof system of ascertaining the alcoholic strength of spirits and other liquid by the OIML (International Organisation of Legal Metrology) system of measurement by reference to percentages of alcohol by volume.

CIDER AND PERRY (EXEMPTION FROM REGISTRATION) ORDER 1976 (AMENDMENT) ORDER 1979 (No. 1218) [10p], made under the Alcoholic Liquor Duties Act 1979, s. 62 (3); operative on January 1, 1980; amends S.I. 1976 No. 1206 by replacing the units of measurement expressed in Imperial terms by metric units of measurement.

WINE AND MADE-WINE REGULATIONS 1979 (No. 1240) [40p], made under the Alcholic Liquor Duties Act 1979, ss. 56 (1), 61 (1), 62 (5); operative on November 1, 1979; revoke and replace with certain amendments S.I. 1975 No. 1790.

617. Car tax—conversion of vehicles

H.M. Customs and Excise have issued Notice No. 672 (January 1979): Car tax—conversion of vehicles.

618. Customs and Excise Duties (General Reliefs) Act 1979 (c. 3)

This Act consolidates certain enactments relating to reliefs and exemptions from customs and excise duties, s. 7 of the Finance Act 1968 and other related enactments.

S. 1 provides for reliefs from customs duty for conformity with EEC and other international obligations; s. 2 deals with reliefs from customs duty referable to EEC practices; s. 3 gives power to exempt particular importations of certain goods from customs duty; s. 4 concerns the administration of reliefs under s. 1 and similar EEC reliefs; s. 5 gives relief from customs duty of certain goods from Channel Islands; s. 6 gives relief from duty of certain goods from Isle of Man; s. 7 deals with duty on imported legacies; s. 8 gives relief from duty on trade samples, labels, etc.; s. 9 provides for relief from duty on antiques and prizes; s. 10 gives relief from duty on certain U.K. goods re-imported; s. 11 gives relief from excise duty on certain foreign goods re-imported; s. 12 deals with supply of duty-free goods to naval ships; s. 13 enables Commissioners to provide for reliefs from duty and VAT for persons entering the U.K.; s. 14 concerns produce of the sea or continental shelf; s. 15 relates to false statements in connection with reliefs from customs duties; s. 16 provides for annual reports to Parliament; s. 17 gives power to make orders and regulations; s. 18 is the interpretation provision; s. 19 contains consequential amendments, repeals and transitional provisions; s. 20 deals with citation and commencement.

This Act received the Royal Assent on February 22, 1979, and came into force on April 1, 1979.

619. Customs and Excise Management Act 1979 (c. 2)

This Act consolidates the enactments relating to the collection and management of customs and excise revenues.

Pt. I (ss. 1–5) contains preliminary provisions: s. 1 is the interpretation section; s. 2 applies this Part to hovercraft; s. 3 relates to pipe-lines; s. 4 applies the Act to certain Crown aircraft; s. 5 relates to the time of importation and exportation.

Pt. II (ss. 6–18) provides for the administration of the Act: s. 6 relates to the appointment and duties of Commissioners; s. 7 sets out the privileges of Commissioners; s. 8 defines the exercise of powers and duties of Commissioners; s. 9 deals with EEC obligations; s. 10 concerns the disclosure by the Commissioners of information as to imports; s. 11 relates to police assistance; s. 12 gives the Commissioners power to hold inquiries; s. 13 sets out offences for unlawfully assuming character of officer; s. 14 deals with the failure to surrender a commission; s. 15 concerns offences of bribery and collusion; s. 16 contains offences regarding the obstruction of officers; s. 17 provides for the disposal of customs duties; s. 18 relates to the remuneration and expenses of Commissioners.

Pt. III (ss. 19–34) sets out control areas: s. 19 confers power to appoint ports; s. 20 relates to wharves; s. 21 deals with control of aircraft into and out of the U.K.; s. 22 gives power to name examination stations; s. 23 refers to control of hovercraft; s. 24 controls the movement of goods by pipe-line; s. 25 relates to transit sheds; s. 26 concerns the movement of goods into and out of Northern Ireland by land; s. 27 gives officers powers of boarding; s. 28 confers powers of access; s. 29 gives officers powers of detention of ships, etc.; s. 30 deals with the control of movement of uncleared goods; s. 31 relates to movement of goods to and from inland clearance depot; s. 32 gives the penalty for carrying away officers; s. 33 confers power to inspect aircraft, aerodromes, records etc.; s. 34 allows officers to prevent flight of aircraft.

Pt. IV (ss. 35–51) relates to the control of importation: s. 35 provides for reporting by inwards vehicles; s. 36 makes provision as to naval ships; s. 37 concerns the entry of goods on importation; s. 38 deals with entry by bill of sight; s. 39 relates to entry of surplus stores; s. 40 makes provision for removal of uncleared goods to Queen's warehouse; s. 41 states the penalty for failing to comply with entry provisions; s. 42 regulates unloading and removal of goods; s. 43 relates to the duty on imported goods; s. 44 excludes importers keeping standing deposits from the provisions of s. 43 (1); s. 45 concerns deferred payment of duty; s. 46 permits goods to be warehoused without payment of duty; s. 47 exempts from payment goods entered for transit; s. 48 exempts goods temporarily imported; s. 49 deals with forfeiture of goods improperly imported; s. 50 gives the penalty for improper importation of goods; s. 51 makes special provisions as to proof in Northern Ireland.

Pt. V (ss. 52–68) provides for the control of exportation: s. 52 defines " dutiable or restricted goods "; s. 53 concerns the entry outwards of such goods; s. 54 deals with the entry outwards of goods which are not dutiable or restricted; s. 55 provides for a register of exporters and assignment of identifying numbers; s. 56 makes alternative provisions to entry for registered exporters; s. 57 relates to the specification of certain goods; s. 58 relaxes the requirements of s. 57 where particulars of goods are recorded by computer; s. 59 makes restrictions on putting export goods alongside for loading; s. 60 makes additional restrictions as to certain goods; s. 61 sets out provisions as to stores; s. 62 gives the requirements as to information and documentation regarding export goods; s. 63 deals with entry outwards of exporting ships; s. 64 concerns the clearance outwards of ships and aircraft; s. 65 gives power to refuse or cancel clearance of ship or aircraft; s. 66 enables the Commissioners to make regulations as to exportation; s. 67 sets out offences in relation to exportation of goods; s. 68 deals with exporting prohibited or restricted goods.

Pt. VI (ss. 69–74) provides for control of coastwise traffic: s. 69 defines a coasting ship; s. 70 makes exceptional provisions for the coasting trade; s. 71

deals with the clearance of coasting ships and transire; s. 72 gives additional powers to officers in relation to coasting ships; s. 73 confers power to make regulations as to carriage of goods coastwise; s. 74 sets out offences in connection with carriage of goods coastwise.

Pt. VII (ss. 75–91) makes supplementary provisions as to customs and excise control: s. 75 relates to movement of explosives; s. 76 gives power to require pre-entry and clearance of goods; s. 77 makes further requirements as to information on goods; s. 78 deals with the customs and excise control of persons entering or leaving the U.K.; s. 79 confers power to require evidence in support of information; s. 80 relates to information and documents of goods evidenced under EEC law or practice; s. 81 gives power to regulate small craft to prevent smuggling; s. 82 confers power to haul up revenue vessels and patrol coasts; s. 83 states the penalty for removing seals or locks; s. 84 gives the penalty for signalling to smugglers; s. 85 states the penalty for interfering with revenue vessels; s. 86 makes special penalty provisions for armed or disguised offenders; s. 87 sets out the penalty for offering goods for sale as smuggled goods; s. 88 provides for the forfeiture of ship, aircraft or vehicle constructed for concealing goods; s. 89 concerns the forfeiture of a ship jettisoning or destroying cargo to prevent seizure; s. 90 deals with forfeiture of ship or aircraft unable to account for missing cargo; s. 91 relates to ships failing to bring to.

Pt. VIII (ss. 92–100) makes provisions as to warehouses and pipe-lines: s. 92 gives Commissioners power to approve warehouses; s. 93 enables Commissioners to regulate warehouses and goods; s. 94 concerns deficiency in warehoused goods; s. 95 deals with deficiency in goods occurring during removal from warehouse without payment of duty; s. 96 relates to deficiency in certain goods moved by pipe-line; s. 97 restricts compensation for loss or damage to goods in warehouse or pipe-line; s. 98 sets out the procedure on warehouse ceasing to be approved; s. 99 makes provisions as to deposit in Queen's warehouse; s. 100 states general offences relating to warehouses and warehoused goods.

Pt. IX (ss. 101–118) provides for the control of excise licence trades and revenue traders: s. 101 deals with excise licences; s. 102 allows for payment of excise licences by cheque; s. 103 concerns renewal of excise licences; s. 104 regulates the transfer and removal of excise licence trades and licences; s. 105 permits certain sales without an excise licence; s. 106 specifies offences in connection with certain excise licences; s. 107 gives power to require person carrying on excise licence trade to display sign; s. 108 concerns the making of entries; s. 109 relates to new or further entries of same premises; s. 110 sets out proof as to entries; s. 111 states offences in connection with entries; s. 112 gives officers power of entry upon premises of revenue traders; s. 113 enables officers to search for concealed pipes; s. 114 gives Commissioners power to prohibit use of certain substances in exciseable goods; s. 115 enables officers to keep a specimen on premises of revenue traders; s. 116 provides for payment of excise duty by revenue traders; s. 117 makes traders liable for execution and distress; s. 118 relates to the liability of ostensible owner or principal manager.

Pt. X (ss. 119–137) makes general provisions for duties and drawbacks: s. 119 allows the delivery of imported goods on giving security for duty; s. 120 empowers the Secretary of State to make regulations determining origin of goods; s. 121 gives power to impose restrictions where duty depends on certain matters other than use; s. 122 concerns regulations where customs duty depends on use; s. 123 provides for repayment of duty where goods returned or destroyed by importer; s. 124 concerns forfeiture for breach of certain conditions; s. 125 deals with valuation of goods for purpose of *ad valorem* duties; s. 126 imposes excise duty on manufactured or composite imported articles; s. 127 sets out method of determining disputes as to duties on imported goods; s. 128 enables Commissioners to restrict delivery of goods; s. 129 gives power to remit duty on denatured goods; s. 130 provides for repayment of duty on goods lost or destroyed; s. 131 allows for enforcement of bond in respect of goods removed without payment of duty; s. 132 permits an extension of drawback; s. 133 makes general provisions as to claims for drawback; s. 134 deals with drawback and allowance on goods damaged or destroyed after shipment; s. 135 sets time limits on payment of drawback or allowance; s. 136 relates to offences in connection with claims for drawback; s. 137 provides for recovery and calculation of duties and drawbacks.

Pt. XI (ss. 138–156) makes provision for detention of persons, forfeiture and legal proceedings: s. 138 relates to detention; s. 139 concerns seizure and condemnation of goods; s. 140 provides for forfeiture of spirits; s. 141 deals with forfeiture of ships, etc., used in connection with goods liable to forfeiture; s. 142 makes special provision as to forfeiture of larger ships; s. 143 gives a penalty in lieu of forfeiture of larger ships where officer implicated in offence; s. 144 protects officers in relation to seizure and detention of goods; s. 145 deals with institution of proceedings; s. 146 is a service of process provision; s. 147 specifies the proceedings for offences; s. 148 determines the place of trial; s. 149 relates to non-payment of penalties and maximum terms of imprisonment; s. 150 makes incidental provisions as to legal proceedings; s. 151 provides for the application of penalties; s. 152 enables Commissioners to mitigate penalties; s. 153 sets out proof requirements for certain documents; s. 154 contains general provisions as to proof; s. 155 states the persons who may conduct proceedings; s. 156 is a saving provision for outlying enactments.

Pt. XII (ss. 157–178) contains general and miscellaneous provisions: s. 157 relates to bonds and security; s. 158 gives power to require provision of facilities; s. 159 enables officers to examine and take account of goods; s. 160 gives power to take samples; s. 161 empowers officers to search premises; s. 162 gives power to enter land in connection with access to pipe-lines; s. 163 enables officers to search vehicles or vessels; s. 164 gives power to search persons; s. 165 gives power to pay rewards; s. 166 deals with agents; s. 167 relates to untrue declarations; s. 168 concerns counterfeiting documents; s. 169 deals with false scales, etc.; s. 170 states the penalty for fraudulent evasion of duty; s. 171 contains general provisions as to offences and penalties; s. 172 concerns the making of regulations; s. 173 relates to the giving of directions; s. 174 deals with removal of goods to and from the Isle of Man; s. 175 has special provisions for Scotland; s. 176 concerns game licences; s. 177 contains consequential amendments, repeals and saving and transitional provisions; s. 178 deals with citation and commencement.

The Act received the Royal Assent on February 22, 1979, and came into force on April 1, 1979.

620. —— guide to legislation

H.M. Customs and Excise have issued Notice No. 250 (March 1979): Guide to Customs and Excise consolidation.

621. Customs documents

H.M. Customs and Excise have issued Notice No. 37 (January 1979): coding lists used in completion of customs documents.

622. Customs duties

Customs Duties (ECSC) Provisional Anti-Dumping (No. 2) Order 1979 (No. 191), [20p], made under the Finance Act 1978 (c. 42), s. 6 (1) and (2); operative on February 27, 1979; imposes a provisional anti-dumping duty on imports into the U.K. from February 16, 1979, of certain haematite pig iron and cast iron as described in the Order, originating in Brazil, at a rate equal to the amount by which the price paid by the importer for the goods inclusive of insurance and freight and the duty under the ECSC unified tariff is lower than the price last published by the E.C. Commission at the time of importation.

Customs Duties (ECSC) (Quota and Other Reliefs) (Revocation) Order 1979 (No. 1142) [10p], made under the Customs and Excise Duties (General Reliefs) Act 1979 (c. 3), s. 1; operative on September 13, 1979; revokes S.I. 1978 No. 1933, which provided for exemption from duty for certain iron and steel products originating in Brazil.

Customs Duties (Greece) Order 1979 (No. 1649) [10p], made under the European Communities Act 1972 (c. 68), ss. 5 (2) and (3); operative on January 1, 1980; amends regulations relating to certain fruit and vegetables originating in Greece, and substitutes metric for imperial measures.

CUSTOMS DUTIES (QUOTA RELIEF) (PAPER, PAPERBOARD AND PRINTED PRO-
DUCTS) ORDER 1979 (No. 1717) [70p], made under the Customs and Excise
Duties (General Reliefs) Act 1979, ss. 1, 4; operative on January 1, 1980;
provides for the opening of duty-free tariff quotas for paper, paperboard and
printed products originating in certain non-EEC countries.

CUSTOMS DUTIES (QUOTA RELIEF) (PAPER, PAPERBOARD AND PRINTED PRO-
DUCTS) (AMENDMENT) ORDER 1979 (No. 1718) [10p], made under the Customs
and Excise Duties (General Reliefs) Act 1979; operative on December 21,
1979; increases the duty-free tariff quota which the U.K. is entitled to open
under an agreement between EEC and Finland for certain types of coated
mechanical printing paper.

CUSTOMS DUTIES (ECSC) (QUOTA AND OTHER RELIEFS) ORDER 1979 (No.
1747) [40p], made under the Customs and Excise Duties (General Reliefs)
Act 1979, ss. 1, 4; operative on January 1, 1980; provides for reliefs from
customs duty on certain iron and steel products originating in the developing
countries named in Sched. 2 to the Order. Provision is also made for exemption
from duty and for duty-free quotas in respect of certain goods for the Sched.
2 countries.

623. Dumping

ANTI-DUMPING DUTY (REVOCATION) ORDER 1979 (No. 104) [10p], made
under the Customs Duties (Dumping and Subsidies) Act 1969 (c. 16), ss. 1, 2,
10 (3), 15 (4) and the Finance Act 1978 (c. 42), s. 6 (7); operative on February
27, 1979; removes the anti-dumping duty on imports of certain angles, shapes
and sections of non-alloy iron or steel originating in Japan imposed by S.I.
1977 No. 1134.

CUSTOMS DUTIES (ECSC) ANTI-DUMPING (AMENDMENT) ORDER 1979 (No.
155) [10p], made under the European Communities Act 1972 (c. 68), s. 5 (1)
(3); operative on February 17, 1979; provides no anti-dumping duty shall be
charged on imports of certain iron and steel products originating in Bulgaria
where such duty was imposed by S.I. 1978 Nos. 641, 698.

CUSTOMS DUTIES (ECSC) PROVISIONAL ANTI-DUMPING ORDER 1979 (No.
181) [20p], made under the Finance Act 1978, s. 6 (1) (2); operative on
February 23, 1979; imposes a provisional anti-dumping duty on imports of
certain angles, shapes and sections of iron and steel originating in Spain at a
rate equal to the amount by which the price paid by the importer is lower
than the price last published by the Commission of the European Communities.
The duty will not be collected if the importer gives security for that duty.

CUSTOMS DUTIES (ECSC) PROVISIONAL ANTI-DUMPING (No. 4) ORDER 1979
(No. 314) [20p], made under the Finance Act 1978, s. 6 (1) and (2);
operative on March 16, 1979; imposes a provisional anti-dumping duty on
imports into the U.K. from March 15, 1979, of certain iron or steel coils for
re-rolling as described in the Order, originating in Greece, at a rate equal to
the amount by which the price paid by the importer for the goods inclusive
of insurance and freight and the duty under the ECSC unified tariff is lower
than the price last published by the Commission of the European Communities
at the time of importation.

CUSTOMS DUTIES (ECSC) PROVISIONAL ANTI-DUMPING (REVOCATION) (No. 1)
ORDER 1979 (No. 492) [10p], made under the Finance Act 1978,
s. 6 (1) (2); operative on April 24, 1979; revokes S.I. 1979 No. 191 in relation
to imports into the United Kingdom of certain haematite pig iron and cast iron
originating in and consigned from Brazil.

CUSTOMS DUTIES (ECSC) PROVISIONAL ANTI-DUMPING (REVOCATION) (No. 2)
ORDER 1979 (No. 510) [10p], made under the Finance Act 1978, s. 6 (1) (2);
operative on May 3, 1979; revokes S.I. 1979 Nos. 181 and 231 in relation
to imports into the United Kingdom of certain angles, shapes and sections
and certain sheets and plates of iron or steel originating in and consigned from
Spain.

CUSTOMS DUTIES (ECSC) DEFINITIVE ANTI-DUMPING ORDER 1979 (No. 566)
[20p], made under the Finance Act 1978, s. 6 (1), (2); operative on May
24, 1979; imposes a definitive anti-dumping duty on imports into the U.K. of
certain angles, shapes and sections of iron or steel as described in the Order.
originating in Spain and consigned to the U.K. from another country, at a rate

equal to the amount by which the price paid by the importer for the goods inclusive of insurance and freight and the duty under the ECSC unified tariff is lower than the price last published by the Commission of the European Communities at the time of importation.

CUSTOMS DUTIES (ECSC) DEFINITIVE ANTI-DUMPING (No. 2) ORDER 1979 (No. 567) [20p], made under the Finance Act 1978, s. 6 (1) and (2); operative on May 24, 1979; imposes a definitive anti-dumping duty on imports into the U.K. of certain haematite pig iron and cast iron as described in the Order, originating in Brazil and consigned to the U.K. from another country.

CUSTOMS DUTIES (ECSC) DEFINITIVE ANTI-DUMPING (No. 3) ORDER 1979 (No. 627) [20p], made under the Finance Act 1978, s. 6 (1) and (2); operative on June 8, 1979; imposes a definitive anti-dumping duty on imports into the U.K. of certain sheets and plates of iron or steel as described in the Order, originating in Spain and consigned to the U.K. from another country, at a rate equal to the amount by which the price paid by the importer for the goods inclusive of insurance and freight and the duty under the ECSC unified tariff is lower than the price last published by the Commission of the EEC at the time of importation.

ANTI-DUMPING DUTY (TEMPORARY SUSPENSION) ORDER 1979 (No. 842) [10p], made under the Customs Duties (Dumping and Subsidies) Act 1969, ss. 1, 10 (3) (4), 15 (4) and the Finance Act, s. 6 (7); operative on July 18, 1979; suspends for a period of three months the anti-dumping duty imposed by S.I. 1977 No. 716 on certain stainless steel, in so far as it consists of products covered by the ECSC Treaty, originating in Spain.

CUSTOMS DUTIES (ECSC) PROVISIONAL ANTI-DUMPING (REVOCATION) (No. 3) ORDER 1979 (No. 1148) [10p], made under the Finance Act 1978, s. 6 (1) (2); operative on September 15, 1979; removes the anti-dumping duty on imports of certain iron or steel coils for rerolling originating in Greece imposed by S.I. 1979 No. 314.

ANTI-DUMPING DUTY (TEMPORARY SUSPENSION) (No. 2) ORDER 1979 (No. 1182) [10p], made under the Customs Duties (Dumping and Subsidies) Act 1969, ss. 1, 10 (3), 15 (4) and the Finance Act 1978, s. 6 (7); operative on October 18, 1979; suspends for a further period of three months the anti-dumping duty imposed by S.I. 1977 No. 716 on certain stainless steel originating in Spain.

624. Exchange control. See REVENUE AND FINANCE.

625. Excise Duties (Surcharges or Rebates) Act 1979 (c. 8)
This Act consolidates s. 9 of and Scheds. 3 and 4 to the Finance Act 1961 with the provisions amending them.

S. 1 provides for surcharges or rebates of amounts due for excise duties; s. 2 deals with orders under s. 1; s. 3 concerns the application of certain enactments; s. 4 contains interpretation, consequential amendments, repeals and saving provisions; s. 5 deals with citations and commencement.

The Act received the Royal Assent on February 22, 1979, and came into force on April 1, 1979.

626. Export and import controls
EXPORT OF GOODS (CONTROL) (AMENDMENT No. 2) ORDER 1979 (No. 164) [10p], made under the Import, Export and Customs Powers (Defence) Act 1939 (c. 69), s. 1; operative on March 19, 1979; further amends S.I. 1978 No. 796 by substituting a new form of control on antiques and other collectors' items. The main change is that the age-limit below which goods may be exported is reduced.

EXPORT OF GOODS (CONTROL) (AMENDMENT No. 3) ORDER 1979 (No. 276) [10p], made under the Import, Export and Customs Powers (Defence) Act 1939, s. 1; operative on April 1, 1979; further amends S.I. 1978 No. 796 by including among the goods of which the export is controlled equipment specially designed for the manufacture or assembly of goods included in the entry relating to centrifuges in Group 2 of Pt. II of Sched. 1 and by deleting the provision that the " United Kingdom " includes the Isle of Man.

EXPORT OF GOODS (CONTROL) (AMENDMENT No. 4) ORDER 1979 (No. 1437) [20p], made under the Import, Export and Customs Powers (Defence) Act

1939, s. 1; operative on November 19, 1979, save for art. 2 (*g*) (*h*) (*i*) which is operative on December 10, 1979; further amends S.I. 1978 No. 796 which provides for goods which are subject to export control.

EXPORT OF GOODS (CONTROL) (AMENDMENT NO. 5) ORDER 1979 (No. 1671) [10p], made under the Import, Export and Customs Powers (Defence) Act 1939, s. 1; operative on December 13, 1979; revoke the provisions of S.I. 1978 No. 796 which prohibited the export of all goods to any destination in Southern Rhodesia. In future the same rules that apply to any other country in Sched. 2 to the Order shall apply to Southern Rhodesia.

627. Export of personal effects

H.M. Customs and Excise have issued Notice No. 290 (February 1979): export of personal and household effects.

628. General reliefs

CUSTOMS DUTIES (STANDARD EXCHANGE RELIEF) REGULATIONS 1979 (No. 554) [25p], made under the Customs and Excise Duties (General Relief) Act 1979 (c. 3), s. 2; operative on June 11, 1979; provide for relief from customs duty on goods imported into the U.K. as replacements for goods exported from the U.K. outside the Community for repair.

629. Hydrocarbon oil

COMPOSITE GOODS ORDER 1968 (REVOCATION) ORDER 1979 (No. 1393) [10p], made under the Customs and Excise Management Act 1979 (c. 2), Sched. 2; operative on December 5, 1979; abolishes the *ad valorem* rates of hydrocarbon oil duty on imported composite goods containing hydrocarbon oil.

630. Hydrocarbon Oil Duties Act 1979 (c. 5)

This Act consolidates the enactments relating to the excise duties on hydrocarbon oil, petrol substitutes, power methylated spirits and road fuel gas.

S. 1 defines hydrocarbon oil; s. 2 contains provisions supplementing s. 1; s. 3 provides for hydrocarbon oil as an ingredient of imported goods; s. 4 deals with petrol substitutes and power methylated spirits; s. 5 defines " road fuel gas "; s. 6 imposes excise duty on hydrocarbon oil; s. 7 imposes excise duty on petrol substitutes and power methylated spirits; s. 8 concerns excise duty on road fuel gas; s. 9 deals with oil delivered for home use for certain industrial purposes; s. 10 places restrictions on the use of duty-free oil; s. 11 provides for rebate of duty on heavy oil; s. 12 exempts fuel for road vehicles from rebate; s. 13 imposes penalties for misuse of rebated heavy oil; s. 14 gives a rebate on light oil for use as furnace fuel; s. 15 provides for drawback of duty on exportation of certain goods; s. 16 gives drawback of duty on exportation of power methylated spirits; s. 17 concerns heavy oil used by horticultural producers; s. 18 relates to fuel for ships in home waters; s. 19 deals with fuel used in fishing boats; s. 10 provides for oil being contaminated or accidentally mixed in warehouse; s. 21 empowers Commissioners to make regulations with respect to commodities dutiable under the Act; s. 22 prohibits use of petrol substitutes on which duty has not been paid; s. 23 prohibits use of road fuel gas on which duty has not been paid; s. 24 controls use of duty-free and rebated oil; s. 25 confers general power to make regulations; s. 26 concerns the giving of directions under the Act; s. 27 is the interpretation section; s. 28 contains consequential amendments, repeals, savings and transitional provisions; s. 29 deals with citation and commencement.

The Act received the Royal Assent on February 22, 1979, and came into force on April 1, 1979.

631. Import duties

CUSTOMS DUTIES (ECSC) (QUOTA AND OTHER RELIEFS) (AMENDMENT) ORDER 1979 (No. 153) [20p], made under the Import Duties Act 1958 (c. 6), ss. 5, 13, Sched. 3, para. 8 (2); operative on February 19, 1979; amends S.I. 1978 No. 1933 by increasing the amounts of the duty-free tariff quotas and the maximum amounts within the quotas listed in the Schedule in accordance with a Decision of the ECSC.

632. —— forfeiture—smuggling coins—whether " goods "

[Customs and Excise Act 1952 (c. 44), s. 44.] Three men were convicted of smuggling Kruggerand into England. The word " goods " in s. 44 of the

Customs and Excise Act 1952 was wide enough to include gold, silver, bullion, and coins including Kruggerand. They were liable to forfeiture under the Act: and the customs authorities had a discretion not to return them to persons claiming to be the true owners of the coins, who had let the smugglers have the coins against an allegedly bad cheque. The fact that they were not " goods " for the purpose of the Treaty of Rome did not mean that they were not goods for the purposes of an English Customs Act: ALLGEMEINE GOLD-UND-SILBERSCHEIDEANSTALT *v.* CUSTOMS AND EXCISE COMMISSIONERS, *The Times,* December 11, 1979, C.A.

633. Import entry procedure
H.M. Customs and Excise have issued Notice No. 465 (June 1979): outline of import entry precedure.

634. Import of goods
H.M. Customs and Excise have published Notice No. 780 (August 1979): imports of goods subject to the Common Agricultural Policy.

635. Isle of Man Act 1979 (c. 58)
This Act amends the law relating to customs and excise, value added tax, car tax and the importation and exportation of goods between the United Kingdom and the Isle of Man.

S. 1 relates to common duties; s. 2 deals with the Isle of Man share of common duties; s. 3 provides for the recovery of common duties chargeable in the Isle of Man; s. 4 makes provision as to the enforcement of Isle of Man judgments for common duties; s. 5 specifies offences relating to common duties, etc.; s. 6 deals with value added tax; s. 7 contains provisions relating to car tax; s. 8 provides for the removal of goods from the Isle of Man to the U.K.; s. 9 deals with the removal of goods from the U.K. to the Isle of Man; s. 10 relates to the exchange of information; s. 11 provides for the transfer of functions to Isle of Man authorities; s. 12 deals with proof of Acts of Tynwald, etc.; s. 13 makes various amendments to customs and excise Acts; s. 14 contains the short title, interpretation, repeals, commencement and extent.

The Act received the Royal Assent on December 20, 1979, ss. 6, 7, 10 and 11 came into force on that date, the remaining provisions came into force on April 1, 1980.

636. Matches and Mechanical Lighters Duties Act 1979 (c. 6)
This Act consolidates the enactments relating to the excise duties on matches and mechanical lighters.

S. 1 imposes excise duty on matches; s. 2 provides for licences to manufacture matches; s. 3 empowers Commissioners to make regulations about matches; s. 4 defines mechanical lighters; s. 5 deals with the prescribed component; s. 6 imposes excise duty on mechanical lighters; s. 7 concerns regulations about mechanical lighters; s. 8 is the interpretation section; s. 9 contains repeals and consequential amendments; s. 10 deals with citation and commencement.

The Act received the Royal Assent on February 22, 1979, and came into force on April 1, 1979.

637. Outward processing relief
OUTWARD PROCESSING RELIEF REGULATIONS 1979 (No. 555) [25p], made under the Customs and Excise Duties (General Reliefs) Act 1979 (c. 3), s. 2 and the European Communities Act 1972 (c. 68), s. 2 (2); operative on June 11, 1979; revoke and replace S.I. 1976 Nos. 838 and 901. They provide for relief from customs duty and agricultural levy on compensating products and intermediate products imported into the U.K. which have been produced or manufactured overseas by outward processing of goods temporarily exported from the U.K. or any other Member State of the Community.

638. Personal reliefs
CUSTOMS DUTY (PERSONAL RELIEFS) (NO. 1) ORDER 1975 (AMENDMENT) ORDER 1979 (No. 655) [10p], made under the Customs and Excise (General Reliefs) Act 1979 (c. 3), s. 13; operative on June 18, 1979; consequent upon the increases in VAT to 15 per cent. this Order increases the aggregate amount payable by way of duty and tax on personal effects imported by passengers.

CUSTOMS DUTY (PERSONAL RELIEFS) (NO. 1) ORDER 1968 (AMENDMENT)

ORDER 1979 (No. 1551) [10p], made under the Customs and Excise Duties (General Reliefs) Act 1979, s. 13; operative on January 1, 1980; consequent upon the introduction within the EEC as from January 1, 1980, of the OIML system for determining the alcoholic strength of spirit, this Order converts to that system the existing references to the present Sykes proof system in S.I. 1968 No. 1558.

639. Pleasure craft

PLEASURE CRAFT (ARRIVAL AND REPORT) REGULATIONS 1979 (No. 564) [20p], made under the Customs and Excise Management Act 1979 (c. 2), ss. 35 (4), 42 (1) and 81 (2); operative on July 1, 1979; require the person responsible (as defined) to cause a yellow flag to be flown on a pleasure craft arriving from abroad; require the notification to the Customs of the arrival of a pleasure craft based in the U.K.; require the person responsible for a pleasure craft to make written report of the vessel on a form directed by the Commissioners; require the person responsible for foreign or certain pleasure craft based in the U.K. to make report by handing the appropriate form to a Customs officer; and require that report may be made two hours after notifying arrival by lodging the completed form in a Customs or Post Office post box.

640. Public notices

H.M. Customs and Excise have issued Notice No. 1000 (April 1979): Public notices obtainable from H.M. Customs and Excise.

641. Quota relief

CUSTOMS DUTIES (QUOTA RELIEF) ORDER 1979 (No. 737) [10p], made under the Customs and Excise Duties (General Reliefs) Act 1979 (c. 3), s. 4; operative on July 1, 1979; provides for the administration of the U.K.'s share of the tariff quota opened for the period July 1, 1979, to February 29, 1980, by the EEC, providing exemption from customs duty on import into the U.K. for home use of rum, arrack and tafia originating in various African, Caribbean and Pacific States.

642. Returned goods relief

H.M. Customs and Excise have issued Notice No. 236 (December 1978): Returned goods relief—EEC 1977.

643. Ship's report

SHIP'S REPORT REGULATIONS 1979 (No. 565) [10p], made under the Customs and Excise Management Act 1979 (c. 2), s. 35 (4); operative on July 1, 1979; prescribe revised procedures for the making of a report for a commercial vessel.

644. Tobacco

TOBACCO PRODUCTS REGULATIONS 1979 (No. 904) [50p], made under the Tobacco Products Duty Act 1979 (c. 7), ss. 2 (2), 7 (1); operative on September 1, 1979; provide the machinery for administration of the excise duty on tobacco products imposed by s. 2 of the 1979 Act. They replace S.I. 1977 No. 1779.

TOBACCO PRODUCTS (AMENDMENT OF UNITS OF MEASUREMENT) ORDER 1979 (No. 1489) [10p], made under the Finance Act 1977 (c. 36), s. 7; operative on January 1, 1980; provides for the rates of excise duty on cigars, hand-rolling tobacco and other smoking and chewing tobacco to be expressed in terms of metric instead of imperial units.

645. Tobacco Products Duty Act 1979 (c. 7)

This Act consolidates the enactments relating to the excise duty on tobacco products.

S. 1 defines tobacco products; s. 2 provides for the charge and remission of tobacco products duty; s. 3 imposes an additional duty on higher tar cigarettes; s. 4 deals with the calculation of duty in case of cigarettes more than 9 cm. long; s. 5 concerns the retail price of cigarettes; s. 6 provides for alteration of rates of duty; s. 7 empowers Commissioners to make regulations for management of duty; s. 8 concerns a charge in cases of default; s. 9 confers general power to make regulations; s. 10 is the interpretation section; s. 11 contains repeals, savings and transitional and consequential provisions; s. 12 deals with citation and commencement.

The Act received the Royal Assent on February 22, 1979, and came into force on April 1, 1979.

646. Vehicles. See ROAD TRAFFIC; TRANSPORT.

647. Warehouses

CUSTOMS WAREHOUSING REGULATIONS 1979 (No. 207) [25p], made under the Customs and Excise Management Act 1979 (c. 2), s. 93; operative on April 1, 1979; prescribe the conditions under which goods may be put into, stored in and removed from a customs warehouse and subjected to operations therein.

EXCISE WAREHOUSING REGULATIONS 1979 (No. 208) [30p], made under the Customs and Excise Management Act 1979, s. 93; operative on April 1, 1979; prescribe the conditions under which goods liable to excise duties may be put into, stored in and removed from an excise warehouse and subjected to operations therein.

ARTICLES. See *post*, p. [20.].

DAMAGES

648. Assessment—deduction of unemployment benefit

[Social Security Act 1975 (c. 14), s. 12 (1) (*a*).] Unemployment benefit received by an injured workman ought to be taken into account in assessing damages against his negligent employers. The amount due should be reduced accordingly (*Parsons* v. *B.N.M. Laboratories* [1963] C.L.Y. 933, disapproved). Leave to appeal granted as the previous damages rule concerning unemployment benefit should be reviewed: NABI v. BRITISH LEYLAND (U.K.), *The Times*, December 1, 1979, C.A.

649. Contract—date of assessment—mitigation and reliance thereon

The plaintiff TL agreed on June 25, 1974, to devise two lots of land to the defendant BL for £61,286 per annum. On July 8, 1974, BL went into occupation and on April 25, 1975, purported to rescind the contract. On May 19, 1975, BL ceased to occupy the premises and on September 29, 1975, gave notice to terminate the tenancies from Christmas 1975. TL relet the premises separately on January 8, 1976, and September 19, 1977, at £28,266 and £24,000 per annum respectively. TL sued BL for damages for breach of contract and on July 6, 1978, Whitford J. gave judgment to TL and ordered an inquiry into damages. TL then contended for assessment as at January 8, 1976, and BL at September 19, 1977. *Held*, assessment would be at September 19, 1977. As TL was under a duty to mitigate his loss by reletting either side was entitled to rely on the result of this mitigation for the purpose of ascertaining the loss; any diminution in TL's loss, even if under no duty to mitigate, should similarly be taken into account (*Wroth* v. *Tyler* [1973] C.L.Y. 3466, *Horsler* v. *Zorro* [1975] C.L.Y. 3547 considered): TECHNO LAND IMPROVEMENTS v. BRITISH LEYLAND (U.K.) (1979) 252 E.G. 805, Goulding J.

650. —— measure of damages—date from which calculated

D contracted to construct and lease to P a warehouse. It was a term of the contract that C should construct a concrete parking area for the warehouse, but C specified tarmacadam to their builders, and this was laid. D had specified concrete because of the very heavy traffic at the warehouse, but C had specified tarmacadam for cheapness. This was hopelessly inadequate, and would need replacing within five years. The only question was the measure of damages. *Held*, the prima facie rule was that P was entitled to such damages as would put him in a position to have the building he contracted for, unless the cost of reinstatement was wholly disproportionate to the advantages of reinstatement. P was entitled to the cost of replacing the tarmacadam with concrete. Damages would be assessed as at the date of the hearing, for the reasons given by Oliver J. in *Radford* v. *De Frobeville* [1977] C.L.Y. 2484: WILLIAM CORY & SONS v. WINGATE INVESTMENTS (LONDON COLNEY); J. H. COOMBS & PARTNERS, THIRD PARTY (1978) 248 E.G. 687, Sir Douglas Franks, Q.C.

651. Fatal accident—dependants' claim

[Law Reform (Miscellaneous Provisions) Act 1934 (c. 41), s. 1 (2) (*c*).] The plaintiff and his wife were elderly. Their two daughters, aged 31 and 27, died in an aircraft crash. They claimed damages for the estate and themselves. The defendants submitted that by virtue of s. 1 (2) (c) of the Law Reform (Miscellaneous Provisions) Act 1934 the estate could not recover damages in respect of moneys that the deceased would have earned in their working lives; since damages had to be calculated without reference to any " gain " to the estate consequent on the deaths. *Held*, following *Rose* v. *Ford* [1937] A.C. 826, that as damages for loss of expectation of life were not within the meaning of the section, neither were damages for loss of earnings. The section applied to those gains to the estate that arose as a result of the death itself and independently of the fact that the death was caused by the defendant's wrongful act. So the section did not prevent the estate recovering damages for the " lost years ": KANDALLA v. BRITISH AIRWAYS CORP. (1979) 123 S.J. 769, Griffiths J.

652. **Foreign currency—frustrated contract—valuation of defendant's benefit.** See B. P. EXPLORATION CO. (LIBYA) v. HUNT (NO. 2), § 334.

653. **Inconvenience factor—measure of damages.** See DUNN v. DISC JOCKEY UNLIMITED CO., § 328.

654. **Interest—earning capacity—future effect—South Australia**
[Supreme Court Act 1935–1974, s. 30C; Supreme Court Amendment Act 1974, s. 3 (b).]
Interest may not be awarded in respect of compensation for future loss.
The plaintiff was awarded some $65,000 damages in respect of injuries sustained in an accident, the award including $21,500 for future loss of earning capacity. The trial judge, upheld by the full court, awarded the plaintiff a lump sum in lieu of interest, such sum being calculated by reference to the total award of damages. *Held*, allowing the defendant's appeal, that it offended against principle to award interest upon that element of the damages which reflected future loss. (*Cookson* v. *Knowles* [1978] C.L.Y. 713 applied.)
THOMPSON v. FARAONIO [1979] 1 W.L.R. 1157, P.C.

655. —— **variation of judgment—differing House of Lords decisions.** See DENT v. LEVI STRAUSS (U.K.), § 2150.

656. **Loss of expectation of life—whether prospective earnings recoverable—interest on general damages**
A plaintiff whose life expectation is shortened by injury is entitled to damages reflecting his prospective loss of earnings during the " lost years."
At the age of 51, in 1974, the plaintiff contracted mesothelioma due to exposure to asbestos dust at work. At the trial in 1976 (liability being admitted) it appeared that the plaintiff's life expectancy had been reduced to one year, whereas without the disease he could have worked until 65. He was awarded £7,000 as general damages with interest from the date of service of the writ, £1,508 in respect of loss of earnings and £500 for loss of expectation of life. The Court of Appeal held that no sum was payable in respect of loss of prospective earnings during the " lost years " but increased the amount of general damages to £10,000, without interest, and the amount for loss of expectation of life to £750. (Prior to the appeal the plaintiff had died but the proceedings were conducted by his widow as administratrix.) *Held*, allowing the appeal and cross-appeal of the administratrix and the employers, that (1) (Lord Russell of Killowen dissenting) damages for loss of prospective earnings during the lost years were recoverable, being computed by deduction of the plaintiff's likely living expenses had he lived, and that the case would be remitted for such damages to be assessed; (2) the Court of Appeal had erred in ordering that no interest was payable upon the general damages; and (3) that since the trial judge had made no error of principle in assessing the amount of general damages, the Court of Appeal had no jurisdiction to substitute its own figure therefor and the original award would be restored. (*Pope* v. *D. Murphy & Son* [1960] C.L.Y. 859, *Skelton* v. *Collins* [1967] C.L.Y. 1043 and *Davies* v. *Powell Duffryn Associated Collieries* [1942] A.C. 601 applied; *Harris* v. *Brights Asphalt Contractors* [1953] C.L.Y. 392 and *Oliver* v. *Ashman* [1961] C.L.Y.

2311 overruled; dictum of Lord Denning M.R. in *Cookson* v. *Knowles* [1978] C.L.Y. 713 disapproved.)

PICKETT (ADMINISTRATRIX OF THE ESTATE OF RALPH HENRY PICKETT, DECD.) *v.* BRITISH RAIL ENGINEERING [1978] 3 W.L.R. 955, H.L.

657. Measure of damages—repair of building—delay in repair—date when cost calculated

The plaintiffs owned a building from which they operated a garage business, and in 1968 the defendants, in erecting a multi-storey car park next door, caused damage to that building. The plaintiffs, through lack of finance, had not effected repairs by date of hearing in 1978. Cantley J. held that judgment had to be given on the 1970 basis. On appeal, *held,* allowing the appeal, that where there was serious structural damage to a building it was wrong that a plaintiff, in a time of inflation, should be limited to recovery on the basis of the prices of repair at the time of the wrongdoing. The plaintiffs had delayed the repairs for good commercial reasons and 1978 figures should be used in calculating the cost of repairs: DODD PROPERTIES (KENT) *v.* CANTERBURY CITY COUNCIL, *The Times,* December 27, 1979, C.A.

658. Mitigation—appropriate time for measuring damages

[Can.] It has been *held,* that after a breach of an obligation to redeliver shares arising out of a contract of bailment, P must mitigate his loss by purchasing like shares in the market on the date he knows of the breach or within a reasonable period thereafter. Only where there is such a substantial and legitimate interest in specific delivery of the shares that the court would order specific performance of the defendant's obligation is the plaintiff excused from mitigating his loss. The reasonable time will take into account the practical difficulties of purchasing large blocks of shares and the conduct of the defendant. It may be reasonable for the plaintiff to refrain from replacing the shares during reasonably speedy and prompt litigation, or if litigation is postponed at the defendant's request. The fact that the plaintiff has obtained an injunction to restrain the defendant from disposing of the shares does not excuse his duty to mitigate. (*British Westinghouse* v. *Underground Electric Railway Co.* [1912] A.C. 673 applied; *Victoria Laundry (Windsor)* v. *Newman Industries* (1948) C.L.C. 2565, *Parsons (H.) (Livestock)* v. *Uttley Ingham & Co.* [1978] C.L.Y. 789, *Pilkington* v. *Wood* (1953) C.L.C. 3775, *Wroth* v. *Tyler* [1973] C.L.Y. 3466, *White and Carter (Councils)* v. *McGregor* [1962] C.L.Y. 501 referred to): ASAMERA OIL CORP. *v.* SEA OIL & GENERAL CORP. (1978) 89 D.L.R. (3d) 1, Can.Sup.Ct.

659. Personal injuries—expert evidence—lodging agreed reports. See PRACTICE DIRECTION, § 1274.

660. —— master and servant—injury to seaman—quantum. See O'KEEFE *v.* JOHN STEWART & CO. SHIPPING; THE YEWKYLE, § 2474.

661. —— quantum—ankle

[Scot.] Male aged 52 at date of accident and 56 at date of hearing. Fell while descending short flight of stairs, causing severe fracture, dislocation of right ankle. Fracture was reduced by open operation and the fragments were held in place by internal fixation using three screws. A low-grade infection developed in the ankle. He was in plaster for three months; off work for six months. After his return to work one of the pins worked its way out through the skin: he was off work for a further five weeks. Four years after the accident he still could not walk long distances; the ankle became swollen at times; he lost 50 per cent. of normal range of ankle movement. It was likely traumatic arthritis would develop. Solatium (general damages) £2,000: KOPANSKI *v.* NAIRN FLOORS, 1979 S.L.T. 86, Outer House.

662. —— —— back

[Scot.] A man, aged 55, ducked to pass under a fixed scaffolding tube. He straightened up too quickly and struck his left shoulder against the tube. He felt slight pain but carried on working for two hours, until the end of the working day. Next morning he woke with severe pain in his neck and shoulder which radiated down his left arm to the wrist. Before the accident he suffered for at least seven years from cervical spondylosis; this accident accelerated the degenerative change in his back by about two years. After the accident he was no longer fit for his previous employment, but was capable of some employment. Solatium assessed at £1,200: CHARLES *v.* CONCRETE (SCOTLAND), 1979 S.L.T. 57, Outer House.

663. —— —— brain damage—cost of future care—principles applicable
[Law Reform (Personal Injuries Act) 1948 (c. 41), s. 2 (4).]
In a "catastrophic" case, care must be exercised to avoid duplication in awards for loss of earnings and for the cost of future care; the living expenses should be taken into account in assessing the multiplicand.
The plaintiff doctor suffered extensive and irremediable brain damage due to the defendants' admitted negligence. She was reduced to a barely sentient existence and was totally dependent upon others for care. Her expectation of life (she was 36 at the time of the injury) was unaffected. Bristow J. awarded her £243,000 including £20,000 for pain, suffering and loss of amenities, £84,500 for loss of future earnings, £105,000 for the cost of future care and £8,000 for loss of pension. The Court of Appeal upheld the award. *Held*, that (1) £20,000 was appropriate for pain, suffering and loss of amenities; the fact that the plaintiff was unaware of such loss notwithstanding; (2) in such a case sums for expenses which would have been incurred in earning a living and living expenses fell to be deducted: where there was a cost of care claim living expenses should be deducted as "the domestic element" in calculating the multiplicand; (3) the risk of inflation was of little account where a large sum was payable; and (4) having considered fresh evidence as to the cost of care, the appropriate multiplicand was £6,400 with a multiplier of 12 years' purchase; accordingly the total award was reduced to some £229,000. (Decision of Court of Appeal varied; *H. West & Son.* v. *Shephard* [1963] C.L.Y. 952, *Shearman* v. *Folland* (1950) C.L.C. 2554 and *Pickett* v. *British Rail Engineering* [1979] C.L.Y. 656 applied.)
LIM POH CHOO *v.* CAMDEN AND ISLINGTON AREA HEALTH AUTHORITY [1979] 3 W.L.R. 44, H.L.

664. —— —— effect of inflation—paraplegia
In the most serious cases damages awarded since 1973 have generally failed to keep pace with inflation.
The appellants appealed against a sum of £35,000 awarded to a boy aged 16 at the date of an accident in respect of pain, suffering and loss of amenities, the accident having rendered him paraplegic. *Held*, dismissing the appeal, that such a sum should be regarded as realistic in the more serious cases: previous awards had failed to take account of the lessening value of money. (*Senior* v. *Barker & Allen* [1965] C.L.Y. 1007 considered.)
WALKER *v.* JOHN MCLEAN & SONS [1979] 1 W.L.R. 760, C.A.

665. —— —— knee
[Scot.] Apprentice electrician aged 18 at time of accident, stumbled on some rocks and stones in an underground passageway. The medial cartilage of the right knee was torn. Subsequent operation to remove cartilage: arthritis developed subsequently in site from which cartilage removed. Some mental depression because of "long" period before return to work (about a year). *Solatiur*: £1,800, being £1,200 for past solatium and £600 for present: CONNOLLY *v.* NATIONAL COAL BOARD, 1979 S.L.T. 24, Outer House.

666. —— —— passenger on ship struck by mooring wire. See DALY *v.* GENERAL STEAM NAVIGATION CO.; THE DRAGON, § 1869.

667. Personal injuries or death—accident to child—mother's contemplation of child's illness
[Scot.] A child aged eight was seriously injured when he fell from a window of a third-floor flat occupied by his mother as tenant of the local authority. After proof (the evidence was heard), the local authority was held liable in damages. The child died after the action was raised, but before the evidence was heard, and his mother thereafter sued also as executrix. *Held*, the mother was awarded £12,000 as executrix and £1,250 as an individual for solatium. She was not entitled to an award for suffering caused to her by seeing her child as a quadraplegic over the four years between the accident and his death.

But she was entitled to a larger award than usual because of her special attachment to the child, which had resulted from his condition: PARKE v. GLASGOW DISTRICT COUNCIL, 1979 S.L.T. 45, Outer House.

—— quantum of damages

Details have been received of the following cases in which damages for personal injuries or death were awarded. The classifications and sequence of the classified awards follow that adopted in Kemp and Kemp, *The Quantum of Damages,* 4th ed., Vol. 2. Unless there is some statement to the contrary the age of an applicant is his age at the time of the court hearing. The damages are stated on the basis of full liability, *i.e.* ignoring any reduction made for contributory negligence. The sum is the amount of the general damages awarded unless otherwise stated.

Reports from practitioners of awards of which they have knowledge will be gratefully received, particularly where they relate to unusual injuries or to a subject matter which is not adequately covered in recorded cases. Awards in Fatal Accident claims will be most welcome, since so many of these are settled without going to trial.

Occasionally, we are unaware that awards already reported at first instance have been altered on appeal. If practitioners observe any case of this nature, we would be grateful for information about the award so that the correct position can be stated in a later issue of Current Law.

Injuries of Maximum Severity
(a) *Quadriplegia*

668. HYDE v. TAMESIDE AREA HEALTH AUTHORITY (*Daily Telegraph* and *Daily Express,* October 30, 1979; Anthony Lincoln J.; Manchester). Male, aged about 38 at date of accident in February 1972 and 45 at date of trial. Married. Admitted to hospital with painful neck and shoulder. Wrongly believed he had cancer and became acutely depressed and distressed as result of which he attempted to commit suicide by jumping through first-floor ward window. Fractured spine causing quadriplegia. Would now have to spend rest of life in bed or in a wheelchair. Permanently unemployable. Defendant held liable for negligence in failing to diagnose his condition. *Agreed damages*: £200,000.

669. CHAMBERS v. KARIA (February 2, 1979; O'Connor J.). Male, aged 30 at date of accident in September 1975 and nearly 34 at date of trial. Married, with three children aged 11, nine and seven. Leading hand at furniture manufacturers, almost certain to be supervisor by date of trial and probably senior foreman at about 40. Fracture dislocation of C5 vertebrae with associated tetraplegia which was almost complete. Paralysis from elbows down. Severe spasticity for which future operation might effect moderate improvement. Required constant care and attendance and heated accommodation at constant temperature. Life expectancy about 20 years. Loss of earnings: " lost years " case under *Pickett* v. *British Rail Engineering* [1978] C.L.Y. 720a, dealt with by applying a multiplier of 15 to loss of earnings at £4,800 net p.a., two of the 15 applicable to " lost years " from which discounted his own expenses and keep and a further discount for accelerated payment, giving total of £68,000 (£4,800 × 13 + £2,800 × 2). Future nursing and wife's services: £40,000 on a multiplier of 13 for 20-year life expectancy. Pain, suffering and loss of amenity, £40,000. House extensions: cost agreed at £11,000 but claim rejected as would enhance capital value of property; instead £6,500 awarded under *George* v. *Pinnock* [1973] C.L.Y. 862 to represent annual loss of interest on capital expended on own house and extension; capital calculated as £38,500, *i.e.* £27,500 purchase price plus £11,000 cost of extension less annual rent and rates on previous council house; interest of £6,500 apparently calculated as £500 p.a. on multiplier of 13. Future running costs of house agreed at £500 p.a. to cover extra rates, telephone, heating and maintenance, again giving £6,500 on multiplier of 13. Two interim payments made—£10,000 in March 1976 and £27,500 in July 1977. Judge rejected approach in Ord. 29, rr. 9–17; interim payments to be applied to extinguish special damages claim and then to be set against award for pain, suffering and loss of amenity. *Agreed special* *damages*: £14,000, including £1,800 awarded by judge to cover wife's nursing services for two-and-a-half years to date of trial. *Total award*: £183,650. (*Ex rel. D. J. Brennan, Esq., Barrister.*)

(b) Paraplegia

670.   CASEY *v.* HEANEY (June 19, 1979; Smith J.). Male, aged about 19 at date of accident in May 1976 and 22 at date of hearing. Former trainee accountant. Spinal injuries resulting in paraplegia from chest and elbows down. Would spend rest of life in wheelchair. Estimated life expectancy of 20 years. Incapable of work of any kind, let alone chosen profession. Loss of future earnings assessed at £58,000 based on multiplier of 20. Cost of future care assessed at £35,000 based on payments to family friends and nurses who would help look after plaintiff and taking into account possibility that he would survive his parents and have to be cared for in a home. Pain and suffering and loss of amenities assessed at £40,000. " Miscellaneous " damages (including special damages) assessed at £8,000. *Total damages*: £141,000.

671.   ANGUS *v.* JONES (March 16, 1979; Stocker J.). Male, aged about 25 at date of accident in June 1975 and 29 at date of trial. Batchelor. Former spring maker who would have been earning about £89 per week at date of trial. Fractures of fifth, sixth and seventh thoracic vertebrae resulting in complete paraplegia from mid-chest downwards. No prospect of any significant recovery and would probably be confined to wheelchair for life. Unusual feature of case was that plaintiff suffered from constant, disabling pain, necessitating controlling injections and drugs, which was likely to continue to greater or lesser extent. Great many of pleasures of life now closed to him. Prospects of marriage remote, if they existed at all. Now lived alone in council bungalow assisted by home help and visiting district nurse. In receipt of supplementary benefit and invalidity benefit of £25 per week. Now capable of only sedentary work and even this made more difficult by pain suffered. Future loss of earnings assessed at £50,000 based on net continuing loss of £3,350 per annum and multiplier of 16, giving £53,600 which was " rounded down," presumably for accelerated receipt of capital sum. Expenses related to car conversion, travelling for future treatment, contributions to local authority assistance and gardening help assessed at £2,638. Pain and suffering and loss of amenities assessed at £40,000. *Special damages*: £10,734 (consisting of £734 agreed special damages and £10,000 part loss of earnings). *Total general damages*: £92,638.

(c) Very severe brain damage

672.   TAYLOR *v.* GLASS (May 23, 1979; Smith J.; Middlesbrough). Boy, aged almost 9. Father, aged 39, director of and majority shareholder in building company employing some 20 men with gross salary of £10,000 p.a. Mother housewife, aged 40. Formerly bright, happy, healthy and normal child who was more intelligent than his elder brother had been at similar age. Then aged 12 months developed haemophilus meningitis. Owing to failure of defendant general practitioner to treat condition promptly, he suffered severe, irreversible, global brain damage resulting in gross mental handicap and permanent and highly disabling physical disabilities: (1) he was totally deaf; (2) he had right-sided hemiplegia; could not use right arm at all and hence could not wash or dress himself, and walked with bizarre gait, rolling unsteadily and swinging right leg as if he had wooden leg below knee; (3) he could not talk or communicate in any way, save that parents thought they could understand him to say a few simple words, but he tried hard to do so through grunts, shouts and gestures; became very frustrated when these were not understood and would strike his head very forcibly with his left hand; (4) there was complete and permanent loss of right-sided vision in both eyes with result that he could not see things on his right side and constantly bumped into objects; (5) he was incontinent of faeces and urine. He had to be put on a commode every hour, but invariably soiled himself when he got off it; he soiled his bed frequently at night; (6) his I.Q. and level of mental development were those of a child aged 12 to 15 months and would never improve. As a result he was ineducable and would never be able to acquire any skill, however slight.

At time of hearing he was a weekly boarder at school for deaf children where he required constant supervision and attendance; headmaster of school considered plaintiff was most handicapped child he had ever been responsible for; school could do nothing more for him and he would shortly have to leave it; (7) he had developed epilepsy and had suffered major fits in spite of taking drugs; since February 1979, when mix of drugs was changed, there had been great improvement in this respect: he seemed brighter, more alert, ate better and was happier and only very minor fits had been witnessed since then.

He was "neither a cripple nor a cabbage." He was vigorous, sturdy and physically healthy, had a will and something of a mind of his own and could enjoy his small world to a limited extent. He would take things and run away, hoping to be chased which he showed he enjoyed by giggling. He was extremely mobile and for this reason had to be constantly watched in case he got into mischief or danger. He could play, but his playing skills were "pathetically" limited. In this respect the most he could do was to play peg-board, throw a soft ball in the air and avoid it falling on him and play a kind of football with his father which consisted of his father running about and kicking a ball to him, which he could sometimes kick back. He had his good days and his bad days. On bad days nobody could do anything right and he became very naughty when not understood. On his goods days he was happy and giggled a lot. He was sentient with a limited perception of his disabilities, which might increase in adult life. Apart from his disabilities, he would grow up to be a physically strong and normally healthy man. His life expectancy was reduced by 10 to 15 years. He would never be capable of working. His parents, who adored him, were determined that he should stay with them as long as they lived, but the strain of looking after him was almost intolerable and the help of an auxiliary nurse was essential. Due to the risk of his falling downstairs it was necessary for the family to move to a bungalow. This was being built by his father at an estimated cost of £25,000 to £30,000. It had been necessary to buy a car to enable his mother to take him around with her. Smith J. awarded damages as follows: (1) agreed damages of £26,000 (consisting of £15,000 towards cost of building bungalow, £500 towards cost of car, £1,800 in respect of running costs of car to date of hearing, £7,500 in respect of its future running costs and £1,200 in respect of damage done by plaintiff to home and contents); (2) £20,000 in respect of parents' services to date of hearing (based on agreed cost of such services on open labour market of £50 p.w.); (3) £104,500 in respect of cost of future care by nursing auxiliary (based on multiplicand of £4,180 and multiplier of 25, taking into account plaintiff's reduced life expectancy, future inflation and probability that, as parents likely to pre-decease him, he would have to go into an institution); (4) £32,500 in respect of value of parents' services in future (based on multiplier of 13 and multiplicand of £2,500); (5) £50,000 in respect of future loss of earnings based on multiplier of 10 (taking account of plaintiff's youth, uncertainty of future, general uncertainty as to employment prospects, accelerated payment and future inflation) and multiplicand of £5,000 (discounted by £428 because of "overlap" between this head of damage and agreed damages in respect of bungalow and car, cost of which would have had to have been met out of plaintiff's earnings had he lived a normal life); (6) £60,000 in respect of pain and suffering and loss of amenities. *Total damages*: £293,000.

673. CROKE v. BRENT AND HARROW AREA HEALTH AUTHORITY (*Daily Telegraph* and *Daily Mail*, November 6, 1979; Michael Davies J.) Boy aged 21 months at date of accident in 1973 and seven at date of hearing. Clever bright little boy with lovely personality. Developed croup which was diagnosed as teething troubles." Whilst undergoing treatment in hospital suffered cardiac arrest resulting in severe brain damage. Now quadriplegic, almost blind and mentally retarded. Mental development below that of normal 12-month-old baby. Could not speak, although he did respond to his parents' voices by making noises. Totally dependent on others. Could not sit up by himself and if he rolled over on the floor could not roll back. Had sleeping and feeding difficulties. Took an hour to get him up and dress him in morning. Could just catch hold of rattle with left hand, but could not release it. By no means a "cabbage" and liked to be picked up and cuddled. "A shadow of the fine boy and later man he would have become." Lived with parents who gave him loving care. Father self-employed builder aged 32 and mother, former teacher, aged 41. Mother had given up career to look after him. Life expectancy reduced to about 33 years. Mother's loss of earnings, cost of home help and other expenses assessed at £35,000; cost of future care assessed at £130,000; future loss of earnings assessed at £45,000. Cost of new bungalow to better accommodate plaintiff agreed at £15,000. *Total damages*: £269,698.

674. SHEWMAN *v.* KENSINGTON, CHELSEA AND WESTMINSTER AREA HEALTH AUTHORITY (*Evening Standard,* October 29, 1979; Griffiths J.) Female, aged 25 at date of accident and 30 at date of hearing. Accomplished teacher with promising future. Had teaching job in Japan at time of accident. While undergoing routine operation was given nitrous oxide instead of oxygen owing to defect in anaesthetic equipment resulting in severe brain damage. Underwent intensive care initially, when her condition was critical, followed by four years treatment. Now virtually a "cabbage". Severe intellectual impairment and partial blindness. Such of the qualities of normal life as she was able to enjoy were "fleeting and transient episodes in a shadowy and confused existence." Incapable of independent existence. Needed constant care, kindness and guidance. Her father, a businessman, aged 59, had cared for her with utmost devotion and was planning to spend rest of his life looking after her. *Agreed damages* of £262,500 approved by judge.

675. LANGLEY *v.* DEPARTMENT OF THE ENVIRONMENT (*The Guardian,* March 27, 1979; Chapman J.). Male, aged 27 at date of accident and 33 at date of hearing. Happily married with two children, girl aged six and boy aged five. Had established successful retail fitted-furniture business. Severe brain injuries causing gross intellectual damage and mental disturbance. On leaving hospital mental condition was terrifying and he was given to bouts of physical violence. Now separated from wife and children and marriage was at an end. Spent part of his time with his parents in Malta, where he was cared for by his mother, and remainder attending head injuries work centre in this country. Mother described caring for him as being like "bringing him up as a child all over again." *Agreed damages* of £187,500 (including £8,362 in respect of loss and/or expense incurred by his father who had looked after plaintiff's business until it was sold) were approved by Chapman J.

676. WHITEHOUSE *v.* BIRMINGHAM AREA HEALTH AUTHORITY (*Daily Telegraph,* December 2, 1978; Bush J.; Birmingham). Boy, aged 9. Suffered severe brain damage at birth as result of negligence of obstetric surgeon in course of attempted "forceps" delivery. "Helpless cripple" with mental age of 17 months. Mother, who was now divorced from father, had looked after him at home for 4½ years and has determined to continue to do so. But possible that at some stage he would have to be admitted to an institution. *Damages*: £100,000. (*Note*: This award was set aside by the Court of Appeal, which by a majority held that the surgeon had not been negligent: [1979] C.L.Y. 1883.)

677. SHADLOCK *v.* NEWMAN (January 19, 1979; Tudor-Evans J.). Female, aged 65 at date of accident on April 5, 1976. Nearly 68 at date of trial. Prior to accident had led an active life, very well read, lively, good memory, intelligent, forthright in her opinions and good sense of humour. Catastrophic injuries. Severe head injury causing brain damage. Dense right-sided hemiplegia with right-sided facial weakness. Spinal cord intact but total paralysis of both legs and useless right arm with right hand permanently clenched. Tardive-dyskinesis. Virtually incapable of speech and could not enjoy normal communication. Immobile and incontinent. Requires total care throughout 24 hours. Danger of pressure sores and urinary tract infection developing. Various orthopaedic injuries—compound fracture of left tibia and fibula and fracture of medial tibial table of right leg. Can turn over pages of a book and occasionally feed herself by hand. Has understanding of her misfortune but no capacity to communicate the emotions she feels. Life expectancy of five years. Damages for pain and suffering £17,500. There were also nursing expenses and other miscellaneous special damages. (Total reduced by 50 per cent. for contributory negligence.) (*Ex rel. R. Walker, Esq., Barrister.*)

Mutiple Injuries

678. CLARKE *v.* ESTATE OF LOWE (DECD.) (December 1, 1978; Judge Lewis Hawser, Q.C.). Male, aged 27 at date of accident, 31 at date of hearing. Production engineer with British Leyland. Injured in March 1975 in head-on collision between his car and van driven by the deceased. Serious fractures of all four limbs (injuries from which " he could well have perished "), broken shoulder-blade, shock, bruising and cuts. In hospital for five months and underwent a number of operations. Back at work part-time by November 1975; employed full-time by February 1976. Suffered the following permanent disabilities: limited movement of left wrist, aching and risk of arthritis; half the normal rotation of his right arm, limited elbow movement and an inability to flex his little finger which made taking change awkward; limited movement in both knees which rendered it impossible for him to squat; right leg was two-thirds of an inch shorter than his left, and although he wore a built-up heel, he walked with a slight limp. Severe unattractive scarring, most of which was hidden by his clothing. One of his eyelashes grew inward, which was an irritation. Married in June 1978 a young lady whom he had known before the accident. Became tired easily, which affected his work prospects. *General damages*: £7,500. (*Ex rel. Robert Thoresby, Esq., Barrister.*)

679. WILLIAMS *v.* NEWTON (March 26, 1979; Ackner J.; Winchester). Male, aged 22. Right handed. Injured in road accident in January 1975. Severe head injury and oblique, slightly comminuted fracture of shaft of right radius. Unconscious two days. In hospital five weeks, of which five days spent in intensive care unit. Now suffered from headaches almost daily, irritability, poor memory and inability to concentrate, *e.g.* he could put down tools at work and forget where he had left them. Could no longer go out for drink at night due to nocturnal incontinence. Had post-traumatic amnesia. Slight permanent disability in right arm consisting of some limitation of movement and discomfort on heavy use. Possibility of degenerative arthrosis in wrist joint in future. Still played football but had had to give up goalkeeping. *Special damages*: £167. *General damages*: £5,000. (*Ex rel. Stephen Parish, Esq., Barrister.*)

680. EVERETT *v.* F. MONK AND SONS (November 13, 1979; Deputy Judge Roy Beldam Q.C.). Male aged about 45 at date of accident and 48 at date of hearing. Whilst working on cupola, section of cupola broke away and he was thrown about five feet into air and fell to ground. Suspected fracture of lumbar vertebra aggravating pre-existing degenerative changes in lower lumbar spine and lumbo-sacral joint; contusion to left forearm; minor fracture or severe sprain of left wrist; contusions to left side of trunk; bruising to ribs and left knee. Subsequently developed anxiety condition and became nervous and irritable. Left wrist and forearm in plaster about five weeks. Wore spinal corset intermittently. Full recovery from injury to left wrist within five months. Injury to spine accelerated onset of pain in lower back by about three years. Unable to do work requiring bending, stooping, heavy lifting or climbing ladders. Full recovery from effects of accident by time of trial: now in same anxious condition and suffering from same low back pains as if accident had not occurred. Unable to resume pre-accident work and fit only for light duties. Had been unemployed since accident. *Special damages*: £8,842·32 (based upon three years' past loss of earnings). *General damages*: £1,500 (based upon three years' pain and suffering and loss of amenities resulting from acceleration of onset of back complaints). (*Ex rel. Frank R. Moat, Esq., Barrister.*)

Brain and Skull

681. SETON *v.* ELLIOT (April 6, 1979; Mustill J.; *Daily Telegraph, Daily Express, Daily Mail,* April 7, 1979). Male aged 36 years. Chartered surveyor and estate agent with his own business before the accident, now employed part-time. Injured in an accident in 1977 when his car was hit by another car and forced into a bus stop which collapsed and pierced his skull. Now registered as blind.

Imperfect tunnel vision. His face was disfigured and his senses of smell and taste were substantially reduced. There was some brain damage. No longer able to play golf. Had lost his independence and had much time on his hands which he could not occupy. *Total damages*: £205,786, £144,000 of which was for loss of future earnings.

682.   HUET *v.* CUDDEFORD (December 20, 1978; Michael Davies J.; Exeter). Male, aged 51 at date of accident in November 1974 and 55 at date of hearing. Former foreman writer in dockyard earning about £40 p.w. net. Suffered severe head injury, minor degree of aggravation of pre-existing injury to cervical spine and other relatively minor injuries, including some damage to eye which initially caused double vision and bruising and cuts to legs. Some 12 months after accident developed post-traumatic epilepsy. However, this was controlled by drugs and possibility of further fits not great. Had some difficulty in writing with right hand. Now psychologically dependent to substantial extent on his wife who had given up work to look after him. Evidence given that psychological treatment would be of assistance, but possibility remained that he would be dependent on wife for some time. Unable to resume work except in some sheltered capacity, possibility of obtaining which was remote. Unable to do own home decorating and gardening on which he had been keen. Pain and suffering and loss of amenities assessed at £20,000. Plaintiff's future pecuniary loss assessed at £14,568 consisting of: (1) loss of future earnings of £9,930 (based on multiplier of 5 and multiplicand of £1,986); (2) loss of pension rights assessed at £3,638 of which £2,910 was in respect of periodic pension payments (based on multiplier of 6 and agreed multiplicand of £485) and £728 in respect of lump sum payment entitlement (after reduction by one half for accelerated receipt); (3) future cost of home decorating of £500; and (4) future cost of gardening of £500. Plaintiff's wife's future pecuniary loss assessed at £7,470 consisting of (1) future loss of earnings of £7,228 (based on multiplier of 4, although, if psychiatric assistance to plaintiff was successful, wife would be able to resume work); and (2) £242 in respect of her entitlement to one half of husband's pension in event of his death (representing one half of one yearly periodic payment). *Agreed special damages*: £9,085 (consisting of £5,805 in respect of wife's and £3,180 in respect of plaintiff's past loss of earnings and £1,000 in respect of miscellaneous out-of-pocket expenses). *Total general damages*: £42,038. (*Ex rel. Messrs. Bond Pearce and Co., solicitors*).

683.   BASTIEN *v.* WOOD (April 24, 1979; Judge Hawser, Q.C.). Boy, aged two at date of accident in November 1974 and six at date of trial. West Indian from disadvantaged home background. Both parents had low I.Q.s Mother an epileptic who had been paralysed and unable to speak since 1977. Father in full-time employment as labourer. Head injury resulting in left-sided brain damage. Unconscious eight days. Detained in hospital three months. Suffered epileptiform attack after 12 months. After 18 months still suffered from unsteadiness of gait, continuous dribbing, hyperactivity, lack of concentration, delayed speech development, bed-wetting and disturbed sleep. Thereafter made steady progress so that by February 1979 only residual clinical symptoms were hyperactivity, lack of concentration and bed-wetting. Judge accepted medical evidence that there was impairment of intellectual capacity associated with organic brain damage which would make plaintiff " an odd lot on the labour market " in future. Now attended special school for physically handicapped children. Risk of epilepsy developing assessed at 5 per cent. Taking into account that home background might in any event have resulted in psychological disturbance and consequential difficulties on labour market, loss of earning capacity assessed at £3,000. Pain and suffering and loss of amenities assessed at £7,500. *Total general damages*: £10,500 (*Baker* v. *Willoughby* [1970] C.L.Y. 1862 followed; *Hodgson* v. *General Electric* [1978] C.L.Y. 718 not followed). (*Ex rel. Jonathan Sofer, Esq., Barrister.*)

684.   WATSON *v.* CHICHESTER DISTRICT COUNCIL (July 3, 1979; Judge Edgar Fay Q.C.). Male, aged 35 at date of accident and 40 at date of trial. Work study officer. Fell from rear platform of refuse vehicle. Fracture of right occipital bone. Unconscious a matter of minutes. In hospital five weeks. Suffered from headaches, vomiting and photophobia which were slow to improve. Returned to work on part-time basis after five months and gradually built up to full-time work over 18 months. After five years still suffered from regular headaches, though these were relieved by drugs. Some continuing impairment of memory, giddiness and slight imbalance which would gradually improve. No loss of future earnings or loss of earning capacity. *Special damages*: £41·60. *General damages*: £3,000. (*Ex rel. Kenneth Gillance, Esq., Barrister.*)

Face

685.   PLATT *v.* ZEHETNER (January 10, 1979; Judge Curtis; Stockport County Ct.). Married woman, aged 43. Typist. In November 1977 metal fish tank hood fell from shelf and hit her on head causing laceration above left eyebrow. No loss of consciousness. Required three or four stitches under local anaesthetic and given anti-tetanus injection. Not detained in hospital. Face and eyelids swelled and became discoloured over next few days and remained so for about a fortnight. Left with 2 cm. long scar at outer end of eyebrow which was white, slightly depressed and cross-hatched by suture marks and noticeable particularly in oblique lighting. It was not amenable to improvement by plastic surgery and was difficult to hide with make-up. Plaintiff was embarrassed by its appearance. Off work about a week. No special damages. *General damages*: £750. (*Ex rel.Messrs. Norton & Co., plaintiff's solicitors.*)

Teeth

686.   MACK *v.* PORT (February 21, 1979; Master Creightmore). Girl aged 18 at time of accident in 1977 was kicked in face by horse. Judgment by default of appearance against stable owner. Damages assessed by Master. Upper and lower lip cut requiring 10 stitches leaving minimal scarring. Bridge and crown work required to replace two upper teeth and for restoration of two lower teeth. Treatment started 10 months after accident. Seen 14 times at dental school. Five more visits required. Bridge in upper jaw completed 18 months after accident. Until this completed plaintiff lisped and felt uncomfortable. Crown still to be fitted to lower teeth. Further therapy may be needed in future. Will have to pay special attention to teeth in future. Plaintiff injured towards beginning of two-week summer holiday which was spoilt by injury. No loss of earnings. *Special damages*: £17·50. *General damages* (inclusive of small amount of interest for five months and taking into account spoilt holiday): £2,300. (*Ex rel. Neil Kaplan, Esq., Barrister.*)

Burns and Scars

687.   ROBINSON *v.* AUTOMATIC BOILER CO. (*Daily Telegraph,* March 24, 1979; Peter Pain J.). Girl, aged four at date of accident in 1976 and eight at date of trial. Suffered severe and extensive burns when, owing to defects in central heating system, scalding water escaped, came through the ceiling of her bedroom, bringing part of it down onto her bed, and poured onto her as she slept. Was initially at " death's door " and spent days in hospital intensive care unit. Left with hideous scars on her arms, body and legs. Would require two plastic surgery operations when she was aged 15 to minimise scarring. One in five chance that operations would not be successful. *Damages*: £17,750 (including £150 for " horrifying experience ").

688.   BARNES *v.* ROSEACRE LAUNDRY (May 11, 1979; Deputy Judge Honig). Male, aged about 61 at date of accident and 64 at date of hearing. Former laundryman. Suffered severe burns when boiling water erupted over him. Underwent extensive skin grafts. Left with extensive scarring to body which constituted very severe disfigurement. There were extensive signs of skin grafting which resulted in very severe cosmetic damage. Permanent limitation of movement in right hand which had robbed him of hobby of gardening. Suffered from irritation of skin. Since accident had not felt urge for sexual intercourse and wife had reciprocated that feeling because found him moody and bad-tempered. Judge concluded that this was psychological in origin and that plaintiff would get over it once case over. Had been unable to do any kind of work since accident. *Agreed special damages*: £4,988. *General damages*: £7,000.

689.   WOODGATES *v.* MINISTRY OF DEFENCE (March 9, 1979; Park J.; Exeter). Male, aged 61 at date of accident in November 1977. Slipped on loose mat when carrying kettle of freshly boiled water. Suffered burns to right wrist, back of right hand and right side of body from chest to hip and injury to shoulder. Burns very painful for first four or five weeks, during which time he attended hospital twice a week for dressings, and his sleep was greatly disturbed. Returned to work after five months, throughout which period he received full pay. By time of hearing he had made excellent recovery. Left with minor disfigurement of chest, due to uneven pigmentation of skin, and scar on hip. No scars could be seen on right hand, but fingers were still slightly swollen, grip was weak and knuckles were painful. Movements of shoulder not restricted, but suffered occasional pain. Because of injury to hand not allowed to work with chemicals for at least two years and so had taken slightly less well-paid job. *Agreed special damages*: £500 (including future loss of earnings). *General damages*: £2,000. (*Ex rel. Robert Thoresby, Esq., Barrister.*)

690.   HORMAN *v.* STEEL (October 4, 1979; Boreham J.; Newcastle-upon-Tyne). Male, aged 15 at date of accident and 19 at date of trial. Struck by car while crossing road. Deep cut on left side of neck involving external jugular vein, which required surgical repair, and minor injuries including black eye, abrasions to fingers and knees and slight concussion. Left with quite significant scar on left side of neck about 4in. long which was not particularly vivid, but when visible was quite disfiguring. This would be improved by surgery after which disfigurement was likely to be insignificant. Plaintiff's claim dismissed. *General damages*: £1,500. *Per curiam*: Scar not as serious a feature as it would be in case of a young woman. (*Ex rel. Kenneth Gillance, Esq., Barrister.*)

Sight

691.   VANDOME *v.* JONES (May 25, 1979; Deputy Judge Lipfriend). Girl aged two or three at date of accident and five at date of hearing. Right eye pierced by sharpened hacksaw blade resulting in total loss of sight in that eye. Her prospects of marriage and position on labour market could be adversely affected by disability. No special damage. *General damages*: £10,000.

Hearing

692.   *Re* FULLER (September 3, 1979; Criminal Injuries Compensation Board). Male, aged 38 at date of accident in June 1975 and about 42 at date of assessment. Former HGV driver. Struck over head and fell to ground, fracturing skull and suffering immediate total loss of hearing. Complete loss of sense of smell and effective loss of sense of taste, continuing tinnitus and occasional loss of balance. Had suffered headaches following accident, but these had now diminished. Now very much more tired at end of day. As result of disabilities had lost HGV licence and pre-accident job. Now a dustman, a job which he was likely to retain. No award for loss of earnings as benefits received and to be received (including disablement pension for life) exceeded loss of earnings. *Total assessment*: £40,000. (*Ex rel. Geoffrey Nice, Esq., Barrister.*)

693.   BAILEY *v.* I.C.I. (May 14, 1979; Caulfield J.; Manchester). Male, aged 35. As result of his employment from about age of 30 had suffered from tinnitus and bilateral high tone hearing loss which averaged 15 to 18 decibels at 1/2/3 kHz and was severe at 3 kHz. Tinnitus would continue for rest of life. Would continue to suffer degree of social embarrassment, some loss of enjoyment of music and would have to make effort when trying to listen to competing sounds. Possibility of deafness worsening with age. Loss of earning capacity assessed at £1,500 and pain and suffering and loss of amenities at £7,000. No special damages. *Total general damages*: £8,500. (*Ex rel. Messrs. Brian Thompson and Partners, Solicitors.*)

694.   ALLESBROOK *v.* BUTCHER (July 23, 1979; Deputy Judge Hayman). Male, aged 23. Former refuse collector. As result of road accident in March 1976 suffered perforation of left ear drum with haemorrhage from ear resulting in presence of blood in auditory canal, temporary left-sided deafness and slight bilateral deafness, mild degree of tinnitus, dizziness and headaches for about two months and irritability which caused strain on marriage and continuing

tension headaches after first two-months. Left-sided hearing loss initially severe —in March 1976 it was estimated at 65 to 70 decibels and he was unable to hear his baby cry or to hear television properly, it gradually improved. In October 1976 it was 50 to 60 decibels and in April 1977 30 to 40 decibels which was described as "mild." From about October 1978 namely some two and a half years after accident he had no further complaints. For all practical purposes had made full recovery. Now self-employed chain-link fencer. No continuing loss of earnings. Off work about five months. *Special damages*: £301·58. *General damages*: £1,300. (*Ex rel. Frank Moat, Esq., Barrister.*)

Neck

695. GUEST *v.* BREARLEY (March 13, 1979; Comyn J.). Male, aged 29 at date of trial. Ambulance driver. "Moderate to serious" whiplash injury to cervical spine as result of road accident on September 25, 1975. In hospital for three days and off work initially for six weeks and thereafter intermittently for a further 10 days. Pain in neck extending into shoulder for period of almost three and a half years to date of trial. Ability to play football restricted and social life affected by injury. Unable to bend down and pick up step-daughter. Difficulty in sleeping. Regularly prescribed distalgesics by general practitioner. Intermittent use of cervical collar, described as "uncomfortable and unsightly." Two collars discarded through regular use and using third collar at date of trial. Last wore collar two weeks before date of trial. Element of continuing disability. *Agreed special damages*: £240. *General damages*: £2,100. (*Ex rel. Frank R. Moat, Esq., Barrister.*)

Spine

696. SIMMONDS *v.* HOLLINGSBEE (January 29, 1979; Judge Edgar Fay Q.C.). Female, aged 23. Unmarried. Former calculating machine operator. Lively, vigorous and ambitious. As result of accident in February 1977 portion of muscle torn out of back and spine chipped. Now suffered considerable pain in back due to muscle loss and tired very easily. Found difficulty keeping house and coping with a job because of strain. Would have difficulty having children and in coping with them afterwards. Registered as disabled. Unable to continue her pre-accident job and considerably restricted as to alternative jobs. Now faced with "lifetime of frustration." Loss of future earnings assessed at £4,000 based on multiplicand of £400 and multiplier of 10. Pain and suffering and loss of amenities assessed at £5,000. *Special damages*: £1,440·43. *Total general damages*: £9,000.

697. CHILDS *v.* CRAWLEY BOROUGH COUNCIL (October 12, 1979; Michael Davies J.). Married woman, aged 58. Housewife. As result of coach in which she was travelling overturning suffered shock, very severe bruising and minor injuries (from all of which she made complete recovery) and compression fractures of two thoracic vertibrae resulting in local kyphus and narrowing of intervertebrae discs. After about six months resumed light housework. Unable to stand for more than five to 10 minutes without pain. Always conscious of back. Avoided bending, lifting or carrying. Wore surgical corset "98 per cent. of the time" and took analgesics once or twice a week. No longer able to play golf and curling restricted, but able to swim comfortably. *Special damages*: £1,057·51. *General damages*: £8,500. (*Ex rel. Roger Eastman, Esq., Barrister.*)

698. HUNTER *v.* TRAVENOL LABORATORIES (November 9, 1979: Neill J.). Male, aged 32 at date of accident and 34 at date of hearing. Former chemical production services operator. Whilst pulling loaded skid slipped and fell heavily on back. Compression fracture of 12th dorsal vertebra resulting in permanent disability. Stooping, bending and lifting at speed more likely to precipitate backache than in normal person. Unable to perform heavy manual work which involved repetitious lifting and stooping. Unable to continue pre-accident work. At date of hearing employed on lighter work as paint sprayer. Off work one year. Damages for loss of earning capacity assessed at £4,000 and for pain and suffering and loss of amenities at £3,000. *Agreed special damages*: £2,368. *Total general damages*: £7,000. (*Ex rel. L. Bingham and Co., Solicitors.*)

699. CLARKE *v.* HOME OFFICE (April 5, 1979; Bush J.; Sheffield). Male, aged 44. Former painter and decorator at a Borstal whose duties involved giving instruction to trainees. Suffered from pre-existing degenerative condition of spine which caused him to have short periods off work. As result of accident in March 1974 sustained mid-lumbar intervertebral disc lesion. Due to increasing pain had to stop working after about a month. After about five months fitted with canvas belt, but this produced little relief in symptoms. After about eight months fitted with plaster jacket which he continued to wear for about three months. Thereafter underwent course of physiotherapy, including traction. Last in hospital in September 1975. Became very depressed when realised that unlikely to be able to return to pre-accident work, had crying fits of which he was ashamed and his sexual life was impaired. In April 1976 was sent on course to retrain as instrument mechanic, but because of depression was unable to cope with course and had to give it up. In February 1977 obtained light job as boilerman on permanent basis. As result depression immediately reduced. Still had discomfort in thigh, groin and back if attempting heavy tasks about the house, such as home decorating and motor mechanics. Permanently unfit for heavy work involving lifting and bending and would never be able to resume pre-accident work. Found present job, which made few mental demands upon him, boring, whereas had found pre-accident work, which he had done all his life, enjoyable and satisfying. Judge concluded that there was risk that eventually he might have had to give up latter in any event due to pre-existing back condition. No award for loss of future earnings or loss of earning capacity. *Special damages*: £445·48. *General damages*: £2,500. (*Ex rel. D. R. Bentley, Esq., Barrister.*)

700.   BULLOCK v. NATIONAL COAL BOARD (May 17, 1979; Woolf J.; Sheffield). Male, aged 28. Fitter. Injury to lumbar spine. Discharged from hospital after four days wearing plaster jacket. Thereafter attended as out-patient for physiotherapy for five months, during which time he was re-admitted to hospital for investigation for four weeks. During 18 months after accident twice returned to light work but had to stop work due to back pain, on first occasion after four months and on second occasion after one month. 18 months after accident resumed pre-accident work and thereafter only had little time off work. Effects of accident spent after two years. *Special damages*: £1,200. *General damages*: £1,500. (*Ex rel. D. R. Bentley, Esq., Barrister.*)

701.   GRAY v. NATIONAL COAL BOARD (July 25, 1979; Reeve J.; Sheffield). Male, aged 49 at date of accident in November 1971 and 57 at date of trial. Underground diesel engine driver. Fell backwards out of cab and struck back on hydraulic ram resulting in acute lumbar strain. Initially in considerable pain. Returned to work after four months, but back pain continued and in December 1972 had to stop work again for this reason. Effects of accident spent by January 1973, viz. after about 14 months. *Special damages*: £68·40. *General damages*: £1,250. (*Ex rel. D. R. Bentley, Esq., Barrister.*)

Respiratory Organs

702.   SHEARS v. MINISTRY OF DEFENCE (March 9, 1979; Park J.; Exeter). Male, aged 56. Fit and active. Lifelong non-smoker. Contracted asbestosis in course of his employment. First suffered from bouts of coughing and general pain in lungs and chest in mid-1960's. Since then condition had progressively deteriorated. By time of hearing so racked with coughing that he found it difficult to sleep and had to use aerolyser. In the mornings was liable to vomit. Both his own and his wife's nerves were affected. No longer able to tend his garden. Condition would grow steadily worse. Expectation of life reduced to 10 years. Did not know gravity of his condition. Forced to retire at age of 53 and had not been able to work since. Would otherwise have worked until 65. Loss of future earnings agreed at £13,500 (based on multiplier of $4\frac{1}{2}$ and multiplicand of £3,000), loss of pension rights at £2,000 and loss of expectation of life at £500. Pain and suffering and loss of amenities assessed at £16,000. *Agreed special damages*: £6,000 (representing past loss of earnings). *Total general damages*: £32,000. (*Smith* v. *Central Asbestos* [1971] C.L.Y. 6830; *Jenks* v. *Court Works* and *Buick* v. *Cape Insulation* both reported in Kemp and Kemp, *The Quantum of Damages*, Vol. 2, para. 7014/1; *Pickett* v. *British Rail Engineering* [1978] C.L.Y. 720a; *Shaw* v. *Cape Insulation* [1977] C.L.Y.

781; *Hembry* v. *Ministry of Defence* [1978] C.L.Y. 748; *Crossman* v. *British Rail Engineering* [1978] C.L.Y. 747; and *Paten* v. *Paten* (unreported) considered). *Per* Park J.: The awards in previous cases were no more than signposts of the appropriate bracket of awards. The plaintiff was in the higher bracket signposted by such cases. (*Ex rel. Robert Thoresby, Esq., Barrister.*)

703. SPENCER v. BRITISH STEEL CORP. (November 2, 1978; Neill J.; Liverpool). Male aged 65, foundry worker, disabled partly by pneumoconiosis and partly by unrelated heart condition. Made redundant by employers as no suitable alternative work available. Redundancy expressed as being on health grounds and employers contended that paid in lieu of wages. *Held,* redundancy payment not deductible from special damage as redundancy payment nothing to do with recipient's injury or incapacity and redundancy payment can only be made in circumstances laid down in Redundancy Payments Act 1965. General damages of £14,000 appropriate if all disability due to inhalation of dust but reduced to £7,000 on account of heart condition. (*Ex rel. Messrs. Brian Thompson & Partners, Solicitors.*)

704. POOLE v. NATIONAL COAL BOARD (December 15, 1978; Kenneth Jones J.; Sheffield). Miner aged 42; hit by jib of loading machine; fractures of fourth, fifth and sixth left ribs, twisted neck, severe shock; returned to light work six months after accident; suffered pain in neck for 18 months after accident; suffered pain in chest of diminishing severity brought on by exertion for five years later accident; left with defect of function of left lung of 22 per cent., of which 13 per cent. attributable to accident and 9 per cent. to pre-accident bronchitis; this caused breathlessness and prevented him continuing with his pre-accident work on the coal face although he was still able to do reasonably heavy work. Due to his bronchitis he would in any event have had to give up work on coal face five years earlier than a man in sound health. Continuing loss of earnings of £686·40 per annum. Award—general damages for pain and suffering £2,000; damages for future loss of earnings £5,491·20. *Agreed special damages*: £2,221·27. *Total general damages*: £7,491·20. (*Ex rel. D. R. Bentley, Esq., Barrister.*)

Reproductive Organs

705. CAUGHLIN v. JONESCO (PRESTON) (June 7, 1979; Talbot J.; Preston). Male, aged 33. Former sheet metal worker. Hit by large piece of flying metal causing injuries to left upper thigh and groin and loss of one tooth. Large lump of flesh taken out of thigh. Left testicle had to be removed. No reduction in reproductive capacity and still able to perform sexual act, though occasionally trapped nerve led to sharp pain during intercourse resulting in loss of erection. After three years thigh still tender; was left with scarred area which was adherent to underlying tissues and bad scarring in area of hip which was not of major cosmetic importance because of its position; suffered aching in left leg when bent, burning sensation in leg after walking two or more miles or running and numbness after sitting cross-legged for some time. Divorced shortly before hearing and found injuries embarrassing and handicap in intimate relations with girl friends. Had given up playing snooker because of discomfort when pressure put on scarred area. Had given up pre-accident work and become paint-sprayer to avoid bending. No loss of earnings and no reduction in value on labour market. Off work eight months. No special damages. *General damages*: £4,000. (*Ex rel. Gerard F. McDermott, Esq., Barrister.*)

Hip

706. MORIARTY v. J. CAPELLA & SONS (January 20, 1979; T. P. Russell, Q.C.). Female, aged 62 at date of accident and 64 at date of trial. Part-time waitress earning £15 per week at time of accident. Fracture of hip. Hip replacement advisable sooner rather than later because of considerable pain which would be largely eliminated by this operation. *General damages*: £8,000 of which £2,000 for cost of hip replacement, £4,000 pain and suffering and loss of amenities, £2,000 loss of future wages at £20 per week. *Special damages*: £1,113. (*Ex rel. Jonathan Sofer, Esq., Barrister.*)

Wrist

707. BENTLEY *v.* KEELING (February 9, 1979; C.A.) Male aged 18 at time of accident, 25 at date of trial. Fracture of right scaphoid, not treated for three months. Bone graft from right radius. Off work 20 weeks. Right-handed. Unable to resume pre-accident work as apprentice engineer. Restriction of movement and 25 per cent. loss of grip. Osteo-arthritis already present; arthrodesis might be necessary in distant future. Damages for pain and suffering and loss of amenity £3,750. (There was no appeal against this). Continuing loss of earnings of £800 a year: award of £11,200, applying multiplier of 14. The Court of Appeal dismissed the defendants' appeal against this award. *Special damages*: £1,842. Total award of £16,792 was affirmed by Court of Appeal. (*Ex rel. Adam Pearson, Esq., Barrister.*)

708. SEWELL *v.* HUBBARD (July 20, 1979; Deputy Judge Lipfriend). Female, aged 69. Retired concert pianist who before accident had practised three to four hours daily for pleasure. Severe Colles' fracture of left wrist resulting in reduction of power in wrist and of span of hand. Now unable to play for more than half an hour at most and then only simple pieces. Had thus effectively lost her main pleasure in life. *Special damages*: £145. *General damages*: £3,500. (*Ex rel. Jonathan Sofer, Esq., Barrister.*)

Hand

709. BOWDEN *v.* THAMES BOARD MILLS (October 25, 1979; O'Connor J.). Male, aged 42 at date of accident in August 1977 and 44 at date of trial. Former finisher on board making machine, skilled work which he enjoyed. Right handed. Right hand trapped in rollers resulting in degloving of dorsum of hand as far as wrist. Complete loss of index, middle and ring fingers and partial loss of thumb and little finger. Underwent six major operations including skin grafts and attaching hand to groin flap for three weeks. Had had much pain and suffering. Only real function remaining in hand was gripping selected objects between stumps of thumb and little finger. Left with severe cosmetic disability, including obvious blemish with contour depression at donor site on right groin and thigh, and mild and superficial scarring on both upper arms and left thigh at donor sites. Scarring liable to breakdown and susceptible to minor trauma. Now unable to do car repairs, much restricted in jobs at home and unable to play cricket. Unable to resume pre-accident work, but had been kept on by defendant employers at same rate of pay operating fork-lift truck to move pallets. As result had lost job satisfaction. No continuing loss of earnings and job reasonably secure. But plaintiff concerned about his future, as there had been significant closures and redundancies in industry. Judge *held*, that his job security could not be considered by reference to defendant company alone and that other factors, such as possibility of change of management and other injury to plaintiff and illness, should be taken into account. Plaintiff now permanently unfit for many jobs and would be at considerable disadvantage on labour markets. Loss of earning capacity assessed at £6,000 and pain and suffering and loss of amenities at £15,000. No special damage. *Total general damages*: £21,000. (*Ex rel. Robin Thompson and Partners, Solicitors.*)

710. LANGTON *v.* M. TUGS (November 2, 1979; Judge Edgar Fay Q.C.). Male, aged 36 at date of accident in November 1974 and 41 at date of hearing. Former Thames lighterman. Right handed. Left hand caught in lifting tackle. Crush injuries to index, middle, ring and little fingers. Underwent surgical amputation of distal phalanx of index finger, of middle and ring fingers through proximal interphalangeal joint and of little finger to middle phalanx. As result of there being exposed bone in index, middle and ring fingers admitted to hospital for skin grafting operation to provide full thickness cover to these areas with flap from right upper arm. Underwent unpleasant experience of having arms joined together for three weeks. Readmitted to hospital in April 1975 because little finger not progressing and underwent further surgery to make stumps more presentable and useful. Left with permanent reduction of power in left hand of 30–40 per cent. Unable to pick up small objects from flat surface, had difficulty cutting up food and sometimes dropped fork. Suffered occasional "phantom" pains. Left with ugly $3\frac{1}{2}$ in. × $2\frac{1}{2}$ in. scar at donor site. Now often depressed and smoked and drank more than previously. Unable to row or play golf and had difficulty in making models with his children. Because of embarrassment no longer sunbathed or went swimming and tried to avoid eating out. Unable to resume pre-accident work and had suffered loss of job satisfaction through having to work ashore. Now employed as local authority refuse vehicle driver. Loss of earning capacity assessed at £1,500 and pain and suffering and loss of amenities and loss of enjoyment of work assessed at £7,500. Off work about nine months. *Special damages*: £947·35. *Total general damages*: £9,000. (*Ex rel. G. N. Webber, Esq., Barrister.*)

Fingers and Thumb

711.   HAMKALO v. BRITISH STEEL CORP. (April 2, 1979; Willis J.; Birmingham). Male, aged 26 at date of accident in September 1977 and nearly 28 at date of trial. Partially ambidextrous. Trainee spark tester. Right hand caught between rollers of steel mill and trapped for several minutes before release could be effected. Complete loss of ring and middle fingers, index finger amputated at proximal interphalangeal joint and little finger disarticulated at distal interphalangeal joint with fixed flexion of 90° at proximal interphalangeal joint. Thumb undamaged. Extensive scarring on palm and back of hand where skin rubbed off by rollers. Both remaining stumps numb. Retained power 4 grip for wrist, pencil, hook and pinch between index finger stump and thumb. Now unable to play golf, tennis or darts. Agreed continuing loss of earnings of £1,171 per annum to which multiplier of 17 applied, giving loss of future earnings of £19,907. Pain and suffering and loss of amenities assessed at £10,000. No special damages. Credit given for amount by which relevant statutory benefits exceeded past loss of earnings, viz. £128. *Total general damages*: £29,779. (*Ex rel. John Ungley, Esq., Barrister.*)

712.   HOWDEN v. BRITISH RAIL ENGINEERING (June 13, 1979; Balcombe J.; Newcastle-upon-Tyne). Male, aged 27. Machine operator. Left handed. Left hand glove caught on revolving tool and hand dragged on to tool resulting in traumatic amputation of left thumb through interphalangeal joint and loss of about $1\frac{1}{4}$ inch of that digit. Continuing pain in stump, particularly in cold weather. Able to resume pre-accident work and, although injury slowed him down, was able to earn his normal wage. Job reasonably secure. Loss of earning capacity assessed at £750 and pain and suffering and loss of amenities at £4,000. Minimal special damages. *Total general damages*: £4,750. (*Ex rel. Messrs. Evill and Coleman, Solicitors.*)

713.   ISAAC v. CHEMETRON (December 19, 1978; Comyn J.; Cardiff). Male aged 33 at date of accident, 36 at hearing. Machine operator, right handed. Left hand came into contact with grinding wheel injuring index finger. Surgical amputation at the level of the end joint leaving finger 1 in. short. Detained in hospital four days and then three months' physiotherapy. 18 months after accident second operation to remove a small nail remnant and a small neuroma, which involved four more days in hospital. Thereafter tip well healed, featureless and painless. Able to continue pre-accident employment but some handicap and awkwardness in certain activities connected with employment. Snooker playing made difficult. Comyn J. found no liability on the defendants but if he had would have awarded £2,000 general damages plus £950 agreed special damages. (*Ex rel. T. Tucker, Esq., Barrister.*)

714.   SMITH v. WAVIN PLASTICS (June 13, 1979; Judge White sitting as High Court Judge). Male, aged 53. Weighbridge operator. Apparently right-handed. Crushing injury to right index and middle fingers. Some scarring of both fingers and nails of each left shortened and deformed, though not very noticeable cosmetically. Some loss of grip and now unable to carry out intricate manipulation with injured fingers. Able to continue pre-accident work. No loss of earnings. No special damages. *General damages*: £1,400.

715. WOODESON *v.* BOVIS CIVIL ENGINEERING (September 26, 1979; Judge Garfitt; Cambridge County Ct.). Male, aged 23 at date of accident and 25 at date of hearing. Right handed. Builder's labourer. Right little finger trapped whilst stacking drainage pipes. Lacerations and contusions of proximal half of finger. Lacerations lightly sutured and sutures removed after two days. After three and a half weeks good range of mobility had returned and he resumed work after six weeks. After one week's work he was absent for further one and a half weeks due to strain imposed on finger. At date of hearing only residual disabilities were extensive scarring about one inch in length on palmar aspect of finger, lesser scarring of about half an inch in length on dorsal aspect, slight thickening of skin around joint and loss of extremes of flexion and extension. Loss of mobility of finger and scarring would improve in short term and prognosis was good. Development of degenerative changes unlikely. *Agreed special damages*: £184·77. *General damages*: £600. (*Ex rel. Simon Tattersall, Esq., Barrister.*)

Leg

716. DUFFY *v.* VIBIXA (July 26, 1979; Kenneth Jones J.; Bristol). Male, aged 40 at date of accident in March 1973 and 46 at date of hearing. Machine minder. Suffered severe injuries to left leg and foot when work set on pallets fell on him. Compound fractures of left tibia and fibula, cuboid and cuneiform bones, third, fourth and fifth metatarsals and dislocation of second metatarso-phalangeal joint. Plating and screwing of tibial fracture and wire fixation of foot bones required. Eventually returned to work wearing leg caliper, but treatment to save limb continued until October 1975 when below-knee amputation performed. Subsequently had nine prostheses made and required further trimming of stump. About six months after amputation returned to work again, but had further lengthy absences. Judge found that plaintiff would be able to work as trained estimator and accordingly assessed loss of future earnings at £23,810 based on multiplier of 10 and agreed partial continuing net loss of earnings of £2,381 p.a. Damages for loss of earning capacity assessed at £3,450 and for pain and suffering and loss of amenities at £16,000. *Agreed special damages*: £7,450. *Total general damages*: £43,260. (*Ex rel. Messrs. Brian Thompson and Partners, Solicitors.*)

717. MARTIN *v.* HALL (February 7, 1979; Deputy Judge Bruce Griffiths, Q.C.; Swansea). Male, aged about 43 at date of accident in March 1976 and 46 at date of hearing. Former site manager for major poultry producer. Fractures to both femoral shafts, right tibia and fibula and brain damage due to subsequent development of fat embolism in bloodstream which passed into brain. Owing to latter development whilst being prepared for operation for fractures he became unconscious and his general condition was considered critical. Remained unconscious for three weeks. In hospital for total period of some nine months, where he underwent conservative treatment to fractures. Fat embolism had caused some form of damage to fluid-carrying section of brain and widening of cerebral sulci which were found to be far wider than normal for man of his age. Brain scan showed evidence of small areas of atrophy which were present in body of brain tissue in areas which were not regenerative, especially the temples, and which were likely to affect hearing and speech. His speech was now slow and hesitant and he paused to a noticeable extent. He experienced lack of concentration which was reflected in deterioration in his ability at chess. His personality had been blunted and flattened. He had lost zest for life due to brain damage and overlay from other injuries. Left leg shortened by ¼″. Left with severe limitation of movement in both knees and possible minor limitation of movements in left hip. Maximum distance which he would be capable of walking would be in region of a quarter of a mile. Unable to squat or adopt full kneeling position and would experience great difficulty in cramped spaces. Arthritic changes likely to develop in both knees and in years to come joint replacement might be necessary. Would probably never drive again and would have to travel on public transport. Unable to resume pre-accident job. Now fit only for sedentary work. Had been unemployed since accident, but it was agreed that within 18 to 24 months he would obtain employment of some kind in Civil Service. Loss of future earnings assessed at £15,000 based on multiplier of 10 and taking account of fact that in his pre-accident job: (1) he had lived in tied house, rent and rates-free (whereas he now had to pay both); (2) he had received a regular Christmas bonus award; (3) he had received a chicken and two-and-a-half dozen eggs a week free; and (4) and he had free use of telephone. Pain and suffering and loss of amenities assessed at £17,500. *Agreed special damages*: £5001·25. *Total general damages*: £32,500. *Per curiam*: It was not right to assess general damages for pain and suffering and loss of amenities for leg injuries as a percentage of what the courts award for a below-knee amputation. (*Ex rel. Messrs. Brian Thompson and Partners*, Solicitors.)

718.   CHARLES v. HOLMES (July 12, 1979; Deputy Judge Sir Basil Nield; Lincoln). Female, aged 16 at date of accident and almost 18 at date of hearing. Former student at College of Technology doing one-year course in office studies with view to obtaining clerical job. Multiple crush injuries of right leg, splitting laceration of right groin and numerous deep abrasions on outer aspect of left leg. In hospital seven weeks. After six days right leg amputated at mid-shaft of thigh level. After discharge from hospital received out-patient treatment for about eight months during which time she was fitted with prosthesis. Did not resume pre-accident course, but in January 1979 started similar course instituted by Department of Employment. Had made good physical and mental recovery from effects of injuries, but remained concerned over restrictions upon her mobility. Left with extensive scarring of right thigh and of left leg involving lateral aspect of knee in two areas and lateral malleolus also in two areas, latter amounting to serious cosmetic disability in view of judge. Deprived of her previous enjoyment of all forms of sport and outdoor activities. Engaged to be married to second defendant, but there had been difficulties between them and future of relationship uncertain. Claim for partial loss of future earnings rejected. Loss of earning capacity assessed at £4,500. Pain and suffering and loss of amenities assessed at £22,000, taking into account scarring. £1,500 awarded as contribution towards cost of purchasing specially adapted car with accelerator pedal moved to left of foot-brake pedal and having automatic transmission. *Total general damages*: £28,000. (*Ex rel. Messrs. John Latham & Co., Solicitors.*)

719.   LEWIS v. GRAY (November 11, 1979; Boreham J.; Teesside). Male, aged 48. Foreman. As result of accident in January 1977 sustained comminuted fracture of upper third of shaft of left femur and bruising to neck and left shoulder. In hospital three months. Still suffered minor discomfort in form of aching and some slight·loss of movement in neck and shoulder. Fracture had united soundly with minimal shortening of about 1·5 cms. Now wore permanent raise in left shoe. Some continuing pain in left hip from time to time. Left knee now hyperextended due to ligaments being stretched and he had been advised to wear knee brace to prevent deterioration. Slight possibility of late arthritic changes in left knee, but these would not affect his work until he was 60. Off work nine months. *General damages*: £5,500 (including £500 for loss of earning capacity due to handicap on labour market after age of 60). (*Ex rel. P. H. Bowers, Esq., Barrister.*)

720.   HOPKINS v. McCLUSKIE-BEATTIE (February 2, 1979; Master Lubbock). Female, aged 21, housewife, injured, whilst pregnant, in road collision with lorry in February 1977. Laceration to the nose. Closed fracture of the mid-shaft of the left femur. Kuntschner nail inserted and shunted up the femur through an exit wound in the buttock and back past the point of fracture. Detained for three weeks in hospital. Suffered discomfort about the left hip until nail removed in April 1978. Unable to bear weights for six months. Child born unharmed after normal labour. Substantial recovery although some difficulty in negotiating stairs and walking distance restricted to 1½ miles due to ache about the knee. This would improve with time. No limp. Left with noticeable scarring around site of nail, 8 in. long and ½ in. wide and 2½ in. red scar on left hip. Embarrassed to go swimming and to undress in front of husband. Scarring could be improved with operation costing £600. Also scarring along bridge of nose ¾ in. but not obstrusive. Shortening of left leg by ½ in. warranting use of raised shoe to avoid back trouble later on. Function of left leg will always be restricted to a minor degree. Capacity to play tennis a little restricted and will never be very athletic again. No loss of earnings. Master Lubbock approved overall settlement by consent of £5,000 (*Ex rel. Keith Hornby, Esq., Barrister.*)

721. HOLDEN *v.* BEADSMORE (July 27, 1979; Deputy Judge Hayman). Male, aged 18 at time of accident in February 1975 and 22 at date of hearing. Skilled borer with machine-tool company. Comminuted and slightly displaced fracture of right patella and transverse fracture of second metatarsal shaft of left ankle. Not detained in hospital initially. Left foot supported by crepe bandage for a time and right leg in plaster for a month. Then underwent physiotherapy. Left ankle injury cleared up, but in April 1976 ankle gave way, he fell and re-fractured right patella. Right leg again in plaster for a month after which underwent further physiotherapy. Continued to suffer persistent pain in knee and injury pre-disposed him to develop osteo-arthritis. As result in April 1978 underwent operation for removal of right patella. Now left with distinct weakness of right knee, which might improve as thigh muscles strengthened, and residual pain in damp weather and after prolonged standing or exercise. There was medical evidence that due to traumatic neurosis he was maximising his symptoms. Compelled to give up previous hobbies of football, tennis and dancing. Off work for total of 28 weeks. *Agreed special damages*: £134·83. *General damages*: £4,000. *Per curiam*: General damages award reflected fact that scale of damages had gone up and awards were being increased across the board. (*Ex rel. Miss Rozanna Malcolm, Barrister.*)

722. MULLALY *v.* BROMLEY LONDON BOROUGH (June 20, 1979; Deputy Judge Oddie). Male, aged about 18 at date of accident and 23 at date of hearing. Student. Fractured femur and other injuries. In hospital 20 weeks. Underwent operation for insertion of pin in femur. In traction 16 weeks during which time had good deal of pain and suffering. Almost complete recovery by time of hearing, but hobbies of walking and sailing curtailed. Likely to develop osteo-arthritis in his forties. Now studying to become a dentist. Although much of this work could be done in seated position, would be required to stand for about 25 per cent. of time. Expected onset of osteo-arthritis would make work awkward for him, but would not stop him working. *Agreed special damages*: £980. *General Damages*: £2,750.

Knee

723. BALL *v.* VAUGHAN BROS. (DROP FORGINGS) (June 26, 1979; Hodgson J.; Birmingham). Male, aged 20 at the date of accident, and 22 at the date of hearing. Employed in defendants' forging bay. In about August or September 1976 suffered torn cartilage in left knee as result of accident whilst playing football. In consequence would inevitably have had to undergo operation for removal of cartilage within very near future if he had continued playing any type of sport and within a few years or even a few months if he had stopped playing all types of sport. In January 1977 slipped on snow and slush at place of work and fell to ground, twisting left knee. Suffered pain in knee for a few weeks after which underwent meniscotemy. *Agreed special damages*: £500·32. *General damages* (for slight acceleration of cartilage operation and pain and suffering caused by relevant accident): £500. (*Ex rel. Rowleys & Blewitts, Solicitors.*)

Ankle

724. EATON *v.* CONCRETE NORTHERN (January 11, 1979; C.A.). Male aged about 44 at date of accident in April 1972 and 50 at date of trial. Former crane driver. Fracture dislocation of right ankle involving lateral malleolus, anterior articular surface of lower end of tibia and outer surface of talus. Underwent nine surgical operations and manipulations, including arthrodesis of ankle in November 1973. Degenerative changes in tarsal area had permanently reduced movements of foot and tarsal joint to one-half of normal. Now restricted in running, walking over uneven ground and weight bearing and suffered aching pain in foot after exertion and following rest. Incapable of resuming pre-accident work. Able to work as van driver or clerical assistant, but, owing to fact that lived in area of high unemployment, no such work was available. At date of trial employed as cleaner. Payne J.

(October 31, 1977; Liverpool) assessed loss of future earnings at £2,808 based on multiplicand of £312 and multiplier of 9 and pain and suffering and loss of amenities at £4,500. Court of Appeal increased award in respect of future loss of earnings to £7,000. *Agreed special damages*: £7,068. *Total general damages*: £11,500. (*Ex rel. Marilyn Mornington, Barrister.*)

725. FRANCIS *v.* BRITISH RAILWAYS BOARD (November 8, 1979; Kenneth Jones J.). Female, aged 58 at date of accident in October 1977 and 61 at date of hearing. Pre-existing Halix Valgus condition which had been treated by bilateral Kellers operation leaving deformation in both feet and slight pre-existing osteo-arthritis in both knees which accentuated walking difficulties. Struck by mechanical trolley when disembarking from train. Pott's fracture to right ankle with fracture of medial malleolus. In plaster from three weeks initially then underwent operation under general anaesthetic for fixing of fracture of malleolus with screw. Moderate to good recovery. One inch thickening of ankle. About 10 per cent. restriction of ankle movement. Possibility of development of osteo-arthritis in ankle within 10 years. Had ceased work shortly after accident, but this unrelated to injuries. *Special damages*: £190. *General damages*: £3,000. (*Ex rel. Stephen Rubin, Esq., Barrister.*)

726. GRAINGER *v.* BRITISH STEEL CORP. (November 9, 1978; Park J.; Birmingham). Male aged 24, sustained fracture to the inner side of the left ankle joint. The plaintiff was an in-patient in hospital for four days and, in that time, whilst under a general anaesthetic, he had a pin inserted into the fracture of the ankle joint. The plaintiff was not in plaster of Paris; he was on crutches for three weeks and he was attending hospital as an out-patient for eight or nine weeks; he then returned to work. The medical evidence concluded that the plaintiff was doing extremely well from a fracture on the inner side of the ankle joint, and from an examination of the ankle and the state of the X-rays the plaintiff will recover completely. The fracture was reduced to an absolutely excellent position and the clinical state likewise was excellent. The plaintiff had made a good recovery from the injuries and the outlook for the future was absolutely excellent. The effects of the injury had long since passed by and the plaintiff had a highly satisfactory ankle. *General damages*: £1,250. *Agreed special damages*: £211. (*Ex rel. Messrs. Rowleys & Blewitts, Solicitors.*)

Foot

727. BERRY *v.* FORD MOTOR CO. (June 22, 1979; Caulfield J.). Male, aged 22 at date of accident and 26 at date of hearing. Roof repairer. Fracture of navicular bone and oscalcis of left foot, fracture of ribs on right side resulting in surgical emphysema in right lung and partial severing of tendon in right thumb. In hospital three weeks. Underwent underwater drainage of right side of chest. Wore arch support for left foot three months. Complete recovery from chest injuries. Had regained almost complete use of right hand and full use of left foot. But foot tended to ache after walking long distances or digging garden and he had difficulty in walking on sloping roofs. Osteo-arthritis had developed in foot and operation might be necessary in future. Had obtained better paid job with defendant employers, but change of job might be necessary in future as osteo-arthritis worsened. No longer able to play rugby. Loss of earning capacity assessed at £1,500 and pain and suffering and loss of amenities at £8,000. *Special damages*: £196·08. *Total general damages*: £9,500. (*Ex rel. Messrs. Evill and Coleman, Solicitors.*)

728. FISK *v.* LAWRENCE HEYS (May 9, 1979; Bush J.; Manchester). Male, aged 37 at date of accident in August 1971 and 44 at date of hearing. Former television aerial rigger. As result of collapse of ladder on which descending suffered serious injuries to both feet consisting of fractures of left cuboid and right os calcis. Left foot in plaster for one year in all. After seven and a half months underwent arthrodesis of joint between cuboid and os calcis. Had eventually made substantial recovery from injury to right foot, but had continuing severe pain in left foot. Although now did more sedentary job, was still in great pain and difficulty at end of day, feeling drained of energy, and needed much more sleep. Had been taking pain killing drugs and sleeping tablets, but sleep regularly disturbed by burning sensation in left foot. Unable to pursue pre-accident activities of walking, shooting, camping and home decorating. Serious possibility of future triple arthrodesis of left foot and consequent lengthy absence from work. No evidence of any substantial risk that would lose job. Out of work nearly three years. *Agreed special damages:* £749·14. *General damages:* £6,500. (*Ex rel. A. Vos, Esq., Barrister.*)

729.   SAMUELS *v.* SMITH FOUNDRIES (November 1979; Forbes J.; Birmingham). Male, aged 56 at date of accident. Stacka-truck driver. Heavy casting fell on left foot causing fracture of terminal phalanx of left great toe. Subsequently adhesions had developed in toe, but plaintiff had not received any further treatment. Continuing moderate pain in toe for which he took mild pain killing tablets. Unable to walk normally and tended to avoid pressure on toe by walking on outside of foot. Pain might subside a little in time. Had resumed his pre-accident employment. Slight risk that might lose this job in future. If so, would be at some disadvantage on open labour market. Loss of earning capacity assessed at £250 and pain and suffering and loss of amenities at £3,500. Off work 12 weeks. *Agreed special damages:* £330·44. *Total general damages:* £3,750. (*Ex. rel. Nicholas J. Worsley, Esq., Barrister.*)

730.   IVES *v.* NEWMAN AND HIGGENS (April 5, 1979; Michael Davies J.). Male, aged 46 at date of accident and 48 at trial. Plumber. As result of fall from unfooted ladder suffered fracture of navicular bone of right foot. In below-knee plaster for six weeks. No residual limitation of movement and no risk of osteo-arthritis. Still had occasional twinges of pain when walking on rough ground or climbing ladder. In five to 10 years might have some slight increase in symptoms, particularly when walking on rough ground, but not sufficient to disturb his work pattern. No continuing loss of earnings or loss of earning capacity. Off work three months in all. *Special damages:* £460. *General damages:* £2,500 (*Gardener v. Fishel* reported in Kemp and Kemp, *Quantum of damages* (4th ed.), Vol. 2, para. 10–519 referred to). (*Ex rel. Jonathan Sofer, Esq., Barrister.*)

Miscellaneous Injuries

731.   SCURIAGA *v.* POWELL (*Daily Telegraph* and *Daily Mail,* May 19, 1979; Watkins J.). Female, aged 22 at date of operation and 29 at date of trial. Unmarried. Disabled by polio. Former trainee teacher. Became pregnant and underwent lawful abortion operation which, owing to negligence of defendant surgeon, was unsuccessful. Five weeks after operation plaintiff discovered she was still pregnant. After seven months gave birth to healthy son, now aged six. Now lived alone with son whom she was bringing up. Future loss of earnings assessed at £7,500; ruined marriage prospects at £3,500 and pain and suffering at £750. *Special damages:* £7,000. *Total general damages:* £11,750.

Minor Injuries

732.   CUST *v.* MILLIGAN (November 6, 1979; Judge Chapman Q.C.; York County Ct.). Girl, aged 14 at date of accident in March 1978. Knocked off her bicycle by car and sustained fracture to right ankle, multiple lacerations on left side of face and two lacerations on forehead at hair line. Ankle in plaster five weeks during which she was absent from school and lost opportunity of visit to Germany on exchange basis. In considerable pain for two weeks and underwent course of pain killing tablets. Suffered mild pain in ankle in damp weather for a year. Full recovery from ankle injury, but slight risk of osteo-arthritis in later life. Left with three small gouge marks on left side of face by ear, measuring $\frac{3}{4}$in., $\frac{1}{8}$in. and $\frac{1}{2}$in. in diameter, two 1in. scars and $\frac{1}{2}$in. scar on forehead at hair line. Only gouges would be permanent. Judge described scars as only " blemishes," but *held*, that they had produced slight change in appearance. Plaintiff had altered her hair style because felt self-conscious of scars. Cosmetic disability assessed at £400, pain and suffering from ankle injury at £400 and loss of amenities at £600. *Agreed special damages:* £97·94. *Total general damages:* £1,400. (*Ex rel. George M. Marriott, Esq., Barrister.*)

733.   CORDING *v.* BRITISH STEEL CORP. (November 16, 1979; Deputy Judge G. J. Jones; Newport County Ct.). Male, aged 58. Carpenter. Fracture of terminal phalanx of left great toe. Very painful injury. Returned to work after

nine weeks. During absence from work unable to drive, work in garden or pursue hobby of old-time and sequence dancing. Complete recovery. *Agreed special damages*: £121·38. *General damages*: £450. (*Ex rel. Charles S. Welchman, Esq., Barrister.*)

734. PENFOLD *v.* ABBOTT AND FORD MOTOR CO. (February 7, 1979; Mr. Registrar Nicholson; Canterbury). Schoolboy, aged 16, knocked off bicycle by defendant's van. Temporary concussion; abrasions to eyebrow, cheek, left knee and shin; suspected fracture of right wrist not confirmed by X-ray. "Tubigrip" support fitted. Sporting activity and writing inhibited for three weeks. Pain in wrist and persistent headaches for 10 months. Epilepsy risk not more than 1 per cent. *Agreed special damages*: £43·22. *General damages*: £350 (£50 for increased epilepsy risk). (*Ex rel. D. Smart, Esq., Barrister.*)

735. EDMOND *v.* SHIPPEY (November 13, 1979; Judge Lauriston Q.C.; Whitby County Ct.). Male in his 30s. Police sergeant. Attacked by alsatian dog and suffered single, severe bite to top of leg causing puncture marks and bruising. "Very frightening incident" in which dog hanging on to leg for some time before being beaten off. Required hospital out-patient treatment, including injections. Leg painful and for about six weeks unable to sit comfortably, after which there was full recovery. No time off work. *General damages*: £175. (*Ex rel. Kenneth Gillance, Esq., Barrister.*)

736. HINKLEY *v.* HALL (July 24, 1979; His Honour Judge Sumner; Canterbury County Ct.). Male in his 30s. Injured in a road accident. Some bruising of left knee, which lasted a fortnight, and shock. Walked with a limp, suffered pain in knee and did not feel well enough to drive for a week. Took pain-killing drugs which he already had, but did not see doctor until 3½ weeks after accident by which time had made full recovery. *General damages*: £150. (*Ex rel. Nicholas Davidson, Esq., Barrister.*)

Osteo-Arthritis

737. STEWART *v.* NATIONAL COAL BOARD (November 11, 1979; Waterhouse J.; Sheffield). Male, aged 39 at date of accident and 42 at date of trial. Former colliery face worker who would probably have continued this work until aged 60 and then retired under defendant's early retirement scheme. As result of being struck by mine car suffered cut to finger, injury to back and injury to right knee resulting in development of osteo-arthritis in knee. Full recovery from injuries to finger and back within a fortnight. Off work for 10 months, then returned to light work underground. After two years underwent exploratory operation on knee followed by course of physiotherapy involving further three months off work. Then resumed light work underground. Left with 2½in. operation scar on inner side of knee. Still had some pain on inner side of knee every day for a few hours which was made worse by walking which job involved. Knee felt liable to give way and there was crepitus on full flexion. Permanently unfit for face work, but would probably be able to manage present light job for foreseeable future. Risk that might have to transfer to work on colliery surface towards end of working life due to progress of degenerative changes in knee which would involve loss of earnings. Present continuing loss of earnings £354·48 a year. Had had to give up previous pastimes as member of Territorial Army and training alsatian dogs, now had difficulty with gardening and ability to go on long walks affected. Future loss of earnings assessed at £3,750 based on multiplier of about 10½. Pain and suffering and loss of amenities assessed at £4,000. No award for loss of earning capacity as employment secure. *Special damages*: £2,110. *Total general damages*: £7,750. (*Ex rel. D. R. Bentley, Esq., Barrister.*)

738. BROOKES *v.* BRISTOL OMNIBUS CO. (October 26, 1979; Lawson J.). Male, aged 55 at date of accident and 57 at date of trial. Public service vehicle driver. Wife crippled with arthritis and depended upon him for care and assistance. Worked special hours by arrangement with employers. Multiple abrasions, contusions and lacerations of both legs causing infra-patellar bursitis in right knee and effusion and extensive subcutaneous haematoma in ecchymosis formation about left lower thigh and knee. Pre-existing osteo-arthritis aggra-

vated by factor of two to three years. Aggravation most severe in left knee and leg. Small degree of aggravation, not exceeding two to three years, in varicose vein condition. Left with pigmented scar on right calf. Right knee seat of variable pain and occasional swelling with some local radiation of symptoms and tendency to morning stiffness. Left knee also seat of variable pain, grating, swelling and morning stiffness. Injuries more serious because now less able to care for wife, *e.g.* by carrying her up and down stairs. Effective working life as vehicle driver shortened by estimated two to three years, Would probably be able to obtain other work when unable to continue vehicle driving, but probably at lower rate of pay. Future loss of earnings assessed at £3,000 and pain and suffering and loss of amenities at £3,000. *Agreed special damages*: £155. *Total general damages*: £6,000. (*Ex rel. Brian Thompson and Partners, Solicitors.*)

739. Sale of land—repudiation—date damages calculated. See WOODFORD ESTATES *v.* POLLACK, § 2776.

740. Spoilt holiday—racial discrimination
Defendant landlady refused accommodation to the plaintiff, a Pakistani. As a result he was unable to join his white *de facto* wife and family in a holiday flat and had to take accommodation with his wife in a nearby hotel leaving the two children with the grandparents in the flat. *Held,* that (1) the refusal was the result of the defendant's consideration of her other customers' likely prejudices rather than her own views; (2) she did not know the plaintiff was the husband to the family; (3) the last two days of their holiday had been spoilt, although it was not the same as the case of a ruined holiday abroad in a bad hotel. The defendant had made a very handsome apology to the plaintiff in court. Award: alternative accommodation £15; additional meals £10; spoilt holiday £25; hurt feelings £25. Total award: £75: WEBSTER *v.* JOHNSON, November 28, 1979, Leeds County Ct., Judge Nevin. (*Ex rel. S. Grenfell, Esq., Barrister.*)

741. Trespass—provocation—exemplary damages. See TAYLOR *v.* REES, § 2733.

ARTICLES. See *post*, p. [20.].

DEATH DUTIES

742. Estate duty
ESTATE DUTY (INTEREST ON UNPAID DUTY) ORDER 1979 (No. 1690) [10p], made under the Finance Act 1970 (c. 24), s. 30; operative on January 1, 1980; increases to 9 per cent. the rate of interest paid on unpaid estate duty and repayments of overpaid estate duty.

743. —— armed forces—exemption—whether wound cause of death
[Finance Act 1952 (c. 41), s. 71 (1).]
Construing s. 71 (1) of the Finance Act 1952, a person "died from a wound" if as a result of the wound he died earlier than he would have done had he not sustained the wound.
In 1944 the deceased was wounded on active service; he died of cancer in 1967. The executors claimed exemption from estate duty on the basis that he had "died from a wound inflicted" on active service. The council that heard the application found as a fact that the septicaemia he had developed as a result of the wound was a significant condition which had contributed to his death, but refused the application. The executors sought a declaration that the council should have issued the appropriate exemption certificate. *Held,* making the declaration, that given the findings of fact and applying a true construction of s. 71 (1) to those facts, the inevitable conclusion was that the wound was a cause of death. (Dictum of Megaw J. in *R.* v. *Criminal Injuries Compensation Board, ex p. Ince* [1973] C.L.Y. 506 applied.)
BARTY-KING *v.* MINISTRY OF DEFENCE [1979] 2 All E.R. 80, May J.

744. —— controlled company—shares—benefit accruing
[Finance Act 1940 (c. 29), ss. 46, 47, 58 (3).] At the date of his death the deceased held 40 per cent of the ordinary shares of a company which at all material times had been controlled by not more than five persons including the deceased. The Crown claimed to value the shares by reference to the assets of the company, and for this purpose it became necessary to determine the

proportion that the aggregate amount of the benefits accruing to the deceased from the company bore to the net income of the company. *Held*, affirming the decision of Sir Robert Megarry V.-C., that benefits accruing to the deceased included not only dividends received by him but also the increase in the value of his shares resulting from the retention of income by the company: I.R.C. *v.* STANDARD INDUSTRIAL TRUST [1979] S.T.C. 372, C.A.

745. —— **discretionary trust—power to accumulate income after settlor's death.** See BAIRD *v.* LORD ADVOCATE, § 2416.

746. —— **income—power to accumulate**
[Scot.] [Finance Act 1894 (c. 30), s. 2 (1) (*b*) (iv); Trusts (Scotland) Act 1961 (c. 57), s. 5; Law Reform (Miscellaneous Provisions) (Scotland) Act 1966 (c. 19).] In 1958 the deceased settled property on discretionary trusts, the trustees being given a power to accumulate income arising during the trust period. As at the date of the deceased's death in 1972 the trust deed had not been terminated nor had the trust period expired. The Inland Revenue maintained that estate duty was chargeable on the value of the trust fund under F.A. 1894, s. 2 (1) (*b*) (iv). *Held*, that by virtue of s. 5 of the Trusts (Scotland) Act 1961, the power to accumulate terminated on the death of the truster, and that the settled property was accordingly chargeable to estate duty: TRUSTEES OF THE LATE SIR JAMES DOUGLAS WISHART THOMSON *v.* I.R.C. [1978] T.R. 171, Ct. of Session.

DEEDS AND BONDS

747. Rectification—conveyance—mistake by solicitor
W owned a half-acre plot with a house on the southern part. He divided it into two parts with a fence, and put the southern part up for sale. B inspected the property, and it was made clear at all times that only the southern part and the house were being sold. B bought the property, but by mistake W's solicitors negligently included the whole property in the contract and the conveyance. W obtained rectification of the conveyance. B appealed. *Held*, dismissing the appeal, rectification can be granted even when there is a negligent mistake by the solicitor of one of the parties. There had been a common intention and the instruments did not carry it out. If B had noticed the mistake before signing but had carried on without telling W, rectification would still be granted. (*Barrow* v. *Isaacs & Son* [1891] 1 Q.B. 417 applied): WEEDS V. BLANEY (1977) 247 E.G. 211, C.A.

DIVORCE AND MATRIMONIAL CAUSES

748. Ancillary relief—ex parte orders
Upon W's *ex parte* application, unsupported by sworn evidence and made on terms that W would file a petition for judicial separation within a certain time, the trial judge ordered H to pay W forthwith half of the moneys in their building society joint account. *Held*, allowing H's appeal, that the order made was wholly wrong and quite contrary to the concept of justice. *Ex parte* orders should only ever be made after careful deliberation about what effect they would have. Order discharged: JACKSON V. JACKSON (1978) 9 Fam. Law 56, C.A.

749. Appeals—from Registrars—procedure
The following Practice Direction was issued by the Family Division on February 26, 1979:
1. As from March 12, 1979, on entering an appeal to a judge from a judgment, order or decision of a Registrar exercising Family Division jurisdiction in the High Court or in the county court the following procedure will apply.
2. Where the appellant is represented by a solicitor, he shall—
    (a) at the time of entering the appeal, certify (if this is the case) that it has been agreed with the solicitor for the respondent that nothing in any oral evidence taken before the Registrar is relevant to any issue arising on the appeal, and that no notes of evidence will be lodged, and

(b) unless otherwise directed, and subject as aforesaid, lodge prior to the hearing of the appeal a copy of the Registrar's notes of evidence and judgment (if any) or a copy of any such notes as have been prepared and agreed by the parties' legal advisers and approved by the Registrar.

3. Where the appellant is acting in person, he should lodge a copy of any notes of evidence and judgment that are available to him. If none are available the respondent's solicitor (if any) shall, after service of the notice of the appeal, comply with the obligations imposed by para. 2 (a) and (b) above as if he were acting for the appellant and inform the appellant of the lodging of such notes and (if so requested) supply to him a copy thereof on payment of the usual copying charges.

4. Where both parties to the appeal are acting in person, the Registrar shall, where possible, make a note for the assistance of the judge hearing the appeal and shall, prior to the hearing, furnish each party with a copy of that note or certify that no note can be made.

[1979] 1 W.L.R. 284.

750. Conflict of laws. See CONFLICT OF LAWS.

751. Costs

MATRIMONIAL CAUSES (COSTS) RULES 1979 (No. 399) [40p], made under the Matrimonial Causes Act 1973 (c. 18), s. 50; operative on April 24, 1979; introduces a new composite scale (" the matrimonial scale ") for the taxation of costs in matrimonial proceedings in the High Court, in a divorce county court or in both.

752. —— matrimonial causes

The following Practice Direction was issued by the Family Division on April 11, 1979:

1. The amendment to Ord. 62, App. 2, provided by the Rules of the Supreme Court (Amendment) 1979, has been accompanied by the introduction of a new " Matrimonial Scale," contained in the Matrimonial Causes (Costs) Rules 1979, applicable to the costs of matrimonial proceedings both in the divorce county court and in the Family Division. The new App. 2 will apply to all taxations governed by R.S.C., Ord. 62 other than matrimonial proceedings, with effect from April 24, 1979. The matrimonial scale will apply with effect from the same date to all matrimonial proceedings. As from April 24, 1979, therefore the position with regard to taxations in the Family Division and the divorce county courts will be as follows: —

(a) the costs of matrimonial proceedings in a divorce county court will be governed by the Matrimonial Causes (Costs) Rules 1979 and the County Court Rules (as applied by the Matrimonial Causes Rules 1977) and may be taxed in accordance with the matrimonial scale,

(b) the costs of matrimonial proceedings in the High Court (Family Division) will be governed by the Matrimonial Causes (Costs) Rules 1979 and the Rules of the Supreme Court (as applied by the Matrimonial Causes Rules 1977) and may be taxed in accordance with the matrimonial scale,

(c) the costs of non-matrimonial proceedings assigned to the Family Division (for example, applications in respect of wardship, guardianship, adoption, under the Inheritance Act, etc.) will be governed by the Rules of the Supreme Court and may be taxed in accordance with the new App. 2,

(d) the costs of an appeal to the Court of Appeal from a decision of a Judge of the Family Division will also be governed by the Rules of the Supreme Court and may be taxed in accordance with the new App. 2.

(*Note*: (i) " matrimonial proceedings " are defined by r. 2 (2) of the Matrimonial Causes Rules 1977 as " any proceedings with respect to which rules may be made under section 50 of the Matrimonial Causes Act of 1973."

(ii) the High Court business assigned to the Family Division is set out in Sched. 1 to the Administration of Justice Act 1970.)

in Sched. 1 to the Administration of Justice Act 1970)

2. The new App. 2 has been designed to simplify the process of drawing, reading and taxing a contentious bill of costs and thereby to reduce the time

and expense of the taxation procedure. The matrimonial scale, with the same objective in view, follows the form of the new App. 2 as closely as possible, consistent with the particular requirements of the proceedings to which it is to be applied. It follows that for the first time matrimonial proceedings in the divorce county court and in the High Court will be subject to a common scale of costs, the items in the present divorce scale having been converted into their High Court equivalents, although the amount of the allowance will for the most part remain different. The new scales have been constructed by merging items which are similar in nature and by abandoning other items which are either obsolete or which ought properly to be considered as part of a solicitor's normal overhead costs and as such provided for in his expense rate. The two Tables set out in Scheds. 1 and 2 hereto show (i) how the items in the former App. 2 have been assimilated to the items in the new Appendix or abolished and (ii) how the items in the divorce county court scale have been assimilated to the items in the matrimonial scale or abolished.

Division into parts

3. The new scales will apply, subject to the transitional provisions, to all bills lodged after the appointed day no matter when the work was done so that it will not usually be necessary to divide bills into separate parts for work done before and after that day. It will still be necessary to divide bills into parts, as at present to show separately work done before and after the introduction of VAT and before and after the issue of a civil aid certificate. Also, because the allowance for the various items will vary in amount as between work done in the divorce county court and in the High Court, there must still be a division of the work into parts as between the different courts.

Block allowance

4. The one major difference between the new App. 2 and the matrimonial scale is that in the new App. 2 a new procedure has been introduced in the form of the block allowance prescribed in Part II item 5. This will apply to all actions for personal injury and may, if the party entitled to the costs so elects, apply to any other action or proceedings, subject, in either case, to a direction to the contrary made by taxing officer. It was considered that the block allowance procedure generally would not be appropriate in respect of matrimonial proceedings and it has not been included in the matrimonial scale.

5. The object of the block allowance is to simplify and hasten taxation. It is intended to provide reasonable allowance for the items in Part 1 taken as a whole. It would not be appropriate to elect to insert a block allowance and then on taxation to seek to apply under R.S.C., Ord. 62, r. 32 (2) for a large increase over the permitted maximum. If the case warrants substantial Part 1 charges beyond the maximum, the new procedure should not be chosen. If a block allowance is included in a divided bill it must be apportioned between the several parts but the total allowed by the taxing officer will not exceed the amount which would have been allowed if the bill had not been divided.

6. The lodging of a bill which includes a block allowance will in general be taken as a sufficient election but since the taxing officer may, of his own motion, refuse to accept the election without affording the elector the right to be heard, a preliminary application may if so desired be made *ex parte* by letter in cases in which there is real doubt or difficulty.

7. When it is intended to make use of the block allowance procedure in non-matrimonial proceedings, the bill is to be drawn in the usual form, that is to say the various items for which a charge would normally have been made should continue to be set out in chronological order. However, no profit cost allowances should be included in respect of those items which fall within the scope of items comprised in Part I of App. 2 and the claim for the block allowance under Part II should be inserted just before the claim in respect of item 10, preparation for trial.

Miscellaneous provisions in respect of App. 2 and the matrimonial scale

8. Preparation of proofs of evidence should be charged under Item 10 and not under Item 3.

9. In cases to which the Part II block allowance does not apply, copy documents required to be exhibited to an affidavit should be charged under Item 4 and the collating time under Item 10 (see note (a)). There will no longer be a separate charge for marking exhibits.

10. Attendance in Court or in chambers should appear with a note of the time engaged. Similarly attendances on Counsel in conference or consultation should have the time noted.

11. It is intended that an attendance for directions only in the course of an ancillary application shall be charged under Item 6, not Item 8, of the matrimonial scale. Similarly, an attendance on a pre-trial review hearing will be allowed under Item 6, not Item 8, of the scale.

12. There is no longer a separate profit charge for service of any process. Where a solicitor makes use of a process server, that process server's charges should be shown as a disbursement. Where another solicitor is instructed solely to serve process, his charge also may be included as such a disbursement.

13. Accounts must accompany the bill for all payments claimed (other than court fees or minor out of pocket disbursements) whether or not these payments have later to be vouched. In the case of professional fees (other than fees to Counsel or to medical experts) over £25, the account must be accompanied by details showing the work done and the computation of the charge. Where fees claimed are substantial, copies of the accounts should be annexed to the copy bill served on a paying party.

14. Where allowable travelling expenses are claimed they would be shown as a disbursement and details supplied. Local travelling expenses claimed by a solicitor will not be allowed. The definition of " local " is a matter for the discretion of the taxing officer; in cases proceeding in a District Registry or a divorce county court inquiry should be made of the registrar concerned. As a matter of guidance only and subject to the discretion of the taxing officer concerned in cases proceeding in the Divorce Registry in London, whether in the High Court or the divorce county court, " local " will, in general, be taken to mean within a radius of 10 miles from the Divorce Registry. When considering whether to allow travelling expenses the taxing officer will take into account whether it would have been reasonable to employ an agent residing or carrying on business nearer the court or court office.

15. Conduct money paid to witnesses who attend a trial or hearing should be shown as part of the expenses claimed at the trial or hearing and not included in the bill at the date of the service of a subpoena.

16. Part IV, Item 10, Preparation for Trial. This item should be prefaced by a brief narrative indicating the issues, the status of the fee-earner concerned and the expense rates claimed. It is stressed that this statement should be short and to the point. Because normally the official file will be available to the taxing officer, a long statement is unnecessary, nor does it assist the assessment of an allowance which depends partly on an arithmetical computation and partly on a judgment of value and it may lead to a reduction in the amount claimed for the costs of taxation. The narrative should be followed by a statement in two parts (i) setting out a breakdown of the work done in relation to the relevant sub-paragraphs of paragraph (a) of the note to item 10 and (ii) a statement in relation to care and conduct under paragraph (b) of the note referring to the relevant factors relied on. The amount claimed for care and conduct should be expressed as a separate monetary amount as well as a percentage of the work figure.

17. Telephone calls will be allowed as a time charge if, but only if, they stand in place of an attendance whereby material progress has been made and the time has been recorded or can otherwise be established. A notional conversion into a time charge of letters and routine telephone calls will not be accepted.

18. It is provided in the note to Item 10 of the matrimonial scale (sub-para. (a) (xi)) that the preparation and service of miscellaneous notices are to be charged under that Item instead of under Item 3. For guidance it is stated that the following documents in matrimonial proceedings will be regarded as coming within this category:

Notice of change of solicitor.

Notice of issue amendment, discharge or revocation of civil aid certificate.
Praecipe to writ of execution.
Certificate as to reconciliation.
Notice under Matrimonial Causes Rule 34 (3).
Notice of abatement.
Penal notice (in the High Court).
Notice under Matrimonial Causes Rule 96.
Application for Directions for Trial (Matrimonial Causes Rule 33).
The list is not exhaustive.

19. Claims under Item 10 (b) may be made in respect of each separate ancillary application.

20. Charges as between a principal solicitor and a solicitor agent will continue to be dealt with on the established principle that such charges form, where appropriate, part of the principal solicitor's profit costs. Where these charges relate to the items comprised in Parts I, II or III of App. 2, or Parts I or III of the matrimonial scale, they should be included in their chronological order. Where they relate to work done under Part IV, Item 10, para. (xi) (App. 2) or Item 10, para. (x) (matrimonial scale) either they may be included in the principal solicitor's, Item 10 or they may be shown as a separate item, properly detailed, following afterwards. Solicitors are reminded however that agency charges for advising the principal how to proceed are not recoverable inter partes.

21. Taxation of costs (Item 12, App. 2; Item 11, matrimonial scale). No narrative will be required for this item but on taxation the party entitled to the costs must justify the amount claimed. The costs of ancillary applications made in the course of matrimonial proceedings should so far as possible be included in the bill of costs of the cause or matter.

22. The power given to a taxing officer to exercise a discretion to allow a larger sum than appears in the matrimonial scale in respect of the costs of proceedings in a divorce county court has now been extended to cover all the items in the scale. In line with the exercise of a similar general discretion in respect of matrimonial proceedings in the High Court under R.S.C., Ord. 62, r. 32 (2), it is intended that such a power should not be used save where in the opinion of the taxing officer the costs which may be allowed under the scale may be inadequate in all the circumstances by reason of the work done having been unusually heavy or important. There is no justification for basing any increase in the allowance on a time charge where the scale item itself is not calculated on such a basis.

23. Occasionally it happens that proceedings are commenced in a court which is not a divorce county court nor the Family Division of the High Court and they are subsequently transferred so as to become matrimonial proceedings and remain such up to the time when the costs have to be taxed. Although all the costs of such proceedings will be taxed in accordance with the procedure laid down in the Matrimonial Causes (Costs) Rules 1979, the costs of that part of the proceedings which was carried on otherwise than as matrimonial proceedings will be taxed and allowed by reference to the scale of costs which would be applicable had the proceedings not become matrimonial proceedings.

24. When bills are lodged for taxation they should be supported by the relevant papers arranged as below:

(i) The bill of costs;

(ii) Counsel's fee notes and accounts for other disbursements;

(iii) Cases to Counsel to advise with his advices; opinions and instructions to Counsel to settle documents; briefs to Counsel, all arranged in chronological order;

(iv) Reports and opinions of medical and other experts arranged in chronological order (unless they have been previously lodged in court);

(v) The solicitor's correspondence and attendance notes. Files should be left intact and not for the purpose of taxation divided into different sections to relate to different portions of the bill;

(vi) Any additional papers, bundled and labelled.

TABLE 1

1. Assimilation of Appendix 2 Items

After April 1979 Item	Prior to April 1979 Items
1	1, 2, 3, 4 (b), 6 (a), 6 (b)
2	5, 13, 14 (a), 14 (b), 15, 40, 41
3	6 (c), 7, 8, 9, 10, 11, 12 (a), 12 (b) 16, 22 (a), 22 (b), 22 (c), 25 (a), 25 (b), 25 (c), 28, Part 30, 72, 73, 74, 75, 76, 77, 78, 79.
4	82 (a), 82 (b)
5	No corresponding item
6	19, 20 (a), 20 (b), 21, 32, 33 (a), 34
7	29
8	33 (b), 33 (c)
9	61, 62, 63, 64, 65, 66, 67, 68, 69, 70, 71
10	23, 24 (a), 24 (b), 26 (a–j), 27, Part 30, 40, 41, 52, 53, 54, 56, 57, 60, 80, 81, 84, 86, 87, 98, 99, 100
11	90, 91, 92, 93 (a), 94, 95, 96 (a), 96 (b), 97
12	36, 37, 38, 39

2. *Items in Appendix 2 prior to April 1979 for which no item is provided in the Appendix from April 1979*
4 (a), 17, 18, 31, 35, 42 (a), 42 (b), 43, 44, 45 (a), 45 (b), 46, 47, 48, 49, 50 (a), 50 (b), 50 (c), 50 (d), 51, 55, 58, 59, 83, 85, 88 (a), 88 (b), and 89 (a), 38 (b)

TABLE 2.

Assimilation of Divorce Scale Items

Divorce Scale Item	Matrimonial Scale
1 (i) (ii) (iii)	10
2	1 or 3
3 (a)	3
3 (b)	2 or 3
4 (a) (b) (c)	4
5	10
6 (a)	10 (a)
6 (b)	10 (b)
7 (i) (ii)	8
8 (i) (ii)	8
9	6 and 2 (also 3 if Counsel is briefed)
10	6
11	10
12 (a) (b) (c)	10
12 (d)	7
13 (a) (b)	8
14	6
15	10
16	1, 2 or 3 (otherwise 10)
17	1, 2 or 3 (otherwise 10)
18	1, 2 or 3
19	1, 2 or 3
20	3
21	3 and disbursements

Divorce Scale Item	Matrimonial Scale
22	10
23	10
24 (a) (b) (c)	11 (a) (b)
25 (a) (b)	5 (a)
26	5 (d)
27	5 (e)
28 (a)	5 (b)
28 (b)	5 (c)
29 (a)	5 (f)
29 (b)	5 (g)
30	No item provided.
31 (a) to (f)	
32	
33	No item provided.
34a	
35a	
36a	
37a	
34b	
35b	10
36b	
37b	

[1979] 2 All E.R. 150; 123 S.J. 287.

753. The following Practice Direction was issued by the Family Division on November 12, 1979:

In the Practice Note of April 11, 1979 ([1979] C.L.Y. 752) on the new practice on taxation it was laid down that bills must be divided into parts to show, *inter alia,* the work done in the High Court and the divorce county court.

There appears to be some degree of misunderstanding about the method of setting out the work in the two courts and the object of this note is to clarify this method.

Where work is begun in the county court and transferred to the High Court (or, rarely, vice versa) items 10 (*a*) and 10 (*b*) relating to that work must be set out at the end of that part of the bill. In any subsequent transfer between the High Court and the county court the same procedure will apply.

The Family Division has not been asked to approve any form of bill and will not accept as correct any form of bill that does not conform with the Practice Note of April 11, 1979, as explained in the present Practice Note. [1979] 3 All E.R. 896.

754. —— **taxation—injunction proceedings by wife—costs of service on husband** [Matrimonial Causes Rules 1973 (S.I. 1973 No. 2016), r. 119.] W had petitioned for divorce and had issued proceedings for a non-molestation injunction. The documents were personally served upon H by inquiry agents since he was not legally represented at that stage. At court both parties were legally represented and H entered into the usual undertaking not to assault, molest or otherwise interfere with W. H later broke this undertaking and at the subsequent hearing gave a second undertaking to the judge in similar terms. The court order on this occasion was again served upon H by inquiry agents. H broke this undertaking as well but on this occasion his solicitors refused to accept service, claiming that they no longer had contact with H. The matter was finally adjourned generally when attempts to effect service were abandoned and it became apparent that H was now leaving W alone. On taxation of W's party and party bill for costs the registrar disallowed the costs of service by inquiry agents as being not reasonably incurred within the meaning of r. 119. *Held*, allowing W's appeal, that when approaching the taxation of the costs of service in this type of case the registrar should always consider the merits of the individual case and the difficulties facing the petitioner's solicitors. Solicitors were under a particularly onerous duty to

protect their client in the most efficient manner possible and should not be
subjected to the risk of having costs reasonably incurred disallowed on some
technical ground. Here service of proceedings and knowledge of them by H
were of fundamental importance to the successful outcome of W's application
for an injunction, or more so, her application to commit: JACOB *v.* JACOB
(1978) 9 Fam. Law 57, C.A.

755. —— —— **power to allow objection to taxation out of time.** See THORNE *v.*
THORNE, § 2188.

756. Decree absolute—satisfactory arrangements for children—delay
    [Matrimonial Causes Act 1973 (c. 18), s. 41.] Following the pronouncement
of the decree nisi upon W's divorce petition H attended the appointment for
consideration of arrangements for the children with counsel and indicated that
he proposed to claim custody. The judge adjourned W's application for a
declaration under s. 41 and for custody to a later date. On that occasion He
appeared in person and said that he was applying for legal aid to claim
custody. The judge being in difficulty only as to H's lack of representation again
adjourned the s. 41 declaration and custody to another date to be fixed. *Held,*
allowing W's appeal, that H's dilatory approach had succeeded in witholding
W's decree absolute indefinitely. The primary purpose of s. 41 was to ensure
that the judge was seized of the question of the interests of the children. If
there was no issue between the parties a declaration under one of the alternatives to s. 41 should be made unless there were specific matters about which the
judge required to be satisfied in the immediate future, or for some other
reason the sanction of witholding the decree absolute was likely to be useful.
At that stage he could and should order a welfare report and give directions
as to any further steps to be taken, and, if possible, fix the date of a further
hearing. If there was an issue as to custody the s. 41 proceedings could be
deferred provided the delay was likely to be fairly short. If considerable time
was likely to elapse then consideration should be given to existing *de facto*
arrangements. If these appeared reasonably satisfactory, though not necessarily
the best that could be made, for that would be decided at the custody hearing,
a declaration in the form of s. 41 (1) (*b*) (i) or s. 41 (1) (*c*) could be made. Here
a declaration under s. 41 (1) (*b*) (ii) would be made, *i.e.* that W's arrangements
were the best that could be devised in the circumstances. An interim custody
order in favour of W would also be made and an order for H to file an
application for custody and evidence in support within 28 days, if so advised,
with liberty to W to apply for a full order if no such application was filed
within that time limit: ASHLEY *v.* ASHLEY (1979) 9 Fam. Law 219, C.A.

757. Domestic courts. See § 1719.

758. Domicile. See CONFLICT OF LAWS.

759. Fees
    MATRIMONIAL CAUSES FEES (AMENDMENT) ORDER 1979 (No. 966 (L.10))
[10p], made under the Matrimonial Causes Act 1973 (c. 18), s. 51 and the
Public Offices Fees Act 1879 (c. 58), ss. 2, 3; operative on September 3, 1979;
amends S.I. 1975 No. 1346 by increasing the fee payable on the presentation
of a petition to £25.

760. Financial provision—consent order—jurisdiction to vary—Hong Kong. See DE
LASALA *v.* DE LASALA, § 2200.

761. —— **periodical payments—finality**
    Following their divorce, W remained in the matrimonial home with the
two children while H moved to lodgings. H was ordered to transfer his
interest in the home to W, and to pay periodical payments of £7.50 per week
for the children and 5p per annum for W. The house was to be charged with
payment to H of 25 per cent. of the net proceeds of sale, when sold or on
W's death. On appeal, *held,* the periodical payments were inconsistent with the
" clean break " principle and the order would be varied to that extent (*Minton*
v. *Minton* [1979] C.L.Y. 766 applied): DUNFORD *v.* DUNFORD (1979) 123 S.J.
585, C.A.

762. —— —— **variation of previous consent order**
    Following the parties' divorce a consent order was made in April 1977

giving W £1 per week maintenance on the basis that she was working and earned £30 per week. In fact, although those concerned with the consent order were unaware of it, W had stopped work in February 1977 because she was pregnant by another man. The child was born in August 1977 and W now lived on social security. Upon H's appeal against the judge's order increasing W's weekly sum from £1 to £10, *held*, allowing H's appeal, that £10 per week was too much in the particular circumstances of this case. Whatever the court ordered would make no difference at all to the amount of money available to W because her sole income came from social security benefits and none of these amounts would make any difference to the amount which she would actually have in her hand. The court had therefore to consider what would be fair in the circumstances. Order reduced, accordingly, from £10 to £3 per week: WAGNER *v.* WAGNER (1978) 9 Fam. Law 183, C.A.

763. —— **sale of house—practice**
The following Practice Note was issued by the Family Division on December 4, 1979:
On May 1, 1979, in *Ward* v. *Ward & Greene* [1979] C.L.Y. 764 the Court of Appeal held that judges and registrars have power to order sale of property under s. 24 of the Matrimonial Causes Act 1973 and without specific application under s. 17 of the Married Women's Property Act 1882 or s. 30 of the Law of Property Act 1925.

764. —— —— —— **whether pro forma summons necessary**
Having dismissed an appeal from the decision of Dunn J., where the judge had suggested that the husband should issue a *pro forma* summons under s. 17 of the Married Women's Property Act 1882, the Court of Appeal *held*, that there was no need to multiply pieces of paper; it was not necessary to institute proceedings as being under the Married Women's Property Act 1882 or the Law of Property Act 1925 (s. 30) or to issue a *pro forma* summons to enable the court to exercise its powers under one or other of those Acts: WARD *v.* WARD AND GREENE (1979) 123 S.J. 838, C.A.

765. —— **short marriage—cohabitation for long period before marriage**
[Matrimonial Causes Act 1973 (c. 18), s. 25.] In 1947 the parties started living together and a son was born in 1950. From 1955 W worked full time in H's factory and came to occupy a responsible position. The parties married in 1971 but the marriage lasted only four months when H refused to cohabit with W. A decree nisi was granted to W in 1977. *Held*, that it was important for the court not to limit its discretion by a narrow construction of the guidelines provided by s. 25 of the 1973 Act and a broad approach should be adopted in considering the words " to have regard to all the circumstances of the case " and " to their the parties conduct." An order for a lump sum of £8,000 was made in favour of W: K. *v.* K., *The Times*, December 4, 1979, Wood J.

766. —— **variation of order—finality**
[Matrimonial Causes Act 1973 (c. 18), s. 23.]
The court has no power to make a second or subsequent maintenance order after an earlier application has been dismissed.
By a consent order H, the husband, was to convey the matrimonial home to W, the wife, and pay her nominal maintenance which would cease on completion of the conveyance. After completion and when maintenance had ceased, W sought to " vary " the periodical payments to her and the children. The order was varied in respect of the children but not W. The Court of Appeal affirmed this decision. On appeal, *held,* the Matrimonial Causes Act 1973, s. 23 (1) and (4), conferred jurisdiction to make subsequent orders in respect of the children but not W. The consent order had effected a clean break between the parties. The court could not make a future order on a subsequent application by W after H had complied with his obligations.
MINTON *v.* MINTON [1979] 2 W.L.R. 31, H.L.

767. —— —— **nature of particulars sought**
[Matrimonial Causes Rules 1977 (S.I. 1977 No. 344), r. 100 (5).] W applied to vary a maintenance agreement made in 1962 and sought very detailed particulars of H's income and property described by Stamp L.J. as " extremely

oppressive." The registrar made the order sought but this was set aside on H's appeal by the judge. *Held*, allowing W's appeal, H should be ordered to file an affidavit containing full particulars of property and income pursuant to r. 100 (5): SMITH v. SMITH (1978) 8 Fam. Law. 245, C.A.

768. Five years apart—whether " visits " amount to " living together "
[Matrimonial Causes Act 1973 (c. 18), s. 2 (5) (6).] The parties separated in February 1970 but H visited W regularly at her address spending weekends, sometimes several nights a week, and on three occasions a whole week, with her. Between January and May 1975 H lived continuously with W for four-and-a-half months. In September 1975 H petitioned for divorce under s. 1 (2) (*e*) of the 1973 Act but W denied the five years' separation alleged. *Held*, dismissing W's appeal from the judge's order of decree nisi, the relationship subsisting between the parties after their separation in 1970 until September 1975 did not amount to " living together " within the meaning of s. 2 (6) such as to disentitle H to a decree. He was merely visiting W regularly and they kept separate households. (*Santos* v. *Santos* [1972] C.L.Y. 1087 considered: PIPER v. PIPER (1978) 8 Fam. Law 243, C.A.

769. Foreign decree—recognition—Malaysian law
[Recognition of Divorce and Legal Separation Act 1971 (c. 53).] H and W had married in Ceylon in 1955. From 1961 until 1975 they had lived together in Malaysia. H, a Hindu, had remained behind whilst W, an Anglican, had come to England with the children but intended to return to Malaysia once their education was completed. In 1977 W heard that H had become a Muslim a year earlier. She began divorce proceedings. H filed an answer to the petition claiming that the marriage had automatically terminated upon his conversion to Islam. In March 1978 H obtained a fatwa, or binding declaration on a point of Muslim law, to the effect that W was not a " Kitabiyya," or non-Muslim woman whom H was now permitted to marry. The judge held that the marriage had ended under Malaysian law but that the court could not recognise such a termination. *Held*, dismissing H's appeal against the grant of a decree nisi to W, that the 1971 Act did not apply to the case because the events in Malaysia neither constituted a divorce nor a legal separation; and a fatwa was not a " judicial proceeding " in the meaning of that Act. On the common law rules there should be recognition unless English notions of substantial justice would be offended. This was not the case here for a 20-year marriage should not be ended by a religious conversion. The definition given of " Kitabiyya " was arbitrary and historically inaccurate, and W, being in ignorance of H's moves, had not been given the opportunity of making representations herself. (Decision of Wood J. upheld): VISWALINGHAM v. VISWALINGHAM (1979) 123 S.J. 604, C.A.

770. —— —— nullity—New Jersey decree
A foreign decree of nullity based on residence of sufficient quality will be recognised by the English courts even though not recognised by the country of origin of one of the parties.

The respondent, an Italian, married on American woman in Italy. She returned to the U.S.A. without consummating the marriage. She later obtained a decree of nullity from a New Jersey court, whose jurisdiction was based on her residence. The decree was not recognised in Italy. The respondent later remarried in England and when subsequently the wife brought a petition for divorce the question arose as to whether the English marriage was a valid and subsisting one. *Held*, that the court would recognise the New Jersey decree affecting the status of both parties and accordingly the second marriage was valid and subsisting. (*Indyka* v. *Indyka* [1967] C.L.Y. 551, *Robinson-Scott* v. *Robinson-Scott* [1958] C.L.Y. 513, *Law* v. *Gustin* [1975] C.L.Y. 367 applied; *Padolecchia* v. *Padolecchia* [1967] C.L.Y. 1319 not followed.)
PERRINI v. PERRINI [1979] 2 W.L.R. 473, Sir George Baker P.

771. —— —— test to be applied
[Recognition of Divorces and Legal Separations Act 1971 (c. 53), s. 8 (2).]
An " opportunity to take part " in foreign divorce proceedings under s. 8 (2) (*a*) (ii) of the Recognition of Divorces and Legal Separations Act 1971

means an adequate and effective opportunity of presenting a party's views, and asserting any rights he may have, not merely an opportunity to take part in formalities.

H left W. W obtained a magistrates' order for custody of the children and maintenance on the grounds of H's adultery and desertion. H went to live in Canada, where he filed a divorce petition alleging mental cruelty against W. The petition was served on W, informing her that she had 60 days to file an appearance. The whole of that period was occupied with W's attempts to obtain legal aid in England and in Canada to contest the action. H's lawyers in Canada were told what was happening and also of the English maintenance order, but before an appearance was entered, W was sent the decree nisi. W filed a divorce petition in England, praying for financial relief. Then the Canadian decree nisi was made absolute. H filed an answer in the English proceedings, seeking a declaration that the Canadian decree had already dissolved the marriage. *Held,* W had not been given a reasonable opportunity to take part in the Canadian proceedings and the court would refuse recognition of the Canadian decree. (*Torok* v. *Torok* [1973] C.L.Y. 894, *Kendall* v. *Kendall* [1977] C.L.Y. 835 and *Newmarch* v. *Newmarch* [1977] C.L.Y. 854 considered.)

JOYCE *v.* JOYCE AND O'HARE [1979] 2 All E.R. 156, Lane J.

772. —— whether obtained by judicial or other proceedings
[Recognition of Divorces and Legal Separations Act 1971 (c. 53), s. 2 (*a*).]
The words " other proceedings " in the Recognition of Divorce Act 1971 are not limited solely to quasi-judicial proceedings, but refer to any proceedings, such as divorce by talaq, officially recognised in the country in which they are taken.

The parties, who married in India in 1963, were Muslims, born in India and nationals of Pakistan. In 1968 while living in Thailand they made a khula, recognised as a form of divorce under Muslim law, terminating the marriage. In 1973 the husband came to England, bought a house, and was joined by his family, including, against his wishes, his wife. The husband returned to Pakistan and purported to divorce his wife again by pronouncing the talaq in accordance with the laws of Pakistan. The husband presented a petition for a declaration that the marriage had been lawfully dissolved by either the khula or talaq or both. Wood J. held that both proceedings would be recognised by the court as dissolving the marriage. The Court of Appeal allowed the wife's appeal. On appeal, *held,* allowing the husband's appeal, that the words " other proceedings " applied to any proceedings officially recognised by the country in which they were taken, and that a divorce obtained by talaq was a divorce obtained by such " other proceedings."

QUAZI *v.* QUAZI [1979] 3 W.L.R. 833, H.L.

773. Irretrievable breakdown—dismissal of petition—second petition based on respondent's subsequent behaviour—whether petitioner entitled to decree
[Matrimonial Causes Act 1973 (c. 18), s. 1 (2) (*b*).]
A petitioner is entitled to a decree on a second petition if it is shown that the marriage remains irretrievably broken down and that the respondent's subsequent behaviour was such that the petitioner could not reasonably be expected to live with him.

W petitioned for divorce alleging that the marriage had broken down irretrievably and that H's behaviour was such that W could not reasonably be expected to live with him. The judge found that it was W's behaviour that had caused the breakdown and dismissed the petition. Thereafter H made life unpleasant for W to make her leave the matrimonial home. W petitioned a second time relying on H's subsequent behaviour. *Held,* granting the decree, W was entitled to a decree because the marriage remained irretrievably broken down and H's subsequent behaviour had been such that W could not reasonably be expected to live with him.

STEVENS *v.* STEVENS [1979] 1 W.L.R. 885, Sheldon J.

774. —— parties living together after divorce
Parties had married in 1940. W petitioned for divorce on the ground of

H's behaviour. The trial judge, who heard evidence over a period of two days, did not accept H's evidence where it differed from that given by W and her witnesses, and found in favour of W. H, who was not in good health, and was still being looked after by W, appealed and appeared in person. *Held*, dismissing H's appeal, that the court could do no more than look at the judge's findings of fact and, if there was evidence to support those findings, to accept them. Nevertheless, it was reasonably clear from the context of this case that W had been looking after H for a long time now as an act of kindness and it would be wrong to treat these two people as if they were living together in an ordinary married situation. H obviously required help but there was in fact no ground for allowing this appeal: JUDGE *v.* JUDGE (1978) 9 Fam. Law 154, C.A.

775. Maintenance

RECIPROCAL ENFORCEMENT OF MAINTENANCE ORDERS (DESIGNATION OF RECIPROCATING COUNTRIES) ORDER 1979 (No. 115) [20p], made under the Maintenance Orders (Reciprocal Enforcement) Act 1972 (c. 18), ss. 1, 24, 45 (1); operative on April 1, 1979; designates as reciprocating countries for the purposes of Pt. I of the 1972 Act certain specified countries.

MAINTENANCE ORDERS (FACILITIES FOR ENFORCEMENT) (REVOCATION) ORDER 1979 (No. 116) [10p], made under the Maintenance Orders Act 1958 (c. 39), s. 19; operative on April 1, 1979; revokes S.I. 1959 No. 377 and S.I. 1964 No. 696 in so far as they extend the Maintenance Orders (Facilities for Enforcement) Act 1920 to specified countries. These countries are designated as reciprocating countries for the purposes of Pt. I of the Maintenance Orders (Reciprocal Enforcement) Act 1972 by S.I. 1979 No. 115.

RECOVERY OF MAINTENANCE (UNITED STATES OF AMERICA) ORDER 1979 (No. 1314) [10p], made under the Maintenance Orders (Reciprocal Enforcement) Act 1972, s. 40; operative on January 1, 1980; applies the provisions of Pt. II of the 1972 Act to the American states specified in the Order.

RECIPROCAL ENFORCEMENT OF MAINTENANCE ORDERS (HAGUE CONVENTION COUNTRIES) ORDER 1979 (No. 1317) [£1·25], made under the Maintenance Orders (Reciprocal Enforcement) Act 1972, s. 40; operative on March 1, 1980; provides for the implementation in the U.K. of the Convention on the Recognition and Enforcement of Decisions Relating to Maintenance Obligations concluded at the Hague on October 2, 1973. The effect is to provide for the transmission of U.K. orders to Convention countries for recognition and enforcement and to enable maintenance proceedings to be taken in the U.K. against persons resident in Convention countries.

MAGISTRATES' COURTS (RECOVERY ABROAD OF MAINTENANCE) (AMENDMENT) RULES 1979 (No. 1561 (L. 22)) [10p], made under the Justices of the Peace Act 1949 (c. 101), s. 15 as extended by the Magistrates' Courts Act 1952 (c. 55), s. 122, the Justice of the Peace Act 1968 (c. 69), s. 5 (1) and the Maintenance Orders (Reciprocal Enforcement) Act 1972, ss. 27 (8)–(10), 32 (1)–(3) (6) (8), 33 (4) (5), 35 (4), 38 (2); operative on January 1, 1980; apply the provisions of S.I. 1975 No. 488 to the American States specified in S.I. 1979 No. 1314.

776. —— circumstances justifying order against mother

F had been given custody of the three children of the marriage following M's departure to live with another man. Upon F's subsequent application to vary the order to include maintenance M had been ordered by the local justices to pay £4 per week for each child. *Held,* that the justices had misdirected themselves in thinking that they were entitled to take into account the earnings of the man with whom M was living. M could only pay if she had her own means or was put in funds by that other person which was not the case here. Appeal allowed: *Re* L. (MINORS) (1979) 123 S.J. 404, Dunn J.

777. —— remission of arrears—hindrance of access

[Magistrates' Courts Act 1952 (c. 55), s. 76.] The fact that a wife has hindered a husband's access to the children is not a ground for remitting arrears of maintenance under s. 76 of the Magistrates' Courts Act 1952: R. *v.* HALIFAX JUSTICES, *ex p.* WOOLVERTON (1978) 123 S.J. 80, D.C.

778. —— **tracing of husband—procedure**

The following Practice Direction was issued by the Family Division on June 26, 1979:

The Practice Note of November 28, 1972 [1973] 1 W.L.R. 60; [1972] C.L.Y. 1059 is hereby amended by deleting para. (3) thereof under the heading " Ministry of Defence " and by substituting the following: —

In cases where the person sought is known to be serving or to have recently served in any branch of H.M. Forces, the solicitor representing the applicant may obtain the address for service of maintenance or wardship proceedings direct from the appropriate Service Department. In the case of Army service-men the solicitor can obtain a list of Regiments and of the various Manning and Record Offices from the Officer in Charge, Central Clearing Wing, Higher Barracks, Exeter, EX4 4ND.

The solicitor's request should be accompanied by a written undertaking that the address will be used solely for the purpose of service of process in the proceedings and that so far as is possible the solicitor will disclose the address only to the Court and not to the applicant or any other person, except in the normal course of the proceedings.

Alternatively if the solicitor wishes to serve process on the person's Com-manding Officer under the provisions contained in s. 101 of the Naval Dis-cipline Act 1957, s. 153 of the Army Act 1955 and s. 153 of the Air Force Act 1955 (all of which as amended by s. 62 of the Armed Forces Act 1971) he may obtain that Officer's address in the same way.

Where the applicant is acting in person the appropriate Service Department is prepared to disclose the address of the person sought, or that of his Com-manding Officer, to a Registrar on receipt of an assurance that the applicant has given an undertaking that the information will be used solely for the purpose of serving process in the proceedings.

In all cases the request should include details of the person's full name, service number, rank or rating, and his Ship, Arm or Trade, Corps, Regiment or Unit or as much of this information as is available. Failure to quote the service number and the rank or rating may result in failure to identify the serviceman or at least in considerable delay.

Enquiries should be addressed as follows:

(a) Officers of Royal Navy and Women's Royal Naval Service	Ministry of Defence (Naval Secretary), Old Admiralty Building, Whitehall, London, SW1A 2BD.
Ratings in the Royal Navy WRNS Rating QARNNS Ratings	The Commodore, (Naval Drafting Division), HMS Centurion, Grange Road, Gosport, Hants, PO13 9XA.
RN Medical and Dental Officers	Ministry of Defence, Medical Director General (Naval), First Avenue House, High Holborn, London, WC1V 6HE.
Officers of Queen Alexandra's Royal Naval Nursing Service	Ministry of Defence, The Matron-in-Chief, QARNNS, First Avenue House, High Holborn, London, WC1V 6HE.
Naval Chaplains	Ministry of Defence, Chaplain of the Fleet, Lacon House, Theobalds Road, London, WC1T 8RY.

(b) Royal Marine Officers	The Commandant-General Royal Marines (MS Branch), Old Admiralty Building, Whitehall, London, SW1A 2BE.
Royal Marine Ranks	The Commodore (DRORM), HMS Centurion, Grange Road, Gosport, Hants, PO13 9XA.
(c) Army Officers (Including WRAC and QARANC)	Ministry of Defence, Army Officers' Documentation Office, Government Buildings (F Block), Stanmore, Middlesex, HA7 4PZ.
Other Ranks, Army	The Manning & Record Office which is appropriate to the Regiment or Corps.
(d) Royal Air Force and Women's Royal Air Force Officers (Including PMRAFNS)	Ministry of Defence, AR8b (RAF), Eastern Avenue, Barnwood, Gloucester, GL4 7PN.
Other Ranks, RAF and WRAF	Ministry of Defence, RAF Personnel Management Centre, RAF Innsworth, Gloucester, GL3 1E2.

[1979] 1 W.L.R. 925.

779. Matrimonial Causes Rules

MATRIMONIAL CAUSES (AMENDMENT) RULES 1979 (No. 400) [10p], made under the Matrimonial Causes Act 1973 (c. 18), s. 50; operative on April 24, 1979; amend S.I. 1977 No. 344 so as: (a) to provide the same procedure for the rescission of decrees of judicial separation by consent, following a reconciliation, as is already provided for the rescission of decrees nisi of divorce or nullity; and (b) to allow the petitioner who is proceeding in person to give as the address for service the name and address of a solicitor from whom the petitioner is receiving advice.

780. Matrimonial home. See HUSBAND AND WIFE.

781. Nullity—conduct of husband—whether grant of decree injustice to wife

[Matrimonial Causes Act 1973 (c. 18), s. 13 (1).]

Since the Nullity of Marriage Act 1971 approbation of a marriage has ceased to be a bar to the grant of a decree of nullity and the question whether public policy requires the marriage to be continued is no longer a relevant factor.

The parties' marriage had never been consummated because W refused to undergo an operation for a physical impediment. H and W nevertheless agreed to adopt two children. Months later H left home to live with another woman. In an undefended suit H prayed for a decree of nullity on the ground of W's refusal to consummate the marriage. On the question whether H's approbation of the marriage and the provisions of the 1973 Act prevent a decree being granted, *held*, granting the decree, that approbation of a marriage no longer was a bar to the grant of a decree of nullity and the question of whether public policy required the marriage to be continued was no longer a relevant factor. In the circumstances it would not be unjust to grant the decree so there was no statutory bar to the grant of a decree.

D. *v.* D. (NULLITY: STATUTORY BAR) [1979] 3 W.L.R. 185, Dunn J.

782. —— wilful refusal—Muslim parties—failure to go through religious ceremony

H and W were both strict Muslims. A week after H's arrival in England from Pakistan in November 1975, the parties underwent a ceremony of marriage at a registry office, for the primary purpose of enabling H to remain in

England. It was understood by both parties that a Muslim ceremony would take place in the future when H had organised his financial affairs in England on a secure footing. The parties both lived in separate bedrooms in W's family's house and without consummation until March 1978. In the meantime H's financial position improved and arrangements were in hand by W's family for a religious ceremony to take place in April or May 1978. In March 1978 it was discovered that there had been, as H agreed, a romantic liaison between H and one of W's younger sisters; even after discovery of the relationship H expressed a wish to marry the sister and not W. H was thrown out of W's family's house and the arrangements for a religious ceremony cancelled. *Held*, that H, by his conduct, made it clear that he did not wish to go through a religious ceremony of marriage and thereby made it impossible for the marriage to be consummated. Such conduct is equivalent to wilful refusal: MALIK *v.* MALIK, September 21, 1979, Stephen Brown J. (*Ex rel. C. Limb, Esq., Barrister.*)

783. Petition—leave to present within three years of marriage—exceptional hardship

[Matrimonial Causes Act 1973 (c. 18), s. 3 (2).] Parties had married in September 1976 when W was 22 years and H 23 years. The marriage proved to be unhappy and W left to live with her mother in February 1978. In May 1978 W applied for leave to petition under s. 3 on the grounds of exceptional hardship. W alleged that her health had suffered in a serious way and that she had a severe reactive depression. Her work had suffered and there had been a severe setback in her career because of the unhappiness in the marriage. The judge refused her application, the case being one of normal upset. *Held*, allowing W's appeal, that this case was clearly over the law of normal hardship into the area of exceptional hardship although it was not by any means one of the worst cases that had come before the court. " Exceptional hardship " meant hardship which was more extensive and more serious than that which one would normally expect to follow from the events concerned. It was not necessary to show something quite abnormal in the consequences to the applicant. It was sufficient to show that what the applicant had suffered in the circumstances was more than what ordinary people would expect in an ordinary case of that kind: WOOLF *v.* WOOLF (1978) 9 Fam. Law 216, C.A.

784. —— petitioner's address for service

The following Practice Direction was issued by the Family Division on April 12, 1979 :

Para. 5 (*c*) of App. 2 to the Matrimonial Causes Rules 1977 is amended by S.I. 1979 No. 400 with effect from April 24, 1979.

As from that date a petitioner, though acting in person, may give as his address for service the name and address of a solicitor, providing that (a) that solicitor has given him legal advice and assistance and (b) agrees. The petitioner, however, will remain on the record as acting in person.

Where a solicitor has agreed to his name and address being used as the address for service of the petitioner but subsequently wishes to withdraw his agreement, he should notify the court to this effect, give the petitioner's last known address and certify that he has notified the petitioner of the withdrawal of his agreement.

[1979] 1 W.L.R. 533.

785. —— procedural ban—diplomatic immunity from suit

[Diplomatic Privileges Act 1964 (c. 81), Sched. 1, art. 31 (1).]

The court will hear a petition brought against a party with diplomatic immunity, if that immunity has been lost by the time its existence is brought to the court's attention.

H was a U.S. diplomat in Britain. H and W were married in the U.S.A. W issued a petition for divorce against H whilst he still enjoyed diplomatic immunity. H issued a summons to strike out the petition on the ground that he was immune from suit under the Diplomatic Privileges Act 1964. He then ceased to be a member of the diplomatic staff and returned to the U.S.A. Subsequently, at the hearing of the summons, *held*, the immunity was not from legal liability but from suit, and the suit was only a nullity when set aside. The petition was a valid petition, and since H had now lost his immunity, there was no bar to the proceedings. (*Empson* v. *Smith* [1965] C.L.Y. 2052 applied.)

SHAW *v.* SHAW [1979] 3 W.L.R. 24, Balcombe J.

786. —— **within three years of marriage—exceptional hardship and depravity** [Matrimonial Causes Act 1973 (c. 18), s. 3 (2).]

It is not exceptional depravity for one spouse to abandon sexual interest in the other in favour of members of their own sex; it may, however, amount to exceptional hardship upon the other spouse.

H and W were married after having had a heterosexual relationship for 3 years. During that time H had had homosexual relationships as well, but he led W to believe that they would have a perfectly normal sexual relationship. H lost interest in her sexually immediately after they were married and the marriage broke up. On W's application for leave to present a petition within three years, the judge held that it was not a case either of exceptional hardship or of exceptional depravity. On appeal by W, *held*, allowing the appeal, that in the great majority of cases it was unnecessary to rely upon exceptional depravity, since the judge could take into account hardship arising from the conduct of the other spouse, and hardship in having to wait until a petition could be presented. In the present case W had made out a case of exceptional hardship.

C. *v.* C. (DIVORCE: EXCEPTIONAL HARDSHIP) [1979] 2 W.L.R. 95, C.A.

787. Practice—appeal—leave out of time

W's notice of appeal against the registrar's judgment reached the court one day out of time on a five-day notice. The judge refused her an extension of time for filing her notice of appeal. *Held,* allowing W's appeal, that the objection that the appeal was out of time was the most naked formality and the judge should have extended the time immediately because to do anything else would be to penalise W in the most unreasonable and unjust manner. It was a total denial of justice if W was to be precluded from challenging the registar's order on an important matter like a lump sum order: WILLIAMS *v.* WILLIAMS (1978) 9 Fam. Law 153, C.A.

788. —— **consent summonses and notices of application**

The following Practice Direction was issued by the Family Division on March 5, 1979:

Where a consent summons or notice of application seeks an order which includes agreed terms for periodical payments direct to a child in excess of the amounts qualifying for the time being as " small maintenance payments " under s. 65 of the Income and Corporation Taxes Act 1970, it is no longer necessary for the solicitor to certify whether the child is or is not living with the party who will be making the payments under the proposed terms.

Para. (2) of the Registrar's Direction of December 22, 1975 ([1975] C.L.Y. 952) is accordingly hereby cancelled.

[1979] 1 W.L.R. 290.

789. —— **special procedure—criticism**

Having refused a husband's appeal to be allowed to file an answer out of time and to rescind a decree of divorce granted under the special procedure, Goff L.J. said that he dismissed the appeal with reluctance; the matter could have been dealt with properly under the ordinary procedure and that the rule-making committee should consider revision of the rules relating to the special procedure: SANDHOLM *v.* SANDHOLM, *The Times,* December 21, 1979, C.A.

790. Special procedure list

The following note was issued by the Family Division on December 5, 1979:

The hearing numbers of the above causes run from 1 to 9999 with a prefix letter. The prefix letter at present in use is " D." In order to clear the lists of cases which have been set down for trial for some time but in respect of which the date fixed to the court for pronouncement of the decree has been vacated, those cases listed with a prefix " B " have now been struck out of the lists.

Causes struck out of the special procedure lists under this direction may be restored to the current lists by filing Notice to Restore (Form D435A) in the Divorce Registry.

791. Undefended petition—custody order—estoppel per rem judicatem—father denying that children are children of family

An estoppel *per rem judicatam* does not arise in respect of a custody order made when granting a decree nisi in an undefended suit.

Per curiam: The Matrimonial Causes Rules Committee should be invited to consider what changes should be made in the printed form of acknowledgment of service of a divorce petition.

W presented a petition for divorce on the ground of two years' separation and H's consent. In the petition W alleged that there were two children of the family of whom H was not the father. On the printed form of acknowledgment H did not seek to defend the petition, did not seek to be heard on the claim for custody of the children and did not apply for access to or custody of the children. The Registrar ordered H to pay maintenance in respect of the two children. On appeal by H, Balcombe J. affirmed the order, holding that although he found as a fact that H had never accepted the children as members of the family, H was estopped by the custody order from denying that they were children of the family. On appeal, *held*, allowing the appeal, that estoppel was based on public policy and there was no public advantage in requiring the issue whether a child was a child of the family to be determined before the decree was pronounced, so estoppel *per rem judicatam* did not arise in respect of a custody order made when granting a decree nisi in an undefended suit. (*Lindsay* v. *Lindsay* [1934] P. 162 and *Gower* v. *Gower* [1971] C.L.Y. 3476 overruled; *Carl Zeiss Stiftung* v. *Rayner & Keeler (No. 2)* [1966] C.L.Y. 1665 considered.)

ROWE v. ROWE [1979] 3 W.L.R. 101, C.A.

792. —— special procedure—application to set aside registrar's certificate

[Matrimonial Causes Act 1973 (c. 18), s. 1 (4); Matrimonial Causes Rules 1977 (S.I. 1977 No. 344), r. 48 (1) (*a*), (2).]

A certificate of the registrar that a petitioner has proved the contents of a petition and is entitled to a decree under r. 48 (1) (*a*) of the Matrimonial Causes Rules 1977 is tantamount to a decree nisi, and any application to set it aside must be dealt with as an application to set aside a decree nisi.

W petitioned for divorce. H gave notice of his intention to defend but did not file an answer. The suit was apparently undefended, the registrar gave the appropriate directions under r. 33 of the Matrimonial Causes Rules 1977, and the cause was entered for trial in the special procedure list. After considering W's evidence, the registrar granted a certificate under r. 48 (1) (*a*) that W had proved the contents of her petition and was entitled to a decree. On H's application, the judge then took the case out of the special procedure list, and granted H leave to file an answer out of time. W appealed. *Held*, allowing the appeal, that once a registrar's certificate was issued under r. 48 (1) (*a*) the court was bound to grant a decree. Any application for a rehearing must be dealt with as an application for rehearing after a decree nisi, *i.e.* it should be refused unless there were substantial grounds for the belief that the decree would have been obtained contrary to the justice of the case. H had had ample opportunity to file an answer and the justice of the case did not require a rehearing. (*Owen* v. *Owen* [1964] C.L.Y. 1195 applied.)

DAY v. DAY [1979] 2 All E.R. 187, C.A.

BOOKS AND ARTICLES. See *post*, pp. [4], [20].

EASEMENTS AND PRESCRIPTION

793. Claim—whether a "pending land action." See ALLEN v. GREENHI BUILDERS, § 1554.

794. Limitation of actions. See LIMITATION OF ACTIONS.

795. Right of way—obstruction by adjoining tenants of common landlord—whether landlord liable. See HILTON v. JAMES SMITH AND SONS (NORWOOD), § 1601.

796. —— public policy

[Law of Property Act 1925 (c. 20), s. 62 (1).]

Any transaction which without good reason appears to deprive land of a suitable means of access will, if it is possible, be construed so as to avoid that result.

Building land was conveyed in 1908 subject to certain building regulations. The plan on the conveyance showed proposed roads, though the vendor specifically did not undertake to make them, nor did he create any right of way, until the roads should be made. The plot was therefore without access to the highway. In 1922 the plot was enlarged by a further purchase, but the land remained in agricultural and recreational use. In 1973 D, the then owners of adjoining land, attempted to prevent P, the then owner of the enlarged plot, from exercising a right of way over the adjoining land. P claimed a declaration that he was entitled to a right of way of necessity of the land. *Held*, since the public interest required that land should not be made unusable, it was a rule of public policy that no transaction should be construed where the alternative was possible as depriving land without reason of a suitable means of access. Since the land had been conveyed as building land, the conveyance should be construed as freeing the vendor from any obligation to make new roads, rather than as negating a right of way of necessity. (Dictum of Glynne C.J. in *Packer* v. *Wellstead* (1658) 2 Sid. at 112 applied; *North Sydney Printing Pty.* v. *Saberno Investment Corp. Pty.* [1971] 2 N.S.W.R. 150 and *Harris* v. *Flower* (1904) 74 L.J.Ch. 127 distinguished.)

NICKERSON *v.* BARRACLOUGH [1979] 3 All E.R. 312, Megarry V.-C.

797. Right to light—greenhouse—extraordinary light and sun's warmth—whether capable of acquisition by prescription

[Prescription Act 1832 (c.71), s. 3.]

The measure of light which can be acquired by prescription can, in the case of a greenhouse used for its normal purposes, include the right to an extraordinary amount of light and to the benefits of that light including the rays of the sun.

After the plaintiffs had used a greenhouse in their garden for over 20 years as a normal domestic greenhouse, the defendants so obstructed the light to it that it became impossible for the plaintiff to grow various plants therein, although there remained sufficient light to work in the building. The plaintiffs brought an action for nuisance and for injunctions. The action was dismissed. On appeal, *held*, allowing the appeal, that the measure of light which could be acquired by prescription was the light required for the beneficial use of the building for its ordinary purpose, and in the case of a greenhouse this could include the right to an extraordinary amount of light, and the benefits of that light including the sun's rays. (*Colls* v. *Home and Colonial Stores* [1904] A.C. 179, applied.)

ALLEN *v.* GREENWOOD [1979] 2 W.L.R. 187, C.A.

ARTICLES. See *post*, p. [20.].

ECCLESIASTICAL LAW

798. Faculty—title to painting—removal of goods on loan to church

Where a person, without a specific intention of giving goods to a church, delivers them to the custody of the wardens intending to dedicate them to God's service, property in the goods passes to the wardens.

Following restoration in 1977 of a picture hanging for some years in a parish church, the petitioner, whose family had built and furnished the church, sought a faculty for its return, claiming it to be a loan. On the petition, *held*, dismissing the petition, that on the evidence the painting had been delivered into the custody of the church wardens with the intention that it should be dedicated to God's service, and property accordingly passed to the wardens.

Re ESCOT CHURCH [1979] 3 W.L.R. 339, Calcutt Ch.

799. Marriage. See DIVORCE AND MATRIMONIAL CAUSES; HUSBAND AND WIFE.

800. Parochial fees

PAROCHIAL FEES ORDER 1979 (No. 194) [10p], made under the Ecclesiastical Fees Measure 1962 (No. 1), s. 2 (1); operative on July 1, 1979; amends S.I. 1976 No. 1112 by substituting a new Pt. 1 of the Schedule to that Order which sets out various fees payable on specified occasions.

801. Rating—rateable valuation. See RATING AND VALUATION.

802. Redundant churches

PAYMENTS TO REDUNDANT CHURCHES FUND ORDER 1979 (No. 195) [10p], made under the Pastoral Measure 1968 (No. 1), s. 53 (1); operative on April 1, 1979; provides for the maximum payment to the fund between April 1, 1979, to March 31, 1984, to be £1,450,000.

GRANTS TO REDUNDANT CHURCHES FUND ORDER 1979 (No. 478) [10p], made under the Redundant Churches and Other Religious Buildings Act 1969 (c. 22), s. 1 (1) (2); operative on April 18, 1979; specifies April 1, 1979, to March 31, 1984, as a later period for the purposes of s. 1 of the 1969 Act, thus enabling grants to be made to that Fund by the Secretary of State for the Environment to a maximum of £1,450,000.

803. —— disposal of chattels

Following a declaration of redundancy, during the waiting period before the confirmation of a scheme, the contents of a church must be dealt with on proper advice and their disposal authorised by faculty or an archdeacon.

A church was declared redundant. The rector on behalf of the churchwardens, but without a faculty, disposed of the bells to the bell-ringers of a church in another parish, for £20, believing mistakenly that they only had scrap value. The bells turned out to be medieval, and the bell-ringers of the second parish wished to sell one for £250. The rector of the first parish protested, and the incumbent of the second parish petitioned for custody. That petition was opposed by the first parish. A third parish, to whom the bell was to be sold, petitioned for its introduction into their church. *Held*, as the churchwardens of the first parish had no proper advice, and the disposal of the bells was not authorised by faculty or by an archdeacon, title remained vested in the churchwardens.

Re WEST CAMEL CHURCH; *Re* YATTON CHURCH [1979] 2 W.L.R. 501, Newsom Ch.

804. Registration of births, deaths and marriages. See REGISTRATION OF BIRTHS, DEATHS AND MARRIAGES.

EDUCATION

805. Awards

LOCAL EDUCATION AUTHORITY AWARDS REGULATIONS 1979 (No. 889) [£1·25], made under the Education Act 1962 (c. 12), ss. 1, 4 (2), Sched. 1, paras. 3, 4; operative on September 1, 1979; consolidate with amendments the Local Education Authority Awards Regulations 1978; the principal changes increase awards and relax the means tests applicable to the maintenance element.

STUDENTS' DEPENDANTS ALLOWANCES REGULATIONS 1979 (No. 900) [30p], made under the Education Act 1973 (c. 16), s. 3; operative on September 1, 1979 consolidate S.I. 1978 No. 1098 with amendments.

806. Direct grant schools

DIRECT GRANT GRAMMAR SCHOOLS (CESSATION OF GRANT) (AMENDMENT) REGULATIONS 1979 (No. 1552) [10p], made under the Education Act 1944 (c. 31), s. 100; operative on January 1, 1980; modify reg. 3 (2) of S.I. 1975 No. 1198 in its application to pupils admitted in 1980 so as to permit the payment of the grant where the intention of the proprietors that the school should become a maintained school had become conditional on statutory provision not being made for a scheme for assisted places at independent schools.

807. Education Act 1979 (c. 49)

This Act repeals ss. 1–3 of the Education Act 1976 and makes provision as to certain proposals submitted to the Secretary of State under s. 2 of that Act. S. 1 abolishes the duty to give effect to the comprehensive principle by repealing ss. 1–3 of the Education Act 1976, and provides for proposals submitted to the Secretary of State under s. 2 of that Act; s. 2 contains the short title. The Act does not extend to Scotland or Northern Ireland.

The Act received the Royal Assent on July 26, 1979, and came into force on that date.

808. Industrial training. See TRADE AND INDUSTRY.

809. Meals

PROVISION OF MILK AND MEALS (AMENDMENT) REGULATIONS 1979 (No. 695) [20p], made under the Education Act 1944 (c. 31), s. 49; operative on August 1, 1979; increase the dinner charge in nursery, county and voluntary schools from 25p to 30p, and raise the levels of net weekly income below which a parent qualifies for remission of the charge.

PROVISION OF MILK AND MEALS (AMENDMENT) (No. 2) REGULATIONS 1979 (No. 1686) [10p], made under the Education Act 1944, s. 49; operative on February 4, 1980; raise charges for certain school dinners from 30p to 35p.

810. Minister's powers—submission of proposals—form of comprehensive schooling to be adopted

[Education Act 1944 (c. 31), s. 13, as amended by the Education Act 1968 (c. 17), s. 1 (1), and the Education Act 1976 (c. 81), ss. 1 (1), 2 (1) (4).]

The words of s. 2 (4) of the 1976 Act are unambiguous, and where a local authority submits education proposals those proposals must (a) give effect to the comprehensive principle, and (b) be capable of being approved by the Secretary of State who has the power to dictate the type of comprehensive education to be adopted.

In 1977 the Secretary of State required a local authority to submit proposals concerning two local schools. The proposals were considered unsatisfactory and further proposals were required. The authority issued a summons seeking a declaration that the further requirement was *ultra vires. Held*, dismissing the summons, that the Secretary of State had power to require further proposals and to dictate the type of comprehensive education to be adopted. (*Secretary of State for Education and Science* v. *Tameside Metropolitan Borough Council* [1976] C.L.Y. 829 considered.)

NORTH YORKSHIRE COUNTY COUNCIL v. DEPARTMENT OF EDUCATION AND SCIENCE (1978) 77 L.G.R. 457, Browne-Wilkinson J.

811. Northern Ireland. See NORTHERN IRELAND.

812. Remuneration of teachers

REMUNERATION OF TEACHERS (PRIMARY AND SECONDARY SCHOOLS BURNHAM COMMITTEE) (VARIATION) ORDER 1979 (No. 339) [10p], made under the Remuneration of Teachers Act 1965 (c. 3), s. 1 (3) (4); operative on April 23, 1979; ends the representation of three teachers' organisations on the Burnham Committee concerned with the remuneration of teachers in schools maintained by local education authorities.

REMUNERATION OF TEACHERS (PRIMARY AND SECONDARY SCHOOLS) (AMENDMENT) ORDER 1979 (No. 428) [10p], made under the Remuneration of Teachers Act 1965, ss. 2, 7 (3); operative on April 4, 1979; gives effect to the recommendations which increase London Area payments to teachers.

REMUNERATION OF TEACHERS (PRIMARY AND SECONDARY SCHOOLS) ORDER 1979 (No. 1193) [10p], made under the Remuneration of Teachers Act 1965, ss. 1, 2 (2)–(4); operative on September 25, 1979; brings into operation the scales and other provisions relating to the remuneration of teachers in primary or secondary schools maintained by local authorities set out in a document published by HMSO.

813. —— designation of priority schools—validity of order

[Remuneration of Teachers Act 1965 (c. 3), ss. 1, 2; Remuneration of Teachers (Primary and Secondary Schools) (Amendment) Order 1975 (S.I. 1975 No. 152), art. 3.]

Statutory instruments should be construed in the light of their particular purpose and the situation with which they have to deal.

To combat the problem of the high turnover of teachers in stress areas of the country the Government decided that additional remuneration should be given to teachers employed in certain schools. The Burnham Committee received lists of such social priority schools from local authorities and from these lists drew up a revised final list. The defendant county council considered the scheme bad and divisive and passed a resolution to withdraw its list of schools already submitted to the Burnham Committee, but the revised list had already been finalised. In 1975 the Order was made to enable local authorities to pay increased remuneration to teachers in schools designated as social priority schools by the Designating Committee (made up of the members of the Burnham Committee), but the defendants refused to implement the Order. L brought an action to recover the remuneration withheld. At first instance, D's claim that the Order had not been validly implemented because the Designating Committee had merely rubber-stamped the Burnham Committee's final list and that the Secretary of State had acted *ultra vires* in creating a new committee called the Designating Committee, failed before O'Connor J. On appeal, *held,* that a loose rather than a strict construction of the words of the Order should be adopted so as to give effect to the proved intention of the makers of it. The validity of the Order should be upheld. *Per* Lord Denning M.R. and Brandon L.J.: Every statute and statutory instrument must be interpreted in the light of its particular purpose.

LEWIS *v.* DYFED COUNTY COUNCIL (1978) 77 L.G.R. 339, C.A.

814. Scholarships

SCHOLARSHIPS AND OTHER BENEFITS (AMENDMENT) REGULATIONS 1979 (No. 260) [10p], made under the Education Act 1944 (c. 31), s. 81; operative April 6, 1979; amend the 1977 (No. 1443) Regulations concerning clothing expenses of children attending county, voluntary and special schools.

STATE AWARDS (STATE BURSARIES FOR ADULT EDUCATION) (WALES) REGULATIONS 1979 (No. 333) [20p], made under the Education Act 1962 (c. 12), ss. 3 (c) (d), 4 (2) as amended by the Education Act 1975 (c. 2), s. 2; operative on April 17, 1979; consolidate specified Regulations with certain modifications relating to state scholarships for mature students.

SCHOLARSHIPS AND OTHER BENEFITS (AMENDMENT) (No. 2) REGULATIONS 1979 (No. 542) [10p], made under the Education Act 1944, s. 81; operative on June 14, 1979; revoke reg. 5 of S.I. 1977 No. 1443 so that a local authority will no longer require the approval of the Secretary of State before paying fees in respect of children attending non-maintained schools.

815. Schools—choice—suitability of education

[Education Act 1944 (c. 13), ss. 8, 36, 76; Pupils Registration Regulations 1956 (S.I. 1956 No. 357), para. 4 (a) (x).]

While a local education authority is obliged to provide suitable full-time education for a child, there is no duty to keep the child at a school preferred by the parents if the education provided is not suitable for him.

The child suffered from both mental and physical disabilities. The parents wished the child to be educated at the local primary school, which had no special facilities for such children. The local authority agreed to a trial period, but education in an ordinary school proved to be unsuitable. The parents refused a place in a school two miles away which had a class for the mentally handicapped. The local authority obtained a school attendance order for the child to attend a special school, and the child was excluded from the primary school. The parents sought, *inter alia*, an injunction restraining the authority from excluding the child from the primary school and a declaration that the school attendance order was invalid. *Held,* refusing the relief sought, that s. 8 of the Education Act 1944 did not oblige a local education authority to keep a child at an unsuitable school, and in those circumstances s. 76, which provided that the child should be educated in accordance with the wishes of the parents, did not apply. (*Gateshead Union v. Durham County Council* [1918] 1 Ch. 146 applied.)

WINWARD *v.* CHESHIRE COUNTY COUNCIL (1978) 77 L.G.R. 172, Judge Mervyn Davies.

816. Statutory duty of authority—closure of schools through strike

[Education Act 1944 (c. 31), ss. 8, 99 (1).]

Although s. 99 (1) of the 1944 Education Act provides a statutory remedy for an interested person complaining of breach of statutory duty, this does not exclude any other remedy available in the courts for an interested party who has suffered special damage as the result of a positive (*ultra vires*) act resulting in breach of statutory duty.

Due to an industrial dispute involving non-teaching staff, all the borough's schools were closed. The local authority continued negotiating with the unions. Various parents complained to the Secretary of State under s. 99 (1) of the authority's failure to comply with their statutory duty to provide schools and education. The reply was to the effect that there had been no such failure. One parent then issued a writ (on behalf of the others) requiring mandatory injunctions and a declaration. The application was refused. On appeal, *held*, dismissing the appeal (the schools having reopened), that although a statutory avenue of complaint was provided this did not exclude any other remedy available in the courts for a person who had suffered special damage by a breach of statutory duty from a positive act which was for some reason *ultra vires*.

MEADE *v.* HARINGEY LONDON BOROUGH COUNCIL [1979] 1 W.L.R. 637, C.A.

817. Superannuation

TEACHERS' SUPERANNUATION (POLICY SCHEMES) REGULATIONS 1979 (No. 47) [25p], made under the Superannuation Act 1972 (c. 11), ss. 9, 12; operative on February 19, 1979; provide for those teachers who are subject to the Federated Superannuation Scheme for Universities. The teachers' policy scheme service shall be reckonable service for the purposes of S.I. 1976 No. 1987 and shall count as to nine-tenths for the purposes of calculating benefit.

818. Teacher—church school—dismissal

[Education Act 1944 (c. 31), ss. 17 (3), 24 (2).] The appellant was the head teacher of a Roman Catholic voluntary aided primary school. After his divorce and remarriage, the managers suspended him from duty, reported the matter to the bishop, and acted as prosecutors at a tribunal set up by the bishop; the tribunal reported that the appellant should be dismissed and he was summarily dismissed by the managers. *Held*, that (1) the managers had erred in referring the matter to the bishop; they were the proper people to exercise the power of dismissal; (2) there had been a failure to make rules of management containing safeguards with regard to dismissal, in accordance with ss. 17 (3) and 24 (2) of the Education Act 1944; and (3) the dismissal should be prevented by the grant of an injunction: JONES *v.* LEE, *The Times*, November 21, 1979, C.A.

819. —— employment—compensation—whether loss of employment attributable to " direction " of Secretary of State

[Further Education Regulations 1975 (S.I. 1975 No. 1054), reg. 3 (2); Colleges of Education (Compensation) Regulations 1975 (S.I. 1975 No. 1092), regs. 7, 11.]

A teacher engaged upon a fixed term contract may claim compensation for loss of employment if a cause of the employment being of limited duration is a direction by the Secretary of State discontinuing courses.

The applicant teacher was employed as a college lecturer initially part-time, but from September 1, 1976, until August 31, 1977, full-time as a "temporary lecturer" under a contract which stated that after August 1977 her services would not be required "because of the reduction in the number of students attending the college." Such reduction was pursuant to an earlier direction of the Secretary of State that no further students were to be admitted to the college. After expiry of her contract, the teacher unsuccessfully claimed entitlement to compensation, asserting that her loss of employment was "attributable to" the direction of the Secretary of State. *Held*, allowing her appeal, that since entitlement to compensation did not depend upon the loss being solely or proximately attributable to the direction, the applicant was so entitled since the direction was clearly a cause of her not continuing in employment; that she was not disentitled by reason of being told of the reason for not extending her period employment at the time of making of her contract of employment. (*Walsh* v. *Rother District Council* [1978] C.L.Y. 1885, applied.)

PEARSON *v.* KENT COUNTY COUNCIL (1979) 77 L.G.R. 604, Forbes J.

820. Universities. See UNIVERSITIES.

BOOKS AND ARTICLES. See *post,* pp. [4], [21].

ELECTION LAW

821. Boundary Commission—new proposals—objective of electoral equality—ratio of electors to councillors. See ENFIELD LONDON BOROUGH COUNCIL *v.* LOCAL GOVERNMENT BOUNDARY COMMISSION FOR ENGLAND, § 1679.

822. Broadcast—no consent by candidate—whether unlawful
[Representation of the People Act 1969 (c. 15), s. 9 (1).]

S. 9 (1) of the Representation of the People Act 1969 is directed at protecting a candidate "actively participating in" a programme, not one who is merely "shown or recorded or co-operates" in an item to be broadcast.

During the General Election campaign of 1979, the B.B.C. sent a camera crew to film all four candidates in a constituency. The Labour candidate refused to take part in the programme which included the National Front candidate. The plaintiff protested, and claimed that the broadcast would be made without his consent and sought an injunction restraining the B.B.C. from broadcasting the film. The injunction was granted by Lloyd J. On appeal, *held,* allowing the appeal, that the words "takes part in" in s. 9 (1) mean "actively participates in" and not "is shown or recorded or co-operates in." MARSHALL *v.* BRITISH BROADCASTING CORP. [1979] 1 W.L.R. 1071, C.A.

823. Election petition
EUROPEAN ASSEMBLY ELECTION PETITION RULES 1979 (No. 521) [25p], made under the Representation of the People Act 1949 (c. 68), s. 160; operative on June 7, 1979; regulate the presentation and hearing of an election petition to the High Court which questions the declared result of any election to the European Assembly.

ELECTION PETITION (AMENDMENT) RULES 1979 (No. 543) [10p], made under the Representation of the People Act 1949, s. 160; operative on June 15, 1979; amend r. 6 of S.I. 1960 No. 543, which is concerned with security for cost given by means of a recognisance. The amendment makes it clear that persons before whom recognisances may be acknowledged include solicitors.

824. European assembly
EUROPEAN ASSEMBLY ELECTIONS (DAY OF ELECTION) ORDER 1979 (No. 219) [10p], made under the European Assembly Elections Act 1978 (c. 10), Sched. 1, para. 3 (1); operative on March 31, 1979; appoints June 7, 1979, as the day on which the first general election of representatives to the European Assembly shall be held.

EUROPEAN ASSEMBLY ELECTIONS (RETURNING OFFICERS) (ENGLAND AND WALES) ORDER 1979 (No. 220) [20p], made under the European Assembly Elections Act 1978, Sched. 1, para. 4 (1); operative on March 28, 1979; designates the parliamentary constituencies whose returning officers at parliamentary elections are to be returning officers at European Assembly elections.

EUROPEAN ASSEMBLY ELECTIONS REGULATIONS 1979 (No. 338) [80p], made under the European Assembly Elections Act Act 1978, Sched. 1, para. 2; operative on April 3, 1979; provide for the conduct of the election of representatives to the Assembly of European Communities in England, Scotland and Wales. Such elections will be conducted in accordance with the simple majority system.

EUROPEAN ASSEMBLY ELECTIONS (WELSH FORMS) ORDER 1979 (No. 368) [25p], made under the Welsh Language Act 1967 (c. 66), s. 2 (1); operative on May 1, 1979; prescribes in Welsh and English, the form of official poll card of an elector or proxy to be used for a European Assembly election in Wales.

ELECTION (WELSH FORMS) REGULATIONS 1979 (No. 434) [40p], made under the Representation of the People Act 1949 (c. 68), ss. 42, 171 (5) and the Welsh Language Act 1967, s. 2 (2); operative on April 18, 1979; amends S.I. 1975 No. 1329 and prescribe a new form of proxy paper which must be used in connection with elections in Wales.

EUROPEAN ASSEMBLY ELECTIONS (DAY OF BY-ELECTION) (LONDON SOUTH WEST CONSTITUENCY) ORDER 1979 (No. 1021) [10p], made under the European Assembly Elections Act 1978, Sched. 1, para. 3 (3); operative on August 16, 1979; appoints September 20, 1979, as the day for the by-election in the European Assembly Constituency of London South West.

825. Northern Ireland. See NORTHERN IRELAND.

826. Representation of the people

REPRESENTATION OF THE PEOPLE (AMENDMENT) REGULATIONS 1979 (No. 1679) [10p], made under the Representation of the People Act 1949 (c. 68), ss. 42 and 171 (5); operative on December 27, 1979; reg. 3 amends reg. 10 of S.I. 1974 No. 648 so as to remove the requirement that in the electors lists and the register of electors the name of any elector who is a service voter shall be marked with an " S " and the name of any elector who is a merchant seaman shall be marked with an " M." Reg. 5 adds a provision whereby the electoral registration officer is required to supply without fee to a parish or community council one copy of so much of the register as relates to the area of that parish or community.

827. Representation of the People Act 1979 (c. 40)

This Act facilitates polling on the same day at a general election and district council elections and postpones certain parish or community council elections.

S. 1 provides for modification of election rules; s. 2 postpones polling at parish or community council elections; s. 3 deals with citation.

The Act received the Royal Assent on April 4, 1979, and came into force on that date.

828. Returning officers' expenses

RETURNING OFFICERS' EXPENSES (ENGLAND AND WALES) REGULATIONS 1979 (No. 429) [25p], made under the Representation of the People Act 1949 (c. 68), s. 20 (2); operative on April 11, 1979; revoke and replace S.I. 1974 Nos. 179 and 1497 and prescribe a new scale of charges and expenses.

RETURNING OFFICERS' EXPENSES (SCOTLAND) REGULATIONS 1979 (No. 430) [25p], made under the Representation of the People Act 1949, s. 20 (2); operative on April 11, 1979; revoke and replace S.I. 1974 Nos. 180 and 1497 and prescribe a new scale of charges and expenses.

EUROPEAN ASSEMBLY ELECTIONS (RETURNING OFFICERS' EXPENSES) REGU-LATIONS 1979 (No. 588) [25p], made under the Representation of the People Act 1949, s. 20 (2), as applied by S.I. 1979 No. 338 Reg. 3 (1), Sched. 1; operative on May 28, 1979; prescribe the maximum charges in respect of services rendered and expenses incurred by returning officers for the purpose of or in connection with the European Assembly Elections.

ARTICLES. See *post*, p. [21].

ELECTRICITY

829. Electricity (Scotland) Act 1979 (c. 11)

This Act consolidates certain enactments relating to electricity Boards in Scotland and to functions of the Secretary of State in relation to the generation and distribution of electricity in Scotland.

Pt. I (ss. 1–31) deals with the constitution, functions and duties of Boards: s. 1 provides for the constitution of Boards; s. 2 defines the districts of the Boards, s. 3 sets out the functions of the Boards; s. 4 specifies the general duties of the Boards in exercising their functions; s. 5 lists the duties of the Boards in relation to the amenity of the environment; s. 6 sets out the duty of the North Board in relation to economic development; s. 7 gives the Boards ancillary powers; s. 8 empowers the Boards to enter into agreements with each other, and with other persons; s. 9 governs the purchase and supply of electri-city; s. 10 deals with constructional schemes; s. 11 authorises the acquisition of land for constructional schemes; s. 12 relates to the compulsory purchase of land; s. 13 gives ancillary powers in relation to land; s. 14 empowers the Boards to conduct experiments; s. 15 provides for research into heating from electricity; s. 16 enables the Boards to enter into agreements for technical assistance overseas; s. 17 deals with the establishment of Consultative Councils; s. 18 relates to the general fund; s. 19 concerns the general reserve fund of the South Board; s. 20 sets out sums which are to be chargeable by the South Board to revenue account; s. 21 provides for application of surplus revenues of the South Board; s. 22 deals with the fixing and variation of tariffs; s. 23 concerns the maximum charges for reselling electricity supplied by the Boards; s. 24 authorises Exchequer advances to the Boards; s. 25 empowers the Treasury to guarantee loans to the Boards; s. 26 authorises the Boards to issue stock; s. 27 gives the Boards power to borrow; s. 28 deals with the application of money borrowed; s. 29 places a limit on the aggregate of amount outstanding; s. 30 deals with accounts and audit; s. 31 relates to exemption from taxes.

Pt. II (ss. 32–38) defines the powers of the Secretary of State: s. 32 relates to the Secretary's powers; s. 33 empowers Secretary to give directions; s. 34 authorises transfer orders; s. 35 concerns control of new private hydro-electric generating stations; s. 36 deals with compensation for members and officers of the Boards; s. 37 empowers the Secretary to make regulations concerning pension rights; s. 38 deals with inquiries.

Pt. III (ss. 39–47) contains general and miscellaneous provisions: s. 39 relates to disputes between the Boards; s. 40 provides for the making of orders and regulations; s. 41 sets out offences and penalties; s. 42 deals with annual reports, statistics and returns; s. 43 empowers Boards to promote and oppose private legislation; s. 44 concerns service of notices; s. 45 is the interpretation section; s. 46 contains transitional and saving provisions and consequential amendment and repeals; s. 47 contains the short title, extent and commencement. The Act extends to Scotland only, except for para. 1 (*b*) of Sched. 3 which extends also to England and Wales.

The Act received the Royal Assent on March 22, 1979, and came into force on April 22, 1979.

830. Northern Ireland. See NORTHERN IRELAND.

EMERGENCY LAWS

831. Northern Ireland. See NORTHERN IRELAND.

EMPLOYMENT

832. Baking and sausage making

BAKING AND SAUSAGE MAKING (CHRISTMAS AND NEW YEAR) REGULATIONS 1979 (No. 1298) [10p], made under the Health and Safety at Work etc. Act 1974 (c. 37), ss. 11 (2) (*d*), 15 (1) (5) (*a*), 50 (3); operative on November 16, 1979; enable women who have reached the age of eighteen to be employed on specific Saturday afternoons and Sundays in December 1979 and January 1980 in the manufacture of meat pies, sausages or cooked meats, or in the prepacking of bacon, and in the manufacture of bread or flour confectionery.

833. Compensation—compulsory transfer—whether " worsening of position." See TUCK *v.* NATIONAL FREIGHT CORP., § 2728.

834. Constructive dismissal—breach of duty of mutual trust and confidence

[Trade Union and Labour Relations Act 1974 (c. 52), Sched. 1, para. 5 (2) (*c*).] A resigned as CNT Co.'s overseer after 18 years' service, after an argument with an assistant manager, S, during which S told A that A could not " do the bloody job anyway." *Held,* dismissing CNT Co.'s appeal against a finding of constructive dismissal, that A was entitled to treat S's comment, which was not a true expression of S's opinion, as conduct justifying resignation and a claim of constructive dismissal since the comment was in fundamental breach of the implied term in a contract of employment that the employers will not without reasonable and proper cause conduct themselves in a manner calculated to destroy or seriously damage the relationship of confidence and trust between the parties: COURTAULDS NORTHERN TEXTILES *v.* ANDREW [1979] I.R.L.R. 84, E.A.T.

835. —— change in pay—date of termination

H was dismissed as from June 24, 1977, following a disciplinary hearing after H's altercation with two members of the public. He appealed in accordance with the agreed procedure in his contract and three weeks' loss of pay and transfer to another area was substituted for the dismissal. When H reported to the new area he discovered that he would not get shift work or Sunday working allowance and would thus earn £10–£11 per week less. *Held,* dismissing H's appeal, that the tribunal had correctly decided that (1) H had not been dismissed from June 24, 1977, having successfully appealed under his contract of employment; (2) H had not been constructively dismissed. The new job was in the same grade and there was nothing in the B.R.B.'s offer to suggest they were breaking the contract or intending to break it or not to be bound by it: HIGH *v.* BRITISH RAILWAYS BOARD [1979] I.R.L.R. 52, E.A.T.

836. —— conduct of employee—reporting for duty after unfair dismissal complaint

H was demoted following a disciplinary hearing held when he was off sick. He issued an application before the tribunal but later when fit for work reported to do his original job. After being told to report for duty in his demoted position he kept refusing and eventually stopped reporting anywhere. *Held,* dismissing H's appeal against dismissal of his complaint of constructive dismissal, that his behaviour in reporting for duty was inconsistent with the view that he had treated the contract as at an end by reason of B.R.B.'s conduct: HUNT *v.* BRITISH RAILWAYS BOARD [1979] I.R.L.R. 379, E.A.T.

837. —— duty to hear evidence on both sides—whether inflexible rule

R alleged constructive dismissal. At the end of R's case the tribunal invited GEC Co. to make a submission of no case to answer and upheld the submission. *Held,* that (1) the ordinary general practice should be to hear what has to be said on both sides; (2) there may be exceptional cases where it is unnecessary to call on the respondents; (3) this was not such an exceptional case; (4) accordingly the case would be remitted for rehearing (*Buskin* v. *Vacutech Successors* [1977] C.L.Y. 933 considered and explained): RIDLEY *v.* G.E.C. MACHINES (1978) 13 I.T.R. 195, E.A.T.

838. —— employee's repudiation—change of emphasis in duties

P was appointed to the post of bar steward/catering assistant, his letter of appointment stating that his duties would primarily be related to bar steward's work but that when he was not required for such work the catering officer would assign him other catering duties. When in 1977 bookings dropped in the Assembly Rooms where P was bar steward other catering duties were found for him for much of the time. *Held,* allowing the L.B.C.'s appeal against a finding of constructive dismissal, that the change in emphasis in P's duties from those of bar steward to those of catering assistant was not a significant breach going to the root of the contract. It was within the terms of his letter of appointment (*Western Excavating (E.E.C.)* v. *Sharp* [1978] C.L.Y. 900 applied): CAMDEN LONDON BOROUGH *v.* PEDERSEN [1979] I.R.L.R. 377, E.A.T.

839. —— failure to pay salary on due date

[Trade Union and Labour Relations Act 1974 (c. 52), Sched. 1, para. 5 (1) (c).] A, a senior consultant for CZA Co., management consultants, and other staff members were given salary cheques at the end of February 1977 which the bank refused to meet until third presentation on March 29, 1977. In April, A was told that April salaries were due to be paid from moneys due from an Argentinian company. The money was delayed. On April 29, 1977, A asked when he would be paid and was asked to wait until May 2, 1977, when he was assured that the money was on its way. On May 9, 1977, the money not having arrived, A resigned. CZA's problems arose from their reliance sometimes on income from abroad. *Held,* dismissing A's appeal, that the tribunal had not erred in holding that CZA's breach of contract was not so serious as to justify A in resigning and claiming constructive dismissal under Sched. 1, para. 5 (2) (c), of the 1974 Act and that CZA's actions did not show an intention no longer to be bound by an essential term of the contract: ADAMS *v.* CHARLES ZUB ASSOCIATES [1978] I.R.L.R. 551, E.A.T.

840. —— fundamental breach—burden of proof

An employer has an obligation to provide reasonable support to ensure that an employee can work without undue harassment from fellow employees; the burden of proving that such support was given rests upon the employer.

The employee was unpopular with fellow employees at an old people's home since she failed to support their industrial action against the warden. The employers tried unsuccessfully to find her employment elsewhere and she agreed to remain at the home after her employers' assurance that they would give all reasonable support so as to enable her to work without disruption. Nothing was apparently done to remove the fellow-employees' continued hostility towards the employee who in due course left. An industrial tribunal found that she had been unfairly dismissed. *Held*, dismissing the employers' appeal, that the burden had been upon the employers to establish that they had taken all reasonable steps; and that the tribunal had been entitled to conclude upon the evidence that the burden of proof had not been discharged. (*Nimmo* v. *Alexander Cowan & Sons* [1967] C.L.Y. 1653 considered.)

WIGAN BOROUGH COUNCIL v. DAVIES [1979] I.C.R. 411, E.A.T.

841. —— —— failure to invoke grievance procedure—whether failure to mitigate loss

When S & L Co. took over a hairdressing business they re-engaged H, a ladies' hairdresser, on terms stipulated to be no less favourable than those which applied to her previous employment in the business. It was a term of H's previous contract that she had a junior to assist her. When her junior left, S & L Co. failed to appoint another. When she said she could not continue without a junior she was told "either you do your work or else you go." *Held*, dismissing S & L Co.'s appeal, that the tribunal were entitled to find that H had been constructively dismissed. Furthermore, H's failure to invoke the company's grievance procedure could not amount to failure to mitigate loss since once there has been a fundamental breach which has been accepted the contract is ended and it cannot be said that the grievance procedure should have been invoked: SELIGMAN & LATZ v. McHUGH [1979] I.R.L.R. 130, E.A.T.

842. —— overtime worked—employer refusing payment

S and HW Co. agreed that S could claim for all hours overtime which she worked over Christmas 1977. She worked 88 hours overtime during the period. However, despite promises she was not paid for these hours until February 24, 1978, when she was paid for 40 hours. The secretary at the head office and the area manager then told her that this was all she was getting. The assistant area manager told S that he would sort it out and ring her back but S said that she would resign if she did not receive the money on the following day. The assistant manager did not ring back and S resigned. The tribunal invited HW Co.'s counsel at the end of S's evidence to consider whether he would call evidence or submit that there was no case to answer, although he was told that he could call evidence if a submission failed. He announced that he would call no evidence. *Held*, that (1) the tribunal erred in finding that there was no case of constructive dismissal to answer. HW Co. were in fundamental breach of contract and S had acted reasonably; (2) the case would not be remitted for HW Co. to call evidence as their counsel's announcement that he would call no evidence was binding: STOKES v. HAMPSTEAD WINE CO. [1979] I.R.L.R. 298, E.A.T.

843. —— reasons—duty of tribunal to inquire

[Trade Union and Labour Relations Act 1974 (c. 52), Sched. 1, para. 5 (2) (*c*), 6 (1) (8).]

If an employer wishes to contend that if there was a dismissal it was fair, he must say so, and if he does not, an industrial tribunal need not inquire into the question.

P was the warden of a group of council dwellings for old people. She was expected to be on call for five full days a week, but if she wished to go out she could find a stand-in. Her working week was supposed to be 37 hours under a collective agreement. She was told that she must remain on the premises for five full days a week. She tried to do so, and her health suffered. She terminated her employment. The industrial tribunal found that there had been a constructive dismissal, under para. 5 (2) (*c*) of Sched. 1 to the Trade Union and Labour Relations Act 1974. The council appealed, contending that although at prior instance they had only argued that there was no dismissal, the tribunal should have inquired into the fairness of the dismissal which they had found had taken place. *Held*, dismissing the appeal, that there was no such duty upon the tribunal, and there had been a constructive dismissal.

DERBY CITY COUNCIL *v.* MARSHALL [1979] I.C.R. 731, E.A.T.

844. —— termination by consent or dismissal

When L Co. began negotiations for a takeover by M Co., M, a fleet organiser, sought alternative employment as M Co. would not need a fleet organiser. M's contract required six months' notice of termination on either side and prevented him from working in the same field for six months after termination. When the take-over was confirmed, M wrote a letter of resignation asking to be released immediately. He then wrote a second letter stating that he wished to terminate his employment with L Co. " and would request that in view of my future employment, I be released at your earliest convenience." L Co.'s personnel manager replied that " by mutual agreement your employment will terminate with effect from September 6, 1977." *Held*, that the tribunal had erred in finding M to have been constructively dismissed. Termination had been by agreement: L. LIPTON *v.* MARLBOROUGH [1979] I.R.L.R. 179, E.A.T.

845. —— test—contractual not reasonableness test

P was employed on general garage duties. When PC Co. removed him from work as a receptionist, his favourite duty, upon which he had spent 25 per cent. of his time, he resigned. *Held*, allowing PC Co.'s appeal, that P had not been constructively dismissed as P was not contractually entitled to insist on doing receptionist's duties. The tribunal had wrongly applied a reasonableness rather than a contractual test: PETER CARNIE & SON *v.* PATON [1979] I.R.L.R. 260, E.A.T.

846. —— whether contract affirmed—lapse of time between repudiation and acceptance

Following a disturbance B was suspended and later offered a non-supervisory job in another department with reduced wages. B then remained off work for about two and a half months claiming sick pay under BM Co.'s sickness scheme. The rate of sick pay was the same for his old job and the new job offered. B's solicitors corresponded with BM Co. during this period making it clear that he would not accept the alternative offered. Eventually, B's solicitor wrote to BM Co. stating that B was treating his contract as ended and claiming constructive dismissal. *Held*, allowing B's appeal, that the tribunal had erred in finding that B had affirmed the contract and lost his right to claim constructive dismissal. Since B had not returned and worked for a time in the new job without indicating acceptance of BM Co.'s repudiation and since his position was throughout made clear to BM Co., he could still claim constructive dismissal. The drawing of sick pay did not indicate acceptance of the new job (*Western Excavating (E.C.C.)* v. *Sharp* [1978] C.L.Y. 900 distinguished): BASHIR *v.* BRILLO MANUFACTURING CO. [1979] I.R.L.R. 295, E.A.T.

847. Continuity of employment—transfer of business—meaning of time of transfer

[Contracts of Employment Act 1972 (c. 53), Sched. 1, paras. 3, 4, 9.] There was continuity of employment where an employee dismissed by the transferor company was employed later in the same week by the transferee company. The legislation never intended that an employee should lose his statutory protections over redundancy or unfair dismissal because of such a short gap between employment on the transfer of a business: TEESSIDE TIMES *v.* DRURY, *The Times*, December 19, 1979, C.A.

848. —— working alternate weeks

[Employment Protection Act 1975 (c. 71), s. 35 (2); Contracts of Employment Act 1972 (c. 53), Sched. 16, Pt. II, para. 15.]

If an employee is contracted to work alternate weeks, she is " absent from work" by arrangement with her employers, and there is therefore no break in her continuity of employment.

A woman employee, by the terms of her employment, worked alternate weeks only. She became pregnant and was paid maternity pay by her employers. The employers' claim for a rebate was rejected on the ground that the woman had not been continuously employed for the appropriate time, and the employers were not obliged to pay her. The industrial tribunal upheld the Secretary of State's decision. On appeal, *held*, allowing the appeal, that since the employee was absent on alternate weeks by arrangement with her employers, there was no break in the continuity of her employment, and the employers were entitled to a rebate (*Fitzgerald* v. *Hall, Russell and Co.* [1969] C.L.Y. 1281, *R.* v. *Schildkamp* [1970] C.L.Y. 303, *Wishart* v. *National Coal Board* [1974] C.L.Y. 1242 applied.)

LLOYDS BANK v. SECRETARY OF STATE FOR EMPLOYMENT [1979] I.C.R. 258, E.A.T.

849. Contracts of employment—breach by employer—whether employee bound to mitigate loss by continuing employment

[Can.] A community college employed P for five years as director of curriculum. After an administrative reorganisation, the college assigned to P the task of acquiring instructional space. *Held*, (1) in the circumstances, the college was assigning to P substantially different duties from those agreed; (2) P could treat the college's conduct as a repudiation of the contract of employment, even though the college offered the same salary; (3) P need not accept continued employment with the college doing work for which she was not qualified nor where she would suffer a loss of prestige, in mitigating her loss (*Re Rubel Bronze & Metal Co. and Vos* [1918] 1 K.B. 315, *Brace* v. *Calder* [1895] 2 Q.B. 253, *British Westinghouse* v. *Underground Electric* [1912] A.C. 673 referred to): HERRSCHAFT v. VANCOUVER COMMUNITY COLLEGE (1978) 91 D.L.R. (3d) 328, Brit.Col.Sup.Ct.

850. —— implied term—employee's responsibility for cash deficiencies

When cash deficiencies arose at the petrol station where L was a forecourt attendant BG Co. concluded that they were due to dishonesty and deducted a proportion of the loss from L's wages. L resigned and claimed constructive dismissal. The tribunal held that it was an oral term of L's contract that she was responsible for any discrepancies in cash whilst she was on duty. *Held*, dismissing BG Co.'s appeal against a finding of constructive dismissal, that the tribunal had correctly found that it was an implied term that L should not be responsible for losses caused by dishonesty. It was necessary to imply this limitation on the express oral term to give ordinary business efficacy to the contract: BRISTOL GARAGE (BRIGHTON) v. LOWEN [1979] I.R.L.R. 86, E.A.T.

851. —— lay-off—estoppel—acceptance of previous lay-off

In 1974 W was laid off for two days and signed on for statutory benefit for two days at O Co.'s request. In 1976 he was laid off again and claimed to have been dismissed and to be entitled to a redundancy payment. *Held*, allowing W's appeal, that (1) there was no implied contractual right to lay off an employee unless that would be expected according to the customs of the particular trade concerned; (2) W was not estopped from denying such a right by his previous acquiescence in a lay-off, since such acquiescence was not a representation accepted and acted upon by O Co. to their detriment: WAINE v. R. OLIVER (PLANT HIRE) [1977] I.R.L.R. 434, E.A.T.

852. —— scope of " general clerical duties "

G was employed as a " copy typist/general duties clerk." Later a duplicating machine was bought by WE Co. and eventually WE Co. made its operator redundant owing to a redundancy situation amongst clerical staff and asked G to take on the additional duty of operating the machine. G agreed at first but soon had to be taken off such work as vapour from the machine gave her headaches. She rejected a suggestion that she apply for a job in the accounts department and was dismissed. *Held*, dismissing G's appeal, that (1) operation of a duplicating machine fell within the scope of " general clerical duties "; (2) in any event G had agreed to work the machine; (3) the dismissal was fair

385

as G could not work the machine and G had refused to apply for the only alternative job available: GLITZ *v*. WATFORD ELECTRIC CO. [1979] I.R.L.R. 89, E.A.T.

853. —— terms—constructive dismissal

R, a heavy goods vehicle driver, was employed by W Co. in 1973. Soon afterwards he signed a contract of employment form indicating that he would be liable to travel all over the country. R said at the hearing that the manager of W Co. had told him that as R's wife suffered from a nervous condition he would not be required to work outside southern England if he signed the agreement. W Co. was taken over by H.S.P.E. Co. who issued R with a further document in 1976 under the Contracts of Employment Act. This document expressly stated that R may be required to transfer to another workplace on H.E.P.E. Co.'s instruction in accordance with the appropriate Working Agreement. On March 16, 1978, H.S.P.E. Co. instructed R to go to Scotland and when he refused wrote to him confirming that by virtue of his refusal R was terminating his employment. *Held*, dismissing H.S.P.E. Co.'s appeal, that (1) it was an oral term of R's contract that he would not be required to work outside Southern England and on the facts this term had not been varied; (2) even if the term had been varied H.S.P.E. Co. should have given R an opportunity to consider the position and should not have taken action immediately upon his refusal to move; (3) the tribunal has not erred in inviting H.S.P.E. Co. to begin; (4) nor did the tribunal have a duty to invite H.S.P.E. Co.'s representative to ask for an adjournment to call further evidence when R gave vital evidence for the first time: HAWKER SIDDELEY POWER ENGINEERING *v*. RUMP [1979] I.R.L.R. 425, E.A.T.

854. —— —— duration

W replied to HC Co.'s advertisement for " a qualified concrete technician to operate the site lab for 15 months commencing mid-June." HC Co. sent a letter confirming their offer of employment and stating that the contract would run for 15–18 months. He was dismissed as redundant after just over 13 months. *Held*, dismissing HC Co.'s appeal, that the tribunal had not erred in finding the dismissal unfair on the ground that it was a term of the contract that its minimum duration would be 15 months. The dismissal might not have been unfair if HC Co. had shown that they had made every effort to find alternative employment: HOLLIDAY CONCRETE (TESTING) *v*. WOODS [1979] I.R.L.R. 301, E.A.T.

855. Contract of service—eclesiastical office holder—jurisdiction of industrial tribunal

B, a licensed reader in the Church of England, was engaged for one year as a full-time reader on a monthly stipend. He was dismissed, and submitted a complaint of unfair dismissal. The industrial tribunal stated that they had no jurisdiction, as, following *Re National Insurance Act 1911; Re Employment of Church of England Curates* [1912] 2 Ch. 563, B was in the same position as a curate, *i.e.* the holder of an ecclesiastical office, and therefore was not an employee, within the Trade Union and Labour Relations Act 1974. On appeal, *held*, that the fact that B was an office holder did not mean that he could not be employed under a contract of service. The question was whether his appointment to that office was made by, or co-existent with, a contract of service. It was for the tribunal to decide whether or not there was a contract of service, and the case would be remitted to them: BARTHORPE *v*. EXETER DIOCESAN BOARD OF FINANCE (1979) 123 S.J. 585, E.A.T.

856. Counter inflation. See REVENUE AND FINANCE.

857. Discrimination—application

An applicant for relief for unlawful discrimination may be allowed to amend his application to include a complaint of unfair dismissal, particularly where the employer is not prejudiced thereby.

The employee applied to an industrial tribunal for a decision as to whether he had been unlawfully discriminated against because of his race, his application setting out that after two years secondment from the Inland Revenue to the Home Office during which no complaint was made as to his performance, he had been returned to the Revenue at a lesser salary. Subsequently an industrial tribunal gave leave to the employee to amend his application by inclusion of a claim for unfair dismissal. *Held*, dismissing the employer's appeal, that the facts stated in the original application sufficed to support a claim for unfair dismissal and that accordingly no injustice was done by permitting the amendment.

HOME OFFICE *v.* BOSE [1979] I.C.R. 481, E.A.T.

858. **Dockworkers—work performed by registered dockworkers—position of " listed weekly workers " under scheme.** See E.C.C. PORTS *v.* NATIONAL DOCK LABOUR BOARD, § 2467.

859. **Employment agencies**

EMPLOYMENT AGENCIES AND EMPLOYMENT BUSINESSES LICENCE FEE REGULATIONS 1979 (No. 770) [10p], made under the Employment Agencies Act 1973 (c. 35), ss. 2 (2), 12 (1)–(3); operative on August 1, 1979; revoke S.I. 1978 No. 390 and prescribe increased fees payable on the grant or renewal of a licence under the 1973 Act to carry on an employment agency or an employment business.

EMPLOYMENT AGENCIES ACT 1973 (EXEMPTION) (NO. 2) REGULATIONS 1979 (No. 1741) [10p], made under the Employment Agencies Act 1973, ss. 12 (1), 13 (7) (i); operative on February 4, 1980; exempt from the licensing and other provisions of the Employment Agencies Act 1973 certain named organisations.

860. **Employment Agencies Act 1973—exemption**

EMPLOYMENT AGENCIES ACT 1973 (EXEMPTION) REGULATIONS 1979 (No. 342) [20p], made under the Employment Agencies Act 1973 (c. 35), ss. 12 (1) (2), 13 (7) (i); operative on May 1, 1979; exempt from the licensing and other provisions of the 1973 Act certain named organisations providing services for their members and registered students.

861. **Employment Appeal Tribunal—costs—delay in withdrawing notice of appeal**

[Employment Appeal Tribunal Rules 1976 (S.I. 1976 No. 322), r. 21.] On February 10, 1978, TVR Co. entered a notice of appeal against a finding of unfair constructive dismissal. They requested notes taken of the evidence which were sent to their solicitors on April 19, 1978. On July 12, 1978, notice of withdrawal of the appeal was sent, the date for hearing of the appeal having been fixed for July 21, 1978. *Held*, awarding costs incurred as a result of the appeal subsequent to June 15, 1978, against TVR Co., that there had been unreasonable delay in communicating the decision to withdraw the appeal within r. 21 of the 1976 Rules. Such communication should not be left until a few days before the date fixed for the hearing: T.V.R. ENGINEERING *v.* JOHNSON [1978] I.R.L.R. 555, E.A.T.

862. —— **jurisdiction—new ground for complaint—whether to remit case for rehearing**

Where a completely new point is raised before the appeal tribunal on which there are no findings of fact to support the claim, the appeal tribunal will not remit the case for rehearing nor itself consider the point.

J complained of unfair dismissal on the grounds of wrong selection for redundancy; his complaint was dismissed. He appealed on the new ground that the employers had not complied with the Code of Practice. *Held*, dismissing the appeal, that since the new point could have been taken before the tribunal it would be wrong to remit the case, and since there were no findings of fact to support the new point the appeal tribunal could not consider it.

JONES *v.* R.M. DOUGLAS CONSTRUCTION [1979] I.C.R. 278, E.A.T.

863. —— **practice—fresh evidence**

[Employment Protection Act 1975 (c. 71), Sched. 6, paras. 19, 20.]

The Employment Appeal Tribunal has a discretion to admit fresh evidence relating to the matters in issue on an appeal from an industrial tribunal.

An industrial tribunal ruled that an employee's dismissal was unfair having regard to the apparent knowledge of the employers at the time of dismissal and their failure to permit the employee to explain his conduct. The employers at the appeal hearing sought to adduce further evidence upon these issues. *Held*, that the appellate tribunal had a discretion whether to admit such evidence; that it would be admitted since there was a reasonable explanation as to why it had not been adduced at the original hearing, it was credible and might have a decisive effect on the result of the appeal. (*Bagga* v. *Heavy Electricals (India)* [1972] C.L.Y. 1223 considered.)

INTERNATIONAL AVIATION SERVICES (U.K.) *v.* JONES [1979] I.C.R. 371, E.A.T.

864. —— —— listing of appeals

The following Practice Direction was issued by the Employment Appeal Tribunal on February 22, 1979:

Para. 10A of the Practice Direction dated March 3, 1978 [1978] C.L.Y. 921, is revoked.

As from the date hereof the following Practice Direction is substituted. 10A. ENGLAND AND WALES

(a) When the respondent's answer has been received and a copy served on the appellant, the case will be put in the list of cases for hearing. At the beginning of each calendar month a list will be prepared of cases to be heard on specified dates in the next following calendar month. That list will also include a number of cases which are liable to be taken in each specified week of the relevant month. The parties or their representatives will be notified as soon as the list is prepared. When cases in the list with specified dates are settled or withdrawn cases warned for the relevant week will be substituted and the parties notified as soon as possible.

(b) A party finding that the date which has been given causes serious difficulties may apply to the Listing Officer before the 15th of the month in which the case first appears in the list. No change will be made unless the Listing Officer agrees, but every reasonable effort will be made to accommodate parties in difficulties. Changes after the 15th of the month in which the list first appears will not be made other than on application to the President of the Employment Appeal Tribunal; arrangements for the making of such an application should be made through the Listing Officer.

(c) Other cases may be put in the list by the Listing Officer with the consent of the parties at shorter notice, *e.g.* where other cases have been settled or withdrawn or where it appears that they will take less time than originally estimated. Parties who wish their cases to be taken as soon as possible and at short notice should notify the Listing Officer.

(d) Each week an up-to-date list for the following week will be prepared including any changes which have been made (in particular specifying cases which by then have been given fixed dates).

(e) The monthly list and the weekly list will appear in the Daily Cause List and will also be displayed in Room 6 at the Royal Courts of Justice and at No. 4, St. James's Square, London, S.W.1. It is important that parties or their advisers should inspect the weekly list as well as the monthly list.

(f) If cases are settled or to be withdrawn notice should be given at once to the Listing Officer so that other cases may be given fixed dates.

[1979] 1 W.L.R. 289.

865. —— —— point of law not taken below

[Employment Protection Act 1975 (c. 71), s. 88 (1).]

Although it is not prevented from so doing, the Employment Appeals Tribunal will only in exceptional circumstances permit a point of law to be taken which was not taken below.

An employee was dismissed for refusing to work at an alternative site, although he was contractually obliged to work where directed. Having failed in a complaint of unfair dismissal he sought to argue on appeal that it was an implied term of his contract that any other site at which he was required to work would be similar to that at which he had previously worked. *Held*, dismissing the appeal, that only if, for example, a party was prevented by deception or through some other exceptional circumstance from taking a point of law at the first hearing, would the Appeals Tribunal entertain such a point on appeal.

KUMCHYK *v.* DERBY CITY COUNCIL [1978] I.C.R. 1116, E.A.T.

866. —— sittings

The following Practice Direction was issued by the President of the E.A.T. on October 11, 1979:

Pursuant to para. 14 of Sched. 11 to the Employment Protection (Consolidation) Act 1978, and to the powers vested in me by r. 25 (1) of the Employment Appeal Tribunal Rules 1976 (S.I. 1976 No. 332) I direct that

1. The sittings of the Employment Appeal Tribunal for the year 1980 shall be: Friday, January 11 to Wednesday, April 2; Monday, April 14 to Thursday, May 22; Monday, June 2 to Thursday, July 31; Monday, September 1 to Tuesday, September 30; Wednesday, October 1 to Friday, December 19.

2. The central office of the Tribunal in London will be closed on the following days: Saturdays and Sundays; Tuesday, January 1; Easter, Friday, April 4 and Monday, April 7; May Day, Monday, May 5; Friday, May 23 and Spring Bank Holiday, May 26; late summer holiday, Monday, August 25; Christmas, Wednesday, Thursday and Friday, December 24, 25 and 26.

3. The Glasgow office of the Tribunal will be closed on the following days: Saturdays and Sundays; Tuesday and Wednesday, January 1 and 2; Easter, Friday, April 4 and Monday, April 7; May Day, Monday, May 5; H.M. The Queen's Birthday Holiday, Monday, May 26; summer holiday, Monday, July 21; autumn holiday, Monday, September 29; Christmas, Thursday and Friday, December 25 and 26.

The hours during which the offices of the Employment Appeal Tribunal shall be open to the public shall, subject to paras. 2 and 3 above, be 10 a.m. until 4.30 p.m. except during the month of August when they shall be 10 a.m. until 2.30 p.m.

123 S.J. 724.

867. Employment protection

EMPLOYMENT PROTECTION (VARIATION OF LIMITS) ORDER 1979 (No. 1722) [20p], made under the Employment Protection (Consolidation) Act 1978 (c. 44), ss. 15 (5), 122 (6), 148, 154 (3); operative on February 1, 1980; varies certain limits set by ss. 15 (1), 122 of the Employment Protection (Consolidation) Act 1978.

868. —— maternity leave—notice of intention to return not given in time

[Employment Protection Act 1975 (c. 71), s. 35 (2).]

In considering whether or not it was reasonably practicable for an employee to give notice (three weeks before leaving her employment) of her intention to return to work after the birth of her child, the relevant question is whether she knew or ought to have known of her rights.

An employee informed her employers she was pregnant. She was repeatedly asked whether she intended to return to work after the baby's birth, but was uncertain and indicated she probably would not. She eventually changed her mind and gave notice but failed to give the notice three weeks before leaving her employment as required by s. 35 (2). An industrial tribunal found that her anxiety concerning the baby's health had made it not " reasonably practicable." On appeal by the employers, *held*, allowing the appeal, that the test was whether she knew of her rights; and since she clearly did, the tribunal had erred in law in saying it was " not reasonably practicable." (*Dedman* v. *British Building and Engineering Appliances* [1974] C.L.Y. 1316 applied.)

NU-SWIFT INTERNATIONAL v. MALLINSON [1979] I.C.R. 157, E.A.T.

869. —— working paper

The Secretary of State for Employment has published a working paper proposing amendments to unfair dismissal provisions, industrial tribunal procedures, maternity provisions and guarantee pay provisions. Among the proposals is that new firms of less than 20 employees should be exempt from the unfair dismissal provisions for the first two years of trading.

870. Equal pay—genuine material difference—employee voluntarily working fewer hours

[Equal Pay Act 1970 (c. 41), s. 1 (3) (as amended by the Sex Discrimination Act 1975 (c. 65), s. 8 (1)); EEC Treaty 1972 (Cmnd. 5179–11), art. 119.]

The fact that a female employee is required to work fewer hours than her male counterpart may justify payment of a lower hourly rate.

Male and female employees working a basic 40 hours per week received the same hourly remuneration. But female employees had the option of working only 26 hours per week at a lower rate of pay; one such employee sought equality of pay with a male, full-time, machinist. An industrial tribunal rejected her claim. *Held*, dismissing the employee's appeal, that (1) the tribunal had been entitled to conclude that the difference in total hours worked was a "material difference" justifying a variation in pay rates; (2) that art. 119 of the EEC Treaty did not require that the same rate of pay was allowed when employees worked a different number of hours. (*Shields* v. *E. Coomes* (*Holdings*) [1978] C.L.Y. 943 and *Clay Cross* (*Quarry Services*) v. *Fletcher* [1978] C.L.Y. 945 applied.)

HANDLEY *v.* H. MONO [1979] I.C.R. 147, E.A.T.

871. —— —— grading

P, a female lecturer employed on point 5 of the salary scale at the University of Sussex, was paid more than X, a male lecturer also employed on point 5. P complained under the Equal Pay Act 1970 that she should have been graded higher than X since she was older and better qualified. *Held*, dismissing P's appeal, that there was no term in P's contract that was less favourable than the equivalent term in X's contract. The "age wage" norm, whereby under the ordinary arrangements in the University older persons are given higher points, was not a contractual term but an internal system for guidance which formed no part of the official appointing procedure: POINTON *v.* THE UNIVERSITY OF SUSSEX [1979] I.R.L.R. 119, C.A.

872. —— job evaluation study—validity—scheme not yet applied

[Equal Pay Act 1970 (c. 41), s. 1 (2) (*b*) (as amended by Sex Discrimination Act 1975 (c. 65), s. 8).]

A merit assessment scheme is not part of a job evaluation scheme and if there has been a valid job evaluation scheme the employees are entitled to a salary appropriate to the grade for their job.

A job evaluation scheme was carried out and the applicants were informed of their new job grade and salary range for the grade. Before the scheme and the new gradings were applied a merit assessment scheme was to be introduced. Because of the Government's pay policy the employees were never remunerated on the new salary range. The applicants claimed an entitlement to equal pay because the evaluation scheme had been completed and had rated their jobs as equivalent to those of men who were paid more. An industrial tribunal dismissed the application. On appeal, *held*, that a merit assessment scheme was not part of a job evaluation scheme and if there was a valid job evaluation scheme the applicants were entitled to a salary appropriate to the grade for their job. The phrase "determined by the rating of the work" was limited to mean that the term of the woman's contract of employment must be of such a kind that the rating of the job is relevant to its application.

O'BRIEN *v.* SIM-CHEM [1979] I.C.R. 13, E.A.T.

873. —— like work—distinction between nature of duties

[Equal Pay Act 1970 (c. 41), s. 1 (4) as amended by Sex Discrimination Act 1975 (c. 65), s. 8.]

Where the nature of employment of male and female employees is considered, if there is a distinction to be drawn between the nature of part of the duties undertaken, they are not employed on "like work" for the purposes of equal pay legislation.

M, a woman, who was employed as a clerk and packer, sought equality of pay with a male employee employed as a storeman and packer. Each was primarily engaged in packing work. H sought equality with a male machine operator, the only difference between their work being that the male was trained to set his own machine whereas H's machine had to be set for her. An industrial tribunal dismissed both applications. *Held*, dismissing the appeals of M and H, that there were differences of practical importance between the work undertaken in each case; and that accordingly the tribunal had no power to assess whether the differences were such as to warrant the particular wage differentials.

MAIDMENT v. COOPER & CO. (BIRMINGHAM) [1978] I.C.R. 1094, E.A.T.

874. —— —— **genuine material difference**
[Equal Pay Act 1970 (c. 41), s. 1 (3), as amended by the Sex Discrimination Act 1975 (c. 65), s. 8 (1).]
Where a company relies on a " material " difference to justify the variation between a man's and a woman's contract, the tribunal must be satisfied that the man's job is not reserved exclusively for men, and that the reason the man was given the job with better terms is not just because he is a man.

M was transferred to a clerical job within the company because of age and ill-health. He was given staff status which he had not previously enjoyed and the same wages as his predecessor. These were lower than his previous wages but more than two women employees doing like work. The women applied for a declaration that they were entitled to equal pay; the tribunal refused the declaration. On appeal, *held*, dismissing the appeal, that the tribunal having found that the reason for the difference in contracts was due to his age and ill-health they were entitled to hold that the variation was due to a material difference other than sex. (*Snoxell and Davies* v. *Vauxhall Motors; Charles Early & Marriott (Witney)* v. *Smith* [1977] C.L.Y. 1257 applied.)
METHVEN v. COW INDUSTRIAL POLYMERS [1979] I.C.R. 613, E.A.T.

875. —— —— **reference to European Court.** See MACARTHYS v. SMITH, § 1237.

876. —— **pension scheme—Community law**
[Equal Pay Act 1970 (c. 41), s. 6 (1A) (*b*); Treaty of Rome, art. 119.]
LB Co. require all clerical officers to join their pension scheme. The women's scheme is non-contributory until the age of 25. The men's is contributory throughout and in order to equalise their position with the women their gross pay is increased by the amount of their contribution. Contributions are returned to those leaving LB Co. *Held*, that the tribunal were excluded from considering the women's complaints of discrimination in pay by s. 6 (1A) (*b*) of the 1970 Act which excludes " terms related to death or retirement, or to any provision made in connection with death or retirement." Nevertheless, the case would be referred to the European Court of Justice for determination of whether the claim could succeed under art. 119 of the Treaty of Rome, which provides for equal pay for equal work with no pension exclusion. It seemed that the claim probably would succeed under art. 119: WORRINGHAM AND HUMPHREYS v. LLOYDS BANK [1979] I.R.L.R. 440, C.A.

877. —— **rates of pay differing for part-time worker—reference to EEC court**
[Equal Pay Act 1970 (c. 41), s. 1; EEC Treaty 1972, art. 119.] The Employ-ment Appeal Tribunal agreed to submit a schedule of questions to the European Court concerning the effect of art. 119 on part-time workers: JENKINS v. KINGSGATE (CLOTHING PRODUCTIONS), *The Times*, November 15, 1979, E.A.T.

878. —— **sex discrimination—less favourable terms—removal expenses—genuine material difference**
[Equal Pay Act 1970 (c. 41), s. 1 (3); Sex Discrimination Act 1975 (c. 65), s. 1 (1) (*b*).] The agreement for the Health Services Whitley Councils provides that removal expenses are payable only if the employee was employed full time prior to moving. D, a clinical psychologist who had transferred from a part-time to a full-time post, claimed to have been discriminated on grounds of sex, contrary to the 1975 Act, s. 1 (1) (*b*), since fewer women can be employed full time while carrying out their domestic duties. She claimed under the Equal Pay Act since the claim related to payment of money. *Held*, that as a part-time woman was in exactly the same position as a part-time man and the N.Y.A.H.A. had shown that the variation between D's contract and that of the man with whom she had compared herself, who had transferred from full-time employment, was genuinely due to a material difference other than that of sex within s. 1 (3) of the 1970 Act, the claim failed. Clauses cannot be transposed directly from the 1975 Act to the 1970 Act: DURRANT v. NORTH YORKSHIRE AREA HEALTH AUTHORITY AND SECRETARY OF STATE FOR SOCIAL SERVICES [1979] I.R.L.R. 401, E.A.T.

879. Factories. See FACTORIES.

880. Guarantee payments

GUARANTEE PAYMENTS (EXEMPTION) (NO. 19) ORDER 1979 (No. 1403) [20p], made under the Employment Protection (Consolidation) Act 1978 (c. 44), ss. 12, 18 (1) (4), Scheds. 1, 2, 3; operative on December 14, 1979; excludes from the operation of s. 12 of the 1978 Act employees to whom the agreements of the National Joint Council for the Motor Vehicle Retail and Repair Industry on the pay, classification and working conditions of skilled and other workers and on the procedure for the avoidance of disputes and related matters relate.

881. —— Industrial Tribunal decisions

GARVEY v. J. & J. MAYBANK (OLDHAM) [1979] I.R.L.R. 408 (during a national road haulage strike pickets at J & J Co.'s works refused to let J & J Co.'s own lorries in or out. J & J Co.'s own drivers disobeyed orders to cross the picket lines. 50 other employees were therefore laid off as a result of lack of waste paper supplies. *Held*, that G was not entitled to a guaranteed payment under s. 12 (1) of the Employment Protection (Consolidation) Act 1978 because the lay-off was occasioned by a trade dispute involving other employees of J & J Co. within s. 13 (1). "Trade dispute" under s. 153 (1) and s. 29 (1) includes a dispute on a matter of discipline. The drivers' disobedience was a matter of discipline).

NAMYSLO v. SECRETARY OF STATE FOR EMPLOYMENT [1979] I.R.L.R. 333 (N, a weekly paid staff employee, was laid off on February 3, 1978, and made redundant on February 24, 1978, his employers having gone into receivership. *Held*, that (1) N was not entitled to claim from the Secretary of State for Employment under s. 122 of the Employment Protection (Consolidation) Act 1978 a sum equal to his salary for the period when he was laid off without pay prior to dismissal. It is now an implied term in the contract of every weekly paid employee that he may be laid off without pay, even if he is a staff employee with a yearly salary and entitled to salary if off work owing to illness; (2) in calculating N's entitlement to salary in lieu of notice his weekly pay should be based on a 40-hour week and not the 48-hour week which N normally worked with overtime. N's earnings and unemployment benefit during the notice period fell to be deducted from the salary in lieu of notice).

882. Health and safety at work

HEALTH AND SAFETY (FEES FOR MEDICAL EXAMINATIONS) REGULATIONS 1979 (No. 1553) [20p], made under the Health and Safety at Work, etc. Act 1974 (c. 37), ss. 43 (2)–(6) and 60 (5) (b); operative on January 7, 1980; fix the fees payable by employers to the Health and Safety Executive for work done by employment medical advisers appointed under s. 56 (1) of the 1979 Act for "conducting various medical examinations of employees under the Factories Act 1961.

883. —— improvement notice—appeal—whether tribunal has power to amend notice to include alleged breach of other provisions

[Health and Safety at Work, etc. Act 1974 (c. 37), s. 24 (2).]

The tribunal may modify the requirements of safety measures to be taken but has no power to amend the notice to include an alleged breach of other provisions.

H served an improvement notice on B. B appealed to the industrial tribunal and H sought to amend the notice to include allegations of a breach of a further provision of the Act. *Held*, that the tribunal had no power under s. 24 (2) to amend the notice to include an alleged breach of other provisions of the Act.

BRITISH AIRWAYS BOARD v. HENDERSON [1979] I.C.R. 77, Industrial Tribunal.

884. —— Industrial Tribunal decision

ASSOCIATED DAIRIES v. HARTLEY [1979] I.R.L.R. 171 (following an accident, an improvement notice was issued under the Health and Safety at Work Act 1974 requiring AD Co. to provide protective footwear to all employees involved in operating hydraulic trolley jacks free of charge. *Held*, allowing AD Co.'s appeal, that the expense of providing the footwear free of charge

was disproportionate to the risk to employees in requiring AD Co. merely to
ensure that it was available in accordance with existing arrangements whereby
it could be purchased by employees at cost price by instalments. Accordingly
the existing arrangements satisfied the requirement under s. 2 to secure
employees' safety " so far as is reasonably practicable ").

885. Industrial injuries benefit. See SOCIAL SECURITY.

886. Industrial organisation and development. See TRADE AND INDUSTRY.

887. Industrial relations. See TRADE UNIONS.

888. Industrial training. See TRADE AND INDUSTRY.

889. Industrial tribunals—costs—adjournment of hearing
    Where an adjournment of proceedings before an industrial tribunal is ordered,
the tribunal has power to grant costs against the party responsible.
    Shortly before the hearing of a complaint of unfair dismissal the employee's
counsel was handed a substantial bundle of documents by the employer's representative and was granted an adjournment so as to consider the same. The
industrial tribunal ordered the employer to pay the cost of the adjournment.
Held, dismissing the employer's appeal, that it is not necessary in relation to
the costs of an adjournment for the tribunal to find the party against whom
they are awarded to have acted frivolously or vexatiously.
    LADBROKE RACING *v.* HICKEY [1979] I.C.R. 525, E.A.T.

890. —— **discovery—complaints of sex and racial discrimination.** See SCIENCE
RESEARCH COUNCIL *v.* NASSE; LEYLAND CARS (B.L. CARS) *v.* VYAS, § 940.

891. —— **evidence—discretion to admit hearsay evidence**
    A tribunal, when deciding whether an employer has acted reasonably in a
dismissal case, needs to know what information was before the employers,
and ought therefore to relax the rules of evidence to admit hearsay evidence,
even though a criminal offence is alleged.
    The employees, manager and cashier of a squash club were dismissed
following complaints that they were breaching the licensing laws. The
employers called a temporary manager to give evidence of complaints made
by customers to him. The tribunal refused to admit the evidence, and found
for the employees. On appeal, *held*, allowing the appeal, that since it was
necessary for the tribunal to know what information was before the employers
they ought to have admitted the evidence.
    CORAL SQUASH CLUBS *v.* MATTHEWS [1979] I.C.R. 607, E.A.T.

892. —— **High Court action pending—tribunal's discretion to postpone hearing**
    [Industrial Tribunal (Labour Relations) Regulations 1974 (S.I. 1974 No.
1386), 11 (2) (*b*).] A tribunal postponed the hearing of C's complaint of
unfair dismissal pending the outcome of C.C. Co's action in the High Court
against C for breaches of contract and serious misconduct. *Held*, allowing
C's appeal, that r. 11 (2) (*b*) of the 1974 Regulations gives tribunal chairmen
a wide discretion as to whether to postpone proceedings in the interests of
justice. The E.A.T. had erred in holding that a tribunal must hear a claim
before the High Court proceedings unless there were special reasons or
unusual circumstances: CARTER *v.* CREDIT CHANGE [1979] I.R.L.R. 361, C.A.

893. —— **jurisdiction—complaint presented before termination of contract**
    [Trade Union and Labour Relations Act 1974 (c. 52), Sched. 1, para. 21 (4A),
as added by Employment Protection Act 1975 (c. 71), Sched. 16, Pt. III, para.
21.]
    Para. 21 (4A) of Sched. 1 to the Trade Union and Labour Relations Act
1974, which permits an industrial tribunal to consider a complaint even though
presented before the effective date of termination, is not limited by paras. (*a*)
to (*d*) of sub-para. (4A) so as to exclude a case where notice is given by an
employee as opposed to an employer.
    On February 13, E wrote to his employers terminating his employment as
from March 20 on the grounds of their conduct. On February 23 he presented
a complaint of unfair dismissal. The industrial tribunal held that it had no
jurisdiction on the ground that the power to present a complaint before the

effective date of termination under para. 21 (4A) of Sched. 1 to the Trade Union and Labour Relations Act 1974 was limited by paras. (*a*) to (*d*) so as to exclude cases where notice was given by the employer. On appeal by E, *held*, allowing the appeal, that " dismissal " in para. 5 (2) (*c*) of Sched. 1 included constructive dismissal, " dismissal with notice " in para. 21 (4A) included notice by employer or employee; para. 21 (4A) referred simply to " notice," and accordingly the tribunal had jurisdiction to hear the complaint.

PRESLEY *v.* LLANELLI BOROUGH COUNCIL [1979] I.C.R. 419, E.A.T.

894. —— —— **transfer of case to Scotland**
[Industrial Tribunals (Labour Relations) Regulations 1974 (S.I. 1974 No. 1386), reg. 3.]

Registration under the Companies Act 1948 is sufficient to satisfy the requirement of residence in reg. 3 (*a*) of the Regulations.

Per curiam: Such problems will be more conveniently solved in future if the appropriate rule-making body makes a simple provision in the rules for transfer between England and Scotland where justice and convenience or agreement between the parties suggests that this is the right thing to do.

The employers were a foreign corporation having a registered office in London but operating from a base in Scotland. The employee was dismissed, and he made an application claiming compensation for unfair dismissal in London. The application was registered as the employers had a registered office in London, thereby satisfying the residence requirement of reg. 3 (*b*) of the Industrial Tribunals (Labour Relations) Regulations 1974. The employers asked for the case to be transferred to Scotland and the matter was referred to the regional chairman of tribunals who decided that there was no machinery for transfer and that the registration in England was valid. *Held*, dismissing the employers' appeal, that as the employers were a company registered in London that was sufficient to satisfy the requirement of residence in reg. 3 (*a*) of the 1974 Regulations.

ODECO (U.K.) INC. *v.* PEACHAM [1979] I.C.R. 823, E.A.T.

895. —— —— **transfer of proceedings for rehearing—whether tribunal functus officio**
An industrial tribunal has inherent power to transfer a case to a differently constituted tribunal for rehearing if they consider that their own findings are inconclusive.

Three employees applied to an industrial tribunal alleging unfair dismissal and redundancy. One tribunal member found unfair dismissal, another redundancy, and the third neither of these. The chairman proposed to transfer the case to another tribunal for rehearing. The employers sought orders of prohibition and mandamus to compel the tribunal to enter a decision dismissing the employees' claim. *Held*, dismissing the application, that if the tribunal's decision was, in its view, inconclusive, it had the inherent power to transfer the proceedings to another tribunal. (*Fussell* v. *Somerset Justices Licensing Committee* (1947) C.L.C. 5143 applied.)

R. *v.* INDUSTRIAL TRIBUNAL, *ex p.* COTSWOLD COLLOTYPE [1979] I.C.R. 191, D.C.

896. —— **practice—adjournment of proceedings—chairman's discretion**
The Employment Appeal Tribunal will only interfere with a chairman's discretion to adjourn proceedings at an industrial tribunal if it is shown that he has improperly taken some matter into account, or that he has failed to take a relevant matter into account, or that his decision is perverse.

P, the employee, was manager of D Co.'s bookmakers shop. He was dismissed for swindling the company and complained of unfair dismissal. He was charged with theft and elected for trial at the Crown Court. He applied for the industrial tribunal hearing to be adjourned on the ground, *inter alia,* that evidence he wanted to give at the tribunal would be prejudicial to the hearing at the Crown Court. D Co. argued that the issues were different, and the adjournment would cause unacceptable delay. The chairman refused the application. On appeal against that decision by P, *held,* dismissing the appeal, that the chairman had considered all relevant matters, there was no matter which he had improperly taken into consideration, his decision was not perverse, and there was no ground for interfering with his discretion. (*Butler* v. *Sabah Timber South-East* (*Merchants*) (unreported), July 25, 1978, E.A.T. considered.)

BASTICK *v.* JAMES LANE (TURF ACCOUNTANTS) [1979] I.C.R. 778, E.A.T.

897. —— —— **grounds for rehearing—loss of confidence in tribunal**

A lack of confidence in the fairness of the proceedings by a party before an industrial tribunal is of itself insufficient to form a ground for a rehearing.

An industrial tribunal heard the employee's complaint of unfair dismissal over two days. In the afternoon of the second day, the employee applied through his counsel for the matter to be heard *de novo* by a different tribunal. He was dissatisfied with the way counsel conducted his case, and he had no confidence in the fairness of the tribunal, which he alleged to be biased. The tribunal, notwithstanding having considered the allegation of bias to be groundless, decided they could not proceed if the employee had no confidence in them, and ordered a rehearing before a different tribunal. *Held*, allowing the employer's appeal, that (1) the tribunal misdirected themselves in law in deciding that they were obliged, because of the employee's lack of confidence in them, to discontinue the hearing; lack of confidence in the proceedings by itself was insufficient to form a ground to order a rehearing; (2) even if the tribunal had a discretion in such circumstances to order a rehearing, there was no basis in the present case for so doing.

AUTOMOBILE PTY. *v.* HEALY [1979] I.C.R. 809, E.A.T.

898. —— —— **inherent jurisdiction to reconsider judgment**

Industrial tribunals have an inherent jurisdiction, to be sparingly exercised, to reopen proceedings prior to the reasons for their decisions being drawn up.

After announcing the tribunal's decision, but prior to the written reasons being drawn up, the chairman, realising that full consideration had not been given to an authority which had been cited, invited the parties to return for further argument. An employee in whose favour the original decision had been, appealed on the grounds that the tribunal had exhausted its jurisdiction. *Held,* dismissing the appeal, that tribunals shared the inherent jurisdiction of the civil courts to reconvene prior to judgment being drawn up, such a power being exercised, however, only in cases of simple errors. (*Earl of Bradford* v. *Jowett* [1978] C.L.Y. 1021, considered.)

HANKS *v.* ACE HIGH PRODUCTIONS [1978] I.C.R. 1155, E.A.T.

899. —— —— **originating application—whether applicant's telephone number sufficient without address**

[Rules of Procedure, r. 1 (1).] Mr. and Mrs. T sent originating applications on one form to the central office of the Industrial Tribunals. The form stated their telephone number but not the address. They sent no copy to the respondents. *Held*, that the applications were valid: GOSPORT WORKING MEN'S AND TRADE UNION CLUB *v.* TAYLOR (1978) 13 I.T.R. 321, E.A.T.

900. —— —— **power to order new hearing**

An industrial tribunal has an inherent power, to be sparingly exercised, to order a rehearing before a differently constituted tribunal.

During the hearing of the employee's complaint of unfair dismissal the chairman adjourned the proceedings after inviting the employee to take professional advice on a matter of law and then reconsider or withdraw the proceedings. A solicitor consulted by the employee later applied for a rehearing before a differently constituted tribunal on the grounds that the tribunal had prematurely decided the point against his client. *Held*, dismissing the employee's appeal against the tribunal's refusal to order a rehearing, that the tribunal's power to regulate its own procedure entitled it to order a rehearing; but that in the present case there were no grounds for so acting.

CHARMAN *v.* PALMERS SCAFFOLDING [1979] I.C.R. 335, E.A.T.

901. —— —— **review—failure to give notice to respondent**

Held, that as a matter of ordinary practice on an application for a review regarding a question of substance made under the Industrial Tribunals (Labour Relations) Regulations (S.I. 1974 No. 1386, as amended), no final order can be made in the absence of a party who has not received notice of the proceedings. Accordingly, since in this case the application was made in the absence of NF who had not been given notice, the matter would be remitted for a fresh review before a different tribunal: ALI *v.* NILGUN FASHIONS (1978) 13 I.T.R. 443, E.A.T.

902. —— **review of decision—notice of proceedings incorrectly addressed—subsequent notices correct—whether presumption that received**

[Industrial Tribunals (Labour Relations) Regulations 1974 (S.I. 1974 No. 1386), Sched, 9, r. 9 (1) (*b*); Interpretation Act 1889 (c. 63), s. 26.]

In considering whether a notice of proceedings has been " received " within the meaning of r. 9 (1) (*b*) of the Schedule to the 1974 Regulations, regard should be paid to both the regulations and s. 26 of the 1889 Act, the effect of which is that a document sent through the post is deemed to be received unless the contrary is proved.

A group of companies in financial difficulties entered into a hiving-down agreement with M Ltd. The staff were sub-contracted to that company. M Ltd. itself then went into voluntary liquidation. The T.G.W.U. made an application on behalf of the staff of one of the other companies in the group for a protective award against M Ltd. The award was granted but M Ltd., who did not attend the hearing, asked for a review on the grounds that no notice had been received. The tribunal found that the first notice was incorrectly addressed but that subsequent notices were correctly addressed but no replies had been received. They refused the review. On appeal, *held*, dismissing the appeal, that a document sent through the post was deemed to have been received unless the contrary was proved.

MIGWAIN *v.* TRANSPORT AND GENERAL WORKERS' UNION [1979] I.C.R. 597, E.A.T.

903. —— **service outside jurisdiction—whether jurisdiction to hear complaint.** See KNULTY *v.* ELOC ELECTRO-OPTIEK AND COMMUNICATIE B.V., § 2182.

904. Job Release Act 1977—continuation

JOB RELEASE ACT 1977 (CONTINUATION) ORDER 1979 (No. 957) [10p], made under the Job Release Act 1977 (c. 8), s. 1 (4) (*b*) (5); operative on September 30, 1979; continues in force for a further year the provisions of s. 1 of the 1977 Act.

905. Local authority—discretionary payment—implied term

P was headmaster of a junior school. The Burnham Primary and Secondary Committee reports, which are given force of law by statutory instruments governed his salary and provided for a mandatory additional payment to teachers of special classes and for a discretionary payment to headteachers if the authority consider his salary is not adequate having regard to his special duties and responsibilities. A discretionary payment of 62 per cent. of the assistant teachers' payment was made to P by virtue of the special class attached to his school. In 1975, when the assistant teachers' payment increased, P's payment was not increased proportionally. P brought an action for a declaration that D should continue to pay 62 per cent. of the assistant teachers' payment until his retirement. *Held*, that (1) there was no evidence to show that the exercise of the discretion by making payment in favour of the plaintiff was sufficient to convert the discretion into a contractual obligation to continue the payments beyond the next Burnham scale and therefore there should be judgment for the defendants; (2) although a local authority cannot enter into a contract which imposes restraints upon the local authority which are incompatible with the exercise of some power or discretion invested by statute, had the payments to the plaintiff been converted into a contractual obligation this would not have been incompatible with the exercise of the local authority's statutory power and therefore it would not have been *ultra vires* and would have bound the defendants: SMITH *v.* STOCKPORT METROPOLITAN BOROUGH COUNCIL, August 8, 1979, Deputy Judge Bloom, Stockport County Ct. (*Ex rel.* K. A. G. Platts, *Solicitor.*)

906. Local employment

DERELICT LAND CLEARANCE AREAS ORDER 1979 (No. 334) [10p], made under the Local Employment Act 1972 (c. 5), ss. 8 (6), 18; operative on April

17, 1979; specifies as derelict land clearance areas the areas specified in the Order and deletes from S.I. 1978 No. 691 otiose references to certain employment office areas which were specified as derelict land clearance areas by that Order but are now, as part of the City of Birmingham Special Area, so specified by this Order.

ASSISTED AREAS (AMENDMENT) ORDER 1979 (No. 1642) [20p], made under the Local Employment Act 1972, ss. 1 (1) and (4) and 18 (1) and the Industry Act 1972 (c. 63), ss. 1 (4), as 5 (3) and Sched. 2 (2); operative on December 12, 1979; amends the Assisted Areas Order 1979 by changing certain areas from development to special development areas.

907. Master and servant. See NEGLIGENCE.

908. —— vicarious liability—servant acting contrary to instructions. See PORTSEA ISLAND MUTUAL CO-OPERATIVE SOCIETY v. LEYLAND, § 608.

909. Maternity pay—dates—contractual provision—limitation on statutory provision
[Employment Protection Act 1975 (c. 71), s. 36 (2).]

A contractual term purporting to limit a woman's right to choose the commencement date of her paid maternity leave within s. 36 (2) of the Employment Protection Act 1975 is void.

N, a teacher, wrote to her employers indicating her intention to start her paid maternity leave some three weeks before her expected confinement. The employers pointed out that she was contractually bound to start her leave on the 11th week before confinement. On a complaint to the industrial tribunal, the tribunal held that N was entitled to choose when to start her maternity leave. On appeal, *held*, dismissing the appeal, that s. 36 (2) of the Act, by implication, gave an employee the right to choose when, following the 11th week before the expected confinement, she wished to commence her leave.

INNER LONDON EDUCATION AUTHORITY v. NASH [1979] I.C.R. 229, E.A.T.

910. National insurance. See NATIONAL INSURANCE.

911. Northern Ireland. See NORTHERN IRELAND.

912. Police. See POLICE.

913. Racial discrimination—discovery—confidential reports

In a complaint of racial discrimination, discovery of confidential reports should be ordered where they appear prima facie to be relevant and then only subject to the chairman's discretion.

The Indian applicant complained that his employers practised racial discrimination in their assessment of his performance. He sought discovery of records of the appraisals made of other staff and of the personal file of one employee. An industrial tribunal ordered discovery in relation only to a limited number of time sheets and progress reports. Both parties appealed. *Held*, that (1) discovery of confidential reports should be ordered only if it appears that their contents might be relevant to the issues and then in the discretion of the chairman if he determined to examine their contents; (2) wider discovery than that ordered by the tribunal was not justified. (*Science Research Council* v. *Nassé* [1978] C.L.Y. 1034 applied.)

BRITISH RAILWAYS BOARD v. NATARAJAN; NATARAJAN v. BRITISH RAILWAYS BOARD [1979] I.C.R. 326, E.A.T.

914. [Race Relations Act 1976 (c. 74), s. 68 (1).] J claimed to have been discriminated against on grounds of colour or race when his request for transfer to a new position was turned down. He sought particulars of the number of staff and payroll coloured employees of I.M.I. Co. at the time in the rolled metal division and the strip mill together with details of education, qualifications, age, length of service, race, colour and ethnic origin of those who had been selected for vacancies for which J had applied since joining I.M.I. Co. in 1969. He also sought discovery of part of a letter regarding a previous vacancy for which he had applied. *Held*, dismissing J's appeal, that, *inter alia*, the tribunal had correctly refused orders for the particulars or discovery since the request was wholly unreasonable, irrelevant and should not be answered. The particulars requested went only to credit and not to the question of whether there was discrimination on the occasion in question. In relation to the education, qualifications, age and length of service of successful candidates it would also be wrong to require I.M.I. Co. to break their confidence with those persons by disclosing the information. Since J could not show that the part of the letter not discovered was relevant and I.M.I. Co. denied that it was, discovery could not be ordered: JALOTA *v.* IMPERIAL METAL INDUSTRY (KYNOCH) [1979] I.R.L.R. 313, E.A.T.

915. —— Industrial Tribunal decisions

BOHON-MITCHELL *v.* COMMON PROFESSIONAL EXAMINATION BOARD AND COUNCIL OF LEGAL EDUCATION [1978] I.R.L.R. 525 (the respondents' requirements provided that an applicant without a degree in law could only complete the academic stage of training for the Bar by taking a one-year diploma course (as opposed to a 21-month course) if he had a degree from a university or body authorised by the Council of National Academic Awards in the U.K. or the Irish Republic. *Held,* that (1) B-M had shown that the proportion of persons not from the U.K. or Irish Republic who could comply with this requirement was considerably smaller than the proportion of persons from those countries who could comply with it; (2) the respondents had not shown the requirement to be " justifiable " within s. 1 (1) (*b*) (ii) of the Race Relations Act 1976 as its purpose, namely to ensure that all barristers have a knowledge of the English way of life, could be achieved by allowing overseas students to make individual representations that they already have sufficient knowledge of the English way of life; (3) it would be recommended under s. 56 (1) (*c*) that the respondents' regulations be amended accordingly for implementation before September 1979 as the existing requirement amounted to unlawful discrimination contrary to ss. 12 and 1 (1) (*b*) of the Act).

HUSSEIN *v.* SAINTS COMPLETE HOUSE FURNISHERS [1979] I.R.L.R. 337 (S.C.H.F.'s practice in employing staff for their household furnishers' store in the centre of Liverpool was not to employ youths from the " city centre " since experience had shown that such youths attracted their unemployed friends who stood in front of the shop. Accordingly, S.C.H.F. did not interview H because he lived in the city centre. *Held,* that S.C.H.F. had unjustifiably indirectly discriminated against H contrary to ss. 1 (1) (*b*) and 4 (1) (*a*) of the Race Relations Act 1976 since in the city centre 50 per cent. of the population was black or coloured whereas outside the city centre in the Merseyside area no more than 2 per cent. was black or coloured. Thus S.C.H.F.'s policy excluded a large number of black and coloured people in comparison with the proportion of white people liable to be affected. A recommendation would be made under s. 56 that S.C.H.F. cease their existing practice and take such steps as were practicable to obviate the adverse effect of their pre-selection methods).

916. —— requirement regarding beards—whether justifiable—test

[Race Relations Act 1976 (c. 74), s. 1 (1).]

A rule in a food factory that employees may not wear beards upon grounds of hygiene may be justifiable notwithstanding that it discriminates against Sikhs.

The applicant, a Sikh whose religion debarred him from removing facial hair, was unsuccessful in his application for employment at the employer's sweet factory, since he refused to comply with the rigidly enforced rule at that factory that no employee was permitted to have a beard on grounds of hygiene. His complaint of racial discrimination was dismissed on the ground that the rule resulting in discrimination was " justifiable " under s. 1 (1) of the Act. *Held,* dismissing his appeal, that the industrial tribunal had applied the correct test in that the rule was not merely one of convenience but one which was generally equitable and reasonable in all the circumstances (*Steel v. Union of Post Office Workers* [1978] C.L.Y. 1040 considered).

SINGH *v.* ROWNTREE MACKINTOSH [1979] I.C.R. 554, E.A.T.

917. [Race Relations Act 1976 (c. 74), s. 1 (1) (*b*).] Although there was discrimination against prospective Sikh employers, the Court of Appeal found that the factory rule forbidding beards was " justifiable " in the interests of hygiene and safety: PANESAR *v.* NESTLÉ Co., *The Times,* December 5, 1979, C.A.

918. Redundancy

EMPLOYMENT PROTECTION (HANDLING OF REDUNDANCIES) VARIATION ORDER 1979 (No. 958) [10p], made under the Employment Protection Act 1975 (c. 71), s. 106 (4) (5); operative on October 1, 1979; varies the provisions of ss. 99 (3) and 100 (1) of the 1975 Act by reducing to 30 days the period which must elapse after the commencement of consultation with trade union representatives and notification to the Secretary of State before the first of the dismissals takes effect in cases where the employer is proposing to dismiss as redundant 10 to 99 employees at one establishment within a period of 30 days or less. Also varies the 60-day period specified in s. 101 (5) (*b*) by reducing it to 30 days.

919. —— consultation with unions—whether reasonably practicable—test—application for Government loan

[Employment Protection Act 1975 (c. 71), s. 99.] B.S. Co. received a Government loan to help them out of financial difficulties. In December 1977 a second loan was refused but it was suggested that the Scottish economic planning department might help. The workforce was laid off on February 3, 1978, when B.S. Co. heard that no help would be given. H.A. dismissed the workforce forthwith on February 7, 1978, when he was appointed receiver. *Held*, dismissing B.S. Co.'s appeal, that (1) an application for a Government loan by a company which had already received substantial Government assistance is a circumstance special enough to make it not reasonably practicable to issue the formal written details required by the consultation provisions of s. 99 (5) of the 1975 Act; (2) the tribunal had erred in substituting their own business and commercial judgment for B.S. Co.'s and attempting to assess the prospects of a loan being granted; (3) however, B.S. Co. had not shown that they took all reasonably practicable steps towards complying with s. 99 since the position and circumstances should have been disclosed to responsible union officials even on a confidential basis at least when it was decided to ask for a second loan: HAMISH ARMOUR (RECEIVER OF BARRY STAINES) *v.* ASSOCIATION OF SCIENTIFIC, TECHNICAL AND MANAGERIAL STAFFS [1979] I.R.L.R. 24, E.A.T.

920. —— continuity of employment—unincorporated bodies—whether associated employers

[Contracts of Employment Act 1972 (c. 53), Sched. 1, para. 10 (as substituted by Employment Protection Act 1975 (c. 71), Sched. 16, Pt. II, para. 19).]

The expression " company " though not expressly defined in the Employment Protection Act 1975 retains the same meaning as in the Redundancy Payments Act 1965, namely a body corporate and does not include an unincorporated body.

The employee was employed by the area probation committee before he became a deputy warden at a residential hostel not connected with the probation service in the employment of the hostel management committee. He was made redundant and was given a redundancy payment which included the period of his employment with the hostel but not his previous employment with the probation service. He successfully applied for an additional redundancy payment. The tribunal found that there was continuity of employment by reason that both the probation service and the hostel management committee were companies over which a third person, the Home Office, had control, and accordingly were associated employers within the meaning of para. 10 of Sched. 1 to the Contracts of Employment Act 1972 as amended. *Held*, allowing the employer's appeal, that (1) the expression " company " in the Employment Protection Act 1975 retained the same meaning as in the Redundancy Payments Act 1965, namely, a body corporate, and does not include an incorporated body; (2) the two committees were incorporated bodies, and accordingly were not associated employers within the meaning of para. 10 (2) of Sched. 1; (3) alternatively, even if the two committees were companies within the meaning of the paragraph, the funding of the two committees by the Home Office did not amount to control by a third party so as to bring them within the meaning of associated employers in para. 10 (2).

SOUTHWOOD HOSTEL MANAGEMENT COMMITTEE *v.* TAYLOR [1979] I.C.R. 813, E.A.T.

921. —— dismissal—employee agreeing to become self-employed

[Redundancy Payments Act 1965 (c. 62), s. 3 (2) (as amended by the Employment Protection Act 1975 (c. 71), Sched. 16, Pt. 1 para. 3).]

An employee told that his employers' business is closing and who enters into an agreement with the employers to continue work in a self-employed capacity may be regarded as dismissed.

The employee motor mechanic was told by his employers of their intention to close the motor repair section of their business; he refused employment in a less senior position. After he had told the employers that they would have to dismiss him for redundancy, they suggested and he agreed that he would become self-employed, using their premises for his business. After he began so to work, the employers gave notice terminating his right to occupy the premises. An industrial tribunal awarded the employee a redundancy payment. *Held,* dismissing the employers' appeal, that the employee had been dismissed as from the date of his status changing from employed to self-employed.

GLENCROSS v. DYMOKE [1979] I.C.R. 536, E.A.T.

922. —— dismissal for misconduct during notice period

[Redundancy Payments Act 1965 (c. 62), s. 10 (3).] K was dismissed during the period of his redundancy notice after being convicted of theft. He applied under s. 10 (3) of the 1965 Act for a determination whether he should receive the whole or part of the redundancy payment to which he would have been entitled but for the dismissal for misconduct. *Held,* dismissing L.P. Co.'s appeal against a finding that K should receive 60 per cent. of the payment, that the E.A.T. could only interfere when there has been some error in principle. The tribunal had borne in mind all relevant considerations: LIGNACITE PRODUCTS v. KROLLMAN [1979] I.R.L.R. 22, E.A.T.

923. —— dismissal or resignation—date of dismissal not ascertainable—cross-notice during notice period

[Redundancy Payments Act 1965 (c. 62), ss. 4, 21.] P-R Co. sent B and M letters stating that " the job which you are currently undertaking will last for at least seven months from March 1, 1977." B and M gave notice of termination in May 1977 and claimed redundancy pay. *Held,* allowing P-R Co.'s appeal, that, *inter alia,* (1) the letter could not be construed as notice of dismissal as facts from which the date of dismissal could be ascertained were not given. It was a warning of possible termination with a guarantee of employment for seven months; (2) even if B and M had been dismissed with notice, they had served their cross-notices of termination earlier than the date permitted by virtue of s. 4 of the 1965 Act and accordingly had to be regarded as having left voluntarily; (3) in any event the applications were ineffective, having been made before the date of termination of the contract: PRITCHARD-RHODES v. BOON AND MILTON [1979] I.R.L.R. 19, E.A.T.

924. —— failure to consult trade union—protective award—basis

[Employment Protection Act 1975 (c. 71), ss. 101, 102 (3).] S-F announced on April 7, 1978, without prior consultation with the recognised unions, that 36 of their bakeries would be closed down on April 26, 1978. Thirteen of the bakeries were sold to other companies as going concerns and most employees in those bakeries continued to work for the new owners without any break in their employment. *Held,* dismissing S-F's appeal, that the tribunal had correctly decided that it had jurisdiction to make a protective award under s. 101 of the 1975 Act where a union complained of non-consultation about proposed redundancies even in cases where employees had suffered no loss by reason of the lack of consultation. It is the loss of days of consultation rather than the loss or potential loss of actual remuneration during the relevant period which has to be considered. The provision in s. 102 (3) that "any payment" to an employee by an employer under his contract of employment during the relevant period shall go towards discharging the employer's liability to pay money under a protective award, only relates to payments by the employer in default: SPILLERS-FRENCH (HOLDINGS) v. UNION OF SHOP, DISTRIBUTIVE AND ALLIED WORKERS [1979] I.R.L.R. 339, E.A.T.

925. —— **failure to give notice to trade union—part-time employees**
[Employment Protection Act 1975 (c. 71), s. 119 (7).]

The provisions of s. 99 of the Employment Protection Act 1975 apply to employment under a fixed term contract in excess of 12 weeks, irrespective of the number of weekly hours worked.

Members of the appellant union were employed as part-time teachers under a fixed term contract for an academic year; they in fact worked less than 16 hours per week. The council decided not to re-engage them at the end of the contract since fewer pupils than anticipated required teaching in the next session; discussions were held with the union prior to dismissal. The union sought a declaration that the council had breached s. 99 (5) of the 1975 Act in failing to give written notice of the redundancies and a protective award. An industrial tribunal ruled, *inter alia*, that the employees did not fall within s. 119 (7) of the Act since they were employed for less than 16 hours per week; it also held that the reason for dismissal was " some other substantial reason " (*i.e.* the shortfall of pupils) and not redundancy. *Held*, allowing the union's appeal, that the tribunal erred in applying s. 119 (7) to the exclusion of the employees, their weekly working hours being irrelevant thereunder; the tribunal should not have ruled that the employees were not dismissed for redundancy; but that since the tribunal had indicated that if it had been wrong in construing the law, it would in its discretion refuse a protective award, the case would not be remitted. (*Terry* v. *East Sussex County Council* [1976] C.L.Y. 876 considered).

NATIONAL ASSOCIATION OF TEACHERS IN FURTHER AND HIGHER EDUCATION *v.* MANCHESTER CITY COUNCIL [1978] I.C.R. 1190, E.A.T.

926. —— **illegal contract—jurisdiction to entertain complaint—where employee innocent party**

P employed D to run a dry-cleaning establishment. D drew her cash weekly from the till, no deductions being made from her wages. The tribunal found that it could not entertain D's claims for a redundancy payment and unfair dismissal compensation as the contract of employment was illegal. *Held*, allowing D's appeal, that the tribunal had erred in failing to consider whether D was a party to the illegality. If D was a party neither to the illegal act nor the illegal intention, she could make a statutory claim and rely on the contract. (*Tomlinson* v. *Dick Evans* " *U* " *Drive* [1978] C.L.Y. 912 distinguished): DAVIDSON *v.* PILLAY [1979] I.R.L.R. 275, E.A.T.

927. —— **Industrial Tribunal decisions**

Failure to consult union—commencement of protective period

GENERAL AND MUNICIPAL WORKERS' UNION (MANAGERIAL, ADMINISTRATIVE, TECHNICAL AND SUPERVISORY ASSOCIATION SECTION) *v.* BRITISH URALITE [1979] I.R.L.R. 409 (on January 1, 1979, during discussions as to a wage claim, BU Co. mentioned intended redundancies. On February 5, 1979, the claim was settled and BU Co. decided to draw up proposals for redundancies to reduce overheads by £100,000 per annum. The union was verbally informed on February 14, 1979, that there would be redundancies affecting 15 employees and were told that if no reasonable counter proposals were received by the next morning the employees would be dismissed. Notices of dismissal and a memorandum to the union setting out details of the redundancies were sent the next morning. Three employees were given 60 days' notice and the remainder three months. On February 19, 1979, the union raised seven questions which were answered by BU Co. on February 26, 1979. *Held*, that consultations within s. 99 (3) (*b*) of the Employment Protection Act 1975 cannot be held to have begun earlier than the date on which the union is given the information required by s. 99 (5) in writing. Accordingly, consultations had not begun before the notices of dismissal had been dispatched. The memorandum had complied with s. 99 (5) save that it referred to actual rather than proposed dismissals. Neither the effect on the morale of employees nor BU Co.'s financial circumstances amounted to " special circumstances " in this case rendering it not reasonably practicable to comply with s. 99 by beginning consultations with the union at least 60 days before the proposed redundancies).

GENERAL AND MUNICIPAL WORKERS' UNION (MANAGERIAL, ADMINISTRATIVE,

TECHNICAL AND SUPERVISORY ASSOCIATION SECTION) *v.* BRITISH URALITE [1979] I.R.L.R. 413 (BU Co. had failed to comply with the redundancy consultation requirements in the Employment Protection Act 1975, s. 99. *Held*, that (1) a protective award of 14 days' remuneration would be made in favour of the relevant employees. The purpose of the Act is to compensate for the failure to consult. Meaningful consultations began four days after issue of the notices of dismissal but BU Co. failed to answer important questions until 12 days after consultations should have begun. There was a loss of 12 days' consultation due to the breach; (2) the breach of s. 99 by informing the union of actual rather than proposed dismissals was not one purely of form. Had proposals been made voluntary redundancies may have been secured; (3) although employees were given permission to leave before expiry of their notices, the protected period would begin on the date on which the first dismissal took effect in accordance with BU Co.'s notice. The protected period under s. 101 (5) begins on the date on which the employer proposes to dismiss any of the relevant employees and not on any other date which may subsequently be agreed with any particular employees as the date of termination of their contracts. The relevant date is not the same as " the effective date of termination " as defined in s. 55 (4) of the Employment Protection (Consolidation) Act 1978).

Selection

GREIG *v.* SIR ALFRED MCALPINE & SON (NORTHERN) [1979] I.R.L.R. 372 (G, an electrician, was selected for redundancy. AM Co.'s notice of redundancy stated that selection would be based upon service/performance/attendance record. Selection was made by the site electrical supervisor, on no formal or structural basis. G claimed to have been selected because he was a communist and chairman of the unofficial shop committee. *Held*, that the selection was unfair since AM Co. had not shown that they had an objective system of assessment for deciding not to retain G. Where criteria other than " last in, first out " are adopted the employer must show that his criteria are reasonable and have been reasonably and objectively applied on a reasonably structured and comparative basis. It is insufficient to say that selection was based upon the management, skill and judgment of one person. Management must take steps to ensure that selection is as objective and unbiased as possible).

928. —— **lay-offs—rejection of offers of employment—counter-notice**
[Redundancy Payments Act 1965 (c. 62), ss. 6, 53 (1).]
To be valid, a counter-notice served after receipt of an employee's notice of claim for a redundancy payment must state that the employers deny liability to make such a payment.

After being laid off for four months, the employee bricklayers gave written notice of intention to claim a redundancy payment. They refused a later offer of employment by the employers and orally gave notice asking for their P45s and holiday pay. The employers posted letters to the men confirming the offer of employment, but such letters were found by the tribunal not to have been received. The tribunal awarded the employees a redundancy payment on the grounds, *inter alia,* that since the employers' letters had not been received, no counter-notice under s. 6 (5) of the Act had been served. *Held*, dismissing the employers' appeal, that (1) the employees' oral notice complied with s. 6 (3) of the Act; (2) by virtue of s. 53 (1), the tribunal should have found that the notice given by the employer was served when posted; but (3) the notice was defective in that it did not state that the employers contested liability to make a redundancy payment.
FABAR CONSTRUCTION *v.* RACE [1979] I.C.R. 529, E.A.T.

929. —— **offer of alternative employment—lower wage**
[Redundancy Payments Act 1965 (c. 62), s. 2 (as amended by the Employment Protection Act 1975 (c. 71), Sched. 16, Pt. 1, para. 2).]
Prima facie, an offer of alternative employment at a lower wage is unsuitable employment for the purposes of determining entitlement to a redundancy payment.

Having been made redundant the employee agreed to work for a trial period at a nearby factory at a lower wage, but he left soon thereafter complaining of the working conditions. An industrial tribunal rejected his claim for a redundancy payment on the grounds that the employee had indicated that had working conditions been to his liking, he would not have been concerned at the lower wage. *Held*, allowing the employee's appeal, that since the employee's willingness to accept the lower pay was conditional upon his satisfaction with the other aspects of the job, he was not debarred from contending that it was not suitable alternative employment. (*Taylor* v. *Kent County Council* [1967] C.L.Y. 1274 applied.)

HINDES v. SUPERSINE [1979] I.C.R. 517, E.A.T.

930. —— —— **reasonable refusal—relevance of employee's age and employer's viability**

[Redundancy Payments Act 1965 (c. 62), s. 2.] After issuing redundancy notices to all their staff, but before the notices had expired, PC & Co. obtained a Government subsidy and wrote to their staff offering them re-instatement and stating that trading conditions were difficult but they hoped that there would be greater job security in the future. Only W, who had obtained employment elsewhere commencing on expiry of the redundancy notice, rejected the offer. *Held*, dismissing PC & Co.'s appeal, that the tribunal had not erred in law in finding W's refusal of the offer reasonable. W was 61 and had obtained another job which avoided the risk of future unemployment. An employee's age and the apparent viability of the employers are capable of creating exceptional cases (*Pilkington* v. *Pickstone* [1967] C.L.Y. 1450 and *Morganite Crucible* v. *Street* [1972] C.L.Y. 1233 considered): PATON CALVERT & CO. v. WESTERSIDE [1979] I.R.L.R. 108, E.A.T.

931. —— —— **trial period—whether employee dismissed**

[Redundancy Payments Act 1965, s. 3 (2) (c) (3), as amended by Employment Protection Act 1975 (c. 71), Sched. 16, Pt. 1.]

An employee, not contractually bound so to do, who moves to a new location for a trial period exceeding four weeks prior to leaving may be regarded as dismissed for redundancy.

The employee's contract did not require her to work at other than her current location. When the employees were forced to move offices, the employee complained at the proposal that she should work in basement accommodation which she found claustrophobic but agreed so to move for a trial period. After some two months she left and complained of unfair dismissal. An industrial tribunal upheld her complaint on the grounds that the employers had not shown that other sites or alternative employment were not available. *Held*, allowing the appeal, that in the absence of evidence that the employer could have made more suitable arrangements, the dismissal was not unfair; but that the fact that the employee deferred for a trial period her right to accept the employers' repudiation of her contract did not disentitle her to a redundancy payment. (*Shields Furniture* v. *Goff* [1973] C.L.Y. 1095, followed.)

AIR CANADA v. LEE [1978] I.C.R. 1202, E.A.T.

932. —— —— **whether employee dismissed**

[Redundancy Payments Act 1965 (c. 62), s. 3 (2) (3), as amended by Employment Protection Act 1975 (c. 71), Sched. 16, Pt. I, para. 3.]

Employees who agree to try alternative employment are entitled to a reasonable period in which to decide whether to accept new terms; only thereafter does the four-week period under s. 3 (3) of the Redundancy Payments Act 1965 commence.

The employees were offered alternative employment in lieu of redundancy; they agreed to a trial period. More than four weeks later they rejected the alternative positions and claimed a redundancy payment. An industrial tribunal dismissed their claims on the grounds that by remaining in the alternative jobs for more than four weeks they were not to be treated as dismissed by reason of s. 3 (3) of the 1965 Act. *Held*, allowing their appeals, that the tribunal had erred in assuming that the four-week period commenced as soon as the alternative employment was taken up; the employees were first entitled to a reasonable period to decide whether to accept new contracts; and the case would accordingly be remitted for reconsideration. (*Air Canada* v. *Lee* [1979] C.L.Y. 931 applied.)

TURVEY v. C. W. CHEYNEY & SON [1979] I.C.R. 341, E.A.T.

933. —— payment—calculation—normal working hours—whether regular overtime included

[Employment Protection Act 1975 (c. 71), s. 85, Sched. 4, paras. 1, 2.]

In assessing whether certain overtime fell within the "normal working hours" of an employee regard should be had to any local arrangement between employer and union having the effect of rendering overtime compulsory.

The employee worked as a fan attendant at a colliery. Cl. 2 of his contract provided for a normal working week of 40 hours, but for many years the employee regularly worked a 56 hour week since it was necessary for safety reasons for the ventilation equipment to be manned continuously. The agreement also provided that local "arrangements" could be made between the Board and trade union to provide for regular working of additional shifts. Following the employee being made redundant, an industrial tribunal assessed compensation upon the basis of a 40 hour week since it could find no evidence of an "agreement" rebutting the express provision in cl. 2. *Held*, allowing the employee's appeal and remitting the case for reconsideration, that the tribunal should look for an arrangement, possibly an informal one, and not a formal agreement. (*Saxton* v. *National Coal Board* [1970] C.L.Y. 918, considered.)

BARRETT v. NATIONAL COAL BOARD [1978] I.C.R. 1101, E.A.T.

934. —— —— fixed term contract—temporary lecturer

[Redundancy Payments Act 1965 (c. 62), s. 1 (2) (*b*).]

An employee who at the time of accepting a temporary contract knew that the existing work would decline and that it was unlikely that there would be a continuing need for his services was not entitled to a redundancy payment.

The employee was employed as a teacher by the local authority before he accepted a job with the same employers as a lecturer in a teacher training college for a period of one year. His employment was extended for one year but he was dismissed after the extended period. He successfully applied for a redundancy payment. The tribunal found that the employers had a policy of reducing the number of students in teacher training in anticipation of a reduction in the number of children in schools, and that the employee had known of the diminishing need for lecturers when he accepted the post. The tribunal, while accepting that the employee had only a temporary contract, rejected the employers' contention that s. 1 (2) (*b*) of the Redundancy Payments Act 1965 did not apply where the employee was engaged for a fixed term knowing that the work he was engaged to do would no longer be available at the end of the period. *Held*, allowing the employers' appeal, that a redundancy payment was payable where the requirements of the business had ceased or diminished or were expected to cease or diminish but not where the employee accepted the temporary contract knowing that the existing work would decline and that it was unlikely that there will be a continuing need for his services, thereby not satisfying s. 1 (2) (*b*).

NOTTINGHAMSHIRE COUNTY COUNCIL v. LEE [1979] I.C.R. 818, E.A.T.

935. —— —— "normal" working hours—employee on stand-by duty

[Trade Union and Labour Relations Act 1974 (c. 52), Sched. 1, paras. 9, 10; Contracts of Employment Act 1972 (c. 53), s. 11, Sched. 1, para. 4.]

When considering the "normal" hours of employment, regard should be had to such time during which the employee is contractually required to be available for duty.

As a part-time fireman, the employee on average attended for duty for some 10½ hours per week, but he was contractually required to be available for duty at four minutes' notice for 102 hours per week, and was subject to disciplinary measures if he was not so available. Following his dismissal an industrial tribunal declined jurisdiction to hear his claims for unfair dismissal and/or a redundancy payment upon the grounds that his "normal" hours of employment were less than 21 hours per week in accordance with para. 4 of Sched. 1

to the 1972 Act. The employers appealed against the E.A.T.'s reversal of such decision. *Held,* dismissing the appeal, that the period of stand-by duty for which the employee was contractually required to be available was to be considered in computing his normal working hours. (Decision of E.A.T. [1978] C.L.Y. 1009 affirmed.)

BULLOCK v. MERSEYSIDE COUNTY COUNCIL [1979] I.C.R. 79, C.A.

936. —— —— **rebate—continuity of employment—whether entitled to rebate**
[Redundancy Payments Act 1965 (c. 62), ss. 1 (1), 9, 30 (1).]

The fact that an employer may be estopped from denying liability to make a redundancy payment to an employee does not entitle him to a rebate in respect of a payment for which he was not otherwise liable under the statute.

After working for a company from 1948 to 1970 an employee agreed in lieu of redundancy to transfer to the respondent company (in which his then employers held shares but in relation to which they were not an associated company within the meaning of the Contracts of Employment Act 1972) after assurances from, *inter alia,* the respondents that his employment would be regarded as continuous from 1948. In 1975 the employee was made redundant and the respondents paid him a redundancy payment based upon five years' service. The employee applied to an industrial tribunal which ruled that although his service was not continuous, the respondents were estopped by reason of the 1970 assurance from denying continuity and were accordingly liable to make a payment based upon continuous service from 1948. The respondents successfully applied under s. 34 (2) of the 1965 Act for a declaration that they were entitled to a rebate upon the full amount paid by them, the industrial tribunal's decision being upheld by the Employment Appeal Tribunal and the Court of Appeal. *Held,* allowing the appeal of the Secretary of State, that such a rebate was payable only in respect of a redundancy payment for which an employer was liable under the 1965 Act; and that the payment ordered by the industrial tribunal was not one due under that Act but was due by reason of the respondents being estopped from denying the continuity of service. (Decision of C.A. [1978] C.L.Y. 1016 and *Evenden* v. *Guildford City Association Football Club* [1975] C.L.Y. 1147 overruled.)

SECRETARY OF STATE FOR EMPLOYMENT v. GLOBE ELASTIC THREAD CO. [1979] 3 W.L.R. 143, H.L.

937. —— **selection procedure—failure to follow—whether unfair dismissal**
[Scot.] [Trade Union and Labour Relations Act 1974 (c. 52), Sched. 1, para. 6 (7) (*b*).]

In applying the principle of last in, first out, continuous, not cumulative, employment should be considered. The employer cannot agree privately with an employee to treat his employment as continuous where other employees' rights will be affected by the agreement.

E was dismissed for redundancy, on the principle of last in, first out. E's cumulative service was 18 months less than another employee who was not dismissed, but the other driver had had a period of four weeks working for another company. He had then been asked by D Co. to return on the basis that his employment remained continuous. *Held,* an employee who broke his employment must be treated as beginning his employment after the last break for the purposes of the last in, first out principle, and the employers could not privately agree to treat an employee's periods of employment as continuous where to do so would affect the rights of other employees. Accordingly the dismissal was unfair. (*Clyde Pipeworks* v. *Foster* [1978] C.L.Y 1017, *Dorrell and Ardis* v. *Engineering Developments (Farnborough)* [1975] C.L.Y. 1147, and *Sudders* v. *Prestige Group* [1975] C.L.Y. 934 considered.)

INTERNATIONAL PAINT CO. v. CAMERON [1979] I.C.R. 429, E.A.T.

938. Restraint of trade—restrictive covenant—wide geographical operation
The plaintiff had worked for the defendant since 1924. In 1974, on becoming a director, the plaintiff had given the defendant a covenant "not within 12 months from the termination of his contract to engage in any part of the U.K. in any business which is similar to any business involving such trade secrets carried on by [the defendant]." The plaintiff sought a declaration that the

covenant was unenforceable. On appeal, *held*, the clause was invalid and unreasonably wide in its geographical application: GREER *v.* SKETCHLEY [1979] F.S.R. 197, C.A.

939. Sex discrimination—benefits continuing after retirement—whether provisions " in relation to retirement "

[Sex Discrimination Act 1975 (c. 65), ss. 1 (1) (*a*), 6 (2) (*a*) (*b*), (4).]

" Provision in relation to death or retirement " in s. 6 (4) of the Sex Discrimination Act 1975 means provision " about " death or retirement.

In the first case, the employers had a policy whereby the normal retirement age for women was 60, and for men, 65. E, a woman cleaner, was dismissed at the age of 60. In the second case, British Rail gave concessionary travel facilities to employees and their families. After retirement men and their families continued to benefit; women also did, but their families did not. In the third case, the employers operated a redundancy scheme whereby employees between 50 and 59 received an extra six weeks' pay. Those over 60 received an extra 10 weeks' pay. The retiring age for men was 65, and for women, 60. E complained that as a woman she would have to retire at 60, and therefore could never qualify for the extra 10 weeks' pay on redundancy. *Held*, the exemption in favour of " provisions in relation to death or retirement " under s. 6 (4) of the Sex Discrimination Act 1975 was an exemption in favour of provisions " about " death or retirement, and in each case s. 6 (4) applied. There had been no unlawful discrimination. (Decision of E.A.T. in *Roberts v. Cleveland Area Health Authority* [1978] C.L.Y. 1028 affirmed; decision of E.A.T. in *Garland* v. *British Rail Engineering Ltd.* [1978] C.L.Y. 1031 and *MacGregor Wallcoverings Ltd.* v. *Turton* [1978] C.L.Y. 1041 reversed.)

ROBERTS *v.* CLEVELAND AREA HEALTH AUTHORITY; GARLAND *v.* BRITISH RAIL ENGINEERING; MACGREGOR WALLCOVERINGS *v.* TURTON [1979] 1 W.L.R. 754, C.A.

940. —— discovery—confidential documents

[County Court Rules, Ord. 14, rr. 1, 2; Industrial Tribunals (Labour Relations) Regulations 1974 (S.I. 1979 No. 1386), Sched., r. 4 (2) (*a*) (*b*).]

General discovery of confidential documents, such as reports on fellow employees, should not be made on the ground of relevance alone, instead, whether discovery was necessary for disposing fairly of the proceedings and, in deciding whether it was necessary, the tribunal should inspect the documents and consider whether " covering up " or hearing in camera should be adopted.

In one case a married woman trade unionist complained of discrimination and in the other an Asian made a similar claim. Both cases were heard together. Both sought discovery of confidential reports on fellow employees who might have benefited from the alleged discrimination. The Court of Appeal allowed the employers' claim of privilege. On the employees' appeal to the House of Lords, *held*, dismissing the appeals, that, although public interest immunity does not extend to such confidential documents and confidentiality alone is insufficient for immunity, discovery should not be allowed on the ground of relevance alone unless it was necessary for disposing fairly of the proceedings and, to decide whether discovery was necessary, the tribunal should inspect the documents and consider adopting " covering up " or a hearing *in camera*.

SCIENCE RESEARCH COUNCIL *v.* NASSÉ; LEYLAND CARS (B.L. CARS) *v.* VYAS [1979] 3 W.L.R. 762, H.L.

941. —— extra payment for dirty work given to men

[Sex Discrimination Act 1975 (c. 65), s. 6 (2) (*b*).] J, an examiner grade 1, worked on rota with 11 other examiners to supervise production in a group of shops. The colour bursting shop was dirty and and required the wearing of protective clothing and taking of showers after work. 4p per hour extra pay was given for working in this shop. Women were not required to work in this shop but J was so required occasionally if he volunteered to work overtime. *Held*, dismissing the Ministry's appeal, that J had been treated less favourably on grounds of his sex than the Ministry had treated a woman. The requirement to work in this shop was a detriment for J within s. 6 (2) (*b*) of the 1975 Act. Allegations that women objected to working in this shop,

that the facilities did not exist for them to do so and it would be unfair and
likely to lead to unrest to require them to do so were irrelevant to the issue
in question (*Peake* v. *Automotive Products* [1977] C.L.Y. 1077 not followed):
JEREMIAH v. MINISTRY OF DEFENCE [1979] I.R.L.R. 436, C.A.

942. —— Industrial Tribunal decision
THORNDYKE v. BELL FRUIT (NORTH CENTRAL) [1979] I.R.L.R. 1 (B.F.'s local
director rejected T for a post because " I was unaware that you had three
children and I do feel that with the job involvement necessary for this
particular type of work it could prove difficult for you to run your home and
also give full justice to the job." *Held*, that T had been discriminated against
on grounds of her married status since the proportion of married persons,
particularly women, who could comply with the condition of not having young
and/or dependent children was considerably smaller than the proportion of
unmarried persons who could comply with the condition).

943. —— justice of the peace—selection procedure
[Sex Discrimination Act 1975 (c. 65), ss. 6 (1), 85 (2) (*a*) (*b*), 86 (2).]
An industrial tribunal has no jurisdiction to hear a complaint under the
Sex Discrimination Act 1975 by a justice of the peace alleging discrimination
in relation to her appointment.
The applicant, wishing to become a justice of the peace, was interviewed
by the appropriate company, but was not recommended for appointment. She
complained to an industrial tribunal alleging, from questions at interview,
discrimination on the grounds of sex. The tribunal held they had no jurisdiction because a justice of the peace was not " employed " and as a statutory
office holder was expressly excluded from the provisions of the Act. On appeal,
held, dismissing the appeal, that (1) a justice of the peace was not " employed "
but appointed to hold office; (2) a justice did not serve a Minister of the Crown
within s. 85 (2) (*a*) but rather the Crown itself, and accordingly the tribunal
had no jurisdiction to hear the complaint. (*I.R.C.* v. *Hambrook* [1956] C.L.Y.
1427 applied.)
KNIGHT v. ATT.-GEN. [1979] I.C.R. 194, E.A.T.

944. —— motive
Miss G and another woman were due to join CI's painting and decorating
team on the same day. A, CI's personnel officer, told G, however, that since
the other woman had not reported, G could not be accepted as problems had
arisen in the past when there had been only one female member of the team.
Held, allowing G's appeal, that G had been unlawfully discriminated against
and a declaration would be granted to such effect. Good motive was no
defence. (*Peake* v. *Automotive Products* [1977] C.L.Y. 1077 distinguished):
GRIEG v. COMMUNITY INDUSTRY AND Z. AHERN [1979] I.R.L.R. 158, E.A.T.

945. —— services on behalf of the Crown—rent officer
[Sex Discrimination Act 1975 (c. 65), s. 85 (2) (*b*).]
The post of rent officer is not one over which the industrial tribunal has
jurisdiction for the purposes of a complaint of unfair discrimination on the
ground of sex.
P, a woman, applied for the job of rent officer and was turned down. She
complained of unlawful discrimination on the ground of sex under s. 6 (1) of
the Sex Discrimination Act 1975. The industrial tribunal held that it had
jurisdiction to hear the complaint under s. 85 (2) (*b*) of the Sex Discrimination
Act 1975. On appeal by the Department of the Environment, *held*, allowing the
appeal, that on the true construction of s. 85 (2) (*b*) a rent officer was not
giving service for the purposes of " a person holding a statutory office," who
must be someone apart from the statutory office holder himself; nor was he
engaged in service " for purposes of a statutory body."
DEPARTMENT OF THE ENVIRONMENT v. FOX [1979] I.C.R. 736, E.A.T.

946. —— tribunal recommendation—delay in implementing
[Sex Discrimination Act 1975 (c. 65), s. 65 (3).]
It is reasonable to expect that employers recommended by an industrial
tribunal to avoid sexual discrimination will need some time to implement the
recommendation.

Having found that the female applicants had been discriminated against by reason of their sex, an industrial tribunal in November 1976 recommended that the employer " within six months " seriously considered the applicants for promotion upon the same basis as their male counterparts. When, in August, 1977, vacancies for promotion arose the applicants applied and were required, *inter alia*, to take a written test; one was successful. Some male employees were promoted without being required to take a test. The remaining two applicants sought compensation for the employers' failure to implement the recommendation. The industrial tribunal found that the employers had reasonable justification for non-compliance with the recommendation. *Held*, dismissing the applicants' appeals, that the tribunal had been entitled to consider the practical realities of the situation; it was not realistic to expect discriminatory practices to be eliminated immediately.

NELSON *v.* TYNE & WEAR PASSENGER TRANSPORT EXECUTIVE [1978] I.C.R. 183, E.A.T.

947. —— university—fellowships offered to men only

[Sex Discrimination Act 1975 (c. 65), ss. 6, 43, 51.] Under a university college statute, research fellowships were available to men only, a position the college conceded was discriminatory. The applicant complained she had been unlawfully discriminated against. *Held*, dismissing the appeal, the tribunal had correctly held that the meaning of " employment " as defined in s. 82 (1) was wide enough to include a research fellowship but that s. 43 applied to exclude liability since college statutes were charitable instruments. Liability was also excluded in that s. 51 applied, the discriminatory acts complying with an enactment passed before the 1975 Act, namely the college statute: HUGH-JONES *v.* ST. JOHN'S COLLEGE, CAMBRIDGE (1979) 123 S.J. 603, E.A.T.

948. —— woman wrestler

[Sex Discrimination Act 1975 (c. 65), s. 51.] A woman professional wrestler was refused employment with a promotions company because the G.L.C. expressly prohibited women's wrestling in their licences. She claimed unlawful discrimination. *Held*, there was no discrimination, the tribunal accepting the G.L.C.'s defence under s. 51 (1) (*b*) that the discrimination was necessary in order to comply with the licence, an instrument made under a previous statute: GREATER LONDON COUNCIL *v.* FARRAR, *The Times*, November 21, 1979, E.A.T.

949. Superannuation. See PENSIONS AND SUPERANNUATION.

950. Teachers. See EDUCATION.

951. Terms of employment—remuneration " fixed in pursuance of an enactment " —whether Central Arbitration Committee has jurisdiction

[National Health Service Reorganisation Act 1973 (c. 32), Sched. 1, para. 10; Employment Protection Act 1975 (c. 71), Sched. 11, para. 3.]

The remuneration of ambulancemen agreed under the Whitley Council rules is remuneration " fixed in pursuance of an enactment," thereby excluding it from the jurisdiction of the Central Arbitration Committee.

A trade union complained to ACAS that the applicant health authority were observing less favourable terms for ambulancemen than those contained in the Whitley Council agreement which had been approved in accordance with Sched. 1, para. 10, to the 1973 Act. Upon referral by ACAS to the Central Arbitration Committee, the applicants unsuccessfully contended that the committee had no jurisdiction by virtue of para. 3 of Sched. 11 to the 1975 Act, the terms of employment being fixed in accordance with an " enactment," namely the 1973 Act. *Held*, granting the authority's application for an order to quash the committee's award and to prohibit further hearings, that the ambulancemen's remuneration was fixed in accordance with an enactment and the committee's jurisdiction was therefore excluded.

R. *v.* CENTRAL ARBITRATION COMMITTEE, *ex p.* NORTH WESTERN REGIONAL HEALTH AUTHORITY [1978] I.C.R. 1228, D.C.

952. Trade disputes—research study

The Department of Employment has published a research study, " Strikes in Britain," which looks at the nature and extent of strikes during the period 1966–1973. The study shows that strike activity is concentrated in a relatively small number of larger plants in certain geographical areas and contrary to popular belief is not widespread throughout British industry. The study is available from HMSO [£6].

953. Trade unions. See TRADE UNIONS.

954. Trade union activities—Industrial Tribunal decisions

CARTER *v.* WILTSHIRE COUNTY COUNCIL [1979] I.R.L.R. 331 (W.C.C. rejected a request for C and other members of the British Fire Service Federation, an independent trade union not recognised by the W.C.C., to hold a meeting outside working hours in the social club at W.C.C.'s fire station. When the union members convened the meeting anyway, W.C.C. threatened to take disciplinary action against them if the meeting continued. *Held,* that " appropriate time " under s. 53 (1) of the Employment Protection Act 1975 included time when the worker was, and was entitled to be, on the employer's premises. Accordingly, since C was entitled to be in the social club at the relevant time, W.C.C.'s threat constituted a contravention of his right under s. 53 (1) not to have action taken against him for the purpose of deterring him from or penalising him for taking part in the activities of an independent trade union at an appropriate time).

DAVIES AND ALDERTON *v.* HEAD WRIGHTSON TEESDALE [1979] I.R.L.R. 170 (D and A, as officials of a recognised independent trade union, were allowed three days off work to attend a course, in accordance with s. 27 of the 1978 Act. For some years they had usually worked two hours' overtime on two of these days each week. *Held,* that they were not entitled to be paid for the overtime they would have been able to work if they had not attended the course since they were not contractually bound to work overtime and accordingly the overtime hours were not their " working hours " within s. 32 (1) (*b*)).

DUNCAN *v.* WEIR PACIFIC VALVES [1978] I.R.L.R. 523 (WPV Co., a subsidiary of the W group, refused D, a convenor of shop stewards at WPV Co.'s works and a shop steward of the AUEW, paid time off to attend a meeting of stewards from subsidiaries of the W group to discuss a joint approach to the Group to have sick pay policy negotiated on a group basis. *Held,* that as D was at the material time involved in collective bargaining about sick pay in WPV Co.'s plant attendance at the meeting was a duty of D as a union official under s. 57 of the Employment Protection Act 1975 rather than a trade union activity under s. 58. Although WPV Co. claimed to have autonomy for sick pay negotiations, if the Group adopted a certain policy, WPV Co. would be required to comply. Accordingly it was not unreasonable for shop stewards also to consult on matters concerning industrial relations and D was entitled to paid time off to attend the meeting).

McCORMACK *v.* SHELL CHEMICALS U.K. [1979] I.R.L.R. 40 (under McC's contract of employment he was entitled to £97 per week as a senior operator. When he was elected full-time convener with the T.G.W.U., a union recognised by SC Co., SC Co. proposed to apply an agreed rule covering transfers from shifts to days for operational or medical reasons, under which shift payments were gradually reduced to equal day work rates. *Held,* that by virtue of s. 57 of the Employment Protection Act 1975 McC was entitled to £97 per week whilst on trade union work and SC Co. were not entitled to reduce his wage).

955. —— paid time off—course on pension rights

[Employment Protection Act 1975 (c. 71), s. 57.] Y, a shop steward, sought paid time off under s. 57 of the 1975 Act to attend a course at his union's college on Pensions and Participation, CF Co. having set up a pension scheme as a result of the 1975 Social Security Act. *Held,* allowing Y's appeal, that the first question was whether Y was seeking to undergo training in aspects of industrial relations relevant to the carrying out of his duties concerned with industrial relations between CF Co. and its employees. The tribunal had erred in finding that the fact that there was no agreed procedure or customary arrangement for union officials to be concerned with administration, alteration or management of the pension scheme meant that the course was not concerned with industrial relations between CF Co. and its employees. Negotiation and advice regarding pension rights are a part of industrial relations: YOUNG *v.* CARR FASTENERS [1979] I.R.L.R. 420, E.A.T.

956. —— —— meeting of advisory committee
[Employment Protection Act 1975 (c. 71), s. 57.] S, an ASTMS official, sought paid time off to attend a meeting of a Product Advisory Committee with union representatives from other subsidiary companies within the G.E.C. group, S being employed by a particular G.E.C. subsidiary, the purpose of such meeting being merely to exchange information and experience. *Held,* dismissing S's appeal, that he was not entitled to the paid time off under s. 57 (1) (*a*) of the 1975 Act since it was not required to enable him to carry out his duties in relation to a matter which arose in relations between employees and management, since the committee had no power to negotiate with any of the companies in the group or to represent anyone: SOOD *v.* G.E.C. ELLIOTT PROCESS AUTOMATION [1979] I.R.L.R. 416, E.A.T.

957. Trusts. See SETTLEMENTS AND TRUSTS.

958. Unemployment benefit. See SOCIAL SECURITY.

959. Unfair dismissal
UNFAIR DISMISSAL (VARIATION OF QUALIFYING PERIOD) ORDER 1979 (No. 959) [10p], made under the Employment Protection (Consolidation) Act 1978 (c. 44), s. 149 (4); operative on October 1, 1979; varies the qualifying period of 26 weeks for unfair dismissal complaints to an industrial tribunal to 52 weeks where the effective date of termination falls on or after October 1, 1979.
UNFAIR DISMISSAL (INCREASE OF COMPENSATION LIMIT) ORDER 1979 (No. 1723) [10p], made under the Employment Protection (Consolidation) Act 1978, s. 75 (2); operative on February 1, 1980; increases to £6,250 the limit on the amount of compensation awarded by an industrial tribunal in claims for unfair dismissal.

960. —— adjournment of proceedings—concurrent High Court proceedings—order for private hearing
[Industrial Tribunals (Labour Relations) Regulations 1974 (S.I. 1974 No. 1386), Sched. 6 (1).]
Where there are pending concurrent High Court proceedings relating to the same subject matter as a complaint of unfair dismissal, it is proper that the latter proceedings be adjourned pending determination of the High Court action.
The employee was dismissed for alleged misappropriation of copies of confidential documents. He was charged with theft and was awaiting trial therefor. The employers also instituted High Court proceedings for breach of confidence. An industrial Tribunal to whom the employee complained of unfair dismissal ordered that the hearing thereof be adjourned pending determination of the outstanding civil and criminal proceedings and further ordered that the eventual hearing of the complaint should be in private because of the confidential nature of the documents. Before the appeal the employee was acquitted upon the criminal charges. *Held,* allowing the employee's appeal in part, that (1) it was appropriate to await the outcome of the civil proceedings before determining the complaint, since similar issues arose in both sets of proceedings; and (2) as the High Court would need to decide whether or not the hearing should be in private, consideration of whether the tribunal proceedings would be private or not should be deferred pending the High Court ruling thereon.
CAHM *v.* WARD AND GOLDSTONE [1979] I.C.R. 574, E.A.T.

961. —— capability—conduct—opportunity to state case
[Trade Union and Labour Relations Act 1974 (c. 52), Sched. 1, para. 6.]
Even where an employee is incapable of doing his work properly he ought not to be dismissed without any warning.
Complaints were received of B's workmanship, and while he was away on holiday his employers dismissed him. The industrial tribunal found that he had

not been given the opportunity of explaining his poor work, that he should have been given a final warning and that the dismissal was unfair. On appeal by the employers, *held*, that tribunals should distinguish clearly between an employee's incapability due to an inherent incapacity and his failure to make use of his ability which might more properly be regarded as misconduct; even where an employee was incapable he ought not to be dismissed without any warning, and the employee ought to have been given a chance to explain his conduct. The appeal was dismissed. (Dictum in *Kraft Foods* v. *Fox* [1978] C.L.Y. 1118 explained.)

SUTTON & GATES (LUTON) v. BOXALL [1979] I.C.R. 67, E.A.T.

962. —— —— **mental illness**

[Trade Union and Labour Relations Act 1974 (c. 52), Sched. 1, paras. 6 (1) (*b*) (2) (*a*) (8).] O'B was employed by PA Co. as a district agent after a medical examination in which he falsely led the examiner to believe that he had no history of mental illness. In fact he had a long such history which came to light when he applied to PA Co. for a life insurance policy. A report was obtained from his doctor after which he admitted giving false information because he thought that otherwise he would not have been appointed. Two of O'B's superiors recommended that a further report be obtained from a consultant psychiatrist. However, O'B was dismissed following a recommendation by PA Co.'s principal medical adviser. *Held,* that the tribunal had not erred either in finding the dismissal to have been " for some other substantial reason " within the 1974 Act, Sched. 1, para. 6 (1) (*b*), rather than " capability " in view of O'B's deliberate deception or in finding the dismissal fair. Failure to obtain a consultant psychiatrist's report did not affect the decision since it would have made no difference to PA Co.'s decision: O'BRIEN v. PRUDENTIAL ASSURANCE CO. [1979] I.R.L.R. 140, E.A.T.

963. —— **clocking-in offence—warning—meaning of " liable to instant dismissal "**

C was dismissed for clocking-in a fellow worker half an hour before he in fact attended for work. At first he denied the offence, accusing another of lying. EB Co.'s induction booklet provided that clocking or signing in for someone else would render an employee " liable to " instant dismissal. *Held,* allowing EB Co.'s appeal, that the tribunal had erred in finding the dismissal unfair because clocking-in offences had not been specifically defined as inevitably resulting in dismissal. All the circumstances had to be taken into account, including C's false denials and accusations. (*Dalton* v. *Burton's Gold Medal Biscuits* [1974] C.L.Y. 1325 and *Meridian* v. *Gomersall* [1977] C.L.Y. 1105 distinguished): ELLIOTT BROTHERS (LONDON) v. COLVERD [1979] I.R.L.R. 92, E.A.T.

964. —— **closed shop agreement—failure to join union—employer not following proper procedure**

[Trade Union and Labour Relations Act 1974 (c. 52), Sched. 1, para. 6 (5).] P Co. made a post-entry closed shop agreement with certain unions. E was subsequently dismissed for failing to join the relevant union. P Co. could have relied upon Sched. 1, para. 6 (5), of the 1974 Act if they had followed the prescribed procedure to ensure that E had an opportunity of joining the union and was made aware of the implications of refusing to join. *Held*, dismissing E's appeal against an award of compensation based upon loss of wages for three months, that the tribunal had correctly assessed E's compensation by assessing the loss suffered by him. It was incorrect to suggest that compensation in such a case should be generous or exemplary. The first question is what would have been likely to have happened if the proper steps had been taken. The maximum period for which compensation should be awarded is that between dismissal and the estimated date of re-employment. Having assessed that period the tribunal decide whether to award compensation in respect of the whole period or a portion only which is reasonable having regard to the assessment of probabilities: EDWARDS v. PETBOW (1978) 13 I.T.R. 431, E.A.T.

965. —— **company director—whether an employee—jurisdiction of tribunal**

[Trade Union and Labour Relations Act 1974 (s. 52), s. 30 (1); Companies Act 1948 (c. 28), s. 196 (2); Companies Act 1967 (c. 81), s. 26 (1).] Where a working director has no express contract of service and there is insufficient evidence to infer a contract of service, where his remuneration is described as " directors' emoluments," he may not be an " employee " and entitled to complain of unfair dismissal.

P was one of four directors of a family company with subsidiaries for which he worked full time. He received equal remuneration with the others voted by resolution at the end of each financial year and described as " directors' emoluments." There was no written contract of service or memorandum of an oral contract. P was removed as director and applied to an industrial tribunal for unfair dismissal. The tribunal held that he was not an " employee." The appeal tribunal ordered the remission of the case to another tribunal. On appeal, *held,* allowing the appeal, and restoring the tribunal's decision, that it was clear that P was regarded and remunerated as a director, was not employed under a contract of service and could not complain to an industrial tribunal of unfair dismissal.

PARSONS *v.* ALBERT J. PARSONS AND SONS [1979] I.C.R. 271, C.A.

966. —— company in voluntary liquidation—some employees retained to achieve orderly winding up
[Employment Protection Act 1975 (c. 71), s. 64.]
A claim for wrongful dismissal is not synonymous with a claim for unfair dismissal.
Per curiam: It is doubtful whether there can be an unfair dismissal in the case of a properly conducted entry into liquidation.
F Ltd. was in financial difficulties and gave three months' notice to B and others. One month later F Ltd. went into liquidation and B and others were instantly dismissed although some employees were kept on to fulfil outstanding orders. The industrial tribunal held B had been unfairly dismissed. On appeal by the liquidator, *held,* that the expressed instant dismissal was a breach of contract giving rise to a claim for damages for wrongful dismissal but this was not synonymous with a claim for unfair dismissal. Although only some of the employees had been retained, it did not follow that the others had been unfairly dismissed. (*Pambakian* v. *Brentford Nylons* [1978] C.L.Y. 910 distinguished.)
FOX BROTHERS (CLOTHES) (IN LIQUIDATION) *v.* BRYANT [1979] I.C.R. 64, E.A.T.

967. —— compensation—apportionment of blame—reduction of compensation
A tribunal when assessing compensation could consider the employee's contribution to his own dismissal, and in the exceptional case deduct 100 per cent. of the compensatory award.
The employee was employed on the understanding that he would join the appropriate trade union. He joined but as a result of a disagreement over industrial action he stopped paying his subscriptions. His fellow employees refused to work with him and he was dismissed. The tribunal had to disregard pressure on the employers to dismiss the employees when considering whether or not the dismissal was fair (as required by para. 15 of Sched. 1 to the Trade Union and Labour Relations Act 1974) and accordingly held that the dismissal was unfair. The tribunal made no compensatory award on the ground that the employee was wholly to blame for his dismissal except for the minimum basic award of compensation. *Held,* dismissing the appeal, that (1) it was open to a tribunal when assessing compensation to consider the employee's contribution to his own dismissal; (2) in the exceptional case a tribunal could deduct 100 per cent. of the compensatory award; (3) having regard to its finding that the employee had known that he would be unable to work unless he belonged to the union, the tribunal were justified in concluding that his conduct was the sole reason for the dismissal.
SULEMANJI *v.* TOUGHENED GLASS [1979] I.C.R. 799, E.A.T.

968. —— —— assessment—payment by employers in lieu of notice
Where an employee has by his own conduct contributed to his dismissal, payments made by the employer should be deducted after the net amount of compensation has been calculated and not as part of those calculations.
M was suspended for breaches of discipline, and then dismissed, receiving 10 weeks' wages in lieu of notice. The industrial tribunal held he was unfairly dismissed but was 50 per cent. responsible. In assessing compensation they

deducted the payments made to M and halved the result because of M's contributory responsibility. On appeal by the employer, *held*, that M was unfairly dismissed but the assessment of compensation was wrong. The deduction for the employer's payment should be made after the net figure for compensation had been calculated, otherwise the employer would be worse off when the employee was at fault than when the employee was blameless.

CLEMENT-CLARKE INTERNATIONAL *v.* MANLEY [1979] I.C.R. 74, E.A.T.

969. —— —— **deduction of sickness benefit**

[Social Security Act 1975 (c. 14), ss. 14 (1) (*b*), 17 (1) (*c*).]

An employee who, having been unfairly dismissed, is compensated for the period between employments, and who during that same period is unwell and claiming sickness benefit, is entitled to compensation without deduction of the received benefit.

F was found to be unfairly dismissed and the tribunal awarded her compensation for a 13-week period between jobs. F had been unwell during those weeks and claiming sickness benefit. On the employer's appeal, *held*, dismissing the appeal, that F was entitled to receive benefit regardless of whether she was receiving payment under her contract of employment, and that she was therefore entitled to compensation without deduction of the benefit.

SUN AND SAND *v.* FITZJOHN [1979] I.C.R. 268, E.A.T.

970. —— —— **delay in providing written reference**

[Employment Protection Act 1975 (c. 71), s. 76.] A tribunal awarded G £208·85 compensation for unfair dismissal, including £50 in respect of W Co.'s delay in giving a written reference. No award as to loss of earnings was made since W Co. had given G the chance to apply for two vacancies. *Held,* that (1) the tribunal had no jurisdiction to award compensation for a loss consequent upon failure to give a written reference, rather than upon the dismissal itself; (2) the tribunal had correctly made no award for loss of earnings as G had unreasonably failed to mitigate his loss: GALLEAR *v.* J. F. WATSON & SON [1979] I.R.L.R. 306, E.A.T.

971. —— —— **failure to mitigate loss**

An unfairly dismissed employee whose loss of pension rights is properly attributable to his unreasonable refusal to accept an offer of reinstatement rather than to the original dismissal is not entitled to compensation in respect thereof.

The employee was dismissed for refusing to obey instructions. A week later the employers offered to reinstate him but he refused. His claim for unfair dismissal succeeded, but the tribunal found that his refusal of the offer of re-instatement was unreasonable and that since he had suffered no loss attributable to the dismissal, he was entitled only to the basic award. *Held*, dismissing his appeal (by a majority), that the employee's loss of pension rights flowed from his refusal to accept the offer of reinstatement and was therefore not recoverable; and such refusal also amounted to a failure by the employee to mitigate his loss as required by s. 76 (4) of the Employment Protection Act 1975.

SWEETLOVE *v.* REDBRIDGE AND WALTHAM FOREST AREA HEALTH AUTHORITY [1979] I.C.R. 477, E.A.T.

972. [Employment Protection Act 1975 (c. 71), s. 76 (4).]

In assessing the amount to be deducted for failure to mitigate loss, the tribunal should not reduce the whole compensatory award by a percentage but should decide on a date by which the employee should have found work and assess his loss up to that date.

The employee was dismissed on November 8, 1977, and he remained unemployed until April 1978. During the period of unemployment he tried for 10 or 12 jobs. The tribunal found that he was unfairly dismissed, and that had he tried harder, he would have found suitable employment much earlier than April 1978. Therefore he had failed to mitigate his loss. The tribunal awarded compensation by assessing his total loss of earnings and then deducted 40 per cent. for failure to mitigate his loss before making other deductions.

Held, allowing the employee's appeal and remitting the case back to the tribunal, that the amount of deduction for failure to mitigate loss should not reduce the whole compensatory award by a percentage. Instead a date by which the employee should have found work should be fixed and his loss up to that date assessed.

PEARA *v.* ENDERLIN [1979] I.C.R. 804, E.A.T.

973. ——— ——— ——— procedure and test on appeal

PP Co. claimed that the tribunal had erred (1) in finding that R had not failed to mitigate his loss following his dismissal in view of his failure to register as unemployed; and (2) in ignoring sums earned by R as a freelance journalist in assessing compensation. *Held,* that (1) these were questions of fact and the tribunal were entitled to find that in view of the nature of R's employment as an editor registration as unemployed would have little point and that his free-lance earnings should be ignored since he was entitled to make such earnings under his contract of employment; (2) if an appeal against an award of compensation can only succeed by asking the tribunal to elaborate part of its decision, the inquiry should be put in before the appeal comes for hearing: PENTHOUSE PUBLICATIONS *v.* RADNOR (1978) 13 I.T.R. 528, E.A.T.

974. ——— ——— fresh employment—permanent or temporary

G was unfairly dismissed in January 1976. Compensation was assessed in July 1977, by which time G had taken a fresh job but lost it after four weeks. *Held,* that in assessing compensation the whole period from dismissal to the date of assessment had to be taken into account. Earnings during that period had to be brought into the calculation but it was irrelevant whether the fresh employment was regarded at the time as temporary or permanent: GING *v.* ELLWARD LANCS. (1978) 13 I.T.R. 265, E.A.T.

975. ——— ——— loss of pension rights—employers' contribution

An unfairly dismissed employee is entitled to compensation for loss of pension rights, regard being had to the employers' contribution notwithstanding that no specific part thereof was allocated to a particular employee.

Prior to his unfair dismissal the employee contributed to his employers' contributory pension scheme. The employers' contribution was not allocated to each employee but was paid on an actuarial basis and in fact amounted to some 14 per cent. of the total annual salaries of all contributing members. Upon leaving the employee opted to take a lump sum as the surrender value of his pension rights. It was established that the longer an employee was employed the less he effectively paid for his share of pension rights. An industrial tribunal awarded him compensation for loss of such rights and for future loss, taking account, *inter alia,* of the possibility of the employee having no or less favourable pension rights in subsequent employment and of his in any event voluntarily leaving his employment. *Held,* dismissing the employers' appeal, that all relevant factors had been considered by the tribunal; and that the tribunal had been entitled to deem the annual percentage paid into the fund by the employers as being attributable to a particular employee.

WILLMENT BROTHERS *v.* OLIVER [1979] I.C.R. 378, E.A.T.

976. ——— ——— pension contributions

An employee who, on leaving a company, has a choice as to the method of return of his pension contributions, is under no obligation, when unfairly dismissed, to choose that method which mitigates his loss.

Under the employer's contributory pension scheme B had a choice as to whether to take a lump sum or a deferred pension when leaving the company. B was dismissed and elected to take the lump sum rather than the deferred pension which would have produced more money. The industrial tribunal found he had been unfairly dismissed, and in assessing compensation found that he was entitled to receive the employer's contributions to the scheme as well as his own. On appeal, *held,* dismissing the appeal, that the fact that B had the choice of taking the deferred pension did not prevent him from claiming he had received less than his entitlement by going for a lump sum.

STURDY FINANCE *v.* BARDSLEY [1979] I.C.R. 249, E.A.T.

977. —— —— pension rights—employee never likely to qualify for pension
[Employment Protection Act 1975 (c. 71), s. 76.]
Where an employee who has been unfairly dismissed would never have qualified under a pension scheme, his pension rights will be limited to his contractual rights under the scheme.
E was unfairly dismissed. There was a pension scheme which required five years' service before pensions could be drawn. The industrial tribunal found the E's employment would in any case have ended before the five-year period ended. E had the contractual right under the scheme to have his own contributions refunded, and that was done. The tribunal awarded no sum representing the loss of benefit of employers' contributions during his employment. On appeal by E, *held,* dismissing the appeal, that as E would never have qualified for a pension, his rights were limited to his contractual entitlement to the return of his own contributions.
MANNING *v.* R. & H. WALE (EXPORT) [1979] I.C.R. 433, E.A.T.

978. —— complaint—right to make—settlement of claim—action by ACAS
[Trade Union and Labour Relations Act 1974 (c. 52), Sched. 1, paras. 26, 32, as amended by Employment Protection Act 1975 (c. 71), Sched. 16, Pt. III, para. 24.]
Where ACAS has been asked to intervene in a dispute, and in consequence a settlement is concluded, the employee is prevented from bringing a complaint of unfair dismissal.
The employee was suspended on suspicion of theft. A conciliation officer was asked to intervene and a settlement " in final settlement of all claims, etc." was duly signed. The employee subsequently applied to an industrial tribunal for unfair dismissal. The tribunal held that they had jurisdiction to hear the complaint. On appeal, *held*, allowing the appeal, that the settlement was " action in accordance with " para. 26 (4) of the Schedule and that accordingly para. 32 (1) did not apply so as to render the agreement void.
DUPORT FURNITURE PRODUCTS *v.* MOORE [1979] I.C.R. 165, E.A.T.

979. —— —— time limit
[Trade Union and Labour Relations Act 1974 (c. 52), Sched. 1, para. 21 (4).]
The question whether it has been " reasonably practicable " for the complaint to be presented in time or within a further reasonable period is essentially one of fact for the industrial tribunal to decide.
K was summarily dismissed and went to draw unemployment pay. He was told the matter would go to a tribunal and he would not get it for six weeks. He knew unfair dismissal proceedings must be commenced within three months but mistakenly believed the same tribunal would deal with his unfair dismissal claim as was already dealing with his unemployment pay claim. When he learned the true position he acted with all speed but was by then outside the time limit. The industrial tribunal found it was not reasonably practicable for K to have presented the complaint in time and that the complaint had been presented within a further period which was reasonable in the circumstances. The appeal tribunal dismissed the employers' appeal but granted leave to appeal. *Held*, dismissing the appeal, that the question whether it was " reasonably practicable " for the complaint to be presented within the time limit or within a further reasonable period was essentially one of fact for the industrial tribunal. *Per* Lord Denning M.R.: industrial tribunals should be fairly strict in enforcing the three months' time limit. (*Dedman* v. *British Building and Engineering Appliances* [1974] C.L.Y. 1316 applied; *Norgett* v. *Luton Industrial Co-operative Society* [1976] C.L.Y. 969; *Union Cartage Co.* v. *Blunden* [1977] C.L.Y. 1185 and *Porter* v. *Bandridge* [1978] C.L.Y. 1084 considered.)
WALL'S MEAT CO. *v.* KHAN [1979] I.C.R. 52, C.A.

980. —— —— upper age limit—normal retirement age—effect of employer/union agreement
[Trade Union and Labour Relations Act 1974 (c. 52), Sched. 1, para. 10 (*b*).]
When the Post Office changed from a Government department to a public corporation in 1969, its employees were given assurances to the effect that their

security of employment and retirement conditions or benefits would not be adversely affected. Since some employees had been allowed to work beyond the age of 60, N and W assumed that the assurance meant that they would be entitled to do so. Meanwhile the Post Office and unions reached agreement recognising that the normal retiring age was 60. *Held,* dismissing N's and W's appeals, that they were disqualified from making complaints of unfair dismissal by Sched. 1, para. 10 (*b*) of the 1974 Act as they were over the normal retiring age for employees holding positions similar to theirs. There had never been more than an understanding that, at the Post Office's discretion, good and experienced employees could in some circumstances be retained beyond 60. Furthermore, the fact that the agreement between the Post Office and the unions was not approved by each individual member did not prevent it from binding every member: NELSON AND WOOLLETT *v.* THE POST OFFICE [1978] I.R.L.R. 548, E.A.T.

981. —— **complaint of indiscipline—officer making complaint also assisting tribunal —whether breach of natural justice**
The fact that an education officer initiates a complaint of indiscipline against a group of teachers, submits a report on the matter, and subsequently assists a disciplinary tribunal deciding the case, does not of itself amount to a fundamental breach of the rules of natural justice provided it is evident that the tribunal acted fairly and justly.

As a result of disquiet at a school and an ensuing strike, an education officer made complaints of indiscipline against a group of teachers arising out of the strike and their refusal to work. The officer wrote a report for the disciplinary tribunal and attended to assist the tribunal. The tribunal found the charges proved and dismissed the teachers. The teachers then applied to an industrial tribunal alleging unfair dismissal. On appeal by the teachers, *held,* dismissing the appeals, that (1) the employers by waiting until all the facts were known had not waived their right to dismiss for breach of contract; (2) though the officer acted as prosecutor and as consultant to the disciplinary tribunal this did not, in this case, where the tribunal had clearly acted fairly and justly, involve a fundamental breach of the rules of natural justice. (*Simmons* v. *Hoover* [1977] C.L.Y. 1058 considered; *Ward* v. *Bradford Corporation* [1971] C.L.Y. 21 applied.)
HADDOW *v.* INNER LONDON EDUCATION AUTHORITY [1979] I.C.R. 202, E.A.T.

982. —— **complaint out of time—skilled advice followed**
[Trade Union and Labour Relations Act 1974 (c. 52), Sched. 1, para. 21 (4).]
Where a dismissed employee consults a citizens' advice bureau, the bureau is considered to be a skilled adviser. Where after such consultation a complaint is not presented within the three months' limit, the tribunal is entitled to infer that it was " reasonably practicable " to present the complaint in time.

R was dismissed on suspicion of theft. She consulted a citizens' advice bureau which advised her to await the outcome of that case before commencing unfair dismissal proceedings. She was acquitted on the theft charge, but presented her complaint outside the time limit. The tribunal found that she knew of her right to complain, though not of the time limit, and dismissed the claim for want of jurisdiction. On appeal, *held,* dismissing the appeal, that the bureau was acting as a skilled adviser, and the tribunal, in the absence of contrary evidence, was entitled to infer that it was therefore " reasonably practicable " for her complaint to be presented in time. (*Dedman* v. *British Building and Engineering Appliances* [1974] C.L.Y. 1316 applied.)
RILEY AND GREATER LONDON CITIZENS' ADVICE BUREAU *v.* TESCO STORES [1979] I.C.R. 223, E.A.T.

983. —— **conduct—belief of employer**
[Trade Union and Labour Relations Act 1974 (c. 52), Sched. 1, para. 6 (8).]
An industrial tribunal has to decide whether the employer has established the fact of his belief that the employee was guilty of misconduct, whether he had reasonable grounds to sustain that belief and whether at the stage at which he had formed that belief he had carried out as much investigation as was reasonable in the circumstances: W. WEDDEL & CO. *v.* TEPPER, *The Times,* December 22, 1979, C.A.

984. —— —— **criminal offence unconnected with work**
B, an advisory drama teacher, was dismissed following his conviction of possession and cultivation of cannabis. *Held,* dismissing the NCC's appeal against a finding of unfair dismissal and an order of reinstatement, that each case depended on its own facts where a teacher is convicted of such an offence. (*Nottinghamshire County Council* v. *Bowly* [1978] C.L.Y. 1100 applied): NORFOLK COUNTY COUNCIL *v.* BERNARD [1979] I.R.L.R. 220, E.A.T.

985. —— —— **disciplinary procedures not followed**
S, a public service vehicle driver, was nowhere to be found by the inspector at 7.00 p.m. though S's shift was due to end at 9.45 p.m. On the following night two inspectors watched him and saw him hand in his cash and time card much earlier than he should have. The same happened a few days later. A report was submitted to the district traffic superintendent and following a meeting S was dismissed. *Held,* dismissing S's appeal, that the tribunal were entitled to find the dismissal fair despite the fact that WS Co. had not followed their disciplinary procedure in that they did not challenge S after the first incident rather than watch him commit further offences without saying anything to him. False clocking in and false claims about hours worked are serious offences of dishonesty which can justify instant dismissal: STEWART *v.* WESTERN S.M.T. Co. [1978] I.R.L.R. 553, E.A.T.

986. —— —— **disciplinary rules expressly providing for instant dismissal—minor breaches**
L.R. Co.'s disciplinary rules and conditions of employment prohibited employees from placing bets or allowing other staff to do so. During an investigation arising from suspicions of fraud and dishonesty during which no such fraud or dishonesty was revealed, it was discovered that A and others had committed minor breaches of the prohibition. *Held,* that the tribunal had not erred in finding the dismissals of the employees concerned unfair notwithstanding that the disciplinary rules specifically stated that a breach of the relevant rule would result in immediate dismissal: LADBROKE RACING *v.* ARNOTT [1979] I.R.L.R. 182, E.A.T.

987. —— —— **dishonesty—obligation to make inquiries—dismissal pending trial**
[Trade Union and Labour Relations Act 1974 (c. 52), Sch. 1, para. 6 (8).]
An honest and reasonable belief that an employee has stolen from his employer may justify the latter in dismissing him; the employee's subsequent acquittal would not render the dismissal unfair.
In November, the employee was suspended with pay after he had been charged with stealing his employer's property which was found on his premises. The following February the employers, upon hearing that the employee had elected jury trial, without previously consulting the employee dismissed him. Later the employee was acquitted of theft. An industrial tribunal found that the dismissal was unfair since the immediate reason was not the employee's dishonesty but the likely delay pending the outcome of the trial. *Held,* allowing the employers' appeal in part, that the employers might have been justified in dismissing the employee upon honestly and reasonably believing him to have stolen company property without awaiting the outcome of the criminal trial, but that having suspended the employee pending resolution thereof, they acted unreasonably in dismissing him without some further consultation with him, there being no reason why, if such consultation was handled with care, a fair trial should have been prejudiced; but that the tribunal should reconsider the effect of both parties' conduct on the amount of compensation payable. (*Alidair* v. *Taylor* [1978] C.L.Y. 1096 applied.)
HARRIS (IPSWICH) *v.* HARRISON [1978] I.C.R. 1256, E.A.T.

988. —— —— —— **opportunity to state case**
[Trade Union and Labour Relations Act 1974 (c. 52), Sched. 1, para. 6 (8).]
A dismissal without opportunity to state a case may nevertheless be fair, even though it cannot be said that such an opportunity would have made no difference.
One of the terms of E's employment gave D Co. the right to dismiss instantly any employee responsible for theft of the company's property. The

police told D Co. that E had admitted stealing from them. When the managing director spoke to E about the matter, he made no attempt to deny it. E was dismissed. He complained of unfair dismissal on the ground that he had had no opportunity to explain why the provision for instant dismissal should not operate. The application was dismissed. On appeal by E, *held*, dismissing the appeal, that although the circumstances fell short of those where an opportunity to explain could have made no difference, the industrial tribunal were entitled to find that the dismissal was fair, in particular, since E had made no denial. (*Carr* v. *Alexander Russell* (*Note*) [1979] C.L.Y. 992 followed; *Budgen & Co.* v. *Thomas* [1976] C.L.Y. 976 doubted.)
PARKER v. CLIFFORD DUNN [1979] I.C.R. 463, E.A.T.

989. —— —— gross misconduct—dismissal without warning
C was employed by a veterinary practice as an animal nursing auxiliary. She had completed almost two years working in veterinary practices and, at the time of her dismissal, was shortly due to take final examinations which, if she passed, together with the two years' practice would enable her to become a registered animal nursing auxiliary approved by the Royal College of Veterinary Surgeons. Although her employer, K, felt that C was not as efficient as she ought to have been he had never warned her that her work was unsatisfactory and her conduct had never been questioned before the date of her dismissal. Following an altercation with the veterinary surgeon employed by the practice C left the operating theatre during an operation on a dog and a replacement nurse had to be found. *Held*, C was dismissed because she left the theatre during an operation. The altercation in the theatre did not justify C in deserting her post. K reasonably believed that the life of the animal was or may have been placed at risk by her action and K was entitled to regard this conduct as gross misconduct justifying C's immediate dismissal without warning: CLARKE v. KYDD, September 4, 1979; Industrial Tribunal. (*Ex rel. R. J. Terry, Esq., Barrister.*)

990. —— —— natural justice—no opportunity to cross-examine
[Trade Union and Labour Relations Act 1974 (c. 52), Sched. 1, para. 6.]
Natural justice requires not only that a man should have a chance to state his own case but also that he should know what is being said against him.
M was involved in a fight with S at the company's premises. Statements were taken from witnesses and both M and S were interviewed separately. M was dismissed. He appealed and was allowed to give his own evidence but not to question S or the witnesses. The appeal panel confirmed the dismissal. On application to an industrial tribunal he was held to have been unfairly dismissed. *Held*, dismissing the company's appeal, that natural justice required not only that a man be able to state his own case, but also that he should know what was being said against him so that he could put forward his own case properly.
BENTLEY ENGINEERING CO. v. MISTRY [1979] I.C.R. 47, E.A.T.

991. —— —— senior employee—assisting potential competitor of employer
L, a warehouse manager, was dismissed because GCH Co.'s managing director believed L to be going into business with an ex-employee of GCH Co. in competition with GCH Co. and to have done work for his new business on GCH Co.'s premises and to have lied about this when challenged. *Held*, allowing an appeal against a finding of unfair dismissal, that where a senior employee has set out to assist a potential competitor of his employer and has used his employer's premises for that purpose and then lied about it, no reasonable tribunal could find his dismissal unfair: GOLDEN CROSS HIRE CO. v. LOVELL [1979] I.R.L.R. 267, E.A.T.

992. —— —— theft from employers' premises—employee charged—summary dismissal
[Scot.] [Industrial Relations Act 1971 (c. 72), s. 24.]
In some circumstances, instant dismissal for gross misconduct without an opportunity to explain will not be considered unfair.
C was employed by A Co. Some of A Co.'s property was stolen, and C was charged with the offence. A Co. were told that C had been caught red-

handed. As C was off work at the time, A Co. wrote to him dismissing him on the ground of gross misconduct. C made no protestation of innocence and did not implement the grievance procedure under his contract of employment. *Held,* an internal inquiry would have been improper, because proceedings were pending, suspension was impractical for the length of the wait involved before trial; and in the circumstances, the dismissal was fair. (*Earl* v. *Slater & Wheeler (Airlyne)* [1973] C.L.Y. 1184 considered.)

CARR v. ALEXANDER RUSSELL (NOTE) [1979] I.C.R. 469, Ct. of Session.

993. —— —— theft of company property—failure to make sufficient inquiries or follow correct procedure—test

Where employers have summarily dismissed an employee, the onus is on them to establish that the employee would still have been dismissed even if they had investigated the matter fully.

The employee was dismissed after having knowingly shared in the proceeds of sale of goods stolen from his employers. He asked for a union official to speak on his behalf but he was dismissed before representations could be made. An industrial tribunal found that the employers should have convened a disciplinary committee to consider the matter and that had they done so they might have considered the employee's conduct to be insufficient to warrant dismissal; accordingly the dismissal was unfair. *Held,* dismissing the employers' appeal, that the tribunal was entitled to conclude that the employers had failed to prove on a balance of probabilities that they would have acted in the same way after a full investigation had been held.

BRITISH LABOUR PUMP CO. v. BYRNE [1979] I.C.R. 347, E.A.T.

994. —— —— theft of employer's property—duty to investigate

The appellant roof insulators were dismissed summarily after being charged by police with theft from a house where they were working. They were subsequently acquitted. *Held,* dismissing S.S.H.A.'s appeal against finding of unfair dismissal, that in such circumstances a reasonable employer must have sufficient information to entitle him to assume reasonably that the employee was guilty. Although the prospect of criminal proceedings may limit investigation, some enquiry may at least disclose the information upon which the police were acting. The fact of a charge alone was insufficient. Furthermore, it was unreasonable not to consider the case of each appellant separately. (*Monie* v. *Coral Racing* [1979] C.L.Y. 1053 applied): SCOTTISH SPECIAL HOUSING ASSOCIATION v. COOKE [1979] I.R.L.R. 264, E.A.T.

995. L was dismissed after being charged by police with theft of copper from S.S.H.A. Copper belonging to S.S.H.A. which had been burnt off was found in L's garden. He was subsequently convicted. *Held, inter alia,* allowing an appeal against a finding of unfair dismissal, that in such a case an employer must act fairly towards the employee but must equally do nothing which might cause prejudice in subsequent criminal proceedings. Where an employee appears to have been caught red-handed in possession of his employer's goods, summary dismissal without further investigation might be appropriate: SCOTTISH SPECIAL HOUSING ASSOCIATION v. LINNEN [1979] I.R.L.R. 265, E.A.T.

996. —— —— verbal warning only

McC, a salesman, was summarily dismissed for persistent dealing in other manufacturers' goods contrary to an express prohibition and repeated verbal warnings. *Held,* dismissing McC's appeal, that (1) the tribunal had not erred in finding the dismissal fair; (2) it was not necessary for C.C. Co. to show serious loss to their business resulting from the misconduct; (3) in this case failure to give McC an opportunity to state his case did not render the dismissal unfair; (4) nor did the lack of a written warning. To an intelligent man a verbal warning should be equally effective: MCCALL v. CASTLETON CRAFTS [1979] I.R.L.R. 218 E.A.T.

997. —— continuity of employment—absence " on account of a temporary cessation of work "

[Contracts of Employment Act 1972 (c. 53), Sched. 1, paras. 5, 10.] L, a bus driver with EAB Co., wished to move to Bristol and requested a transfer to an associated company in Bristol. He was not transferred but moved to Bristol and five and a half weeks later he obtained a driving job with WN Co., an associated company of EAB Co. He was dismissed seven weeks later. *Held*, allowing WN Co.'s appeal, that the five and a half week period could not be regarded as an absence from work " on account of a temporary cessation of work " within para. 5, Sched. 1, to the 1972 Act. Accordingly, L's continuity of employment had been broken and he did not qualify for a complaint of unfair dismissal: WESSEX NATIONAL *v.* LONG (1978) 13 I.T.R. 413, E.A.T.

998. —— —— **dismissal for poor attendance—subsequent re-engagement**
[Contracts of Employment Act 1972 (c. 53), Sched. 1, para. 5 (1) (*a*).]
An employee dismissed when, to his employers' knowledge, he was ill, and subsequently re-engaged may be regarded as having been continuously employed from the date of his original employment.
The employee was frequently absent from work due to ill-health. On June 30 the employee was taken ill at work and went home and remained there ill, although he did not so inform his employers. On July 6 the employers dismissed him by reason of his poor attendance record. On August 1 he was re-engaged, but was dismissed again 3 weeks later. An industrial tribunal dismissed his complaint of unfair dismissal on the grounds that by reason of the July 6 dismissal and subsequent break in employment, the employee had not been continuously employed for 26 weeks. *Held*, allowing the employee's appeal, that since the employee's absence in July was in fact due to illness, the earlier dismissal was therefore sufficiently related to para. 5 (1) (*a*) of Sched. 1 to the 1972 Act to enable the employee's employment to be regarded as continuous. (*Fitzgerald* v. *Hall, Russell & Co.* [1969] C.L.Y. 1281 considered.)
SCARLETT *v.* GODFREY ABBOTT GROUP [1978] I.C.R. 1106, E.A.T.

999. —— —— **" normal " hours of employment—no contractual provision**
[Contracts of Employment Act 1972 (c. 53), Sched. 1, para. 4; Trade Union and Labour Relations Act 1974 (c. 52), Sched. 1, para. 10 (*a*).]
Where there is no express contractual provision as to the hours of work, regard should be had to the hours actually and usually worked in order to ascertain the hours of employment normally required by the contract.
Between June 1975 and January 1977 the employee worked as a cleaner. There was no contractual provision as to the hours of work. Initially she worked only a few hours but later increased her hours, reverting on occasion to 14 hours a week, which hours she worked in the last six weeks prior to her dismissal. Overall, out of the 80 weeks of her employment, she worked some for 30 hours during 47 weeks and for less than 21 hours during 30 weeks. An industrial tribunal held that she could not complain of unfair dismissal since her employment was not under a contract normally involving employment for 21 hours a week, as required under para. 4 of Sched. 1 to the 1972 Act. (*Note*: the minimum number of hours is now reduced to 16 under the Employment Protection Act 1975, Sched. 16, Pt. II, paras. 13.) Further the tribunal ruled that since the last six weeks involved less than 21 hours work, she was not " employed," within the meaning of para. 10, Sched. 1 to the 1974 Act, continuous for 26 weeks ending with the effective date of termination. *Held*, allowing the employee's appeal, that the tribunal had erred in placing undue reliance on the last six weeks involving less than 21 hours' work; that the correct approach was to look at the hours normally worked; and that overall the employment normally involved more than 21 hours work per week. (*Dean* v. *Eastbourne Fishermen's and Boatmen's Protection Society and Club* [1977] C.L.Y. 1051 applied.)
LARKIN *v.* CAMBOS ENTERPRISES (STRETFORD) [1978] I.C.R. 1247, E.A.T.

1000. —— —— **normal weekly hours**
[Contracts of Employment Act 1972 (c. 53), Sched. 1, para. 4A (1).] During part of O's employment she worked $20\frac{1}{4}$ and $13\frac{1}{2}$ hour weeks alternatively. From December 1975 she worked $13\frac{1}{2}$ hours only every week. *Held,* that, although up to December 1975 O worked an average of over 16 hours per week, her contract did not normally involve work for 16 hours or more weekly. Accordingly, para. 4A (1) of Sched. 1 to the 1972 Act, which pre-

serves continuity of employment where an employee's normal contractual weekly hours are varied from 16 or more to less than 16 but at least eight, did not apply and O had sufficient continuous service to qualify her to make a complaint of unfair dismissal: OPIE v. JOHN GUBBINS (INSURANCE BROKERS) [1978] I.R.L.R. 541, E.A.T.

1001. —— —— **whether area health authorities " associated employers "**
[Contracts of Employment Act 1972 (c. 53), Sched. 1, para. 10 (1) (2), as amended by Employment Protection Act 1975 (c. 71), Sched. 16, Pt. II, para. 19.]

Employers do not have to be companies to be "associated" within para. 10 (1) of Sched. 1 to the Contracts of Employment Act 1972 for the purposes of computing 26 weeks' continuous employment.

E was a health visitor. She worked first for one area health authority, then another, both being controlled by the same regional authority. She complained to an industrial tribunal of unfair dismissal. The tribunal held that the two area health authorities were " associated employers " under para. 10 (1) of Sched. 1 to the Contracts of Employment Act 1972 for the purposes of computing the 26-week period of continuous employment. On appeal by the employers, *held*, dismissing the appeal, that para. 10 (1) was in wide terms and not limited by the definition of associated employer in para. 10 (2). (*Southern Electricity Board* v. *Collins* [1969] C.L.Y. 1275 and *Re Stanley* [1906] 1 Ch. 131 considered.)

HILLINGDON AREA HEALTH AUTHORITY v. KAUDERS [1979] I.C.R. 472, E.A.T.

1002. —— **continuous service minimum—inclusion of statutory week's notice**
[Trade Union and Labour Relations Act 1974 (c. 52), Sched. 1, paras. 5 (6), 10 (a), 30 (1A), (as added by Employment Protection Act 1975 (c. 71), Sched. 16, Pt. III, paras. 10, 29); Contracts of Employment Act 1972 (c. 53), Sched. 1, paras. 4, 11.]

The week's statutory notice under s. 1 of the Contracts of Employment Act 1972, being the week ending with a Saturday under paras. 4 and 11 (1) of Sched. 1 to that Act, counts as part of the 26-week period of continuous employment under para. 10 (a) of Sched. 1 to the Trade Union and Labour Relations Act 1974.

E worked for D Co. under a contract of employment normally involving employment for over 16 hours a week, from Tuesday, August 30, 1977, until his dismissal without notice on Wednesday, February 15, 1978. On E's complaint of unfair dismissal, the tribunal held that E was entitled to a week's notice, and that the date of termination was the expiration date of such a notice under para. 5 (6) of Sched. 1 to the Trade Union and Labour Relations Act 1974, which took the dismissal date up to February 22. This was still not a period of 26 weeks. But the tribunal held that by paras. 4 and 11 (1) of Sched. 1 to the Contracts of Employment Act 1972, the right date then was the end of the last week or part week for which E was employed for 16 hours, *i.e.* the Saturday, which was February 25. Taking that date as the date of termination, E had been employed for 26 weeks, and the tribunal held that it had jurisdiction to hear the complaint. D Co. appealed. *Held*, dismissing the appeal, that the tribunal's computation was correct.

COOKSON & ZINN v. MORGAN [1979] I.C.R. 425, E.A.T.

1003. —— —— **transfer of business—partnership**
[Employment Protection (Consolidation) Act 1978 (c. 44), Sched. 13, para. 17 (2).] In July 1978 the entire equity in A & Son, solicitors, was transferred to L, the surviving partner on the death of the other partner, G. C, a solicitor employed by the firm, was dismissed shortly afterwards. *Held*, dismissing A & Son's appeal, that there had been a transfer of the business to " another " within Sched. 13, para. 17 (2), to the 1978 Act. The substance of the transaction was that L and G as joint proprietors had transferred the whole of the business to L alone. Accordingly C's continuity of employment was preserved and he had the necessary 26 weeks' service to make a complaint of unfair dismissal: ALLEN & SON v. COVENTRY [1979] I.R.L.R. 399, E.A.T.

1004. —— contract of employment—absences through ill-health

[Scot.] L, a steel fixer, was dismissed following frequent absences due to ill-health. His contract provided, *inter alia*, for dismissal following frequent absences on medical grounds. *Held, inter alia,* that the E.A.T. had not erred in finding that FHCE Co. were entitled to dismiss L in accordance with his contract and that the tribunal was entitled to find the dismissal reasonable, in the light of the contractual provision, despite the fact that FHCE Co. had not consulted with L or inquired into the nature of his incapacity to discover whether he was likely to be fit for work in the future (*East Lindsey District Council* v. *Daubney* [1977] C.L.Y. 1142 distinguished): LEONARD v. FERGUS & HAYNES CIVIL ENGINEERING [1979] I.R.L.R. 235, Ct. of Session.

1005. —— —— musician—shareholder in orchestra

[Trade Union and Labour Relations Act 1974 (c. 52), s. 30 (1).]

A musician who is a shareholder in an orchestra, his engagement being based on a gentleman's agreement, and paying national insurance at the self-employed rate is not an employee within s. 30 of the Trade Union and Labour Relations Act 1974.

P, the principal oboist of the London Philharmonic Orchestra was given three months' notice of termination of his engagement. The orchestra was a registered company whose shareholders comprised the members of the orchestra and the manager. There was no written contract, and on engagement P was referred to a long standing gentleman's agreement between the players and the orchestra. P paid national insurance contributions at the self-employed rate. He sought compensation for unfair dismissal and the application was dismissed on the ground that P was not engaged under a contract of service. On appeal by P, *held*, dismissing the appeal, that the tribunal was entitled to look at the reality of the matter and was entitled on the facts to reach the conclusion that P was not an employee.

WINFIELD v. LONDON PHILHARMONIC ORCHESTRA [1979] I.C.R. 726, E.A.T.

1006. —— contributory fault—computation of compensatory award

S's dismissal was found to have been unfair but the tribunal held that his compensatory award should be reduced by 25 per cent. for contributory fault. Before reducing the award by 25 per cent. the tribunal deducted the payment in lieu of notice which S had received. *Held,* dismissing P. & F. Co.'s appeal, that the tribunal was correct and it would have been wrong to reduce the compensatory award by 25 per cent. before deducting the payment in lieu of notice: PARKER & FARR v. SHELVEY [1979] I.R.L.R. 434, E.A.T.

1007. —— —— test—relevance of tribunal's previous findings—res judicata—interest on compensation

[Trade Union and Labour Relations Act 1974 (c. 52), Sched. 1, para. 19 (3).]

The E.A.T. had dismissed N's appeal against a tribunal's finding that he had been fairly dismissed. The E.A.T. had doubts about the tribunal's finding that N had been dismissed on grounds of redundancy but found the dismissal fair as being for " some other substantial reason," N having unreasonably refused an offer of alternative work. The Court of Appeal had allowed N's appeal on the ground that the E.A.T. should not have given effect to an unpleaded defence and remitted the case to the same tribunal. N now appealed, *inter alia*, from the tribunal's finding that his compensation should be reduced by 60 per cent. on grounds of contributory fault in rejecting the alternative work. The E.A.T. had made an interim decision that the findings of the tribunal at its first hearing were admissible and conclusive as *res judicata* on the issue of contributory fault. *Held*, allowing N's appeal, that (1) the tribunal's findings at the first hearing were inadmissible on the question of contributory fault as they had not been incorporated into its second decision and had not been made in relation to the issue of contribution; (2) there had to be culpability or blameworthiness on an employee's part before a reduction under Sched. 1, para. 19 (3) of the 1974 Act could be made. Not all unreasonable conduct is culpable or blameworthy; (3) the tribunal had erred in law in failing to take into account the Court of Appeal's decision that N had not been made redundant as his job had continued to exist. Accordingly, the offer of other work was in reality a proposal to reassign him to other work within his contractual terms, which the

B.B.C. were entitled to do; (4) the tribunal's finding of 60 per cent. fault would accordingly be set aside. It was unnecessary to decide what reduction should have been made because even with a 60 per cent. reduction compensation exceeded the maximum award by reason of the E.A.T.'s decision on other aspects of the case; (5) neither the tribunal, nor the E.A.T., nor the Court of Appeal had jurisdiction to award interest on compensation: NELSON v. BRITISH BROADCASTING CORP. [1979] I.R.L.R. 346, C.A.

1008. —— disciplinary hearing—appeal—employee not present throughout hearing or on appeal

At a disciplinary hearing M gave his version of events. His foreman then gave his version in the absence of M and his union representatives and then again in front of M's representatives. Other witnesses then gave evidence in front of the representatives. At the hearing of M's appeal against the decision to dismiss him he was not present but was represented by two shop stewards and a full-time union official. *Held, inter alia,* that the tribunal had erred in deciding that the fact that M was not present when important evidence was given or at the appeal constituted a breach of the rules of natural justice: PIRELLI GENERAL CABLE WORKS v. MURRAY [1979] I.R.L.R. 190, E.A.T.

1009. —— —— right to be represented

G and four others were dismissed for altering petrol receipts to make false expenses claims. They were told of their right to appeal but not of their right under R.X. Co.'s disciplinary procedure to be represented at the hearing. Requests at the hearing for a union representative to make representations and for solicitors to attend were refused. *Held, inter alia,* that the tribunal had not erred in finding the breach of the disciplinary rules to have made the dismissals unfair, even though it occurred after the dismissals: RANK XEROX (U.K.) v. GOODCHILD [1979] I.R.L.R. 185, E.A.T.

1010. —— —— rules of natural justice

[Trade Union and Labour Relations Act 1974 (c. 52), Sched. 1, para. 6.]

In domestic proceedings natural justice requires that the employee should know the accusation made, should be given an opportunity to state her case and that the adjudicators should act in good faith.

Complaints against a nursing sister, K, were the subject of a disciplinary inquiry. The patients who complained were not called as witnesses though their statements were admitted. Neither side asked for them to be called and neither side could compel their attendance. K was dismissed and her appeals to an appeals panel and an industrial tribunal were rejected. K appealed that there had been a breach of natural justice. *Held,* that in such proceedings natural justice required that the employee should know the complaints made against her, that she be given an opportunity to state her case and that those adjudicating should act in good faith. These three requirements had been satisfied and the appeal would be dismissed. (*Byrne* v. *Kinematograph Renters Society* [1958] C.L.Y. 2778 applied.)

KHANUM v. MID-GLAMORGAN AREA HEALTH AUTHORITY [1979] I.C.R. 40, E.A.T.

1011. —— dismissal during strike—letter offering re-engagement not received by employee

[Trade Union and Labour Relations Act 1974 (c. 52), Sched. 1, para. 7 (2) (*b*).] M and 35 others went on strike. FS Co. then wrote letters to all of them dismissing them and offering to re-engage them provided that the offer was accepted by a certain date. M's letter was wrongly addressed and he did not receive it. *Held,* that the tribunal correctly decided that they had no jurisdiction to consider the fairness of M's dismissal, by virtue of the 1974 Act, Sched. 1, para. 7 (2) (*b*) since (1) he had been dismissed whilst on strike; (2) on the evidence M, who was an active shop steward, knew of the offer and its terms although he had not received the letter; (3) it could not be said that para. 7 does not apply where a strike is " engineered " by the employers. (*Thompson* v. *Eaton* [1976] C.L.Y. 982 distinguished; *Wilkins* v. *Cantrell and Cochrane (G.B.)* [1978] C.L.Y. 1168 considered): MARSDEN v. FAIREY STAINLESS [1979] I.R.L.R. 103, E.A.T.

1012. —— dismissal or resignation

An employee who resigns not by reason of threats made but by mutual agreement subject to satisfactory financial settlement is not to be regarded as dismissed.

In a small company the employee's family had held half the shares until the other shareholders increased their holding. The employee's wife, who was also employed by the company, was threatened with dismissal by the controlling shareholders and the employee threatened to resign; he was told that if he did not, he would be dismissed. Negotiation followed as a result of which the employee resigned after agreeing financially advantageous terms. His complaint of unfair dismissal was rejected by an industrial tribunal. *Held*, dismissing his appeal, that on the facts the threat of dismissal had not been the ultimate cause of the employee's resignation, it following the conclusion of a financially acceptable settlement.

SHEFFIELD *v.* OXFORD CONTROLS CO. [1979] I.C.R. 396, E.A.T.

1013. S, a fitter and turner, falsely told A.B. Co. that he was off sick with a medical certificate. He was asked to send in a certificate but did not have one. A.B. Co.'s rules stated that medical certificates were required wthin three days of commencement of an illness and that employees failing to comply with the requirement may be considered to have dismissed themselves. S later produced a certificate stating that he had taken a holiday to rest and improve his condition of ischaemic heart disease. *Held,* dismissing S's appeal, that the tribunal had not erred in finding that S had terminated his own employment and that his conduct amounted to a repudiation of his contract of employment justifying A.B. Co. in treating him as having terminated his contract: SMITH *v.* AVANA BAKERIES [1979] I.R.L.R. 423, E.A.T.

1014. —— exclusions—normal retiring age—distinction from pensionable age

[Trade Union and Labour Relations Act 1974 (c. 52), Sched. 1, para. 10 (*b*).]

In 1973, when M was 57, and the normal retiring age for SCS Co.'s employees was 65, M agreed to enter a new pension scheme which, *inter alia*, reduced the pensionable age to 62. He signed a form of consent and waiver. The scheme provided that M could remain in employment after 62 by arrangement with the trustees. Before dismissal M indicated to the trustees that he wished to remain employed. *Held*, that the tribunal had correctly held that M had not reached normal retirement age, which was different from " pensionable age." The pension scheme was between M and the trustees. If the new scheme did become part of M's contract of employment, he had a contractual right thereunder to opt for later retirement by arrangement with the trustees (*Ord* v. *Maidstone and District Hospital Management Committee* [1974] C.L.Y. 1328 applied): STEPNEY CAST STONE CO. *v.* MACARTHUR [1979] I.R.L.R. 181, E.A.T.

1015. —— failure to comply with agreed procedure

Para. C4 of the agreed procedure provided that BP Co. " will inform the appropriate full-time official as soon as possible of any case in which dismissal is contemplated." Before B was dismissed BP Co.'s industrial relations officer attempted to contact the appropriate full-time union official and left a message with the official's secretary for him to telephone on his return to his office. The works manager proceeded to consider the matter and dismissed B before the union official had telephoned. *Held*, allowing B's appeal, that in view of the failure to comply with para. C4 the tribunal had erred in finding the dismissal fair: BAILEY *v.* B.P. OIL (KENT REFINERY) [1979] I.R.L.R. 151, E.A.T.

1016. —— failure to pursue application—two-year delay—whether to dismiss for want of prosecution

[Industrial Tribunals (Labour Relations) Regulations 1974 (S.I. 1974 No. 1386), Sched., r. 11 (2) (*f*), as amended by Industrial Tribunals (Labour Relations) (Amendment) Regulations 1978 (S.I. 1978 No. 991), reg. 9.]

A two-year delay in pursuing a complaint for unfair dismissal may be excused where no prejudice had resulted to the employers from the delay.

After his dismissal in January 1976, the employee presented a complaint of unfair dismissal to an industrial tribunal. Family illness required his return to

India and when the complaint was listed for hearing in May 1976 he was not present and the complaint was adjourned *sine die.* He returned a year later, could not afford to instruct solicitors and in November 1977 informed the tribunal that he would conduct the case himself. He was then in hospital from January to May 1978. In June 1978 he replied immediately to the tribunal's query as to his intentions, stating that he wished the matter to proceed. The employers thereupon applied to dismiss the complaint for want of prosecution. *Held*, refusing the application, that although it was desirable for such matters to be dealt with expeditiously, there was some excuse for the employee's delay and further the employers, who had not so applied earlier, were not prejudiced by the delay in answering the complaint.

RAHI v. H.M. LAND REGISTRY [1979] I.C.R. 93, E.A.T.

1017. —— failure to return to work after strike—illness

On February 20, 1978, shop stewards sent telegrams to J.C. Co.'s striking plumbers advising them to return to work on the following day and that failure to do so could result in dismissal. D did not return because he was ill. He went to the site and saw his shop steward and later, on the afternoon of February 22, 1978, contacted J.C. Co., who had sent his letter of dismissal on February 21. *Held*, dismissing D's and J.C. Co.'s appeals against a finding of unfair dismissal with 60 per cent. reduction in compensation for D's contribution to his dismissal, that with a little diligence J.C. Co. could have found out that D was ill before he was dismissed. There may also be circumstances in which employers may reasonably be expected to reconsider a dismissal if an explanation is given shortly after the letter is sent, although the tribunal may have gone a little too far in suggesting that J.C. Co. should have rescinded the decision as soon as they heard D was ill. (*Devis & Sons* v. *Atkins* [1977] C.L.Y. 1160 and *Chrystie* v. *Rolls Royce* [1976] C.L.Y. 979 considered): JOHN CRAWFORD & CO. (PLUMBERS) v. DONNELLY [1979] I.R.L.R. 9, E.A.T.

1018. —— fixed-term contract—agreement to accept ex gratia payment on expiry

[Trade Union and Labour Relations Act 1974 (c. 52), Sched. 1, paras. 5 (2), 32.] W, a researcher taxed as self-employed under Sched. D, worked on fixed, term contracts for TT Co. for specific programmes. In July 1977 she was appointed a reporter for a fixed term expring on January 1, 1978. She was eventually notified that her contract would not be renewed on its expiry and was given the option of returning to the rank of researcher or receiving an *ex gratia* payment when her contract ended. She chose the latter. *Held*, dismissing TT Co.'s appeal, that (1) the tribunal had not erred in finding that W was employed by TT Co. under a contract of employment. The fact that she had elected to be taxed as self-employed was not conclusive. The question was whether an ordinary person looking at the contract would say it was a contract of service; (2) agreement to accept an *ex gratia* payment at the end of a fixed-term contract after being informed that the contract would not be renewed did not amount to agreement that the contract should not be renewed: THAMES TELEVISION v. WALLIS [1979] I.R.L.R. 136, E.A.T.

1019. —— —— meaning

[Trade Union and Labour Relations Act 1974 (c. 52), Sched. 1, para. 5 (2) (*b*).]

On a true construction of Sched. 1 to the 1974 Act, a contract for a stated period, even though determinable by either party on notice, is a "contract for a fixed term."

D was employed by the B.B.C. for a number of years on a temporary contract for an indefinite period, determinable on notice. The B.B.C., thinking they would not need his services much longer, gave D a new contract for a new stated short term, determinable on one week's notice. The contract was not renewed and D claimed unfair dismissal. The tribunal said it had no jurisdiction, and the Appeal Tribunal allowed the appeal; on the B.B.C.'s appeal, *held*, dismissing the appeal, that D's contract was for a "contract for a fixed term" and the industrial tribunal had jurisdiction to hear the complaint. (*British Broadcasting Corp.* v. *Ioannou* [1975] C.L.Y. 1091 not followed.)

DIXON v. BRITISH BROADCASTING CORP. [1979] 2 All E.R. 112, C.A.

1020. —— illegal contract of employment—employee's failure to disclose benefits to Inland Revenue

Following an award to B for unfair dismissal it was discovered that B had failed to reveal to the Inland Revenue his income derived from the sale of two calves given to him by McC. *Held,* dismissing McC's appeal against the finding of unfair dismissal, that an employee's whole contract of service is not necessarily made illegal so that the tribunal has no jurisdiction to deal with it because the employee fails to disclose to the Inland Revenue a benefit he has received. There was no evidence that McC was a party to any arrangement to defraud the revenue and the contract was thus legal: McCONNELL *v.* BOLIK [1979] I.R.L.R. 422, E.A.T.

1021. —— industrial tribunal—continuing absenteeism—firm in liquidation

B was employed by WW as a machinist for 16 years, the last two years of which he had suffered ill health. He was absent from work for 12 consecutive weeks in 1976, four weeks in 1977 and from early May onwards in 1978. In July 1978 a notice of dismissal was sent effective in October, the reason given being continuing absenteeism. B was given no warning about the possibility of dismissal. On August 18, 1978, WW went into voluntary liquidation and its workforce, save B, were declared redundant. On B's application for unfair dismissal and redundancy payment, *held,* WW acted reasonably in dismissing B for " severe incapacity." B was, however, entitled to redundancy payment because (1) the contract of employment actually terminated on August 18; (2) termination on that date was due to redundancy; (3) voluntary liquidation overtook and superseded notice of dismissal: BARRY *v.* WESTERN WOODCRAFT (IN LIQUIDATION), December 4, 1978. Industrial Tribunal, Cardiff. (*Ex rel. Messrs. Hugh James, Jones & Jenkins, Solicitors.*)

1022. —— Industrial Tribunal decisions

Conduct—whether taking part in trade union activities

STOKES AND ROBERTS *v.* WHEELER-GREEN [1979] I.R.L.R. 211 (an agreement between W-G Co. and full-time S.O.G.A.T. officials provided that if there were a breakdown of the company's rules, custom and practices the London Women's Branch should use their offices to bring a speedy and satisfactory resolution of any problem within the spirit of the agreement. S and R, print finishers and chapel officers, following a culmination of incidents in which they had been obstructive and unco-operative culminating in their refusal to operate particular machines and walking out, were dismissed. *Held,* that the dismissals were by reason of conduct and it had not been shown that the dismissals were for taking part in the activities of an independent trade union. Although S and R were acting together to promote what they thought were their members' interests, they did so on their own initiative, without endorsement of a chapel meeting, in an unconstitutional manner and possibly without the support of the majority of their members. In all the circumstances of the case the dismissals were fair).

Continuous service minimum—pregnant employee

SINGER *v.* MILLWARD LADSKY & Co. [1979] I.R.L.R. 217 (S claimed to have been dismissed because she had become pregnant. *Held,* that the tribunal had no jurisdiction to hear the complaint as S did not have 26 weeks' continuous service. The only exception to the 26 weeks' service requirement in s. 64 (1) (*a*) of the Employment Protection (Consolidation) Act related to " inadmissible " reasons, which concern, under s. 58, trade union membership).

Time-limits—advice of union official

SYED *v.* FORD MOTOR Co. [1979] I.R.L.R. 335 (S was sent a letter of dismissal. He was in Pakistan where the letter was forwarded to him. On December 4, 1978, he saw the full-time union convenor, who said he would take up S's case for him. At the end of December or beginning of January S went to a job centre and was advised to take his case to an industrial tribunal and to act quickly. He submitted his application on January 1, 1979, three weeks after the expiry of the statutory time period. *Held,* that S's claim for unfair dismissal compensation could not be heard. It could not be said that it had not been reasonably practicable for S's complaint to be presented in time as he had engaged a skilled adviser, namely the convenor, to act for him in the matter of dismissal, although S personally had not known of his right to complain of unfair dismissal or the time-limit).

1023. —— **interim relief—form of application—whether strict compliance with requirements necessary**

[Employment Protection (Consolidation) Act 1978 (c. 44), s. 77 (2) (*b*).]

Strict compliance with the formal requirements concerning the documentation to be produced upon an application for interim relief may be waived where the application substantially complies with the statute.

The employee sought interim relief pending determination of his complaint of unfair dismissal, contending that he had been dismissed by reason of his trade union activities. On the same date as his application a letter from a trade union official was sent to the tribunal supporting his application, but it omitted to state (as required by s. 77 (2) (*b*) of the Act) that there were reasonable grounds for supposing that the reason for dismissal was the one alleged in the complaint of unfair dismissal. An industrial tribunal ruled that such omisison deprived them of jurisdiction on the application for interim relief. *Held*, allowing the employee's appeal, that it was clear that the official's letter was intended to be linked to the employee's complaint and that there was accordingly substantial compliance with s. 77 (2) (*b*).

BRADLEY *v.* EDWARD RYDE & SONS [1979] I.C.R. 488, E.A.T.

1024. —— **jurisdiction—" piece-work " outworker—whether an employee**

[Trade Union and Labour Relations Act 1974 (c. 52), s. 30 (1).]

A factory " outworker " employed on a regular basis may be regarded as an employee for the purposes of unfair dismissal.

The applicant had for some seven years been engaged by the respondents as an outworker; she being remunerated as a piece-worker. She was not guaranteed any quantity of work and such quantity varied seasonally, but usually she worked five days a week. Upon her engagement being terminated and she complaining of unfair dismissal, an industrial tribunal ruled as a preliminary issue that she was an " employee " within the meaning of s. 70 (1) of the 1974 Act. *Held*, dismissing the appeal, that on the facts the tribunal were entitled to conclude that a contract of employment was in existence.

AIRFIX FOOTWEAR *v.* COPE [1978] I.C.R. 1210, E.A.T.

1025. —— **lock-out—" relevant employees "—jurisdiction**

[Contracts of Employment Act 1972 (c. 53), Sched. 1, para. 11 (1); Trade Union and Labour Relations Act 1974 (c. 52), Sched. 1, para. 7 (as amended by Employment Protection Act 1975 (c. 71), Sched. 16, Pt. III, para. 13).]

On a true construction " relevant employees " are not confined to those employees who are actually locked out but include those who are directly involved in a trade dispute.

34 employees were asked to give an undertaking that they would work at the normal pace or they would be suspended. The employees did no work the following day but held a meeting and thereafter all but seven of them signed the undertaking. The seven were treated as suspended and were dismissed after failing to give the undertaking following a second request. On their applications claiming unfair dismissal, the tribunal found that there had been a lock-out but the seven employees were the only employees directly interested in the dispute and, therefore, were the only " relevant employees " within para. 7, Sched. 1, but as all seven had been dismissed there was no jurisdiction to hear the complaints. On the employees' appeal, *held,* allowing the appeal, that (1) the seven employees had been dismissed after the second request; (2) the dispute was a trade dispute over the terms and conditions of employment within s. 29 (1) of the 1974 Act, and as the suspension was in consequence of that dispute there was a lock-out within para. 11 (1) of Sched. 1 to the 1972 Act; (3) the tribunal has jurisdiction as " relevant employees " were not confined to those who were actually locked out but included those who were directly interested in the dispute and here not all 34 employees had been dismissed.

FISHER *v.* YORK TRAILER CO. [1979] I.C.R. 834, E.A.T.

1026. —— **normal retiring age—civil servant over 60**

[Trade Union and Labour Relations Act 1974 (c. 52), Sched. 1, para. 10 (*b*).]

Where a tribunal, in considering the position of an employee for the purposes of Sched. 1, para. 10 (*b*) to the 1974 Act, having taken into account not just his rank but his duties and status, concludes that it was permissible, at its discretion, for his employers not to extend his employment between the ages of 60 and 65, then the tribunal is entitled to conclude that his normal retiring age is 60 years.

A civil servant's employment was subject to rules that provided for a minimum age of retirement between the ages of 60 and 65. Retention beyond 60 years was discretionary but the intention was to allow the employee to stay until 20 years' service was completed. H was retired at the age of 61 after 19 years' service. He complained of unfair dismissal but the tribunal found he was excluded from bringing a complaint. On appeal, *held,* dismissing the appeal, that since, having regard to his position and status, it was permissible for the employers not to extend his employment beyond 60 years, the tribunal were entitled to conclude the normal retiring age was 60 years. (Dictum of Lawton L.J. in *Nothman* v. *Barnet London Borough Council* [1978] C.L.Y. 1146, applied.)

HOWARD *v.* DEPARTMENT FOR NATIONAL SAVINGS [1979] I.C.R. 584, E.A.T.

1027. —— —— woman over 60
[Trade Union and Labour Relations Act 1974 (c. 52), Sched. 1, para. 10 (*b*).]
On a true construction of para. 10 (*b*) of Sched. 1 to the Trade Union and Labour Relations Act 1974, which removes the right to complain for unfair dismissal from an employee who has attained the normal retiring age, the normal retiring age in a particular profession is the age at which an employee normally must retire in that profession, and only in the absence of such a requirement with the statutory restriction of 60 for women and 65 for men apply.

A, a woman, was employed as a teacher under a contract of employment which provided for automatic retirement at the age of 65. She was dismissed at the age of 61, and she brought a complaint for unfair dismissal. The tribunal held that it had no jurisdiction to hear the complaint under para. 10 (*b*) of Sched. 1 to the Trade Union and Labour Relations Act 1974. The Employment Appeal Tribunal dismissed A's appeal, holding that para. 10 (*b*) presented a double barrier, and that although A had not reached normal retiring age, she was a woman and had reached 60. The Court of Appeal allowed her appeal, holding that the age restrictions of 65 and 60 only came into operation where there was no normal retiring age to be considered. On appeal by the employers to the House of Lords, *held,* dismissing the appeal, (Lords Diplock and Fraser of Tullybelton dissenting), that para. 10 (*b*) enacted only one barrier; either that normal retiring age, or, if none, 65 or 60.

NOTHMAN *v.* BARNET LONDON BOROUGH COUNCIL [1979] 1 W.L.R. 67, H.L.

1028. —— opportunity to state case—relevance of " expediency "
If the Appeal Tribunal remits to an industrial tribunal a case of unfair dismissal for consideration of ordering reinstatement, the tribunal is to consider reinstatement having regard to the circumstances prevailing at the time of its original decision.

An employee was found to have been unfairly dismissed but reinstatement was not ordered upon the grounds that it was " not expedient." On appeal, *held,* that (1) expediency was not a proper ground for refusing to order reinstatement; and (2) the case would be remitted to the industrial tribunal who should consider reinstatement as at the date of the original decision, although they would refer to subsequent matters but only in so far as the true position at the original date was clarified thereby.

QUALCAST (WOLVERHAMPTON) *v.* ROSS [1979] I.C.R. 386, E.A.T.

1029. —— other substantial reason—business reorganisation—refusal to accept changes
[Trade Union and Labour Relations Act 1974 (c. 52), Sched. 1, paras. 6 (1), 8.]
Dismissal may be justified where employers need to reorganise their business and the employee declines to co-operate with such reorganisation.

The employee was a local secretary employed in Cornwall by the Farmers' Union, his main remuneration arising from his agency for a local insurance company. Other Cornwall secretaries complained to the union that they fared worse than their counterparts over the rest of the country whose insurance agency was for a national company offering scope for earning greater commission. Without further consultation the Union decided to re-organise its Cornwall business to bring it into line with the remaining parts of the country. The employee objected thereto, declined to accept a new contract of employment based upon the revised terms and was accordingly dismissed. His claim for unfair dismissal was rejected by an industrial tribunal on the grounds that the reorganisation amounted to "some other substantial reason" justifying dismissal within the meaning of para. 6 (1) (b) of Sched. 1 to the 1974 Act. The E.A.T. ordered the tribunal to reconsider the matter on the grounds, *inter alia,* that the employers' failure to consult the employee showed that they had not acted reasonably. *Held,* allowing the employers' appeal, that the reorganisation of the business was properly held to be capable of being a reason justifying dismissal; and that the tribunal's finding that there was no necessity for the employer, to consult the employee in these circumstances, rendered it impossible to say that the employers had acted unreasonably in not so consulting. (Dictum in *Lowndes* v. *Specialist Heavy Engineering* [1977] C.L.Y. 1137 doubted; decision of E.A.T. [1978] C.L.Y. 1147 reversed.)
HOLLISTER v. NATIONAL FARMERS' UNION [1979] I.C.R. 542, C.A.

1030. —— —— **policy and advice**
[Trade Union and Labour Relations Act 1974 (c. 52), Sched. 1, para. 6 (1) (b) (8).] The respondents employed two consultant surgeons, B for three half-days per week and X for six. When X resigned, it was decided to appoint one consultant for all nine sessions as suggested by two advisory bodies in accordance with the respondents' policy of rationalisation and practice of amalgamating part-time posts. *Held,* allowing B's appeal, that (1) the tribunal had erred in holding the dismissal fair; (2) that the employers were acting in accordance with a policy or upon a recommendation does not amount to "some other substantial reason" for dismissal within the 1974 Act, Sched. 1, para. 6 (1) (b), unless some evidence is adduced to show what advantages the policy had or was hoped to have or as to what importance was attached to it; (3) nor could acting in accordance with policy or advice *per se* show a dismissal to have been fair without further evidence; (4) there was no evidence to indicate that dismissal was on grounds of redundancy: BANERJEE v. CITY AND EAST LONDON AREA HEALTH AUTHORITY [1979] I.R.L.R. 147, E.A.T.

1031. —— —— **scientist—funds for research withdrawn**
[Trade Union and Labour Relations Act 1974 (c. 52), Sched. 1, paras. 6 (1) (b), (2) (8); Redundancy Payments Act 1965 (c. 62), s. 1 (2) (b).] P, a research scientist, was paid from funds provided by a research council and a research campaign. In April 1977 he was promoted to grade IIS officer. A joint committee of the two bodies later ruled that a grade II officer only was justified on the project on which P was engaged. *Held,* allowing P's appeal, that (1) the tribunal had erred in finding the dismissal to have been for redundancy. The requirement for the type of work done by P had not ceased or diminished. The grade II scientist envisaged would have done the same work; (2) the tribunal found alternatively that there was another substantial reason justifying dismissal and that the dismissal was fair. Where an employer is dismissing because funds from another body are withdrawn it is essential that the reason for withdrawal be ascertained and explained to the employee. The M.A.H.A. should have asked the committee if they would accept P in a more junior position and should have enquired whether some other research by P might be financed: PILLINGER v. MANCHESTER AREA HEALTH AUTHORITY [1979] I.R.L.R. 430, E.A.T.

1032. —— **part-time employee—entitlement to notice—statutory reduction in minimum hours—effect**
[Contracts of Employment Act 1972 (c. 53), Employment Protection Act 1975 (c. 71), Sched. 16, Pt. II.] S worked for AEHA, normally 16 hours per

week, from May 1974 until June 1977. *Held*, dismissing the AEHA's appeal, that Sched. 16, Pt. II, to the 1975 Act, which came into force on February 1, 1977, and reduced the minimum hours for a week to count in computing the period of an employee's employment to 16, meant that all weeks involving 16 hours' work or more, whether before or after February 1, 1977, should count. Accordingly, S was entitled to three weeks' notice at the date of dismissal: ACTIVE ELDERLY HOUSING ASSOCIATION *v.* SPARROW (1978) 13 I.T.R. 395, E.A.T.

1033. —— parties agreeing tribunal wrong—procedure to be followed
Where both parties agree that the decision of an industrial tribunal is in error, the proper course is for the parties to draw up a formal order and submit it to the Employment Appeal Tribunal sitting in open court for ratification.
At a hearing for unfair dismissal, the tribunal, by a majority, found that the applicant had been unfairly dismissed. After the decision both parties came to the conclusion that the tribunal was in error, and drew up a document which was submitted to the registrar. The registrar took the view that he was not empowered to accept it and referred it to the E.A.T. *Held*, that this was the correct procedure to follow and the request for ratification would be granted.
COMET RADIOVISION SERVICES *v.* DELAHUNTY [1979] I.C.R. 182, E.A.T.

1034. —— professional footballer—contract not renewed
A football club employer may be justified in dismissing a player upon the team manager's advice.
The employee had been engaged as a footballer for some seven years under a series of annual contracts, his abilities as a player having never been called into doubt. During his last season he suffered from injuries. After the club was relegated, a new manager wished to restructure the team, leaving no place for the employee whose contract was not renewed without prior warning and without any medical report on the player. *Held*, upholding an industrial tribunal's rejection of a claim for unfair dismissal, that the club had been entitled to act upon the advice of its manager that a player of different aptitudes to those of the employee was required.
GRAY *v.* GRIMSBY TOWN FOOTBALL CLUB [1979] I.C.R. 364, E.A.T.

1035. —— qualifying period of employment—effective date of termination—domestic appeals procedure
[Trade Union and Labour Relations Act 1974 (c. 52), Sched. 1, para. 10 (*a*).]
Where an employee unsuccessfully pursues a domestic appeals procedure against his dismissal, the effective date of termination is that of the original dismissal.
The employee commenced employment in October 1977. In February 1978 he was dismissed for misconduct, and he appealed against such decision to a director of the employers under an internal procedure which provided that pending the director's decision the employee would be suspended without pay, receiving back-pay if later re-instated. The employee was told of the rejection of his appeal on June 1, 1978. The employee then complained to an industrial tribunal of unfair dismissal and succeeded upon a preliminary point in contending that he had been employed for the qualifying period of 26 weeks, his employment not terminating until the dismissal of the internal appeal. *Held*, allowing the employers' appeal, that the effective date of termination was that of the original dismissal.
J. SAINSBURY *v.* SAVAGE [1979] I.C.R. 96, E.A.T.

1036. —— reasonableness—fixed term contract—employer innocently overlooking employee's qualification
[Trade Union and Labour Relations Act 1974 (c. 52), Sched. 1, para. 6.]
An employer who innocently overlooks that a fixed term employee is eligible for alternative available employment at the end of such term may be regarded as acting unreasonably in not considering such employee for re-employment prior to dismissing him.
The employee was temporarily engaged as a needlework teacher for two

terms. Prior to expiry thereof, the employer advertised for a teacher to teach that subject and, preferably, to assist with languages or religious education. The employee applied for such post, referring to her qualification also to teach languages; the employer innocently overlooked her application and she was not considered for the post. Upon expiry of the fixed term she complained of unfair dismissal, but an industrial tribunal ruled that since the employer had innocently overlooked her application, the employer's conduct was not unreasonable. *Held*, allowing the employee's appeal, that since the employers knew of the employee's qualification, albeit that they overlooked it, they were unreasonable within para. 6 (8) of Sched. 1 to the Act in not adequately considering her application.

BEARD *v.* ST. JOSEPH'S SCHOOL GOVERNORS [1978] I.C.R. 1234, E.A.T.

1037. —— redundancy—appeals—costs—unreasonable conduct in appealing
[Employment Appeal Tribunal Rules 1976 (S.I. 1976 No. 322), r. 21 (1).] Mrs. E, an office manager who had started with RRT Co. as a clerk/typist 19 years previously, was made redundant in January 1977. The tribunal found the dismissal was unfair in view of the way in which she had been treated since 1975 when Mr. T became works manager, and after she had refused an offer of the job of administration officer. She and T did not get on and her position had therefore been made less important. *Held*, dismissing RRT Co.'s appeal, that (1) the tribunal were entitled to find the dismissal unfair whether or not a genuine redundancy situation had arisen in view of E's length and quality of service and RRT Co.'s treatment of her; (2) RRT Co.'s conduct in appealing was unreasonable under r. 21 (1) of the 1976 Rules since if counsel's opinion had been taken he would have advised that there was no prospect of success: REDLAND ROOF TILES *v.* EVELEIGH [1979] I.R.L.R. 11, E.A.T.

1038. —— —— failure to consider for alternative employment—poor work record —no warning
M was dismissed on grounds of redundancy. She was not considered for alternative employment with PRS Co. because of her poor work record. *Held*, allowing M's appeal, that the dismissal was unfair because PRS Co. had not warned M that she would be dismissed for redundancy if her work did not improve: MAGRO *v.* PERFORMING RIGHTS SOCIETY (1978) 13 I.T.R. 198, E.A.T.

1039. —— —— failure to offer alternative employment
AC Co. reorganised its business so that S, one of two senior agents, was no longer required. They failed to offer S the job of site agent thinking that he would not accept it as it constituted a demotion. *Held*, dismissing AC Co.'s appeal, that the tribunal were entitled to find that AC Co.'s failure to offer the alternative job, which would have been accepted in fact, rendered the dismissal unfair: AVONMOUTH CONSTRUCTION CO. *v.* SHIPWAY [1979] I.R.L.R. 14, E.A.T.

1040. —— —— failure to pay more compensation than required
A dismissal for redundancy is not normally unfair where the propriety of the dismissal is not in question, and the employee has received the notice and payments to which he is statutorily and contractually entitled.

A chief executive of a local council was appointed in 1974. Following reorganisation and a political complexion change, the executive was dismissed in 1977, with three months notice, on the grounds of redundancy. The tribunal found that redundancy was the true reason for dismissal, and that the employers had acted reasonably, but concluded that this was a case of unfair dismissal as the council should have been more generous in their severance terms. On appeal, *held*, allowing the appeal, that a dismissal for redundancy cannot normally be unfair where the propriety of the dismissal is not in question and the notice and payments to which the employee is entitled are received.

HINCKLEY & BOSWORTH BOROUGH COUNCIL *v.* AINSCOUGH [1979] I.C.R. 590, E.A.T.

1041. —— —— overmanning
[Employment Protection (Consolidation) Act 1978 (c. 44), s. 81 (2) (*b*).] An employer increased his workforce in anticipation of expanding business. These

hopes proved too optimistic and so the workforce was then cut by 10 per cent. because of the overmanning. *Held*, the dismissed employees were not entitled to redundancy payments, unless the requirements of their business as employees to carry out their particular work had ceased or diminished within the meaning of s. 81 (2) (*b*): O'HARE *v.* ROTAPRINT, *The Times*, November 22, 1979, E.A.T.

1042. —— —— **selection—test where union consulted**

F.W.C. Co. made nine out of 30 workers redundant after consultations with their union. *Held*, dismissing H's appeal against a finding that his selection was fair, that, *inter alia*, although the tribunal had erred in declining to consider whether F.W.C. Co. had adequately investigated alternatives to compulsory redundancies, taking the view that the tribunal should not interfere since the union had not suggested short-time working or voluntary redundancies, the error made no difference since it was clear that the union and F.W.C. Co. had considered the alternatives and adopted the only proper course: HASSALL *v.* FUSION WELDING AND CONSTRUCTION (BIRKENHEAD) CO. [1979] I.R.L.R. 13, E.A.T.

1043. —— **refusal to accept change in workplace**

D, a senior sales engineer, became ill when working in the Middle East and could not say when he would recover. B.R.E. therefore required D to return, to work at home instead of in the export field. *Held*, allowing D's appeal, that though under D's terms and conditions of employment he was obliged to work " as required " by B.R.E., some restriction on the requirements must be implied and it was clear that his obligation was to work in the export field. Thus the dismissal was unfair: DEELEY *v.* BRITISH RAIL ENGINEERING [1979] I.R.L.R. 5, E.A.T.

1044. —— **refusal to join trade union—religious beliefs**

[Trade Union and Labour Relations Act 1974 (c. 52), Sched. 1, para. 6 (5).]

An employee may legitimately object to joining a union on the grounds of his personal religious beliefs, notwithstanding that the tenets of the religious sect to which he belongs do not require him to abstain from membership.

Employers and a trade union entered a closed shop agreement, pursuant to which the employee was dismissed for refusing to join the union. The employee had previously told his employers of his objections to joining the union by reason of his Christian convictions; he was a member of the Jehovah's Witness sect, which did not forbid union membership. His initial claim for unfair dismissal was dismissed but a rehearing was ordered on appeal upon the grounds that the pertinent consideration was the employee's own religious beliefs and not those of the sect to which he belonged. At the rehearing the tribunal accepted that the employee honestly believed his objections to be based upon religious beliefs but held, by a majority, that they were not in fact so based. *Held*, allowing the employee's appeal, that in view of their acceptance of the employee's beliefs, the tribunal's decision was unreasonable; the employee had accordingly been unfairly dismissed. SAGGERS *v.* BRITISH RAILWAYS BOARD (No. 2) [1978] I.C.R. 1111, E.A.T.

1045. —— —— **union membership agreement—compliance of employer**

[Employment Protection (Consolidation) Act 1978 (c. 44), s. 58 (3).]

It is not enough to justify dismissal under s. 58 (3) of the Employment Protection (Consolidation) Act 1978 merely to identify failure to belong to a union as a reason for dismissal; the onus is on the employers to show that they complied with the essential provisions of the union membership agreement before dismissal.

A union membership agreement provided that an employee could belong to one of four specified unions. The agreement provided that an employee was liable to be dismissed (1) if he was an existing employee and decided not to join one of the specified unions; or (2) if he was excluded or expelled from one of the unions. There were different appeal and dismissal procedures. E was dismissed for not belonging to a union. The industrial tribunal found that E was not a member of one of the four unions and held that the dismissal was fair. On appeal by E, *held*, allowing the appeal, that the tribunal had erred in failing to consider the detailed provisions of the union membership agreement and the onus was on the employers to show that they had complied with it and the procedures it laid down. The case would be remitted to another tribunal to consider those matters. (*Jeffrey* v. *Laurence Scott & Electromotors* [1978] C.L.Y. 903, considered.)

CURRY v. HARLOW DISTRICT COUNCIL [1979] I.C.R. 769, E.A.T.

1046. —— refusal to work overtime—lack of warning

Throughout his employment with S.S., M was reluctant to agree to work overtime but did so on some occasions after persuasion. He was dismissed after being asked to work on the evening of Friday, February 24, 1978, and Saturday, February 25, 1978, and refusing to work even on the Saturday evening alone. His written terms of employment provided that " you will be expected to work such overtime as is necessary to ensure continuity of service." *Held*, dismissing M's appeal, that the dismissal, for refusing to comply with what was a contractual term, was fair, even though S.S. had not sought to force M to work overtime before and had condoned previous refusals. No warning was necessary as M was determined to go on in his own way. Nor was further inquiry or investigation by S.S. Co. into the reasons for refusal necessary in this case: MARTIN v. SOLUS SCHALL [1979] I.R.L.R. 7, E.A.T.

1047. —— re-organisation—refusal to accept change in terms of employment

M, X and Y, R.A.C. emergency controllers, worked a 31½ hour week. A re-organisation instituted by the R.A.C. to deal with increased numbers of emergency calls involved M, X and Y working a 42 hour week. The R.A.C. reached an agreement with the staff association which was acceptable to the majority of staff. M, X and Y were dismissed for refusing to accept the change. *Held*, allowing M, X and Y's appeals, that the tribunal had erred in finding the dismissals fair merely because the proposed changes had been agreed with the staff association. This was just one matter to be considered in deciding whether the R.A.C. had acted reasonably. The case would be remitted to a differently constituted tribunal for consideration of whether the R.A.C. had demonstrated to M, X and Y with patience and understanding that the re-organisation was sensible and in the interests of employees generally, had listened to and weighed up their representations, had exercised managerial judgment as to whether exceptions could be made in their cases, etc. and were therefore fair in requiring a change in the original terms of employment: MARTIN v. AUTOMOBILE PROPRIETARY [1979] I.R.L.R. 64, E.A.T.

1048. —— seaman—continuous service minimum—computation of 26-week period

[Trade Union and Labour Relations Act 1974 (c. 52), Sched. 1, para. 10 (*a*).]

A seaman's paid leave after completion of his voyage is not part of his employment for the purposes of computing the qualifying period of employment for a claim for unfair dismissal.

P, a seaman, was dismissed. He claimed compensation for unfair dismissal. The industrial tribunal dismissed the claim on the ground that P had not completed 26 weeks' continuous employment, P concluded that he had if his paid leave was taken into account. On appeal by P, *held*, dismissing the appeal, that although voyage leave was calculated by reference to the length of the voyage, and although national insurance contributions were deducted from leave pay, P was free to sign off as soon as the voyage ended, and was no longer subject to the discipline of the master, and the industrial tribunal had correctly ruled that it had no jurisdiction.

DUFF v. EVAN THOMAS RADCLIFFE & Co. [1979] I.C.R. 720, E.A.T.

1049. —— —— employment ceasing at conclusion of voyage

A seaman who is entitled to look for other employment during leave after a voyage, has no continuing employment with the company.

P was engaged by D Co. as a third engineer officer for a six month voyage ˙with three months' leave on D Co.'s ship. His letter of appointment did not offer a service contract, but there was a national agreement for full pay between voyages, save in exceptional circumstances. P completed the voyage, signed on for another voyage but had to return to his sick father. Then the company was unable to offer him work. He sought compensation for unfair dismissal. The tribunal held that P was entitled to look for other work during his leave, and that that was inconsistent with the notion of continuing employment. On appeal by P, *held*, dismissing the appeal that the employment had been terminated either by mutual consent or under the terms of the new agreement, and that therefore there was no dismissal.

STEWART *v.* GRAIG SHIPPING CO. [1979] I.C.R. 713, E.A.T.

1050. —— **strike—all employees dismissed for taking part—some on leave**

[Employment Protection (Consolidation) Act 1978 (c. 44), ss. 57 (1) (3), 62 (1) (*b*).]

An employee's assent or participation in a strike cannot be vicarious through the strike being organised by his shop stewards.

D Co.'s employees who worked on an oil rig went on strike. D Co., believing that all the employees had taken part, dismissed the entire workforce. In fact, some employees had been on leave and knew nothing about the strike. They complained of unfair dismissal. *Held*, that the dismissal was unfair. The fact that the applicants' shop stewards organised the strike did not mean that they had assented or participated. D Co.'s bona fide belief that they had taken part would not be a substantial reason for dismissal.

DIXON *v.* WILSON WALTON ENGINEERING [1979] I.C.R. 438, Industrial Tribunal.

1051. —— —— **offer of re-employment to one—test to be applied in relation to others**

[Trade Union and Labour Relations Act 1974 (c. 52), Sched. 1, para. 7 (3).] CCC dismissed employees taking part in a strike but made an offer of re-engagement to one of them. The tribunal construed para. 7 (3), Sched. 1 to the 1974 Act as requiring them to decide whether the CCC had acted reasonably in treating their reason for not re-engaging the other employees as a sufficient reason for dismissing them. *Held*, allowing the employees' appeals, that the test was whether the employer acted reasonably, in treating the reason given for not offering re-engagement as a sufficient reason for not offering re-engagement: EDWARDS *v.* CARDIFF CITY COUNCIL [1979] I.R.L.R. 303, E.A.T.

1052. —— **sub-postmaster—whether " employed " by Post Office**

A sub-postmaster, although subject to rules of guidance issued by the Post Office, which in that respect exercised a degree of control over him, is not " employed " by the Post Office. There is little day-to-day supervision and the sub-postmaster's power to employ and dismiss staff was inconsistent with a contract of service. The tribunal therefore had no jurisdiction to hear a complaint of unfair dismissal: HITCHCOCK *v.* POST OFFICE, *The Times*, December 19, 1979, E.A.T.

1053. —— **suspicion of dishonesty—reasons for dismissing internal appeal different from original reasons**

Where an employee is dismissed for one reason and his internal appeal is dismissed for another, the employer is entitled to rely on the subsequent reasons as justifying dismissal even though different from the initial reasons.

Money was stolen from an employer's safe in circumstances in which one of two employees must have been responsible. M was dismissed for dishonesty, and his internal appeal was dismissed not for dishonesty but because of misconduct in failing to exercise authorised cash procedures. On a complaint the tribunal found the dismissal fair both on the dishonesty and misconduct grounds. On appeal, *held*, dismissing the appeal, that the employers were entitled to rely on the reasons given for dismissing the internal appeal, which the tribunal had found to be fair. (*Ferodo* v. *Barnes* [1976] C.L.Y. 991 applied.)

MONIE *v.* CORAL RACING [1979] I.C.R. 254, E.A.T.

1054. —— **test**

BMSF Co. were unsatisfied with R's output and gave her six weeks to improve, after which they dismissed her, there being no improvement. The tribunal held that BMSF Co. had acted " in some way reasonably " but had not gone quite far enough as a reasonable employer would have allowed three months. *Held*, allowing BMSF Co.'s appeal, that employers were either reasonable or not, but could not be in some way reasonable but not reasonable enough: British Man-Made Stable Fibres v. Robinson (1978) 13 I.T.R. 241, E.A.T.

1055. —— —— **lack of grievance procedure and higher impartial investigative authority**

H, a housemistress at a girls' public school, was dismissed following warnings. *Held,* dismissing the R.N.S.'s appeal against a finding of unfair dismissal, that the tribunal had not fallen into the error of substituting their own view of what should have been done for an evaluation of what a reasonable employer might reasonably have done. *Obiter*: There is no requirement in law that a grievance procedure must be provided so that when disputes arise between employee and immediate superior it may be taken to a higher impartial authority. The Code of Practice is not necessarily apt in the context of a private school with a staff of 40. Neither the absence of a " buffer " between H and the headmistress nor the absence of an appeal body other than a Board of Governors biased in favour of the headmistress would in themselves have made the dismissal unfair: The Royal Naval School v. Hughes [1979] I.R.L.R. 383, E.A.T.

1056. —— **time limit—effective date of termination—relevance of internal appeal**

[Trade Union and Labour Relations Act 1974 (c. 52), Sched. 1, para. 21 (4).]

Pursuing a domestic appeals procedure against dismissal does not postpone the effective date of dismissal but merely suspends the dismissal pending determination of the appeal.

Per curiam: Normally an employee who pursues a domestic appeals procedure against dismissal, and by reason of that alone fails to present a complaint to the industrial tribunal within the prescribed time limit, should be able to satisfy the tribunal that it had not been reasonably practicable for him to have lodged the complaint within the time limit.

In January the employee was told that he was to be retired for ill-health. He pursued a domestic appeals procedure, appealing to a medical board against the decision, which board rejected his appeal at the end of May. He presented a complaint of unfair dismissal to an industrial tribunal in June: the tribunal assumed jurisdiction, rejecting the employers' contention that the effective date of dismissal was in January and that therefore the complaint had been presented outside the prescribed time limit. *Held,* allowing the employer's appeal, that the employer's contention was correct: pursuing a domestic appeals procedure whether on medical or other grounds did not postpone the effective date of termination; and the case would be remitted for consideration as to whether it had not been " reasonably practicable " for the complaint to be presented within the three-month period. (*J. Sainsbury* v. *Savage* [1979] C.L.Y. 1035 applied.)

Crown Agents for Overseas Governments and Administration v. Lawal [1979] I.C.R. 103, E.A.T.

1057. —— **trade union activities—employer's consent to union meeting**

[Trade Union and Labour Relations Act 1974 (c. 52), Sched. 1, para. 6 (4A).]

A shop steward, whose status was not accepted by the management, could not, in the absence of a general arrangement, be regarded as having the implied consent to call such a meeting. Consent could not be implied either, when he indicated his intention to call a meeting and the employers remained silent: Marley Tile Co. v. Shaw, *The Times,* November 21, 1979, C.A.

1058. —— —— **threat to picket**

[Trade Union and Labour Relations Act 1974 (c. 52), Sched. 1, paras. 6 and 7, as amended by Employment Protection Act 1975 (c. 71), Sched. 16, Pt. III, para. 13.]

A shop steward dismissed upon indicating his intention not to work when next contractually required to do in protest against the dismissal of a colleague, is not dismissed for the inadmissible reason of taking part in trade union activities.

The employee, a shop steward, and others met with management to discuss a problem relating to another employee. During the meeting another shop steward in temper assaulted or threatened to assault the managing director and was sacked. The employee who was due next to work the following day stated that he would not do so but would join a picket instead. He was dismissed. He complained of unfair dismissal alleging (since he had been employed for less than 26 weeks) that his dismissal was due to the inadmissible reason of his having taken part in union activities. An industrial tribunal in rejecting his claim found that his dismissal was due to his taking industrial action. *Held*, dismissing the employee's appeal, that there had been evidence justifying the tribunal's conclusion that the dismissal was not due to the employee's prior participation in union activities.

WINNETT *v.* SEAMARKS BROTHERS [1978] I.C.R. 1240, E.A.T.

1059. —— —— **union activities during lunch and tea breaks—whether within working hours**

[Trade Union and Labour Relations Act 1974 (c. 52), Sched. 1, para. 6 (4), as amended by Employment Protection Act 1975 (c. 71), Sched. 16, Pt. III, para. 11.]

Trade union activities conducted during lunch and tea breaks at work may be held " outside working hours."

Per curiam: It is very desirable that the substantive hearing of a complaint where interim relief has been granted should be heard as a matter of extreme urgency.

The employee complained of unfair dismissal based upon the inadmissible reason of participation in trade union activities. Interim relief was granted in July 1977. At the final hearing in December 1977, the industrial tribunal dismissed her complaint on the grounds that since her union activities were conducted during lunch and tea breaks on the employer's premises, such activities did not occur at "any appropriate time" in accordance with para. 6 (4) of Sched. 1 to the 1974 Act since they were neither outside working hours or at a time agreed with the employers, in accordance with para. 6 (4A) of the Schedule. *Held*, allowing the employee's appeal and ordering the tribunal to reconsider, that simply because the employee was required to be on the employer's premises during breaks, it did not follow that such breaks were part of her "working hours"; the tribunal might further consider whether there was any implied agreement with the employers for such activities to be conducted during meal breaks. (*Post Office* v. *Union of Post Office Workers* [1974] C.L.Y. 3850 and *Marley Tile Co.* v. *Shaw* [1978] C.L.Y. 1131 applied.)

ZUCKER *v.* ASTRID JEWELS [1978] I.C.R. 1088, E.A.T.

1060. —— **variation of contract—whether dismissal and re-employment**

[Trade Union and Labour Relations Act 1974 (c. 52), Sched. 1, paras. 5 (2) (*a*), 6 (1).]

The termination of a sufficiently important part of an employee's duties may change the whole nature of the contract so as to amount to a dismissal within para. 5 (2) (*a*) of Sched. 1 to the Trade Union and Labour Relations Act 1974.

L and W were full-time firemen employed by the council. They were also retained for additional on-call duty in their spare time for which they were paid extra. Those duties were voluntary under the contract of employment. The union decided to abolish part-time duties and move to a 24-hour shift system. L and W refused to accept the union's decision and were expelled. The council agreed with the union and offered new contracts to the firemen. A minority refused the new contracts. The council then sent notices that retained duties would cease in three months. L and W complained to an industrial tribunal of unfair dismissal. The tribunal held that there was a variation of the contract which L and W, by continuing to perform their full-time duties, had accepted, and there was no dismissal. On appeal by the employees and the employers' cross-appeal, *held*, allowing the appeal and the cross-appeal, that the retained duties were so important a part of the contract as a whole, that the whole nature of the contract was changed so as to amount to a dismissal within para. 5 (2) (*a*) of Sched. 1 to the Act of 1974; however, having regard to the union's decision to move to the shift system and the acceptance of that decision by the majority of firemen, the dismissals were not unfair. (*Marriot* v. *Oxford and District Co-operative Society* (*No.* 2) [1970] C.L.Y. 915 distinguished.)

LAND v. WEST YORKSHIRE METROPOLITAN COUNTY COUNCIL [1979] I.C.R. 452, E.A.T.

1061. —— **victimisation—racial discrimination by employer against third parties**
[Race Relations Act 1976 (c. 74), ss. 1 (1), 4 (2), 30, 54 (1), 63.]

Where white bar staff are dismissed for refusing to obey their employer's orders not to serve coloured customers they are entitled to present a complaint to the industrial tribunal.

A white barmaid refused to obey her employer's instructions not to serve coloured customers and was sacked. She presented a complaint under s. 54 of the 1976 Act on the grounds that she had been discriminated against. The industrial tribunal held that they had no jurisdiction to hear the complaint. On appeal, *held,* allowing the appeal, that by dismissing her for refusal to obey his unlawful instructions her employer had treated her less favourably on racial grounds, and she was therefore entitled to present a complaint notwithstanding that the employer might also be in breach of s. 30. (Dicta of Lord Denning M.R. in *Race Relations Board* v. *Applin* [1973] C.L.Y. 20 applied.)

ZARCZYNSKA v. LEVY [1979] 1 W.L.R. 125, E.A.T.

1062. —— **warning—failure to warn specifically—failure to confront employee with those making complaints**

Dr. MacK took over a medical practice from a retired doctor. B, the receptionist, worked between 8.30 and 11.30 a.m. and between 4.00 and 6.00 p.m. and could not work longer owing to family commitments. She repeatedly misled Dr. MacK as to the need for extending surgery hours. Certain patients complained of B's behaviour and difficulty in getting appointments within a reasonable time and B's attention was drawn to the complaints. When B was on holiday Dr. MacK found her filing system was kept negligently and that she had been brusque to patients. Upon her return Dr. MacK said he would extend his morning surgery. B therefore went home and did not return and Dr. MacK wrote terminating her employment. *Held,* allowing Dr. MacK's appeal, that the dismissal was fair despite the failure to warn explicitly as to dismissal and the failure to confront B with the patients who had complained:

MACKELLAR v. BOLTON [1979] I.R.L.R. 59, E.A.T.

1063. —— **whether dismissed—employee expressly " resigns "**

Where an employee has clearly and unequivocally indicated his wish to resign, it is difficult to criticise the employer for unreasonably not giving him a chance to reconsider.

A long-standing employee somewhat prone to fits of temper told his employer after an altercation, " I am leaving . . . I want my cards." His wish was granted. But subsequently he successfully complained to an industrial tribunal that he had been unfairly dismissed as the employer should not have taken words spoken in temper as his resignation. *Held,* allowing the employer's appeal, that if the words used had been less clear, it may be that an employer ought reasonably to have afforded the employee an opportunity to reconsider, but in view of the words actually used it was irrelevant to consider how a reasonable employer ought objectively to have acted.

B. G. GALE v. GILBERT [1978] I.C.R. 1149, E.A.T.

1064. —— **working hours per week—computation—additional preparation at home**
[Trade Union and Labour Relations Act 1974 (c. 52), Sched. 1, para. 9 (1) (*f*).]

In determining the weekly hours required to be worked by an employee, provision relating thereto in a written contract is normally conclusive.

The employee worked as a part-time teacher under a contract specifying her weekly hours of duty as 19 hours, 25 minutes; she was paid at an hourly rate. Upon termination of her employment she complained of unfair dismissal, but the industrial tribunal declined to entertain it on the grounds that her normal weekly hours were less than the 21 hours minimum stipulated in para. 9 (1) (*f*) of Sched. 1 to the 1974 Act. The E.A.T. allowed her appeal, remitting the case for reconsideration, upon the grounds that the employee was contractually obliged to work such additional hours as might properly be necessary in preparation for her school work. *Held,* allowing the employer's appeal, that the employee had a certain amount of " free time " during her express contractual hours and that there were no grounds for implying a term that she was to work outside those hours. (Decision of E.A.T. [1978] C.L.Y. 1187 reversed; *Bullock* v. *Merseyside County Council* [1979] C.L.Y. 935 distinguished.)

LAKE v. ESSEX COUNTY COUNCIL [1979] I.C.R. 577, C.A.

1065. —— written reasons—reference back to letter of dismissal

[Employment Protection Act 1975 (c. 71), s. 70 (4).] On June 28, 1978, ETC sent M a letter of notice setting out in detail the reasons for his dismissal. When he later asked for a written statement of reasons for dismissal ETC referred him back to their letter. *Held,* dismissing M's appeal, that although ETC had refused to comply with M's request for a written statement of reasons they had not unreasonably done so in the circumstances within s. 70 (4) of the 1975 Act (*Horsley Smith & Sherrey* v. *Dutton* [1977] C.L.Y. 1198 considered): MARCHANT v. EARLEY TOWN COUNCIL [1979] I.R.L.R. 311, E.A.T.

1066. —— —— unreasonable refusal to supply

[Employment Protection Act 1975 (c. 71), s. 70 (1) (4).]

A simple failure to supply written reasons for dismissal does not necessarily amount to an " unreasonable refusal " entitling the employee to an award.

After his dismissal the employee requested his employers to provide a written statement of reasons for his dismissal. Because of a failure of communication between the employers and their solicitors, such statement was supplied long after the 14-day period stipulated in s. 70 (1) of the Act. In adjudicating upon the claim for unfair dismissal, the tribunal made no finding in respect of the employee's claim for an award under s. 70 (4) of the Act. *Held,* that " failure " is not synonymous with " refusal "; some unreasonable conduct on the part of the employer is necessary before the penal provisions of s. 70 may be invoked. (*Joines* v. *B. & S. (Burknall)* [1977] C.L.Y. 1154 and *Keen* v. *Dymo* [1977] C.L.Y. 1154 disapproved; *Charles Lang & Sons* v. *Aubrey* [1978] C.L.Y. 1188 applied.)

LOWSON v. PERCY MAIN & DISTRICT SOCIAL CLUB AND INSTITUTE [1979] I.C.R. 568, E.A.T.

1067. Wages—award—whether to award up to amount of unnotified deductions

[Employment Protection Act 1975 (c. 71), ss. 81, 84 (5).]

An industrial tribunal is justified in not making a penal award where unnotified deductions have been made if it finds that the employer was busy and unaware of his statutory obligation.

An employee was engaged on terms that she would receive £30 net per week, which sum she received in cash. No itemised pay slips were supplied. The employee applied under s. 84 of the Act for itemised pay statements showing all unnotified deductions and for payment of the aggregate thereof. At the hearing the parties agreed that the employee should be treated as having been entitled to £40 per week gross. The tribunal found on that basis that there had been a net underpayment totalling some £54 and made an award accordingly; no additional penalty was ordered. *Held,* (1) dismissing the employer's appeal, that the award was correctly calculated; and (2) dismissing the employee's appeal, that the tribunal had a discretion whether to add a penalty to their award.

SCOTT v. CREAGER [1979] I.C.R. 403, E.A.T.

1068. —— road haulage—Central Arbitration Committee—correct approach

[Road Haulage Wages Act 1938 (c. 44), ss. 4 (1) (3), 5 (3), as amended by Employment Protection Act 1975 (c. 71), Sched. 16, Pt. IV, para. 4.]

Where a reference is made to the Central Arbitration Committee alleging unfair remuneration, the Committee must make overall comparisons of remuneration, not just restrict itself to consider only one element of the remuneration (*e.g.* overtime payments).

A company which employed a number of goods vehicle drivers entered into an agreement with the union to pay overtime at the rate of time and a half. Under a local scheme the company operated a scheme of incentive plus overtime payments. On its own the overtime portion of the scheme was less than time and a half. On a complaint by the union the matter was referred to a Central Arbitration Committee which considered that it was concerned only with the overtime payments element of the scheme and upheld the complaint. On application to quash the award, *held,* granting the application, that the Central Committee had misdirected themselves that on a reference alleging unfair remuneration they were concerned strictly with the overtime payments.

R. v. CENTRAL ARBITRATION COMMITTEE, *ex p.* R.H.M. FOODS [1979] I.C.R. 657, Mocatta J.

1069. —— unnotified deductions—award

The applicants were employed as steward and stewardess of the Roath Labour Club, Cardiff, between March 5, 1979, and June 25, 1979. They applied to the Industrial Tribunal under s. 11 of the Employment Protection (Consolidation) Act 1978 for a declaration that the respondents had failed to provide an itemised pay statement in accordance with s. 8 of the Act and sought an order for compensation as provided by the statute. *Held,* that from early April 1979 until the applicants' employment terminated, itemised pay statements had not been provided and that the respondents were negligent in not supplying itemised pay statements, particularly after requests for same had been made on more than one occasion. A declaration was therefore made under s. 8 of the Employment Protection (Consolidation) Act 1978. With regard to the question of compensation the tribunal calculated that for the period of non-compliance Mr. Davies's unnotified deductions amounted to £181·35 and for Mrs. Davies, unnotified deductions amounted to £62·30. The applicants suffered no loss as a result of the unnotified deductions made by the respondents and those deductions were only in respect of income tax and national insurance contributions. It was, therefore, argued on behalf of the respondents that an award, if made, would be of a penal nature. The tribunal rejected the argument that the applicants had suffered no loss but the tribunal held that from the section and two decided cases, *Milsom* v. *Leicestershire County Council* [1978] C.L.Y. 927 and *Scott* v. *Creager* [1979] C.L.Y. 1067, the question of an award is entirely discretionary and made an award for Mr. Davies in the sum of £150 and for Mrs. Davies in the sum of £50: DAVIES v. ROATH LABOUR CLUB, August 10, 1979, Industrial Tribunal, Cardiff. (*Ex rel. Vivian J. Du-Feu, Solicitor.*)

1070. Wages councils

RETAIL TRADES WAGES COUNCILS (FOOD AND ALLIED TRADES) (ABOLITION AND ESTABLISHMENT) ORDER 1979 (No. 862) [30p], made under the Wages Councils Act 1959 (c. 69), s. 4, Sched. 1, para. 5 (*b*) as amended by the Employment Protection Act 1975 (c. 71), s. 89 (1) (3), Sched. 7, Pt IV and the Wages Councils Act 1979 (c. 12), s. 4 (1) (5), Sched. 1, para. 5; operative on September 1, 1979; abolishes specified wages councils and establishes in their place a new wages council for the whole of Great Britain, namely, the Retail Food and Allied Trades Wages Council (Great Britain).

RETAIL TRADES WAGES COUNCIL (NON-FOOD) (ABOLITION AND ESTABLISHMENT) ORDER 1979 (No. 863) [40p], made under the Wages Councils Act 1959, s. 4, Sched. 1, para. 5 (*b*) as amended by the Employment Protection Act 1975, s. 89 (1) (3), Sched. 7, Pt. IV and the Wages Councils Act 1979, s. 4 (1) (5), Sched. 1, para. 5; operative on September 1, 1979; abolishes the specified wages councils and establishes in their place a new wages council for the whole of Great Britain, namely, the Retail Trades (Non-Food) Wages Council (Great Britain).

DRESSMAKING AND WOMEN'S LIGHT CLOTHING WAGES COUNCIL (ENGLAND AND WALES) (VARIATION) ORDER 1979 (No. 864) [20p], made under the Wages Councils Act 1979 (c. 12), s. 4 (2); operative on September 1, 1979; varies the Dressmaking and Women's Light Clothing Wages Council (England and Wales) by the exclusion therefrom of workers employed in the altering, repairing, renovating or re-making of any article of apparel the making of which is included in the Dressmaking and Women's Light Clothing Trade, where such work is carried on, in or about a shop or other place of retail sale, for the purpose of or in connection with such sale.

DRESSMAKING AND WOMEN'S LIGHT CLOTHING WAGES COUNCIL (SCOTLAND) (VARIATION) ORDER 1979 (No. 865) [10p], made under the Wages Councils Act 1979, s. 4 (2); operative on September 1, 1979; varies the Dressmaking and Women's Light Clothing Wages Council (Scotland) by the exclusion therefrom of workers employed in the altering, repairing, renovating or re-making any article of apparel the making of which is included in the Dressmaking and Women's Light Clothing Trade, where such work is carried out, in or about a shop or other place of retail sale for the purpose of or in connection with such sale.

1071. Wages Councils Act 1979 (c. 12)

This Act consolidates the enactments relating to wages councils and statutory joint industrial councils.

Pt. I (ss. 1–9) deals with wages councils: s. 1 provides for the establishment of wages councils; s. 2 concerns the making of applications for wages council orders; s. 3 deals with proceedings on references as to establishment of wages councils; s. 4 provides for the abolition of, or variation of field of operation of, wages councils; s. 5 relates to applications for abolition of wages councils; s. 6 governs references to the Service as to variation or revocation of wages council orders; s. 7 contains supplemental provisions; s. 8 provides for advisory committees; s. 9 sets out the general duty of wages councils to consider references by government departments.

Pt. II (ss. 10–13) provides for statutory joint industrial councils: s. 10 deals with the conversion of wages councils to statutory joint industrial councils; s. 11 concerns disputes between employers' and workers' representatives; s. 12 provides for the abolition of statutory joint industrial councils; s. 13 contains supplemental provisions.

Pt. III (ss. 14–20) deals with orders regulating terms and conditions of employment: s. 14 empowers councils to fix terms and conditions of employment; s. 15 sets out the effect and enforcement of orders under s. 14; s. 16 allows for permits to infirm and incapacitated persons; s. 17 concerns computation of remuneration; s. 18 deals with apportionment of remuneration; s. 19 states that employers are not to receive premiums; s. 20 relates to records and notices.

Pt. IV (ss. 21–32) contains miscellaneous provisions: s. 21 states the criminal liability of agent and superior employer, and special defence open to employer; s. 22 relates to officers; s. 23 gives penalties for false entries in records, producing false records or giving false information; s. 24 empowers Secretary of State to obtain information; s. 25 establishes central co-ordinating committees; s. 26 provides for reports by Service on regulation of terms and conditions of employment; s. 27 authorises the extension of this Act and Northern Ireland legislation; s. 28 is the interpretation section; s. 29 concerns the making of orders and regulations; s. 30 relates to expenses; s. 31 contains transitional provisions, amendments and repeals; s. 32 deals with citation, commencement and extent. This Act, except s. 27, paras. 4 and 5 of Sched. 6 and the repeal of s. 127 (1) (a) of the Employment Protection Act 1975 provided for in Sched. 7, does not extend to Northern Ireland.

The Act received the Royal Assent on March 22, 1979, and came into force on April 22, 1979.

1072. Workmen's compensation. See WORKMEN'S COMPENSATION.

BOOKS AND ARTICLES. See *post,* pp. [4], [21].

EQUITY

1073. Advancement—husband and wife—property registered in joint names. See HEBERT *v.* FOULSTON, § 1396.

1074. Confidential information—injunction—tribal secrets

[Aust.] The plaintiffs, members of an Aboriginal council, moved *ex parte* to restrain an anthropologist from revealing information imparted to him in confidence many years previously by an Aboriginal tribe. *Held,* granting the injunction, that (1) the information was of a confidential character and had been revealed in circumstances giving rise to a duty of confidence; (2) damages would be of no use to the plaintiffs: FOSTER v. MOUNTFORD AND RIGBY [1978] F.S.R. 582, Sup.Ct. of the Northern Territory.

1075. —— reasonable belief of plaintiff—abuse of process
Actions for breach of confidence of a merely speculative character should not be brought. The action should not be allowed to go forward unless the plaintiff can show that he has some basis for a reasonable belief in his assertion: REINFORCED PLASTICS APPLICATIONS (SWANSEA) v. SWANSEA PLASTICS AND ENGINEERING CO. [1979] F.S.R. 182, Whitford J.

1076. —— whether breach governed by arbitration clause. See PACZY v. HAENDLER & NATERMANN GmbH, § 97.

1077. Mistake of fact—moneys paid—tracing
A person who paid another moneys under a mistake of fact is entitled to trace and recover that mistaken payment since he retains an equitable property in it and the payee is under a fiduciary duty to respect that continuing proprietary interest.
The plaintiff, a New York bank, was instructed to pay US $2m. to another New York bank to the account of the defendants. The sum was paid, but later in the day a second payment was made due to a clerical error. The defendants were wound up and the plaintiffs could not recover the whole sum without claiming a declaration that the defendants received the moneys as trustees for the plaintiffs, thus entitling them to trace the mistaken payment. At trial, it was agreed that the mistaken payment was governed by the law of the State of New York but the procedural rights and remedies had to be ascertained by the laws of England. *Held,* the plaintiffs were entitled to trace and recover the mistaken payment on the grounds, that (1) under English law the payer of a mistaken payment retained an equitable property in it and the payee was subjected to a fiduciary duty to respect that continuing proprietary interest; (2) on the evidence, a similar equitable interest exists under the laws of New York State; (3) the moneys in the defendant's hands at the commencement of the winding up did not belong to the defendants beneficially and never formed part of its property.
CHASE MANHATTAN BANK v. ISRAEL-BRITISH BANK (LONDON) [1979] 3 All E.R. 1025, Goulding J.

1078. Priorities—loan for purchase of securities—securities charged to another bank—whether equitable interest at date of charge. See SWISS BANK CORP. v. LLOYDS BANK, § 153.

1079. Rectification—conveyance—mistake by solicitor. See WEEDS v. BLANEY, § 747.

1080. —— whether tax advantage a bar
The court will not refuse rectification of a document merely because the Crown will thereby be deprived of tax.
As a result of various arrangements of family trusts and interests, A, the mother, wished by deed to surrender her life interest in the proceeds of the sale of some property to B and C, her two children, in order to save tax on her death. Because of a misunderstanding by the solicitor the deed failed to release the beneficial interest in the proceeds of sale. A, B and C sought rectification of the deed to give effect to their common intention. *Held,* the transaction was legal, the parties were entitled to avoid payment of tax if they legitimately could, and the Crown was not in any privileged position. The deed would accordingly be rectified to give effect to the attention of the parties. (*Re Colebrook's Conveyance* [1972] C.L.Y. 2909 applied; *Whiteside* v. *Whiteside* [1949] C.L.C. 9380 and dictum of Graham J. in *Re Colebrook's Conveyance* [1972] C.L.Y. 2909 explained.)
Re SLOCOCK'S WILL TRUSTS [1979] 1 All E.R. 358, Graham J.

1081. Tracing—resin used for chipboard—whether right to trace void against creditors. See BORDEN (U.K.) v. SCOTTISH TIMBER PRODUCTS, § 2390.

BOOKS AND ARTICLES. See *post,* pp. [5], [21].

ESTOPPEL

1082. Contract of employment—lay off—acceptance of previous lay-offs. See WAINE *v.* OLIVER (PLANT HIRE), § 851.

1083. Imperfect gift of house to cohabitee—expenditure of money—conduct and expectation of parties

Expenditure of money in reliance on the encouragement and acquiescence of another party may create a proprietary estoppel.

P and D lived as man and wife for some 10 years in a house which P had bought for them in his own name. When P left D for a new mistress, he assured her that the house and its contents would be hers. Relying on this declaration D spent money on redecorations, improvements and repairs. There was no written agreement and P did not convey the house to D. A possession action in the county court was dismissed. On appeal, *held*, that D occupied under a bare licence and the gift of the house remained imperfect. No trust could be inferred from the circumstances but P had encouraged D to improve the house and to believe it was hers and this gave rise to a proprietary estoppel. A mere licence might be defeated by a sale of the house. P must execute a conveyance. (*Dillwyn* v. *Llewelyn* (1862) 4 De G. F. & J. 517, *Inwards* v. *Baker* [1965] C.L.Y. 1487, and *Crabb* v. *Arun District Council* [1975] C.L.Y. 1191 applied.)

PASCOE *v.* TURNER [1979] 1 W.L.R. 431, C.A.

1084. Representation—as to fact—membership of association. See REEL *v.* HOLDER, § 248.

1085. —— financial expenditure—grant of long lease

W had lived most of her life with C, her mother, at 21 Green Street, Hereford. C always assured W that W could live in the house for the rest of her life. W looked after C, especially towards the end of C's life, when she was often ill and in pain. In 1971 C made a will leaving the house to W, but she revoked it by a later one in 1974, in which she left it to G, W's daughter. C died in 1975, and G claimed possession of the house, on the ground that W only had a licence to occupy the house. W contended that the conduct of the parties had raised an equity in favour of W, enabling her to remain in the property. The equity arose because of C's assurances, on the faith of which W had expended money on the premises which she would not otherwise have done. The county court judge granted possession, and W appealed. *Held*, allowing the appeal, there was an equity when one has made a representation on the strength of which another has expended money, the former will not, to the prejudice of the latter, be able to go back and assert his strict legal rights, if to do so would be unconscionable. As W had been promised that she could live rent free for the rest of her life, G was directed to grant W a long lease, determinable on G's death, at a nominal rent. There would be an absolute covenant not to assign. This would avoid giving W a life interest, which could give her greater powers over the property than were originally intended (*Crabb* v. *Arun District Council* [1975] C.L.Y. 1191, *Inwards* v. *Baker* [1965] C.L.Y. 1487, *Binions* v. *Evans* [1972] C.L.Y. 1996, *Bannister* v. *Bannister* (1948) C.L.C. 9341, *Dodsworth* v. *Dodsworth* [1974] C.L.Y. 3144 applied): GRIFFITHS *v.* WILLIAMS (1977) 248 E.G. 947, C.A.

1086. Representations by council—planning permission—existing use rights. See WESTERN FISH PRODUCTS *v.* PENWITH DISTRICT COUNCIL, § 2651.

1087. Res judicata—undefended divorce—custody order—father denying that children are children of family. See ROWE *v.* ROWE, § 791.

ARTICLES. See *post*, p. [21].

EUROPEAN COMMUNITIES

1088. Administrative law—staff agencies—different tenders

The European Court considered an action brought under art. 178 EEC by a staff agency seeking annulment of a Commission decision to contract with another agency for the supply of temporary staff and for damages. *Held*, in dismissing the action, the court found that the non-acceptance by the Commission of a tender need not be on the basis of art. 190 EEC. The Commission may pay more to such agencies to take into account national wage conditions. Provided it has used similar ways of judging all tenders these ways cannot be questioned and in assessing them price need not be the sole criterion, even bearing in mind Art. 59 (2) of Financial Reg., April 25, 1973.

AGENCE EUROPÉENNE D'INTERIMS S.A. *v.* E.C. COMMISSION [1979] 2 C.M.L.R. 57, European Ct.

1089. Agriculture

COMMON AGRICULTURAL POLICY (AGRICULTURAL PRODUCE) (PROTECTION OF COMMUNITY ARRANGEMENTS) (AMENDMENT) ORDER 1979 (No. 1541) [10p], made under the Agriculture Act 1957 (c. 57), ss. 5, 35 (3) and the European Communities Act 1972 (c. 68), s. 6 (3); operative on December 6, 1979; amends S.I. 1973 No. 288 by extending the powers for the protection of the Community support system to cover Community arrangements in respect of pure-breed breeding animals of the domestic bovine species, brought into the common organisation of the market in beef and veal under Council Regulation (EEC) No. 425/77.

1090. —— benefits for cattle producers—corporate bodies excluded

The European Court considered a reference to it by the Pretura di Cecina under art. 177 EEC, of several questions concerning the interpretation of Reg. 2902/77 EEC. The case concerned the restriction by Italian legislation of the benefits of this Regulation in Italy to persons devoting two-thirds of their working to farming and deriving two-thirds of this total income from farming. The defendant was a limited partnership (società in accomandita semplice) and thus excluded from the benefit of the Regulation. *Held*, the power in this Regulation, art. 1, given to Italy to legislate in the context of a policy to help certain agricultural producers of cattle permitted the Member States to limit benefits to natural persons and exclude legal or corporate bodies.

BARDI *v.* AZIENDA AGRICOLA PARADISO (No. 121/78) [1979] 2 C.M.L.R. 599, European Ct.

1091. —— common organisation of market—licence applications

The European Court considered several questions referred to it by the Bundesverwaltungsgericht for a preliminary ruling under art. 177 EEC. The case concerned the interpretation of art. 16 of Reg. No. 19/62 EEC on the progressive establishment of a common organisation of the market in cereals. *Held*, whether an application for the grant of an import licence under the first sentence of art. 16 (1) of Reg. 19/62 EEC can be cancelled and the effect of cancellation must be decided on the basis of community law and take into account Reg. 130/62 EEC. The effective management of common market in cereals would be made unreliable if errors made by traders were taken into consideration. An importer cannot within the context of the organisation of the market established by Regs. 19 and 130 EEC rely on an error made by him concerning the choice of rate of levy operative on the date when he lodges the application, to allow cancellation of an application for an import licence.

BUNDESANSTALT FÜR LANDWIRTSCHAFTLICHE MARKTORDNUNG *v.* JACOB HIRSCH & SÖHNE GMBH (No. 85/78) [1978] E.C.R. 2517, European Ct.

1092. —— —— national boards—licensing

The European Court considered several questions referred to it by the resident magistrate, County Armagh, for a preliminary ruling under art. 177 EEC. The case concerned the prosecution of a lorry driver for conveying pigs without the Pig Marketing Board's authorisation. The court interpreted arts. 177, 28 (2), 30, 34 and 90 EEC and art. 60 (2) of the Act of Accession. *Held*, as there is an EEC common organisation within its Common Agricultural Policy for the pig meat market, national rules must not infringe or contradict this organisation. Member States must not obstruct free access to the market for all producers within the Community. The power to grant licences for the transport of pigs which involves the right to prohibit the transport of pigs, if exercised by a Member State, infringes the EEC rules. The State may not escape this conclusion by the claim that their Pig Marketing Board which issued these licences was a " State monopoly of a commercial character " or a " public undertaking."

PIGS MARKETING BOARD (NORTHERN IRELAND) *v.* REDMOND (No. 83/78) [1979] 1 C.M.L.R. 177, European Ct.

1093. The Armagh Magistrates' Court considered a summons brought by the Pigs Marketing Board (Northern Ireland) against the defendant for unlawfully transporting 75 bacon pigs. *Held*, the magistrate, having read several European Court decisions, decided that as there is a common EEC organisation in the marketing of pig meat, national marketing systems may not use compulsory powers to enforce national marketing. Compulsory registration of producers, monopoly trading rights for such a marketing board and transporting restrictions imposed by such a board are no longer lawful. (*Pigs Marketing Board* (*Northern Ireland*) v. *Redmond* (No. 83/78) [1979] C.L.Y. 1092 applied.)

PIGS MARKETING BOARD (NORTHERN IRELAND) *v.* REDMOND [1979] 3 C.M.L.R. 118, Armagh Magistrates' Ct.

1094. —— —— **sugar**

The European Court considered several questions referred to it by the Finanzgericht, Hamburg, for a preliminary ruling under art. 177 EEC. The case concerned the validity and interpretation of Reg. 837/68, art. 7 (2) as amended by Reg. 878/69. The case concerned the sucrose and malto-dextrine contents of certain products. *Held*, subject to two conditions, the flat-rate methods to test the sucrose content of certain products were valid. This was a test for the purposes of calculating the levy. Where the duty existed to make a statement of reasons, as a result of art. 190 the extent of the duty depends on the nature of the Regulation in question.

WELDING & CO. *v.* HAUPTZOLLAMT HAMBURG-WALTERSHOF (No. 87/78) [1979] E.C.R. 2457, European Ct.

1095. —— **compensatory amounts—currency changes**

The European Court considered several questions referred to it by the Tribunal d' Instance at Lille for a preliminary ruling under art. 177 EEC. The case concerned a manufacturer of starch products from maize who claimed the obligation under Reg. 652/76 to pay large compensatory amounts following the decision of the French Government to take the French franc out of the " European currency snake," was illegal. *Held*, the E.C. Commission may find that a risk of a disturbance in trade may be caused by currency changes and may set out its reasons under Reg. 974/71 (art. 1 (1)). In these circumstances the administration has a wide discretion and the court will only inquire if there has been a manifest error or a misuse of power or if it clearly exceeded its discretion. The Community Institutions may take note general factors in assessing risk of trade disturbance and must ensure permanent harmonisation between the objectives of the agricultural policy.

S.A. ROQUETTE FRÈRES *v.* FRENCH STATE ADMINISTRATION DES DOUANES (No. 29/77) [1977] E.C.R. 1835, European Ct.

1096. —— —— **preserved meat**

The European Court considered several similar questions posed in Case 137/77 (above). In this case the reference was also from the Bundesverwaltungsgericht and the judgment of the Court was to the same effect except that in this case it was *held* that the health charges on bovine meat could not be extended by analogy to preserved meat.

FIRMA HERMANN LUDWIG *v.* FREE AND HANSEATIC CITY OF HAMBURG (No. 138/77) [1978] E.C.R. 1645. European Ct.

1097. —— **definition of—German mark revaluation**

The Finanzgericht at Münster referred several questions to the European Court for a preliminary ruling under art. 177 EEC on the interpretation of art. 39 and art. 40 (3) EEC and arts. 1 (1) and (3) of Reg. No. 2464/69. The case concerned the German decision to revalue the German Mark in 1969 which caused losses in agriculture which was linked to the European agricultural prices. The difficulties in this case arose from the interpretation of Community law and the German law giving compensation. *Held*, although art. 38 EEC does define agricultural provisions to be defined to some extent, the concept of agriculture is not defined in the Treaty and so it is for the competent authority to define it within the context of the agriculture rules derived from the Treaty.

DENKAVIT FUTTERMITTEL GMBH *v.* FINANZAMT WARENDORF (No. 139/77) [1978] E.C.R. 1317, European Ct.

1098. —— discrimination—common organisation

The European Court considered several questions referred to it by the Finanzgericht, Baden-Württemburg for a preliminary ruling under art. 177 EEC. The case concerned the validity of Reg. No. 725/74/EEC in respect of the altering of monetary compensatory amounts and the interpretation of subpara. (2) of art. 40 (3) EEC and the judgment in case 28/78. In particular the court examined the principle of non-discrimination in art. 40 (3). *Held*, this principle does not prohibit different treatment of products that are not the same in every respect unless this results in discrimination between consumers or producers. Nothing affecting the validity of Reg. 725/74 had been raised before the court.

MILAC GMBH GROSS- UND AUSSENHANDEL *v.* HAUPTZOLLAMT FREIBURG [1978] E.C.R. 1721, European Ct.

1099. —— export licences—alteration in calculation of compensation

The applicant sought the annulment of E.C. Commission Reg. No. 1583/77 of July 14, 1977, which altered from July 1, 1977, the calculation of compensation fixed by art. 2 of Reg. EEC No. 937/77, or alternatively damages. The applicant was a trader in sugar and held export certificates entitling it to compensation from the EEC when exports were effected. It argued that as a result of Reg. 1583/77 it would receive less compensation per 100 kg. of white sugar, and thus the regulation was of direct and individual concern to it. *Held*, (1) the application was admissible as the Regulation was of direct and individual concern to the applicant; (2) the application for annulment or damages would be dismissed as there had been no infringements of the basic EEC agricultural rules. Further, the contested Regulation applied solely to white sugar in respect of which the customs export formalities were completed after the entry into force of the Regulation. Thus the Regulation in question did not amount to an amendment having retroactive effect.

AUGUST TÖPFER & CO. GMBH *v.* E.C. COMMISSION (No. 112/77) [1978] E.C.R. 1019, European Ct.

1100. —— export refunds—levy on pigs

The European Court considered several questions referred to it by the High Court of Ireland under art. 177 for a preliminary ruling. The case concerned the Irish scheme for marketing pigs and bacon by which a levy was imposed on all pig carcasses intended for bacon and a bonus was paid to exporters who marketed through the Pigs and Bacon Commission. *Held*, the bonus paid for export infringed EEC law (art. 40 EEC and Reg. 2759/75) in that it infringed the rule that trade barriers should be abolished. EEC refund rules cannot be used to give such a bonus to exporters whether these were exporting to non-Member States or Member States. Similarly a levy on certain producers was unlawful by infringing the principle of open market on which the EEC is based.

PIGS AND BACON COMMISSION *v.* MCCARREN & CO. (No. 177/78) [1979] 3 C.M.L.R. 389, European Ct.

1101. —— health charges—bovine animals

The European Court considered several questions referred to it by the Bundesverwaltungsgericht for a preliminary ruling under art. 177 EEC. The case concerned the interpretation of Council Directive No. 72/462/EEC on the health and veterinary inspection of bovine animals imported from third countries and the interpretation of Reg. 950/68. *Held*, the former Directive cannot be applied by analogy to the import of products such as game which are not directly covered by it, namely, bovine animals, swine and fresh meat.

CITY OF FRANKFURT-AM-MAIN *v.* FIRMA MAX NEUMANN (No. 137/77) [1978] E.C.R. 1623, European Ct.

1102. —— hill farm subsidies—maladministration

The British Ombudsman considered a complaint, by a farmer, that the Department of Agriculture and Fisheries for Scotland was guilty of maladministration because it had reclaimed cattle subsidies and allowances previously paid to him. These subsidies were payable under the implementing legislation following EEC Directive 75/268. The Ombudsman reported that although the complainant was dissatisfied he found the Department had dealt fairly with his case. There was no evidence of maladministration on the facts of the case.

Re SLAUGHTER OF HILL CATTLE IN SCOTLAND [1979] 2 C.M.L.R. 505, Parliamentary Commissioner for Administration.

1103. —— imports—U.K. national laws

The European Court considered an application by the E.C. Commission under art. 169 EEC for a declaration that the United Kingdom had failed to fulfil an obligation under the EEC Treaty by not repealing or amending the provisions of its national law which restrict imports of certain potatoes before the end of 1977. *Held*, the United Kingdom by failing to remove the total import ban on potatoes from other Member States after the end of 1977 had defaulted under and infringed its treaty obligations imposed under art. 30 EEC and arts. 9 and 42 of the Act of Accession.

Re IMPORT OF POTATOES; E.C. COMMISSION *v.* UNITED KINGDOM (No. 231/78) [1979] 2 C.M.L.R. 427, European Ct.

1104. —— import and export securities

The Tribunal Administratif, Paris, requested the European Court of Justice to give a preliminary ruling under art. 177 EEC as to validity and interpretation of art. 3 of Commission Reg. No. 499/76 which required proof of completion of import or export formalities within six months of the expiry of the import or export licence otherwise the importer's or exporter's security would be forfeited. *Held*, art. 3 of Reg. No. 499/76 was invalid. Although the Commission was entitled to stipulate a period within which proof of completion of import or export formalities was to be given, forfeiture of security was too harsh a penalty for non-compliance. In any event, it would be rare for there to be non-compliance, as it would be contrary to the interests of the importer or exporter to delay seeking release of his security.

BUITONI S.A. *v.* FONDS D'ORIENTATION ET DE REGULARISATION DES MARCHÉS AGRICOLES (No. 122/78) [1979] 2 C.M.L.R. 665, European Ct.

1105. —— interim application—regulation—urgency

An Italian company applied to the European Court for certain interim measures in its action against the E.C. Commission. They sought suspension of an invitation by the Commission for certain tenders concerning the purchase and import licences in respect of certain quantities of frozen beef. The company also sought the suspension until publication of judgment in Case 92/78 of certain import arrangements for frozen beef. *Held*, in respect of the first application there were no circumstances of urgency which prima facie justified it. In the case of the second application no circumstances were shown that demonstrated the individual interests of the applicant that would justify the application.

SIMMENTHAL S.P.A. *v.* E.C. COMMISSION (No. 243/78R) [1979] E.C.R. 2391, European Ct.

1106. —— —— suspension regulation—damage

The European Court considered an interim application by the Italian Republic in an action, brought under art. 173 EEC, for the annulment of Reg. 1125/78 concerning the common organisation of the cereal market. Italy sought an interim suspension of this Regulation pending the hearing of the action. *Held*, Italy failed to show that the interim suspension was necessary because of the imminence of serious and irreparable damage to the cereal starch manufacturing industry if the suspension was not ordered.

ITALIAN REPUBLIC *v.* E.C. COUNCIL (No. 166/78R) [1978] E.C.R. 1745, European Ct.

1107. —— monetary compensatory amounts—compensation

The applicant sought (1) the annulment of an E.C. Commission Decision taken under art. 4 (2) of Reg. No. 1608/74. The applicant alleged that the Decision excluded certain contracts from exemption from the French monetary compensatory amounts for the sole reason that they were concluded before May 1975, in other words, at a date when monetary compensatory amounts were applicable in France with regard to sugar; alternatively (2) compensation under para. 2 of art. 215 EEC for the damage which it had suffered, since it alleged that refusal of the French authorities to grant exemption from the monetary compensatory amounts was the result of the wrongful act of the E.C. Commission. *Held*, (1) the application for annulment was inadmissible as in the present case there was no Decision taken under art. 4 of Reg. No. 1608/74 by the E.C. Commission within the meaning of art. 173 EEC; (2) the application for compensation was inadmissible as the refusal by the national authorities to grant exemption from the monetary compensatory amounts in the case of the contracts in question stemmed from an independent decision made by those authorities. Thus, this case did not involve conduct on the part of the E.C. Commission such as to entail liability under para. 2 of art. 215 EEC.

SOCIÉTÉ POUR L'EXPORTATION DES SUCRES S.A. *v.* E.C. COMMISSION (No. 132/77) [1978] E.C.R. 1061, European Ct.

1108. —— —— discretion—date of publication of Regulations

The Bundesfinanzhof referred several questions to the European Court for a preliminary ruling under art. 177 EEC, on the validity of Regs. 649/73. 741/73, 811/73, and the interpretation of art. 191 EEC. The case concerned the use by the EEC administration of its powers of discretion to counter and avoid the harmful consequences on the common agriculture policy, of an economic crisis. *Held*, the administration in such circumstances has wide discretion and Regs. 649/73, 741/73 and 811/73 were valid in so far as they fixed monetary compensatory amounts applicable to red and white wine falling within tariff heading 22.05CI and CII from non-member countries and in respect of their dates of applicability. Art. 191 EEC must be interpreted to mean that a Regulation is to be regarded as published throughout the Community on the date borne by the issue of the *Official Journal* containing the text of that Regulation, in the absence of evidence to the contrary.

FIRMA A. RACKE *v.* HAUPTZOLLAMT MAINZ (No. 98/78) [1979] E.C.R. 69, European Ct.

1109. —— —— effective date of regulation

The Bundesfinanzhof referred several questions to the European Court for a preliminary ruling under art. 177 EEC, on the interpretation of art. 191 EEC, and asking from what date Regs. 649/73 and 741/73 are to be applied. *Held*, a regulation is officially published on the date borne by the issue of the *Official Journal* containing the text of the Regulation. The date of actual publication may in certain circumstances be different. The principle of legal certainty precludes a measure from taking effect from a point of time before its publication; however, it may sometimes be otherwise where the purpose of the measure necessitates it. The monetary compensatory amount system in Reg. 974/71 implies that in principle measures adopted take effect from the occurrence of the date of the events which give rise to them, even events preceding the publication of the Regulation in the *Official Journal*.

WEINGUT GUSTAV DECKER A.G. *v.* HAUPTZOLLAMT LANDAU (No. 99/78) [1979] E.C.R. 101, European Ct.

1110. —— —— imports

The Hessisches Finanzgericht referred several questions to the European Court under art. 177 EEC, for a preliminary ruling concerning the validity of Reg. 3092/76. The case involved the charging of monetary compensatory amounts in respect of imports of, *inter alia,* forequarters of bovine animals within tariff sub-heading 16.02BIII(6)1 of the Common Customs Tariff. *Held*, art. 1 (1) of Reg. 974/71 (amended by Reg. 509/73) does not decide that it is a condition for the application of monetary compensatory amounts that there should have been a recent alteration in the exchange rate of the Member State involved. Nor does this article mean that monetary compensatory amounts should be applied simultaneously in intra-Community trade and in trade with non-member countries even when the situations are different.

HANS SPITTA & CO. *v.* HAUPTZOLLAMT FRANKFURT AM MAIN-OST (No. 127/78) [1979] E.C.R. 171, European Ct.

1111. —— —— **Irish pound**

The European Court considered several questions referred to it by the College van Beroep voor het Bedrijfsleven for a preliminary ruling under art. 177 EEC. The case concerned the validity of the Commission Regulation (EEC) No. 1356/76 on the monetary compensation amounts and the differential amounts applicable in respect of movements in the Irish pound and the pound sterling. *Held,* art. 3 of Reg. 974/71 may be interpreted to mean that the exchange rates taken into account there must be assessed on the basis of economically justified criteria. The Commission can therefore leave out of account rates which it considers unrepresentative. The absence of an opinion of the Committee acting under art. 26 of Reg. 2727/75 does not affect the validity of the measures adopted by the Commission.

N. G. J. SCHOUTEN B.V. *v.* HOOFDPRODUKTSCHAP VOOR AKKERBOUWPRO-DUKTEN (No. 35/78) [1979] E.C.R. 2543, European Ct.

1112. —— —— **powdered whey**

The Finanzgericht de Saarlandes requested a preliminary ruling under art. 177 EEC on the validity of art. 1 of EEC Reg. No. 539/75 fixing the monetary compensatory amounts and on the interpretation of EEC Reg. No. 974/71 in relation to powdered whey. *Held,* the monetary compensatory amounts provided for in art. 1 of Reg. No. 974/71 did not apply to powdered whey. Thus, art. 1 of Reg. No. 539/75 was invalid in so far as it fixed compensatory amounts in respect of trade in powdered whey.

FIRMA MILAC, GROSS- UND AUSSENHANDEL ARNOLD NÖLL *v.* HAUPTZOLLAMT SAARBRÜCKEN (No. 131/77) [1978] E.C.R. 1041, European Ct.

1113. —— —— **sugar**

The Finanzgericht Hamburg requested the European Court of Justice under art. 177 EEC for a preliminary ruling on (1) the validity of art. 4 (3) of EEC Reg. No. 1380/75, and (2) whether art. 4 (3) of Reg. No. 1380/75 together with Reg. No. 2101/75 is to be interpreted as meaning that the export refund for sugar fixed in national currency for each exporter individually, on the basis of tender, should be multiplied by the monetary coefficient fixed by the E.C. Commission, which is derived from the percentage used to calculate the monetary compensation. *Held,* that (1) art. 4 (3) of Reg. No. 1380/75 was valid and did not infringe the principle of non-discrimination; (2) art. 4 (3) of Reg. No. 1380/75 together with Reg. No. 2101/75 is to be interpreted as meaning that the export refund for sugar, fixed in national currency for each exporter individually, on the basis of tender, is not to be multiplied by the monetary coefficient fixed by the E.C. Commission, which is derived from the percentage used to calculate the monetary compensation.

HANS-OTTO WAGNER GMBH AGRARHANDEL KG *v.* HAUPTZOLLAMT HAMBURG-JONAS (No. 108/77) [1978] E.C.R. 1187, European Ct.

1114. —— —— **wine**

The Finanzgericht Rheinland-Pfalz referred two questions to the European Court under art. 177 EEC for a preliminary ruling on the validity of EEC Reg. No. 722/75 amending EEC Reg. No. 539/75 fixing the monetary compensatory amounts and certain rates for their application in so far as it excepts the import into Germany of wines falling within tariff sub-heading 22.05 C 1 of the CCT from the discontinuance of the monetary compensatory amounts. *Held,* consideration of the questions raised has disclosed no factors of such a kind as to affect the validity of the Regulations in so far as the import into German of wine falling within tariff sub-heading 20.05 V 1 is excepted from the discontinuance of the monetary compensatory amounts.

FIRMA A. RACKE *v.* HAUPTZOLLAMT MAINZ (No. 136/77) [1978] E.C.R. 1245, European Ct.

1115. The European Court considered several questions referred to it for a preliminary ruling under art. 177 EEC by the Bundesfinanzhof. The case concerned the interpretation of Reg. 945/70, the validity of Reg. 2448/75 concerning the suspension of monetary compensatory amounts on certain wines. *Held*, the distinction between various types of table wine made in accordance with Reg. 945/70 is based on the characteristics of price formation on the various markets of the Community. Blended wine that cannot be described as Type AII cannot benefit on export to a non-member country from monetary compensatory amounts in respect of the Type AII which it contains. This is so by virtue of the combined effect of Art. 6 of Reg. 1380/75 and Art. 8 of Reg. 192/75.

HAUPTZOLLAMT HAMBURG-JONAS *v.* HERMANN KENDERMANN O.H.G. (No. 88/78) [1979] E.C.R. 2477, European Ct.

1116. —— national law—unilateral action

The Danish Supreme Court referred several questions to the European Court for a preliminary ruling under art. 177 EEC. The case concerned the special rules for the purchase of sugar beet and the quota system for sugar manufacturers. The Court was asked to interpret Reg. 741/75. *Held*, under this Regulation Member States may intervene in cases defined by the Regulation to adopt unilateral measures.

SUKKERFABRIKEN NYKØBING LIMITERET *v.* MINISTRY OF AGRICULTURE (No. 151/78) [1979] E.C.R. 1, European Ct.

1117. —— national rules—egg labels

The European Court considered several questions referred to it by the Pretura di Venasca for a preliminary ruling under art. 177 EEC. The case concerned the interpretation and validity of Reg. 1619/68 arising from an action brought by an Italian whose firm traded as an egg packing centre. *Held*, this Regulation on egg standards, replaced by Regs. 2772/75 and 95/69 allows public authorities in Member States to be entrusted with the preparation and distribution of bands and labels for egg packing. Member States may make charges for the issue of bands and labels and it is for the national court if the charge was justified. A directly applicable regulation precludes any other legislation which is incompatible with it. Art. 7 EEC, does not apply to national rules which are not applicable on the basis of the nationality of the traders concerned.

BUSSONE *v.* ITALIAN MINISTRY FOR AGRICULTURE AND FORESTRY (No. 31/78) [1978] E.C.R. 2429, European Ct.

1118. —— suspension of import licences—interim measures—beef and veal

The Italian applicant sought (1) the suspension on an interim basis of the effectiveness of Commission Decision 78/258 and that the Commission be ordered to instruct the national authorities to suspend the issue of import licences corresponding to the contracts of purchase of frozen beef entered into by successful tenderers with the intervention agencies; and (2) the suspension until publication of the final judgment of the application of the special arrangements for the importation of frozen meat intended for the processing industry. *Held*, the applications would be dismissed; (1) as regards the first application, even if the European Court had power to make an interim order entailing such serious effects on the rights and interests of third parties, not parties to the dispute and whose views had not been expressed, such an order would only be justified if, in its absence, the applicant would be placed in a situation which threatened its very existence. Such a situation did not exist in this case; (2) as regards the second application, such a measure might entail grave consequences on the beef and veal market and adversely affect the interests of innumerable agricultural producers and traders. The possible effects of such a measure would be disproportionate to the individual interests which the applicant sought to safeguard.

SIMMENTHAL S.P.A. *v.* E.C. COMMISSION (No. 92/78 R) [1978] E.C.R. 1129, European Ct.

1119. —— temporary measures—force majeure—compensatory amounts

The European Court considered several questions referred to it by the Finanzgericht at Hamburg for a preliminary ruling under art. 177 EEC. The case concerned the interpretation of art. 5 (2) of Reg. 269/73 in respect of the payment of compensatory amounts payable under a temporary system decided upon because of the accession of new Member States. *Held*, this system was intended, *inter alia*, to safeguard the principle of Community preference continued between the original Member States and the new members until full integration of the latter. Art. 5 (2) (269/73) should be interpreted by analogy with art. 6 (1) of Reg. 192/75 that if goods being exported from an original member to a new member perish by *force majeure*, then the exporter is entitled to a compensatory amount.

UNION FRANÇAISE DE CÉRÉALES *v.* HAUPTZOLLAMT HAMBURG-JONAS (No. 6/78) [1978] E.C.R. 1675, European Ct.

1120. Coinage—import—export—public policy

The European Court considered several questions referred to it by the English Court of Appeal (Criminal Division) for a preliminary ruling under art. 177 ([1978] C.L.Y. 672). The case concerned a prosecution for the unlawful import of Krugerrands into the U.K. and the export of English silver alloy coins some of which were and others which continue to be legal tender in the U.K. *Held*, coinage which is a means of payment is not deemed to be goods within the meaning of arts. 30–37 EEC. Thus the current British coinage and the krugerrands were covered by arts. 30–37 EEC but not the coins that were no longer legal tender. A Member State may prohibit the melting down of its coinage and may prohibit their export so as to prevent their destruction abroad. This may be justified on grounds of public policy under art. 36 EEC.

R. *v.* JOHNSON, THOMPSON AND WOODIWISS (No. 7/78) [1979] 1 C.M.L.R. 47, European Ct.

1121. Common customs tariff—agriculture—milk products

The European Court considered several questions referred to it for a preliminary ruling under art. 177 EEC by the Finanzgericht at Munster. The case concerned the interpretation of certain regulations for the calculation of levies in the milk and milk product market and for the determination of the lactose content of the compound feeding stuffs imported from third countries. *Held*, the Common Customs Tariff should be applied uniformly unless there is express provision to the contrary. The "milk product" context is calculated by applying art. 11 (1) of Reg. No. 823/68. This method of calculation is decisive when the amounts of monetary compensatory amounts are charged on feedstuffs under tariff heading 23.07 BI a 3 or 23.07 BI a 4. Tariff classification of the exporting State is only binding in this context where Community law makes a similar rule for the importing State.

MILCHFUTTER GMBH & CO. KG *v.* HAUPTZOLLAMT GRONAU [1978] E.C.R. 1597, European Ct.

1122. Community law—failure to implement tachographs

The European Court considered an allegation made by the E.C. Commission, initiated under the art. 169 EEC procedure, that the United Kingdom had infringed the provisions of the EEC Treaty in failing to introduce legislation to apply Reg. 1463/70 which required certain motor vericles to be fitted with and use tachographs. *Held*, the United Kingdom was in breach of its treaty obligations by its failure to enforce or adopt legislation to enforce the EEC Regulation. A "directive" clause in an EEC Regulation imposes an absolute obligation on Member States to comply with it which cannot be excused by political opposition, for example, trade unions.

Re TACHOGRAPHS; E.C. COMMISSION *v.* UNITED KINGDOM (No. 128/78) [1979] 2 C.M.L.R. 45, European Ct.

1123. —— national law—constitutional law

The European Court considered observations submitted by the Italian Government in accordance with art. 169 EEC, following a request by the E.C. Commission. Italy had failed to implement nine Council Directives and one Commission Directive within the time allowed. These were 71/316–318, 71/347, 71/349, 71/354, 73/360, 73/362 and 74/148 of the Council and 74/331 of the Commission. *Held*, no Member State may allow domestic difficulties, national laws or its constitution to prevent the implementation of Community Directives within the time allowed.

Re MEASURING INSTRUMENTS; E.C. COMMISSION *v.* ITALY (No. 100/77) [1979] 2 C.M.L.R. 655, European Ct.

1124. Community legislation—declaration—locus standi of applicants

A number of undertakings brought an action before the European Court for a declaration under art. 173 EEC; that an application to annul Reg. 298/78 (amending Reg. 3331/74) was admissible. This Regulation concerned the allocation and alteration of the basic quotas for sugar. *Held,* as this Regulation that was amended was not a decision, the Regulation which amended it was in the nature of a Regulation. The conditions in the second paragraph of art. 173 are not fulfilled when only the Regulations challenged and adopted by a Member State can be of direct and individual concern to the applicants.

SOCIÉTÉ DES USINES DE BEAUPORT *v.* E.C. COUNCIL (Nos. 103–109/78) [1979] E.C.R. 17, European Ct.

1125. —— validity challenged—dumping from Japan

The European Court considered a series of actions by four Japanese manufacturers of ball bearings that challenged the validity of Reg. 1778/77 of the Council directed against the dumping of ball bearings, originating in Japan. These actions were brought under art. 173, second paragraph, and in one claimed compensation under arts. 178 and 215, second paragraph, EEC. *Held,* the Court annulled this Regulation but refused compensation. A Regulation, where specifically directed at dumping by named enterprises, can be directly challenged by individuals under art. 173 EEC. Where national governments automatically implement a Community rule, it is proper for those immediately affected to challenge it before the European Court. It is not lawful for the Commission and Council to halt anti-dumping proceedings by accepting undertakings by the foreign exporter to cease its activities. Where the Council have legislated to implement a treaty object in art. 113 EEC, it may not then make subsequent legislation, for individual cases, which derogated from this implementation.

NTN TOYO BEARING CO. *v.* E.C. COUNCIL (No. 113/77); IMPORT STANDARD OFFICE (I.S.O.) *v.* E.C. COUNCIL (No. 118/77); NIPPON SEIKO K.K. *v.* E.C. COUNCIL (No. 119/77); KOYO SEIKO CO. *v.* E.C. COUNCIL (No. 120/77); NACHI FUJIKOSHI CORP. *v.* E.C. COUNCIL (No. 121/77) [1979] 2 C.M.L.R. 257, European Ct.

1126. Competition—effect of art. 85 EEC in municipal law

A French licensee appealed against a judgment ordering it to pay a sum to its English licensor in respect of royalties in accordance with a minimum royalty clause in the licence agreement between the parties. The licensee argued that the royalty clause was void and/or other clauses in the agreement made the agreement void in view of the prohibition in art. 85 EEC. *Held,* the appeal would be dismissed as the royalty clause was not contrary to art. 85 EEC; the clause was valid and enforceable against the licensee. Even if other clauses in the agreement were contrary to art. 85 EEC, they did not affect the validity of the royalty clause or the rest of the agreement. Where certain clauses of an agreement were void under art. 85 (2) EEC it was a matter of municipal law as to whether, or the extent to which, the rest of the contract would remain valid.

CHEMIDUS WAVIN *v.* SOCIÉTÉ POUR LA TRANSFORMATION ET L'EXPLOITATION DES RESINES INDUSTRIELLES S.A. [1978] 3 C.M.L.R. 514, C.A.

1127. —— trade associations

The E.C. Commission considered certain decisions taken by FEDETAB (the Tobacco Trade Association in Belgium) and certain agreements made between FEDETAB and other tobacco trade associations. *Held,* (1) the approval and categorisation of the wholesalers and retailers by FEDETAB, in order to establish different profit margins for each category, the restrictions set down by FEDETAB on the approval of certain categories of wholesalers, the resale price maintenance by manufacturers arranged by FEDETAB and another tobacco trade association, the ban on resales to other wholesalers, the application to wholesalers and retailers of standard terms of payment, and FEDETAB's decision to oblige retailers to stock a minimum number of brands of tobacco infringed art. 85 (1) EEC and were not notified to the Commission. In view of the non-notification, an exemption under art. 85 (3) EEC was not considered; (2) the FEDETAB recommendation of December 1, 1975, for cigarette sales in Belgium was a decision by an association of undertakings and an agreement between the undertakings that agreed to it within art. 85 (1) EEC and was contrary to art. 85 (1) EEC in that its object and effect were to restrict competition in the Common Market as (a) it divided the Belgian wholesalers and retailers into different categories and established different profit margins for the latter; (b) it applied standard terms of payment to wholesalers and retailers; and (c) it gave wholesalers and retailers end-of-year rebates. The Commission refused to exempt the recommendation under art. 85 (3) EEC; (3) the Commission stated that where a trade association with power to act on its members' behalf, entered into an agreement with another association, its members were individually bound by that agreement even though they did not sign it, if they carried it out and did not show their opposition to it; (4) the Commission issued a cease and desist order.

GB-INNO-BM S.A. *v.* FEDERATION BELGO-LUXEMBOURGEOISE DES INDUSTRIES DU TABAC (FEDETAB) [1978] 3 C.M.L.R. D524, E.C. Commission Decision.

1128. **Constitutional law—directives—implementation**

The European Court considered an application under art. 169 EEC by the E.C. Commission for a declaration concerning the failure by a Member State (Italy) to implement certain EEC directives concerning the elimination of technical barriers to trade between Member States. *Held*, the duty to implement EEC directives within the specified time limits is absolute. Italy had failed to implement Directives 74/151–2/EEC and 74/346–7/EEC and was in breach of this rule. Italy was not excused by reason of any constitutional difficulties from obeying it.

Re TRACTOR TYPE-APPROVAL DIRECTIVE 1974; E.C. COMMISSION *v.* ITALY (No. 69/77) [1979] 1 C.M.L.R. 206, European Ct.

1129. ——— **implementation—Community legislation**

The European Court considered an application by the Commission for a declaration under art. 169 EEC in respect of the Italian Republic's failure to adopt law to comply with Directive 75/324 concerning aerosol dispensers. *Held*, no provisions, practices or facts about the Italian national internal legal system justify such a failure to implement Community directives.

Re AEROSOL DISPENSERS; E.C. COMMISSION *v.* ITALY (No. 163/78) [1979] 2 C.M.L.R. 394, European Ct.

1130. **Convention on Jurisdiction and Enforcement of Judgments—freezing matrimonial property**

The European Court considered a question referred to it under the Brussels Convention on Jurisdiction and Enforcement of Judgments 1968, by the Bundesgerichtshof. The case concerned a divorce action in which it was sought to freeze the assets of the couple. The parties brought divorce proceedings in France and the assets in question were in Germany. The question asked whether this convention extended to cover such protective orders. *Held*, art. 1 (1) of this Convention should be interpreted to the effect that enforcement of such an order in Germany is not covered by the Convention unless the assets are unconnected with the marriage.

DE CAVEL *v.* DE CAVEL (No. 143/78) [1979] 2 C.M.L.R. 547, European Ct.

1131. **Copyright—freedom of information—details of broadcasting programmes**

Details of future broadcasting programmes constitute information within the meaning of art. 10 of the European Convention on Human Rights. The grant by legislation of a monopoly right to publish broadcasting schedules to belong to the broadcasting companies does not infringe art. 10. Publication in programme magazines by broadcasting companies with a copyright monopoly does not infringe arts. 10 and 14, where the broadcasting companies are performing a public service, and profits from the programme magazines finance

their broadcasting activities: DE GEILLUSTREERDE PERS N.V. *v.* THE NETHER-
LANDS [1979] F.S.R. 173, European Commission of Human Rights.

1132. —— imports—free trade agreement

The High Court, Chancery Division, considered an interlocutory injunction
prohibiting the distribution of a circular by the plaintiffs in an action concerning imports from Portugal of gramophone records lawfully made there. *Held,*
the injunction was refused to prevent the circular from being distributed.
The circular's inaccurate claim that such records were unlawfully made in
Portugal did not entitle the applicants for the injunction, the defendants to
the main action, to the injunction.

POLYDOR AND RSO RECORDS INC. *v.* HARLEQUIN RECORD SHOPS AND SIMONS
RECORDS [1979] 3 C.M.L.R. 432, Megarry V.-C.

1133. —— royalties—quantitative restrictions—competition

The Cour d'Appel de Bruxelles considered a case in which the plaintiff had
sought a declaration that a royalty he had been required to pay to the Belgian
performing rights society (SABAM) was devoid of consideration or at least
should be reduced. The court considered arts. 30 and 85 EEC. *Held,* the
royalty was a violation of these articles in the circumstances. It had been
levied on the hiring out in Belgium of musical tapes, manufactured in Britain,
where a manufacturing royalty had already been paid. The property rights in
a musical work do not include the right to lay down territorial limits. The
royalties in the circumstances of this case amounted to a quantitative restriction
on an import within the meaning of art. 30 EEC, and are also void under
art. 85 (2) where it is shown various national societies are acting in concert
to protect their own territories. A tacit or express agreement by a performing
right society with similar organisation in the European Community, *inter alia,*
to prohibit exports of recordings is likely to affect trade in the Common
Market in breach of art. 85 EEC.

S.A. ETABLISSEMENTS BELGES DU TIME LIMIT *v.* SOCIÉTÉ BELGE DES
AUTEURS, COMPOSITEURS ET EDITEURS (SABAM) [1979] 2 C.M.L.R. 578, Cour
d'Appel de Bruxelles.

1134. Customs—force majeure—date of import

The European Court considered several questions referred to it by the
College van Beroep voor het Bedrijfsleven in the Netherlands for a preliminary
ruling under art. 177 EEC. The case concerned an importer whose ship was
delayed at the port of arrival, Rotterdam, so that it entered its customs-
appointed mooring a day late and therefore had to pay additional charges.
Held, under art. 15 (1) of Reg. 120/67 the date of import cannot be earlier
than the date of arrival at the designated place of arrival. Where such a criteria
is in force no principle such as *force majeure* applies. The importer in the
circumstances must bear the loss.

N. G. J. SCHOUTEN B.V. *v.* HOOFDPRODUKTSCHAP VOOR AKKERBOUWPRODUKTEN
(No. 113/78) [1979] 2 C.M.L.R. 720, European Ct.

1134a. Designation of Ministers

EUROPEAN COMMUNITIES (DESIGNATION) ORDER 1979 (No. 1704) [10p], made
under the European Communities Act 1972 (c. 68), s. 2 (2); operative on
January 24, 1980; designates the Secretary of State to exercise powers to make
regulations relating to sea-going tankers entering or leaving U.K. ports.

1135. Directives, decisions and regulations

Court of Justice

Amendments to the Rules of Procedure of the Court of Justice of the European Communities of September 12, 1979. (O.J. 1979 L238/1.)

European Parliament

1136. Decision of the European Parliament of December 13, 1978, on the discharge
to be granted to the Commission in respect of the implementation of the
budget of the European Communities for the 1976 financial year. (O.J. 1979
L18/16.)

Decision of the European Parliament of December 13, 1978, on the discharge to be granted to the Commission in respect of the implementation of the activities of the Fourth European Development Fund for the 1976 financial year. (O.J. 1979 L18/22.)

ECSC, EEC, Euratom

1137. 79/81/ECSC, EEC, Euratom:
Final adoption of the general budget of the European Communities for the financial year 1979. (O.J. 1979 L23/1.)
79/167/ECSC, EEC, Euratom:
Council recommendation of February 5, 1979, on the reduction of energy requirements for buildings in the Community. (O.J. 1979 L37/25.)
79/172/ECSC, EEC, Euratom:
Decision of the Representatives of the Governments of the Member States of the European Communities of February 6, 1979, appointing a judge to the Court of Justice. (O.J. 1979 L37/33.)
79/476/ECSC, EEC, Euratom:
Final adoption of amending and supplementary budget No. 1 of the European Communities for the financial year 1979 (O.J. 1979 L124/1.)
79/568/ECSC, EEC, Euratom:
Final adoption of supplementary budget No. 2 of the European Communities for the financial year 1979. (O.J. 1979 L157/1.)
79/868/ECSC, EEC, Euratom:
Rules of procedure adopted by the Council on July 24, 1979, on the basis of art. 5 of the Treaty of April 8, 1965, establishing a single Council and a single Commission of the European Communities. (O.J. 1979 L268/1.)
79/1000/ECSC, EEC, Euratom:
Decision of the Representatives of the Governments of the Member States of the European Communities of July 24, 1979, appointing Judges and Advocates-General to the Court of Justice. (O.J. 1979 L308/19.)
79/1001/ECSC, EEC, Euratom:
Decision of the Representatives of the Governments of the Member States of the European Communities of November 22, 1979, appointing a Judge to the Court of Justice. (O.J. 1979 L308/20.)
Council Regulation (Euratom, ECSC, EEC) No. 3084/78 of December 21, 1978, adjusting the remuneration and pensions of officials and other servants of the European Communities and the weightings applied thereto. (O.J. 1978 L369/1.)
Council Regulation (Euratom, ECSC, EEC) No. 3085/78 of December 21, 1978, amending, with particular reference to the monetary parities to be used, Regulation (EEC, Euratom, ECSC) No. 259/68 laying down the Staff Regulations of officials of the European Communities and the conditions of employment of other servants of these Communities, Regulation (Euratom, ECSC, EEC) No. 2530/72 and Regulation (ECSC, EEC, Euratom) No. 1543/73 concerning certain special measures. (O.J. 1978 L369/6.)
Council Regulation (Euratom, ECSC, EEC) No. 3086/78 of December 21, 1978, adjusting the weightings applicable to the remuneration and pensions of officials' and other servants of the European Communities following the amendment of the provisions of the Staff Regulations concerning the monetary parities to be used in implementing the Staff Regulations. (O.J. 1978 L369/8.)
Council Regulation (ECSC, EEC, Euratom) No. 1252/79 of June 25, 1979, amending the Financial Regulation of December 21, 1977, applicable to the general budget of the European Communities. (O.J. 1979 L160/1.)
Council Regulation (ECSC, EEC, Euratom) No. 1793/79 of August 9, 1979, adjusting the weightings applied to the remuneration and pensions of officials and other servants of the European Communities. (O.J. 1979 L206/1.)

EEC, Euratom

1138. 79/2/EEC, Euratom:
Council Decision of December 12, 1978, appointing a member of the Economic and Social Committee. (O.J. 1979 L5/27.)

79/665/EEC, Euratom:
Council Decision of July 24, 1979, appointing a member of the Economic and Social Committee. (O.J. 1979 L197/40.)

79/965/EEC, Euratom:
Council Decision of November 12, 1979, appointing two members of the Economic and Social Committee. (O.J. 1979 L293/14.)

79/966/EEC, Euratom:
Council Decision of November 12, 1979, appointing three members of the Economic and Social Committee. (O.J. 1979 L293/15.)

79/1002/Euratom:
Council Decision of November 22, 1979, approving an amendment to the statutes of the joint undertaking 'Schnell-Brüter-Kernkraftwerksgesellschaft mbH' (SBK). (O.J. 1979 L308/21.)

Euratom

1139. Decision of the Council of the European Communities of May 24, 1979, on the admission of the Hellenic Republic to the European Economic Community and to the European Atomic Energy Community. (O.J. 1979 L291/7.)

79/312/Euratom:
Council Decision of March 19, 1979, appointing a member of the Advisory Committee of the Euratom Supply Agency. (O.J. 1979 L73/22.)

79/343/Euratom:
Council Directive of March 27, 1979, amending Directive 76/579/Euratom laying down the revised basic safety standards for health protection of the general public and workers against the dangers of ionizing radiation. (O.J. 1979 L83/18.)

79/344/Euratom:
Council Decision of March 27, 1979, adopting a research programme concerning the decommissioning of nuclear power plants. (O.J. 1979 L83/19.)

79/345/Euratom:
Council Decision of March 27, 1979, adopting a programme of research on the safety of thermal water reactors (indirect nuclear action). (O.J. 1979 L83/21.)

79/346/Euratom:
Council Decision of March 27, 1979, appointing a member of the Advisory Committee of the Euratom Supply Agency. (O.J. 1979 L83/23.)

79/492/Euratom:
Council Decision of May 15, 1979, appointing the members of the Advisory Committee of the Euratom Supply Agency (O.J. 1979 L127/42.)

79/520/Euratom:
Commission decision of May 16, 1979, relating to the setting-up of a group of high-level independent experts in the field of nuclear safety. (O.J. 1979 L141/26.)

79/720/Euratom:
Council Decision of August 3, 1979, approving amendments to the statutes of the " Joint European Torus (Jet), Joint Undertaking." (O.J. 1979 L213/9.)

79/828/Euratom:
Commission Decision of October 2, 1979, amending Decision 79/520/Euratom as regards the term of office of a group of high-level independent experts in the field of nuclear safety. (O.J. 1979 L251/26.)

EEC

1140. 78/1026/EEC:
Council Directive of December 18, 1978, concerning the mutual recognition of diplomas, certificates and other evidence of formal qualifications in veterinary medicine, including measures to facilitate the effective exercise of the right of establishment and freedom to provide services. (O.J. 1978 L362/1.)

78/1027/EEC:
Council Directive of December 18, 1978, concerning the co-ordination of

provisions laid down by law, regulation or administrative action in respect of the activities of veterinary surgeons. (O.J. 1978 L362/7.)

78/1028/EEC:
Council Decision of December 18, 1978, setting up an Advisory Committee on Veterinary Training. (O.J. 1978 L362/10.)

78/1029/EEC:
Council recommendation of December 18, 1978, concerning nationals of the Grand Duchy of Luxembourg who hold a diploma in veterinary medicine conferred in a third country. (O.J. 1978 L362/12.)

78/1031/EEC:
Council Directive of December 5, 1978, on the approximation of the laws of the Member States relating to automatic checkweighing and weight grading machines. (O.J. 1978 L364/1.)

78/1032/EEC:
Third Council Directive of December 19, 1978, on the harmonisation of provisions laid down by law, regulation or administrative action relating to the rules governing turnover tax and excise duty applicable in international travel. (O.J. 1978 L366/28.)

78/1033/EEC:
Fourth Council Directive of December 19, 1978, amending Directive 69/169/EEC on the harmonisation of provisions laid down by law, regulation or administrative action relating to exemption from turnover tax and excise duty on imports in international travel. (O.J. 1978 L366/31.)

78/1034/EEC:
Second Council Directive of December 19, 1978, amending Directive 74/651/EEC on the tax reliefs to be allowed on the importation of goods in small consignments of a non-commercial character within the Community. (O.J. 1978 L366/33.)

78/1035/EEC:
Council Directive of December 19, 1978, on the exemption from taxes of imports of small consignments of goods of a non-commercial character from third countries. (O.J. 1978 L366/34.)

78/1036/EEC:
Council Decision of December 18, 1978, amending Decision 75/459/EEC on action by the European Social Fund for persons affected by employment difficulties. (O.J. 1978 L374/37.)

78/1041/EEC:
Council Decision of December 21, 1978, amending Decision 71/143/EEC setting up machinery for medium-term financial assistance. (O.J. 1978 L379/3.)

79/3/EEC:
Council recommendation of December 19, 1978, to the Member States regarding methods of evaluating the cost of pollution control to industry. (O.J. 1979 L5/28.)

79/4/EEC:
Council Decision of December 19, 1978, on the collection of information concerning the activities of carriers participating in cargo liner traffic in certain areas of operation. (O.J. 1979 L5/31.)

79/5/EEC:
Council Directive of December 19, 1978, amending Directive 75/130/EEC on the establishment of common rules for certain types of combined road/rail carriage of goods between Member States. (O.J. 1979 L5/33.)

79/7/EEC:
Council Directive of December 19, 1978, on the progressive implementation of the principle of equal treatment for men and women in matters of social security. (O.J. 1979 L6/24.)

79/8/EEC:
Decision of the representatives of the Governments of the Member States of the European Economic Community, meeting within the Council, of December 18, 1978, on the abolition of certain postal charges for customs presentation. (O.J. 1979 L6/26.)

79/19/EEC:
Council Decision of December 18, 1978, adopting the annual report on the

economic situation in the Community and laying down the economic policy guidelines for 1979. (O.J. 1979 L8/16.)

79/32/EEC:
Second Council Directive of December 18, 1978, on taxes other than turnover taxes which affect the consumption of manufactured tobacco. (O.J. 1979 L10/8.)

79/33/EEC:
Council Decision of December 18, 1978, concerning the conclusion of the Fifth International Tin Agreement. (O.J. 1979 L10/11.)

79/37/EEC:
Commission Decision of December 7, 1978, relating to a proceeding under art. 85 of the EEC Treaty (IV/93—EMO). (O.J. 1979 L11/16.)

79/40/EEC:
Council Directive of December 18, 1978, amending for the 14th time Directive 65/54/EEC on the approximation of the laws of the Member States concerning the preservatives authorised for use in foodstuffs intended for human consumption. (O.J. 1979 L13/50.)

79/41/EEC:
Council Decision of December 21, 1978, concerning the conclusion of the Agreement in the form of an exchange of letters extending the Trade Agreement between the European Economic Community and the Argentine Republic. (O.J. 1979 L13/51.)

79/42/EEC:
Council Decision of December 21, 1978, concerning the conclusion of the Agreement in the form of an exchange of letters extending and amending, for the year 1977, the Convention between the European Economic Community and the United Nations Relief and Works Agency for Palestine Refugees (UNRWA). (O.J. 1979 L13/53.)

79/43/EEC:
Council Decision of December 21, 1978, concerning the conclusion of the Agreement in the form of an exchange of letters extending and amending until June 30, 1978, the Convention between the European Economic Community and the United Nations Relief and Works Agency for Palestine Refugees (UNRWA) and laying down transitional measures with a view to the conclusion of a new Convention. (O.J. 1979 L13/56.)

79/68/EEC:
Commission Decision of December 12, 1978, relating to a proceeding under art. 85 of the EEC Treaty (IV/29.430—Kawasaki). (O.J. 1979 L/16/9.) (O.J. 1979 L16/9.)

79/73/EEC:
Commission Decision of December 21, 1978, concerning the appointment of members and observers of the Advisory Committee on Industrial Research and Development. (O.J. 1979 L17/13.)

79/76/EEC:
Commission Directive of December 21, 1978, adapting to technical progress Council Directive 72/276/EEC on the approximation of the laws of the Member States relating to certain methods for the quantitative analysis of binary textile fibre mixtures. (O.J. 1979 L17/17.)

79/82/EEC:
Statement of revenue and expenditure of the European Centre for the Development of Vocational Training (Cedefop) for the financial year 1979. (O.J. 1979 L24/1.)

79/83/EEC:
Statement of revenue and expenditure of the European Foundation for the Improvement of Living and Working Conditions for the financial year 1979. (O.J. 1979 L24/23.)

79/84/EEC:
Council Decision of January 15, 1979, appointing the members of the Management Board of the European Centre for the Development of Vocational Traning. (O.J. 1979 L18/23.)

79/85/EEC:
Council Decision of January 15, 1979, appointing the members and alternates of the Advisory Committee on Training in Nursing. (O.J. 1979 L18/25.)

79/86/EEC:
Commission Decision of January 10, 1979, relating to a proceeding under art. 85 of the EEC Treaty (IV/C-29.290 Vaessen/Moris). (O.J. 1979 L19/32.)

79/90/EEC:
Commission Decision of December 12, 1978, on proceeding under art. 85 of the EEC Treaty (IV/29.535—white lead). (O.J. 1979 L21/16.)

79/95/EEC:
Commission Decision of December 29, 1978, amending Decisions 75/578/EEC, 76/221/EEC, 77/145/EEC and 78/124/EEC. (O.J. 1979 L22/21.)

79/112/EEC:
Council Directive of December 18, 1978, on the approximation of the laws of the Member States relating to the labelling, presentation and advertising of foodstuffs for sale to the ultimate customer. (O.J. 1979 L33/1.)

79/113/EEC:
Council Directive of December 19, 1978, on the approximation of the laws of the Member States relating to the determination of the noise emission of construction plant and equipment. (O.J. 1979 L33/15.)

79/114/EEC:
Council recommendation of December 21, 1978, on the ratification of the 1978 International Convention on standards of training, certification and watchkeeping for seafarers. (O.J. 1979 L33/31.)

79/115/EEC:
Council Directive of December 21, 1978, concerning pilotage of vessels by deep-sea pilots in the North Sea and English Channel. (O.J. 1979 L33/32.)

79/116/EEC:
Council Directive of December 21, 1978, concerning minimum requirements for certain tankers entering or leaving Community ports. (O.J. 1979 L33/33.)

79/126/EEC:
Commission Decision of January 29, 1979, making trade in crude oil and/or petroleum products between Belgium and other Member States, France and other Member States and the Netherlands and other Member States subject to a system of authorisation to be granted automatically by the exporting Member State. (O.J. 1979 L30/19.)

79/136/EEC:
Council Decision of February 6, 1979, amending Decision 74/120/EEC on the attainment of a high degree of convergency of the economic policies of the Member States of the European Economic Community. (O.J. 1979 L35/8.)

79/137/EEC:
Council Decision of February 6, 1979, amending Decision 75/185/EEC setting up a Regional Policy Committee. (O.J. 1979 L35/9.)

79/168/EEC:
Council Directive of February 5, 1979, amending Directive 75/726/EEC on the approximation of the laws of the Member States concerning fruit juices and certain similar products. (O.J. 1979 L37/27.)

79/169/EEC:
Council Decision of February 5, 1979, replacing a member and an alternate member of the Advisory Committee on Vocational Training. (O.J. 1979 L37/29.)

79/170/EEC:
Council Decision of February 5, 1979, appointing a full member of the Advisory Committee on Social Security for Migrant Workers. (O.J. 1979 L37/30.)

79/195/EEC:
Council Decision of December 21, 1978, concerning the conclusion of the Agreement between the European Economic Community, the Member States and the International Development Association. (O.J. 1979 L43/13.)

79/196/EEC:
Council Directive of February 6, 1979, on the approximation of the laws of

the Member States concerning electrical equipment for use in potentially explosive atmospheres employing certain types of protection. (O.J. 1979 L43/20.)

79/197/EEC:
Council Directive of February 6, 1979, on a programme to promote drainage in catchment areas including land on both sides of the border between Ireland and Northern Ireland. (O.J. 1979 L43/23.)

79/236/EEC:
Commission Decision of February 8, 1979, extending for certain third countries the period provided for in art. 21 (2) of Directive 70/457/EEC and in art. 32 (2) of Directive 70/458/EEC. (O.J. 1979 L52/20.)

79/253/EEC:
Commission Decision of January 31, 1979, relating to an investigation on the basis of art. 14 (3) of Council Regulation No. 17 at the undertaking Fides, Milan (Case AF/IV/372). (O.J. 1979 L57/33.)

79/267/EEC:
First Council Directive of March 5, 1979, on the co-ordination of laws, regulations and administrative provisions relating to the taking up and pursuit of the business of direct life assurance. (O.J. 1979 L63/1.)

79/270/EEC:
Council Decision of March 5, 1979, replacing a full member of the Committee of the European Social Fund. (O.J. 1979 L62/7.)

79/279/EEC:
Council Directive of March 5, 1979, co-ordinating the conditions for the admission of securities to official stock exchange listing. (O.J. 1979 L66/21.)

79/280/EEC:
Council Decision of March 5, 1979, on the provisional application to St. Lucia after its independence of the arrangements provided for in Decision 76/568/EEC on the association of the overseas countries and territories with the European Economic Community. (O.J. 1979 L66/33.)

79/281/EEC:
Council Decision of March 5, 1979, concerning the conclusion of a Financial Protocol between the European Economic Community and Turkey. (O.J. 1979 L67/14.)

79/298/EEC:
Commission Decision of January 17, 1979, relating to proceedings under art. 85 of the EEC Treaty (IV/28.796—Beecham/Parke, Davis). (O.J. 1979 L70/11.)

79/309/EEC:
Council Decision of March 19, 1979, adjusting the amounts made available to the European Development Fund (1975) for the ACP States and for the overseas countries and territories and the French overseas departments. (O.J. 1979 L72/31.)

79/310/EEC:
Council Decision of March 19, 1979, adjusting Decision 76/568/EEC on the association of the overseas countries and territories with the European Economic Community. (O.J. 1979 L72/33.)

79/311/EEC:
Council Decision of March 19, 1979, concerning the conclusion of the Agreement on a concerted action project in the field of treatment and use of sewage sludge (COST Project 68 *bis*). (O.J. 1979 L72/35.)

79/370/EEC:
Commission Directive of January 30, 1979, on the second adaptation to technical progress of Council Directive 67/548/EEC on the approximation of laws, regulations and administrative provisions relating to the classification, packaging and labelling of dangerous substances. (O.J. 1979 L88/1.)

79/382/EEC:
Council Decision of April 9, 1979, replacing a member of the Advisory Committee on Vocational Training. (O.J. 1979 L93/39.)

79/397/EEC:
Commission Decision of March 29, 1979, extending the period of application of systems of authorisation for trade in crude oil and/or petroleum

products between certain Member States provided for by Decision 79/126/
EEC and 79/135/EEC. (O.J. 1979 L97/15.)

79/409/EEC:
Council Directive of April 2, 1979, on the conservation of wild birds. (O,J.
1979 L103/1.)

79/463/EEC:
Council Decision of May 8, 1979, replacing an alternative member of the
Advisory Committee on Vocational Training. (O.J. 1979 L120/17.)

79/464/EEC:
Council Decision of May 8, 1979, appointing two alternate members of the
Advisory Committee on Safety, Hygiene and Health Protection at Work.
(O.J. 1979 L120/18.)

79/465/EEC:
Council Decision of May 8, 1979, replacing a member of the Advisory Committee on Freedom of Movement for Workers. (O.J. 1979 L120/19.)

79/466/EEC:
Council Decision of May 8, 1979, amending the quotas for imports into Italy
and France of certain products originating in Romania. (O.J. 1979 L120/20.)

79/467/EEC:
Council Decision of May 8, 1979, giving a discharge to the Commission in
respect of the implementation of the operations of the Development Fund
for the overseas countries and territories (First Fund) for the financial year
1977. (O.J. 1979 L120/21.)

79/468/EEC:
Council Decision of May 8, 1979, giving a discharge to the Commission in
respect of the implementation of the operations of the European Development Fund (1963) (Second EDF) for the financial year 1977. (O.J. 1979
L120/22.)

79/469/EEC:
Council Decision of May 8, 1979, giving a discharge to the Commission in
respect of the implementation of the operations of the European Development Fund (1969) (Third EDF) for the financial year 1977. (O.J. 1979
L120/23.)

79/470/EEC:
Council Decision of May 8, 1979, on the Community financing of certain
expenditure relating to food aid in the form of cereals supplied under the
1979 Programme. (O.J. 1979 L120/24.)

79/477/EEC:
Council Decision of May 14, 1979, appointing a member of the Advisory
Committee on Training in Nursing. (O.J. 1979 L123/16.)

79/478/EEC:
Council Decision of May 14, 1979, appointing an alternate member of the
Advisory Committee on Training in Nursing. (O.J. 1979 L123/17.)

79/486/EEC:
Council Decision of May 14, 1979, applying Decision 78/870/EEC empowering the Commission to contract loans for the purpose of promoting investment within the Community. (O.J. 1979 L125/16.)

79/487/EEC:
Council recommendation of May 15, 1979, on the ratification of the International Convention for Safe Containers (CSC). (O.J. 1979 L125/18.)

79/488/EEC:
Commission Directive of April 18, 1979, adapting to technical progress
Council Directive 74/483/EEC on the approximation of the laws of the
Member States relating to the external projections of motor vehicles. (O.J.
1979 L128/1.)

79/489/EEC:
Commission Directive of April 8, 1979, adapting to technical progress
Council Directive 71/320/EEC on the approximation of the laws of the
Member States relating to the braking devices of certain categories of motor
vehicles and their trailers. (O.J. 1979 L128/12.)

79/490/EEC:
Commission Directive of April 18, 1979, adapting to technical progress Coun-

cil Directive 70/221/EEC on the approximation of the laws of the Member States relating to the liquid fuel tanks and rear underrun protection of motor vehicles and their trailers. (O.J. 1979 L128/22.)

79/493/EEC:
Council Decision of May 17, 1979, replacing an alternate member of the Advisory Committee on Freedom of Movement for Workers. (O.J. 1979 L127/46.)

79/494/EEC:
Council Decision of May 17, 1979, replacing a full member and an alternate member of the Commitee of the European Social Fund. (O.J. 1979 L127/47.)

79/496/EEC:
Commission Decision of May 2, 1979, on the United Kingdom scheme of assistance in the form of interest relief grants in favour of the offshore supplies industry (offshore supplies interest relief grant, OSIRG). (O.J. 1979 L127/50.)

79/505/EEC:
Council Decision of May 8, 1979, on the conclusion of the Protocol to the Agreement on the importation of educational, scientific and cultural materials. (O.J. 1979 L134/13.)

79/506/EEC:
Council Decision of May 24, 1979, amending the Decision of December 18, 1978, laying down the schedule for Member States' contributions to the Third European Development Fund (1969) for the financial year 1979. (O.J. 1979 L132/20.)

79/507/EEC:
Council Decision of May 24, 1979, amending the Decision of December 18, 1978, laying down the schedule for Member States' contributions to the Fourth European Development Fund (1975) for the financial year 1979. (O.J. 1979 L132/22.)

79/508/EEC:
Council Decision of May 24, 1979, amending Decision 78/476/EEC on the equivalence of checks on practices for the maintenance of varieties carried out in non-member countries. (O.J. L133/25.)

79/530/EEC:
Council Directive of May 14, 1979, on the indication by labelling of the energy consumption of household appliances. (O.J. 1979 L145/1.)

79/531/EEC:
Council Directive of May 14, 1979, applying to electric ovens Directive 79/530/EEC on the indication by labelling of the energy consumption of household appliances. (O.J. 1979 L145/7.)

79/534/EEC:
Commission opinion of May 23, 1979, on the regional development programmes. (O.J. 1979 L143/7.)

79/535/EEC:
Commission recommendation of May 23, 1979, to the Member States on the regional development programmes. (O.J. 1979 L143/9.)

79/545/EEC:
Commission Decision of June 8, 1979, nominating members of the Advisory Committee on Customs Matters. (O.J. 1979 L146/34.)

79/548/EEC:
Commission Decision of May 31, 1979, extending the period of application of the systems of authorisation for trade in crude oil and/or petroleum products between certain Member States provided for by Decisions 79/126/EEC, 79/135/EEC and 79/397/EEC. (O.J. L148/52.)

79/557/EEC:
Council Decision of June 12, 1979, replacing a full member of the Committee of the European Social Fund. (O.J. 1979 L152/16.)

79/558/EEC:
Council Decision of June 12, 1979, replacing a full member of the Advisory Committee on Freedom of Movement for Workers. (O.J. 1979 L152/17.)

79/581/EEC:
Council Directive of June 19, 1979, on consumer protection in the indication of the prices of foodstuffs. (O.J. 1979 L158/19.)

79/589/EEC:
Commission Decision of June 15, 1979, making trade in crude oil and/or petroleum products between Italy and other Member States subject to a system of authorisation to be granted automatically by the exporting Member State. (O.J. 1979 L160/41.)

79/607/EEC:
Commission Decision of May 30, 1979, amending Decision 77/190/EEC implementing Council Directive 76/491/EEC regarding a Community procedure for information and consultation on the prices of crude oil and petroleum products in the Community. (O.J. 1979 L170/1.)

79/608/EEC:
Commission Directive of June 7, 1979, fixing standard rates of yield for certain inward processing operations. (O.J. 1979 L170/5.)

79/623/EEC:
Council Directive of June 25, 1979, on the harmonization of provisions laid down by law, regulation or administrative action relating to customs debt. (O.J. 1979 L179/31.)

79/639/EEC:
Commission Decision of June 15, 1979, laying down detailed rules for the implementation of Council Decision 77/706/EEC. (O.J. 1979 L183/1.)

79/640/EEC:
Commission Directive of June 21, 1979, amending the Annexes to Council Directive 77/576/EEC on the approximation of the laws, regulations and administrative provisions of the Member States relating to the provision of safety signs at places of work. (O.J. 1979 L183/11.)

79/642/EEC:
Council Decision of July 16, 1979, establishing a second joint programme to encourage the exchange of young workers within the Community. (O.J. 1979 L185/24.)

79/643/EEC:
Council Decision of July 16, 1979, appointing a full member of the Advisory Committee on Safety, Hygiene and Health Protection at Work. (O.J. 1979 L185/27.)

79/644/EEC:
Council Decision of July 16, 1979, replacing a full member of the Advisory Committee on Freedom of Movement for Workers. (O.J. 1979 L185/28.)

79/659/EEC:
Commission Decision of July 18, 1979, fixing the time limit by which the Governments of certain Member States must adopt decisions relating to the establishment of reference tariffs for the carriage of goods by road to and from Denmark. (O.J. 1979 L187/17.)

79/661/EEC:
Council Directive of July 24, 1979, amending Directive 76/768/EEC on the approximation of the laws of the Member States relating to cosmetic products. (O.J. 1979 L192/35.)

79/663/EEC:
Council Directive of July 24, 1979, supplementing the Annex to Council Directive 76/769/EEC on the approximation of the laws, regulations and administrative provisions of the Member States relating to the restrictions on the marketing and use of certain dangerous substances and preparations. (O.J. 1979 L197/37.)

79/691/EEC:
Council Decision of August 3, 1979, applying Regulation (EEC) No. 1736/79 on interest subsidies for certain loans granted under the European monetary system. (O.J. 1979 L200/18.)

79/695/EEC:
Council Directive of July 24, 1979, on the harmonization of procedures for the release of goods for free circulation. (O.J. 1979 L205/19.)

79/696/EEC:
Council Decision of July 24, 1979, on the conclusion of the Agreement between the European Economic Community and the Hellenic Republic on a concerted action project in the field of registration of congenital abnormalities (medical and public health research). (O.J. 1979 L205/27.)

79/707/EEC:
Commission Decision of July 26, 1979, appointing the Deputy-Director of the European Foundation for the Improvement of Living and Working Conditions. (O.J. 1979 L209/24.)

79/719/EEC:
Council Decision of August 1, 1979, on the provisional application to the Republic of Kiribati (formerly the Gilbert Islands) of the arrangements provided for in Decision 76/568/EEC. (O.J. 1979 L208/23.)

79/721/EEC:
Council Decision of August 16, 1979, concerning the conclusion of the Agreement in the form of an exchange of letters between the European Economic Community and the Swiss Confederation on the extension of the Community network for data transmission (Euronet) to the territory of Switzerland. (O.J. 1979 L214/18.)

79/783/EEC:
Council Decision of September 11, 1979, adopting a multiannual programme (1979 to 1983) in the field of data processing. (O.J. 1979 L231/23.)

79/784/EEC:
Council Decision of September 11, 1979, setting up an Advisory Committee for the Management and Coordination of Data-Processing Programmes. (O.J. 1979 L231/29.)

79/785/EEC:
Council Decision of September 11, 1979, adopting an energy research and development programme 1979 to 1983. (O.J. 1979 L231/30.)

79/793/EEC:
Council Decision of September 11, 1979, replacing a member of the Committee of the European Social Fund. (O.J. 1979 L233/28.)

79/794/EEC:
Council Decision of September 11, 1979, replacing a member of the Advisory Committee on Vocational Training. (O.J. 1979 L233/29.)

79/795/EEC:
Commission Directive of July 20, 1979, adapting to technical progress Council Directive 71/127/EEC on the approximation of the laws of the Member States relating to the rear-view mirrors of motor vehicles. (O.J. 1979 L239/1.)

79/796/EEC:
First Commission Directive of July 26, 1979, laying down Community methods of analysis for testing certain sugars intended for human consumption. (O.J. 1979 L239/24.)

79/802/EEC:
Commission Directive of September 6, 1979, on goods entered for inward processing which, if imported for release into free circulation, would benefit from a favourable tariff arrangement by reason of their end-use. (O.J. 1979 L237/29.)

79/810/EEC:
Council Decision of September 18, 1979, appointing an alternate member of the Advisory Committee on Training in Nursing. (O.J. 1979 L240/27.)

79/827/EEC:
Council Decision of September 25, 1979, on the notification of the Community's intention to continue to participate in the International Coffee Agreement 1976. (O.J. 1979 L248/10.)

79/830/EEC:
Council Directive of September 11, 1979, on the approximation of the laws of the Member States relating to hot-water meters. (O.J. 1979 L259/1.)

79/831/EEC:
Council Directive of September 18, 1979, amending for the sixth time Directive 67/548/EEC on the approximation of the laws, regulations and adminis-

trative provisions relating to the classification, packaging and labelling of dangerous substances. (O.J. 1979 L259/10.)

79/841/EEC:
Council Decision of October 9, 1979, reviewing the second multiannual research and development programme for the European Economic Community in the environmental field (indirect action) adopted by Decision 76/311/EEC. (O.J. 1979 L258/29.)

79/842/EEC:
Council Decision of October 9, 1979, adopting a research and development programme in the field of reference materials and methods (Community Bureau of Reference—BCR) and applied metrology (non-nuclear indirect action) (1979 to 1982). (O.J. 1979 L258/32.)

79/843/EEC:
Council Decision of October 9, 1979, appointing a member of the Advisory Committee on Training in Nursing. (O.J. 1979 L260/9.)

79/844/EEC:
Council Decision of October 9, 1979, appointing a member of the Committee of the European Social Fund. (O.J. 1979 L260/10.)

79/846/EEC:
Council Decision of October 9, 1979, appointing the members and alternate members of the Advisory Committee on Medical Training. (O.J. 1979 L260/12.)

79/857/EEC:
Council Decision of October 15, 1979, appointing members and alternate members of the Advisory Committee on Social Security for Migrant Workers. (O.J. 1979 L265/12.)

79/858/EEC:
Commission Decision of September 28, 1979, extending the period of application of the system of authorisation for trade in crude oil and/or petroleum products between Italy and other Member States provided for by Decision 79/589/EEC. (O.J. 1979 L265/12.)

79/859/EEC:
Commission Decision of September 28, 1979, extending the period of application of the systems of authorisation for trade in crude oil and/or petroleum products between certain Member States provided for by Decisions 79/126/EEC, 79/135/EEC, 79/397/EEC and 79/548/EEC. (O.J. 1979 L265/13.)

79/869/EEC:
Council Directive of October 9, 1979, concerning the methods of measurement and frequencies of sampling and analysis of surface water intended for the abstraction of drinking water in the Member States. (O.J. 1979 L271/44.)

79/871/EEC:
Commission opinion of October 10, 1979, addressed to the United Kingdom Government pursuant to art. 3 of Council Directive 76/914/EEC of December 16, 1976, on the minimum level of training for some transport drivers. (O.J. 1979 L269/27.)

79/878/EEC:
Council Decision of October 22, 1979, adopting a European Economic Community concerted research project on the effects of thermal processing and distribution on the quality and nutritive value of food. (O.J. 1979 L270/53.)

79/879/EEC:
Council Decision of October 22, 1979, amending Decision 77/186/EEC on the exporting of crude oil and petroleum products from one Member State to another in the event of supply difficulties. (O.J. 1979 L270/58.)

79/881/EEC:
Council Decision of October 23, 1979, appointing an alternate member of the Advisory Committee on Training in Nursing. (O.J. 1979 L270/72.)

79/921/EEC:
Council Decision of October 29, 1979, amending the import arrangements applied in Italy and the Federal Republic of Germany for tractors, foot-

wear, umbrellas and wrought plates of aluminium, originating in Romania. (O.J. 1979 L281/42.)

79/922/EEC:

Council Decision of October 29, 1979, on the granting of support for Community projects in the hydrocarbons sector. (O.J. 1979 L281/43.)

79/946/EEC:

Commission Decision of October 25, 1979, approving food-aid operations carried out by a charitable organisation and thereby exempting it from payment of monetary compensation amounts. (O.J. 1979 L288/39.)

79/947/EEC:

Commission Decision of October 25, 1979, appointing replacement members and observers of the Advisory Committee on Industrial Research and Development. (O.J. 1979 L 288/40.)

79/962/EEC:

Council Decision of November 12, 1979, replacing a member of the Advisory Committee on Vocational Training. (O.J. 1979 L293/11.)

79/963/EEC:

Council Decision of November 12, 1979, replacing full member and an alternate member of the Committee of the European Social Fund. (O.J. 1979 L293/12.)

79/964/EEC:

Council Decision of November 12, 1979, appointing a full member and an alternate member of the Advisory Committee on Social Security for Migrant Workers. (O.J. 1979 L293/13.)

79/968/EEC:

Council Decision of November 12, 1979, adopting a multiannual research and development programme (1979 to 1982) for the European Economic Community in the field of the recycling of urban and industrial waste (secondary raw materials). (O.J. 1979 L293/19.)

79/989/EEC:

Council Decision of November 20, 1979, replacing an alternate member of the Committee of the European Social Fund. (O.J. 1979 L297/26.)

79/1003/EEC:

Council Decision of November 23, 1979, appointing a member of the Advisory Committee on Social Security for Migrant Workers. (O.J. 1979 L308/23.)

79/1004/EEC:

Council Decision of November 23, 1979, appointing an alternate member of the Advisory Committee on Social Security for Migrant Workers. (O.J. 1979 L308/24.)

79/1005/EEC:

Council Directive of November 23, 1979, amending Directive 75/106/EEC on the approximation of the laws of the Member States relating to the making-up by volume of certain prepackaged liquids. (O.J. 1979 L308/25.)

79/1032/EEC:

Council Decision of December 3, 1979, replacing a member of the Advisory Committee on Vocational Training. (O.J. 1979 L312/30.)

Council Regulation (EEC) No. 3039/78 of December 18, 1978, on the creation of two new types of aid for young people from the European Social Fund. (O.J. 1978 L361/3.)

Council Regulation (EEC) No. 3061/78 of December 19, 1978, amending Regulation (EEC) No. 1544/69 on the tariff treatment applicable to goods contained in travellers' personal luggage. (O.J. 1978 L366/3.)

Council Regulation (EEC) No. 3062/78 of December 19, 1978, amending Regulation (EEC) No. 3164/76 on the Community quota for the carriage of goods by road between Member States. (O.J. 1978 L366/5.)

Council Regulation (EEC) No. 3141/78 of December 18, 1978, on the conclusion of the Agreement in the form of an exchange of letters between the European Economic Community and the People's Democratic Republic of Algeria concerning the import into the Community of preserved fruit salads originating in Algeria (1979). (O.J. 1978 L373/1.)

Council Regulation (EEC) No. 3142/78 December 18, 1978, on the conclusion of the Agreement in the form of an exchange of letters between the European Economic Community and the People's Democratic Republic of Algeria on the importation into the Community of tomato concentrates originating in Algeria (1979). (O.J. 1978 L373/4.)

Council Regulation (EEC) No. 3143/78 of December 18, 1978, on the conclusion of the Agreement in the form of an exchange of letters between the European Economic Community and the Kingdom of Morocco concerning the import into the Community of preserved fruit salads originating in Morocco (1979). (O.J. 1978 L373/7.)

Council Regulation (EEC) No. 3144/78 of December 18, 1978, on the conclusion of the Agreement in the form of an exchange of letters between the European Economic Community and the Republic of Tunisia concerning the import into the Community of preserved fruit salads originating in Tunisia (1979). (O.J. 1978 L373/10.)

Council Regulation (EEC) No. 3165/78 of December 19, 1978, concerning the application of Decision No. 1/78 of the EEC–Austria Joint Committee replacing the unit of account by the European unit of account in Article 8 of Protocol 3 concerning the definition of the concept of " originating products " and methods of administrative co-operation. (O.J. 1978 L376/1.)

Council Regulation (EEC) No. 3166/78 of December 19, 1978, concerning the application of Decision No. 1/78 of the EEC–Finland Joint Committee replacing the unit of account by the European unit of account in Article 8 of Protocol 3 concerning the definition of the concept of " originating products " and methods of administrative co-operation. (O.J. 1978 L376/4.)

Council Regulation (EEC) No. 3167/78 of December 19, 1978, concerning the application of Decision No. 1/78 of the EEC–Iceland Joint Committee replacing the unit of account by the European unit of account in Article 8 of Protocol 3 concerning the definition of the concept of " originating products " and methods of administrative co-operation. (O.J. 1978 L376/7.)

Council Regulation (EEC) No. 3168/78 of December 19, 1978, concerning the application of Decision No. 1/78 of the EEC–Norway Joint Committee replacing the unit of account by the European unit of account in Article 8 of Protocol 3 concerning the definition of the concept of " originating products " and methods of administrative co-operation. (O.J. 1978 L376/10.)

Council Regulation (EEC) No. 3169/78 of December 19 1978, concerning the application of Decision No. 1/78 of the EEC–Portugal Joint Committee replacing the unit of account by the European unit of account in Article 8 of Protocol 3 concerning the definition of the concept of " originating products " and methods of administrative co-operation. (O.J. 1978 L376/13.)

Council Regulation (EEC) No. 3170/78 of December 19, 1978, concerning the application of Decision No. 1/78 of the EEC–Sweden Joint Committee replacing the unit of account by the European unit of account in Article 8 of Protocol 3 concerning the definition of the concept of " originating products " and methods of administrative co-operation. (O.J. 1978 L376/16.)

Council Regulation (EEC) No. 3171/78 of December 19, 1978, concerning the application of Decision No. 1/78 of the EEC–Switzerland Joint Committee replacing the unit of account by the European unit of account in Article 8 of Protocol 3 concerning the definition of the concept of " originating products " and methods of administrative co-operation. (O.J. 1978 L376/19.)

Council Regulation (EEC) No. 3180/78 of December 18, 1978, changing the value of the unit of account used by the European Monetary Co-operation Fund. (O.J. 1978 L379/1.)

Council Regulation (EEC) No. 3181/78 of December 18, 1978, relating to the European monetary system. (O.J. 1978 L379/2.)

Council Regulation (EEC) No. 214/79 of February 6, 1979, amending Regulation (EEC) No. 724/75 establishing a European Regional Development Fund. (O.J. 1979 L35/1.)

Council Regulation (EEC) No. 327/79 of February 19, 1979, on the organization of a sample survey of manpower in spring 1979. (O.J. 1979 L45/6.)

Council Regulation (EEC) No. 337/79 of February 5, 1979, on the common organization of the market in wine. (O.J. 1979 L54/1.)

Council Regulation (EEC) No. 469/79 of March 5, 1979, concerning the conclusion of the Agreement in the form of an exchange of letters relating to art. 9 of Protocol 1 to the Agreement between the European Economic Community and the State of Israel and concerning the import into the Community of preserved fruit salads originating in Israel (1979). (O.J. 1979 L59/1.)

Commission Regulation (EEC) No. 526/79 of March 20, 1979, amending for the second time Reg. (EEC) No. 223/77 on provisions for the implementation of the Community transit procedure and for certain simplifications of that procedure. (O.J. 1979 L74/1.)

Council Regulation (EEC) No. 527/79 of March 19, 1979, amending the list of countries and territories in Reg. (EEC) No. 706/76 on the arrangements applicable to agricultural products and certain goods resulting from the processing of agricultural products originating in the African, Caribbean and Pacific States or in the overseas countries and territories, concerning the list of countries and territories. (O.J. 1979 L71/1.)

Council Regulation (EEC) No. 528/79 of March 19, 1979, derogating from certain provisions concerning the definition of the concept of originating products contained in the Cooperation Agreement between the European Economic Community and the Kingdom of Morocco (O.J. 1979 L71/2.)

Council Regulation (EEC) No. 560/79 of March 5, 1979, on the application of EEC-Israel Joint Committee Decision No. 1/78 amending the Protocol on the definition of the concept of originating products and methods of administrative co-operation to the Agreement between the European Economic Community and the State of Israel. (O.J. 1979 L80/1.)

Council Regulation (EEC) No. 561/79 of March 5, 1979, on the application of EEC-Tunisia Co-operation Council Decision No. 3/78 amending the Protocol on the definition of the concept of originating products and methods of administrative co-operation to the Co-operation Agreement between the European Economic Community and the Republic of Tunisia. (O.J. 1979 L80/44.)

Council Regulation (EEC) No. 590/79 of March 26, 1979, amending Regulation No. 136/66/EEC on the establishment of a common organization of the market in oils and fats. (O.J. 1979 L78/1.)

Commission Regulation (EEC) No. 708/79 of April 9, 1979, amending Regulation (EEC) No. 1380/75 laying down detailed rules for the application of monetary compensatory amounts. (O.J. 1979 L88/9.)

Council Regulation (EEC) No. 725/79 of April 9, 1979, fixing the maximum amount of aid to be made available pursuant to Council Regulation (EEC) No. 1303/78 on the granting of financial support for demonstration projects in the field of energy saving. (O.J. 1979 L93/1.)

Council Regulation (EEC) No. 726/79 of April 9, 1979, fixing the maximum amount of aid to be made available pursuant to Council Regulation (EEC) No. 1302/78 on the granting of financial support for projects to exploit alternative energy sources. (O.J. 1979 L93/2.)

Council Regulation (EEC) No. 727/79 of April 9, 1979, on the implementation in the solar energy sector of Council Regulation (EEC) No. 1302/78 on the granting of financial support for projects to exploit alternative energy sources. (O.J. 1979 L93/3.)

Council Regulation (EEC) No. 728/79 of April 9, 1979, on the implementation in the solid fuel liquefaction and gasification sectors of Council Regulation (EEC) No. 1302/78 ond the granting of financial support for projects to exploit alternative energy sources. (O.J. 1979 L93/5.)

Council Regulation (EEC) No. 729/79 of April 9, 1979, on the implementation in the geothermal energy sector of Council Regulation (EEC) No. 1302/78 on the granting of financial support for projects to exploit alternative energy sources. (O.J. 1979 L93/7.)

Council Regulation (EEC) No. 954/79 of May 15, 1979, concerning the ratification by Member States of, or their accession to, the United Nations Convention on a Code of Conduct for Liner Conferences. (O.J. 1979 L121/1.)

Council Regulation (EEC) No. 955/79 of May 15, 1979, imposing a definitive anti-dumping duty on a certain herbicide originating in Romania. (O.J. 1979 L121/5.)

Council Regulation (EEC) No. 983/79 of May 14, 1979, amending Regulation (EEC) No. 222/77 on Community transit. (O.J. 1979 L123/1.)

Council Regulation (EEC) No. 987/79 of May 15, 1979, amending Regulation (EEC) No. 974/71 with regard to the calculation of monetary compensatory amounts in the wine sector. (O.J. 1979 L123/9.)

Council Regulation (EEC) No. 1038/79 of May 24, 1979, on Community support for a hydrocarbon exploration project in Greenland. (O.J. 1979 L132/1.)

Council Regulation (EEC) No. 1384/79 of June 25, 1979, amending Regulation (EEC) No. 1108/70 introducing an accounting system for expenditure on infrastructure in respect of transport by rail, road and inland waterway. (O.J. 1979 L167/1.)

Council Regulation (EEC) No. 1517/79 of July 16, 1979, amending Regulations (EEC) No. 1408/71 and (EEC) No. 574/72 on the application of social security schemes to employed persons and their families moving within the Community (O.J. 1979 L185/1.)

Council Regulation (EEC) No. 1736/79 of August 3, 1979, on interest subsidies for certain loans granted under the European monetary system. (O.J. 1979 L 200/1.)

Council Regulation (EEC) No. 1893/79 of August 28, 1979, introducing registration for crude oil and/or petroleum product imports in the Community. (O.J. 1979 L220/1.)

Commission Regulation (EEC) No. 1964/79 of September 6, 1979, amending for the third time Regulation (EEC) No. 223/77 on provisions for the implementation of the Community transit procedure and for certain simplifications of that procedure. (O.J. 1979 L227/12.)

Council Regulation (EEC) No. 1996/79 of September 11, 1979, on a Community support mechanism in the field of data processing. (O.J. 1979 L231/1.)

Council Regulation (EEC) No. 2143/79 of September 18, 1979, adjusting the national shares in respect of certain quantitative limits on imports of textile products originating in third countries. (O.J. 1979 L248/1.)

Council Regulation (EEC) No. 2342/79 of October 9, 1979, on the application of EEC-Cyprus Association Council Decision No. 1/79 amending the Protocol concerning the definition of the concept of originating products and methods of administrative co-operation, to the Agreement establishing an association between the European Economic Community and the Republic of Cyprus. (O.J. 1979 L271/1.)

Council Regulation (EEC) No. 2384/79 of October 29, 1979, amending both the Common Customs Tariff in respect of wines and Annex V to Regulation (EEC) No. 337/79 on the common organisation of the market in wine. (O.J. 1979 L274/9.)

Council Regulation (EEC) No. 2397/79 of October 30, 1979, amending Regulation (EEC) No. 337/79 on the common organisation of the market in wine and Regulation (EEC) No. 338/79 laying down special provisions relating to quality wines produced in specified regions. (O.J. 1979 L275/4.)

Council Regulation (EEC) No. 2436/79 of October 9, 1979, on the application of the system of certificates of origin provided for under the International Coffee Agreement 1976 when quotas are in effect. (O.J. 1979 L282/1.)

Commission Regulation (EEC) No. 2467/79 of October 29, 1979, on applications for aid from the European Agricultural Guidance and Guarantee Fund, Guidance Section, for projects to improve public amenities in certain rural areas. (O.J. 1979 L286/1.)

Council Regulation (EEC) No. 2557/79 of October 30, 1979, concerning the conclusion of the Agreement between the European Economic Community and the Argentine Republic on trade in textile products. (O.J. 1979 L298/1.)

Council Regulation (EEC) No. 2558/79 of October 30, 1979, concerning the conclusion of the Agreement between the European Economic Community and the People's Republic of Bangladesh on trade in textile products. (O.J. 1979 L298/38.)

Council Regulation (EEC) No. 2559/79 of October 30, 1979, concerning the conclusion of the Agreement between the European Economic Community and the Republic of Korea on trade in textile products. (O.J. 1979 L298/67.)

Council Regulation (EEC) No. 2560/79 of October 30, 1979, concerning the conclusion of the Agreement between the European Economic Community and Macao on trade in textile products. (O.J. 1979 L298/106.)

Council Regulation (EEC) No. 2561/79 of October 30, 1979, concerning the conclusion of the Agreement between the European Economic Community and the Islamic Republic of Pakistan on trade in textile products. (O.J. 1979 L298/143.)

Council Regulation (EEC) No. 2562/79 of October 30, 1979, concerning the conclusion of the Agreement between the European Economic Community and the Democratic Socialist Republic of Sri Lanka on trade in textile products. (O.J. 1979 L298/184.)

Council Regulation (EEC) No. 2563/79 of October 30, 1979, concerning the conclusion of the Agreement between the European Economic Community and the Kingdom of Thailand on trade in textile products. (O.J. 1979 L298/223.)

Council Regulation (EEC) No. 2592/79 of November 20, 1979, laying down the rules for carrying out the registration of crude oil imports in the Community provided for in Reg. (EEC) No. 1893/79. (O.J. 1979 L297/1.)

Council Regulation (EEC) No. 2594/79 of November 22, 1979, amending Reg. (EEC) No. 337/79 on the common organisation of the market in wine and Reg. (EEC) No. 338/79 laying down special provisions relating to quality wines produced in specific regions. (O.J. 1979 L297/4.)

Council Regulation (EEC) No. 2615/79 of November 23, 1979, amending Art. 107 of Reg. (EEC) No. 574/72 fixing the procedure for implementing Reg. (EEC) No. 1408/71 on the application of social security schemes to employed persons and their families moving within the Community. (O.J. 1979 L301/5.)

ECSC

1141. Decision of the Council of the European Communities of May 24, 1979, on the accession of the Hellenic Republic to the European Coal and Steel Community. (O.J. 1979 L291/5.)

78/1037/ECSC:
Decision of the representatives of the Governments of the Member States of the European Coal and Steel Community, meeting within the Council, of December 29, 1978, opening, allocating and providing for the administration of tariff quotas for certain steel products originating in developing countries. (O.J. 1978 L375/163.)

78/1038/ECSC:
Decision of the representatives of the Governments of the Member States of the European Coal and Steel Community, meeting within the Council, of December 29, 1978, opening tariff preferences for certain steel products originating in developing countries. (O.J. 1978 L375/169.)

78/1039/ECSC:
Decision of the representatives of the Governments of the Member States of the European Coal and Steel Community, meeting within the Council, of December 19, 1978, establishing supervision for imports of certain products originating in Austria (1979). (O.J. 1978 L377/35.)

78/1040/ECSC:
Decision of the representatives of the Governments of the Member States of the European Coal and Steel Community, meeting within the Council, of December 19, 1978, establishing supervision for imports of certain products originating in Sweden (1979). (O.J. 1978 L377/37.)

79/23/ECSC:
Commission Decision of December 7, 1978, approving aids from the U.K. for the coal-mining industry during the coal marketing year 1978–79. (O.J. 1979 L9/33.)

79/34/ECSC:
Decision of the representatives of the Government of the Member States of

the European Coal and Steel Community, meeting within the Council, of December 18, 1978, relating to the Common Customs Tariff nomenclature of the Member States (subheading 73.12 B I) and determining the conditions under which certain ECSC products are eligible upon importation for a favourable tariff arrangement by reason of their end-use. (O.J. 1979 L10/12.)

79/35/ECSC:

Decision of the representatives of the Governments of the Member States of the European Coal and Steel Community, meeting within the Council, of January 13, 1975, on the nomenclature and rates of conventional duty for certain products and the general rules for interpreting and applying the said nomenclature and duties. (O.J. 1979 L10/13.)

79/36/ECSC:

Decision of the representatives of the Governments of the Member States of the European Coal and Steel Community, meeting within the Council, of December 20, 1977, on the nomenclature and the rate of conventional duties for certain products. (O.J. 1979 L10/14.)

79/38/ECSC:

Supplementary Protocol to the Agreement of July 28, 1956, between the Federal Council of the Swiss Confederation, of the one part, and the Governments of the Member States of the European Coal and Steel Community and the High Authority of the European Coal and Steel Community, of the other part, on the introduction of through international railway tariffs for the carriage of coal and steel through Swiss territory. (O.J. 1979 L12/15.)

79/39/ECSC:

Supplementary Protocol to the Agreement of July 26, 1957, between the Austrian Federal Government, of the one part, and the Governments of the Member States of the European Coal and Steel Community and the High Authority of the European Coal and Steel Community, of the other part, on the introduction of through international railway tariffs for the carriage of coal and steel through the territory of the Republic of Austria. (O.J. 1979 L12/27.)

79/87/ECSC:

Commission Decision of January 12, 1979, authorising an agreement strictly analogous to a specialisation agreement between Cockerill SA and Klöckner-Werke AG in respect of wire rod and stainless steel sheet and plate. (O.J. 1979 L19/37.)

79/88/ECSC:

Commission Decision of January 12, 1979, authorising an agreement strictly analogous to a specialisation agreement between Cockerill SA and Estel NV in respect of wire rod. (O.J. 1979 L19/41.)

79/89/ECSC:

Commission Decision of January 15, 1979, authorising the acquisition of the coal wholesale firm Lange, Kühl & Co. KG, Kiel (KGH), by Hugo Stinnes AG, Mülheim (Ruhr). (O.J. 1979 L19/44.)

79/91/ECSC:

Commission Decision of December 22, 1978, derogating from High Authority recommendation No. 1–64 concerning an increase in the protective duty on iron and steel products at the external frontiers of the Community (97th derogation). (O.J. 1979 L21/25.)

79/269/ECSC:

Council Decision of March 5, 1979, appointing a member of the Consultative Committee of the European Coal and Steel Community. (O.J. 1979 L62/6.)

79/411/ECSC:

Commission Decision of March 27, 1979, extending for the second time Decision 75/356/ECSC authorising the application of special tariff measures to the carriage by rail of iron ore from Lorraine and western France to Belgium, Luxembourg and the Saar. (O.J. 1979 L103/25.)

79/412/ECSC:

Commission Decision of March 27, 1979, authorising a specialisation agreement concerning rolled steel products between Irish Steel Holdings Ltd. and

Société métallurgique et navale Dunkerque-Normandie SA. (O.J. 1979 L103/27.)

79/603/ECSC:

Decision of the representatives of the Governments of the Member States of the European Coal and Steel Community, meeting within the Council, of July 2, 1979, extending Decision 77/419/ECSC opening tariff preferences for products covered by that Community and originating in Egypt. (O.J. 1979 L169/14.)

79/604/ECSC:

Decision of the representatives of the Governments of the Member States of the European Coal and Steel Community, meeting within the Council, of July 2, 1979, extending Decision 77/422/ECSC opening tariff preferences for products covered by that Community and originating in Jordan. (O.J. 1979 L169/16.)

79/605/ECSC:

Decision of the representatives of the Governments of the Member States of the European Coal and Steel Community, meeting within the Council, of July 2, 1979, extending Decision 77/420/ECSC opening tariff preferences for products covered by that Community and originating in Syria. (O.J. 1979 L169/17.)

79/606/ECSC:

Decision of the representatives of the Governments of the Member States of the European Coal and Steel Community, meeting within the Council, of July 2, 1979, extending Decision 77/421/ECSC opening tariff preferences for products covered by that Community and originating in Lebanon. (O.J. 1979 L169/18.)

79/666/ECSC:

Council Decision of July 24, 1979, appointing a member of the Consultative Committee of the European Coal and Steel Community. (O.J. 1979 L197/41.)

79/818/ECSC:

Commission Decision of July 26, 1979, authorising British Steel Corporation to acquire the share capital of Dunlop & Ranken Ltd., the Hall Brothers group of companies and Herringshaw Steels Ltd. (O.J. 1979 L245/30.)

79/983/ECSC:

Commission Decision of November 6, 1979, extending the authorisation of the joint selling of fuels for Houillères du Bassin de Lorraine and Saarberg-werke AG by ' Saarlor.' (O.J. 1979 L295/24.)

Commission Decision No. 3071/78/ECSC of December 21, 1978, amending for the third time Decision No. 3002/77/ECSC requiring dealers of iron and steel products to comply with pricing rules. (O.J. 1978 L366/20.)

Commission Decision No. 3097/78/ECSC of December 22, 1978, fixing the rate of the levies for the 1979 financial year and amending Decision No. 3/52/ECSC on the amount of and methods for applying the levies provided for in arts. 49 and 50 of the ECSC Treaty. O.J. 1978 L369/31.)

Commission Decision No. 3139/78/ECSC of December 29, 1978, fixing minimum prices for hot-rolled wide strip, merchant bars and concrete reinforcing bars. (O.J. 1978 L370/79.)

Commission Recommendation No. 3140/78/ECSC of December 29, 1978, concerning the anti-dumping duties imposed on certain iron and steel products. (O.J. 1978 L372/1.)

Commission Decision No. 106/79/ECSC of January 19, 1979, extending for a further year the prohibition on alignment on offers of iron and steel products originating in certain third countries. (O.J. 1979 L14/10.)

Commission recommendation No. 158/79/ECSC of January 29, 1979, amending recommendations 77/329/ECSC on protection against dumping or the granting of bounties or subsidies by countries which are not members of the European Coal and Steel Community. (O.J. 1979 L21/14.)

Commission recommendation No. 165/79/ECSC of January 30, 1979, providing for the suspension of definitive anti-dumping duties established in relation to imports of steel products originating in Bulgaria. (O.J. 1979 L22/11.)

Commission Decision No. 200/79/ECSC of January 31, 1979, further amending Decision No. 527/78/ECSC prohibiting alignment on offers of iron and steel products originating in certain third countries. (O.J. 1979 L28/13.)

Commission recommendation No. 220/79/ECSC of February 5, 1979, amending recommendation 77/330/ECSC establishing Community surveillance in respect of imports into the Community of certain iron and steel products covered by the Treaty establishing the European Coal and Steel Community, originating in third countries. (O.J. 1979 L31/20.)

Commission recommendation 267/79/ECSC of February 9, 1979, imposing a provisional anti-dumping duty on certain angles, shapes and U, I or H sections of iron or steel, not further worked than hot-rolled or extruded, originating in Spain. (O.J. 1979 L37/21.)

Commission recommendation No. 294/79/ECSC of February 13, 1979, imposing a provisional anti-dumping duty on certain hematite pig iron originating in Brazil. (O.J. 1979 L41/29.)

Commission Decision No. 303/79/ECSC of February 15, 1979, further amending Decision No. 527/78/ECSC prohibiting alignment on offers of iron and steel products originating in certain third countries. (O.J. 1979 L42/5.)

Commission Decision No. 421/79/ECSC of February 28, 1979, fixing minimum prices for hot-rolled wide strip, merchant bars and concrete reinforcing bars. (O.J. 1979 L50/49.)

Commission recommendation No. 433/79/ECSC of February 27, 1979, imposing a provisional anti-dumping duty on certain sheets and plates of iron or steel originating in Spain and repealing certain suspended anti-dumping duties. (O.J. 1979 L53/21.)

Commission recommendation No. 496/79/ECSC of March 13, 1979, imposing a provisional anti-dumping duty on iron and steel coils for re-rolling originating in Greece. (O.J. 1979 L65/16.)

Commission Decision No. 503/79/ECSC of March 14, 1979, further amending Decision No. 527/78/ECSC prohibiting alignment on offers of iron and steel products originating in certain third countries. (O.J. 1979 L66/10.)

Commission Decision No. 689/79/ECSC of April 5, 1979, further amending Decision No. 527/78/ECSC prohibiting alignment on offers of iron and steel products originating in certain third countries. (O.J. 1979 L86/21.)

Commission recommendation No. 720/79/ECSC of April 9, 1979, providing for the termination of the application of the provisional anti-dumping duty established in relation to imports of certain hematite pig iron originating in Brazil. (O.J. 1979 L92/10.)

Commission recommendation No. 787/79/ECSC of April 20, 1979, providing for the termination of the provisional anti-dumping duties established in relation to imports of certain steel products originating in Spain. (O.J. 1979 L99/31.)

Commission Decision No. 934/79/ECSC of May 8, 1979, further amending Decision No. 527/78/ECSC prohibiting alignment on offers of iron and steel products originating in certain third countries. (O.J. 1979 L117/15.)

Commission Recommendation No. 935/79/ECSC of May 8, 1979, imposing a definitive anti-dumping duty on certain angles, shapes and U, I or H sections of iron or steel, not further worked than hot-rolled or extruded, originating in Spain but imported from some other non-member country. (O.J. 1979 L117/16.)

Commission Recommendation No. 950/79/ECSC of May 14, 1979, imposing a definitive anti-dumping duty on certain hematite pig iron originating in Brazil but coming from another third country. (O.J. 1979 L120/11.)

Commission recommendation No. 1083/79/ECSC of May 30, 1979, imposing a definitive anti-dumping duty on certain plates of iron or steel originating in Spain but imported from some other non-member country. (O.J. 1979 L135/54.)

Commission recommendation No. 1145/79/ECSC of June 11, 1979, extending the provisional anti-dumping measures established in relation to imports of iron or steel coils for re-rolling originating in Greece. (O.J. 1979 L143/6.)

Commission recommendation No. 1218/79/ECSC of June 19, 1979, supplementing recommendations No. 935/79/ECSC, No. 950/79/ECSC and No. 1083/79/ECSC concerning anti-dumping duties on certain steel products. (O.J. 1979 L153/17.)

Commission Decision No. 1371/79/ECSC of June 27, 1979, amending for the second time Decision No. 3139/78/ECSC fixing minimum prices for hot-rolled wide strip, merchant bars and concrete reinforcing bars. (O.J. 1979 L165/7.)

Commission Decision No. 1687/79/ECSC of July 27, 1979, amending for the second time Decision No. 3017/76/ECSC concerning the obligation of undertakings pursuing a production activity in the steel sector to supply certain data on deliveries of steel. (O.J. 1979 L196/17.)

Commission recommendation No. 2002/79/ECSC of September 6, 1979, to the Member States relating to Community monitoring of imports into the Community of certain iron and steel products covered by the Treaty, establishing the European Coal and Steel Community and originating in third countries. (O.J. 1979 L231/15.)

Commission Decision No. 2651/79/ECSC of November 29, 1979, establishing the final closure of the winding up of the imported ferrous scrap equalisation scheme. (O.J. 1979 L304/13.)

Agriculture

1142. 79/45/EEC:

Commission Decision of December 8, 1978, on the implementation of the reform of agricultural structures in the United Kingdom pursuant to Directives 72/159/EEC and 75/268/EEC. (O.J. 1979 L13/60.)

79/51/EEC:

Commission Decision of December 11, 1978, on the granting by the Guidance Section of the EAGGF to the United Kingdom of a payment on account in respect of expenditure incurred during 1977 on aids relating to the provision of socio-economic guidance for and the acquisition of occupational skills by persons engaged in agriculture. (O.J. 1979 L13/66.)

79/92/EEC:

Commission Decision of December 29, 1978, authorising the Federal Republic of Germany to restrict the marketing of seed of certain varieties of agricultural plant species. (O.J. 1979 L22/14.)

79/93/EEC:

Commission Decision of December 29, 1978, authorising the United Kingdom to restrict the marketing of seed of certain varieties of agricultural plant species. (O.J. 1979 L22/17.)

79/94/EEC:

Commission Decision of December 29, 1978, authorising the French Republic to restrict the marketing of seed of certain varieties of agricultural plant species. (O.J. 1979 L22/19.)

79/108/EEC:

Commission Decision of January 17, 1979, on the reimbursement by the Guidance Section of the EAGGF to the United Kingdom of expenditure incurred during 1976 on aids for the less-favoured farming areas. (O.J. 1979 L28/31.)

79/117/EEC:

Council Directive of December 21, 1978, prohibiting the placing on the market and use of plant protection products containing certain substances. (O.J. 1979 L33/36.)

79/138/EEC:

Commission Directive of December 14, 1978, amending Directive 77/535/EEC on the approximation of the laws of the Member States relating to methods of sampling and analysis of fertilisers. (O.J. 1979 L39/3.)

79/139/EEC:

Twenty-sixth Commission Directive of December 18, 1978, amending the Annexes to Council Directive 70/524/EEC cooncerning additives in feedstuffs. (O.J. 1979 L39/11.)

79/151/EEC:
Commission Decision of December 21, 1978, on the reimbursement by the Guidance Section of the EAGGF to the United Kingdom of premiums paid during 1977 for the non-marketing of milk and milk products and for the conversion of dairy herds. (O.J. 1979 L39/25.)

79/157/EEC:
Commission Decision of December 21, 1978, on the granting by the Guidance Section of the EAGGF to the United Kingdom of a payment on account in respect of expenditure incurred during 1977 on aids and premiums relating to the modernisation of farms including those in the less-favoured farming areas. (O.J. 1979 L39/33.)

79/166/EEC:
Commission Decision of December 22, 1978, on the reimbursement by the Guidance Section of the EAGGF to the United Kingdom of expenditure incurred during 1976 on aids relating to the provision of socio-economic guidance for and the acquisition of occupational skills by persons engaged in agriculture. (O.J. 1979 L39/44.)

79/198/EEC:
Council Decision of February 12, 1979, concerning the conclusion of the International Cocoa Agreement 1975. (O.J. 1979 L44/13.)

79/268/EEC:
Council Directive of March 5, 1979, amending Directive 77/504/EEC on pure-bred breeding animals of the bovine species. (O.J. 1979 L62/5.)

79/372/EEC:
Council Directive of April 2, 1979, amending Directive 77/101/EEC on the marketing of straight feedingstuffs. (O.J. 1979 L86/29.)

79/373/EEC:
Council Directive of April 2, 1979, on the marketing of compound feeding-stuffs. (O.J. 1979 L86/30.)

79/379/EEC:
Commission Decision of March 26, 1979, on the reimbursement by the Guidance Section of the EAGGF to the United Kingdom of aids granted to producers' organisations in the fishing industry during 1977. (O.J. 1979 L87/34.)

79/380/EEC:
Commission Decision of March 26, 1979, on the reimbursement by the Guidance Section of the EAGGF to the United Kingdom of aids granted to producers' organisations in the fishing industry during 1977. (O.J. 1979 L87/35.

79/383/EEC:
Council Decision of April 9, 1979, under the Treaties, concerning fishery activities in waters under the sovereignty or jurisdiction of Member States, taken on a temporary basis pending the adoption of permanent Community measures. (O.J. 1979 L93/40.)

79/430/EEC:
Commission Decision of April 17, 1979, on the implementation of the reform of agricultural structures in the United Kingdom pursuant to Directive 72/159/EEC. (O.J. 1979 L106/44.)

79/532/EEC:
Council Directive of May 17, 1979, on the approximation of the laws of the Member States relating to the component type-approval of lighting and light-signalling devices on wheeled agricultural or forestry tractors. (O.J. 1979 L145/16.)

79/533/EEC:
Council Directive of May 17, 1979, on the approximation of the laws of the Member States relating to the coupling device and the reverse of wheeled agricultural or forestry tractors. (O.J. 1979 L145/20.)

79/553/EEC:
Twenty-Seventh Commission Directive of June 7, 1979, amending the Annexes to Council Directive 70/524/EEC concerning additives in feeding-stuffs. (O.J. 1979 L148/58.)

79/556/EEC:
Council Decision of June 12, 1979, concerning the signing and the deposit of a declaration of provisional application of the Protocols for the fifth extension of the Wheat Trade Convention and the Food Aid Convention constituting the International Wheat Agreement 1971. (O.J. 1979 L152/8.)

79/569/EEC:
Council Decision of June 12, 1979, concerning the conclusion of the Agreement in the form of an exchange of letters on the provisional application of the Agreement between the Government of the Republic of Senegal and the European Economic Community on fishing off the coast of Senegal and of the Protocol and the exchanges of letters relating thereto. (O.J. 1979 L154/25.)

79/572/EEC:
Commission Decision of June 8, 1979, relating to the institution of a Scientific and Technical Committee for Fisheries. (O.J. 1979 L156/29.)

79/590/EEC:
Council Decision of June 25, 1979, under the Treaties, concerning fishery activities in waters under the sovereignty or jurisdiction of Member States, taken on a temporary basis pending the adoption of permanent Community measures. (O.J. 1979 L161/46.)

79/613/EEC:
Commission Decision of June 22, 1979, on the reimbursement by the Guidance Section of the EAGGF to the United Kingdom of expenditure incurred during 1977 on aids for the less-favoured farming areas. (O.J. 1979 L172/15.)

79/622/EEC:
Council Directive of June 25, 1979, on the approximation of the laws of the Member States relating to the roll-over protection structures of wheeled agricultural or forestry tractors (static testing). (O.J. 1979 L179/1.)

79/641/EEC:
Commission Directive of June 27, 1979, amending Council Directives 66/401/EEC, 66/402/EEC, 69/208/EEC and 70/458/EEC on the marketing of fodder plant seed, cereal seed, seed of oil and fibre plants and vegetable seed. (O.J. 1979 L183/13.)

79/692/EEC:
Council Directive of July 24, 1979, amending Directives 66/401/EEC, 66/402/EEC, 70/458/EEC and 70/457/EEC on the marketing of fodder plant seed, cereal seed and vegetable seed and on the common catalogue of varieties of agricultural plant species. (O.J. 1979 L 205/1.)

79/693/EEC:
Council Directive of July 24, 1979, on the approximation of the laws of the Member States relating to fruit jams, jellies and marmalades and chestnut purée. (O.J. 1979 L205/5.)

79/694/EEC:
Council Directive of July 24, 1979, amending Directive 74/150/EEC on the approximation of the laws of the Member States relating to the type-approval of wheeled agricultural or forestry tractors. (O.J. 1979 L205/17.)

79/697/EEC:
Twenty-Eighth Commission Directive of July 20, 1979, amending the Annexes to Council Directive 70/524/EEC concerning additives in feedingstuffs. (O.J. 1979 L207/19.)

79/736/EEC:
Commission Decision of August 2, 1979, on the reimbursement by the Guidance Section of the EAGGF to the United Kingdom of expenditure incurred during 1975 on aids and premiums relating to the modernization of farms. (O.J. 1979 L216/23.)

79/738/EEC:
Commission Decision of August 2, 1979, on the reimbursement by the Guidance Section of the EAGGF to the United Kingdom of expenditure incurred during 1977 on aids relating to the provision of socio-economic guidance for and the acquisition of occupational skills by persons engaged in agriculture. (O.J. 1979 L216/25.)

79/774/EEC:
Commission Decision of August 28, 1979, on the granting by the Guidance Section of the EAGGF to the United Kingdom of a payment on account in respect of expenditure incurred during 1978 on aids relating to the provision of socio-economic guidance for and the acquisition of occupational skills by persons engaged in agriculture. (O.J. 1979 L230/10.)

79/797/EEC:
First Commission Directive of August 10, 1979, amending the Annex to Council Directive 77/101/EEC on the marketing of straight feedingstuffs. (O.J. 1979 L239/53.)

79/832/EEC:
Commission Decision of September 7, 1979, setting out the tables relating to the classification of agricultural holdings on the basis of a Community typology, the method of their transcription on to magnetic tape and the deadline for their transmission for the purposes of the survey on the structure of agricultural holdings for 1977. (O.J. 1979 L259/29.)

79/833/EEC:
Commission Decision of September 7, 1979, laying down, for the purposes of the survey on the structure of agricultural holdings for 1979/80, the Community outline of the schedule of tables, the standard code and the detailed rules for the transcription on to magnetic tape of the data contained in such tables. (O.J. 1979 L259/45.)

79/901/EEC:
Commission Decision of October 12, 1979, concerning the clearance of the accounts presented by the United Kingdom in respect of the European Agricultural Guidance and Guarantee Fund, Guarantee Section, expenditure for 1973. (O.J. 1979 L278/25.)

79/905/EEC:
Council Decision of October 29, 1979, under the Treaties, concerning fishery activities in waters under the sovereignty or jurisdiction of Member States, taken on a temporary basis pending the adoption of permanent Community measures. (O.J. 1979 L277/10.)

79/920/EEC:
Council Directive of October 29, 1979, amending Directive 76/630/EEC concerning survey of pig production to be made by Member States. (O.J. 1979 L281/41.)

79/923/EEC:
Council Directive of October 30, 1979, on the quality required of shellfish waters. (O.J. 1979 L 281/47.)

79/941/EEC:
Commission Decision of October 22, 1979, on the reimbursement by the Guidance Section of the EAGGF to the United Kingdom for aid granted to producers in the hop sector during 1975 and 1976. (O.J. 1979 L288/31.)

79/942/EEC:
Commission Decision of October 22, 1979, on the reimbursement by the Guidance Section of the EAGGF to the United Kingdom of expenditure incurred during 1977 on aids and premiums relating to the modernisation of farms including those in the less-favoured farming areas. (O.J. 1979 L288/33.)

79/943/EEC:
Commission Decision of October 22, 1979, on the reimbursement by the Guidance Section of the EAGGF to the United Kingdom of expenditure incurred during 1977 on annuities relating to measures to encourage the cessation of farming and the reallocation of utilized agricultural area for the purpose of structural improvement. (O.J. 1979 L288/35.)

79/967/EEC:
Council Directive of November 12, 1979, amending Directives 66/403/EEC, 70/457/EEC and 70/458/EEC on the marketing of seed potatoes, the common catalogue of varieties of agricultural plant species and the marketing of vegetable seed. (O.J. 1979 L293/16.)

79/988/EEC:
Council Decision of November 20, 1979, concerning the conclusion of the

Agreement in the form of two exchanges of letters, one providing for the provisional application of the Agreement between the European Economic Community and the Government of Sweden on certain measures for the purpose of promoting the reproduction of salmon in the Baltic Sea, and one concerning the application in 1979 of that Agreement. (O.J. 1979 L297/23.)

79/998/EEC:
Commission Decision of November 12, 1979, on the reimbursement by the Guidance Section of the EAGGF to the United Kingdom of expenditure incurred during 1978 in connection with Community measures for the eradication of brucellosis, tuberculosis and leucosis in cattle. (O.J. 1979 L301/29.)

79/1011/EEC:
Twenty-ninth Commission Directive of November 15, 1979, amending the Annexes to Council Directive 70/524/EEC concerning additives in feeding-stuffs. (O.J. 1979 L310/24.)

79/1033/EEC:
Council Decision of December 3, 1979, under the Treaties, concerning fishery activities in waters under the sovereignty or jurisdiction of Member States, taken on a temporary basis pending the adoption of permanent Community measures. (O.J. 1979 L312/31.)

Council Regulation (EEC) No. 292/78 of December 19, 1978, on the granting of aid from the Guidance Section of the European Agricultural Guidance and Guarantee Fund, in 1978 and 1979, pursuant to Regulation No 17/64/EEC. (O.J. 1978 L357/3.)

Commission Regulation (EEC) No. 3019/78 of December 21, 1978, amending Regulation No. 91/66/EEC as regards the typology of reference for the selection of holdings and the number of returning holdings per division. (O.J. 1978 L359/18.)

Council Regulation (EEC) No. 3040/78 of December 18, 1978, amending Regulation (EEC) No. 2327/78 laying down certain measures for the conservation and management of fishery resources applicable to vessels flying the flag of Spain for the period October 1 to December 31, 1978. (O.J. 1978 L361/5.)

Council Regulation (EEC) No. 3149/78 of December 21, 1978, laying down certain interim measures for the conservation and management of fishery resources applicable to vessels registered in the Faroe Islands. (O.J. 1978 L374/1.)

Council Regulation (EEC) No. 3150/78 of December 21, 1978, laying down certain interim measures for the conservation and management of fishery resources applicable to vessels flying the flag of Norway. (O.J. 1978 L374/9.)

Council Regulation (EEC) No. 3151/78 of December 21, 1978, laying down certain interim measures for the conservation and management of fishery resources applicable to vessels flying the flag of Sweden. (O.J. 1978 L374/18.)

Council Regulation (EEC) No. 3152/78 of December 21, 1978, laying down certain interim measures for the conservation and management of fishery resources applicable to vessels flying the flag of Spain for the period January 1–31, 1979. (O.J. 1978 L374/24.)

Council Regulation (EEC) No. 3153/78 of December 21, 1978, laying down certain interim measures for the conservation and management of fishery resources applicable to vessels flying the flag of certain non-member countries in the 200 nautical-mile zone off the coast of the French department of Guyana. (O.J. 1978 L374/31.)

Council Regulation (EEC) No. 3179/78 of December 28, 1978, concerning the conclusion by the European Economic Community of the Convention on Future Multilateral Co-operation in the North-West Atlantic Fisheries. (O.J. 1978 L378/1.)

Commission Regulation (EEC) No. 137/79 of December 19, 1978, on the institution of a special method of administrative co-operation for applying intra-Community treatment to the fishery catches of vessels of Member States. (O.J. 1979 L20/1.)

Council Regulation (EEC) No. 215/79 of February 5, 1979, regarding the application of Decision No. 4/78 of the ACP-EEC Council of Ministers derogating from the definition of the concept of " originating products " to take into account the special situation of Kenya with regard to certain items of fishing tackle (fishing flies). (O.J. 1979 L31/1.)

Council Regulation (EEC) No. 216/79 of February 5, 1979, regarding the application of Decision No. 5/78 of the ACP-EEC Council of Ministers derogating from the definition of the concept of " originating products " to take into account the special situation of Malawi with regard to certain items of fishing tackle (fishing flies). (O.J. 1979 L31/3.)

Council Regulation (EEC) No. 235/79 of February 5, 1979, amending Regulation (EEC) No. 1696/71 on the common organisation of the market in hops as regards the verification of the equivalence of attestations accompanying hops imported from non-member countries. (O.J. 1979 L34/4.)

Council Regulation (EEC) No. 395/79 of February 28, 1979, laying down for the period January 1 to March 31, 1979, certain interim measures for the conservation and management of fishery resources applicable to vessels flying the flag of Norway. (O.J. 1979 L51/1.)

Council Regulation (EEC) No. 396/79 of February 28, 1979, laying down for the period January 1 to March 31, 1979, certain interim measures for the conservation and management of fishery resources applicable to vessels flying the flag of Sweden. (O.J. 1979 L51/10.)

Council Regulation (EEC) No. 397/79 of February 28, 1979, laying down certain interim measures for the conservation and management of fishery resources applicable to vessels registered in the Faroe Islands. (O.J. 1979 L51/18.)

Council Regulation (EEC) No. 586/79 of March 26, 1979, laying down for 1979 certain measures for the conservation and management of fishery resources applicable to vessels flying the flag of Spain. (O.J. 1979 L81/1.)

Council Regulation (EEC) No. 587/79 of March 26, 1979, laying down for 1979 certain measures for the conservation and management of fishery resources applicable to vessels flying the flag of Norway. (O.J. 1979 L81/9.)

Council Regulation (EEC) No. 588/79 of March 26, 1979, laying down for 1979 certain measures for the conservation and management of fishery resources applicable to vessels flying the flag of Sweden. (O.J. 1979 L81/18.)

Council Regulation (EEC) No. 589/79 of March 26, 1979, laying down for 1979 certain interim measures for the conservation and management of fishery resources applicable to vessels registered in the Faroe Islands. (O.J. 1979 L81/26.)

Council Regulation (EEC) No. 643/79 of March 29, 1979, amending, as regards the French franc, the Italian lira, the pound sterling and the Irish pound, Regulation (EEC) No. 878/77 on the exchange rates to be applied in agriculture. (O.J. 1979 L83/1.)

Council Regulation (EEC) No. 652/79 of March 29, 1979, on the impact of the European monetary system on the common agricultural policy. (O.J. 1979 L84/1.)

Commission Regulation (EEC) No. 706/79 of April 9, 1979, laying down detailed rules for the application of Regulation (EEC) No. 652/79 on the impact of the European monetary system on the common agricultural policy. (O.J. 1979 L89/3.)

Commission Regulation (EEC) No. 707/79 of April 9, 1979, amending Regulation (EEC) No. 1054/78 following the fixing of new exchange rates to be applied in France, Ireland, Italy and the United Kingdom in agriculture. (O.J. 1979 L89/7.)

Council Regulation (EEC) No. 927/79 of May 8, 1979, on the application of Decision No. 2/79 of the ACP–EEC Council of Ministers derogating from the concept of " originating products " to take account of the special situation of Mauritius with regard to its production of canned tuna. O.J. 1979 L117/1.)

Council Regulation (EEC) No 929/79 of May 8, 1979, amending Regulation (EEC) No. 729/70 concerning the amount allotted to the Guidance Section of the European Agricultural Guidance and Guarantee Fund. (O.J. 1979 L117/4.)

Council Regulation (EEC) No. 1030/79 of May 24, 1979, amending Regulation (EEC) No. 1883/78 laying down general rules for the financing of interventions by the European Agricultural Guidance and Guarantee Fund, Guarantee Section. (O.J. 1979 L130/4.)

Council Regulation (EEC) No. 1177/79 of June 12, 1979, laying down for 1979 certain measures for the conservation and management of fishery resources applicable to vessels flying the flag of Spain. (O.J. 1979 L151/1.)

Council Regulation (EEC) No. 1178/79 of June 12, 1979, laying down for 1979 certain interim measures for the conservation and management of fishery resources applicable to vessels registered in the Faroe Islands. (O.J. 1979 L151/9.)

Council Regulation (EEC) No. 1179/79 of June 12, 1979, allocating catch quotas between Member States for vessels fishing in Swedish waters (O.J. 1979 L151/17.)

Council Regulation (EEC) No. 1180/79 of June 12, 1979, allocating certain catch quotas between Member States for vessels fishing in the Norwegian exclusive economic zone. (O.J. 1979 L151/19.)

Council Regulation (EEC) No. 1181/79 of June 12, 1979, allocating catch quotas between Member States for vessels fishing in Faroese waters. (O.J. 1979 L151/21.)

Council Regulation (EEC) No. 1208/79 of June 19, 1979, supplementing Annex I to Regulation (EEC) No. 1035/72 on the common organisation of the market in fruit and vegetables. (O.J. 1979 L153/1.)

Council Regulation (EEC) No. 1264/79 of June 25, 1979, amending Regulation (EEC) No. 652/79 on the impact of the European monetary system on the common agricultural policy. (O.J. 1979 L161/1.)

Council Regulation (EEC) No. 1266/79 of June 25, 1979, amending with respect to the pound sterling and the French franc, Regulation (EEC) No. 878/77 on the exchange rates to be applied in agriculture. (O.J. 1979 L161/4.)

Commission Regulation (EEC) No. 1363/79 of June 29, 1979, amending Regulation (EEC) No. 1054/78 following the fixing of a new exchange rate to be applied in agriculture. (O.J. 1979 L163/23.)

Council Regulation (EEC) No. 1547/79 of July 24, 1979, amending Regulation (EEC) No. 2727/75 on the common organisation of the market in cereals. (O.J. 1979 L188/1.)

Council Regulation (EEC) No. 1552/79 of July 24, 1979, amending Regulation (EEC) No. 1418/76 on the common organisation of the market in rice. (O.J. 1979 L188/9.)

Council Regulation (EEC) No. 1579/79 of July 24, 1979, amending, as regards the mechanism of market management, Regulation (EEC) No. 727/70 on the common organisation of the market in raw tobacco. (O.J. 1979 L189/1.)

Commission Regulation (EEC) No. 1598/79 of July 26, 1979, amending Regulation No. 184/66/EEC as regards the procedures and time limits for forwarding farm returns and the standard fee per farm return. (O.J. 1979 L189/50.)

Council Regulation (EEC) No. 1639/79 of July 24, 1979, amending Regulation (EEC) No. 516/77 on the common organisation of the market in products processed from fruit and vegetables. (O.J. 1979 L192/3.)

Council Regulation (EEC) No. 2047/79 of September 18, 1979, amending, with respect to the German mark and the currencies of the Benelux countries, Regulation (EEC) No. 878/77 on the exchange rates to be applied in agriculture. (O.J. 1979 L237/1.)

Commission Regulation (EEC) No. 2093/79 of September 26, 1979, amending Regulation (EEC) No. 2036/74 fixing prices for the sale at reduced prices to certain institutions and bodies of a social character of hindquarters of adult bovine animals held by the intervention agencies. (O.J. 1979 L245/10.)

Council Regulation (EEC) No. 2139/79 of September 28, 1979, amending, with respect to the French franc, the Italian lira, the pound sterling, the Irish pound and the Danish krone, Regulation (EEC) No. 878/77 on the exchange rates to be applied in agriculture. (O.J. 1979 L246/76.)

Commission Regulation (EEC) No. 2141/79 of September 28, 1979, amending Regulation (EEC) No. 1054/78 following the fixing of new rates of exchange to be applied in agriculture for Denmark, France, Ireland, Italy and the United Kingdom. (O.J. 1979 L247/37.)

Council Regulation (EEC) No. 2227/79 of October 9, 1979, amending Regulations (EEC) No. 587/79 and (EEC) No. 1178/79 laying down for 1979 certain measures for the conservation and management of fishery resources applicable to vessels flying the flag of Norway and vessels registered in the Faroe Islands respectively. (O.J. 1979 L257/3.)

Council Regulation (EEC) No. 2285/79 of October 15, 1979, amending Regulation (EEC) No. 1117/78 on the common organisation of the market in dried fodder. (O.J. 1979 L263/1.)

Council Regulation (EEC) No. 2298/79 of October 15, 1979, on the conclusion of the Agreements in the form of exchanges of letters between the European Economic Community and Barbados, the People's Republic of the Congo, Fiji, the Co-operative Republic of Guyana, Jamaica, the Republic of Kenya, the Democratic Republic of Madagascar, the Republic of Malawi, Mauritius, the Republic of Surinam, the Kingdom of Swaziland, the United Republic of Tanzania, Trinidad and Tobago, the Republic of Uganda, and also the Republic of India, on the guaranteed prices for cane sugar for 1979/80. (O.J. 1979 L264/1.)

Council Regulation (EEC) No. 2299/79 of October 15, 1979, fixing the guaranteed prices applicable for cane sugar originating in the overseas countries and territories (OCT) for 1979/80. (O.J. 1979 L264/6.)

Commission Regulation (EEC) No. 2468/79 of October 29, 1979, on applications for aid from the European Agricultural Guidance and Guarantee Fund, Guidance Section, for special forestry programmes in certain Mediterranean zones of the Community. (O.J. 1979 L286/14.)

Council Regulation (EEC) No. 2622/79 of November 23, 1979, laying down certain technical measures for the conservation of fishery resources applicable to vessels flying the flag of a Member State and fishing in the Regulatory Area defined in the NAFO Convention. (O.J. 1979 L303/1.)

Council Regulation (EEC) No. 2754/79 of December 3, 1979, on the conclusion of the Agreement on fisheries between the European Economic Community and the Government of Canada and of the Agreement in the form of an exchange of letters concerning that Agreement. (O.J. 1979 L312/1.)

1143. Discrimination—freedom to provide services—employment agencies—European Court

The Court of First Instance of Tournai referred several questions to the European Court under art. 177 for a preliminary ruling. The case concerned the interpretation of Directive 67/43/EEC of 1967 and arose out of criminal proceedings in respect of alleged breaches of the Belgian Arrêté Royal 1975 concerning fee-charging by employment agencies for entertainers. *Held,* the European Court under the art. 177 procedure may take or extract from the questions asked the elements of Community law necessary for the national court to determine the legal problem. Art. 59 EEC requires the abolition of all discrimination against persons providing services, in respect of nationality, or place of establishment within the Community. When employment agencies which charge fees are state licensed, the state must not demand of persons established in another state who provide services, that they must, *inter alia,* act through those licensed agencies.

MINISTÈRE PUBLIC AND CHAMBRE SYNDICALE DES AGENTS ARTISTIQUES ET IMPRESARII DE BELGIQUE A.S.B.L. *v.* VAN WESEMAEL. (Nos. 110 and 11/78) [1979] E.C.R. 35, European Ct.

1144. ECSC

EUROPEAN COMMUNITIES (IRON AND STEEL EMPLOYEES RE-ADAPTATION BENEFITS SCHEME) REGULATIONS 1979 (No. 954) [70p], made under the European Communities Act 1972 (c. 68), s. 2 (2); operative on August 5, 1979; consolidate with amendments S.I. 1974 No. 908, S.I. 1976 No. 1265 and S.I. 1978 No. 1122 which provide for the payment of benefits to certain steelworkers who are made redundant or transferred to less well paid employment.

1145. ——— financial penalties

The E.C. Commission gave a decision which imposed large financial penalties on eight iron and steel undertakings found to have infringed the ECSC under the rules implementing arts. 61 and 47 ECSC and Decisions thereunder.

THE COMMUNITY v. SOCIÉTÉ ACIERIES DE MONTEREAU [1979] 1 C.M.L.R. 561, E.C. Commission.

1146. E.C. Commission—enforcement of directives—reason for delay

The European Court considered an action for damages against the E.C. Commission for delay in taking steps to compel Italy to end restrictions on feed-stuff imports that contained a certain concentration of nitrates. *Held,* the Commission was reasonable in the circumstances in not taking enforcement action on Directive 74/63 and to wait for the standing committee established by the Directive to obtain a scientific opinion on the harmful effects of these chemicals.

DENKAVIT S.R.L. AND DENKAVIT B.V. v. E.C. COMMISSION (No. 14/78) [1979] 2 C.M.L.R. 135, European Ct.

1147. ——— powers—ultra vires—regulations

Yoshida GmbH brought a similar case in the Federal Republic of Germany to that noted at [1979] C.L.Y. 1148 and following a reference to the European Court by the Verwaltungsgericht at Kassel the matter was decided in a similar way.

YOSHIDA GMBH v. INDUSTRIE-UND HANDELSKAMMER KASSEL (No. 114/78) [1979] E.C.R. 151, European Ct.

1148.

The College van Beroep voor het Bedrijfsleven at The Hague referred several questions to the European Court on the interpretation and validity of Reg. 2067/77 concerning the origin of slide fasteners. *Held,* the adoption of this Regulation by the Commission was made in excess of the Commission's powers granted under Reg. 802/68 and thus was invalid.

YOSHIDA NEDERLAND B.V. v. KAMER VAN KOOPHANDEL EN FABRIEKEN VOOR FRIESLAND (No. 34/78) [1979] E.C.R. 115, European Ct.

1149. Enforcement of judgments—Convention—interpretation

The European Court considered several questions for a preliminary ruling under the Protocol of June 3, 1971, on the interpretation of by the Court of Justice of the Convention of September 27, 1968, on Jurisdiction and the Enforcement of Judgments in Civil and Commercial Matters. The reference was made by the Oberlandesgericht and Saarbrücken. *Held,* the 1968 Convention, must be interpreted with regard to its objectives and relationship to the Treaty and so as to ensure that the Convention is fully effective in achieving its objects. The concepts in art. 5 (5) of this Convention must be given an independent interpretation that is common to all contracting states. The concept of "operations" includes actions relating to rights and contractual or non-contractual obligations concerning the management of the agency, branch or other establishment.

SOMAFER S.A. v. SAAR-FERNGAS A.G. (No. 33/78) [1978] E.C.R. 2183, European Ct.

1150. European Assembly—constituencies. See § 824.

1151. European Assembly (Pay and Pensions) Act 1979 (c. 50)

This Act provides for the payment of salaries and pensions, allowances and facilities, to Representatives to the European Assembly.

S. 1 provides for salaries to be paid to Representatives; s. 2 empowers the Secretary of State to make provision regarding allowances and facilities; s. 3 relates to grants to Representatives who lose their seats; s. 4 deals with pensions; s. 5 sets out the method of calculating pension benefits; s. 6 provides for the payment of block transfer value into another pension scheme; s. 7 deals with expenses and receipts; s. 8 contains definitions; s. 9 gives the short title. The Act extends to Northern Ireland.

The Act received the Royal Assent on July 26, 1979, and came into force on that date.

1152. European Communities (Greek Accession) Act 1979 (c. 57)

This Act provides for the accession of the Hellenic Republic to the European Communities.

S. 1 extends the meaning of " the Treaties " and " the Community Treaties " to include the Hellenic Republic; s. 2 contains the short title.

The Act received the Royal Assent on December 20, 1979, and came into force on that date.

1153. European Court—action for damages—references to

The European Court considered several questions referred to it by the Beroep voor het Bedrijfsloven for a preliminary ruling under art. 177 EEC on the interpretation of arts. 177 and 215 (2). The case concerned an allegation of loss suffered by a Dutch importer of animal foodstuffs following the introduction of a system under Reg. 563/76 for " protein certificates," a system later found to be invalid. *Held,* until a court of competent jurisdiction has declared community legislation invalid it is presumed valid. Art. 215 (2) proceedings cannot be determined during art. 177 proceedings. The first of the cases are solely within the jurisdiction of the European Court where damage is alleged to be caused by the Community. Where national agencies are alleged to be to blame the appropriate forum is the national court.

GRANARIA B.V. *v.* HOOFDPRODUKTSCHAP VOOR AKKERBOUWPRODUKTEN (No. 101/78) [1979] 3 C.M.L.R. 124, European Ct.

1154. —— contracts—termination of contract

The European Court considered several questions referred to it by the Amtsgericht at Essen, under art. 177 EEC concerning the interpretation of arts. 177 and 237 EEC. The case involved a contract which allowed for its termination if the European Court ruled that the accession to the EEC of Spain and Portugal were not practicable in law. *Held,* contracts cannot impede the division of powers between the European Court of Justice and the national courts. A clause making a contract terminable upon a ruling of the European Court might be void because it appeared to circumvent this division of powers.

LOTHAR MATTHEUS *v.* DOEGO FRUCHTIMPORT UND TIEFKUHLKOST EG (No. 93/78) [1979] 1 C.M.L.R. 551, European Ct.

1155. —— reference—adequate information

The European Court considered several questions referred to it under art. 177 EEC for a preliminary ruling, by the Pretore of Reggio Emilia. The case concerned the Italian levy on sugar held in store. The Italian court supplied few facts to the European Court. *Held,* where questions refer to matters on which the Court has previously ruled and where there are no facts to raise new issues the Court will merely refer to and repeat its earlier ruling. (*Rey Soda* v. *Cassa Conguaglio Zucchero* [1976] C.L.Y. 1029, *Ditta Frattelli Cucchi* v. *Avez* [1978] C.L.Y. 1260 referred to). Where the national court gives inadequate material information for the European Court to focus its answer, the Court will refuse to reply.

I.C.A.P. DISTRIBUTION S.R.L. *v.* BENEVENTI (FEDERGROSSISTI INTERVENING) (No. 222/78) [1979] C.M.L.R. 475, European Ct.

1156. European Court arbitration—transport tariffs

The E.C. Commission considered the adjustment of tariff schedules for the carriage of goods by road between Germany, the Netherlands and Belgium. It decided that under an arbitration clause in art. 4 (2) (*b*) of Reg. 1174/68 EEC (now art. 13 of Reg. 2831/77) the base rates should be increased by 15 per cent. to enable the proper management of this service.

Re CARRIAGE OF GOODS BY ROAD; GERMANY *v.* BELGIUM AND THE NETHERLANDS [1979] 1 C.M.L.R. 597, E.C. Commission.

1157. European Court references—agriculture—common organisation—equality

The European Court considered a reference under art. 177 EEC from the High Court of Justice, Queen's Bench Division (Commercial Court) for a preliminary ruling on the interpretation and validity of Regs. 2472/75, 1862/76, 2158/76, 1110/77 and 1111/77 EEC. The case concerned the common organisation of the market in cereals. A number of actions were commenced against the Intervention Board for Agricultural Produce maintaining that the U.K.

Government was not entitled to implement various of these Regulations. *Held*, where the wording of the court's reference under art. 177 is short and uninformative the European Court may reply on the basis of the parties' submissions. If the preamble to a regulation is unhelpful the purpose of the regulation may be found by looking at the series of rules of which it is part. The general principle of equality is fundamental to Community law. The Council may in certain circumstances delegate legislation to itself. This is so where it has power to make legislation under art. 43 (2) EEC and has followed certain procedure. Where Community tax is levied on one product but not on a similar product this is discriminatory treatment under art. 40 (3) EEC unless it is justified by taking an over-all regard to all the economic circumstances. Practical difficulties in implementing the principle of equality do not justify unequal treatment. It is not a misuse of power when fixing subsidies for a product for the Council or Commission to take into account the effects of these on other products.

ROYAL SCHOLTEN-HONIG (HOLDINGS) *v.* INTERVENTION BOARD FOR AGRI-CULTURAL PRODUCE (Nos. 103/77, 145/77, and 125/77) [1979] 1 C.M.L.R. 675, European Ct.

1158. Euratom—convention—Member States—jurisdiction

The European Court considered the draft Convention on the Physical Protection of Nuclear Materials, Facilities and Transport negotiated with the International Atomic Energy Agency. The application was made under art. 103 of Euratom Treaty and concerned the jurisdiction of Euratom and Member States as regards this Convention. *Held,* some of the matters covered in this Convention were within the jurisdiction of the Member States and some matters were within that of Euratom. Art. 195 of Euratom does not deal with the relation between the power of the Community and the Member States. It does not limit the Community's power to take action to ensure safety for the materials or installations. The Community has the power to enter into international Conventions covering such matters when participation by Member States alone would hinder the functioning of the Euratom Treaty.

Re THE DRAFT CONVENTION ON THE PHYSICAL PROTECTION OF NUCLEAR MATERIALS, FACILITIES AND TRANSPORT [1979] 1 C.M.L.R. 131, European Ct.

1159. Exports—customs duties—charges having equivalent effect

The Copenhagen City Court referred to the European Court of Justice four questions for a preliminary ruling under art. 177 EEC on the interpretation of the concepts of charge having an effect equivalent to a customs duty on exports within the meaning of art. 16 EEC and of internal taxation within the meaning of art. 95 (1) EEC, having regard to the Danish legislation on the control of articles of precious metal. Two Danish goldsmiths asserted that the Statens Kontrol med Aedle Metaller (National Authority for the Control of Precious Metals) had acted contrary to the EEC Treaty in levying a charge on them to cover expenses connected with the supervision of undertakings which manufacture, import or deal in precious metals. *Held*, (1) with regard to the interpretation of art. 16 EEC, a charge which is imposed on undertakings manufacturing, importing or dealing in articles of precious metal to meet the costs of supervising such undertakings and which is calculated on the basis of the undertakings' consumption of precious metals is not in the nature of a customs duty on exports. This is so, provided the charge applies in accordance with the same criteria to all undertakings which are subject to such supervision, whatever the origin or destination of the products; (2) with regard to the interpretation of art. 95 EEC, a system of internal taxation, including a system intended to finance the supervision of the production and marketing of articles of precious metal, must be applied without discrimination, without regard to the origin or destination of the products. The Court noted that the EEC Treaty did not prohibit the following situation of double taxation occurring, *viz.* an article of precious metal could be manufactured by an undertaking in one Member State and be included in calculating the charge for supervision payable by that undertaking; then the article could be exported to another Member State which could levy a further charge in respect of its system of control or supervision.

STATENS KONTROL MED AEDLE METALLER *v.* LARSEN; KJERULFF *v.* STATENS KONTROL MED AEDLE METALLER (No. 142/77) [1979] 2 C.M.L.R. 680, European Ct.

1160. —— licences—change of rules—damages

The European Court considered an action for damages under art. 215 EEC for loss suffered by a number of malt exporters when the terms of their barley export operations under licence were changed by the Commission. *Held*, advance fixing of export subsidies for malt and barley are wholly different from advance payment of subsidies under Reg. 441/69. If the rules of the latter are changed this cannot give rise to a cause of action for damages for loss of expectation of profit. Exporters could not rely on existing rules to continue, especially not in the crisis situation caused by massive Russian purchases and remedial action by the Commission did not make it liable under art. 215 EEC to pay damages.

GROUPEMENT D'INTERET ECONOMIQUE UNION MALT *v.* E.C. COMMISSION (Nos. 44–51/77) [1978] 3 C.M.L.R. 702, European Ct.

1161. —— restrictions—plant breeders' rights

The E.C. Commission issued a statement concerning the head licensee for a number of U.K. cereal seed breeders following the latter's agreement to lift restrictions on export from the U.K. to France of certain seeds. In this statement the Commission stated that plant breeders' rights may not be used prima facie to prevent genuine seed being exported between Member States.

Re THE PLANT ROYALTY BUREAU [1979] 3 C.M.L.R. 42, E.C. Commission.

1162. Foreign trade—protective measures—notification

The Corte di Cassazione referred several questions to the European Court for preliminary ruling under art. 177 EEC. The case concerned the import of Japanese tape recorders into Italy from Belgium. The Court interpreted art. 115 EEC and Council Directive 66/532. *Held*, the EEC customs union, which was established on July 1, 1968, did not affect the duration of the transitional period in art. 8 EEC. Although art. 115 (2) EEC obliges Member States to notify urgent protective measures against foreign imports to the Commission and to other Member States, failure to notify does not invalidate those measures.

AMMINISTRAZIONE DELLE FINANZE DELLO STATO *v.* DITTA RASHAM (No. 27/78) [1979] 1 C.M.L.R. 1, European Ct.

1163. Free movement of services—national rules—judgments

The Cour d'Appel de Mons considered the case of a French construction company that was building in Belgium and using workers employed by them in France. The workers included a number of persons who were not nationals of Member States. This infringed Belgian law but not French law. *Held*, in accordance with art. 60 (3) EEC, which provides that national rules should apply to the person who supplies services, the law of the *situs*, in this case Belgian law, applies so that the supplier of services was open to prosecution there. The Brussels Convention on Enforcement of Judgments does not apply in such a case.

Re TRANSNATIONAL CONSTRUCTION WORKERS [1979] 1 C.M.L.R. 217, Cour d'Appel, Mons.

1164. Freedom of movement—car licences—European Court

The European Court considered several questions referred to it by the Amtsgericht at Reutlingen concerning the interpretation under art. 177 EEC of arts. 48, 52, 59 EEC. The case involved a French national who was convicted in a German court for not having a German driving licence although he had a valid French licence. He had become resident in Germany. *Held*, although there is no community law on this matter, if a case involves one of four freedoms then the European Court will hear references under art. 177 EEC. This requirement for a licence may amount to an indirect restriction on the freedom of movement of labour, and incompatible with the above articles.

Re CHOQUET (No. 16/78) [1979] 1 C.M.L.R. 535, European Ct.

1165. —— restrictions within a Member State's own territory
[EEC Treaty, art. 48.]
Art. 48 of the EEC Treaty does not restrict the power of a Member State to restrict freedom of movement of persons subject to its jurisdiction within its own territory in implementation of domestic criminal law.

D, who was a citizen of the U.K., pleaded guilty to theft in the Crown Court. She was bound over on her own recognisance to go to Northern Ireland and not to enter England or Wales for three years. She was found in Wales. The prosecution queried whether the order infringed art. 48 of the EEC Treaty giving workers the right of free movement within the Community. The Crown Court referred the question to the European Court. *Held,* the rules for the freedom of movement of workers did not affect a wholly domestic situation. They were intended to place a worker of one Member State in the same situation as nationals of the state laying down restrictions, not to restrict a Member State's power to lay down restrictions in its own territory on persons subject to its jurisdiction in the implementation of its domestic criminal law.

R. *v.* SAUNDERS [1979] 2 All E.R. 267, European Ct.

1166. —— right of establishment—veterinary medicine
The European Court considered several questions referred to it under art. 177 for a preliminary ruling on the interpretation of art. 52 EEC. The case concerned an Austrian national who qualified in veterinary medicine in Italy, became a naturalised French citizen but was refused permission to practise in France on the ground that his Italian qualifications did not comply with French requirements. Until the expiry of the implementation period for the Veterinary Medicine Directives 1978 (78/1026 and 78–27) nationals cannot enjoy, because of art. 52 EEC, a complete freedom of establishment but must comply with national rules.

MINISTERE PUBLIC *v.* AUER (No. 136/78) [1979] 2 C.M.L.R. 373, European Ct.

1167. —— self employed—nationality
The European Court considered several questions referred to it by the College van Beroep voor het Bedrijfsleven for a preliminary ruling under art. 177 EEC. The case involved a Dutch plumber who traded in Belgium for seven years. He applied to have a permit to trade in the Netherlands even though he had inadequate qualifications for a Dutch permit. *Held,* in considering Directive 64/427 which sets out rules for the right of movement for self-employed persons, the requirement in this Directive that a Member State should recognise the practice of a trade for a certain period in another Member State as sufficient qualification to practise in another Member State applied to a national of the Netherlands (the host state) who traded in Belgium, (a foreign Member State), and who wished to return home and trade there.

KNOORS *v.* SECRETARY OF STATE FOR ECONOMIC AFFAIRS (No. 115/78) [1979] 2 C.M.L.R. 357, European Ct.

1168. Full Faith and Credit Convention—civil and commercial matters—bankruptcy excluded
The European Court considered a question referred to it by the order of the Bundesgerichtshof under the Protocol to the Full Faith and Credit Convention 1968. The question asked for a preliminary ruling on the interpretation of art. 1, para. 2 (2) of the Convention which stated, *inter alia,* that the Convention should not apply to bankruptcy proceedings relating to the winding-up of insolvent companies. *Held,* the concept of "civil and commercial matters" to which this Convention applies can only be fully understood in the light of the Convention's objectives and the general principles embodied in the national legal systems. An order of a national court, here the Cour d'Appel, Paris, under a provision of the French bankruptcy law ordering a manager of a company to pay certain assets to the company, were excluded from this Convention under art. 1 (2) (11). Following this decision, the case was referred back to the Bundesgerichtshof, who *held* that it was binding upon them to find the Full Faith and Credit Convention inapplicable and that national law for enforcement of judgments could not in such circumstances be used.

GOURDAIN *v.* NADLER (No. 133/78) [1979] 3 C.M.L.R. 180 and 202, European Ct. and Bundesgerichtshof.

1169. —— split jurisdiction

The European Court considered several questions referred to it by the Bundesgerichtshof under the Protocol to the Full Faith and Credit Convention. The case concerned a dispute over a contract between a German firm and a French firm which contained a clause conferring jurisdiction on the national courts of the defendant in any action. There was a claim by the French party and a counterclaim by the German party. *Held*, art. 17 (1) of this Convention allows a contract to provide for a split jurisdiction. In these circumstances it is for the national court to decide if it can hear both claim and counterclaim.

MEETH *v.* GLACETAL S.A.R.L. (No. 23/78) [1979] C.M.L.R. 520, European Ct.

1170. Human rights—court—procedure

The European Court of Human Rights considered an application on behalf of an Irish national, The Irish Government raised various preliminary objections and questions of procedure. *Held*, the Court had no power to determine the Rules of Procedure of the Human Rights Commission. The Commission was entitled to send its Report to the applicant, telling him it must not be published. The Court should know of the applicant's views, in the Commission Report, the observations of the Commission delegates and the applicant himself. The merits of the case must be examined before any decision could be made in the case.

LAWLESS *v.* IRELAND (No. 1) (1960) 1 E.H.R.R. 1, European Ct. of Human Rights.

1171. Following the preliminary procedural questions in *Lawless* v. *Ireland* (*No.* 1) [1979] C.L.Y. 1170, the Principal Delegate of the Commission of Human Rights asked the Court to include in their considerations the applicant's observations set out in the Commissions reports, to make known the applicant's views and to consider a person proposed by the applicant to give assistance. *Held*, the Court was free to use whatever means it felt right to contact the applicant.

LAWLESS *v.* IRELAND (No. 2) (1961) 1 E.H.R.R. 13, European Ct. of Human Rights.

1172. —— imprisonment without trial—emergency laws

In *Lawless* v. *Ireland* (*No.* 2) [1979] C.L.Y. 1171 above, the Court of Human Rights considered the merits of the application involving the fact that the applicant was detained without trial for five months in prison under the Irish Offences against the State Act. He claimed violation of his right of liberty (art. 5 Human Rights Convention), violation of the rule against retro-active criminal law or punishment (art. 6) and infringement of his right to a fair trial (art. 7). *Held*, although art. 17 was intended to deprive extremists of the advantages of the Convention, this did not exclude a person from his fundamental Convention rights. As no criminal charge was made art. 6 was irrelevant. Art. 5 could not be excluded by use of art. 5 (1) (*c*). It was a fundamental right that persons must be tried within a reasonable time. Art. 7 had no bearing on the case. The Court held that a public emergency entitled measures derogating from fundamental Convention obligations (art. 15). As the ordinary law was unable to cope with the national situation in question, the emergency law was justified in this case (art. 15). In the circumstances there was no breach of the Convention.

LAWLESS *v.* IRELAND (No. 3) (1961) 1 E.H.R.R. 15, European Ct. of Human Rights.

1173. —— inhuman and degrading treatment—birching

The Court of Human Rights considered the case of a juvenile (15) who was birched by order of a juvenile Court in the Isle of Man. The complaint was that this action infringed art. 3 of the Human Rights Convention, a provision against torture or inhuman treatment. This was sought to be withdrawn. *Held*, the withdrawal could not be made in the circumstances except that it made unnecessary an award of damages (art. 50). Thus punishment did not constitute torture or inhuman treatment. Excessive humiliation would have involved a breach of art. 3. This could not have been excused because it was an effective deterrent, or because there was an absence of publicity. Judicial corporal punishment did constitute an assault on a person's dignity and physical integrity, involved mental anguish, was aggravated by the fact it was performed on a bare posterior and was a humiliation sufficient to infringe art. 3. It was not excused because it was for an act of violence. Art. 63 (3), designed to cover certain colonial territories did not exclude the Isle of Man from the application of the Convention.

TYRER *v.* UNITED KINGDOM (1978) 2 E.H.R.R. 1, European Ct. of Human Rights.

1174. —— jurisdiction

The Confédération Française Démocratique du Travail (C.F.D.T.) alleged violations of arts. 11, 13 and 14 of the European Convention on Human Rights in that it was not designated as a member of the Consultative Committee of the ECSC despite being the second largest representative organisation in the relevant sector in France. Designation to the Committee is made by the Governments of the Member States and adopted by the E.C. Council. France did not designate the C.F.D.T. but did designate other organisations. The Council adopted the other organisations. C.F.D.T. argued that, in so doing, the Council had not acted in accordance with art. 18, ECSC. *Held*, the Commission dismissed the complaints as inadmissible. The Commission had no jurisdiction *ratione personae* to examine the complaint against the European Communities as such, since the European Communities were not a Contracting Party to the Convention; the Commission had no jurisdiction *ratione personae* to examine the complaint against "the Member-States" taken together as it was really aimed at the E.C. Council. Further, the Commission considered that the question mould arise as to whether the contested act, performed by the E.C. Council, was capable of involving the liability of the E.C. Member States individually under the Convention. It stated that whatever was the answer to that question, it did not have jurisdiction *ratione personae* with regard to France as France had not recognised the right of individual petition under art. 25 of the Convention. With regard to the other Member States, the Commission had no jurisdiction *ratione personae* as those States had not, by their participation in the decisions of the E.C. Council, exercised their "jurisdiction" within the meaning of art. 1 of the Convention.

CONFEDERATION FRANÇAISE DEMOCRATIQUE DU TRAVAIL *v.* THE EUROPEAN COMMUNITIES, THE MEMBER STATES OF THE EUROPEAN COMMUNITIES COLLECTIVELY AND THE MEMBER STATES OF THE EUROPEAN COMMUNITIES INDIVIDUALLY (No. 8030/77) [1979] 2 C.M.L.R. 229, European Commission of Human Rights.

1175. —— Northern Ireland—torture—emergency detention

Ireland alleged that the United Kingdom's detention of I.R.A. suspects involving detaining of prisoners and their treatment; wall-standing, hooding and deprivation of sleep and food infringed art. 3 of the Convention of Human Rights, as torture, and also art. 5 and was not excused by art. 15 as an emergency, was discriminatory under art. 14 because it singled out one group, the I.R.A. The Commission of Human Rights supported the allegations of breaches of the Human Rights Convention. The court regretted the British Government's failure to assist the commission in breach of art. 28 and *held,* that detention without trial did infringe art. 5 (1)–(4) but was permitted because of the public emergency (art. 15) and that there was no discrimination under art. 14. The five interrogation techniques did constitute an infringement of art. 3 as a form of inhuman or degrading treatment.

REPUBLIC OF IRELAND *v.* UNITED KINGDOM (1978) 2 E.H.R.R. 25, European Ct. of Human Rights.

1176. —— right to vote—European Parliament

The European Commission of Human Rights considered an allegation that the restriction of sufferage in the European Parliamentary elections to Belgians resident in Belgium was an infringement by Belgium of art. 3 of Protocol 1 of the European Convention on Human Rights. *Held*, as in *Re an Expatriate United Kingdom Citizen* [1979] C.L.Y. 1177, this was not an infringement.

ALLIANCE DES BELGES DE LA COMMUNAUTÉ EUROPÉENNE *v.* BELGIUM (No. 8612/79) [1979] 3 C.M.L.R. 175, European Commission of Human Rights.

1177. The European Commission of Human Rights considered the allegation of denial of franchise to United Kingdom nationals not residents in the United Kingdom. *Held*, this restriction of sufferage is not an infringement of art. 3 of Protocol 1 of the European Convention on Human Rights.

Re AN EXPATRIATE UNITED KINGDOM CITIZEN (No. 8611/79) [1979] 3 C.M.L.R. 172, European Commission of Human Rights.

1178. The European Commission of Human Rights considered the introduction of simple majority system of voting for the United Kingdom, excluding Northern Ireland, for the European Elections. *Held,* neither the Northern Ireland system, the single transferable vote nor the simple majority system infringed art. 5 of Protocol 1 of the European Convention on Human Rights nor was it discrimination under art. 14 of the Convention. The voting system must ensure the free expression of opinion of people.

LINDSAY *v.* UNITED KINGDOM (No. 8364/78) [1979] 3 C.M.L.R. 167, European Commission of Human Rights.

1179. Imports—health charges—ex parte proceedings—reference to European Court
The European Court considered several questions referred to it by the Pretura, Alessandria for a preliminary ruling under art. 177 EEC. The case concerned the importation of frozen beef into Italy from Uruguay which was subject to a health inspection by the Italian authorities. The Court interpreted arts. 12 of Reg. 14/64, 20 of Reg. 805/68, 9 of Dir. 64/433, 6 of Dir. 77/98 and 8, 12, 16, 23, 26 and 33 of Dir. 72/462. *Held*, in the circumstances these health charges had the effect that they were equivalent to customs duties and were prohibited under Reg. 805/68. Dir. 72/462 provided a general exception but had not yet come into effect because of failure to implement this Directive. However as the failure to permit these inspections would be a discrimination against Community traders under Dir. 64/433 they would be allowed. The European Court will not consider the motive behind a reference to it. It may however be in the best interests of the administration of justice if a reference does .not take place until both sides have been heard and not after an *ex parte* application.

SIMMENTHAL SpA *v.* AMMINISTRAZIONE DELLE FINANZE DELLO STATO (No. 3) (No. 70/77) [1978] 3 C.M.L.R. 670, European Ct.

1180. —— **pornographic materials—public policy**
The House of Lords referred several questions to the European Court under art. 177 (3) EEC in a case concerning the import restrictions on pornographic materials. *Held*, seven questions would be asked as to whether such restrictions infringed arts. 30 and/or 36 EEC. *Inter alia*, it was asked in particular if such import restrictions could be justified on grounds of public morality or public policy or under the Geneva Convention 1923 and the Universal Postal Convention 1974 bearing in mind art. 234 of the treaty.

R. *v.* HENN AND DARBY [1979] 2 C.M.L.R. 495, H.L.

1181. —— **quality designation—restrictions on trade**
The European Court considered several questions referred to it by the Verwaltungsgericht at Bremen under art. 177 EEC. The case concerned the interpretation of arts. 30 and 36 EEC involving quality designations on certain alcoholic drinks. *Held*, only where measures are likely to hinder imports between Member States, directly or indirectly, actually or potentially, are they prohibited by art. 30. Quality designation must depend on intrinsic characteristics that are also objective and cannot depend on geographical locality. The provisions of art. 36 do not cover a restriction imposed on trade, which is attached to the right to use a national quality designation.

FIRMA JOH. EGGERS SOHN & CO. *v.* FREIE HANSESTADT BREMEN (No. 13/78) [1979] 1 C.M.L.R. 562, European Ct.

1182. —— **transitional provisions—national law**
The European Court considered several questions referred to it by the High Court (Commercial Division) under art. 177 EEC, concerning the interpretation of art. 60 (2) of the Act of Accession. The case involved the refusal by the United Kingdom Government to abolish a quantitative restriction at the end of the " transitional period." *Held*, this article in the Act of Accession ceases

to have any effect after December 31, 1977. The power to ban potatoes from being imported from the Netherlands had been lawful under this article.

C. J. MEIJER B.V. *v.* DEPARTMENT OF TRADE, MINISTRY OF AGRICULTURE, FISHERIES AND FOOD AND COMMISSIONERS OF CUSTOMS AND EXCISE (No. 118/78) [1979] 2 C.M.L.R. 398, European Ct.

1183. Inter state trade—customs declaration—restrictions

The European Court considered several questions referred to it under art. 177 EEC for a preliminary ruling on the interpretation of art. 115 EEC. The case concerned the import of Spanish grapes into France from Italy. These grapes came into France accompanied by a certificate that they were of Italian origin. *Held,* that as France had not followed the procedure under art. 115 EEC the inaccuracy of the customs certificate should not attract criminal penalties under the French Customs Code. As art. 115 EEC had not been fulfilled imports from non-Member States could not be prevented from free circulation, after gaining access to the Common Market through a Member State.

PROCUREUR DE LA REPUBLIQUE (ADMINISTRATION DES DOUANES FRANÇAISES INTERVENING) *v.* MICHELANGELO, RIVOIRA AND GIOVANNI RIVOIRA & FIGLI S.N.C. (No. 179/78) [1979] 3 C.M.L.R. 456, European Ct.

1184. Interlocutory order—suspension of regulation—customs charges

The European Court heard an interlocutory application for the suspension of art. 3 of Reg. 1778/77 (EEC) until final judgment in this case in respect of the plaintiff companies and in particular that it need not pay certain sums of money to the customs authorities in Britain, France and Germany. *Held,* allowing the suspension requested, that the applicants substantiated their case that there was urgency and on factual and legal grounds that there was a prima facie case for suspension. It was not established conclusively that if successful in the action that the applicants could recoup charges payable to these customs authorities.

NIPPON SEIKO K.K. *v.* E.C. COUNCIL AND COMMISSION (No. 119/77R) [1977] E.C.R. 1867, European Ct.

1185. International trade—EEC countries—discrimination

The Finanzgericht at Hamburg referred several questions to the European Court under art. 177 EEC on the interpretation of arts. 227 and 95 EEC and a preliminary ruling was given. The case concerned the application of monopoly equalisation duty to imports from a French overseas department, an associated EEC territory and a foreign country now a Lomé Convention country. *Held,* Guadeloupe, as a French overseas department, should not suffer discriminatory treatment against her exports. Unless there is an international treaty which prevents preferential treatment or discrimination, it is not illegal for Member States to discriminate against imports from non-Member States.

H. HANSEN JUN. & O. C. BALLE GmbH & Co. *v.* HAUPTZOLLAMT FLENSBURG (No. 148/77) [1979] 1 C.M.L.R. 604, European Ct.

1186. Migrant workers—social security benefits. See GIULIANI *v.* LANDESVERSICHERUNG-SANSTALT SCHWABEN, § 1245.

1187. Municipal law—communicating business secrets to the EEC Commission

The appellant was an employee of F. Hoffman-La Roche & Co. A.G. Basle (" Roche ") who informed the E.C. Commission of the contents of several of Roche's documents. He appealed against his conviction in Switzerland of making available business secrets to a foreign public body contrary to the Swiss Criminal Code. The appellant argued, *inter alia,* that Roche's conduct was incompatible with the Free Trade Agreement (" FTA ") between the EEC and Switzerland. The Swiss Supreme Court dismissed the appeal, and *held,* that the FTA excluded any obligation to harmonise the laws of the EEC and Switzerland; it merely set out those practices which were incompatible with the FTA, but did not prohibit them or declare them illegal or void (*cf.* arts. 85 & 86 EEC). The FTA did not create any right of action for private individuals in the Swiss courts, nor did it provide a defence to private individuals, charged with contravening the Swiss Criminal Code on unlawfully communicating business secrets, to assert that the principles in the FTA concerning competition had been infringed.

ADAMS *v.* STAATSANWALTSCHAFT DES KANTONS BASEL-STADT [1978] 3 C.M.L.R. 480, Swiss Supreme Ct.

1188. National Courts—references to the European Court of Justice—company law

The Gooiland Chamber of Commerce appealed against Kantonrechter Magistrate of Hilversum's refusal to amend an entry in the Trade Register kept by the Chamber. The Chamber wished the entry in the case of Cetra Nederland N to state that for a particular period E. Ponten was alone authorised to represent the company *vis-à-vis* third parties. *Held,* the appeal would be dismissed for various reasons. The court stated that the aim and scope of the First EEC Council Directive on Companies of March 9, 1968, operated against the assumption that a "single person" as envisaged in art. 9/3/ of the EEC Directive could be a legal person, *i.e.* a private or public limited company. The court refused to ask for a preliminary ruling from the European Court of Justice as such a ruling on the interpretation of art. 9/3/ of the EEC Directive and other provisions could not, in the sense desired by the Chamber of Commerce, result in the appeal directed at quashing the judgment being judged to be well founded.

KAMER VAN KOOPHANDEL EN FABRIEKEN VOOR GOOILAND *v.* CETRA NEDERLAND N.V. [1979] 2 C.M.L.R. 189, Hoge Raad, Netherlands.

1189. National legislation—television—advertising

The Tribunal Correctionel, Liège, considered a prosecution on several Belgian cable television rediffusion companies. The offence alleged under Belgian law was that these companies had retransmitted the advertising material contained in the broadcasts, from neighbouring countries. Belgian law makes it illegal to broadcast advertisements on television. *Held,* a question would be referred to the European Court under art. 177 EEC for a preliminary ruling whether art. 59 EEC prohibits a Member State from passing laws to prevent advertising by cable television in such circumstances.

PROCUREUR DU ROI *v.* DEBAUVE [1979] 2 C.M.L.R. 592, Tribunal Correctionel, Liège.

1190. National rules—criminal record— E.C. Transport Directive

The European Court considered several questions referred to it under art. 177 EEC for a preliminary ruling from the Copenhagen Byrett (City Court). The case involved the interpretation of arts. 2, 4 and 5 of Directive 74/562 concerning the refusal of the Danish road passenger authority to renew the operator's licence of the plaintiff in the action because of his criminal record. *Held,* the directive was valid but that it did not prevent Member States refusing to renew such a licence when the operator was no longer a person of good character. This was so despite art. 4 of this Directive which prohibits a national transport authority from requiring an existing transport operator to furnish proof of his good repute.

DELKVIST *v.* ANKLAGEMYNDIGHEDEN, *ex p.* LANDSNAEVNET FOR OMNIBUSKORSEL (No. 21/78) [1979] 1 C.M.L.R. 372, European Ct.

1191. Officials—appointment—qualifications

An official of the E.C. Commission applied to the European Court to annul a decision appointing another man to the post for which the applicant had also been a candidate. *Held,* it is for the appointing authority, in this case the Commission, to decide if professional experience may be taken as an equivalent to a university degree.

MULCAHY *v.* E.C. COMMISSION (No. 110/77) [1978] E.C.R. 1287, European Ct.

1192. —— candidate competition—refusal on health grounds—rights of candidate

A candidate for an Open Staff Competition held by the E.C. Commission applied to the European Court for the annulment of an implied decision by the Commission rejecting a complaint by the applicant concerning a medical report on him. *Held,* where a candidate is refused employment on medical grounds, that is a decision adversely affecting him within art. 25 of the Staff Regulations and the reason must be stated. However this must be reconciled with professional secrecy. In such a case the administrative body must allow the individual affected to have an opportunity to express his point of view. The court has no jurisdiction to declare that its decision is equivalent to making an appointment.

MOLI *v.* E.C. COMMISSION (No. 121/76) [1977] E.C.R. 1971, European Ct.

1193. —— **competition—advisory examiners—reasons for decision**
The European Court considered an application for the annulment of the refusal of the selection board for a staff competition to admit the applicants to the competition. *Held,* if a complaint is made through an official channel to the appointing authority of a selection board, this is outside the scope of the Staff Regulations but cannot preclude the person concerned also making an application to the court. Art. 3, para. 2 of Annex III of these Regulations does not preclude a selection board seeking the help of advisory examiners provided it does not surrender its ultimate control over proceedings. The board must give reasons for refusing applications. The bald statement that an applicant does not fulfil a condition for admission is an inadequate reason as it does not enable the candidate to know if the refusal was well founded.

SALERNO, AUTHIÉ AND MASSANGIOLI *v.* E.C. COMMISSION (NOS. 4, 19 and 28/78) [1978] E.C.R. 2403, European Ct.

1194. —— **installation allowance**
The European Court considered an application by an official of the E.C. Commission for an annulment of certain decisions of the Commission refusing an installation allowance. *Held,* the competent employing authority has the power to take into account, and to enable an official to overcome, personal difficulties. The installation allowance is to enable an official to pay both removal expenses and the cost of integration in a new environment.

VERHAAF *v.* E.C. COMMISSION (No. 140/77) [1979] E.C.R. 2117, European Ct.

1195. ——**probationary employment—termination**
The European Court considered an application of a former probationary official of the E.C. Commission, requesting an annulment of implied and express decisions of the Commission concerning his dismissal and his probationary employment. *Held,* art. 32 (2), sub-para. (1), does not specify a time in which a decision to terminate an employment at the end of a probationary period must be adopted. The employing authority must adopt the decision within a reasonable period, running from the date of the report at the end of the probationary period.

D'AURIA *v.* E.C. COMMISSION (No. 99/77) [1978] E.C.R. 1267, European Ct.

1196. —— **promotion**
The applicant sought the annulment of vacancy Notice No. COM/267/76 relating to a post in Grade B1 assigned to the Delegation of the Commission in Washington, of the decisions not to accept the applicant's application for that post and to appoint another candidate to it, and of the implied decision rejecting the applicant's complaint. The applicant argued that the contested measures contravened arts. 45 (1) & 7 (1) of the Staff Regulations and were vitiated by misuse of powers. *Held,* the application would be dismissed as unfounded. The applicant's age and seniority though greater than that of the successful candidate's should not prevail over the type of duties that the post required.

DE ROUBAIX *v.* E.C. COMMISSION (No. 25/77) [1978] E.C.R. 1081, European Ct.

1197. —— **reasons for decision—communicating decision**
The European Court considered an application by an official of the E.C. Commission for the annulment of proposals for his promotion and a decision to transfer him. *Held,* the second paragraph of art. 25 of the Staff Regulations does not set out a way of communicating a decision to an individual. It is deemed to reach him when it does so. It is deemed to adequately state the grounds on which it is based if the memorandum in support has been brought to the attention of the individual and clearly states the reasons for the decision.

DITTERICH *v.* E.C. COMMISSION (No. 86/77) [1978] E.C.R. 1855, European Ct.

1198. —— **reinstatement—compensation**

An official of the E.C. Commission applied to the European Court for either reinstatement and salary or compensation for damages for loss of employment. *Held,* dismissing the applications with costs, that following the applicant's absence on leave on personal grounds that there was doubt as to the genuineness of his desire to make himself available for the Commission, there was doubt as to what loss or damage he suffered and that he had no legal interest in seeking the annulment of a decision of the Commission reinstating him three years after he wished to be reinstated.

GIRY *v.* E.C. COMMISSION (Nos. 126/75, 34 and 92/76) [1977] E.C.R. 1937, European Ct.

1199. —— **retirement**

The applicant sought the annulment of the decision of the E.C. Commission retiring the applicant from his post as Director of Directorate A of Directorate General XVI of the Commission and not assigning the applicant to another post in his category of a comparable grade. *Held,* the decision would be annulled in so far as it decided that it was not appropriate to re-assign the applicant to another post in his category corresponding to his grade. The applicant should have been given an opportunity of defending his interests.

OSLIZLOK *v.* E.C. COMMISSION (No. 34/77) [1978] E.C.R. 1099, European Ct.

1200. —— **severance pay—weighting**

A former official of the E.C. Commission applied to the European Court for a declaration that the applicant was entitled to an increased amount of severance pay. He challenged the method of its calculation. *Held,* the Council is at liberty to raise the level of remuneration by applying a weighting to the amounts in art. 66 of the Staff Regulations providing that the pecuniary rights of officials do not become incompatible with those intended by art. 65 of these Regulations. The basic salary in art. 66 is the amount in the table therein, subject where proper to certain weighting.

JACQUEMART *v.* E.C. COMMISSION [1978] E.C.R. 1697, European Ct.

1201. Practice—non-contractual liability—regulation void

The applicants sought an order from the European Court that the EEC should compensate them for the damage which they claim to have suffered as a result of Council Reg. No. 563/76 on the compulsory purchase of skimmed-milk powder held by intervention agencies for use in feeding stuffs. The European Court had previously declared Reg. No. 563/76 null and void. *Held,* the application would be dismissed. A ruling that a legislative measure, such as the Reg. at issue, is null and void does not of itself suffice to give rise to non-contractual liability on the part of the Community under the second paragraph of art. 215 EEC in respect of damage suffered by individuals. The Community does not incur liability by reason of a legislative measure involving choices of economic policy, unless the EEC Institution concerned has manifestly and gravely disregarded the limits on the exercise of its powers, which is not the case here.

BAYERISCHE HNL VERMEHRUNGSBETRIEBE GMBH & Co. KG *v.* E.C. COUNCIL AND COMMISSION (Nos. 83 and 94/76, 4, 15 and 40/77) [1978] E.C.R. 1209, European Ct.

1202. Restrictive practices—discovery—sufficient particularity of request. See BRITISH LEYLAND MOTOR CORP. *v.* WYATT INTERPART CO., § 348.

1203. —— **distribution system—technical qualifications—wholesalers**

The European Court considered an application for the annulment of the decision of the E.C. Commission of December 15, 1975, concerning the procedure to be followed under art. 85 EEC. The case concerned a distribution system of the applicant that before this decision had been given negative clearance under art. 85 EEC. *Held,* natural or legal persons who may by virtue of art. 3 (2) (*b*) of Reg. 17 request the Commission to find an infringement of arts. 85 or 86 EEC must be regarded as directly and individually concerned under art. 173 (second paragraph) by the decision of the Commission. Shares of between 5 per cent. and 10 per cent. of a market in technical products which appear to consumers to be readily interchangeable rule out the existence of a dominant position except in exceptional circumstances. There must always be workable competition though its intensity may vary. This is so by virtue of arts. 3 and 85 EEC. If a distribution system is based on the technical qualifications of the reseller not discrimination it does not infringe art. 85 (1) for this reason. Price competition is not the only form of competition. A marketing system which involves the right of certain producers to check the technical qualifications of the appointed resellers does not necessarily restrict competition. Obligations entered into by a wholesaler that limit his freedom to provide the retail trade with supplies amount to restrictions on competition within art. 85 (1) but this is not so where a nonspecialist wholesaler is obliged to open a special department. Where the latter must achieve a certain turnover this must be appraised in the light of art. 85 (3).

METRO SB-GROSSMÄRKTE GMBH & CO. KG *v.* E.C. COMMISSION (No. 26/76) [1977] E.C.R. 1875, European Ct.

1204. —— dominant position—abuse

The European Court considered an application by a Swiss Pharmaceutical Company for an annulment of a Commission Decision made under art. 86 EEC and a fine imposed thereunder. The company, the world's largest in its field, had concluded 26 agreements with 22 undertakings involving the sale and distribution of seven groups of vitamins and the allegation that the company abused a dominant position. *Held,* parties to proceedings where penalties may be imposed have a right to be heard. In proceedings brought upon this right, a former defect whereby the Commission failed to produce facts, can be cured by production of that information. The concept of " relevant market " in the context of art. 86 implies that there can be effective competition between those products which form part of it. In this article " dominant position " refers to the economic strength of the undertaking and whether it has the economic strength to prevent competition in the relevant market and to act appreciably with disregard to competitors, customers and consumers. The importance of a large market share varies from market to market and the retention of market shares, the production of many interrelated products and the fact that the undertaking is the world's largest in its field is not necessarily indicative of a dominant position. However, *inter alia,* the relationship between the market of one undertaking and its competitors and its technological lead were relevant in indicating this position. In certain markets the market share ranged from 47 to 97 per cent. In these a dominant position was held to exist but in others, market shares from 10 to 51 per cent. did not in themselves constitute a dominant position. Lively competition may not preclude the existence of a dominant position in a market. An undertaking in a dominant position which required purchasers to obtain all or most of their goods from that undertaking abused that position within art. 86 EEC. The concept of " abuse " in this context implies that the presence of an undertaking in a dominant position weakens competition. If it takes steps to further weaken competition this constitutes an abuse of its position and in affecting trade art. 86 EEC includes indirect prejudice to consumers.

HOFFMANN-LA ROCHE & CO. A.G. *v.* E.C. COMMISSION (No. 85/76) [1979] 3 C.M.L.R. 211, European Ct.

1205. —— —— interstate trade

The European Court considered an application by a Swedish company with a British subsidiary for the annulment of a Commission Decision in respect of art. 86 proceedings or for a cancellation or reduction of the fine imposed. The case concerned the refusal by the Swedish plaintiffs and its subsidiary in the United Kingdom from supplying spare parts for the plaintiffs' machines, to another British undertaking. *Held,* although the plaintiffs were in a dominant position in the relevant market in their spare parts within the meaning of art. 86 EEC their conduct had no actual or potential effect on inter-State trade in the context of a restriction to the manufacturer or its subsidiaries of the servicing of its products; here, Hugin cash registers.

HUGIN KASSAREGISTER AB AND HUGIN CASH REGISTERS *v.* E.C. COMMISSION (No. 22/78) [1979] 3 C.M.L.R. 345, European Ct.

1206. —— —— performing rights society

The French Cour de Cassation heard an appeal in case concerning SACEM, the French performing rights society. A film company entered into contract with two composers who had joined SACEM. The latter insisted on fees in respect of world wide rights that they claimed they owned. *Held,* the question whether art. 86 EEC applies to contracts such as these concluded in Member States by parties belonging to that state but purporting to effect their execution in non-Member States was referred to the European Court for a preliminary ruling under art. 177 EEC.

GREENWICH FILMS S.A. *v.* LA SOCIÉTÉ DES AUTEURS ET COMPOSITEURS ET EDITEURS DE MUSIQUE (SACEM) AND LA SOCIÉTÉ DES EDITIONS LABRADOR [1979] 2 C.M.L.R. 535, Cour de Cassation.

1207. —— exclusive buying and selling—resale price maintenance

The E.C. Commission issued a statement on February 10, 1978, concerning cartels, exclusive buying and selling, and resale price maintenance involving a Dutch pharmaceutical association. This statement gave the Commission's decision that this association restricted competition between affiliated manufacturers, importers and dealers and completely prevented competition between. them and those who were not affiliated and thereby infringed art. 85 (1) EEC. This was so in the circumstances where the association controlled 80–90 per cent. of the pharmaceutical sales in the Netherlands. In these circumstances the resale price maintenance imposed by the association also infringed art. 85 (1) EEC.

Re THE PHARMACEUTISCHE HANDELSCONVENTIE [1978] 1 C.M.L.R. 509, E.C. Commission.

1208. —— exclusive distribution—abuse of dominant position

The E.C. Commission considered the voluntary deletion of total exclusivity clauses in distribution contracts by a French publishing distributor, following a Commission statement. The undertaking ran a chain distribution for newspapers, journals and books. It also desisted voluntarily from charging its Belgian supplier French VAT on the export price of its books. *Held,* the undertaking was in a dominant position and such clauses were an abuse of a dominant position within the meaning of art. 86 EEC. However, in view of the voluntary termination of the use of these clauses the E.C. Commission would not proceed with its action against the undertaking.

THE COMMUNITY *v.* HACHETTE AND NOUVELLES MESSAGERIES DE LA PRESSE PARISIENNE [1979] 2 C.M.L.R. 78, E.C. Commission.

1209. —— —— infringements

The Landgericht at Nuremberg-Fürth considered a case in which a manufacturer of electronic leisure equipment sought an interim injunction restraining the acquisition, sale and marketing of the plaintiff's equipment by the defendant, a wholesale retailer. It was alleged that the defendant's unauthorised sales infringed the plaintiff's exclusive EEC distribution system. *Held,* an agreement of this kind to create an exclusive distributorship is provisionally valid when it has been notified to the E.C. Commission but has not received a final answer, unless it clearly breaches a rule against restraint of competition. The exclusion of a major distributor (though not one in a dominant position) from a selective distribution system did not infringe arts. 85 or 86. Violations of an exclusive distribution system involving a breach of contract by an authorised dealer to sell or supply an unauthorised dealer can be restrained under national law.

GRUNDIG A.G. *v.* METRO-SB-GROSSMÄRKTE GMBH & CO. K.G. [1979] 2 C.M.L.R. 564, Landgericht, Nuremberg-Fürth.

1210. —— existing agreements—notification

The European Court considered several questions referred to it by the Cour d'Appel, Mons, for a preliminary ruling under art. 177 EEC. The case concerned a dispute between the grantee and the grantor of an exclusive sales concession and alleged infringement of art. 85 EEC. *Held,* an existing agreement already notified or exempted from notification between undertakings must be allowed to have its legal effect under the law of the contract in the period between its notification to the Commission in accordance with

Reg. 17 and art. 85 EEC and the time when the Commission takes its decision on the agreement.

ESTABLISSEMENTS A. DE BLOOS SPRL. *v.* BOUYER SCA (No. 59/77) [1978] 1 C.M.L.R. 511, European Ct.

1211. —— **export prohibition—third party benefits**
The E.C. Commission considered an export ban imposed by an English motor cycle company. This ban affected its dealers and was in respect of exports to Germany. *Held*, the firm's reliance on wrong legal advice, quickly corrected upon more senior and reliable advice, did not remove the serious nature of the conduct. An export ban restricts competition in the Community and infringes art. 85 (1) EEC. Further a German company, that was not party to the agreement but benefited from it, also infringed art. 85 (1). However, dealers who had to be coerced into the agreement against their interests would not be subject to proceedings by the Commission. The company was fined for this infringement of competition law.

PUTZ (M.) *v.* KAWASAKI MOTORS (U.K.); THE COMMUNITY *v.* KAWASAKI MOTOREN GMBH [1979] 1 C.M.L.R. 448, E.C. Commission.

1212. —— **guarantees—territoriality**
The E.C. Commission considered revised terms of guarantee given by a manufacturer of domestic electrical appliances which replaced an earlier guarantee which had in effect restricted service of the guarantee to the territory into which the appliance had been officially imported. *Decision*, in these circumstances supply contracts are agreements between undertakings within the meaning of art. 85 (1) EEC. Where such a guarantee would be honoured only by the subsidiary company which had imported the appliance into the territory, there was a restriction or distortion of competition in that it hindered cross-frontier trading in the appliances to the detriment of the dealers.

Re THE GUARANTEE GIVEN BY INDUSTRIE A. ZANUSSI SpA [1979] 1 C.M.L.R. 81, E.C. Commission.

1213. —— **interlocutory injunction**
A plaintiff in an action against a number of petrol wholesalers, alleged two infringements of the Restrictive Trade Practices Act 1976 and also violation of arts. 86 and 85 EEC. The plaintiff sought an interlocutory injunction to restrain certain of the defendants alleged restrictive practices from which he suffered, in particular price cutting support. *Held*, refusing the injunction, that, *inter alia*, damages could be sufficient remedy at trial.

CHELMKARM MOTORS *v.* ESSO PETROLEUM CO. [1979] 1 C.M.L.R. 73, D.C.

1214. —— **investigation—privilege in respect of documents**
The E.C. Commission considered several alleged infringements of Community competition law. The case concerned suspicion that certain zinc producers were in breach of art. 85 EEC and Reg. 17/62. *Held*, the Commissioner ordered the production and examination of legal papers written with a view to seeking or giving opinions on points of law despite the privilege claimed in respect of them.

Re AN INVESTIGATION AT A.M. & S. EUROPE [1979] 3 C.M.L.R. 376, E.C. Commission.

1215. —— **joint distribution—joint sales**
The E.C. Commission considered an agreement between 31 Italian steel undertakings which established an office to co-ordinate and allocate supply orders. It also dealt with administrative and statistical work and tried to find new sales outlets for the firm. *Decision*, this agreement was analogous to the creation of a joint selling organisation which restricted normal competition between the undertakings involved. This restriction infringed art. 65 (1) ECSC in that it involved joint selling, distribution and administration.

Re THE UFFICIO COORDINAMENTO E RIPORTIZIONE ORDINI (UCRO) [1979] 1 C.M.L.R. 302, E.C. Commission.

1216. —— **joint research and development—prohibited agreement**
The E.C. Commission considered the provisions of a joint research and development agreement between two companies, one British and one American

pharmaceutical company. *Held,* three clauses were prohibited by art. 85 (1) EEC and were not curable by art. 85 (3) EEC. These clauses included the prohibition of one Member State from the grant of licences, in respect of this Member State a profit-sharing scheme and in respect of the parties to the agreement a royalty-sharing scheme. The joint research and development envisaged therefore went beyond the scope of the Co-operation between Enterprises Notice 1968.

Re THE AGREEMENT BETWEEN BEECHAM GROUP AND PARKE DAVIS AND CO. [1979] 2 C.M.L.R. 157, E.C. Commission.

1217. —— joint sales—authorisation

The E.C. Commission considered its authorisation of a joint sales agreement by certain Belgian mining companies. The agreement concerned solid fuels. It was decided that the existing authorisation should continue as the agreements continued to comply with the requirements of art. 65 (2) ECSC.

Re THE COMPTOIR BELGE DES CHARBONS (COBECHAR) [1979] 1 C.M.L.R. 462, E.C. Commission.

1218. —— —— information exchange

The E.C. Commission considered a Dutch joint sales agency for nitrogenous fertilisers in respect of arts. 85 (1) and (3) EEC. *Held,* the question whether an agreement has an appreciable effect on competition in the EEC need not be answered where the trade involved consists simply and solely of making certain products available for agents for sale in non-member countries. The undertakings involved having a 16 per cent. share of the Community Market and 67 per cent. of the Dutch production and competitors having a smaller share. The joint sales agreement which involved the exchange and joint discussion of information infringed art. 85 (1) and no exemption would be granted under art. 85 (3) EEC.

THE COMMUNITY *v.* CENTRAL STIKSTOF VERKOOPKANTOOR NV [1979] 1 C.M.L.R. 11, E.C. Commission.

1219. —— joint venture—prohibited features

The E.C. Commission considered an agreement for joint participation in a joint venture company which would manufacture and market blackpowder, an explosive substance. Co-ordination of manufacture, research, planning and sales, the elimination of effective competition between owners of a substantial market share and the likelihood of further reduction of competition in markets where these companies made other products were features of the agreement. *Held,* this agreement infringed art. 85 (1) EEC because of the inclusion of these factors and it could not be granted exemption under art. 85 (3) EEC.

Re WANO SCHWARZPULVER GMBH [1979] 1 C.M.L.R. 403, E.C. Commission.

1220. —— —— specialisation agreement

S.A. Cockerill sought authorisation under art. 65/2/ECSC of a specialisation and joint venture agreement made with Klöckner-Werke A.G. and which related to wire rod and stainless steel. *Decision,* the agreement restricted competition but would be authorised as it provided for a substantial improvement in the production of wire rod and stainless steel sheet and plate, which could not have been accomplished to the same extent by each firm operating independently. The agreement was authorised subject to certain conditions; that the firms were not to co-ordinate their distribution activities; that the firms would report to the Commission every two years and that the Commission's approval would be sought to any additions or amendments to the agreement.

Re THE APPLICATION BY SA COCKERILL-OUGRÉE-PROVIDENCE ET ESPERANCE-LONGDOZ (No.1) [1979] 2 C.M.L.R. 236, E.C. Commission.

1221. SA Cockerill sought authorisation under art. 65/2/ECSC of a specialisation and joint venture agreement made with Estel NV and which related to wire rod. *Decision,* the agreement restricted competition but would be authorised subject to similar conditions as those laid down in the E.C. Commission decision with regard to the specialisation agreement between Cockerill and Klöckner-Werke A.G.

Re THE APPLICATION BY SA COCKERILL-OUGRÉE-PROVIDENCE ET ESPERANCE-LONGDOZ (No. 2) [1979] 2 C.M.L.R. 243, E.C. Commission.

1222. —— **national proceedings—stay, reasons for**

The High Court, Chancery Division, considered an action for infringement of design copyright in which a defence included the claim that the plaintffs were in breach of art. 86 EEC for abuse of a dominant position. *Held*, proceedings should be stayed pending a determination by the Commission of a complaint under this article. A decision by either the Court of Justice or the Commission that there had been an abuse of a dominant position would be a good defence in the circumstances. Such a plea as an infringement of art. 86 could not be adjudicated by the national court where the plaintiffs were able to conceal essential facts behind a claim for privilege.

BRITISH LEYLAND MOTOR CORP., BRITISH LEYLAND U.K., PRESSED STEEL FISHER AND BRITISH LEYLAND (AUSTIN MORRIS) *v.* WYATT INTERPART CO. [1979] 3 C.M.L.R. 79, Graham J.

1223. —— **negative clearance**

The Tribunal de Commerce at Paris referred a question under art. 177 EEC on the interpretation of Reg. 17 EEC to the European Court. The case concerned an application by a perfume and cosmetic retail shop to require a wholesale manufacturer with 400 outlets in France to supply it. The question asked by the Court was whether a letter sent by the E.C. Commission stating that certain practices were not a contravention of art. 85 constituted a negative clearance and if so whether it was binding on the national court.

ANNE MARTY S.A. *v.* ESTEE LAUDER S.A. [1979] 3 C.M.L.R. 58, Tribunal de Commerce, Paris.

1224. —— **notice of penalties**

The E.C. Commission imposed fines on four iron and steel undertakings in Germany, France and Italy for infringements of art. 61 ECSC and Decision 3000/77/ECSC in one case and Decision 962/77/ECSC in three cases and published a notice to this effect.

THE COMMUNITY *v.* SACILOR-ACIERIES ET LAMINOIRS DE LORRAINE [1979] 2 C.M.L.R. 513, E.C. Commission.

1225. —— **quantitative restriction**

The European Court considered several questions referred to the Court by the Finanzgericht at Hessen under art. 177 for a preliminary ruling. The case concerned the interpretation of art. 30 EEC involving the refusal by the German Spirits Monopoly to permit the import into Germany of a certain French liqueur because of its insufficient alcoholic strength. *Held*, as there are no common rules yet in force regulating the manufacture and sale of alcohol it is for Member States to control these matters in their own countries and so the interruption of free movement of goods must be accepted in order to ensure fiscal control, the maintenance of health standards, commercial fairness and consumer protection; but the imposition of a rule laying down a minimum content of alcohol in one Member State infringes art. 30 EEC. There can be no reason why goods made and sold in one Member State cannot be sold in another.

REWE-ZENTRAL A.G. *v.* BUNDESMONOPOLVERWALTUNG FÜR BRANNTWEIN (No. 120/78) [1979] 3 C.M.L.R. 494, European Ct.

1226. —— **search—exempt company**

The E.C. Commission, in considering the activities of an independent company in respect of its inquiries into price fixing agreements between manufacturers in different Member States, *held*, that the company would be ordered to give access to its premises and papers to Commission officials even though the company was not part of the industry being investigated but which was performing services for that industry. The status of this company as a *società fiduciaria* (a trust company) does exempt it from investigation and search.

Re THE BUSINESS RECORDS OF FIDES, UNIONE FIDUCIARIA, S.P.A. [1979] 1 C.M.L.R. 650, E.C. Commission.

1227. —— **specialisation agreements—prohibited features**

The E.C. Commission considered various specialisation agreements between two French steel companies principally concerning stainless steel products. The abandonment of production of certain items in favour of others, supply preference, information exchange and agreement to refrain from certain company acquisition were features of these agreements. *Held*, because these matters were included in the agreements between the firms the agreements were prohibited under art. 65 (1) ECSC but authorisation would be granted under art. 65 (2).

Re THE AGREEMENTS BETWEEN CREUSOT-LOIRE S.A. AND UGINE ACIERS S.A. [1979] 1 C.M.L.R. 349, E.C. Commission.

1228. The E.C. Commission considered its own authorisation of specialisation agreements between two Italian steel enterprises which involved the joint buying and joint selling between these firms. *Held*, this agreement restricted competition in that the undertakings had agreed to co-ordinate investments, production plans, supply and sales. However, although such agreements infringe art. 65 (1) ECSC authorisation would be granted subject to conditions.

Re THE AGREEMENTS OF ACCIAIERIE E FERRIERE LOMBARDE FALCK SpA AND GIUSEPPE & FRATELLO REDAELLI SpA [1979] 1 C.M.L.R. 357, E.C. Commission.

1229. ——— ——— **steel products**

The E.C. Commission considered a specialisation agreement concerning steel products. Several undertakings applied to the Commission for authorisation for an agreement that, *inter alia*, renounced or abandoned the production of certain products in favour of another party to the agreement, nominated each other as main distributor both for specialisation and other products and assist each others' sales in their own areas of market influence. The Commission held these agreements to be prohibited under art. 65 (1) ECSC but that they would authorise a specialisation agreement relating to steel products under art. 65 (2).

Re THE AGREEMENT OF IRISH STEEL HOLDINGS AND THE SOCIÉTÉ METALLURGIQUE ET NAVALE DUNKERQUE-NORMANDIE S.A. [1979] 2 C.M.L.R. 527, E.C. Commission.

1230. ——— **takeover**

Hugo Stinnes AG, a subsidiary of VEBA, engaged like its parent company in the distribution of solid fuels, applied to the E.C. Commission for authorisation to acquire Lange, Kühl & Co. KG, a coal wholesaler (both Hugo Stinnes AG and Lange, Kühl & Co. KG are undertakings within the meaning of art. 80 ECSC). The Government of the Federal Republic of Germany objected to the merger. *Decision*, the takeover would lead to a concentration within the meaning of art. 66/1/ECSC but it would be authorised as the merger was not likely to give VEBA the power to evade the ECSC competition rules since it would not have an artificially privileged position involving a substantial advantage in access to markets and the impact of the merger on competition occurred in a limited geographical area which did not constitute a substantial part of the Common Market.

Re THE TAKEOVER OF LANGE, KÜHL & Co. KG BY HUGO STINNES AG (79/89/ECSC) [1979] 2 C.M.L.R. 207, E.C. Commission.

1231. ——— **trade association—supply prohibition—parchment—trade confidence**

The E.C. Commission considered the actions of the members of the vegetable parchment association, in engaging in concerted practices to allow and encourage one member to keep exclusive control of a large part of the market. *Decision*: where the sole parchment manufacturer in Britain agreed with European manufacturers that the latter should supply the former with any demand in production it could not meet itself but the European supplier would not sell direct to the public, this was a concerted practice which infringed art. 85 (1) EEC. However, the collection and analysis of statistical data in an industry to determine output and sales was a proper activity of a trade association. But the dissemination of business confidences to competitors will amount to a prohibited concerted practice. In the circumstances the E.C. Commission fined a Finnish undertaking for violation of art. 85 EEC.

THE COMMUNITY *v.* MEMBERS OF THE GENUINE VEGETABLE PARCHMENT ASSOCIATION [1978] 1 C.M.L.R. 534. E.C. Commission.

1232. —— trade fairs—rules for exhibitors

The E.C. Commission considered the rules which governed official CECIMO trade fairs. These rules related to exhibitors in the machine tool industry's trade fairs (EMO) which occur biennially. A requirement that exhibitors at EMO should undertake not to exhibit their machines again that year except in certain circumstances; an exclusion of manufacturers from the EMO who infringe this rule; and, *inter alia*, the agreement by the CECIMO General Secretariat that tools exhibited at an EMO may be made available to exhibitors at other fairs in CECIMO member countries without the manufacturer's label were all features of these rules. *Held*, these rules restricted competition within the meaning of art. 85 (1) EEC and were prohibited but subject to certain conditions would be exempted for 10 years under art. 85 (3) EEC.

Re THE APPLICATION BY THE EUROPEAN COMMITTEE FOR CO-OPERATION OF THE MACHINE TOOL INDUSTRY (CECIMO) [1979] 1 C.M.L.R. 419, E.C. Commission.

1233. —— trade marks—similarity

The E.C. Commission considered the circumstances of a German chemical undertaking obtaining a court injunction against a Japanese undertaking preventing the latter from marketing its chemical products under its own trade mark. There was a close similarity between the two. The Commission issued a statement which stated that an agreement between the two parties to a three-year period, in which the Japanese undertaking could freely use its mark in Germany, provided that its name was printed close to it, did not restrict trade and did not infringe art. 85 EEC.

TANABE SEIYAKU CO. *v.* BAYER A.G. [1979] 2 C.M.L.R. 80, E.C. Commission

1234. —— trade secrets—quotas—extraterritoriality

The E.C. Commission considered a practice carried on between a British, a Dutch and a German enterprise which involved commercial co-operation in the white lead industry. This co-operation continued voluntarily after it had been formally terminated. Included in this procedure was exchange of information and trade secrets, and a quota delivery system. *Held*, continuation of the agreement in this way was a concerted practice infringing art. 85 (1) EEC. Such information exchange restricts competition and is similarly prohibited. The delivery quota system limits or controls markets under art. 85 (1) (*b*) EEC and firms in non-Member States who collaborate with an EEC enterprise(s) in any of these matters are subject to art. 85 EEC.

THE COMMUNITY *v.* ASSOCIATED LEAD MANUFACTURERS [1979] 1 C.M.L.R. 464, E.C. Commission.

1235. Sale of goods—instalment credit terms

The Cour de Cassation asked the European Court to give a preliminary ruling under art. 177 EEC on whether the sale of a machine by one company to another company for a price to be paid by way of two equal bills of exchange payable at 60 and 90-day intervals can be interpreted as a sale of goods on instalment credit terms within art. 13 of the Brussels Convention on Jurisdiction 1968 (Full Faith and Credit Convention) (" Convention "). *Held*, the concept of a contract on instalment credit terms varies from one Member State to another, but as used in art. 13 of the Convention it should be given a unified Community interpretation. The concept of the sale of goods on instalment credit terms within the meaning of art. 13 of the Convention is not to be interpreted as extending to the sale of a machine by one company to another for a price which is to be paid by way of bills of exchange spread over a period.

SOCIÉTÉ BERTRAND *v.* PAUL OTT KG (150/77) [1978] 3 C.M.L.R. 499, European Ct.

1236. Services—banking—national law

The European Court considered several questions referred to it by the Oberlandesgericht for a preliminary ruling under art. 177 EEC. The case concerned a German national who, while resident in France, had engaged a French bank to invest on the Paris Stock Exchange in speculative ventures.

The German did not pay his debts incurred on this speculation and the French Bank tried to recover these debts. *Held*, the plaintiff bank was not being discriminated against in being met with the plea in bar under German law, that the debts were irrecoverable as they arose from illegal consideration, gambling. This was so because German plaintiffs would be equally unsuccessful before a German court. Such stock exchange dealings for a client were the provision of services within the meaning of art. 60 (1) EEC.

SOCIÉTÉ GÉNÉRALE ALSACIENNE DE BANQUE S.A. *v.* KOESTLER (No. 15/78) [1979] 1 C.M.L.R. 89, European Ct.

1237. Sex discrimination—equal pay—reference to European Court
The case concerned a woman employed in a broadly similar job to a man. There was a gap of four months since the man had left his employment. *Held*, that the question would be referred to the European Court as to whether in these circumstances the woman was entitled to the same pay as the man on the interpretation of art. 119 EEC.

MACARTHYS *v.* SMITH [1979] 3 C.M.L.R. 44, C.A.

1238. Social security—accident in West Berlin—industrial benefit
The National Insurance Commissioner for the United Kingdom considered a claim by a plumber who worked at the British Embassy in West Berlin and who had an accident while being driven during his work in West Berlin. *Held*, by virtue of the provisions of art. 56 of Reg. 1408/71 EEC he would receive industrial injury benefit as if the accident had happened in the United Kingdom.

Re A CAR ACCIDENT IN WEST BERLIN [1979] 2 C.M.L.R. 42, U.K. National Insurance Commissioner.

1239. —— advance old age—pensions of ex-prisoners of war—discrimination
The Cour d'Appel Nancy referred several questions to the European Court under art. 177 EEC concerning the interpretation of EEC Regulation No. 1408/71 in the light of an application made by a Belgian ex-prisoner of war resident in France for an early pension. French law granted an advance old-age pension to certain ex-prisoners of war. The applicant argued that he was entitled to such a pension on the basis of the principles of equality of treatment between workers of EEC Member States. *Held*, the early pension provided by French law for certain ex-prisoners of war did not possess the characteristics of a social security benefit within the meaning of art. 4 (1) of EEC Reg. No. 1408/71. Art. 4 (4) of EEC Reg. No. 1408/71 provided that the Reg. did not apply to benefit schemes for victims of war or its consequences. Thus, the Reg. did not apply to social benefits for ex-prisoners of war such as the early pension provided by French law and the applicant could not invoke the protection of EEC Law.

DIRECTEUR RÉGIONAL DE LA SÉCURITÉ SOCIALE DE NANCY *v.* GILLARD (9/78) [1978] 3 C.M.L.R. 554, European Ct.

1240. —— aggregation of benefits—community nationality
The European Court considered a reference to it made under art. 177 EEC from the Sozialgericht at Gelsenkirchen for a preliminary ruling on the interpretation of arts. 2 (1) and 94 (2) of Reg. 1408/71. The case concerned a claimant working in France for 13 years and Germany for two years. For these years he was a French national. At the end of this period he became an Algerian national. *Held*, as he was a Community national for these periods they could and should be aggregated for the purpose of a claim for social security benefits.

TAYEB BELBOUAB *v.* BUNDESKNAPPSCHAFT (No. 10/78) [1979] 2 C.M.L.R. 23, European Ct.

1241. —— discrimination—benefits in prison
The European Court considered several questions referred to it by the National Insurance Commissioner (U.K.) for a preliminary ruling under art. 177 EEC. The case concerned a person who while in prison in Ireland became ill and received hospital treatment. Subsequently he claimed National Insurance benefit for this period of illness. The court interpreted arts. 7 and 48 EEC and arts. 3 (1), 19 (1) and 22 (1) of Reg. 1408/71 in the context of these

facts. *Held*, art. 7 (1) EEC of Reg. 1408/71 is directly applicable in Member States in the circumstances. British courts can disqualify a national of another Member State or its own national from benefits for a reason, in this case being in prison, which would disqualify him if it had occurred in Britain. There is no express or implicit discrimination in such a decision. Subject to the application of art. 18 of Reg. 1408/71 such rules should be made by national legislation.

KENNY *v.* INSURANCE OFFICER (No. 1/78) [1978] 3 C.M.L.R. 651, European Ct.

1242. —— East Germany—industrial injury during war
The European Court considered several questions referred to it by the Regional Social Court at Baden Württemburg for a preliminary ruling under art. 177 EEC. The case concerned an Italian worker who received an industrial injury in Strassfurt, in what is now the German Democratic Republic in 1944, and who now claimed benefit in the Federal Republic of Germany. *Held*, art. 50 and Annex G1A of Reg. 3 EEC and art. 89 and Annex VC 1 (6) of Reg. 1408/71 EEC were valid. West German legislation granting benefit to EEC nationals following events occurring in parts of Germany no longer part of the Federal Republic in connection, *inter alia*, with the Second World War was discretionary in the case of non-residents and did not fall within the definition of "social security." It was outside the protection of the EEC rules on social security.

TINELLI *v.* BERUFSGENOSSENSCHAFT DER CHEMISCHEN INDUSTRIE (No. 114/78) [1979] 2 C.M.L.R. 735, European Ct.

1243. —— family allowances—overlapping
The European Court considered several questions referred to it by the Tribunal du Travail at Charleroi for a preliminary ruling under art. 177 EEC. The case concerned the interpretation of art. 79 (3) of Reg. 1408/71 in respect of an Italian worker who was in receipt of a Belgian disability pension and whose wife continued to work in Italy. *Held*, as the Italian authorities took the man still to be head of the family, in these circumstances and as his wife therefore had no Italian allowance, the husband was entitled to Belgian allowances. Belgian allowances could be cut only by the actual allowance paid to the wife. The rule in art. 79 (3) only operates to suspend allowances to the extent to which such further allowance is paid.

ROSSI *v.* CAISSE DE COMPENSATION POUR ALLOCATIONS FAMILIALES DES REGIONS DE CHARLEROI ET NAMUR (No. 100/78) [1979] 3 C.M.L.R. 544, European Ct.

1244. —— invalidity and unemployment benefit—overlapping benefits
The National Insurance Commissioner for the United Kingdom considered a claim by an Irishman who suffered industrial disablement in Ireland. When he was certified capable of work this benefit was stopped and the claimant sought unemployment benefit. *Held*, until the time when he was held fit so as to entitle him to unemployment benefit he would be paid arrears of unfitness benefit. Art. 12 (2) of Reg. 1408/71 EEC does not extend national rules on overlapping benefits to payments in other Member States although it may be lawful for this to be done by the Member States themselves.

Re INDUSTRIAL DISABLEMENT [1979] 1 C.M.L.R. 653, U.K. National Insurance Commissioner.

1245. —— migrant workers—aggregation of benefit
The European Court considered several questions referred to it by the Sozialgericht at Augsburg for a preliminary ruling under art. 177 EEC. The case concerned an Italian national residing in Italy who had worked towards his pension in both Italy and Germany but who claimed that his benefit should be determined exclusively by German legislation. *Held*, art. 46 (3) of Reg. 1408/71, which allows certain persons to be entitled to the total sum of benefits calculated in accordance with the Regulation but which allows the institution in some circumstances to adjust this payment, is only applicable where it is necessary in certain cases to have recourse to the aggregation

rules for insurance benefit. Waiving the residence clauses under art. 10 of this Regulation does not involve the application of the said art. 46 (3).

GIULIANI *v.* LANDESVERSICHERUNGSANSTALT SCHWABEN (No. 32/77) [1977] E.C.R. 1857, European Ct.

1246. —— —— **unemployment benefit**

A claimant claimed unemployment benefit for a period in 1975 and claimed that contributions that he had made during three years' work in Germany should be included in his eligibility for unemployment benefit. The British National Insurance Commissioner *held,* that art. 71 (1) of Reg. 1408/71 EEC applied in this case and accordingly the period of work in Germany should be counted in the assessment.

Re WORK IN GERMANY (No. 2) [1979] 1 C.M.L.R. 267, National Insurance Commissioner.

1247. —— **overlapping benefits**

The National Insurance Commissioner considered an application of a claimant for benefit who had worked and paid contributions in Germany from 1934 to 1938 and thereafter in Great Britain. Because of EEC rules he was entitled to a German pension and claimed British sickness benefit in 1976 and 1977. *Held,* art. 12 (2) of Reg. 1408/71 does not justify a reduction in benefit payable under British law alone by reference to entitlement to a German pension payable by virtue of EEC rules.

Re GERMAN RETIREMENT PENSION (No. 905/78) [1979] 3 C.M.L.R. 382, National Insurance Commissioner.

1248. —— —— **most favourable procedure**

The European Court considered several questions referred to it by the Cour du Travail at Mons on the interpretation of arts. 27 and 28 of Reg. 3. The case concerned a claim by an Italian who had worked in Belgium for a Belgian invalidity pension. He had also worked in Italy and was entitled to an invalidity pension there. *Held,* these articles allowed entitlements under both states to be put together so that each state, Italy and Belgium, would pay the proportion of the pension that was due following the applicant's periods of work and social security contributions in each country, provided this procedure was more favourable to the applicant than by assessing his pension using national Belgian rules on the overlapping of benefits.

INSTITUT NATIONAL D'ASSURANCE MALADIE-INVALIDITÉ (I.N.A.M.I.) AND UNION NATIONAL DES FEDERATIONS MUTUALISTES NEUTRES *v.* VIOLA (No. 26/78) [1979] 1 C.M.L.R. 635, European Ct.

1249. —— **residence—convalescence**

The U.K. National Insurance Commissioner considered the case of an Italian worker who had lived and worked in England for 25 years when he became totally disabled, received sickness benefit here and returned for convalescence for six weeks to Italy. *Held,* during the six-week period of return to Italy he was not entitled to benefit and that although he always intended to return ultimately to Italy at the end of his life he was not resident there and was not covered by the exception allowing retention of benefit when authorised to return to the Member State where he resides (art. 22 (1) of Reg. 1408/71).

Re AN ITALIAN WORKER (No. 622/78) [1979] 2 C.M.L.R. 441, Monroe J.

1250. —— **rest cure in Member State—sickness benefits**

The National Insurance Commissioner (U.K.) considered a claim for sickness benefit on behalf of a sick person who had been advised she should go away for a rest and she accordingly spent a fortnight in West Germany. *Held,* travel to another Member State for a rest and change of air without medical treatment did not allow the person to claim the exemption of art. 22 of Reg. 1408/71. Only if the European Court permits such a course can a national court declare an EEC rule invalid. Therefore the fortnight in Germany did not entitle the claimant to sickness benefit.

Re CONVALESCENCE IN GERMANY [1979] 1 C.M.L.R. 390, National Insurance Commissioner (U.K.).

1251. —— **sickness benefit—pensionable age**

The National Insurance Commissioner considered an application on behalf of an Irish woman, insured in Ireland who came to the U.K. after she was 60 years of age, this being the upper limit for entering the British national insurance scheme. In particular the case concerned the question whether this woman was entitled to British sickness benefit which is pension related. *Held*, this question would be referred to the European Court for a preliminary ruling under art. 177 EEC in respect of the interpretation of Reg. 1612/68 and Reg. 1408/71.

Re SICKNESS BENEFIT FOR AN ELDERLY IRISH WOMAN (No. 26/77) [1979] 3 C.M.L.R. 442, National Insurance Commissioner.

1252. —— **stateless persons—forms**
The Ombudsman considered a complaint against the Department of Health and Social Security that a form E.111 had been delayed following a request from Germany. The case concerned a stateless employee temporarily resident in Germany who had fallen ill there. The Department admitted they thought the man was a Chilean national, and was not therefore entitled to EEC social security benefits. The Report stated that the Department's apology for not reading the note on the back of this form referring to stateless persons was an adequate response and that the proper course for the applicant would have been to have applied for the form E.111 before he left Britain for Germany, as he was advised to do.

Re MEDICAL TREATMENT IN GERMANY [1979] 1 C.M.L.R. 369, Parliamentary Commissioner for Administration.

1253. —— **territory—continental shelf**
The National Insurance Commissioner (U.K.) referred several questions to the European Court for a preliminary ruling under art. 177 EEC. The case concerned an employee of an English company working on a Panamian registered oil rig and operating off Holland under licence from the Dutch Government. *Held*, the questions to be asked were whether the continental shelf of a Member State on which an oil rig rested was part of the territory of the Member State for EEC social security rules and which state should pay the benefits in an industrial injury claim.

Re THE KEY GIBRALTAR OIL RIG [1979] 1 C.M.L.R. 362, European Ct.

1254. —— **unemployment benefit—absence in another Member State**
The European Court considered several cases referred to it by the Sozial-gericht at Hildesheim under art. 177 E.E.C. for a preliminary ruling on the interpretation of art. 69 of Reg. 1408/71 E.E.C. The case concerned an Italian worker, domiciled in Germany and registered unemployed there, who went to Italy to work but fell ill there, and thus was prevented from returning to Germany within a three-month period, so losing certain unemployment benefits. *Held*, this regulation permits absence from one Member State of a person regis-tered unemployed there, for him to seek employment in another Member State. Extension of a three-month period for such absence is permissible but the national authorities in using their discretion in granting this extension may take into account all the factors they think are relevant.

COCCIOLI *v.* BUNDESANSTALT FÜR ARBEIT (No. 139/78) [1979] 3 C.M.L.R. 144, European Ct.

1255. The National Insurance Commissioner considered an application for unemployment benefit for a claimant for the period between ending his job in the Netherlands and registration as unemployed in the U.K. This intervening period was two and a half months spent mostly in the Netherlands though he made a few weekend trips to the U.K. to arrange house removal. *Held*, he was not entitled to benefit in the U.K. because he was abroad at the relevant time and had failed to register as unemployed within the requirements of EEC rules.

Re UNEMPLOYMENT BENEFITS (No. 6/79) [1979] 3 C.M.L.R. 449, National Insurance Commissioner.

1256. —— —— **seeking employment abroad**
The National Insurance Commissioner (U.K.) considered a claim by a farm manager for unemployment benefit while he was looking for a job in France for seven days. *Held*, as the manager was registered as unemployed in England and did not register as unemployed while in France for the seven-day period,

he did not lose his right to benefit under national law and was entitled to unemployment benefit in England for the period.

Re A FARM MANAGER [1979] 1 C.M.L.R. 445, National Insurance Commissioner.

1257. Trade marks—relabelling products—parallel imports

The Arrondissementsrechtbank at Rotterdam considered a case involving a plaintiff, a manufacturer of pharmaceutical products, who sought to exercise exclusive trade mark rights against the defendant, a parallel importer of these products who had illegally attached labels of the plaintiffs to these products. *Held*, the plaintiff was entitled to exercise these rights against the defendant. Parallel importers must abide by national rules on repacking if it complied with art. 36 but must not reattach the manufacturer's trade mark without permission.

THE BOOTS CO. *v.* CENTRAFARM B.V. (No. 2) [1979] 2 C.M.L.R. 497, Arrondissementsrechtbank, Rotterdam.

1258. —— right to use—partitioning market

The European Court considered several questions referred to it by the Arrondissementsrechtbank (District Court) Amsterdam for a preliminary ruling under art. 177 EEC. The case concerned the interpretation of art. 36 where an import into Holland from Britain by the plaintiff company of medicine involved the substitution of a Dutch trade mark for a British trade mark without perimssion. *Held*, that the only exception allowed under this article to the principle of free movement of goods, are measures or actions which safeguard the right of the owner of the trade mark to exclusive use of it. The owner of a trade mark had the exclusive right to determine the mark attached to the product and it is consistent with art. 36 EEC that he may prohibit other marks being affixed. But he may not use different marks in different parts of the market so as to partition it. National law will decide this. It is assumed that national law on the use of such names does not amend Community law on the subject.

CENTRAFARM B.V. *v.* AMERICAN HOME PRODUCTS CORP. (No. 3/78) [1979] 1 C.M.L.R. 326, European Ct.

1259. Transport—operator's licence—qualifications

The European Court considered several questions referred to it by the Raad van State, Afdeling Rechtspaak, under art. 177 EEC for a preliminary ruling. The case concerned two brothers who jointly managed a road haulage firm for more than three years and another man who had many years' experience in this field. The former were proposing to split into two firms and the latter's experience was managing his father's firm during the latter's retirement. The problem was whether these men could be exempt from the need to obtain a formal diploma and hence an operating licence in respect of business as transport operators because of their running their own firms for three years. *Held*, by splitting a firm into two and by one man each taking one of the two parts there was no change in the continuity of identity (Directive 74/561, s. 4 (2)) and this three-year exception could be used. S. 4 (2) does not allow exemption to be given in the case of retirement, an expected event, but only to such incidents as death or incapacity, unexpected events.

A. P. AUGUSTIJN *v.* STAATSSECRETARIS VAN VERKEER EN WATERSTAAT (No. 145/78) [1979] 3 C.M.L.R. 516, European Ct.

1260. —— regulations—ultra vires

The European Court considered several questions referred to it by the Oberlandesgericht at Düsseldorf for a preliminary ruling under art. 177 EEC. The case concerned the validity of Reg. 543/69 on the harmonisation of certain social legislation governing road safety. *Held*, the council has wide powers under art. 74 EEC to legislate and establish common rules. The above regulation was made under this article and merely implements this policy in part. There was no case here of the council exceeding its powers.

Re SCHUMALLA (No. 97/78) [1979] E.C.R. 2311, European Ct.

1261. —— state aids—railway tariffs—community obligations

The European Court considered an application for a declaration that Belgium had failed to comply with a Commission Decision. The applicant, the E.C. Commission, alleged non-compliance with its Decision of May 4, 1976, on aid from the Belgian Government for the Belgian Railway and international railway tariffs on coal and steel. *Held*, under art. 77 EEC, state aid to transport is not permitted for any aid that is not clearly for well-defined instances in the general interests of the Community. A Member State cannot use art. 184 EEC to object to the legality of Community legislation unless a regulation is in issue. It is inapplicable where a Decision addressed to that Member State is in issue. Art. 93 (2) EEC allows a declaration that a Member State has failed to comply with a Commission Decision and arts. 169 and 170 EEC allow a declaration concerning failure to fulfil treaty obligations.

E.C. COMMISSION *v.* KINGDOM OF BELGIUM (No. 156/77) [1978] E.C.R. 1881, European Ct.

1262. —— support tariffs for coal and steel producers
The Government of the Federal Republic of Germany requested the E.C. Commission to authorise the continuation of special German railway tariffs in favour of coal and steel producers in the Saar. The Federal Government supported its request with reference to the unfavourable competitive position of the Saar's coal and steel producers *vis-à-vis* their competitors in the Ruhr, Lorraine and Luxembourg who had benefited from improved transportation facilities. *Decision*, the Commission authorised under art. 70 ECSC the continuation of support tariffs for the transport of coal and steel out of the Saar until 1983. Such support tariffs in the Saar were unlikely to create disturbances in the functioning of the coal and steel market and did not appreciably affect competition in the corresponding transport markets. In view of the unfavourable location of the Saar and of its economic situation, the amount of the tariff aids was only such as was strictly necessary to encourage the recipient firms to adjust to new economic conditions.

Re GERMAN RAILWAY TARIFFS FOR COAL AND STEEL PRODUCERS IN THE SAAR [1979] 2 C.M.L.R. 210, E.C. Commission.

1263. Treaties, conventions and regulations
Act concerning the conditions of accession of the Hellenic Republic and the adjustments of the Treaties. (O.J. 1979 L291/17).

EUROPEAN COMMUNITIES (DEFINITION OF TREATIES) (ECSC DECISION ON SUPPLEMENTARY REVENUES) ORDER 1979 (No. 292) [10p], made under the European Communities Act 1972 (c. 68), s. 1; operative on March 15, 1979; declares the Decision of the Representative of the Governments of the Member States of the ECSC meeting within the Council, of October 30, 1978, allocating to that Community supplementary revenues for 1978 (Cmnd. 7464) to be a Community Treaty as defined in s. 1 (2) of the 1972 Act.

EUROPEAN COMMUNITIES (DEFINITION OF TREATIES) (ECSC DECISION OF 9TH APRIL 1979 ON SUPPLEMENTARY REVENUES) ORDER 1979 (No. 932) [10p], made under the European Communities Act 1972, s. 1; operative on a date to be published; declares the Decision of the Representatives of the Governments of the Member States of the ECSC to be a Community Treaty.

EUROPEAN COMMUNITIES (DEFINITION OF TREATIES) (INTERNATIONAL WHEAT AGREEMENT) Order 1979 (No. 1446) [10p], made under the European Communities Act 1972, s. 1 (3); operative on a date to be notified in the *London Gazette*; declares the 1979 Protocols for the Fifth Extension of the Wheat Trade Convention and the Food Aid Convention constituting the International Wheat Agreement 1971 to be Community treaties as defined in s. 1 (2) of the 1972 Act.

BOOKS AND ARTICLES. See *post*, pp. [5], [21].

EVIDENCE

1264. Admissibility—co-accused's statement. See R. *v.* TAYLOR, § 445.

1265. —— non-attendance—affidavits—examination outside jurisdiction
A debtor who fails to attend for cross-examination runs the risk of having his affidavit evidence excluded at the discretion of the trial judge.

The petitioning creditor presented a petition in bankruptcy against the debtor who was living in Spain, and who claimed that he had acquired there a domicile of choice. The debtor disputed the court's jurisdiction, but after the affidavit evidence was filed, and with various warrants for corrupt practices having been issued in England against him, he applied for leave to give his evidence in Spain. That application was dismissed. The creditor made an application for a direction that the debtor's affidavit evidence should not be admitted if he did not attend, and this application was refused as premature. Both parties appealed. *Held,* dismissing both appeals, that (1) although the debtor's liability to arrest was a factor to be considered in deciding whether to allow examination outside the jurisdiction, it should not be allowed to prejudice the creditor; and (2) that the debtor, in failing to attend, ran the risk of having his affidavit evidence excluded by the trial judge at the hearing.

Re A DEBTOR (No. 2283 OF 1976) [1978] 1 W.L.R. 1512, C.A.

1266. Blood tests
BLOOD TESTS (EVIDENCE OF PATERNITY) (AMENDMENT) REGULATIONS 1979 (No. 1226) [10p], made under the Family Law Reform Act 1969 (c. 46), s. 22; operative on November 1, 1979; increase the fees payable under S.I. 1971 No. 1861 in respect of blood tests carried out for the purpose of determining paternity in civil proceedings.

1267. Contract. See CONTRACT.

1268. Criminal cases. See CRIMINAL LAW; MAGISTERIAL LAW.

1269. Cross-examination—affidavits—proceedings for judicial review. See GEORGE *v.* SECRETARY OF STATE FOR THE ENVIRONMENT, § 307.

1270. Discovery. See PRACTICE.

1271. Divorce cases. See DIVORCE AND MATRIMONIAL CAUSES.

1272. Estoppel. See ESTOPPEL.

1273. Expert evidence—disclosure—substance of evidence. See OLLETT *v.* BRISTOL AEROJET (NOTE), § 2167.

1274. —— personal injury actions—lodging agreed reports
The following Practice Direction was issued by the Queen's Bench Division on February 15, 1979:

1. In personal injury actions, it would be of great convenience and assistance to the trial judge to have the opportunity before the trial to read the reports of the experts, both medical and other experts, which have been agreed between the parties.

2. Accordingly, in personal injury actions, a copy of the reports of the medical and other experts which have been agreed between the parties must be lodged by the plaintiff with the proper officer (as defined in R.S.C., Ord. 34, r. 3 (5)) at the place where the action has been set down for trial, within 14 days after such reports have been agreed or as soon after setting down as is practicable.

3. These reports will be placed by the proper officer with the documents required to be lodged with him when setting an action down for trial under R.S.C., Ord. 34, r. 3 and they will accompany such documents for the use of the trial judge.

4. Each such report should state on the face of it the name of the party on whose behalf the expert has given that report and the date on which it was given.

[1979] 1 W.L.R. 290; [1979] 1 All E.R. 818.

1275. —— subpoena of opponent's witness
The principle as to there being no property in a witness extends to expert witnesses as to any witness of fact.

Since the genuineness of a disputed document was crucial to their case, the plaintiffs approached a handwriting expert for his opinion. It was to be inferred that such opinion was unfavourable. The expert informed the plaintiffs' representatives that he would not act for the other side. Some time later the same expert was approached on behalf of the defendants, whom he advised, forgetting the previous consultation; as soon as he realised that the document was the same, he told the defendants that he could no longer act. At the trial the defendants having procured the expert's attendance by *subpoena* successfully contended that he was a compellable witness, notwithstanding the plaintiffs' objection. *Held*, dismissing the plaintiffs' appeal, that expert witnesses formed no exception to the rule against there being no property in a witness; and that even if the plaintiffs had established that the expert had contractually agreed not to testify for the defendants, such a contract would have been unenforceable as contrary to public policy.

HARMONY SHIPPING CO. S.A. *v.* DAVIS [1979] 3 All E.R. 177, C.A.

1276. —— whether appropriate
[R.S.C., Ord. 38, r. 36.]

The court will not give leave to adduce as " expert evidence " in negligence proceedings, evidence which in fact does no more than rehearse the arguments as to negligence and causation.

The plaintiff was injured after a collision between his moped and the defendant's bus; the defendants denied negligence. The plaintiffs sought leave to adduce as expert evidence a report from consulting engineers who gave an opinion as to how the accident occurred. The Master on the summons for directions refused leave. *Held*, dismissing the plaintiff's appeal, that the report was not truly expert evidence, as opposed to argument; that in any event expert evidence was not needed in such a case.

HINDS *v.* LONDON TRANSPORT EXECUTIVE [1979] R.T.R. 103, C.A.

1277. Extradition—committal proceedings—substantive law of evidence to be applied.
See R. *v.* GOVERNOR OF PENTONVILLE PRISON, *ex p.* KIRBY (NOTE) § 1292.

1278. —— —— witness refreshing memory. See R. *v.* GOVERNOR OF GLOUCESTER PRISON, *ex p.* MILLER, § 1293.

1279. Foreign tribunals
EVIDENCE (PROCEEDINGS IN OTHER JURISDICTIONS) (ISLE OF MAN) ORDER 1979 (No. 1711) [20p], made under the Evidence (Proceedings in Other Jurisdictions) Act 1975 (c. 34), s. 10 (3); operative on February 1, 1980; provides for the Evidence (Proceedings in Other Jurisdictions) Act 1975 to be extended to the Isle of Man, subject to certain modifications.

1280. Hearsay—discretion of industrial tribunal to admit. See CORAL SQUASH CLUBS *v.* MATTHEWS, § 891.

1281. Negligence. See NEGLIGENCE.

1282. Witnesses—public inquiry—whether absolutely privileged
Where a public inquiry is set up by statutory authority and conducted judicially, witnesses giving evidence before it may be absolutely immune from civil proceedings arising from their evidence.

The appellant was dismissed as a headmaster by the local education authority, of which the respondent was chairman. Pursuant to the appellant's petition, the Secretary of State set up an inquiry, with Queen's Counsel as commissioner, under the Education (Scotland) Act 1946 to investigate the dismissal. The inquiry was held in public, the procedure adopted being similar to that in a court of law; evidence was given, *inter alia*, by the respondent. The commissioner concluded that the dismissal was reasonably justifiable and reported accordingly to the Minister who accepted such conclusion. (As a matter of practice although such a report's conclusion was not binding upon the Minister, it was rare for him not to accept it.) The appellant brought proceedings against the respondent alleging that he had given maliciously false evidence to the inquiry thereby influencing its decision. The respondent succeeded in having the action dismissed on the grounds of this evidence being absolutely privileged. *Held*, dismissing the appellant's appeal, that absolute privilege could apply to evidence given in proceedings which, although they did not finally determine the issues raised, formed part of the decision-making process; the nature of this inquiry indicated that such privilege would apply. (*Dawkins* v. *Lord Rokeby* (1873) L.R. 8 Q.B. 255 and dictum of Lord Atkin in *O'Connor* v. *Waldron* [1934] All E.R.Rep. 281 at 283 applied.)

TRAPP *v.* MACKIE [1979] 1 All E.R. 489, H.L.

BOOKS AND ARTICLES. See *post*, pp. [5], [22].

EXECUTORS AND ADMINISTRATORS

1283. Confirmation to Small Estates (Scotland) Act 1979 (c. 22)

This Act amends the law relating to confirmation to small estates in Scotland.

S. 1 amends the Intestates Widows and Children (Scotland) Act 1875 and the Small Testate Estates (Scotland) Act 1876 in relation to the confirmation of small estates; s. 2 repeals various enactments; s. 3 contains the short title, extent, construction and commencement. The Act extends to Scotland only.

The Act received the Royal Assent on March 29, 1979, and comes into force on a day to be appointed.

1284. Intestacy—surviving spouse—matrimonial home—appropriation

[Administration of Estates Act 1925 (c. 23), s. 41; Intestates' Estates Act 1952 (c. 64), Sched. 2, para. 1 (1), 5 (2).]

A widow may require the appropiation to her of a former matrimonial home upon her husband's intestacy, notwithstanding that the value thereof exceeds the value of the widow's interest in the estate, if she will pay the balance to the personal representatives.

A widow gave notice to her deceased intestate husband's personal representatives requiring them to appropriate to her the former matrimonial home, the value of which exceeded that of her absolute interest in the estate: she undertook to pay the difference in value to the representatives. Foster J. held that she could not require them to appropriate the home under para. 1 (1) of Sched. 2 to the 1952 Act, since such requirement could only be made if the value of the matrimonial home was less than that of her absolute interest. *Held*, allowing her appeal, that para. 1 (1) is to be construed so as to include a transaction which is partly appropriation and partly sale. (Decision of Foster J. [1978] C.L.Y. 1438, reversed.)

Re Phelps (decd.); Wells *v.* Phelps [1979] 3 All E.R. 373, C.A.

1285. Liability—plene administravit—defence after judgment—whether too late

[R.S.C., Ord. 24, r. 17, Ord. 35, r. 2.]

The court has no jurisdiction to allow a personal representative to enter a defence pleading *plene administravit* after judgment has been given against a deceased's estate.

A son commenced an action against his father. The father died. E, the executrix, became the defendant under an order to carry on the proceedings. Due to inadvertence, E failed to plead *plene administravit* in her defence. E's defence was struck out under R.S.C., Ord. 24, r. 16, for failure to comply with an order for discovery; judgment was entered in default of defence, an inquiry into damages was ordered, and costs were awarded against E. The damages and costs amounted to £100,000; the assets of the estate amounted to £9,000. Since E had not pleaded *plene administravit*, she was personally liable for the balance. E sought leave to serve a defence pleading *plene administravit praeter*. *Held*, dismissing the application, that when judgment had been given, the court had no jurisdiction under R.S.C., Ord. 24, r. 17 to revoke a previous order made under Ord. 24, r. 16, even though the inquiry into damages was still outstanding. There was no defence on the record to be amended under R.S.C., Ord. 20, r. 5, and R.S.C., Ord. 35, r. 2 could not be used to set aside the order giving judgment. Furthermore, after judgment had been given, a party in contempt by failure to comply with an order for discovery could not invoke the court's inherent jurisdiction. (*Haigh* v. *Haigh* (1885) 31 Ch.D. 478 applied; *The Duke of Buccleuch* [1892] P. 201 distinguished.)

Midland Bank Trust Co. *v.* Green (No. 2) [1979] 1 All E.R. 726, Oliver J.

1286. Northern Ireland. See Northern Ireland.

1287. Practice—engrossments—facsimile copies

The following Practice Direction was issued by the Family Division on November 8, 1979.

To assist in the preparation of fiat copies of testamentary documents, it has been decided that, subject to the Registrar's discretion, as an alternative to typewritten engrossments, facsimile copies produced by photography may be used in the following circumstances:

1. Where a complete page or pages are to be excluded.
2. Where words on the same page below the testator's signature can be excluded by masking out.
3. Where the original has been altered but not re-executed or re-published and there exists a photocopy of the original executed document.

This extended practice will apply in the District Probate Registries and Sub-Registries as well as in the Principal Registry.

[1979] 3 All E.R. 859.

Books and Articles. See *post*, pp. [5], [23].

EXPLOSIONS AND EXPLOSIVES

1288. Health and safety at work

Explosives Act 1875 (Exemptions) Regulations 1979 (No. 1378) [10p], made under the Health and Safety at Work etc. Act 1974 (c. 37), ss. 11 (2) (*d*), 15 (1) (5) (*b*), 50 (3); operative on December 31, 1979; provide for the granting of exemptions from any requirements and prohibitions imposed under the 1875 Act or any regulation or Order made under that Act.

1289. Northern Ireland. See NORTHERN IRELAND.

1290. Unlawful possession—pyrotechnic effect only

[Explosives Act 1875 (c. 17), s. 3; Explosive Substances Act 1883 (c. 3), s. 4 (1).]

A substance used or manufactured to produce a pyrotechnic effect is an " explosive substance " for the purposes of s. 4 (1) of the Explosive Substances Act 1883.

The appellant was charged with possession of an explosive substance contrary to s. 4 (1) of the 1883 Act; the only issue at this trial was whether the substance in his possession was an explosive substance, the defence expert gave evidence that the substance would produce a pyrotechnic but not an explosive effect. The trial judge directed the jury that no defence had been raised. *Held*, dismissing the appeal, that it was right to construe s. 4 (1) of the 1883 Act by reference to the definition of " explosive " (which induced pyrotechnic effects) contained in s. 3 of the 1875 Act.

R. *v*. WHEATLEY [1979] 1 W.L.R. 144, C.A.

EXTRADITION

1291. Fugitive offenders

Fugitive Offenders (Designated Commonwealth Countries) Order 1979 (No. 460) [10p], made under the Fugitive Offenders Act 1967 (c. 68), s. 2 (1); operative on May 30, 1979; designates Saint Lucia for the purposes of s. 1 of the 1967 Act.

Norway (Extradition) (Amendment) Order 1979 (No. 913) [20p], made under the Extradition Act 1870 (c. 52), ss. 2, 17, 21; operative on August 24, 1979; amends the application of the Extradition Acts in the case of Norway so as to reserve the right of the requested Government not to extradite its nationals in accordance with the Treaty between the U.K. and Norway for the mutual surrender of fugitive criminals which was signed on June 26, 1873.

Denmark (Extradition) (Amendment) Order 1979 (No. 1311) [20p], made under the Extradition Act 1870, ss. 2, 17, 21; operative on November 19, 1979; applies the Extradition Act to Denmark as amended by Notes exchanged on August 24, 1979.

Fugitive Offenders (Designated Commonwealth Countries) (No. 2) Order 1979 (No. 1712) [10p], made under the Fugitive Offenders Act 1967, s. 2 (1); operative on January 24, 1980; designates Kiribati and Saint Vincent and the Grenadines for the purposes of s. 1 of the Fugitive Offenders Act 1967.

1292. —— evidence
[Fugitive Offenders Act 1967 (c. 68), ss. 7 (5), 11 (1).]
A magistrate must apply the English substantive law of evidence on proceedings under s. 7 of the Fugitive Offenders Act 1967.
The Canadian Government requested the return of D for offences of fraud.
During committal proceedings under s. 7 of the Fugitive Offenders Act 1967.
the magistrate heard the evidence of a chartered accountant of the contents
of accounts which were not themselves produced, and should have been
excluded from consideration unless properly proved. On D's application for a
writ of habeas corpus, *held*, that the committal in respect of charges relying
upon such evidence would be set aside. (*R.* v. *Brixton Prison Governor, ex p.
Sadri* [1962] C.L.Y. 1236 considered.)
R. *v.* GOVERNOR OF PENTONVILLE PRISON, *ex p.* KIRBY (NOTE) [1979] 1
W.L.R. 541, D.C.

1293. —— —— witness refreshing memory from non-contemporaneous statement
[Fugitive Offenders Act 1967 (c. 68), ss. 7 (5), 11 (1).]
A magistrate must apply the English substantive law of evidence on proceedings under s. 7 of the Fugitive Offenders Act 1967; but this does not
prevent him from allowing a witness to refresh his memory from a non-
contemporaneous statement.
The Government of Australia requested the return of D for offences of
obtaining money by deception. During committal proceedings under s. 7 of
the Fugitive Offenders Act 1967, the magistrate permitted a witness to refresh
her memory from statements not made contemporaneously with the alleged
incidents. D was committed in custody to await the decision of the Secretary
of State. On D's application for a writ of habeas corpus, *held*, refusing the
application, that although the magistrate had to observe the rules of evidence,
the rule as to refreshing memory from a contemporaneous note was a rule of
practice and the order made was valid. (*R.* v. *Governor of Pentonville Prison.
ex p.* KIRBY (NOTE) [1979] C.L.Y. 1292 considered.)
R. *v.* GOVERNOR OF GLOUCESTER PRISON, *ex p.* MILLER [1979] 1 W.L.R.
587, D.C.

1294. Habeas corpus—definitions of crime not identical
[Extradition Act 1870 (c. 52).] Where the facts of a case disclose a prima
facie case according to English law and the crime is substantially similar in
concept both in England and a country requesting extradition from England,
the request cannot be refused on the ground that the definitions of the crime
are not identical in both countries. The Divisional Court refused habeas corpus
where burglary in America was defined as not requiring entry as a trespasser.
The offence alleged here was not of a political character, and in those circumstances the court would not allow allegations of bad faith against the requesting
country: *Re* BUDLONG; *Re* KEMBER, *The Times*, December 7, 1979, D.C.

1295. —— fugitive offender—renewal of application—what constitutes fresh evidence
[Administration of Justice Act 1960 (c. 65), s. 14 (2); Fugitive Offenders
Act 1967 (c. 68), s. 8 (3) (*b*).]
An applicant is not precluded from renewing an application for habeas
corpus but the " fresh evidence " in support must be evidence that the applicant
could not have put forward on the first application.
In December 1975 the Singapore Government brought charges against T who
resided in England. In 1977, T was committed to custody for extradition on
some of the charges. T applied for a writ of habeas corpus on the grounds, *inter
alia*, under s. 8 (*a*) that it would be unjust and oppressive to return him, by
reason of the triviality of the alleged offences. The Divisional Court upheld
the committal of some of the charges but dismissed the others. On appeal a
further charge was dismissed in April 1978. T then petitioned the Secretary
of State but his petition failed. T applied to the Divisional Court a second
time for a writ of habeas corpus relying this time (i) on s. 8 (*a*) in the light of
" fresh evidence "; (ii) on s. 8 (*b*) in that it would be unjust and oppressive by
reason of the time that had now elapsed since the alleged offences were committed; and (iii) on the court's general powers because of the fresh evidence.
Held, (1) " fresh evidence " must be evidence which T could not have, or been

reasonably expected to, put forward on the first application otherwise *res judicata* applied; (2) the reasons under s. 8 (3) for discharge from custody were " grounds " for the purpose of a renewed application for habeas corpus; (3) the Secretary of State's decision did not preclude T from issuing a second application; (4) the evidence put forward did not constitute " fresh evidence " and the passage of time would not make it oppressive to return T for trial. (*Johnson* v. *Johnson* [1900] P. 19, *R.* v. *Medical Appeal Tribunal (North Midland Region), ex p. Hubble* [1959] C.L.Y. 2147, *Yat Tung Investment Co.* v. *Dao Heng Bank* [1975] C.L.Y. 211, and dictum of Lord Diplock in *Kakis* v. *Government of Cyprus* [1978] C.L.Y. 1451 applied; *R.* v. *Governor of Brixton Prison, ex p. Savakar* [1908–10] All E.R.Rep. 603 distinguished.)

Re TARLING [1979] 1 All E.R. 981, Gibson J.

1296. Internationally protected persons

EXTRADITION (INTERNATIONALLY PROTECTED PERSONS) ORDER 1979 (No. 453) [30p], made under the Extradition Act 1870 (c. 52), ss. 2, 17, and the Internationally Protected Persons Act 1978 (c. 17), ss. 3 (2), 4 (1); operative on May 24, 1979; applies the Extradition Acts 1870 to 1895 so as to make offences against internationally protected persons mentioned in the 1978 Act extraditable.

INTERNATIONALLY PROTECTED PERSONS ACT 1978 (OVERSEAS TERRITORIES) ORDER 1979 (No. 456) [25p], made under the Internationally Protected Persons Act 1978, s. 4 (2) and the Fugitive Offenders Act 1967 (c. 68), s. 17; operative on May 24, 1979; extends ss. 1–3 of the 1978 Act to certain specified territories.

1297. Suppression of terrorism

SUPPRESSION OF TERRORISM ACT 1978 (DESIGNATION OF COUNTRIES) ORDER 1979 (No. 497) [10p], made under the Suppression of Terrorism Act 1978 (c. 26), s. 8; operative on May 27, 1979; designates the Republic of Cyprus for the purposes of the 1978 Act so that it becomes a convention country within the meaning of the Act.

ARTICLES. See *post*, p. [23].

FACTORIES

1298. Breach of statutory duty—incorrect replacement of guard—negligence

[Horizontal Milling Machine Regulations 1928 (S.I. 1928 No. 548), regs. 3, 6.] The plaintiff lost his middle finger and suffered severe damage to his ring finger when his hand came into contact with the cutter on the horizontal milling machine, which he was operating at the time. It was found by the judge that immediately before the accident the cutter had been renewed and that the accident occurred as a result of the guard being improperly replaced. Park J. held that (1) there was a breach of reg. 3 of the Horizontal Milling Machine Regulations 1928, but that the breach did not cause the accident; and (2) although the plaintiff had no training in changing the cutter and replacing the guard, there were trained personnel available to do the job: the plaintiff knew that he ought not to have attempted to change the cutter. Thus his claim of common law negligence failed. On appeal, *held*, dismissing the appeal, that (1) in view of the judge's finding that the plaintiff could see that the guard was loose, it was impossible for the plaintiff to succeed in his claim of breach of statutory duty. The defendants had provided an ideally designed guard and the accident would have happened anyway; (2) the argument that, where the plaintiff established that an employer is in breach of statutory duty and the plaintiff is injured, there is something like a *res ipsa locquitur* position, is totally unfounded; (3) there was ample evidence for the finding that the plaintiff was negligent and he himself in breach of the regulations. Therefore the defendants were not in breach of their common law duty: LINEKER v. RALEIGH INDUSTRIES, July 17, 1979, C.A. (*Ex rel. Browne, Jacobson & Roose, Solicitors.*)

1299. —— slipping on snow and slush—previous injury

[Factories Act 1961 (c. 34), s. 29 (1).] The plaintiff was employed by the defendants in their forging bay. At 11.00 a.m. when crossing an open yard from the forging bay to the stores, the plaintiff slipped on the snow and slush and twisted his left knee. Some four to five months previously the plaintiff had severely injured his left knee and would have needed to have had an operation for the removal of a torn cartilage quite soon. *Held*, that (1) there was a breach of s. 29 (1) of the Factories Act 1961 in that the defendants failed to clear the yard; (2) on the same facts, the defendants were in breach of their common law duty, as they were negligent in not clearing the yard before 11.00 a.m.; (3) the plaintiff should be compensated for the pain and suffering caused by the accident and for the slight acceleration of his cartilage operation: BALL *v.* VAUGHAN BROS. (DROP FORGINGS), June 26, 1979, Hodgson J., Birmingham Crown Ct. (*Ex rel. Rowleys & Blewitts, Solicitors.*)

1300. Building operations. See BUILDING AND ENGINEERING, ARCHITECTS AND SURVEYORS.

1301. Fencing of machinery—whether machinery being cleaned is being "worked"
[Scot.] P was injured when he came into contact with a dangerous part of machinery within the meaning of reg. 42 of the Construction (General Provisions) Regulations 1961. At the time the machinery was being cleaned, which process necessitated the machine being put and kept in motion. The employers were charged with a breach of reg. 3 (1) in that they failed to fence securely the dangerous part. *Held*, the words "works or uses" in reg. 3 (1) embraced not only the commercial or industrial operation of a machine for its designed purpose, but any operation that involved its activation. Cleaning the machine was an integral part of its normal daily working. (*Knight* v. *Leamington Spa Courier* [1961] C.L.Y. 3457 considered): SMITH *v.* W. J. R. WATSON, 1977 J.C. 52, Ct. of Justiciary.

1302. Harbours and docks. See SHIPPING AND MARINE INSURANCE.

1303. Northern Ireland. See NORTHERN IRELAND.

1304. Shops. See SHOPS.

FAMILY ALLOWANCES

1305. Child benefit
CHILD BENEFIT AND SOCIAL SECURITY (FIXING AND ADJUSTMENT OF RATES) AMENDMENT REGULATIONS 1979 (No. 998) [10p], made under the Child Benefit Act 1975 (c. 61), s. 5; operative on November 12, 1979; amend the 1976 (No. 1267) Regulations by increasing the weekly rate of child benefit in respect of a child living with one parent by £0·50.

1306. —— "living with"—divorced parents—entitlement to claim
[Child Benefit Act 1975 (c. 61), s. 3.] M and F were divorced in 1975: on July 30, 1975, the parents were given joint custody of the two children, S and D, and it was ordered that they should not be removed from M's care and control. The claimant F was to have reasonable access. M received family allowance throughout the period of entitlement. F paid all boarding school fees and met a much larger proportion of the cost of S and D's maintenance than M. The local tribunal found that greater periods of time had been spent by the children with M and their home was with her. Both parties claimed child benefit for S and D. The local tribunal held that the claimant was not entitled to claim. On appeal the Commissioner held that, in construing s. 3 of the Child Benefit Act 1975, "living with" could not be looked at in the light of the family allowances cases, as child benefit is not limited to a parent, it is obtainable by any person responsible for the child. The expression should be given its ordinary and natural meaning in the context in which it occurs. It would be dangerous and unnecessary to define its meaning as involving *de facto* care and control, or the satisfaction of some other test. The test in each case is whether a child can be said to be "living with" the claimant at the relevant time: each case depends upon its own particular facts. "Living with" is not synonymous with "residing together" nor with "presence under the same roof." Care and control is not a necessary factor, but is of importance if it is in fact exercised by the person with whom the child is staying. When S and D were spending part of their holidays with F, who had lawful rights of access, and

was paying for their education, and exercising care control during their stay, F was entitled to claim during that period: DECISION NO. R (F) 2/79.

1307. —— parent of child—stepfather—death of mother

[Child Benefit Act (c. 61), s. 24 (3).] The claimant, who married S's mother, claimed child benefit in respect of S from the date of his wife's death. S's father was still alive. The Commissioner *held*, that (1) the claimant became S's stepfather on marriage to her mother (*I.R.C.* v. *Russell* [1955] C.L.Y. 1311 applied); (2) the claimant did not cease to be S's stepfather on the death of his wife, S's mother, although that event deprived him of his status as a married man. It was unnecessary to consider whether, if the marriage had been terminated by divorce, the status of stepfather would have continued (*Mander* v. *O'Toole* [1948] N.Z.L.R. 909 and *Re N. (Minors) (Parental Rights)* [1973] C.L.Y. 2183 considered): DECISION NO. R (F) 1/79.

1308. Family income supplements

FAMILY INCOME SUPPLEMENTS (GENERAL) AMENDMENT REGULATIONS 1979 (No. 160) [10p], made under the Family Income Supplements Act 1970 (c. 55), s. 10 (2) (*a*); operative on April 3, 1979; further amend S.I. 1971 No. 226 to provide that for the purposes of s. 1 (1) (*a*) of the 1970 Act a single person with at least one dependent child is treated as being engaged and normally engaged in remunerative full-time work if he is engaged in remunerative work for not less than 24 hours per week.

FAMILY INCOME SUPPLEMENTS (COMPUTATION) REGULATIONS 1979 (No. 939) [10p], made under the Family Income Supplements Act 1970, ss. 2 (1), 3 (1) (1A), 10 (1) (3) (4); operative on November 13, 1979; specify the prescribed amount for any family and the weekly rate of benefit under the 1970 Act in accordance with the amendments made to that Act by the Child Benefit Act 1975.

FAMILY INCOME SUPPLEMENTS (COMPUTATION) (No. 2) REGULATIONS 1979 (No. 1430) [10p], made under the Family Income Supplements Act 1970 ss. 2 (1), 3 (1), (1A), 10 (1), (3) and (4); operative on November 13, 1979; specify the prescribed amount for any family and the weekly rate of benefit under the 1970 Act in accordance with the amendments made by the Child Benefit Act 1975.

FAMILY INCOME SUPPLEMENTS (GENERAL) AMENDMENT (No. 2) REGULATIONS 1979 (No. 1504) [20p], made under the Family Income Supplements Act 1970, ss. 4 (1) (2), 6 (2), 10; operative on December 31, 1979; further amends S.I. 1971 No. 226.

FAMILY INCOME SUPPLEMENTS (CLAIMS AND PAYMENTS) (AMENDMENT REGULATIONS 1979 (No. 1505) [10p], made under the Family Income Supplements Act 1970, s. 10 (2) (*i*); operative on December 31, 1979; further amends S.I. 1971 No. 227. Reg. 8 of that Instrument is amended to provide that payment of family income supplement may be suspended by the Secretary of State pending the outcome of an appeal.

1309. National insurance. See NATIONAL INSURANCE.

FIRE SERVICE

1310. Disciplinary proceedings—charge referred to committee—chief fire officer in committee—rules of natural justice

[Fire Services Act 1947 (c. 41), s. 17; Fire Services (Discipline) Regulations 1948 (S.I. 1948 No. 545), reg. 5.]

Where a chief fire officer has been called into a disciplinary committee while sentence is being considered but has not participated in the deliberations, there has been a breach of the principle that justice must manifestly be seen to have been done.

Per curiam: There might be circumstances in which a declaration that the decision was the committee's own would suffice to expiate the breach, but the present was not such a case.

T, a station officer in a fire brigade, was charged with disobeying an order. The chief fire officer intended to hear the charge himself together with two other officers, but T sent a letter to the county council accusing the chief fire officer of victimisation so the chief fire officer referred the charge to the fire authority. At the hearing the charge was found proved. The committee cleared the room to consider sentence but called in the chief fire officer to advise on the practical implications of the various sentences available. The sentence was to reduce T's rank. The chairman stated that the chief fire officer had not participated in the committee's deliberations. On an application for certiorari to quash the award on the grounds that (1) the committee had no jurisdiction, and (2) there had been a breach of the rules of natural justice, *held*, granting the application, that (1) it was not necessary under the Regulations for the chief fire officer to begin to hear a case before referring it to the fire authority and the committee therefore did have jurisdiction; (2) there had been a breach of the principle that justice must manifestly be seen to have been done even though the chief fire officer had not, in fact, participated in the deliberations as to sentence. (*R.* v. *Bodmin Justices, ex p. McEwen* (1947) C.L.C. 6049 and *Ward* v. *Bradford Corporation* [1971] C.L.Y. 21 applied.)

R. *v.* LEICESTERSHIRE FIRE AUTHORITY, *ex p.* THOMPSON (1978) 77 L.G.R. 373, D.C.

1311. Pensions

FIREMEN'S PENSION SCHEME (AMENDMENT) (No. 2) ORDER 1979 (No. 855) [20p], made under the Fire Services Act 1947 (c. 41), s. 26 as amended and extended by the Reserve and Auxiliary Forces (Protection of Civil Interests) Act 1951 (c. 65), s. 42 and the Superannuation Act 1972 (c. 11), ss. 12, 16; operative on August 20, 1979; amends S.I. 1973 No. 966 to extend the definition of infirmity occasioned by a particular injury to include cases where an injury which became apparent only after retirement so aggravated an infirmity as to result in death or disablement; and to give widows of firemen an option to take a smaller pension and a lump sum in lieu of the pension currently provided.

FIREARMS

1312. Fees

FIREARMS (VARIATION OF FEES) ORDER 1979 (No. 86) [10p], made under the Firearms Act 1968 (c. 27), s. 43; operative on May 1, 1979; increases fees in respect of firearm certificates, shot gun certificates and in respect of the registration of firearms dealers.

FIREARMS (VARIATION OF FEES) ORDER 1979 (REVOCATION) ORDER 1979 (No. 459) [10p], made under the Firearms Act 1968, s. 43 (3) and the Statutory Instruments Act 1946 (c. 36), s. 5 (1); revokes S.I. 1979 No. 86.

1313. Northern Ireland. See NORTHERN IRELAND.

1314. Possession—forfeiture—binding over. See GOODLAD *v.* CHIEF CONSTABLE OF SOUTH YORKSHIRE, § 1714.

1315. ——— whether antique—burden of proof—evidence
[Firearms Act 1968 (c. 27), ss. 1 (1) (*a*), 2 (1), 58 (2).]
Where a defendant charged with possession of firearms without a licence claims that he bought them as antiques, there is some burden upon him to show that that is the case; but the question is one of fact for the jury.

D was charged with various offences under the Firearms Act 1968 relating to his possession of a ·303 rifle and a 12-bore shotgun without a firearms certificate. When questioned by the police, D said he thought they were antiques. At his trial, no expert evidence was called. The judge directed the jury that they must convict. On appeal by D, *held*, allowing the appeal, that the judge should have left to the jury the question whether they were sure as a matter of fact that the firearms were not antiques.

R. *v.* BURKE (1978) 67 Cr.App.R. 220, C.A.

BOOKS AND ARTICLES. See *post*, pp. [5], [23].

FISH AND FISHERIES

1316. Fishery limits

HADDOCK (WEST OF SCOTLAND AND ROCKALL) LICENSING ORDER 1979 (No. 71)

[20p], made under the Sea Fish (Conservation) Act 1967 (c. 84), ss. 4, 15 and S.I. 1978 No. 272; operative on February 12, 1979; prohibits the fishing for haddock in the specified areas by fishing boats registered in the U.K.

1317. Fishing boats

FISHING BOATS (FAROE ISLANDS) DESIGNATION ORDER 1979 (No. 256) [20p], made under the Fishery Limits Act 1976 (c. 86), s. 2 (1); operative on March 10, 1979; designates the Faroe Islands as a country whose registered fishing boats may fish in the areas specified for the descriptions of sea fish indicated in relation to those areas.

FISHING BOATS (SPECIFIED COUNTRIES) DESIGNATION ORDER 1979 (No. 504) [25p], made under the Fishery Limits Act 1976, ss. 2 (1), 6 (2); operative on April 30, 1979; revokes and supersedes S.I. 1977 No. 1084 as amended and S.I. 1979 No. 252. It designates the Faroe Islands, Norway, Spain and Sweden as countries whose registered fishing boats may fish for certain species of sea fish in certain areas of British fishery limits outside the area within 12 miles from the baselines from which the breadth of the territorial sea is measured.

MERCHANT SHIPPING (FISHING BOATS REGISTRY) (AMENDMENT) ORDER 1979 (No. 1455) [10p], made under the Merchant Shipping Act 1894 (c. 60), s. 373 (5) (d); operative on January 1, 1980; amends S.R. & O. 1927 No. 642 by increasing the penalties specified therein.

1318. Fishing vessels

FISHING VESSELS (ACQUISITION AND IMPROVEMENT) (GRANTS) (VARIATION) SCHEME 1979 (No. 1692) [10p], made under the Sea Fish Industry Act 1970 (c. 11), ss. 44, 45, 57; operative on December 15, 1979; further varies S.I. 1976 No. 304 by substituting January 1, 1981, as the date by which applications for grants must have been received by the White Fish Authority and the Herring Industry Board.

1319. Illegal fishing—contravention of by-law—meaning of " fishing "

[Sea Fisheries Regulation Act 1966 (c. 38), s. 11 (2) (as amended by Fishery Limits Act 1976 (c. 86), Sched. 1, para. 1 (2)).]

" Fishing " continues after fish are caught in a net and until such time as they are reduced into useful possession.

The defendant was convicted of two offences of using in fishing a purse seine net within the three-mile limit. On each occasion at the time of discovery the net had been " pursed " so that fish could no longer be caught but the catch had yet to be pumped aboard. The defendant claimed that on one occasion the vessel had drifted within the limit after the net had been pursed and that on the other the net had been accidentally shot while fish were being sought within the limit. *Held*, dismissing the defendant's appeal, that (1) the fishing operation did not end until the fish were pumped aboard; and (2) in relation to the second occasion, it sufficed that the vessel was searching for fish within the limit. (*R.* v. *The Frederick Gerring Jnr.* [1895] 5 Exch.C.R. 164 applied.)

ALEXANDER v. TONKIN [1979] 1 W.L.R. 629, D.C.

1320. Northern Ireland. See NORTHERN IRELAND.

1321. Offences—increase in penalty—offence occurring before new Act. See R. v. PENRITH JUSTICES, *ex p.* HAY, § 1742.

1322. Safety of fishermen—report and revised safety code

Recommendations aimed at improving the safety of fishermen are contained in the recently published " Report of the Working Group on the Occupational Safety of Fishermen." The group's main task was the revision of the existing Code of Safety and it recommends that the revised Code be adopted by all sea-going sectors of the U.K. fishing industry. The report is available from HMSO [50p]. The " Recommended code of safety for fishermen " is also available [£1·50].

1323. Sea fishing

COD AND WHITING (LICENSING) ORDER 1979 (No. 268) [20p], made under the Sea Fish (Conservation) Act 1967 (c. 84), ss. 4, 15; operative on March 26, 1979; prohibits fishing by boats registered in the U.K. for cod and whiting in the North Sea and specified areas off the west coast of Scotland.

HERRING BY-CATCH (RESTRICTIONS ON LANDING) (NO. 2) (VARIATION) ORDER 1979 (No. 398) [10p], made under the Sea Fish (Conservation) Act 1967, ss. 6, 15, 20 (1); operative on April 23, 1979; amends S.I. 1976 No. 2094. A "herring by-catch" is now defined as any quantity of herring in a catch of which more than 50 per cent. consists of other species of sea fish.

WHITE FISH SUBSIDY (DEEP SEA VESSELS) (SPECIFIED PORTS) SCHEME 1979 (No. 421) [20p], made under the Sea Fish Industry Act 1970 (c. 11), s. 49; operative on April 4, 1979; the scheme provides for the payment of grant to the owners or charterers of fishing vessels to which the scheme applies in respect of dock dues levied at certain specified ports in relation to voyages made during 1978 (the subsidy period) for the purpose of catching white fish.

SEA FISHING (SPECIFIED FOREIGN BOATS) LICENSING ORDER 1979 (No. 503) [25p], made under the Sea Fish (Conservation) Act 1967, ss. 4, 15, 20 (1); operative on April 30, 1979; supersedes and revokes S.I. 1977 No. 942. It prohibits fishing except under the authority of a licence, by fishing boats registered in the Faroe Islands, Spain and Sweden within certain areas within British fishery limits for certain species of sea fish for a period expiring on December 31, 1979.

IMMATURE SEA FISH ORDER 1979 (No. 741) [20p], made under the Sea Fish (Conservation) Act 1967, ss. 1 (1) (4) (5), 15; operative on July 1, 1979; supersedes S.I. 1968 No. 1618. It continues the provisions of the previous order setting minimum sizes for specified sea fish landed or sold in Britain. It also extends the provisions to foreign fishing boats within British fishery limits the statutory provisions against the carriage of undersize fish.

IMMATURE NEPHROPS ORDER 1979 (No. 742) [10p], made under the Sea Fish (Conservation) Act 1967, ss. 1 (1) (4) (5), 15; operative on July 1, 1979; prescribes for the purposes of s. 1 (1) of the 1967 Act a minimum size for nephrops, of 25 mm determined by reference to the length of the carapace. As a result the landing, sale or possession for the purposes of sale of nephrops of less than the prescribed size is prohibited.

NEPHROPS TAILS (RESTRICTIONS ON LANDING) ORDER 1979 (No. 743) (10p], made under the Sea Fish (Conservation) Act 1967, ss. 6, 15; operative on July 1, 1979; prohibits the landing of nephrops tails in the U.K., except where the landing consists of a quantity of not more than 290 tails per kilogram of the landed weight.

FISHING NETS (NORTH-EAST ATLANTIC) (VARIATION) ORDER 1979 (No. 744) [30p], made under the Sea Fish (Conservation) Act 1967, ss. 3, 20 (1); operation on July 1, 1979; varies S.I. 1977 No. 440 by providing a new definition of "the Irish Sea" modifying the orders provisions about fishing nets, and by adding sea bass to the list of fish named in Sched. 3.

IRISH SEA HERRING (PROHIBITION OF FISHING) ORDER 1979 (No. 1176) [20p], made under the Sea Fish (Conservation) Act 1967, ss. 5 (1) (2), 15; operative on September 22, 1979, save for art. 2 (2) which is operative on November 17, 1979; prohibits fishing for herring in specified parts of the Irish Sea.

THIRD COUNTRY FISHING (ENFORCEMENT) REGULATIONS 1979 (No. 1205) [20p], made under the European Communities Act 1972 (c. 68), s. 2 (2); operative on October 6, 1979; make breaches of certain Community regulations relating to third countries fishing offences for the purposes of U.K. law where they occur within British fishery limits.

SEA FISHING (NORTH-WEST SCOTTISH COAST WATERS) (PROHIBITION OF FISHING METHODS) ORDER 1979 (No. 1422) [20p], made under the Sea Fish (Conservation) Act 1967, ss. 5 (1) (2), 15; operative on November 12, 1979; prohibits fishing by trawls, ring nets and purse seine nets in specified areas adjacent to the north-west Scottish coast.

SEA FISH INDUSTRY ACT 1970 (RELAXATION OF TIME LIMITS) ORDER 1979 (No. 1691) [10p], made under the Sea Fish Industry Act 1973 (c. 3) , s. 1 (2); operative on December 15, 1979; relaxes time limits contained in certain provisions of the 1970 Act by providing that references to 1972 shall be read as references to 1980.

1324. Shell fish

POOLE FISHERY (VARIATION) ORDER 1979 (No. 38) [10p], made under the Sea Fisheries (Shellfish) Act 1967 (c. 83), Sched. 1; operative on February 13, 1979; varies the Poole Fishery Order 1915 by deleting art. 5 (2).

BRANCASTER STAITHE FISHERY ORDER 1979 (No. 1066) [10p], made under the Sea Fisheries (Shellfish) Act 1967, s. 1; operative on September 20, 1979; confers upon the Brancaster Staithe Fishermen's Society the right of several or exclusive fishery for oysters, mussels and cockles on a portion of the sea bed in Brancaster Staithe harbour.

CONWY MUSSEL FISHERY (VARIATION) ORDER 1979 (No. 1087) [10p], made under the Sea Fisheries (Shellfish) Act 1967, s. 1 (1) (6); operative on September 28, 1979; transfers regulation of the Conwy Mussel Fishery to Local Fisheries Joint Committee of the Lancashire and Western Sea Fisheries District.

STANSWOOD BAY OYSTER FISHERY (EXTENSION OF PERIOD) ORDER 1979 (No. 1137) [10p], made under the Sea Fisheries (Shellfish) Act 1967, Sched. 1; operative on June 1, 1980; continues S.I. 1973 No. 861 in operation for a further 15 years.

ARTICLES. See *post*, p. [23].

FOOD AND DRUGS

1325. Bread

BREAD PRICES (NO. 2) ORDER 1976 (REVOCATION) ORDER 1979 (No. 384) [10p], made under the Prices Act 1974 (c. 24), s. 2 (1) (6) (8); operative on April 2, 1979; revokes S.I. 1976 No. 2128 which regulated the maximum retail price of most bread loaves of 800g. or less.

1326. Butter

BUTTER PRICES (AMENDMENT) ORDER 1979 (No. 34) [10p], made under the Prices Act 1974 (c. 24), s. 2 (1) (6) (8); operative on February 5, 1979; varies S.I. 1978 No. 97 by increasing the maximum retail prices of butter.

BUTTER SUBSIDY (PROTECTION OF COMMUNITY ARRANGEMENTS) (AMENDMENT) REGULATIONS 1979 (No. 1175) [10p], made under the European Communities Act 1972 (c. 68), s. 2 (2); operative on September 27, 1979; amend S.I. 1979 No. 586.

1327. Dangerous drugs. See CRIMINAL LAW; MEDICINE.

1328. Hygiene

FOOD HYGIENE (SHIPS) REGULATIONS 1979 (No. 27) [20p], made under the Food and Drugs (Control of Food Premises) Act 1976 (c. 37), s. 7 (2); operative on February 19, 1979; apply the provisions of ss. 1–6 of the 1976 Act to the carrying on of a catering business or other retail food business in boats or craft which are moored or which are plying exclusively in inland waters or engaged exclusively in coastal excursions.

POULTRY MEAT (HYGIENE) (AMENDMENT) REGULATIONS 1979 (No. 693) [50p], made under the European Communities Act 1972 (c. 68), s. 2 (2) and the Food and Drugs Act 1955 (c. 16), ss. 13 and 123; operative on July 18, 1979; prescribe the conditions which must be satisfied when poultry meat is immersed in water to meet the washing or cooling requirements of item 8 of Sched. 4 to S.I. 1976 No. 1209; set down the conditions under which poultry carcases, which are dispatched from licensed slaughter houses in large packages, are exempt from the need for individual health marking; and amend reg. 24 of S.I. 1976 No. 1209 to clarify the status of official veterinary surgeons.

1329. Import of food

IMPORTED FOOD (AMENDMENT) REGULATIONS 1979 (No. 1426) [50p], made under the European Communities Act 1972 (c. 68), s. 2 (2) and the Food and Drugs Act 1955 (c. 16), ss. 13 and 123; operative on January 1, 1980; amend S.I. 1968 No. 97.

1330. —— official certificates

The Ministry of Agriculture, Fisheries and Food has issued the following circulars under the Imported Food Regulations 1968, as amended: 1/79 (Republic of Ireland); 2/79 (Paraguay); 3/79 (Denmark); 4/79 (Belgium); 5/79 (Singapore); 6/79 (France); 7/79 (Republic of Ireland); 8/79 (Federal

Republic of Germany); 9/79 (Netherlands); 10/79 (France); 11/79 (New Zealand); 13/79 (Canada); 14/79 (Australia); 15/79 (Federal Republic of Germany); 16/79 (Netherlands); 17/79 (Yugoslavia); 18/79 (Switzerland); 19/79 (Belgium); 20/79 (Republic of Ireland); 21/79 (New Zealand); 22/79 (Norway); 23/79 (Uruguay); 24/79 (Republic of Ireland); 25/79 (France); 27/79 (Australia); 28/79 (Federal Republic of Germany).

1331. Labelling of food

LABELLING OF FOOD (AMENDMENT) REGULATIONS 1979 (No. 1570) [20p], made under the Food and Drugs Act 1955 (c. 16), ss. 7 and 123; operative on January 1, 1980; amend S.I. 1970 No. 400.

1332. Lead

LEAD IN FOOD REGULATIONS 1979 (No. 1254) [40p], made under the Food and Drugs Act 1955 (c. 16), ss. 4, 123; operative on April 12, 1980; re-enact with amendments S.I. 1961 No. 1931 which restrict the amount of lead which may be present in food intended for sale for human consumption. The regs. amend certain definitions and reduce the general limit on lead in food to 1·0 mg. per kg.

1333. Milk

MILK (GREAT BRITAIN) (AMENDMENT) ORDER 1979 (No. 604) [20p], made under the Emergency Laws (Re-enactments and Repeals) Act 1964 (c. 60), ss. 6 and 7; operative on June 1, 1979; increases by 1½p per pint the maximum retail prices of milk.

MILK (GREAT BRITAIN) (AMENDMENT) (No. 2) ORDER 1979 (No. 700) [10p], made under the Emergency Laws (Re-enactments and Repeals) Act 1964, ss. 6, 7; operative on June 24, 1979; brings forward from July 15, 1979, to June 24, 1979, increases of 1½p per pint in the maximum retail prices of milk on sales in Scotland.

MILK (NORTHERN IRELAND) (AMENDMENT) (No. 2) ORDER 1979 (No. 1289) [10p], made under the Emergency Laws (Re-enactments and Repeals) Act 1964, ss. 6, 7, 22 (3); operative on November 1, 1979; increases by 3·358p per litre the maximum prices for the sale in Northern Ireland of raw milk for heat treatment.

MILK (GREAT BRITAIN) (AMENDMENT) (No. 3) ORDER 1979 (No. 1290) [10p], made under the Emergency Laws (Re-enactments and Repeals) Act 1964, ss. 6, 7; operative on November 1, 1979; increases by 1·1p per litre the maximum prices for sale in Great Britain of raw milk for heat treatment.

MILK AND DAIRIES (GENERAL) (AMENDMENT) REGULATIONS 1979 (No. 1567) [10p], made under the Food and Drugs Act 1955 (c. 2), ss. 29, 30 and 123; operative on January 1, 1980; convert the references to temperatures in reg. 17 of S.I. 1959 No. 277 to °C from °F.

MILK (EXTENSION OF PERIOD OF CONTROL OF MAXIMUM PRICES) ORDER 1979 (No. 1602) [10p], made under the Emergency Laws (Re-enactments and Repeals) Act 1964, s. 6; operative on December 31, 1979; continues for a further period of five years the power of the Minister of Agriculture, Fisheries and Food or the Secretary of State to control by order the maximum prices to be charged for liquid milk.

1334. Milk marketing

MILK MARKETING SCHEME (AMENDMENT) REGULATIONS 1979 (No. 249) [20p], made under the European Communities Act 1972 (c. 68), s. 2 (2); operative on April 4, 1979; amends S.R. & O. 1933 No. 789, for the purpose of putting the Board and their milk purchasers on an equal footing when negotiating prices.

1335. Northern Ireland. See NORTHERN IRELAND.

1336. Poisons. See MEDICINE.

1337. Preservatives

PRESERVATIVES IN FOOD REGULATIONS 1979 (No. 752) [£1·25], made under the Food and Drugs Act 1955 (c. 16), ss. 4, 7, 123 and 123A; operative on July 31, 1979; permit for the first time the use of sorbic acid as a preservative in or on specified foods.

1338. Sale—food not of substance demanded—prejudice to purchaser

[Food and Drugs Act 1955 (c. 16), s. 2 (1).] LF Co. manufactured and sold a can of strawberries which contained a beetle. At the hearing, the information alleged sale of the can which was not of the substance demanded, to the prejudice of the purchaser, contrary to s. 2 (1) of the 1955 Act. Justices dismissed the information on the ground that LF Co. had taken all reasonable care and that the beetle's presence was an unavoidable consequence of the process of collection or preparation within s. 3 (3). *Held,* allowing an appeal, that the presence of the beetle could not, in ordinary language, be said to be a consequence of the process of collection or preparation (*Smedleys* v. *Breed* [1974] C.L.Y. 1651 applied): GREATER MANCHESTER COUNCIL v. LOCKWOOD FOODS [1979] Crim.L.R. 593, D.C.

1339. Welfare food

WELFARE FOOD (AMENDMENT) ORDER 1979 (No. 1568) [10p], under the Emergency Laws (Re-enactments and Repeals) Act 1964 (c. 60), ss. 4 and 7; operative on January 1, 1980; amends S.I. 1977 No. 25.

FORESTRY

1340. By-laws

DEAN FOREST AND NEW FOREST ACTS (AMENDMENT) REGULATIONS 1979 (No. 836) [20p], made under the Forestry Act 1979 (c. 21), s. 2 (2) (5); operative on August 16, 1979; amend enactments relating to the Dean Forest and the New Forest by the substitution of metric for imperial measurements.

1341. Felling

FORESTRY (FELLING OF TREES) REGULATIONS 1979 (No. 791) [80p], made under the Forestry Act 1967 (c. 10), ss. 10 (1), 11 (2), 14 (3), 15 (2), 16 (2), 19 (3), 20 (1), 21 (2) (3) (5), 23 (1), 24 (2), 25 (1), 26 (2), 32 (1, (2); operative on August 9, 1979; revoke and re-enact S.I. 1951 No. 1726 and make provision for various procedural matters under the 1967 Act.

FORESTRY (EXCEPTIONS FROM RESTRICTION ON FELLING) REGULATIONS 1979 (No. 792) [20p], made under the Forestry Act 1967, ss. 9 (5) (*a*), 32 (1); operative on August 9, 1979; s. 9 (1) of the 1967 Act requires a felling licence to be granted by the Forestry Commissioners for the felling of growing trees except where by or under that Act, the subsection does not apply. Exceptions from its application are contained in s. 9 (2) (3) (4) of the Act and additional exceptions can be added under s. 9 (5). This order adds five further exceptions to the requirements of s. 9 (1).

1342. Forestry Act 1979 (c. 21)

This Act restates the power of the Forestry Commissioners to make grants and loans and provides for the metrication of enactments relating to forestry and forest lands.

S. 1 empowers the Forestry Commissioners to provide finance for forestry; s. 2 introduces the metrication of measurements; s. 3 contains the short title. commencement, etc. The Act does not extend to Northern Ireland.

The Act received the Royal Assent on March 29, 1979, and came into force on May 29, 1979.

FRAUD, MISREPRESENTATION AND UNDUE INFLUENCE

1343. Damages—innocent breach of law

[Exchange Control Act 1947 (c. 14), s. 7.] Plaintiff, who wished to buy a house in Spain, was entirely ignorant of the provisions of the Exchange Control Act 1947; she paid the price to the defendants in breach of the provisions of s. 7. The defendants were unable to give any title to the house and the plaintiff claimed her money back as damages for fraud. The judge found that the defendants had swindled her from the beginning. *Held,* that the parties were not *in pari delicto* and the plaintiff was entitled to recover notwithstanding the breach of exchange control: SHELLEY v. PADDOCK (1979) 123 S.J. 706, C.A.

1344. Innocent misrepresentation—specific performance—purchase of land

[Eire] During negotiations for the purchase of the defendant's lands, an agent for the plaintiff told the defendant that if she did not sell to the plaintiff the local authority would acquire the lands under compulsory powers. This was not true but the agent believed it to be true and the defendant believed it to be true. *Held*, that by reason of the plaintiff's misrepresentation the defendant had been under a fundamental misapprehension about the true facts and that it would be unjust to grant a decree of specific performance in the circumstances: SMELTER CORP. *v.* O'DRISCOLL [1977] I.R. 305, Eire Sup.Ct.

1345. Insurance—agent using undue influence—whether contract concluded

P wished to invest the £90,000 standing in her bank account, and it was recommended that she put her money in the property bonds of D1, an insurance company. Accordingly, P met D2, D1's agent, who explained the nature and advantages of the property bond policy, and offered P D1's "liquidity facility." P then arranged a meeting between her accountant and D2, who explained the property bond and the liquidity facility, to which the accountant gave his approval. P and D2 then went to P's bank and P, after a discussion with the bank manager, handed over a cheque for £91,600 in D1's favour. Five or six months later, P requested that £50,000—£60,000 of her investment be returned to her. She was unwilling to accept a surrender value, and D1 were unwilling to return all the money P had paid to them. P claimed that she never intended to make this investment, but a short-term deposit with a similarly named building society; that D2 had misrepresented the nature of property bonds and had exercised undue influence to obtain P's application; and that no binding contract was ever concluded. *Held*, dismissing P's appeal, that (1) in the light of the trial judge's finding that P had had the basic terms of D1's usual form of property bond policy fully explained to her, and in the light of the authorities, the trial judge's analysis that D1's conduct constituted acceptance of P's offer was correct and justifiable in law (*Adie & Sons* v. *The Insurance Corp.* (1898) 14 T.L.R. 544; *General Accident Insurance Corp.* v. *Cronk* (1901) 17 T.L.R. 233 considered); (2) if that was wrong, having regard to the circumstances of the case, there was an inevitable inference from P's conduct in doing and saying nothing for seven months that she accepted the policy as a valid contract between herself and D1; (3) accordingly on one basis or the other there was a concluded contract between P and D1 on the terms of the policy: RUST *v.* ABBEY LIFE ASSURANCE Co. [1979] 2 Lloyd's Rep. 334, C.A.

BOOKS. See *post*, p. [5].

FRIENDLY SOCIETIES

1346. Dissolution—disposal of assets—surplus

[Friendly Societies Act 1896 (c. 25), s. 49 (1).]

If no provision has been made by the rules of a friendly society as to the distribution of surplus funds on the society's termination, normally such funds will be divided among the existing members in equal shares and will not go to the Crown as *bona vacantia*.

The object of a friendly society was to provide by voluntary contributions from members for the relief of widows and orphans of deceased members of the Bucks Constabulary. The society's rules made no provision for the distribution of its assets in the event of the society's dissolution. When the Bucks Constabulary was merged with the Thames Valley Constabulary, the society resolved that it should be wound up and an attempt was made to transfer the surplus assets to the Thames Valley Fund and to a fund for serving members of the former Bucks Constabulary. That disposal was ruled invalid by the court as being unauthorised. The trustees then asked the court to determine whether the surplus assets should be distributed among the members, and if so how, or whether, as the Crown claimed, they should go to the Crown as *bona vacantia*. *Held*, the surplus would be held on trust to be distributed amongst the existing members at the time of dissolution in equal shares and to the total exclusion of the Crown. (*Tierney* v. *Tough* [1914] I.R. 142

applied; *Cunnack* v. *Edwards* [1896] 2 Ch. 679, *Braithwaite* v. *Att.-Gen.*
[1909] 1 Ch. 510 and *Re West Sussex Constabulary's Widows, Children and
Benevolent* (1930) *Trusts* [1970] C.L.Y. 2632 distinguished.)
    Re BUCKS CONSTABULARY WIDOWS' AND ORPHANS' FUND FRIENDLY SOCIETY;
THOMPSON *v.* HOLDSWORTH (NO. 2) [1979] 1 All E.R. 623, Walton J.

1346a. Fees
    FRIENDLY SOCIETIES (FEES) REGULATIONS 1979 (No. 1555) [20p], made
under the Friendly Societies Act 1974 (c. 46), s. 104 (1) and S.I. 1971 No.
1900; operative on January 1, 1980; increases the fees payable for registration
and sundry other matters and for the inspection of documents.

GAME

1347. Northern Ireland. See NORTHERN IRELAND.

GAMING AND WAGERING

1348. Lottery—cigarette cards—no payment for chance of winning
    [Lotteries and Amusements Act 1976 (c. 32), ss. 1, 14 (1).]
    A game of chance offered free to participants is not an unlawful lottery or
competition.
    In November 1978, after complaints had been made by the plaintiffs' com-
petitors, the Director of Public Prosecutions caused summonses to be issued
against the plaintiffs and their directors alleging that they were operating
an unlawful lottery and/or competition. It was intimated that the director
would seek trial on indictment: an assurance was sought that the scheme would
be discontinued pending the outcome of the trial. The scheme operated was
known as "Spot Cash": the plaintiffs, tobacco manufacturers, inserted in
cigarette packets a card with a number of boxes thereon. If the same figure
appeared in at least three boxes the holder won a prize, either cash or free
cigarettes. No extra charge was made for packets containing the cards, many
of which were distributed free of charge without any purchase of cigarettes.
The plaintiffs sought a declaration that the scheme was lawful and did not
contravene the 1976 Act. Donaldson J. entertained the application but ruled
that the scheme was an unlawful lottery and competition. *Held*, allowing the
appeal, that (1) considering, *inter alia*, the likely delay in the trial of the
criminal offences the court had rightly assumed jurisdiction to entertain the
application; (2) no payment or contribution was exacted from potential prize-
winners and accordingly the scheme was not a lottery within the meaning of
s. 1 of the Act; and (3) the absence of any "entrance charge" and of the need
for any purposeful striving on the part of entrants meant that the scheme was
not an unlawful competition within the meaning of s. 14 (1) (*b*) of the Act.
(*Atkinson* v. *Murrell* [1972] C.L.Y. 1611 and dicta of Lord Widgery C.J. in
Reader's Digest Association v. *Williams* [1976] C.L.Y. 1316 applied; *Whitbread & Co.* v. *Bell* [1970] C.L.Y. 1172 disapproved in part; *Willis* v. *Young*
[1907] 1 K.B. 448 and *Kerslake* v. *Knight* (1925) 41 T.L.R. 555, overruled.)
    IMPERIAL TOBACCO *v.* ATT.-GEN. [1979] 2 W.L.R. 805, C.A.

1349. Pool Competitions Act 1971—continuance
    POOL COMPETITIONS ACT 1971 (CONTINUANCE) ORDER 1979 (No. 763) [10p],
made under the Pool Competitions Act 1971 (c. 57), s. 8 (2) (3); operative on
July 26, 1979; continues in force the 1971 Act until July 26, 1980.

    BOOKS AND ARTICLES. See *post*, pp. [5], [23].

GAS AND GASWORKS

1350. Meters
    MEASURING INSTRUMENTS (EEC REQUIREMENTS) (GAS VOLUME METERS)
(AMENDMENT) REGULATIONS 1979 (No. 1224) [20p], made under the European
Communities Act 1972 (c. 68), s. 2 (2); operative on October 25, 1979; amend
S.I. 1975 No. 1873 in consequence of Commission Directive No. 78/365/EEC.

1351. Northern Ireland. See NORTHERN IRELAND.

1352. Rating. See RATING AND VALUATION

GIFTS

1353. Imperfect gift—house given to co-habitee—expenditure of money—estoppel.
See PASCOE *v.* TURNER, § 1083.

GOODWILL

1354. Appropriation—agency—passing off
The plaintiffs, a U.S. company, published periodicals sustained by advertising
revenue and distributed to likely purchasers of scientific instruments. P was the
agent, earning commission, and pursued another business. P compiled a list of
the identity and requirements of customers. In 1974 P launched a periodical for
the U.K. market called *Labmate*. In October 1975 the plaintiffs determined P's
agency. The defendants had previously launched another magazine. The plaintiffs alleged an intention to appropriate goodwill amounting to passing off.
Held, (1) it was a term of P's contract that he would not promote a competing
periodical during his agency; (2) the lists of customers satisfied the criteria for
confidential information; (3) the plaintiffs were entitled to a copy of the defendant's promotion list. Either party could use the list in his own business; (4) the
defendants were in breach of duty for publication of *Labmate* but on account
of their delay the plaintiffs were not entitled to an account of profits; (5) the
plaintiffs were entitled to compensatory damages for passing off since P had
appropriated the plaintiff's goodwill: INTERNATIONAL SCIENTIFIC COMMUNICA-
TIONS INC. *v.* PATTISON [1979] F.S.R. 429, Goulding J.

GUARANTEE AND INDEMNITY

**1355. Guarantee—duty of creditor to guarantor—sale of security—duty to obtain best
price**
P were T's bankers. D agreed to guarantee payment of all T's debts to the
bank. From 1971 onwards, any sums outstanding from T were secured in
P's favour by a charge over T's leasehold interest in certain premises. In
1975 P exercised rights of sale and realised £6,500 on the property, and then
claimed a further £11,000 from D. D said that P had not obtained the best
possible price for the security, and had a duty to D to do so. Cl. 10 of the
guarantee authorised P to " realise any securities in such manner as you may
think expedient." *Held*, there is no general duty of a creditor towards a
guarantor to obtain the best price reasonably available for a security. Cl. 10
expressly gave P certain rights and did not give D a right to complain about
P's dealings with the property (*Cuckmere Brick Co.* v. *Mutual Finance* [1971]
C.L.Y. 7479 distinguished): BARCLAYS BANK *v.* THIENEL (1978) 247 E.G. 385,
Thesiger J.

1356. —— subrogation—loan
A, on behalf of their Dutch subsidiary D, were provided by M with a one
million guilder loan. The loan was guaranteed by P, who took a counter
guarantee from A. The A group met financial difficulties in November 1975,
and when D defaulted an interest payment, M called upon P to pay under the
guarantee. P in their turn gave A formal notice that A, on February 25, 1976,
would owe them 1,043,166.67 guilders under the counter guarantee, with
interest at 6½ per cent. in case of delay. A replied on March 1 acknowledging
the request, and asking for a loan of the requisite sum. On February 25, P
paid M under the guarantee, but received nothing from A or D. P claimed that
they were subrogated to all M's right against D, and to be entitled to the
principal sum lent, with interest. *Held*, that (1) on February 25 P made a payment on their own behalf at a time when they had no authority from A to make
the payment or to make a loan to A to enable A to pay M; (2) at the close
of business on February 25, P had paid M under the guarantee and were
subrogated to M's right against D; and P, having demanded of A payment
under the counter guarantee, could also look to A for payment; (3) but after
P's ratification of A's application for a loan on March 1, P had a new right
against A, *i.e.* to be paid 1,043,166.67 guilders with 6½ per cent. interest;
nothing was agreed whereby P's rights under the counter guarantee were

preserved, and P had inadvertently and by operation of law lost their right against D; (4) P had not paid off M, and so were not subrogated to M's rights against D; but even if they were, those rights were transferred to A by operation of law when A with the aid of a loan from P met their liabilities under the counter guarantee; and P's claim failed: BROWN SHIPLEY & CO. v. AMALGAMATED INVESTMENT (EUROPE) B.V. [1979] 1 Lloyd's Rep. 488, Donaldson J.

1357. Joint guarantors—one released with knowledge and consent of other—no prejudice to other's position—whether released

[Can.] It has been *held,* that where a debt is guaranteed by two guarantors, the release of one with the knowledge and consent of the other, does not have the effect of releasing the other unless the latter's position is prejudiced by the release. Moreover, effect will be given in such circumstances to a clause in the guarantee empowering the creditor to grant releases and discharges to other persons without prejudice to the liability of the guarantor. (*Cutler* v. *McPhail* [1962] C.L.Y. 1753 referred to): CANADIAN IMPERIAL BANK OF COMMERCE v. VOPNI (1978) 86 D.L.R. (3d) 383, Manitoba Q.B.

1358. Letter of lien—construction. See GENERAL PRODUCE CO. v. UNITED BANK, § 154.

HAWKERS AND PEDLARS

1359. Northern Ireland. See NORTHERN IRELAND.

HIGHWAYS AND BRIDGES

1360. Bridges

COUNTY COUNCIL OF HAMPSHIRE (BASINGSTOKE CANAL—ODIHAM BYPASS BRIDGE) SCHEME 1978 CONFIRMATION INSTRUMENT 1979 (No. 606) [20p], made under the Highways (Miscellaneous Provisions) Act 1961 (c. 63), s. 3; confirms a scheme for the construction of the Basingstoke Canal Odiham Bypass Bridge.

COUNTY OF SOUTH GLAMORGAN (SOUTHERN ACCESS ROAD–ELY SECTION BRIDGE) SCHEME 1978 CONFIRMATION INSTRUMENT 1979 (No. 1260) [20p], made under the Highways (Miscellaneous Provisions) Act 1961, s. 3; operative on a date to be published; gives effect to a scheme for the construction of a bridge over the River Ely.

NORTHAMPTONSHIRE COUNTY COUNCIL (NORTHAMPTON TO WELLINGBOROUGH NEW A45 CLASSIFIED ROAD (GREAT DODDINGTON TO LITTLE IRCHESTER SECTION) (NEW BRIDGES) SCHEME 1979 CONFIRMATION INSTRUMENT 1979 (No. 1664) [40p], made under the Highways (Miscellaneous Provisions) Act 1961, s. 3 and the Highways Act 1971 (c. 41), s. 11; operative on a date to be published; confirms a scheme for the construction of a bridge over the River Nene.

BUCKINGHAMSHIRE COUNTY COUNCIL (H10 BLETCHLEY TO CALDECOTTE ROAD MILTON KEYNES CANAL BRIDGE) SCHEME, 1979 CONFIRMATION INSTRUMENT 1979 (No. 1674) [40p], made under the Highways (Miscellaneous Provisions) Act 1961, s. 3; operative on a date to be published; confirms a scheme for the construction of a bridge over the British Waterways Board's canal at Simpon, Milton Keynes, Buckinghamshire.

BUCKINGHAMSHIRE COUNTY COUNCIL (OLD WINDMILL FOOTBRIDGE MILTON KEYNES) SCHEME, 1979 (CONFIRMATION INSTRUMENT 1979 (No. 1675) [40p], made under the Highways (Miscellaneous Provisions) Act 1961, s. 3; operative on a date to be published; confirms a scheme for the construction of a footbridge over the British Waterways Board's canal at the Old Windmill site, Bradwell, Buckinghamshire.

1361. Duty to maintain roads—road subject to flooding

[Highways (Miscellaneous Provisions) Act 1961 (c. 63), s. 1.]

A highway authority may be liable for failure to take steps to drain part of a roadway which it ought reasonably to have known amounted to a potential danger by reason of flooding.

The defendant motorist lost control of his car and collided with that of the plaintiff after driving into a pool of water on the roadway. The plaintiff claimed damages from both the defendant motorist and the highway authority. *Held*, that the motorist and the authority were liable in equal proportions; on the evidence the authority ought reasonably to have known of the potential hazard and to have taken steps by way of drainage to prevent its occurrence; but the defendant motorist was not exonerated since in driving in wet conditions he had evidently driven too fast in order to see such a hazard as might have been anticipated. (*Burnside* v. *Emerson* [1968] C.L.Y. 1762 considered.)

TARRANT v. ROWLANDS [1979] R.T.R. 144, Cantley J.

1362. Footpath—conflicting evidence as to use—map conclusive
[National Parks and Access to the Countryside Act 1949 (c. 97), ss. 27 (*b*), 32 (4) (*a*).]
The showing of a right of way as a " footpath " on a definitive map is conclusive as to its status.

The definitive map published by P in 1961 showed a lane as a footpath. D wished to use the lane for vehicular access to their caravan site and produced evidence that the land had formerly been used as a public cartway. P sought a declaration that the lane was a footpath only. The judge held that rights of way additional to that shown on the definitive map were not precluded. The Court of Appeal allowed an appeal by P. On appeal, *held*, that on a literal reading of the section the definitive map was conclusive and precluded more extensive rights. A literal reading was consistent with a purposive construction of the Act and P was entitled to the declaration. (*Att.-Gen.* v. *Honeywill* [1972] C.L.Y. 2540 and *R.* v. *Secretary of State for the Environment, ex p. Hood* [1975] C.L.Y. 2462 considered. Decision of C.A. [1978] C.L.Y. 1545 affirmed.)

SUFFOLK COUNTY COUNCIL v. MASON [1979] 2 W.L.R. 571, H.L.

1363. —— diversion order—retroactive power
The development of a new residential estate required that a public footpath be diverted. A diversion order was made, after the development had commenced, but a new order was drawn up in 1976 and confirmed by the minister, after the original order was rejected by a public meeting. The plaintiffs appealed against the order on the ground that it was *ultra vires*, as s. 209 of the Town and Country Planning Act 1971 did not include power for the Secretary of State to make a retrospective diversion order in respect of a new route for a footpath. *Held*, dismissing the appeal, that s. 209 did apply here, but it could not be made to cover all retrospective orders. If the work had been finished, ss. 209 and 210 did not apply: ASHBY v. SECRETARY OF STATE FOR THE ENVIRONMENT, *The Times*, December 21, 1979, C.A.

1364. —— evidence of use as bridleway—definitive map
[National Parks and Access to the Countryside Act 1949 (c. 97), ss. 32 (4) (*a*), 33 (1) (*c*), Sched. 1, Pt. III, paras. 9 (1), 10; Highways Act 1959 (c. 25), s. 34 (1) (2).]
New evidence of user prior to a definitive map should be considered as if the authority had been preparing a draft map.

In the definitive map a highway was shown as a footpath. At the second and special review of the map and statement, pursuant to claims made by the parish council and the applicant, part of the highway was upgraded to bridleway. Objections were raised and at the inquiry the applicant gave evidence of former use of the highway by riders which ceased because of determined obstruction. The Inspector concluded in his findings of fact that there was no evidence of such user since the definitive map had been published, and recommended that the objection be allowed. He regarded the evidence of user prior to the definitive map as not relevant. His report was adopted by the Minister. The applicant sought orders of certiorari and mandamus to quash his decision and to direct him to hear and determine the objections according to law. *Held*, granting the orders, that (1) there had been an " event " in the discovery by the authority of new evidence as a result of the information provided by the applicant and that this evidence should have been considered as if the authority had then been preparing the draft map and not excluded as not relevant; (2) it was not correct to argue that the matter of the right of the public to use the highway had not been brought into question until the second review since this had been done at the time of making the definitive map; (3) the applicant was not questioning the validity of the map but the validity of the decision of the Secretary of State to exclude admissible evidence necessary for the proper determination of the matters in question. (*Suffolk County Council* v. *Mason* [1978] C.L.Y. 1545 applied.)

R. v. SECRETARY OF STATE FOR THE ENVIRONMENT, *ex p.* STEWART (1979) 37 P. & C.R. 279, D.C.

1365. —— upgrading—objections
[National Parks and Access to the Countryside Act 1949 (c. 97).] Two paths were designated as a bridleway and a road used as a public path, in the definitive map. Later both paths were designated as a " byway open to all traffic." Objectors argued that confirmation of these upgradings by the Secretary of State was invalid on the ground that there was insufficient evidence to justify such a finding. *Held,* there was sufficient evidence to justify the Secretary of State's decision. The inspector had looked at the paths and formed a view: R. v. SECRETARY OF STATE FOR THE ENVIRONMENT, *ex p.* PEARSON [1979] J.P.L. 765, D.C.

1366. Local authority—statutory power to repair highways—duty of care. See BARRATT v. DISTRICT OF NORTH VANCOUVER, § 1866.

1367. Motorways—inquiry—rules of evidence—cross-examination
[Highways Act 1959 (c. 25), Sched. 2.] At a motorway inquiry the inspector refused to allow cross-examination of evidence given on behalf of the department on future traffic predictions. He later recommended that the schemes be made. The Minister refused the objector's request that the inquiry be reopened because of change of circumstances relating to the need for the motorway, stating that he had taken such matters into account. *Held* (Templeman L.J. dissenting), that in a proper case cross-examination should be allowed and the objectors had not had " a fair crack of the whip." (*Re the Trunk Roads Act 1936 and re the London–Portsmouth Trunk Road (Surrey) Compulsory Purchase Order (No. 2) 1938* [1939] 2 K.B. 515 not followed; *Fairmount Investments* v. *Secretary of State for the Environment* [1976] C.L.Y. 305 applied; decision of Sir Douglas Frank [1978] C.L.Y. 1551 reversed): BUSHELL v. SECRETARY OF STATE FOR THE ENVIRONMENT (1979) 123 S.J. 605, C.A.

1368. Negligence. See NEGLIGENCE.

1369. Northern Ireland. See NORTHERN IRELAND.

1370. Obstruction—legal proceedings—discretion of Council
[Highways Act 1959 (c. 25), s. 116.] Frontagers blocked a path over which it was alleged the public had a right of way. The Parish Council urged the County Council to take legal proceedings to remove the obstructions. Ultimately they sought an order of mandamus to carry out their obligations under the Highways Act 1959, s. 116. *Held,* s. 116 imposed duties and not powers. The County council had no discretion whether to act and an order of mandamus would go, but the council had a discretion as to the way in which and extent to which the proceedings should be prosecuted: R. v. SURREY COUNTY COUNCIL, *ex p.* SEND PARISH COUNCIL [1979] J.P.L. 613, D.C.

1371. Public inquiry—objections—discretion of inspector
[Highways Act 1959 (c. 25), ss. 7, 9, 13, Sched. I; Highways Act 1971 (c. 41), s. 4.]
Where evidence having been heard and objections noted at a first public inquiry, an inspector excludes or gives no opportunity for such objections to be reopened at a second local inquiry, he is acting within his discretion and such action is not a breach of the rules of natural justice.

A scheme for the orbital M25 motorway proposed that the line of the motorway should pass close to the applicant's home. At a first public inquiry the applicant called evidence objecting to the motorway in principle. The scheme was approved by the Minister save for details of a road interchange. The Minister later opened a second local inquiry regarding this interchange. At the second inquiry the applicant sought to reopen her objections of the first inquiry and with others disrupted the hearing. The objectors were excluded, but later permitted to return, a fact which did not come to the applicant's attention. The applicant's motion to quash the scheme was dismissed at first instance. On appeal, *held*, dismissing the appeal, that the inspector would have been entitled to exclude objections to the principle of the motorway canvassed at the first hearing, and there was no breach of natural justice. (*The "Ace of Spades" Case* [1939] 2 K.B. 515, *Franklin* v. *Minister of Town and Country Planning* (1947) C.L.C. 7724 applied.)

LOVELOCK v. SECRETARY OF STATE FOR TRANSPORT [1979] R.T.R. 250, C.A.

1372. Road Traffic. See ROAD TRAFFIC.

1373. Special roads
S.I. 1979 Nos. 126 (M4–Reading South-East and Wokingham North-West Link) [10p]; 127 (A329(M) Reading South-East and Wokingham North-West Link) [10p]; 520 (M20–Legworth–Lenham) [10p]; 640 (A1(M) Blackfell Link Road) [10p]; 856 (M25–Wisley Section) [10p]; 857 (M25–Wisley Interchange) [10p]; 1246 (M65–Calder Valley Route, Hyndburn to Burnley) [10p]; 1247 (M65–Calder Valley Route, Hyndburn to Burnley) [10p]; 1377 (A146 Beccles Bypass–River Waveney Bridge) [20p]; 1697 (M55 Preston Northern Bypass Motorway–Squires Gate Link) [10p]; 1733 (M25 Yeoveney to Poyle Section) [10p]; 1735 (M25 Poyle Interchange) [10p].

1374. Street trading. See HAWKERS AND PEDLARS.

1375. Tolls
SEVERN BRIDGE TOLLS ORDER 1979 (No. 883) [20p], made under the Severn Bridge Tolls Act 1965 (c. 24), s. 2; operative on August 29, 1979; revokes and replaces S.I. 1966 No. 813, S.I. 1973 No. 120 and S.I. 1974 No. 745 and increases specified toll fees.

1376. Town and country planning. See TOWN AND COUNTRY PLANNING.

1377. Trunk roads
S.I. 1979 Nos. 66 (Levins Bridge–Greenodd–Barrow-in-Furness) [10p]; 89 (London–Fishguard) [10p]; 96 (Liverpool–Leeds) [10p]; 108 (London–Holyhead) [10p]; 150 (Folkestone–Honiton) [10p]; 327 (Princess Parkway, Princess Road (A5103) Manchester Section, Altrincham Road to Riverside Avenue, Northbank Walk) [20p]; 336 (Exeter–Leeds) [10p]; 388 (Llandeilo–Carmarthen) [10p]; 397 (Shreswbury–Dolgellau) [10p]; 526 (Swansea–Manchester) [10p]; 556 (Folkestone–Honiton) [20p]; 609 (Barnet Way, A1) [10p]; 610 (London–Portsmouth) [10p]; 626 (London–Penzance) [20p]; 634 (London–Edinburgh–Thurso) [10p]; 635 (Gateshead Western Bypass) [10p]; 636 (A1 Tyne Tunnel Road) [10p]; 637 (Carlisle–Sunderland) [10p]; 650 (Swansea–Manchester) [10p]; 764 (Bath–Lincoln) [10p]; 810 (Exeter–Leeds) [10p]; 814 (Folkestone–Honiton). [10p]; 827 (A249—Stockbury to Chestnut Street) [10p]; 833 (Swansea–Manchester) [10p]; 834 (Swansea–Manchester) [10p]; 835 (London–Carlisle–Glasgow–Inverness) [10p]; 848 (A41 Rock Ferry Bypass) [10p]; 849 (A570 Scarisbrick New Road) [10p]; 850 (Shrewsbury–Whitchurch–Warrington–Preston) [10p]; 851 (Manchester–Hyde–Mottram) [10p]; 852 (A565 Water Lane) [10p]; 835 (A565) Formby Bypass) [10p]; 854 (Shrewsbury–Whitchurch–Warrington–Preston) [10p]; 858 (A3 London–Portsmouth) [10p]; 859 (A3 London–Portsmouth) [10p]; 871 (Liverpool–Skegness) [10p]; 872 (Edgware Road, Barnet and Brent) [10p]; 873 (North Circular Road, Barnet and Brent) [10p]; 874 (Western Avenue Hillingdon) [10p]; 935 (London–Fishguard) [20p]; 962 (Birmingham–Great Yarmouth) [10p]; 986 (London–Fishguard) [10p]; 987 (Fishguard–Bangor) [10p]; 1029 (Folkestone–Honiton [10p]; 1035 (Newport–Monmouth–Ross-on-Wye–Worcester) [10p]; 1046 (Sheffield–Grimsby) [20p]; 1050 (Nottingham–Widmerpool) [10p]; 1051 (Bath–Lincoln) [10p]; 1059 (Exeter–Leeds) [10p]; 1060 (Birmingham–Great Yarmouth) [10p]; 1061 (Winchester–Preston) [10p]; 1082 (London–Birmingham) [40p]; 1121 (Great West Road, Hounslow) [10p]; 1126 (North of Westhoughton Link) [10p]; 1156 (Western Avenue, Ealing) [10p]; 1188 (Bilston Link Trunk Road and Slip Roads–revocation) [10p]; 1229 (Cardiff–Llangurig) [20p]; 1245 (Manchester–Burnley) [10p]; 1248 (Leeds–Halifax–Burnley–Blackburn–East of Preston) [10p]; 1255 (Western Avenue, Ealing) [20p]; 1272 (Folkestone–Honiton) [10p]; 1300 (Newport–

Shrewsbury–Warrington) [10p]; 1302 (Carlisle–Sunderland) [10p]; 1370 (Fishguard–Bangor) [10p]; 1380 (Fishguard–Bangor) [10p]; 1381 (Fishguard–Bangor) [10p]; 1386 (London–Fishguard) [10p]; 1433 (Great West Road, Hounslow) [10p]; 1469 (Taunton–Fraddon) [10p]; 1479 (London–Penzance) [10p]; 1480 (Winchester–Preston) [10p]; 1481 (Winchester–Preston) [10p]; 1482 (Winchester–Preston) [10p]; 1497 (London–Edinburgh–Thurso) [40p]; 1503 (London–Edinburgh–Thurso) [10p]; 1665 (Liverpool–Warrington–Stockport–Sheffield–Lincoln–Skegness) [10p]; 1666 (Liverpool–Leeds–Hull) [10p]; 1734 (M25 Poyle Interchange to Heathrow) [10p]; 1739 (North Circular Road, Brent) [10p]; 1762 (New Road, Barking) [20p]; 1763 (Liverpool–Preston–Leeds) [20p].

BOOKS AND ARTICLES. See *post,* pp. [5], [23].

HIRE PURCHASE

1378. Minimum deposit

HIRE-PURCHASE AND CREDIT SALE AGREEMENTS (CONTROL) (AMENDMENT) ORDER 1979 (No. 1223) [10p], made under the Emergency Laws (Re-enactments and Repeals) Act 1964 (c. 60), ss. 1, 7; operative on October 29, 1979; varies the exemption from control under S.I. 1976 No. 1135 relating to credit sale agreements in certain cases where the cash price is paid by way of agreement for running-account credit.

HOUSING

1379. Compulsory purchase. See COMPULSORY PURCHASE.

1380. Control order—certiorari to quash order—alternative remedy

H served notice on H to reduce the number of people living in M's property to one family. W was the only lawful occupier, and M sought possession against her on the ground of unlawful sub-letting. Possession suspended for 28 days was obtained, but within that time H served a control order on M under s. 73 of the Housing Act 1964, H applied for an order of certiorari to quash the order, saying that s. 73 only applied to lawful occupiers. *Held,* dismissing the application, s. 82 gave M power to appeal against the notice, and the court would not grant a prerogative order where it was shown that there was an alternative remedy: MINFORD PROPERTIES *v.* HAMMERSMITH LONDON BOROUGH (1978) 247 E.G. 561, D.C.

1381. Council tenancy—notice to quit—repairing covenant

[Housing Act 1961 (c. 65), s. 32.] Notice to quit was served on a council tenant. The house had been classified as unfit, because of defects in structure and damp. Alternative accommodation had been found. P defended the possession action and counterclaimed for breach of the repairing covenant. P appealed against the order and dismissal of counterclaim. *Held,* the prospective life of the house affected the duty of the council and repairs would be useless. Appeal dismissed: NEWHAM LONDON BOROUGH *v.* PATEL [1979] J.P.L. 303, C.A.

1382. Fitness for habitation—intention—" back to back houses "—" intended for the working classes "

[Housing Act 1957 (c. 56), s. 5.]

There must be an intention, either actual or implied, to erect " back to back houses " for " the working classes " for a building to contravene the Housing Act 1957, s. 5.

Per curiam: The court did not find it necessary to define the modern meaning of " the working classes."

B Co. built different types of housing, including two blocks of four one-bedroomed houses. Each house had two outside walls with windows and two inside walls so that the houses were back to back as well as side by side. They were relatively inexpensive, intended for sale at a price below £10,000. The purchasers came from various occupations, including a doctor, a professional ice-skater and a nurse. The local authority alleged that the houses were " back to back houses intended to be used as dwellings for the working classes " and were prohibited by s. 5 (1) of the Housing Act 1957. As the houses were relatively inexpensive, they were intended for the lower income groups and thus " the working classes." *Held*, dismissing the summons, that (1) as the houses being constructed did not fall within the popular and general meaning of " back to back houses," in other words terraces of houses where all the houses, except those at the end of the terrace, had three inside walls and only one outside wall, they were not prohibited by s. 5; (2) B Co. did not have the necessary intention, either actual or implied, to erect the houses " for the working classes " since there was no intention to sell the houses to any particular income group but to purchasers who tended to be single people or couples without children rather than people with low incomes.

CHORLEY BOROUGH COUNCIL *v.* BARRATT DEVELOPMENTS (NORTH WEST) [1979] 3 All E.R. 634, Blackett-Ord V.-C.

1383. —— repairs—reasonable expense—demolition order
[Housing Act 1957 (c. 56), ss. 16, 20 and 39 (1).] The appellant authority made a demolition order on a house in 1976 as unfit and not capable of being made fit at reasonable cost. Agreed costs of reinstatement were £1,400–£1,500. Demolition would cost £500. The house was fully tenanted by tenants who were not prepared to co-operate with the carrying-out of major works. The authority valued the house at a nominal £50 with sitting tenants and £1,000 as reinstated. The county court judge quashed the order. *Held*, dismissing the appeal, the judge had properly exercised his discretion without recourse to strict mathematical calculation. He had to consider the " open market value " which might or might not be the " sitting tenant " value, depending on the situation as to security of tenure and so on. He was entitled to take into account the expense of demolition in favour of the owners. (*Victoria Square Property Co.* v. *Southwark London Borough Council* [1978] C.L.Y. 276, *Inworth Property Co.* v. *Southwark London Borough Council* [1978] C.L.Y. 1574 and *Hillbank Properties* v. *Hackney London Borough Council* [1978] C.L.Y. 1573 applied): DUDLOW ESTATES *v.* SEFTON METROPOLITAN BOROUGH COUNCIL (1979) 249 E.G. 1271, C.A.

1384. —— works in default under statutory notice—appeal—discretion of local authority
[Housing Act 1957 (c. 56), ss. 9–11.] The appellants were the freehold owners of a large early-Victorian terraced property. In February 1978 the respondent council, being satisfied that the tenanted basement flat at the premises was unfit for human habitation, served a notice on the appellants under s. 9 (1) requiring them to execute works recited in the schedule to the notice. The appellants did not carry out the works within the time limit and in October the council instructed a building contractor to execute the works in default. A demand for the recovery of expenses incurred was rendered to the appellants in December; the appellants then appealed under s. 11 (1) (*b*). The grounds of appeal included, *inter alia*, that the respondent had a discretion under s. 10 (1) as to whether or not they should themselves do the work required to be done by the notice and that this discretion had not been exercised properly. The council argued that the word " may " in s. 10 (1) conferred an enabling power which the local authority were bound to exercise as their power was coupled with a duty under s. 9 (1). Consequently the council had no discretion in the matter and were not obliged to consult further before undertaking the default works. *Held*, (1) on appeal under s. 11 (1) (*a*), the court in considering the validity and reasonableness of a notice served under s. 9 (1), has jurisdiction to consider all relevant surrounding circumstances including, for example, the personal circumstances of the owner or the person having control of the premises. On the other hand, on an appeal under s. 11 (1) (*b*), the court cannot consider such matters (s. 11 (2) and *Hillbank Properties* v. *Hackney London Borough Council* [1978] C.L.Y. 1573 applied); (2) the word " may " in s. 10 (1) does not confer a discretion which must be exercised: it is an enabling provision giving an absolute discretion. The council was therefore not subject to a duty to investigate further or to consult with the recipient of the statutory notice. The council was under a duty to ensure that a house unfit for human habitation was rendered fit; (3) the construction of the word " may " adopted by the court made sense

of the legislation under review and would not lead to injustice. The appeal, which then proceeded solely on the question of quantum of costs and quality of workmanship, was dismissed with costs. Demand upheld: ELLIOTT *v.* BRIGHTON BOROUGH COUNCIL, June 13 and July 16, 1979, Judge Brian Grant, Brighton County Ct. (*Ex rel. Jonathan Teasdale, Esq., Barrister.*)

1385. Homeless persons—statutory duty to provide accommodation—breach of duty—action for damages

[Housing (Homeless Persons) Act 1977 (c. 48), s. 3 (4).]

A homeless person may bring an action for damages in tort against a housing authority for breach of its statutory duty to provide accommodation for him under s. 3 (4) of the Housing (Homeless Persons) Act 1977.

P brought an action against the housing authority for damages and an injunction for breach of duty under s. 3 (4) of the Housing (Homeless Persons) Act 1977, in that, having reason to believe that he was homeless and had a priority need, it had failed to secure accommodation for him to occupy pending his application for accommodation under the Act. The county court judge ordered the particulars of claim to be struck out on the ground that a civil action for damages did not lie. On appeal by P, *held*, allowing the appeal, that an action for damages in tort lay, and the action would proceed to that (*Guardians of the Poor of Gateshead Union* v. *Durham County Council* [1918] 1 Ch. 146 and *Cutler* v. *Wandsworth Stadium* (1949) C.L.C. 4241 applied).

THORNTON *v.* KIRKLEES METROPOLITAN BOROUGH COUNCIL [1979] 2 All E.R. 349, C.A.

1386. —— —— date of duty

[Housing (Homeless Persons) Act 1977 (c. 48).] In an application for an order of mandamus to compel the council to carry out their statutory duty to rehouse homeless persons, the question arose as to the time at which the duty arose. *Held*, that the duty arose as soon as the council were satisfied that the person was homeless. There was no postponement of the duty until the council had complied with the statutory requirement to notify the person applying for assistance: R. *v.* BEVERLEY BOROUGH COUNCIL, *ex p.* McPHEE [1979] J.P.L. 94, D.C.

1387. —— —— Irish applicant

[Housing (Homeless Persons) Act 1977 (c. 48), ss. 5, 6 (1) (c).]

A housing authority may discharge its statutory obligation to provide accommodation for a homeless person by advising and assisting such a person to accept the offer of accommodation outside the area of the authority's jurisdiction.

The applicant and her seven children left her matrimonial home in Tralee, Eire, because of her husband's violence. She went to Bristol and there sought accommodation as a homeless person. The respondent authority contacted the welfare officer in Tralee, he being aware of the applicant's domestic circumstances: that officer assured the authority that suitable accommodation would be provided for the applicant if she returned to Tralee. The authority accepted their obligation to the applicant under the 1977 Act, but considered that such obligation would be discharged by advising the applicant to return to Tralee (and paying her expenses of so doing); they advised her accordingly. The applicant sought an order of mandamus compelling the authority to provide accommodation in Bristol. *Held*, refusing the application, that (1) the " some other person," by whom accommodation could be provided under s. 6 (1) (c) of the Act, did not need to be within the authority's area; (2) if s. 5 of the Act was applicable, the authority had acted properly in concluding on the advice of the Tralee Welfare Officer that the applicant would not run the risk of domestic violence if she returned; and (3) it mattered not that the Tralee Welfare Officer had not specified the particular accommodation to be provided. R. *v.* BRISTOL CITY COUNCIL, *ex p.* BROWNE [1979] 3 All E.R. 344, D.C.

1388. —— —— whether intentionally homeless

[Housing (Homeless Persons) Act 1977 (c. 48), s. 3 (4).] Italian workers came to the U.K., stayed for a short while with relatives, and then became homeless. They applied for housing to the local authority, pursuant to s. 3 (4) of the Housing (Homeless Persons) Act 1977. *Held,* that the authority was, on the facts, entitled to conclude that the workers became homeless intentionally " by coming to this country without having ensured that they had permanent accommodation to come to " and, accordingly, to refuse the applications: DE FALCO *v.* CRAWLEY BOROUGH COUNCIL; SILVESTRI *v.* SAME, *The Times,* December 13, 1979, C.A.

1389. Housing Act 1974—commencement
HOUSING ACT 1974 (COMMENCEMENT NO. 6) ORDER 1979 (No. 1214 (C. 32)) [20p], made under the Housing Act 1974 (c. 44), s. 131; operative on October 9, 1979; brings into force s. 130 of and Scheds. 13 and 15 to the 1974 Act so far as they relate to specified repeals.

1390. Housing associations—non-compliance with objects—eligibility to remain on register
[Housing Act 1974 (c. 44), ss. 13, 15.]
S. 13 (6) of the Housing Act 1974 raises a statutory conclusive presumption, except in the case of rectification of the register, that once a housing association is on the register and is an association within s. 13 (1) (*b*), it has complied with the conditions of s. 13 (2) and (3); if those conditions are not complied with then the Divisional Court may compel the Housing Corporation to take proper steps by one of the prerogative orders.
The Dolphin Square Trust was registered under the Industrial and Provident Societies Act 1965 and was on the register of the Housing Corporation as a housing association under s. 13 of the Housing Act 1974. The Trust's objects was to carry on the business of providing houses for letting; profits were not allowed to be distributed among members; they were to be used for rent rebates and improvements. The Trust sought an order for possession against P, a tenant. P issued a writ against the Trust and the Housing Corporation claiming a declaration that the Trust was ineligible to be on the register because it had let some flats as offices and some as holiday accommodation, and rectification of the register to remove the Trust's name. The judge at first instance struck out P's claim. On appeal by P, *held,* dismissing the appeal, (1) s. 13 (6) raised a statutory conclusive presumption that the Trust was an association within s. 13 (1) (*b*) and had complied with the conditions under s. 13 (2) and (3); s. 15 excluded rectification except in certain circumstances which did not apply, so that the declaration could not be granted; the Trust was unable to trade for profit since its objects prevented distribution, and any complaint should be remedied by the Housing Corporation under ss. 20 and 22. If necessary the Divisional Court could compel the Housing Corporation to act by way of judicial review under one of the prerogative orders. (Dictum of Fletcher Moulton L.J. in *Re Spanish Prospecting Co.* [1911] 1 Ch. 92, 98–99 applied.)
GOODMAN *v.* DOLPHIN SQUARE TRUST (1979) 38 P. & C.R. 257, C.A.

1390a. Housing Corporation
HOUSING CORPORATION ADVANCES (INCREASE OF LIMIT) ORDER 1979 (No. 1586) [10p], made under the Housing Act 1974 (c. 44), s. 7 (5); operative on December 3, 1979; specifies the aggregate amount outstanding by way of principal shall not exceed £750 million.

1391. Housing subsidies
ASSISTANCE FOR HOUSE PURCHASE AND IMPROVEMENT (VARIATION OF SUBSIDY) ORDER 1979 (No. 894) [20p], made under the Housing Subsidies Act 1967 (c. 29), s. 28 (3) (4) (5) as inserted by the Housing Act 1969 (c. 33), s. 78; operative on September 1, 1979; provides a new scale of percentages in relation to option mortgage subsidy payable under Pt. II of the 1967 Act in respect of interest payable under option mortgages where the rate of interest for the time being exceeds 6·7 per cent. per annum.
ASSISTANCE FOR HOUSE PURCHASE AND IMPROVEMENT (TRANSITIONAL PROVISIONS) REGULATIONS 1979 (No. 1515) [40p], made under the Housing Act 1974 (c. 44), s. 119 (4) (*a*), (5) (6); operative on January 1, 1980; make transitional provisions to secure the proper application of Pt. II of the Housing Subsidies Act 1967 after April 5, 1980, to certain existing option mortgages for which

the option notice was signed on or before June 26, 1974, or the loan was made in pursuance of an offer made before that date.

1392. Northern Ireland. See NORTHERN IRELAND.

1393. Rent allowance subsidy

HOUSING FINANCE (RENT ALLOWANCE SUBSIDY) ORDER 1979 (No. 234) [10p], made under the Housing Finance Act 1972 (c. 47), s. 8 (4); operative on March 31, 1979; substitutes 100 per cent. for 80 per cent. in s. 8 (3) of the 1972 Act which fixes the amount of rent allowance subsidy payable to a local authority for the year 1979–80.

1394. Rent rebates

RENT REBATES AND RENT ALLOWANCES (STUDENTS) (ENGLAND AND WALES) REGULATIONS 1979 (No. 1014) [10p], made under the Housing Finance Act 1972 (c. 47), s. 25 (3) (c); operative on September 1, 1979; increased to £8·75 the amount prescribed as the deduction to be made in calculating the rent which is eligible to be met by a rent rebate or a rent allowance under Pt. II of the 1972 Act, as amended, in the case of tenants who are students who have grants from public funds for the purpose of their full-time education.

RENT REBATE AND RENT ALLOWANCE SCHEMES (AND SERVICES AMENDMENT) (ENGLAND AND WALES) REGULATIONS 1979 (No. 1319) [20p], made under the Housing Finance Act 1972, s. 25 (3); operative on November 12, 1979; make provision concerning the variations of Sched. 3 to the 1972 Act with which every rent rebate scheme and every rent allowance scheme under Pt. II of the Act must conform.

1395. Town and country planning. See TOWN AND COUNTRY PLANNING.

BOOKS AND ARTICLES. See *post*, pp. [5], [23].

HUSBAND AND WIFE

1396. Advancement—property registered in joint names—considerations

[Can.] Where property is registered in the joint names of a husband and wife, the presumption of advancement arises and can only be rebutted by evidence of the most cogent nature. The presumption is not rebutted by evidence that H only intended to bestow a limited estate on W in the event of his death, and accordingly W acquires a half interest in the property and is entitled to an order for partition and sale. (*Falconer* v. *Falconer* [1970] C.L.Y. 1234 considered and distinguished): HEBERT v. FOULSTON (1978) 90 D.L.R. (3d) 403, Alta.Sup.Ct.

1397. Ancillary relief—matrimonial home—partial property adjustment order unsatisfactory

Following the parties' divorce various ancillary relief orders were made and it was agreed that H should transfer the home, which was in his sole name, into the joint names of W and himself. The judge made no provision as to the right of occupation of the house. H was employed in Kuwait with a contract lasting until the mid-1980s. *Held*, allowing W's cross-appeal, that the situation with the matrimonial home was anything but satisfactory. Judges dealing with property matters must deal with them in full at the time when the issue was before the court. It was quite plain from the Matrimonial Causes Act 1973 that the court was required to make the appropriate property adjustment order at the time it dealt with the matter. The order as it stood, therefore, was wrong in principle and would be varied by means of a *Mesher* type of order (see [1973] C.L.Y. 1615), *i.e.* that W should have the right to occupy the house until the younger of the two children of the family was 18, whereupon it should be sold and the proceeds divided equally. That at least tied up the property position and did not leave it in a state of doubt: RUSHTON v. RUSHTON (1978) 9 Fam. Law 218, C.A.

1398. Children. See MINORS.

1399. Civil liability—action for damages for conspiracy—whether spouses one person in law

The court will hear a motion to set aside judgment by default where the substance of the application goes to the court's jurisdiction and finality has not been reached in the proceedings. Spouses are not immune from civil liability in circumstances where the unmarried would be liable.

H granted his son an option to purchase a farm, but in breach of contract and with the intent to defeat the option conveyed the farm to W. The son brought an action seeking an order for specific performance, damages in lieu of or in addition to specific performance and damages for conspiracy. After the death of the three parties the action was continued by the personal representatives. After D failed to comply with an order for discovery Hs defence was struck out. At the trial all claims against W's estate were dropped but an inquiry as to damages against H's estate was ordered. On D's motion to set aside judgment on the basis that P's claim disclosed no reasonable cause of action and that D had a good defence in that H and W being married were incapable in law of conspiring together, *held*, that (1) the court would hear the motion on its merits since the substance of the application went to the court's jurisdiction and since finality had not yet been reached in the proceedings; (2) the common law rule that spouses could not be guilty of the crime of conspiracy was based on public policy; but public policy did not require that immunity from civil liability should be given to spouses in circumstances where the unmarried would be liable. (*Gordon* v. *Gordon* [1940] P. 163 applied; *Re Barraclough, decd.* [1965] C.L.Y. 1617 and *Hadkinson* v. *Hadkinson* [1952] C.L.Y. 2648 distinguished; *Anon.* (1345) Y.B. (R.S., ed. Pike) 19 Edw. 3 Mich. 24, *Phillips* v. *Barnet* (1876) 1 Q.B.D. 436, *D.P.P.* v. *Blady* [1912] 2 K.B. 89, *Gottliffe* v. *Edelston* [1930] 2 K.B. 378, *Broom* v. *Morgan* [1953] C.L.Y. 1309 and *Mawji* v. *The Queen* [1957] C.L.Y. 694 considered.) MIDLAND BANK TRUST CO. *v.* GREEN (No. 3) [1979] 2 W.L.R. 594, Oliver J.

1400. Couple living together as man and wife—injunction—jurisdiction

[Domestic Violence and Matrimonial Proceedings Act 1976 (c. 50), s. 1 (2).] M and N had lived together as man and wife between October and December 1978 during which time N had been violent. N had continued to make threats after this time. M obtained an injunction under the 1976 Act in February 1979. She then sought to add a power of arrest in April 1979. The judge, however, decided that he had no jurisdiction, refused M's application and discharged the injunction. *Held*, allowing M's appeal, that since N had not made application to set aside the injunction or even participated in the proceedings the judge had been wrong to set aside the injunction. On the question of jurisdiction, it was not necessary to show that the man and the woman were living together at the time of the application so long as they had lived together as husband and wife. There was no doubt on these facts that M and N had fulfilled this qualification (*Davis* v. *Johnson* [1978] C.L.Y. 1590 applied; *B.* v. *B.* [1978] C.L.Y. 1591 considered): McLEAN *v.* NUGENT (1979) 123 S.J. 521, C.A.

1401. Divorce. See DIVORCE AND MATRIMONIAL CAUSES.

1402. Financial provision—application after long period of separation

Parties had married in 1935. H was now aged 65 and W was 62. In 1956 W had left to live with another man. She now lived with her son, by that other relationship, in a flat. H lived in the former matrimonial home, worth £26,500. In April 1978 W was granted a decree nisi under s. 1 (2) (*e*) of the Matrimonial Causes Act 1973. She now sought a lump sum order and under s. 17 of the Married Women's Property Act 1882 also sought an order for the sale of the former matrimonial home and a division of the proceeds of sale. *Held*, that after a long lapse of time a party to a marriage should be entitled to take the view that there would be no revival or initiation of financial claims against him. The longer the lapse of time the more secure he should feel and the less should any claim be encouraged or entertained. The court was satisfied that W was in no danger of losing occupation of her present home and was not in need. Even if it could be assumed that W was entitled to the £5,000 she sought it was unreasonable to expect H to raise the amount by the sale of the house or to raise a loan on the equity existing in the premises: CHAMBERS *v.* CHAMBERS (1979) 123 S.J. 689, Wood J.

1403. —— **conduct of parties**
[Matrimonial Causes Act 1973 (c. 18), ss. 10 (2) (3), 25 (1).]
When dealing with conduct, it is essentially to the conduct of the party claiming financial relief that attention must be paid, though the general context and the behaviour of the other party cannot be ignored.
H and W were married in 1957, and they lived abroad until the breakdown of the marriage in 1972. H was Southern Irish and W was Northern Irish. There were many rows, two of which resulted in W injuring H, the second time by stabbing him in the chest. After that the parties lived apart. W also accused H of preferring his career to his family, and on occasions made damaging remarks in letters and telephone calls about him to his superiors. By the time of the hearing the parties' three children had left home. W could have got a job but pursued the policy that she was entitled to be a lady of leisure by reason of her contribution to the marriage and her right to call upon H for support. *Held*, the court should take into account W's conduct in such a way as to reduce the amount of relief she obtained, but by no means to extinguish it, which would amount to ignoring her valuable contribution to the marriage and also H's shortcomings.
BATEMAN *v.* BATEMAN [1979] 2 W.L.R. 377, Purchas J.

1404. —— **court order—enforcement**
In order to enforce a lump sum award the court may appoint a receiver of a husband's equitable interest in property.
A husband paid nothing under an order for payment of £2,000 as lump sum maintenance. His only apparent asset was an interest shared with his brother under a trust for sale of a house. The brother would not agree to sell. *Held*, that a receiver would be appointed, the receiver having power to take proceedings in the husband's name so as to enforce a sale of the house. (*Stevens v. Hutchinson* [1953] C.L.Y. 1598 considered.)
LEVERMORE *v.* LEVERMORE [1979] 1 W.L.R. 1277, Balcombe J.

1405. —— **house bought after divorce in hope of reconciliation**
The parties jointly purchased a house after they had been divorced in the hope of effecting a reconciliation. The reconciliation failed. W appealed against the judge's order giving her slightly less than one-third of the net proceeds of sale. *Held*, dismissing the appeal, the judge was right in deciding that the purchase was a joint purchase venture and to begin the division of proceeds on a basis of equality. His subsequent calculations which gave H a larger share could not be faulted because of the large sums H had spent on the property after the failure of reconciliation: WOODGATE *v.* WOODGATE (1978) 8 Fam. Law 244, C.A.

1406. —— **lump sum—considerations**
Parties had married in 1945. W, now aged 54 years, was unemployed and had no capital. H, now aged 57, earned £7,152 per annum and was entitled to retire at 60 and to receive a lump sum payment of £9,000. Had the marriage continued W would have been entitled to a pension of £1,000 per annum if she survived H. The matrimonial home had been sold upon the breakdown of the marriage and the proceeds, some £22,500, had been placed on deposit in the parties' joint names. In addition H had investments amounting to £2,290 and a monthly saving plan scheme to the value of £4,400. *Held*, allowing W's appeal and increasing the lump sum payment from £7,750 to £12,000, that the order of the judge was insufficient in three respects. He was wrong to omit the monthly savings scheme since this was to provide a sum to supplement H's pension. He was also wrong not to take account of W's loss of pension rights and should have had regard to the lump sum retirement payment of £9,000. However, W's share should not be greater than one-third: RICHARDSON *v.* RICHARDSON (1978) 9 Fam. Law 86, C.A.

1407. —— **maintenance of child—suitability of order**
At the time of the parties' divorce H was ordered to pay £3 per week for the child of the family, now aged five years. The order was subsequently varied by the local magistrates' court to £2 per week, where it was registered. Upon W's application for an " upwards " variation the amount was raised back

to £3 per week. W now appealed stating that £6 was a more suitable figure. *Held*, that in restoring the weekly sum to the original figure of £3 the justices had not taken inflation into account; for W had been put back into the position she had once occupied. The question to be asked was, what was the money available, and what the need? The amount would therefore be increased to £5 per week, but this was no more than an attempt to get justice for the child regarding the parties' respective obligations to that child; for it was now generally accepted that there should be no order under £5 per week. However, although it could also be argued that the current subsistence level for a child of five years plus is £5·30 per week this was not the way to look at the problem: *Re* L. (1979) 9 Fam. Law 152, Sir George Baker P.

1408. —— periodical payments
    H worked as a lorry driver paying keep to his mother with whom he now lived. W and the child of the marriage were living wholly upon social security. *Held*, dismissing H's appeal against the maintenance order, that the first charge on a husband's income was his wife and child even though the effect of such an order would be to reduce his income below a tolerable, but not subsistence, level: CLARKE *v.* CLARKE (1979) 9 Fam. Law 15, C.A.

1409.   Following W's petition for divorce W now lived with the two children of the marriage in a council flat whilst H lived with a Mrs. J and her two children from a previous marriage. H, in his appeal against the maintenance order, argued that both on the " liable relative " formula adopted by the Supplementary Benefits Commission and on the terms of the order he was less well-off whilst remaining in employment than if he were receiving supplementary benefits. *Held*, allowing H's appeal in part, that in this context the " liable relative " formula would provide nothing more than a ranging shot and that what was relevant here was that H's income would, in fact, be reduced below subsistence level. Order varied accordingly. (*Smethurst* v. *Smethurst* [1977] C.L.Y. 1541 considered; *Ashley* v. *Ashley* [1968] C.L.Y. 1297 and *Shallow* v. *Shallow* [1978] C.L.Y. 818 applied): FITZPATRICK *v.* FITZPATRICK (1979) 9 Fam. Law 16, C.A.

1410. —— —— jurisdiction to vary agreement not to increase
    [Matrimonial Causes Act 1973 (c. 18), ss. 31, 34.]
    An agreed order for maintenance reciting the wife's agreement not to apply for any increase but which is expressed to be " until further order " does not preclude a later application by the wife.
    After their separation the parties in 1972 reached agreement conditional upon approval by the court for the payment of periodical maintenance to the wife who agreed not to make any further claim for financial provision. A judge approved the agreement and an agreed order was drawn up reflecting the same but including the words " until further order." In 1978 the wife's application for an increase was struck out on the grounds that jurisdiction was excluded by the 1972 agreement. *Held*, allowing the wife's appeal, that the 1972 order was not genuinely a final order, and the court accordingly had jurisdiction to entertain an application for variation. (*Hyman* v. *Hyman* [1929] A.C. 601 applied; *Minton* v. *Minton* [1979] C.L.Y. 766 distinguished.)
    JESSEL *v.* JESSEL [1979] 1 W.L.R. 1148, C.A.

1411. —— second wife's income and capital
    [Matrimonial Causes Act 1973 (c. 18), s. 25 (1).] Following the parties' divorce in 1977 H remarried. W applied for periodical payments for herself and the two children, and sought a transfer of property order in respect of the former matrimonial home. W maintained that H's new wife had a substantial earning capacity and invited the registrar to make an order requiring the second wife to file an affidavit of means in addition to that of H. *Held*, allowing W's appeal against the registrar's refusal, that it was material for the court to know how the means of the second wife were deployed within H's household. Such information must be forthcoming for the court to discharge its duty properly under s. 25 (1) of the 1973 Act. Having regard to the duties placed upon the court by that section, W had not to go so far as to show gifts of money or property made by the second wife to H

before the means of the second wife became a relevant consideration (*Grainger* v. *Grainger* [1954] C.L.Y. 1026 applied): WILKINSON v. WILKINSON (1979) 123 S.J. 752, Booth J.

1412. —— **wealthy father—provision for children—settlement—age of children**
[Matrimonial Causes Act 1973 (c. 18), ss. 24 (1) (*b*), 25 (2).]
There is power under s. 24 (1) (*b*) of the Matrimonial Causes Act 1973 to order a settlement which by its nature will continue to benefit a child after the age of 18, but it is not right to order a settlement which will provide income for children who are subject to no disability and whose maintenance and education are secure.

H and W were divorced. They had two daughters. H was a millionaire. H was ordered to pay the daughters' entire school fees, to make periodical payments for each of them of £1,812 per year until the age of 18, and to settle £25,000 on trust for each of them for life, and thereafter for the benefit of her children, and failing children, to the other surviving daughter. H had set up a trust under a prior order to pay the school fees, which had become inadequate. On appeal by H, *held*, allowing the appeal, (1) that the order to pay school fees would defeat the object of the earlier trust, and the court would accept H's undertaking to make up the amount outstanding; (2) the court should not regard any father, however rich, as having financial responsibilities and obligations to provide a settlement for a child who was under no disability and whose maintenance and education is secure, and the order for the settlements of £25,000 would be set aside. (Dicta of Scarman L.J. in *Chamberlain* v. *Chamberlain* [1974] C.L.Y. 1799 and of Bagnall J. in *Harnett* v. *Harnett* [1974] C.L.Y. 1026 applied.)
LILFORD (LORD) v. GLYNN [1979] 1 W.L.R. 78, C.A.

1413. Marriage—discretion to refuse declaration of validity
[Matrimonial Causes Act 1973 (c. 18), s. 45; Domicile and Matrimonial Proceedings Act 1973 (c. 45), s. 1.]
Although a marriage by licence is not invalidated by false declarations made by one of the parties, it may be unjust for the court to make a declaration as to its validity.

Having absconded whilst on bail for criminal offences in her native country, West Germany, the petitioner entered the U.K. by use of a false passport. In England she married at a register office an English-domiciled man, giving false details as to her identity and residence in the notice of marriage. After her arrest on an extradition warrant she claimed registration as a British citizen and in support thereof sought a declaration that the English marriage was valid and subsisting. *Held*, refusing the declaration, that (1) the false details given in the notice did not invalidate the marriage; but (2) by obtaining residence in England by lies and fraud, the petitioner was barred from obtaining a domicile of choice in England; and (3) in the light of the petitioner's conduct, it was not just to make the declaration sought. (*Plummer* v. *Plummer* [1917] P. 163 followed; *R.* v. *Secretary of State for Home Affairs, ex p. Hussain* [1977] C.L.Y. 12 considered.)
PUTTICK v. ATT.-GEN. [1979] 3 W.L.R. 542, Sir George Baker P.

1414. Matrimonial causes. See DIVORCE AND MATRIMONIAL CAUSES.

1415. Matrimonial home—assessing respective shares
Following divorce proceedings H, a bus driver, now lived in a bed-sitting room whilst W lived with a daughter aged 12 in the home. W worked in part-time employment and also provided bed and breakfast accommodation in the summer months. The judge order the transfer of the home into equal shares with a postponement of sale until daughter was aged 17 or ceased full-time education. W appealed, contending that the sum she would receive upon sale would be insufficient for her to obtain secure accommodation. *Held*, allowing the appeal, that a just result could better produced by a two-thirds division of the proceeds to W with one-third to H. Order varied accordingly. (*Hanlon* v. *Hanlon* [1978] C.L.Y. 1616 and *Martin* v. *Martin* [1977] C.L.Y. 1559 considered): CAWKWELL v. CAWKWELL (1979) 9 Fam. Law 25, C.A.

1416. —— **equitable interest—failure to register whether wife in " actual occupation."**
See WILLIAMS & GLYN'S BANK v. BOLAND, § 1826.

1417. —— **exclusion of husband—injunction**

Before the parties' marriage the matrimonial home was a council house in W's sole name; after the marriage it was put in their joint names. In December 1977 W left the matrimonial home because of H's violence and went to live in a battered wives' home. W appealed from the judge's refusal to grant her an injunction excluding H from the matrimonial home, notwithstanding his finding that it was unreasonable for W to live with H. *Held*, allowing the appeal, that although there were no children, W was entitled to a peaceful existence in the house which was her home before she married H, and she did not have to live in a battered wives' home. (*Walker* v. *Walker* (1978) C.L.Y. 1611 considered): PEKESIN v. PEKESIN [1978] 8 Fam. Law 244, C.A.

1418. Parties had lived together in a small house consisting of two bedrooms and a living room with their child, a girl, now aged 17 months, until January 1978 when H left and went to live with his parents. In February W applied for judicial separation alleging extreme unkindness by H but no violence or drunkenness. W went on a four-week holiday upon H's undertaking that he would remove himself from the house before W's return. H did not honour this undertaking. *Held*, allowing W's appeal, that it was simply not viable for two parties who had quarrelled and were in the process of separating to live in such extremely cramped conditions. It would be wholly wrong and bad for the child. It was quite plain that if an exclusion order were not made W would not return to the house and she and the child would have to live somewhere else, no doubt back in her parents' home. The proper order was, therefore, that H should be excluded from the house until the matrimonial proceedings had come for trial and the disposition of the matrimonial home had been decided upon: SPEARING v. SPEARING (1978) 9 Fam. Law 153, C.A.

1419. —— —— —— **evidence**

Upon the hearing of the petitioner, W's application for an order excluding H from the matrimonial home, H offered non-molestation undertakings whereupon the judge declined to hear any further evidence from W and, in particular, from a social worker, that these undertakings were insufficient for her protection. *Held*, allowing W's appeal and ordering a new trial, that the circumstances of this case required the hearing of all relevant evidence including that based upon the adequacy of H's undertakings. (*Bassett* v. *Bassett* [1975] C.L.Y. 1617 considered; *Walker* v. *Walker* [1978] C.L.Y. 1611 applied): DIRIR v. DIRIR [1979] 9 Fam. Law 20, C.A.

1420. —— —— —— **jurisdiction**

The former wife (W) applied after decree absolute for a non-molestation order and an order excluding her former husband (H) from the matrimonial home. There was one child of whom W had custody. The home was in joint names of H and W. W intended to apply for a property transfer order but had not done so. H was willing to give a non-molestation undertaking. *Held*, there was no jurisdiction after decree absolute to make an order requiring H to leave the matrimonial home unless the welfare of the child so required (*Montgomery* v. *Montgomery* [1964] C.L.Y. 1140 applied): FOSTER v. FOSTER, May 30, 1979, Croydon County Ct., Judge Perks. (*Ex rel. R. W. Spon-Smith, Esq., Barrister.*)

1421. —— —— —— **power of arrest**

[Domestic Violence and Matrimonial Proceedings Act 1976 (c. 50), s. 2.] Upon W's application the judge had granted W, *inter alia*, injunctions restraining H from molesting her and the three children of the family, two girls and a boy, and from entering the matrimonial home. H had made threats against W whilst in the witness-box and the judge had added a power of arrest although there was no evidence of violence by H. *Held*, that a power of arrest could only be attached to one or other of those three types of injunction referred to in s. 2 of the 1976 Act. It could not be attached to an injunction not to interfere with the children. The judge's power only arose if two conditions were satisfied. First, that he (the judge) was satisfied that the other party had caused actual bodily harm to the applicant or, as the case may be, to the children; secondly, that it was considered that he was likely to do so again.

In the circumstances the only such evidence was for present purposes quite irrelevant as it had occurred in 1976 and the parties had hardly been in contact over the intervening two years. Appeal of H allowed to the extent of deleting the power of arrest in so far as it attached to the injunction: MCLAREN *v.* MCLAREN (1978) 9 Fam. Law 153, C.A.

1422. —— —— —— **test**

W petitioned for divorce on the grounds of H's unreasonable behaviour. In affidavit evidence W alleged that she was unable to return to the home whilst H remained in occupation, H having broken his promise to move out earlier. Upon H's appeal against an order requiring him to so vacate, *held,* that in such circumstances the test to be applied was whether there was any prima facie good reason why W should not go back. On the totality of the evidence the test had not been satisfied here. Appeal allowed (*Walker* v. *Walker* [1978] C.L.Y. 1611 considered): ELSWORTH *v.* ELSWORTH (1979) 9 Fam. Law 21, C.A.

1423. —— **joint tenancy—legal charge by one tenant—validity.** See CEDAR HOLDINGS *v.* GREEN, § 1827.

1424. —— **property adjustment order**

Parties had married in 1953. Following the divorce in 1975 W now lived with the child of the marriage, a son aged 18, in the matrimonial home worth £11,000 with an equity of £10,000. H lived in an alcoholic's hospital. *Held,* on appeal, that the order made at first instance, which provided for H to obtain a share of the proceeds of sale, to take place after a lapse of five years, was not the right order in the circumstances of the case. W would be 65 years old by the time the period elapsed. She was living in a house which was near the bottom of the housing market. It would therefore be impossible to satisfy the charge without selling the house. The right solution was for H's interest only to become effective on W's death. The house should accordingly be held on trust for sale not be sold during W's lifetime, with a right of occupation to W. After her death the net proceeds of sale were to be held on trust as to two-thirds for W, her executors and administrators, and the remaining third to H if he survived W: KURYLOWICZ *v.* KURYLOWICZ (1978) 9 Fam. Law 119, C.A.

1425. —— **transfer of property—background information**

Parties, now both aged 50, married in 1952 with two children of university age. In February 1977 W obtained a decree nisi on the grounds of H's adultery with NM with whom he now lived in a house bought by her. H, having formerly earned around £7,000 per year, was now unemployed having been obliged to resign from a company in April 1976 after 19 years' service. W was receiving salary of £3,000 per year plus some investment income. H was ordered, inter alia, to transfer the matrimonial home to W. *Held,* allowing H's appeal, that the judge at first instance had failed to have sufficient regard to H's difficulties in obtaining alternative employment and that if H did obtain employment at £6,000 per year or less W would only be able to receive nominal periodical payments. Order substituted that home should be sold and that W should receive two-thirds of the net proceeds of sale after discharging the mortgage debt or a capital sum: BENNETT *v.* BENNETT (1979) 9 Fam. Law 19, C.A.

1426. —— **wife's equitable interest—whether " in actual occupation "**

[Land Registration Act 1925 (c. 21), s. 70 (1) (*g*).]

A wife who has an equitable interest in property of which the husband is the sole legal owner is not " in actual occupation " of the property for the purposes of s. 70 of the Land Registration Act 1925.

Prior to her marriage, the defendant wife contributed some 20 per cent. of the purchase price of the lease of a flat which was to be the matrimonial home. Most of the balance was obtained by way of an interest-free mortgage by the husband from trustees of a fund of which he was the future beneficiary. The flat was registered in the husband's name alone. After two years, in 1974, the husband became bankrupt and was later imprisoned. Upon the trustees seeking possession of the flat in which the wife still lived, she having obtained a divorce, the wife contended that although her interest had not been registered, she had

in relation to the mortgage an overriding interest, in that she had been in actual occupation within the meaning of s. 70 (1) (*g*) of the 1925 Act. *Held*, allowing the plaintiff's claim, that an equitable tenant in common was not " in actual occupation " under s. 70 (1) (*g*); that in any event it was equitable that the lease be sold, the proceeds being divided between those equitably entitled.
BIRD *v.* SYME THOMPSON [1978] 3 All E.R. 1027, Templeman J.

1427. —— wife's rights of occupation
[Matrimonial Homes Act 1967 (c. 75), s. 1 (5).] Upon an interlocutory application by the landlords the registrar had made an order for possession against H, the tenant, who had left the matrimonial home. The subsequent defended action against W was stood over by the judge, upon undertakings, so that an application for leave to appeal out of time could be made against the registrar's order, it becoming apparent that her claim to a subsequent contractual tenancy would fail and that if the possession order against H stood W would lose her defence under the 1967 Act. A further application to enlarge the time for appealing was refused. *Held*, allowing W's appeal, that there would be no injustice in allowing her appeal out of time so as to enable her defence under the Act to be fully raised and argued. In the circumstances the registrar's order clearly ought not to have been made. Normally, cogent reasons were required to justify an appeal out of time but here the registrar's inter-locutory order was not made against the intending appellant but against a co-defendant and it affected her only by a side wind. The action was intended to continue against W and it must have been in the contemplation of the parties that her defences would be dealt with on their merits. (*Middleton* v. *Baldock* (1950) C.L.C. 8897; *Penn* v. *Dunn* [1970] C.L.Y. 2439 considered): GRANGE LANE SOUTH FLATS *v.* COOK, *The Times*, November 28, 1979, C.A.

1428. Matrimonial property—petitioners' conjectural needs—respondent's ability to pay
Parties married 1955, divorced 1975. Three children all over 17 years of age and working. During the marriage the petitioner, besides bringing up the three children, assisted on the respondent's father's farm and caravan and camp site which subsequently became the respondent's property. At date of hearing respondent's farm, camp site and stock worth in region of £225,000 and pro-duced annual gross income of £10,400. Petitioner had remarried another farmer who owned no land but was a tenant in partnership with his brother. He earned in the region of £4,800 per annum. On his death the petitioner, who was the sole beneficiary under his will, had expectations of £14,000–£15,000. She would not be able to continue to reside in her current home. *Held*, the petitioner's position with her second husband was very largely the same as with the first. Her main difficulty would be if her second husband died before her. For the foreseeable future she would continue to enjoy a similar standard of living, but on his death would be in real difficulties. The respondent was currently paying off at the rate of £250 per month the purchase price of £17,000 for additional land. When that was repaid he would be able to raise further moneys. The court had to balance the conjectural needs of the petitioner against the respondent's ability to pay. The appropriate order was one in the sum of £15,000 to be paid on or before December 31, 1981: MUDD *v.* DINSDALE, June 28, 1979, Reeve J. (*Ex rel. A. R. D. Stuttard, Esq., Barrister.*)

1429. —— valuation—date of valuation
Parties had married in 1951 and from 1956 onwards H had started various successful businesses and W had assisted him. In 1970 the marriage broke up and was dissolved in 1976. W now appealed against the judge's award of £10,000 on the basis of the 1970 value of the property in question. *Held*, allowing W's appeal, that on the professional valuation evidence before the judge it was apparent that there had been a considerable rise in values between 1970 and 1977. However, there was no evidence that this rise was due to any additional expenditure by way of improvement on the part of H. In these cir-cumstances there was no reason why these values should not be adapted for present purposes in preference to the 1970 values. Sum of £20,000 substituted: WALLHEAD *v.* WALLHEAD (1978) 9 Fam. Law 85, C.A.

1430. —— —— disclosure of valuation report

At the hearing of W's application for a lump sum order representing her interest in the matrimonial home both parties gave oral evidence as to the value of the house. W had instructed a surveyor but had chosen not to disclose the contents of his report either to H or to the registrar as she disagreed with his valuation. *Held,* that the duty of disclosure applied equally to both H and W in this type of case. The evidence before the registrar had been inadequate to enable him to proceed. He would have been wiser to adjourn and even appoint a valuer himself. Although it was expensive to obtain valuations the sums involved were large, and in particular, in relation to the parties concerned. It was thus very difficult for registrars to make accurate property adjustment orders without having the benefit of a professional valuation, even in these smaller cases. H's appeal allowed on terms: CHAND *v.* CHAND (1978) 9 Fam. Law 84, C.A.

1431. —— —— expert valuation required under court order—effect

Following W's presentation of her divorce petition and application for ancillary relief, the registrar ordered that a valuation of certain property " be agreed if possible and that if not a valuation be obtained by a valuer to be agreed between the solicitors for the parties at the joint expense of the parties." H disagreed with the valuation in question and wished to adduce further evidence. *Held,* that the court could not order parties to be bound, without their consent, by an arbitration to any other third person being, or purporting to be, an expert. Therefore, the registrar's order could not bind the parties to accept the valuation contemplated as being conclusive unless there was agreement, at that point, to such effect. This was not the case. It was not precluded by the order from adducing further evidence as to the value of the properties in question. This decision applied equally to the furtherance of W's case: BRENT *v.* BRENT (1979) 9 Fam. Law 59, C.A.

1432. Northern Ireland. See NORTHERN IRELAND.

1433. Practice—ex parte injunction—time limit

[Domestic Violence and Matrimonial Proceedings Act 1976 (c. 50), s. 2.] On W's *ex parte* application under the 1976 Act the judge granted a non-molestation injunction and attached a power of arrest. It was made to operate " until further order." At the *inter partes* hearing the injunction, as previously made, was continued and various other orders made. *Held*, on appeal, that it was wholly unjustifiable and improper to make an injunction *ex parte* " until further order" (*Ansah* v. *Ansah* [1977] C.L.Y. 1567 applied): MORGAN *v.* MORGAN (1979) 9 Fam. Law 87, C.A.

1434. Widow's benefit. See SOCIAL SECURITY.

BOOKS AND ARTICLES. See *post,* pp. [5], [23].

INCOME TAX

1435. Additional rate—non-resident trustee company

[Finance Act 1973 (c. 51), s. 16 (1).] A discretionary settlement fund, established under the law of Jersey, was vested solely in a non-resident trustee company for the benefit of the settlor's family, who were U.K. residents. The fund included U.K. company shares, dividends from which had been received by the trustee company; the company was assessed to income tax at the additional rate on " distributions " received from U.K. companies. The company argued that (1) s. 16 (1) only applied to income which was " chargeable to income tax at basic rate "; and (2) the relevant income was not chargeable to basic rate tax (s. 87 (5) of the Finance Act 1972). Both points had to be established for the company to succeed. *Held,* that the phrase in s. 16 (1) " in addition to being chargeable to income tax at basic rate " was not intended to make a charge to tax at the additional rate conditional on the income being assessable at the basic rate. The addtional rate was not intended to supersede the basic rate charge. That being so, there was no need to consider the company's second argument: I.R.C. *v.* REGENT TRUST Co., *The Times,* November 30, 1979, Slade J.

1436. Appeal—determination—validity

[Taxes Management Act 1970 (c. 9), ss. 31, 50, 55.]

An appeal is finally determined when the Commissioners have given their decision on all of the issues raised.

Estimated assessments to income tax and profits tax were made upon the taxpayer company. It appealed against the assessments, and the Commissioners decided the appeals by stating the amount of income assessable to tax but without stating the amount of tax actually payable. The taxpayer company sought a declaration that until the Commissioners had amended the assessments by stating the tax actually payable, the appeals had not been finally determined and there was no liability to tax. *Held*, (1) for a tax assessment to be valid it had to include a statement of the amount of tax payable, but the Inspector could make the necessary amendments to the assessments; and (2) the Commissioners had determined the appeals by determining the issues raised thereon (*Income Tax General Purposes Commissioners for City of London* v. *Gibbs* [1942] A.C. 402, considered).

HALLAMSHIRE INDUSTRIAL FINANCE TRUST v. I.R.C. [1979] 1 W.L.R. 620, Browne-Wilkinson J.

1437. Artificial transactions in land—opportunity of realising gain

[Income and Corporation Taxes Act 1970 (c. 10), ss. 488, 489.]

Assessment under I.C.T.A. 1970, s. 488, can be made only in respect of gains actually received or immediately receivable.

Two Guernsey companies owned by the trustees of settlements established by the taxpayer purchased land from Y Ltd., a company in which the taxpayer had a substantial shareholding. The land was purchased without the benefit of planning permission. After planning permission had been obtained, the land was sold back to Y Ltd. at an enhanced price. Only part of the purchase price was paid, the balance being left outstanding. The taxpayer was assessed to tax under I.C.T.A. 1970, s. 488, on the ground that he had provided the Guernsey companies with the opportunity of realising a gain. *Held*, that (1) the case must be remitted to the Commissioners for them to find the facts necessary for determining whether the taxpayer had provided the opportunity to the Guernsey companies; and (2) the gain was able to be assessed only as moneys were received (or immediately receivable) by the Guernsey companies.

YUILL v. WILSON [1979] 1 W.L.R. 987, C.A.

1438. Assessment—estimated—irregularities in proceedings

[Taxes Management Act 1970 (c. 9), s. 56.] Estimated assessments were made against the taxpayer in respect of fees from work as a freelance draughtsman carried on from his home and in respect of untaxed interest. At the hearing of the appeal he admitted the receipt of interest, but in respect of the fees claimed to deduct 25 per cent. of the cost of running his home and an unquantified amount of the monthly mortgage payments. No evidence was given to justify the deductions. The Commissioners allowed only £10 as deductible expenditure. The taxpayer appealed, and at the hearing of the appeal alleged that the hearing had not been properly conducted. *Held*, dismissing the appeal, that where irregularities in proceedings were alleged the correct procedure was to apply to the Divisional Court for a prerogative order, and that there was no ground on which the court could interfere with the Commissioners' decision as to the amount of the deductible expenditure: THOMAS v. INGRAM [1979] S.T.C. 1, Fox J.

1439. Back duty—hearing—taxpayer not present—finding of fraud

Although the court is normally reluctant to interfere with the exercise of the Commissioners' discretion, where the charges are serious and refusal of an adjournment could have caused injustice, it will remit the case.

Back duty assessments were made on the taxpayer for the years 1963–64 to 1975–76. The taxpayer appealed, but at the hearing of the appeal he was not present and was not represented. However, by letter he requested an adjournment on the ground that he had consulted counsel. At the hearing the Crown made allegations of fraud or wilful default under the Taxes Management Act 1970, s. 36, or alternatively neglect under s. 37 of that Act. The

Commissioners refused the adjournment and found the taxpayer guilty of fraud for certain of the years. The taxpayer appealed, alleging breach of the rules of natural justice. *Held*, that while the question of adjournment was a question for the Commissioners, having regard to the nature of the charges refusal of the adjournment seriously prejudiced the taxpayer. The appeal was allowed and the appeal remitted to be heard by different Commissioners. (*Rose* v. *Humbles* [1970] C.L.Y. 1260 applied.)

OTTLEY v. MORRIS [1979] 1 All E.R. 65, Fox J.

1440. Bonus—P.A.Y.E.—payment

[Income and Corporation Taxes Act 1970 (c. 10), s. 204.]

A bonus credited to a director's account with a company is a " payment " for P.A.Y.E. purposes.

In March 1975 bonuses voted to directors were in part paid over to them and, as to the balance, were credited to their accounts with the company, on which accounts the directors were free to draw. The company was notified that it should have accounted for tax under the P.A.Y.E. Regulations on the whole amounts of the bonuses. *Held*, allowing the Crown's appeal from the decision of the Special Commissioners, that the placing of moneys unreservedly at the disposal of the directors by crediting them to their accounts with the company amounted to a " payment " for P.A.Y.E. purposes.

GARFORTH v. NEWSMITH STAINLESS [1979] 1 W.L.R. 409; [1979] S.T.C. 129, Walton J.

1441. Capital allowances—boat converted into floating restaurant—whether " plant "

[Capital Allowances Act 1968 (c. 3), s. 18; Finance Act 1971 (c. 68), s. 41.]

A floating restaurant is not " plant " for the purposes of capital allowances.

The taxpayer company bought a vessel and converted it into a floating restaurant at a total cost of approximately £78,000. It claimed that the vessel was " plant " and that the money spent on the purchase and conversion qualified for capital allowances. *Held*, dismissing the taxpayer company's appeal, that the vessel was the structure within which the business was carried on and did not constitute the apparatus or plant by means of which the business was carried on. Therefore, the expenditure did not qualify for capital allowances. (*Yarmouth* v. *France* (1887) 19 Q.B.D. 647; *I.R.C.* v. *Barclay, Curle & Co.* [1969] C.L.Y. 1659 applied.)

BENSON v. YARD ARM CLUB [1979] 1 W.L.R. 347, C.A.

1442. —— false ceilings—plant

[Finance Act 1971 (c. 68), ss. 41, 42.] A company which operated restaurants installed false ceilings in three of their premises. In the cavity between the ceilings were electrical conduits, fire detectors and other equipment. The company claimed that the ceilings fell within the term " plant " in F.A. 1971, s. 41, and that it was entitled to capital allowances in respect of the cost. *Held*, allowing the Crown's appeal from the decision of the general commissioners, that the ceilings were not plant: HAMPTON v. FORTES AUTOGRILL, *The Times*, December 4, 1979, Fox J.

1443. —— industrial building—coins

[Capital Allowances Act 1968 (c. 3), ss. 1, 7.] Currency used as a means of exchange (coins) were held not to be " goods," for the purposes of s. 7 of the Capital Allowances Act 1968; so that a building in which coins were sorted into specified quantities was not a building in which goods were subjected to a process. Therefore, no allowance was available under s. 1 of the Capital Allowances Act 1968, in respect of the cost of construction of the building: BUCKINGHAM v. SECURITIES PROPERTIES, *The Times*, December 7, 1979, Slade J.

1444. Capital gains

CAPITAL GAINS TAX (GILT-EDGED SECURITIES) (NO. 1) ORDER 1979 (No. 1231) [10p], made under the Capital Gains Tax Act 1979 (c. 14), Sched. 2, para. 1; specifies gilt-edged securities which are exempt from tax on capital gains if held for more than 12 months.

CAPITAL GAINS TAX (GILT-EDGED SECURITIES) (NO. 2) ORDER 1979 (No. 1676) [10p], made under the Capital Gains Tax Act 1979, Sched. 2, para. 1; operative on December 7, 1980; specifies gilt-edged securities which are exempt from tax on capital gains if held for more than 12 months.

1445. —— avoidance scheme—base cost—wholly and exclusively
[Finance Act 1965 (c. 25), Sched. 6, para. 4 (1) (*a*).] The taxpayer entered into a capital gains tax avoidance scheme with a Jersey company as part of which he purchased for £543,600 the reversionary interest in a Gibraltar settlement, which sum represented the market value of the reversionary interest. Funds were then moved from the Gibraltar settlement to another settlement in which the taxpayer was interested. The reversionary interest was then sold at a price which showed a loss. The Crown contended that the sum of £543,600 paid by the taxpayer for the reversion under the Gibraltar settlement was not given " wholly and exclusively " for the acquisition of the reversion, and so was not admissible in computing the capital gains tax base cost of the reversion. *Held*, allowing the Crown's appeal from the decision of the General Commissioners, that the taxpayer was under a contractual obligation to the promoters of the scheme to complete all stages of the scheme, including the purchase of the reversion at £543,600. The purchase of the reversion was in part fulfilment of that obligation. Therefore, the sum of £543,600 was not paid wholly and exclusively for the acquisition of the reversion, and so was not deductible in computing the allowable loss on the subsequent disposal of the reversion: EILBECK *v.* RAWLING [1979] S.T.C. 16, Slade J.

1446. —— " pension "
[Finance Act 1965 (c. 25), Sched. 7, para. 15.]
Sched. 7, para. 15 (2), to the Finance Act 1965 (Capital Gains Tax Act 1979, s. 25 (2)) extends to the concerted exercise of collective control.
The vendors wished to sell their shares in Company A to Company B. They created Company C, to which they sold the shares in Company A in exchange for the issue of shares in Company C. Immediately thereafter Company C sold the shares in Company A to Company B. A fourth company registered in the Cayman Islands subsequently acquired shares in Company C, and then took up preferred ordinary shares, commanding the greater part of the value of Company C, on a rights issue, the controlling shareholders not taking up their entitlement to the shares and not otherwise being actively involved in relation to the rights issue. *Held*, affirming the decision of the Court of Appeal (Lord Wilberforce and Lord Keith of Kinkel dissenting), that the scheme failed at the second stage of value-shifting, the provisions of F.A. 1965, Sched. 7, para. 15 (2), extending to a case where two or more persons had control of a company, and the making and implementation of the scheme amounting to the exercise of control. (*Blue Metal Industries* v. *Dilley* [1969] C.L.Y. 137 considered.)
FLOOR *v.* DAVIS [1979] 2 W.L.R. 830, H.L.

1447. —— chargeable gains—sale of land
[Finance Act 1965 (c. 25), Sched. 6, para. 14 (5).] Before the introduction of capital gains tax in 1965 the taxpayer sold 47 acres for £47,040 to a development company and arranged for future payment to be made to the taxpayer of £7,500 for each acre developed. The agreement also provided for the taxpayer to receive compensation should the land be compulsorily acquired. In 1976 the taxpayer was paid £348,250 in settlement. *Held*, that the taxpayer's rights under the agreement constituted a chargeable asset that was deemed to have been disposed of when he received the payment in 1976 (*Marren* v. *Ingles* [1979] C.L.Y. 1452 applied): MARSON *v.* MARRIAGE, *The Times*, December 22, 1979, Fox J.

1448. —— exemption—annual payments due under a covenant
[Finance Act 1965 (c. 25), Sched. 7, para. 12 (*c*).] The taxpayer company, which had a licence to exploit the xerographic process throughout the world except in the U.S.A. and Canada, by agreements under seal surrendered its rights in respect of certain countries in consideration of a royalty of 5 per cent. on the sales in those countries. It then resolved to pay a dividend to its shareholders to be satisfied by the distribution of its rights to royalty payments. It claimed that the royalty payments were " annual payments due under a covenant " within the Finance Act 1965, Sched. 7, para. 12 (*c*), and that the disposal of those rights did not give rise to a liability for corporation tax on chargeable gains. *Held*, allowing the Inland Revenue's appeal, that the

exemption applied only to unilateral obligations of a voluntary character, so that the disposal in this case was not exempt: RANK XEROX *v.* LANE (1979) 123 S.J. 736, H.L.

1449. —— land—development value
[Finance Act 1965 (c. 25), Sched. 6, para. 23 (1) (*b*).]
Absence of planning permission does not exclude the application of the valuation provisions in para. 23 of Sched. 6 to the Finance Act 1965.

The taxpayer had inherited in 1962 22 acres of agricultural land which had a value for tax purposes of £11,581. He sold it in 1972 for £264,000, the price reflecting the hope or expectation that planning permission would be granted. He appealed against an assessment to capital gains tax in respect of the sale for the year 1971–72, contending that para. 23 of Sched. 6 to the Finance Act 1965 (which prescribes April 1965 value as the capital gains tax base cost) had no application where land was sold without planning consent, and that para. 24 (time-apportionment of gain) was the more appropriate method of computation. *Held,* affirming the decision of the Court of Appeal, that the land had to be valued as at April 6, 1965, since the application of the statutory hypothesis was not restricted to cases where planning permission existed at the date of sale.

WATKINS *v.* KIDSON [1979] 1 W.L.R. 876, H.L.

1450. —— loans—debt on security
[Finance Act 1965 (c. 25), Sched. 7, paras. 7 and 11.]
A debt having all the characteristics of loan stock and evidenced by a statutory declaration is a " debt on a security."

With a view to creating a capital gains tax allowable loss the taxpayer effected the following transactions: (1) it purchased all of the shares in C Ltd.; (2) it made two loans of £218,750 each (L1 and L2) to C Ltd. for 30 and 31 years respectively each loan carrying interest at 11 per cent.; (3) it agreed to interest on L1 being reduced to nil and interest on L2 being increased to 22 per cent.; (4) it sold L2 to M Ltd. for £393,750; (5) C Ltd. was wound up, L1 becoming repayable at par and L2 at £394,673. The taxpayer claimed that (a) it made a loss in respect of the shares in C Ltd., and (b) the gain on the disposal of L2 was exempt, L2 not being a " debt on a security." *Held,* reversing the decision of Goulding J., that L2 displayed all the essential characteristics of loan stock, and, having been evidenced by a statutory declaration recording the transactions, was a " debt on a security." (*Dicta* of Lord Wilberforce and Lord Russell in *Aberdeen Construction Group* v. *I.C.R.* [1978] C.L.Y. 358 applied; *Cleveleys Investment Trust Co.* v. *I.R.C.* [1971] C.L.Y. 1915 distinguished.)

W. T. RAMSAY *v.* I.R.C. [1979] 1 W.L.R. 974, C.A.

1451. —— reorganisation of share capital—shares of the same class
[Scot.] [Finance Act 1965 (c. 25), Sched. 6, para. 27 (3).] In 1956 the taxpayer's wife acquired 10,000 ordinary shares of £1 each in S Ltd.; a private company which, by its articles of association, restricted the transfer of its shares. In March 1965 the taxpayer's wife acquired a further 10,000 shares on a bonus issue. On April 2, 1965, she sold 1,000 shares. In 1967 L Ltd. took-over S Ltd; the taxpayer's wife received 253,330 shares of 25p. each in L Ltd. by way of share exchange. The articles of association of L Ltd. did not impose any restriction on the transfer of its shares. In March 1974 the taxpayer's wife sold 100,000 of her shares in L Ltd. The point in issue depended upon whether F.A. 1965, Sched. 6, para. 27 (3), applied in relation to the shares. This in turn depended upon whether the shares in L Ltd. were shares " of the same class " as the shares in S Ltd. The taxpayer contended that para. 27 (3) had no application. *Held,* that as the shares in L Ltd. were free from restrictions on transfer, they were not shares " of the same class " as the shares in S Ltd. Therefore, para. 27 (3) had no application: I.R.C. *v.* BEVERIDGE [1979] S.T.C. 592, Ct. of Session.

1452. —— sale of shares—deferred consideration
[Finance Act 1965 (c. 25), s. 22 (1) (3), and Sched. 7, para. 11.]
Receipt of a deferred consideration involves the disposal of an asset for capital gains tax purposes.

In 1970 the taxpayers sold shares in a private company at a price of £750 per share with provision for a further deferred payment to be based on the market price of the shares on the first day of dealing following the flotation of the company. In December 1972 the deferred consideration (amounting to £2,825 per share) became payable. *Held,* reversing in part the decision of Slade J., that (1) the receipt of the deferred payment constituted a "disposal" of an asset for capital gains tax purposes within F.A. 1965, s. 22 (3); and (2) the right to the deferred consideration was not a "debt" within F.A. 1965, Sched. 7, para. 11.

MARREN *v.* INGLES [1979] 1 W.L.R. 1131, C.A.

1453. —— settlement—tax avoidance

[Finance Act 1965 (c. 25), ss. 20 (1), 25 (1) (3), 42 (2).]

A scheme for appointing shares through non-resident trustees, made to avoid capital gains tax, has been held not to constitute a "settlement" for the purposes of F.A. 1965, s. 42.

Trustees wished to appoint shares in Lex Garages in favour of two beneficiaries absolutely. To avoid the capital gains tax liability of some £170,000 which would arise under F.A. 1965, s. 25 (3), they adopted the following avoidance scheme: (1) appointment of non-resident trustees; (2) appointment in favour of each beneficiary of half of the shares contingent upon his surviving for three days; (3) sale of contingent interests to Jersey company; (4) contract by Jersey company to sell Lex Garages shares to beneficiaries; (5) completion of sale of shares to beneficiaries after three-day period. The beneficiaries were assessed to capital gains tax under F.A. 1965, s. 42. *Held,* allowing the taxpayers' appeals, that (1) notwithstanding the contract for the sale on of the shares, on the termination of the settlement the Jersey company, and not the beneficiaries, became absolutely entitled against the trustees, and (2) as the arrangement did not involved any bounty, it was not a "settlement" for the purposes of F.A. 1965, s. 42. (*I.R.C.* v. *Plummer* [1978] C.L.Y. 1680 applied.)

CHINN *v.* HOCHSTRASSER; CHINN *v.* COLLINS [1979] 2 W.L.R. 411, C.A.

1454. —— —— trustees—liability for tax

[Finance Act 1965 (c. 25), s. 25, and Sched. 10, para. 12.] In 1975, by virtue of first an appointment and then an arrangement sanctioned by the court, a trust fund was effectually divided into two parts. Non-resident trustees were appointed of one part and the original trustees remained as the trustees of the other part. A tax avoidance scheme was then carried out in the course of which chargeable gains accrued to the non-resident trustees. The question was whether the capital gains tax could be recovered from the original trustees resident in the U.K. who remained trustees of one part of the fund. *Held,* dismissing the Crown's appeal, that the 1955 appointment resulted in two separate settlements for capital gains tax purposes, and that such tax was recoverable only from the trustees to whom the gain actually accrued: ROOME *v.* EDWARDS, *The Times,* December 5, 1979, C.A.

1455. —— valuation—lands tribunal

Between 1971 and 1973 some 375 acres of agricultural land were compulsorily acquired from the taxpayer. He elected that for capital gains tax purposes valuation should be made as at April 6, 1965, in accordance with Finance Act 1965, Sched. 6, para. 23. The valuation of the land was referred to the Lands Tribunal which heard evidence from both the taxpayer and the Revenue, the taxpayer contending for a figure of approximately £1,000,000, and the Revenue for the District Valuer's figure of £650,000, which allowed, in particular, £100,000 for abnormal drainage costs. *Held,* that a prudent developer would have allowed for drainage costs, and the costs of acquiring necessary incidental easements, and that the value of the land should be determined at the District Valuer's figure of £650,000: HALLEY *v.* WEIGHTMAN (1978) 249 E.G. 547, Lands Tribunal.

1456. Capital Gains Tax Act 1979 (c. 14)

This Act consolidates Pt. III of the Finance Act 1965 with related provisions in that Act and subsequent Acts.

Pt. I (ss. 1–18) contains general provisions: s. 1 imposes tax in respect of capital gains; s. 2 defines persons chargeable under the Act; s. 3 sets out the rate of tax; s. 4 specifies gains chargeable to tax; s. 5 gives relief for gains less than £9,500; s. 6 relates to small gifts; s. 7 concerns the time for payment of tax; s. 8 deals with postponement of payment of tax; s. 9 contains further provisions regarding postponement; s. 10 gives double taxation relief; s. 11 makes allowance for foreign tax; s. 12 concerns non-residents with U.K. branch or agency; s. 13 deals with foreign assets and delayed remittances; s. 14 relates to foreign assets of persons with foreign domicile; s. 15 contains provisions as to non-resident companies; s. 16 concerns non-resident groups of companies; s. 17 deals with non-resident trusts; s. 18 defines residence and location of assets.

Pt. II (ss. 19–43) relates to gains and losses: s. 19 concerns disposal of assets; s. 20 deals with capital sums derived from assets; s. 21 makes provision for compensation and insurance moneys; s. 22 provides for assets lost or destroyed, or whose value becomes negligible; s. 23 concerns mortgages and charges; s. 24 has provisions relating to hire-purchase; s. 25 relates to value shifting; s. 26 contains further provisions as to value shifting; s. 27 gives the time of disposal and acquisition where asset disposed of under contract; s. 28 defines chargeable gains; s. 29 defines losses; s. 30 has introductory provisions; s. 31 relates to consideration chargeable to tax on income; s. 32 contains general provisions as to expenditure; s. 33 excludes expenditure by reference to tax on income; s. 34 restricts losses by reference to capital allowances and renewals allowances; s. 35 concerns part disposals; s. 36 deals with assets derived from other assets; s. 37 defines wasting assets; s. 38 provides for straightline restriction of allowable expenditure attributable to wasting assets; s. 39 deals with wasting assets qualifying for capital allowances; s. 40 concerns consideration due after time of disposal; s. 41 provides for contingent liabilities; s. 42 relates to expenditure reimbursed out of public money; s. 43 contains supplemental provisions.

Pt. III (ss. 44–63) deals with persons and trusts: s. 44 deals with married persons; s. 45 imposes tax on married women's gains; s. 46 relates to nominees and bare trustees; s. 47 gives allowances for expenses in administration of estates and trusts; s. 48 defines liability for tax; s. 49 makes general provisions as to death; s. 50 applies the Act to the law of Scotland; s. 51 defines settled property; s. 52 concerns trustees of settlements; s. 53 defines gifts in settlement; s. 54 relates to persons becoming absolutely entitled to settled property; s. 55 provides for the termination of life interest; s. 56 excludes chargeable gain on death of life tenant; s. 57 deals with the death of annuitants; s. 58 concerns disposal of interests in settled property; s. 59 provides for recovery of tax from donee of gifts; s. 60 makes provisions as to partnerships; s. 61 deals with insolvents' assets; s. 62 provides for transactions between connected persons; s. 63 interprets connected persons.

Pt. IV (ss. 64–100) relates to shares and securities: s. 64 is an interpretation section; s. 65 concerns pooling; s. 66 deals with disposal on or before day of acquisition; s. 67 exempts long-term gains; s. 68 makes general provisions as to identification; s. 69 concerns disposal to husband or wife and third person; s. 70 relates to reacquisition after sale at a loss; s. 71 exempts Government non-marketable securities; s. 72 concerns distribution which is not a new holding within ss. 77–91; s. 73 makes provisions as to disposal of right to acquire shares; s. 74 grants relief in respect of income tax consequent on shortfall in distributions in the disposal of shares; s. 75 deals with shares in close company transferring assets at an undervalue; s. 76 provides for calculation of the consideration for acquisition of shares under share option schemes; s. 77 concerns the application of ss. 78–81; s. 78 deals with the equation of original shares and new holding; s. 79 relates to the consideration given or received by holder; s. 80 provides for part disposal of new holding; s. 81 specifies composite new holdings; s. 82 concerns equation of converted securities and new holding; s. 83 deals with premiums on conversion of securities; s. 84 makes provisions as to compensation stock; s. 85 deals with the exchange of securities for those in another company; s. 86 provides for the reconstruction or amalgamation involving issue of securities; s. 87 restricts the application of ss. 85 and 86; s. 88 sets out the procedure for clearance in advance; s. 89 provides for consideration for new holding in relation to stock dividends; s. 90 deals with capital gains on certain stock dividends; s. 91 applies ss. 77–91 to quoted options; s. 92 is an interpretation section; s. 93 applies the Act to unit trusts; s. 94 concerns reduction of tax liability on disposal of units or shares; s. 95 relates to the valuation of assets and rights; s. 96 deals with unit trusts for exempt unit holders; s. 97 provides for unit trusts for pension schemes; s. 98 concerns the transfer of a company's assets to unit trust which later comes within s. 96 or 97; s. 99 deals with funds in court; s. 100 reduces the rate of tax payable on chargeable gains accruing to a court investment fund.

Pt. V (ss. 101–114) contains provisions relating to land: s. 101 grants relief on disposal of private residence; s. 102 specifies the amount of relief; s. 103 makes further provisions as to the amount of relief; s. 104 deals with private residences occupied under terms of settlement; s. 105 concerns private residences occupied by dependent relative; s. 106 applies Sched. 3 to leases of land and other assets; s. 107 relates to small part disposals; s. 108 concerns part disposal to authority with compulsory powers; s. 109 concerns part disposal where consideration exceeds allowable expenditure; s. 110 provides for situations where compensation is paid on compulsory acquisition; s. 111 specifies the time of disposal and acquisition; s. 112 relates to grants for giving up agricultural land; s. 113 deals with woodlands; s. 114 concerns the interaction with development land tax and other taxation.

Pt. VI (ss. 115–139) makes future provisions as to property: s. 115 grants roll-over relief; s. 116 relates to assets only partly replaced; s. 117 concerns new assets which are depreciating assets; s. 118 states the relevant classes of assets; s. 119 deals with assets of Class 1; s. 120 states that where a trade is carried on by a family company a reference to the person carrying on the trade shall include a reference to that individual; s. 121 concerns activities other than trades; s. 122 deals with appropriations to and from stock; s. 123 grants roll-over relief on transfer of business; s. 124 gives relief on transfer; s. 125 deals with transfer by way of capital distribution from family company; s. 126 grants relief for gifts of business assets; s. 127 concerns movable property and wasting assets; s. 128 exempts chattels under a certain value; s. 129 applies Sched. 3 to leases of property other than land; s. 130 relates to passenger vehicles; s. 131 concerns decorations for valour or gallant conduct; s. 132 deals with commodities and other assets without earmark; s. 133 exempts gains on foreign currencies for personal expenditure; s. 134 applies to debts; s. 135 concerns foreign currency bank accounts; s. 136 grants relief in respect of loans to traders; s. 137 relates to options and forfeited deposits; s. 138 states the application of rules as to wasting assets regarding options; s. 139 provides for quoted options to be treated as part of new holdings.

Pt. VII (ss. 140–149) contains miscellaneous provisions: s. 140 deals with policies of insurance; s. 141 provides for disallowance of insurance premiums as expenses; s. 142 concerns underwriters; s. 143 relates to life assurance and deferred annuities; s. 144 exempts superannuation funds, annuities and annual payments; s. 145 exempts charities and property held on charitable trusts; s. 146 concerns gifts to charities; s. 147 relates to works of art etc.; s. 148 deals with maintenance funds for historic buildings; s. 149 makes provision as to employee trusts.

Pt. VIII (ss. 150–155) contains supplemental provisions; s. 150 deals with valuation of property; s. 151 concerns assets disposed of in a series of transactions; s. 152 relates to unquoted shares and securities; s. 153 determines the time of valuation on the death of a person; s. 154 states that decisions on assessments or appeals shall be conclusive; s. 155 is the interpretation section.

Pt. IX (ss. 156–160) contains general provisions: s. 156 provides for commencement of the Act; s. 157 makes savings, transitory provisions and consequential amendments; s. 158 repeals certain enactments; s. 159 deals with the continuity and construction of references to old and new law; s. 160 contains the short title.

The Act received the Royal Assent on March 22, 1979, and came into force on April 6, 1979.

1457. Charities—transfers from one charity to another—" charitable purposes "
[Income and Corporation Taxes Act 1970 (c. 10), s. 360 (1); Finance Act

1965 (c. 25), s. 35 (1).] An outright transfer of money between charities is to be regarded as income applied for charitable purposes although the money stays undistributed without showing how it is to be applied by the transferee: I.R.C. *v.* HELEN SLATER CHARITABLE TRUST, *The Times*, December 1, 1979, Slade J.

1458. Child allowance—custody of adult in full-time education
[Income and Corporation Taxes Act 1970 (c. 10), s. 10.] In 1975 the taxpayer's sister was of full age and was receiving full-time education. The taxpayer provided for her, and was regarded as being *in loco parentis* in relation to her. *Held*, that as the sister was an adult she could not be in the "custody" of the taxpayer, so that he was not entitled to a child allowance in respect of her. (*Nwagbo* v. *Rising* . [1978] C.L.Y. 1647 applied): ASPDEN V. BAXI [1979] S.T.C. 566, Brightman J.

1459. Construction industry—deductions by contractors—exemption—powers of Commissioners on appeal
[Finance (No. 2) Act 1975 (c. 45), s. 70, Sched. 12, Pt. I.] An applicant for a sub-contractor's tax certificate failed to satisfy the conditions in Finance (No. 2) Act 1975, Sched. 12. The inspector refused to grant the certificate. The applicant appealed, and, prior to the hearing before the General Commissioners, rectified his position so that the statutory conditions were satisfied. The Commissioners decided that he should be granted a certificate. *Held,* allowing the Crown's appeal, that the Commissioners should consider the position as it was when the applicant applied for the certificate (or when the inspector made his decision). As the statutory conditions were not then satisfied, the Commissioners were not entitled to decide that the applicant should be granted a certificate: KIRVELL *v.* GUY [1979] S.T.C. 312, Walton J.

1460. Double taxation
DOUBLE TAXATION RELIEF (TAXES ON INCOME) (AUSTRIA) ORDER 1979 (No. 117) [25p], made under the Income and Corporation Taxes Act 1970 (c. 10), s. 497, the Finance Act 1972 (c. 41), s. 98 (2) and the Finance Act 1965 (c. 25), s. 39; the Protocol scheduled to the Order alters the Convention set out in S.I. 1970 No. 1947. These alterations follow from the introduction of the new U.K. corporation tax system which came into operation, in part, on April 6, 1973.

DOUBLE TAXATION RELIEF (TAXES ON INCOME) (NORWAY) ORDER 1979 (No. 118) [25p], made under the Income and Corporation Taxes Act 1970, s. 497, the Finance Act 1972, s. 98 (2) and the Finance Act 1965, s. 39; the Protocol scheduled to this Order amends the Convention with Norway, signed January 22, 1969, by, *inter alia,* providing rules for avoidance of the double taxation of U.K. and Norwegian residents in respect of income and profits from activities connected with offshore oil and gas exploration or exploitation on the U.K. and Norwegian continental shelves.

DOUBLE TAXATION RELIEF (SHIPPING AND AIR TRANSPORT PROFITS) (JORDAN) ORDER 1979 (No. 300) [10p], made under the Income and Corporation Taxes Act 1970, s. 497 and the Finance Act 1965 (c. 25), s. 39; sets out the arrangements made with Jordan under which profits, income and capital gains derived from all shipping and air transport operations, by an undertaking of one of the countries are to be exempt from tax in the other country.

DOUBLE TAXATION RELIEF (SHIPPING AND AIR TRANSPORT PROFITS) (VENEZUELA) ORDER 1979 (No. 301) [20p], made under the Income and Corporation Taxes Act 1970, s. 497 and the Finance Act 1965, s. 39; exempts from tax the shipping and air transport profits derived by an undertaking of one of the countries from the other country.

DOUBLE TAXATION RELIEF (TAXES ON INCOME) (MALAWI) ORDER 1979 (No. 302) [20p], made under the Income and Corporation Taxes Act 1970, s. 497, the Finance Act 1972, s. 98 (2), and the Finance Act 1965, s. 39; the Supplementary Agreement scheduled to the Order makes certain alterations to the Agreement signed in November 1955 between the U.K. and the Federation of Rhodesia and Nyasaland. The main alteration follows from the introduction of the new U.K. corporation tax system.

DOUBLE TAXATION RELIEF (TAXES ON INCOME) (NORWAY) (No. 2) ORDER

1979 (No. 303) [30p], made under the Income and Corporation Taxes Act 1970, s. 497, as amended by the Finance Act 1972, s. 98; the Protocol scheduled to the Order makes certain alterations to the Convention set out in S.I. 1970 No. 154. These alterations follow from the introduction of the new U.K. corporation tax system which came into operation on April 6, 1973.

DOUBLE TAXATION RELIEF (TAXES ON ESTATES OF DECEASED PERSONS AND ON GIFTS) (UNITED STATES OF AMERICA) ORDER 1979 (No. 1454) [70p], made under the Finance Act 1975 (c. 7), by Sched. 7, para. 7; operative on November 14, 1979; the Double Taxation Convention with the U.S.A. which forms the Schedule to this Order applies to death duties and gift taxes. The taxes covered are capital transfer tax, and in the U.S.A. estate and gift taxes.

1461. Farming—profits—subsidy

Payment from an EEC grant for undertaking to carry on a farming business in a particular way, amounts to a premium paid to make good temporary losses, and the payment is accordingly an income profit and liable to tax.

Per curiam: As a matter of morality it seems unfair to tax compensation more heavily than the income (if received) would have been.

Pursuant to an EEC regulation introducing the Dairy Herd Conversion Scheme, D undertook not to supply or sell milk for a period of four years and instead to use their land for keeping beef cattle or sheep. In return D received a grant. D credited the payment as capital but were taxed on it as a trading receipt. On appeal the General Commissioners held the payment was capital On appeal by the Crown, *held*, allowing the appeal, that D received the money for undertaking to carry on the business in a particular way and the payment did arise from the carrying on of D's trade. The payment amounted to a premium paid to make good temporary income losses and was itself income liable to tax. (*Higgs* v. *Olivier* [1952] C.L.Y. 1669 distinguished: dictum of Diplock L.J. in *London and Thames Haven Oil Wharves* v. *Attwooll* [1967] C.L.Y. 1943 applied.)

WHITE v. G. AND M. DAVIES [1979] 1 W.L.R. 908, Browne-Wilkinson J.

1462. Interest

INCOME TAX (INTEREST ON UNPAID TAX AND REPAYMENT SUPPLEMENT) ORDER 1979 (No. 1687) [10p], made under the Finance Act 1967 (c. 54), s. 40 (2), the Taxes Management Act 1970 (c. 9), s. 89 (2) and the Finance (No. 2) Act 1975 (c. 45), ss. 47 (7) (10), 48 (6); operative on January 1, 1980 (arts. 1 and 2) and January 6, 1980 (art. 3); provides for the rate of interest payable on certain unpaid taxes to be raised to 12 per cent., and also for the supplement on repayments of certain taxes to be increased to 12 per cent.

1463. Malaysia—loss—double taxation agreement

[Income Tax Act 1967 (No. 47 of 1967), s. 3; Double Taxation Relief (Republic of Singapore) Order 1967 (P.U. 385) art. xvii. 1].

Where a double taxation treaty gave exemption from tax for profits but made no reference to losses, the taxpayer was entitled to set off losses against its other income.

The taxpayer company was resident in Malaysia, and carried on business there and through a branch in Singapore. By the Double Taxation Relief (Republic of Singapore) Order 1966, it was exempt from Malaysian tax in respect of the profits from its Singapore branch. The tax treaty made no provision for losses. In 1968 the company made a profit in Malaysia and a loss in Singapore. Under the Income Tax Act 1967 losses were deductible in computing income. *Held* (Lord Russell of Killowen dissenting), that the losses sustained in Singapore were able to be set off against the profits arising in Malaysia.

HOCK HENG CO. SDN. BHD. v. DIRECTOR-GENERAL OF INLAND REVENUE [1979] 2 W.L.R. 788, P.C.

1464. Northern Ireland. See NORTHERN IRELAND.

1465. P.A.Y.E.

INCOME TAX (EMPLOYMENTS) (No. 9) REGULATIONS 1979 (No. 747) [10p] made under the Income and Corporation Taxes Act 1970 (c. 10), s. 204; operative on October 6, 1979; raise the limit of weekly or monthly pay above which an employer has to operate the P.A.Y.E. scheme for every employee, to take account of the increased income tax allowances for 1979/80.

1466. Precept—failure to comply—penalty

[Taxes Management Act 1970 (c. 9), s. 51.] The taxpayer failed to comply with a precept requiring him to produce certain bank and building society passbooks. The General Commissioners imposed a penalty of £50. The taxpayer appealed against the penalty, and explained that following the issue of the precept he had written to the Inspector, and was awaiting a reply. *Held*, that the excuse put forward by the taxpayer was " exceptionally thin," and that in the absence of reasonable excuse, justification or explanation the appeal must be dismissed: GALLERI v. WIRRAL GENERAL COMMISSIONERS [1979] S.T.C. 216, Walton J.

1467. Reliefs

INCOME TAX (LIFE ASSURANCE PREMIUM RELIEF) REGULATIONS 1979 (No. 346) [10p], made under the Finance Act 1976 (c. 40), Sched. 4, para. 16; operative on April 6, 1979; amend S.I. 1978 No. 1159 by dispensing the requirement contained in Reg. 3 (5) (a) of the 1978 Regs. that the life assurance office obtained certain information from a person paying premiums before it can accept payment of premiums under deduction.

1468. Rent—mineral royalties

[Income Tax Act 1952 (c. 10), s. 175.]

Royalties payable under a licence agreement are income derived from the use of land within the charge to tax on excess rents.

In 1957 and 1960 the taxpayer company, by separate documents executed contemporaneously, granted to W Ltd. leases and licences of certain land. The leases excluded mineral rights; the licences conferred rights to take minerals. The question was whether the royalties payable under the licence agreements were " rent payable under a lease " within s. 175 of the Income Tax Act 1952. Goulding J. held that the royalties were not within the charge, on the ground that rent bore its strict legal meaning of payments issuing out of land and recoverable by distress. *Held*, allowing the Crown's appeal, that the object and effect of s. 175 was to tax moneys of an income character derived from land, and the royalties were within the charge.

T. & E. HOMES v. ROBINSON [1979] 1 W.L.R. 452, C.A.

1469. Returns—default—penalty

[Taxes Management Act 1970 (c. 9), s. 8.] The appellant failed to supply completed tax returns for the years 1972–73, 1973–74, 1974–75. He complained of misconduct on the part of the Inspector of Taxes and his staff, and claimed that there was reasonable excuse for his non-compliance. The General Commissioners found that there was no sufficient reason for the failure and awarded a penalty of £25 for each year. *Held*, upholding the judgment of Brightman J., that the application for the penalties to be discharged should be refused: NAPIER v. I.R.C. [1978] T.R. 403, C.A.

1470. Schedule D—furnished lettings—expenses—question of fact

The taxpayer was assessed to income tax in respect of profits on rents from furnished lettings. Before the Commissioners he failed to produce receipts or vouchers in respect of expenses which he claimed had been incurred by him in respect of the properties. The Commissioners accepted the taxpayer's oral evidence that a somewhat larger sum had been expended on decoration for certain of the years than had been allowed by the inspector, but otherwise confirmed the assessments. *Held*, dismissing the taxpayer's appeal, that the matter turned wholly upon acceptance by the Commissioners of the taxpayer's evidence as to expenditure which had been incurred by him, and that no question of law arose in respect of which the court could interfere with the Commissioners' decision: ABIDOYE v. HENNESSEY [1979] S.T.C. 212, Walton J.

1471. —— payment for newspaper story—annual profits

[Income and Corporation Taxes Act 1970 (c. 10), s. 108.]

The proceeds of sale of a story to a newspaper are taxable income.

The taxpayer, the wife of one of the " Great Train Robbers," was resident in Canada. Through an " agent " in the U.K. she entered into an agreement whereby she sold " her story " to the *News of the World* for £39,000. She was assessed to income tax under Case VI of Sched. D. *Held*, that (1) on the evidence the Commissioners were entitled to hold that the sum was received as income; and (2) the sum was derived by the taxpayer from property (the contract) in the U.K., and, accordingly was within the charge to tax under Case VI of Sched. D.

ALLOWAY *v.* PHILLIPS [1979] 1 W.L.R. 564, Brightman J.

1472. Schedule E—deductible expenditure

[Income and Corporation Taxes Act 1970 (c. 10), s. 189 (1).] The taxpayer was employed as an assistant surveyor by the G.L.C. He incurred expenditure on cleaning and repairing clothes which had become dirty and damaged during visits to construction sites. *Held,* allowing the Crown's appeal, that the expenditure was not deductible in computing his taxable emoluments, as it was not incurred wholly in the performance of his duties (*Woodcock* v. *I.R.C.* [1977] C.L.Y. 1593 followed): WARD *v.* DUNN [1979] S.T.C. 178, Walton J.

1473. The taxpayer incurred costs seeking new employment, and in paying for legal representation before an industrial tribunal in a claim for unfair dismissal. He was successful before the tribunal but no order as to costs was made in his favour. The taxpayer contended that the costs thus incurred were deductible from the tribunal's award. *Held,* that the court was not at liberty to disregard the clear words of taxing statutes so as to achieve what it thought to be a fair result. No provision existed to support the view that Schedule E tax was payable only in respect of the " profit " that resulted to the taxpayer following his dispute with his former employer. Therefore, by virtue of s. 187 (1) and (4) the full sums, less the exemption on the first £5,000, fell to be treated as earned income assessable under Sched. E: WARNETT *v.* JONES, *The Times,* November 30, 1979, Slade J.

1474. ―― emoluments—employment—gold sovereigns

[Income and Corporation Taxes Act 1970 (c. 10), s. 183 (1); Coinage Act 1971 (c. 24), s. 2.]

Tax under Sched. E is chargeable on the full amount of the emoluments of employment and where these are paid in gold sovereigns it is the amount realised on the sovereigns and not their nominal value.

J asked his employer to pay him in gold sovereigns. Under the scheme the employer purchased sovereigns from X, paid the necessary number to J to pay his wages and J sold the sovereigns back to X for £1 less than his employer had paid for them. J was assessed to income tax under Sched. E on the value that he received for the sovereigns. J appealed contending that sovereigns were legal tender and he should only be charged to tax on their nominal value of £1 sterling each. *Held,* the assessment was correct. Tax under Sched. E was chargeable on the amount of the emoluments falling under that Schedule which was the amount J realised on the sovereigns not their nominal value. This was not inconsistent with the provisions of the Coinage Act 1971 because that provided that gold coins were not to have a value less than their face value and did not prevent them being treated as having a greater value than their nominal face value. Appeal dismissed.

JENKINS *v.* HORN [1979] 2 All E.R. 1141, Browne-Wilkinson J.

1475. ―― ―― ―― shares

[Finance Act 1956 (c. 54), Sched. 2, para. 1 (1).]

Where Commissioners have found that shares were obtained as an emolument of employment and there is evidence warranting such finding, their decision cannot be upset by a court.

A company sought a public quotation for its shares by offering shares for sale through a bank, but reserved 10 per cent. of the shares for certain of its employees at a fixed price. The taxpayer, being one of the employees in question, applied for and obtained 5,000 shares. On the first day of dealing, the shares commanded a price in excess of the cost to the taxpayer. He was assessed to tax under Sched. E in respect of the profit. The Special Commissioners held that the shares were an emolument of the taxpayer's employment. *Held,* allowing the Crown's appeal from the decision of the Court of Appeal, that there was evidence to justify the Special Commissioners' conclusions and their decision should not be interfered with.

TYRER *v.* SMART [1979] 1 W.L.R. 113, H.L.

1476. —— office

[Income and Corporation Taxes Act 1970 (c. 10), s. 181.]

A person appointed by the Secretary of State for the Environment to hold a public local inquiry is the holder of an office for tax purposes.

The taxpayer, a distinguished chartered civil engineer, was invited from time to time to act as an inspector at a public local inquiry under the Acquisition of Land (Authorisation Procedure) Act 1946. Until 1973 he had been assessed to tax under Case II of Sched. D on the fees he received in this capacity; but the practice was then changed and P.A.Y.E. deductions were made from his fees on the basis that he was the holder of an office within I.C.T.A. 1970, s. 204. *Held*, allowing the Crown's appeal, that the taxpayer was the holder of an office and therefore the fees were taxable under Sched. E. EDWARDS *v.* CLINCH [1979] 1 W.L.R. 338, Walton J.

1477. —— pension payments

[Finance Act 1970, (c. 65), Sched. 5, Part II, para. 1 (1).] The taxpayer retired at the age of 62. Under the rules of his employer's pension scheme be became entitled to a " temporary pension " until he attained 65 years of age. The pension scheme was being considered for approval under F.A. 1970. The trustees deducted income tax from the payments made to the taxpayer. *Held*, that the payments were of an income character, and as the scheme was being considered for approval under F.A. 1970, they were subject to Sched. 5. Therefore, the trustees had properly deducted income tax on making the payments: ESSLEMONT *v.* ESTILL [1979] S.T.C. 624, Oliver J.

1478. Settlement—accumulation of income—beneficiaries' liability

[Income Tax Act 1952 (c. 10), s. 412 (as amended by Finance Act 1969 (c. 32), s. 33).] In 1942 overseas property was settled on accumulation trusts. The accumulations formed a capital fund, which was divided equally between two branches of the family. Income from each moiety of the fund was accumulated and reinvested. Between 1962 and 1966 the non-resident trustees made capital appointments to discretionary beneficiaries, who were assessed to income tax pursuant to subss. (1) and (2) of s. 412 of the Income Tax Act 1952 (see now Income and Corporation Taxes Act 1970, s. 478) on *pro rata* parts of the income which had arisen to the non-resident trustees. Appeals and cross-appeals from the decision of Walton J. were made direct to the House of Lords under the Administration of Justice Act 1969. *Held*, dismissing the Crown's appeals and allowing the taxpayers' cross-appeals, and overruling the decision in *Congreve* v. *I.R.C.* (1948) C.L.C. 4824, that no assessment could be made under s. 412 on beneficiaries of a trust who had not made, or been associated with, the transfer of the funds into the settlement: VESTEY *v.* I.R.C., *The Times*, November 24, 1979, H.L.

1479. Singapore—profits—capital allowances—exempt profits

[Income Tax Act, s. 32; The Economic Expansion Incentives (Relief from Income Tax) Act 1967, s. 32.] The appellant company was entitled to exemption from tax in respect of certain " export profits " and also claimed tax relief for capital allowances. The Comptroller of Income Tax claimed to restrict the relief for capital allowances by apportioning a pro rata part of the allowances to the exempt export profits. *Held*, allowing the company's appeal, that the company was entitled to full relief for its capital allowances, there being no justification for any rateable apportionment of the allowances to the exempt profits: UNION CARBIDE SINGAPORE PRIVATE *v.* THE COMPTROLLER OF INCOME TAX [1979] T.R. 51, P.C.

1480. Sub-contractors—failure to make deduction

[Finance Act 1971 (c. 68), ss. 29, 30; Taxes Management Act 1970, (c. 9), s. 50 (6); Income Tax (Payments to Sub-Contractors in the Construction Industry) Regulations 1971 (S.I. 1971 No. 1779), regs. 6 (3), 11 (1).] R & B Ltd. engaged individual sub-contractors for construction work. They had exemption certificates under F.A. 1971, s. 30. After the certificates had expired, payments were made by R & B Ltd., but no deduction was made. The Inspector of Taxes declined to exonerate R & B Ltd. from the failure to make the deduction and made an assessment on it to recover the sum which should have been deducted. The General Commissioners discharged the assessment on the ground that R & B Ltd. had taken reasonable care to comply with its obligations. *Held,* that the General Commissioners had no power to override the Inspector's determination and to discharge the assessment: SLATER *v.* RICHARDSON AND BOTTOMS [1974] S.T.C. 630, Oliver J.

1481. Surtax—close company apportionment—commissioners' jurisdiction

[Income and Corporation Taxes Act 1970 (c. 10), ss. 296, 298.] The taxpayer company was a non-trading close company; its shares were largely held by members of one family, and it was indebted to two members of the family in the sums of £30,000 and £200,000. It held shares in a public company. For its accounting periods ended March 1970 and March 1971, it waived dividends on the shares; the loan creditor for £200,000 waived interest on the loan. The Inland Revenue apportioned the company's income for the two periods among the participators according to their respective interests on winding up. On appeal, the commissioners held that they could not substitute their view as to the proper manner of apportionments for the decision of the Revenue, where the Revenue had not exceeded it powers or failed to exercise any discretion. *Held,* that (1) the Commissioners had jurisdiction to review the Revenue decision; but (2) as neither party wished the matter to be remitted to the commissioners, the apportionment should stand and the appeal be dismissed: LOTHBURY INVESTMENT CORP. *v.* I.R.C. (1979) 123 S.J. 720, Goulding J.

1482. —— restrictive covenants—inducement to give up profession

[Income and Corporation Taxes Act 1970 (c. 10), s. 34.]

Where restrictions upon an individual's activities arise from acceptance of an employment and not from any specific covenant to that effect, a payment made to induce him to accept the employment is not taxable under I.C.T.A. 1970, s. 34.

A barrister was offered employment with a large construction company, the acceptance of which necessarily precluded him from continuing to practise at the bar. He was offered a payment of £40,000 as " an inducement to him to give up his status as a practising barrister with the consequent loss of those advantages he now enjoys." *Held,* allowing the taxpayer's appeal from the decision of the Special Commissioners, that the sum of £40,000 was not taxable under s. 34 of the Income and Corporation Taxes Act 1970 as it was not paid " in respect of the giving of an undertaking " the tenor or effect of which was to restrict him as to his conduct or activities. (*Pritchard* v. *Arundale* [1971] C.L.Y. 5762, applied.)

VAUGHAN-NEIL *v.* I.R.C. [1979] 1 W.L.R. 1283, Oliver J.

1483. Tax advantage—transactions in securities

[Income and Corporation Taxes Act 1970 (c. 10), ss. 460–468.] The taxpayers and companies which they controlled entered into a tax avoidance scheme having three stages: (1) property transactions implemented by K Ltd.; (2) the exchange by the taxpayers of their shares in K Ltd. for the issue to them of shares in G Ltd. and the payment of a large dividend by K Ltd. to G Ltd.; and (3) the making of loans by D Ltd. to the taxpayers, and the subsequent purchase of the shares in D Ltd. by G Ltd. The Inland Revenue challenged stages (2) and (3) of the scheme under I.C.T.A. 1970, ss. 460–468. *Held,* that stage (2) fell within both circumstances D and E of s. 461, and E (2) prevented counteraction until the shares in G Ltd. were repaid; but that stage (3) fell within paras. C and D, and the "tax advantage" obtained by the taxpayers from the loans ("transactions in securities") was able to be counteracted under s. 460: WILLIAMS *v.* I.R.C. [1979] T.R. 39, C.A.

1484. [Income and Corporation Taxes Act 1970 (c. 10), ss. 460–468.]

The receipt of purchase moneys on the scale of shares may constitute a tax advantage for the purposes of I.C.T.A. 1970, s. 460.

W Ltd. carried on the business of making and dealing in picture frames. In 1955 it bought a frame for 48 guineas. Seven years later it transpired that the frame held a very valuable painting. In 1967 the shareholders of W Ltd. caused the major part of its stock to be transferred to another of their companies. They then sold the shares in W Ltd., which still owned the valuable painting, to K Ltd. for £45,000. *Held*, allowing the Crown's appeal, that the transactions were caught by I.C.T.A. 1970, s. 460, the shareholders having obtained a "tax advantage" from a "transaction in securities" in s. 461D circumstances.

I.R.C. *v.* WIGGINS [1979] 1 W.L.R. 325, Walton J.

1485. —— —— bona fide commercial reasons

[Income and Corporation Taxes Act 1970 (c. 10), s. 460.]

A commercial reason extrinsic to the actual transactions may be a bona fide commercial reason for the purposes of I.C.T.A. 1970, s. 460.

The taxpayer, a farmer, wished to purchase a farm adjoining his own, being of the opinion that the resulting entity could be farmed more efficiently. To this end he decided to raise the necessary moneys by selling his shares in H Ltd., a private investment company the assets of which consisted mainly of shares in C Ltd., a public quoted company of which the taxpayer's father was chairman and managing director. So that control of C Ltd. would not pass from the family, the taxpayer sold his shares in H Ltd. to E Ltd., a family investment company in which the taxpayer held shares. The Inland Revenue contended that the foregoing transactions gave rise to a tax advantage for the taxpayer, which tax advantage could be counteracted under I.C.T.A. 1970, s. 460. The taxpayer contended that the transactions were motivated by his need to obtain moneys to purchase the farm, and that this was a bona fide commercial reason which prevented s. 460 from applying. *Held*, allowing the taxpayer's appeal from the decision of the Special Commissioners, that the commercial reason need not be connected with the companies concerned with the transactions. On the facts, the predominant reason for the transaction was the taxpayer's wish to acquire the adjoining farm; this was a commercial reason which prevented s. 460 from operating (dictum of Lord Pearce in *I.R.C.* v. *Brebner* [1967] C.L.Y. 1978 applied).

CLARK *v.* I.R.C. [1979] 1 All E.R. 385, Fox J.

1486. Tax avoidance—artificial transactions in land—information required—validity of notice

[Income and Corporation Taxes Act 1970 (c. 10), s. 490.] Notices were served on two individuals and two companies under I.C.T.A. 1970, s. 490, requiring information in respect of categories of transactions and arrangements which were not specifically identified. The taxpayers challenged the validity of the notices on the grounds that (a) the transactions and arrangements should have been identified, and (b) the notices were inordinately burdensome and oppressive. *Held*, that (1) under the section the Commissioners were empowered to seek information as to unidentified transactions or arrangements; (2) oppression by itself did not render the notices invalid, for they could only be challenged on grounds of issue in bad faith; and (3) the terms of the notices were not so ambiguous and obscure that no reasonable inspector could have thought it necessary to require the information. (*Royal Bank of Canada* v. *I.R.C.* [1972] C.L.Y. 1697 and *Clinch* v. *I.R.C.* [1973] C.L.Y. 1689 followed): ESSEX *v.* I.R.C. [1979] S.T.C. 525, Slade J.

1487. —— settlement

[Income and Corporation Taxes Act 1970 (c. 10), ss. 52, 109, 434, 457.] The taxpayer entered into an arm's-length transaction with a charitable company whereby in consideration of the payment to him of a capital sum he covenanted to make payments to the company over a number of years. He claimed to deduct these payments in arriving at his total income for the purposes of surtax. The Crown disallowed the deduction, claiming that the arrangements constituted a settlement for the purposes of I.C.T.A. 1970, s. 457, of which the taxpayer was the settlor. *Held* (Viscount Dilhorne and Lord Diplock dissenting), that an arrangement in which no element of bounty existed was not a "settlement" within s. 457: I.R.C. *v.* PLUMMER (1979) 123 S.J. 769, H.L.

1488. Tax fraud—Inland Revenue officers—powers of search and seizure. See I.R.C. *v.* ROSSMINSTER, § 2279.

1489. Trade—appeal

The taxpayer, a builder, appealed against a decision of the Special Commissioners that certain land acquired in the name of his wife in 1957 and ultimately sold in 1973, had been acquired by the wife as nominee for the taxpayer and formed part of his trading stock. *Held*, dismissing the appeal, that no question of law was involved and that on the evidence before them the Special Commissioners were justified in coming to the conclusion that the land formed part of the taxpayer's trading stock: SMART *v.* LOWNDES [1978] S.T.C. 607, Fox J.

1490. —— business—objects of company—whether carrying on a business. See AMERICAN LEAF BLENDING CO. SDN. BHD. *v.* DIRECTOR-GENERAL OF INLAND REVENUE, § 270.

1491. —— land—isolated transaction

[Malaysian Income Tax Ordinance 1947, s. 10 (1).] The appellant company's objects included dealing in land and buildings. In 1962/63 it purchased several pieces of land in Penang with a view to building a shopping arcade and hotel. Preliminary negotiations for the letting of the hoted proved abortive, and in 1963 the company transferred the land and the building works to another company in exchange for the issue of shares in that company. The company had not otherwise dealt in land. The Malaysian Special Commissioners held that the acquisition and the disposal of the land amounted to trade and that the profits were taxable accordingly. *Held*, that the isolated character of the transaction did not prevent it from being by way of trade, and that the Special Commissioners were justified in reaching their conclusion that the transactions amounted to trade: INTERNATIONAL INVESTMENT *v.* THE COMPTROLLER-GENERAL OF INLAND REVENUE [1978] T.R. 247, P.C.

1492. —— share dealings

[Income and Corporation Taxes Act 1970 (c. 10), s. 168.] From 1969 the taxpayer (a mathematics graduate and a freelance operational research consultant) bought and sold shares on the Stock Exchange on a large scale and using borrowed moneys. In the year ending March 31, 1973, he made a loss, and claimed that this was a loss in a trade in respect of which he was entitled to relief under I.C.T.A. 1970, s. 168. The Commissioners found that the activity did not amount to a trade. *Held*, dismissing the taxpayer's appeal, that there is a presumption that speculative dealings in shares by an individual is not trading, and that the Commissioners' conclusion on this question of fact should not be disturbed: SALT *v.* CHAMBERLAIN (1979) 123 S.J. 490, Oliver J.

1493. Unpaid tax—recovery—appeal—enforcement proceedings

The taxpayer was assessed to income tax for several years of assessment in respect of his profits as a property consultant. His appeal against the assessments was dismissed; he demanded a case stated, which was duly filed, but not set down for hearing. The taxpayer then unsuccessfully challenged in the High Court the validity of a writ claiming the tax assessed and interest, the challenge being based on the ground that the writ had not been signed by the person purporting to sign it. The Inland Revenue then issued a summons for summary judgment. The taxpayer was refused leave to defend, and so appealed to the Judge in Chambers, raising an additional point that final judgment on the writ could not be entered until the tax appeal had been determined. *Held*, that (1) the validity of the writ had previously been affirmed by the High Court; and (2) notwithstanding the tax appeal, as the assessments raised against him had been affirmed by the Commissioners, the taxpayer could not resist recovery proceedings (*I.R.C.* v. *Pearlberg* [1953] C.L.Y. 1670 followed): I.R.C. *v.* SOUL (1976) 51 T.C. 86, C.A.

BOOKS AND ARTICLES. See *post*, pp. [10], [23].

INDUSTRIAL SOCIETIES

1494. Credit unions

CREDIT UNIONS (AUTHORISED INVESTMENTS) ORDER 1979 (No. 866) [20p], made under the Credit Unions Act 1979 (c. 34), ss. 13 (1), 29; operative on

August 20, 1979; prescribes the manner in which credit unions may invest funds not immediately required for their purposes.

INDUSTRIAL AND PROVIDENT SOCIETIES (CREDIT UNIONS) REGULATIONS 1979 (No. 937) [£1·50], made under the Industrial and Provident Societies Act 1965 (c. 12), ss. 70 (1), 71 (1), as applied by the Industrial and Provident Societies Act 1967 (c. 48), s. 7 (2), and the Credit Unions Act 1979, s. 31 (2); operative on August 20, 1979; prescribe the forms of application for registration of societies as credit unions under the 1979 Act, make provision for the keeping of documents by the Central Office of the Registry of Friendly Societies and the public inspection of such documents, and prescribe fees payable in connection with the 1965, 1967 and 1979 Acts.

1495. Credit Unions Act 1979 (c. 34)

This Act enables certain societies to be registered under the Industrial and Provident Societies Act 1965 as credit unions and makes further provision with respect to the societies so registered.

S. 1 provides for the registration of credit unions under the Industrial and Provident Societies Act 1965; s. 2 makes supplementary and transitional provisions as to registration; s. 3 concerns the use of the name " credit union "; s. 4 relates to the form and amendment of rules of a credit union; s. 5 contains provisions as to membership and voting rights; s. 6 specifies the minimum and maximum number of members; s. 7 deals with shares of a credit union; s. 8 places a general prohibition on deposit-taking; s. 9 places restrictions on deposits by persons too young to be members; s. 10 gives credit unions power to borrow money; s. 11 enables credit unions to make loans to their members; s. 12 empowers credit unions to hold land for limited purposes; s. 13 relates to investments; s. 14 makes provisions as to the computation and application of profits; s. 15 states that credit unions must insure against fraud or other dishonesty; s. 16 concerns guarantee funds; s. 17 gives power to the registrar to require information; s. 18 empowers the chief registrar to appoint an inspector and call meetings; s. 19 gives power to the chief registrar to suspend the operations of a credit union; s. 20 deals with the cancellation or suspension of registration and a petition for winding up; s. 21 concerns amalgamations and transfers of engagements; s. 22 disallows conversion of a credit union into a company; s. 23 sets out the conditions for the conversion of a company into a credit union; s. 24 modifies the requirements as to audit of accounts; s. 25 inserts a new s. 340A into the Income and Corporation Taxes Act 1970 with respect to the taxation of credit unions; s. 26 places a prohibition on subsidiaries; s. 27 places restrictions on undischarged bankrupts and other persons; s. 28 contains provisions as to offences; s. 29 concerns the making of orders under the Act; s. 30 relates to the expenses of the chief registrar and assistant registrars; s. 31 is the interpretation section; s. 32 contains provisions relating to the application of the Act in Northern Ireland; s. 33 deals with the short title, commencement and extent. Except for ss. 25 and 32 (4), this Act does not extend to Northern Ireland.

The Act received the Royal Assent on April 4, 1979, and ss. 32 and 33 came into force on that date; the remaining provisions come into force on a day to be appointed.

1496. —— commencement

CREDIT UNIONS ACT 1979 (COMMENCEMENT NO. 1) ORDER 1979 (No. 936 (C. 25)) [10p], made under the Credit Unions Act 1979 (c. 34), s. 33 (2); brings into force on August 20, 1979, ss. 1, 2, 3 (1) (4), 4–14, 16–31 of and Scheds. 1–3 to the 1979 Act.

1496a. Fees

INDUSTRIAL AND PROVIDENT SOCIETIES (CREDIT UNIONS) (AMENDMENT OF FEES) REGULATIONS 1979 (No. 1556) [20p], made under the Industrial and Provident Societies Act 1965 (c. 12), ss. 70 (1) and 71 (1) as applied by the Industrial and Provident Societies Act 1967 (c. 48), s. 7 (2) and the Credit Unions Act 1979 (c. 34), s. 31 (2); operative on January 1, 1980; increase the fees payable in connection with matters to be transacted and for the inspection of documents.

INDUSTRIAL AND PROVIDENT SOCIETIES (AMENDMENT OF FEES) REGULATIONS

1979 (No. 1558) [20p], made under the Industrial and Provident Societies Act 1965, s. 70 (1) as applied by the Industrial and Provident Societies Act 1967, s. 7 (2); operative on January 1, 1980; increase the fees to be paid for matters to be transacted and for the inspection of documents.

1497. Industrial assurance

INDUSTRIAL ASSURANCE (FEES) REGULATIONS 1979 (No. 1549) [20p], made under the Industrial Assurance Act 1923 (c. 8), s. 43; operative on January 1, 1980; increase the fees payable in connection with the exercise by the Industrial Assurance Commissioner of his functions under the 1923 Act, except in relation to disputes, where the fees payable remain unchanged.

INNKEEPERS

BOOKS. See *post*, p. [6].

INSURANCE

1498. Accident insurance—driver killed while intoxicated—whether death caused by " accident "

[Can.] It has been *held*, that an injury may be accidental even though it was caused by conduct that was dangerous and grossly negligent. Thus, where D dies as a result of driving while severely intoxicated, the death occurs " from accidental bodily injuries " within the meaning of an accident insurance policy. (*Fenton* v. *Thorly* [1903] A.C. 443 referred to): MUTUAL OF OMAHA INSURANCE COMPANY v. STATS (1978) 87 D.L.R. (3d) 169, Sup.Ct. of Canada.

1499. Agent—failure to warn of lack of coverage

[Can.] An insurance agent knew of his client's needs, but failed to secure the appropriate insurance policy. *Held*, he was liable to his client for the failure to warn of the lack of coverage. Thus, where an agent knows his client carries on business in part of the premises to be insured, but takes out a policy excluding business use, the agent is liable to the client for the uninsured loss: MCCANN v. WESTERN FARMERS MUTUAL INSURANCE (1978) 87 D.L.R. (3d) 135, Ontario High Ct. Justice.

1500. —— implied authority. See STOCKTON v. MASON, § 39.

1501. —— oral assurance—no notification of exclusion—liability

[Can.] D rented a crane from P. Before taking possession, D telephoned their insurance agents to place insurance on the crane. The agents' representative gave an oral assurance that the crane would be insured forthwith. The next day the crane collapsed because it was overloaded. The agents claimed that their representative had been in error and that coverage had not been placed, but that as damage caused by overloading would have fallen within an exclusion clause in any event, D had not suffered any loss. D claimed that the exclusion clause could not be raised as a defence because they had no knowledge of it. *Held*, that D were entitled to a 50 per cent. contribution from the agents. D must be taken to have sought the best coverage reasonably obtainable in the circumstances, namely coverage including the exclusion clause. However, D were entitled to a policy of insurance with a reputable insurer, and had suffered damage in that they had lost their chance of settling by compromise. A reputable insurer would have compromised at 50 per cent., and D would have been advised to accept such compromise. (*Fraser* v. *Furman* (*Productions*) [1967] C.L.Y. 2037 applied): L. MARTIN CONSTRUCTION v. GAGLARDI [1979] 1 W.W.R. 171, Bt.Col.Sup.Ct.

1502. —— theft—moneys received on account of another—agent using insurance premiums for own purposes. See R.v. BREWSTER, § 596.

1503. —— undue influence—whether contract concluded. See RUST v. ABBEY LIFE ASSURANCE CO., § 1345.

1504. British Honduras—limitation of liability—construction of ordinance—personal injuries

H received fatal injuries in a motor accident in British Honduras, and P, H's executor, obtained judgment for BH$175,000 against the driver responsible, Y, who was unable to pay any part of that sum. Y was insured by D under a policy issued in accordance with the British Honduras Motor Vehicles Insurance (Third Party Risks) Ordinance 1958, which provided, *inter alia,* by s. 4 (1), for compulsory third party insurance " provided that such a policy shall not be required to cover liability in respect of any sum in excess of $4,000 arising out of any one claim by any one person "; and, by s. 20, that the insurer would be liable " in respect of any such liability as is required to be covered by a policy under " s. 4 (1) to the person entitled to the benefit of a judgment. D paid P $4,000 and the question arose whether they were liable for the balance of $171,000. *Held,* dismissing P's appeal, that (1) the ordinance had to be construed as it stood, and not by reference to different language in different legislation; (2) the word " liability " had the same meaning throughout s. 4 (1), and there was no reason in principle why the legislation should not have provided for total or partial or limited exemption of liability; (3) the construction of s. 20 was clear in that it applied to liability under s. 4 (1), including the limit of liability: HARKER *v.* CALEDONIAN INSURANCE CO. [1979] 2 Lloyd's Rep. 193, C.A.

1505. Contract of insurance—necessary elements

[Insurance Companies Act 1974 (c. 49), ss. 12 (1), 85 (1).]

One of the necessary elements of a contract of insurance is that the assured becomes entitled to something on the occurrence of some event, and that " something " must be of the nature of money or its equivalent. Accordingly, membership of the Medical Defence Union is not a contract of insurance.

The Medical Defence Union sought a declaration that it did not carry on the business of insurance. It had 80,000 members who paid subscriptions. The union existed to advise members on such matters as employment, defamation, professional and technical matters. It had power, entirely at its own discretion, to conduct any proceedings on behalf of a member, relating to his profession or to grant him indemnity in any such proceedings. *Held,* granting the declaration sought, that a member only became entitled, in certain events, to the right to have his application for indemnity or to have proceedings conducted on his behalf considered fairly by the union. That was not money or money's worth, and therefore that element of a contract of insurance was lacking. (*Prudential Insurance Co.* v. *I.R.C.* [1904] 2 K.B. 658, *Gould* v. *Curtis* [1913] 3 K.B. 84, C.A., *West Wake Price & Co.* v. *Ching* [1956] C.L.Y. 4423 and *Department of Trade and Industry* v. *St. Christopher Motorists Association* [1974] C.L.Y. 1900 considered.)

MEDICAL DEFENCE UNION *v.* DEPARTMENT OF TRADE [1979] 2 W.L.R. 686, Megarry V.-C.

1506. Contribution—professional indemnity—exclusion clause—double insurance

C, solicitors, were insured by P under a policy (the NEM policy), which provided, *inter alia,* by cl. 3, that C were to give immediate written notice to P of any occurrence which might subsequently give rise to a claim, and that such notice having been given, any subsequent claim would be deemed to have been made during the subsistence of the policy. The policy further provided, " This policy does not indemnify [C] in respect of any claim made against him for which [C] is entitled to indemnity under any other policy except in respect of any excess beyond the amount payable by such other policy." The NEM policy expired at midnight on March 24–25, 1976, and on the day of expiry C gave written notice of an occurrence which might give rise to a claim in the future. Subsequently, D, underwriter, insured C with effect from midnight on March 24–25, 1976, under a policy (the master policy), which provided, *inter alia,* " This insurance shall indemnify the assured in respect of any loss arising out of any claim in respect of any circumstance or occurrence which has been notified under any other insurance attaching prior to the inception of this [cover]." P claimed a declaration that as this was a case of double insurance, they were entitled to a contribution from D. *Held,* that (1) while it was true that the exclusion clause in the master policy was narrower than that in the NEM policy, they were both exclusion clauses, and even if they were clauses which limited the cover, it would still be impossible to distinguish between them; (2) in order to see whether a claim was covered by another policy within the meaning of the NEM exclusion clause, the time when the claim was made had to be looked at and not when it was deemed to be made; the deeming provision in cl. 3 merely extended cover so as to bring subsequent claims within its purview; (3) each policy was to be looked at separately, and if each would be liable but for the existence of the other, the exclusion clauses would be treated as cancelling each other out, and P and D were liable on the policies, and P entitled to a contribution (*Weddell* v. *Road Transport and General Insurance* [1932] 2 K.B. 563 and *Austin* v. *Zurich General Accident and Liability Co.* [1945] 1 K.B. 250, applied). Judgment for P: NATIONAL EMPLOYERS MUTUAL GENERAL INSURANCE ASSOCIATION *v.* HAYDEN [1979] 2 Lloyd's Rep. 235. Lloyd J.

1507. Employers' liability—personal injury—whether accident occurred " in course of employment "

P, an employee of D, was injured whilst a passenger in a vehicle owned by D due to negligent driving by D's driver. The vehicle was on its way from D's office to their construction site where P was told he was required, it being D's practice to transport their employees to the site in their vehicles. D were insured with T under an employers' liability insurance policy covering them in respect of bodily injury suffered by an employee " caused and arising out of and in the course of employment by [D]." D settled P's claim, and sought an indemnity from T. *Held*, dismissing T's appeal, that (1) on the facts, P was in D's office in the course of his employment; (2) P was therefore in the course of his employment in that he was in D's vehicle under an obligation to go to the site in obedience to which he had been told (*Vandyke* v. *Fender* [1970] C.L.Y. 1366 distinguished); (3) accordingly, the liability to indemnify D fell within the terms of T's policy: PATERSON *v.* COSTAIN & PRESS (OVERSEAS) [1979] 2 Lloyd's Rep. 204, C.A.

1508. Exclusion clause—causal connection between accident and death

[Can.] The deceased was insured under a life insurance policy with an exclusionary clause which read " if death results directly or indirectly from operating, riding in or descending from any kind of aircraft, if the insured has any duties aboard the aircraft." While flying an aircraft alone, the deceased crashed in mountains in November 1975. He left a note stating he was not injured and would attempt to walk out. The evidence showed that in all probability he slipped on a creek bank, fell into an icy pool, and drowned. As to whether the death was " indirectly " the result of operating the aircraft, *held*, there was not a consequent or causative relationship between the flying and the death by drowning, and judgment was granted to the executor of the deceased's estate (*Coxe* v. *Employers Liability Ass. Corp.* [1916] 2 K.B. 629 applied): ROYAL TRUST CO. *v.* GREAT WEST LIFE [1979] 2 W.W.R. 177, Brit.Col.Sup.Ct.

1509. Fire—actual loss or replacement value

Where a policy of house insurance provides that the house is insured for its " full value," the full value being the amount which it would cost to replace the property in its existing form should it be totally destroyed, and that the insurers provide insurance and indemnity at their option by payment, reinstatement or repair, the sum payable on total loss will be the market value or actual loss, as opposed to full reinstatement loss if the latter is greater.

P bought a house from his parents-in-law for £1,500. He put it up for sale for £12,500, then insured it with D Co. for £10,000. That figure was under the policy " the full value," *i.e.* " the amount which it would cost to replace the property in its existing form should it be totally destroyed." Under the policy D Co. agreed to provide insurance and indemnity " at their option by payment, reinstatement or repair." P increased the sum insured, as the cost of rebuilding the house, to £14,000. However, its actual value had dropped, and P had to reduce the asking price to £4,500. Then the house burnt down. D Co. repudiated liability. The judge at first instance held D Co. liable, and held that under the terms of the policy P was entitled to the full cost of replacement, namely £8,694. On appeal as to quantum by D Co., *held*, that " full value " was the maximum amount recoverable, and there was nothing in the policy to the effect that the amount recoverable was full reinstatement value. P could recover only his actual loss, which was the market value—£4,500—less the site value of £1,500. (*Castellain* v. *Preston* (1883) 11 Q.B.D. 380 and *British Traders' Insurance Co.* v. *Monson* (1964) 111 C.L.R. 86 applied.)

LEPPARD v. EXCESS INSURANCE CO. [1979] 1 W.L.R. 512, C.A.

1510. —— **non-disclosure—method of evaluating loss—effect of spent conviction**

P1 and P2, whose premises had been partially destroyed by fire in November 1973, brought an action against the insurers, D, on the question of quantum under a policy issued in August 1973, which provided, *inter alia*, " The Insurers agree that if the property insured or any part of such property be destroyed or damaged by fire the Insurers will pay to the Insured the value of the property at the time of the happening of its destruction or the amount of such damage or the Insurers at their option will reinstate or replace such property or any part thereof." The agreed settlement of £243,000 fell through, D contending that it was only justified if P intended to reinstate the damage, and P contending that reinstatement of the premises by the terms of the contract was the responsibility of D if they so elected. *Held*, that (1) the cost of reinstatement was not the inevitable contractual method of giving an indemnity, although it remained a possible method of doing so even though prior agreement to that effect could not be found in the contract; (2) P's claim for replacement damages was not a mere pretence; they had a genuine intention to reinstate if given the insurance moneys, and would not otherwise be properly indemnified; (3) the fact that an allegation of conspiracy to defraud had been made against P1 was not a material fact which he was bound to disclose, since the material circumstance was the commission of an offence, and not that an allegation had been made; (4) D had failed to prove that P1's conviction in 1961 for receiving property, which had also not been disclosed to them, was a material fact which could have affected the judgment of a reasonable or prudent insurer; (5) if D had proved that the conviction was a material fact, there would have been no real injustice in requiring the conviction to be disclosed because P1 would have been bound to disclose it when obtaining the policy (before the Rehabilitation of Offenders Act 1974) which he would otherwise not have been entitled to obtain and D would have been entitled to avoid; (6) P were entitled to be put in the position in which they would have been had D not refused to pay under the contract three and three-quarter years previously, and the proper sum for unliquidated damages was £343,320. (*Murphy* v. *Wexford County Council* (1921) 2 I.R. 230 applied): REYNOLDS AND ANDERSON v. PHOENIX ASSURANCE Co. [1978] 2 Lloyd's Rep. 440, Forbes J.

1511. —— **premium—" cost of reinstatement "—date of calculation**

In construing a lease in accordance with commercial good sense the words " the full cost of reinstatement " must cover the cost at the time when reinstatement took place.

By an underlease made between P and D, D covenanted, *inter alia*, to pay to P a sum equivalent to the premium paid for keeping the premises " insured for the full cost of reinstatement against loss or damage by fire." D contended " the full cost " was to be calculated as at the date each annual insurance premium was paid, P contended " the full cost " was to be calculated by reference to a prospective date of reinstatement. *Held*, the lease was to be construed as a whole in accordance with commercial good sense and that the words " the full cost of reinstatement " must cover the cost of reference to the date at which reinstatement could reasonably be completed, bearing in mind the possible effects of inflation. The maximum period to be allowed was approximately two-and-a-half years from the date on which the annual premium was payable. (Dictum of Megaw L.J. in *C. H. Bailey* v. *Memorial Enterprises* [1974] C.L.Y. 2122 applied; *Finchbourne* v. *Rodrigues* [1976] C.L.Y. 1521 considered.)

GLENIFFER FINANCE CORP. v. BAMAR WOOD AND PRODUCTS (1979) 37 P. & C.R. 208, Forbes J.

1512. —— **reinstatement—market value—measure of damages**

In November 1972, P's premises, which were insured by D, were extensively damaged by fire. The policy provided, *inter alia*, " Professional fees . . . the insurance on fees applies only to those necessarily incurred in the reinstatement of the property consequent upon its destruction or damage" and "Public authorities requirements . . . the insurance extends to include such additional cost of reinstatement as may be incurred solely by reason of the necessity to comply with building or other Regulations provided that the work of reinstatement must be commenced and carried out with reasonable despatch." The sum of £163,000 being the cost of reinstatement, was agreed between the parties, but D paid only £117,585, contending that the professional fees and public authorities requirements clauses rendered the amount of the deductions not payable until incurred in the reinstatement of the premises, and further, that the amount paid more than fairly represented the amount of the damage, being the difference in the market value of the premises immediately before and after the fire. P replied that D could not propound a new measure of damages, but that if the new basis alleged was correct, there was still an underpayment exceeding £30,000. *Held*, that (1) in the absence of a concluded agreement between the parties, although P were led to believe that only points of construction were going to be taken, D were not prevented from setting up a new plea with a new measure of damages; (2) there were not special facts which justified departing from the primary measure of damage under the policy, *i.e.* the cost of reinstatement; (3) the wording of the public authorities requirements clause made it clear that the costs to be recovered were not notional or estimated costs, but the actual costs of reinstatement carried out within a specified time; and P's claim in respect of this deduction failed; (4) the professional fees clause contained a proviso relating to commencement and completion of reinstatement; there was no distinction between fees and other building costs in the absence of plain words; the words "necessarily incurred" were words of description of type of cost and not of limitation by event; and P were entitled to recover £13,228·02: PLEASURAMA v. SUN ALLIANCE AND LONDON INSURANCE [1979] 1 Lloyd's Rep. 389, Parker J.

1513. Friendly societies. See FRIENDLY SOCIETIES.

1514. Indemnity assurance—fire extinguishers—to be available at "any place" where work carried out—construction

[Scot.] Fire damage was caused to a church allegedly by negligence of contractors in the use of a blow-lamp. The church trustees sued the contractors, who in turn alleged they were entitled to be indemnified by their insurers who they sued as a third party. The policy provided, *inter alia*, that "where blow-lamps are used away from the insured's premises the insured shall arrange for portable fire extinguishing appliances to be available at any place where work is to be carried out." *Held*, the word "place" meant the actual place where a burning appliance was being used by its operator and not the "premises" in which such work was being done. (*Fowkes* v. *Manchester Assurance Assoc.* (1863) 32 L.J.Q.B. 153 referred to): LAIDLAW v. MONTEATH & Co., 1979 S.L.T. 78, Outer House.

1515. Insurance Brokers Registration Council

INSURANCE BROKERS REGISTRATION COUNCIL (INDEMNITY INSURANCE AND GRANTS SCHEME) RULES APPROVAL ORDER 1979 (No. 408) [40p], made under the Insurance Brokers (Registration) Act 1977 (c. 46), ss. 27 (1), 28 (1); operative on July 1, 1979; require practising insurance brokers and enrolled bodies corporate to take out professional indemnity insurance and also to provide for the making of grants to persons who have suffered loss as a result of negligence, fraud or other dishonesty of insurance broking firms or their employees.

INSURANCE BROKERS REGISTRATION COUNCIL (ACCOUNTS AND BUSINESS REQUIREMENTS) RULES APPROVAL ORDER 1979 (No. 489) [50p], made under the Insurance Brokers (Registration) Act 1977, ss. 27 (1) and 28 (1); operative on July 1, 1979; approves rules made by the Council in exercise of their powers under s. 11 of the 1977 Act. These rules lay down requirements for the carrying on of business by practising insurance brokers and enrolled bodies corporate.

INSURANCE BROKERS REGISTRATION COUNCIL (REGISTRATION AND ENROLMENT) (AMENDMENT) RULES APPROVAL ORDER 1979 (No. 490) [10p], made under the Insurance Brokers (Registration) Act 1977, ss. 27 (1), 28 (1); operative on July 1, 1979; amends S.I. 1978 No. 1395 by revoking r. 3.

1516. Lloyd's underwriters

LLOYD'S (GENERAL BUSINESS) REGULATIONS 1979 (No. 956) [20p], made under the European Communities Act 1972 (c. 68), s. 2 (2); operative on August 1, 1979; implement provisions relating to Lloyd's that are contained in EEC Council Directive No. 73/239/EEC on the taking up and pursuit of the business of direct insurance other than life insurance.

1517. National insurance. See NATIONAL INSURANCE; SOCIAL SECURITY.

1518. Non-disclosure—previous conviction—duty of brokers

In April 1974, T, brokers, insured P's home with D, insurers. In August 1974, the house was destroyed by fire. D denied liability because of P's non-disclosure of his criminal record, which P admitted but claimed that T knew about. *Held,* on T's appeal, that (1) the factors which influenced the trial judge in assessing the credibility of two witnesses and deciding that T knew of P's criminal record were misconceived; there was a real risk that he might be wrong and that substantial injustice might have been done, and it was unsafe to maintain his conclusion on this issue of fact; (2) if T did know about P's criminal record, D were to be deemed to have had that knowledge and could not rely upon P's non-disclosure even if P did not know that D or T had that knowledge; (3) T were not entitled to judgment in their favour, but to allow the decision against them to stand would be a departure from the court's duty on a rehearing, and T were entitled to an order for a new trial: WOOLCOTT *v.* EXCESS INSURANCE CO. AND MILES, SMITH, ANDERSON AND GAME [1979] 1 Lloyd's Rep. 231, C.A.

1519. In April 1974 T, brokers, insured P's house with D, insurers. In August 1974 the house was destroyed by fire. D denied liability because of P's non-disclosure of his criminal record, which P admitted but claimed that T knew about. On a retrial of the issue whether T had such knowledge, *held,* that on review of the evidence T knew that P had a serious criminal record, but had failed to pass this information on to D. Judgment for P against D, and for D against T on their claim for an indemnity: WOOLCOTT *v.* EXCESS INSURANCE CO. AND MILES, SMITH, ANDERSON AND GAME (No. 2) [1979] 2 Lloyd's Rep. 210, Cantley J.

1520. Non-life insurance services

The Law Commission and the Scottish Law Commission have published a private international law report prepared by a Joint Working Group on the choice of law rules in the Draft Non-Life Insurance Services Directive. The Report is available from HMSO [£2·50].

1521. Overlapping policies—whether liability attaching to insured as " owner " or " occupier "

The defendant company insured the plaintiff house-owner against "liability at law attaching solely as owner, not occupier, of the house." He was also covered on a secondary policy for all third party claims by another company, NIG. The plaintiff was sued in nuisance by a neighbour for damages caused by tree roots on the plaintiff's premises. The issue was between the defendant and NIG (who indemnified the plaintiff as to the costs) as to liability. *Held,* liability for " passive " nuisance where ownership and occupation were undivided could not be said to attach only to the owner *qua* owner rather than, in any degree, to the occupier. Accordingly the defendant was not liable for this damage (*Sturge* v. *Hackett* [1962] C.L.Y. 1575 considered): RIGBY *v.* SUN ALLIANCE AND LONDON INSURANCE (1979) 252 E.G. 491, Mustill J.

1522. Road traffic. See ROAD TRAFFIC.

1523. Unemployment benefit. See SOCIAL SECURITY.

1524. Value added tax. See VALUE ADDED TAX.

BOOKS AND ARTICLES. See *post,* pp. [6], [24].

INTERNATIONAL LAW

1525. Aviation. See AVIATION.

1526. Common market. See EUROPEAN COMMUNITIES.

1527. Conflict of laws. See CONFLICT OF LAWS.

1528. Consuls

CONSULAR FEES REGULATIONS 1979 (No. 875) [20p], made under the Consular Fees and Salaries Act 1891 (c. 36), s. 2 (2) and the Fees (Increase) Act 1923 (c. 4), s. 8 (2); operative on August 6, 1979; replace S.I. 1978 No. 692 and prescribe the manner in which consular officers should carry out duties relating to the levying, accounting for and application of fees.

1529. Diplomatic privileges—immunity—divorce petition. See SHAW *v.* SHAW, § 785.

1530. Extradition. See EXTRADITION.

1531. Fisheries. See FISH AND FISHERIES.

1532. Foreign compensation

FOREIGN COMPENSATION (FINANCIAL PROVISIONS) ORDER 1979 (No. 109) [10p], made under the Foreign Compensation Act 1950 (c. 12), s. 7 (2) and the Foreign Compensation Act 1962 (c. 4), s. 3 (3); operative on March 20, 1979; directs the Foreign Compensation Commission to pay into the Exchequer, out of funds paid to the Commission for the purpose of being distributed under the Acts, amounts in respect of the Commission's expenses during the period October 1, 1977, to September 30, 1978, in relation to the distribution of those funds.

1533. Immunities and privileges

INTELSAT (IMMUNITIES AND PRIVILEGES) ORDER 1979 (No. 911) [30p], made under the International Organisations Act 1968 (c. 48), s. 10 (1); operative on a date to be published; confers privileges and immunities on the International Telecommunications Satellite Organisation "INTELSAT," on representatives of its members and of signatories of its Operating Agreement, on its officers and on certain persons participating in arbitration proceedings.

INTERNATIONAL OIL POLLUTION COMPENSATION FUND (IMMUNITIES AND PRIVILEGES) ORDER 1979 (No. 912) [30p], made under the International Organisations Act 1968, s. 10 (1); operative on a date to be published; confers privileges and immunities on the International Oil Pollution Compensation Fund, on representatives of its members and on its officers and experts.

OSLO AND PARIS COMMISSIONS (IMMUNITIES AND PRIVILEGES) ORDER 1979 (No. 914) [20p], made under the International Organisations Act 1968, s. 10 (1); operative on a date to be published; confers privileges and immunities upon the Oslo and Paris Commissions and their officers.

1534. International carriage of perishable foodstuffs

INTERNATIONAL CARRIAGE OF PERISHABLE FOODSTUFFS REGULATIONS 1979 (No. 415) [30p], made under the International Carriage of Perishable Foodstuffs Act 1976 (c. 58), ss. 1–3, 4 (6), 20; operative on October 1, 1979; provide for the specified types of food covered by the Act, temperatures, machinery and designation marks.

INTERNATIONAL CARRIAGE OF PERISHABLE FOODSTUFFS (FEES) REGULATIONS 1979 (No. 416) [20p], made under the International Carriage of Perishable Foodstuffs Act 1976, ss. 3 (1), 4 (2), 20; operative on October 1, 1979; for the purposes of the 1976 Act these Regulations prescribe fees in respect of tests, type approval examinations and certification of transport equipment used or intended to be used for the international carriage of perishable foodstuffs.

1535. International Carriage of Perishable Foodstuffs Act 1976—commencement

INTERNATIONAL CARRIAGE OF PERISHABLE FOODSTUFFS ACT 1976 (COMMENCEMENT) ORDER 1979 (No. 413 (C. 12)) [10p], made under the International Carriage of Perishable Foodstuffs Act 1976 (c. 58), s. 21 (2); brings the 1976 Act into force on October 1, 1979.

1536. International Maritime Satellite Organisation

INMARSAT (IMMUNITIES AND PRIVILEGES) ORDER 1979 (No. 454) [10p], made under the International Organisations Act 1968 (c .48), s. 10 (1); operative on a date to be notified; confers the legal capacities of a body corporate and certain fiscal privileges on the International Maritime Satellite Organisation (INMARSAT).

1537. Internationally Protected Persons Act 1978

INTERNATIONALLY PROTECTED PERSONS ACT 1978 (GUERNSEY) ORDER 1979 (No. 573) [10p], made under the Internationally Protected Persons Act 1978 (c. 17), s. 4 (2); operative on May 24, 1979; extends the 1978 Act to Guernsey.

INTERNATIONALLY PROTECTED PERSONS ACT 1978 (ISLE OF MAN) ORDER 1979 (No. 574) [20p], made under the Internationally Protected Persons Act 1978, s. 4 (2); operative on May 24, 1979; extends the 1978 Act to the Isle of Man.

INTERNATIONALLY PROTECTED PERSONS ACT 1978 (JERSEY) ORDER 1979 (No. 575) [10p], made under the Internationally Protected Persons Act 1978 s. 4 (2); operative on May 24, 1979; extends the 1978 Act to Jersey.

1538. —— commencement

INTERNATIONALLY PROTECTED PERSONS ACT 1978 (COMMENCEMENT) ORDER 1979 (No. 455 (C. 14)) [10p], made under the Internationally Protected Persons Act 1978 (c. 17), s. 5 (5); operative on May 24, 1979; brings into force the whole of the 1978 Act.

1539. Overseas aid

CARIBBEAN DEVELOPMENT BANK (FURTHER PAYMENTS) ORDER 1979 (No. 1160) [20p], made under the Overseas Aid Act 1968 (c. 57), s. 2 (1); operative on September 17, 1979; provides for the payment to the Caribbean Development Bank of a subscription to the increased authorised capital stock of the Bank, and for the payment of an additional contribution to the Special Development Fund of the Bank, in accordance with the arrangements made with the Bank in accordance with a Resolution adopted by the Board of Governors of the Bank in 1979, and two pledges given to the Bank in 1978 and 1979.

1540. Rhodesia. See BRITISH COMMONWEALTH.

1541. State immunity

STATE IMMUNITY (FEDERAL STATES) ORDER 1979 (No. 457) [10p], made under the State Immunity Act 1978 (c. 33), s. 14 (5); operative on May 2, 1979; applies the provisions of Pt. I of the 1978 Act to the constituent territories of the Republic of Austria.

STATE IMMUNITY (OVERSEAS TERRITORIES) ORDER 1979 (No. 458) [20p], made under the State Immunity Act 1978, s. 23 (7); operative on May 2, 1979; extends to the specified dependent territories the provisions of the 1978 Act.

BOOKS AND ARTICLES. See *post,* pp. [6], [24].

INTOXICATING LIQUORS

1542. Licensing

LICENSING (REPEAL OF STATE MANAGEMENT PROVISIONS) ORDER 1979 (No. 977) [10p], made under the Licensing (Abolition of State Management) Act 1971 (c. 65), s. 5 (1) (2); operative on September 1, 1979; repeals provisions of the Licensing Act 1964 following disposal of property in the Carlisle State Management District under the 1971 Act.

LICENSING ACT 1964 (AMENDMENT) REGULATIONS 1979 (No. 1476) [10p], made under the European Communities Act 1972 (c. 68), s. 2 (2); operative on January 1, 1980; amend s. 167 (1) of the Licensing Act 1964, which excludes liqueur chocolates from the Act, provided that the proportion of intoxicating liquor in the confectionery does not exceed the amount specified in the section. The Regulations replace the reference to proof spirit with a reference to the quantity of alcohol contained in the liquor expressed as a percentage of the volume of the liquor, so as to conform with Council Directive 76/766.

1543. —— occasional licence—selling outside permitted hours

[Licensing Act 1964 (c. 26), s. 160 (1) (a), as amended by Finance Act 1967 (c. 54), Sched. 16.] S had an occasional licence for certain premises. Sales of intoxicating liquor took place on the premises outside the hours specified in the licence. *Held,* allowing S's appeal against conviction of selling intoxicating liquor, he not then being the holder of a justices' licence authorising the sale, contrary to s. 160 of the 1964 Act, that s. 160 (1) (a) did not cover a sale of liquor outside hours when a licence which had been granted permitted sales: SOUTHALL v. HAIME [1979] Crim.L.R. 249, D.C.

1544. —— supply by persons not servants or agents of defendant licensee

[Licensing Act 1964 (c. 26), s. 59 (1) (*a*).] D held a justices' licence for the sale of intoxicating liquor. X Co. were using the premises as a restaurant but had not obtained authority to sell intoxicating liquors. The magistrate found that D was unconnected with X Co. and absent when the alleged offences of supplying intoxicating liquor outside the permitted hours were committed. *Held*, allowing D's appeal, that D could not be guilty in the absence of evidence that the drinks were supplied by his servants: TAYLOR *v.* SPEED [1979] Crim.L.R. 114, D.C.

1545. Licensing hours—permitted hours—" special occasion "—sporting club

[Licensing Act 1964 (c. 26), s. 74 (4).]

In relation to a special order of exemption under s. 74 (4) of the Licensing Act 1964, it is not essential that there is some event completely external to the applicant in order for there to be a special occasion.

A golf club, registered under the Licensing Act, applied to justices for special orders of exemption to extend drinking hours on certain annual sporting occasions organised by the club. The justices refused the application on the grounds that the occasions were not " special " within the meaning of s. 74 (4). On appeal by case stated, *held*, allowing the appeal, that it was not essential that there was some event completely external to the applicant in order for there to be a special occasion. (Dictum of Widgery J. in *Lemon* v. *Sargent* [1967] C.L.Y. 2167 applied.)

KNOLE PARK GOLF CLUB *v.* CHIEF SUPERINTENDENT, KENT COUNTY CONSTABULARY [1979] 3 All E.R. 829, D.C.

1546. —— special order of exemption—discretion of justices

[Licensing Act 1964 (c. 26), s. 74 (4).]

For an occasion to be " special," when justices are considering a special order of exemption, it must be special from a national or local point of view, and not too frequent. The justices must first decide whether the occasion is capable of being special, and then decide whether to grant the special order.

The secretary of a Victuallers' Association applied to the justices for special orders of exemption for December 22–26, and December 31, 1978, and January 1, 1979, which dates were to cover the Christmas and New Year festivities. The justices decided that December 22 and 23 were not special occasions and refused the special order. On appeal, *held*, dismissing the appeal, that the question whether an occasion is special is one of fact for the justices to decide, but it must be essentially special from a national or local point of view and not one which occurs too frequently. (*Devine* v. *Keeling* (1886) 50 J.P. 551 applied.)

MARTIN *v.* SPALDING [1979] 2 All E.R. 1193, D.C.

BOOKS AND ARTICLES. See *post*, pp. [7], [24].

JURIES

1547. Challenge—defendant's right—jury empanelled to try whether accused mute of malice

[Juries Act 1974 (c. 23), s. 12.]

There is no right of challenge of juries empanelled to try whether an accused is mute of malice.

D was charged with various assaults. He refused to plead, and a jury was empanelled to try whether he was mute of malice. They held that he was, he was tried and convicted. When the jury that tried the preliminary matter was sworn, D was not offered the right of challenge. He appealed against conviction contending that he had had the right of challenge, and that therefore all subsequent proceedings were a nullity. *Held*, dismissing the appeal, that under s. 12 of the Juries Act 1974 that was no right of challenge until the trial had begun, *i.e.* the defendant had been arraigned and pleaded to the charge.

R. *v.* PALING (1978) 67 Cr.App.R. 299, C.A.

1548. Coroner—duty to summon jury—purpose of inquest. See R. v. H.M. CORONER AT HAMMERSMITH, *ex p.* PEACH, § 367.

1549. Discharge of juror—not in open court—whether effective
[Juries Act 1974 (c. 23), s. 16 (1).]
A trial judge is entitled, if he has good reason, to discharge a juror otherwise than in open court.
On the second day of a trial a juror notified the court that she was unable to attend as her husband had died. The judge discharged her but made no mention of the fact in open court or to counsel in chambers. R appealed against conviction on the grounds of material irregularity. *Held,* dismissing the appeal, that by s. 16 (1) of the 1974 Act the judge had power, if he had good reason, to discharge a juror otherwise than in open court.
R. v. RICHARDSON [1979] 3 All E.R. 247, C.A.

1550. Jurors—employer dismissing juror—contempt of court. See ROONEY v. SNARES-BROOK CROWN COURT, § 2119.

1551. Retirement—policy on overnight accommodation
Juries are spending too many nights in hotels while they devote prolonged consideration to their verdicts; apart from the cost to the public, it is to be remembered that the time needed to make a decision tends to expand with the time available for making it, and this puts a strain on defendants. Juries should, where appropriate, retire shortly after the court sits in the morning so as to obviate the need for overnight accommodation: R. v. WOODING, *The Times,* December 4, 1979, C.A.

1552. Trial—discharge of juror—whether necessary to re-swear entire jury. See R. v. PAYNE, § 600.

BOOKS AND ARTICLES. See *post,* pp. [7], [24].

JURISPRUDENCE

BOOKS AND ARTICLES. See *post,* pp. [7], [24].

LAND CHARGES

1553. Local land charges
LOCAL LAND CHARGES (AMENDMENT) RULES 1979 (No. 1404) [10p], made under the Local Land Charges Act 1975 (c. 76), s. 14; operative on December 3, 1979; increase the fees payable in connection with the registration of Local Land Charges.

1554. Registration—" pending land action "—existence of easement
[Land Charges Act 1972 (c. 61), s. 1 (1).]
An action in which an easement over land is directly in issue is a " pending land action " for the purposes of the Land Charges Act 1972.
The plaintiffs were owners of a number of houses adjoining the land which the defendants acquired for development. The plaintiffs sought damages and injunctions in respect of the defendant's working claiming easements of support and wrongful interference with their rights. The plaintiffs then registered a caution against the company's land, and the company moved for an order that the registration be vacated. *Held,* refusing the order, that an action in which an easement is directly in issue is a " pending land action," since it is a claim to a right over land which affects the title to that land and will operate as an incumbrance on the land.
ALLEN v. GREENHI BUILDERS [1978] 3 All E.R. 1163, Browne-Wilkinson J.

1555. Right of pre-emption—whether an interest in land
The grant of a right of pre-emption did not create an interest in land as it gave no present right to call for a conveyance of the land, the subject of the right, but merely a contractual right. A registered option to purchase, being an interest in land therefore took priority over the prior right of pre-emption. *Per* Templeman and Stephenson L.JJ.: the grant of a right of pre-emption could bind a grantor's successor in title: PRITCHARD v. BRIGGS (1979) 123 S.J. 705, C.A.

1556. Unregistered option—conveyance at undervalue to defeat option
[Land Charges Act 1925 (c. 22), s. 13 (2).]
The conveyance of land at a gross undervalue is not a purchase " for money or money's worth " within the meaning of s. 13 of the Land Charges Act 1925.
A father granted a 10-year option to his son to purchase the farm which the son farmed as tenant. The option was not registered and the father to defeat the option conveyed the farm some six years later to the mother for £500. The farm was worth £40,000. When the son discovered what had happened he sought to register the option and to give notice exercising it. In proceedings commenced after the mother's death against, *inter alia,* her estate and carried on after the son's death by his executors, a declaration was sought that the option was binding on the mother's estate. Oliver J. held that the mother was a purchaser of a legal estate for money or money's worth against whom the unregistered option was void. On appeal, *held,* allowing the appeal (Sir Stanley Rees dissenting), that the court could inquire into the adequacy of the consideration and the genuineness of the transaction and that a conveyance at a gross undervalue was not a purchase for money or money's worth. *Per* Lord Denning M.R.: Fraud in this context covers any dishonest dealing done so as to deprive unwary innocents of their rightful dues. *Per* Sir Stanley Rees: Unless fraud is proved or the conveyance is a sham or the consideration nominal or illusory then an unregistered estate contract is void against the purchasers. (Decision of Oliver J. [1978] C.L.Y. 1415 reversed.)
MIDLAND BANK TRUST CO. *v.* GREEN [1979] 3 W.L.R. 167, C.A.

LAND DRAINAGE

1557. Drainage authorities
ANGLIAN WATER AUTHORITY (VALUATION OF THE LONGSTANTON AND SWAVESEY AWARDS) ORDER 1978 (No. 1980) [20p], made under the Land Drainage Act 1976 (c. 70), ss. 25 (4) and 109 (6); operative on March 12, 1979; confirms a scheme for varying the land drainage provisions of the Awards so far as they relate to certain watercourses.
ANGLIAN WATER AUTHORITY (VARIATION OF THE GAMLINGAY AWARD) ORDER 1979 (No. 511) [20p], made under the Land Drainage Act 1976, s. 25 (1); operative on April 30, 1979; confirm a scheme for varying the land drainage provisions of the Award so far as they relate to a certain watercourse shown on a special map.
NORTH WEST WATER AUTHORITY (ABOLITION OF THE PILLING AND WINMARLEIGH DRAINAGE DISTRICT) ORDER 1979 (No. 579) [20p], made under the Land Drainage Act 1976, s. 11 (1); operative on May 21, 1979; confirms a scheme for the abolition of the Pilling and Winmarleigh Drainage District.
ANGLIAN WATER AUTHORITY (ABOLITION OF THE CLEY AND WIVETON AND THE SALTHOUSE AND KELLING INTERNAL DRAINAGE DISTRICTS) ORDER 1979 (No. 1243) [20p], made under the Land Drainage Act 1976, s. 11 (1); operative on September 26, 1979; transfers all the rights and property of the Drainage Boards for the said Districts to the Anglian Water Authority.

1558. Drainage order
Order made under the Land Drainage Act 1976 (c. 70), ss. 11 (4) and 109 (6): S.I. 1979 No. 266 (Elloughton and Welton Internal Drainage District) [20p].

1559. Flood barriers
BENFLEET CREEK (BARRIER) AND THE HADLEIGH RAY, EASTHAVEN, LEIGH AND VANGE CREEKS (TIDAL DEFENCES) (AMENDMENT) ORDER 1979 (No. 696) [80p], made under the Thames Barrier and Flood Prevention Act 1972 (c. xiv), ss. 56 and 59; operative on June 20, 1979; empowers the Anglian Water Authority to construct a flood barrier with movable gates across Benfleet Creek and to execute ancillary works.

1560. Lands tribunal decision
STRUTTS KINGSTON ESTATE SETTLEMENT TRUSTEES *v.* KINGSTON BROOK INTERNAL DRAINAGE BOARD (Ref./138/1977) (1979) 251 E.G. 577 (claim under s. 17 (5) of the Land Drainage Act 1976 for compensation for collapse of bridge over stream on the claimant trust's land in Nottinghamshire caused by

works of improvement to the stream carried out by the respondent board. *Held,* the collapse had been caused by the works and compensation would be awarded in the full rebuilding cost of the bridge at £18,090).

1561. Northern Ireland. See NORTHERN IRELAND.

1562. Sewerage. See PUBLIC HEALTH.

LAND REGISTRATION

1563. District registries

LAND REGISTRATION (DISTRICT REGISTRIES) ORDER 1979 (No. 1019) [30p], made under the Land Registration Act 1925 (c. 21), ss. 132, 133; operative on November 19, 1979; replaces S.I. 1978 No. 1162 and constitutes a new district land registry at Weymouth, which includes the counties of Hampshire and Isle of Wight.

1564. Land Registration (Scotland) Act 1979 (c. 33)

This Act provides a system of registration of interests in land in Scotland in place of the recording of deeds in the Register of Sasines; it also simplifies certain deeds relating to land, and enables tenants-at-will to acquire their landlords' interests.

Pt. I (ss. 1–11) relates to the registration of interests in land: s. 1 sets up the Land Register of Scotland; s. 2 lists the circumstances in which an unregistered interest in land shall be registered; s. 3 deals with the effect of registration; s. 4 relates to the acceptance of applications for registration; s. 5 deals with completion of registration; s. 6 provides for the title sheet to be made up and maintained; s. 7 provides for the ranking of titles; s. 8 relates to the continuing effectiveness of recording in the Register of Sasines; s. 9 deals with rectification of the register; s. 10 relates to positive prescription in respect of registered interests; s. 11 makes transitional provisions.

Pt. II (ss. 12–14) deals with indemnity: s. 12 provides for a person suffering loss to be indemnified by the keeper; s. 13 contains supplementary provisions; 14 relates to interests in land consisting wholly or partly of foreshore or a right in foreshores.

Pt. III (ss. 15–19) relates to the simplification and effect of deeds: s. 15 provides for deeds relating to registered interests to be in a simplified form; s. 16 states that certain clauses may be omitted from deeds; s. 17 relates to the registration of land obligations; s. 18 deals with variations and discharges of land obligations; s. 19 provides for agreements as to a common boundary to be recorded or registered.

Pt. IV (ss. 20–30) contains miscellaneous provisions: s. 20 gives a tenant-at-will the right to acquire his landlord's interest in that land; and sets out the basis on which compensation is calculated; s. 21 contains provisions supplementary to s. 20; s. 22 contains supplementary provisions regarding heritable creditors; s. 23 relates to fees for registration; s. 24 provides for expenses incurred by the keeper to be defrayed out of money provided by Parliament; s. 25 sets out the circumstances in which appeals may be made to the Lands Tribunal for Scotland; s. 26 extends the application of this Act to the Crown; s. 27 empowers the Secretary of State to make rules relating to the register; s. 28 contains definitions; s. 29 contains amendments and repeals; s. 30 gives the short title. The Act extends to Scotland only.

The Act received the Royal Assent on April 4, 1979, and ss. 1, 16–23 and 30 came into force on that date; the remaining provisions come into force on a day to be appointed.

1565. Overriding interest—matrimonial home—possession—whether wife in " actual occupation." See WILLIAMS & GLYN'S BANK *v.* BOLAND, § 1826.

1566. —— wife's equitable interest—whether " in actual occupation." See BIRD *v.* SYME THOMPSON, § 1426.

1567. Transfer of title—claim by third party—solicitor's undertaking on registration —Malaysia

A solicitor's undertaking may be enforced notwithstanding that the interests of persons not party to agreement pursuant to which it was given may be adversely affected.

Land which was contracted to be sold " free from all encumbrances " was at all material times the subject of a *lis pendens* entry on the register in respect of a claim for a half share therein. A solicitor received the purchase price from the purchaser and undertook to pay the same to the vendor upon registration of transfer of the land. The vendor procured such registration but the solicitor refused to pay the money. On the vendor's application to enforce the undertaking, the judge ordered that the money to be paid into court so as to safeguard the claimant's interest should he succeed in this claim for a half share. The Federal Court upheld the order but on the grounds that the solicitor should be protected against a later claim from the purchaser by reason of the land being encumbered. *Held*, allowing the vendor's appeal, that the interests of persons not party to the undertaking were irrelevant to the question of enforcement thereof.

DAMODARAN S/O RAMAN v. CHOE KUAN HIM [1979] 3 W.L.R. 383, P.C.

1568. Water. See WATER AND WATERWORKS.

BOOKS AND ARTICLES. See *post*, pp. [7], [25].

LANDLORD AND TENANT

1569. Agreement for lease—specific performance—draft lease annexed to agreement
The grant of a right of way for any particular purpose does not place the grantor under any obligation to make it suitable for use, nor is there any warranty that the property is physically fit for the purpose the grant is made.

L agreed in writing to grant a lease of land to T for 21 years. T was going to build a factory. By cl. 5 T was entitled to determine the agreement if planning approval was refused within 12 months from March 25, 1974. By the draft lease attached to the agreement L granted T a right of way along the road or similar rights over a reasonable alternative roadway. Planning permission was applied for on February 12, 1975, and refused on April 10. Meanwhile, L had had difficulties with the planning authority who had served enforcement notices requiring the removal of both the original roadway and the alternative roadway. However, L appealed successfully against the latter notice. L had, however, asked T not to execute the lease because of those difficulties. Then L obtained an order for specific performance against T who claimed that he was entitled to a suitable roadway. On appeal by T, *held,* the grant of a right of way for any particular purpose did not place the grantor under any obligation to make it suitable for use, there was no warranty that the property was physically fit for the purpose the grant was made, and there was nothing to show any contract, warranty or condition that the right would fit the needs of T. (*Hill* v. *Harris* [1965] C.L.Y. 2197 applied.)

STOKES v. MIXCONCRETE (HOLDINGS) (1978) 38 P. & C.R. 488, C.A.

1570. Agricultural holdings. See AGRICULTURE.

1571. Assignment—conditional assent—revocation on subsequent discovery of material facts
M held a baker's shop on a seven-year lease from F. A clause in the lease prohibited assignment without F's consent. M sought F's leave to assign to H, and on March 29, 1977, F gave his consent, conditional upon M's paying one-third of the cost of replacing a blind in the shop, £100 for repairs to the forecourt, and arrears of rent. This money was all paid by May 23, 1977. On May 24, 1977, F's solicitors wrote to M enclosing a newspaper cutting relating to 39 offences committed by H against the Food Hygiene Regulations 1970, for which he had been fined a total of £1,560. The offences all related to a baker's shop, and M had had no knowledge of them until he received F's letter. F withdrew his consent to the assignment. M sought a declaration that he was entitled to assign. *Held*, granting the declaration, a tenant seeking a licence to assign could not have done more than M had done. Full references had been given, and it was up to F to take them up or make further inquiries of M. M was quite without fault, and had incurred expense

as the result of F's consent; though that consent was given in ignorance of a material fact, F could not withdraw it: MITTEN v. FAGG (1978) 247 E.G. 901, Goulding J.

1572. —— consent of landlord—whether refusal reasonable—landlord's objection to user

The tenant wanted to assign his lease to a large firm of bookmakers, and the landlord refused leave to assign, having moral objections to gambling. The tenant contended that as the proposed assignee's trade was a lawful one, and as there was no possible objection to the assignee on any other ground, the landlord's refusal was unreasonable, being based on mere caprice. *Held*, the landlord was not being unreasonable. There were many activities now lawful which were unlawful a short while ago—prostitution, abortion, and bookmaking were examples—and although the law might have changed, there was no reason for a person's own morality to do so. It could not possibly be held that an objection to gambling was an unreasonable attitude: RODNEY v. AUSTER-FIELD, June 6, 1979; Judge Perks; Croydon County Ct.

1573. —— National Conditions of Sale—purchaser unable to gain landlord's assent

[National Conditions of Sale (18th ed.), Condition 10 (5).] S contracted to sell leasehold property to B for £8,000. A deposit of £850 was paid. The National Conditions of Sale were expressly incorporated into the contract. Condition 10 made the sale conditional on the reversioner's licence being obtained. The purchaser had a duty to supply all information demanded, and the vendor had a duty to obtain the reversioner's licence. The reversioner refused assent until further references were received. B had provided impeccable character references, and was unable to provide more. S sued B for breach of contract for sale, and B counterclaimed for the return of the £850 deposit. On appeal, *held,* the vendor had a positive duty to get the reversioner's assent, subject to the purchaser's supplying all information reasonably demanded of him to satisfy the reversioner. There was no implied or express absolute duty on the purchaser to provide whatever the vendor or reversioner might reasonably require. Condition 10 (5) was not a covenant; it was a condition affecting the vendor's covenant. The purchasers had done all that was required of them, and the contract would be avoided, because the sale was subject to the reversioner's license being obtained. It had not been, and could not be, obtained. B was therefore entitled to a return of the deposit. Alternatively, S was in default, albeit innocently, and was unable to perform his part of the contract, and the court would exercise its discretion under s. 49 (2) of the Law of Property Act 1925, and order a return of the deposit. (*Elfer* v. *Beynton-Lewis* [1972] C.L.Y. 1960 distinguished): SHIRES v. BROCK (1977) 247 E.G. 127, C.A.

1574. —— surrender-back proviso—whether valid or contrary to statute

[Landlord and Tenant Act 1927 (c. 36), s. 19 (1).]

S. 19 (1) of the Landlord and Tenant Act 1927 does not seek to limit the freedom of contract of the parties to agree to a lease which forbids altogether assignments by a tenant, and consequently a covenant which forbids assignment unless a condition precedent is fulfilled (surrender of the lease) is perfectly valid.

The first defendants, a company, were tenants of a flat under a six-year lease. The second defendant was a director of the company occupying the flat as sub-tenant or licensee. The lease contained a " no assignment without consent " covenant with a proviso that if the tenant wanted to assign the whole of the flat he should first offer to surrender his lease. The defendant company was wound up and the landlords claimed forfeiture of the lease. The tenants applied for relief and for a declaration that by virtue of s. 19 (1) of the 1927 Act the proviso was void. The master refused relief and the declaration. On appeal, *held*, dismissing the appeal, that there was no reason for invalidating a covenant which effectively prohibited assignment unless a condition precedent was fulfilled. The proviso was valid. (*Adler* v. *Upper Grosvenor Street Investment* [1957] C.L.Y. 1913 applied; *Creer* v. *P. & O. Lines of Australia* (1971) 45 A.L.J.R. 697 adopted.)

BOCARDO S.A. v. S. & M. HOTELS [1979] 3 All E.R. 737, C.A.

1575. —— without consent—no restriction on assignment in terms

Whilst a landlord is required to express any restriction on alienation in clear terms, covenants not to assign, underlet or part with possession are not mutually exclusive and breach of one can constitute a breach of another.

W, assigned his tenancy to M, without obtaining the consent of his landlord. The tenancy agreement provided that W was "not to underlet or part with possession of the premises without the landlord's previous consent in writing which [shall] not be unreasonably withheld." M decided he did not wish to accept the assignment and sought repayment of the amount he had paid W. The question whether W had been free to assign without the landlord's consent was tried as a preliminary issue. *Held*, the landlord must express any restriction on alienation in clear terms but covenants not to assign, underlet or part with possession were not mutually exclusive and breach of one could constitute breach of another. Since the assignment necessarily involved a parting of possession it followed that W had been in breach.

MARKS *v.* WARREN [1979] 1 All E.R. 29, Browne-Wilkinson J.

1576. Business tenancies—application for new tenancy—break clause—rebuilding— considerations

L owned a row of 12 shops, of one of which T was the tenant. T applied for a new tenancy. L asked that it be for 14 years subject to the right of the landlord for the time being to determine at any time on two years' notice if he wished to rebuild or reconstruct the premises. Seven of the 11 other shops had similar clauses in their leases. L would probably not be able to redevelop, but wished to be free to sell to a prospective developer. The county court judge refused to include such a clause in the lease, saying that the terms of the new lease must depend on its facts, and he found that the premises were not yet ripe for development. He granted a seven-year lease with no break clause. L appealed. *Held*, allowing the appeal, the judge had failed to consider the following: (1) there could be no certainty regarding the future. Market conditions could change dramatically, and it was impossible to say what might be a profitable investment in five years' time; (2) the 1954 Act was not intended to give tenants security of tenure at the expense of preventing redevelopment; (3) L would only be able to use the break clause if he were actually going to redevelop, and T would still be protected if L's notice were not bona fide. Moreover, T would be entitled to the compensation provided in the Act. L would suffer greater hardship if the break clause were not granted, and accordingly the appeal would be allowed (*Reohorn* v. *Barry Corporation* [1956] C.L.Y. 4852 applied): ADAMS *v.* GREEN (1978) 247 E.G. 49, C.A.

1577. —— —— evidence

T was the tenant of No. 7, The Arcade; he failed to agree with L, his landlord, about the rent for the property under a new lease. The county court judge heard evidence on T's behalf from the tenants of Nos. 6 and 9, The Arcade, who said that The Arcade was a bad trading area, that their rent was too high at £2,500 per annum each, and that a fair rent would be £1,800–£2,000. T's surveyor also gave evidence, mostly based on hearsay (although this was not apparent at the time) of comparables. The judge, relying heavily on the evidence of the neighbours, and of the surveyor, concluded that a proper rent was £2,000. L appealed. *Held*, ordering a new trial, the evidence given by the neighbours was only relevant to show that the trading position of the shops was less advantageous than might otherwise have been expected, and the judge had been wrong to rely on their evidence for any other purpose. Their Lordships would probably not have granted a new trial on the hearsay point alone, because it had not been taken in the county court below, and it was not clear what the effect of its having been taken would have been: ROGERS *v.* ROSEDIMOND INVESTMENTS (BLAKES MARKET) (1978) 247 E.G. 467, C.A.

1578. —— —— interim rent—date from which payable

[Landlord and Tenant Act 1954 (c. 56), s. 24A, as amended by the Law of Property Act 1969 (c. 59), s. 3.]

On the granting of an interim rent in proceedings for a new tenancy under the Landlord and Tenant Act 1954, the interim rent is payable from the date of the summons for the determination of the interim rent under s. 24A.

A lease of business premises was determinable at six months' notice. L, the landlords, gave notice under s. 25 of the Landlord and Tenant Act 1954 to determine the tenancy on November 14, 1975. T Co. issued a counter notice and an originating summons for an order for a new tenancy. Negotiations followed. On June 20, 1977, L issued a summons under s. 24A for the determination of an interim rent. Ultimately the tenancy came to an end on May 3, 1978. The interim rent was payable until May 3 but L contended that it was payable from November 14, 1975, the date of the s. 25 notice; T Co. contended that it was payable from June 20, 1977, the date of the summons under s. 24A. *Held*, the interim rent became payable on the date of the s. 24A summons. (*Stream Properties* v. *Davis* [1972] C.L.Y. 1962 applied; dictum of Lord Denning M.R. in *Secretary of State for Social Services* v. *Rossetti Lodge Investment Co.* [1975] C.L.Y. 1851 considered.)

VICTOR BLAKE (MENSWEAR) v. WESTMINSTER CITY COUNCIL (1979) 38 P. & C.R. 448, Deputy Judge Michael Wheeler, Q.C.

1579. —— —— structural repairs necessary—whether need for legal possession
[Landlord and Tenant Act 1954 (c. 56) (as amended by Law of Property Act 1969 (c. 59), s. 7 (1)), ss. 30 (1) (f), 31A (1) (a).]

In having regard to the words "with the use of the holding" in s. 31A of the 1954 Act, the court has to look to the physical effects of the work and not the consequences from a business point of view.

T occupied business premises under a lease which allowed L to enter on to the premises to carry out structural repairs. T applied under s. 24 for a new lease and L opposed the grant on the ground, *inter alia,* that he intended to reconstruct the premises and could not reasonably do so without obtaining possession of them. T stated, pursuant to s. 31A, that she would give L access to carry out the work. At the trial it was found that T would have to be out of occupation for two to four months to allow the works to be done. The deputy judge found in favour of T on the basis that the interference with her business would not be substantial and that she would be able to carry on the business upon her return. On appeal, *held,* allowing the appeal, that for s. 31A to apply it had to be shown that L could carry out the work without interfering with T's use of the holding for the purpose of the business carried on by her, and not that the work could be done without interfering to a substantial extent with T's business or the goodwill of T's business. (*Heath* v. *Drown* [1972] C.L.Y. 1983 applied.)

REDFERN v. REEVES (1978) 37 P. & C.R. 364, C.A.

1580. —— —— withdrawal of application—effect on landlord's application under s. 24A
[Landlord and Tenant Act 1954 (c. 56), s. 24A; County Court Rules, Ord. 13, r. 1.] K had a tenancy of premises in Regent Street for seven years at £2,800 per annum rent. The lease expired on September 28, 1974. On March 29, 1974, A (the landlord) served notice under s. 25 to determine the tenancy from October 9. K served a counter-notice under s. 24. A applied for determination of an interim rent, under Ord. 13, r. 1, of the County Court Rules, on April 30. Six weeks later, K discontinued its application. The county court judge held that the s. 24A application was distinct from the application for a new tenancy, and determined the interim rent at £9,000 per annum, to run from April 30. K appealed, saying that an application under Ord. 13, r. 1 must be discontinued if the original s. 24 application is discontinued. *Held*, dismissing the appeal, that the s. 24A application was not " parasitic," but was in the nature of a counterclaim, and did not die when K's application was withdrawn (*McGowan* v. *Middleton* (1883) 11 Q.B.D. 464 applied): MICHAEL KRAMER & CO. v. AIRWAYS PENSION FUND TRUSTEES (1976) 246 E.G. 911, C.A.

1581. —— contracting out—penalty for applying for new tenancy
[Landlord and Tenant Act 1954 (c. 56), s. 38 (1).]

A covenant in a business tenancy for the tenant to pay the landlord's expenses on an application by the tenant for a new tenancy is void as being the imposition of a penalty under s. 38 (1) of the Landlord and Tenant Act 1954.

By a lease of business premises T, the tenant, covenanted to " pay to the landlord, all costs, charges and expenses, including legal costs and charges payable to a surveyor which may be incurred by the landlord, of any incidental to the preparation and service of any notice by either party on the other under Part II of the Landlord and Tenant Act 1954 and all negotiations subsequent thereto and of all proceedings thereunder and to keep the landlord fully and effectually indemnified against all costs, proceedings, expenses, claims and demands whatsoever in respect of the said applications, notices, negotiations and proceedings." T made such an application. Proceedings took place and were concluded by a consent order. L Co. sought their costs of £1,072. The judge found for L Co. On appeal by T, *held*, allowing the appeal, that the provision was a threat of a financial sanction unrelated in its imposition to any question of the merits of its imposition; it therefore amounted to " the imposition of a penalty " in the event of an application for a new lease under s. 38 (1) of the Landlord and Tenant Act 1954, and was void.

STEVENSON & RUSH (HOLDINGS) *v.* LANGDON (1979) 38 P. & C.R. 208, C.A.

1582. —— holding over paying rent—whether new periodic tenancy to be inferred
The respondent tenant held a lease of business premises with a flat above. He ceased business use shortly before expiry of the term and claimed to hold over as a Rent Act protected tenant. Rent was paid and accepted for three years after expiry of the term. The appellant landlords asked for possession consistently from signing until proceedings were issued. The county court judge found a new periodic tenancy by payment and acceptance of rent and refused to order possession. *Held*, allowing the appeal, the old common law presumption of a tenancy from payment and acceptance of rent " no longer holds." In the circumstances the respondent remained in occupation merely because he declined to go and could not be removed except by proceedings. The respondent had been in occupation for " very many years " and one of the appellants' witnesses had indicated that the money had been accepted as mesne profits. No new tenancy was to be inferred as having been in the minds of the parties: possession ordered (*Lewis* v. *M.T.C.* (*Cars*) [1975] C.L.Y. 1880, *Marcroft Wagons* v. *Smith* (1951) C.L.C. 8831 considered): LONGRIGG, BURROUGH AND TROUNSON *v.* SMITH (1979) 251 E.G. 847, C.A.

1583. —— interim rent—whether disrepair to be considered
[Landlord and Tenant Act 1954 (c. 56), ss. 24A, 34.]
Assessment of an interim rent for business premises should take account of actual condition of the premises on the date for commencement of such rent.
From 1970 onwards the tenant carried on his business in premises at an annual rent of £2.750: after 1975 the tenancy subsisted by virtue of s. 24 of the Act. In 1975 the premises were twice flooded due to a blocked drainpipe. In 1976 the landlord determined the tenancy but the tenant made application for a new tenancy for a term of 14 years from June 1976 at an annual rental of £3,600. In 1977 it became clear that major repairs were required to both the interior and exterior of the premises due to dry rot caused by neglect of the exterior. The landlord did not object to a new tenancy but opposed the proposed terms and sought an interim rent. At the hearing in 1978 the tenant proposed an interim rent of £1,000 on the basis that the premises were not of use, save for storage, until the repairs were completed. The judge ruled that, although the landlord was liable to repair the exterior, the lack of repair was not relevant to the assessment of an interim rent, which he fixed at £3,450. For the new tenancy the rent was fixed at £3,950 with no reduction, temporary or otherwise, to allow for completion of repairs. *Held*, allowing the tenant's appeal, that (1) the present state of repair to the premises was relevant to the assessment of an interim rent; (2) the court has power, albeit one rarely to be exercised, to fix a differential rent pending completion of necessary repairs, such power extending to the fixing of an interim rent. (*English Exporters (London)* v. *Eldonwall* [1973] C.L.Y. 1902 and *Regis Property Co.* v. *Lewis and Peat* [1970] C.L.Y. 1530 considered.)

FAWKE *v.* VISCOUNT CHELSEA [1979] 3 W.L.R. 508, C.A.

1584. —— landlord's interest partly beneficial—intention to occupy for his business
[Landlord and Tenant Act 1954 (c. 56), s. 41 (2).] Upon the tenant

company applying for a new lease of its premises, the landlord opposed on
the ground of intention to occupy for its own business (s. 30 (1) (*g*)). The
landlord's interest was vested in the respondents C and H in equal shares. H
claimed to be entitled to occupy as beneficiary by s. 41 (2) of the Act. C's
interest was to be conveyed to him for consideration. The county court
judge allowed the application for a new tenancy. *Held*, dismissing the appeal,
the landlord could occupy only *qua* beneficiary to satisfy s. 41 (2). Half his
interest was here by purchase contrary to s. 30 (2) and the trust would fail
upon conveyance. (*Frish* v. *Barclays Bank* [1955] C.L.Y. 1520 applied):
CARSHALTON BEECHES BOWLING CLUB v. CAMERON (1979) 249 E.G. 1279, C.A.

**1585. —— licensed premises—whether substantial proportion of business other than
alcoholic**
[Landlord and Tenant Act 1954 (c. 56), s. 43 (1) (*d*) (i).] The appellant tenant
held a public-house upon a lease which she claimed to be able to renew under
the statute on the basis that the business involved the provision of overnight
accommodation and meals to a " substantial " extent other than the sale of
alcohol. This would have brought the tenancy within the protection of the Act
by s. 43 (1) (*d*) (i) despite the general exception of licensed premises. At its
highest her non-alcoholic proportion of sales was only 16–18 per cent. of the
total takings. *Held*, dismissing her appeal, the proportion of non-alcoholic
transactions was not substantial and the appellant was unprotected. (*Re Net
Book Agreement 1957* [1962] C.L.Y. 3017 approved; *J. G. Swales & Co.* v.
H. S. Mosley [1968] C.L.Y. 2187 doubted): GRANT v. GRESHAM (1979) 252
E.G. 55, C.A.

1586. —— notice to quit—validity—wrong date
A notice to quit will be valid despite a wrong date if no reasonable tenant
would in the circumstances have been misled.
P granted a seven-year lease of business premises to D. P wished to bring
the tenancy to an end at the expiry of the term and served a s. 25 notice.
This first notice was wrongly dated, and a second s. 25 notice was sent. This
second notice, although in other respects correct, gave the year of termination
as 1976 instead of 1977, but the covering letter that accompanied gave the
correct date. No counter-notice was received and P sought a declaration that
the notice was good and effective. The county court judge so held and D
appealed. *Held*, dismissing the appeal, that the test was whether a reasonable
tenant would have been misled reading the notice. In the instant case no
reasonable tenant could have been misled by reading the notice and covering
letter. (*Carradine Properties* v. *Aslam* [1976] C.L.Y. 1551 applied; *Hankey*
v. *Clavering* [1942] 2 K.B. 326 distinguished.)
GERMAX SECURITIES v. SPIEGAL (1979) 37 P. & C.R. 204, C.A.

1587. —— obligations under lease—date arising
Although a term of years under a lease can only run from the date of
execution of the lease, obligations under the lease may be made to run from a
date prior to its execution.
L let business premises to T on a lease of 21 years less a day, expiring on
March 24, 1974, at a rent of £312 per annum. Between that date and January
11, 1977, T was seeking a new tenancy under Pt. II of the Landlord and
Tenant Act 1954. Finally a consent order was made creating a new term of
10 years from March 25, 1974, at a rent of £1,750 per annum. T had continued
to pay rent at the old figure of £312 per annum. T concluded that the rent
remained payable at that rate, since his obligation to pay rent did not arise
until the new lease was executed. *Held*, although the term of years could not
run from a date earlier than the execution of the lease, its obligations could.
Accordingly, rent was payable from March 25 at the new rate of £1,750 per
annum.
BRADSHAW v. PAWLEY [1979] 3 All E.R. 273, Megarry V.-C.

1588. —— " occupied for the purpose of business "—premises used for dumping waste
[Landlord and Tenant Act 1954 (c. 56), s. 23.] Tenants of shop premises
used by them for dumping waste material taken from two nearby shops which
were being altered. At the end of the contractual term, *held*, that the premises
were not occupied for the purpose of a business carried on by the tenants

within s. 23 of the Landlord and Tenant Act 1954 and, accordingly, the Act did not apply to them: HILLIL PROPERTY & INVESTMENT CO. *v.* NARAINE PHARMACY (1979) 123 S.J. 437, C.A.

1589. —— —— tenant and associated company
[Landlord and Tenant Act 1954 (c. 56), s. 23 (1).]
Upon the plaintiff tenant's application for a new tenancy of a shopping precinct the landlord contended that the business was carried on by D, an associated company of the tenant's. The tenant claimed that D merely managed the premises while the tenant retained possession and control thereof and carried on the business of granting licences to stall-holders and providing a variety of services to them. *Held,* the tenant did occupy the premises for the purposes of a business carried on by it within the meaning of the section and was entitled to a new tenancy: ROSS AUTO WASH *v.* HERBERT (1979) 250 E.G. 971, Fox J.

1590. —— possession—landlord requiring premises for his company
[Landlord and Tenant Act 1954 (c. 56), s. 30 (1) (*g*), (3).] The plaintiff HT Ltd. was served with a notice to terminate its business tenancy under s. 25 by the defendant landlord specifying ground (*g*) of s. 30 (1), in that he intended to occupy the premises for the purposes of a business carried on by him. In fact the business was to be that of a company in which he had a controlling interest. On trial of a preliminary issue as to the validity of the notice, *held,* the notice was valid. Had ground (*g*) been cited *simpliciter* the notice would have been good—see s. 30 (3). There was no hardship on the plaintiff and s. 30 (3) covered the point: HARVEY TEXTILES *v.* HILLEL (1979) 249 E.G. 1063, Whitford J.

1591. —— rent review clause—counternotice—what constitutes counternotice
L granted T a 14-year business lease of premises, at £1,500 per annum with a rent review clause in the seventh year. The provisions for reviewing the rent were subject to a clause saying that time was to be of the essence. An open market rental was to be determined either (1) by L's specifying in a recorded delivery letter sent six clear months before the review date; or (2) by agreement between the parties within three months thereafter; or (3) at election of L, made by a counternotice in writing served within three months thereafter, by an independent surveyor appointed jointly by L and T. A formal notice was served within time on March 20, 1978, telling T that the new rent was to be £5,250 per annum. This was acknowledged by T on March 31, 1978, which said "we would hardly need to add that we do not accept your revised figure." There was no further communication until July 24, 1978. The question arose of whether the words quoted formed a counternotice, duly served. *Held,* they did not. It was a pure question of construction whether or not the words told L that T wanted the market rental value to be determined by an independent surveyor. The words were no more than a refusal of L's proposal, leaving T with a number of options; they did not commit T to any of the three means of determining the market rental, and accordingly the rent should stand at £5,250 per annum: BELLINGER *v.* SOUTH LONDON STATIONERS (1979) 252 E.G. 699, Goulding J.

1592. —— request for new tenancy—second request made after expiry of time for application
[Landlord and Tenant Act 1954 (c. 56), s. 29 (3).] On August 11, 1978, the appellant business tenant served a request under s. 26 of the Act for a new tenancy to commence on July 16, 1979. The respondent landlord served a counternotice within two months but no application was made to the court for a new tenancy within four months as prescribed by s. 29 (3). On January 12, 1979, the tenant purported to serve a second request for a new tenancy on July 16, 1979, the same date as in the first request. The landlord argued that the tenancy determined according to the first request, that the second request was of no effect and accordingly that the tenant had lost its rights under the Act. The county court judge upheld the landlord. *Held,* dismissing the tenant's appeal, the failure to apply to the court under the first request under s. 29 (3) initiated the second request. (*Stile Hall Properties* v. *Gooch* [1968] C.L.Y. 2189 followed): POLYVIOU *v.* SEELEY (1979) 252 E.G. 375, C.A.

1593. —— **right of way—whether use amounted to occupation in course of business**
[Landlord and Tenant Act 1954 (c. 56), s. 23 (1).]
A so-called " lease " conferring a right of way over land is not a business tenancy within the terms of the Landlord and Tenant Act 1954.
The plaintiff land-owners were granted a " lease " by the defendant council granting them for a term of years the right of way over a roadway which formed the sole means of access to their business premises. Prior to expiry of the term the plaintiffs applied for a new tenancy under the 1954 Act. On a preliminary issue Brightman J. held that the right of way was not capable of occupation within the meaning of s. 23 (1) of the Act. *Held*, dismissing the plaintiffs' appeal, that the Act was not applicable to such a right of way. (Decision of Brightman J. [1958] C.L.Y. 1174 affirmed; *Whitley* v. *Stumbles* [1930] A.C. 544 considered.)
LAND RECLAMATION CO. *v.* BASILDON DISTRICT COUNCIL [1979] 1 W.L.R. 767, C.A.

1594. —— **s. 26 request defective—whether landlord waived defect**
[Landlord and Tenant Act 1954 (c. 56), s. 26 (2).]
A tenant's failure to comply with the provisions of s. 26 (2) of the Landlord and Tenant Act 1954 is capable of being waived by the landlord's subsequent conduct.
T Co. gave L Co. a notice requesting a new tenancy under the Landlord and Tenant Act 1954. The notice was dated February 4 and requested a tenancy commencing on February 16. By s. 26 (2) of the Act the date should have been at least six months ahead and not earlier than the date when the tenancy should have come to an end. The correct date would have been October 31. Neither L Co. nor T Co. noticed the mistake, and L Co. indicated that they would not oppose the new tenancy and they gave no notice under s. 26 (6). L Co. applied to the court for an interim rent. They then sold the reversion to P Co. who at first continued the negotiations for an interim rent, but later asserted that the tenants' request was bad, and served notice purporting to terminate the tenancy. They then applied for T Co.'s application for a new tenancy to be struck out on the ground of the defective request. The county court judge held that the landlords had waived the defect and that T Co. were entitled to a new tenancy. On appeal by P Co., *held*, dismissing the appeal, that in any event, the landlords having led the tenants to expect that the application would not be opposed, P Co. were estopped from denying the validity of T Co.'s request; alternatively, P Co.'s application for an interim rent amounted to a waiver of any defect in the tenants' notice. (*Tennant* v. *London County Council* [1957] C.L.Y. 1961 and *Kammin's Ballrooms Co.* v. *Zenith Investments* (*Torquay*) [1970] C.L.Y. 1525 applied.)
BRISTOL CARS *v.* R.K.H. (HOTELS) (IN LIQUIDATION) (1979) 38 P. & C.R. 411, C.A.

1595. —— **terms of new tenancy—clear leases**
[Landlord and Tenant Act 1954 (c. 56), s. 35.] The plaintiffs, in applying for a new lease of office premises, contended for terms requiring the defendant landlord to repair and maintain the premises in return for a fixed rent, as under their current lease. The landlord required a lower rent plus variable service charges consisting of all its maintenance costs, the rent being clear profit. It was agreed that clear leases increased the tenanted freehold value of the premises. On application to the court to determine the terms of the new lease under s. 35, the plaintiffs argued that (1) the variation of maintenance costs should fairly be borne by the landlord; (2) clear leases allowed the landlord to effect surreptitious improvements; (3) the challenge and estimate provisions thereunder were unfair. *Held*, the terms were to be the landlords, being reasonably required. providing compensation to the tenants and not interfering with their security: O'MAY *v.* CITY OF LONDON REAL PROPERTY Co. (1979) 249 E.G. 1065, Goulding J.

1596. —— —— **whether option to purchase may be imposed on landlord**
[Landlord and Tenant Act 1954 (c. 56), ss. 32 (3), 35.]
Where on an application for a new tenancy under the Landlord and Tenant

Act 1954 the original lease contained an option to purchase the freehold which has expired, the court cannot enlarge the holding by creating a new option.

L granted T a lease of business premises for five years which contained an option to purchase the freehold by notice to be given not less than three months prior to the expiration of the term. T did not exercise the option, the option expired, and then L gave T notice under s. 25 of the Landlord and Tenant Act 1954 terminating the tenancy. T applied under s. 26 for a new tenancy. The deputy judge ordered the grant of a new lease containing an option to purchase in similar terms but at an increased price. On appeal by L, *held*, allowing the appeal, that the court could not, when ordering a new tenancy, create a new saleable asset for the tenant, nor enlarge the holding, nor confer rights on the tenant which he did not previously enjoy; the order of a fresh option created a new saleable asset, and enlarged the tenant's holding and should therefore be deleted from the order. (*G. Orlik (Meat Products)* v. *Hastings and Thanet Building Society* [1975] C.L.Y. 1870 and dictum of Denning L.J. in *Gold* v. *Brighton Corporation* [1956] C.L.Y. 4862 applied; *Re No.* 1, *Albermarle Street* [1959] C.L.Y. 1827 distinguished.)
KIRKWOOD v. JOHNSON (1979) 38 P. & C.R. 392, C.A.

1597. Covenant—breach of—permitting nuisance—persistent admirer of actress

The actress Sally Thomsett held a statutory tenancy of the appellant company. One of the terms thereof required her " not to do or permit to be done on the premises anything which may be or become a nuisance or annoyance or be injurious or detrimental to the reputation of the premises." An over-persistent admirer caused annoyance to adjoining occupiers by telephoning, ringing the entry phone and shouting. The respondent held rowdy parties. She gave interviews to newspapers which, said the appellant, " lowered the tone." The county court judge dismissed the appellant's possession action. *Held*, dismissing the appeal, the judge had applied the correct test and acted reasonably upon it. " Permit " means " to give leave for an act which without that leave could not be legally done, or to abstain from taking reasonable steps to prevent the act where it is within a man's power to prevent it." She had installed an Ansafone, disconnected the entry phone, called the police to eject partygoers and conducted interviews *off* the premises. Accordingly " valiant " and " courageous " counsel was without an argument (*Berton* v. *Alliance Economic Investment Co.* [1922] 1 K.B. 742 applied): COMMERCIAL GENERAL ADMINISTRATION v. THOMSETT (1979) 250 E.G. 547, C.A.

1598. —— oral assurance by landlord—collateral contract or promissory estoppel

A landlord's oral waiver of his strict rights under a lease is and remains enforceable.

L Co., landlords of a flat-roofed block of flats, granted 99-year leases of the flats and at the same time sought planning permission to build more flats on the existing roof. The leases contained a stipulation that the tenants would contribute to the maintenance of the roof. A tenants' association was formed whilst the flats were still on offer. The roof was in a state of disrepair and L Co. gave an oral assurance that they would carry out those repairs at their own cost, unless planning permission was granted. Some prospective lessees obtained the waiver in writing; other executed leases relying on the oral assurance. Planning permission was refused, and the work was done at a cost of £15,000. L Co. tried to recover contributions from the tenants, and in some cases from assignees. In an action in the county court against, *inter alia*, A, an original lessee who relied on the oral assurance, B, an assignee from an original lessee who was told of the assurance before the assignment, and C, an assignee from a first assignee who entered after the repairs and whose assignor knew of the assurance before the assignment, the judge held that in each case there was an estoppel against L Co. from claiming any contribution. On appeal by L Co., *held*, dismissing the appeals (*per* Roskill and Cumming-Bruce L.JJ.) (1) the oral assurances to original lessees created collateral contracts upon which the lessees could rely; and (2) although assignees could not rely on the collateral contracts, the assurances were a waiver of L Co.'s rights which survived the assignments, so that what was assigned was a lease free of the waived obligation (*per* Lord Denning M.R.) each defendant was entitled to rely on the doctrine of promissory estoppel, the benefits and burdens of which passed to assignors and assignees. (*Hughes* v. *Metropolitan Railway Co.* (1877) 2 App.Cas. 439 applied; *Central London Property Trust* v. *High Trees House* (1947) C.L.C. 5601 considered.)

BRIKOM INVESTMENTS *v.* CARR; SAME *v.* RODDY; SAME *v.* HICKEY [1979] 2 W.L.R. 737, C.A.

1599. —— to repair—inherent defect—changes in building practice since building erected—liability of tenant

It is a question of degree whether work done constitutes repair or the creation of a wholly different thing from that demised.

D was the tenant of a 16-storey block of maisonettes constructed of reinforced concrete and stone claddings but without expansion joints as was then the building practice. D covenanted with P " to repair " and to repay to P costs of executing works to remedy want of reparation. In 1973 the stone claddings became loose and because of the urgency of securing the stone claddings P did the work, reinstating the cladding and adding expansion joints which had been found to be necessary and was by then standard building practice. The cost of the repairs was £55,000 of which £5,000 was attributable to the cost of expansion joints. The cost of erecting the building in 1973 would have exceeded £3 million. P sought the whole cost of the repairs, D denied liability for the cost of the expansion joints. *Held*, D was liable for want of repair due to an inherent defect. It was a question of degree whether the work done constituted repair or the creation of a wholly different thing from that demised. The cost of inserting the joints was trivial compared to the value of the building. D was liable for the whole cost. (Dictum of Lord Esher M.R. in *Lister* v. *Lane and Nesham* [1893] 2 Q.B. 212, *Lurcott* v. *Wakeley and Wheeler* [1911–13] All E.R.Rep. 41, *Pembery* v. *Lamdin* [1940] 2 All E.R. 434, *Sotheby* v. *Grundy* (1947) C.L.C. 5413 and *Brew Brothers* v. *Snax (Ross)* [1969] C.L.Y. 2024 applied; *Collins* v. *Flynn* [1963] C.L.Y. 1958 doubted.)

RAVENSEFT PROPERTIES *v.* DAVSTONE (HOLDINGS) [1979] 1 All E.R. 929, Forbes J.

1600. Conveyancing. See REAL PROPERTY AND CONVEYANCING.

1601. Derogation from grant—right of way—obstruction by adjoining tenants of common landlord—whether landlord liable

The respondent tenants of an antique shop in London were granted a right of way over a private roadway occupied by their landlord behind the shop, together with the grant of sole use of a parking space. Other tenants of the same landlord obstructed the roadway so that both parking space and easement became unusable to the respondents. The county court judge held, following *Sedleigh-Denfield* v. *O'Callaghan* [1940] A.C. 880, that the landlord was liable for the acts of the other tenants and their licensees although it was not itself guilty of any culpable act. *Held*, dismissing the landlord's appeal, the landlord was continuing or adopting acts within the principles of the cited authority. There was a breach of the covenant for quiet enjoyment, derogation from grant and/or nuisance. Injunction and damages upheld: HILTON *v.* JAMES SMITH AND SONS (NORWOOD) (1979) 251 E.G. 1053, C.A.

1602. Distress

DISTRESS FOR RENT (AMENDMENT) RULES 1979 (No. 711) [20p], made under the Law of Distress Amendment Act 1888 (c. 21), s. 8; operative on July 16, 1979; amend the provisions of S.I. 1953 No. 1702 as to the requirement of a security for a certificate to act as a bailiff, and prescribes revised fees, charges, and expenses recoverable in respect of the levying of distress for rent under those Rules.

1603. Forfeiture of lease—relief—sub-tenant—unfurnished prohibited, furnished permitted

[Law of Property Act 1925 (c. 20), s. 146 (4).] A lease granted in 1959 of a shop with a flat above prohibited sub-letting of the flat except on a furnished basis. Until 1974 furnished lettings of residential premises did not attract full Rent Act protection. Upon a claim for relief from forfeiture by an unfurnished sub-tenant it was argued that, since a furnished sub-tenancy would now be protected in any event, the appellant's unfurnished sub-tenancy should be preserved. The county court judge refused relief. *Held,* dismissing the appeal, the landlord would be saddled with a protected tenant of the flat if relief were given. It was irrelevant that a lawful furnished sub-letting would now be protected also: CLIFFORD v. PERSONAL REPRESENTATIVES OF JOHNSON DECD. (1979) 251 E.G. 571, C.A.

1604. Holiday letting—sham—licence or tenancy

[Rent Act 1977 (c. 42), s. 9.] The plaintiff, McH, let a flat to seven people in June 1977 for a fixed term of six months. All the occupants were overseas visitors. The agreement signed by all seven was headed " Temporary Holiday Accommodation Hire Agreement " and contained a clause reciting that the agreement was for " temporary holiday accommodation only." The term expired and the occupants, only three of whom were by then of the original group, were granted a number of short extensions. The plaintiff sued for possession alleging that (1) the agreement was a licence; (2) alternatively it was a holiday letting within s. 9. The defendants alleged that the agreement was a sham and that they were protected tenants under the Act. *Held,* granting an order for possession, the agreement was more like a tenancy than a licence but it was sufficient to hold that it was a holiday letting. There was no common intention to deceive and therefore no sham. Furthermore, a " working holiday " was contemplated by s. 9 and the present agreement fell within it. (*Buchmann* v. *May* [1978] C.L.Y. 1783 considered): McHALE v. DANEHAM (1979) 249 E.G. 969, Judge Edwards.

1605. Joint tenancy—liability for part of rent only—whether tenancy or licence

D and A went to S's agent, saying they wanted to rent a flat. They each signed an agreement, which purported to grant them only a licence of the property, determinable on a week's notice by the landlord, and if not determined, to last for a year. Each was to be liable only for his share of the rent, and a year's rent was taken from each of them in a number of post-dated cheques. The county court judge found that D and A had together exclusive occupation of the flat. He concluded that they were joint tenants, and were entitled to the protection of the Rent Acts. The landlords appealed. *Held,* dismissing the appeal, a joint tenancy with each of the tenants paying only one half of the total amount of the rent due for the joint tenancy could create a logical inconsistency, but it did not rule out a joint tenancy. In particular, in the present case the landlord had in any case secured the whole of his year's rent from D and A. (*Somma* v. *Hazlehurst* [1978] C.L.Y. 1797 and *Aldrington Garages* v. *Fielder* [1979] C.L.Y. 1616 considered and distinguished): DEMUREN v. SEAL ESTATES (1978) 249 E.G. 440, C.A.

1606. Leasehold reform—application for freehold—whether two tenancies to be treated as a single tenancy

[Leasehold Reform Act 1967 (c. 88) (as amended by Housing Act 1974 (c. 44), s. 118 (1)), ss. 1 (6) (*c*), 3 (2) (3).]

Where a lease is granted and then vests in another person who obtains a renewal, the two tenancies are to be treated as a single tenancy for the purposes of Pt. I of the Leasehold Reform Act 1967.

In 1961 B's mother was granted a lease for 27¼ years at a rent of less than two-thirds of the rateable value of the house. In 1964 the lease vested in B. In 1973, B surrendered the lease and was immediately granted a new lease for 29¼ years from September 29, 1973, at the same rent. When in 1975 B applied under the 1967 Act for the freehold of the house it was agreed that the tenancy was a long tenancy at a low rent and that she satisfied the five years' residence provision. However, the deputy judge held that s. 1 (6) (*c*) was not satisfied because the tenancy had not been created on or before February 1966 but in 1973 and the house was then outside the permitted rateable value. On appeal, *held,* allowing the appeal, that s. 3 (3) of the 1967 Act provided that the 1961 and 1973 tenancies were to be treated for the purposes of Pt. I of the Act as a single tenancy granted in 1961. Thus s. 1 (6) (*c*) had been satisfied and the application was within the 1967 Act. (Dicta of Russell and Stamp L.JJ. in *Roberts* v. *Church Commissioners for England* [1971] C.L.Y. 6638 considered.)

BATES v. PIERREPOINT (1978) 37 P. & C.R. 420, C.A.

1607. —— conveyance to lessee—meaning of " appurtenant "

[Leasehold Reform Act 1967 (c. 88), s. 2 (3).]

" Appurtenances " within s. 2 (3) of the Leasehold Reform Act 1967 include land within the curtilage of the house.

Property consisting of a house, garden and paddock was assigned to a lessee for a term of 64 years in 1929. The plan showed an unbroken line between garden and paddock. On the tenant serving a notice under the Act for the conveyance of the freehold of the house and premises the landlord sought a declaration that premises did not include the paddock. At first instance it was held that " appurtenances " included the paddock. On appeal, *held,* allowing the appeal, that though " appurtenances " included land within the curtilage of the house, the paddock could not be so described, and that where premises included a cultivated garden and an area of rough pasture, the latter did not come within the definition of " garden." (*Trim* v. *Sturminster R.D.C.* [1938] 2 K.B. 508 applied.)

METHUEN-CAMPBELL v. WALTERS [1979] 2 W.L.R. 113, C.A.

1608. —— enfranchisement—tenant separating demised premises

[Landlord and Tenant Act 1954 (c. 56), s. 3; Leasehold Reform Act 1967 (c. 88), s. 1 (1).]

When a tenant relinquishes occupation of part of the premises and never re-occupies, a claim to conveyance of the freehold will be barred.

Premises consisting of a ground floor shop and flat above were demised in 1876 for 99 years. The premises were undivided until 1956, when the tenant separated the shop from the flat, and sub-let the shop for 14 years. That sub-lease terminated in 1972, whereafter the shop was let on short tenancies. The head lease expired in March 1973. The tenant died in 1974. Rent was accepted from March 1973 until 1975. The tenant's wife then sought the conveyance of the freehold to her under the Leasehold Reform Act 1967. *Held,* that the shop premises had been relinquished in 1956 and were reoccupied, and the tenant's wife could not claim conveyance of the freehold of the premises. Although the landlord had received rent, the intention of the parties had not been to create a new tenancy.

BARON v. PHILLIPS (1979) 38 P. & C.R. 91, C.A.

1609. —— Lands Tribunal decisions

BAKER v. COX (LR/22/1978) (1979) 250 E.G. 1094 (upon a reference for the determination under the 1967 Act of the price to be paid for the freehold interest in a terraced house in Grays, Essex, the tribunal took a middle course between the tenant's cleared site figure of £775 and the landlord's figure of £1,750 based on other settlements in the same street. Award £1,300. No deduction for the effect in *Delaforce* v. *Evans* [1971] C.L.Y. 6633 appropriate).

BURTON v. KOLUP INVESTMENTS (LR/19/1978) (1979) 251 E.G. 1289 (reference by occupier to determine purchase price under Leasehold Reform Act 1967. Mews flat in Paddington, London. Disadvantages included office block opposite. Accordingly, percentage for site value would be 30 per cent. only. Entirety value £21,000. Price to be paid £5,325).

EMBLING v. WELLS AND CAMPDEN CHARITY'S TRUSTEES (LR/19/1977) (1978) 247 E.G. 909 (in a reference to determine the price which the tenant should pay to acquire the freehold of a four-storey house in Hampstead, in the initial valuation of which both parties had adopted the " standing house " approach, *held,* the " standing house " approach was not a satisfactory one, being arbitrary and artificial, but the tribunal would have to adopt it here, because although the valuers had sought local evidence of a market in land for residential development, they had found none. The tribunal rejected the applicant's use of differential percentage rates, which he claimed should have been employed because modern ground rents are less secure than actual rents).

1610. —— price payable—clause in current lease purporting to affect value of freehold—whether void

[Leasehold Reform Act 1967 (c. 88), ss. 9 (1), 23 (1).]

Where a long lease is granted by the freeholder to the reversioner subject to an existing lease but before notice is served by that existing tenant under the Leasehold Reform Act 1967, the rights so granted to the freeholder by that intermediate lease cannot be disregarded when assessing the price of the freehold under s. 9 (1) (*a*) of the Act.

The tenant, occupier of the house, was granted a lease for 87 years in 1961. In 1973 the tenant gave notice of her intention to acquire the freehold. Two days before service of the notice the freeholders granted a concurrent lease to a property company subject to the existing lease. On the tenant's application to determine the price of the freehold two alternative valuations were agreed; one where the intermediate lease was left out of account, and one where it was taken into consideration. The Lands Tribunal found that regard should be paid to the concurrent lease in assessing the freehold price. The Court of Appeal reversed the decision. On appeal by the freeholders, *held,* allowing the appeal, that the rights granted to the freeholders by the intermediate lease could not be ignored, but the modifications as to calculation of price did not affect or exclude the tenant's other rights regarding purchase of the freehold. (Decision of Court of Appeal [1978] C.L.Y. 1793 reversed.)

JONES *v.* WROTHAM PARK SETTLED ESTATES [1979] 2 W.L.R. 132, H.L.

1611. Leasehold Reform Act 1979 (c. 44)

This Act provides further protection, for a tenant in possession claiming to acquire the freehold under the Leasehold Reform Act 1967, against artificial inflation of the price he has to pay.

S. 1 deals with the price to the tenant on enfranchisement by stating that the price payable on a conveyance for giving effect to s. 8 of the Leasehold Reform Act 1967 cannot be made less favourable by reference to a transaction since February 15, 1979, involving the creation or transfer of an interest superior to his own; s. 2 deals with citation and extent. The Act extends to England and Wales only.

The Act received the Royal Assent on April 4, 1979, and came into force on that date.

1612. Leases—change of user—consent of landlord

[Landlord and Tenant Act 1954 (s. 56), s. 23 (4).] Premises were used for business purposes despite such a prohibtion in the lease. On expiry of the lease the defendant company became yearly tenants. The plaintiff landlord unsuccessfully brought an action for possession, although his predecessor in title knew of the prohibited use and never objected or asked that such use be discontinued. *Held*, allowing the plaintiff's appeal, there had been no consent to the business use. Mere acquiesence was not sufficient consent: BELL *v.* FRANKS (ALFRED) & BARTLETT CO. (1979) 123 S.J. 804, C.A.

1613. —— interpretation of clause—prohibition of offensive trade

[Can.] It has been *held*, that where a lease prohibits the carrying on of an offensive trade or business the word " offensive " must take its meaning from the context of the lease. Where a lease had other provisions relating to physical emissions resulting from a business, it is not incorrect for a trial judge to come to the conclusion that the word " offensive " encompasses nude dancing and topless waitresses: *Re* KOUMOUDOUROS & MARATHON REALTY CO. (1978) 89 D.L.R. (3d) 551, Ontario H.C.J.

1614. Licence—question of lease raised—Ord. 14 proceedings

Judgment under R.S.C., Ord. 14 was granted against the defendant G, the manager of club premises. The plaintiff company had granted him what purported to be a licence by a written agreement which had governed the relationship of the parties since 1972. The defendant appealed, alleging a tenancy. *Held*, dismissing the appeal, there was nothing in the agreement to raise a triable issue or defence. It was clearly a licence: ROSSVALE *v.* GREEN (1979) 250 E.G. 1183, C.A.

1615. Licence or tenancy—non-exclusive—sham

The appellant landlord granted the respondent a six-month term of a London flat. A written agreement was signed by the parties which purported to create a licence but contained many clauses consistent with a tenancy. The appellant claimed possession on the grounds that the agreement created a mere licence, as in *Somma* v. *Hazelhurst* [1978] C.L.Y. 1797 and *Aldrington Garages* v. *Fielder* [1979] C.L.Y. 1616. The county court judge dismissed the claim, holding the agreement to be a sham to disguise a tenancy. *Held,* dismissing the appeal and distinguishing the above authorities, the agreement was for a tenancy. There had been a prior oral agreement for a tenancy inconsistent with the agreement. Although the agreement, as in the other cases, contemplated sharing the premises with others the landlord did not in fact contemplate requiring the respondent to share with any other people. Each case of this sort depends on its own particular facts: O'MALLEY v. SEYMOUR (1979) 250 E.G. 1083, C.A.

1616. —— two occupiers of same flat—separate identical agreements expressly avoiding exclusive possession

Where the parties succeed in producing an agreement which is in fact a licence and not a tenancy they should not be prevented from that course by the courts.

P allowed D to occupy a flat by an agreement in writing which described D as " the licensee " and granted D " the right to use in common with others . . . the premises," D also agreed not to assign or permit any other person to sleep or reside in or share occupation of the rooms except as licensed by P. D was given a letter expressly stating that the relationship created by the agreement was intended to avoid a tenancy being granted and that D had no right of control over the person to whom P might decide to grant licences. On the same occasion another occupier had executed a similar agreement and received a similar letter. After this second occupier had terminated the agreement and left the flat D remained, paying the same rent as before. P sought possession, but the judge held that in reality the agreements between P and D and the other occupier were a single transaction creating a joint tenancy and found for D. On appeal, *held,* allowing the appeal, that where the parties had succeeded in producing an agreement which was in fact a licence and not a tenancy they should not be prevented from that course by the courts. (*Somma* v. *Hazlehurst* [1978] C.L.Y. 1797 applied; *Wimbush* v. *Cibulia* [1949] C.L.C. 8496 distinguished.)

ALDRINGTON GARAGES v. FIELDER (1979) 37 P. & C.R. 461, C.A.

1617. Northern Ireland. See NORTHERN IRELAND.

1618. Notice to quit—validity—fixed term tenancy

The defendant was granted a tenancy for a term of two years to expire on December 31, 1979. The tenancy agreement provided that the lease could be determined by either party giving the other one calendar month's notice expiring on the 27th day of any month. The landlord served a notice to quit on October 2, 1978, to determine the tenancy on November 1, 1978. The notice to quit contained the proviso " or the day on which a complete period of your tenancy expires next after the end of four weeks from the service of this notice." On a preliminary point, *held,* the notice to quit was invalid to terminate the tenancy as it was not served in acordance with the express terms of the tenancy agreement, nor could it be saved by the proviso since being a fixed term tenancy for two years the only complete period expired on December 31, 1979. The proceedings would therefore be dismissed with costs: PAREKH v. CHUAH, April 4, 1979, Judge Granville Slack, Willesden County Ct. (*Ex. rel. M. McH. George, Esq., Barrister.*)

1619. Option to renew—unregistered—landlord alleging invalidity—whether estoppel

Tenants of two adjoining shops claimed specific performance of options to renew in their leases which the landlord disclaimed for lack of registration under the Land Charges Act 1925. Both tenants had carried out substantial improvements in reliance on the option. *Held,* options are registrable, following *Beesly* v. *Hallwood Estates* [1961] C.L.Y. 2430. However, the doctrine of acquiescence or equitable estoppel will bind the landlord if it would be " dishonest or unconscionable " for him to argue otherwise: *per* Buckley L.J. in

Shaw v. *Applegate* [1977] C.L.Y. 2485. In *Taylor's* case the landlord had arrived on the scene after the work had been done and it was not possible to say that the works would not have been done had the tenant known that the option was void: specific performance refused. In *Old's* case the landlord had encouraged the tenant to carry out works, to take another lease of adjoining premises and had fixed the value of the freehold with the burden of the option: specific performance granted. *Per curiam,* it is not an essential element of this category of estoppel that the party estopped, although he must have known of the other party's belief, must have known that that belief was mistaken: TAYLOR FASHIONS *v.* LIVERPOOL VICTORIA FRIENDLY SOCIETY; OLD & CAMPBELL *v.* SAME (1979) 251 E.G. 159, Oliver J.

1620. Overcrowding—exclusion of Rent Acts—meaning of " room "

P sued for possession of a dwelling-house consisting of two rooms and a kitchen cum bathroom. The tenant G had living with him his wife, two teenage daughters and a child under 10. One of the two rooms was found to be unfit for human habitation by reason of lack of ventilation and natural light. It was contended that this room should not be taken into account for the purposes of calculating, by the table in Sched. 6 to the Housing Act 1957, the number of " units " permitted to occupy the premises without overcrowding. The room had been a storage room at the commencement of the tenancy but had been slightly altered by the addition of glazing in a door and making the door able to open. It was used at the time of trial for sleeping in. There were in the locality other rooms unfit for human habitation being used for sleeping in, but no evidence of any room with such inadequate lighting being so used. *Held,* that (1) this " room " was not a room of a type generally used in the locality as a living room or bedroom; (2) further, the real meaning of the word " room " in this context is a room suitable to be used for the purpose of sleeping. This " room " was to be excluded: it was not habitable; (3) without including this " room " in the reckoning, the premises were overcrowded and there was no Rent Act protection: PATEL *v.* GODAL, December 5, 1979, Judge Curtis-Raleigh, Bloomsbury & Marylebone County Ct. (*Ex rel. Stephen Zollner, Esq., Barrister.*)

1621. Possession—application to set aside judgment—delay

The defendant tenant lawfully sub-let his property and went abroad making no arrangements for the payment of rent. The plaintiff landlords obtained possession of the flat on the ground of non-payment of rent, leasing it to a third party. On his return, the defendant successfully applied to have the judgment set aside. *Held,* allowing the plaintiffs' appeal, the defendant had created a situation whereby any reasonable landlord would suppose that the premises had been abandoned. Delay over all was a material factor to be considered. Further, the rights of the third party should have weighed heavily with the trial judge. They held the lease in good faith and had acted upon it by effecting improvements (*Grimshaw* v. *Dunbar* [1953] C.L.Y. 709 applied): RHODES TRUST *v.* KHAN (1979) 123 S.J. 719, C.A.

1622. —— assignment in breach of covenant—service of notice of breach

[Law of Property Act 1925 (c. 20), s. 146.]

Where a lessee assigns the remainder of the term in breach of covenant, the assignment is effective, and the proper recipient of a s. 146 notice under the Law of Property Act 1925 is the assignee, not the original lessee.

The plaintiffs granted a lease of business premises to the defendant for a period of three years with a " no assignment without consent " covenant. The lease was assigned without consent, and a s. 146 notice was served on the original lessee. The question arose as to who was the correct recipient of the notice. *Held,* that the s. 146 notice should have been served on the assignee who is the person concerned to avoid forfeiture, and not on the original lessee.

OLD GROVEBURY MANOR FARM *v.* W. SEYMOUR PLANT SALES AND HIRE (No. 2) [1979] 3 All E.R. 504, C.A.

1623. —— interim payment—bona fide counterclaim

[R.S.C., Ord. 29, r. 18.]

It is not appropriate to grant to a plaintiff in forfeiture proceedings, an order for interim payment in respect of the defendant's use of the land where there is a bona fide cross-claim for an amount in excess of the interim payment sought.

The plaintiffs claimed forfeiture of land used as a petrol station and occupied by the defendants to whom the lease had been assigned without the plaintiff's consent as required under the lease. The lease was due shortly to expire; the defendants claimed to have exercised an option to renew and/or relied upon the Landlord and Tenant Act 1954; they also claimed £20,000 damages for harm done to their business by the plaintiffs. The plaintiffs sought an interim payment of £11,400 under R.S.C., Ord. 29, r. 18. *Held,* that in view of the counterclaim, an interim payment order was inappropriate: OLD GROVEBURY MANOR FARM *v.* W. SEYMOUR PLANT SALES & HIRE [1979] 1 W.L.R. 263, Brightman J.

1624. —— recovery—claim by one of two owner-occupiers
[Rent Act 1968 (c. 23), s. 10, Sched. 3, Pt. II, Case 10.]
Case 10 of Pt. II of Sched. 3 to the Rent Act 1968 applies where joint owner-occupiers are reclaiming possession of premises for a residence for only one of them.

Per curiam: Preliminary points of law should only be decided in courts of first instance in exceptional cases, in particular when the fact was complicated and the legal issue short and easily decided.

A and B, joint owner-occupiers, let their house to C furnished and on a regulated tenancy for two years. The agreement contained a notice that the landlord might recover possession under Case 10 of Pt. II of Sched. 3 to the Rent Act 1968. C remained in possession and A and B brought proceedings under Case 10 on the ground that the premises were required as a residence for A only. As a preliminary issue, the county court judge held that Case 10 did not apply where the house was required as a residence for one joint owner only. The Court of Appeal affirmed the decision. On appeal to the House of Lords, *held,* allowing the appeal, that A was a person who had occupied the premises as a residence, she had let it on a regulated tenancy and was therefore an owner-occupier, and the dwelling-house was required as a residence for her. Case 10 accordingly applied, and the matter would be remitted to the county court to be decided on that basis. (*McIntyre* v. *Hardcastle* (1948) C.L.C. 8434 distinguished.)

TILLING *v.* WHITEMAN [1979] 2 W.L.R. 401, H.L.

1625. —— —— whether reasonably required by landlord
The landlord claimed possession of the basement and ground floor of a house which were let on separate tenancies on the grounds that (1) he was resident within s. 12 of the Rent Act 1977, and (2) under Case 9 of Pt. 1 of Sched. 15. At the commencement of the tenancies the landlord was not physically living in the house and during the tenancies he had negotiated with the local Council to sell the house to them. He contended, however, that he always intended to return to live in the house, and secondly, that throughout the lettings the attic of the house was empty and furnished and was therefore a symbol of occupation (*Brown* v. *Brash* (1948) C.L.C. 8853 referred to). On Case 9 the evidence was that by the commencement of proceedings the landlord already occupied the first and second floors and the attic. He claimed he needed the first floor to give his family more room including the only bathroom in the house and needed the basement as a flat for his daughter who intended to marry, although possibly not for two years. *Held,* (1) the negotiations to sell the house were clear evidence that the landlord had not always had an intention to return; (2) accepting the tenant's evidence that the attic was in fact let during their tenancies and that therefore there was no symbol of occupation, that even on the landlord's evidence to have held that in such circumstances a landlord could claim to be resident would allow any landlord who owned two houses and kept one room vacant with a few items of furniture in it to claim he was resident and thereby undermine the policy of the Rent Acts and the intention of Parliament. The landlord was not within s. 12 of the Act; (3) granting an order for possession of the ground floor and refusing an order in respect of the basement that it could not be said that the landlord reasonably required

the basement when the sole purpose for which it would be used was as a home for his daughter in the event of her marriage which might be two years hence: KISSIAS *v.* LEHANY, March 2, 1979, Judge Dow, Clerkenwell County Ct. (*Ex rel. M. McH. George, Esq., Barrister.*)

1626. —— trespass—damages

Where a plaintiff has established that the defendant has remained on residential property as a trespasser he is entitled to damages for trespass without bringing evidence that he could or would have let the property to someone else.

The plaintiffs let the flat to T for a fixed term; T then introduced M and S as licensees. T left before the expiry of the fixed term but M and S remained. The plaintiffs sued for possession and for damages for trespass. The judge gave them possession but found that they were not entitled to damages for trespass. On appeal, *held,* allowing the appeal, that the plaintiffs were entitled to damages for trespass notwithstanding the fact that they had not adduced evidence that they could or would have relet the premises; the measure of damages was the letting value of the premises. (*Whitwham* v. *Westminster Brymbo Coal and Coke* [1896] 2 Ch. 538 and *Penarth Dock Engineering* v. *Pounds* [1963] C.L.Y. 514 applied.)

SWORDHEATH PROPERTIES *v.* TABET [1979] 1 All E.R. 240, C.A.

1627. Protected tenancies—action for possession—resident landlord—whether tenant's flat part of landlord's premises

[Rent Act 1977 (c. 42), s. 12.] The plaintiff was the owner of Nos. 4–6 Moreton St., London. These premises were erected at the same time but were constructed as two separate shops. Each half of the premises consisted of a basement, a ground floor with shop-front and door on to the street and living accommodation on the first floor. At some time a hole had been made in the wall dividing the two basements; most of the wall dividing the ground floor rooms had been demolished so that one large room was formed spanning both parts; a doorway had been made connecting the flat on the first floor at No. 4 with that at No. 6. The plaintiff lived in the flat at No. 4 but the door connecting his flat to No. 6 was locked and partly sealed up. He used the ground floor and basement of both parts of the premises as a potter's studio and showroom. In 1975 the flat at No. 6 was let to the defendant. Her contractual tenancy ended and she claimed to be a protected tenant. The plaintiff sought an order for possession relying on s. 12 as a resident landlord *Held,* that the defendant's flat formed part of a building and that building was the whole premises, 4–6 Moreton St. The plaintiff also occupied a dwelling-house which formed part of that building and was accordingly a resident landlord within s. 12. Order for possession made: GUPPY *v.* O'DONNELL, July 27, 1979, Judge Rowland, Westminster County Ct. (*Ex rel. Daniel Pearce-Higgins, Esq., Barrister.*)

1628. —— divorced ex-wife of tenant in possession—whether statutory tenant

[Rent Act 1977 (c. 42), s. 2.] The first defendant was the sole tenant of residential premises. He left in 1970 with no intention of returning. In 1976 he and the second defendant, who continued to reside in the premises, were divorced. No transfer of the tenancy to her was made or applied for under s. 7 of the Matrimonial Homes Act 1967. Notice to quit was served. The county court judge ordered possession as against the second defendant. *Held,* dismissing the appeal, in the absence of a statutory transfer or a joint tenancy a divorced ex-spouse of a statutory tenant had no rights where the tenant had no intention to return. Furthermore in the instant case there had on the facts been no surrender and re-grant to the second defendant by acceptance of rent. (*Robson* v. *Headland* (1948) C.L.C. 8840 followed; *Wiles* v. *Morse* (1950) 155 E.G. 290 explained; *Clarke* v. *Grant* (1950) C.L.C. 5551 considered): HEATH ESTATES *v.* BURCHELL (1979) 251 E.G. 1173, C.A.

1629. —— let as a separate dwelling—students

[Rent Act 1977 (c. 42), ss. 1, 8.]

An arrangement in which an owner lets his house to a college which in turn lets it to students, and covenants only so to do, and in which the students have separate and exclusive use of a room (though bathroom and kitchen are shared) is inconsistent with the concept of a building which can itself be described as a separate dwelling.

With a view to taking advantage of s. 8 (1) of the 1977 Act and to making accommodation more generally available to students in Oxford, a scheme was devised where owners of houses let them to colleges which then made them available to undergraduates. A suitable house was found, was let to St. Catherine's College and five students applied for accommodation. Each student had his own room, paid his share of the rent, but shared the kitchen and bathroom. After signing the agreement the college applied for a fair rent and a declaration that the tenancy was protected. This was refused on the grounds that the house was not let as a separate dwelling. On appeal, *held*, dismissing the appeal, that on a true construction of the agreement the phrase "used as private residence" meant "for residential purposes" and what was being granted was the tenancy of a building containing a number of units of habitation. (*Horford Investments* v. *Lambert* [1973] C.L.Y. 2823 considered.)

St. Catherine's College v. Dorling [1979] 3 All E.R. 250, C.A.

1630. —— succession—male friend of female tenant—whether member of "family"
[Rent Act 1977 (c. 42), Sched. 1, para. 3.]

A lover who has lived for some years with a statutory tenant is not to be treated upon the tenant's death as a member of her "family" for the purposes of his succeeding to the statutory tenancy.

In 1972 the defendant moved into the flat of which Miss T was the statutory tenant, and lived with her thereafter as her lover. For the three years prior to her death in 1977, the defendant cared for the ailing Miss T as a husband would have done. The couple did not pretend to be married and there was evidence that Miss T wished to preserve her independence by remaining single. The defendant claimed to be a member of Miss T's "family" within the meaning of Sched. 1, para. 3 to the 1977 Act. The plaintiff landlady successfully claimed possession. *Held*, dismissing the appeal, that on the evidence the relationship lacked the degree of permanence to warrant describing the parties as members of a single family. (*Dyson Holdings* v. *Fox* [1975] C.L.Y. 1909 applied.)

Helby v. Rafferty [1978] 3 All E.R. 1016, C.A.

1631. Regulated tenancy—increased rent—registration—whether tenant subsequently entitled to reopen financial calculations
[Housing Finance Act 1972 (c. 47), s. 90 (1) (4) (12).]

A tenant who is being sued for a rent which has been increased and registered by the rent officer cannot on discovery seek to reopen the rent officer's financial calculations.

D paid rent under a tenancy of his flat of £830 per year. L Co. covenanted to supply hot water, heating, light, and cleaning of the common parts of the building, which was all included in the rent. L Co. applied to the rent officer for an increased rent, up to £2,000 per year. They attached to their application calculations showing that £840 per year was attributable to the provision of services. The rent office registered a rent of £1,670 and T refused to pay it. When P Co. brought proceedings for the rent in the county court, T sought specific discovery of accounts for the service charges for the previous three years. The judge made the order, with reference to s. 90 of the Housing Finance Act 1972. On appeal by L Co. *held*, allowing the appeal, that (1) s. 90 permitted a tenant to obtain a summary of costs of services in writing only where there was a service charge payable as part of or in addition to the rent. In the present case the fact that the rent included certain services did not mean that a "service charge" was payable; (2) T could not reopen the financial calculations applicable to the registration of the rent in the county court. No valid issue was raised in the action to which the documents were relevant, and the order for discovery should have been refused.

Legal and General Assurance Society v. Keane (1978) 38 P. & C.R. 399, C.A.

1632. Rent—arrears—Order 14 proceedings. See Asco Developments v. Gordon, § 2166.

1633. —— building in disrepair—set off—unliquidated damages

An equitable set-off for an unquantified amount may be allowed against a claim for rent if it arises out of a transaction closely connected with the lease.

The plaintiffs agreed with the defendants to build and in due course lease to the defendants certain warehouses. The agreement provided that the plaintiffs would at their own expense remedy any defects in the floors of the buildings caused by their default in design or construction. The subsequently entered lease contained no such provision, nor did it contain a covenant to repair. The defendants later commenced actions claiming damages in excess of £1 million for alleged defects in the floors and they refused to pay further rent. The plaintiffs claimed possession of the premises and arrears of rent and mesne profits of some £570,000, of which £540,000 was admitted to be due by the defendants subject to a set-off in respect of their counterclaim. On a preliminary issue as to whether the defendants were entitled to set off their unliquidated demand, *held*, that (1) a bona fide claim for unliquidated damages could amount to an equitable set-off affording a complete defence if its amount exceeded that of the plaintiffs' claim; (2) the defendants could not rely upon any common law right of set-off against rent; but (3) the doctrine of equitable set-off applied since the defendants had no common law right and since, although their claim did not arise out of the lease, it arose from an agreement closely connected therewith, and because it would be manifestly unjust to allow the plaintiffs to recover without taking account of their breaches of the original agreement. (*Lee-Parker* v. *Izzet* [1971] C.L.Y. 6656 considered; dicta of Parker J. in *The Teno* [1977] C.L.Y. 2753, and of Lord Denning M.R. in *Henriksen's Rederi A/S* v. *T.H.Z. Rolimpex*; *The Brede* [1973] C.L.Y. 3103 applied.)

BRITISH ANZANI (FELIXSTOWE) *v.* INTERNATIONAL MARINE MANAGEMENT (U.K.) [1979] 2 All E.R. 1063, Forbes J.

1634. Rent Acts—tenant holding over—new tenancy

T had a six-month tenancy, which expired in October 1975. Shortly before this expiry, T asked L if he could stay, and L agreed, on condition that T paid an extra £10 per month. There was no discussion about any of the other terms in the lease. In proceedings for possession on the ground of the expiry of the six-month tenancy, T alleged that a fresh or continuation tenancy had been agreed between the parties and that this had not been terminated. The county court judge concluded that a new contractual tenancy had not been granted, and gave possession. T appealed. *Held*, dismissing the appeal, if no question had arisen as to the Rent Acts the only inference that could have been drawn on the facts would have been that there was a renewal of the contractual tenancy, but the fact that there was a rent restriction background to what was done was a matter which both could and ought to have been taken into account. If the acceptance of rent could be explained on some other footing than that a contractual tenancy existed (as, for example, that T had an existing or statutory right to remain) the creation or otherwise of a new agreement was a matter of inference to be drawn by the judge, and it was impossible to say that the county court judge had erred. (*Cole* v. *Kelly* [1920] 2 K.B. 106 considered; *Morrison* v. *Jacobs* [1945] K.B. 577 and *Marcroft Wagons* v. *Smith* (1951) C.L.C. 8831 applied): HARVEY *v.* STAGG (1977) 247 E.G. 463, C.A.

1635. Rent restriction. See RENT RESTRICTION.

1636. Rent review—disregarding tenant's improvements—factors and methods of valuation

A 21-year lease of business premises allowed for rent reviews at the seventh and fourteenth years. The tenant had entered an empty shell and completed the fitting-out at its own cost and at a peppercorn rent for the first six months. The arbitrator on first review stated a case as to the valuation method to be adopted: the review clause required that any effect on the rental value of any improvements carried out by the tenant should be disregarded. *Held*, the effect of inflation on rental values and building costs might differ substantially. Subject to that, the tenant must be credited with the rental equivalent of the works which it carried out, taking into account that they are a wasting asset which will enure to the benefit of the landlord at the end of the term and are devalued by obsolescence at each review. General survey in judgment of valuation methods and factors to be taken into account: GREA REAL PROPERTY INVESTMENTS v. WILLIAMS (1979) 250 E.G. 651, Forbes J.

1637. The applicant landlord applied to set aside the award of an arbitrator appointed under a rent review clause. The subject property was a terrace of four buildings of which the covenanted user of ground and upper floors were, or might be different. The tenant had carried out improvements which, pursuant to the rent review clause in the lease, fell to be ignored in calculating the reviewed rent. The arbitrator found the ground floor rent on the basis of comparables but assessed the upper floor rent, in the absence of comparables, by decapitalising the costs of the improvements, adjusted for inflation, in order to arrive at an " unimproved " rent. *Held,* in valuing the upper floor the arbitrator had used a method which was probably not in accordance with the intentions of the parties. Accordingly, there was an error of law on the face of the record. Case remitted to the arbitrator for reassessment. General remarks as to valuation, the *Grea* case and the role of arbitrators. (*Grea Real Property Investments* v. *Williams* [1979] C.L.Y. 1636 considered): ESTATES PROJECTS v. GREENWICH BOROUGH COUNCIL (1979) 251 E.G. 851, Forbes J.

1638. —— **failure to serve arbitration notice in time—whether time of the essence**
    Under rent review clauses time is presumed not to be of the essence and it is for a tenant to show that this presumption is rebutted in a particular case.
    A 21-year lease provided, *inter alia,* that the landlord would be entitled to call for a rent review within the last six months before the expiration of the seventh and 14th year of the term. If within three months after the notice calling for a rent revision there was no agreement the matter " shall if the landlord shall so require by notice in writing given to the tenant within three months thereafter but not otherwise be referred to " arbitration. The landlord did not give an arbitration notice until almost 18 months after the review notice. The tenant objected and the landlord sought a declaration that it was entitled to require the matter to be referred to arbitration. *Held,* dismissing the summons, that (1) under the rent review clauses time was presumed not to be of the essence but the tenant could show that the presumption was rebutted in a particular case; (2) the wording of the clause, especially " but not otherwise," did make time of the essence for the arbitration notice and the landlord was no longer entitled to serve notice. (*United Scientific Holdings* v. *Burnley Borough Council* [1977] C.L.Y. 1758 applied.)
    DREBBOND v. HORSHAM DISTRICT COUNCIL (1979) 37 P. & C.R. 237, Megarry V.-C.

1639. —— **strict user covenant—valuation of hope of relaxation—whether relevant**
    An arbitrator who is called upon to determine a rent arrear does so on the basis that the parties' rights will be enforced and their duties performed,
    L sublet office premises to T. The underlease contained a covenant to use the premises only for the purposes of the business of consulting civil engineers. There was a rent review clause, the rent in default of agreement to be determined by an arbitrator, and to represent a fair rack rent market value. It was agreed that without the restrictive covenant the premises were worth £130,455, and that with it, they were worth £89,200. The arbitrator found for the lower sum. On a special case stated, the High Court held that the arbitrator could not take into account the fact that the landlord might consent to a change of user and that the arbitrator's award was correct. On appeal by L, *held,* dismissing the appeal, that the arbitrator must look at the legal position of the parties and nothing else; he must assume that the rights of the parties would be enforced and their obligations performed.
    PLINTH PROPERTY INVESTMENTS v. MOTT, HAY & ANDERSON (1978) 38 P. & C.R. 361, C.A.

1640. Statutory tenancy—action for possession—purported assignment to son during winter—intention of father to move back in spring
    [Rent Act 1977 (c. 42), s. 2 (1) (*a*), Sched. 1, para. 13 (1) (2).]
    An assignment which is a nullity can have no effect in law on the position of a statutory tenant.

F was the statutory tenant of a bungalow. Because of the condition of the bungalow and his wife's ill health he wished to move out during the winter months and return in the spring. His son was to move into the bungalow during the winter and effect repairs and decoration to make it more habitable. Acting, as he thought, on advice F purported to assign his statutory tenancy to his son. The plaintiff landlord was not a party to that agreement as the 1977 Act requires. The plaintiff sought possession. The deputy judge held that F retained the intention to return to the bungalow but that as a matter of law he had lost the *corpus possessionis* by purporting to assign the tenancy. On appeal, *held,* allowing the appeal, that the purported transfer being in law a nullity, it could have no effect in law on the position of F. The deputy judge had been satisfied that but for the purported transfer F would have retained the *corpus possessionis*; accordingly F remained the statutory tenant and P was not entitled to possession.

ATYEO *v.* FARDOE (1978) 37 P. & C.R. 494, C.A.

1641. —— rent deemed to be registered under Pt. IV of 1968 Act—whether calculated exclusive of rates

[Rent Act 1968 (c. 23), s. 47 (2) (3); Rent Act 1974 (c. 51), s. 5 (1).]

A rent deemed to be registered under Pt. IV of the 1968 Act is not deemed to be an exclusive rent if it was not such a rent in fact.

In 1972 M went into occupation of a furnished flat at a rent inclusive of rates. The rent tribunal reduced the rent to £52 per month and in 1973 the landlords granted M a further term at the reduced rent of £52 per month still with the landlords liable for the rates. In 1974 under the new Act the tenancy became protected and in 1976 after receiving a notice to quit M became a protected tenant. The landlords claimed that the effect of the 1974 Act was to convert the former inclusive rent into an exclusive rent and claimed arrears of rates. The judge found for the landlords. On appeal by M, *held,* allowing the appeal, that the rent was deemed to be registered under Pt. IV of the 1968 Act, but it was not deemed to be that which it was not, *i.e.* an exclusive rent. Thus the landlords were not entitled to recover payment for the rates.

DOMINAL SECURITIES *v.* McLEOD (1978) 37 P. & C.R. 411, C.A.

1642. —— tenancy by succession—whether friend member of tenant's family

[Rent Act 1968 (c. 23), Sched. I, para. 3.]

It is not possible for two people, who are not in fact related, to establish a familial nexus for the purposes of the Rent Acts by acting as or calling themselves " aunt " and " nephew."

The defendant, then aged 24, lived with an old lady for many years, and there developed between them a close platonic relationship. They treated each other as aunt and nephew. The contractual tenancy ended in 1973 and the old lady remained in the flat until her death in 1976. In an action for possession, the defendant, who had remained in the flat, claimed he had been a member of the deceased's family and was therefore the statutory tenant. The defendant succeeded at first instance, the landlord on appeal, and on appeal by the defendant, *held,* dismissing the appeal, that two people who were not in fact related could not establish a familial nexus merely by acting as aunt and nephew. (*Ross* v. *Collins* [1964] C.L.Y. 3153 applied.)

JORAM DEVELOPMENTS *v.* SHARRATT [1979] 1 W.L.R. 928, H.L.

1643. —— undisclosed principal—parol evidence varying terms of lease

Miss G and Miss C were tenants under a five-year lease which expired in 1972, when they became statutory tenants. Mrs. G, Miss G's mother, had lived with them throughout the tenancy, and stayed on when they left in 1976. She claimed that she had obtained the tenancy for the three of them, but had been unable to attend the signing of the lease, so the other two signed on her behalf, although none of this appeared on the face of the lease. *Held,* the question was, is the identity of the people named as lessees of such importance as a term of the contract that it cannot properly be taken that some other person could be regarded as an undisclosed principal? In the present case, the landlord should know on whom he could rely for performance of covenants, and who might become statutory tenants, and accordingly the defendant was not a statutory tenant (*Drughorn (Fred)* v. *Rederiaktiebolaget Transatlantic* [1919] A.C. 203 considered; *Danziger* v. *Thompson* [1944] K.B. 654 distinguished): HANSTOWN PROPERTIES *v.* GREEN (1977) 246 E.G. 917, C.A.

1644. Sub-lease—consent—reasonableness of landlord's refusal to grant
In considering whether a landlord has unreasonably withheld consent to a sub-lease or assignment, " unreasonably " depends upon all the circumstances of the case, and the question is not whether the proposed sub-letting is "normal" or "abnormal," but what was the true purpose of the covenant.
T Co. were tenants by an assignment dated March 1974 of a lease dated June 1971 for a term of 14 years. The premises were business premises with a self-contained furnished flat above. L, the landlord, acquired the reversion in November 1976. At that time no sub-tenant occupied the furnished flat, then T Co. sought consent to sub-let to Mr. and Mrs. X. L refused consent on the ground that the proposed tenants would become protected tenants which would reduce the value of the premises. By the lease, T Co. had covenanted not to assign or underlet without L's consent, such consent not to be unreasonably withheld. The county court judge held that the sub-tenancy was a normal one, and declared that consent had been unreasonably withheld. On appeal by L, *held*, allowing the appeal, that the question was not whether the sub-lease was normal or abnormal, but what was the true purpose of the covenant. That purpose was to enable T Co. to give living accommodation to its staff, or create no more than a furnished tenancy with L's consent. The clear intention of the parties was that L could recover possession at the end of the term unfettered by any statutory protection of the occupiers, and the withholding of consent was reasonable. (*Norfolk Capital Group* v. *Kitway* [1976] C.L.Y. 1519 and *Bickel* v. *Duke of Westminster* [1978] C.L.Y. 1763 applied; *Swanson* v. *Forton* (1949) C.L.C. 5345 considered.)
WEST LAYTON *v.* FORD (EXECUTRIX OF THE ESTATE OF JOSEPH, DECD. [1979] 3 W.L.R. 14, C.A.

1645. —— **unlawful—whether knowledge of landlord's agents waives breach**
The respondent granted a tenancy of one of a block of 120 flats to S who in 1975 sub-let the flat to the appellant in breach of covenant. In 1978 the appellant brought herself to the notice of the respondent's head office and she was sued successfully for possession, the county court judge holding her sub-tenancy to be unlawful and therefore unprotected by s. 137 of the Rent Act 1977. The appellant contended that the breach of covenant had been waived by the knowledge of the porters of the block of her existence from 1975 to 1978. It was agreed that the porters had had regular dealings with the appellant before 1978 and that rent had been accepted from S at all times until the respondent's manager became directly aware of the appellant's existence in 1978. *Held*, allowing the appeal, the respondent company would be deemed to have knowledge of the appellant's status and of the breach of covenant and had waived the latter. The evidence showed that it was part of the duty of the porters to inform the respondent of changes in occupation of the flats. Art. 106, r. 2, in *Bowstead on Agency* (14th ed.) applied to fix the respondent with deemed knowledge as principal of the porter agents: METROPOLITAN PROPERTIES CO. *v.* CORDERY (1979) 251 E.G. 567, C.A.

1646. Unlawful eviction—harassment of non-tenant
[Rent Act 1965 (c. 75), s. 30.] B's house was shared by several people, not including B but including McP, who lived in several different rooms during her period of occupation. In September 1976 B gave the occupants notice to leave by the end of the year. In January 1977 McP went into hospital for three weeks, during which time B turned McP's belongings out of the house and locked the door. *Held*, that McP was not protected by s. 30 of the 1965 Act since McP was merely a contractual licensee, not a tenant, and had been given reasonable notice. Thus there was no case for B to answer on charges of unlawful eviction and harassment: R. *v.* BLANKLEY [1979] Crim.L.R. 166, Knightsbridge Crown Ct.

1647. —— **tenant deserting wife—landlord refusing access to wife—whether claim in trespass—damages.** See TAYLOR *v.* REES, § 2733.

BOOKS AND ARTICLES. See *post*, pp. [7], [25].

LAW REFORM

1648. Contract—implied terms

The Law Commission has published a " Report on Implied Terms in Contract for the Supply of Goods." One of its principal recommendations is that a customer's rights should be the same whether his contract is one of sale, hire-purchase, hire, exchange or for work and materials. The Report is available from HMSO (Law Com. No. 95) [£2·50].

1649. Criminal law—comparative research

The Home Office has published a report by John Croft, the head of the Home Office Research Unit, which examines the relevance of comparative research to the study of crime, and the problems that will confront policy makers in the 1980s. The report entitled " Crime and comparative research " Home Office Research Study 57 is available from HMSO [£1·00].

1650. Illegitimacy

The Law Commission has published Working Paper No. 74 on Illegitimacy to promote wide public discussion of the issues. The paper makes proposals designed to eliminate the legal discrimination and to help remove the stigma of illegitimacy. The paper is available from HMSO [£2·75].

1651. Insurance

The Law Commission has published Working Paper No. 73 on the reform of the law relating to non-disclosure and breach of warranty by the insured. The Working Paper is available from HMSO [£2·50].

1652. Interference with the course of justice

The Law Commission has published a report on Offences Relating to Interference with the Course of Justice, in which it recommends the abolition of the present law in this area. In its place it suggests a new scheme of individual crimes, each with its own maximum sentence. The report is available from HMSO (Law Com. No. 96) [£4·50].

1653. Personal injuries litigation

The Report of the Personal Injuries Litigation Procedure Working Party has been published. It makes various recommendations for reducing the delay in disposing of personal injury cases. The report is available from HMSO (Cmnd. 7476) [£1].

ARTICLES. See *post*, p. [25].

LEGAL HISTORY

BOOKS AND ARTICLES. See *post*, pp. [8], [26].

LIBEL AND SLANDER

1654. Blasphemous libel—mens rea. See R. *v.* LEMON; R. *v.* GAY NEWS, § 409.

1655. Fair comment—relevance of evidence as to honest belief of authors

[Can.] P, a city alderman, claimed he had been libelled by a letter written by two law students and published by D in their newspaper. The students were not sued, nor were they called as witnesses, so no evidence as to their honest beliefs was presented. D's testimony showed they did not agree with the students' opinions, but they argued they were entitled to enter the defence of fair comment as they believed the letter reflected the students' honest beliefs. *Held*, as there was no evidence as to the honest beliefs of the writers of the letter, and as D did not agree with the contents of the letter, the defence of fair comment should not properly be put to the jury. (" *Truth* " (*N.Z.*) v. *Holloway* [1960] C.L.Y. 1803; *Arnold* v. *King-Emperor* [1914] A.C. 664 applied): CHERNESKEY v. ARMADALE PUBLISHERS [1978] 6 W.W.R. 618, Can. Sup.Ct.

1656. Interim injunction—principles

An overseas company controlled by one Sheik Khojabi bought the block of flats in which S lived. The managing agents were T. S believed that T were harassing the long-term tenants in the block, and told T of his intention to call a press conference, at which he would make public his allegations. T obtained an *ex parte* injunction preventing S from making statements to the effect that T were (a) unmitigated scoundrels and gangsters, (b) harassing tenants, and (c) working in conjunction with the Arabs against the British. When the summons came for rehearing, S offered an undertaking not to accuse T of (a). The judge continued the whole injunction. S appealed. *Held*, allowing the appeal, freedom of speech is so important that if a person is only saying or repeating what he believes to be true, an interim injunction will not be given against him. S should be allowed to say publicly what he honestly believed. The injunction would be discharged and the undertaking continued. (*Bonnard* v. *Perryman* [1891] 2 Ch. 269 applied; *American Cyanamid Co.* v. *Ethicon* [1975] C.L.Y. 2640 distinguished): J. TREVOR & SONS v. SOLOMON (1977) 248 E.G. 779, C.A.

1657. Interlocutory injunction—husband and wife—breach of confidence
The plaintiff sought to restrain the first defendant, his ex-wife, from publishing in a newspaper details of his former married life. *Held*, (1) no injunction to restrain the libel would be granted since the defendants intended to justify their allegations; (2) the plaintiff and his ex-wife had themselves made public intimate details in the past and for profit and no relief would be granted for the alleged breach of confidence: LENNON v. NEWS GROUP NEWSPAPERS AND TWIST [1978] F.S.R. 573, C.A.

BOOKS AND ARTICLES. See *post*, pp. [8], [26].

LIEN

1658. Exercise—advance payment of contract—repairs to ship. See FRASER v. EQUITORIAL SHIPPING CO. AND EQUITORIAL LINES, § 340.

1659. General lien—warehouseman—whether effective against non-contracting owners. See CHELLARAM & SONS (LONDON) v. BUTLERS WAREHOUSING & DISTRIBUTION, § 144.

1660. Information—amendment—defective tyre wrongly described. See R. v. SANDWELL JUSTICES, *ex p.* WEST MIDLANDS PASSENGER TRANSPORT EXECUTIVE, § 2293.

1661. Solicitors—unpaid fees—client's documents
Finding themselves in difficulties, solicitors discharged themselves and sought to recover unpaid fees. *Held*, having discharged themselves so, in the course of an action, a solicitor loses his possessory lien over the client's documents in his possession, for unpaid fees (*Robins* v. *Goldingham* (1872) L.R. 13 Eq. 440 followed): GAMLEN CHEMICAL CO. (U.K.) v. ROCHEM, *The Times*, December 6, 1979, C.A.

LIMITATION OF ACTIONS

1662. Acknowledgment—of indebtedness—action to safeguard property of missing person
[Limitation Act 1939 (c. 21), s. 23 (4); R.S.C., Ord. 20, r. 5.]
An acknowledgment that money might be due is not an admission of indebtedness within s. 23 (4) of the Limitation Act 1939.
X rendered services to D Co. in 1967. In May 1967 D Co. recognised that he was out of pocket to the extent of £100,000. In March 1970 D Co. wrote to X denying that there was any agreement to pay him, and saying that although substantial sums had been paid for out-of-pocket expenses, no account had been delivered in respect of them, and that no further payment would be made unless such an account supported by evidence was delivered. X then disappeared. His brother, P, the plaintiff, was appointed under Lebanese law as his judicial administrator and authorised to bring an action against D Co. A writ was issued in 1975. *Held*, (1) P's title to sue was not recognised in the English courts since English law did not provide for the safeguarding of the property and affairs of absent persons; (2) the letter of March 1970 could not be construed with the letter of May 1967 as an acknowledgment that D Co.

owed X remuneration and expenses, and it did not amount to an admission of indebtedness (*Good* v. *Parry* [1963] C.L.Y. 2020 applied; *Dungate* v. *Dungate* [1965] C.L.Y. 2274 distinguished; *Didisheim* v. *London and Westminster Bank* [1900] 2 Ch. 15 considered.)

KAMOUH v. ASSOCIATED ELECTRICAL INDUSTRIES INTERNATIONAL [1979] 2 W.L.R. 795, Parker J.

1663. Action out of time—prejudice to defendant

[Limitation Act 1939 (c. 21), s. 2D (1) (*b*).] When a plaintiff in a personal injuries action seeks leave to proceed notwithstanding that three years has elapsed since the accrual of the cause of action, the prejudice to the defendant which falls for consideration under s. 2D (1) (*b*) of the Limitation Act 1939 is the prejudice flowing from the decision of the court to allow the action to proceed; the prejudice which has accrued to the defendant by the delay of the plaintiff within the normal period of limitation cannot be said to be prejudice caused by the decision of the court: DEEMING v. BRITISH STEEL CORP. (1978) S.J. 303, C.A.

1664. Concealment of right of action—building contract—severe defects in construction

[Limitation Act 1939 (c. 21), s. 26.] The respondent builders constructed four tower blocks for the appellants' predecessor in title in 1961. In 1971 very severe defects were found therein due to faulty construction. The repairs cost £150,000. The appellants sued for breach of contract in 1976. The respondents pleaded the Act and the Official Referee struck out the statement of claim on the ground that there could be no " concealed fraud " within s. 26 of the Act where the parties were of equal weight and unable to take advantage of each other. *Held*, allowing the interlocutory appeal, the claim should be restored, at least for a preliminary issue as to the applicability of the Act. There is for these purposes no difference between a building contract for a small house and one for a large block. Although the appellants' predecessor doubtless employed a team of experts to supervise the site at the time of building, the respondents could easily still have concealed the defects from them. Accordingly, it was wrong to hold at this stage that the appellants' predecessor or its agent must or should with reasonable diligence have discovered the defect in 1961 (*King* v. *Victor Parsons* [1973] C.L.Y. 29 applied). *Per curiam*: if a claim for negligence were to be added the test for limitation would be very different: LEWISHAM LONDON BOROUGH v. LESLIE & Co. (1979) 250 E.G. 1289, C.A.

1665. Dismissal of action—relevance of previous action within time limit

[Limitation Act 1939 (c. 21) (as amended by Limitation Act 1975 (c. 54), s. 1), s. 2D.]

Only in the most exceptional case could a plaintiff rely upon s. 2D of the Limitation Act 1939 (as amended) where he had issued an earlier writ on the same cause of action within the limitation period but not proceeded therewith.

In 1971 the plaintiff issued and served a writ claiming damages for injury sustained during his employment by the defendants between 1966 and 1971. No statement of claim was served. New solicitors consulted by the plaintiff wrote in 1973 to the defendants alleging that they were liable and were told by the defendants' insurers that any attempt to proceed would be met with a summons to strike out for want of prosecution. Further solicitors were eventually consulted and they in December 1976 issued a new writ based upon the same cause of action; the defendants entered a conditional appearance thereto and successfully applied to the Master for the striking out of the second writ. Swanwick J., upheld by the Court of Appeal, restored the action upon the plaintiff's undertaking to discontinue the original proceedings, the appellate court considering that the plaintiff was entitled to have tried whether he could rely upon the proviso in s. 2D of the 1939 Act. *Held*, allowing the defendants' appeal, that the plaintiff having originally started an action within the primary limitation period, any application by him to bring himself within the terms of s. 2D failed *in limine*; only in the most exceptional circumstances, such as where the original action had not been proceeded with due to some impropriety

on the part of the defendants, could such a plaintiff succeed under s. 2D. (Decision of Court of Appeal [1978] C.L.Y. 1845 reversed; *Birkett* v. *James* [1977] C.L.Y. 2410 considered.)
WALKLEY *v.* PRECISION FORGINGS [1979] 1 W.L.R. 606, H.L.

1666. Expiry of time—negligence of solicitors—whether plaintiff prejudiced
[Limitation Act 1939 (c. 21), s. 2 D.] Plaintiff's cause of action for damages for negligence against D2 became statute-barred by the negligence of his solicitors D1; he issued a writ against D1 and later added D2, relying on the " disapplying " provisions of s. 2D of the Limitation Act 1939. It was conceded that plaintiff had not suffered prejudice by D1's negligence since he had a cause of action against them as well as against D2. *Held*, that the action should not be allowed to continue against D2. (*Firman* v. *Ellis* [1978] C.L.Y. 1848 considered): BROWES *v.* JONES & MIDDLETON (A FIRM) (1979) 123 S.J. 489, C.A.

1667. —— second plaintiff added—Hague Rules
[Can.] An action arose out of alleged damage to cargo while in transit, which was commenced within the one-year period limited by the Hague Rules. *Held*, an order could be made to add another party as plaintiff (who was in fact the owner of the goods for a certain period of the time of carriage) (*Marubeni* v. *Pearlstone Shipping* [1977] C.L.Y. 2350 applied): BALFOUR GUTHRIE (CANADA) *v.* VICTORIA SHIPPING (1978) 91 D.L.R. (3d) 88, Brit.Col.Sup.Ct.

1668. Extension of time limit—personal injuries
[Limitation Act 1975 (c. 54), s. 2.]. The appellant was a labourer who, between 1972 and 1974, was employed by the respondents in work which brought him into contact with epoxy resin, a notorious substance likely to cause dermatitis, which in fact the appellant contracted. By December 1973 he knew that he had dermatitis and by May 1974, he knew that this was because of his contact with epoxy resin during this work. The appellant did not know until February 1979 that he might in law, have a cause of action. A writ was issued forthwith and the question of whether the claim was statute barred was tried by consent as a preliminary issue upon affidavits. Boreham J. held that the claim was statute barred. S. 2A (vi) repealed the previous state of the law so that his lack of knowledge that in law he had a claim no longer prevented the running of the three-year limitation period. Although it was held that s. 2D and the court's power to override the time limits could be relied upon, in accordance with s. 2D (iii) (a) the reasons for the delay on the part of the appellant in this case meant that it would be inequitable to allow the action to proceed, having regard to the prejudice to the plaintiff arising from s. 2A being outweighed by the prejudice to the employers because of the delay. The Court of Appeal *held*, dismissing the appeal although section 2D (iii) still enabled a plaintiff to rely on his lack of knowledge that in law there might be a cause of action, and while each case had to be decided on its own facts, in this case the employee's own knowledge of the nature and cause of his dermatitis (in respect of which, generally, there has been previous litigation so it was not an uncommon circumstance), and the fact that he was a member of a union and therefore had access to legal advice even if he did not take it, did not justify the delay in comparison to the prejudice resulting to the employers, albeit that the intention of the 1975 Act was primarily to assist potential plaintiffs: CASEY *v.* J. MURPHY & SONS, December 13, 1979, C.A. (*Ex rel. R. Thorn, Esq., Barrister.*)

1669. —— —— alternative action available
On October 15, 1974, P injured his back when moving tools. He consulted solicitors in June 1977, and a letter before action dated June 14, 1977, was sent to the defendants. Considerable correspondence took place between June 1977 and June 1978 between the plaintiff's solicitors and the defendants' insurers but at no time did the insurers admit or deny liability. In March 1978 the insurers stated in a letter that they had completed their investigations. By an oversight the plaintiff's solicitors failed to issue a protective writ prior to October 14, 1977. The plaintiff applied to override the normal limitation period under s. 2D of the Limitation Act 1975. At the trial the plaintiff gave evidence

to the effect that he would not wish to sue his solicitors because they had done conveyancing transactions for him previously and he did not think it right for him to sue them. The defendants admitted that they had not been prejudiced but contended that the plaintiff had not either as he had a remedy against his solicitors. *Held,* the court would exercise its discretion in favour of P. He had been prejudiced in that he would have to start a new action against his solicitors and he did not wish to do so (dictum of Ormrod L.J. in *Firman* v. *Ellis* [1978] C.L.Y. 1848 applied): RIGBY v. SMITH & JOHNSON, October 17, 1979; Mais J.; Leeds Crown Ct. (*Ex rel. J. Behrens, Esq., Barrister.*)

1670. Unreasonable delay—action in negligence against solicitors
[Limitation Act 1939 (c. 21), s. 2D.] In May 1975 the plaintiff sustained personal injuries when he was a passenger in a car being driven by the defendant. In March 1978 he consulted solicitors who notified the insurers of his claim for damages. No admission of liability was made by the insurers, nor were there any negotiations for settlement. The solicitors failed to issue a writ within the three-year period. The plaintiff then consulted fresh solicitors, who issued and served a writ on the defendant. The defendant applied for the action to be dismissed on the ground that it was statute-barred and at about the same time the plaintiff made an application for leave to proceed with the action pursuant to s. 2D of the Limitation Act 1975. *Held,* that it would not be equitable to exercise discretion under s. 2D in favour of the plaintiff, who appeared to have an unanswerable case in negligence against the first solicitors. There was therefore no prejudice to the plaintiff, but there would be prejudice to the defendant if the action were to be allowed to continue. Action accordingly dismissed: MEAD v. MEAD, September 18, 1979; Milmo J.; Cardiff Crown Ct. (*Ex rel. Messrs. Swain & Co., Solicitors.*)

1671. —— defence of limitation—prejudice to defendants
[Limitation Act 1939 (c. 21), s. 2D (as inserted by Limitation Act 1975 (c. 54), s. 1).] The plaintiff claimed damage for personal injuries sustained in an accident at his place of work on September 22, 1974. He consulted a solicitor in February 1975 who advised him that he had three years in which to make up his mind whether to proceed. He returned to work although severely incapacitated and took no action hoping that he would recover from his injuries. In August 1976 he was informed by the D.H.S.S. Board that he was 70 per cent. disabled. He did not tell his employers of the extent of his injuries until February 1977, because he was fearful of losing his job. In March 1977 he again saw the solicitor who had advised him in 1975 and applied for legal aid. In June 1977 he instructed his solicitor "to do whatever was necessary." Although the solicitor sent a letter to the defendants' solicitors in June 1977, he took no further action until September 1978. A writ was issued on November 10, 1978. The Statement of Claim was served on April 5, 1979, by new solicitors. The defence was served on August 8, 1979, contending that the action was statute barred. The defendants deposed on affidavit that they would be prejudiced and their evidence less cogent, *inter alia,* because documents had been destroyed or lost, witnesses might not be found and the *locus in quo* had been altered, although the insurers had inspected the *locus in quo* and taken a statement from a witness in October 1974. Counsel for the defendants made the insurance file available to the court. *Held,* on a preliminary point, that it would be equitable to allow the action to proceed and that the paragraph in the defence relying upon the Limitation Act was to be struck out. It was not clear that the plaintiff could succeed against his former solicitor as there was a possibility of a misunderstanding and the prejudice to the plaintiff, if s. 2A was not disapplied was likely to be serious. Although the plaintiff had not acted promptly he had acted reasonably in all the circumstances. The defendants were not likely to be so prejudiced as they had investigated the accident within five weeks of its occurrence. There was a reasonable likelihood of witnesses being traced and of them having good recollections as the accident was a memorable one (*Buck* v. *English Electric* [1977] C.L.Y. 1802 considered; *Firman* v. *Ellis* [1978] C.L.Y. 1848 followed): STANNARD v. STONAR SCHOOL, August 13, 1979, Judge Hawser. (*Ex rel. Keith Hornby, Esq., Barrister.*)

LITERARY AND SCIENTIFIC INSTITUTIONS

1672. British Museum

BRITISH MUSEUM (AUTHORISED REPOSITORIES) ORDER 1979 (No. 1086) [10p], made under the British Museum Act 1963 (c. 24), s. 10 (2); operative on September 25, 1979; adds certain adjacent premises to the authorised repository of the British Museum in Orsman Road.

1673. Public Lending Right Act 1979 (c. 10)

This Act provides for public lending right for authors.

S. 1 deals with the establishment of public lending right; s. 2 relates to the Central Fund; s. 3 provides for the administration of the scheme; s. 4 establishes a register of books and their authors; s. 5 deals with citation and interpretation. The Act extends to Northern Ireland.

The Act received the Royal Assent on March 22, 1979, and comes into force on a day to be appointed.

ARTICLES. See *post*, p. [26].

LOANS

1674. Moneylenders. See MONEYLENDERS.

LOCAL GOVERNMENT

1675. Allowances to members

LOCAL GOVERNMENT (ALLOWANCES TO MEMBERS) (PRESCRIBED BODIES) REGULATIONS 1979 (No. 1122) [10p], made under the Local Government Act 1972 (c. 70), s. 177 (2) (c); operative on October 5, 1979; prescribe the Clifton Suspension Bridge Trust for the purposes of ss. 173, 174 and 176 of the 1972 Act.

LOCAL GOVERNMENT (ALLOWANCES) (AMENDMENT) REGULATIONS 1979 (No. 1565) [10p], made under the Local Government Act 1972, ss. 173, 178; operative on December 29, 1979; increase the maximum rate of attendance allowance payable to members of a local authority for the performance of an approved duty.

1676. Armorial bearings

LOCAL AUTHORITIES (ARMORIAL BEARINGS) ORDER 1979 (No. 909) [10p], made under the Local Government Act 1972 (c. 70), s. 247; operative on August 14, 1979; confers on the Town Council of Hexham the right to bear and use the armorial bearings formerly borne and used by the Hexham U.D.C.

1677. Bailiffs—powers—distress for rates—damages. See MUNROE AND MUNROE *v.* WOODSPRING DISTRICT COUNCIL, § 2226.

1678. Boundaries

HARFORD AND IVYBRIDGE (AREAS) ORDER 1979 (No. 90) [10p], made under the Local Government Act 1972 (c. 70), ss. 47, 48 (8), 51 (1) (2); operative for the purposes of art. 2 on February 14, 1979, and operative for all other purposes on April 1, 1979; transfers part of the Parish of Harford in the District of South Hams to the Parish of Ivybridge in the same district.

1679. —— new proposals—objective of electoral equality—ratio of electors to councillors

[Local Government Act 1972 (c. 70), s. 47 (1), Sched. 11, para. 3 (2) (a).]

The only proposals for change the boundary commission are authorised to make are those which appear desirable in the interests of effective and convenient local government; the commission must first make a decision on these grounds and only then give effect to the requirements of Sched. 11, para. 3 (2) to the Local Government Act 1972 to secure, as nearly as possible, electoral equality.

The Local Government Boundary Commission in making proposals for electoral changes in a London borough adopted a scheme put forward by a local political party in preference to one put forward by the borough council. The council's scheme was reasonably practicable and provided for a greater degree of electoral equality. The council applied for a declaration that the proposals were invalid as they did not comply with the requirement in para. 3 (2) (*a*) of Sched. 11. The judge granted the declaration, he was reversed on appeal, and on further appeal, *held*, dismissing the appeal, it was the duty of the commission first to consider a scheme and make proposals in the interests of effective and convenient local government, and subsequently to give effect to para. 3 (2) as far as practicable.

ENFIELD LONDON BOROUGH *v.* LOCAL GOVERNMENT BOUNDARY COMMISSION FOR ENGLAND [1979] 3 All E.R. 747, H.L.

1680. Breach of statutory duty—remedy. See WYATT *v.* HILLINGDON LONDON BOROUGH COUNCIL, § 1854.

1681. By-laws—parks regulations—no dogs allowed—whether oppressive. See BURNLEY BOROUGH COUNCIL *v.* ENGLAND, § 2010.

1682. Compulsory purchase. See COMPULSORY PURCHASE.

1683. Diseases of animals. See ANIMALS.

1684. Education. See EDUCATION.

1685. Electoral divisions

Orders made under the Local Government Act 1972 (c. 70), s. 51 (1): S.I. 1979 Nos. 710 (Borough of Great Yarmouth) [30p]; 1015 (District of North Wiltshire) [20p]; 1016 (District of Waverley) [20p]; 1027 (Borough of Doncaster) [20p]; 1028 (Borough of Trafford) [20p]; 1071 (District of Wealden) [20p]; 1107 (District of Newbury) [20p]; 1108 (District of West Wiltshire) [20p]; 1109 (District of Teesdale) [20p]; 1110 (District of Ryedale) [20p]; 1111 (District of Lewis) [20p]; 1112 (District of Harborough) [20p]; 1113 (City of Kingston upon Hull) [20p]; 1131 (City of Carlisle) [20p]; 1264 (District of Sedgefield) [20p]; 1265 (District of Wear Valley) [20p]; 1266 (Borough of Worthing) [20p]; 1295 (District of West Norfolk) [20p]; 1320 (Borough of Calderdale) [20p]; 1321 (Borough of Bolton) [20p]; 1322 (City of Coventry) [20p]; 1323 (Borough of Rotherham) [20p]; 1324 (Borough of Stockport) [20p]; 1327 (Borough of Harrogate) [40p]; 1328 (District of Warwick) [20p]; 1341 (Borough of Rochdale) [20p]; 1346 (Borough of Reading) [20p]; 1347 (Borough of Poole) [10p]; 1348 (Borough of St. Helens) [20p]; 1349 (District of East Devon) [10p]; 1368 (Borough of Tameside) [20p]; 1411 (City of Liverpool) [20p]; 1472 (Borough of Walsall) [20p]; 1473 (City of Exeter) [20p]; 1474 (City of Leicester) [40p]; 1494 (City of Portsmouth) [20p]; 1495 (District of Stroud [40p]; 1496 (Borough of Torbay) [20p]; 1523 (Borough of Wirral) [20p]; 1524 (Borough of Wigan) [20p]; 1685 (Borough of Cheltenham) [20p]; 1615 (City of Sheffield) [20p]; 1616 (City of Leeds) [20p]; 1663 (Borough of North Bedfordshire) [20p]; 1670 (Borough of Restormel) [20p]; 1695 (Borough of Wellingborough) [20p].

1686. Gypsies

GYPSY ENCAMPMENTS (DESIGNATION OF THE LONDON BOROUGH OF LAMBETH) ORDER 1979 (No. 419) [10p], made under the Caravan Sites Act 1968 (c. 52), s. 12 (1); operative on April 26, 1979; designates Lambeth as an area to which s. 10 of the 1968 Act applies.

GYPSY ENCAMPMENTS (DESIGNATION OF THE LONDON BOROUGH OF LEWIS-HAM) ORDER 1979 (No. 420) [10p], made under the Caravan Sites Act 1968, s. 12 (1); operative on April 26, 1979; designates Lewisham as an area to which s. 10 of the 1968 Act applies.

1687. Highways. See HIGHWAYS AND BRIDGES.

1688. Housing. See HOUSING.

1689. Land drainage. See LAND DRAINAGE.

1690. Local authorities

LOCAL AUTHORITIES (MISCELLANEOUS PROVISION) ORDER 1979 (No. 1123) [40p], made under the Local Government Act 1972 (c. 70), s. 254 (1) (*a*) and (2) (*a*)–(*c*), operative on October 5, 1979; provides for the amendment of certain Acts, the variation of orders for grouping parishes and communities, the admissibility as prima facie evidence of copies of or extracts from maps relating to changes of areas, certain franchise rights and the transfer of certain property.

1691. —— **contracts—repudiation of contract by newly elected council.** See DEVON-PORT BOROUGH COUNCIL v. ROBBINS, § 342.

1692. —— **salary—discretionary payment—implied term.** See SMITH v. STOCKPORT METROPOLITAN BOROUGH COUNCIL, § 905.

1693. Local commissioner—complaint—jurisdiction
    [Children and Young Persons Act 1963 (c. 37), s. 1; Local Government Act 1974 (c. 7), ss. 26, 34.]
    The Local Commissioner is entitled to investigate a complaint of injustice as a result of inefficient or improper administration and it is sufficient for a complainant to specify the action of the local authority in connection with which the complaint of maladministration was made.
    The two children of M were taken into care by the local authority in 1975. The father of the children, F, with whom M had been living, was sent to prison. M subsequently lost touch with F but formed an attachment with F's father H who divorced his wife and married M in 1977. M's earlier attempts to get her children back had failed and in 1977 she complained about the local authority's actions, first to a local councillor and secondly to the Local Commissioner, who decided to investigate them and who formulated four grounds of complaint. The local authority applied for an order of prohibition. A declaration was granted that the Local Commissioner was entitled to continue grounds 1, 2, and 4 but not 3. On appeal by the local authority and cross appeal by the Local Commissioner, *held,* dismissing the appeal and allowing the cross appeal, that the Local Commissioner had properly exercised his over-riding discretion to investigate the complaints; that M had no "remedy by way of proceedings in any court of law"; and that it was sufficient for M to specify the action of the local authority in connection with which the complaint of maladministration was made.
    R. v. LOCAL COMMISSIONER FOR ADMINISTRATION FOR THE NORTH AND EAST AREA OF ENGLAND, *ex p.* BRADFORD METROPOLITAN CITY COUNCIL [1979] 2 W.L.R. 1, C.A.

1694. Local enactments
    CITY OF DERBY (LOCAL ACT REPEALS) ORDER 1979 (No. 805) [10p], made under the Local Government (Miscellaneous Provisions) Act 1976 (c. 57), s. 81; operative on August 13, 1979; Pt. II of the 1976 Act having been adopted by the Derby City Council, those provisions of the Derby Corporation Act 1972 that are specified as being inconsistent with it or unnecessary are repealed.
    CITY OF LIVERPOOL (LOCAL ACTS REPEALS) ORDER 1979 (No. 806) [20p], made under the Local Government (Miscellaneous Provisions) Act 1976, s. 81; operative on August 13, 1979; Pt. II of the 1976 Act having been adopted by the Liverpool City Council, those provisions of the Liverpool Corporation Act 1972 that are specified as being inconsistent with it or unnecessary are repealed.

1695. London. See LONDON.

1696. Metropolitan counties
    METROPOLITAN COUNTIES (LOCAL STATUTORY PROVISIONS) ORDER 1979 (No. 969) [10p], made under the Local Government Act 1972 (c. 70), s. 262 (9) (b); operative on August 30, 1979; postpones to December 31, 1980, the date on which local statutory provisions applying to metropolitan counties cease to have effect.

1697. National health service. See NATIONAL HEALTH.

1698. Negligence—exercise of statutory powers—inspection of foundations. See MARSH v. BETSTYLE CONSTRUCTION AND THE GREATER LONDON COUNCIL, § 1875.

1699. —— **statutory duty—remoteness of damage.** See TRAPPA HOLDINGS v. DISTRICT OF SURREY, § 1890.

1700. Northern Ireland. See NORTHERN IRELAND.

1701. Pensions. See PENSIONS AND SUPERANNUATION.

1702. Public health. See PUBLIC HEALTH.

1703. Rating. See RATING AND VALUATION.

1704. Rent. See RENT RESTRICTION.

1705. Reorganisation—contract with transport company—whether implied term as to termination—whether contract frustrated. See KIRKLEES METROPOLITAN BOROUGH COUNCIL *v.* YORKSHIRE WOOLLEN DISTRICT TRANSPORT CO., § 345.

1706. Scilly Isles
ISLES OF SCILLY (FUNCTIONS) ORDER 1979 (No. 72) [20p], made under the Local Government Act 1972 (c. 70), ss. 265, 266 (2); operative on March 1, 1979; makes provision for the exercise and performance of functions contained in existing orders made under the Local Government Act 1933 and provides for the exercise and performance by the Council of the Scilly Isles of the functions imposed on district councils by the Local Land Charges Act 1975.

1707. Sewerage. See PUBLIC HEALTH.

1708. Shops. See SHOPS.

1709. Town and country planning. See TOWN AND COUNTRY PLANNING.

1710. Water. See WATER AND WATERWORKS.

BOOKS AND ARTICLES. See *post*, pp. [8], [26].

LONDON

1711. Greater London Council
GREATER LONDON COUNCIL HOUSING (STAFF TRANSFER AND PROTECTION) ORDER 1979 (No. 1737) [50p], made under the London Government Act 1963 (c. 33), ss. 84, 85; operative on January 2, 1980; makes general provisions for the transfer of certain employees of the Greater London Council to certain other authorities.

1712. Justices of the Peace Act 1979. See § 1732.

MAGISTERIAL LAW

1713. Application for summons—locus standi of defendant—whether magistrate has discretion to hear him
[Magistrates' Courts Act 1952 (c. 55), s. 1 (1).]
A proposed defendant to a summons has no *locus standi* on the application for the summons, but the justices may, in the exercise of their discretion under s. 1 (1) of the Magistrates' Courts Act 1952 as to whether to issue the summons, hear representations from the proposed defendant if they consider it necessary.

A, the applicant, was a solicitor who had represented X as plaintiff in a county court action against C, the complainant. X won the action. C brought an action against X alleging conspiracy to injure him by giving false evidence. C sought to join A, and the application was dismissed with costs as disclosing no cause of action. C then applied to the metropolitan stipendiary magistrate for a summons against A, alleging perjury. A applied to be heard on the application. The magistrate took the view that he had no power to hear A, and even if he had, he would not have done so. A sought an order of mandamus directed to the magistrate to hear and determine A's objection to the issue of the summons. *Held*, refusing the application, that although the magistrate had a residual discretion to hear the proposed defendant when considering in his discretion whether to issue the summons, the proposed defendant had no *locus standi* and no right to be heard. (Dictum of Lord Goddard C.J. in *R.* v. *Wilson, ex p. Battersea Borough Council* (1947) C.L.C. 5952 applied.)

R. *v.* WEST LONDON JUSTICES, *ex p.* KLAHN [1979] 2 All E.R. 221, D.C.

1714. Binding over—common law—firearms—forfeiture or disposal
[Highways Act 1959 (c. 25), s. 140; Firearms Act 1968 (c. 27), ss. 52 (1) (*b*); Justices of the Peace Act 1361 (c. 1).] G was convicted of discharging a firearm within 50 feet of the highway contrary to s. 140 of 1959 Act. He was bound over under the 1361 Act on condition that he did not possess, carry or use a firearm, and arms and ammunition seized were ordered to be

forfeited and sold under s. 52 (1) (*b*) of the 1968 Act, which permits such an order where a condition of not possessing, using or carrying a firearm is attached to a binding over. *Held*, deleting the condition and revoking the forfeiture and sale orders, that s. 52 (1) (*b*) was applicable only to a common law binding over as a binding over under the 1361 Act could not have conditions attached (*Lister* v. *Morgan* [1978] C.L.Y. 1896 considered): GOODLAD *v.* CHIEF CONSTABLE OF SOUTH YORKSHIRE [1979] Crim.L.R. 51, Sheffield Crown Ct.

1715. Committal for sentence—child attaining 15 between dates of finding of guilt and committal
[Magistrates' Courts Act 1952 (c. 55), s. 28.] T attained 15 years of age between the date of his being found guilty and the date of his committal to the Crown Court for sentence with a recommendation for Borstal training under s. 28 of the 1952 Act. *Held*, that the committal was defective as there was only power to commit under s. 28 if T was 15 at the date of conviction. The date of conviction was the date of the finding of guilt, not the date of committal. (*S.* (*An Infant*) v. *Manchester City Recorder* [1969] C.L.Y. 2189 considered): R. *v.* T. (A JUVENILE) [1979] Crim.L.R. 588, Snaresbrook Crown Ct.

1716. Committal proceedings—criminal libel—evidence of bad reputation of prosecutor—whether admissible. See R. *v.* WELLS STREET STIPENDIARY MAGISTRATE, *ex p.* DEAKIN, § 451.

1717. ⸺ driving whilst disqualified—when proceedings " commenced "
[Criminal Law Act 1977 (c. 45), ss. 16, 65; Criminal Law Act (Commencement No. 5) Order 1978 (S.I. 1978 No. 712), para. 2 (2).]
Proceedings are " commenced," in the case of an arrest without warrant, when the detainee is charged at a police station and not upon his first court appearance.
In May 1978 the defendant was arrested and charged at a police station with driving whilst disqualified; he was bailed therefrom to appear at court in August 1978. Upon that occasion the justices committed him for sentence to the Crown Court, being of the opinion that the proceedings had been " commenced " at the hearing and that their powers under the 1977 Act which came into force in July 1978 were applicable. The Crown Court declined jurisdiction to hear the committal. The justices thereupon declined to sentence on the grounds that the committal was valid. *Held*, ordering the justices to sentence the defendant, that the proceedings had been commenced when the defendant was charged and that accordingly the court's powers were restricted to those under the 1952 Magistrates' Courts Act.
R. *v.* BRENTWOOD JUSTICES, *ex p.* JONES [1979] R.T.R. 155, D.C.

1718. ⸺ prior reading of papers by magistrate
[Magistrates' Courts Act 1952 (c. 55), s. 4 (3); Magistrates' Courts Rules 1968 (S.I. 1968 No. 1920), r. 58 (2).]
There is no provision in either the Magistrates' Courts Act or Rules which forbids the supply of the prosecution statements to the court before committal proceedings commence, nor is it in breach of the rules of natural justice.
The applicants were charged with various offences, and during the committal proceedings the magistrate stated that he had been supplied with and read the prosecution statements before the proceedings began. The documents contained matters highly prejudicial to the defendants. The magistrate refused to discharge himself and committed the defendants for trial. On application for certiorari, *held*, dismissing the application, that (1) perusal of the documents in advance was not a tendering of evidence in the absence of the accused; and (2) such practice was perfectly valid and not in breach of the rules of natural justice. (*Metropolitan Properties* v. *Lannon* [1968] C.L.Y. 3372 applied.)
R. *v.* COLCHESTER STIPENDIARY MAGISTRATE, *ex p.* BECK [1979] 2 W.L.R. 637, D.C.

1719. Domestic courts
DOMESTIC COURTS (CONSTITUTION) RULES (No. 757 (L. 6)) [20p], made under the Justices of the Peace Act 1949 (s. 101), s. 15, as extended by the

Magistrates' Courts Act 1952 (c. 55), s. 56A; operative on July 27, 1979; provide for setting up domestic court panels in arcas outside inner London.

DOMESTIC COURTS (CONSTITUTION) (INNER LONDON) RULES 1979 (No. 758 (L. 7)) [30p], made under the Justices of the Peace Act 1949, s. 15, as extended by the Magistrates' Courts Act 1952, s. 56A; operative on July 27, 1979; provide for setting up domestic court panels for the inner London boroughs and the City of London.

1720. Domestic Proceedings and Magistrates' Courts Act 1978—commencement
DOMESTIC PROCEEDINGS AND MAGISTRATES' COURTS ACT 1978 (COMMENCEMENT NO. 3) ORDER 1979 (No. 731 (C. 15)) [30p], made under the Domestic Proceedings and Magistrates' Courts Act 1978 (c. 22), s. 89 (3) and (4); brings into operation s. 40 of the 1978 Act and the provisions of that Act mentioned in Sched. 1, on September 17 and November 1, 1979.

1721. Food and drugs. See FOOD AND DRUGS.

1722. Forms
MAGISTRATES' COURTS (FORMS) (AMENDMENT) RULES 1979 (No. 1220 (L. 16)) [40p], made under the Justices of the Peace Act 1949 (c. 101), s. 15 as extended by the Magistrates' Courts Act 1952 (c. 55), s. 122 and the Domestic Proceedings and Magistrates' Courts Act 1978 (c. 22), s. 17 (2); operative on November 1, 1979; amend S.I. 1968 No. 1919 in consequence of ss. 16 to 18 of the 1978 Act.

1723. Gaming. See GAMING AND WAGERING.

1724. Highways. See HIGHWAYS AND BRIDGES.

1725. Indictable offences. See CRIMINAL LAW.

1726. Information—wrong section referred to—validity of conviction. See LEE *v.* WILTSHIRE CHIEF CONSTABLE, § 2313.

1727. Jurisdiction—common law offence—obscene publications—effect of 1977 Act
[Criminal Law Act 1977 (c. 45), s. 53; Obscene Publications Act 1959 (c. 66), s. 1.] G was served in November 1977 with a summons for keeping a disorderly house contrary to the common law. On December 1, 1977, s. 53 of the 1977 Act which converted the offence into a statutory one and provided that a person "shall not be proceeded against" for common law offences involving obscene cinematograph publications, came into effect. *Held*, that the stipendiary magistrate was correct in holding that since there were no transitional provisions in the Act he had no jurisdiction to hear the information: R. *v.* WELLS STREET STIPENDIARY MAGISTRATES, *ex p.* GOLDING [1979] Crim.L.R. 254, D.C.

1728. Justices—committal proceedings—review by Divisional Court—lower court proceedings incomplete
The Divisional Court has no jurisdiction to review a decision of justices in committal proceedings until the termination of such proceedings.

During committal proceedings the prosecution sought to adduce, as similar fact evidence, evidence of other offences allegedly committed by the defendant. The justices declined to admit such evidence and adjourned the proceedings. The prosecution sought to quash such ruling during the adjournment. *Held*, refusing the application, that until the committal proceedings had been terminated, the court had no jurisdiction to review decisions made during the course thereof. (*R.* v. *Carden* (1879) 5 Q.B.D. 1, applied.)
R. *v.* ROCHFORD JUSTICES, *ex p.* BUCK (1978) 68 Cr.App.R. 114, D.C.

1729. —— prison disciplinary hearing—whether visiting justice's decision reviewable. See DAEMAR *v.* HALL, § 535.

1730. —— selection procedure—complaint of sex discrimination. See KNIGHT *v.* ATT.-GEN., § 943.

1731. Justices' clerks
JUSTICES' CLERKS (QUALIFICATIONS OF ASSISTANTS) RULES 1979 (No. 570 L. 5)) [20p], made under the Justices of the Peace Act 1949 (c. 101), s. 15, as extended by the Justices of the Peace Act 1968 (c. 69), s. 5 (2); operative on October 1, 1980; make provision for the qualifications required for a person to be employed to assist a justices' clerk as a clerk in a magistrates' court.

1732. Justices of the Peace Act 1979 (c. 55)

This Act consolidates certain enactments relating to justices of the peace (including stipendiary magistrates), justices' clerks and the administrative and financial arrangements for magistrates' courts.

Pt. I (ss. 1–16) contains general provisions: s. 1 defines commission areas; s. 2 specifies London commission areas; s. 3 gives power to adjust London commission areas; s. 4 outlines petty sessions areas; s. 5 relates to general form of commissions of the peace; s. 6 provides for the appointment and removal of justices of the peace; s. 7 sets out residence qualifications; s. 8 provides for the keeping of a supplemental list for England and Wales; s. 9 deals with the removal of a name from the supplemental list; s. 10 outlines the effect of the entry of a name in the supplemental list; s. 11 deals with records of justices of the peace; s. 12 makes provision for travelling, subsistence and financial loss allowances; s. 13 relates to the appointment and removal of stipendiary magistrates; s. 14 provides for the retirement of stipendiary magistrates; s. 15 authorises the appointment of acting stipendiary magistrates; s. 16 outlines the place of sitting and powers of stipendiary magistrates.

Pt. II (ss. 17–30) provides for the organisation of functions of justices: s. 17 deals with the appointment of a chairman and deputy chairmen of justices; s. 18 sets out rules as to chairmanship and size of bench; s. 19 contains general provisions as to magistrates' courts committees; s. 20 sets out the constitution of magistrates' courts committees; s. 21 specifies the powers of the Secretary of State in relation to magistrates' courts committees; s. 22 contains supplementary provisions as to such committees; s. 23 outlines the powers and duties of a committee as to petty sessional divisions; s. 24 deals with the procedure relating to s. 23; s. 25 provides for the appointment and removal of justices' clerks; s. 26 sets out the qualifications for appointment as justices' clerk; s. 27 deals with the conditions of service and staff of justices' clerks; s. 28 outlines the general powers and duties of justices' clerks; s. 29 specifies the functions of justices' clerks as collecting officers; s. 30 relates to a person acting as substitute clerk to justices.

Pt. III (ss. 31–38) deals with the inner London area: s. 31 provides for the appointment, removal and retirement of metropolitan stipendiary magistrates; s. 32 relates to the allocation and sittings of metropolitan stipendiary magistrates; s. 33 sets out the jurisdiction of metropolitan stipendiary magistrates and lay justices; s. 34 provides for an acting metropolitan stipendiary magistrate; s. 35 deals with the setting up of a committee of magistrates for the inner London area; s. 36 makes provision for petty sessional divisions in the inner London area; s. 37 deals with justices' clerks and other officers; s. 38 outlines other functions for which the committee is or may be responsible.

Pt. IV (ss. 39–43) deals with the City of London: s. 39 provides for *ex officio* and appointed justices; s. 40 relates to the chairman and deputy chairmen of justices; s. 41 deals with application of enactments to the City; s. 42 states that there shall be no petty sessional divisions in the City; s. 43 provides for the keeping of records of appointed justices for the City.

Pt. V (ss. 44–54) provides for the protection of justices and indemnification of justices and justices' clerks; s. 44 relates to acts done within jurisdiction; s. 45 deals with acts outside or in excess of jurisdiction; s. 46 makes provision as to warrants granted on a conviction or order made by another justice; s. 47 deals with the exercise of discretionary powers; s. 48 provides for compliance with, or confirmation on appeal to, a superior court; s. 49 deals with distress warrants for rates; s. 50 provides that where action is prohibited, proceedings may be set aside; s. 51 states that no action shall be brought in the county court if the defendant justice objects; s. 52 imposes a limitation on damages; s. 53 relates to indemnification of justices and justices' clerks; s. 54 contains provisions as to prerogative proceedings and membership of Crown Court.

Pt. VI (ss. 55–62) makes administrative and financial arrangements: s. 55 outlines the duties of local authorities outside Greater London; s. 56 contains provisions supplementary to s. 55; s. 57 deals with the application of ss. 55 and 56 to outer London areas and the City of London; s. 58 makes corresponding arrangements in the inner London area; s. 59 deals with grants by the Secretary of State to responsible authorities; s. 60 makes special provision as to grants to the Greater London Council; s. 61 deals with the application of fines and fees; s. 62 relate to defaults of justices' clerks and their staffs.

Pt. VII (ss. 63–72) contains miscellaneous and supplementary provisions: s. 63 provides for courses of instruction; s. 64 outlines the disqualification in certain cases of justices who are members of local authorities; s. 65 states that justices are not disqualified by reason of their being ratepayers; s. 66 deals with acts done by justices outside their commission area; s. 67 relates to the promissory oaths of certain justices; s. 68 contains provisions relating to Greater Manchester, Merseyside and Lancashire; s. 69 relates to the Isles of Scilly; s. 70 is the interpretation section; s. 71 contains transitional provisions and savings, amendments and repeals; s. 72 contains the short title, commencement and extent.

The Act received the Royal Assent on December 6, 1979, and came into force on March 6, 1980.

1733. Juvenile courts
JUVENILE COURTS (CONSTITUTION) (AMENDMENT) RULES 1979 (No. 952 (L. 8)) [10p], made under the Justices of the Peace Act 1949 (c. 101), s. 15 as extended by the Children and Young Persons Act 1969 (c. 54), s. 61; operative on October 1, 1979; amend S.I. 1954 No. 1711 by providing that members of a juvenile court panel shall commence their service from January 1 instead of November 1, following the date of their appointment.

1734. —— evidence—cross-examination by parent. See R. *v.* MILTON KEYNES JUSTICES, *ex p.* R., § 1791.

1735. Maintenance orders
MAGISTRATES' COURTS (RECIPROCAL ENFORCEMENT OF MAINTENANCE ORDERS) (AMENDMENT) RULES 1979 (No. 170 (L. 4)) [10p], made under the Justices of the Peace Act 1949 (c. 101), s. 15, as extended by the Magistrates' Courts Act 1952 (c. 55), s. 122, and the Maintenance Orders (Reciprocal Enforcement) Act 1972 (c. 18), s. 18 (1); operative on April 1, 1979; amend S.I. 1974 No. 668.

1736. Matrimonial causes. See DIVORCE AND MATRIMONIAL CAUSES.

1737. Northern Ireland. See NORTHERN IRELAND.

1738. Petty Sessional divisions
PETTY SESSIONAL DIVISIONS (ESSEX) ORDER 1979 (No. 1284) [20p], made under the Justices of the Peace Act 1949 (c. 101), s. 18 (1) (3)–(7); operative on January 1, 1980, save for para. 2 to the Sched. which is operative immediately; provides for the petty sessional divisions of Halstead and North Hinckford to be combined to form the new division of Halstead and Hedingham.

1739. Probation
COMBINED PROBATION AND AFTER-CARE AREAS (ESSEX) ORDER 1979 (No. 1285) [10p], made under the Powers of Criminal Courts Act 1973 (c. 62), s. 54 (4), Sched. 3, para. 1, as extended by S.I. 1974 No. 529; operative on January 1, 1980, save for art. 3 which is operative immediately; amends S.I. 1974 No. 529 to take account of the combination of the petty sessional divisions of Halstead and North Hinckford in the new division of Halstead and Hedingham.

1740. Procedure
MAGISTRATES' COURTS (AMENDMENT) RULES 1979 (No. 1221 (L. 17)) [40p], made under the Justices of the Peace Act 1949 (c. 101), s. 15 as extended by the Magistrates' Courts Act 1952 (c. 55), s. 122 and the Domestic Proceedings and Magistrates' Courts Act 1978 (c. 22), s. 17 (2); operative on November 1, 1979; amends S.I. 1968 No. 1920 in consequence of ss. 16 to 18 and s. 77 of the 1978 Act. The provisions relate to the powers of the court to make orders for the protection of a party to a marriage or a child of the family and payments required to be made to a child, etc.

1741. Prosecution—store detective—prosecutor and main witness—failure to take oath —whether justices under duty to assist prosecutor
A store detective appeared in a magistrates' court to prosecute D for shoplifting. She was the only witness for the prosecution. She related the facts from

the witness box and when the chairman asked if she realised she had not been sworn she said she understood she was not giving evidence on oath. A submission of no case to answer was upheld. *Held*, refusing orders of mandamus directing the justices to hear the charge and certiorari to quash their decision, that the justices had power but no duty to rehear the case or remit it to another bench for rehearing in the light of the material irregularity. They had to be careful not to seem to be leaning towards the prosecution: R. *v.* UXBRIDGE JUSTICES, *ex p.* CONLON [1979] Crim.L.R. 250, D.C.

1742. Sentence—increase in penalty after offence

Magistrates fined the defendant for fisheries offences contrary to the Sea Fisheries Regulation Act 1966. After the offences were committed the Fishery Limits Act 1976 was passed, increasing the maximum penalty provided by the 1966 Act. The magistrates purported to apply the new penalty even though the offences took place before the new Act came into force. It was held, that applying *D.P.P.* v. *Lamb* [1941] 2 K.B. 89, they were wrong to do so since in criminal matters the principle was that without clear words new legislation was not retroactive. The matter was remitted to the magistrates for them to impose sentences within their powers: R. *v.* PENRITH JUSTICES, *ex p.* HAY (1979) 123 S.J. 621, D.C.

1743. —— non-payment of fines—defendant in prison—whether notice of hearing necessary

[Criminal Justice Act 1967 (c. 80), s. 44 (6).]

Where an offender is already serving a term of imprisonment, the justices have express authority under the 1967 Act to issue a warrant of commitment without a hearing at which the offender is present.

P was sentenced to a term of imprisonment for failing to pay compensation to the Department of Health and Social Security, but the warrant of commitment was postponed so long as he continued to pay instalments. P was also liable for fines for motoring offences and he was in arrears with both weekly instalments. After P had been convicted at the Crown Court of burglary and sentenced to a term of imprisonment, the justices sentenced him in his absence to terms of imprisonment for default in payment of the fines. On an application for certiorari to quash the order on the ground that it was contrary to natural justice for P not to have been heard or have been legally represented, *held*, dismissing the application (Robert Goff J. dissenting), that since P was already serving a term of imprisonment the justices had express authority under the 1967 Act to issue a warrant of commitment without a hearing at which P was present. *Per* Robert Goff J.: it is fundamental that unless a statute provides otherwise, a citizen should have the opportunity to be heard before a sentence of imprisonment is imposed on him.

R. *v.* DUDLEY JUSTICES, *ex p.* PAYNE [1979] 1 W.L.R. 891, D.C.

1744. Stannaries Court—jurisdiction—power of justices to try tinner. See R. *v.* EAST POWDER JUSTICES, *ex p.* LAMPSHIRE, § 1776.

1745. Sunday trading—moveable market—whether stall a " place " where retail trade is carried on. See NEWARK DISTRICT COUNCIL *v.* E. & A. MARKET PROMOTIONS, § 2503.

1746. Weights and measures. See WEIGHTS AND MEASURES.

BOOKS AND ARTICLES. See *post*, pp. [8], [26].

MARKETS AND FAIRS

1747. Rival market—within seven miles on same day—whether nuisance

There is an irrebuttable presumption that a new market set up to be held on the same day as a franchise market, and within the common law distance of seven miles, is *per se* an actionable nuisance.

T borough had held a franchise of a market from time immemorial. A neighbouring town began to hold a market on the same day within one and a half miles from the franchise market. T borough's application for an injunction was refused on the ground that they had failed to show they had suffered any loss as a result. On a trial on the point as to whether the nuisance was actionable *per se*, *held*, granting the injunction, that the cause of action was complete when the franchise owner established there was a same day market within the common law distance. (*Re Islington Market Bill* (1835) 3 Cl. & F. 513, *Dorchester Corporation* v. *Ensor* (1869) L.R. 4 Exch. 335, *Hammerton* v. *Earl of Dysart* [1916] 1 A.C. 57 applied.)

TAMWORTH BOROUGH COUNCIL *v.* FAZELY TOWN COUNCIL (1978) 77 L.G.R. 238, Vivian Price, Q.C.

ARTICLES. See *post*, p. [26].

MEDICINE

1748. Dangerous drugs

MISUSE OF DRUGS (LICENCE FEES) REGULATIONS 1979 (No. 218) [10p], made under the Misuse of Drugs Act 1971 (c. 38), ss. 30 and 31; operative on April 1, 1979; prescribe the fee payable in relation to a licence to produce, supply, offer to supply or possess controlled drugs.

MISUSE OF DRUGS (AMENDMENT) REGULATIONS 1979 (No. 326) [10p], made under the Misuse of Drugs Act 1971, ss. 7, 10, 31; operative on May 14, 1979; amend S.I. 1973 No. 797 by adding phencyclidine to Sched. 2 to those Regulations.

1749. Dental and surgical materials

MEDICINES (COMMITTEE ON DENTAL AND SURGICAL MATERIALS) AMENDMENT ORDER 1979 (No. 1535) [20p]; made under the Medicines Act 1968 (c. 67), ss. 4, 129 (4); operative on January 1, 1980; amends S.I. 1975 No. 1473 by extending the Committee's functions to cover certain substances and fluids for use with contact lens for human use or the blanks from which such lenses are prepared.

1750. Dentists—disciplinary action—negligence

[Dentists Act 1957 (c. 28), s. 25 (1) (*b*).] A dentist charged with " infamous or disgraceful conduct in a professional respect " should only be found guilty if his conduct deserves the strongest reprobation; mere negligence does not suffice. The penalty provisions of the Act, whereby the only punishment is the erasing of the offender's name from the register, need to be reconsidered (*Felix* v. *General Dental Council* [1960] C.L.Y. 1958 followed): MCENIFF *v.* GENERAL DENTAL COUNCIL, *The Times*, December 1, 1979, P.C.

1751. Fees

MEDICINES (FEES) AMENDMENT REGULATIONS 1979 (No. 899) [20p], made under the Medicines Act 1971 (c. 69), s. 1 (1) (2); operative on September 1, 1979; amend S.I. 1978 No. 1121 so as to increase the fees payable in connection with licenses granted and certificates issued under the Medicines Act 1968.

1752. Food and drugs. See FOOD AND DRUGS.

1753. General Medical Council

GENERAL MEDICAL COUNCIL (REVIEW BOARD FOR OVERSEAS QUALIFIED PRACTITIONERS RULES) ORDER OF COUNCIL 1979 (No. 29) [20p], made under the Medical Act 1978 (c. 12), s. 27; operative on February 15, 1979; the Rules approved by this Order prescribe the constitution, quorum and procedure of the Review Board established to hear applications by medical practitioners with qualifications obtained overseas for a review of certain decisions made by the GMC under s. 28 of the 1978 Act relating to their registration.

GENERAL MEDICAL COUNCIL (CONSTITUTION) ORDER 1979 (No. 112) [20p], made under the Medical Act 1978, s. 1; operative on March 7, 1979; provides for the reconstitution of the General Medical Council on September 27, 1979.

GENERAL MEDICAL COUNCIL (REGISTRATION REGULATIONS) ORDER OF COUNCIL 1979 (No. 844) [40p], made under the Medical Act 1969 (c. 40), s. 4; operative on August 1, 1979; prescribes the conditions under which persons may be included in the Overseas List of the register of medical practitioners maintained by the G.M.C.

GENERAL MEDICAL COUNCIL (QUORUM RULES) ORDER OF COUNCIL 1979 (No. 1358) [10p], made under the Medical Act 1978, s. 1 (14), Sched. 1, para. 4;

operative on November 8, 1979; prescribes the quorum of the G.M.C. as reconstituted under the 1978 Act.

1754. Medical Act 1978—commencement
MEDICAL ACT 1978 (COMMENCEMENT No. 2) ORDER 1979 (No. 920 (C. 24))
[20p], made under the Medical Act 1978 (c. 12), s. 32 (2); brings into force on September 27, 1979, ss. 1 (13) (14), 3, 5, 15, 16, 31 (1) (2) (3) of and Scheds. 1, 6, paras. 1–3, 5–12, 14, 19, 37, 48 (a), 49, 56, 59; 7 to the Act.

1755. Medical practitioners
IRISH REPUBLIC (TERMINATION OF 1927 AGREEMENT) ORDER 1979 (No. 289)
[25p], made under the Medical Act 1978 (c. 12), s. 4; operative on April 30, 1979; make consequential repeals or modifications of legislation concerning doctors and dentists following the termination of the 1927 Agreement that related to reciprocal recognition of qualifications.

1756. —— psychiatrist—report in access proceedings—disagreement with solicitors.
See NOBLE *v.* ROBERT THOMPSON & PARTNERS, § 2163.

1757. —— registration—termination of contract of employment
[Medical Act 1956 (c. 76), s. 28 (1).] Under s. 28 (1) of the Medical Act 1956 no person can hold an appointment as a medical officer in a hospital unless he is fully registered. Accordingly, if a doctor is suspended by the G.M.C. his contract of employment is frustrated and is at an end: TARNESBY *v.* KENSINGTON, CHELSEA & WESTMINSTER AREA HEALTH AUTHORITY (TEACHING) (1978) 123 S.J. 49, Neill J.

1758. Medicinal products
MEDICINES (GENERAL SALE LIST) AMENDMENT ORDER 1979 (No. 315) [50p], made under the Medicines Act 1968 (c. 67), ss. 51, 129 (4); operative on April 12, 1979; amends S.I. 1977 No. 2129 which specifies medical products which can be sold or supplied otherwise than by a pharmacist. The amendments are to include additions to the list.

MEDICINES (CHLOROFORM PROHIBITION) ORDER 1979 (No. 382) [20p], made under the Medicines Act 1968, s. 62; operative on March 28, 1979; prohibits, subject to certain exemptions, the sale or supply of medicinal products which are for human use and which consist of or contain chloroform.

MEDICINES (PRESCRIPTION ONLY) AMENDMENT (No. 2) ORDER 1979 (No. 1040) [10p], made under the Medicines Act 1968, ss. 58 (1), 129 (4); operative on September 7, 1979; amends S.I. 1977 No. 2127 excludes medicinal products containing Tylosin Phosphate from the class of prescription only medicines where the product is sold for incorporation in feed as a growth promoter for pigs.

MEDICINES (EXEMPTION FROM LICENCES) (ASSEMBLY) ORDER 1979 (No. 1114) [20p], made under the Medicines Act 1968, s. 15 (1) and (2); operative on October 2, 1979; exempts certain medicinal products for human use from the restrictions imposed by s. 8 (2) of the 1968 Act on the labelling without a manufacturer's licence of any medicinal product. The Order specifies the persons to whom and the conditions upon which exemption is granted, its duration in certain cases and the circumstances in which it may be terminated by the licensing authority.

MEDICINES (PHENACETIN PROHIBITION) ORDER 1979 (No. 1181) [20p], made under the Medicines Act 1968, s. 62; operative on March 27, 1980; prohibits the sale supply or importation of medicinal products which consist of or contain phenacetin. There are certain specified exceptions to the general prohibition.

MEDICINES (CONTACT LENS FLUIDS AND OTHER SUBSTANCES) (APPOINTED DAY) ORDER 1979 (No. 1539) [10p], made under the Medicines Act 1968, s. 16 (1); appoints January 1, 1980, as the day from which the licensing restrictions on marketing, manufacture and wholesale dealing imposed by ss. 7 and 8 of the 1968 Act and the restrictions imposed by clinical trials imposed by s. 31 of the Act shall apply to certain substances and fluids for use with contact lenses.

MEDICINES (CONTACT LENS FLUIDS AND OTHER SUBSTANCES) (EXEMPTION FROM LICENCES) ORDER 1979 (No. 1585) [20p], made under the Medicines

Act 1968, ss. 13 (2), 15 (1), (2), 23 (4), 35 (8), 129 (4); operative on January 1, 1980; gives exemption from the restriction imposed by s. 8 (2) of the 1968 Act on the labelling of certain fluids for use with contact lenses or blanks.

MEDICINES (CONTACT LENS FLUIDS AND OTHER SUBSTANCES) (EXEMPTION FROM LICENCES) AMENDMENT ORDER 1979 (No. 1745) [20p], made under the Medicines Act 1968, ss. 15 (1), (2), 129 (4); operative on January 1, 1980; provides a definition of "contact lens" for the purposes of the Medicines (Contact Lens Fluids and Other Substances) (Exemption from Licences) Order 1979 (No. 1585).

MEDICINES (CONTACT LENS FLUIDS AND OTHER SUBSTANCES) (LABELLING) REGULATIONS 1979 (No. 1759) [75p], made under the Medicines Act 1968, ss. 85 (1), 86 (1), 91 (2) (3), 129 (5); operative on February 1, 1980; provide special requirements as to the particulars to be furnished with certain substances and fluids for use with contact lenses or blanks which are for sale or supply.

MEDICINES (CONTACT LENS FLUIDS AND OTHER SUBSTANCES) (ADVERTISING AND MISCELLANEOUS AMENDMENTS) REGULATIONS 1979 (No. 1760) [75p], made under the Medicines Act 1968, ss. 18, 36, 95, 96 (6), 129 (1) (5); operative on February 1, 1980; provide requirements as to certain advertisements relating to certain substances and fluids for use with contact lenses or blanks.

1759. National health. See NATIONAL HEALTH.

1760. Northern Ireland. See NORTHERN IRELAND.

1761. Nurses

NURSES AND ENROLLED NURSES (AMENDMENT) RULES APPROVAL INSTRUMENT 1979 (No. 49) [25p], made under the Nurses Act 1957 (c. 15), s. 32; operative on February 22, 1979; amend S.I. 1969 No. 1675, and provide for, *inter alia*, the cessation of reduction in training for the general part of the register or roll, or the part of the register for sick children's nurses in the case of holders of the Thoracic Nursing Certificate.

NURSING QUALIFICATIONS (EEC RECOGNITION) ORDER 1979 (No. 1604) [60p], made under the European Communities Act 1972 (c. 68), s. 2 (2); operative on January 1, 1980; amends the Nurses Act 1957, the Nurses (Scotland) Act 1951 and the Nurses and Midwives Act (Northern Ireland) 1970 taking into account provisions of EEC Directives relating to the rights of nurses who obtain qualifications in a member State other than the United Kingdom to be established and to render nursing services in the United Kingdom.

1762. Nurses, Midwives and Health Visitors Act 1979 (c. 36)

This Act establishes a Central Council for Nursing, Midwifery and Health Visiting and makes new provision as to the education, training and regulation of nurses, midwives and health visitors.

S. 1 sets out the constitution of the Central Council; s. 2 specifies the functions of the Council; s. 3 relates to standing committees of the Council; s. 4 establishes a Midwifery Committee; s. 5 provides for the constitution of National Boards; s. 6 sets out the functions of the Boards; s. 7 deals with standing committees of the Boards; s. 8 relates to the establishment of joint committees of Council and Boards; s. 9 concerns local training committees; s. 10 states that the Central Council has a duty to prepare and maintain a register of qualified nurses, midwives and health visitors; s. 11 deals with admission to the register; s. 12 provides for removal from, and restoration to, the register; s. 13 relates to appeals; s. 14 concerns the making of a false claim of professional qualification; s. 15 empowers the Council to make rules as to midwifery practice; s. 16 relates to local supervision of midwifery practice; s. 17 prohibits attendance by unqualified persons at childbirth; s. 18 exempts practising midwives from jury service in Scotland; s. 19 deals with the finances of Council and Boards; s. 20 relates to the accounts of Council and Boards; s. 21 provides for the dissolution of existing bodies; s. 22 empowers the Council to make rules for the purpose of giving effect to the Act; s. 23 is the interpretation section; s. 24 deals with short title, commencement and extent. The Act extends to Northern Ireland.

The Act received the Royal Assent on April 4, 1979, and ss. 21 (2) and 24 came into force on that date; the remaining provisions come into force on a day to be appointed.

1762a. Opticians

GENERAL OPTICAL COUNCIL (REGISTRATION AND ENROLMENT RULES) (AMENDMENT) ORDER OF COUNCIL 1979 (No. 1638) [20p], made under the Opticians Act 1958 (c. 32), s. 7; operative on April 1, 1980; requires registered opticians and enrolled bodies corporate carrying on business as opticians to show all practice addresses in the registers and lists maintained by the General Optical Council; also increases certain fees.

1763. Professions supplementary to medicine

PROFESSIONS SUPPLEMENTARY TO MEDICINE (REGISTRATION RULES) (AMENDMENT) ORDER OF COUNCIL 1979 (No. 365) [10p], made under the Professions Supplementary to Medicine Act 1960 (c. 66), s. 2; increase with effect from April 1, 1979, the registration fees and retention fees payable to the Boards established under the 1960 Act.

1764. Sale

MEDICINES (PRESCRIPTION ONLY) AMENDMENT ORDER 1979 (No. 36) [10p], made under the Medicines Act 1968 (c. 67), ss. 58 (1) (4) (a), 129 (4); operative on February 10, 1979; amend S.I. 1977 No. 2127 by postponing until February 11, 1980, the termination of the temporary exemption from the restriction imposed by s. 58 (2) (b) of the 1968 Act. The exemption relates to certain injectable medicinal products.

1765. Veterinary drugs

MEDICINES (EXEMPTIONS FROM RESTRICTIONS ON THE RETAIL SALE OR SUPPLY OF VETERINARY DRUGS) ORDER 1979 (No. 45) [60p], made under the Medicines Act 1968 (c. 67), ss. 57 (1) (2), 129 (4); operative on February 11, 1979; consolidated S.I. 1977 No. 2167 and S.I. 1978 No. 1001 and replaces their schedules with up-dated schedules.

MEDICINES (EXEMPTIONS FROM RESTRICTIONS ON THE RETAIL SALE OR SUPPLY OF VETERINARY DRUGS) (AMENDMENT) ORDER 1979 (No. 1008) [£1·00], made under the Medicines Act 1968, ss. 57 (1) (2), 129 (4); operative on September 1, 1979; amends S.I. 1979 No. 45 by replacing all the Schedules in that Order with updated new Schedules.

ARTICLES. See *post*, p. [26].

MEETINGS

BOOKS. See *post*, p. [8].

MENTAL HEALTH

1766. Assault on patient—single act—whether ill-treatment

[Mental Health Act 1959 (c. 72), s. 126.] H was charged with ill-treating a patient contrary to s. 126 of the 1959 Act by slapping the patient's face on one occasion. *Held*, rejecting a submission of no case to answer, that a single act would constitute ill-treatment in law. (*R.* v. *Hayles* [1968] C.L.Y. 1947 considered): R. *v.* HOLMES [1979] Crim.L.R. 52, Bodmin Crown Ct.

1767. Hospital order—unreasonable objection—application for substitution of acting nearest relative—evidence

[Mental Health Act 1959 (c. 72), s. 52 (3) (c); C.C.R., Ord. 46, r. 18 (5).]

When considering medical evidence in support of a s. 52 application under the Mental Health Act, the judge is concerned with the medical content not the statutory form of the reports, and it matters not if there are defects in the reports for the purposes of a subsequent s. 26 application.

Mrs. B's daughter entered hospital as a voluntary patient. While she was there an order was obtained for her compulsory detention. On the expiry of that order the doctors considered that she ought to remain in hospital and took appropriate steps. The mother, her "nearest relative" refused her consent to the s. 26 application. An application was then made under s. 52 of the Act that the mental welfare officer be appointed to exercise the mother's function as her objection was unreasonable. At the s. 52 hearing two medical reports were handed to Mrs. B's solicitor (she did not see them) recommending the daughters' continued stay in hospital. The judge ordered that the health authority exercise the function of the nearest relative. Mrs B. appealed. On appeal, *Held*, dismissing the appeal, that (1) it was a sufficient compliance with C.C.R., Ord. 46, r. 18 (5), that reports were handed to Mr. B's legal advisor in these circumstances; (2) any defects in medical reports for the purposes of s. 26 were irrelevant for the purposes of a s. 52 application.

B. v. B. (MENTAL HEALTH PATIENT) [1979] 3 All E.R. 494 C.A.

1768. Insanity. See CRIMINAL LAW; DIVORCE AND MATRIMONIAL CAUSES.

ARTICLES. See *post*, p. [26].

MINING LAW

1769. Coal industry

MINEWORKERS' PENSION SCHEME (LIMIT ON CONTRIBUTIONS) ORDER 1979 (No. 374) [10p], made under the National Coal Board (Finance) Act 1976 (c. 1), s. 2 (4); operative on March 28, 1979; increases to £36,480,000 the maximum expenditure that the Secretary of State may incur to reimburse the N.C.B. for expenditure in eliminating deficiencies in the Pension Scheme.

REDUNDANT MINEWORKERS AND CONCESSIONARY COAL (PAYMENTS SCHEMES) (AMENDMENT) ORDER 1979 (No. 385) [30p], made under the Coal Industry Act 1977 (c. 39), s. 7 (7) (10); operative on March 31, 1979; amends S.I. 1973 No. 1268 and S.I. 1978 No. 415, the principal change is the addition to the 1978 Scheme of a new table of basic weekly benefit for those who became redundant on or after April 6, 1979.

1770. Coal mines

MINES (PRECAUTIONS AGAINST INRUSHES) REGULATIONS 1979 (No. 318) [25p], made under the Health and Safety at Work etc. Act 1974 (c. 37), ss. 11 (2) (*d*), 15 (1) (2) (3) (*a*), 50 (3), 82 (3) (*a*), Sched. 3, paras. 1 (1) (*c*), 8 (2), 9, 15 (1), 16, 18 (*a*); operative on April 9, 1979; impose on owners and managers of mines duties to take precautions against inrushes of gas, water and material which flows or is likely to flow when wet.

1771. Ironstone mining

IRONSTONE RESTORATION FUND (STANDARD RATE) ORDER 1979 (No. 211) [10p], made under the Mineral Workings Act 1971 (c. 71), ss. 3 and 5; operative on April 1, 1979; raises the rate of payment out of the Ironstone Restoration Fund, made to ironstone operators, in respect of all work completed after March 31, 1979, to £782 per acre.

1772. Mines and quarries

COAL AND OTHER MINES (ELECTRIC LIGHTING FOR FILMING) REGULATIONS 1979 (No. 1203) [50p], made under Health and Safety at Work, etc., Act 1974 (c. 37), ss. 11 (2) (*d*), 15 (1) (2) (3) (*a*) (*b*) (4) (*a*), 50 (3), Sched. 3, paras. 1 (1) (*a*) (*c*) (2), 4 (1), 6 (1), 8 (2); operative on October 20, 1979; make provision for electric lighting for filming in mines of coal, stratified ironstone, shale and fireclay.

1773. National Coal Board

COAL INDUSTRY (LIMIT ON GRANTS) ORDER 1979 (No. 1011) [10p], made under the Coal Industry Act 1977 (c. 39) s. 5 (3); operative on August 7, 1979; increases the limit of grants which may be made by the Secretary of State to the National Coal Board.

COAL INDUSTRY (BORROWING POWERS) ORDER 1979 (No. 1012) [10p], made under the Coal Industry Act 1965 (c. 82), s. 1 (3) as substituted by the Coal Industry Act 1977, s. 1 (1); operative on August 7, 1979; increases by £400 million the limit on the borrowing powers of the National Coal Board.

1774. Opencast coal-mining

OPENCAST COAL (RATE OF INTEREST ON COMPENSATION) ORDER 1979 (No. 942) [10p], made under the Opencast Coal Act 1958 (c. 69), ss. 35 (8), 49 (4); operative on September 4, 1979; increases to 14½ per cent. per annum the interest payable on compensation in certain circumstances and revokes S.I. 1978 No. 1802.

1775. —— application—authorisation—modification—ultra vires decision

[Opencast Coal Act 1958 (c. 69), s. 7 (2), Sched. 1.] The Coal Board applied for the authorisation of opencast coal mining. A public inquiry was held into the objections. The inspector recommended refusal of authorisation but the Secretary of State granted the authorisation for an area substantially different from that the subject of the original application. Wigan Council applied for the authorisation to be quashed on the ground that it was *ultra vires. Held*, there was sufficient of the earlier proposal in the later authorisation for it to be a modification and not a replacement. There was no breach of natural justice because there was no real risk of injustice. (*Legg* v. *Inner London Education Authority* [1972] C.L.Y. 1122 applied): WIGAN BOROUGH COUNCIL v. SECRETARY OF STATE FOR ENERGY AND THE NATIONAL COAL BOARD [1979] J.P.L. 610, Deputy Judge Michael Kempster, Q.C.

1776. Stannaries Court—criminal jurisdiction—power of justices to try tinner

[Stannaries Court (Abolition) Act 1896 (c. 45), s. 1 (1); Magistrates Courts Act 1952 (c. 55), s. 2 (1).]

S. 2 (1) of the Magistrates Courts Act 1952 gives jurisdiction to the justices to hear all summary offences committed within their jurisdiction without any limitation whatsoever.

The respondent, a privileged tinner, was charged with a summary motoring offence. He claimed to be entitled to be tried by the court now exercising the old Stannaries Court jurisdiction, namely the county court. The justices held they had no jurisdiction. On a judicial review on applications for certiorari and mandamus, *held*, granting the application, that it was only the civil jurisdiction of the old Stannaries Court that was transferred to the county court, and the respondent could not therefore claim to be entitled to a trial at the county court.

R. v. EAST POWDER JUSTICES, *ex p.* LAMPSHIRE [1979] 2 W.L.R. 479, D.C.

MINORS

1777. Access

MAGISTRATES' COURTS (GUARDIANSHIP OF MINORS) (AMENDMENT) RULES 1979 (No. 953 (L. 9)) [10p], made under the Justices of the Peace Act 1949 (c. 101), s. 15 as extended by the Magistrates' Courts Act 1952 (c. 55), s. 122 and the Guardianship of Minors Act 1971 (c. 3), s. 16 (5); operative on September 17, 1979; amend S.I. 1974 No. 706 in consequence of s. 40 of the Domestic Proceedings and Magistrates' Courts Act 1978 (access to minors by grandparents).

1778. —— court's responsibility

A former husband's application for access was adjourned and in the interim period the husband was allowed such supervised access as the welfare officer should determine. On appeal by the former wife, *held*, that the welfare officer was in a difficult position, and should not have the responsibility of deciding the issue of access: the courts should make the decision, it being wrong in principle to place the responsibility elsewhere: MNGUNI v. MNGUNI, *The Times*, November 30, 1979, C.A.

1779. —— denied to father

F, a Pakistani, and M, an English woman, married in 1970. They had a boy and a girl now aged five and seven years respectively. In 1974 M left taking the children with her. She obtained an order for custody in the magistrates' court. There were difficulties over access and F had even taken the children back to Pakistan without informing M for a month in 1976. Thereafter F was denied access both by M and later by the divorce court judge. *Held*, dismissing F's appeal, that what had to be considered, and what was the paramount consideration, was the benefit of the children. F had broken every access order made by the court. He had failed to pay maintenance and contrary to the magistrates' order had taken the children out of the country without even getting them vaccinated. F was now a stranger having not seen the children for two years. At their present ages, therefore, access would not benefit the children: RASHID *v.* RASHID (1978) 9 Fam. Law. 118, C.A.

1780. —— order refusing access in perpetuity
The parties had a grown-up son, and a daughter aged seven. In November 1974 the father left home, in 1975 he went to Saudi Arabia and in August 1976 he returned to England and sought access to the girl. The judge refused access and also terminated all rights of- access in the father in perpetuity. *Held*, allowing the father's appeal in part, whilst no access arrangements would work at present, it was clearly wrong to deprive the father of all rights of access in perpetuity: MURDOCH *v.* MURDOCH (1978) 8 Fam. Law 247, C.A.

1781. —— psychiatrist's report on mother—solicitors asking for amended report.
See NOBLE *v.* ROBERT THOMPSON & PARTNERS, § 2163.

1782. —— sexual misconduct of husband against daughter
The husband applied for access to his two children. The wife strongly objected as it was alleged that the husband had been involved in sexual misconduct with his three-year-old daughter. The county court judge adjourned for medical evidence to be taken of the risk to the children if allegations eventually found true. An answer was filed denying the allegations. On application to a High Court judge, medical evidence was filed of the husband's therapy for psycho-sexual disorders and of admission of sexual attraction to his daughter. Two specialists advised no risk to the children if access was supervised and the husband's mother was willing to undertake this. *Held*, that an order should be made for reasonable access supervised by a welfare officer: C. *v.* C., March 21, 1979, Bush J., Leeds. (*Ex rel. Messrs. Lester & Hatch, Solicitors.*)

1783. —— simultaneous adoption application—jurisdiction of justices
[Guardianship of Minors Act 1971 (c. 3), s. 9 (1); Children Act 1975 (c. 72), s. 85 (7).] F and M had lived together with their illegitimate son for the first six months following the birth before F had moved out. During 1977 F had paid occasional visits to see his son but after M's marriage to another man in June 1978 F was denied access completely. In November 1978 F applied in the magistrates' court for access under s. 9 (1) of the 1971 Act. In December 1978 M and the stepfather applied to the same court for an adoption order. Both proceedings were heard together but only F's access application was successful. M and the stepfather appealed against both decisions. *Held*, allowing the appeal, that although the justices had used the right procedure they had adopted the wrong test. As the evidence was the same for both applications it was possible to make an access order under s. 9 (1) of the 1971 Act without there being a custody order in existence, by reason of s. 85 (7) of the 1975 Act. However, the justices had erred by their consideration of the question of access first rather than adopting a balancing test and dealing with the two applications at one and the same time: C. *v.* H. (1979) 123 S.J. 537, D.C.

1784. Adoption
ADOPTION (COUNTY COURT) (AMENDMENT) RULES 1979 (No. 978 (L. 13)) [10p], made under the Adoption Act 1958 (c. 5), s. 9 (3), as amended by the Children Act 1975 (c. 72), Sched. 3, para. 22; operative on September 3, 1979; amend the 1976 (No. 1644) Rules so as to allow an adoption application in respect of a child whose parents are divorced to be made to the divorce county court in which the divorce was obtained.
MAGISTRATES' COURTS (ADOPTION) (AMENDMENT) RULES 1979 (No. 1222 (L. 18)) [10p], made under the Justice of the Peace Act 1949 (c. 101), s. 15, as extended by the Magistrates' Courts Act 1952 (c. 55), s. 122 and the Adoption Act 1958, s. 9; operative on November 1, 1979; amend S.I. 1976 No. 1768 in consequence of ss. 79, 80 and 81 of the Domestic Proceedings and Magistrates' Courts Act 1978 having come into force.

1785. —— **foster parents—wardship—white foster parents fostering children of Nigerian parents**

The natural parents were Nigerian and had two children, aged respectively 12½ years and nine years now, born to them when they were visiting the U.K. for work and educational purposes. These children were fostered out to a white woman now aged 58 and her common law husband aged 48, when the children were aged two years and six weeks respectively. The natural parents now lived permanently in Nigeria with two further children in prosperous surrounding; the parents were aged 40 and 31. They sought an order that the children be returned to them in Nigeria. The foster parents applied for an adoption order and later made a wardship application. *Held*, (1) adoption was inappropriate as there was no justification for cutting these children off from their natural parents; (2) the children would continue to be wards of court with care and control to the foster mother and regular and defined access to the natural parents, but they were not to leave the jurisdiction without further order: *Re* A. (MINORS) (1978) 8 Fam. Law 247, Comyn J.

1786. —— **perfection of order—judge's refusal**

Following a hearing at the local county court the judge pronounced an adoption order. Subsequently, the applicants were informed, via the Essex County Council, that the judge had reconsidered the case and had felt obliged to ask the clerk to the court not to issue the order until he had thoroughly considered the advantages of wardship proceedings. A subsequent application to perfect the order was dismissed; and the applicants then applied to the High Court for an order of mandamus. *Held*, that although the judge was entitled at any time until the order was perfected to vary or alter the order he originally expressed there must be a valid reason for altering or varying that order. The sole question in this case was whether the judge had expressed his discretion judicially. Unfortunately, the judge had expressed no reason why the child should be made a ward of court and was, therefore, not justified in making the variation or alteration. Application allowed. Order to stand and judge directed that his original order should be perfected: R. *v.* COLCHESTER AND CLACTON COUNTY COURT, *ex p.* A. D. W. AND B. A. W. (1979) 9 Fam. Law 155, C.A.

1787. —— **stepfather—dispensing with father's consent**

[Children Act 1975 (c. 72), s. 10 (3).] F and M married in April 1973 but separated in July 1973. M gave birth to the boy in question in January 1974. In August 1976 the marriage was dissolved and M married a Mr. G by whom she had a child in July 1977. They also applied to adopt the boy. F, whose only contact had been for a few moments during a visit three weeks after the birth, gave his formal written consent to the adoption but subsequently withdrew it. At the hearing the judge refused the application on the ground that adoption would not in any way safeguard or promote the welfare of the boy better than the existing arrangement and in view of s. 10 (3) of the 1975 Act. *Held*, allowing the applicants' appeal, that s. 10 (3) was directed to requiring the court to consider in such circumstances, where a stepfather came on the scene, whether adoption was really the right way of dealing with that situation or whether it was better dealt with under the Matrimonial Causes Act 1973. Here the boy was a *de facto* member of Mr. G's family. This was really a case of integrating this child legally and bringing the legal situation into direct relationship with the human situation which should be the objective in most of these cases. F, in this case was also unreasonably withholding his consent to the adoption. A reasonable father should give great weight to the nature of the relationship existing between him and the child, what it had been, was and was likely to be in the future. If that test applied, there could only be one answer. S. 10 (3) was accordingly satisfied. (*Re S.* [1977] C.L.Y. 1923 and *Re L.* [1962] C.L.Y. 1550 applied): *Re* S. (1978) 9 Fam. Law 88, C.A.

1788. Borstal detention—sentence. See CRIMINAL LAW.

1789. Care and control—father unable to exercise proper discipline—discretion of judge to see child

In divorce proceedings in 1975 a joint custody order was made concerning the three daughters of the marriage, with care and control being given to the father.

The father was unable to exercise proper discipline over the children with the result that the eldest girl, aged 15, was having an undesirable relationship with a 30-year-old man and was completely uncontrollable. It was agreed that she could stay with the father. The middle child, aged 13, wanted to go and live with her mother and had been bullied by the eldest girl and it was agreed that care and control of her should be transferred to the mother. Dispute arose as to the youngest child, aged 11, who wanted to stay with the father. She had been six when the mother left the matrimonial home and her behaviour to date indicated that she was following in the footsteps of her eldest sister, under whose influence she was. The judge had been invited to see the child by the father's counsel to ascertain her wishes and had declined to do so. On appeal, *held*, granting care and control of the youngest child to the mother, that it is not incumbent upon a judge to see a child of the family to ascertain his or her wishes before making an order regarding its care and control and that if there ever was a matter of personal discretion it was whether or not to see a child and a judge is fully entitled to make up his own mind without criticism from the Court of Appeal: D. *v.* D., June 22, 1979, C.A. (*Ex rel. Messrs. Godfrey Leighton & Co., Solicitors.*)

1790. Care order—evidence of threat to proper development

[Children and Young Persons Act 1969 (c. 54), s. 1 (2) (*a*).] F, a serving soldier, was granted custody of the two children of the family in divorce proceedings. The children were voluntarily put into care of foster parents whilst F was serving abroad. F, following a second marriage, now wished for the children to be returned. *Held*, s. 1 (2) (*a*) of the 1969 Act was only concerned with presently existing events and not with future events no matter how imminent those events might be. On the facts, there was no evidence of existing circumstances preventing the proper development of these two children. Application of council refused accordingly: ESSEX COUNTY COUNCIL *v.* T. L. R. AND K. B. R. (MINORS) (1979) 9 Fam. Law 15, D.C.

1791. —— juvenile court—cross-examination of witnesses of local authority

[Magistrates' Courts (Children and Young Persons) Rules 1970 (S.I. 1970 No. 1792), r. 14B, as added by the Magistrates' Courts (Children and Young Persons) (Amendment) Rules 1976 (S.I. 1976 No. 1769), Sched., r. 5.]

As a parent is permitted by the 1970 rules to meet any allegation made against him in care proceedings by calling or giving evidence, he is of necessity able to cross-examine witnesses.

A local authority applied to take a child into care, alleging that the mother had attempted to poison the child. The mother applied to cross-examine the witnesses called by the authority. The justices ruled it would not be right to permit cross-examination. On application for orders of mandamus, prohibition or certiorari, *held*, granting certiorari, that although the rules were silent regarding a parent's right to cross-examine in care proceedings, the right of a parent to meet any allegation against him by calling evidence required that the parent must be allowed to cross-examine the local authority's witnesses. R. *v.* MILTON KEYNES JUSTICES, *ex p.* R. [1979] 1 W.L.R. 1062, D.C.

1792. Children and Young Persons Act 1969—modification

CHILDREN AND YOUNG PERSONS ACT 1969 (TRANSITIONAL MODIFICATIONS OF PART I) ORDER 1979 (No. 125) [10p], made under the Children and Young Persons Act 1969 (c. 54), ss. 34, 69; operative on March 1, 1979; excludes the application of s. 23 (2) (3) of the 1969 Act, which enables a young person to be committed to a prison, in relation to girls under 17 and thus revokes S.I. 1977 No. 420, which related to girls under 15.

1793. Community homes

REVOCATION OF INSTRUMENTS OF MANAGEMENT (ST. VINCENT'S HOME) ORDER 1979 (No. 285) [10p], made under the Children and Young Persons Act 1969 (c. 54), s. 47 (4); operative on April 11, 1979; revokes the said instrument and makes provision for the London Borough of Bexley to run the home as if it were a community home provided by the borough.

1794. Criminal offenders—presumption of doli incapax. See R. *v.* B; R. *v.* A., § 465.

1795. —— **taking a conveyance—joint responsibility.** See C. (A MINOR) v. HUME, § 577.

1796. Custody—appeal from justices—reasons for decision
[Guardianship of Minors Act 1971 (c. 3).] In October 1978, following the parties' divorce and F's remarriage, M found herself in financial straits. Accordingly, she handed the children of the family, two boys aged six and four, to F and his new wife; and the local justices duly made an order under the 1971 Act giving custody to F. In 1979, M resumed living with her parents and sought a variation of the order to enable her to have custody. *Held,* dismissing F's appeal against the justices' decision in favour of M, that the justices had come to the right decision. However, in giving their reasons they had wrongly endeavoured to answer criticisms in the grounds of appeal. By attempting to answer points they were entering the arena. Such a practice was thoroughly bad. There was no need for them to see the grounds of appeal when formulating their reasons; and if they did they should not be influenced by them: FAULKNER v. FAULKNER (1979) 123 S.J. 751, D.C.

1797. —— **breach of order—effect on father's appeal**
In March 1978 care of the eldest three children of the family, all boys, was committed to F and of the youngest two boys to M. The five children were made wards of court and it was ordered that they should not be taken out of the jurisdiction without the authority of the court or the consent of the parents. In June 1978 F took all the children overseas to Sicily and there was no indication that he intended to bring them back. F now appealed in respect of the order as to the elder of the two boys in the care of M. *Held,* that in taking the children to Sicily F was in flagrant breach of the order. Accordingly there could really be no purpose in allowing the appeal to continue since, inevitably, the welfare of the children now required that there should be a full investigation of the circumstances in which F came to take the children overseas. Appeal dismissed: *Re* A MINOR (1978) 9 Fam. Law 151, C.A.

1798. —— **decision for the foreseeable future**
In dealing with a custody matter the judge treated the case as an interim application and made an order allowing F to keep the children. *Held,* allowing M's appeal, that although the judge's order preserving the situation was perfectly correct, it involved putting off a decision as to the permanent future of the children for an indefinite and, perhaps, a prolonged time. In the circumstances a new trial was required at the earliest possible moment: DAVIS v. DAVIS (1979) 9 Fam. Law 26, C.A.

1799. —— **declaration as to welfare**
[Matrimonial Causes Act 1973 (c. 18), s. 41 (1).]
Where an issue as to custody is likely to cause more than a short delay in proceedings under s. 41 of the Matrimonial Causes Act 1973, the appropriate declaration as to welfare should be made under s. 41 (1) (*b*) (i) or (*c*) on the basis of the existing *de facto* arrangements.
W was granted a decree nisi on her undefended petition. There were four children. W applied for custody and a declaration of satisfaction under s. 41 (1) of the Matrimonial Causes Act 1973. H did not file a statement of proposed arrangement, nor did he claim custody. At the hearing H indicated that he wished to claim custody. On the second adjourned hearing, when H said he still wanted to apply for legal aid, the judge said that he was satisfied as to the arrangements for the children, but would not make a declaration under s. 41 until the custody application had been heard. W appealed against that refusal. *Held,* allowing the appeal, that in view of H's dilatory approach, a declaration should be made under s. 41 (1) (*b*) (i) that W's arrangements were the best that could be devised in the circumstances.
A. v. A. (CHILDREN: ARRANGEMENTS) [1979] 1 W.L.R. 533, C.A.

1800. —— **hearing an " informal discussion "—new trial**
On a custody application relating to two children aged eight and five, after counsel for the father had outlined the facts, the judge stated he proposed to deal with the application by means of an informal discussion. No evidence was given on oath and custody was given to the mother. The father appealed.

Held, allowing the appeal and ordering a retrial, there was no reason why the judge could not have dealt with the application by means of a trial and counsel should have objected when the judge did not do so: JENKINS *v.* JENKINS (1978) 8 Fam. Law 246, C.A.

1801. —— impressive father—reason for award against mother
Parties had married in 1973 when F was 19 years and M was 16 years old. They had one child, a girl, now aged four and a half years. The marriage broke down in 1977 and M had taken the child to live together with her parents in their home. F was in the Army but planned to obtain a discharge as soon as he could in about 18 months' time. He had had difficulty in obtaining access to the child. The judge awarded custody to F because first, he was greatly impressed with F and, secondly, he thought that access was more likely to be effective and good if custody were given to F. *Held*, allowing M's appeal, that the judge had come to the wrong conclusion. However good a sort of man he may be, F could not perform the functions which a mother performed by nature in relation to a little girl. As to the second reason, access could be dealt with if there were difficulties by appropriate orders of the court: M. *v.* M. (1978) Fam. Law 92, C.A.

1802. —— jurisdiction of court—local authority care orders still in force
[Children and Young Persons Act 1969 (c. 54).] F had brought his two children to this country from Rhodesia. This necessitated their being taken in to care by the local authority and in November 1976 the juvenile court made care orders under s. 1 of the 1969 Act. In March 1977 F filed a divorce petition which included a prayer that he be granted custody of the two children. The judge held that he had no jurisdiction in law to entertain such an application whilst there were care orders still in force. *Held*, allowing F's appeal, that the judge was wrong in saying that he had no jurisdiction. There was now no appreciable difference between the powers of a judge in the divorce court and the powers of a judge exercising wardship jurisdiction. The case fell to be dealt with on the principles set out in *Re* H. [1978] C.L.Y. 2002. This meant that although the divorce court had jurisdiction to interfere with a care order, *i.e.* to supersede it by an order of its own, on general principles the court would not entertain an application to do that unless there were strong reasons which indicated that the welfare of the child required the court to take that course. The matter would be referred back to the judge for him to look at the merits, if so required by F. (*H.* v. *H.* [1973] C.L.Y. 2189 also considered): E. *v.* E. AND CHESHIRE COUNTY COUNCIL (INTERVENER) (1978) 9 Fam. Law 185, C.A.

1803. —— " toddler " left with father pending welfare report
The parties had one child aged 16 months at the date of the appeal. In January 1978 the mother left the matrimonial home leaving the child behind. in order to live with another man and his 13-year-old son. The judge adjourned the custody dispute pending a welfare report and gave interim care and control to the father. *Held*, allowing the mother's appeal, it was very distressing to separate a child of this age from its mother unless there were strong reasons for doing so: SOUTHGATE *v.* SOUTHGATE (1978) 8 Fam. Law 246, C.A.

1804. —— welfare officer—court's attitude to advice
Parties had married in 1971 and had one child, a boy now aged five years. In 1975 M left to live with another man P whom she proposed to marry when she was free to do so. F was granted custody of the boy by the local magistrates' court. They both lived with F's parents. The grandmother was the female influence in the boy's life on a day-to-day basis but F proposed getting married again to a young lady. The judge gave custody to M despite the welfare officer's recommendation in favour of F. *Held*, dismissing F's appeal, that the judge's decision on the evidence should remain unaltered for that very reason. He had been struck by the bitterness and unfairness which he thought he detected in F's attitude towards M. He felt that F was not concerned primarily with the interests of the child, a view which differed from that of the welfare officer. They had many other advantages, but one dis-

advantage so far as judges were concerned was that they did not have the benefits of hearing people cross-examined. The welfare officer was there to help but, of course, not to control. The judge thought that the situation had markedly changed since the magistrates' court hearing. M's position was now stable and it was F's future which looked a bit uncertain. Both M and P had impressed the judge very favourably. There was no doubt that he had come to the right conclusion: J. v J. (1978) 9 Fam. Law 91, C.A.

1805. ——— ——— whether decision should be postponed for further report

The judge had given custody of the two children of the marriage, who were in Australia with M, and were very distressed, to F and had ordered M to hand over the children within a certain time to enable them to travel to England. M appealed contending, *inter alia*, that the decision as to custody should be postponed for evidence from a further welfare report. *Held*, dismissing the appeal, that on the facts and the additional evidence the situation of the children was such that it ought not to be allowed to continue for a moment longer than was necessary. Although the report from Australia had been made when the children had only recently gone to their new home and new schools in Adelaide there was more recent affidavit evidence which took the matter no further. The children on the face of it appeared to be very, very distressed and unhappy. There were also proceedings due to be heard shortly in Australia. If further evidence before that court showed that the children were no longer unhappy, effective action would, no doubt, be taken by the Australian court: CORBET v. CORBET (1978) 9 Fam. Law 119, C.A.

1806. Juvenile courts. See MAGISTERIAL LAW.

1807. Local authorities, children in care of—access—wardship proceedings—jurisdiction to review merits of authority's decision

[Children and Young Persons Act 1969 (c. 54), s. 1.]

The court's jurisdiction over a statutory body exercising a statutory power is supervisory not appellate, and the court will not entertain an "appeal" from a local authority's decision based solely on the merits of the case.

A juvenile court made orders committing two children into care. Initially the mother had access to the children placed with foster parents, but her visits tailed off. The authority decided to end the access. The mother issued a wardship summons seeking an order that she be granted reasonable access. The judge declined the order. On appeal, *held*, dismissing the appeal, that the sole discretionary power to decide on the child's best interests was with the local authority; the court's jurisdiction was supervisory not appellate. *Re M. (An Infant)* [1961] C.L.Y. 4336, and *Re T. (A. J. J.) (An Infant)* [1970] C.L.Y. 1360 applied; *Re H. (A Minor) (Wardship: Jurisdiction)* [1978] C.L.Y. 2002 distinguished.)

Re W. (MINORS) (WARDSHIP: JURISDICTION) [1979] 3 W.L.R. 252, C.A.

1808. ——— consistent failure of parents to discharge obligations

[Children Act 1948 (c. 43), s. 2 (1) (b) (v), as substituted by Children Act 1975 (c. 72), s. 57.]

The " failure to discharge obligations " of s. 2 (1) (b) (v) of the Children Act 1948 requires culpability of a high degree, and evidence of behaviour over a period which constantly adheres to the pattern of which complaint is made, is required.

The parents, married in 1968, had three children. During each pregnancy the mother suffered from hypertension. During the fourth pregnancy the same condition prevailed and the three children were taken into care, as was the new born baby. During the fifth pregnancy, the parents returned the children to the local authority and were extremely unenthusiastic about weekend visits. The fifth child was immediately taken into care. The local authority passed a resolution vesting the parental rights in themselves (s. 57 of the 1975 Act) on the grounds of consistent failure to discharge obligations. The juvenile court confirmed the resolution and on appeal, *held*, dismissing the appeal, that the " failure " had to be culpable to a high degree to come within the section, but there was ample evidence of consistent neglect here.

M. v. WIGAN METROPOLITAN BOROUGH COUNCIL [1979] 2 All E.R. 958, D.C.

1809. —— **duty of care—escape of child with fire-raising propensities—church destroyed by fire.** See VICAR OF WRITTLE *v.* ESSEX COUNTY COUNCIL, § 1865.

1810. —— **mother's request for return of child—whether child remains in care thereafter**
    [Children Act 1948 (c. 43), ss. 1 (3) (3A), 2 (1), as amended and substituted by Children Act 1975 (c. 72), ss. 56, 57.]
    On the true construction of s. 1 (3) of the Children Act 1948, a request made by a parent for the return of a child in the care of a local authority does not terminate the care.
    M, the mother, placed her child in the care of the local authority voluntarily. A year later she gave the authority written notice of her desire to resume care of the child. The authority passed a resolution under s. 2 (1) of the Children Act 1948 vesting all parental rights and duties in it on the ground that M had so consistently failed to discharge her parental obligations as to be unfit to have the care of the child. M objected, and the authority made a complaint under s. 2. The court, following *Johns* v. *Jones* [1978] C.L.Y. 1994 held that they had no jurisdiction to hear the complaint on the ground that on receipt of the parent's notice the authority no longer had care of the child. The Divisional Court refused leave to apply for a review and the Court of Appeal refused to make an order of mandamus. On appeal by the authority, *held,* allowing the appeal, that s. 1 (3) of the Act did not have the effect that upon receipt of a parent's notice the local authority no longer had care of the child under s. 1, and the case would go back to the juvenile court to be determined (*Johns* v. *Jones* [1978] C.L.Y. 1994 overruled; *Halvorsen* v. *Hertfordshire County Council* [1975] C.L.Y. 2193 disapproved; *Wheatley* v. *Waltham Forest London Borough Council* (*Note*) [1979] C.L.Y. 1811 considered.)
    LEWISHAM LONDON BOROUGH COUNCIL *v.* LEWISHAM JUVENILE COURT JUSTICES [1979] 2 W.L.R. 513, H.L.

1811.   [Children Act 1948 (c. 43), ss. 1 (3) (3A), 2 (1), as amended and substituted by Children Act 1975 (c. 72), ss. 56, 57.]
    S. 1 (3) of the Children Act 1948 must be read in conjunction with s. 3A, and a parent's request for the return of a child in the care of a local authority does not terminate the care.
    M, the mother, disappeared, leaving her child with her sister. The sister was unable to cope with the child. She approached the local authority who took the child into care under s. 1 of the Children Act 1948. M re-appeared, and some months later gave notice in writing of her intention to remove the child from care. The local authority assumed parental rights over the child under s. 2 on the ground that M had so consistently failed without reasonable cause to discharge her parental obligation as to be unfit to have the care of the child. M objected and the local authority sought and were granted an order by justices. On appeal by M, *held,* allowing the appeal on the facts, that s. 1 (3) of the Act must be read with s. 3A, and the child was still in the care of the authority under s. 1 when the parental rights resolution was passed. (*Re D.* (*Minors*) (*Adoption by Parent*) [1973] C.L.Y. 2164 and *Watson* v. *Nikolaisen* [1955] C.L.Y. 1314, considered.)
    WHEATLEY *v.* WALTHAM FOREST LONDON BOROUGH COUNCIL (NOTE) [1979] 2 W.L.R. 543, D.C.

1812. —— **need for independent welfare report**
    M had led an unstable life since the age of 16 and had borne seven children by five different men. All the children had been taken into the care of the local authority at an early age. M was now concerned about the two youngest children. She had seen them regularly in a residential home and the local authority had found foster parents who were prepared to accept both children and M as a visitor. M thereupon made the children wards of court and invited the court to grant their care and control to her. *Held,* that in view of M's former mode of life, the court's doubts as to her future, and the fact that the bond between M and the children would not be broken if the proposal of the local authority were to be carried out, the children should remain wards of court, be in the care of the local authority and that M's access

should be at their discretion. The court had also taken account of the views of the children. It was always important in such cases for the court to have a reliable account if weight were to be placed upon them and if the children were of a suitable age to give them. This could not be provided through the local authority's social workers since they were party to the action. The interests of the children were best served, therefore, by an independent welfare report: *Re* A. (MINORS) (1979) 123 S.J. 553, Dunn J.

1813. Maintenance. See DIVORCE AND MATRIMONIAL CAUSES.

1814. Northern Ireland. See NORTHERN IRELAND.

1815. Social security. See SOCIAL SECURITY.

1816. Taking out of jurisdiction—conditions—reasonable security

M was given leave to take the only child of the marriage to America, having now married an officer in the American Air Force. The judge attached conditions to the leave to be supported by a bond " to be agreed in the sum of £10,000." No bond was agreed although the parties were well off and M had assets of £50,000. *Held* allowing M's appeal, that the order as it stood was to all intents and purposes unenforceable because the parties had failed to come to an agreement. The bond was therefore of little value. In the circumstances the whole concept of it was inappropriate, ineffective, and undesirable. If some form of security for the performance of the order was required, then that proposed in the notice of appeal requiring a deposit of £1,000 in the joint names of the parties' solicitors was more appropriate: BOYD (FORMERLY BICKERDIKE) *v.* BICKERDIKE (1979) 9 Fam. Law 122, C.A.

1817. Ward of court—jurisdiction of High Court—child subject of juvenile court case proceedings

Only in exceptional circumstances will the High Court exercise its wardship jurisdiction in respect of a child already the subject of care proceedings in a juvenile court.

The father of the child left its mother in 1976 shortly after the child's birth. In September 1978 the child was injured by his mother and was detained by the local authority in a place of safety under a 28-day order, the authority also instituting care proceedings in the juvenile court. An interim order was made. Thereafter the father (who had unsuccessfully attempted to obtain a magistrates' summons for custody of the child) applied for the child to be made a ward of court and for custody, care and control to be given to him. The mother and the local authority opposed his application. *Held*, refusing the application, that where a lower court and/or local authority had statutory powers the High Court would exercise its wardship jurisdiction only if the lower court's powers were inadequate or if the local authority had improperly exercised its powers or if there was some exceptional feature requiring intervention by the High Court; that no such feature existed here. (*Re T. (A. J. J.)* (*an infant*) [1970] C.L.Y. 1360 applied; *Re H. (a minor) (Wardship: jurisdiction)* [1978] C.L.Y. 2002 distinguished.)

M. *v.* HUMBERSIDE COUNTY COUNCIL [1979] 2 All E.R. 744, Sir George Baker P.

1818. —— jurisdiction to grant injunctions

[Matrimonial Homes Act 1967 (c. 75); Domestic Violence and Matrimonial Proceedings Act 1976 (c. 50).] H and W married in February 1976. V who was not H's child, was born in March 1976. V was made a ward of court. In subsequent proceedings care and control of V was given to W plus an order for H not to molest W. H assaulted W who then sought an injunction in the proceedings excluding H from the matrimonial home. H also sought an order in the same terms. *Held*, that under the wardship jurisdiction the court had, in appropriate circumstances, the power to grant a non-molestation injunction against either party if it was in the interests of the child. However, there was no jurisdiction to make an exclusion order against a mother; that remedy lay under the 1967 Act or the 1976 Act. Here H had assaulted W and it was in the interests of V and H be excluded for a period of three months: *Re* V. (A MINOR) (WARDSHIP) (1979) 123 S.J. 201, Sir George Baker P.

1819. —— order for care and control in favour of local authority

Under the wardship jurisdiction the issue of the care and control of two children, a boy now aged 14 and a girl aged seven, was contested by the mother and the maternal grandfather. The House of Lords ([1979] C.L.Y. 1820) had allowed the grandfather's appeal to the extent of restoring the judgment at first instance committing the care of the minors to the local authority but said that the matter should be restored to a judge of the Family Division for reconsideration. *Held*, that with the passing of time the mother was now a more stable and mature person and that, in consequence, the interests of the children would be best served by allowing them to live with the mother with reasonable access to the grandparents. If a court committed the care of minors to a party to the litigation a care order in favour of the local authority was inappropriate; and if a party was capable of exercising care and control, it was preferable for the local authority to intervene by way of a supervision order. Order accordingly: B. *v.* W. (1979) 123 S.J. 704, Dunn J.

1820. —— —— Court of Appeal varying order

The Court of Appeal should not vary the order of a judge unless the variation is justified on material which was not before the judge.

Lane J. made an order committing two wards of court to the care of the local authority and made detailed provisions as to access to the children's maternal grandparents. The grandfather (B) appealed against this order, seeking care and control himself. His appeal was dismissed and in addition the Court of Appeal varied the provisions relating to access by making the extent of access in the discretion of the local authority. No party to the proceedings sought such a variation, but the court was influenced by a letter from the social worker in the case which was on the court file, but which neither B nor his advisers had ever seen. On appeal, *held*, allowing the appeal in part, that (1) there were no grounds for concluding that the judge had erred in exercising her discretion. The judge had had the benefit of seeing B in the witness box and the Court of Appeal should not have varied her order unless the variation was justified on materials which were not before her; (2) failing to let B and his advisers see a document the court had regarded as important was a breach of the rules of natural justice. Order of Lane J. restored in full. *Per* Lord Diplock: In cases dealing with the custody of children, an appellate court ought to be particularly chary of interfering with the exercise of a judge's discretion. *Per* Lord Scarman: The Court of Appeal has three courses open to it when varying a custody order: (1) if on the evidence the order is demonstrably wrong, the appeal should be allowed and the appropriate order made; (2) if satisfied the order is wrong but unsure on the evidence what order ought to be made, the case should be remitted; (3) exceptionally, the court may hear evidence to resolve its doubts.

B. *v.* W. (WARDSHIP: APPEAL) [1979] 1 W.L.R. 1041, H.L.

BOOKS AND ARTICLES. See *post*, pp. [8], [27].

MONEY

1821. Banking. See BANKING.

1822. Exchange control. See REVENUE AND FINANCE.

1823. Loans. See MONEYLENDERS.

1824. Mortgages. See MORTGAGES.

MORTGAGES

1825. Building societies. See BUILDING SOCIETIES.

1826. Equitable interest—matrimonial home—whether wife in "actual occupation"
[Land Registration Act 1925 (c. 21), ss. 3 (xv) (*a*) (xvi), 20 (1), 70 (1) (*g*), 74.]

Wives who contribute to the purchase of the matrimonial home hold overriding interests. Wives who are in "actual occupation" of the land hold overriding interests and are entitled to protection.

Per curiam: Lenders of money on the security of matrimonial homes should realise that most wives now have proprietary interests and should make the necessary inquiries.

In two appeals H was registered as the sole proprietor of the matrimonial home. W had made a substantial contribution to the purchase price but no caution, restriction or notice was registered. H had charged the house, unknown to W, to the bank to secure business loans. In an action for possession brought by the bank in the first appeal Templeman J. held that the bank was not affected by W's minor interest, and in the second appeal the county court judge followed this ruling. On appeal, *held,* (1) that W's interests were minor interests capable of being overriding interests; (2) W was in actual occupation of the land and held overriding interests to which the charges were subject; (3) the bank's claim should be investigated under s. 36 of the Administration of Justice Act 1970. (*Bull* v. *Bull* [1955] C.L.Y. 2313, *Elias* v. *Mitchell* [1972] C.L.Y. 1954, *Hodgson* v. *Marks* [1971] C.L.Y. 6487, *Irani Finance* v. *Singh* [1970] C.L.Y. 2277 considered; *Caunce* v. *Caunce* [1969] C.L.Y. 2286 and *Bird* v. *Syme-Thomson* [1979] C.L.Y. 1426 not followed.)

WILLIAMS & GLYN'S BANK v. BOLAND [1979] 2 W.L.R. 550, C.A.

1827. Joint tenancy—matrimonial home—legal charge by one tenant—validity
[Law of Property Act 1925 (c. 20), s. 63 (1).]

A purported legal charge by one of two joint tenants of land held on trust for sale is not effectual to charge the charger's beneficial interest.

The defendants were joint legal and beneficial owners of their former matrimonial home. After their divorce the first defendant and a woman posing as the second defendant purported to execute a legal charge by way of mortgage on the house in favour of the plaintiffs. After discovering the deception, the plaintiffs sought, *inter alia,* a declaration that the first defendant had charged his beneficial interest in the house in their favour and an order for its sale. *Held,* dismissing the plaintiffs' appeal against the rejection of their claim, that the mortgage was not effective to charge the first defendant's beneficial interest in the proceeds of sale, it being expressed to be a charge on land. (*Irani Finance* v. *Singh* [1970] C.L.Y. 2277 considered.)

CEDAR HOLDINGS v. GREEN [1979] 3 W.L.R. 31, C.A.

1828. Possession—action not bona fide—brought by wife as mortgagee
The court is entitled to look behind the formal legal relationship of the parties, and a mortgagee will not be granted possession of property unless it is sought bona fide for the purpose of enforcing the security.

The landlord, the mortgagor, owned a valuable house which he mortgaged to the bank to secure an overdraft. Without the bank's consent he let the house to a tenant who became a statutory tenant. The landlord, wishing to regain possession, approached the bank to take action but they refused. The landlord's wife then paid off the bank, the mortgage was transferred to her name, and she brought an action for possession on her husband's behalf. The judge upheld her claim. On appeal, *held,* allowing the appeal, that the wife had brought the action for the ulterior motive of assisting her husband obtain vacant possession, and she would therefore be treated as the landlord's agent in the action. (*Dudley and District Benefit Society* v. *Emerson* (1949) C.L.C. 8835 distinguished.)

QUENNELL v. MALTBY [1979] 1 All E.R. 568, C.A.

1829. —— order—indefinite loan—equitable discretion to suspend execution
[Administration of Justice Act 1970 (c. 31), s. 36; Administration of Justice Act 1973 (c. 15), s. 8.]

For the purposes of s. 36 and s. 8 of the 1970 and 1973 Administration Acts the court has to take into account not merely the legal stipulations in a mortgage deed but their practical effect in equity, and where the parties contemplate an indefinite loan, despite the legal provisions for single repayment of principal, the court may exercise its discretion to suspend the operation of an order for possession. The defendant mortgaged his house to the plaintiffs for £27,500. The deed provided for the repayment of the principal sum in six months, with provisions as to the payment of interest by instalments, and provisions as to immediate possession in default. The defendant fell into arrears with his interest payments and the plaintiffs obtained an order for possession. The defendant applied for a suspension of the order under s. 36 (2) of the 1970 Act, contending that s. 8 of the 1973 Act applied. The plaintiffs argued that s. 8 did not apply as the principal was to be repaid in a single sum on a specified date which had passed. *Held*, on its true construction, the mortgage contemplated an indefinite loan with the right of redemption being kept alive indefinitely in equity unless the mortgagee took foreclosure proceedings and accordingly s. 8 applied, and the court could exercise its discretion to suspend the order.

CENTRAX TRUSTEES *v.* ROSS [1979] 2 All E.R. 952, Goulding J.

1830. Rating surcharge—priority of local authority charge

[General Rate Act 1967 (c. 9), ss. 17A, 17B.] Business premises were charged with a legal mortgage to secure the company's debts to the bank. Subsequently, the bank demanded payment under their charge and the local authority demanded a rating surcharge under ss. 17A and 17B, which charge was registered as a local land charge. The bank, as mortgagees sold the premises to the defendants. The local authority claimed the surcharge, and a declaration that it was charged on the land and that it took priority over all the interests in the land. *Held,* granting the declarations sought, the words " charged on the land " imported a charge on all the interests in the land: WESTMINSTER CITY COUNCIL *v.* HAYMARKET PUBLISHING (1979) 123 S.J. 804, Dillon J.

1831. Redemption—figure wrongly calculated by mortgagee—effect of endorsed receipt

In 1974 Mr. and Mrs. T mortgaged their house to the plaintiff Council. On December 8, 1976, the Council informed T's solicitors at their request that the amount required to redeem the mortgage on December 6, 1976, would be £2,667·25. They paid this sum; the Council endorsed a receipt on the mortgage deed pursuant to the Law of Property Act 1925, s. 115, and T sold the house free of the mortgage and purchased another. The receipt was under seal and stated, *inter alia*, " received the sum of £2,667·25 representing the balance remaining owing in respect of the principal sum secured by the within written Legal Charge together with all interest and costs." On January 26, 1977, the Council repaid £34·40 stated to be an overpayment on the mortgage account, being one month's repayment received after the redemption figure had been calculated. On March 22, 1977, the Council informed T's solicitors that the redemption figure had been calculated wrongly and that a further £1,000 was due from T. T's solicitors advised them not to pay and the Council issued proceedings. *Held*, (1) an endorsed receipt under s. 115 releases the property from the charge, and in the absence of fraud releases the mortgagor from all liability under the covenant to repay the principal. Although the 1925 Act refers to " discharge of the mortgaged property " whereas s. 42 of the Building Societies Act 1874 referred to the effect of a receipt to " vacate the mortgage or further charge or debt ", *Harvey* v. *Municipal Permanent Building Society* (1884) 26 Ch.D. 273 and *London & County United Building Society* v. *Angell* (1896) 65 L.J.Ch. 194 decided on the 1874 Act applied to the position under the 1925 Act. The Council could not go behind the receipt to question the sufficiency of the repayment; (2) if the receipt under s. 115 was under the seal of the mortgagee, then it operated separately as a release of the debt, and, being under seal, consideration was unnecessary; (3) on the facts, Mr. and Mrs. T had relied upon the Council's representations and had changed their position so that the Council was estopped from recovering the money claimed to be outstanding: EREWASH BOROUGH COUNCIL *v.* TAYLOR, October 16, 1978, Judge Brooke-Willis, Ilkeston County Ct. (*Ex rel. Messrs. Freeth, Cartwright & Sketchley, Solicitors*).

1832. Second charge—non est factum—lack of independent advice

The defendants, an elderly couple, left all the arrangements for the purchase of a new house to their son, a chartered accountant who was in financial difficulties. The son borrowed from the plaintiffs to pay the outstanding balance of the purchase price after mortgage of the house to a building society, and agreed to procure a second charge on the house for this sum. The son, saying that the defendants had to sign further mortgage documents, effected this second charge. On the disappearance of the son, the plaintiffs claimed the sum plus possession of the house. *Held,* dismissing the plaintiffs' appeal, the following factors made the transaction voidable: (1) the plaintiffs approached the son to procure the transaction; (2) relationship between son and elderly parents; (3) lack of independent advice (*Chaplin & Co.* v. *Brammall* [1908] 1 K.B. 233, citing *Turnbull & Co.* v. *Duval* [1902] A.C. 429). *Per* Brandon and Brightman L.JJ.: the defendants failed to exercise reasonable care in the circumstances and could not succeed on the defence of *non est factum*: AVON FINANCE CO. *v.* BRIDGER (1979) 123 S.J. 705, C.A.

ARTICLES. See *post,* p. [27].

NAME

1833. **Trade name.** See TRADE MARKS AND TRADE NAMES.

ARTICLES. See *post,* p. [27].

NATIONAL HEALTH

1834. **Charges**

NATIONAL HEALTH SERVICE (DENTAL AND OPTICAL CHARGES) AMENDMENT REGULATIONS 1979 (No. 677) [10p], made under the National Health Service Act 1977 (c. 49), ss. 78 (1), 79, Sched. 12, paras. 2 (1) (2), 3 (1)–(3); operative on July 16, 1979; increase the charges for the supply of certain dental appliances and the provision of dental treatment under the 1977 Act.

NATIONAL HEALTH SERVICE (CHARGES FOR DRUGS AND APPLIANCES) AMENDMENT REGULATIONS 1979 (No. 681) [10p], made under the National Health Service Act 1977, ss. 77 (1) (2) and 83 (*a*); operative on July 16, 1979; amend S.I. 1974 No. 285.

1835. **Contributions.** See SOCIAL SECURITY.

1836. **Family Practitioner Committees**

NATIONAL HEALTH SERVICE (FAMILY PRACTITIONER COMMITTEES: MEMBERSHIP AND PROCEDURE) REGULATIONS 1979 (No. 739) [40p], made under the National Health Service Act 1977 (c. 49), s. 16 (1), Sched. 5, paras. 6 (1), 12; operative on July 27, 1979; consolidate with amendments the Regulations which provide for the appointment and term of office of members of, and the procedure of, Family Practitioner Committees.

1837. **Health authorities**

NATIONAL HEALTH SERVICE (HEALTH AUTHORITIES: MEMBERSHIP) REGULATIONS 1979 (No. 738) [40p], made under the National Health Service Act 1977 (c. 49), Sched. 5, paras. 1 (2), 2 (1) (*b*), 12 (*a*); operative on July 27, 1979; consolidate with amendments the Regulations which provide for the appointment and tenure of office of chairmen and members of Regional and Area Health Authorities and alter the dates of termination of office of certain members of Health Authorities in England from July 31 to September 30 and adjust appropriately the tenures of office of the original members.

NATIONAL HEALTH SERVICE (HEALTH AUTHORITIES AND FAMILY PRACTITIONER COMMITTEES: MEMBERSHIP) REGULATIONS 1979 (No. 897) [30p], made under the National Health Service Act 1977, s. 16 (1), Sched. 5, paras. 1 (2), 2 (1) (*b*), 6 (1), 12; operative on July 27, 1979; make minor drafting amendments to S.I. 1979 Nos. 738 and 739.

1838. ——— **employment—whether " associated employers."** See HILLINGDON AREA HEALTH AUTHORITY *v.* KAUDERS, § 1001.

1839. **Health services—duty to provide facilities—breach of duty**

[National Health Service Act 1977 (c. 49), ss. 1, 3.] Hospital patients waited for treatment for periods longer than was advisable because of a shortage of facilities; they sought declarations that the respondent authorities were in breach of their duties under ss. 1 and 3 of the National Health Service Act 1977 to provide the necessary facilities and health service. *Held,* dismissing the application, that it was not the court's function to direct Parliament what funds to make available and how to allocate them, and the court could interfere with the Secretary of State's conduct only if he had acted so as to frustrate the policy of the Act, or in a manner in which no reasonable minister could have acted: R. *v.* SECRETARY OF STATE FOR SOCIAL SERVICES, *ex p.* HINCKS (1979) 123 S.J. 436, Wien J.

1840. **Medical practitioners—wages paid to ancillary staff—exclusion of wives and dependants**
[Health Services and Public Health Act 1968 (c. 46), s. 29.] The provisions of the scheme for reimbursing general medical practitioners part of the cost of ancillary workers, which exclude reimbursement in respect of salaries paid to wives or dependants, are (by virtue of s. 29 of the Public Health Act 1968) not *ultra vires*; nor can it be said that the Minister must have been unreasonable to make such provisions: GLANVILL *v.* SECRETARY OF STATE FOR SOCIAL SERVICES, *The Times,* November 20, 1979, C.A.

1841. **National insurance.** See NATIONAL INSURANCE.

1842. **Northern Ireland.** See NORTHERN IRELAND.

1843. **Pensions.** See PENSIONS AND SUPERANNUATION.

1844. **Teaching hospitals**
NATIONAL HEALTH SERVICE (PRESERVATION OF BOARDS OF GOVERNORS) ORDER 1979 (No. 51) [25p], made under the National Health Service Reorganisation Act 1973 (c. 32), s. 15 (1) (2) (3) (5A) as amended by the National Health Service Act 1977 (c. 49); operative on February 22, 1979; takes effect upon the expiration of S.I. 1974 No. 281 and preserves from abolition under s. 14 of the 1973 Act the Boards of Governors of the specified Teaching Hospitals until March 31, 1982.

BOOKS. See *post,* p. [9].

NATIONAL INSURANCE

1845. **Family allowances.** See FAMILY ALLOWANCES.

1846. **National health service.** See NATIONAL HEALTH.

1847. **Northern Ireland.** See NORTHERN IRELAND.

1848. **Social security.** See SOCIAL SECURITY.

1849. **Supplementary benefit.** See SOCIAL SECURITY.

NEGLIGENCE

1850. **Architects—planning permission—validity—failure to advise client**
[Town and Country Planning Act 1971 (c. 78), s. 74 (1).] An architect, C, designed an office building under 10,000 square feet which therefore did not require an office development permit (ODP). Additional basement car parking and a caretaker's flat were to C's surprise excluded from the computation of office space and planning permission was granted. Potential tenants later questioned the lack of an ODP and the deal fell through. At first instance C was found to be negligent in failing to warn the plaintiffs that the planning permission may be void. *Held,* allowing C's appeal, it was impossible to say C was negligent. Although surprised at the attitude taken by the planning officer, it was C's view that the final decision would be made by the planning committee and that decision would be conclusive. It did not matter whether C was right or wrong in law in his view, the question was whether he was negligent in holding that view: B. L. HOLDINGS *v.* ROBERT J. WOOD AND PARTNERS (1979) 123 S.J. 570, C.A.

1851. **Auctioneers—vanishing purchaser—failure to secure name and address.** See HARDIAL SINGH *v.* HILLYER AND HILLYER, § 134.

1852. **Bailment—bailee—duty—vehicle immobilized—theft.** See IDNANI *v.* ELISHA (TRADING AS GRAFTON SERVICE STATION), § 143.

1853. **Breach of statutory duty—factory—incorrect replacement of guard.** See LINEKER *v.* RALEIGH INDUSTRIES, § 1298.

1854. —— **local authority—statutory remedy**
[National Assistance Act 1948 (c. 29), ss. 29 (1) (as amended by the Mental Health (Scotland) Act 1960, ss. 113 (1), 114 and Sched. 4), (2), 36; Chronically Sick and Disabled Persons Act 1970 (c. 44), ss. 1, 2 (1).]
Where a local authority fails to discharge its functions under the Chronically Sick and Disabled Persons Act 1970, the remedy lies with the default powers of the Minister under s. 36 of the National Assistance Act 1948, not by action.
P suffered from disseminated sclerosis. She was registered with the local authority as a disabled person under the Chronically Sick and Disabled Persons Act 1970. She claimed damages from the local authority for negligence and breach of statutory duty under s. 2 of the Act, in failing to meet her need for adequate home help or to provide practical assistance in her home. The master and the judge struck out P's statement of claim as disclosing no cause of action. On appeal by P, *held*, dismissing the appeal, that P's sole remedy was by representation to the Minister under s. 36 of the National Assistance Act 1948. (Dicta of Veale J. in *Reffell* v. *Surrey County Council* [1964] C.L.Y. 2570 and of Lord Denning M.R. in *Southwark London Borough Council* v. *Williams* [1971] C.L.Y. 9950 applied.)
WYATT v. HILLINGDON LONDON BOROUGH COUNCIL (1978) 76 L.G.R. 727, C.A.

1855. —— **slipping on snow and slush—previous injury.** See BALL v. VAUGHAN BROS. (DROP FORGINGS), § 1299.

1856. Contributory negligence—seat belts—failure to wear. See HOADLEY v. DARTFORD DISTRICT COUNCIL, § 2367.

1857. Damages. See DAMAGES.

1858. Defective premises—work done before commencement of 1972 Act
[Defective Premises Act 1972 (c. 35), s. 1 (1).]
The relevant date for the purposes of the duty owed under the Defective Premises Act 1972 is the date that work was taken on and not that upon which it is completed.
In 1972 the defendants agreed to arrange the sale to the plaintiff of a dwelling and to arrange for its conversion into two flats. The work was effectively completed in February 1974. The plaintiff being dissatisfied with the conversion work sought to rely upon the 1972 Act which imposed a duty upon persons "taking on" such conversion work. The Act came into force on January 1, 1974. Walton J. found for the defendants upon a preliminary issue as to the applicability of the Act. *Held*, dismissing the plaintiff's appeal, that the duty imposed by the statute arose at the date of the agreement to take on the work or, at the latest, at the date of commencement thereof, and that the Act could not be construed so as to have retrospective effect.
ALEXANDER v. MERCOURIS [1979] 1 W.L.R. 1270, C.A.

1859. Defence—negligence of Post Office—inaccurate plan of underground cables
[Telegraph Act 1878 (c. 76), s. 8.]
The duty of the post office when indicating the position of underground cables on a plan, even when they know that the plan will be used and relied on by contractors, is to provide a rough plan, not a blue print.
The post office supplied the local authority with a plan on which the various underground cables in the area were marked. With the plan came a disclaimer as to its accuracy. The plan was in fact inaccurate, and contractors relying upon it, struck and injured telegraphic lines. The contractors conceded liability by virtue of s. 8, but counterclaimed for negligence of the post office in supplying an inaccurate plan knowing that the plan would be used for the proposed works. *Held*, dismissing the counterclaim, that, leaving aside the disclaimer, the post office was under a duty to do no more than supply a plan indicating roughly where the cables lay. (*Hedley Byrne & Co.* v. *Heller & Partners* [1963] C.L.Y. 2416 applied; *Postmaster-General* v. *Liverpool Corporation* [1923] A.C. 587 distinguished.)
POST OFFICE v. MEARS CONSTRUCTION [1979] 2 All E.R. 814, Willis J.

1860. —— **statutory liability—circuity of action**
[Telegraph Act 1878 (c. 76), s. 8.]
An action may be dismissed on the ground of circuity of action.

The council wished to drain a flooded road. The Post Office's employee indicated the position of a cable. The council's employee dug into the ground three feet away and hit the cable. It cost the Post Office £718 to repair it. The Post Office claimed the cost from the council under s. 8 of the Telegraph Act 1878. The judge held that the cause of the injury was the negligence of the Post Office in misinforming the council. On appeal by the Post Office, *held,* dismissing the appeal, that the cause of the injury was the voluntary act of the council's employee; however, the council had a good claim in damages for negligent misinformation for whatever sum they were liable for under the statute. The Post Office's action should therefore be dismissed on the grounds of circuity of action. (*Postmaster-General* v. *Liverpool Corporation* [1923] A.C. 587, *Workington Harbour and Dock Board* v. *Towerfield* (1950) C.L.C. 9609 and *Ginty* v. *Belmont Building Supplies* [1959] C.L.Y. 2191 considered.)
POST OFFICE *v.* HAMPSHIRE COUNTY COUNCIL [1979] 2 W.L.R. 907, C.A.

1861. Driving instructor—failure to advise about seat belts. See GIBBONS *v.* PRIESTLEY, § 2368.

1862. Duty of care—builders—third parties or purchasers
[Can.] It has been *held,* that the Canadian courts have not as yet extended the principle of liability for negligence of the builder to third persons or subsequent purchasers for damages suffered by the goods or the building itself. A builder who sells a house in the course of construction is held to impliedly warrant that the house has not been constructed negligently and that it is fit and suitable for habitation. The vendor of a house that has been completely constructed, however, is protected by the principle of *caveat emptor* except as modified by express warranties or where there has been fraudulent misrepresentation. (*Dutton* v. *Bognor Regis Urban District Council* [1972] C.L.Y. 2352 not followed; *Perry* v. *Sharon Development Co.* [1937] 4 All E.R. 390 referred to): THOMAS *v.* WHITEHOUSE (1979) 95 D.L.R. (3d) 762, New Brunswick Sup.Ct.

1863. —— car driver—passenger tripping over loose seatbelt
The driver of a car has a duty to take reasonable care to provide a vehicle which is safe for his passenger.
D drove a four-seater mini-cab with seat-belts on the front seats. It was usual practice among mini-cab drivers to tie their seat-belts up, so that they did not endanger passengers. P, who hired the mini-cab at night, caught her foot in a seat-belt as she got out, fell and broke her ankle. The interior light had not been switched on. The judge at first instance dismissed P's claim on the ground that it was her duty to guard against any possible obstruction by the seat-belt. On appeal by P, *held,* allowing the appeal, that any driver had a duty to take care to provide a vehicle which was safe for his passengers and to prevent its equipment for increasing safety from becoming a danger. P, who was unfamiliar with the car, had not contributed to her fall, and judgment would be entered for P. (*Donn* v. *Schachter* [1975] C.L.Y. 2322 distinguished.)
McCREADY *v.* MILLER [1979] R.T.R. 186, C.A.

1864. —— foreseeability—economic loss not consequence of damage to person or property
[Aust.] In the course of its operations a dredge fractured an oil pipeline laid in the bed of a bay which connected an oil refinery on one shore with an oil terminal on the other. The refinery and pipeline were owned by A, the terminal by B. There was an arrangement between A and B whereby B supplied crude oil to A for processing, and the refined product was delivered through the pipeline to the terminal. The refined oil carried through the pipeline was B's property, but the arrangement provided that risk of loss or damage remained with A. The damage to the pipeline was attributable to the negligent navigation of the dredge and to defects in a chart prepared by a marine surveyor. B incurred expense in transporting refined oil from the refinery to the terminal while the pipeline could not be used. *Held,* B was entitled to recover that expense from the owner of the dredge and marine surveyor as damages for negligence. Although as a general rule damages are not recoverable for economic loss which is not consequential upon injury to person or property,

even if the loss is forseeable, damages are recoverable when **D** has knowledge (or the means of knowledge) that a particular person, not merely a member of an unascertained class, will be likely to suffer economic loss as a result of his negligence (*Hedley Byrne* v. *Heller* [1963] C.L.Y. 2416, *Weller* v. *Foot & Mouth D.R.I.* [1965] C.L.Y. 2671, *Margarine Union* v. *Cambay Prince* [1967] C.L.Y. 3608, and *Spartan Steel* v. *Martin & Co.* [1972] C.L.Y. 2341 considered): CALTEX OIL (AUSTRALIA) *v.* THE DREDGE WILLEMSTAD (1976) 136 C.L.R. 529, Aust.High.Ct.

1865. —— **local authority—escape of child in care—church destroyed by fire**

A local authority in whose care a child is placed owes a duty of care to those with whom a sufficient relationship of neighbourhood exists; the duty is that of a reasonable parent to control his child, and responsibility extends to the consideration of the consequences of failure to exercise that parental control.

A 12-year-old boy was remanded in care by a juvenile court as he was known to have been responsible for starting a number of fires in the area. He was placed in a community home, but the head of the home was not informed of his fire-raising propensities. The boy walked out of the home in broad daylight and set fire to a local church. The plaintiffs brought an action in negligence against the local authority. *Held,* giving judgment for the plaintiffs, (1) a relationship of neighbourhood existed between the parties sufficient to establish a duty of care; (2) a wide discretion existed which served to limit the local authority's duty of care; (3) the duty of care owed was the ordinary duty of a reasonable parent to control his child. (*Home Office* v. *Dorset Yacht Co.* [1970] C.L.Y. 1849, *Anns* v. *Merton London Borough Council* [1977] C.L.Y. 2030 applied.)

VICAR OF WRITTLE *v.* ESSEX COUNTY COUNCIL (1979) 77 L.G.R. 656, Forbes J.

1866. —— **power, not duty, to repair highways**

[Can.] P was injured when thrown from a bicycle as a result of riding into a deep pothole in the road. The municipality had a statutory power to repair highways but no duty to do so. *Held,* as the municipality had undertaken to exercise its statutory powers to maintain the road in question by making regular inspections and repairs, a prima facie duty of care to the users of the highways in the exercise of the powers arose. However, the powers and duties of the municipality were definable in terms of public and not private law. For a civil action based on negligence against it to succeed, there must be acts or omissions taken outside the limits of the discretion delegated to it or its officers. The municipality did not in fact know of the existence of this particular pothole. Liability can only arise if it should have known of its existence. The frequency of inspection of roads is a matter of policy to be decided by the municipality in its discretion. The circumstances negatived the duty which it prima facie owed to P as a user of the road in question (*Donoghue* v. *Stevenson* [1932] A.C. 562, *Anns* v. *Merton London Borough Council* [1977] C.L.Y. 2030, *Home Office* v. *Dorset Yacht Co.* [1970] C.L.Y. 1849, and *Dutton* v. *Bognor Regis Urban District Council* [1972] C.L.Y. 2352 referred to): BARRATT *v.* DISTRICT OF NORTH VANCOUVER (1978) 89 D.L.R. (3d) 473, Brit.Col.C.A.

1867. —— **seller of dangerous car—liability to third party—car sold " as seen with all its faults "**

The seller of a car in a dangerous condition may discharge his duty of care towards third parties by selling the same " as seen with all its faults and without warranty."

The respondents acquired a motor-car, the chassis of which was in such a dangerous condition through corrosion that the car was not safe to drive. The respondents entered the car in an auction, offering it " as seen with all its faults and without warranty." The successful bidder resold the car at the auction to C. Some eight days later the appellant was a passenger in the car being driven by C when the chassis collapsed causing the car to crash, killing C and severely injuring the appellant. who subsequently alleged that the respondents were negligent in failing to warn any potential purchaser of the car's dangerous condition. Kenneth Jones J. found for the appellant, but a majority of the Court of Appeal reversed that decision. *Held,* affirming the Court of Appeal decision, that the warning subject to which the car was sold sufficed to discharge the duty owed by the respondents. (*Ward* v. *Hobbs* (1878) 4 App.Cas. 13 doubted.)

HURLEY *v*. DYKE [1979] R.T.R. 265, H.L.

1868. —— subterranean water—draining of pond and lake
The plaintiff owned farmland at the head of a valley with ponds and an ornamental lake. An oil company was granted statutory powers to construct an oil refinery and a railway track. In doing so they fissured the rock strata causing the water table to be lowered and so draining the ponds and lake. *Held*, that at common law an owner of land could, when acting lawfully, abstract subterranean water whether to secure some benefit to himself or for no good reason. New duties of care might arise in the proper circumstances, but here the company acted within its statutory powers and owed no duty of care to preserve the quantity of subterranean water: THOMAS *v*. GULF OIL REFINING (1979) 123 S.J. 787, Watkins J.

1869. Exemption clause—personal injury—quantum of damages
In January 1971, P's husband, H, booked passage on D's ship, the D, for himself and his family from Rosslare to Le Havre on July 7. Neither at the time of booking nor on payment of the balance was H's attention drawn to D's conditions of carriage. H's ticket arrived through the post in a folder on which were set out D's conditions of carriage, which provided, by cl. 3, that D " shall not be liable for any injury or accident to passengers wheresoever and howsoever caused and whether by negligence of their servants or agents or otherwise." H did not notice the conditions. On July 7, while the D was unberthing, P was on the after part of the main deck when the port stern mooring wire suddenly whiplashed forward and struck P, causing severe injuries to her right arm and shoulder. Contrary to normal practice, there was no rope stretched across the deck to indicate that passengers were not supposed to go further aft. On P's action for damages, *held*, that (1) P's accident was solely caused by the negligence of D's servants in not erecting a rope barrier and allowing P to be on the after deck without indicating that it was unsafe to be there during the unmooring operation; and not any want of care for her own safety on her own part; (2) the contract of carriage was concluded in January when the booking was made and confirmed, and D could not subsequently introduce conditions into the contract when it was not subject to them originally; (3) it could not be said that the contract was only concluded after H had received and accepted the ticket after payment of the balance, and accordingly D could not rely on cl. 3 as a defence to P's claim; (4) P as a housewife was as much disabled from doing her unpaid job as an employed person from doing a paid job and was entitled to be compensated in a similar way; (5) P's life expectancy at the date of judgment was 30 years or more, and the appropriate multiplier was 15; and P was entitled to special damages of £1,689; partial loss of house-keeping capacity assessed at £2,691 for past loss and £8,736 for future loss; £8,000 for pain and suffering and loss of amenities; total damages £21,116, with interest on £4,380 at half the short term investment rate from the date of the accident to the date of judgment (*The Eagle* [1977] C.L.Y. 2035 applied): DALY *v*. GENERAL STEAM NAVIGATION CO; THE DRAGON [1979] 1 Lloyd's Rep. 257, Brandon J.

1870. Foreseeability—contributory negligence—spectator injured by hockey stick during game
[Can.] P lost the sight of one eye as the result of being struck by a hockey stick while watching a hockey game. P was standing in an aisle next to the sideboards at the time of injury. Spectators were not required to be seated, nor were there protective shields above the boards. The aisle in question was the only means of entrance and exit to spectator areas. *Held*, D was liable for one-third of the damages, P for two-thirds. The likelihood of a spectator being hit with a hockey stick was to be anticipated; D was negligent by not providing protective guards above the sideboards. P was contributorily negligent by standing beside the boards. It could not be said that by merely attending the game, P consented to the risk of injury. (*Murray* v. *Harringay Arena* (1951)

C.L.C. 6698 considered): KLYNE v. BELLEGARDE (1978) 6 W.W.R. 743, Sask.
Q.B.

1871. Liability—admission of negligence—entry of judgment. See RANKINE v. GARTON
SONS & CO., § 2146.

1872. —— barristers—immunity—settlement of proceedings. See BIGGAR v. McLEOD,
§ 2111.

1873. —— car chase—police officer injured—liability of driver. See ATT.-GEN. FOR
ONTARIO v. KELLER, § 2089.

**1874. —— of manufacturer, retailer, owner and agent respectively—sale of defective
towing coupling**
     A manufacturer of a defectively designed part for a motor vehicle may be
liable to a third party injured due to the failure of such part.
     A trailer coupling advertised by its manufacturers as foolproof and needing
no maintenance was fitted to a Land Rover supplied by retailers. Unbeknown
to them the coupling was defective in that its safe use depended upon the
integrity of a spindle. After the fitting the spindle went missing and the coupling
was plainly damaged. During servicing of the vehicle the retailers did not
report on the coupling. Some three to six months after the damage to the
coupling, the vehicle was being driven by the owner's employee when the
coupling failed, causing a trailer to detach and collide with the plaintiffs'
vehicle, killing two of the occupants. The plaintiffs claimed damages against the
owner, driver, manufacturers and retailers. The owner joined as third parties
the retailers who in turn joined the manufacturers. *Held,* that (1) the owner
and driver were liable as to 25 per cent. for using the vehicle in a damaged state
without repairing the coupling or ascertaining whether it was safe to use; (2)
the manufacturers were liable as to 75 per cent. for putting into circulation a
defectively designed and dangerous coupling; (3) the retailers were not liable
as they had no reason to know of the design defect nor any duty to inspect the
coupling when servicing the vehicle; (4) since the owner knew or ought to have
known of the dangerous state of the coupling, this continued use of it in such
condition was not in the contemplation of the parties at the time of sale and
this claim against the retailers accordingly failed. (*Mowbray* v. *Merryweather*
[1895] 2 Q.B. 640, applied.)
     LAMBERT v. LEWIS; LEXMEAD (BASINGSTOKE), THIRD PARTY; B. DIXON-BATE;
FOURTH PARTY [1979] R.T.R. 61, Stocker J.

1875. Local authority—exercise of statutory powers—inspection of foundations
     [London Building Acts (Amendment) Act 1939 (c. xcvii), s. 82.] In 1974 the
first defendants began work extending and converting a house in Inner London
into flats: the extension required foundations. The G.L.C.'s district surveyor
visited the site pursuant to s. 82 of the 1939 Act: but he failed to notice defects
in the damp-proofing which involved non-compliance with the bylaws. In 1976
the plaintiff entered into a 99-year lease from the first defendants of the semi-
basement flat. Water entered the flat through the floor: the walls were damp.
The plaintiff sued the first defendants for damages under the Defective Premises
Act 1972, s. 1 (1) and for negligence and the G.L.C. for damages for breach
of statutory duty under s. 82 of the 1939 Act and for negligence: the first
defendants did not appear at the hearing. The G.L.C. contended that s. 82 was
not actionable in civil proceedings, alternatively it imposed a duty only to take
reasonable care: the plaintiff contended s. 82 imposed an absolute duty to cause
the bylaws to be duly observed. *Held,* that, (1) the bylaws had not been complied
with; (2) the first defendants were negligent; (3) the district surveyor had been
negligent in not detecting the defects in damp proofing; (4) s. 82 of the 1939
Act was actionable in civil proceedings; (5) the G.L.C. were liable both at
common law and under the 1939 Act for a failure to take reasonable care; (6)
therefore it was unnecessary to decide whether the duty under s. 82 was absolute:
MARSH v. BETSTYLE CONSTRUCTION CO. AND THE GREATER LONDON COUNCIL,
August 6, 1979, Judge Lewis Hawser, Q.C. (*Ex rel. Graeme Williams, Esq.,
Barrister.*)

1876. Master and servant—duty of care—injury in warship during sea trials
     In November 1975 P, a fitter employed by V Ltd., was working aboard a

warship taken over by a foreign navy. The ship was built by V Ltd. under contract with the Ministry of Defence according to drawing and design of V Ltd. which had been approved by the Ministry of Defence. The ship was undergoing various sea trials under command of the owner, V Ltd. having provided some personnel to assist. In the area around the interior of the aft end of the ship there was a walk way for personnel with a hand guard rail on the inward side and low toe board on the hull side. Also on the hull side hand holds could be used on beams mechanism or equipment. On the hull side of the walk way there were gaps of various dimensions between the hull and the tow boards. P lurched off balance and his left foot went over the tow board into the gap. He fell on his right hand and injured his right shoulder. P sued V Ltd. in negligence arguing that the gap was uncovered or his employers failed to provide a hand rail on the hull side of the walk way thereby exposing him to a forseeable risk. *Held,* that the employer's duty is to take reasonable care for the safety of its employees but it is wrong to equate and demand the same high standard in a warship undergoing sea trials as in a factory. The standard of design and construction was high. The employers had not been incompetent in their duties and the claim failed: PARKER *v.* VICKERS, June 18, 1979; Talbot J.; Preston Crown Ct. (*Ex rel. Noel J. Noble, Solicitor.*)

1877. **employee robbed—duty of employer**
    C, a chemist and manager at Barking factory, was attacked by robbers when collecting the workforce's wages. In 1974 F.P.I. Co. had reviewed their policy re collection of wages due to a wages snatch. *Held,* that F.P.I. Co. were liable to C for the injuries in negligence since (1) an employer has a duty to take reasonable steps to ensure employees are not subjected to any unnecessary risks of injury, including injury by criminals; and (2) any reasonable employer with F.P.I. Co.'s history would have employed a professional firm, at a virtually trivial cost, to collect wages. On the facts of this case, the difficulties preventing employing a professional firm having been eliminated three years previously, failure to do so constituted negligence: CHARLTON *v.* THE FORREST PRINTING INK CO. [1978] I.R.L.R. 559, Forbes, J.

1878. **fire on vessel—deck hand washed from liferaft and drowned—whether skipper negligent**
    [Scot.] After her steering mechanism had failed due to the spread of a stove fire, the fishing vessel N was out of control and steaming at about her full speed of 10 to 10½ knots, in a force 3 or 4 wind with a 3 to 4 foot swell. The skipper was informed that a lifeboat was on its way, and then agreed to a liferaft being launched. This was done by the mate, who secured the raft by means of a rope attached to its grabline. The skipper did not check that the rope was properly secured; and, further, allowed each man to decide whether to take to the raft. R, a deckhand, had entered the raft when the grabline parted, as a result of which R was swept overboard and drowned. P1, P2 and P3 (R's widow, father and mother) claimed damages from D, the owners of the N, alleging that the skipper had been negligent, and the stove faulty. *Held,* that (1) a reasonably competent skipper would have checked the lashing on a liferaft being towed at speed by a ship out of control before permitting men to enter it; accordingly the skipper was guilty of negligence, and this had caused the accident; (2) the skipper had failed to take reasonable care for the safety of his crew in not ordering them to remain on board, and this was also a direct cause of the accident; (3) it was not negligent to permit the launching of the liferaft; (4) it was not clear how the stove caught fire, and no fault had been established; (5) £11,800 plus interest would be awarded to P1, £500 to P2 and £700 to P3: RUSSELL *v.* BRITISH UNITED TRAWLERS (GRANTON) [1978] 2 Lloyd's Rep. 579, Ct. of Session.

1879. **injury to seaman—liability—quantum of damages.** See O'KEEFE *v.* JOHN STEWART & CO. SHIPPING; THE YEWKYLE, § 2474.

1880. **safe system of working—foreseeable risk of injury—docker lifting heavy weight**
    Employers may be negligent in failing to provide a safe system of working where there is a foreseeable risk of an uneven sharing of a load between two

employees even though the load itself is the maximum safe weight in the circumstances.

The plaintiff, a docker, injured his back while engaged in unloading cases of tobacco from a ship on to a barge. The plaintiff and a fellow employee had begun to lift one end of a case when the case caught on a band securing a case in the lower layer. They then lowered the case and, putting more effort into it, lifted again hoping to overcome the obstruction. This extra strain caused injury to the plaintiff's back and a severe depressive illness resulted. Subsequently he accepted a voluntary severance payment as his injuries made him less suited to dock work. *Held,* that (1) even though the weight which each man was bearing was the maximum safe weight that a man should be asked to lift in such circumstances, the operation involved a foreseeable risk because of the uneven sharing of the load between the two men when the load caught the obstruction; (2) the employers were liable accordingly to the plaintiff for having failed to provide a safe system of working; and (3) the voluntary severance payment received by the plaintiff should be deducted from damages awarded for future loss of earnings.

FRICKER *v.* BENJAMIN PERRY & SONS (1973) 16 K.I.R. 356, Bridge J.

1881. Medical practitioner—duty to patient—injury in descent from examination table

[Aust.] A woman patient aged 63 but not disabled was examined by a doctor on an examination table at a surgery. When the examination was completed and while descending from the table the patient slipped, fell and was injured. The doctor had turned away and had his back to the patient when she was descending from the table. *Held,* the doctor did not owe a duty of care to the patient to assist her in or advise her about her descent from the examination table: ROBERTSON *v.* SMYTH (1979) 20 S.A.S.R. 184, Sth.Aust.Sup.Ct.

1882. —— failure to terminate pregnancy

The defendant doctor agreed to perform a legal abortion on the plaintiff which failed to terminate her pregnancy. He was negligent in doing so. The plaintiff did not learn that she could have had another such operation until it was too late and she gave birth to a healthy child. She was entitled to damages for loss of earnings, for diminution of her marriage prospects and for pain and suffering: SCURIAGA *v.* POWELL (1979) 123 S.J. 406, Watkins J.

1883. —— obstetrician—infant plaintiff injured at birth

The plaintiff, an infant suing by his mother, was awarded £100,000 damages against the defendant obstetrician for severe brain damage suffered during birth. It was alleged that the defendant had pulled too long and too hard with the forceps during the delivery and that this amounted to a want of skill and care resulting in the baby's cerebral haemorrhage. On appeal, *held,* allowing the appeal, that an error of judgment by doctors is not the same as negligence and the defendant could not be held liable for the brain damage suffered by the plaintiff: WHITEHOUSE *v.* JORDAN, *The Times,* December 6, 1979, C.A.

1884. Negligent misstatement—auditors—liability to third parties for error in certified accounts

[N.Z.] A relied, *inter alia,* on the accounts of D in making a takeover offer for the shares of D. By an elementary error, the assets of D were overstated. The same kind of error had been made in some previous years. R, who were D's auditors, were aware of some discrepancy but did not investigate any at the time and issued the relevant Companies Act certificate. Soon after the takeover was completed, the nature and extent of the error was discovered. A brought an action against R; R admitted negligence in giving the certificate but denied any duty of care to A, and in any event denied that any recoverable damage had resulted. *Held,* R were not liable for damages for negligent misstatement. *Per* Richmond P.: a " special relationship " should not be found to exist (*i.e.* where responsibility for advice exists) unless the maker of the statement was or ought to have been aware that his advice would be made available to and be relied upon by a particular person for a particular transaction. (*Anns* v. *Merton London Borough Council* [1977] C.L.Y. 2030; *Derry* v. *Peek* (1887) 37 Ch.D. 541; *Dorset Yacht Co.* v. *Home Office* [1970] C.L.Y.

1849; and *Hedley Byrne & Co.* v. *Heller* [1963] C.L.Y. 2416 referred to): SCOTT GROUP v. MACFARLANE [1978] 1 N.Z.L.R. 553, N.Z.C.A.

1885. Northern Ireland. See NORTHERN IRELAND.

1886. Patent agents—breach of contract. See ANDREW MASTER HONES v. CRUICK-SHANK AND FAIRWEATHER, § 2052.

1887. Product liability—cost of repair of defective vehicle recoverable from manufacturer

[Can.] It has been *held*, that where a defect in a motor vehicle causes an accident that damages the vehicle, both the manufacturer and the retail seller are liable to the buyer for the cost of repair. Liability may be based on breach of the manufacturer's express warranty and on negligence (*Dutton* v. *Bognor Regis Urban District Council* [1972] C.L.Y. 2352 referred to): FULLER v. FORD MOTOR CO. OF CANADA (1978) 94 D.L.R. (3d) 127, York County Ct., Ontario.

1888. Railways—duty of care—involuntary fall of passenger onto railway line

[Aust.] While awaiting a train, P, an intending passenger, suffered an epileptic attack and fell unconscious onto the rails, where she was struck by a train. P obtained judgment at first instance. On appeal, *held*, (1) by majority, a carrier by rail owes a duty to take reasonable care for the safety of the passenger, whether that passenger is in the course of being carried or is standing on a platform waiting for a train; (2) by majority, P's involuntary fall from the platform onto the rails did not make her a trespasser and absolve D from its duty to take reasonable care for her safety. (*Hillen and Pettigrew* v. *I.C.I.* [1936] A.C. 65, *Commissioner for Railways* v. *Quinlan* [1969] C.L.Y. 2516, *Commissioner for Railways* v. *McDermott* [1966] C.L.Y. 838, *Herrington* v. *British Railways Board* [1972] C.L.Y. 2344 and *Southern Portland Cement* v. *Cooper* [1974] C.L.Y. 2574 considered): PUBLIC TRANSPORT COMMISSION OF N.S.W. v. PERRY (1977) 137 C.L.R. 107, Aust.High Ct.

1889. Solicitors—duty of care—beneficiary's claim under will. See ROSS v. CAUNTERS, § 2570.

1890. Statutory duty—remoteness of damage—local authority

[Can.] D1 was a local authority which embarked upon reconstruction of a street. It engaged the services of D2 who were contractors. P carried on a nursery business in the street. When D1 contracted with D2 for D2 to carry out the building works, there was no suggestion that the road would be wholly or partially closed: both D1 and D2 intended there would be reasonable access to all shops and businesses in the street. However, signs were placed indicating the street was closed, and D2's employees operated flags to preclude motorists from having access to the street. *Held*, if D1 had given notice to the businesses in the street that there would be an absolute closure for a certain period of time, then the businesses rights would have been confined to seeking compensation by arbitration, as provided by statute. However, as D1 had elected to keep access to the businesses open, it was under a duty to provide such access as was reasonably possible. The failure to properly sign the approaches, or to maintain the road directly caused loss of business to P. Such loss was not beyond D1's contemplation (or D2's) but on the contrary was always in their minds: TRAPPA HOLDINGS v. DISTRICT OF SURREY (1978) 95 D.L.R. (3d) 107, Brit.Col.Sup.Ct.

BOOKS AND ARTICLES. See *post*, pp. [9], [27].

NORTHERN IRELAND

1891. Administrative law

LANDS TRIBUNAL (SALARIES AND SUPERANNUATION) ORDER (NORTHERN IRELAND) 1979 (No. 50) [10p], made under the Lands Tribunal and Compensation Act (Northern Ireland) 1964 (c. 29), s. 2 (5); operative on April 9, 1979; increases the salaries of members of the Lands Tribunal; revokes the 1978 (No. 305) Order.

SALARIES (COMPTROLLER AND AUDITOR-GENERAL AND OTHERS) ORDER

(NORTHERN IRELAND) 1979 (No. 220) [10p], made under S.I. 1973 No. 1086 (N.I. 14), art. 4; operative on August 6, 1979; increases the salaries of the comptroller and auditor-general, the parliamentary commissioner and the commissioner for complaints; revokes the 1978 (No. 303) Order.

LANDS TRIBUNAL (SALARIES) ORDER (NORTHERN IRELAND) 1979 (No. 221) [10p], made under the Lands Tribunal and Compensation Act (Northern Ireland) 1964, s. 2 (5); operative on August 6, 1979; increases the salaries of members of the lands tribunal; revokes arts. 3 and 4 of the 1979 (No. 50) Order.

1892. —— discrimination

[Northern Ireland Constitution Act 1973 (c. 36), ss. 19, 23.] A district council prepared a scheme to provide coaching for young persons in various sports including Gaelic football and later deleted Gaelic football from the scheme. On an application for a declaration that this was unlawful discrimination under s. 19 of the Northern Ireland Constitution Act 1973, *held,* granting the application, that (1) the decision to delete Gaelic football from the scheme was taken on political grounds and adversely affected the plaintiffs; (2) the decision constituted discrimination as defined in s. 23 (2) of the 1973 Act as it was the duty of the council to provide adequate recreational and physical facilities and no distinction can be drawn between different sports; (3) while the Gaelic Athletic Association, which is the controlling body for Gaelic football, is itself a body which discriminates, the scheme was to be run under the control of the district council and not the Association: PURVIS *v.* MAGHERAFELT DISTRICT COUNCIL [1978] N.I. 26, Murray J.

1893. Agriculture

MILK MARKETING (AMENDMENT) REGULATIONS (NORTHERN IRELAND) 1978 (No. 366) [20p], made under the European Communities Act 1972 (c. 68) s. 2 (2); operative on January 1, 1979; amend the 1955 (No. 43) scheme as respects provisions relating to the manner in which the price of milk sold to the milk marketing board is established.

MOVEMENT OF PIGS (REVOCATION) REGULATIONS (NORTHERN IRELAND) 1979 (No. 13) [10p], made under the Agricultural Marketing Act (Northern Ireland) 1964 (c. 13), s. 17 (1), as amended by the Agriculture (Miscellaneous Provisions) Act (Northern Ireland) 1970 (c. 20), s. 9; operative on March 7, 1979; revoke the 1972 (No. 90) Regulations.

EMPLOYMENT IN AGRICULTURE (AMENDMENT) SCHEME (NORTHERN IRELAND) 1979 (No. 22) [10p], made under the Agriculture (Temporary Assistance) Act (Northern Ireland) 1954 (c. 31), s. 1, as amended by the Agriculture (Temporary Assistance) (Amendment) Act (Northern Ireland) 1957 (c. 3); operative on January 30, 1979; increases the amount payable under, and extends the duration of, the 1972 (No. 230) Scheme.

PIGS (CARCASE CLASSIFICATION) (AMENDMENT) SCHEME ORDER (NORTHERN IRELAND) 1979 (No. 41) [10p], made under S.I. 1975 No. 1038 (N.I. 8), art. 2; operative on April 1, 1979; makes detailed amendments of the 1977 (No. 335) Order.

PIGS (FEED PRICE ALLOWANCE) (REVOCATION) SCHEME (NORTHERN IRELAND) 1979 (No. 42) [10p], made under the Agriculture (Temporary Assistance) Act (Northern Ireland) 1954, s. 1, as amended by the Agriculture (Temporary Assistance) (Amendment) Act (Northern Ireland) 1957; operative on April 1, 1979; revokes the 1972 (No. 86), 1973 (No. 106), 1975 (No. 220), 1976 (No. 26), 1977 (No. 88) and 1978 (No. 47) Orders.

BULK MILK TANKS (ASSISTANCE) SCHEME (NORTHERN IRELAND) 1979 (No. 96) [10p], made under the Agriculture (Temporary Assistance) Act (Northern Ireland) 1954, s. 1, as amended by the Agriculture (Temporary Assistance) (Amendment) Act (Northern Ireland) 1957; operative on April 1, 1979; provides for the payment by the Department of Agriculture of grants to the Milk Marketing Board in respect of expenditure incurred by the Board in the purchase and installation on dairy farms of bulk milk tanks.

POULTRY (FEED PRICE ALLOWANCE) (AMENDMENT) SCHEME (NORTHERN IRELAND) 1979 (No. 100) [10p], made under the Agriculture (Temporary Assistance) Act (Northern Ireland) 1954, s. 1; operative on April 1, 1979;

specifies the total maximum amount payable under the poultry, eggs and pigs feed price allowance schemes to June 30, 1979; revokes the 1978 (No. 49) Scheme.

EGGS (FEED PRICE ALLOWANCE) (AMENDMENT) SCHEME (NORTHERN IRELAND) 1979 (No. 101) [10p], made under the Agriculture (Temporary Assistance) Act (Northern Ireland) 1954, s. 1; operative on April 1, 1979; specifies the total maximum amount payable under the eggs, poultry and pigs feed price allowance schemes to June 30, 1979; revokes the 1978 (No. 48) Scheme.

MILK AID SCHEME (NORTHERN IRELAND) 1979 (No. 127) [10p], made under the Agriculture (Temporary Assistance) Act (Northern Ireland) 1954, s. 1; operative on April 1, 1979; provides for the payment of aid to the Milk Marketing Board for Northern Ireland to compensate it partially for lower net returns for milk sold by it compared to the net returns received by the Milk Marketing Board of England and Wales.

CHAFF-CUTTING MACHINES (ACCIDENTS) ACT 1897 (REPEAL) ORDER (NORTHERN IRELAND) 1979 (No. 128) [10p], made under the Agriculture (Safety, Health and Welfare Provisions) Act (Northern Ireland) 1959 (c. 24), s. 1 (6); appoints May 1, 1979, as the day for the repeal of the Chaff-Cutting Machines (Accidents) Act 1897 (c. 60).

AGRICULTURE (SAFETY, HEALTH AND WELFARE PROVISIONS) ACT (NORTHERN IRELAND) 1959 (REPEALS AND MODIFICATION) REGULATIONS (NORTHERN IRELAND) 1979 (No. 129) [20p], made under S.I. 1978 No. 1039 (N.I. 9), arts. 17 (3) (a) (b), 46; operative on June 1, 1979; repeal ss. 1–4 (part), 5, 7–11, 13–16, and modify s. 18 of the Agriculture (Safety, Health and Welfare Provisions) Act (Northern Ireland) 1959.

AGRICULTURE (POISONOUS SUBSTANCES) ACT (NORTHERN IRELAND) 1954 (REPEALS AND MODIFICATIONS) REGULATIONS (NORTHERN IRELAND) 1979 (No. 130) [20p], made under S.I. 1979 No. 1039, arts. 17 (3) (a) (b), 46; operative on June 1, 1979; repeal ss. 1–3, 4 (part), 5, 9, 10, and modify s. 6 of the Agriculture (Poisonous Substances) Act (Northern Ireland) 1954 (c. 5).

IMPORTATION AND PLANTING OF POTATOES (AMENDMENT) ORDER (NORTHERN IRELAND) 1979 (No. 138) [10p], made under the Plant Health Act (Northern Ireland) 1967 (c. 28), ss. 2, 3A; operative on May 21, 1979; amends the definition of " importer " in the 1972 (No. 24) Order and the procedure to be adopted when potatoes are landed in contravention of that Order.

SEED POTATO (IMPROVEMENT) SCHEME (NORTHERN IRELAND) 1979 (No. 166) [20p], made under the Agriculture (Temporary Assistance) Act (Northern Ireland) 1954, s. 1, as amended by the Agriculture (Temporary Assistance) (Amendment) Act (Northern Ireland) 1957; operative on June 13, 1979; provides for the payment of grants, not exceeding £30,000 in total, to the Seed Potato Marketing Board in respect of measures designed to increase the efficiency of the seed potato industry.

EGGS (FEED PRICE ALLOWANCE) (AMENDMENT No. 2) SCHEME (NORTHERN IRELAND) 1979 (No. 217) [10p], made under the Agriculture (Temporary Assistance) Act (Northern Ireland) 1954, s. 1; operative on July 1, 1979; specifies the total maximum amount payable under the eggs, poultry and pigs feed price allowance schemes to March 31, 1980; revokes the 1979 (No. 101) Scheme.

POULTRY (FEED PRICE ALLOWANCE) (AMENDMENT No. 2) SCHEME (NORTHERN IRELAND) 1979 (No. 218) [10p], made under the Agriculture (Temporary Assistance) Act (Northern Ireland) 1954, s. 1; operative on July 1, 1979; specifies the total maximum amount payable under the poultry, eggs and pigs feed price allowance schemes to March 31, 1980; revokes the 1979 (No. 100) Scheme.

SEEDS (FEES) REGULATIONS (NORTHERN IRELAND) 1979 (No. 285) [50p], made under the Seeds Act (Northern Ireland) 1965 (c. 22), ss. 1, 2 (2) (4); operative on September 27, 1979; increase fees payable under certain Regulations dealing with seeds; revoke the 1978 (No. 226) Regulations.

MARKETING OF POTATOES (AMENDMENT) REGULATIONS (NORTHERN IRELAND) 1979 (No. 298) [10p], made under the Marketing of Potatoes Act (Northern Ireland) 1964 (c. 8), ss. 3 (3), 7 (2), 11; operative on October 1, 1979; amend the 1964 (No. 112) Regulations by increasing the fee payable for the inspection of potatoes to 99p per tonne.

AGRICULTURAL TRUST (MARKET DEVELOPMENT) (REVOCATION) SCHEME (NORTHERN IRELAND) 1979 (No. 357) [10p], made under the Agriculture (Temporary Assistance) Act (Northern Ireland) 1954 (c. 31), s. 1 (4); operative on November 12, 1979; revokes the 1971 (No. 106) Scheme.

AGRICULTURAL RETURNS (AMENDMENT) REGULATIONS (NORTHERN IRELAND) 1979 (No. 376) [10p], made under the Agricultural Returns Act (Northern Ireland) 1939 (c. 35), s. 1 (6); operative on December 21, 1979; amend the 1966 (No. 47) Regulations by adding the last week-day of January in each year as a prescribed day for the furnishing of returns containing the particulars mentioned in reg. 1 (d).

1894. Animals

WELFARE OF LIVESTOCK (INTENSIVE UNITS) REGULATIONS (NORTHERN IRELAND) 1978 (No. 360) [10p], made under the Welfare of Animals Act (Northern Ireland) 1972 (c. 7), s. 2; operative on January 1, 1979; provide for the welfare of agricultural livestock kept in intensive units.

TRANSPLANTATION OF OVA (ANIMALS) REGULATIONS (NORTHERN IRELAND) 1978 (No. 368) [20p], made under S.I. 1975 No. 1834 (N.I. 17), art. 5; operative on January 16, 1979; provide for the licensing of private ova transplantation centres and for the collection, preparation, storage, distribution and sale of ova.

EXPORTED ANIMALS (CHARGES AND COMPENSATION) (AMENDMENT) ORDER (NORTHERN IRELAND) 1979 (No. 12) [10p], made under the Exported Animals (Compensation) Act (Northern Ireland) 1952 (c. 24), ss. 5, 10, as extended by S.I. 1972 No. 964 (N.I. 7), arts. 3, 4; operative on February 19, 1979; increases the levy on exported cattle, sheep and pigs and the limit on compensation payable for an animal slaughtered or lost at sea.

ANIMALS AND POULTRY QUARANTINE FEES ORDER (NORTHERN IRELAND) 1979 (No. 64) [20p], made under the Diseases of Animals Act (Northern Ireland) 1958 (c. 13), s. 43A, as inserted by the Agriculture (Miscellaneous Provisions) Act (Northern Ireland) 1965 (c. 3), s. 13, and amended by S.I. 1977 No. 1245 (N.I. 12), art. 12; operative on April 9, 1979; increases fees payable for the care and housing of imported animals, poultry and hatching eggs including, in the case of animals, feeding in a quarantine station; revokes the 1978 (No. 58) Order.

BRUCELLOSIS CONTROL (AMENDMENT) ORDER (NORTHERN IRELAND) 1979 (No. 126) [10p], made under the Diseases of Animals Act (Northern Ireland) 1958, ss. 13, 53; operative on April 30, 1979; amends the 1972 (No. 94) Order in relation to the movement of eligible animals and animals being returned to the herd from which they came.

IMPORTATION OF BEES (PROHIBITION) REGULATIONS (NORTHERN IRELAND) 1979 (No. 184) [10p], made under the Bee Pest Prevention Act (Northern Ireland) 1945 (c. 1), s. 4A (1) (a) (c); operative from June 1, 1979, until December 31, 1979; prohibit the importation of bees into Northern Ireland from specified countries and from other countries unless certain requirements are met.

HORSE BREEDING SCHEME (NORTHERN IRELAND) 1979 (No. 260) [40p], made under the Agriculture Act (Northern Ireland) 1949 (c. 2), s. 9; operative on August 22, 1979; provides for the registration of non-thorough-bred mares, the approval of stallions considered suitable for breeding purposes and the making of payments to encourage the keeping and use of good quality stallions; revokes the 1969 (No. 49) Scheme.

EUROPEAN COMMUNITIES POULTRY MEAT (HYGIENE) (AMENDMENT) REGULATIONS (NORTHERN IRELAND) 1979 (No. 261) [50p], made under the European Communities Act 1972 (c. 68), s. 2 (2); operative on September 1, 1979; implement EEC directives on the immersion chilling process and on the health marking of large packages of fresh poultry meat.

DISEASES OF ANIMALS (EXPORT HEALTH CERTIFICATES) ORDER (NORTHERN IRELAND) 1979 (No. 267) [40p], made under the Diseases of Animals Act (Northern Ireland) 1958, s. 24A; operative on August 20, 1979; makes the exportation of bovine animals, swine and fresh poultry meat from Northern Ireland to EEC Member States other than the United Kingdom, subject to certain exceptions, conditional upon the existence of an appropriate health certificate.

DISEASES OF ANIMALS (IMPORTATION OF MACHINERY) ORDER (NORTHERN IRELAND) 1979 (No. 281) [40p], made under the Diseases of Animals Act (Northern Ireland) 1958, ss. 5, 13, 18, 23, 53, as extended by S.I. 1975 No. 1307 (N.I. 12); operative on September 1, 1979; prohibits the importation of machinery which has been used on land in any country outside Northern Ireland and the Republic of Ireland unless it has been thoroughly cleansed and disinfected.

WELFARE OF ANIMALS (FEES) ORDER (NORTHERN IRELAND) 1979 (No. 289) [10p], made under the Welfare of Animals Act (Northern Ireland) 1972, s. 8 (3); operative on November 15, 1979; increases fees payable for licences to keep pet shops, animal boarding establishments and riding and zoological establishments; revokes the 1972 (No. 335) Order.

TRANSPLANTATION OF OVA (ANIMALS) (AMENDMENT) REGULATIONS (NORTHERN IRELAND) 1979 (No. 326) [10p], made under S.I. 1975 No. 1834 (N.I. 17), art. 5; operative on October 29, 1979; amend the 1978 (No. 368) Regulations to enable the Department of Agriculture to approve the use of vehicles for the collection, preparation and storage of ova.

RABIES VIRUS ORDER (NORTHERN IRELAND) 1979 (No. 374) [20p], made under the Diseases of Animals Act (Northern Ireland) 1958, ss. 5, 13 (1), 18 (1), 23 (1), 53 (1), and S.I. 1975 No. 418 (N.I. 3), art. 8A; operative on November 26, 1979; prohibits the importation, keeping or deliberate introduction into animals of rabies virus except under the authority of a licence.

IMPORTATION OF BEES (PROHIBITION) (AMENDMENT) REGULATIONS (NORTHERN IRELAND) 1979 (No. 395) [10p], made under the Bee Pest Prevention Act (Northern Ireland) 1945, s. 4A (1) (a) (c); operative on January 1, 1980; extend the operation of the 1979 (No. 184) Regulations until June 30, 1980, and add certain countries to those from which the importation of bees into Northern Ireland is prohibited.

1895. Armed forces

RESERVE AND AUXILIARY FORCES (PROTECTION OF CIVIL INTERESTS) (NORTHERN IRELAND) ORDER 1979 (No. 291) [40p], made under the Reserve and Auxiliary Forces (Protection of Civil Interests) Act 1951 (c. 65), s. 65; operative on April 12, 1979, save for arts. 6 (2), 43 (2) (a) (d) which are operative on the day appointed for the commencement of the Consumer Credit Act 1974, Sched. 4, paras. 12, 14; extends the 1951 Act to Northern Ireland. It also modifies that Act, in its application to Northern Ireland, to take account of Northern Ireland law.

1896. Bankruptcy—after-acquired property

[Irish Bankrupt and Insolvent Act 1857 (c. 60), s. 267.] In 1970, K entered into an arrangement with his creditors under which his estate vested in the official assignee (" O.A. "). K held a house under a long lease, subject to a mortgage for £50 less than its value. O.A. elected not to take the house, but agreed that K should buy the equity of redemption in it. In 1971 K was adjudicated bankrupt. O.A. did not elect to take the house, which K sold in 1975. After discharging the mortgage, £3,257 was left, which O.A. claimed. *Held*, under s. 267 of the Irish Bankrupt and Insolvent Act 1857, O.A. was entitled to the net proceeds: *Re* KEANEY [1977] N.I. 67, Murray J.

1897. Building and engineering, architects and surveyors

BUILDING (AMENDMENT) REGULATIONS (NORTHERN IRELAND) 1979 (No. 79) [30p], made under S.I. 1972 No. 1996 (N.I. 19), arts. 3, 5; operative on May 1, 1979; amend the 1977 (No. 149) Regulations but not in relation to work completed, or for which plans have been deposited, before the operative date.

BUILDING REGULATIONS (1978 ORDER) (COMMENCEMENT NO. 1) ORDER (NORTHERN IRELAND) 1979 (No. 327) (C. 15) [20p], made under S.I. 1978 No. 1038 (N.I. 8), art. 1 (2), and the Northern Ireland Act 1974 (c. 28), Sched. 1, para. 2 (1) (2); brings specified provisions of the S.I. into operation on November 1, 1979.

1898. —— right to challenge the nomination of an architect

A local authority's edition of a standard form of building contract gave the contractor a right to object to a successor to the architect nominated under the contract but a footnote directed that this right was to be struck out where the original architect was an officer of a local authority. The relevant words were, however, not physically struck out. On an originating summons to determine whether the contractor was entitled to object to the nomination of an officer of the Northern Ireland Housing Executive as successor to the original architect, *held,* that the Housing Executive was to be treated for the purposes of the contract as a local authority and the footnote had the effect of deleting from the contract the contractor's right to object: NORTHERN IRELAND HOUSING EXECUTIVE *v.* McTAGGART & Co. [1978] N.I. 87, Murray J.

1899. Building societies

BUILDING SOCIETIES (FEES) (AMENDMENT) REGULATIONS (NORTHERN IRELAND) 1979 (No. 73) [20p], made under the Building Societies Act (Northern Ireland) 1967 (c. 31), s. 123 (1); operative on May 1, 1979; increase the fees payable in connection with the exercise by the Registrar of his functions under the 1967 Act and for the inspection and copying of documents; revoke the 1978 (No. 28) Regulations.

1900. Capital taxation

CAPITAL TRANSFER TAX (NORTHERN IRELAND CONSEQUENTIAL AMENDMENT) ORDER 1979 (No. 927) [10p], made under the Northern Ireland Constitution Act 1973 (c. 36), s. 38 (2); operative on July 26, 1979; amends s. 122 of the Finance Act 1976 dealing with the consequences for capital transfer tax of court orders under the Inheritance (Provision for Family and Dependants) Act 1975.

1901. Charities—cy-près doctrine—consent of beneficiary necessary—whether general charitable intention

A testatrix left the residue of her estate to her executors and trustees upon trust for a named church and referred in her will to the wish of her late mother and sister that the bequest be used for the installation of bells at that church. The church decided not to install the bells. On a summons to determine whether the residue should devolve as on intestacy or be applied *cy-près*, *held*, that (1) the trust was initially impossible of performance as the consent of the church was essential for its fulfilment; and (2) the residue should be applied *cy-près* as the testatrix had a general charitable intention to advance religion through the work of that church: *Re* DUNWOODIE (DECD.); NORTHERN BANK EXECUTOR AND TRUSTEE Co. *v.* MOSS [1977] N.I. 141, Murray J.

1902. Chronically Sick and Disabled Persons (Northern Ireland) Act 1978 (c. 53)—commencement

CHRONICALLY SICK AND DISABLED PERSONS (1978 ACT) (COMMENCEMENT No. 1) ORDER (NORTHERN IRELAND) 1978 (No. 365 (C. 19)) [10p], made under the Chronically Sick and Disabled Persons (Northern Ireland) Act 1978 (c. 53), s. 21 (2); brings that Act, except s. 14, into operation on December 28, 1978.

CHRONICALLY SICK AND DISABLED PERSONS (1978 ACT) (COMMENCEMENT No. 2) ORDER (NORTHERN IRELAND) 1979 (No. 364) (C. 16) [10p], made under the Chronically Sick and Disabled Persons (Northern Ireland) Act 1978, s. 21 (2); brought s. 14 of the Act into operation on October 31, 1979.

1903. Company law

COMPANIES (1978 ORDER) (COMMENCEMENT No. 2) ORDER (NORTHERN IRELAND) 1979 (No. 191) (C. 8) [50p], made under S.I. 1978 No. 1042 (N.I. 12), art. 1 (1), read with the Northern Ireland Act 1974 (c. 28), Sched. 1, para. 2 (1) (*b*); bring specified provisions of that S.I. into operation on June 18, 1979, in so far as they confer power to make regulations and orders, and into operation on July 31, 1979, for other purposes.

COMPANIES (FEES) REGULATIONS (NORTHERN IRELAND) 1979 (No. 210) [10p], made under the Companies Act (Northern Ireland) 1960 (c. 22), s. 373 (1) (*a*); operative on July 31, 1979; require specified fees to be paid to the registrar of companies on the re-registration of a company as unlimited or limited.

COMPANIES (DISCLOSURE OF DIRECTORS' INTERESTS) (EXCEPTIONS) No. 1

REGULATIONS (NORTHERN IRELAND) 1979 (No. 226) [10p], made under S.I. 1978 No. 1042 (N.I. 12), art. 37 (1); operative on July 31, 1979; relieve a director of a company from the obligation to notify it of certain interests where the interest arises solely from a constraint imposed by the company's memorandum or articles of association on a person's right to dispose of a share.

COMPANIES (DISCLOSURE OF DIRECTORS' INTERESTS) (EXCEPTIONS) No. 2 REGULATIONS (NORTHERN IRELAND) 1979 (No. 227) [10p], made under S.I. 1978 No. 1042, art. 37 (1); operative on July 31, 1979; relieve a director of a company of the obligation to notify it of certain interests where the interest is in securities of an industrial or provident society or arises in relation to the director's holding of office as a trustee or as a beneficiary under certain pension schemes.

COMPANIES (DISCLOSURE OF DIRECTORS' INTERESTS) (EXCEPTIONS) No. 3 REGULATIONS (NORTHERN IRELAND) 1979 (No. 228) [10p], made under S.I. 1978 No. 1042, art. 37 (1); operative on July 31, 1979; in certain circumstances relieve a director of a company of the obligation to notify it of certain interests where the interest is in the securities of a body corporate incorporated outside Northern Ireland or of a holding company required to keep a register of directors' interests in securities by that S.I.

LISTED COMPANIES (DISCLOSURE OF SHARE INTERESTS) (EXCLUSIONS) REGU-LATIONS (NORTHERN IRELAND) 1979 (No. 229) [10p], made under S.I. 1978 No. 1042, art. 114 (5) (f); operative on July 31, 1979; prescribe interests which need not be notified under art. 114 of that S.I. to a company listed on a recognised stock exchange.

COMPANIES (FORMS) REGULATIONS (NORTHERN IRELAND) 1979 (No. 231) [£1·75], made under the Companies Act (Northern Ireland) 1960, ss. 93 (1) (5) (8), 95 (1), 191 (6), 358, 399 (1) and S.I. 1978 No. 1042, arts. 36 (3), 39 (9), 57 (1), 118 (1) (3) (a), 119 (1), 121 (3), 131 (3); operative on July 31, 1979; prescribe the forms to be used by companies when providing the registrar of companies with information under certain provisions of that Act and S.I. and prescribe a time within which a company incorporated outside Northern Ireland but with a place of business in it must notify the registrar of a change in its name.

COMPANIES (FORMS) (AMENDMENT) REGULATIONS (NORTHERN IRELAND) 1979 (No. 232) [60p], made under the Companies Act (Northern Ireland) 1960, ss. 15 (2), 52 (2), 399 (1); operative on July 31, 1979; amend the 1961 (No. 83) Regulations by prescribing a new form of declaration of compliance for production to the registrar on application for the registration of a company and a new form giving particulars of a contract relating to shares allotted as fully or partly paid up otherwise than in cash where the contract is not in writing.

COMPANIES (1978 ORDER) (COMMENCEMENT NO. 3) ORDER (NORTHERN IRELAND) 1979 (No. 325) (C. 14) [10p], made under S.I. 1978 No. 1042 (N.I. 12), art. 1 (1), and the Northern Ireland Act 1974 (c. 28), Sched. 1, para. 2 (1) (b); bring specified provisions of the S.I. into operation, so far as they confer power to make regulations, on October 8, 1979, and for other purposes, on November 12, 1979.

COMPANIES (FORMS No. 2) REGULATIONS (NORTHERN IRELAND) 1979 (No. 355) [20p], made under S.I. 1978 No. 1042 (N.I. 12), art. 4 (1); operative on November 12, 1979; prescribe the forms to be used by companies when notifying the registrar of companies of their accounting reference date.

1904. Compulsory purchase

COMPULSORY ACQUISITION (INTEREST) (No. 2) ORDER (NORTHERN IRELAND) 1978 (No. 353) [10p], made under the Administrative and Financial Provisions Act (Northern Ireland) 1956 (c. 17), s. 14 and the Local Government Act (Northern Ireland) 1972 (c. 9), Sched. 6, para. 18; operative on December 22, 1978; increases to 12½ per cent. per annum the rate of interest on compensation payable under specified Acts for compulsorily acquired land; revokes the 1978 (No. 248) Order.

COMPULSORY ACQUISITION (INTEREST) ORDER (NORTHERN IRELAND) 1979 (No. 33) [10p], made under the Administrative and Financial Provisions Act

(Northern Ireland) 1956, s. 14 and the Local Government Act (Northern Ireland) 1972 (c. 9), Sched. 6, para. 18; operative on March 29, 1979; increases to 14 per cent. per annum the rate of interest on compensation under certain enactments for compulsorily acquired land; revokes the 1978 (No. 353) Order.

COMPULSORY ACQUISITION (INTEREST) (NO. 2) ORDER (NORTHERN IRELAND) 1979 (No. 287) [10p], made under the Administrative and Financial Provisions Act (Northern Ireland) 1956, s. 14, and the Local Government Act (Northern Ireland) 1972, Sched. 6, para. 18; operative on September 26, 1979; reduces to 13 per cent. per annum the rate of interest on compensation payable under certain enactments for compulsorily acquired land; revokes the 1979 (No. 33) Order.

1905. —— **Lands Tribunal decisions**

ALLEN AND HANNA v. NORTHERN IRELAND HOUSING EXECUTIVE, R/4/1978 and R/5/1978 (compensation for land in Kilkeel, Co. Down).

COOPER v. NORTHERN IRELAND HOUSING EXECUTIVE, R/18/1978 (compensation for land at Enniskillen, Co. Fermanagh, held by two claimants as tenants in common but no compensation for injurious affection to other land in which only one of the claimants had an interest).

O'DONNELL v. NORTHERN IRELAND ELECTRICITY SERVICE, R/12/1977 (compensation for damages, loss and injurious affection due to siting of electricity pylons on farming land).

1906. Coroners

CORONERS (SALARIES) (AMENDMENT) RULES (NORTHERN IRELAND) 1979 (No. 18) [10p], made under the Coroners Act (Northern Ireland) 1959 (c. 15), s. 36 (1) (a); operative on March 1, 1979; increase coroners' salaries and allowances; revoke the 1976 (No. 203), 1977 (No. 206) and 1978 (No. 227) Rules.

CORONERS (SALARIES, FEES AND EXPENSES) (AMENDMENT) RULES (NORTHERN IRELAND) 1979 (No. 82) [10p], made under the Coroners Act (Northern Ireland), 1959, s. 36 (1) (a); operative on April 17, 1979, with effect from September 1, 1977; increase the maximum fee payable to persons assisting at post-mortem examinations.

1907. County court practice

COUNTY COURT (AMENDMENT) RULES (NORTHERN IRELAND) 1978 (No. 370) [40p], made under the County Courts Act (Northern Ireland) 1959 (c. 25), s. 146; operative on February 1, 1979; amend Ord. 12 in the 1976 (No. 374) Rules as to the procedure in default and summary actions and Ord. 5 by deleting r. 2 (6) (money-lenders' actions); insert a new Ord. 28A for applications under s. 139 (1) (a) of the Consumer Credit Act 1974 for the re-opening of credit agreements because they are extortionate.

COUNTY COURT (BLOOD TESTS) RULES (NORTHERN IRELAND) 1978 (No. 378) [20p], made under the County Courts Act (Northern Ireland) 1959, s. 146; operative on March 1, 1979; prescribe county court practice and procedure in relation to the use of blood tests in paternity proceedings.

COUNTY COURT (MENTAL HEALTH ACT) RULES (NORTHERN IRELAND) 1978 (No. 380) [20p], made under the County Courts Act (Northern Ireland) 1959, s. 146 and the Mental Health Act (Northern Ireland) 1961 (c. 15), s. 44; operative on March 1, 1979; set out the procedure for applications to county courts under Pt. II of the 1961 Act.

COUNTY COURT (RENT ORDER) RULES (NORTHERN IRELAND) 1978 (No. 407) [90p], made under the County Courts Act (Northern Ireland) 1959, s. 146; operative on February 1, 1979; prescribe county court procedure under the Rent (Northern Ireland), Order 1978.

COUNTY COURT DIVISIONS ORDER (NORTHERN IRELAND) 1979 (No. 31) [10p], made under the County Courts Act (Northern Ireland) 1959, s. 1 (1), as substituted by the Judicature (Northern Ireland) Act 1978 (c. 23), s. 95; operative on the day appointed for the coming into force of s. 95 of the 1978 Act; divides Northern Ireland into eight county court divisions, each division comprising specified petty sessions districts.

COUNTY COURT (CRIMINAL DAMAGE COMPENSATION) (AMENDMENT) RULES (NORTHERN IRELAND) 1979 (No. 106) [10p], made under the County Courts

Act (Northern Ireland) 1959, s. 146 and S.I. 1977 No. 1247 (N.I. 14), arts. 12, 14, 15; operative on April 18, 1979; amend the 1978 (No. 135) Rules by substituting for references to the clerk of the Crown and peace references to the chief clerk and circuit registrar.

COUNTY COURT (FAIR EMPLOYMENT ACT) (AMENDMENT) RULES (NORTHERN IRELAND) 1979 (No. 107) [10p], made under the County Courts Act (Northern Ireland) 1959, s. 146, and the Fair Employment (Northern Ireland) Act 1976 (c. 25), s. 45; operative on April 18, 1979; amend the 1978 (No. 151) Rules by substituting for references to the clerk of the Crown and peace references to the chief clerk.

COUNTY COURT (CRIMINAL INJURIES TO THE PERSON) (COMPENSATION) (AMENDMENT) RULES (NORTHERN IRELAND) 1979 (No. 108) [10p], made under the County Courts Act (Northern Ireland) 1959, s. 146, and S.I. 1977 No. 1248 (N.I. 15), arts. 13–15, 20; operative on April 18, 1979; amend the 1977 (No. 313) Rules by substituting for references to the clerk of the Crown and peace references to the chief clerk and circuit registrar.

COUNTY COURT (COMMISSIONER FOR COMPLAINTS) (COMPENSATION) (AMENDMENT) RULES (NORTHERN IRELAND) 1979 (No. 109) [10p], made under the County Courts Act (Northern Ireland) 1959, s. 146; operative on April 18, 1979; amend the 1971 (No. 178) Rules by substituting for references to the clerk of the Crown and peace references to the chief clerk.

COUNTY COURT (CRIMINAL INJURIES TO PROPERTY) (COMPENSATION) (AMENDMENT) RULES (NORTHERN IRELAND) 1979 (No. 110) [10p], made under the County Courts Act (Northern Ireland) 1959, s. 146, and the Criminal Injuries to Property (Compensation) Act (Northern Ireland) 1971 (c. 38), ss. 5 (3), 6 (3), 8 (1) (2); operative on April 18, 1979; amend the 1973 (No. 166) Rules by substituting for references to the clerk of the Crown and peace references to the chief clerk and circuit registrar.

COUNTY COURT (AMENDMENT) RULES (NORTHERN IRELAND) 1979 (No. 111) [30p], made under the County Courts Act (Northern Ireland) 1959, s. 146; operative on April 18, 1979; amend the 1976 (No. 374) Rules to make new provision in respect of the civil jurisdiction exercisable by circuit registrars and for an arbitration procedure for small claims.

COUNTY COURT (AMENDMENT NO. 2) RULES (NORTHERN IRELAND) 1979 (No. 112) [30p], made under the County Courts Act (Northern Ireland) 1959, s. 146; operative on April 18, 1979; amend the 1976 (No. 374) Rules by substituting for references to the clerk of the Crown and peace and county court registrar references to the circuit registrar and chief clerk and make other incidental amendments.

COUNTY COURT (ELECTORAL REGISTRATION APPEAL) (AMENDMENT) RULES (NORTHERN IRELAND) 1979 (No. 113) [10p], made under the County Courts Act (Northern Ireland) 1959, s. 146; operative on April 18, 1979; amend the 1969 (No. 345) Rules by substituting for references to the clerk of the Crown and peace reference to the chief clerk.

COUNTY COURT (BLOOD TESTS) (AMENDMENT) RULES (NORTHERN IRELAND) 1979 (No. 114) [10p], made under the County Courts Act (Northern Ireland) 1959, s. 146; operative on April 18, 1979; amend the 1978 (No. 378) Rules by substituting for references to the clerk of the Crown and peace references to the chief clerk.

COUNTY COURT (RENT ORDER) (AMENDMENT) RULES (NORTHERN IRELAND) 1979 (No. 115) [10p], made under the County Courts Act (Northern Ireland) 1959, s. 146; operative on April 18, 1979; amend the 1978 (No. 407) Rules by substituting for references to the clerk of the Crown and peace references to the chief clerk.

COUNTY COURT (LICENSING) (AMENDMENT) RULES (NORTHERN IRELAND) 1979 (No. 116) [10p], made under the County Courts Act (Northern Ireland) 1959, s. 146, and the Licensing Act (Northern Ireland) 1971 (c. 13), Sched. 1, para. 2; operative on April 18, 1979; amend the 1971 (No. 174) Rules by substituting for references to the clerk of the Crown and peace references to the chief clerk.

COUNTY COURT (ADOPTION) (AMENDMENT) RULES (NORTHERN IRELAND) 1979 (No. 117) [10p], made under the County Courts Act (Northern Ireland), 1959, s. 146, and the Adoption Act (Northern Ireland) 1967 (c. 35), s. 45; operative on April 18, 1979; amend the 1969 (No. 279) Rules by substituting for references to the clerk of the Crown and peace references to the chief clerk.

COUNTY COURT (MENTAL HEALTH ACT) (AMENDMENT) RULES (NORTHERN IRELAND) 1979 (No. 118) [10p], made under the County Courts Act (Northern Ireland) 1959, s. 146, and the Mental Health Act (Northern Ireland) 1961 (c. 15), s. 44; operative on April 18, 1979; amend the 1978 (No. 380) Rules by substituting for references to the clerk of the Crown and peace references to the chief clerk.

COUNTY COURT FEES ORDER (NORTHERN IRELAND) 1979 (No. 154) [30p], made under the Judicature (Northern Ireland) Act 1978 (c. 23), s. 116 (1) (4); operative on April 18, 1979; fixes the fees to be taken in the county courts and the fees payable to process servers and provides for the manner in which such fees are to be taken and applied.

1908. Criminal law

PERJURY (NORTHERN IRELAND) ORDER 1979 (No. 1714 (N.I. 19)) [70p], made under the Northern Ireland Act 1974 (c. 28), Sched. 1, para. 1; operative on January 20, 1980; consolidates the Perjury Act (Northern Ireland) 1946 and other related enactments.

TREATMENT OF OFFENDERS (1976 ORDER) (COMMENCEMENT NO. 2) ORDER (NORTHERN IRELAND) 1979 (No. 60) (C. 3) [10p], made under S.I. 1976 No. 226 (N.I. 4), art. 1 (2); brings arts. 7–11 of that S.I. into operation on April 1, 1979.

TREATMENT OF OFFENDERS (1968 ACT) (COMMENCEMENT NO. 3) ORDER (NORTHERN IRELAND) 1979 (No. 149) (C. 8) [20p], made under the Treatment of Offenders Act (Northern Ireland) 1968 (c. 29), s. 36 (3); brings into operation on June 1, 1979, ss. 1, 5, 7, 8, 12, 14, 34 of, and Sched. 3, Pt. II to, and parts of ss. 2, 3, 18–21, 26, 28, 29 of, and Sched. 3, Pt. III to, the Act.

YOUNG OFFENDERS CENTRE RULES (NORTHERN IRELAND) 1979 (No. 155) [60p], made under the Prison Act (Northern Ireland) 1953 (c. 18), s. 13, as extended by the Treatment of Offenders Act (Northern Ireland) 1968, s. 2; operative on June 1, 1979; regulate the management of young offenders centres and set out conditions for the treatment and control of inmates.

REHABILITATION OF OFFENDERS (1978 ORDER) (COMMENCEMENT) ORDER (NORTHERN IRELAND) 1979 (No. 194) (C. 9), made under S.I. 1978 No. 1908 (N.I. 27), art. 1; brings the provisions of that S.I. into operation on July 1, 1979.

REHABILITATION OF OFFENDERS (EXCEPTIONS) ORDER (NORTHERN IRELAND) 1979 (No. 195) [30p], made under S.I. 1978 No. 1908, arts. 5 (4), 8 (4); operative on July 1, 1979; provides that art. 5 (1) of the S.I. shall not apply in relation to certain proceedings, that art. 5 (2) shall not apply in relation to certain questions and that art. 5 (3) (*b*) shall not apply in relation to certain professions, offices, employments and action for the purpose of safeguarding national security or of protecting public safety or public order.

1909. —— criminal damage—building demolished—compensation for loss of rent

B's property, an industrial building, was criminally damaged and later demolished. B owned adjoining property which had been cleared of buildings. The entire area was suitable for redevelopment as a single unit. The value of the site after demolition was therefore as high as its value before the building was damaged. B claimed compensation for the loss of rent for 18 months—the time required to rebuild. *Held*, B was entitled to compensation for the loss of rent, but that this should allow for hazards of vacancies, partial occupancies, bad debts, and other matters: BAMBER *v.* SECRETARY OF STATE [1977] N.I. 35, Gibson L.J.

1910. —— —— compensation for interest on overdraft

[Criminal Injuries Acts (Northern Ireland) 1956 to 1970.] M Co.'s premises were destroyed by a fire started maliciously. H Co. claimed compensation. The amount awarded included a sum for interest paid by it on money which it was compelled to borrow to meet the additional costs of carrying on its business. On appeal, *held,* that the sum of interest was correctly awarded since the general principle of foreseeability applied to awards of compensation under the

Criminal Injuries Acts (Northern Ireland) 1956 to 1970: JOHN HARKNESS & CO. *v.* SECRETARY OF STATE [1977] N.I. 43, C.A.

1911. —— criminal injury—failure to give information to police

[Criminal Injuries to Persons (Compensation) Act (Northern Ireland) 1968 (c. 9), s. 1 (3) (*e*).] M was beaten up in a club and then shot. He made an inaccurate and incomplete statement to the police about the incident. M applied for compensation. In his evidence, M admitted that he recognised his attackers, but said that he did not know their names. *Held*, M was not entitled to compensation, since he had not made a full and true disclosure, as required by s. 1 (3) (*e*) of the Criminal Injuries to Property (Compensation) Act (Northern Ireland) 1968, of all the relevant circumstances relating to his injury. The fear of reprisals did not constitute a reasonable cause for failing to make the necessary disclosure: MOORE *v.* SECRETARY OF STATE [1977] N.I. 14, McGonigal L.J.

1912. —— —— offence arising from use of a motor vehicle

[Criminal Injuries to Persons (Compensation) Act (Northern Ireland) 1968 (c. 9), s. 11 (1).] The applicant was injured when his car collided with another car which had been hijacked a short time earlier and was being driven to some place either for the commission by the occupants of a terrorist offence or for the purpose of facilitating the commission of such an offence either immediately or at some future date. On a case stated, *held*, that the phrase " facilitating the commission of some other offence " in s. 11 (1) of the Criminal Injuries to Persons (Compensation) Act (Northern Ireland) 1968 is capable of including an act facilitating the commission of an unidentifiable offence by unspecified persons at an indefinite time in the future: CREGAN *v.* SECRETARY OF STATE [1978] N.I. 159, C.A.

1913. —— —— whether compensation payable to adherent to illegal organisation

[Criminal Injuries to Persons (Compensation) Act (Northern Ireland) 1968 (c. 9), s. 1 (2).] C was injured in an attack. He claimed, and was awarded compensation. S appealed to the High Court, which allowed the appeal, since C was proved to be an adherent to or member of the provisional Irish Republican Army. On appeal, *held*, dismissing the appeal, that under s. 1 (2) of the Criminal Injuries to Persons (Compensation) Act (Northern Ireland) 1968 the court could take into account circumstances other than the activities which the claimant was involved in when he was injured: CAHILL *v.* SECRETARY OF STATE [1977] N.I. 53, C.A.

1914. —— Crown witness suspected of complicity

On appeal against conviction it was contended that a Crown witness should not have been put forward because the Crown knew that he was going to tell a story which a police witness knew was wrong. *Held,* dismissing the appeal, that as the Crown had a suspicion, but no evidence to prove, that the witness was an accomplice to the commission of the offence and had nothing against him by way of record, the Crown could not properly have suggested that he was of bad character: R. *v.* McGUIGAN [1978] N.I. 14, C.C.A.

1915. —— duress—whether defence available to member of terrorist organisation

F was convicted of murder and robbery, which he committed as a member of the Irish Republican Army (" the IRA "). He had tried to leave the IRA, but had been told that he could not do so and threatened. On appeal, *held*, that the defence of duress was not available to F as he had associated himself with violent criminals and voluntarily exposed himself to the risk of compulsion to commit criminal acts: R. *v.* FITZPATRICK [1977] N.I. 20, C.C.A.

1916. —— evidence—admissibility—confession

[Northern Ireland (Emergency Provisions) Act 1973 (c. 53), s. 6.] The accused, after being interviewed by the police for 39 hours out of a total of 72 hours, made a statement that he had taken part in the commission of a murder. Remarks by the accused shortly before making the statement indicated that he may have been mixed up and confused. *Held*, that the court has a discretion whether to admit a statement otherwise admissible under s. 6 of the Northern Ireland (Emergency Provisions) Act 1973 and, as the Crown had not discharged its onus to show that the statement was voluntary, it should not be admitted: R. *v.* MILNE [1978] N.I. 110, McGonigal L.J.

1917. —— evidence—admissibility of statements by accused

[Northern Ireland (Emergency Provisions) Act 1973 (c. 53), s. 6.] The admissibility of statements made by the accused who were charged with a series of offences ranging from murder to membership of a proscribed organisation, was challenged on the ground that they had been subjected to torture or to inhuman or degrading treatment in order to induce them to make the statements. *Held*, that (1) a statement made by an accused as a result of such treatment will be excluded under s. 6 of the Northern Ireland (Emergency Provisions) Act 1973 if he was subjected to such treatment in order to induce him to make the statement; (2) treatment of a less severe degree or treatment which was not used in order to induce the accused to make the statement will not exclude it under that section but the court has a discretion to exclude it; (3) the court's discretion should only be exercised where failure to do so might cause injustice by the admission of a statement which was suspect because of the method by which it was obtained; and (4) where an accused has made out a prima facie case of maltreatment the onus is on the prosecution to prove that the statement was taken in a manner which does not require its exclusion either under the section or in the exercise of the court's discretion: R. *v.* McCORMICK [1977] N.I. 105, McGonigal L.J.

1918. —— habeas corpus—certiorari—legal aid

[S.I. 1976 No. 226 (N.I. 4), art. 15 (1).] On the hearing of a charge of tampering with a motor vehicle the applicant was informed of his right to apply for legal aid in accordance with art. 15 (1) of S.I. 1976 No. 226. He did not apply, pleaded guilty and was ordered to attend an attendance centre. He was subsequently charged with failing to attend the attendance centre but was not during the hearing of that charge informed of his right to apply for legal aid. He was then ordered to attend a training school. On an application for habeas corpus and certiorari, *held*, that the proceedings for failing to attend the attendance centre were fresh proceedings and, as art. 15 (1) applied to those proceedings because a sentence of detention in a young offenders centre is wide enough to include a training school order, the applicant should have been again informed of his right to apply for legal aid. The order directing the applicant to attend the training school was accordingly quashed: R. (McCANN) *v.* BELFAST JUSTICES [1978] N.I. 153, Lowry L.C.J.

1919. —— murder—death caused by bomb explosion—warning given—driver of getaway car

The accused waited in a car while two men planted a bomb at an inn and carried out a robbery there. They warned the occupants that a bomb had been planted. The accused then drove the two men away. A police constable was killed by the explosion. The accused was charged with murder and robbery. *Held*, that (1) the accused was not guilty of murder as although he knew the bomb was to be planted he also knew that a warning was to be given and it had not been proved beyond a reasonable doubt that he knew that it was probable that serious personal injury would result; (2) as the unlawful acts of the two men involved a risk of injury and as death had resulted, the accused was guilty of manslaughter; and (3) he was not guilty of robbery as he did not know that robbery was contemplated or would occur: R. *v.* McFEELY [1977] N.I. 149, Lowry L.C.J.

1920. —— offence committed in one county—committal for trial in another

[Criminal Justice Act (Northern Ireland) 1945 (c. 15), s. 7 (1); Magistrates' Courts Act (Northern Ireland) 1964 (c. 21), s. 47 (2).] C was arrested in Co. Armagh on suspicion of having committed a customs offence. He was taken into custody and brought to Belfast where he was charged before the magistrates' court there and remanded on bail. He elected to go for trial on indictment and after the preliminary investigation was committed for trial on bail to the Belfast City Commission. On C's application for an order of certiorari and mandamus to quash the order of committal and to direct that he be committed for trial in Co. Armagh, *held*, that as the effect of bail was to release C from custody of the law to the custody of his sureties he was in custody in Belfast and could, by virtue of s. 7 (1) of the Criminal Justice Act (Northern Ireland) 1945 under which an offence is deemed to have been committed in any county or place in which a person is in custody and by virtue of s. 47 (2) of the Magistrates' Courts Act (Northern Ireland) 1964 which provides that a person may be committed for trial in a county in which an offence was committed or is deemed to have been committed, be committed for trial in Belfast: R. (CAHERTY) v. BELFAST JUSTICES [1978] N.I. 94, Gibson L.J.

1921. —— possession of firearms—penalties increased between date of offence and date of trial—whether retrospective
[Firearms Act (Northern Ireland) 1969 (c. 12), s. 19A; S.I. 1976 No. 1341 (N.I. 24), art. 3.] The appellant was convicted in January 1977 of two offences under s. 19A of the Firearms Act (Northern Ireland) 1969 committed in April 1976. The maximum penalty for these offences was increased in August 1976 from five to 10 years' imprisonment by art. 3 of S.I. 1976 No. 1341. The appellant was sentenced to six years' imprisonment for each offence. On appeal, *held*, that art. 3 is ambiguous but that it should be construed as not having retrospective effect as the presumption against retrospection and the presumption of adherence to treaty obligations had not been rebutted by express language or necessary implication: R. v. DEERY [1977] N.I. 164, C.C.A.

1922. —— procedure—joint or several offence
Y was charged with assault on a police constable while acting together and in concert with C. A similar complaint against C was dismissed. The case against Y was then dismissed on the ground that while it had been proved that he assaulted the constable, it had not been proved that he had acted together with C. On appeal by way of case stated, *held*, that a charge alleging that two or more jointly committed a crime is, unless the joint action is an essential ingredient of the crime, a charge against each accused jointly and severally. The case was remitted to the resident magistrate with a direction to convict: HARKNESS v. YOUNG [1977] N.I. 173, C.A.

1923. —— statements—whether obtained as result of torture or inhuman or degrading treatment
[Northern Ireland (Emergency Provisions) Act 1973 (c. 53), s. 6 (2).] T was convicted of murder and of belonging to the Irish Republican Army. At his trial, statements made by T were admitted in evidence since it had been proved that T had not been subjected to torture or to inhuman or degrading treatment in order to induce him to make them. On appeal, *held*, dismissing the appeal, that under s. 6 (2) of the Northern Ireland (Emergency Provisions) Act 1973, the Crown need only produce prima facie evidence of the making of a statement by the accused and that he must then, to exclude it from evidence, raise a prima facie case that he was subjected to torture or to inhuman or degrading treatment in order to make it: R. v. THOMPSON [1977] N.I. 74, C.C.A.

1924. Death duties
ESTATE DUTY (NORTHERN IRELAND) (INTEREST ON UNPAID DUTY) ORDER 1979 (No. 1689) [10p], made under the Finance Act (Northern Ireland) 1970 (c. 21 (N.I.)), s. 1 (2) as amended by the Northern Ireland (Modification of Enactments—No. 1) Order 1973 (No. 2163), Sched. 3 art. 5 (3); operative on January 1, 1980; increases the rate of interest on unpaid estate duty to 9 per cent. Interest will also be at 9 per cent. when overpaid estate duty is repaid.

1925. Divorce and matrimonial causes
MATRIMONIAL CAUSES (1978 ORDER) (COMMENCEMENT No. 2) ORDER 1978 (No. 396) (C. 22) [10p], made under S.I. 1978 No. 1045 (N.I. 15), art. 1 (2); bring arts. 1, 2, 4 (7), 9, 28 (2), 43, 48, 53 (2) (4), 54 of, and Scheds. 2, 3 (pt.) to, that S.I. into operation on January 15, 1978.
MATRIMONIAL CAUSES RULES (NORTHERN IRELAND) 1979 (No. 89) [£1·50], made under S.I. 1978 No. 1045 (N.I. 15), art. 54; operative on April 18, 1979; replace, with a few exceptions and several amendments, all previous rules relating to matrimonial causes and make provision for the procedure on the coming into force of that S.I. The main changes relate to applications for leave

to present petitions, discontinuances of causes before service of a petition, signing of petitions, filing of children's birth certificates, conciliation of the parties where children are involved, service of petitions, medical examinations in nullity proceedings, evidence of marriages outside Northern Ireland, rescission of decrees of judicial separation by consent, making decrees absolute on lodging notice, applications for ancillary relief, care and supervision of children, alteration of maintenance agreements and judgment summonses for the enforcement of orders.

MATRIMONIAL CAUSES (1978 ORDER) (COMMENCEMENT NO. 3) ORDER (NORTHERN IRELAND) 1979 (No. 99) (C. 4) [10p], made under S.I. 1978 No. 1045; brings the remaining provisions of that S.I. into operation on April 18, 1979.

1926. Education

TEACHERS' SUPERANNUATION (AMENDMENT NO. 2) REGULATIONS (NORTHERN IRELAND) 1978 (No. 351) [30p], made under S.I. 1972 No. 1073 (N.I. 10), arts. 11, 14, Sched. 3; operative on December 29, 1978; amend the 1977 (No. 260) and 1978 (No. 147) Regulations so that they meet the contracting-out requirements of S.I. 1975 No. 1503 (N.I. 15).

STUDENTS AWARDS REGULATIONS (NORTHERN IRELAND) 1978 (No. 357) [70p], made under S.I. 1972 No. 1263 (N.I. 12), arts. 39, 40, 125; operative on November 24, 1978; govern the making of awards which boards must make to students; revoke the 1977 (No. 312) Regulations.

EDUCATION AND LIBRARY BOARDS (PAYMENTS TO BOARD MEMBERS) REGULATIONS (NORTHERN IRELAND) 1979 (No. 44) [20p], made under S.I. 1972 No. 1263 (N.I. 12), arts. 67 (3), 125; operative on March 26, 1979; provide for the payment of attendance and financial loss allowances to members of education and library boards; revoke the 1976 (No. 130) and 1977 (Nos. 57, 328) Regulations.

GRAMMAR SCHOOL PUPILS (ADMISSIONS, GRANTS AND ALLOWANCES) (AMENDMENT) REGULATIONS (NORTHERN IRELAND) 1979 (No. 219) [10p], made under S.I. 1972 No. 1263 (N.I. 12), arts. 105 (1), 125 (1); operative on August 1, 1979; revoke reg. 7 (2) (*b*) of the 1978 (No. 217) Regulations which provided for the inclusion in the grant payable under reg. 7 (2) of the amount of examination fees of non-fee paying pupils enrolled in voluntary grammar schools.

TEACHERS' SALARIES (AMENDMENT) REGULATIONS (NORTHERN IRELAND) 1979 (No. 245) [90p], made under S.I. 1972 No. 1263, arts. 57, 125; operative on July 30, 1979; introduce revised scales of salary for certain teachers.

SECONDARY SCHOOLS (GRANT CONDITIONS) (AMENDMENT) REGULATIONS (NORTHERN IRELAND) 1979 (No. 249) [10p], made under S.I. 1972 No. 1263, arts. 105 (1), 125 (1); operative on August 1, 1979; increase the base figure used in the calculation of the annual rate of salary grant payable in respect of certain teachers.

MAINTENANCE ALLOWANCES (PUPILS OVER COMPULSORY SCHOOL AGE) (AMENDMENT) REGULATIONS (NORTHERN IRELAND) 1979 (No. 283) [20p], made under S.I. 1972 No. 1263 (N.I. 12), arts. 39 (1) (2), 125 (1); operative on September 1, 1979; introduce improved rates of maintenance allowances for certain pupils over compulsory school age; revoke the 1978 (No. 214) Regulations

STUDENTS AWARDS REGULATIONS (NORTHERN IRELAND) 1979 (No. 291) [£1·25], made under S.I. 1972 No. 1263 (N.I. 12), arts. 39 (1) (2), 40 (2), 125 (1); operative on September 1, 1979; govern the making of awards which it is the duty of boards to make to specified persons and provide for the making of awards to specified persons for teacher-training courses and for long-term residential courses of full-time education for adults at certain specified colleges; revoke the 1978 (No. 357) Regulations.

INSTITUTIONS OF FURTHER EDUCATION SALARIES (AMENDMENT) REGULATIONS (NORTHERN IRELAND) 1979 (No. 297) [40p], made under the Administrative and Financial Provisions Act (Northern Ireland) 1962 (c. 7), s. 18 and S.I. 1972 No. 1263 (N.I. 12), arts. 57, 125; operative on September 24, 1979; provide, with effect from April 1, 1979, for revised salary scales and allowances for teachers in further education institutions.

COLLEGE OF EDUCATION SALARIES (AMENDMENT) REGULATIONS (NORTHERN IRELAND) 1979 (No. 315) [40p], made under S.I. 1972 No. 1263 (N.I. 12), arts. 57 (1), 125 (1), and the Administrative and Financial Provisions Act (Northern Ireland) 1962, s. 18; operative on September 28, 1979; revise scales of salaries for teachers in colleges of education; revoke the 1978 (No. 216) Regulations.

1927. Election law

EUROPEAN ASSEMBLY ELECTIONS (NORTHERN IRELAND) REGULATIONS 1979 (No. 322) [90p], made under the European Assembly Elections Act 1978 (c. 10), Sched. 1, para. 2; operative on March 29, 1979; provide for the conduct of the election of representatives to the Assembly of the European Communities from Northern Ireland which forms a single constituency for the purpose of such an election.

RETURNING OFFICERS' EXPENSES (NORTHERN IRELAND) REGULATIONS 1979 (No. 431) [20p], made under the Representation of the People Act 1949 (c. 68), s. 20 (2); operative on April 11, 1979; revoke and replaces S.I. 1974 Nos. 181 and 1497 and prescribe a new scale of charges and expenses.

EUROPEAN ASSEMBLY ELECTIONS (RETURNING OFFICERS' EXPENSES) (NORTHERN IRELAND) REGULATIONS 1979 (No. 589) [20p], made under the Representation of the People Act 1949, s. 20 (2), as applied by S.I. 1979 No. 322 Reg 3 (1), Sched. 1; operative on May 28, 1979; prescribe for Northern Ireland the maximum charges in respect of expenses incurred by the Chief Electoral Officer for Northern Ireland for the European Assembly Elections.

REPRESENTATION OF THE PEOPLE (NORTHERN IRELAND) (AMENDMENT) REGULATIONS 1979 (No. 1657) [10p], made under the Representation of the People Act 1949, ss. 42 and 171 (5); operative on December 25, 1979; remove the requirement that in the electors lists and the register of electors the name of any elector who is a service voter shall be marked with " S " and the name of any elector who is a merchant seaman shall be marked with an " M."

EUROPEAN ASSEMBLY ELECTION PETITION RULES (NORTHERN IRELAND) 1979 (No. 179) [20p], made under the Representation of the People Act 1949, s. 160; operative on June 7, 1979; make provision for petitions to the High Court which question the declared results of elections to the European Assembly.

1928. Electricity—Lands Tribunal decision

REID *v.* NORTHERN IRELAND ELECTRICITY SERVICE, R/7/1979 (compensation for damage caused to two trees by workmen of the Northern Ireland Electricity Service when repairing an electricity transmission line).

1929. Emergency laws

EMERGENCY REGULATIONS (NORTHERN IRELAND) 1979 (No. 1) [40p], made under the Emergency Powers Act (Northern Ireland) 1926 (c. 8), s. 1, as amended by the Emergency Powers (Amendment) Act (Northern Ireland) 1964 (c. 34); operative from January 11, 1979 to January 14, 1979; provide for securing the essentials of life to the community.

MOTOR FUEL (FILLING STATIONS) ORDER (NORTHERN IRELAND) 1979 (No. 9) [20p], made under S.R. 1979 No. 1, reg. 22 (1); operative on January 12, 1979; 1979; prohibits the acquisition of motor fuel from filling stations except for specified purposes.

MOTOR FUEL (BULK SUPPLIES) ORDER (NORTHERN IRELAND) 1979 (No. 10) [20p], made under S.R. 1979 No. 1, reg. 22 (1); operative on January 12, 1979; prohibits the acquisition of bulk supplies of motor fuel except for specified purposes.

OIL FUEL ORDER (NORTHERN IRELAND) 1979 (No. 11) [20p], made under S.R. 1979 No. 1, reg. 22 (1); operative on January 12, 1979; prohibits the acquisition or supply of oil fuel except for specified purposes.

1930. —— interference with property rights—compensation

[Northern Ireland (Emergency Provisions) Act 1973 (c. 53), s. 25.] The applicant, who carried on a garage and service station business, claimed compensation under s. 25 of the Northern Ireland (Emergency Provisions) Act 1973 for loss to his business caused by the erection of security barriers which did not prevent passage from his premises to the street but had the effect of diverting passing traffic away from the premises. The county court judge refused to appoint an arbitrator to determine the question of compensation but an order of certiorari was granted to remove the order of the county court judge for the purpose of being quashed. *Held*, allowing an appeal from this order, that even if the owner of premises on a highway can show that he has sustained particular damage following the interference with the public right of passage on the highway this does not convert the public right into a private right and that there was no interference with his private right of access to the highway. He was, therefore, not entitled to compensation under s. 25 of the Act: R. (McCreesh) *v.* County Court Judge for Armagh [1978] N.I. 164, C.A.

1931. Employment

Code of Practice (Time Off) (Commencement) Order (Northern Ireland) 1978 (No. 361) [10p], made under S.I. 1976 No. 1403 (N.I. 16), art. 14A (5); brings the code of practice on time off for trade union duties and activities into operation on January 1, 1979.

Industrial Relations (1976 No. 2 Order) (Commencement No. 4) Order (Northern Ireland) 1978 (No. 362) (C. 18) [10p], made under S.I. 1976 No. 2147 (N.I. 28), art. 1 and the Northern Ireland Act 1974 (c. 28), Sched. 1, para. 2 (1) (2); brings arts. 37 and 38 of that S.I. into operation on January 1, 1979.

Health and Safety at Work (1978 Order) (Commencement) Order 1978 (No. 384) (C. 21) [20p], made under S.I. 1978 No. 1039 (N.I. 9), art. 1 (2); brings arts. 1, 2 (1) (pt.) (2) (pt.) (4) (5), 3, 11–15, 17, 18, 40 (pt.), 46, 47, 52 (1), 53 (pt.), 54, 55, 56 (1) (pt.) (3) of and Scheds. 1–3, 6 (pt.) to, that S.I. into operation on February 1, 1979, and the remaining provisions of that S.I. into operation on May 1, 1979.

Industrial Relations (1976 No. 2 Order) (Commencement No. 5) Order (Northern Ireland) 1978 (No. 406) (C. 23) [10p], made under the Northern Ireland Act 1974, Sched. 1, para. 2 (1) (2) and S.I. 1976 No. 2147 (N.I. 28), art. 1; brings arts. 39 (3) (b) (pt.), 40 (pt.), 42 (pt.), and 43 (2) (c) of that S.I. into operation on January 1, 1979.

Unfair Dismissal (Increase of Compensation Limit) Order (Northern Ireland) 1979 (No. 6) [10p], made under S.I. 1976 No. 1043 (N.I. 16), arts. 37 (2), 80 (3); operative on February 1, 1979; increases to £5,750 the amount of certain compensation which can be awarded by industrial tribunals in claims for unfair dismissal.

Industrial Relations (Variation of Limits) Order (Northern Ireland) 1979 (No. 7) [20p], made under S.I. 1976 No. 1043, arts. 70, 80 (3) and S.I. 1976 No. 2147, arts. 5 (5), 63 (4); operative on February 1, 1979; varies certain financial limits in the Contracts of Employment and Redundancy Payments Act (Northern Ireland) 1965 and those S.I.'s.

Medical Examinations (Fees) Regulations (Northern Ireland) 1979 (No. 171) [20p], made under S.I. 1978 No. 1039 (N.I. 9), arts. 17 (1) (3) (a), 40 (2), 49 (1); operative on June 8, 1979; fix fees payable by employers for work done by medical advisers appointed under that S.I. in conducting various medical examinations of employees in factories and fix fees payable by employers to appointed medical practitioners for work done where the fees had not been previously agreed.

Industrial Relations (Handling of Redundancies) Variation Order (Northern Ireland) 1979 (No. 305) [10p], made under S.I. 1976 No. 1043 (N.I. 16), art. 56 (4); operative on October 1, 1979; reduces to 30 days the period which must elapse after the commencement of consultation with trade union representatives and notifications to the Department of Manpower Services before the first of the dismissals takes effect in cases where the employer is proposing to dismiss as redundant 10 to 99 employees at one establishment within a period of 30 days or less; also reduces to 30 days the period specified in art. 51 (5) (b) of the S.I.

Industrial Tribunals (Industrial Relations) (Amendment) Regulations (Northern Ireland) 1979 (No. 306) [10p], made under S.I. 1976 No. 1043, art. 59; operative on November 1, 1979; amend the 1976 (No. 262) Regulations to give power to a tribunal to require of its own motion a party to furnish further particulars, to review a decision of another tribunal where it is not practicable for that tribunal to review its decision and to strike out any originating application for want of prosecution.

UNFAIR DISMISSAL (VARIATION OF QUALIFYING PERIOD) ORDER (NORTHERN IRELAND) 1979 (No. 307) [10p], made under S.I. 1976 No. 1043, art. 24 (3); operative on October 1, 1979; varies the minimum period of employment necessary to enable an unfair dismissal complaint to be made to an industrial tribunal from 26 weeks to 52 weeks.

INDUSTRIAL TRIBUNALS (IMPROVEMENT AND PROHIBITION NOTICES APPEALS) REGULATIONS (NORTHERN IRELAND) 1979 (No. 324) [40p], made under S.I. 1976 No. 1043, art. 59 (1) (2), and S.I. 1978 No. 1039 (N.I. 9), art. 26 (1); operative on October 22, 1979; set out the rules of procedure of industrial tribunals for the determination of appeals against improvement notices and prohibition notices issued under the 1978 S.I. and prescribe the period under which notice of appeal must be given.

BOILER EXPLOSIONS LEGISLATION (REPEALS AND MODIFICATIONS) REGULATIONS (NORTHERN IRELAND) 1979 (No. 378) [10p], made under S.I. 1978 No. 1039 (N.I. 9), arts. 17 (1) (3) (a), 54; operative on December 1, 1979; repeal and modify provisions of the Boiler Explosions Act 1882 (c. 22) and the Boiler Explosions Act 1890 (c. 35) which are superseded or affected by that S.I.

EMPLOYMENT SUBSIDIES (RENEWAL) ORDER (NORTHERN IRELAND) 1979 (No. 382) [10p], made under the Employment Subsidies Act 1978 (c. 6), s. 3 (2) (b); operative on January 1, 1980; renews until June 30, 1981, the powers of s. 1 of the Act.

1932. —— **health and safety at work**

TRUCK ACTS 1831 TO 1896 (ENFORCEMENT) REGULATIONS (NORTHERN IRELAND) 1979 (No. 239) [20p], made under S.I. 1978 No. 1039 (N.I. 9), art. 54 (1) (3) (4); operative on August 7, 1979; provide for the enforcement of the Truck Acts 1831 to 1896 by officers of the Department of Manpower Services.

OFFICE AND SHOP PREMISES ACT (REPEALS AND MODIFICATIONS) REGULATIONS (NORTHERN IRELAND) 1979 (No. 284) [40p], made under S.I. 1978 No. 1039 (N.I. 9), arts. 17 (1) (3) (a), 55 (2); operative on October 1, 1979; repeal and modify provisions of the Office and Shop Premises Act (Northern Ireland) 1966 (c. 26) and regulations thereunder which are superseded or affected by that S.I.

1933. —— **industrial training**

Orders made under the Industrial Training Act (Northern Ireland) 1964 (c. 18), s. 4:

S.R. 1979 Nos. 143 (engineering industry) [20p]; 144 (textiles industry) [20p]; 172 (road transport industry) [20p]; 182 (construction industry) [20p]; 183 (food and drink industry) [20p]; 203 (clothing and footwear industry) [20p]; 204 (catering industry) [20p].

1934. —— **wages councils**

Orders made under the Wages Councils Act (Northern Ireland) 1945 (c. 21), s. 10:

S.R. 1978 No. 403 (sugar confectionery and food preserving) [20p]; 1979 Nos. 29 (linen and cotton handkerchief and household goods and linen piece goods) [20p]; 35 (readymade and wholesale bespoke tailoring) [20p]; 93 (paper box) [20p]; 94 (dressmaking and women's light clothing) [20p]; 95 (dressmaking and women's light clothing) [10p]; 125 (shirtmaking) [20p]; 207 (road haulage) [30p]; 240 (sugar confectionery and food preserving) [30p]; 247 (boot and shoe repairing) [20p]; 304 (retail bespoke tailoring) [20p]; 311 (readymade and wholesale bespoke tailoring) [30p]; 312 (sugar confectionery and food preserving) [10p]; 347 (shirtmaking) [20p]; 359 (dressmaking and women's light clothing) [20p]; 360 (dressmaking and women's light clothing) [20p].

1935. Evidence

BLOOD TESTS (EVIDENCE OF PATERNITY) REGULATIONS (NORTHERN IRELAND) 1978 (No. 379) [40p], made under S.I. 1977 No. 1250 (N.I. 17); art. 10;

operative on March 1, 1979; prescribe the procedure in relation to blood samples in paternity proceedings.

1936. Executors and administrators

ADMINISTRATION OF ESTATES (NORTHERN IRELAND) ORDER 1979 (No. 1575 (N.I. 14)) [90p], made under the Northern Ireland Act 1974 (c. 28), Sched. 1, para. 1, coming into operation on days to be appointed; restates and modernises to varying extent, *inter alia*, the law relating to the grant of probate of wills, the grant of letters of administration, the rights and duties of personal representatives and others.

1937. Explosions and explosives

COMPRESSED ACETYLENE ORDER (NORTHERN IRELAND) 1979 (No. 290) [10p], made under the Explosives Act 1875 (c. 17), ss. 43, 83, 104; operative on December 1, 1979; exempts from prohibitions under the 1942 (No. 128) Order the keeping, conveyance and sale of compressed acetylene which has been imported under a licence granted under the 1875 Act and which remains in the cylinder in which it was imported.

1938. Factories

NOTICE OF INDUSTRIAL DISEASES ORDER (NORTHERN IRELAND) 1979 (No. 185) [20p], made under the Factories Act (Northern Ireland) 1965 (c. 20), s. 80 (3); operative on June 29, 1979; prescribes the form of notice required by s. 80 of the Act for certain industrial diseases occurring in factories or other places to which that section applies; revokes the 1964 (No. 103) Order.

EMPLOYMENT MEDICAL ADVISORY SERVICE (FACTORIES ACT LEGISLATION AMENDMENT) REGULATIONS (NORTHERN IRELAND) 1979 (No. 187) [50p], made under S.I. 1978 No. 1039 (N.I. 9), arts. 17 (1) (3) (a), 55 (2); operative on July 9, 1979; amend certain instruments made under the Factories Act (Northern Ireland) 1965, in consequence of Pt. III of that S.I.

FACTORIES ACT (ENFORCEMENT OF SECTION 135) REGULATIONS (NORTHERN IRELAND) 1979 (No. 238) [20p], made under S.I. 1978 No. 1039 (N.I. 9), art. 54 (1) (3) (4); operative on August 7, 1979; provide for the enforcement of s. 135 of the Factories Act (Northern Ireland) 1965 by officers of the Department of Manpower Services.

FACTORIES LEGISLATION (REPEALS AND MODIFICATIONS) REGULATIONS (NORTHERN IRELAND) 1979 (No. 246) [80p], made under S.I. 1978 No. 1039 (N.I. 9), arts. 17 (1) (3) (a), 45, 54 (1), 55 (2); operative on September 1, 1979; repeal and modify provisions of the Factories Act (Northern Ireland) 1965 and the Hours of Employment (Conventions) Act 1936 (c. 22) and instruments thereunder consequent upon the coming into operation of the S.I. of 1978.

1939. Family allowances

CHILD BENEFIT (GENERAL) REGULATIONS (NORTHERN IRELAND) 1979 (No. 5) [40p], made under S.I. 1975 No. 1504 (N.I. 16), arts. 2 (2) (3) (5) (6), 4 (2) (3), 5 (3) (c.) (4) (5), 6 (1), 11 (a), 19 (5) (6), 22 (1) (2) (c), Sched. 1, Sched. 2, para. 6; operative on March 5, 1979; consolidate with minor amendments, and revoke, the 1976 (No. 226), 1977 (No. 85) and 1978 (No. 251) Regulations.

FAMILY INCOME SUPPLEMENTS (GENERAL) (AMENDMENT) REGULATIONS (NORTHERN IRELAND) 1979 (No. 45) [10p], made under the Family Income Supplements Act (Northern Ireland) 1971 (c. 8), s. 10 (2) (a); operative on April 3, 1979; specify circumstances in which a single person with at least one dependent child is to be treated as engaged in remunerative full-time work.

FAMILY INCOME SUPPLEMENTS (COMPUTATION) REGULATIONS (NORTHERN IRELAND) 1979 (No. 265) [10p], made under the Family Income Supplements Act (Northern Ireland) 1971, ss. 2 (1), 3 (1) (1A); operative on November 13, 1979; specify the prescribed amount for any family and the weekly rate of benefit under the 1971 Act as amended by S.I. 1975 No. 1504 (N.I. 16), Sched. 4, paras. 5, 6; revoke the 1978 (No. 238) Regulations.

CHILD BENEFIT (GENERAL) REGULATIONS (NORTHERN IRELAND) 1979 (No. 361) [10p], made under S.I. 1975 No. 1504 (N.I. 16), art. 6 (1), Sched. 1, para. 1 (f); operative on November 12, 1979; amend the 1979 (No. 5) Regulations in relation to children in the care of the Department of Health and Social Services or the subject of a parental rights order.

FAMILY INCOME SUPPLEMENTS (COMPUTATION) (No. 2) REGULATIONS (NORTHERN IRELAND) 1979 (No. 393) [10p], made under the Family Income Supplements Act (Northern Ireland) 1971, ss. 2 (1), (3) (1) (1A); operative on November 13, 1979; specify the prescribed amount for any family and the weekly rate of benefit under the 1971 Act in accordance with the amendments made to that Act by S.I. 1975 No. 1504 (N.I. 16).

1940. Fire service

FIRE SERVICES (APPOINTMENTS AND PROMOTION) REGULATIONS (NORTHERN IRELAND) 1979 (No. 167) [30p], made under the Fire Services Act (Northern Ireland) 1969 (c. 13), ss. 16 (2), 40 (1) (a); operative on July 2, 1979; consolidate with amendments and revoke the 1973 (No. 414) and the 1977 (No. 125) Regulations, the principal amendments being in the specifications of examinations leading to certain promotions and the transfer to a central board of responsibility for examinations previously the responsibility of the Fire Authority for Northern Ireland.

FIREMEN'S PENSION SCHEMES (AMENDMENT No. 2) ORDER (NORTHERN IRELAND) 1979 (No. 310) [20p], made under the Fire Services Act (Northern Ireland) 1969, s. 17; operative on October 1, 1979, with effect from December 1, 1978; increase flat rates by which certain amounts under various firemen's pension schemes are determined.

1941. Firearms

FIREARMS (AMENDMENT) (NORTHERN IRELAND) ORDER 1979 (No. 923) (N.I. 7) [50p], made under the Northern Ireland Act 1974 (c. 28), Sched. 1, para. 1; operative on August 27, 1979; amends the Firearms Act (Northern Ireland) 1969 (c. 12) relating to the functions of the Chief Constable under the Act, the issue of firearm certificates and permits, and firearms checks.

FIREARMS (VARIATION OF FEES) ORDER (NORTHERN IRELAND) 1979 (No. 36) [10p], made under the Firearms Act (Northern Ireland) 1969, s. 47; operative on April 1, 1979; increase fees for firearm certificates.

FIREARMS (VARIATION OF FEES) (No. 2) ORDER (NORTHERN IRELAND) 1979 (No. 91) [10p], made under the Firearms Act (Northern Ireland) 1969, s. 47; operative on March 31, 1979; revokes the 1979 (No. 36) Order.

FIREARMS (PRESCRIBED FORMS) REGULATIONS (NORTHERN IRELAND) 1979 (No. 276) [£1·00], made under the Firearms Act (Northern Ireland) 1969, ss. 22, 23, 28, 49; operative on August 27, 1979; consolidate with minor amendments and revoke the 1973 (Nos. 191, 473) and the 1975 (Nos. 254, 255) Regulations.

FIREARMS (AIR WEAPONS LAWFULLY HELD IN GREAT BRITAIN) REGULATIONS (NORTHERN IRELAND) 1979 (No. 277) [20p], made under the Firearms Act (Northern Ireland) 1969, ss. 13B, 49; operative on August 27, 1979; provide that a person resident in Great Britain who may lawfully have an air weapon and ammunition in his possession there without a firearm certificate may, without holding a Northern Ireland firearm certificate, have such a weapon and ammunition in his possession there only if he gives the Chief Constable certain information, obtains his written approval and complies with the conditions of the approval.

1942. Fish and fisheries

HERRING (PROHIBITION OF FISHING) REGULATIONS (NORTHERN IRELAND) 1978 (No. 397) [10p], made under the Fisheries Act (Northern Ireland) 1966 (c. 17), ss. 19, 124; operative on January 1, 1979; prohibit herring fishing until March 31, 1979 in an area off Northern Ireland.

RAINBOW TROUT WATERS BYELAWS (NORTHERN IRELAND) 1978 (No. 404) [10p], made under the Fisheries Act (Northern Ireland) 1966, s. 26; operative on February 1, 1979; designate certain waters so that there is no close season for angling for rainbow trout in them; revoke the 1977 (No. 356) Byelaws.

LOUGH ERNE COMMERCIAL FISHING CONTROL BYELAWS (NORTHERN IRELAND) 1978 (No. 405) [20p], made under the Fisheries Act (Northern Ireland) 1966, s. 26; operative on March 17, 1979; regulate commercial fishing on Lough Erne; revoke the 1977 (No. 59) Byelaws.

EEL FISHING REGULATIONS (NORTHERN IRELAND) 1979 (No. 19) [20p], made under the Fisheries Act (Northern Ireland) 1966, s. 15; operative on April 1, 1979; consolidate, with amendments, and revoke, the 1967 (Nos. 72, 241), 1968 (No. 207), 1969 (Nos. 79, 185, 330), 1970 (Nos. 4, 237), 1971 (No. 369) and 1973 (No. 124) Regulations.

EEL FISHING (LICENCE DUTIES) REGULATIONS (NORTHERN IRELAND) 1979 (No. 20) [20p], made under the Fisheries Act (Northern Ireland) 1966, s. 15; operative on April 1, 1979; increase licence duties on eel fishing engines; revoke the 1975 (No. 344) Regulations.

ANGLING (DEPARTMENT OF AGRICULTURE WATERS) BYELAWS (NORTHERN IRELAND) 1979 (No. 24) [30p], made under the Fisheries Act (Northern Ireland) 1966, s. 26; operative on March 1, 1979; specify permitted angling methods on waters controlled by the Department of Agriculture; revoke the 1977 (No. 239) Byelaws.

FOYLE AREA (PENSION) (AMENDMENT) REGULATIONS 1979 (No. 43) [20p], made under the Foyle Fisheries Act 1952 (Eire No. 5), s. 13, Sched. 3, para. 16, as amended by the Foyle Fisheries (Amendment) Act 1961 (Eire No. 44) and the Foyle Fisheries Act (Northern Ireland) 1952 (c. 5), s. 13, Sched. 3, para. 16, as amended by the Foyle Fisheries (Amendment) Act (Northern Ireland) 1962 (c. 5); operative on January 31, 1979; establish a new pension scheme for staff of the Foyle Fisheries Commission.

HERRING (PROHIBITION OF FISHING) REGULATIONS (NORTHERN IRELAND) 1979 (No. 80) [10p], made under the Fisheries Act (Northern Ireland) 1966, ss. 19, 124, 125; operative on April 1, 1979; prohibit, from April 1 to August 31, 1979, herring fishing by any means in a specified area off Northern Ireland.

PROHIBITION OF INTRODUCTION OF FISH ORDER (NORTHERN IRELAND) 1979 (No. 178) [10p], made under the Fisheries Act (Northern Ireland) 1966, s. 13; operative on August 1, 1979; prohibits the introduction of certain kinds of live fish into inland waters excluding waters in the Londonderry area; revokes the 1977 (No. 209) Order.

SEA FISH (MINIMUM SIZE) (AMENDMENT) ORDER (NORTHERN IRELAND) 1979 (No. 235) [10p], made under the Fisheries Act (Northern Ireland) 1966, s. 127; operative on July 1, 1979; amends the minimum sizes for various species of sea fish which may be landed, sold or used in the course of business in Northern Ireland.

HERRING (PROHIBITION OF FISHING) (NO. 2) REGULATIONS (NORTHERN IRELAND) 1979 (No. 308) [10p], made under the Fisheries Act (Northern Ireland) 1966, ss. 19, 124, 125; operative on September 1, 1979; continue until August 31, 1980, the prohibition on herring fishing by any means in an area off the Northern Ireland coast.

FISHERIES (LICENCE DUTIES) BYELAWS (NORTHERN IRELAND) 1979 (No. 402) [20p], made under the Fisheries Act (Northern Ireland 1966, s. 26; operative on January 1, 1980; increase the duties on certain licences for fishing, fishing engines and dealers; revoke the 1978 (No. 339) Byelaws.

1943. —— **conviction for having nets near a river for an unlawful purpose—forfeiture of vehicle transporting nets**

[Foyle Fisheries Act (Northern Ireland) 1952 (c. 5), ss. 39, 51A (3), 75.] T and another were convicted of an offence under s. 39 of the Foyle Fisheries Act (Northern Ireland) 1952 of having nets in their possession near the banks of a river for the purpose of taking salmon, trout or other fish. T's car was used to transport the nets. On an application for forfeiture of the car the resident magistrate held that it was automatically forfeited by virtue of s. 75 of the Act. On appeal by way of case stated, *held*, dismissing the appeal, that the discretionary power of forfeiture in s. 51A (3) of the Act only applied where an offence under that section had been committed and the car was automatically forfeited under s. 75: FOYLE FISHERIES COMMISSION v. TIMONEY [1978] N.I. 178, C.A.

1944. Food and drugs

MILK (NORTHERN IRELAND) (AMENDMENT) ORDER 1979 (No. 600) [20p], made under the Emergency Laws (Re-enactments and Repeals) Act 1964 (c. 60), ss. 6, 7, 22 (3); operative on June 1, 1979; decreases by 2·486p per litre the maximum prices for the sale of raw milk for heat treatment and increases by 1½p per pint the maximum retail prices of milk on sale.

IMPORTED FOOD (NORTHERN IRELAND) (AMENDMENT) REGULATIONS 1979 (No. 1427) [50p], made under the European Communities Act 1972 (c. 68), s. 2 (2) and the Food and Drugs Act 1955 (c. 16), ss. 13, 82, 123 (1) (2) (5) (6), 134, Sched. 10; operative on January 1, 1980; further amend S.I. 1968 No. 98.

COLOURING MATTER IN FOOD (AMENDMENT) REGULATIONS (NORTHERN IRELAND) 1979 (No. 49) [20p], made under the Food and Drugs Act (Northern Ireland) 1958 (c. 27), ss. 4, 7, 68, 68A; operative on April 9, 1979; amend the 1973 (No. 466) Regulations.

COFFEE AND COFFEE PRODUCTS REGULATIONS (NORTHERN IRELAND) 1979 (No. 51) [40p], made under the Food and Drugs Act (Northern Ireland) 1958, ss. 4, 7, 68, 68A; operative on July 12, 1980, save for Regs. 1, 2 and 15 which are operative on April 11, 1979; implement Council Directive No. 77/436/EEC on the approximation of the laws of the Member States relating to coffee extracts and chicory extracts.

PRICE MARKING (CHEESE) ORDER (NORTHERN IRELAND) 1979 (No. 293) [20p], made under the Prices Act 1974 (c. 24), s. 4; operative on October 1, 1979; requires the price of cheese offered or exposed for retail sale to be indicated.

1945. Forestry

FOREST PARKS AND FOREST RECREATION AREAS BYE-LAWS (NORTHERN IRELAND) 1979 (No. 150) [20p], made under the Forestry Act (Northern Ireland) 1953 (c. 2), s. 14, as amended and extended by S.I. 1977 No. 1245 (N.I. 12), arts. 7, 21, Sched. 2; operative on May 30, 1979; regulate the use by the public of forest parks and forest recreation areas.

Regulation made under the Forestry Act (Northern Ireland) 1953, s. 14: S.R. 1979 No. 145 (Davagh) [10p].

1946. Fraud, misrepresentation and undue influence—widow putting all her money in a joint account with her niece

The deceased, a widow aged 85, was brought back from America to Northern Ireland by the applicant, her niece. Before and after her return to Northern Ireland the deceased had repeatedly stated that she wanted to give all her money to the applicant but the applicant wanted her to keep it while she lived. The deceased and the applicant went to a bank where the deceased said that she wanted to put all her money in the applicant's name. After discussion with the manager, where the applicant's attitude was that it was for the deceased to do what she wished with her money and during which the applicant did not use any influence over the deceased, the deceased opened joint accounts in the names of herself and the applicant. When the bank after the deceased's death refused to pay out the money either to the personal representative, who claimed that it formed part of the deceased's estate, or to the applicant, the matter was referred to the Chief Registrar of Friendly Societies under s. 27 of the Trustee Savings Banks Act 1969. The deputy Registrar held that the exercise of undue influence was to be presumed from the circumstances and that the presumption had not been rebutted. On application for an order of certiorari, *held,* that rebuttable presumptions are rules of evidence which arise only when the facts are not sufficiently known and operate only until the facts become known and that on the facts there was no evidence to justify the finding that a relationship of trust and confidence existed from which the exercise of undue influence could be presumed and there was no room for the presumption here as the exercise of undue influence had been conclusively negatived: R. (PROCTOR) v. HUTTON [1978] N.I. 139, Lowry L.C.J.

1947. Friendly societies

FRIENDLY SOCIETIES (FEES) (AMENDMENT) REGULATIONS (NORTHERN IRELAND) 1979 (No. 72) [20p], made under the Friendly Societies Act (Northern Ireland) 1970 (c. 31), ss. 98, 100; operative on May 1, 1979; increase the fees to be paid for matters transacted, and for the inspection and copying of documents, under the 1970 Act; revoke the 1972 (No. 248) (part) and the 1978 (No. 30) Regulations.

1948. Game

GAME PRESERVATION (HARES) ORDER (NORTHERN IRELAND) 1979 (No. 74) [10p], made under the Game Preservation Act (Northern Ireland) 1928 (c. 25), ss. 7 (3), 7F, and the Northern Ireland Act 1974 (c. 28), Sched. 1, para. 2 (1) (2); operative on May 1, 1979; permits, within orchards and nursery grounds of at least one-half acre in area, the taking, killing or destroying of hares from May 1 to June 30 in 1979 and from February 1 to June 30 in 1980 and 1981.

GAME PRESERVATION (GROUSE, PARTRIDGE AND HEN PHEASANTS) ORDER (NORTHERN IRELAND) 1979 (No. 251) [10p], made under the Game Preservation Act (Northern Ireland) 1928, ss. 7C (1), 7F and the Northern Ireland Act 1974, Sched. 1, para. 2 (1) (2); operative on August 11, 1979; prohibits, subject to exemption, the killing of hen pheasants during the open season, restricts dealing in hen pheasants, prohibits commercial dealings in grouse and prohibits the shooting or taking of partridge.

1949. Highways and bridges

ROADS (CONTROL OF BUILDERS' SKIPS) REGULATIONS (NORTHERN IRELAND) 1979 (No. 85) [20p], made under S.I. 1978 No. 1051 (N.I. 21), art. 3 (2); operative on June 4, 1979; make provision with respect to the depositing, siting, size, markings, guarding, lighting and removal of builders' skips.

ROADS (CONTROL OF BUILDERS' SKIPS) (AMENDMENT) REGULATIONS (NORTHERN IRELAND) 1979 (No. 173) [10p], made under S.I. No. 1051 (N.I. 21), art. 3 (2); operative on June 4, 1979; revoke regs. 3 and 4 of the 1979 (No. 85) Regulations.

Order made under the Special Roads Act (Northern Ireland) 1963 (c. 12), ss. 1, 2, 16, 26:

S.R. 1979 No. 250 (Crosskennan Junction) [10p].

1950. —— statutory duty—ice on road

[Roads (Liability of Road Authorities for Neglect) Act (Northern Ireland) 1966 (c. 11), s. 1.] The plaintiff, whose car was damaged when it skidded on an icy road, claimed that the defendant had failed to remove or reduce the hazard caused by the ice on an otherwise safe and sound road surface. *Held,* that the defendant's statutory duty did not extend beyond a duty to repair and this duty was not affected by s. 1 of the Roads (Liability of Road Authorities for Neglect) Act (Northern Ireland) 1966 as the term " maintain " as used there does not embrace any condition or act which is not covered by " repair." The defendant was, therefore, not liable: LAGAN *v.* DEPARTMENT OF THE ENVIRONMENT [1978] N.I. 120, Gibson L.J.

1951. Housing

HOUSE-BUILDING STANDARDS ORDER (NORTHERN IRELAND) 1979 (No. 120) [20p], made under S.I. 1975 No. 1039 (N.I. 9), art. 4; operative on May 7, 1979; approves the Scheme to be operated by the National House-Building Council in Northern Ireland and the forms of Notice of Insurance Cover issued by the Council in relation to dwellings erected pursuant to the Scheme.

HOUSING (DETERMINATION OF UNFITNESS) ORDER (NORTHERN IRELAND) 1979 (No. 379) [10p], made under the Housing (Ireland) Act 1919 (c. 45), s. 6 (6) and the Planning and Housing Act (Northern Ireland) 1931 (c. 12), s. 29 (7); operative on January 1, 1980; increases from 15 to 21 the figure by which the net annual value is multiplied for the purpose of determining the reasonable expenses of making a house fit for human habitation in accordance with the Acts.

1952. Industrial societies

INDUSTRIAL AND PROVIDENT SOCIETIES (FEES) (AMENDMENT) REGULATIONS (NORTHERN IRELAND) 1979 (No. 52) [20p], made under the Industrial and Provident Societies Act (Northern Ireland) 1969 (c. 24), s. 97; operative on April 2, 1979; increase the fees to be paid for matters transacted or arising under the 1969 Act in relation to industrial and provident societies other than credit unions; revoke the 1978 (No. 29) Regulations.

INDUSTRIAL AND PROVIDENT SOCIETIES (CREDIT UNION FEES) (AMENDMENT) REGULATIONS (NORTHERN IRELAND) 1979 (No. 53) [20p], made under the Industrial and Provident Societies Act (Northern Ireland) 1969, s. 97; operative on April 2, 1979; increase the fees to be paid for matters transacted or arising under the 1969 Act in relation to credit unions; revoke the 1978 (No. 31) Regulations.

1953. Insurance

INDUSTRIAL ASSURANCE (NORTHERN IRELAND) ORDER 1979 (No. 1574) (N.I. 13)) [£1·50], made under the Northern Ireland Act 1974 (c. 28), Sched. 1. para. 1, operative on January 4, 1980; consolidates the Industrial Assurance Acts (Northern Ireland) 1924 to 1958 and related enactments.

1954. Intoxicating liquors—licensing—objections to grant of off-licences for super-markets

[Licensing Act (Northern Ireland) 1971 (c. 15), ss. 2 (3), 7.] The appellants appealed against the grant of provisional off-licences for premises in two supermarkets. *Held*, that (1) as the control of premises for the purposes of s. 2 (3) (*c*) of the Licensing Act (Northern Ireland) 1971 is not affected by a contractual restriction on the user of the premises for a particular purpose, the first respondent was a fit person within the meaning of that section; (2) to come within the terms of s. 7 (2) of that Act an applicant for a provisional licence must propose to carry on the business either personally or through a manager and, therefore, that the second respondent, whose tenant would be carrying on the business, was not competent to apply for a provisional licence under that section; and (3) in determining whether the number of licensed premises in the vicinity was inadequate the court was entitled to have regard to the demand for off-licence facilities created in each vicinity by shoppers from outside those vicinities: CRAZY PRICES (NORTHERN IRELAND) *v.* ROYAL ULSTER CONSTABULARY; STEWART'S SUPERMARKETS *v.* ROYAL ULSTER CONSTABULARY [1977] N.I. 123, C.A.

1955. —— —— whether planning permission required

An application was made for the provisional grant of a licence in respect of premises which had been licensed first under a publican's licence and later under an hotel licence. In 1975 the residential business ceased and the premises therefore ceased to qualify as an hotel. The premises were then closed. The divisional planning officer, in reply to a query from the applicant, confirmed that provided that there was no change of user planning permission would not be required. *Held*, that as the previous use of the premises had not been abandoned, there was no necessity to secure planning permission to resume the business and the premises were, therefore, suitable for the grant of a licence: WHEATFIELD INNS (BELFAST) *v.* CROFT INNS [1978] N.I. 83, Gibson L.J.

1956. Judicature (Northern Ireland) Act 1978—commencement

JUDICATURE (NORTHERN IRELAND) ACT 1978 (COMMENCEMENT NO. 3) ORDER 1979 (No. 124 (C. 3)) [20p], made under the Judicature (Northern Ireland) Act 1978 (c. 23), s. 123 (2) (3); brings into operation s. 122 (1) of the Act in so far as it relates to those parts of Sched. 5, Pt. II, which amend Arts. 2 and 4 of S.I. 1974 No. 2143 on February 21, 1979. Also brings into force s. 122 (1) of the Act in so far as it relates to those parts of Sched. 5, Pt. II, which amend Art. 5 of the 1974 Order on September 1, 1979.

JUDICATURE (NORTHERN IRELAND) ACT 1978 (COMMENCEMENT NO. 4) ORDER 1979 (No. 422 (C. 13)) [10p], made under the Judicature (Northern Ireland) Act 1978, s. 123 (2) (3); operative on April 18, 1979; brings into force the provisions of the Act that are not already in force.

1957. Juries

JURIES (DIVISIONAL JURORS LISTS) REGULATIONS (NORTHERN IRELAND) 1979 (No. 264) [40p], made under S.I. 1974 No. 2143 (N.I. 6), arts. 2 (2), 4 (1) (2) (3) (5) (6), 7; operative on August 17, 1979; prescribe the form and division of the Divisional Jurors Lists and the notice and form of return to be served on persons selected from the register of electors; also prescribe the day to be arranged for the selection of jurors and the day on which public notice shall be given that copies of the Lists are available; revoke the 1975 (No. 22) Regulations.

1958. Land registration

LAND REGISTRY (FEES) ORDER (NORTHERN IRELAND) 1979 (No. 299) [70p], made under the Land Registration Act (Northern Ireland) 1970 (c. 18), s. 84; operative on October 1, 1979; varies certain fees chargeable in the land registry; revokes the 1977 (No. 155) Order.

1959. Landlord and tenant

REGISTERED RENTS (INCREASE) ORDER (NORTHERN IRELAND) 1979 (No. 335) [10p], made under S.I. 1978 No. 1050 (N.I. 20), art. 33 (1); operative on October 15, 1979; increases by 16 per cent. the rents registered under Pt. V of the S.I. for dwelling-houses which are let under regulated tenancies.

1960. —— business tenancies—landlord a public authority

[Business Tenancies Act (Northern Ireland) 1964 (c. 36), s. 2.] The plaintiff, a public authority, acquired the reversion to premises occupied and used by the defendant as a car park. The plaintiff, pursuant to a scheme subsequently prepared by it for the operation of car parks including that of the defendant, served on him a notice to quit. In an action for ejectment, *held*, that as s. 2 (1) (*g*) of the Business Tenancies Act (Northern Ireland) 1964 may apply where a public authority's requirement of possession supervenes at a date subsequent to that of the acquisition of the premises and as the authority had proved its requirement of possession at the date of the hearing, it was entitled to possession of the premises: DEPARTMENT OF THE ENVIRONMENT FOR NORTHERN IRELAND *v.* McCULLY [1977] N.I. 85, Murray J.

1961. —— —— Lands Tribunal decisions

JEFFERSON, POLLIN, DALZELL AND NASH *v.* CHERRY, BT/56/1978 (refusal of application for new tenancy of playing fields on the ground that the landlord intended to use the land for his beef farming business).

KERR *v.* BELFAST CELTIC FOOTBALL AND ATHLETIC Co., BT/25/1978 (application for a new tenancy of a holding used as part of a joinery workshop refused as the landlord genuinely intended to demolish the premises on the holding and to carry out substantial works of construction on it and could not do so without obtaining possession of it).

PAGNI *v.* LOCKHART, BT/57/1978 (grant of a new tenancy of a cafe-restaurant in Dungannon, Co. Tyrone where the application was opposed by the landlord on the ground that the tenant had failed to observe his covenant to repair).

1962. —— Lands Tribunal decision

BURNS *v.* HANLEY, BT/61/1978 (grant of new tenancy of premises in Banbridge, Co. Down for a term of three years at a rent of £1,040 per annum, the former tenancy being for a term of three years at a rent of £520 per annum).

1963. Local government

LOCAL GOVERNMENT (SUPERANNUATION) (AMENDMENT) REGULATIONS (NORTHERN IRELAND) 1978 (No. 386) [40p], made under the Local Government Act (Northern Ireland) 1966 (c. 6), s. 103 and S.I. 1972 No. 1073 (N.I. 10), arts. 9, 14; operative on February 9, 1979; amend certain provisions relating to the superannuation of persons engaged in local government; revoke the 1969 (No. 283) Regulations.

LOCAL GOVERNMENT (SUPERANNUATION) (ACCOUNTS AND AUDIT) REGULATIONS (NORTHERN IRELAND) 1978 (No. 395) [20p], made under S.I. 1972 No. 1073, art. 9; operative on February 23, 1979; provide for the keeping and audit of the local government superannuation fund.

LOCAL GOVERNMENT (GENERAL GRANT) ORDER (NORTHERN IRELAND) 1979 (No. 4) [10p], made under S.I. 1972 No. 1999 (N.I. 22), Sched. 1, Pt. I, para. 3 (1); operative on April 1, 1979; specifies districts to be taken into account in calculating standard rate products for the year ending March 31, 1980.

LOCAL GOVERNMENT (PAYMENTS TO COUNCILLORS) (AMENDMENT) REGULATIONS (NORTHERN IRELAND) 1979 (No. 8) [10p], made under the Local Government Act (Northern Ireland) 1972 (c. 9), s. 36; operative on January 23, 1979; provide for the maximum amount of attendance and financial loss allowances for councillors to be determined by the Department of the Environment; revoke the 1977 (No. 317) Regulations.

LOCAL GOVERNMENT (SUPERANNUATION) (AMENDMENT) REGULATIONS (NORTHERN IRELAND) 1979 (No. 23) [50p], made under S.I. 1972 No. 1073 (N.I. 10), arts. 9, 14; operative on March 16, 1979; introduce into the local government superannuation scheme provisions to allow it to be contracted-out under the Social Security Pensions (Northern Ireland) Order 1975.

COUNCILLORS (TRAVELLING AND SUBSISTENCE ALLOWANCES) (AMENDMENT) REGULATIONS (NORTHERN IRELAND) 1979 (No. 25) [10p], made under the Local Government Act (Northern Ireland) 1972, s. 36; operative on March 16, 1979; amend provisions relating to travelling and subsistence allowances for councillors and committee members of district councils, revoke the 1978 (No. 57) Regulations.

LOCAL GOVERNMENT (SUPERANNUATION) (AMENDMENT) (No. 2) REGULATIONS (NORTHERN IRELAND) 1979 (No. 56) [30p], made under S.I. 1972 No. 1073 (N.I. 10), arts. 9, 14; operative on March 30, 1979; further amend the 1962 (No. 210) Regulations.

LOCAL GOVERNMENT (SUPERANNUATION) (AMENDMENT) (No. 3) REGULATIONS (NORTHERN IRELAND) 1979 (No. 214) [90p], made under S.I. 1972 No. 1073 (N.I. 10), arts. 9, 14; operative on August 1, 1979; amend the 1962 (No. 210) Regulations to enable certain officers to make payments to secure unreduced lump sum retiring allowances and to extend the provisions for the purchase of added years.

1964. Magisterial law

MAGISTRATES' COURTS (AMENDMENT) RULES (NORTHERN IRELAND) 1978 (No. 374) [10p], made under the Magistrates' Courts Act (Northern Ireland) 1964 (c. 21), s. 23; operative on February 1, 1979; amend the 1974 (No. 334) Rules as respects order books, objections to certain written statements and sureties.

MAGISTRATES' COURTS (COSTS IN CRIMINAL CASES) RULES (NORTHERN IRELAND) 1978 (No. 375) [20p], made under the Magistrates' Courts Act (Northern Ireland) 1964, s. 23 and the costs in Criminal Cases Act (Northern Ireland) 1968 (c. 10), s. 7 (3); operative on February 1, 1979; prescribe maximum amounts which may be ordered by courts in criminal cases to be paid for solicitors' or counsel's fees or in connection with the attendance of witnesses; revoke the 1977 (No. 174) and 1978 (No. 194) Rules.

MAGISTRATES' COURTS (BLOOD TESTS) RULES (NORTHERN IRELAND) 1978 (No. 376) [20p], made under the Magistrates' Courts Act (Northern Ireland) 1964, s. 23; operative on March 1, 1979; prescribe magistrates' courts practice and procedure in relation to the use of blood tests in paternity proceedings.

PETTY SESSIONS DISTRICTS ORDER (NORTHERN IRELAND) 1979 (No. 30) [10p], made under the Magistrates' Courts Act (Northern Ireland) 1964, s. 21 (2), as substituted by the Judicature (Northern Ireland) Act 1978 (c. 23), s. 101; operative on the day appointed for the coming into force of s. 101 of the 1978 Act; divides Northern Ireland into 26 petty sessions districts with the same names and boundaries as the local government districts.

MAGISTRATES' COURTS (AMENDMENT) RULES (NORTHERN IRELAND) 1979 (No. 132) [20p], made under the Magistrates' Courts Act (Northern Ireland) 1964, s. 23; operative on April 18, 1979; make amendments to the 1974 (No. 334) Rules consequential upon the implementation of the Judicature (Northern Ireland) Act 1978.

MAGISTRATES' COURTS (LICENSING) (AMENDMENT) RULES (NORTHERN IRELAND) 1979 (No. 133) [10p], made under the Magistrates' Courts Act (Northern Ireland) 1964, s. 23; operative on April 18, 1979; amend r. 13 of the 1975 (No. 349) Rules by substituting for the reference to the clerk of the Crown and peace a reference to the chief clerk.

MAGISTRATES' COURTS (SCHOOL ATTENDANCE PROCEEDINGS) (AMENDMENT) RULES (NORTHERN IRELAND) 1979 (No. 134) [10p], made under the Magistrates' Courts Act (Northern Ireland) 1964, ss. 23, 25 (2); operative on April 18, 1979; amend the 1969 (No. 300) Rules to take account of the re-division of Northern Ireland's petty sessions districts.

MAGISTRATES' COURTS FEES ORDER (NORTHERN IRELAND) 1979 (No. 159) [20p], made under the Judicature (Northern Ireland) Act 1978, s. 116 (1) (4); operative on May 21, 1979; fixes the fees to be taken in the magistrates' courts and the fees payable for service of a summons or process and provides for the manner in which such fees are to be taken and applied.

1965. —— appeal—case stated

[Magistrates' Courts Act (Northern Ireland) 1964 (c. 21), s. 146; Treaty of Rome, art. 177.] R was charged with transporting pigs contrary to the Agricultural Marketing Act (Northern Ireland) 1964 and regulations made under it. On a submission by R that the regulations and the relevant sections of the Act conflicted with the Treaty of Rome the resident magistrate decided to refer the matter to the European Court. On a case stated, *held*, that (1) the court could not entertain the case as the mandatory requirement, laid down by s. 148 (8) of the Magistrates' Courts Act (Northern Ireland) 1964, that the date of the transmission of the case be indorsed on the copy served on R had not been observed; (2) the resident magistrate, once the question as to the interpretation of the Treaty had been raised, had power under art. 177 of the Treaty to refer the matter to the European Court; (3) as the question whether or not a question as to the interpretation of the Treaty had been raised or not was a question of fact the case stated did not involve a decision on a point of law: PIGS MARKETING BOARD (NORTHERN IRELAND) *v.* REDMOND [1978] N.I. 73, C.A.

1966. Medicine

MISUSE OF DRUGS (LICENCE FEES) REGULATIONS (NORTHERN IRELAND) 1979 (No. 57) [20p], made under the Misuse of Drugs Act 1971 (c. 38), ss. 30, 31, 38; operative on April 1, 1979; increase fees for licences under the Act; revoke the 1975 (No. 10) and 1978 (No. 6) Regulations.

MISUSE OF DRUGS (AMENDMENT) REGULATIONS (NORTHERN IRELAND) 1979 (No. 258) [10p], made under the Misuse of Drugs Act 1971, ss. 7, 10, 31, 38; operative on September 1, 1979; add phencyclidine to Sched. 2 to the 1974 (No. 272) Regulations.

1967. Mining law

MINERAL EXPLORATION (NORTHERN IRELAND) ORDER 1979 (No. 1713 (N.I. 18)) [20p], made under the Northern Ireland Act 1974 (c. 28), Sched. 1, para. 1; operative on January 1, 1980; provides for financial assistance by way of grants to persons engaged in mineral exploration.

1968. Minors

TATTOOING OF MINORS (NORTHERN IRELAND) ORDER 1979 (No. 926) (N.I. 10) [10p], made under the Northern Ireland Act 1974 (c. 28), Sched. 1, para. 1; operative on August 27, 1979; make it an offence in Northern Ireland to tattoo a person under the age of 18 unless performed for medical reasons by a medical practitioner.

1969. Mortgages

OPTION MORTGAGE (RATES OF INTEREST) (No. 2) ORDER (NORTHERN IRELAND) 1978 (No. 354) [20p], made under S.I. 1978 No. 457 (N.I. 2), art. 11; operative on January 1, 1979; specifies rates of interest to be used in calculating option mortgage subsidy.

OPTION MORTGAGE (RATES OF INTEREST) ORDER (NORTHERN IRELAND) 1979 (No. 241) [20p], made under S.I. 1978 No. 457 (N.I. 2), art. 11; operative on September 1, 1979; specifies rates of interest to be used in calculating option mortgage subsidy; revokes the 1978 (No. 354) Order.

1970. National health

WELFARE FOODS (AMENDMENT No. 2) REGULATIONS (NORTHERN IRELAND) 1978 (No. 399) [10p], made under the Welfare Foods Act (Northern Ireland) 1968 (c. 26), s. 1 (3); operative on January 15, 1979; increase prices of certain welfare foods.

CHARGES FOR DRUGS AND APPLIANCES (AMENDMENT) REGULATIONS (NORTHERN IRELAND) 1979 (No. 215) [10p], made under S.I. 1972 No. 1265 (N.I. 14), arts. 98, 106, 107, Sched. 15; operative on July 16, 1979; amend the 1973 (No. 419) Regulations to increase charges for the supply of drugs and certain appliances, sums prescribed for the grant of prepayment certificates of exemption from some of these charges and the allowance for exemption from those charges on grounds of low income.

GENERAL DENTAL SERVICES (AMENDMENT) REGULATIONS (NORTHERN IRELAND) 1979 (No. 216) [20p], made under S.I. 1972 No. 1265, arts. 61, 98, 106, 107, Sched. 15; operative on July 16, 1979; amend the 1975 (No. 227) Regulations to increase charges for the supply of certain dental appliances and the provision of dental treatment.

1971. Negligence—street lighting—liability for failure to maintain reasonable standard
P fell in a street and suffered injuries because a street light provided by the defendants under statutory powers was not working. P claimed damages. *Held*, that the defendants were liable since where an authority with power to do so provides street lights to a certain standard, it assumes an obligation to exercise reasonable care in maintaining the lights to that standard and the defendants had not done so: FARRELL *v*. NORTHERN IRELAND ELECTRICITY SERVICE [1977] N.I. 39, Lowry L.C.J.

1972. Northern Ireland Act 1974—extension
NORTHERN IRELAND ACT 1974 (INTERIM PERIOD EXTENSION) ORDER 1979 (No. 816) [10p], made under the Northern Ireland Act 1974 (c. 28), s. 1 (4); operative on July 11, 1979; extends until July 16, 1980 the period specified in s. 1 (4) of the 1974 Act for the operation of the temporary provisions for the government of Northern Ireland.

1973. Northern Ireland (Emergency Provisions) Act 1978—amendment
NORTHERN IRELAND (EMERGENCY PROVISIONS) ACT 1978 (AMENDMENT) ORDER 1979 (No. 746) [10p], made under the Northern Ireland (Emergency Provisions) Act 1978 (c. 5), s. 21 (4); operative on July 3, 1979; adds the Irish National Liberation Army to the list of proscribed organisations.

1974. —— continuance
NORTHERN IRELAND (EMERGENCY PROVISIONS) ACT 1978 (CONTINUANCE) ORDER 1979 (No. 817) [10p], made under the Northern Ireland (Emergency Provisions) Act 1978 (c. 5), s. 33 (3) (*a*); operative on July 25, 1979; continues in force for a further six months the provisions of the 1978 Act.
NORTHERN IRELAND (EMERGENCY PROVISIONS) ACT 1978 (CONTINUANCE) (No. 2) ORDER 1979 (No. 1683) [10p], made under the Northern Ireland (Emergency Provisions) Act 1978, s. 33 (3) (*a*); operative on January 25, 1980; continues in force for a further six months the temporary provisions of the 1978 Act.

1975. Pensions and superannuation
ROYAL IRISH CONSTABULARY (LUMP SUM PAYMENTS TO WIDOWS) REGULATIONS 1979 (No. 1407) [10p], made under the Royal Irish Constabulary (Widows' Pensions) Act 1954 (c. 17), s. 1; operative on December 3, 1979; provide for the payment of an additional £10 in the case of a widow in receipt of an allowance or pension under S.I. 1971 No. 1469 if she is not entitled to a payment under the Pensioners' Payments and Social Security Act 1979, s. 1 (1). Also provide that an allowance or pension may be paid to widows of former members of the R.U.C. supplementary to an existing pension.
CONTRACTED-OUT EMPLOYMENT (MISCELLANEOUS PROVISIONS No. 2) REGULATIONS (NORTHERN IRELAND) 1978 (No. 398) [20p], made under S.I. 1975 No. 1503 (N.I. 15), art. 33 (5), Sched. 2, paras. 1, 9; operative on January 31, 1979; amend the 1976 (No. 5) Regulations as to elections and the 1976 (No. 29) Regulations as to the effect of contracting-out certificates.
JUDICIAL PENSIONS (NORTHERN IRELAND) (WIDOWS' AND CHILDREN'S BENEFITS) (AMENDMENT) REGULATIONS 1979 (No. 67) [10p], made under the Administration of Justice Act 1973 (c. 15), Sched. 3, as adapted by S.I. 1973 No. 2163, art. 3 (1), Sched. 2; operative on April 21, 1979; amend the 1974 (No. 178) Regulations to remove an anomaly relating to deductions from salary for periodical payments and increases from 3 per cent. to 4 per cent. the interest rate for refunds of periodical payments.
FIREMEN'S PENSION SCHEME (AMENDMENT) ORDER (NORTHERN IRELAND) 1979 (No. 88) [70p], made under the Fire Services Act (Northern Ireland) 1969 (c. 13), s. 17; operative on May 1, 1979; amends the 1973 (No. 393) Order to provide a new method for transferring superannuation rights where a person enters the fire brigade from certain other forms of pensionable employment or

enters such employment after leaving the fire brigade; also enables the pension scheme to satisfy the requirements for the issue of a contracting-out certificate under art. 33 of S.I. 1975 No. 1503 (N.I. 15).

SUPERANNUATION (NORTHERN IRELAND ECONOMIC DEVELOPMENT OFFICE) ORDER (NORTHERN IRELAND) 1979 (No. 174) [10p], made under S.I. No. 1073 (N.I. 10), art. 3 (4); operative on June 18, 1979; adds employment in the Northern Ireland Economic Development Office to the employments for which the Department of the Civil Service may make superannuation schemes.

PENSIONS INCREASE (REVIEW) ORDER (NORTHERN IRELAND) 1979 (No. 338) [20p], made under S.I. 1975 No. 1503 (N.I. 15), art. 69 (1)–(5); operative on November 12, 1975; provides for an increase in the rates of public service pensions.

PENSIONS INCREASE (MODIFICATION) REGULATIONS (NORTHERN IRELAND) 1979 (No. 339) [20p], made under the Pensions (Increase) Act (Northern Ireland) 1971 (c. 35), s. 5 (3); operative on November 12, 1979; provide for an increase in the rates of certain pensions payable under the Belfast Corporation Act (Northern Ireland) 1943 (c. i).

TEACHERS' SUPERANNUATION (AMENDMENT) REGULATIONS (NORTHERN IRELAND) 1979 (No. 380) [40p], made under S.I. 1972 No. 1073 (N.I. 10), arts. 11, 14; operative on December 10, 1979; amend the 1977 (No. 260) Regulations in relation to transfer values, pensions increases and the teachers' superannuation account.

FIREMEN'S PENSION SCHEME (AMENDMENT NO. 3) ORDER (NORTHERN IRELAND) 1979 (No. 387) [40p], made under the Fire Services Act (Northern Ireland) 1969, s. 17; operative on December 31, 1979; amends the 1973 (No. 393) Order by extending the definition of infirmity occasioned by a particular injury, by giving widows an option to take a smaller pension and a lump sum and by increasing the rate of interest payable on certain transfer values.

PENSIONS APPEAL TRIBUNALS (NORTHERN IRELAND) (AMENDMENT) RULES 1979 (No. 397) [10p], made under the Pensions Appeal Tribunals Act 1943 (c. 39), Sched. para. 5; operative on December 17, 1979; amend the 1972 (No. 267) Rules to provide that an assessment appeal will be struck out automatically where an offer of an increased assessment is made.

PENSIONS INCREASE (APPROVED SCHEMES) (HEALTH AND PERSONAL SOCIAL SERVICES) REGULATIONS (NORTHERN IRELAND) 1979 (No. 399) [50p], made under the Pensions (Increase) Act (Northern Ireland) 1971, s. 10; operative on December 31, 1979; supersede and revoke the 1974 (No. 94) Regulations.

1976. Petroleum

PRICE MARKING (PETROL PRICE DISPLAY) ORDER (NORTHERN IRELAND) 1979 (No. 294) [40p], made under the Prices Act 1974 (c. 24), s. 4; arts. 2, 3 and 4 operative on November 12, 1979, and the remainder on September 17, 1979; replaces with amendments and revokes the 1977 (No. 293) Order; requires the price of petrol sold by petrol pumps to be indicated.

GAS CYLINDERS (CONVEYANCE) (AMENDMENT) REGULATIONS (NORTHERN IRELAND) 1979 (No. 334) [20p], made under the Petroleum (Consolidation) Act 1929 (c. 13), s. 6, and the Northern Ireland Act 1974 (c. 28), Sched. 1, para. 2 (1); operative on September 21, 1979; make various amendments to the 1936 (No. 113) Regulations.

1977. Police

ROYAL ULSTER CONSTABULARY PENSIONS (LUMP SUM PAYMENTS TO WIDOWS) REGULATIONS 1978 (No. 358) [10p], made under the Police Act (Northern Ireland) 1970 (c. 9), s. 25; operative on December 4, 1978; provide for the payment of £10 to certain widows of policemen.

ULSTER SPECIAL CONSTABULARY PENSIONS (LUMP SUM PAYMENTS TO WIDOWS) REGULATIONS 1978 (No. 359) [10p], made under the Special Constables Act 1914 (c. 61), s. 1 and the Constabulary (Pensions) Act (Northern Ireland) 1949 (c. 9), s. 4 (4); operative on December 4, 1978; provide for the payment of £10 to certain widows of former members of the U.S.C.

ROYAL ULSTER CONSTABULARY PENSIONS (AMENDMENT) REGULATIONS 1979

(No. 209) [10p], made under the Police Act (Northern Ireland) 1970, s. 25; operative on July 16, 1979; make revised arrangements for the calculation of interest on delayed payments of transfer values.

ROYAL ULSTER CONSTABULARY (AMENDMENT) REGULATIONS 1979 (No. 331) [40p], made under the Police Act (Northern Ireland) 1970, s. 25; operative on October 8, 1979, with effect from May 1, 1979; amend the 1973 (No. 31) Regulations by increasing the rates of pay of members of the R.U.C. with ranks not higher than that of chief superintendent.

ROYAL ULSTER CONSTABULARY (AMENDMENT No. 2) REGULATIONS 1979 (No. 406) [40p], made under the Police Act (Northern Ireland) 1970, s. 25; operative on December 3, 1979; increase certain allowances and rates of pay.

ROYAL ULSTER CONSTABULARY PENSIONS (LUMP SUM PAYMENTS TO WIDOWS) REGULATIONS 1979 (No. 411) [20p], made under the Police Act (Northern Ireland) 1970, s. 25; operative on December 3, 1979; provide for the payment of a gratuity of £10 to certain policemen's widows.

1978. Practice

JUDGMENTS ENFORCEMENT AND DEBTS RECOVERY (NORTHERN IRELAND) ORDER 1979 (No. 296) (N.I. 3) [80p], made under the Northern Ireland Act 1974 (c. 28), Sched. 1, para. 1; operative on days to be appointed; makes amendments to the Judgments (Enforcement) Act (Northern Ireland) 1969 (c. 30) including amendments relating to the powers of the Enforcement of Judgments Office to make orders (art. 3), limitations on the enforcement of certain judgments (art. 4), notices and certificates of unenforceability (art. 5), priority of applications (art. 6), taking custody of goods under money judgments (art. 7), attendance and examination of debtors and witnesses (arts. 8–10), seizure of goods (art. 11), enforcement against land (art. 12), delivery of goods (art. 13), vesting orders for funds, stocks or shares (art. 14), appointment of receivers (art. 15), attachment of debts and earnings (arts. 16, 17, Sched. 1), administration orders (art. 18, Sched. 2), recovery of certain debts without judgment (art. 19, Sched. 3), committals for default and contempts (arts. 21, 22), false applications, answers or representations (arts. 24, 25, 27) and creditors (art. 31); amends the Costs in Criminal Cases Act (Northern Ireland) 1968 in relation to orders for costs made in criminal cases by the High Court or Court of Appeal; and makes further provision about the recovery of debts by public bodies.

LEGAL AID, ADVICE AND ASSISTANCE (NORTHERN IRELAND) ORDER 1979 (No. 1572 (N.I. 11)) [40p], made under the Northern Ireland Act 1974; Sched. 1, para. 1; coming into operation on days to be appointed; extends the provisions of the Legal Aid and Advice Act (Northern Ireland) 1965 (c. 8), relating to legal advice and assistance and makes certain other amendments.

NORTHERN IRELAND WINTER ASSIZE ORDER 1978 (No. 356) [20p], made under S.I. 1975 No. 816 (N.I. 7), art. 5; operative from December 15, 1978, to March 31, 1979; constitutes Northern Ireland, except Belfast, a single county for the purposes of winter assizes.

LEGAL AID (FINANCIAL CONDITIONS) REGULATIONS (NORTHERN IRELAND) 1978 (No. 363) [10p], made under the Legal Aid and Advice Act (Northern Ireland) 1965, ss. 2, 3; operative on December 29, 1978; increase income and capital limits for legal aid.

LEGAL AID (ASSESSMENT OF RESOURCES) (AMENDMENT No. 2) REGULATIONS (NORTHERN IRELAND) 1978 (No. 367) [10p], made under the Legal Aid and Advice Act (Northern Ireland) 1965, ss. 4, 14; operative on January 3, 1979; amend the 1965 (No. 218) Regulations by increasing allowances for dependants in assessing disposable capital.

JUDGMENTS ENFORCEMENT (AMENDMENT) RULES 1979 (No. 58) [20p], made under the Judgments (Enforcement) Act (Northern Ireland) 1969, s. 117, as substituted by the Judicature (Northern Ireland) Act 1978 (c. 23), s. 122 (1), Sched. 5; operative on March 27, 1979; provide a new procedure for a notice of intention to enforce a judgment in the Enforcement of Judgments Office.

JUDGMENT ENFORCEMENT (FEES) (AMENDMENT) ORDER (NORTHERN IRELAND) 1979 (No. 59) [10p], made under the Judicature (Northern Ireland) Act 1978, s. 116; operative on March 27, 1979; prescribes the fee payable on the lodgment of a notice of intention to enforce in the Enforcement of Judgments Office.

RULES OF THE SUPREME COURT (NORTHERN IRELAND) (TRANSITIONAL RULES) 1979 (No. 86) [70p], made under the Judicature (Northern Ireland) Act 1978, s. 55; operative on April 18, 1979; amend the 1936 (No. 70) Rules by replacing Ord. 41 with a new Order which does not require the Registrar to countersign all orders and by adding new Orders 94 which provides for the distribution of business among the Divisions of the High Court, 95 which provides for the delegation of jurisdiction to the masters of the Supreme Court, 96 which provides for appeals from the masters, 97 which gives effect to the new judicial review procedure, 98 which replaces existing provisions relating to applications for habeas corpus, 99 which deals with the exercise of jurisdiction in relation to persons under disability, 100 which deals with the powers and duties of the Official Solicitor, 101 which deals with the appointment of commissioners for oaths and notaries public and 102 which lists the surety companies which may give bonds for the purposes of proceedings in the High Court or Court of Appeal; also amend Orders relating to appeals from the Taxing Master on questions of quantum and in relation to the affairs of mental patients.

JUDGMENTS ENFORCEMENT RULES 1979 (No. 87) [90p], made under the Judgments (Enforcement) Act (Northern Ireland) 1969, s. 117 (1); operative on April 18, 1979; prescribe the procedure to be followed by the Enforcement of Judgments Office and the Office of the Master for the Enforcement of Judgments, in particular, the procedure relating to applications for enforcement under s. 18 of the 1969 Act and the ascertainment of debtors' means, the procedure following the examination of a debtor and the enforcement officer's report and the procedure relating to service of documents, notices and certificates of unenforceability, administration orders, staying enforcement, costs, registration of judgments and proceedings under the Payments for Debt (Emergency Provisions) Act (Northern Ireland) 1971 (c. 30); revoke the 1971 (Nos. 5, 335) Rules and the 1971 (No. 1) Regulations.

CROWN COURT RULES (NORTHERN IRELAND) 1979 (No. 90) [50p], made under the Costs in Criminal Cases Act (Northern Ireland) 1968 (c. 10), s. 7, and the Judicature (Northern Ireland) 1978, ss. 48 (5), 51 (5), 52 (1); operative on April 18, 1979; regulate the procedure and practice of the Crown Court with regard to costs between parties, bail, indictments and references to the Court of Justice of the European Communities; repeal the Indictments Act (Northern Ireland) 1945 (c. 16), ss. 1, 2, and revoke the 1977 (No. 191) Rules.

CLERKS OF THE CROWN AND PEACE (TRANSFER OF FUNCTIONS) ORDER (NORTHERN IRELAND) 1979 (No. 103) [20p], made under the Judicature (Northern Ireland) Act 1978, s. 69 (6); operative on April 18, 1979; provides for the transfer to circuit registrars of some of the functions of the office of clerk of the Crown and peace and makes minor amendments consequential upon the establishment of the new Court Service.

JUVENILE COURTS AND ASSESSORS FOR COUNTY COURTS REGULATIONS (NORTHERN IRELAND) 1979 (No. 104) [10p], made under the Children and Young Persons Act (Northern Ireland) 1968 (c. 34), s. 178 (3), Sched. 2; operative on April 18, 1979; designate the areas in which juvenile courts are to exercise jurisdiction, provide for the selection of, and retiring age for, members of a juvenile court panel and make provision for the selection of assessors for county courts and for the payment of allowances to them.

COURT FUNDS RULES (NORTHERN IRELAND) 1979 (No. 105) [60p], made under the Judicature (Northern Ireland) Act 1978, s. 82 (1); operative on April 18, 1979; provide for the management of funds in the High Court and county courts and for the centralisation of funds under the control of the Accountant General of the Supreme Court.

JUDGMENTS ENFORCEMENT AND DEBTS RECOVERY (NORTHERN IRELAND) ORDER 1979 (COMMENCEMENT NO. 1) ORDER 1979 (No. 119) (C. 5) [20p], made under S.I. 1979 No. 296, art. 1 (2); brings arts. 1–18, 20–35, of, and Scheds. 1

(except s. 77D in Pt. I), 2, 4 (except certain amendments) and 5 (except certain repeals) to, that S.I. into operation on April 18, 1979.

JUDGMENT ENFORCEMENT FEES ORDER (NORTHERN IRELAND) 1979 (No. 158) [30p], made under the Judicature (Northern Ireland) Act 1978, s. 116; operative on May 21, 1979; provides a new scale of fees payable in connection with the enforcement of judgments through the Enforcement of Judgments Office; revokes the 1970 (No. 349), 1975 (No. 327) and the 1976 (No. 392) Regulations and the 1979 (No. 59) Order.

SUPREME COURT FEES ORDER (NORTHERN IRELAND) 1979 (No. 160) [50p], made under the Public Offices Fees Act 1879 (c. 58), ss. 2, 3, and the Judicature (Northern Ireland) Act 1978, s. 116; operative on May 21, 1979; replaces the 1977 (No. 103) Order with amendments increasing from £10 to £15 the fee payable on a writ of summons, originating summons and petition.

SUPREME COURT (NON-CONTENTIOUS PROBATE) FEES ORDER (NORTHERN IRELAND) 1979 (No. 161) [20p], made under the Public Offices Fees Act 1879, ss. 2, 3, and the Judicature (Northern Ireland) Act 1978, s. 116; operative on May 21, 1979; replaces the 1976 (No. 205) Order with amendments increasing certain fees payable on, or relating to, applications for grants of probate and letters of administration, and on caveats and settling documents.

LEGAL AID (FINANCIAL CONDITIONS) REGULATIONS (NORTHERN IRELAND) 1979 (No. 175) [10p], made under the Legal Aid and Advice Act (Northern Ireland) 1965 (c. 8), ss. 2, 3; operative on June 15, 1979; increase the financial limits for legal aid.

LEGAL ADVICE AND ASSISTANCE (FINANCIAL CONDITIONS) REGULATIONS (NORTHERN IRELAND) 1979 (No. 176) [10p], made under the Legal Aid and Advice Act (Northern Ireland) 1965, ss. 7C, 14; operative on June 15, 1979; increase to £35 per week the disposable income above which a person receiving legal advice and assistance under the Act is required to pay a contribution and make consequential amendments to the scale of contributions.

LEGAL ADVICE AND ASSISTANCE (FINANCIAL CONDITIONS) (NO. 2) REGULATIONS (NORTHERN IRELAND) 1979 (No. 177) [10p], made under the Legal Aid and Advice Act (Northern Ireland) 1965, ss. 7 (2), 14; operative on June 15, 1979; increase the disposable income limit for the availability of legal advice and assistance under the Act to £75 per week and the disposable capital limit to £600.

LEGAL ADVICE AND ASSISTANCE (AMENDMENT) REGULATIONS (NORTHERN IRELAND) 1979 (No. 188) [10p], made under the Legal Aid and Advice Act (Northern Ireland) 1965, ss. 4, 14; operative on July 6, 1979; amend the 1978 (No. 201) Regulations to increase the allowances for a spouse, dependent child or dependent relative when assessing disposable income.

LEGAL AID (ASSESSMENT OF RESOURCES) (AMENDMENT) REGULATIONS (NORTHERN IRELAND) 1979 (No. 189) [10p], made under the Legal Aid and Advice Act (Northern Ireland) 1965, s. 4; operative on July 6, 1979; amend the 1965 (No. 218) Regulations by removing the disregard of £104 of income, specifying the employment expenses which may be deducted from income, increasing the deductions from income for dependants and removing the deductions from capital for dependants and low income.

RULES OF THE SUPREME COURT (NORTHERN IRELAND) (AMENDMENT No. 1) 1979 (No. 205) [10p], made under the Judicature (Northern Ireland) Act 1978, s. 55; operative on July 2, 1979; amend Ord. 54, r. 13 of the 1936 (No. 70) Rules to remove a restriction on the jurisdiction conferred on Masters by Ord. 95, r. 7, to exercise the powers of a Judge in Chambers; revoke Ord. 60A of the 1936 Rules.

RULES OF THE SUPREME COURT (NORTHERN IRELAND) (AMENDMENT No. 2) 1979 (No. 206) [10p], made under the Judicature (Northern Ireland) Act 1978, s. 55; operative on July 2, 1979; amend Scales I and II of fixed costs in Pt. VI of Appendix S to the 1936 (No. 70) Rules to take account of the increase by the 1979 (No. 160) Order on the court fees payable on a writ of summons.

LEGAL AID (GENERAL) (AMENDMENT) REGULATIONS (NORTHERN IRELAND) 1979 (No. 248) [10p], made under the Legal Aid and Advice Act (Northern Ireland) 1965, s. 14; operative on August 10, 1979; amend the 1965 (No. 217)

Regulations to authorise the Secretary to the Legal Aid Committee or a certifying committee to approve on behalf of the committee an application for a civil aid certificate.

JUDGMENT ENFORCEMENT FEES ORDER (NO. 2) (NORTHERN IRELAND) 1979 (No. 262) [10p], made under the Judicature (Northern Ireland) Act 1978, s. 116; operative on September 1, 1979; applies the 1979 (No. 158) Order with modifications to proceedings in the Enforcement of Judgments Office under the Payments for Debt (Emergency Provisions) Act (Northern Ireland) 1971 (c. 30).

LEGAL AID (FINANCIAL CONDITIONS) (NO. 2) REGULATIONS (NORTHERN IRELAND 1979 (No. 372) [10p], made under the Legal Aid and Advice Act (Northern Ireland) 1965, ss. 2, 3; operative on November 12, 1979; increase the financial limits for legal aid.

LEGAL ADVICE AND ASSISTANCE (FINANCIAL CONDITIONS) (NO. 3) REGULA-TIONS (NORTHERN IRELAND) 1979 (No. 373) [10p], made under the Legal Aid and Advice Act (Northern Ireland) 1965, ss. 7 (2), 7C, 14; operative on November 12, 1979; increase the disposable income limits for the availability of advice and assistance under the Act.

1979. —— **jurisdiction—enforcement of judgments—interpleader proceedings**
    [Enforcement of Judgments Act (Northern Ireland) 1969 (c. 30), s. 8.] The respondent bank advanced money to C on condition that the proceeds of the sale of his house would be lodged with the bank. The solicitors acting for C in the sale gave the bank an undertaking that they would so lodge the proceeds. About two years later the Enforcement of Judgments Office by order appointed a receiver to receive the proceeds of the sale. C's solicitors commenced proceedings by way of interpleader to determine whether they should hold the proceeds for the bank or for the Office. *Held,* that (1) the jurisdiction to hear and determine an application by way of interpleader is not jurisdiction relating to the enforcement of judgments and is not affected by s. 8 of the Enforcement of Judgments Act (Northern Ireland) 1969; and (2) the agreement with the bank amounted to an equitable assignment to the bank of the proceeds and ranked in priority to the interest of the receiver: CARLETON, ATKINSON AND SLOAN v. ALLIED IRISH BANK [1977] N.I. 158, C.A.

1980. —— **new trial—costs**
    In an action for damages for personal injuries sustained by the plaintiff while in the defendant's employment the judge withdrew the case from the jury on the application of the defendant. On appeal a new trial was ordered. *Held,* that, where a new trial is ordered and the relevant error in the first trial was due to the act of the defendant, the plaintiff's costs of the first trial should follow the event of the second and the defendant should bear his own costs of the first trial in any event: MORROW v. MCADAM [1978] N.I. 82, C.A.

1981. —— **want of prosecution—failure to serve notice of intention to proceed on one of joint defendants**
    [R.S.C., Ord. 36, r. 11.] P commenced proceedings against D1 and D2 in 1964. Pleadings were closed in 1964. In June 1975 a notice of intention to proceed was served on D1 and, it was claimed, on D2. D2 moved to have the action dismissed for want of prosecution. His application was dismissed. On appeal, *held*, that (1) notice of intention to proceed was not served on D2; (2) as " the defendant " in Ord. 36, r. 11, does not mean all defendants, D2 was entitled under that rule to have the action dismissed as against him: MCMULLAN v. WALLACE [1977] N.I. 1, C.A.

1982. —— **writs issued but not served—expiry of limitation period**
    [S.I. 1976 No. 1158 (N.I. 18), art. 1.] Two writs claiming damages for personal injuries arising out of an accident in January 1973 were issued in August and September 1974 and a further writ in September 1975. The writs were never issued and the defendant's insurers did not become aware of the third claim until September 1976. On an *ex parte* application for renewal of the three writs, *held*, that (1) the court's discretion under S.I. 1976 No. 1158, art. 1, to disapply the limitation period should not be exercised on an *ex parte* application as the discretion is exercisable only after notice to the defendant

and consideration by the court of various matters including matters likely to be within the exclusive knowledge of the defendant; (2) the application should not be dismissed as that would constitute a final order and prevent fresh applications under that S.I. The applications were, therefore, adjourned: JOHNSTON *v.* MOHAN [1978] N.I. 126, Murray J.

1983. Public health

CONTROL OF FOOD PREMISES (NORTHERN IRELAND) ORDER 1979 (No. 1710 (N.I. 17)) [40p], made under the Northern Ireland Act 1974 (c. 28), Sched. 1, para. 1; operative on January 20, 1980; empowers a court of summary jurisdiction to prohibit the continued use of premises for the purposes of a food business where there is a danger to health in allowing the business to carry on.

POLLUTION CONTROL AND LOCAL GOVERNMENT (NORTHERN IRELAND) (1978 ORDER) (COMMENCEMENT NO. 1) ORDER (NORTHERN IRELAND) 1978 (No. 348) (C. 17) [20p], made under S.I. 1978 No. 1049 (N.I. 19), art. 1 (2) and the Northern Ireland Act 1974, Sched. 1, para. 2 (1) (2); brings Pt. I, arts. 37–42, 49–56, 63–84, 86, 87 of, and Scheds. 3–5, 6 (pt.), 7 (pt.) to, that S.I. into operation on December 18, 1978.

CONTROL OF NOISE (APPEALS) REGULATIONS (NORTHERN IRELAND) 1978 (No. 350) [20p], made under S.I. 1978 No. 1049 (N.I. 19), arts. 50 (1) (2), 86; operative on December 18, 1978; contain provisions as to appeals to courts of summary jurisdiction under arts. 38, 40 and 41 of that S.I.

INTEREST ON RECOVERABLE SANITATION EXPENSES (NO. 2) ORDER (NORTHERN IRELAND) 1978 (No. 352) [10p], made under the Public Health and Local Government (Miscellaneous Provisions) Act (Northern Ireland) 1962 (c. 12), s. 5; operative on December 22, 1978; increases to 12½ per cent. per annum the rate of interest on certain expenses recoverable by district councils under the Public Health (Ireland) Act 1978; revokes the 1978 (No. 249) Order.

OIL FUEL (SULPHUR CONTENT OF GAS FUEL) REGULATIONS (NORTHERN IRELAND) 1979 (No. 21) [20p], made under S.I. 1978 No. 1049 (N.I. 19), art. 55; operative on March 5, 1979; specify the permitted sulphur content for gas oil used in certain furnaces and engines.

INTEREST ON RECOVERABLE SANITATION EXPENSES ORDER (NORTHERN IRELAND) 1979 (No. 34) [10p], made under the Public Health and Local Government (Miscellaneous Provisions) Act (Northern Ireland) 1962 (c. 12), s. 5; operative on March 29, 1979; increases to 14 per cent. per annum the rate of interest on certain expenses recoverable by district councils under the Public Health (Ireland) Act 1878; revokes the 1978 (No. 352) Order.

INTEREST ON RECOVERABLE SANITATION EXPENSES (NO. 2) ORDER (NORTHERN IRELAND) 1979 (No. 288) [10p], made under the Public Health and Local Government (Miscellaneous Provisions) Act (Northern Ireland) 1962, s. 5; operative on September 26, 1979; reduces to 13 per cent. per annum the rate of interest on certain expenses recoverable by district councils under the Public Health (Ireland) Act 1878 (c. 52); revokes the 1979 (No. 34) Order.

1984. Rating and valuation

RATES AMENDMENT (NORTHERN IRELAND) ORDER 1979 (No. 297) (N.I. 4) [30p], made under the Northern Ireland Act 1974 (c. 28), Sched. 1, para. 1; operative on April 1, 1979; art. 3 provides for rate relief on certain hereditaments used for the purposes of a prescribed recreation; under art. 4 certain hereditaments used for the purposes of recreational charities may be distinguished in the valuation lists; art. 5 provides for rate relief on certain hereditaments in which there are special facilities for disabled persons and under art. 6 certain hereditaments used by institutions for the disabled may be distinguished in the valuation lists; arts. 7–10 amend S.I. 1977 No. 2157 (N.I. 28) and the Development of Tourist Traffic Act (Northern Ireland) 1948 (c. 4) and repeal an obsolete enactment.

RATES (REGIONAL RATE AND REDUCTION OF REGIONAL RATE ON DWELLINGS) ORDER (NORTHERN IRELAND) 1979 (No. 26) [10p], made under S.I. 1977 No. 2157 (N.I. 28), arts. 7, 27; operative on April 1, 1979; fixes for the year ending March 31, 1980, the regional rate and the amount by which it is reduced for dwelling-houses.

RECREATIONAL CHARITIES (RECORD OF USE) REGULATIONS (NORTHERN IRELAND) 1979 (No. 156) [20p], made under S.I. 1977 No. 2157 (N.I. 28), arts. 2 (2), 61 (1) (*bb*); operative on June 1, 1979; make provision as to the records of use of premises to be kept for the purpose of ascertaining the eligibility of certain premises to distinguishment in the valuation list as hereditaments used for recreational charity.

RATE REBATE (AMENDMENT) ORDER (NORTHERN IRELAND) 1979 (No. 358) [20p], made under S.I. 1977 No. 2157 (N.I. 28), art. 28; operative on November 12, 1979; revises the scale of needs allowances to be applied in assessing applications for rate rebates; permits the backdating of first applications in exceptional circumstances.

1985. —— Lands Tribunal decisions

ARTHUR *v*. COMMISSIONER OF VALUATION, VR/101/1978 (successful appeal against the valuation of premises in Shipquay Place, Londonderry, occupied by a chartered surveyor and estate agent).

BROOKS *v*. COMMISSIONER, VR/93/1978 (unsuccessful appeal against the valuation of a dwelling house in Hillsborough, Co. Down).

COWAN *v*. COMMISSIONER OF VALUATION, VR/11/1978 (successful appeal against the valuation of a retail discount furniture warehouse in Bangor, Co. Down, the tribunal holding that three other such warehouses in Bangor were comparable hereditaments in the same state and circumstances).

CRAZY PRICES (N.I.) *v*. COMMISSIONER OF VALUATION, VR/81/1978 (unsuccessful appeal against the valuation of a food supermarket in Lisburn, Co. Antrim).

DON *v*. COMMISSIONER OF VALUATION, VR/64/1977 (valuation of market on former airport).

FLETCHER *v*. COMMISSIONER OF VALUATION VR/108/1978 (unsuccessful appeal against the valuation of a dwelling-house in Comber, Co. Down).

HAMPDEN HOMES *v*. COMMISSIONER OF VALUATION, VR/79/1978 (unsuccessful appeal against the valuation of a large retail store in Lisburn, Co. Antrim, selling hardware, garden supplies, household furnishings, textiles and do-it-yourself equipment).

HARPER *v*. COMMISSIONER OF VALUATION, VR/58/1978 (successful appeal against the valuation of a dwelling-house, out-offices and a swimming pool in Comber, Co. Down).

JOHN KELLY CO. *v*. COMMISSIONER OF VALUATION, VR/1/2/1978 (valuation of coal yards, the tribunal holding that by far the greater area in each hereditament, and the deployment of the labour force, was for the processes of adapting the coal for sale, so that each hereditament was used for factory purposes and that the primary use entitled it to be entered as industrial).

KELLY *v*. COMMISSIONER OF VALUATION, VR/76/1978 (appeal against valuation of a dwelling house in Cedar Avenue, Belfast, the tribunal reducing the valuation on account of the unpleasantness of bricked up and vandalised adjoining houses).

MATTOCKS *v*. COMMISSIONER OF VALUATION, VR/47/1978 (unsuccessful appeal against the valuation of a dwelling-house in Belfast).

ROYAL BRITISH LEGION ATTENDANTS CO. (BELFAST) *v*. COMMISSIONER OF VALUATION, VR/47/1977 (car park operated by the company, a registered charity, *held* to be occupied and used for charitable purposes).

SAWERS (BELFAST) *v*. COMMISSIONER OF VALUATION, VR/59/1978 (appeal against the valuation of shop premises in Castle Street, Belfast, the tribunal holding that, where the lessee has covenanted to keep the premises in good and tenantable repair, the doctrine of *rebus sic stantibus* does not include the retention of boarded-up windows and doors following bomb damage).

1986. Registration of births, deaths and marriages

BIRTHS, DEATHS AND MARRIAGES (FEES) ORDER (NORTHERN IRELAND) 1979 (No. 48) [30p], made under the Registration of Births, Deaths and Marriages (Fees, etc.) Act (Northern Ireland) 1955 (c. 29), s. 1, as modified by the Northern Ireland Constitution Act 1973 (c. 36), s. 40, Sched. 5, para. 4, S.I. 1976 No. 1041 (N.I. 14), art. 47 and S.I. 1976 No. 1212 (N.I. 21), art. 15;

operative on April 1, 1979; increases fees relating to the registration of births, deaths and marriages.

1987. Revenue and finance

APPROPRIATION (NO. 2) (NORTHERN IRELAND) ORDER 1979 (No. 922) (N.I. 6) [40p], made under the Northern Ireland Act 1974 (c. 28), Sched. 1, para. 1; operative on July 26, 1979; authorises the issue of sums out of the consolidated fund and appropriates those sums for specified services.

TAX, CONSUMER CREDIT AND JUDICATURE (NORTHERN IRELAND CONSEQUENTIAL AMENDMENTS) ORDER 1979 (No. 1576) [20p], made under the Northern Ireland Constitution Act 1973 (c. 36), s. 38 (2), as extended by the Northern Ireland Act 1974, Sched. 1, para. 1 (7); operative on January 3, 1980, except arts. 2 (3) (*a*) and 4, which come into force on the days appointed under art. 1 (2) of S.I. 1979 No. 1575 for the coming into operation of art. 9 and the definition of "non-contentious probate business" in art. 2 (2) of that order; amends the Income and Corporation Taxes Act 1970, the Finance Act 1975, the Finance Act 1976 and the Judicature (Northern Ireland) Act 1978.

ULSTER SAVINGS CERTIFICATES (EIGHTEENTH ISSUE) REGULATIONS 1978 (No. 373) [10p], made under the Exchequer and Financial Provisions Act (Northern Ireland) 1950 (c. 3), s. 15 (1); operative on January 29, 1979; prescribe terms governing the issue of the 18th issue Ulster savings certificates and a maximum holding.

SELECTIVE EMPLOYMENT PAYMENTS (TERMINATION OF PAYMENT AND CONSEQUENTIAL PROVISIONS) ORDER (NORTHERN IRELAND) 1979 (No. 213) [10p], made under S.I. 1972 No. 1100 (N.I. 11), art. 16 (3) (4) (5) and the Northern Ireland Act 1974, Sched. 1, para. 2 (1) (2); operative on July 31, 1979; appoints July 31, 1979, for the purposes of art. 16 (3) of that S.I. so that selective employment premiums cease to be payable in respect of weeks commencing after that date and appoints July 31, 1980, as the day on which the repeal of statutory provisions relating to the payment of premiums takes effect.

1988. Road traffic

MOTOR VEHICLES (TYPE APPROVAL) (AMENDMENT) REGULATIONS (NORTHERN IRELAND) 1978 (No. 393) [40p]; made under the European Communities Act 1972 (c. 68), s. 2 (2); operative on February 1, 1979; amend the 1973 (No. 408) Regulations as respects information documents, the application of approval marks to components and a revised Sched. 2.

MOTOR VEHICLES (DRIVING LICENCES) (AMENDMENT) (NO. 2) REGULATIONS (NORTHERN IRELAND) 1978 (No. 394) [10p], made under the Road Traffic Act (Northern Ireland) 1970 (c. 2), ss. 2, 189; operative on February 1, 1979; exempt policemen who are 18 or over from the requirement to have heavy goods vehicle driving licences.

ROAD VEHICLES (REAR FOG LAMPS) REGULATIONS (NORTHERN IRELAND) 1979 (No. 65) [20p], made under the Road Traffic Act (Northern Ireland) 1970, ss. 26, 42, 189; operative on April 9, 1979; give effect to Council Directives 76/756/EEC and 77/538/EEC relating to rear fog lamps.

MOTOR VEHICLES (DRIVING LICENCES) (AMENDMENT) REGULATIONS (NORTHERN IRELAND) 1979 (No. 137) [10p], made under the Road Traffic Act (Northern Ireland) 1970, ss. 5, 15, 189; operative on May 28, 1979; amend the 1965 (No. 42) Regulations in relation to mopeds and prescribe the duration of a provisional licence which remains at one year.

DUNDROD CIRCUIT (ADMISSION CHARGES) REGULATIONS (NORTHERN IRELAND) 1979 (No. 196) [10p], made under S.I. 1977 No. 2155 (N.I. 26), art. 4 (3) (*b*); operative on July 24, 1979; set out maximum admission charges to the Dundrod Circuit, Co. Antrim, on race days.

PUBLIC SERVICE VEHICLES (AMENDMENT) REGULATIONS (NORTHERN IRELAND) 1979 (No. 317) [10p], made under the Road Traffic Act (Northern Ireland) 1970, ss. 55, 61, 189; operative on November 1, 1979; increase licence fees for public service vehicles.

MOTOR VEHICLES (DRIVING LICENCES) (AMENDMENT) (NO. 2) REGULATIONS (NORTHERN IRELAND) 1979 (No. 318) [10p], made under the Road Traffic Act (Northern Ireland) 1970, ss. 8, 189; operative on November 1, 1979; increase the fee for a driving test on all vehicles except invalid carriages.

HEAVY GOODS VEHICLES (DRIVERS' LICENCES) (AMENDMENT) REGULATIONS (NORTHERN IRELAND) 1979 (No. 319) [10p], made under the Road Traffic Act (Northern Ireland) 1970, ss. 71, 189; operative on November 1, 1979; increase the fee for a heavy goods vehicle driving test.

MOTOR CARS (DRIVING INSTRUCTION) (AMENDMENT) REGULATIONS (NORTHERN IRELAND) 1979 (No. 320) [10p], made under the Road Traffic Act (Northern Ireland) 1970, ss. 117, 117C, 189; operative on November 1, 1979; amend the 1974 (No. 109) Regulations by requiring a person applying to have his name entered for the first time in the Register of approved driving instructors to pay a fee of £30 and by increasing other fees under these Regulations.

MOTOR VEHICLE TESTING (AMENDMENT) REGULATIONS (NORTHERN IRELAND) 1979 (No. 321) [10p], made under the Road Traffic Act (Northern Ireland) 1970, ss. 29A, 29C, 29D, 189; operative on November 1, 1979; increase fees for vehicle test certificates for motor cars and motor bicycles.

ROAD TRAFFIC (CROWN EXEMPTION) REGULATIONS (NORTHERN IRELAND) 1979 (No. 322) [10p], made under the Road Traffic Act (Northern Ireland) 1970, s. 183 (1); operative on November 1, 1979; exempt from speed limits vehicles, and their drivers, being used by or on behalf of the Department of the Environment to measure the skid resistance of roads; revoke the 1972 (No. 269) Regulations.

'PELICAN' PEDESTRIAN CROSSINGS (AMENDMENT) REGULATIONS (NORTHERN IRELAND) 1979 (No. 362) [20p], made under the Road Traffic Act (Northern Ireland) 1970, s. 25; operative on November 19, 1979; amend the 1970 (No. 83) Regulations to permit the width of a crossing to extend to a maximum of 10 metres without the written authorisation of the Department of Environment and to authorise an alternative phasing of the light signals.

DISABLED PERSONS (BADGES FOR MOTOR VEHICLES) REGULATIONS (NORTHERN IRELAND) 1979 (No. 365) [40p], made under the Chronically Sick and Disabled Persons (Northern Ireland) Act 1978 (c. 53), s. 14; operative on October 31, 1979; make provision for the form and issue of badges to be displayed on motor vehicles driven by or used for the carriage of certain disabled persons and for the exemption from certain provisions of vehicles displaying such badges.

GOODS VEHICLES (CERTIFICATION) (AMENDMENT) REGULATIONS (NORTHERN IRELAND) 1979 (No. 381) [10p], made under the Road Traffic Act (Northern Ireland) 1970, ss. 47, 52, 189; operative on December 3, 1979; increase the fees for test certificates (including duplicates) for all goods vehicles except new ones.

TRAFFIC SIGNS REGULATIONS (NORTHERN IRELAND) 1979 (No. 386) [£5·75], made under the Road Traffic Act (Northern Ireland) 1970, s. 25; operative on December 31, 1979; consolidate with amendments and revoke the 1966 (No. 23), 1967 (Nos. 15, 101), 1968 (Nos. 267, 279), 1969 (Nos. 156, 277, 287) and 1970 (No. 276) Regulations.

ROAD VEHICLES (REAR FOG LAMPS) (AMENDMENT) REGULATIONS (NORTHERN IRELAND) 1979 (No. 389) [10p], made under the Road Traffic Act (Northern Ireland) 1970, ss. 26, 42, 189; operative on December 17, 1979; amend the definition of "approval mark" in the 1979 (No. 65) Regulations.

ROADS (RESTRICTION OF WAITING) ORDER (NORTHERN IRELAND) 1979 (No. 400) [20p], made under the Road Traffic Act (Northern Ireland) 1970, s. 19; operative on December 31, 1979; prohibits, subject to certain exemptions, the waiting of vehicles on any public road in contravention of a traffic sign and provides generally for regulating the waiting of vehicles on any public road or in any area.

Orders made under the Road Traffic Act (Northern Ireland) 1970:

S. 19: S.R. 1978 No. 328 (Downpatrick) [10p]; 1979 Nos. 15 Enniskillen) [20p]; 38 (Larne) [20p]; 69 (Newry) [20p]; 70 Belfast–Newtownabbey) [50p]; 71 (York Street, Belfast) [20p]; 84 (Belfast) [60p]; 146 (Belfast–Newtownabbey) [30p]; 147 (Belfast) [10p]; 162 (Newtownards) [20p]; 163 (Lisburn) [20p]; 164 (Limavady) [20p]; 169 (Strangford) [10p]; 233 (Enniskillen [10p]; 236 (Donaghadee) [20p]; 266 (Belfast) [10p]; 268 (Portrush) [20p]; 316 (Millisle) [10p]; 341 (Banbridge) [10p]; 342 (Portadown) [10p]; 343 (Newry) [10p]; 344 (Lurgan) [10p]; 345 (Banbridge) [10p]; 348 (Craigavon)

[10p]; 349 (Ballymena) [20p]; 350 (Larne) [10p]; 353 (Larne) [10p]; 396 (Newcastle) [20p]; 404 (Lurgan) [20p].

S. 20: S.R. 1979 Nos. 55 (Craigavon) [20p]; 75 (Lurgan) [10p]; 199 (Queen's Square, Belfast) [20p]; 202 (Belfast) [20p]; 330 (The Palms, Portadown) [10p]; 356 (Newcastle, Co. Down) [10p].

S. 43 (4): S.R. 1979 Nos. 61 (Cos. Antrim, Down, Londonderry, Tyrone) [20p]; 62 (Cos. Antrim, Down, Londonderry, Tyrone) [20p]; 351 (Cos. Antrim, Armagh, Down, Londonderry) [40p]; 352 (Cos. Antrim, Armagh, Down) [20p].

S. 89: S.R. Nos. 83 (Belfast)` [20p]; 168 (Larne–Magherafelt) [25p]; 180 (Cos. Armagh and Down) [60p]; 385 (Belfast) [50p].

S. 175 (1): S.R. No. 3 (specified areas) [10p].

Orders made under the Special Roads Act (Northern Ireland) 1963 (c. 12), s. 20 and the Road Traffic Act (Northern Ireland) 1970, s. 22:

S.R. 1978 No. 355 (M1) [10p]; S.R. 1979 Nos. 388 (M1) [10p]; 390 (M1) [10p].

1989. —— driving under influence of alcohol—blood specimen offered by constable
[Road Traffic Act (Northern Ireland) 1970 (c. 2), s. 122 (5).] A doctor took a specimen of blood from the respondent, who was charged with driving, attempting to drive or being in charge of a motor vehicle while under the influence of drink, divided it into two parts, gave them to the constable who made the arrest and he in the presence of the doctor proffered them to the respondent who took one and signed a receipt for it. *Held,* that the analysis of the specimen was admissible notwithstanding that the specimen had not been offered to the respondent by the person who took it as required by s. 122 (5) of the Road Traffic Act (Northern Ireland) 1970: CURRIE v. BEATTIE [1978] N.I. 107, C.A.

1990. Sale of goods
UNSOLICITED GOODS AND SERVICES (1976 ORDER) (COMMENCEMENT) ORDER (NORTHERN IRELAND) 1979 (No. 292) (C. 11) [10p], made under S.I. 1976 No. 57 (N.I. 11), art. 1 (2), and the Northern Ireland Act 1974 (c. 28), Sched. 1, para. 2 (1) (*b*); brings arts. 2 (3) and 5 (4) of the S.I. into operation on September 12, 1979.

UNSOLICITED GOODS AND SERVICES (INVOICES, ETC.) REGULATIONS (NORTHERN IRELAND) 1979 (No. 323) [20p], made under S.I. 1976 No. 57, art. 6 (1) (2) (3); operative on October 15, 1979; set out the requirements with which invoices and similar documents must comply if they are not to be regarded as asserting a right to payment for the purposes of the S.I. and specify the contents required in a note of a person's agreement to a change for an entry in a directory; revoke the 1976 (No. 239) Regulations.

1991. Sheriffs
UNDER-SHERIFFS (DISCHARGE OF DUTIES) ORDER (NORTHERN IRELAND) 1979 (No. 122) [10p], made under the Judicature (Northern Ireland) Act 1978 (c. 23), s. 104 (1); operative on April 18, 1979; authorises a person appointed as an under-sheriff in Northern Ireland to discharge the duties of that office for or in relation to a county court division instead of for or in relation to a county or county borough.

1992. Shipping and marine insurance
LOUGH ERNE (NAVIGATION) (AMENDMENT) BYE-LAWS (NORTHERN IRELAND) 1979 (No. 332) [10p], made under S.I. 1973 No. 69 (N.I. 1), art. 41, Sched. 7; operative on November 1, 1979; extend the area of waterway restricted by speed limit at Carrybridge.

Order made under the Harbours Act (Northern Ireland) 1970 (c. 1), s. 1: S.R. 1979 No. 32 (Belfast) [20p].

1993. Social security
SOCIAL SECURITY (NORTHERN IRELAND) ORDER 1979 (No. 396 (N.I. 5)) [40p], made under the Northern Ireland Act 1974, (c. 28), Sched. 1 (1), as modified by the Social Security Act 1979 (c. 18), s. 19, operative on March 30, 1979; makes provision for Northern Ireland corresponding to certain provisions contained in the Social Security Act 1979.

PNEUMOCONIOSIS, ETC., (WORKERS' COMPENSATION) (NORTHERN IRELAND) ORDER 1979 (No. 925) (N.I. 9) [40p], made under the Northern Ireland Act 1974, Sched. 1, para. 1; operative on days to be appointed; provides for the payment of lump sums to certain persons who are, or were immediately before they died, disabled by pneumoconiosis, byssinosis or diffuse mesothelioma.

SOCIAL SECURITY (CONTRIBUTIONS) (AMENDMENT No. 2) REGULATIONS (NORTHERN IRELAND) 1978 (No. 369) [10p], made under the Social Security (Northern Ireland) Act 1975 (c. 15), ss. 3, 9 (4), Sched. 1, para. 6 (1) (m); operative on November 30, 1978; amend the 1975 (No. 319) Regulations by disregarding certain payments for travelling expenses and earnings from certain profit-sharing schemes; except divers and diving supervisors in specified employment from class 4 contributions.

SOCIAL SECURITY BENEFIT (COMPUTATION OF EARNINGS) REGULATIONS (NORTHERN IRELAND) 1978 (No. 371) [20p], made under the Social Security (Northern Ireland) Act 1975, ss. 3 (2), 66 (3), 82 (4), 119 (3), 126; operative on February 12, 1979; consolidate, with minor amendments, and revoke the 1975 (No. 15) Regulations, as amended.

SOCIAL SECURITY (CONTRIBUTIONS) (EARNINGS LIMITS) (AMENDMENT) REGULATIONS (NORTHERN IRELAND) 1978 (No. 372) [10p], made under S.I. 1975 No. 1503 (N.I. 15), art. 3; operative on April 6, 1979; substitute new earnings limits for class 1 contributions.

SOCIAL SECURITY (NON-CONTRIBUTORY INVALIDITY PENSION) (AMENDMENT No. 2) REGULATIONS (NORTHERN IRELAND) 1978 (No. 385) [10p], made under the Social Security (Northern Ireland) Act 1975, s. 36 (7); operative on January 5, 1979; amend the 1975 (No. 202) Regulations as respect days on which persons are to be regarded as incapable of work.

SOCIAL SECURITY (CONTRIBUTIONS, RE-RATING) (No. 2) ORDER (NORTHERN IRELAND) 1978 (No. 387) [10p], made under the Social Security (Northern Ireland) Act 1975, s. 120; operative on April 6, 1979; raises classes 2 and 3 contributions and the limits of profits between which class 4 contributions are payable.

SOCIAL SECURITY (CONTRIBUTIONS) (MARINERS) (AMENDMENT) REGULATIONS (NORTHERN IRELAND) 1978 (No. 400) [20p], made under the Social Security (Northern Ireland) Act 1975, ss. 3 (2), 124 (1), 128 (6), Sched. 1, para. 6 (1) (d) and the Social Security (Consequential Provisions) Act 1975 (c. 18), Sched. 3, para. 9; operative on April 6, 1979; amend the 1975 (No. 319) Regulations as respects certain employment, transitionals and tax years in respect of which contributions may be treated as paid.

SOCIAL SECURITY (CATEGORISATION OF EARNERS) REGULATIONS (NORTHERN IRELAND) 1978 (No. 401) [40p], made under the Social Security (Northern Ireland) Act 1975, ss. 2 (2), 4 (4) (5), Sched. 1, para. 6 (1) (k); operative on February 13, 1979; consolidate with minor amendments, and revoke, the 1975 (Nos. 27, 55), 1976 (No. 112), 1977 (No. 193) and 1978 (No. 308) Regulations.

SOCIAL SECURITY (CONTRIBUTIONS, RE-RATING) (CONSEQUENTIAL AMENDMENT) REGULATIONS (NORTHERN IRELAND) 1979 (No. 14) [10p]; made under the Social Security (Northern Ireland) Act 1975, s. 124 (1); operative on April 6, 1979; increase the rate of class 2 contributions payable by share fishermen.

SOCIAL SECURITY (MOBILITY ALLOWANCE) (AMENDMENT) REGULATIONS (NORTHERN IRELAND) 1979 (No. 47) [20p], made under the Social Security (Northern Ireland) Act 1975, s. 37A (2) (5); operative on March 21, 1979; prescribe the circumstances in which a person is entitled to mobility allowance and allow that allowance to be paid to persons using certain vehicles which are not power driven road vehicles controlled by the occupants.

SOCIAL SECURITY PENSIONS (1975 ORDER) (COMMENCEMENT No. 13) ORDER (NORTHERN IRELAND) 1979 (No. 54) (C. 2) [10p], made under S.I. 1975 No. 1503 (N.I. 15), art. 1 (3); brings into operation, in relation to men of a specified age group, arts. 24, 74 (1) (part) of, and Sched. 5, paras. 29, 31–33 to, that S.I., for the purposes of certain matters relating to mobility allowance, on March 7, 1979, and, for all other purposes, on June 6, 1979.

SOCIAL SECURITY (HOSPITAL IN-PATIENTS) (AMENDMENT) REGULATIONS (NORTHERN IRELAND) 1979 (No. 68) [10p], made under the Social Security (Northern Ireland) Act 1975, ss. 81 (4) (*d*), 82 (6) (*b*), 85 (1); operative on April 6, 1979; amend the 1975 (No. 109) Regulations in relation to Category A retirement pensions.

SOCIAL SECURITY (INDUSTRIAL INJURIES) (PRESCRIBED DISEASES) (AMENDMENT) REGULATIONS (NORTHERN IRELAND) 1979 (No. 77) [10p], made under the Social Security (Northern Ireland) Act 1975, s. 113 (1) (2); operative on April 6, 1979; amend reg. 48 of the 1977 (No. 272) Regulations with regard to the right of appeal to a medical appeal tribunal against a decision of a medical board on a diagnosis question relating to pneumoconiosis or byssinosis.

SOCIAL SECURITY (INDUSTRIAL INJURIES) (PRESCRIBED DISEASES) (AMENDMENT No. 2) REGULATIONS (NORTHERN IRELAND) 1979 (No. 78) [10p], made under the Social Security (Northern Ireland) Act 1975, ss. 76 (2) (4), 77 (2); operative on April 13, 1979; amend reg. 2 of the 1977 (No. 272) Regulations so that, for the purposes of deciding whether byssinosis is a prescribed disease in relation to a person, it is no longer necessary that he should have been employed for a specific minimum period in an occupation prescribed in relation to byssinosis.

SOCIAL SECURITY (RECIPROCAL AGREEMENTS) ORDER (NORTHERN IRELAND) 1979 (No. 92) [20p], made under the Social Security (Northern Ireland) Act 1975, s. 134 (1); operative on April 6, 1979; modifies certain Orders, which provide for reciprocity in social security matters, to take account of changes made by S.I. 1975 No. 1503 (N.I. 15).

SOCIAL SECURITY (OVERLAPPING BENEFITS AND MISCELLANEOUS AMENDMENTS) REGULATIONS (NORTHERN IRELAND) 1979 (No. 97) [20p], made under the Social Security (Northern Ireland) Act 1975, ss. 3 (2), 66 (3), 85; operative on April 6, 1979; amend the 1975 (No. 94) and the 1978 (No. 371) Regulations.

SOCIAL SECURITY (BENEFIT) (TRANSITIONAL) REGULATIONS (NORTHERN IRELAND) 1979 (No. 98) [20p], made under S.I. 1975 No. 1503 (N.I. 15), art. 72; operative as to reg. 7 on March 30, 1979, and as to remainder on April 6, 1979; provide for transitional matters connected with the coming into force of that S.I.

SOCIAL SECURITY (ATTENDANCE ALLOWANCE) (AMENDMENT) REGULATIONS (NORTHERN IRELAND) 1979 (No. 102) [20p], made under the Social Security (Northern Ireland) Act 1975, s. 35 (2) (*b*), (2A), (5A); operative on April 2, 1979; amend the 1975 (No. 102) Regulations in relation to the qualifying period for entitlement to an allowance after an interval of non-entitlement and in relation to persons suffering from renal failure who are undergoing renal dialysis.

SOCIAL SECURITY BENEFIT (PERSONS ABROAD) (AMENDMENT) REGULATIONS (NORTHERN IRELAND) 1979 (No. 131) [20p], made under the Social Security (Northern Ireland) Act 1975, s. 126; operative on April 17, 1979; amend the 1978 (No. 114) Regulations to relax the restrictions relating to entitlement to industrial injuries benefit under the Act of certain earners employed in Norway or a Member State of the EEC.

SOCIAL SECURITY PENSIONS (1975 ORDER) (COMMENCEMENT No. 14) ORDER (NORTHERN IRELAND) 1979 (No. 135) (C. 6) [10p], made under S.I. 1975 No. 1503, art. 1 (3); operative on April 11, 1979; brings into force provisions of that S.I. dealing with mobility allowance in relation to women born on or after March 23, 1919, but before December 21, 1919.

SOCIAL SECURITY (1979 ORDER) (COMMENCEMENT No. 1) ORDER (NORTHERN IRELAND) 1979 (No. 136) (C. 7) [10p], made under S.I. 1979 No. 396 (N.I. 5), art. 1 (3); operative on April 11, 1979; brings into force provisions of that S.I. dealing with mobility allowance in relation to women born on or after June 7, 1918, but before March 23, 1919.

SOCIAL SECURITY (CONTRIBUTIONS) REGULATIONS (NORTHERN IRELAND) 1979 (No. 186) [£2·00], made under the Social Security (Northern Ireland) Act 1975, ss. 1 (6), 3, 4 (2) (*b*) (5) (6), 7 (5) (6), 8 (1) (2), 9 (7)–(9), 10 (1) (2), 11, 13 (4), 128 (2) (3), 129 (1) (2), 130–132, 134 (6), 146 (5), Sched. 1, paras. 1, 2, 3, 4 (*a*) (*c*) (*d*), 5, 6, the Social Security (Consequential Provisions) Act 1975, Sched. 3, paras. 3, 6, 7, 9 and S.I. 1975 No. 1503 (N.I. 15), arts. 3, 5 (2),

7, 29 (3), 72 (1); operative on August 6, 1979; consolidate and revoke the regulations hitherto in force relating to contributions under the 1975 Acts and S.I.

SOCIAL SECURITY (EARNINGS FACTOR) REGULATIONS (NORTHERN IRELAND) 1979 (No. 193) [20p], made under the Social Security (Northern Ireland) Act 1975, ss. 13 (5), 115 (1), Sched. 13, para. 2; S.I. 1975 No. 1503 (N.I. 15), art. 37 (3), and S.I. 1977 No. 610 (N.I. 11), art. 3 (6); operative on July 9, 1979; consolidate and revoke the 1975 (No. 82) and 1977 (Nos. 332, 333) Regulations.

SOCIAL SECURITY (INDUSTRIAL INJURIES) (PRESCRIBED DISEASES) (AMEND-MENT No. 3) REGULATIONS (NORTHERN IRELAND) 1979 (No. 208) [20p], made under the Social Security (Northern Ireland) Act 1975, ss. 76 (2) (4), 77 (2); operative on August 8, 1979; add nasal carcinoma to Sched. 1, Pt. I, to the 1977 (No. 272) Regulations.

SOCIAL SECURITY (UNEMPLOYMENT, SICKNESS AND INVALIDITY BENEFIT) REGULATIONS (NORTHERN IRELAND) 1979 (No. 211) [70p], made under the Social Security (Northern Ireland) Act 1975, ss. 16 (1), 17 (1) (a) (e) (2), 20, 33 (2) (3), 79 (3) (4), 126 and the Social Security (Consequential Provisions) Act 1975, Sched. 3, paras. 3, 9; operative on August 20, 1979; consolidate and revoke the 1975 (No. 86), 1976 (No. 247), 1977 (No. 25) and 1978 (Nos. 87, 120) Regulations.

SOCIAL SECURITY (OVERLAPPING BENEFITS) REGULATIONS (NORTHERN IRE-LAND) 1979 (No. 242) [70p], made under the Social Security (Northern Ireland) Act 1975, ss. 83 (1), 85 and the Social Security (Consequential Provisions) Act 1975, Sched. 3, paras. 3, 9; operative on September 3, 1979; consolidate provisions relating to adjustment of benefits under the first-mentioned Act of 1975 by reference to other benefits payable for the same period.

SOCIAL SECURITY (WIDOW'S BENEFIT AND RETIREMENT PENSIONS) REGULA-TIONS (NORTHERN IRELAND) 1979 (No. 243) [70p], made under the Social Security (Northern Ireland) Act 1975, ss. 29 (5), 30 (3), 33, 39 (1) (4), 40 (2), 85 (1), 152, Sched. 17 and S.I. 1975 No. 1503, art. 22, Sched. 1, paras. 2 (2) (a), 3; operative on September 4, 1979; consolidate and revoke certain regulations relating to widows' benefits, retirement pensions and age addition for persons not in receipt of retirement pensions.

SOCIAL SECURITY (WIDOW'S BENEFIT, RETIREMENT PENSIONS AND OTHER BENEFITS) (TRANSITIONAL) REGULATIONS (NORTHERN IRELAND) 1979 (No. 244) [70p], made under the Social Security (Consequential Provisions) Act 1975, s. 2, Sched. 3, paras. 3, 4, 5, 7, 9 and S.I. 1975 No. 1503, art. 72; operative on September 5, 1979; consolidate and revoke certain regulations providing for transitional matters connected with that Act and S.I.

SOCIAL SECURITY REVALUATION OF EARNINGS FACTORS ORDER (NORTHERN IRELAND) 1979 (No. 256) [10p], made under S.I. 1975 No. 1503 (N.I. 15), art. 23; operative on July 16, 1979; directs that the earnings factors relevant to calculating the additional component in the rate of any long-term benefit for the 1978–79 tax year are to be increased by 13·3 per cent.

SOCIAL SECURITY (CLAIMS AND PAYMENTS) (AMENDMENT) REGULATIONS (NORTHERN IRELAND) 1979 (No. 259) [10p], made under the Social Security (Northern Ireland) Act 1975, s. 79 (3); operative on September 5, 1979; amend the definition of "medical certificate" in the 1977 (No. 351) Regulations relating to forward allowances and disallowances of incapacity benefits to include a doctor's statement based on a written report from any doctor.

PNEUMOCONIOSIS, ETC. (WORKERS' COMPENSATION) (1979 ORDER) (COM-MENCEMENT) ORDER (NORTHERN IRELAND) 1979 (No. 270) (C. 10) [10p], made under S.I. 1979 No. 925 (N.I. 9), art. 1, and the Northern Ireland Act 1974, Sched. 1, para. 2 (1) (2); brings that S.I. into operation on September 3, 1979.

PNEUMOCONIOSIS, ETC. (WORKERS' COMPENSATION) (DETERMINATION OF CLAIMS) REGULATIONS (NORTHERN IRELAND) 1979 (No. 271) [20p], made under S.I. 1979 No. 925, art. 11 (1); operative on September 3, 1979; prescribe the manner in which claims under the S.I. must be made.

CHILD BENEFIT AND SOCIAL SECURITY (FIXING AND ADJUSTMENT OF RATES) (AMENDMENT) REGULATIONS (NORTHERN IRELAND) 1979 (No. 272) [10p], made under S.I. 1975 No. 1504 (N.I. 16), art. 7; operative on November 12, 1979; increase by 50p the weekly rate of child benefit payable under the S.I. in respect of a child living with one parent.

SOCIAL SECURITY BENEFITS UP-RATING ORDER (NORTHERN IRELAND) 1979 (No. 273) [70p], made under the Social Security (Northern Ireland) Act 1975, s. 120; operative on November 12, 1979; increases certain benefits and allowances and the amount of weekly earnings which must be exceeded before retirement pension is reduced by reference to earnings.

SUPPLEMENTARY BENEFIT (DETERMINATION OF REQUIREMENTS) REGULATIONS (NORTHERN IRELAND) 1979 (No. 274) [20p], made under S.I. 1977 No. 2156 (N.I. 27), art. 4 (2) (3); operative on November 12, 1979; increase the weekly sums allowed in calculating requirements for the purpose of determining entitlement to, and the amount of, supplementary pension or allowance, the weekly amount for attendance requirements and the rent addition for non-householders; revoke the 1978 (No. 204) Regulations.

SOCIAL SECURITY (INDUSTRIAL INJURIES) (PRESCRIBED DISEASES) (AMENDMENT No. 4) REGULATIONS (NORTHERN IRELAND) 1979 (No. 275) [40p], made under the Social Security (Northern Ireland) Act 1975, ss. 76, 77; operative on September 3, 1979; amend the 1977 (No. 272) Regulations in relation to occupational deafness.

SOCIAL SECURITY (UNEMPLOYMENT, SICKNESS AND INVALIDITY BENEFIT) (AMENDMENT) REGULATIONS (NORTHERN IRELAND) 1979 (No. 286) [20p], made under the Social Security (Northern Ireland) Act 1975, s. 20 (3); operative on August 30, 1979; impose an additional condition with respect to the receipt of unemployment benefit by persons following courses of full-time education at certain establishments.

SOCIAL SECURITY (1979 ORDER) (COMMENCEMENT No. 2) ORDER (NORTHERN IRELAND) 1979 (No. 301) (C. 12) [10p], made under S.I. 1979 No. 396 (N.I. 5), art. 1 (3); operative on September 5, 1979; brings into force provisions of that S.I. dealing with mobility allowance in relation to women born on or after November 29, 1914, but before June 7, 1918.

SOCIAL SECURITY PENSIONS (1975 ORDER) (COMMENCEMENT No. 15) ORDER (NORTHERN IRELAND) 1979 (No. 302) (C. 13) [10p], made under S.I. 1975 No. 1503 (N.I. 15) art. 1 (3); operative on September 5, 1979; brings into force provisions of that S.I. dealing with mobility allowance in relation to men born on or after November 29, 1914, but before June 7, 1918.

SOCIAL SECURITY (PORTUGAL) ORDER (NORTHERN IRELAND) 1979 (No. 303) [80p], made under the Social Security (Northern Ireland) Act 1975 (C. 15), s. 134 (1), and S.I. 1975 No. 1504 (N.I. 16), art. 17 (1); operative on October 1, 1979; modifies the Act and S.I. so as to give effect to the Convention on Social Security between the United Kingdom and Portugal.

SUPPLEMENTARY BENEFIT (GENERAL) (AMENDMENT) REGULATIONS (NORTHERN IRELAND) 1979 (No. 313) [10p], made under S.I. 1977 No. 2156 (N.I. 27), art. 19 (1), Sched. 1, para. 13; operative on November 12, 1979; increase to £4·65 the weekly sum taken to be the personal requirements of an applicant for supplementary benefit who is residing in residential accommodation; revoke the 1978 (No. 236) Regulations.

SOCIAL SECURITY (GENERAL BENEFIT) (AMENDMENT) REGULATIONS (NORTHERN IRELAND) 1979 (No. 314) [10p], made under the Social Security (Northern Ireland) Act 1975, s. 119 (3); operative on October 15, 1979; bring within the scope of the 1975 (No. 26) Regulations certain decisions requiring repayment of overpaid benefit.

SOCIAL SECURITY (DETERMINATION OF CLAIMS AND QUESTIONS) (AMENDMENT) REGULATIONS (NORTHERN IRELAND) 1979 (No. 354) [20p], made under the Social Security (Northern Ireland) Act 1975, s. 119 (3) (4); operative on November 5, 1979; amend the 1975 (No. 100) Regulations in relation to certain benefits subsequently found not to have been payable.

SOCIAL SECURITY BENEFITS UPRATING REGULATIONS (NORTHERN IRELAND) 1979 (No. 371) [20p], made under the Social Security (Northern Ireland) Act

1975, ss. 17 (2) (*a*), 36 (9) (*b*), 58 (3), 126, Sched. 14, para. 2 (1); operative on November 12, 1979; make provision consequential upon the 1979 (No. 273) Order; revoke the 1978 (No. 262) Regulations.

SOCIAL SECURITY (UNEMPLOYMENT, SICKNESS AND INVALIDITY BENEFIT) (AMENDMENT NO. 2) REGULATIONS (NORTHERN IRELAND) 1979 (No. 377) [10p], made under the Social Security (Northern Ireland) Act 1975, ss. 17 (1) (*a*), (2) (*a*), 20 (2); operative on October 26, 1979; revoke reg. 6 (1) (*g*) of the 1979 (No. 211) Regulations which provided that a day should not be treated as a day of incapacity for work if a person did any work on that day unless certain conditions were satisfied and provide that in certain circumstances a person who is found to be not incapable of work by reason only of the fact that he has done some work may be deemed to be incapable of work if the work done satisfies specified conditions.

SOCIAL SECURITY (MAXIMUM ADDITIONAL COMPONENT) REGULATIONS (NORTHERN IRELAND) 1979 (No. 391) [20p], made under S.I. 1975 No. 1503 (N.I. 15), art. 11 (3); operative on November 9, 1979; prescribe a maximum additional component for the purposes of art. 11 (3).

SOCIAL SECURITY BENEFIT (PERSONS ABROAD) (AMENDMENT NO. 2) REGULATIONS (NORTHERN IRELAND) 1979 (No. 392) [20p], made under the Social Security (Northern Ireland) Act 1975, s. 126; operative on November 10, 1979; amend the 1978 (No. 114) Regulations in relation to entitlement to basic component and additional component of retirement pension and to the payment of up-rating increases.

SOCIAL SECURITY (EARNINGS-RELATED ADDITION TO WIDOW'S ALLOWANCE) (SPECIAL PROVISIONS) REGULATIONS (NORTHERN IRELAND) 1979 (No. 394) [10p], made under the Social Security (Northern Ireland) Act 1975, s. 125; operative on January 6, 1980; modify Sched. 6, Pt. I, to the Act in cases where the late husband was over pensionable age during the whole or part of the relevant year and would have had liability for Class I contributions but for art. 6 (1) of S.I. 1975 No. 1503 (N.I. 15).

1994. Statutes and orders

STATUTORY RULES (NORTHERN IRELAND) ORDER 1979 (No. 1573 (N.I. 12)) [50p], made under the Northern Ireland Act 1974 (c. 28), Sched. 1, para. 1; operative on January 4, 1980; consolidates the Statutory Rules Act (Northern Ireland) 1958 (c. 18) and the provisions amending it.

1995. Stock exchange

STOCK EXCHANGE (COMPLETION OF BARGAINS) (1977 ORDER) (COMMENCEMENT) ORDER (NORTHERN IRELAND) 1979 (No. 28) (C. 1) [10p], made under S.I. 1977 No. 1254 (N.I. 21), art. 1; brings that S.I. into operation on March 5, 1979.

STOCK TRANSFER (ADDITION OF FORMS) ORDER (NORTHERN IRELAND) 1979 (No. 66) [20p], made under the Stock Transfer Act (Northern Ireland) 1963 (c. 24), s. 3 (1); operative on April 18, 1979; amends s. 1 of, and Sched. 1 to, the 1963 Act in order to facilitate the "Talisman" settlement system for transactions in securities on the Stock Exchange.

STOCK EXCHANGE (DESIGNATION OF NOMINEES) ORDER (NORTHERN IRELAND) 1979 (No. 76) [10p], made under S.I. 1977 No. 1254 (N.I. 21), art. 2 (2); operative on April 18, 1979; designates Sepon Ltd. as a nominee of the Stock Exchange for the purposes of that S.I.

1996. Trade and industry

AIRCRAFT AND SHIPBUILDING INDUSTRIES (NORTHERN IRELAND) ORDER 1979 (No. 294) (N.I. 1) [25p], made under the Northern Ireland Act 1974 (c. 28), Sched. 1, para. 1; operative as to art. 14 (2) (*d*) in so far as it provides for the repeal of art. 4 of S.I. 1975 No. 1309 (N.I. 14) on August 13, 1981, and as to the remainder on April 1, 1979; empowers the Department of Commerce to give financial assistance to Harland and Wolff Ltd., Short Brothers Ltd. and their subsidiary or associated companies (art. 3), to give guarantees to persons entering into contracts with those companies (art. 4), to acquire securities of companies with related undertakings (art. 5), to give directions to those companies (art. 6), to require those companies to furnish information (art. 7) and to review the performance of those companies and to obtain advice and assistance in connection with the exercise of its functions (arts. 8, 9).

CATERING ESTABLISHMENTS (AMENDMENT) REGULATIONS (NORTHERN IRELAND) 1979 (No. 333) [10p], made under the Development of Tourist Traffic Act (Northern Ireland) 1948 (c. 4), ss. 11, 34 (1); operative on November 1, 1979; dispense with the opinion of the Northern Ireland Tourist Board in relation to the qualifications for registration of certain catering establishments.

1997. Transport

COMMUNITY ROAD TRANSPORT RULES (EXEMPTIONS) REGULATIONS (NORTHERN IRELAND) 1979 (No. 121) [20p], made under the European Communities Act 1972 (c. 68), s. 2 (2); operative on May 14, 1979; give effect to exemptions, in respect of certain national transport operations, from provisions of EEC Regulations Nos. 543/69 and 1463/70.

1998. —— European Communities

EUROPEAN COMMUNITIES (INTERNATIONAL PASSENGER SERVICES) REGULATIONS (NORTHERN IRELAND) 1979 (No. 401) [40p], made under the Transport Act (Northern Ireland) 1967 (c. 37), s. 45 (*i*) to (*l*), the Road Traffic Act (Northern Ireland) 1970 (c. 2), s. 61 (1) (*p*) (*q*) (2) and the European Communities Act 1972 (c. 68), s. 2 (2); operative on December 31, 1979; bring certain international passenger services within the scope of the 1973 (Nos. 200, 212) Regulations.

1999. Vendor and purchaser—prior oral agreement that purchaser would transfer part of purchased land

G owned a leasehold interest in land part of which he used as a golf driving range. After an unsuccessful attempt to acquire the freehold interest in the land G orally agreed with C, who owned a licensed restaurant in the neighbourhood, that C would acquire the land, G putting up part of the purchase money, and that C would then transfer the driving range to G. C orally agreed to purchase the land but before signing a written contract informed G that he wished to incorporate in the transfer of the driving range a covenant preventing the use of the range for the purposes of a licensed restaurant. When G did not agree C proceeded with the purchase of the land and refused to transfer the driving range to G. On an application for a declaration and injunction, *held*, that when C offered to purchase the land he was acting as trustee for himself and G and the attempt to introduce the restrictive covenant before the contract of sale was signed was irrelevant. As soon as the vendors signed C had an enforceable right against them which he was bound to exercise for G's benefit as agreed, G being entitled to prove by parol evidence that the land was conveyed to C as trustee, for the Statute of Frauds does not prevent proof of a fraud. (*Rochefoucauld* v. *Boustead* [1897] 1 Ch. 196 and *McGillicuddy* v. *Joy* [1960] C.L.Y. 3275 applied): GILMURRAY v. CORR [1978] N.I. 99, Lowry L.C.J.

2000. Weights and measures

WEIGHTS AND MEASURES (VARIOUS GOODS) (TERMINATION OF IMPERIAL QUANTITIES) ORDER (NORTHERN IRELAND) 1979 (No. 197) [20p], made under the Weights and Measures Act (Northern Ireland) 1967 (c. 6), s. 15 (2) (3) (5); operative on July 31, 1979; provides for the termination on certain dates of the use of imperial quantities in the pre-packing of various goods.

MEASURING INSTRUMENTS (INTOXICATING LIQUOR) (AMENDMENT) REGULATIONS (NORTHERN IRELAND) 1979 (No. 212) [20p], made under the Weights and Measures Act (Northern Ireland) 1967, ss. 5 (3), 7 (1), 8 (1); operative on August 1, 1979; amend the 1967 (No. 230) Regulations and prohibit beer and cider measuring instruments being fitted with sight glasses, windows or other devices for showing that the measuring chamber is properly charged or discharged as an alternative to devices which prevent liquid being discharged until the chamber is full or the chamber being filled until it is properly emptied.

WEIGHTS AND MEASURES (COFFEE EXTRACTS AND CHICORY EXTRACTS) ORDER (NORTHERN IRELAND) 1979 (No. 384) [20p], made under the Weights and Measures Act (Northern Ireland 1967, s. 15 (2) (3) (5); operative on January 1, 1980; implements Council Directive No. 77/436/EEC as to the prescribed range of metric quantities and the quantity marking relating to coffee extracts and chicory extracts.

2001. Wills

INHERITANCE (PROVISION FOR FAMILY AND DEPENDANTS) (NORTHERN IRELAND) ORDER 1979 (No. 924) (N.I. 8) [90p], made under the Northern Ireland Act 1974 (c. 28), Sched. 1, para. 1; operative on September 1, 1979; makes fresh provision for empowering the court to make orders for the making out of the estate of a deceased person provision for the dependants of that person.

FAMILY LAW REFORM (1977 ORDER) (COMMENCEMENT NO. 2) ORDER (NORTHERN IRELAND) 1978 (No. 377) (C. 20) [10p], made under S.I. 1977 No. 1250 (N.I. 17), art. 1 (2); brings Pt. III of that S.I. into operation on March 1, 1979.

2002. —— power to appoint to a child or remoter issue

T had power to appoint property by will to his child or remoter issue, such child or remoter issue to take vested interests within 21 years of T's death. in default of appointment the property was to go to T's next-of-kin. By will T appointed the property to his daughter for life, with remainder to the daughter's issue, and in default of issue to T's wife and certain charities. T's wife predeceased him, and his daughter had no issue. On a previous originating summons it was held that the appointment in favour of the charities was bad as they were not named as objects of the power and that T's daughter became absolutely entitled to the property. On a further originating summons to determine whether she became so entitled on T's death or 21 years after it, *held,* that (1) the power to appoint to a child or remoter issue was not disjunctive and T had power to appoint in favour of his daughter and her issue; and (2) as the daughter could have had a child after T's death, she could not have become absolutely entitled to the property until the expiration of 21 years from T's death: *Re* LOWRY (DECD.); NORTHERN BANK EXECUTOR AND TRUSTEE CO. *v.* STONE [1978] N.I. 17, Murray J.

2003. Workmen's compensation

WORKMEN'S COMPENSATION (SUPPLEMENTATION) (AMENDMENT) REGULATIONS (NORTHERN IRELAND) 1979 (No. 346) [20p], made under the Industrial Injuries and Diseases (Northern Ireland Old Cases) Act 1975 (c. 17), ss. 2, 4 (1); operative on November 14, 1979; make adjustments to the intermediate rates of lesser incapacity allowances consequential upon the increase in the maximum rate of that allowance made by the 1979 (No. 273) Order.

ARTICLES. See *post,* p. [28].

NUISANCE

2004. Earth-fall—duty of defendants

An occupier of land owes a duty of care to his neighbours in relation to hazards arising on his land, even if those hazards arise from the natural condition of the land. The defendants were, accordingly, *held* liable for damages, and injuncted, in respect of falls of earth and tree stumps from a mound on their land (*Goldman* v. *Hargrave* [1966] C.L.Y. 8145 applied; *Giles* v. *Walker* (1890) 24 Q.B.D. 656 overruled; *Pontardawe R.O.C.* v. *Moore-Gwyn* [1929] 1 Ch. 656 not followed; decision of O'Connor J. [1978] C.L.Y. 2201 affirmed): LEAKEY *v.* NATIONAL TRUST FOR PLACES OF HISTORIC INTEREST OR NATURAL BEAUTY (1979) 123 S.J. 606, C.A.

2005. Greenhouse—obstruction of light—prescriptive right. See ALLEN *v.* GREENWOOD, § 797.

2006. Northern Ireland. See NORTHERN IRELAND.

2007. Smell—statutory authorisation of nuisance

[Gulf Oil Refining Act 1965 (c. xxiv), s. 5 (1).]

The defence of statutory authority to a claim in nuisance will succeed only to the extent that the use of the thing complained of is specifically authorised by statute.

The plaintiff's action was taken as a test case concerning complaints by villagers that the use of a nearby oil refinery operated by the defendants constituted a nuisance, by reason of the noise, vibration and noxious substances emanating therefrom. By the Act of 1965 the defendants were authorised to acquire the land and construct certain works thereon. They relied upon the defence of statutory authority. On a trial of a preliminary issue, May J. ruled that the defendants could rely upon such defence. *Held,* allowing the plaintiff's appeal, that the defence was inapplicable, since the authority granted by the Act did not extend to the operation of any specified refinery. (*Jones* v. *Ffestiniog Railway Co.* (1868) L.R. 3 Q.B. 733 and *Hammersmith and City Railway Co.* v. *Brand* (1869) L.R. 4 H.L. 171, applied.)

ALLEN *v.* GULF OIL REFINING CO. [1979] 3 W.L.R. 523, C.A.

2008. Strict liability—natural user of land—defendant's tree causing damage to plaintiff's house

[Can.] A tree on D's property fell onto the roof of P's house during a storm. The reason for its fall was advanced internal decay; the tree, however, had appeared at all times before the accident to be normal and D had no knowledge of the decay prior to the accident. *Held,* (1) there was no reason for D to believe the tree was decayed or dangerous, or should have been cut down; (2) there was no strict liability on D despite the fact the tree was situate on the property when D purchased the same; (3) there was no liability in nuisance where the use of the property was a natural use, such as the growing of a tree. (*Rylands* v. *Fletcher* (1868) L.R. 3 H.L. 330 not applied): BOTTONI *v.* HENDERSON (1978) 90 D.L.R. (3d) 301, Ont.H.C.J.

OPEN SPACES AND RECREATION GROUNDS

2009. Litter—whether " left "

[Litter Act 1958 (c. 34), s. 1 (1).] D was seen sorting through a pile of metal beside his lorry in a lane where he had been living with his family in a tent for at least a day. *Held,* dismissing his appeal against conviction of depositing scrap metal in a public place in circumstances such as to cause defacement by litter contrary to s. 1 (1) of the 1958 Act, that, the court having found that D intended to remove only such metal as was of scrap value, he had " left " the metal within the meaning of the Act. An article deposited with no intention of removing it could be found to have been left after only a short time: WITNEY *v.* CATTANACH [1979] Crim.L.R. 461, D.C.

2010. Parks regulations—no dogs allowed—whether by-law oppressive

A by-law made by a local authority banning dogs from ornamental parks and children's playgrounds is not *per se* unreasonable, nor is it an oppressive or gratuitous interference with the rights of others.

A local authority, in the exercise of powers under a private Act, made by-laws banning dogs from entry into certain pleasure grounds and children's play areas. Protests failed to effect the withdrawal of the by-law and the local residents organised a protest walk. The council sought an injunction. *Held,* granting the injunction, that the by-law was valid. (Dicta of Russell C.J. in *Kruse* v. *Johnson* [1898] 2 Q.B. 91 applied.)

BURNLEY BOROUGH COUNCIL *v.* ENGLAND (1978) 77 L.G.R. 227, Hugh Francis, Q.C.

2011. Sports grounds

SAFETY OF SPORTS GROUNDS (DESIGNATION) ORDER 1979 (No. 1022) [10p], made under the Safety of Sports Grounds Act 1975 (c. 52), s. 1 (1); operative on January 1, 1980; designates certain sports stadia as those requiring safety certificates under the 1975 Act.

PARLIAMENT

2012. Elections. See ELECTION LAW.

2013. House of Commons Members' Fund

Resolution of the House of Commons dated December 10, 1979, passed in pursuance of the House of Commons Members' Fund Act 1948 (c. 36):

S. 3: S.I. 1979 No. 1667 (periodical payments–past members and widows) [10p].

2014. House of Commons (Redistribution of Seats) Act 1979 (c. 15)

This Act increases the number of constituencies in Northern Ireland.

S. 1 provides for the increase in number of Northern Ireland constituencies; s. 2 deals with citation.

The Act received the Royal Assent on March 22, 1979, and came into force on that date.

2015. Ministerial salaries

MINISTERIAL AND OTHER SALARIES AND PENSIONS ORDER 1979 (No. 905) [20p], made under the Ministerial and other Salaries Act 1975 (c. 27), s. 1 (4) and the Parliamentary and other Pensions Act 1972 (c. 48), ss. 4 (3A), 29 (2A); operative on July 26, 1979; increases parliamentary salaries and pensions.

2016. Ministers. See CONSTITUTIONAL LAW.

2017. Northern Ireland. See NORTHERN IRELAND.

2018. Statutes. See STATUTES AND ORDERS.

ARTICLES. See *post*, p. [28].

PARTNERSHIP

2019. Existence—evidence—remission to commissioners

At the hearing before the Commissioners it was necessary to determine whether—and, if so, when—a partnership was entered into. The stated case contained no express finding on this point. *Held*, that the case should be remitted to the Commissioners to express a finding of fact on the date of the partnership formation: SAYWELL *v.* POPE [1978] T.R. 229, Slade J.

BOOKS AND ARTICLES. See *post*, pp. [9], [28].

PATENTS AND DESIGNS

2020. Amendment—disclaimer

Claim 21 of the specification was held untenable. The present application was intended to refer only to a run in each example rather than to the examples at large. D opposed the application to allow amendment. *Held,* (1) the proposed amendment had a disclaiming effect and was allowable by way of disclaimer; (2) the proposed amendment ment the criticisms of the Court of Appeal and was an allowable correction. There was no reason to withhold discretion to allow amendment: IMPERIAL CHEMICAL INDUSTRIES (SMALL'S) PATENT [1979] F.S.R. 78, Patent Office.

2021. —— obvious mistake

[Patents Act 1949 (c. 87), ss. 4, 30, 31.] In an infringement action the patentees sought amendment of the specification on the ground of obvious mistake. The claim related to a projecting, retractable twist-lock device. Claim 1 limited the patent to twist-locks in which the guide member in the retracted position was lying entirely within and flush with a face of the body. The description and drawings of the preferred embodiment showed a system with projection below the bottom of housing. Amendment allowed. On appeal to the House of Lords, *held*, (1) anyone studying the drawings and description and claim would appreciate the discrepancy; (2) the delay should not prevent the application to amend from succeeding. Appeal dismissed: HOLTITE *v.* JOST (GREAT BRITAIN) [1979] R.P.C. 81, H.L.

2022. Appeals from Comptroller-General

The following Practice Direction was issued by the Chancery Division on May 18, 1978:

1. Under Ord. 104, r. 14 (17) the Chief Master had nominated Mr. D. F. James, at present the Registrar of the Patents Appeal Tribunal, to be the " proper officer " of the Patents Court for the purposes of appeals from the Comptroller-General of Patents, Designs and Trade Marks. He will be known

as the Registrar of Patents Appeals. The Registrars of the Chancery Division will continue to perform their present duties in infringement actions and other patent business.

2. (*a*) Appeals from the Comptroller must be brought by originating motion (Ord. 104, r. 14 (1)). The originating motion (in the rule called "notice of appeal" is issued by lodging copies with the Registrar of Patent Appeals (Room 152). If the Registrar of Patent Appeals and his deputy are not available, the copies may be lodged in the Chief Master's Secretariat (Room 169).

(*b*) Two copies of the originating motion (notice of appeal) will be required. one of which must be stamped with a £10 fee (Fee 8) and the other of which will be sealed and returned to the Appellant.

(*c*) A respondent's notice under Ord. 104, r. 14 (9), asking that the decision of the Comptroller be varied, must be stamped £5 (Fee 36).

[1979] R.P.C. 96.

2023. Application—best method

[Patents Act 1949 (c. 87), s. 4 (3) (*a*) (*b*).] The claim in the application failed to disclose the best method known to put the invention into effect. The hearing officer rejected the application. On appeal the applicants argued that in view of the many possible uses of such compositions the best guidance must itself be stated in general terms. *Held*, that (1) the application should not be rejected for failing to comply with s. 4 (3) (*b*); (2) the question of "best method" must be determined on the basis of evidence to support the conclusion that the disclosure was of the best method: GARLOCK INC.'S APPLICATION [1979] F.S.R. 604, Whitford J.

2024. —— convention priority—amendment

[Patents Act 1949 (c. 87), ss. 29, 31.] Application was for a patent claiming priority from two U.S. applications. The applicants sought to amend claim 1 of the application by correction and disclaimer. The evidence showed that the U.K. specification had been drafted by a U.S. patent agent, with the intention of securing Convention priority. There was no evidence from the U.K. agents. *Held*, on appeal by the opponents against the allowal of amendment, the absence of evidence by the U.K. patent agents as to the role they had played was a matter on which the applicants should adduce evidence to satisfy the court that they should exercise their discretion to allow amendment: S.C.M. CORP.'S APPLICATION [1979] R.P.C. 341, C.A.

2025. —— method of identification

The applicants sought to patent a method of identifying diamonds by means of topograms. A number of topograms of a diamond would be made, and used for identification. The examiner refused to proceed. Whitford J. rejected the appeal. *Held*, on appeal, the topograms were to be made in accordance with a prescribed procedure which the applicants claimed was new and adapted for identification: DE BEERS CONSOLIDATED MINES' APPLICATION [1979] F.S.R. 72, C.A.

2026. —— new manufacture—colour

[Patents Act 1949 (c. 47), s. 101.] The application was to register a squash ball coloured blue. The examiner objected that the claim did not relate to a manner of manufacture. *Held*, allowing the appeal, it was arguable that the colouring of the ball improved the article. It was not so plain that it did not relate to a new manner of manufacture that application should be refused: I.T.S. RUBBER'S APPLICATION [1979] R.P.C. 318, Whitford J.

2027. —— opposition—confusion

The applicants sought registration of the mark UNIMAX in respect of electrical apparatus in Class 9. The opponents under ss. 11 and 12 had a reputation in a series of marks with the prefix UNI, in particular UNIVAC, used in the computer field. The applicants showed that they had used the mark UNIMAX for a number of years in respect of electrical switches. *Held*, refusing the application, that if the applicants used UNIMAX in relation to computer installations there was a danger of confusion and deception: UNIMAX TRADE MARK [1979] R.P.C. 469, Trade Marks Registry.

2028. Extension—inadequate remuneration
[S.A.] Extension for a term was sought on the ground of inadequate remuneration. The opponents contended that the remuneration was adequate and some delay in exploitation of pharmaceutical patents was inevitable. The commissioner granted a three-and-a-half year extension. The opponents appealed. *Held,* that the commissioner's assessment and conclusion was correct. HOECHST'S SOUTH AFRICAN PATENT EXTENSION [1979] F.S.R. 486, S.A.Sup.Ct.

2029. —— relevance of loss of expenditure
[Patents Act 1949 (c. 87), s. 23.] On an application to extend for ten years the patent for hovercraft, granting the extension the judge *held,* that (1) the invention subject of the patent was a necessary prerequisite for the manufacture of commercially operable hovercraft; (2) the export markets had conferred exceptional benefit on the public; (3) there was nevertheless a loss of half a million pounds because of research expenditure prior to 1967. Much of the loss was abortive expenditure for types of skirt. Nevertheless it was impossible fairly to discount expenditure so that the patentees' accounts would show a profit; (4) the patentees deserved the extension for which they had applied: HOVERCRAFT DEVELOPMENT'S PATENT EXTENSION [1979] F.S.R. 481, Whitford J.

2030. Infringement—amendment—validity—ambiguity—novelty
[Patents Act 1949 (c. 87), ss. 4, 6, 30, 31, 32. 69.] The plaintiffs manufactured and sold a synthetic suture made from homopolymer PHAE. The defendants manufactured VICRYL in the United States. A *quia timet* injunction was sought. An issue arose as to the construction of the specification in suit. The defendants alleged obviousness, lack of fair basis and insufficiency. The plaintiffs applied to amend the specification in suit. *Held,* (1) the pleas of ambiguity, lack of fair basis and no invention failed; (2) the cited prior documents did not amount to anticipation; (3) the plaintiffs' experiments were preferable to those of the defendant; (4) the defendants failed to establish that the successful commercial articles owed nothing to the original invention; (5) the "best method" attack failed. The amendments were allowable and the patents valid and infringed. Injunction granted. The skilled addressee of the specification was a highly qualified and trained research scientist. The best method rule did not oblige the applicant under the Patents Act 1949, s. 4 (6) to include claims to additions to his original invention: AMERICAN CYANAMID Co. *v.* ETHICON [1979] R.P.C. 215, Graham J.

2031. —— application to strike out—particulars of infringement
[Patents Act 1977 (c. 37), s. 60 (2), Sched. 4, para. 3; R.S.C., Ord. 104, rr. 5 (2), 9 (1).] The plaintiffs were patentees of a diamond grit coated with metal and embedded in resin bond. The defendants sought to strike out the statement of claim and the plaintiffs sought an order for discovery of the names and addresses of the defendants' customers and suppliers. *Held,* on appeal by the defendants, that (1) the first two paragraphs of the particulars of infringement did not conform to R.S.C., Ord. 104, r. 5 (2) and the defendants did not have adequate knowledge of the case against them; (2) the allegation in para. 3, the sale to someone who to the knowledge of the vendor intended to use it in a resin bond, was of itself an infringement or amounted to procuring an infringement. No cause of action was disclosed: BELEGGING-EN EXPLOITATIEMAATSCHAPPIJ LAVENDER B.V. *v.* WITTEN INDUSTRIAL DIAMONDS [1979] F.S.R. 59, C.A.

2032. —— discovery—confidential documents
[Evidence (Proceedings in Other Jurisdictions) Act 1975 (c. 34).] The plaintiffs claimed an injunction for infringement. The defendants contemporaneously brought proceedings in The Netherlands Patent Office opposing applications on the ground of obviousness. The defendants had discovered confidential documents which were shown only to the plaintiffs' legal advisers and independent experts. Certain documents, the red file, were shown to the plaintiffs themselves. The plaintiffs sought an order that these documents be made available in the Dutch action. They denied that the documents were of a confidential nature. *Held,* dismissing the plaintiffs' appeal, that if the "red

file " were put in evidence in the Dutch proceedings the defendants might be forced to put forward further confidential documents to explain the red file documents, and these documents would become public under Dutch law: HALCON INTERNATIONAL INC. v. THE SHELL TRANSPORT AND TRADING CO. [1979] R.P.C. 97, C.A.

2033. —— **estoppel—prior publication**
[Israel] [Patents Law 1967, s. 695 (1); Patents Act 1949 (c. 62), ss. 14, 32, 85.] In U.K. opposition proceedings the opponents succeeded upon the ground of prior user. In the Patent Office the opponent succeeded on the ground of prior user. On appeal the Patent's Appeal Tribunal found against the opponents. The objection of prior user subsequently succeeded but prior publication failed. In Israel the defendants alleged prior publication in the light of the same citation used in the U.K. proceedings. The plaintiffs alleged that the Patents Appeal Tribunal's findings gave rise to an issue estoppel. *Held*, (1) what constituted prior publication in Israel had to be determined in accordance with Israeli law; (2) the law of estoppel in Israel was the same as in England; (3) the Patents Appeal Tribunal and House of Lords findings should be regarded as complementary. The issue of prior publication had been adjudicated and resolved. An issue estoppel was created by this foreign judgment; (4) the Patents Appeal Tribunal findings on the question of prior publication was not essential to the final decision and could not constitute the basis for an issue estoppel: BRISTOL-MYERS CO. v. BEECHAM GROUP [1978] F.S.R. 553, Sup.Ct. of Israel.

2034. —— **importation—interlocutory injunction—whether seller a tortfeasor**
A German manufacturer sold goods in Germany to an American corporation knowing they would be sold or leased to persons who would bring them into the United Kingdom where they would infringe a British patent. There was sufficient common design to make them joint tortfeasors as soon as infringement actually occurred. (*The Koursk* [1924] P. 140; *Morton-Norwich Products Inc.* v. *Intercen* [1976] C.L.Y. 2131 followed.) A seller could only protect himself by emphasising that the goods were not to be sold in any jurisdiction where it would be an infringement. On a balance of convenience, an interlocutory injunction would be granted, if the parties could not agree a method of preventing the import of the goods pending trial: NORTH WESTERN TRAILER CO. v. ITEL CORP. INTERNATIONAL, *The Times*, December 19, 1979, Graham J.

2035. —— **interlocutory injunction**
Graham J. granted interlocutory injunctions in patent infringement actions. In one order the phrase " or otherwise infringing letters patent . . ." was used. The defendants appealed. The Court of Appeal dismissed the appeal but varied the order. The court observed that the words " or otherwise infringing " should not be included in the order. Only the particular infringement should be restrained: HEPWORTH PLASTICS v. NAYLOR BROTHERS (CLAY-WARE) [1979] F.S.R. 521, C.A.

2036. —— **interpleader—innocent carrier**
[Patents Act 1977 (c. 37), s. 60; Community Patent Convention, art. 29.] H ordered from D a drug, which D agreed to ship to London. British Airways carried it from Milan to London, storing it in the bonded warehouse, to the order of H. D, H, and British Airways were joined by the plaintiffs. *Held*, on a proper construction of the Patents Act 1977, ss. 60 (1) and 130 (7) and the Community Patent Convention, art. 29 (*a*), British Airways had not " kept " the goods. As innocent carriers they were not liable and were entitled to relief by way of interpleader: SMITH KLINE & FRENCH LABORATORIES v. R. D. HARBOTTLE (MERCANTILE) [1979] F.S.R. 555, Oliver J.

2037. —— **practice**
The defendants applied for certain questions relating to infringement to be tried as preliminary points. They undertook that if they be answered in the sense the defendants anticipated, they would abandon the claim and counterclaim relating to validity. *Held*, the determination was likely to result in a

substantial saving of time and money. The order should be made: GENERAL
FOAM PRODUCTS *v.* RYBURN FOAM [1979] F.S.R. 477, Whitford J.

2038. [R.S.C. Ord. 25, r. 1, note 25/1/3B.] In an action for infringement the
writ was issued in 1972. The patent expired in 1974. The defendants had ceased
manufacturing the allegedly infringing article. In 1979 the plaintiffs restored
the summons for directions and the defendants applied to have the action
struck out. *Held,* the action would be struck out because the plaintiffs had
been late in commencing proceedings and there were six and a half years of
unexplained delay: HORSTMAN GEAR CO. *v.* SMITHS INDUSTRIES [1979] F.S.R.
461, Graham J.

2039. —— —— **discovery**
[R.S.C. Ord. 104, r. 10, Ord. 24, rr. 7 and 8.] In an action for infringement
the defendant sought discovery of documents which would enable him to assess
the quantum of damages before the trial and before the question of quantum
was in issue. The plaintiffs objected on the grounds that such discovery would
be burdensome and would delay the trial of the action. *Held,* the order would
be burdensome to the plaintiffs and of no substantial benefit to the defendants:
HAZELTINE CORP. *v.* BRITISH BROADCASTING CORP. [1979] F.S.R. 523, Whitford J.

2040. —— —— **expert witness**
[Aust.] In a patent infringement action relating to storage batteries the
question arose whether a letter of request should issue for the examination
in the U.K. of an independent witness. F lived in Sweden and was an expert
in the field. The defendants sought his evidence as to obviousness. *Held,*
that F's invention in 1962 in Sweden arose from common general knowledge
which was more extensive than common general knowledge in Australia in
1966, the date of the patent in suit; (2) the applicant had not established
that F would be able to give relevant and admissible evidence on the issue
of obviousness. The evidence would not assist the Australian judge in his
consideration of the hypothetical Australian technician: LUCAS INDUSTRIES *v.*
CHLORIDE BATTERIES [1979] F.S.R. 322, Fed.Ct. of Australia.

2041. —— —— **inspection**
The patent in suit related to six-inch activators. The plaintiffs contended that
the defendants' six-inch activators contained a cone-shaped device similar to the
baffle member required by the claim. They sought an order for inspection. The
defendants brought a cross-motion to strike out the action as frivolous, vexatious and an abuse of the process of the court. *Held,* (1) there was no supporting evidence for the plaintiffs' suspicion and there was no ground for granting
an order for inspection; (2) it was not clear that there was no case on infringement, and the plaintiffs' claim should not be struck out: WAHL AND SIMON-
SOLITEC *v.* BUHLER-MIAG (ENGLAND) [1979] F.S.R. 183, Whitford J.

2042. —— —— **statement of nature of dependants attack on validity**
In an infringement action the defendants pleaded obviousness and prior
publication. The plaintiffs sought statements as to which items shown in the
advertisements relied on by the defendants corresponded with features of each
patent claim. The plaintiffs sought a further order that the defendants state
which features a man skilled in the art would have used with which other
features. *Held,* such an order could be made, but in view of the simplicity of
the apparatus in issue, it was not appropriate in the present case: POWERSCREEN
INTERNATIONAL *v.* J. FINLAY (ENGINEERING) AND SURE EQUIPMENT [1979]
F.S.R. 108, Whitford J.

2043. Interlocutory injunction—balance of convenience
The plaintiffs were importers of a product made by patented process. The
manufacturers were an Italian company connected with Italian ex-licensees of
the plaintiff. The defendants were importers of square mesh plastic netting.
The plaintiffs claimed that they had recently invented further improvements
and that their planned research and development programme would be jeopar-
dised if the defendants were allowed to sell the imported netting. *Held,* on
appeal, that (1) damages would not be an adequate remedy for the defendants

or the plaintiffs; (2) the balance of convenience lay with the plaintiffs: NETLON *v.* BRIDPORT-GRUNDY [1979] F.S.R. 530, C.A.

2044. Italy—constitution—protection for drugs
[Italy.] The Patents Act forbade the patenting of medicines and processes for their manufacture. The court found that this provision violated art. 9 of the Constitution which related to the encouragement of scientific and technical research, and art. 3 which related to equal protection, in that it discouraged research and placed at an unfair disadvantage those who do nevertheless engage in research as compared with those who merely avail themselves of the research of others: CIBA S.A. *v.* UFFICIO CENTRALE BREVETTI [1979] F.S.R. 505, Italian Constitutional Ct.

2045. Non-infringement—declaration—whether production of article required
[Patents Act 1949 (c. 87), s. 66.] The plaintiffs brought an action for a declaration that the process of which particulars had been supplied by them to the defendants did not infringe any of three patents. *Held*, as a matter of construction the Patents Act 1949, s. 66, requires only provision of particulars to the defendant of the process or article. There is no obligation to provide the article itself: PLASTICISERS *v.* PIXDANE [1978] F.S.R. 595, D. W. Falconer, Q.C.

2046. Objection—invention—method
[Eire] [Patents Act 1964, ss. 2, 6, 9, 18, 19; Patents Rules 1965, rr. 19 (2) 69 and 117.] The application related to naturally occurring micro-organisms and methods of production. Objection was taken that the claim was not an invention. On appeal the further question arose as to whether the claim related to an unaltered substance occurring in nature. *Held*, dismissing the appeal against the refusal to allow the application to proceed, (1) micro-organisms were composed of living cells which had been grown and were not manufactured or composition of matter; (2) they were an unaltered substance occurring in nature: RANK HOVIS MCDOUGALL *v.* THE CONTROLLER OF PATENTS, DESIGNS AND TRADE MARKS [1978] F.S.R. 588, High Ct. of Ireland.

2047. Opposition—appeal—judge entitled to take view on effect of facts
In opposition proceedings, a conflict of evidence had arisen. The hearing officer, and Appeal Tribunal decided for the applicant, on the question of obviousness. The opponents appealed against the finding that the applicant was the first inventor. On appeal the question arose whether the judge could take a view different to that of the hearing officer. *Held*, the judge had not disturbed any findings of fact. He could reconsider the question as to the effect of the evidence and facts: TIEFEBRUN'S APPLICATION [1979] F.S.R. 97, C.A.

2048. —— claim copying—insufficiency
[Patents Act 1949 (c. 87), s. 14 (1) (*g*).] Claim had been copied word for word from a specification of the opponents. The hearing officer held that the objection on the grounds of insufficiency succeeded. *Held*, dismissing the appeal, claim copying was done in order to establish effectively the objection of prior claiming against the later patent where a later application had been published first; (2) the applicant might find that he had not made the same invention and have claims unsupported by the description in the body of the specification: GENERAL TYRE AND RUBBER CO. (HOFELT & CORL'S) APPLICATION [1977] F.S.R. 402, Whitford J.

2049. —— practice
In hearing cases under the Patent Act 1849 in opposition proceedings the patentee or applicant for a patent has the right to open, despite R.S.C., Ord. 104 which did not repeat the terms of R.S.C., Ord. 103, r. 18 (3): E.I. DU PONT DE NEMOURS & CO. (HULL'S) APPLICATION [1979] F.S.R. 128, Patent Office.

2050. —— prior claiming
[Patents Act 1949 (c. 87), s. 9.] Application related to developer compositions for use in copying machines. The hearing officer decided in opposition proceedings that the applicant's claim was in substance the same invention as

the opponent's, and directed that s. 9 reference be inserted into the specification. *Held*, on appeal, that (1) the claims related to properties of materials not an invention; (2) the applicant's claims were of necessary consequences of the opponent's claim: XEROX CORP. (CHATTERJI'S) APPLICATION [1979] R.P.C. 375, Whitford J.

2051. Passing off—injunction—utilitarian features
[H.K.] The plaintiffs alleged patent infringement and passing off of their electric fan. The defendants challenged the validity of the patent and contended that the features of each fan were dictated by functional considerations above. *Held*, granting an interlocutory injunction, that (1) there was a triable issue in relation to patent infringement; (2) there were some visual characteristics not dictated by utilitarian considerations; (3) the appropriation of reputation in get-up may come about by copying of a combination of features: KEMTRON PROPERTIES PTY. *v.* JIMMY'S CO. [1979] F.S.R. 87, Hong Kong High Ct.

2052. Patent agents—breach of contract—negligence
The plaintiffs developed a device which enabled a marine crankshaft to be machined *in situ*. The defendants, agents, failed to put the specification in order by the necessary date because the patent agent had decided the patent was invalid. The plaintiff sued in negligence and contract. The defendants contended that they rightly took the view that the patent was invalid and had acted properly in informing the plaintiffs. *Held*, that the agent had (1) taken a superficial and incorrect view; (2) failed to ascertain from his client the features which in conjunction distinguished it from the prior art.; (3) failed to give the client the opportunity of deciding whether to proceed: ANDREW MASTER HONES *v.* CRUICKSHANK AND FAIRWEATHER [1979] F.S.R. 268, Graham J.

2053. Practice—Anton Piller order
In application for leave to appeal against an Anton Piller order, the defendents, who opposed the application, argued that they were given express right to apply to discharge the order. The court found this irrelevant. The defendants further argued that because the order had been executed an appeal would be of no practical use. The court rejected this argument: BESTWORTH *v.* WEARWELL [1979] F.S.R. 320, Slade J.

2054. —— discovery—experimental work
[R.S.C., Ord. 24, rr. 7, 8.] The plaintiffs brought a *quia timet* action for infringement of two patents. The defendants alleged obviousness, insufficiency and inutility, and sought orders for discovery of documents relating to the research and experiments in the course of which the plaintiffs made the invention. *Held*, discovery ordered of all documents relevant to obviousness, insufficiency and inutility: HALCON INTERNATIONAL INC. *v.* THE SHELL TRANSPORT AND TRADING CO. (DISCOVERY NO. 2) [1979] R.P.C. 459, Whitford J.

2055. —— validity of patent—security for costs of counter-claim
The plaintiffs sought security for costs of a counterclaim. The defendants alleged that the patent was invalid, and also counterclaimed. The defendants were in voluntary liquidation. *Held*, the costs occasioned by putting in issue the validity of the patent were not costs on the counterclaim except to a nominal extent. No order should be made: NORPRINT *v.* S.P.J. LABELS AND LABELPLY [1979] F.S.R. 126, Whitford J.

2056. Registration—refusal—lack of originality
[Registered Designs Act 1949 (c. 88), s. 1.] Application was to register a design in respect of a football shirt bearing the bands and colours of the England football team. Application was refused because of lack of novelty and originality. The applicants appealed. *Held*, although there was prior art as to the striping, having regard to the combination of colours and their location. it would not be appropriate to refuse the application at this stage. The judge observed that the application should proceed with a statement of novelty limited to a claim for the particular stripes of colour applied to the article in the manner shown: COOK & HURST'S DESIGN APPLICATION [1979] R.P.C. 197. Whitford J.

BOOKS AND ARTICLES. See *post*, pp. [9], [28].

PEERAGES AND DIGNITIES

ARTICLES. See *post*, p. [28].

PENSIONS AND SUPERANNUATION

2057. Armed forces

NAVAL, MILITARY AND AIR FORCES ETC. (DISABLEMENT AND DEATH) SERVICE PENSIONS AMENDMENT ORDER 1979 (No. 113) [25p], made under the Social Security (Miscellaneous Provisions) Act 1977 (c. 5), s. 12 (1); operative as to arts. 1, 3, 4 (*a*), (*c*) and (*d*), 5 and 6, on April 2, 1979, and as to arts. 2 and 4 (*b*) on April 6, 1979; amends S.I. 1978 No. 1525 and provides, *inter alia*, for the receipt of an additional component within the meaning of s. 6 (1) (*b*) of the Social Security Pensions Act 1975, or of a graduated retirement benefit under the National Insurance Act 1965, no longer to render a member of the forces ineligible for an award of unemployability allowance under art. 18 of the principal order.

NAVAL, MILITARY AND AIR FORCES ETC. (DISABLEMENT AND DEATH) SERVICE PENSIONS AMENDMENT (No. 2) ORDER 1979 (No. 1312) [70p], made under the Social Security (Miscellaneous Provisions) Act 1977, s. 12 (1); operative on November 12, 1979; amends S.I. 1978 No. 1525 by increasing the rates and scope of certain pensions and allowances.

2058. British Railways

BRITISH RAILWAYS BOARD (FUNDING OF PENSION SCHEMES) (No. 7) ORDER 1979 (No. 1724) [20p], made under the Railways Act 1974 (c. 48), ss. 5, 6; operative on December 31, 1979; reduces the sums which the British Railways Board have to provide for the funding of the British Railways Superannuation Fund (Amalgamated Sections) and also the quarterly interest payments payable by the Board in certain circumstances.

2059. Children's pensions

SUPERANNUATION (CHILDREN'S PENSIONS) (EARNINGS LIMIT) ORDER 1979 (No. 680) [10p], made under the Superannuation (Amendment) Act 1965 (c. 10), Sched. 2, para. 24 (1) and (3) and S.I. 1968 No. 1656; operative on July 16, 1979; increases the limit on emoluments received during training (when the payment of a children's pension continues after the child reaches 16) from £104 to £598 a year.

SUPERANNUATION (CHILDREN'S PENSIONS) (EARNING LIMIT) (No. 2) ORDER 1979 (No. 1275) [10p], made under the Superannuation (Amendment) Act 1965, Sched. 2, para. 24 (1) (3); operative on November 12, 1979; revokes S.I. 1979 No. 680 by increasing the limit on emoluments to £694 a year.

2060. Civil service

INCREASE OF PENSIONS (INDIA, PAKISTAN AND BURMA) (AMENDMENT) REGULATIONS 1979 (No. 1276) [10p], made under the Pensions (Increase) Act 1971 (c. 56), ss. 5 (3), 10, 11A, and the Ministers of the Crown Act 1975 (c. 26), s. 7 (2), Sched. 2, Pt. I; operative on November 12, 1979; amend S.I. 1972 No. 990 so as to provide for increases payable in respect of specified pensions.

SUPERANNUATION (LYON KING OF ARMS AND LYON CLERK) ORDER 1979 (No. 1540) [10p], made under the Superannuation Act 1972 (c. 11), s. 1 (5) (8); operative on January 18, 1980; adds the office of Lord Lyon King of Arms and the office of Lyon Clerk and Keeper of the Records of Court and office of Lyon King of Arms to the offices, listed in Sched. 1 to the 1972 Act, thereby bringing persons holding either of these offices within the principal civil service pension scheme.

2060a. Fees

SUPERANNUATION AND OTHER TRUST FUNDS (FEES) REGULATIONS 1979 (No. 1557) [10p], made under the Superannuation and other Trust Funds (Validation) Act 1927 (c. 41), s. 3 (6); operative on January 1, 1980; increase the fees payable to the Registrar of Friendly Societies in respect of the registration of amendment of rules of funds and other matters.

2061. Fire service

FIREMENS' PENSION SCHEME (AMENDMENT) ORDER 1979 (No. 407) [10p], made under the Fire Services Act 1947 (c. 41), s. 26 as amended and extended by the Reserve and Auxiliary Forces (Protection of Civil Interests) Act 1951 (c. 65), s. 42 and the Superannuation Act 1972 (c. 11), ss. 12, 16; operative on May 1, 1979; amends S.I. 1973 No. 966 by increasing the rate of interest payable by a fire authority on a transfer value in respect of a fireman who has ceased to be a member of that authority's brigade.

FIREMEN'S PENSION SCHEME (AMENDMENT) (No. 3) ORDER 1979 (No. 1286) [40p], made under the Fire Services Act 1947, s. 26 as amended and extended by the Reserve and Auxiliary Forces (Protection of Civil Interests) Act 1951 (c. 65), s. 42 and the Superannuation Act 1972 (c. 11), ss. 12, 16; operative on November 12, 1979; amends S.I. 1973 No. 966 and increases the flat-rate by reference to which certain awards which do not qualify for increases under the Pensions (Increase) Act 1971 are determined.

FIREMEN'S PENSION SCHEME (WAR SERVICE) ORDER 1979 (No. 1360) [50p], made under the Fire Services Act 1947, s. 26, as amended by the Reserve and Auxiliary Forces (Protection of Civil Interests) Act 1951, s. 42, and the Superannuation Act 1972, ss. 12 and 16; operative on December 1, 1979; provides for firemen who have completed a period of war service, as defined, and meet the other requisite qualifications. A qualified fireman may elect to increase his own pension by buying additional years of reckonable service up to half his period of war service or he may pay more and provide also a corresponding increase in the benefits under the pension scheme for widows and children.

2062. Judicial officers

JUDICIAL PENSIONS (WIDOWS' AND CHILDREN'S BENEFITS) (AMENDMENT) REGULATIONS 1979 (No. 210) [20p], made under the Administration of Justice Act 1973 (c. 15), s. 10 (7); operative on April 1, 1979; amend S.I. 1974 No. 44 in relation to periodic payments.

SUPERANNUATION (JUDICIAL OFFICES) (AMENDMENT) RULES 1979 (No. 668) [10p], made under the Superannuation Act 1965 (c. 74), s. 39A, and the Courts Act 1971 (c. 23), Sched. 2, para. 4 (4); operative on July 16, 1979; revoke and replace S.I. 1972 No. 1277.

2063. Local government

LOCAL GOVERNMENT SUPERANNUATION (AMENDMENT) REGULATIONS 1979 (No. 2) [40p], made under the Superannuation Act 1972 (c. 11), ss. 7, 12; operative on February 1, 1979; further amend S.I. 1974 No. 520 in relation to allowances and contributions.

LOCAL GOVERNMENT SUPERANNUATION (AMENDMENT) (No. 2) REGULATIONS 1979 (No. 592) [10p], made under the Superannuation Act 1972, ss. 7 and 12; operative on July 2, 1979; amend S.I. 1974 No. 520, reg. A7 (treatment of certain additional duties of whole-time officers as separate variable-time employment) so that for the purposes of that regulation the duty of an acting returning officer includes duties required to be discharged by such an officer at a European Assembly election.

LOCAL GOVERNMENT SUPERANNUATION (AMENDMENT) (No. 3) REGULATIONS 1979 (No. 1534) [£1·50], made under the National Insurance Act 1965 (c. 51), s. 110 (1) and Superannuation Act 1972, ss. 7, 12; operative on January 1, 1980; make further amendments to the Local Government Superannuation Regulations 1974.

2064. National Freight Corporation

NATIONAL FREIGHT CORPORATION (FUNDING OF PENSION SCHEMES) (No. 3) ORDER 1979 (No. 1416) [10p], made under the Transport Act 1978 (c. 55), ss. 19, 20; operative on December 1, 1979; increases the sum which the National Freight Corporation is to provide for funding certain obligations owed in respect of the NFC (1978) Pension Fund.

2065. National insurance. See NATIONAL INSURANCE.

2066. Northern Ireland. See NORTHERN IRELAND.

2067. Overseas pensions

OVERSEAS SERVICE (PENSIONS SUPPLEMENT) (AMENDMENT) REGULATIONS 1979 (No. 1277) [20p], made under the Pensions (Increase) Act 1971 (c. 56), ss. 11, 11A and the Ministers of the Crown Act 1975 (c. 26), s. 7 (2), Sched. 2, Pt. I; Pt. I of the Order is operative on November 12, 1979, Pt. II of the Order is operative on July 1, 1980; amend S.I. 1977 No. 1675 to provide for the payment of supplements in respect of overseas public service pensions to be calculated by reference to increases payable on a Civil Service pension.

SOCIAL SECURITY BENEFIT (PERSONS ABROAD) AMENDMENT (No. 2) REGULATIONS 1979 (No. 1432) [20p], made under the Social Security Act 1975 (c. 14), s. 131; operative on November 10, 1979; modify the conditions relating to entitlement to basic component and additional component of retirement pension, and to the payment of up-rating increases, in relation to persons absent from and not ordinarily resident in Great Britain.

2068. Pensioners' Payments and Social Security Act 1979 (c. 48)

This Act provides for lump sum payments to pensioners; it also modifies s. 125 of the Social Security Act 1975.

S. 1 provides for a lump sum payment of £10 to pensioners to be made in December 1979; s. 2 contains definitions; s. 3 relates to the administration of payments; s. 4 relates to payments for 1980 and subsequent years; s. 5 modifies s. 125 of the Social Security Act 1975; s. 6 contains financial provisions; s. 7 contains additional provisions relating to Northern Ireland; s. 8 gives the short title.

The Act received the Royal Assent on July 26, 1979, and came into force on that date.

2069. Pensions appeal tribunals

PENSIONS APPEAL TRIBUNALS (ENGLAND AND WALES) (AMENDMENT) RULES 1979 (No. 1744) [10p], made under the Pensions Appeals Tribunals Act 1943 (c. 39), para. 3 of the Sched. as amended by the Administration of Justice Act 1977 (c. 38); operative on January 29, 1980; increase some of the amounts payable by the Pensions Appeal Tribunals by way of allowances and expenses.

2070. Pensions increase

PENSIONS INCREASE (SPEAKERS' PENSIONS) (AMENDMENT) REGULATIONS 1979 (No. 762) [20p], made under the Pensions (Increase) Act 1971 (c. 56), s. 5 (3) and (4); operative on July 30, 1979; provide that the pension of any particular past Speaker or his dependants shall for the purpose of calculating the increase thereto under the 1971 Act be deemed to have begun on the date of the last increase in the pension payable to that person if he should cease to hold that office and not on the date when he actually ceases to hold that office.

PENSIONS INCREASE (PAST PRIME MINISTERS) (AMENDMENT) REGULATIONS 1979 (No. 771) [10p], made under the Pensions (Increase) Act 1971, s. 5 (3) and (4); operative on July 30, 1979; provide that the pension of a past Prime Minister shall for the purpose of calculating the increase thereto under the 1971 Act be deemed to have begun on the date of the last increase in the pension payable to that person if he should cease to hold that office and not on the date when he actually ceases to hold that office.

PENSIONS INCREASE (REVIEW) ORDER 1979 (No. 1047) [20p], made under the Social Security Pensions Act 1975 (c. 60), s. 59; operative on November 12, 1979; provides for an increase in the rates of public service pensions.

2071. Police

POLICE CADETS (PENSIONS) (AMENDMENT) REGULATIONS 1979 (No. 75) [20p], made under the Police Act 1964 (c. 48), s. 35 as extended by the Superannuation Act 1967 (c. 28), s. 13 and the Superannuation Act 1972 (c. 11), ss. 12, 15 and under the Police Act 1969 (c. 63), s. 4 (5); operative on March 1, 1979; amend S.I. 1973 No. 430, so as to apply amendments to the Police Pension Regulations to the cadets pension regulations.

SPECIAL CONSTABLES (PENSIONS) (AMENDMENT) REGULATIONS 1979 (No. 76) [20p], made under the Police Act 1964, s. 34 and read with the Police Pensions Act 1961 (c. 35), s. 1 (2) and extended by the Superannuation Act 1972, ss. 12, 15; operative on March 1, 1979; amend S.I. 1973 No. 431 and apply certain amendments to the Police Pension Regulations to the special constable pension regulations.

POLICE PENSIONS (AMENDMENT) REGULATIONS 1979 (No. 406) [10p], made under the Police Pensions Act 1976 (c. 35), ss. 1, 4; operative on May 1, 1979; amend S.I. 1973 No. 428 by increasing the rate of interest payable by a police authority on a transfer value in respect of a policeman who has retired from the force maintained by that authority.

POLICE PENSIONS (WAR SERVICE) REGULATIONS 1979 (No. 1259) [50p], made under the Police Pensions Act 1976, ss. 1, 3, 4; operative on November 6, 1979; supplement S.I. 1971 No. 232 and S.I. 1973 No. 428 and make special provision for regular policemen who have completed a period of war service. The provisions enable qualified policemen to increase their years of reckonable service.

POLICE PENSIONS (AMENDMENT) (No. 2) REGULATIONS 1979 (No. 1287) [20p], made under the Police Pensions Act 1976, ss. 1, 3, 5; operative on November 12, 1979; amend S.I. 1973 No. 428 and increase the flat rate by reference to which certain widows' pensions and childrens' allowances are determined.

POLICE PENSIONS (LUMP SUM PAYMENTS TO WIDOWS) REGULATIONS 1979 (No. 1406) [10p], made under the Police Pensions Act 1976, ss. 1, 3, 5; operative on December 3, 1979; provide for the payment of a gratuity of £10 in the case of a policeman's widow in receipt of a discretionary increase in her police widow's pension, granted under S.I. 1971 No. 232, during the week beginning December 3, 1979 if she is not entitled to a payment by virtue of the Pensioners' Payments and Social Security Act 1979.

2072. Retirement pension—applicant abroad for certain periods—whether resident in Great Britain

The applicant left Great Britain in 1973 intending to live in Rhodesia. For business and family reasons she returned to Great Britain for part of each year in 1974 and 1975 and claimed that she was entitled to increases in retirement pension introduced during the years 1973–1975. On appeal, *held*, that the applicant was not ordinarily resident during her periods in Great Britain and was accordingly not entitled to the increases: DECISION R(P) 1/78.

2073. —— increase in respect of wife—late claim due to ignorance of regulations

The claimant retired in 1971 and was paid retirement pension at the personal rate. He learned at that time that he was not entitled to an increase in respect of his wife because of her earnings. From April 1976 he became entitled to such an increase when the earnings rule was relaxed. Because of his ignorance of this change he did not make a claim until March 1977, well outside the statutory time limit. The claimant was disqualified from receiving the increase because good cause was not shown for the failure to claim. On appeal, *held*, that (1) failure to make inquiries as to such changes in the law does not of itself defeat a plea of good cause for delay; and (2) there were facts leading to a conclusion that the claimant's ignorance was reasonable. He was accordingly entitled to the increase in benefit: DECISION No. R(P) 1/79.

2074. Surviving spouses

SOCIAL SECURITY (MAXIMUM ADDITIONAL COMPONENT) AMENDMENT REGULATIONS 1979 (No. 1428) [10p], made under the Social Security Pensions Act 1975 (c. 60), s. 9 (3); operative on November 9, 1979; amend S.I. 1978 No. 949, which deals with Category A retirement pensions of surviving spouses.

2075. Teachers

TEACHERS' SUPERANNUATION (AMENDMENT) REGULATIONS 1979 (No. 1206) [40p], made under the Superannuation Act 1972 (c. 11), ss. 9, 12, Sched. 3; operative on November 1, 1979; amend S.I. 1976 No. 1987 in particular reg. 85 and other provisions of Pt. V relating to the keeping of a teachers' superannuation account.

2076. War pensions

PERSONAL INJURIES (CIVILIANS) AMENDMENT SCHEME 1979 (No. 270) [25p], made under the Personal Injuries (Emergency Provisions) Act 1939 (c. 82), s. 2; Arts. 1, 3, 4, 5 (a) (c) (d), 6, 7, operative on April 2, 1979, Arts. 2, 5 (b) operative on April 6, 1979; further amends S.I. 1976 No. 585 which provides for compensation to or in respect of civilians who were killed or injured in the 1939–1945 war.

PERSONAL INJURIES (CIVILIANS) AMENDMENT (No. 2) SCHEME 1979 (No. 1232) [40p], made under the Personal Injuries (Emergency Provisions) Act 1939, s. 2; operative on November 12, 1979; amends S.I. 1976 No. 585 and increases the rates and scope of certain pensions and allowances.

INJURIES IN WAR (SHORE EMPLOYMENT) COMPENSATION (AMENDMENT) SCHEME 1979 (No. 1506) [10p], made under the Injuries in War Compensation Act 1914 (c. 18), s. 1, as amended by S.I. 1964 No. 488, and the Defence (Transfer of Functions) Act 1964 (c. 15), s. 1 (1) (3); operative on November 12, 1979; increases to £38·00 the maximum weekly allowance paid to ex-members of the Women's Auxiliary Forces who suffered disablement from their service overseas during the 1914–18 war.

2077. —— **discrimination—EEC.** See DIRECTEUR RÉGIONAL DE LA SÉCURITÉ SOCIALE DE NANCY *v.* GILLARD, § 1239.

BOOKS AND ARTICLES. See *post*, pp. [9], [28].

PETROLEUM

2078. Enforcing authorities

PETROLEUM (CONSOLIDATION) ACT 1928 (ENFORCEMENT) REGULATIONS 1979 (No. 427) [25p], made under the Health and Safety at Work etc. Act 1974 (c. 37), ss. 11 (2) (*d*), 15 (1) (3) (*a*), 18 (2), 50 (3), 82 (3) (*a*); operative on July 1, 1979; provides that a petroleum-spirit licensing authority will be the enforcing authority in its area for the 1928 Act.

2079. Paraffin

PARAFFIN (MAXIMUM RETAIL PRICES) (THIRD AMENDMENT) ORDER 1979 (No. 193) [10p], made under the Energy Act 1976 (c. 76), ss. 1 (4), 17 (2), (3); operative on February 27, 1979; increases the maximum retail prices for the supply of paraffin intended for use in portable domestic oil burners.

PARAFFIN (MAXIMUM RETAIL PRICES) (REVOCATION) ORDER 1979 (No. 797) [10p], made under the Energy Act 1976, s. 1 (4); operative on July 12, 1979; revokes S.I. 1976 No. 1204 which imposed maximum retail prices in respect of paraffin intended for use in portable domestic oil burners.

PARAFFIN (MAXIMUM RETAIL PRICES) (REVOCATION) (No. 2) ORDER 1979 (No. 1375) [10p], made under the Statutory Instruments Act 1946 (c. 36), s. 5 (1); operative on October 31, 1979; revokes S.I. 1979 No. 797.

PARAFFIN (MAXIMUM RETAIL PRICES) (REVOCATION) (No. 3) ORDER 1979 (No. 1383) [10p], made under the Energy Act 1976, s. 1 (4); operative on October 31, 1979; revokes S.I. 1976 No. 1204 as amended which imposed maximum retail prices in respect of the supply of paraffin intended for use in portable domestic oil burners.

2080. Prices

PETROL PRICES (DISPLAY) (AMENDMENT) ORDER 1979 (No. 4) [10p], made under the Prices Act 1974 (c. 24), s. 4 (3); operative on February 1, 1979; amends S.I. 1978 No. 1389 to substitute a reference to the new British standard specification for petrol for that referred to in art. 2 (*a*).

POLICE

2081. Chief Inspector of Constabulary

Her Majesty's Chief Inspector of Constabulary, Sir Colin Woods, has published his annual report for 1977, which discusses, *inter alia,* the rôle of the police in the heart of the community. The report is available from HMSO (H.C. 1351) [£3.50].

2082. Committee of Inquiry—Report

The third report of the Edmund-Davies Committee of Inquiry on the Police has been published. This report deals with the structure and role of police staff associations and, though recommending improvements, takes the view that no radical changes are needed in the existing arrangements covering the associations. The report is available from HMSO (Cmnd. 7633) [£3·00].

2083. Complaints Board—report

The Police Complaints Board has published its report for 1978, its first full year of operation, which shows that the two largest categories of complaint are irregularity in procedure and assault. The report has been issued by the Home Office and is available from HMSO [80p].

2084. Dog-handler—overtime allowance

[Police Regulations 1971 (S.I. 1971 No. 156), regs. 25, 26, 40; Police (Amendment) Regulations 1973 (S.I. 1973 No. 33), reg. 11 (2); Police Act 1964 (c. 48), s. 33 (4).] P, a police constable, had been a dog-handler since 1965. In 1973 an official of the Home Office purported to give approval to the police authority's proposal to make payments of £165 a year to dog-handlers (being less than would have been payable under reg. 26 of the 1971 Regulations) under reg. 40 of the 1971 Regulations and made the approval retrospective to September 1, 1972. *Held,* dismissing the police authority's appeal, that (1) P's duties in caring for the dog for the accepted period of one hour a day when on mobile patrol and on public holidays and rest days was "a duty" within regs. 25 and 26 of the 1971 Regulations; (2) reg. 40 did not permit the granting of an approval of an allowance; (3) even if the approval were referable to reg. 40 it would be invalid as it purported to be retrospective and in so far as it purported to give a reduced allowance the approval would have been invalid by s. 33 (4) of the Police Act 1964. The authority therefore had to make the payments provided for under the 1971 Regulations as amended: CROSBY *v.* SANDFORD [1979] Crim.L.R. 668, C.A.

2085. Duty to enforce law—failing to carrying out duty—wilful neglect

The offence of a public officer neglecting to perform his duty requires that the neglect be wilful, not merely inadvertent, and culpable, that is without reasonable excuse or justification; an element of corruption or dishonesty is not an essential ingredient.

An officer in uniform was some 30 yards from a club exit when a man was ejected by the bouncers. The man was then beaten and kicked to death in the gutter. The officer made no move to intervene or summon assistance. He was charged with " misconduct of an officer." At his trial he demurred to the indictment on the ground that it disclosed no offence, since misconduct involved malfeasance or misfeasance not mere non feasance. The judge ruled against the demurrer and the defendant was eventually convicted. On appeal, on a point of law concerning the demurrer, *held,* dismissing the appeal, that the neglect had to be wilful and culpable in the sense that the conduct impugned injured the public interest so as to call for condemnation and punishment. (*R.* v. *Wyat* (1705) 1 Salk. 380, *R.* v. *Bembridge* (1783) 3 Doug.K.B. 32, *R.* v. *Llewellyn Jones* [1967] C.L.Y. 841 considered.)

R. *v.* DYTHAM [1979] 3 W.L.R. 467, C.A.

2086. —— pornography

[Obscene Publications Act 1959 (c. 66), ss. 2, 3.] The new arrangements made by the Metropolitan Police Commissioner for proceedings under ss. 2 and 3 of the Obscene Publications Act 1959, under which the D.P.P. no longer normally has the conduct of such proceedings, are within the Commissioner's discretion; it is impossible to say that the Commissioner has " turned his back on his duties ": R. *v.* METROPOLITAN POLICE COMMISSIONER, *ex p.* BLACKBURN, *The Times,* December 1, 1979, D.C.

[For previous proceedings, see [1968] C.L.Y. 1703, 3065; [1973] C.L.Y. 2580.]

2087. Metropolitan police

The annual report of the Commissioner of the Metropolitan Police, Sir David McNee, has been published. The report highlights the large cost of keeping public order at the unprecedented number of demonstrations, industrial disputes and processions. Other points noted were the marginal drop in serious crime, the first reduction in eight years, and the decrease in the overall number of road accidents in London. The report is available from HMSO (Cmnd. 7580) [£2·50].

2088. Police cadets

POLICE CADETS (AMENDMENT) REGULATIONS 1979 (1543) [10p], made under the Police Act 1964 (c. 48), s. 35 and the Police Act 1969 (c. 63), s. 4 (4); operative on January 1, 1980; further amend S.I. 1968 No. 25 by increasing the pay of police cadets and the charges payable by them for board and lodging provided by police authorities.

POLICE CADETS REGULATIONS 1979 (No. 1727) [40p], made under the Police Act 1964, s. 35; operative on February 1, 1980; consolidate (with minor amendments) the Police Cadets Regulations 1968 (No. 25) and other related regulations.

2089. Police officers—injury while chasing car—liability of driver

[Can.] It has been *held*, that where a police officer is injured when his car goes out of control and crashes during a high speed chase of a car whose driver knew he was being chased, and was trying to escape arrest, the officer has a cause of action against the driver and owners of the car. (*Lochgelly* v. *M'Mullan* [1934] A.C. 1; *Grant* v. *Australian Knitting Mills* [1936] A.C. 85 referred to): ATT.-GEN. FOR ONTARIO v. KELLER (1978) 86 D.L.R. (3d) 426, Ontario H.C.J.

2090. —— pay increase

POLICE (AMENDMENT) REGULATIONS 1979 (No. 694) [30p], made under the Police Act 1964 (c. 48), s. 33 and the Police Act 1969 (c. 63), s. 4 (4); operative on July 23, 1979; increase rates of pay for police officers in England and Wales and the London allowance payable to members of the City of London and Metropolitan police forces.

2091. Police regulations

POLICE (AMENDMENT) (No. 2) REGULATIONS 1979 (No. 1216) [20p], made under the Police Act 1964 (c. 48), s. 33 and the Police Act 1969 (c. 63), s. 4 (4); operative on November 1, 1979; amend provisions of S.I. 1971 No. 156 concerning rates of pay for police officers.

POLICE REGULATIONS 1979 (No. 1470) [£1·75], made under the Police Act 1964, ss. 33, 46 (3) and the Police Act 1969, s. 4 (4); operative on January 1, 1980; consolidate with minor amendments S.I. 1971 No. 156 and its amending instruments.

2092. Powers—taking possession of arrested person's jewellery

N was charged with assaulting a police officer causing him actual bodily harm. After being arrested for obstruction, N was placed in a detention room where her rings, a necklace and earrings were forcibly removed, N having refused to hand them over. A policewoman was injured in the struggle whilst N's jewellery was being removed. *Held*, upholding a submission of no case to answer, that the right of police officers to search arrested persons and take possession of their property was very limited. They may search for and remove objects which they reasonably suspect to be connected with a criminal offence committed by the accused, or any object with which a prisoner might do herself or others injury, or any tool which may be used to effect escape. These items of jewellery were not such objects: R. v. NAYLOR [1979] Crim.L.R. 532, Leicester Crown Ct.

2093. Powers of arrest—obstruction in execution of duty

[Police Act 1964 (c. 48), s. 51 (3).]

A policeman has no power of arrest for a "simple" obstruction of him in the execution of his duty where no breach of the peace has occurred or is likely.

Police visited a jeweller's shop upon information that a stolen ring was there offered for sale. The plaintiff, the proprietor's son and a solicitor, was called to the shop and he, not being satisfied that the ring was stolen, told the police that he would not release the ring unless the police gave a receipt therefor. He repeatedly asked for a receipt but was refused. Since the plaintiff would not release the ring otherwise, the police officer arrested him for allegedly obstructing the officer in the execution of his duty and forcibly removed him to a nearby police car and thence to the police station where the plaintiff was confined in the detention room for about an hour. The station sergeant accepted the charge and the plaintiff was released. He was later acquitted of the criminal charge. The plaintiff sought damages for assault, false imprisonment and malicious prosecution. *Held*, that (1) the arrest was unlawful since there was no breach of the peace, actual or likely, and since the plaintiff's refusal to release the ring without a receipt was reasonable, and the plaintiff was entitled to damages for assault and false imprisonment; but (2) the claim for malicious prosecution failed, the officer having acted honestly, if mistakenly, and the station sergeant having accepted the charge. (*Willmott* v. *Atack* [1976] C.L.Y. 527 and *Frank Truman Export* v. *Metropolitan Police Commissioner* [1977] C.L.Y. 2261 applied.)

WERSHOF v. METROPOLITAN POLICE COMMISSIONER (1978) 68 Cr.App.R. 82, May J.

2094. Promotion

POLICE (PROMOTION) REGULATIONS 1979 (No. 991) [40p], made under the Police Act 1964 (c. 48), s. 33; operative on October 1, 1979; consolidate, with amendments, the Regulations which govern promotion to the rank of sergeant or inspector in a police force in England and Wales.

BOOKS AND ARTICLES. See *post*, pp. [9], [28].

POST OFFICE

2095. Damage to telegraph lines—negligence of Post Office—inaccurate plan. See POST OFFICE v. MEARS CONSTRUCTION, § 1859.

2096. Northern Ireland. See NORTHERN IRELAND.

2097. Telecommunications. See TELECOMMUNICATIONS.

2098. Telephones—tapping—whether unlawful

[Convention for the Protection of Human Rights and Fundamental Freedoms (1953) (Cmnd. 8969), arts. 8, 13.]

Telephone tapping by the Post Office by means of recording telephone conversations from wires which, though connected to the subscriber's premises, are not on them, is not against the law of England.

P was charged with handling stolen property. The prosecution admitted that there had been interception of P's telephone conversations on the Secretary of State's authority. P sought declarations against the Metropolitan Police Commissioner to the effect that such conduct was unlawful. *Held*, refusing the declarations sought, that (1) the Convention of Human Rights had the status of a treaty which was not justiciable in England, and the court could only make declarations on legal or equitable rights; (2) although no law authorised telephone tapping, there was no law against it; (3) there was no right of property in words transmitted over a telephone apart from copyright; (4) there was no right of privacy, or of telephonic privacy, in English law; (5) there was no contractual right of confidentiality with the Post Office; (6) in any event it was not the defendant who had intercepted the conversations, it was the Post Office, and there was no law against the Post Office tapping telephones by means of recording from wires which were not on the subscriber's premises. (*Guaranty Trust Co. of New York* v. *Hanning & Co.* [1915] 2 K.B. 536 and *Rhodes* v. *Graham* (1931) 37 S.W. (2d) 46 distinguished; *Hanson* v. *Radcliffe Urban District Council* [1922] 2 Ch. 490, *Katz* v. *United States* (1967) 389 U.S. 347, *Fraser* v. *Evans* [1968] C.L.Y. 3133 and *Initial Services* v. *Putterill* [1967] C.L.Y. 3215 considered.)

MALONE v. METROPOLITAN POLICE COMMISSIONER [1979] 2 W.L.R. 700, Megarry V.-C.

2099. Trade unions. See TRADE UNIONS.

POWERS

2100. Power of appointment—extension by court—power of investment widened by appointment

A clause in a power of appointment whereby the trustees stood possessed of the fund for the beneficiaries' maintenance, education and advancement " and otherwise at the discretion of any person and with such gifts over and generally in such manner for their benefit as shall be appointed," gives the donee of the power a general authority to confer wider powers upon the trustees.

By an arrangement made under the Variation of Trusts Act 1958, P was given a power of appointment over the reversioners' fund. By cl. 5 the trustees were to stand possessed of the fund subject to the power on trust for the beneficiaries " in such shares with such provision for maintenance education and advancement and otherwise at the discretion of any share and with such gifts over and generally in such manner for the benefit of such (beneficiaries) as P should ... appoint." P exercised the power of appointment, purporting in doing so to grant the trustees much wider powers of investment than the original powers. *Held*, the words " and otherwise or the discretion of any person " and " generally in such manner " gave P a general authority to give the trustees any additional powers of investment or otherwise which P in the proper exercise of her discretion thought would enure for the benefit of the appointees. (Dictum of Warrington J. in *Re Falconer's Trusts* [1908] 1 Ch. 410, 414, *Re Mackenzie* [1916] 1 Ch. 125 and *Re Ainsworth* [1921] 2 Ch. 179 considered).

Re RANK'S SETTLEMENT TRUSTS; NEWTON *v.* ROLLO [1979] 1 W.L.R. 1242, Slade J.

PRACTICE

2101. Administration of Justice (Emergency Provisions) (Scotland) Act 1979 (c. 19)

This Act provides for emergency arrangements for the administration of justice in Scotland.

S. 1 deals with the duration and effect of the Act; s. 2 provides for an extension of time limits; s. 3 defines the period of detention of unconvicted prisoners; s. 4 concerns the prosecution of offences and criminal diets; s. 5 makes arrangements for court proceedings during emergency period; s. 6 partially suspends operation of s. 17 of Stamp Act 1891; s. 7 gives short title and extent.

The Act received the Royal Assent on March 22, 1979, and came into force on that date.

2102. Admiralty. See SHIPPING AND MARINE INSURANCE.

2103. Adoption. See MINORS.

2104. Appeal—extension of time—mandamus to Crown Court to allow

The applicant for judicial review was served with a summons to attend a magistrates' court on the hearing of an affiliation application but had mislaid the summons and failed to appear. The magistrates decided in his absence that he was the father of the child and liable for maintenance. The applicant did not receive a copy of the order until three weeks after the time for appealing had expired. The Crown Court judge refused leave to appeal and later refused a request for an oral hearing. On appeal, *held*, that an order of mandamus should go to the Crown Court requiring it to exercise its powers under r. 7 (5) of the Crown Court Rules 1971 to extend the time for the applicant to give notice of appeal from the magistrates' decision. (*R.* v. *Derby Justices, ex p. Kooner* [1970] C.L.Y. 466 referred to): *Re* WORTH'S APPLICATION FOR JUDICIAL REVIEW, January 19, 1979, C.A. (*Ex rel. G. Vos, Esq., Barrister.*)

2105. —— notice of appeal—time for lodgment. See RINGROAD INVESTMENTS AND COURTBURN *v.* SECRETARY OF STATE FOR THE ENVIRONMENT, § 2607.

2106. —— petitions for leave

The following Practice Direction was issued by the House of Lords on March 6, 1979:

1. As from October 1, 1976, petitions for leave to appeal to the House of Lords will be referred to an Appeal Committee consisting of three Lords

of Appeal, who will consider whether the petition appears to be competent to be received by the House and, if so, whether it should be referred for an oral hearing.

For the purposes of this Direction, petitions are incompetent if they fall under one of the following heads:

(a) Petitions for leave to appeal to the House of Lords against a refusal of the Court of Appeal to grant leave to appeal to that court from a judgment of a lower court.

(b) Petitions for leave to appeal to the House of Lords barred by s. 108 (2) (b) of the Bankruptcy Act 1914.

(c) Petitions for leave to appeal to the House of Lords barred by para. 4 of Sched. 4 to the Housing Act 1957.

(d) Petitions for leave to appeal to the House of Lords brought by a petitioner in respect of whom the High Court has made an order under s. 51 of the Supreme Court of Judicature (Consolidation) Act 1925, as amended by the Supreme Court of Judicature (Amendment) Act 1959, unless leave to present such a petition has been granted by the High Court or a judge thereof pursuant to that section.

2. Petitions for leave to appeal will be referred for an oral hearing if any member of the Appeal Committee—

(i) considers that the petition is competent or expresses doubts as to whether it is incompetent; and

(ii) considers that it is fit for an oral hearing.

3. Where a petition is not considered fit for an oral hearing, the Clerk of the Parliament will notify the parties that the petition is dismissed.

4. This Practice Direction supersedes the previous Practice Directions on petitions for leave to appeal.

[1979] 1 W.L.R. 497; [1979] 2 All E.R. 224.

2107. —— —— **out of time**

The following Practice Note was issued by the House of Lords on June 27, 1979:

We have heard this petition for leave to appeal on its merits, and we dismiss it. But I think it is right to point out that it is a matter of indulgence that we have allowed the merits to be gone into at all, because this is a petition which is six and a half months out of time. A wholly inadequate attempt has been made to explain the delay. The excuses offered, even when taken at their face value, explain some three and a half months only of the delay which has occurred, leaving a substantial period of time wholly unexplained.

Laxity in relation to compliance with Standing Orders is increasing, and it must be curbed. Earlier this year, in February, in another case * quite unrelated to the present one, the noble and learned Viscount, Lord Dilhorne, said in words that we respectfully adopt:

" The Standing Orders of this House are meant to be complied with. There are very experienced firms of solicitors acting on both sides, and there is a great deal of money involved. The Standing Orders of this House really cannot be treated as if they meant nothing, so that the parties can ignore them. The fact that there is no excuse for it is a matter we shall have to consider. . . ."

We have considered the non-compliance in this case very carefully, and we want it to become known that laxity of this kind will not be tolerated. If it is persisted in, the day will dawn when parties seeking leave to appeal will find that they are out of court for that reason alone, regardless of the merits. Disobedience to the clear rules as to time disorganises business in this House and shows disrespect if non-compliance occurs which is wholly or (as in the present case) largely unexplained. We refuse leave to appeal.

Note. Standing Order No. II of the Standing Orders of the House Regulating Judicial Business requires a petition for leave to appeal to be lodged within the Parliament Office within one month from the date of the last order or judgment appealed from.

* *Unitramp* v. *Garnac Grain Co. Inc.* (1979) (Unreported) (petition for leave to appeal out of time).
[1979] 1 W.L.R. 884.

2108. —— **point of law—interpretation of ordinary English word.** See A.C.T. CONSTRUCTION CO. v. CUSTOMS AND EXCISE COMMISSIONERS, § 2741.

2109. **Attachment of earnings—pension—whether " in respect of disablement "**
[Attachment of Earnings Act 1971 (c. 32), s. 24.]
An attachment of earnings order may be made in relation to a so-called " ill-health " pension provided that the amount of the pension is calculated according to the length of the employee's service and not to the extent of his disability.
The husband was in receipt of an " ill-health " pension paid by a local authority by whom he had been employed as a fireman until his forced retirement by reason of osteo-arthritis; its amount was slightly more than it would have been had he retired without ill-health, but its amount was fixed by reference to his years of service and not by reference to the extent of his disability. His former wife obtained an attachment of earnings order directed to the local authority to secure maintenance payments. The husband's appeal was dismissed by the Divisional Court. *Held*, dismissing his further appeal, that since it was calculated solely by reference to length of service, the pension fell within the definition of earnings in s. 24 (1) of the 1971 Act.
MILES v. MILES [1979] 1 W.L.R. 371, C.A.

2110. **Barristers—negligence—immunity—acceptance of any client**
[Can.] It has been *held*, that the public interest in the administration of justice does not require that lawyers engaged in court work be immune from action at the suit of their clients for negligence in the conduct of a civil case in court. With respect to the duty of counsel to the court and the risk that, in the absence of immunity, counsel will be tempted to prefer the interest of the client and thereby prolong trials, there is no empirical evidence that it is so serious as to justify rendering the client remediless. Nor is it justified by the undesirability of re-litigating an issue already tried. This contingency already exists in the law. Under the concept of *res judicata* a party to an action *in personam* is precluded from re-litigating the matter only against another party to the action. It is better that re-litigation occur than that the client be without recourse. As to the obligation of a lawyer to accept any client, however difficult, thereby enhancing the risk of an action by an unreasonable person, it is doubtful whether such an obligation has ever been the practice in Ontario, at least in the practice of civil litigation. Nor does it follow from the existence of an absolute privilege with respect to anything said in court that there should be immunity from liability for negligence. (*Rondel* v. *Worsley* [1968] C.L.Y. 3054; *Saif Ali* v. *(Sidney) Mitchell & Co.* [1978] C.L.Y. 2323 referred to): DEMARCO v. UNGARO (1979) 95 D.L.R. (3d) 385, Ont.H.C.J.

2111. —— —— —— **settlement of proceedings—whether action for negligence will lie**
[N.Z.] D, a barrister and solicitor, acted for P in matrimonial proceedings. After oral evidence had been given, D advised P that the proceedings could be settled on terms which he outlined. Later P claimed that D had misinformed her as to the terms of the settlement, and she brought an action for damages alleging negligence by D. On a motion to strike out, the judge at first instance dismissed P's action on the basis of a barrister's immunity from suit for negligence. P appealed. *Held*, the settlement of an action by compromise in court was work related to the contract of litigation which was covered by a barrister's immunity from action by a client. (*Rondel* v. *Worsley* [1968] C.L.Y. 3054; *Saif Ali* v. *Sydney Mitchell and Co.* [1978] C.L.Y. 2323 referred to): BIGGAR v. McLEOD [1978] 2 N.Z.L.R. 9, N.Z.C.A.

2112. **Certiorari—prison disciplinary hearing—whether visiting justice's decision reviewable.** See DAEMAR v. HALL, § 535.

2113. **Chancery Division—Chancery business outside London—long vacation**
The following Practice Direction was issued by the Chancery Division on May 4, 1979:

During the Long Vacation Vice-Chancellor Blackett-Ord or his deputy will sit at the Crown Court, Courts of Justice, Crown Square, Manchester at 11 a.m. on Wednesdays, August 1, 8, 15, 22, 29; September 5, 12, 19 and 26, and on such other days as may be necessary for the purpose of hearing such applications which may require to be immediately or promptly heard as are within his jurisdiction and according to the practice in the Chancery Division are usually heard in court or by the judge in chambers personally.

Papers for use in court. The following papers must reach the cause clerk (Chancery Division) in the Manchester District Registry, Quay Street, Manchester M60 9DJ, before 1 p.m. two days previous to the day on which the application is to be made:

(*a*) a certificate of counsel that the case requires to be immediately or promptly heard and stating concisely the reasons,

(*b*) a copy of the notice of motion bearing the district registry seal,

(*c*) a copy of the writ and of the pleadings (if any),

(*d*) unless the case is proceeding in the Manchester District Registry an extra copy of (*b*) and (*c*) above and office copy affidavits in support and in answer (if any).

If the case is proceeding in a district registry other than the Manchester District Registry, the papers should be lodged at that registry one day prior to the day on which they are to reach the cause clerk at Manchester for transmission to him. In emergencies papers in such cases may be sent to him direct by post.

Solicitors should apply at once to the clerk in court for the return of their papers as soon as the application has been disposed of.

When the vacation judge is not sitting, applications may be made, but only in cases of extreme urgency, to him personally. His address must first be obtained from the officer in charge of his list at the Manchester District Registry and telephonic communication to the vacation judge is not to be made except after reference to that officer, unless the registry is closed when the need first appears.

Application may also be made by prepaid letter, accompanied by counsel's brief, office copy affidavits in support and a minute on a separate sheet of paper signed by counsel, of the order to which he may consider the applicant entitled and also an envelope sufficiently stamped, capable of receiving the papers and addressed to the District Registrar, Manchester District Registry, Quay Street, Manchester M60 9DJ, to whom the papers will be returned by the Vice-Chancellor.

(1979) 123 S.J. 340.

2114. —— summonses for direction adjourned from judge to master

The following Practice Direction was issued by the Chancery Division on January 31, 1979:

1. When a judge, on hearing a motion, directs a speedy trial of the action it is now usual for the judge to treat the summons for directions in the action as before him (subject to the issue of a pro-forma summons) and to give preliminary directions, adjourning the rest of the summons to the Master on a fixed date in order that the Master may consider the progress of the action and give such further directions as may be necessary to enable the action to be set down for hearing without delay.

2. Solicitors are reminded that the Master needs to be supplied with copies of the relevant papers before the date fixed by the judge. The solicitors to the party at whose instance the order for speedy trial was made and who have issued the pro-forma summons (normally the plaintiff's solicitors) must accordingly, not less than two days before the date of the adjourned hearing, lodge with the Master's Summons Clerk:

(a) copies of the writ and all subsequent pleadings and notices,

(b) a copy of the summons for directions issued pro-forma,

(c) a certified or office copy of the judge's order or, if it has not yet been perfected, a copy of the draft order or, if it has not been drafted, counsel's brief endorsed with the judge's directions, and

(d) the duplicate appearance and a copy of any Civil Aid certificate.

3. If the Master has not been supplied with these papers in due time before the adjourned hearing and accordingly has to order a further adjournment it is likely to be at the expense of the party in default.

[1979] 1 W.L.R. 204; [1979] 1 All E.R. 364.

2115. Charging Orders Act 1979 (c. 53)

This Act provides for the imposing of charges to secure payment of money due, or to become due, under judgments or orders of court and related matters.

S. 1 authorises the appropriate court (as defined by subs. (2) to charge property belonging to the debtor, where the debtor is the subject of a judgment or order of the High Court or a county court; s. 2 further defines the property which may be charged; s. 3 orders that the Land Charges Act 1972 and the Land Registration Act 1925 shall apply to charging orders and makes provisions supplementing ss. 1 and 2; s. 4 allows for completion of execution; s. 5 deals with stop orders and notices; ss. 6 and 7 contain an interpretation clause and consequential amendment, repeals and transitional provisions; s. 8 contains short title, commencement and extent.

The Act received the Royal Assent on December 6, 1979, and comes into force on a day to be appointed.

2116. Commercial Court—procedure

The following Practice Statement was issued by the Commercial Court on February 7, 1979:

One of the prime objects of the Commercial Court has always been to provide an efficient service for the resolution of commercial disputes. The Commercial Court Committee, which consists of the Commercial Judges and 16 representatives of the main groups of users of the court, has been considering whether any procedural changes could be introduced in order to further this object.

The court has always adopted a flexible approach and endeavoured to adjust procedures so as to enable each case to be disposed of as speedily and economically as possible. It is therefore the unanimous view of the Committee that it would be a retrograde step to try to lay down any new rules of procedure. There are, however, certain matters to which the Committee feel it desirable to draw the attention of those resorting to the court.

A central feature of the court's practice is the summons for directions which is heard by a judge. It should be issued as early as possible in the action and practitioner should then consider how the twin objectives of speed and economy can best be achieved.

In some cases very considerable savings in time and costs can be made by, for example, dispensing with pleadings and discovery or replacing oral evidence with agreed statements of fact or written evidence. In other cases this is not desirable and the greatest savings in time and money will in the end be achieved by full and accurate pleadings and full discovery, not only of documents but even, if necessary, by way of interrogatories. By such means each party will be forced to make a realistic appraisal of the strength or weakness of its case at a comparatively early stage.

Interlocutory applications in the right case and for the above objects are therefore desirable if initial applications by letter are refused. Parties who refuse such applications may expect to have to pay the costs of an application to the court if they are subsequently ordered to give particulars or discovery which they have refused. On the other hand parties who endeavour to use interlocutory applications for the purposes of delay and seek to obtain unnecessary particulars or discovery, may expect to have to pay the costs on the failure of their applications.

The English tradition is for oral hearings, but there is a body of opinion which favours avoiding unnecessary reading aloud in court as involving a waste of valuable time. Thus, it is said, much time could be saved if the judges were given the pleadings, the correspondence and, in appropriate cases, written summaries of the parties' submissions together with a list of authorities and read them in his room either before or in the course of the hearing. Against this it has been said that oral guidance given by counsel will enable the judge to confine his reading to the essential documents and that the preparation of written submissions takes more time than is saved in court. Further suggestions have been that there should be time limits upon the arguments of counsel and that the examination-in-chief of expert witnesses, whose proofs have been exchanged, should be confined to a few questions designed to enable the witness to confirm his proof and to explain particular points of importance.

Experience has shown that established procedures are generally the most efficient. For example, it has been found in many cases to take more time to remove from the judge's mind an impression mistakenly formed from unguided reading than to present the case in the traditional way. There are however many individual cases when, by agreement between the parties, some parts of the suggested variations are valuable. If requested by both parties to do so the judges frequently read certain documents overnight or before trial in order to save time reading them in court. In suitable cases they will, whenever reasonably possible, continue to co-operate in agreed measures designed to save costs provided that this does not interfere with the need to ensure that justice is administered in public nor involve the infringement of some substantive provision of the law or mandatory rule of procedure.

The judges of the court wish it to be known that they regard it as a very important part of their duty to be available at short notice at any stage in the progress of an action on the initiative of either party. Subject to what has been said above, the costs of attendance at court will be regarded, prima facie, as part of the general costs of the cause.

(1979) 123 S.J. 132.

2117. Companies Court—winding-up—disposition of property with intent to defraud creditors—jurisdiction' to grant relief. See *Re* SHILENA HOSIERY CO., § 286.

2118. Contempt—Anton Piller order—wilful disobedience. See CHANEL *v.* 3 PEARS WHOLESALE CASH AND CARRY CO., § 2699.

2119. —— Crown Court—summary disposal by judge—employer dismissing juror
It is undesirable that, when dealing with an alleged contempt not in the face of the court, a judge should appear to be both judge and prosecutor.

A juror at a Crown Court reported to a court official that he had been dismissed from his employment because of his being called for jury service. The complaint was passed to the judge who required the attendance of the juror's employer, who was called to the witness box by the judge and there questioned by him as to the reason for the juror's dismissal. The employer stated that the reason for the juror's dismissal was that shortly after commencing employment it had become apparent that he was quite unsuitable; his forthcoming jury service was not a factor in the decision to dismiss him. The judge rejected this explanation and fined the employer £250 for contempt. *Held*, allowing the employer's appeal, that the judge had erred in finding contempt to have been proved where there was not clear evidence relating thereto; and that further it was undesirable for the judge to act as instigator and arbitrator of the complaint: another judge or the Divisional Court should have been left to consider it. (*Balogh* v. *St. Alban's Crown Court* [1974] C.L.Y. 2912 considered.)

ROONEY *v.* SNARESBROOK CROWN COURT (1978) 68 Cr.App.R. 78, C.A.

2120. —— deliberate flouting of justice's ruling—identity of witness disclosed
[Official Secrets Act 1920 (c. 75), s. 8 (4).]
Where a court makes a ruling which will be frustrated by an act done outside the courtroom, a person who knowingly commits such an act may be guilty of contempt in interfering with the due administration of justice.

In committal proceedings relating to breaches of the Official Secrets Acts, counsel for the Crown was granted an application that a witness might be referred to as "Colonel B," and his name be written down and shown only to the court, the defendants and their counsel. In cross-examination "Colonel B" gave information whereby his identity could easily be discovered and neither the Crown nor the court objected. Subsequently a number of magazines published "Colonel B's" identity. The magistrates had given no direction against such publication, being under the impression that they had no power to do so. The Attorney-General brought proceedings in the Divisional Court for contempt against the publishers. The publishers were held guilty. On appeal, *held*, allowing the appeal, that although such an activity outside the court might be a contempt if done knowing that it would frustrate the purpose of a ruling in court, in the present case, any intended effect of the magistrates' ruling outside the court was abandoned when information was given by the colonel, without protest, from the Crown or the court, which would readily identify him. *Per* Lords Diplock, Russell of Killowen and Scarman allowing Colonel B to conceal his identity was an acceptable extension of the court's power to control its own proceedings in the interests of this due administration of justice by sitting in private, but in future cases, the court should give a warning as to the intended effect of its ruling and of the risk of proceedings for contempt. (*Scott* v. *Scott* [1913] A.C. 417, *R.* v. *Socialist Worker Printers and Publishers, ex p. Att.-Gen.* [1975] C.L.Y. 2601 and *Taylor* v. *Att.-Gen.* [1975] 2 N.Z.L.R. 675 considered.)

ATT.-GEN. v. LEVELLER MAGAZINE [1979] 2 W.L.R. 247, H.L.

2121. ——— inferior court—local valuation court—whether court for purpose of protection from contempt by High Court

[R.S.C., Ord. 52, r. 1 (2) (*a*) (iii).]

A local valuation court is an inferior court which the High Court in its contempt jurisdiction is concerned to protect.

The Attorney-General sought an injunction to restrain the defendants from broadcasting matters relating to an appeal pending before a local valuation court on the grounds that it would be a contempt of court. The Divisional Court held that it was a court for these purposes. On appeal, *held*, dismissing the appeal, that a local valuation court was an inferior court which the High Court in its contempt jurisdiction was concerned to protect. (Dicta in *Society of Medical Officers of Health* v. *Hope* [1960] C.L.Y. 2705 applied.)

ATT.-GEN. v. BRITISH BROADCASTING CORP. [1979] 3 W.L.R. 312, C.A.

2122. ——— litigation pending—subsequent comment—whether likely to prejudice fair trial

[Aust.] P brought an action against D, the publisher of a newspaper with a wide circulation, alleging he had been defamed by an article in the newspaper about his medical clinic. P's methods of therapy were of much public interest. A fortnight after the alleged defamatory article was published, D published two further articles about P which were largely factual reports of P's affairs, and did not in terms adversely criticise P. P brought proceedings to commit D and its editor on the ground that the two articles were likely to prejudice the fair trial of P's defamation action. *Held*, that neither of the two articles constituted contempt, because (1) it was unlikely the trial of the action would take place for a very considerable time and thus would not then be in a juror's mind; (2) where there is a matter of public interest or concern, the discussion thereof and denunciation of public abuses are not to be suspended merely because, as an unintended by-product, there may be prejudice to someone who happens to be a litigant; (3) nevertheless, when litigation is pending in relation to a matter on which a newspaper comments, it does so at its peril (*Att.-Gen.* v. *Times Newspapers* [1973] C.L.Y. 2618 applied): BRYCH v. THE HERALD & WEEKLY TIMES [1978] V.R. 727, Vict.Sup.Ct.

2123. Costs—estate agents—two agents competing for commission—costs of actions against defendant vendor. See MOSS KAYE & ROY FRANK & CO. v. JONES; ALAN SADICK & CO. v. JONES, § 37.

2124. ——— review of taxation—care order—fee of independent social worker

In the course of *R.* v. *P.*, an appeal by a three-year-old child to the Crown Court against the making of a care order in the Juvenile Court, the child's solicitors employed an independent social worker, who played a major role in the appeal being allowed and the care order being replaced by a supervision order. The solicitors did not seek prior authority from the Crown Court to incur this disbursement. On taxation, the Crown Court disallowed the whole fee of almost £300 for three reasons. First, prior authority had not been granted;

secondly, that the judge had not placed great value on the evidence in court of the independent social worker (in fact the independent social worker was called to give brief evidence as, due to his involvement in negotiations and monitoring of the situation between the Juvenile Court and the Crown Court hearings the case had been largely conceded by the local authority. However, the solicitors had to be prepared for evidence to be given in full by him). Thirdly, the court did not place great store on the use of independent social workers in care cases because of their lack of direct involvement in the case being considered and the necessity of basing their judgments on interim inquiries and hearsay. An appeal against taxation was made to the Supreme Court Taxing Master. *Held,* (1) there is nothing in the Legal Aid Acts or Regulations which give the Crown Court power to give or withhold authority retrospectively or otherwise to employ an expert witness. A prudent solicitor may wish to find out the court's general attitude before incurring the disbursement but any such advice is without prejudice to taxation; (2) if the Crown Court Taxing Officer has adopted a fixed attitude towards the use of independent social workers and is intent on discouraging their use by disallowing their fee this is an improper exercise of the Taxing Officer's judicial discretion as it involves the pre-judgment of an issue which ought to be considered on the facts of each particular case; (3) when considering whether an item in a bill is proper the court should not be affected by hindsight and should be slow to disallow a disbursement bona fide incurred by a solicitor in the interests of a client and which, if disallowed, would fall on the solicitor personally. The test is whether in the light of all the circumstances the disbursement was a reasonable one. In this case the Taxing Master recognised the value of employing an independent social worker as an expert witness and the appeal was allowed: R. *v.* P., May 15, 1979. Master Clews. (*Ex rel. Messrs. Wilford McBain, Solicitors.*)

2125. —— taxation—bill of costs

The following Practice Direction was issued by the Chief Taxing Master on January 29, 1979:

1. The amendment to Ord. 62, App. 2, provided for by the Rules of the Supreme Court (Amendment) 1979, and these Practice Notes will apply with effect from April 24, 1979, to all taxations governed by R.S.C., Ord. 62, other than matrimonial causes as defined by s. 50 of the Matrimonial Causes Act 1973. These notes are intended to supplement and not to supersede the existing practice.

2. The new App. 2 is designed to simplify the process of drawing, reading and taxing a contentious bill of costs and thereby to reduce the time and expense of the taxation procedure. It has been constructed by merging items which are similar in nature and by abandoning other items which are either obsolete or which ought properly to be considered as part of a solicitor's normal overhead cost and as such provided for in his expense rate. (The Table set out in Sched. 1 hereto shows how the items in the former Appendix have been assimilated to the items in the new Appendix or abolished.)

3. In addition to this general simplification a new procedure has been provided in the block allowance prescribed in Pt. II, item 5, which will apply to all actions for personal injury and may, if the party entitled to the costs so elects, apply to any other action subject, in either case, to a direction to the contrary made by the taxing officer.

4. The new Appendix will apply, subject to the transitional provisions included in the Order, to all bills lodged after the appointed day no matter (save as provided in Ord. 62, r. 32 (1)) when the work was done so that it will not usually be necessary to divide bills into separate parts for work done before and after that day. However, it will still be necessary to divide bills into parts, as at present, to show separately work done before and after the introduction of VAT and before and after the issue of a civil aid certificate. If, therefore, a block allowance is included in a divided bill it must be apportioned between the several parts but the total allowed by the taxing officer will not exceed the amount which would have been allowed if the bill had not been divided.

5. The object of this new procedure is to simplify and hasten taxation and the block allowance is intended to provide a reasonable allowance for the items

in Pt. I taken as a whole but if an action for personal injury is of such unusual weight that the block allowance would be wholly inappropriate an application should be made, for leave to deliver an extended bill. Conversely, it will not be appropriate in an action other than one for personal injury to elect to insert a block allowance and then on taxation to seek to apply under r. 32 (2) for a large increase over the permitted maximum: if the case warrants substantial Pt. I charges beyond the maximum, the new procedure should not be chosen.

6. Where, in an action for personal injury, it is desired for proper reasons to avoid the use of the block allowance, the party entitled to the costs should apply for leave to the taxing officer to whom the taxation has been referred. In general, this application may be made *ex parte* and before the bill is drawn by letter setting out the grounds, although the taxing officer may require the applicant to attend him before giving his decision. The lodging of a bill in extended form will in itself be accepted as an application for leave but it must be emphasised that there is no right of election in personal injury cases, and should leave be refused, no extra costs will on taxation be allowed for drawing the rejected bill. The granting of leave is a matter for the taxing officer in the exercise of his discretion, in any particular case, but for the general guidance of the profession it is anticipated that leave will be granted only where it is clearly shown that there are unusual circumstances which would make the use of the block allowance wholly inappropriate or unfair.

7. In cases other than personal injury cases, the lodging of a bill which includes a block allowance will in general be taken as a sufficient election but since the taxing officer may, of his own motion, refuse to accept the election with or without affording the elector the right to be heard, a preliminary application may if so desired be made to him *ex parte* by letter in cases in which there is real doubt or difficulty.

8. In cases to which Pt. II applies the bill is to be drawn in the form prescribed in the Second Sched. In order to facilitate taxation the bill, or each part as the case may be, is to be prefaced by a chronological table setting out all the main events in the action in the relevant part of it. No profit cost allowances should be included for any of these events which fall within the scope of items comprised in Pt. II. Where the events in question relate to attendances covered by Pt. III the profit costs allowances should be set out against each such event in this part of the bill. Where any such event has occasioned a disbursement the amount claimed should be inserted alongside that event. It will be noted that, to conform with the normal practice on taxation, item 10 has been placed after all items other than item 12 (costs of taxation) including attendance at the trial or hearing. This practice should also be followed in bills in which the block allowance is not used, which will otherwise be drawn with the several items in chronological order in the same manner as prior to the Amendment to the Rules.

9. Pt. I, Item 3. A charge for preparing instructions to counsel to settle a document under item 3 (*d*) will be allowed as a separate charge only where there is no charge allowable for preparing the document in question under item 3 (*a*), (*b*) or (*c*). Preparation of proofs of evidence should be charged under item 10 and not under this item. In cases to which a Pt. II block allowance does not apply, copy documents required to be exhibited to an affidavit should be charged under item 4 and the collating time under item 10 (*a*) (ix). There will no longer be a separate charge for marking exhibits. The reference to " additional copies " in the note to item 3 does not include any allowance for copies made for the use of the solicitor, his agent and his client or for counsel to settle.

10. Pt. III. Attendance in court or at chambers should appear with a note of the time engaged and, in the case of summonses, of what order for costs was made. Similarly, attendances on counsel in conference or consultation should have the time noted.

11. There will no longer be a separate profit charge for service of any process. Where, however, a solicitor makes use of a process server, that process server's charges should be shown as a disbursement. Where another solicitor is instructed solely to serve process his charge should be included as such a disbursement.

12. Accounts much accompany the bill for all payments claimed (other than court fees or minor out of pocket disbursements) whether or not these payments have later to be vouched. In the case of professional fees (other than fees to counsel or to medical experts) over £25, the account must be accompanied by details showing the work done and the computation of the charge. Where fees claimed are substantial, copies of the accounts should be annexed to the copy bill served on the paying party.

13. Where allowable travelling expenses are claimed they should be shown as a disbursement and details supplied. Local travelling expenses claimed by a solicitor will not be allowed. The definition of " local " is a matter for the discretion of the taxing officer and in District Registry Cases inquiry should be made of the taxing officer concerned. While no absolute rule can be laid down, as a matter of guidance, in cases proceeding in the High Court in London, " local " will, in general, be taken to mean within a radius of 10 miles from the Royal Courts of Justice.

14. Conduct money paid to witnesses who attend a trial or hearing should be shown as part of the expenses claimed at the trial or hearing and not included in the bill at the date of the service of a subpoena.

15. Pt. IV, item 10. This item should conveniently be prefaced by a brief narrative indicating the issues, the status of the fee-earners concerned and the expense rates claimed. It is stressed that this statement should be short and succinct; the assessment of an allowance which depends partly on an arithmetical computation and partly on a judgment of value is not assisted by prolixity which may lead to a reduction in the amount allowed for taxation. The narrative should be followed by a statement in two parts: (i) setting out a breakdown of the work done in relation to the relevant sub-paragraphs of item 10 (*a*), and (ii) a statement in relation to care and conduct under item 10 (*b*) referring to the relevant factors set out in Pt. VII (formerly Pt. X) relied on. The amount claimed for care and conduct should be expressed as a separate monetary amount as well as a percentage of the work figure. Telephone calls will be allowed as a time charge if, but only if, they stand in place of an attendance whereby material progress has been made and the time has been recorded or can otherwise be established. A notional conversion into a time charge of letters and routine telephone calls will not be accepted.

16. Charges as between a principal solicitor and a solicitor agent will continue to be dealt with on the established principle that such charges form, where appropriate, part of the principal solicitor's profit costs. Where these charges relate to the items comprised in Pts. I, II or III they should be included in their chronological order. Where they relate to work done under Pt. IV, item 10, para. (xi) they may either be included in the principal solicitor's item 10 or they may be shown as a separate item properly detailed following afterwards. Solicitors are reminded, however, that agency charges for advising the principal how to proceed are not recoverable *inter partes.*

17. Item 12. No narrative will be required for this item but on taxation the party entitled to the costs must justify the amount claimed.

18. When bills are lodged for taxation they should be supported by the relevant papers arranged in the order set out below. This requirement will be strictly applied in the Supreme Court Taxing Office and failure to observe it may result in the bill being refused or the allowance for taxation reduced. This practice may, however, vary in District Registries and where necessary guidance should be sought from the taxing officer concerned:

   (i) The bill of costs.

  (ii) A bundle comprising all civil aid certificates and amendments thereto, notices of discharge or revocation and specific legal aid authorities. Copies of the offer and acceptance of a civil aid certificate will no longer be accepted in place of a copy of the actual certificate.

 (iii) A certificate of times or a copy of the associates' certificate unless the relevant information is included in the judgment or order or the parties have agreed the times.

 (iv) A bundle comprising counsel's fee notes and accounts for other disbursements.

(v) One complete set of pleadings arranged in chronological order. Where one is available a bound copy is to be preferred. To this set should be annexed any interlocutory summonses and lists of documents.

(vi) Cases to counsel to advise with his advices; opinions and instructions to counsel to settle documents and briefs to counsel with enclosures, all arranged in chronological order.

(vii) Reports and opinions of medical and other experts arranged in chronological order.

(viii) The solicitor's correspondence and attendance notes. Files should be left intact and not for the purpose of taxation divided into different sections to relate to different portions of the bill.

(ix) Any additional papers should be bundled and so labelled.

TABLE

1. *Assimilation of Appendix 2 Items*

After April 1979 Item	Prior to April 1979 Items
1	1, 2, 3, 4 (*b*), 6 (*a*), 6 (*b*).
2	5, 13, 14 (*a*), 14 (*b*), 15, 40, 41.
3	6 (*c*), 7, 8, 9, 10, 11, 12 (*a*), 12 (*b*), 16, 22 (*a*), 22 (*b*), 22 (*c*), 25 (*a*), 25 (*b*), 25 (*c*), 28, Pt. 30, 72, 73, 74, 75, 76, 77, 78, 79.
4	82 (*a*), 82 (*b*).
5	No corresponding item.
6	19, 20 (*a*), 20 (*b*), 21, 32, 33 (*a*), 34.
7	29.
8	33 (*b*), 33 (*c*).
9	61, 62, 63, 64, 65, 66, 67, 68, 69, 70, 71.
10	23, 24 (*a*), 24 (*b*), 26 (*a–j*), 27, Pt. 30, 40, 41, 52, 53, 54, 56, 57, 60, 80, 81, 84, 86, 87, 98, 99, 100.
11	90, 91, 92, 93 (*a*), 94, 95, 96 (*a*), 96 (*b*), 97.
12	36, 37, 38, 39.

2. Items in Appendix 2 prior to April 1979 for which no item is provided in the Appendix from April 1979 4 (*a*), 17, 18, 31, 35, 42 (*a*), 42 (*b*), 43, 44, 45 (*a*), 45 (*b*), 46, 47, 48, 49, 50 (*a*), 50 (*b*), 50 (*c*), 50 (*d*), 51, 55, 58, 59, 83, 85, 88 (*a*), 88 (*b*), and 89 (*a*), 89 (*b*).

[The second Schedule has not been reproduced here.]
[1979] 1 All E.R. 958.

2126. —— —— **petitions for leave to appeal**
The following Practice Direction was issued by the House of Lords on December 7, 1978:
The Appeal Committee have determined that, where leave to brief Counsel before them has been obtained pursuant to Direction No. 8, agents will be permitted to make a charge for preparing Counsel's Brief.
Item (xvi) on p. 6 of the Forms of Bills of Costs applicable to Judicial Taxations in the House of Lords will be amended accordingly.
[1979] 1 Lloyd's Rep. 443.

2127. —— —— **work undertaken by solicitor before legal aid order issued—claim by solicitor in respect of that work**
[Legal Aid Act 1974 (c. 4), s. 28 (7).]
No payment can be authorised for work undertaken and disbursements incurred prior to the issue of a legal aid order.

R was arrested and charged with illegally importing cannabis. Three applications to the magistrates' court for a legal aid order were refused. After committal to the Crown Court, he applied to that court for a legal aid order and was informed that he would be granted such an order if he deposited £50 towards any contribution order the court might make. His solicitors were already working on his case and after depositing £50 he was issued with a legal aid order. He pleaded guilty at his trial. When his solicitors submitted their bill of costs for taxation no sums were allowed for work done prior to the issue of the legal aid order. The solicitors appealed contending that a legal aid order operated retrospectively. *Held*, no payment could be authorised for the work done and disbursements incurred by R's solicitors prior to the issue of the legal aid order. (*R.* v. *Tullett* [1975] C.L.Y. 491 considered.)

R. v. ROGERS [1979] 1 All E.R. 693, Master Matthews.

2128. Discovery—confidential documents—industrial tribunals. See SCIENCE RESEARCH COUNCIL v. NASSÉ; LEYLAND CARS (B.L. CARS) v. VYAS, § 940; BRITISH RAILWAYS BOARD v. NATARAJAN, § 913 AND JALOTA v. IMPERIAL METAL INDUSTRY (KYNOCH), § 914.

2129. —— government commercial action—whether privileged

Documents should be produced for inspection by the court if without inspection it is not possible to decide whether the balance of public interest lay for or against disclosure.

B Co. brought an action against the Bank concerning the purchase by the Bank shares held by B Co. in an attempt to help B Co.'s financial difficulties. The Bank refused to produce some documents relating to communications between the Bank and the government regarding the transaction. Foster J. upheld the claim for privilege without inspecting the documents. The Court of Appeal, after reading the documents, dismissed B Co.'s appeal. On appeal to the House of Lords, *held*, dismissing the appeal, that (1) where without inspection of the documents the court could not decide whether the balance of public interest lay for or against disclosure, the court should inspect the documents; (2) on inspection, the documents contained no such evidence necessary for disposing fairly of the case; that their relevance was of little significance so as not to override the public service objections. *Per* Lords Keith and Scarman: Where the court inspects a document for which Crown privilege was claimed, there should be a right to appeal before the document is produced. (Dictum of Lord Reid in *Conway* v. *Rimmer* [1968] C.L.Y. 3098 applied.)

BURMAH OIL CO. v. GOVERNOR AND COMPANY OF THE BANK OF ENGLAND [1979] 3 W.L.R. 722, H.L.

2130. —— medical reports—power to impose conditions

[R.S.C., Ord. 24, rr. 9, 13 (1).]

Although a party to an action has prima facie an unrestricted right to inspect the other party's documents, the court can impose conditions to restrict inspection where there is a real risk of disclosure being used for a collateral purpose.

The Church of Scientology brought libel actions against the Department of Health and Social Security and two of its officers, over various letters written by the Department to foreign health authorities and the press about the Scientologists' treatment of mentally sick members. Amongst the Department's documents were medical records of patients and letters written about the Scientologists. The Department objected to disclosure on the grounds of confidentiality. The master restricted disclosure of the letters to the Scientologists' solicitors and counsel, to be used only for the conduct of the action, and of the medical reports to a registered medical practitioner who had undertaken not to disclose their contents. The Scientologists appealed. The Department argued that the Scientologists had begun many actions to suppress their critics and that they would harass the makers of the documents. *Held*, allowing the appeal, that the court had the power to restrict inspection under its inherent jurisdiction to prevent abuse of the process, and in the present case there was a real risk of harassment. However, the terms imposed would be altered and substituted by terms agreed between the parties. (*Alterskye* v. *Scott* (1948) C.L.C. 7656, *Riddick* v. *Thames Board Mills* [1977] C.L.Y. 1368 and *McIvor* v. *Southern Health and Social Services Board, Northern Ireland* [1978] C.L.Y. 2356 considered.)

CHURCH OF SCIENTOLOGY OF CALIFORNIA v. DEPARTMENT OF HEALTH AND SOCIAL SECURITY [1979] 1 W.L.R. 723, C.A.

2131. Evidence. See EVIDENCE.

2132. Exchange controls

The Lord Chancellor's Department has issued the following notice dated November 8, 1979:

1. With certain qualifications, the Treasury have exempted from the provisions of the Exchange Control Act 1947 any payment to or for the credit of or by order or on behalf of persons resident outside the scheduled territories. The major qualification is that the controls have not been lifted in respect of any person resident in Southern Rhodesia.

2. Despite the lifting of exchange controls, a plaintiff must continue to indorse the writ that payment by the defendant should be made into court where the plaintiff, or the person on whose behalf the payment is made, is resident outside the scheduled territories. This is required by R.S.C., Ord. 6, r. 2, and must be observed until such time as the rule and the various prescribed forms of writ are amended.

3. Because of the lifting of exchange controls, R.S.C., Ord. 22, r. 9, and C.C.R., Ord. 46, r. 12 (payment to the plaintiff of money in court); R.S.C., Ord. 45, r. 2 (payment by the defendant under a judgment); R.S.C., Ord. 46, r. 7 (payment of the proceeds of execution); and R.S.C., Ord. 49, r. 7 (order against a garnishee) apply only to cases where the plaintiff is resident in Southern Rhodesia. Further, the Accountant-General has directed, and now requires, that the forms currently used in connection with court funds, and in particular Forms 2, 10, 11 and 13, PF2 and PF3 should be adapted to the current situation by inserting in place of the words " outside the scheduled territories," wherever they appear, the words " in Southern Rhodesia."

2133. Fees

SUPREME COURT FEES (AMENDMENT) ORDER 1979 (No. 968 (L. 12)) [10p], made under the Supreme Court of Judicature (Consolidation) Act 1925 (c. 49), s. 213, the Companies Act 1948 (c. 38), s. 365 (3) and the Public Offices Fees Act 1879 (c. 58), ss. 2, 3; operative on September 3, 1979; increases the fee payable on the issue of a writ or other originating process in the High Court by adding to the existing fee.

2134. —— accident cases—new scales

The following Practice Direction was issued by the Chief Taxing Master on October 30, 1979:

The list of counsel's fees which was last increased in April 1975 has been the subject of discussion between the Chief Taxing Master and the Senate of the Inns of Court and the Bar. New fees relating to such cases will come into operation in respect of instructions and briefs delivered on or after December 1, 1979. The new list is set out below. The Masters of the Supreme Court Taxing Office have said that the fees in the new list would be proper to be allowed upon taxation in the normal run of such cases where the item has been dealt with fully. Each fee is intended to cover any necessary perusal of papers in connection with the item. A lower fee may, however, be appropriate where the item has not been dealt with comprehensively, was unusually simple, or where more than one item has been dealt with simultaneously. If a higher fee has been agreed it will need to be justified upon taxation, as indeed will any fee which is claimed whether included in the list or not.

INTERLOCUTORY FEES: REVISED SCALES FROM DECEMBER 1, 1979

QUEEN'S BENCH DIVISION

ITEMS	*Personal injury cases*	*Running down cases*
Statement of claim	£25	£18
Defence without counterclaim	£20	£15

QUEEN'S BENCH DIVISION ITEMS	*Personal injury cases*	*Running down cases*
Defence plain admission	£ 8	£ 8
Particulars, request and answers	£10	£10
Reply with or without defence to counterclaim	£15	£12
Third party notice (not to stand as statement of claim)	£15	£15
Interrogatories and answers	£20	£20
Advice on evidence	£25	£25
Opinion (including opinion on appeal)	£25	£25
Opinion on liability	£25	£25
Opinion on quantum	£25	£25
Opinion on liability and quantum	£35	£35
Notice of appeal to Court of Appeal and counter notice	£25	£25
Brief on summons before Master	£20	£20

Conference fees

Queen's Counsel	£20 for first ½ hour, £15	} for each succeeding
Junior Counsel	£10 for first ½ hour, £ 8	} half hour

(1979) 123 S.J. 772.

2135. Foreign judgment. See CONFLICT OF LAWS.

2136. Funds

SUPREME COURT FUNDS (AMENDMENT) RULES 1979 (No. 106 (L.3)) [10p], made under the Administration of Justice Act 1965 (c. 2), s. 7 (1); operative on March 1, 1979; raise the rate of interest allowed on money in a short-term investment account to 12½ per cent. per annum.

2137. Industrial tribunals. See EMPLOYMENT; TRADE AND INDUSTRY; TRADE UNIONS.

2138. Injunction—availability—sporting events

[Can.] It has been *held*, that an injunction lies only to restrain injuries to property, the infringement of rights capable of being enforced at law or in equity, or to prevent fraud by a majority of an association on a minority. Here, a baseball club protested against a ruling of an association of which it was a member. It was held not to have any rights in the property of the association, or other rights which could be enforced. The court will not interfere in a sporting event or reverse the decision of officials, particularly when such a decision is based upon highly technical points of eligibility: WEIR *v.* SASKATCHEWAN A.S.A. (1970) 90 D.L.R. (3d) 707, Sask.Q.B.

2139. —— breach of negative covenant—jurisdiction

[N.Z.] Since 1946 A and R had been in contractual relationship as freezing company and exporter respectively. The current contract between the parties was to run for 20 years from October 1968 and provided that either party could request amendments and submit such requests to arbitration on certain conditions at three-yearly intervals. In 1974–5 A was taken over and subsequently merged: instead of waiting to exercise its right to arbitration in October 1977, A purported to determine or repudiate the contract at three days' notice in October 1976. The contract provided, *inter alia*, that A would not handle stock on behalf of anyone apart from B unless compelled by a competent authority so to do. R sought an injunction restraining A from acting in breach of the contract. *Held*, an injunction may be granted to restrain breaches of negative covenants in contracts that are in part contracts for the sale of goods even though this may amount to ordering specific performance in a roundabout way and for a long period. (*Esso Petroleum Co.* v. *Harper's Garage (Stourport)* [1967] C.L.Y. 3906 applied); THOMAS BORTHWICK *v.* SOUTH OTAGO FREEZING Co. [1978] 1 N.Z.L.R. 538, N.Z.Ct. Appeal.

2140. —— confidential information—tribal secrets. See FOSTER *v.* MOUNTFORD AND RIGBY, § 1074.

2141. —— Mareva injunction—defendants resident within jurisdiction—payment into court

P chartered their vessel, the A, to D, an English company resident within the jurisdiction, for the carriage of a cargo of sugar to Lagos. Considerable delay in discharging at Lagos was experienced, and P claimed against D for demurrage or damages for detention. D were granted a stay of the action under s. 1 of the Arbitration Act 1975, and the question arose whether a *Mareva* injunction could be granted against D, and whether the court had power to order a payment into court under s. 12 (6) (*f*) of the Arbitration Act 1950. *Held*, that (1) there was a settled practice which prevented the granting of *Mareva* injunctions against a defendant resident within the jurisdiction, and what was said to the contrary in *Rasu Maritima S.A.* v. *Pertamina* [1977] C.L.Y. 2346 was rather an indication of what the law ought to be than what it was (*The Siskina* [1977] C.L.Y. 2344 considered); (2) there was no power under s. 12 (6) (*f*) to order a payment into court in the course of an arbitration merely because the court might have made such an order as a condition of leave to defend in Ord. 14 proceedings (*The Rena K* [1978] C.L.Y. 91, *Associated Bulk Carriers* v. *Koch Shipping Inc.* [1978] C.L.Y. 2590 considered): GEBR VAN WEELDE SCHEEPVAART KANTOOR B.V. v. HOMERIC MARINE SERVICES; THE AGRABELE [1979] 2 Lloyd's Rep. 117, Lloyd J.

2142. —— —— foreign defendant with overdrawn bank account—whether assets in jurisdiction

The court has jurisdiction to grant a Mareva injunction where there is evidence of assets within the jurisdiction, and that evidence in the case of a commercial undertaking may be evidence of a bank account even though overdrawn.

The plaintiffs, shipowners, had claims against the defendants, a Panamanian corporation with no assets here save an overdrawn bank account. The plaintiffs applied for a Mareva injunction freezing the defendants' assets in the U.K., and were granted the injunction. The defendants appealed contending, *inter alia*, that as the account was overdrawn, the plaintiffs had been unable to prove the existence of assets within the jurisdiction. *Held*, dismissing the appeal, the existence of a bank account, even where overdrawn, was evidence of assets within the jurisdiction in the case of a large overdraft by a commercial undertaking.

THIRD CHANDRIS SHIPPING CORP. v. UNIMARINE S.A. [1979] 2 All E.R. 972, C.A.

2143. —— —— principles applicable

It is possible to grant a *Mareva* injunction restraining the holder of a bill of exchange from removing from the jurisdiction moneys recovered in an action on the bill, but the court ought only to do so where there is good reason to believe the debtor intends to defeat his creditor's claim by removing assets from the jurisdiction.

The plaintiffs, two Italians, sold leather goods to an English defendant company. Payment was by bills of exchange, which were subsequently dishonoured. The defendants counterclaimed for damages alleging the goods were defective. Both plaintiffs obtained summary judgment, but in one the Master granted a stay of execution. On appeal Peter Pain J. removed the stay by Jupp J., granted a stay and a *Mareva* injunction. On appeal, *held*, dismissing one and allowing the other appeal, that (1) a counterclaim for unliquidated damages was no defence to an action on the bill, nor was it a ground for granting a stay of execution; (2) though a *Mareva* injunction was a possibility in these circumstances it should not be granted unless there was good reason to suppose a debtor intended to defeat a claim by removing his assets from the jurisdiction. (Dictum of Lord Denning M.R. in *The Siskina* [1977] C.L.Y. 2344 applied.)

MONTECCHI v. SHIMCO (U.K.); NAVONE v. SAME [1979] 1 W.L.R. 1180, C.A.

2144. —— —— sale of ship

V agreed to sell their vessel, the A, to P by a contract on the Norwegian Sale Form, which provided, *inter alia*, by cl. 17 that the vessel was to be delivered in substantially the same condition as when inspected. A few days before completion of the sale, P discovered a good deal of indentation on the bottom of the A. On the date of completion, P, taking the view that there would be a considerable sum of damages due to them for breach of cl. 17, obtained a *Mareva* injunction restraining V from dealing with the $190,000 deposit which had been paid into a joint account pending completion of the sale, but gave no notice of this to V. On the same day V handed to P the delivery documents and P handed to V the money and a letter authorising the bank to release the deposit. P then advised the bank of the injunction, and the bank refused to release the money to V. V's application to discharge the injunction succeeded. On P's application for leave to appeal, *held*, (1) *Mareva* injunctions should be granted with caution and kept for proper circumstances and not extended so as to endanger the proper conduct of business; (2) the judge would not have granted the injunction if he had known all the circumstances and was right to discharge it; (3) it was right and proper that the $190,000 should not be removed except on two clear business days' notice and V's undertaking to that effect would be accepted; and this was not therefore a case where leave to appeal should be given: NEGOCIOS DEL MAR S.A. *v.* DORIC SHIPPING CORP. S.A.; THE ASSIOS [1979] 1 Lloyd's Rep. 331, C.A.

2145. —— —— transfer of assets in ordinary course of business
The plaintiffs in an action for damages had obtained a *Mareva* injunction. The court held that the fundamental purpose of the injunction was to prevent the defendants as foreign parties from causing assets to be removed from the jurisdiction in order to avoid the risk of having to satisfy any judgment which might be entered against them in a pending action. But the court would allow a variation of the injunction to allow a transfer of assets by the defendant in good faith in the ordinary course of business. In this case the court granted an application by interveners that assets frozen should be used to pay debts owing to them: IRAQI MINISTRY OF DEFENCE *v.* ARCEPEY SHIPPING CO. S.A., *The Times,* December 12, 1979, Goff J.

2146. Judgment—admission of fact—not admission of liability
[R.S.C., Ord. 27, r. 3.]
An admission of negligence is not necessarily an admission of liability, so that a plaintiff must show both components of his cause of action are admitted before he can seek to enter judgment under R.S.C., Ord. 27, r. 3.
The plaintiff, a lorry driver, sued his employers for an injury suffered when dismounting from his lorry. The defendants denied liability in their defence, but later admitted negligence in a letter to the plaintiff. The plaintiff sought an order under R.S.C., Ord. 27, r. 3, for leave to enter judgment with damages to be assessed. On appeal, *held*, allowing the appeal, that the admission was as to negligence only, not as to the plaintiff's injuries resulting from that negligence. The plaintiff could not show that both components of his cause of action were admitted. (*Blundell* v. *Rimmer* [1970] C.L.Y. 2329 followed.)
RANKINE *v.* GARTON SONS & CO. [1979] 2 All E.R. 1185, C.A.

2147. —— in default of defence—claim for Mareva injunction—whether leave should be granted
[R.S.C., Ord. 13, r. 6.] The plaintiffs applied for leave to sign judgment in default of appearance. The defendants were outside the jurisdiction and the writ had been indorsed with a claim for a *Mareva* injunction. *Held*, that in such circumstances the appropriate action was to grant the plaintiffs leave to enter judgment, notwithstanding the claim for the injunction. The court could also order that the *Mareva* injunction continue in force, after the judgment, in aid of execution. If the plaintiffs were unable to obtain a judgment without abandoning their *Mareva* injunction, a defendant could defeat the purpose of the proceedings simply by declining to enter an appearance and such conduct would be an abuse of process of the court: STEWART CHARTERING *v.* C. & O. MANAGEMENTS S.A., *The Times,* December 29, 1979, Robert Goff J.

2148. —— —— form of indorsement
The following Practice Direction was issued by the Queen's Bench Division on May 9, 1979:
Having regard to the abolition of the requirement for the indorsement of

service on the writ of summons, and in order to ensure that a judgment in default of the service of his defence by the defendant is not entered prematurely, the following indorsement must first be signed and dated by the solicitor for the plaintiff, or by the plaintiff if he is acting in person, on the back of the court copy of the judgment which he tenders for entry against the defendant for default of service of his defence.

"I/we, solicitors for the plaintiff certify that the time for service of the defence by the defendant prescribed by the Rules of Court or extended by order of the court or the consent of the parties has expired and that the defendant is in default in serving his defence within such time.

Dated.................   ....
                                       Solicitors for the Plaintiff."

[1979] 1 W.L.R. 851; [1979] 2 All E.R. 1062.

2149. —— —— **motion to set aside—court acting without jurisdiction.** See MIDLAND BANK TRUST CO. *v.* GREEN (No. 3), § 1399.

2150. —— **variation—parties given leave to apply pending House of Lords decision —leave sought on different decision**

On April 21, 1978, Latey J. gave judgment for the plaintiff in her claim for damages for personal injuries in the sum of £8,250, being £7,750 as to general damages for pain suffering and loss of amenity and £500 as to damages for reduced competitiveness in the labour market (see [1978] C.L.Y. 737). No interest was awarded on general damages following the guidelines laid down by the Court of Appeal in *Cookson* v. *Knowles* [1977] C.L.Y. 735a, but full account was taken of the effect of inflation. Since the plaintiff's appeal in *Cookson* v. *Knowles* had already been heard in the House of Lords at the date of the trial, to take account of any possible changes in the law relating to interest and the effects of inflation on general damages Latey J., with the agreement of the parties, gave liberty to apply, to enable the parties to apply to the court following the publication of their Lordships' opinions in *Cookson* v. *Knowles*. In the event, their Lordships in *Cookson* v. *Knowles* [1978] C.L.Y. 713 declined to express any views as to the question of interest on damages for non-economic loss in personal injury actions. On November 2, 1978, in the case of *Pickett* v. *British Rail Engineering* [1979] C.L.Y. 656, the House of Lords disapproved the dictum of Lord Denning M.R. in *Cookson* v. *Knowles* [1977] C.L.Y. 735a that interest should not be awarded on general damages for pain suffering and loss of amenity in personal injury actions and re-instated the guidelines laid down in *Jefford* v. *Gee* [1970] C.L.Y. 603. The plaintiff's solicitors thereupon applied to the court for interest upon the award of £7,750 general damages made by Latey J. on April 21, 1978. *Held,* dismissing the application, that since Latey J. had expressly limited the liberty to apply to take account of any change in the law which might result from the decision of the House of Lords in *Cookson* v. *Knowles*, which was then known to be imminent, the plaintiff was unable, following the decision which was in fact inconclusive on the question of interest, to await for a further case to be decided, possibly at some very distant date in the future, which might reverse the Court of Appeal's decision on interest in *Cookson's* case, in order to found an application for interest to be added to general damages in the instant case; it was purely fortuitous that the decision in *Pickett* v. *British Rail Engineering* had been given within a comparatively short time after the decision of the House of Lords in *Cookson's* case. Applying the maxim *interest reipublicae ut sit finis litium* the defendants were entitled to consider their file was closed after *Cookson's* case had finally been concluded. In the circumstances, therefore, it was unnecessary to decide whether, in any event, "liberty to apply" could enable the court to add interest to damages or alter an award of general damages after judgment had been given, although on behalf of the defendants it had been argued that to do so would, in effect, be to vary a final judgment, which could not be permitted. (*Cristel* v. *Cristel* (1951) C.L.C. 4563 applied): DENT *v.* LEVI STRAUSS (U.K.), May 10, 1978, Balcombe J., Leeds. (*Ex rel. S. Hawkesworth, Esq., Barrister.*)

2151. Judgment debts

JUDGMENT DEBTS (RATE OF INTEREST) ORDER 1979 (No. 1382 (L. 19)) [10p], made under the Administration of Justice Act 1970 (c. 31), s. 44; operative on December 3, 1979; increases to 12½ per cent. per annum the rate of interest on judgment debts under s. 17 of the Judgments Act 1838.

2152. Judicial statistics

The annual report of judicial statistics for 1978 has been published. It contains statistics relating to the House of Lords, Court of Appeal, the High Court and the Judicial Committee of the Privy Council. The report is available from HMSO (Cmnd. 7627) [£4.25].

2153. Juries. See JURIES.

2154. Jurisdiction—service out of jurisdiction—tort—telex sent from abroad

[R.S.C. Ord. 11, r. 1 (1) (h).]

The sending of a telex message from outside the jurisdiction to England, containing allegedly fraudulent or negligent misrepresentation, may result in a tort being committed at the place of receipt of the telex; accordingly it would be a tort committed within the jurisdiction.

The plaintiffs, commodity brokers, negotiated to purchase a large quantity of sugar via some American brokers; in accordance with brokers' practice, confirmation was required of a bank that the transaction was bona fide. The defendant bank by telex from Nassau confirmed the respectability of the American brokers and the existence of documents proving the availability of the sugar, the messages being sent to the plaintiffs of their bank in London. In fact the sugar did not exist. Initially the plaintiffs issued proceedings against the bank for negligent misrepresentation; leave to serve outside the jurisdiction was refused on the ground that the action was founded upon a tort committed outside the jurisdiction. The plaintiffs did not pursue that action but later began new proceedings alleging fraudulent misrepresentation by the bank. Donaldson J. refused leave to serve outside the jurisdiction on similar grounds. *Held*, that the substance of the alleged tort was committed where the messages were received, that is in London; that accordingly the court had jurisdiction to give leave to serve the bank outside the jurisdiction (but in its discretion the court refused leave on the grounds that the plaintiffs had adduced no satisfactory evidence as to their loss). (*Original Blouse Co.* v. *Bruck Mills* [1964] C.L.Y. 534 applied; *Cordova Land Co.* v. *Victor Brothers* [1966] C.L.Y. 9912, distinguished.)

DIAMOND v. BANK OF LONDON AND MONTREAL [1979] 2 W.L.R. 228, C.A.

2155. Legal aid

LEGAL ADVICE AND ASSISTANCE (FINANCIAL CONDITIONS) REGULATIONS 1979 (No. 166) [10p], made under the Legal Aid Act 1974 (c. 4), ss. 4, 20; operative on April 6, 1979; increases to £35 a week the disposable income above which a person receiving legal advice and assistance under the 1974 Act is required to pay a contribution, and makes consequential amendments to the scale of contributions.

LEGAL AID (GENERAL) (AMENDMENT) REGULATIONS 1979 (No. 263) [20p], made under the Legal Aid Act 1974, s. 20; operative on April 6, 1979; amend further the 1971 (No. 62) Regulations by, *inter alia,* empowering local and area secretaries to approve applications for legal aid in all cases.

LEGAL AID (ASSESSMENT OF RESOURCES) (AMENDMENT) REGULATIONS 1979 (No. 280) [10p], made under the Legal Aid Act 1974, ss. 11, 20; operative on April 6, 1979; further amend S.I. 1960 No. 1471 by (1) removing the disregard of £104 of income and making consequential amendments; (2) specifying the employment expenses which may be deducted from income; (3) increasing the deductions from income for dependants; and (4) removing the deductions from capital for dependants and low income.

LEGAL ADVICE AND ASSISTANCE (AMENDMENT) REGULATIONS 1979 (No. 281) [10p], made under the Legal Aid Act 1974, ss. 11, 20; operative on April 6, 1979; further amend S.I. 1973 No. 349 by increasing the allowances for a spouse, dependent child or dependent relative when assessing disposable income.

LEGAL ADVICE AND ASSISTANCE (FINANCIAL CONDITIONS) (No. 2) REGULATIONS 1979 (No. 350) [10p], made under the Legal Aid Act 1974, ss. 1, 20; operative on April 6, 1979; increase the disposable income limit for the availability of legal advice and assistance to £75 a week and increase the disposable capital limit to £600.

LEGAL AID (FINANCIAL CONDITIONS) REGULATIONS 1979 (No. 351) [10p], made under the Legal Aid Act 1974, ss. 6, 9, 20; operative on April 6, 1979; increase the financial limits of eligibility for legal aid so that legal aid is available to those with disposable incomes of up to £3,600 per annum and disposable capital of up to £2,500.

LEGAL AID IN CRIMINAL PROCEEDINGS (FEES AND EXPENSES) (AMENDMENT) REGULATIONS 1979 (No. 360) [20p], made under the Legal Aid Act 1974, s. 39; operative on May 1, 1979; amend S.I. 1968 No. 1230 in relation to the operation of The Law Society's function as a taxing authority in the case of magistrates' courts where a counsel is instructed although the legal aid does provide for the services of a counsel.

LEGAL ADVICE AND ASSISTANCE (FINANCIAL CONDITIONS) (No. 4) REGULATIONS 1979 (No. 1164) [10p], made under the Legal Aid Act 1974, ss. 4, 20; operative on November 12, 1979; increases from £35 to £40 a week the disposable income above which a person receiving legal advice and assistance under the 1974 Act is required to pay a contribution.

LEGAL AID (FINANCIAL CONDITIONS) (No. 2) REGULATIONS 1979 (No. 1394) [10p], made under the Legal Aid Act 1974, ss. 6, 9 (2), 20, as amended by the Legal Aid Act 1979 (c. 26); operative on November 12, 1979; increase the income limits for eligibility for legal aid to those with disposable incomes of not more than £4,075 a year and available without payment of a contribution to those with disposable incomes of not more than £1,700 a year.

LEGAL ADVICE AND ASSISTANCE (FINANCIAL CONDITIONS) (No. 3) REGULATIONS 1979 (No. 1395) [10p], made under the Legal Aid Act 1974, ss. 1, 20, as amended by the Legal Aid Act 1979; operative on November 12, 1979; increase the disposable income limit for eligibility for legal advice and assistance from £75 to £85 a week.

2156. —— annual reports

The Lord Chancellor has laid before Parliament the 28th Annual Reports of the Law Society and of the Lord Chancellor's Advisory Committee on legal aid. The reports cover the operation and finance of Pt. 1 of the Legal Aid Act 1974 for 1977–78 and are available from HMSO [£1·75].

2157. —— costs of counterclaim

[Legal Aid Act 1974 (c. 4), s. 13 (1); Legal Aid (Costs of Successful Un-assisted Parties) Regulations 1964, reg. 2; Legal Aid (General) Regulations 1971, reg. 6 (1) (*b*), (2) (*b*).] The defendants acted as managers for the plaintiffs, semi-professional singers. The plaintiffs started an action seeking a declaration that a contract entered into on the defendant's persuasion, and other transactions, were void. They also sought a full account of all moneys received by the defendants. The defendants obtained legal aid and counter-claimed that the transactions were invalid; they also claimed a *quantum meruit.* The action was settled and the plaintiffs applied for payment of the costs of the counterclaim out of the legal aid fund. *Held,* awarding costs to the plaintiffs, the counterclaim constituted a separate proceeding under s. 13 (3) so the court could make an order if it were just and equitable and no severe hardship would be caused. Severe hardship could not be caused because the costs of a counterclaim were limited to those additional to the costs of the claim. (*Saner* v. *Bilton* (1878) 7 Ch.D. 815). The costs would therefore be limited to the *quantum meruit* issue which would be very small; the costs on issues common to the claim and the counterclaim could not be apportioned. This applies to simple cases, a special order should be made if the rule would produce an unfair result: MILLICAN v. TUCKER (1979) 123 S.J. 860, Browne-Wilkinson J.

2158. —— successful unassisted defendant—legally aided plaintiff—defendant's costs out of legal aid fund—whether " just and equitable "

[Legal Aid Act 1974 (c. 4), s. 13.]

The legal aid fund had brought the defendant before the court and although the cost of the defendant came from public funds it was " just and equitable " that the defendant's costs should come out of the legal aid fund.

Per curiam: Where such an order is made in favour of an unassisted party, 10 weeks' notice should be given to the legal aid committee to enable them to appear and object to the proposed order.

M was granted a legal aid certificate to bring proceedings against his chief constable claiming declarations that he was entitled to legal representation in police disciplinary proceedings that were being brought against him. His claim and subsequent appeal to the Court of Appeal were both dismissed. The defendant applied for costs to be paid out of the legal aid fund under the Legal Aid Act 1974, s. 13. The Court of Appeal granted the order for costs but susended taxation for 21 days to allow The Law Society to apply to the court. *Held*, it was " just and equitable " that the defendant's costs in the Court of Appeal should come out of the legal aid fund.

MAYNARD v. OSMOND (No. 2) [1979] 1 W.L.R. 31, C.A.

2159. —— transfer of matrimonial home—whether Law Society entitled to charge
[Legal Aid Act 1974 (c. 4), s. 9 (6).] Property which is the subject of a property adjustment order under s. 24 of the Matrimonial Causes Act 1973 can be charged as " property recovered or preserved " in proceedings under s. 9 (6) of the Legal Aid Act 1974. Appeal dismissed and leave given to appeal to the House of Lords: HANLON v. THE LAW SOCIETY, *The Times*, December 5, 1979, C.A.

2160. —— unassisted parties' costs—application for payment out of legal aid fund
[Legal Aid Act 1974 (c. 4), ss. 8 (1) (e), 13.] The defendants applied for costs to be enforced against the unsuccessful, legally aided plaintiffs and for costs to be paid out of the legal aid fund. *Held*, with regard to their financial state, the plaintiffs' contributions would, of necessity be modest, but should be divided in per capita shares between the defendants, who should receive all the party and party costs incurred in excess of the sum recoverable from the personal plaintiffs (*Nowotnik* v. *Nowotnik* [1965] C.L.Y. 3180 as modified by *Hanning* v. *Maitland* (*No.* 2) [1970] C.L.Y. 2313, followed): MILLER v. LITTNER (1979) 123 S.J. 473, Oliver J.

2161. Legal Aid Act 1979 (c. 26)
This Act amends certain Acts relating to legal aid and legal advice and assistance.

Pt. I (ss. 1–5) provides for England and Wales: s. 1 extends assistance to representation in any proceedings before a court or tribunal, or in connection with a statutory inquiry; s. 2 imposes financial limits on the prospective cost of advice and assistance; s. 3 relates to contributions from persons receiving advice and assistance; s. 4 relates to contributions from persons receiving legal aid; s. 5 imposes a charge on property recovered for persons receiving legal aid.

Pt. II (ss. 6–10) provides for Scotland: s. 6 extends assistance to representation in any proceedings before a court or tribunal, or in connection with a statutory inquiry; s. 7 places financial limits on the prospective cost of advice and assistance; s. 8 relates to contributions from persons receiving advice and assistance; s. 9 relates to contributions from persons receiving legal aid; s. 10 provides for payments out of property recovered for persons receiving legal aid.

Pt. III (ss. 11–14) contains general provisions: s. 11 provides for increases attributable to this Act to be defrayed out of moneys provided by Parliament; s. 12 contains definitions, and makes special provision for Scotland; s. 13 contains minor amendments and repeals; s. 14 gives the short title. Except for ss. 1 (2) and 6 (2), and Sched. 1, paras. 8 and 19, the Act does not extend to Northern Ireland.

The Act received the Royal Assent on April 4, 1979, and comes into force on days to be appointed.

2162. —— commencement
LEGAL AID ACT 1979 (COMMENCEMENT NO. 1) ORDER 1979 (No. 756 (C. 17)) [10p], made under the Legal Aid Act 1979 (c. 26), s. 14 (3); brings into operation on July 20, 1979, s. 4 of and Sched. 1, para. 13, and part of Sched. 2 to the 1979 Act. S. 4 (1) amends s. 9 (1) of the Legal Aid Act 1974 to enable

the Lord Chancellor to prescribe the maximum contribution payable by those receiving legal aid and to enable him to prescribe different maxima for different classes of case.

2163. Medical reports—access proceedings—disagreement between solicitors and psychiatrist over report

The plaintiff was a consultant psychiatrist and was asked by the defendant firm of solicitors to write a report on Mrs. X for use in access proceedings to her children. He was asked to prepare a report " on her present condition and whether in your opinion her recovery would be assisted by resuming access to her children." The solicitors undertook to pay the reasonable fees of such a report. The plaintiff wrote the report but the defendant firm asked him to exclude certain passages from it in which he had stated that " access should not be enforced against the wishes of the children themselves, who are in a position to express their views." These remarks were considered by the defendant firm of solicitors to be prejudicial. The psychiatrist felt, however, that it would be wrong to exclude certain aspects of a report which were less palatable to those requesting it and refused to amend his report. The solicitors in turn declined to pay his fee saying that he was in breach of the terms of the contract. The fee was agreed to be a reasonable one and it therefore fell to the court to consider whether or not the psychiatrist could insist on his fee or whether the solicitors were right in asking for the report to be amended. *Held,* finding for the psychiatrist, that in the court's view the report was prepared for the purposes of access proceedings. It was therefore right that the report should concern itself with the relationship between a parent and the children. The court felt that the terms of reference allowed the doctor to express the views that he did and it was also against the submission by the defendant firm that he had dealt with matters not strictly medical, but merely an opinion on how the court should approach the question of access. The two matters were entirely interacting and the doctor was being quite proper in his decision refusing to amend the report. It would be of no assistance to the courts if doctors were encouraged to abandon their professional approach and write reports designed to achieve particular objects at the behest of the patient or anyone else: NOBLE *v.* ROBERT THOMPSON & PARTNERS, July 20, 1979; Judge Curtis-Raleigh; Bloomsbury and Marylebone County Ct. (*Ex rel. Messrs. Le Brasseur & Oakley, Solicitors.*)

2164. —— examination—need for presence of party's consultant

The court will not normally make it a condition of the plaintiff's submission to a medical examination by the defendant's medical expert that the plaintiff's consultant should be present; a consultant should be given credit for being fair in conducting the examination. Good reasons will have to be shown to the court for departing from the usual practice. The court should hesitate long before permitting any addition to the time and expense of personal injury actions: HALL *v.* AVON AREA MEDICAL AUTHORITY, *The Times,* December 7, 1979, C.A.

2165. Order 14—building contract—whether leave to defend should be given

In 1977, P entered into two contracts for the construction of two buildings, B1 and B2. In August 1978, P sent in invoices for £52,060 in respect of B1 and £17,269 in respect of B2. D resisted the claims on the ground that they had counterclaims in respect of both contracts, in the case of B1 the estimates ranging between £15,000 and £43,000, the latter sum being acknowledged to be in respect of a drastic and expensive remedy. On P's application for summary judgment under R.S.C., Ord. 14, *held,* on appeal to the Court of Appeal, that (1) in respect of B1, it was not possible to say that there was not at least an arguable case that the seemingly exaggerated larger sum of £43,000 would be needed to effect the necessary repair, and accordingly P were only entitled to leave to sign judgment for the difference between the £52,060 claimed and £43,000; (2) in respect of B2, it was right to say that there was an identifiable sum in respect of which judgment could be given, and to refuse to allow as an equitable set-off against P's claim the shadowy amount due in respect of alleged breaches of the contract: SABLE CONTRACTORS *v.* BLUETT SHIPPING [1979] 2 Lloyd's Rep. 33, C.A.

2166. —— **rent arrears—defence that landlord not complying with covenant to repair**

There were three Ord. 14 summonses in claims for arrears of rent. The defendants contended that they should have unconditional leave to defend. They did not dispute the amount of arrears, but alleged breaches of the landlord's covenants to repair. L had performed the repairs himself, and cross-claimed for his expenditure. O and G had filed affidavits alleging that the repairs had not been carried out and that they therefore had claims against A " for an amount of damages in excess of the amount claimed by way of rent." *Held*, giving all three defendants unconditional leave to defend, the right of recoupment applied to arrears of rent as well as future rent. In showing a defence for Ord. 14 purposes, a defendant has to quantify his set-off (if any), otherwise the court will not know whether it meets all or only a part of the plaintiff's claim. However, his lordship had an uneasy feeling that O and G had simply not presented their cases as well as they could have done, and as a defendant should not be shut out from defending unless it was very clear that he has no case, unconditional leave to defend would be granted to all three (*Lee-Parker* v. *Izzet* [1971] C.L.Y. 6656 applied): Asco DEVELOPMENTS v. GORDON (1978) 248 E.G. 683, Megarry V.-C.

2167. Order 38—disclosure of expert evidence—purpose of rule

[R.S.C., Ord. 38, r. 38.]

The purpose of R.S.C., Ord. 38 is to save expense by dispensing with the calling of experts, and by avoiding parties being taken by surprise, and an order under r. 38 that the substance of expert evidence to be adduced be disclosed should normally be made. The " substance " of the evidence is not confined to factual descriptions but should include the expert's conclusions.

OLLETT v. BRISTOL AEROJET (NOTE) [1979] 1 W.L.R. 1197, Ackner J.

2168. Orders—time for drawing up

The following Practice Direction was issued by the Queen's Bench Division on July 16, 1979:

Attention is especially drawn to the practice that the Master will usually *expressly* specify a time within which certain classes of orders must be drawn up, as, for example, orders relating to the approval of settlements of actions or claims by or on behalf of infants or patients, orders for substituted service and orders for payment into court, and in such cases of course the orders must be drawn up within the time specified by the Master.

On the other hand, for the convenience of the parties and the court, it has been decided that where any order required by the Rules of Court to be drawn does *not* expressly direct that it must be drawn up within a specified time, the parties should be relieved of the obligation to get the leave of the Master before drawing up such an order.

Accordingly, the following words in line 7 of para. (1) of this Practice Direction shall be deleted, namely, " or, if no time is specified, 21 days after the making of the order."

This relaxation of the present practice does not absolve the parties from their obligation to draw up such an order as soon after the making thereof as is reasonably practical.

2169. Parties—plaintiff—valid foreign title to sue—action to safeguard property of missing person. See KAMOUH v. ASSOCIATED ELECTRICAL INDUSTRIES INTER-NATIONAL, § 1662.

2170. Pleading—probate proceedings—plea of want of knowledge or approval

The plaintiff sought to propound a purported will under which she was the sole residuary beneficiary. The third defendant by counterclaim asked the court to pronounce for an earlier will under which he had been named sole residuary beneficiary. Undue influence was not pleaded. The plaintiff applied for a number of allegations to be struck out in accordance with R.S.C., Ord.. 76, r. 9 (3), which debars a party pleading want of knowledge and approval from alleging matters in support which would be relevant in pleas of, *inter alia,* undue influence. *Held*, if the plaintiff's contention was correct the defendant must either abandon completely a number of crucially important allegations or plead undue influence when he had little or no personal knowledge of the circumstances surrounding the execution of the will. An allegation should not be treated as "relevant" for the rule unless, if established, it would prove the relevant alternative plea, either solely or in conjunction with other pleaded facts. The allegations would not be struck out: *Re* STOTT, DECD.; KLOUDA *v.* LLOYDS BANK (1979) 123 S.J. 422, Slade J.

2171. Precedent—House of Lords decisions—Privy Council and colonial courts. See DE LASALA *v.* DE LASALA, § 2200.

2172. Privilege—accident inquiry report

An accident report prepared by defendants to a claim for personal injuries may be disclosable unless its dominant purpose was for it to be used by the defendants' legal advisers.

W, a British Rail employee, died as the result of a collision on their railways. The Board procured a "joint inquiry report" to be prepared, incorporating witness statements to be sent to the railway inspectorate; such report contained the statement that it was finally to be sent to the Board's solicitor for his advice. In W's widow's action against the Board, she sought discovery of the report, but the Board, who denied liability, claimed that it was the subject of legal professional privilege. Donaldson J. and a majority of the Court of Appeal, upheld such claim. *Held,* allowing the plaintiff's appeal, that the interests of justice and the public strongly required the disclosure of such report since it probably contained the best evidence as to the cause of the accident and that such interests should only be overridden if the dominant purpose of the report's preparation was for its submission for legal advice; that, at very most, such purpose was here only equal to the purpose of ensuring the safety on the railways. (*Birmingham and Midland Omnibus Co.* v. *London and North Western Railway* [1917] 3 K.B. 850, *Ankin* v. *London and North Eastern Railways* [1930] 1 K.B. 527 and *Ogden* v. *London Electric Railway Co.* (1933) 49 T.L.R. 542 overruled; dictum of Lord Strathclyde in *Whitehill* v. *Glasgow Corporation* (1915) S.C. 1015 at 1017 applied.)

WAUGH *v.* BRITISH RAILWAYS BOARD [1979] 3 W.L.R. 150, H.L.

2173. Privy Council. See PRIVY COUNCIL PRACTICE.

2174. Probate. See EXECUTORS AND ADMINISTRATORS.

2175. Representative action—tort—suit by minority shareholder—jurisdiction

The court has jurisdiction, in certain carefully defined circumstances, to entertain a representative action by a plaintiff suing on behalf of a class where the cause of action of the plaintiff and each member of the class is alleged to be a separate cause of action in tort.

A company (Newman) proposed to acquired the assets of another company and issued a circular to the shareholders explaining the proposal. The proposal was passed by a majority of shareholders, but the plaintiffs, a company with a minority shareholding in Newman voted against the resolution. The plaintiff brought an action alleging conspiracy against the chairman and claiming damages. The action as orginally framed was in the form of a derivative action claiming damages on behalf of Newman; it was also framed to entitle the plaintiff to bring a personal claim for damages against the defendants. The plaintiff proposed to amend the statement of claim so as to bring a representative action on behalf of the shareholders claiming a declaration they were entitled to damages, and damages on their behalf. *Held,* the court had jurisdiction in certain circumstances to entertain a representative action by a plaintiff suing on behalf of a class where the cause of action of each member was alleged to be a separate cause in tort, and the court would allow the amendments in this case.

PRUDENTIAL ASSURANCE CO. *v.* NEWMAN INDUSTRIES [1979] 3 All E.R. 507, Vinelott J.

2176. Rules of the Supreme Court

RULES OF THE SUPREME COURT (AMENDMENT) 1979 (No. 35) (L.1)) [25p], made under the Supreme Court of Judicature (Consolidation) Act 1925 (c. 49), s. 99 (4); operative on February 5, 1979, except for rr. 4 and 5 which come into operation on April 24, 1979; amend the Rules so as to prevent the plaintiff from obtaining a judgment in default of a defence in a summons under Ord.

86 has been served (c. 2), to allow a respondent the same time for appealing against the decision of the court below as he has, under the existing rules, for serving a respondent's notice (r. 3); to introduce a new and simpler scheme in Appendix 2 to Ord. 62 for the taxation of costs (rr. 4 and 5); to substitute new fixed costs for the basic costs allowable under Appendix 3 to Ord. 62 where the sum recovered is either £350 or between £350 and £1,200 (r. 6); and to extend Ord. 73, r. 10, so as to cover the enforcement of awards under the Arbitration Act 1975 (r. 7).

RULES OF THE SUPREME COURT (AMENDMENT NO. 2) 1979 (No. 402 (L. 5)) [25p], made under the Supreme Court of Judicature (Consolidation) Act 1925, s. 99 (4); operative on April 24, 1979; amends the R.S.C. so as: (a) to allow service by post in many situations in which personal service is required under the existing rules; (b) to change the rules in respect of joinder of parties and the enforcement of a judgment for contribution or indemnity, following the coming into force of the Civil Liability (Contribution) Act 1978; (c) to make minor changes to the rules regarding the taxing of costs; and (d) to allow two months for the service of an application for a new tenancy.

RULES OF THE SUPREME COURT (AMENDMENT NO. 3) 1979 (No. 522) [25p], made under the Supreme Court of Judicature (Consolidation) Act 1925, s. 99 (4); operative on June 7, 1979, save for rr. 4–9 which are operative on a day to be appointed; amend the R.S.C. so as to (a) raise the fees payable to examiners of the court; (b) allow a person making an affidavit to give a work address; (c) make provision for proceedings under the Arbitration Act 1979 once the "case stated" procedure under s. 21 of the Administrative Act 1950 has ceased to be available; (d) make provision for proceedings affecting the International Oil Pollution Compensation Fund; (e) amend the rules applicable to summary proceedings for possession of land so as to require Form No. 11A to be used in every case.

RULES OF THE SUPREME COURT (AMENDMENT NO. 4) 1979 (No. 1542) [40p], made under the Supreme Court of Judicature (Consolidation) Act 1925, s. 99 (4); operative on January 2, 1980; amend the Rules of the Supreme Court dealing with, *inter alia,* enforcement of exchange controls, arbitration proceedings, appeals under the Matrimonial Proceedings (Magistrates' Courts) Act 1960 and injunctions granted under the Domestic Violence and Matrimonial Proceedings Act 1976.

RULES OF THE SUPREME COURT (WRIT AND APPEARANCE) 1979 (No. 1716 (L. 23)) [£1.75], made under the Supreme Court of Judicature (Consolidation) Act 1925, s. 99 (4); operative on June 3, 1980; prescribe new forms of writ of summons and replaces the entry of appearance by acknowledgement of service. Various forms used in the Central Office and district registries and forms of writ in Admiralty actions *in rem* have been revised. A number of related changes have also been made, *inter alia,* the defendant must be served with a sealed instead of a plain copy of the writ and the form of acknowledgement will have to be returned to the court office out of which the writ was issued, except in certain circumstances.

RULES OF THE SUPREME COURT (AMENDMENT NO. 5) 1979 (No. 1725) [10p], made under the Supreme Court of Judicature (Consolidation) Act 1925, s. 99 (4); operative on January 2, 1980; remove all provisions in the Rules of the Supreme Court concerned with the enforcement of exchange controls.

2177. Sentence. See CRIMINAL LAW; MAGISTERIAL LAW.

2178. Service of process—abolition of indorsement

The following Practice Direction was issued by the Queen's Bench Division on April 20, 1979:

1. The present requirement of R.S.C., Ord. 10, r. 1 (4) for the writ of summons to be indorsed with specified particulars within three days after its service has been abolished by R.S.C. (Amendment No. 2) 1979 (S.I. 1979 No. 402 (L. 5)) as from April 24, 1979.

2. Accordingly, the following Practice Forms of Affidavits of Service should be amended by deleting therefrom para. 3 thereof, namely, Nos. PF 122 to PF 130 inclusive.

(1979) 123 S.J. 308.

2179. —— affidavits of service by post

The following Practice Direction was issued by the Queen's Bench Division on April 20, 1979:

The following Practice Forms shall, wherever applicable, be used with such variations as the circumstances of the particular case may require.

No. PF. 122A

Affidavit of Service of Writ on individual by Post

(see Ord. 10, *r.* 1 (3) (*b*))

[*Title as in action*]

I, (state name, address and description of *deponent*) MAKE OATH AND SAY AS FOLLOWS:

1. That I did serve the above-named defendant, C.D. with a true copy of the writ of summons in this action by posting the same on   day, the   day of   19   , by ordinary post first class mail in an envelope duly pre-paid and properly addressed to the said defendant at (*state the address in full*).

2. The said letter or envelope has not been returned by the Post Office through the dead letter service.

3. That in my opinion [*or in the case of posting by the plaintiff's solicitor or any employee in his firm*, in the opinion of the plaintiff] the said writ of summons so posted to the defendant will have come to his knowledge within seven days after the said date of posting thereof.

SWORN etc.

No. PF. 122B

Affidavit of Service of Writ on individual by Insertion through Letter-Box

(see Ord. 10, *r.* 1 (3) (*b*))

[*Title as in action*]

I, (state name, address and description of *deponent*) MAKE OATH AND SAY AS FOLLOWS:

1. That I did serve the above-mentioned defendant, C.D. with a true copy of the writ of summons in this action by inserting the same through the letter-box for the address of the said defendant on   day, the   day of   19   , enclosed in a sealed envelope duly and properly addressed to the said defendant at (*state the address in full*).

2. That in my opinion [*or in the case of such insertion by the plaintiff's solicitor or any employee in his firm* in the opinion of the plaintiff] the said writ of summons so inserted in the letter-box for the address of the defendant will have come to his knowledge within seven days after the said date of such insertion thereof.

SWORN etc.

No. PF. 122C

Affidavit of Service of Writ of Summons on partnership Firm by Post

(see Ord. 81, *r.* 3 (2) (*b*))

[*Title as in action*]

I, (state name, address and description of *deponent*) MAKE OATH AND SAY AS FOLLOWS:

1. That I did serve the above-named defendant firm, C.D. & Co. with a true copy of the writ of summons in this action by posting the same on the   day of   19   , by ordinary post first class mail in an envelope duly pre-paid and properly addressed to the said defendant firm at (*state the address in full of the principal place of business of the defendant firm.*).

2. The said letter or envelope has not been returned by the Post Office through the dead letter service.

3. That in my opinion [*or in the case of posting by the plaintiff's solicitor or any employee in his firm* in the opinion of the plaintiff] the said writ of

summons so posted to the above-named defendant firm will have come to the knowledge of one or more of the partners or a person having at the time of service the control or management of the partnership business there within seven days after the said date of posting thereof.
SWORN etc.

No. PF. 122D
Affidavit of Service of Writ on Body Corporate by Post
(see Ord. 65, r. 3 (2))
[*Title as in action*]

I, (state name, address and description of *deponent*) MAKE OATH AND SAY AS FOLLOWS:
1. That I did serve the above-named defendant corporation, C.D. with a true copy of the writ of summons in this section by posting the same on   day, the   day of   19 , by ordinary post first class mail in an envelope duly pre-paid and properly addressed to the said defendant corporation at (*state the address in full of the registered or principal office of defendant body corporate*).
2. The said letter or envelope has not been returned by the Post Office through the dead letter service.
3. That in my opinion [*or in the case of posting by the plaintiff's solicitor or any employee in his firm* in the opinion of the plaintiff] the said writ of summons so posted to the above-named defendant corporation will have some to the knowledge of [*the Mayor or Chairman, or Town Clerk, or other similar officer of the above-named defendant corporation referred to in R.S.C., Ord. 65, r. 3 (1), as the case may be*] within seven days after the said date of posting thereof.
SWORN etc.

No. PF. 122E
Affidavit of Service of Writ on Body Corporate by
Insertion through Letter-Box
(see Ord. 65, r. 3 (2))
[*Title as in action*]

I, (state name, address and description of *deponent*) MAKE OATH AND SAY AS FOLLOWS:
1. That I did serve the above-named defendant corporation, C.D. with a true copy of the writ of summons in this action by inserting the same through the letter-box for the address of the said defendant corporation on   day, the   day of   19 , enclosed in a sealed envelope duly and properly addressed to the said defendant corporation at (*state the address in full*).
2. That in my opinion [*or in the case of such insertion by the plaintiff's solicitor or any employee in his firm* in the opinion of the plaintiff] the said writ of summons so inserted in the letter-box for the address of the above-named defendant corporation will have come to the knowledge of [*the Mayor or Chairman, or Town Clerk, or other similar officer of the above-named defendant corporation referred to in R.S.C., Ord. 65, r. 3 (1), as the case may be*] within seven days after the said date of such insertion thereof.
SWORN etc.
(1979) 123 S.J. 308.

2180. —— substituted service—defendant out of jurisdiction
[R.S.C., Ord. 65, r. 4 (1).]
An order for substituted service cannot be made unless the defendant was within the jurisdiction at the time of issue of the writ sought to be served.
The plaintiff issued a writ against the defendant who was resident in Jersey claiming relief in respect of wrongs allegedly done to the plaintiff in Jersey. The defendant made frequent visits to England but he successfully avoided service. The plaintiff obtained an order for substituted service under Ord. 65, r. 4, and served the writ upon the London office of a company of which the defendant was a director. The defendant succeeded in having set aside the order for substituted service. *Held*, dismissing the plaintiff's appeal, that since the

defendant had been out of the country at the date of issue of the writ, there was no jurisdiction to order substituted service thereof. (*Porter* v. *Freudenberg* [1915] 1 K.B. 857 and *Laurie* v. *Carroll* [1960] C.L.Y. 2573 followed.)
MYERSON v. MARTIN [1979] 3 All E.R. 667, C.A.

2181. Service out of jurisdiction—agency agreement—whether agreement governed by English law. See ATLANTIC UNDERWRITING AGENCIES AND DAVID GALE (UNDERWRITING) v. COMPAGNIA DI ASSICURAZIONE DI MILANO S.P.A., § 313.

2182. —— industrial tribunals—whether jurisdiction to hear complaint
[Industrial Tribunals (Labour Relations) Regulations 1974 (S.I. 1974 No. 1386) Sched., rr. 3, 14 (1) (e) (f).]
A valid service is effected outside the United Kingdom by sending the document either to the address given in the originating application as being that of the respondent or, if a company, to that company's registered office. The tribunal has jurisdiction to hear a complaint against a non-resident company who carries on business in the United Kingdom.
The respondents were a Dutch company registered in Amsterdam. The originating application stated their address in Amsterdam and a copy was sent to that address. Solicitors acting on behalf of the respondents asked for an extension of time for entering a notice of appearance on the ground that there were High Court proceedings between these same parties. The chairman extended the rule generally and postponed the tribunal hearing until after the High Court hearing. In the High Court proceedings, the respondents entered an appearance and defence stating that the address given in the originating application was that of their registered office and that they had carried on business in the U.K. The employees were awarded damages for wrongful dismissal. They then applied for the tribunal to hear their complaints. The respondents were directed to enter an appearance within 14 days but it was impossible to give notice of that decision to them in this country. The tribunal was asked whether there had been a valid service of the originating application and whether they had jurisdiction to hear the complaint. *Held,* that (1) a valid service could be effected by sending the documents either to the address given in the originating application as that of the respondent or, of a company, to its registered office; (2) there had been a valid service; (3) where a person had carried on business in the U.K. there is jurisdiction to hear complaints against that person.
KNULTY v. ELOC ELECTRO-OPTIEK AND COMMUNICATIE B.V. [1979] I.C.R. 827, Industrial Tribunal.

2183. Set-off—rent arrears—building in disrepair—unliquidated damages. See BRITISH ANZANI (FELIXSTOWE) v. INTERNATIONAL MARINE MANAGEMENT (U.K.), § 1633.

2184. Stay of proceedings—criminal prosecution pending—disclosure of defence
[Supreme Court of Judicature (Consolidation) Act 1925 (c. 49), s. 41.]
A plaintiff in a civil action is not to be barred from pursuing that action merely because the defendant might have to disclose, in contemporaneous criminal proceedings, what his defence is likely to be.
P employed D as a general accounts clerk. She was dismissed and irregularities in the accounts were discovered. P brought Ord. 14 proceedings to recover the £29,190 missing and D was also prosecuted under the Theft Act 1968 in connection with the same matter. D claimed that to swear an affidavit in the Ord. 14 proceedings would necessarily disclose her defence in the criminal proceedings. Forbes J. ordered the proceedings to be adjourned until the conclusion of the criminal proceedings on payment by D of £24,206 into a joint account. On appeal, *held,* that (1) there was no principle of law that a plaintiff in a civil action was to be debarred from pursuing his action merely because the defendant might have to disclose in contemporaneous criminal proceedings what his defence was likely to be (*Wonder Heat Pty.* v. *Bishop* [1960] V.R. 489 considered); (2) the court had a discretion to stay proceedings if justice between the parties so required but there was nothing in the facts of the present case which led to such a conclusion.
JEFFERSON v. BHETCHA [1979] 1 W.L.R. 898, C.A.

2185. Striking-out proceedings—existence of arguable cause of action

Land sold to plaintiffs by the defendant vendor was the subject of a boundary dispute and the plaintiffs brought an action for damages against the vendor and solicitors who had acted for him alleging a duty of care owed to them as they were relying on the accuracy of the answers contained in the requisitions on title. The solicitors applied to strike out the particulars of claim. *Held*, dismissing the solicitors' appeal, where there was an application to strike out the proper course for the court to take was simply to decide whether there was or was not an arguable cause of action and if there were to consider whether it was likely to succeed. The issues being arguable, the particulars of claim did not fall to be struck out: WILSON *v.* BLOOMFIELD (1979) 123 S.J. 860, C.A.

2186. Summons—before Masters—adjournment, restoration and vacation of appointments

The following Practice Direction was issued by the Queen's Bench Division on July 16, 1979:

1. *Summons in the Ordinary List*

A summons in the ordinary list may be adjourned or withdrawn or transferred to Counsel's List or for a special appointment without reference to a Master:

(a) by consent; or

(b) if the summons has not been served.

In all other cases application must be made to the Master to whom the summons has been assigned.

2. A summons may be restored to the ordinary list for hearing:

    (a) without the leave of a Master if for any reason the summons has not been heard, or, if heard, has not been fully disposed of;

    (b) in other cases, by leave of a Master.

3. *Special Appointments before the Masters*

An application for the adjournment of a special appointment given by a Master must be made to the Master who gave the appointment personally.

4. Where the matter involved in a Summons for which a Master has given a special appointment has been settled, it is the duty of solicitors for the parties and particularly the solicitor who obtained that appointment to notify that Master immediately.

[1979] 1 W.L.R. 1039.

2187. —— —— return dates

The following Practice Direction was issued by the Queen's Bench Division on July 16, 1979:

1. The arrangements for return dates for the hearing of summonses before the Queen's Bench Masters in Chambers (Masters' Practice Direction [1977] C.L.Y. 2404) have been revised and the current practice will continue.

2. Masters' Practice Direction 16A (1) (Return Dates for Masters' Summonses) is therefore amended by deleting the first three paragraphs and substituting therefor the following paragraphs:

" 1. The current practice for the hearing of summonses before the Queen's Bench Masters in Chambers will continue.

2. Two Masters will sit each day to hear summonses in Chambers and they will sit as at present in Rooms 95 and 96 at 10.30 a.m.

3. The present 'Supplementary Lists' on Tuesdays and Thursdays will continue but will be listed for hearing before the Master at 2.00 p.m. and the Master will sit in Room 95 or 96, as necessary. If the business before the Masters makes it necessary or desirable, the Masters may take an occasional 'Additional List'."

In all other respects the Practice Direction referred to above will continue to apply.

See Practice Direction (Masters' Summonses) [1975] C.L.Y. 2689; [1975] 2 All E.R. 1136; added October 14, 1977, Masters' Practice Direction [1977] C.L.Y. 2404.

[1979] 1 W.L.R. 1038.

2188. Taxation of costs—power to allow objection to taxation out of time
[R.S.C., Ord. 3, r. 5, Ord. 62, r. 33 (2).]
Notwithstanding the apparently mandatory wording of Ord. 62, r. 33 (1), those provisions are governed by Ord. 3, r. 5, which gives a court power, in a proper case, to extend the time for filing objections to a taxation of costs.
A husband was ordered to pay the wife's cost of divorce and ancillary proceedings. Costs were taxed on July 14, 1978, but due to a solicitor's oversight (the person dealing with the matter having left the firm) no objections were filed until August 15, well out of time. The taxing officer had in the meantime signed the certificate. The registrar refused the application to file objections out of time. On appeal, *held*, allowing the appeal, that the court had inherent jurisdiction under Ord. 3, r. 5, to extend the time for filing objections. (*Re Furber* (1898) 42 S.J. 613, *Brown* v. *Youde* (*Practice Note*) [1967] C.L.Y. 3123 applied.)
THORNE v. THORNE [1979] 1 W.L.R. 659, Comyn J.

2189. Trial—setting down of actions
The following Practice Direction was issued by the Queen's Bench Division on July 16, 1979:
1. Subject to compliance with R.S.C., Ord. 3, r. 6 (requirement of service of notice of intention to proceed after a year's delay), where applicable, the plaintiff need not obtain the leave of the court or the consent of the defendant or the defendants, if there are more than one, before setting an action down for trial after the expiry of the period fixed by an order made under R.S.C., Ord. 34, r. 2 (1).
2. The foregoing change in the practice in no way relieves the plaintiff of his obligation to set the action down for trial within the time fixed by the order of the court, and his failure to do so may entail the dismissal of the action for want of prosecution under R.S.C., Ord. 34, r. 2 (2).
3. The Practice Direction (Setting Actions Down for Trial) dated September 30, 1964 [1964] C.L.Y. 3025 is hereby revoked.
[1979] 1 W.L.R. 1040.

2190. Value added tax—taxation of costs
The following Practice Direction was issued by the Chief Taxing Master on June 14, 1979:
1. Attention is drawn to the Practice Direction issued on March 9, 1973 [1973] 1 W.L.R. 438, [1973] C.L.Y. 2720 as varied by the Practice Direction issued on January 28, 1974 [1974] 1 W.L.R. 217, [1974] C.L.Y. 3030, and Practice Direction (Crown Court) No. 2 of 1973 issued on March 12, 1973 [1973] C.L.Y. 2719.
2. The increase in the rate from 8 per cent. to 15 per cent. which, subject to para. 3 below, will be effective on and after June 18, 1979, will apply to all bills of costs the taxation of which is completed on or after that date.
3. Para. 4 of Motion No. 2 of the Budget Statement, however, provides as follows:
" Where a supply in fact made wholly or partly before the said June 18, or a supply which, apart from the other provisions of the said s. 7, would be treated as so made by subs. (2) or (3) of that section, is treated under those other provisions as made on or after that date, the person making the supply may account for and pay tax on the supply or, as the case may be, on the relevant part of it as if the rate of tax had not been increased by para. (1) (b) above."

4. Where all or a part of work was undertaken prior to June 18, 1979, it will be assumed, unless a contrary indication is given in writing, that an election to charge VAT at 8 per cent. has been made and VAT will be calculated on that part of the bill at 8 per cent. VAT will be calculated at 15 per cent. on all work undertaken on or after that date.
5. In any case in which an election to charge the lower rate is not made such decision must be justified in accordance with the principles of taxation which are applicable to the basis on which the costs are ordered to be taxed.
6. Until a further direction is made all bills of costs, fee notes and dis-

bursements on which VAT is chargeable must be divided into separate parts so as to show the work done on a day to day basis before, and, on and after June 18, 1979. Where, however, a lump sum charge is made for work, any part of which was performed before June 18, 1979, the lump sum must also be apportioned. The totals of profit costs and disbursements in each part must be carried separately to the summary.

7. Where in addition work was undertaken prior to April 1, 1973, the bill must be divided to show work undertaken before that date in accordance with existing practice.

8. With the concurrence of the Senior Registrar of the Family Division and the Admiralty Registrar, this direction is to apply to all costs in the Supreme Court taxed under their respective jurisdictions.

[1979] 1 W.L.R. 927; [1979] 2 All E.R. 1008.

2191. Want of prosecution—infant plaintiff—extended limitation period—right to issue fresh writ

[Limitation Act 1939 (c. 21), s. 22 (as amended by Limitation Act 1975 (c. 54), s. 2).]

Even after inordinate delay, it may be pointless to dismiss an action for want of prosecution where the infant plaintiff can sue in any event within three years of attaining his majority.

In 1964, when aged two, the infant plaintiff was injured in an accident with a car. A writ claiming damages for personal injuries was issued in 1967 and served the following year. No further step was taken until 1977 when notice of intention to proceed was served on the defendant. The Court of Appeal reversed Dunn J.'s decision dismissing the action for want of prosecution. *Held*, dismissing the defendants' appeal (Lord Wilberforce and Viscount Dilhorne, dissenting), that since the plaintiff could start a fresh action within three years of attaining her majority, dismissal of the original action would not avail the defendants. (Decision of Court of Appeal affirmed; *Biss* v. *Lambeth, Southwark and Lewisham Area Health Authority* (*Teaching*) [1978] C.L.Y. 2425 distinguished; *Birkett* v. *James* [1977] C.L.Y. 2410 considered.) *Quaere* whether once an action has been struck out for some contumelious conduct, a second action is an abuse of the process of the court.

TOLLEY v. MORRIS [1979] 1 W.L.R. 592, H.L.

2192. Wards of court. See MINORS

2193. Witnesses. See EVIDENCE.

BOOKS AND ARTICLES. See *post*, pp. [10], [28].

PRESS

2194. Advertising—agents—liability for money had and received. See PRESS AND GENERAL PUBLICITY SERVICES v. PERCY BILTON, § 26.

BOOKS. See *post*, p. [10].

PRISONS

2195. Board of visitors—disciplinary proceedings—subject to judicial review

[Supreme Court of Judicature (Consolidation) Act 1925 (c. 49), s. 31 (1) (*a*), as amended by Criminal Appeal Act 1968 (c. 19), s. 52, Sched. 5; Administration of Justice Act 1960 (c. 65), s. 1 (1) (*a*).]

When a board of prison visitors are adjudicating on charges of offences against disciplinary rules they are performing a judicial act and the proceedings are therefore subject to judicial review by certiorari.

Following a prison riot, a board of visitors heard charges against a number of prisoners alleging indiscipline during the riot. The board found the prisoners guilty and made various disciplinary awards including loss of remission. The prisoners applied to the Divisional Court for certiorari to quash the awards, but their application was dismissed on the grounds that certiorari was not available. On the prisoners' appeal, *held*, that (1) the Court of Appeal had jurisdiction to hear the appeal; (2) the board were performing a judicial act when performing these functions, and had a duty to act judicially, and certiorari was in principle available to review their decisions. (*Amand* v. *Home Secretary and Minister of Defence of Royal Netherlands Government* [1943] A.C. 147 distinguished; *Ridge* v. *Baldwin* [1963] C.L.Y. 2667 applied.)

     R. *v.* BOARD OF VISITORS OF HULL PRISON, *ex p.* ST. GERMAIN [1979] 2 W.L.R. 42, C.A.

2196. —— —— whether bound by rules of criminal procedure
     [Prison Act 1952 (c. 52), s. 47 (2); Prison Rules 1964 (S.I. 1964 No. 388), r. 49 (2).]

     A board of prison visitors is not bound by the technical rules of evidence as applied in the criminal courts, but where hearsay evidence is admitted, the prisoner must be informed of the nature of the evidence and be allowed to cross-examine the witnesses whose evidence was initially before the board in the form of hearsay.

     A riot broke out at a prison and disciplinary proceedings under the Prison Rules 1964 were brought against some prisoners. By virtue of r. 49 (2) every prisoner should be given a full opportunity of hearing the allegations against him and of presenting his own case before the board of visitors. Prior to the hearing, each prisoner was given a booklet stating the procedure laid down in the rules, *inter alia*, that a prisoner has to ask the chairman permission to call a witness, telling him who the witness was and what his evidence would be. If a witness was called, after hearing the evidence the prisoner may add anything further about the case, comment about all the evidence and point out anything in his favour. The prison governor was present at the hearing with a dossier containing the prison officers' account of the part played by the prisoner in the riot, which was given to the board from time to time. Eight prisoners were found guilty and were awarded punishments. On an application of certiorari to quash the award on the grounds that (1) the prisoners had not been given an opportunity of presenting their cases in accordance with r. 49 (2); (2) there had been a breach of natural justice in that the board, *inter alia*, refused to allow them to call witnesses in support of their cases and, had acted upon hearsay evidence from the governor's dossier. *Held*, granting the application, that (1) s. 47 (2) of the 1952 Act and r. 49 (2) of the 1964 Rules were merely declaratory of the basic rule of natural justice; therefore, a person charged with a serious disciplinary offence had the right to be heard himself and to call any evidence which is likely to assist in establishing vital facts in issue; (2) the chairman had the discretion to refuse permission to allow a prisoner to call witnesses but it would be improper to refuse simply on the ground that it would cause considerable administrative inconvenience, though the number of witnesses may be limited where the large attendance was an attempt to render the hearing impracticable; (3) the Board, though not bound by the technical rules of evidence, may only admit hearsay evidence subject to informing the prisoner of the evidence and allowing him to cross-examine the witnesses whose evidence was initially before the Board in the form of hearsay; that where the witness's attendance was not possible, the hearsay evidence should not be admitted, or, if it had already come to the Board's notice, it should be expressly dismissed from consideration. (Dicta of Lord Denning in *Kanda* v. *Government of the Federation of Malaya* [1962] C.L.Y. 254, Lord Atkin in *General Medical Council* v. *Spackman* [1943] A.C. 627; and Lord Jenkins in *Ceylon University* v. *Fernando* [1960] C.L.Y. 3267 applied.)

     R. *v.* HULL PRISON BOARD OF VISITORS, *ex p.* ST. GERMAIN (NO. 2) [1979] 3 All E.R. 545, D.C.

2197. Northern Ireland. See NORTHERN IRELAND.

     BOOKS AND ARTICLES. See *post*, pp. [10], [29].

PRIVY COUNCIL PRACTICE

2198. Appeal—reference from Governor-General of New Zealand—jurisdiction
     [N.Z.] [Crimes Act 1961, s. 406 (*b*); Judicial Committee Act 1833 (*c.* 41), s. 3.]

No appeal lies to the Privy Council from an opinion given by the New Zealand Court of Appeal upon reference being made by the Governor-General on consideration of an application for exercise of the prerogative of mercy.

The defendant applied to the Governor-General to quash his convictions for murder by exercising the prerogative of mercy. The Governor-General referred the case to the Court of Appeal pursuant to s. 406 of the 1961 Act which provides for the Governor-General to seek the opinion of the Court of Appeal should he desire assistance. The court gave an opinion unfavourable to the defendant who sought to appeal to the Privy Council. *Held,* that the "opinion" given under s. 406 was not appealable, it not being a "decision" within the meaning of s. 3 of the 1833 Act and not being binding upon the Governor-General. (*Théberge* v. *Landry* [1876] 2 App.Cas. 102, applied; *Oteri* v. *The Queen* [1970] C.L.Y. 167 distinguished.)

THOMAS *v.* THE QUEEN [1978] 3 W.L.R. 927, P.C.

2199. Cayman Islands—leave to appeal—conditions

[Cayman Islands (Appeal to Privy Council) Order 1965 (No. 1862), s. 5.] Under s. 5 of the Cayman Islands (Appeal to Privy Council) Order 1965, leave is to be granted by the Court of Appeal of Jamaica (*a*) on condition that the appellant give security for costs within a period to be fixed by the court but not exceeding 90 days; and (*b*) on such other conditions as to the time for procuring the dispatch of the record to England as the court thinks reasonable. *Held,* that the period fixed under (*b*) could be extended by the Court of Appeal, either expressly or by implication: ROULSTONE *v.* PANTON (1979) 123 S.J. 735, P.C.

2200. Precedent—House of Lords decisions—whether binding

Colonial courts should treat a House of Lords decision on common legislation as binding although in juristic theory such a decision is persuasive only.

In 1970 H agreed not to defend W's divorce petition and to make certain financial provision for her in return for W consenting to dismiss her claims for financial relief. A consent order was duly made and H executed the financial arrangements agreed. In 1975 W applied for an order to set aside or vary the consent order. Her application was dismissed but her appeal against this judgment was allowed by the Court of Appeal of Hong Kong, holding that it was not bound by English Court of Appeal decisions. H appealed to the Privy Council and by the date of the hearing the House of Lords had given judgment approving the decision in question of the English Court of Appeal. He claimed this was conclusive but W contended that the Hong Kong courts were not bound by House of Lords decisions. *Held,* allowing the appeal, that (1) all Court of Appeal decisions and those House of Lords decisions on common law were of persuasive authority only on a colonial court, though the persuasive authority of the House of Lords was very great (*Robins* v. *National Trust Co.* [1927] A.C. 515 and *Australian Consolidated Press* v. *Uren* [1967] C.L.Y. 3276 applied); (2) in matters of common legislation the colonial courts should treat a House of Lords decision as binding even though in juristic theory such a decision was persuasive only; and (3) the policy of the 1973 Act was to allow the parties to make a clean break from which there was no going back. (*Minton* v. *Minton* [1979] C.L.Y. 766 applied.)

DE LASALA *v.* DE LASALA [1979] 2 All E.R. 1146, P.C.

2201. Registration of title—land in Malaysia

[National Land Code (No. 56 of 1965), s. 327.]

Upon an application for the removal of a caveat, the caveator is obliged to show that there is a serious issue to be tried so as to justify preservation of the status quo.

The respondents entered a caveat after the appellant vendors of land of which they were registered proprietors served notice terminating a contract for sale of the land, the respondents having defaulted in the final payment of the purchase price in accordance with the written contract. The appellants' application for removal of the caveat was supported by an affidavit exhibiting the contract. By their affidavit the respondents raised various assertions conflicting with the appellants' affidavit and the written contract. At first instance the judge rejected the respondents' assertions of fact as, *inter alia*, not being capable of belief. The appellants' appealed against the Federal Courts' reversal of that decision. *Held,* allowing the appeal, that although a conflict of evidence would normally indicate the existence of a serious triable issue, the judge was entitled, as he had done here, to reject the caveator's evidence if after considering it judicially he found it to lack credibility. (*American Cyanamid* v. *Ethicon* [1975] C.L.Y. 2640 applied.)

ENG MEE YONG *v.* LETCHUMANAN S/O VELAYUTHAM [1979] 3 W.L.R. 373, P.C.

PUBLIC ENTERTAINMENTS

2202. Cinema
CINEMATOGRAPH FILMS (LIMITS OF LEVY) ORDER 1979 (No. 395) [10p], made under the Films Act 1970 (c. 26), s. 5 (1); operative on April 1, 1979; amends s. 2 (3) (*b*) of the Cinematograph Films Act 1957 by increasing the maximum limit from £7m. to £12m.

CINEMATOGRAPH FILMS (DISTRIBUTION OF LEVY) (AMENDMENT) REGULATIONS 1979 (No. 1750) [20p], made under the Cinematograph Films Act 1957 (c. 21), s. 3; operative on February 10, 1980; provide a limit on the total payment which may be made to the maker from the British Film Fund, and also amend the rules as to the calculation of such payments.

CINEMATOGRAPH FILMS (COLLECTION OF LEVY) (AMENDMENT No. 7) REGULATIONS 1979 (No. 1751) [20p], made under the Cinematograph Films Act 1957, s. 2; operative on February 10, 1980; alter the rate of the levy and exemptions from payment of levy.

2203. Films Act 1979 (c. 9)
This Act amends the Films Act 1960.
S. 1 substitutes a new s. 6 (1) of the Films Act 1960; s. 2 gives the short title.
The Act received the Royal Assent on February 22, 1979, and came into force on that date.

2204. Ministers, transfer of functions
TRANSFER OF FUNCTIONS (ARTS AND LIBRARIES) ORDER 1979 (No. 907) [20p], made under the Ministers of the Crown Act 1975 (c. 26), ss. 1, 2; operative on September 1, 1979; transfers to the Chancellor of the Duchy of Lancaster functions presently exercised by the Secretary of State for Education and Science relating to the arts, libraries and other specified institutions.

2205. Public lending right. See LITERARY AND SCIENTIFIC INSTITUTIONS.

2206. Television. See TELECOMMUNICATIONS.

ARTICLES. See *post*, p. [29].

PUBLIC HEALTH

2207. Aircraft
PUBLIC HEALTH (AIRCRAFT) (ISLE OF MAN) ORDER 1979 (No. 1315) [40p], made under the Public Health Act 1936 (c. 49), s. 143 (10), operative on December 1, 1979; extends S.I. 1970 No. 1880, as amended, to the Isle of Man.

PUBLIC HEALTH (AIRCRAFT) REGULATIONS 1979 (No. 1434) [90p], made under the Public Health Act 1936, s. 143, as modified by the Civil Aviation Act 1949 (c. 67), s. 69, Sched. 11, the Civil Aviation Act 1971 (c. 75), s. 32, and the Airport Authority Act 1975 (c. 78), s. 15; operative on January 1, 1980; consolidate S.I. 1970 No. 1880, S.I. 1974 No. 268 and S.I. 1978 No. 286.

2208. Building. See BUILDING AND ENGINEERING, ARCHITECTS AND SURVEYORS.

2209. Food and drugs. See FOOD AND DRUGS.

2210. Lands Tribunal decision
GEORGE WHITEHOUSE *v.* ANGLIAN WATER AUTHORITY (Ref./157/1977) 247 E.G. 223 (sewage works were carried out in the road where GW ran their garage business. The works obstructed access to the garages for six months.

Mud and dust were thrown up, some of which settled on GW's cars which were exposed for sale. GW claimed £708 compensation for the cost of cleaning the cars, and £6,848 for loss of profit, under s. 278 of the Public Health Act 1936, alternatively under s. 22 in Sched. 3 to the Water Act 1945. *Held*, all GW needed to show was that if the acts done by the local authority had been done by an individual, there would have been a cause of action against him, and that there had been material interference with their use and enjoyment of their property. GW could rely on s. 22 in addition to s. 278).

2211. Lead pollution

MOTOR FUEL (LEAD CONTENT OF PETROL) (AMENDMENT) REGULATIONS 1979 (No. 1) [10p], made under the Control of Pollution Act 1974 (c. 40), s. 75; operative on February 1, 1979; amend S.I. 1976 No. 1866.

2212. Medicine. See MEDICINE.

2213. National health. See NATIONAL HEALTH.

2214. Northern Ireland. See NORTHERN IRELAND.

2215. Port health authorities

STROUD PORT HEALTH AUTHORITY ORDER 1979 (No. 134) [20p], made under the Public Health Act 1936 (c. 49), ss. 2, 3, 9 (1), as extended by the Control of Pollution Act 1974 (c. 40), s. 108, Sched. 3, para. 6; operative on April 1, 1979; constitutes part of the Port of Gloucester as a port health district and constitutes the District Council of Stroud as port health authority for that district.

FOWEY PORT HEALTH AUTHORITY ORDER 1979 (No. 1085) [40p], made under the Control of Pollution Act 1974, s. 108, Sched. 3, para. 6; operative on October 1, 1979; constitutes the Port of Fowey as a port health authority.

2216. Public Health Laboratory Service Act 1979 (c. 23)

This Act extends the powers conferred by s. 5 (2) (*c*) of the National Health Service Act 1977 and amends provisions relating to the Public Health Laboratory Service Board.

S. 1 amends s. 5 of the 1977 Act to provide for the extension of the public health laboratory service; s. 2 provides for payments to members of Public Health Laboratory Service Board and its committees; s. 3 contains the short title and extent. The Act does not extend to Scotland or Northern Ireland.

The Act received the Royal Assent on March 29, 1979, and came into force on that date.

2217. Sewerage—drainage pipes—whether "public sewer"—whether adjoining houses "one building"

[Public Health Act 1936 (c. 49), s. 343.]

Adjoining semi-detached houses may be regarded as being "one building" for the purposes of s. 343 of the Public Health Act 1936.

In 1954 the local authority, at their expense, laid down pipes for drainage to the main sewer at the back of a house No. 17, with the permission of the then owner of No. 17, the plaintiff's predecessor in title, the drains from Nos. 19 and 21, a pair of semi-detached houses then in common ownership, were connected to those pipes. In 1974 the defendant bought Nos. 19 and 21 and No. 23; he demolished Nos. 21 and 23 and built a new house on the curtilage of No. 23, connecting the drainage pipes to those at the rear of No. 19 and thence into the pipe on No. 17's land. The plaintiff sought injunctions requiring the defendant to disconnect the drainage pipes from Nos. 19 and 23. *Held*, that (1) Nos. 19 and 21 had acquired a permanent right of drainage into the pipe at No. 17 by virtue of the permission given earlier and that they were to be regarded as "one building"; (2) no such right existed in respect of No. 23 and that accordingly the defendant was guilty of trespass; but since no damage was suffered thereby, nominal damages would be given for the past trespass and the plaintiff would be compensated in damages for continuing trespass since it would be oppressive to require the drain's disconnection. (*Ward* v. *Kirkland* [1966] C.L.Y. 4174 considered.)

COOK *v.* MINION (1978) 37 P. & C.R. 58, Goulding J.

2218. Ships

PUBLIC HEALTH (SHIPS) (ISLE OF MAN) ORDER 1979 (No. 1316) [40p], made under the Public Health Act 1936 (c. 49), s. 143 (10); operative on December 1, 1979; extends S.I. 1970 No. 1881, as amended, to the Isle of Man.

PUBLIC HEALTH (SHIPS) REGULATIONS 1979 (No. 1435) [£1], made under the Public Health Act 1936, s. 143; operative on January 1, 1980; consolidate S.I. 1970 No. 1881, S.I. 1974 No. 269 and S.I. 1978 No. 287, which provide for public health control of ships arriving at or leaving ports in England and Wales.

2219. Trade effluent—launderette
[Public Health (Drainage of Trade Premises) Act 1937 (c. 40), s. 14.] The Court of Appeal *held*, allowing the appeal of the Thames Water Authority, that (1) a launderette is trade premises; (2) when deciding whether effluent discharge from trade premises was trade effluent or domestic sewage, one could not just ask whether the trade activity was one which was carried on in the home, but also ask the purpose for which the activity was carried on; (3) the meaning of " domestic sewage " could be derived from the proviso (*a*) (1) to s. 34 of the Public Health Act 1936; (4) the effluent discharged from washing machines on launderette premises is trade effluent: THAMES WATER AUTHORITY *v.* BLUE AND WHITE LAUNDERETTES, *The Times,* December 21, 1979, C.A.

2220. Water. See WATER AND WATERWORKS.

BOOKS AND ARTICLES. See *post,* pp. [10], [29].

RAILWAYS

2221. British Railways Board
BRITISH RAILWAYS BOARD (BORROWING POWERS) ORDER 1979 (No. 944) [10p], made under the Transport Act 1968 (c. 73), s. 42 (6), as amended by the Railways Act 1974 (c. 48), s. 2; operative on August 11, 1979; raises to £900m. the limit on the borrowing powers of the British Railways Board.

2222. Light railways
STEAMTOWN LIGHT RAILWAY ORDER 1979 (No. 317) [20p], made under the Light Railways Act 1896 (c. 48), ss. 7, 9–11, 18 as amended by the Light Railways Act 1912 (c. 19) and the Railways Act 1921 (c. 55), Pt. V; operative on March 24, 1979; makes provisions for the operation of the Steamtown Light Railway.

BRITISH RAILWAYS BOARD (TOTTON HYTHE AND FAWLEY LIGHT RAILWAY) (AMENDMENT) ORDER 1979 (No. 1091) [40p], made under the Light Railways Act 1896, ss. 7, 9, 10, 24; operative on September 7, 1979; amends S.I. 1962 No. 1289 by substituting the Fourth and Fifth Schedules.

YORKSHIRE DALES LIGHT RAILWAY ORDER 1979 (No. 1270) [20p], made under the Light Railways Act 1896, ss. 7, 9, 10, 18; operative on October 14, 1979; transfers the railway from the British Railways Board to the Yorkshire Dales Railway Museum Trust (Holdings) Ltd.

NATIONAL COAL BOARD BUTTERWELL LIGHT RAILWAY ORDER 1979 (No. 1421) [40p], made under the Light Railways Act 1896, ss. 7, 9–11; operative on November 15, 1979; makes provision for the Butterwell Light Railway.

2223. Negligence—duty of care—involuntary fall of passenger onto railway line. See PUBLIC TRANSPORT COMMISSION OF N.S.W. *v.* PERRY, § 1888.

RATING AND VALUATION

2224. Charity—rating relief—licensee occupying house owned by charity. See FORCES HELP SOCIETY AND LORD ROBERTS WORKSHOPS *v.* CANTERBURY CITY COUNCIL, § 244.

2225. Distress
DISTRESS FOR RATES ORDER 1979 (No. 1038) [20p], made under the General Rate Act 1967 (c. 9), s. 101; operative on September 1, 1979; prescribes revised fees, charges, and expenses in respect of the levying of distress for rates; revokes S.I. 1972 No. 820.

2226. —— powers of a local authority bailiff—damages
Council bailiffs, armed with a distress warrant, forcibly entered a garage

situated within the curtilage of, but separated by about a yard from a house which the plaintiff owned and occupied along with her husband. The garage was included in the rating assessment. The bailiffs destrained on the plaintiff's motor-car and subsequently sold it at public auction. The plaintiff claimed damages for trespass and conversion. The council, on the other hand, claimed that distress for rates was analogous to seizure by the sheriff (execution) and that the sheriff's bailiff in execution of a writ of *fieri facias* was entitled to break into outbuildings, but may not break the main door of the dwelling-house. *Held*, (1) the sheriff may not break the door of a dwelling-house or a door within the curtilage of a dwelling-house; (2) in any event there were differences between the powers of a local authority bailiff and of a sheriff's bailiff (*per* Viscount Maugham in *Potts* v. *Hickman* [1941] A.C. 212, 234); (3) s. 99 (7) of the General Rate Act 1967 did not limit the claim to special damages (the cost of a new lock for the garage) because the original entry was an irregularity and not a " subsequent irregularity " for the purposes of the subsection; (4) the council's bailiffs had exceeded their powers, the distress was unlawful and the plaintiff was entitled to damages representing the value of the car, general damages for trespass and loss of use of the car and special damages for the damage to the garage door: MUNROE AND MUNROE v. WOODSPRING DISTRICT COUNCIL, October 4 and 5, 1979, Judge Russell, Bristol County Ct. (*Ex rel. John Bailey, Solicitor and Deputy Clerk, Woodspring District Council.*)

2227. —— **warrants—no notice of proceedings—whether " person aggrieved by distress "**

[General Rate Act 1967 (c. 9), ss. 99 (5), 103 (1).]

Where an attempt has been made to levy distress, and a ratepayer is prejudiced to the extent of having to pay distress fees, and is liable to imprisonment on a commitment warrant, he is a " person aggrieved by a distress " and has a right of appeal to the Crown Court.

A ratepayer, having occupied certain business premises, failed to pay the rates on the authority's demand. The authority applied for distress warrants which were issued in the ratepayer's absence, as he had moved and had not received notice of the proceedings. There were nil returns on the warrants, and commitment warrants were issued. The ratepayer applied for certiorari to quash the warrants and appealed to the Crown Court as a " person aggrieved by a distress." The Crown Court refused jurisdiction on the basis that no distress had actually been levied. On appeal, *held*, that (1) allowing the appeal to the commitment warrants, there had not been a sufficient inquiry into the rate-payer's means; (2) refusing the application on the distress warrants, the authority had done all that was required; (3) where an attempt to levy distress has been made, the Crown Court has jurisdiction to hear an appeal. (*R.* v. *London Justices* [1899] 1 Q.B. 532 distinguished.)

R. v. LIVERPOOL CITY JUSTICES, *ex p.* GREAVES; GREAVES v. LIVERPOOL CITY COUNCIL (1979) 77 L.G.R. 440, D.C.

2228. **Gas boards**

GAS HEREDITAMENTS (RATEABLE VALUES) (AMENDMENT) ORDER 1979 (No. 1516) [10p], made under the Local Government Act 1974 (c. 7), ss. 19, 22 (3), Sched. 3, para. 3, and the General Rate Act 1967 (c. 9), s. 114; operative on November 24, 1979; amends S.I. 1976 No. 490 by substituting a new formula in art. 5 and by applying the provisions of that article to Mid Suffolk.

2229. **Lands Tribunal decisions**

BALFOUR KILPATRICK INTERNATIONAL v. GRIFFITH (Ref. No. LVC/164–165/ 1978) (1979) 250 E.G. 63 (the appellants appealed against assessments on their offices in Hackbridge, Sutton, the bulk of which had been assessed at £15 per m². They contended that two other office blocks in the vicinity, assessed at £11 per m², were fair comparables. The valuation officer contended that the subject property, though not in an " office " area, was of a far higher quality than the other offices and that other more distant premises in more prestigious areas should be compared. *Held*, the subject property was of a high quality and could not be directly compared with the nearer offices: a figure of £13·50 per m² was found).

BARB v. HAYES; RIGBY v. SAME (LVC/754–755/1976) (1978) 247 E.G. 743 (the peace of B's and R's houses in Gerrard's Cross was disturbed by noise from the M40. They were compensated under Pt. 1 of the Land Compensation Act 1973, which assumed a $7\frac{1}{2}$ per cent. reduction in the capital value of the houses. The LVC allowed a reduction by 5 per cent. of the gross values of the houses. B and R appealed, saying that this latter decision did not adequately take into account the exceptional noise pollution from the M40, nor the level of awards made under the 1973 Act. *Held*, allowing the appeals, the percentage amounts of depreciation of capital values were the acceptable guides to the amount of depreciation values, and that the destruction of amenities by noise would affect the rent which a hypothetical tenant would pay. The rateable value would be reduced by $7\frac{1}{2}$ per cent. as the gross value had been).

BARB v. SECRETARY OF STATE FOR TRANSPORT; RIGBY v. SAME (Ref. 147 and 214/1977) (1979) 247 E.G. 473 (on a claim for compensation for disturbance by noise under Pt. I of the Land Compensation Act 1973 the tribunal found depreciation of $7\frac{1}{2}$ per cent. Two houses in the Gerrards Cross area were 620 and 730 metres from the M40 motorway. The claimant relied on local market transactions: the authority upon other compensation settlements. The claimant claimed 15 per cent. depreciation: the authority nil. There was detailed expert acoustic evidence. Compensation settlements provide a more dependable basis of measurement than market transactions).

BEAZLEY v. COOKE-PRIEST (LVC/977–978/1976) (1977) 247 E.G. 139 (unsuccessful appeal against rating assessment on two agricultural dwelling-houses in a pleasant Bedfordshire commuter village which had a high amenity value— s. 26 (2) of the General Rate Act 1967 applied. The valuation officer said that the starting point for rating was the gross value of the properties calculated without any allowances for the effect of s. 26 (2), and with a subsequent deduction of 10 per cent. to take the section into account. The attractive character of the village was a factor that would be reflected in negotiated rents, and therefore in the initial gross value).

BRITISH AIRWAYS BOARD v. RIDGEON, LVC/541–546/1976 (levels of value in the locality for different classes of hereditament were considered acceptable as evidence of value by the Lands Tribunal when arrriving at the correct rating assessment on a large composite hereditament at Heathrow Airport, London, used for aircraft maintenance. The tribunal also held that the value to be ascertained was the value at April 1, 1973, to date no present valuation list came into effect, and that no valuation officer could properly project forward to that date in the light of the evidence available to him at the time when collection of evidence came to an end, *i.e.* anticipated future trends could be taken into account in so far as they appeared to be well established. The tribunal expressed the view that it would be helpful if Parliament would consider the possibility of substituting a precise date of valuation for a new valuation list, *e.g.* 12 months before the list was due to come into operation).

CIVIL AVIATION AUTHORITY v. LANGFORD AND CAMDEN LONDON BOROUGH COUNCIL, LVC/766/1977 (1978) 248 E.G. 957 (two large office blocks joined by a link block in Kingsway, London W.C.2, were completed as a shell in 1966. In mid-1968 a completion notice was served and it was subsequently agreed that the premises were to be treated as completed in December 1968. The premises remained empty until 1975 when the ratepayers began to occupy the building in stages, beginning a massive programme of rehabilitation and fitting out to suit their purposes. Occupation was not complete until 1977. The Lands Tribunal reduced the rating assessment on the premises from £1,042,000 gross value, £868,305 rateable value, to £1 gross value, £1 rateable value, holding that although the hereditament must be deemed to have been completed in December 1968 pursuant to the completion notice and agreement, and be deemed to have been ready for occupation for rating purposes, and although the hypothetical landlord must be deemed to have carried out all reasonable repairs, the structural defects affecting the columns and the high alumina cement beams used in the building, which had appeared between the completion date and the proposal date and upon which work was being carried out on the proposal date, were so substantial that they could not be regarded as being within the hypothetical landlord's repairing obligations, particularly as, when remedied, a building materially and significantly better than and different from that which existed before would result, and also the premises would be unlettable at the proposal date by reason of the general doubt and uncertainty which surrounded all buildings where high alumina cement was present. The work that was going on in regard to these faults at the proposal date together with all necessary consequential disturbance, were material circumstances to be taken into account when valuing the premises *rebus sic stantibus*).

COMMERCIAL UNION ASSURANCE CO. *v.* BURNE, LVC/1/1977 (1979) 249 E.G. 751 (the appellant company occupied offices in High Street, Exeter, and contended for a valuation of the ground floor and basement based on other office comparables occupied by other insurance companies elsewhere in town. The respondent valuation officer based his assessment on bank comparables in the High Street. There were no other office comparables in the High Street. *Held*, the valuation officer's assessment was in line with the basis laid down in *Dawkins* v. *Royal Leamington Spa Borough Council and Warwickshire County Council* [1961] C.L.Y. 7423 and should be upheld).

CORSER *v.* GLOUCESTERSHIRE MARKETING SOCIETY, LVC/955–957/1976 (an auction hall in a fruit and vegetable market was *held* to be an agricultural building and thus to be exempt from rates, where it was occupied by a society formed by local growers for the purpose of marketing their agricultural and horticultural produce collectively, even though a small amount of produce was bought by the society for resale, amounting to a merchandising use independent and distinct from agricultural operations carried out on agricultural land, since such use must be disregarded under the Rating Act 1971, s. 1 (2), as it was not carried out for a substantial part of the time during which the auction hall was used).

CRESSWELL *v.* B.O.C. (LVC/923/1976) (1979) 250 E.G. 1195 (local valuation court upheld in finding that a fish farm was exempt from rates as an agricultural hereditament. "Livestock" in s. 1 of the Rating Act 1971 includes trout. *Quaere* whether a matter of law. *Jones* v. *Bateman* [1975] C.L.Y. 2766 followed).

CUMBER *v.* ASSOCIATED FAMILY BAKERS (SOUTH WEST) (LVC/970/1977) (1979) 252 E.G. 69 (appeal by valuation officer against valuation court finding of rateable value on the basis that a prover and oven in a bakery were items of removable plant to be excluded under Class 4 (*e*) of the Plant and Machinery (Rating) Order 1960 (as amended) pursuant to s. 21 of the General Rate Act 1967. *Held*, the items did not require demolition to be removed. Demolition requires an element of destruction: these items would merely be taken to pieces and re-constructed. Appeal dismissed).

DE ROSE *v.* SMITH AND SOUTHEND-ON-SEA BOROUGH COUNCIL, LVC/183/ 1978 [1979] J.P.L. 623 (a rating assessment of £720 gross value was confirmed on four units in a market in Southend-on-Sea, the tribunal holding that the level of assessment resulting in that figure was well established and that the evidence produced of the assessments on conventional shops opposite the market shops did not render that figure excessive).

ELLESMERE PORT AND NESTON BOROUGH COUNCIL *v.* SHELL U.K.; CHESTER CITY COUNCIL *v.* SHELL U.K. (Ref. 562–614/1977) (1978) 248 E.G. 603 (the question was solely whether the Lands Tribunal had jurisdiction to increase the assessments which were the subject of the appeals. At the local valuation court the ratepayers and the valuation officer announced agreed figures, which the court confirmed and ordered to be listed. The rating authorities appealed. The ratepayers claimed that under s. 76 of the General Rate Act 1967 the Lands Tribunal could only give directions which the local valuations court could give, and that as there had been no issue for the local valuation court to determine, and that all the Lands Tribunal could do was ratify the local court's judgment. *Held*, rejecting this argument, "argument" in s. 76 (4) means the contention in the proposal, not the agreed figures. The effect of ousting persons expressed in the statute to be parties was a fatal flaw in the ratepayers' contention, as this would involve the consequence that in tripartite litigation agreement by two parties would bind the third).

EYSTON *v.* MUNDY, LVC/35/1971 (an agreement to open a country house to the public, in return for grants for its restoration, was held to be nothing more than a personal arrangement between the ratepayer and the Minister and as such was not to be taken into account in arriving at gross value. The agreement to allow public access was not one which as a matter of law the hypothetical landlord must be deemed to have undertaken—still less was it a duty to be imposed on the hypothetical tenant).

HENRIQUES *v.* GARLAND (Ref. No. LVC/63 and 976/1976) (1977) 247 E.G. 55 (until 1973 the appeal property had been used as a shop and store on the ground floor, and as a house on the first and second floors. H bought the property in 1973, and without structural alterations used the whole premises as a house only, getting planning permission for this change of user. Further permission would have been needed to revert to the original user. The valuation officer decided it should be valued as shop, house and premises together. H appealed. *Held*, allowing the appeal, the authorities disclosed three propositions, which held that the rateable value could take into account; (1) any use for which premises are physically suitable; (2) any uses in the same mode as that in actual use; or (3) the actual user only—(1) was too wide, (2) and (3) were in this case the same. The question of hypothetical planning permission would be ignored, and the appeal property would be valued as a house).

JONES *v.* MASON (Ref./58/1978) (1979) 250 E.G. 763 (Inland Revenue reference to determine market value of land in Huddersfield on April 6, 1965. The taxpayer valued the 4·268 acres at £17,600 and the Revenue at £7,500. The Revenue evidence was based on comparable transactions in 1965 and 1966. The taxpayer gave evidence of an offer made for the land in 1963. *Held*, the evidence of the offer in 1963 was not dependable and the Revenue evidence was acceptable. Valuation accordingly at £7,500).

LEICESTER CITY COUNCIL *v.* NUFFIELD NURSING HOMES TRUST AND HEWETT (LVC/251/1977) (1979) 252 E.G. 385 (appeal by rating authority against valuation court reduction of valuation on a private nursing home. The court had taken account of comparable nursing homes elsewhere. *Held*, no discernible pattern in comparables. Accordingly contractor's basis should be used. A reduction could be made for the present surplusage of beds in the home pending full development, but appeal allowed and valuation raised).

LEIGHTON *v.* THOMAS, LVC/927/1976 (the Lands Tribunal confirmed a rating assessment of £109 gross value on a mobile home in Somerset, occupied for eight months each year, holding that comparison with a post-war prefabricated bungalow also occupied only eight months in the year, was logical, but now there could be no valid comparison with a permanent, two-storeyed house. The Tribunal also *held* that depreciation was not a matter to be taken into account when arriving at gross value).

SIR ROBERT MCALPINE & SONS *v.* GILBERT (LVC/552–555/1978) (1979) 251 E.G. 171 (the appeal premises were four contractors' huts on a site in front of Euston Station. The company appealed against valuations on the basis that it had made agreements all over the country at a flat rate of £2·50 per square metre. The valuation officer cited many local settlements at between £5 and £7·50 per square metre. *Held*, dismissing the appeal, the local evidence was to be preferred. The company was the only possible tenant but the market alternatives would produce a rent closer to the officer's valuation (*Tomlinson* v. *Plymouth Argyle Football Co.* [1961] C.L.Y. 7423 considered)).

MARCHANT *v.* SECRETARY OF STATE FOR TRANSPORT (Ref./294/1978) (1979) 250 E.G. 559 (the claimant claimed £2,000 compensation under the Land Compensation Act 1973 for depreciation in the value of his interest in a bungalow 597 metres from the centre-line of the M20 Ditton by-pass. The tribunal heard expert acoustic evidence and heard the " impressive " noise level on a view. *Held*, rejecting the respondent's valuation evidence, compensation of £1,000 would be awarded. Despite the fact that no compensation had been agreed and paid in the locality in other cases further than 244 metres from the road there was an unaccountably high degree of noise which made conversation difficult in the garden on 90 days per year and kept visitors awake at night. Accordingly there was depreciation).

MARSHAL v. EBDON, LVC/1053/1977 [1979] J.P.L. 682 (a valuation officer was *held* to be entitled to make a proposal for the alteration of the valuation list at any time and was not bound to wait until premises were effectively occupied and to be entitled to enter one assessment against an empty property in the valuation list, which had, prior to 1976, been occupied and rated as two hereditaments, since at the relevant date it was unoccupied, in one rating area and formed one geographical unit. There was held to be no support for the contention that no one would give any rent for the property owing to its poor condition, since the repairs, which the valuation officer assumed the hypothetical landlord would have done rather than to reduce the rent further, were capable of being carried out at no great cost).

JOHN MICHAEL v. GARVIE (LVC/930/1976) (1978) 248 E.G. 419 (the premises were Nos. 35–39 Oldham Street, an old-established shopping street in Central Manchester. The accommodation was on six floors. It was agreed that the further along the street one went, the lower the rents were, and the less desirable property was, but it was the rate of decline in the value of property that was in dispute, and its effect on the subject premises. *Held*, there would be an end-allowance for shape, broken space, and superfluity of floors and basement accommodation. A gross value of £18,000 and a rateable value of £14,972 was declared).

MIDLAND BANK v. LANHAM (Ref. No. LVC/28–29/1975) (1977) 246 E.G. 1018, 1117 (the bank used one floor and part of another in a building as a training school. Although adapted for this use, any adaptations necessary to turn these floors into offices would be of a very minor nature. The question of the basis for rating arose. *Held*, the rate is to be measured by the annual value of the hereditament expressed in the form of the rent at which it might reasonably be expected to be let. Every factor, intrinsic or extrinsic was relevant. One should look at a market value which was the result of competition among potential users in the same mode or category of use, and such users must relate to the premises in their existing physical state. Accordingly, the premises would be rated as a training school, and not as offices).

NATIONAL CAR PARKS v. GUDGION; NATIONAL CAR PARKS v. BURROWS; WEST v. NATIONAL CAR PARKS, LVC/65/1976, 715/1975 and 320/1976 (1978) 247 E.G. 565; [1979] J.P.L. 317 (appeals against rating assessment on multi-storey car parks in Reading, Bromley and Weston-super-Mare. The assessment on the car park in Reading, built by the local authority and operated by the ratepayers under a licence, was reduced by the Lands Tribunal when taking into account all the relevant factors, including the fact that the class of hypothetical tenant in the market for the subject hereditament could not exclude the local authority, which was under no requirement to trade at a profit, was not subject to price control in the same way, and might well be expected to overbid any private operator; that the licence provided no dependable evidence of market rental value since the conditions contained in it showed that it was a typical management agreement; and that the contractor's test gave no true indication of rental value since the car park was built by a local authority to fulfil a statutory duty placed upon it and not to provide an economic return on capital invested. The assessment on the car park in Bromley, held on a repairing lease for 99 years, was confirmed, since it was supported by the rent paid under the lease, which provided the best evidence of market value at the relevant date, and it was also supported by the valuation officer's comparables. The assessment on the car park in Weston-super-Mare was increased, the rent payable being regarded as unreliable as it was negotiated as part of a larger business transaction and was no guide to market rental. The contractor's test was unreliable as the car park was operated on an obligation under a much larger agreement and not to provide an economic return on capital invested. The accounts could not necessarily be used to reach a basis of rental value since the test was not whether the property would produce profit but whether it would produce rent, and in that regard the local authority was a possible hypothetical tenant).

PAUL RAYMOND ORGANISATION *v.* PIRIE (LVC/498–499/1978) (1979) 252 E.G. 67 (Raymond's Revuebar in Soho, London consists of two small theatres seating 200 each plus bars and other facilities. Prior to 1970 it had been a club properly so called. Since the change in censorship laws at that date it has been transformed into theatres. The valuation officer assessed gross value of £18,500 as club premises based on local club comparables. The valuation court had reduced it to £12,000. The appellant company claimed that the basis of assessment should be as a theatre. *Held*, reducing the gross value to £10,000, this was a theatre, or rather two theatres, and was not so outstandingly successful as to be an exceptional case. £30 per seat for one and £20 per seat valuation basis found on evidence of profitability. Club basis disapproved).

RYE BAY CARAVAN PARK *v.* MORGAN, LVC/43/1977 (an asssesment of £4,000 gross value, £3,305 rateable value was confined as the residual parts of a caravan park, following separate assessments of 283 caravans and their standings stationed in the park. Although it was agreed that, in such a case as the present one, the hypothetical tenant of the subject hereditament would not necessarily be entitled to receive rents from the caravans, some sensible arrangement would undoubtedly be devised whereby the various amenities and services available on the ratepayers' hereditament could be provided with a proper payment being made to cover the costs. The ratepayers' assumption that the cost of providing services on the residual hereditament was reflected in the gross value of the caravans, was an assumption for which there was no justification in law).

SNOWMAN *v.* McLEAN (LVC/38/1978) (1979) 251 E.G. 859 (factory in Harrow, Middlesex, manufacturing children's clothing. Valuation officer supported valuation court finding of RV at £12,400. Appellant ratepayer argued that there should be 20 per cent. discount by way of disability allowance for state of premises. Cracks in brickwork, etc., caused by "Leave." Valuation officer argued that hypothetical tenant would not require a discount. *Held*, there should be a 10 per cent. discount. Rating value found of £11,160).

VESTA LAUNDERETTES *v.* SMITH (LVC/551/1977) (1979) 251 E.G. 769 (launderette in St. Albans with 25 machines. A launderette was not a "shop" (Town and Country Planning (Use Classes) Order 1972) and the property could only be valued for its lawful use—*rebus sic stantibus.* "Zoning" as a method of valuation was inappropriate as was counsel's novel method of valuation according to the number of machines. However, a launderette is of the same mode or category as a shop, and using other shops as comparables, a gross value of £1,000 and rateable value of £805 were assessed (*Wexler* v. *Playle* [1960] C.L.Y. 2698 applied)).

WEST DORSET DISTRICT COUNCIL *v.* AUTON AND THE POST OFFICE, LVC/205/1976 [1979] J.P.L. 623 (an assessment of £10,000 gross value was confirmed on a building used as a telephone exchange, since, although in arriving at the rent which a hypothetical tenant would pay for the hereditament, it was relevant to consider use of the premises for office purposes, since it was quite proper and indeed necessary in arriving at rental value to consider anticipated events which might be in the mind of the hypothetical tenant in so far as they might influence the rent which he could reasonably be expected to pay, a tenant wishing to use these particular premises as office premises would not pay a rent in excess, in terms of gross value, of £10,000, on account of alterations which would need to be made and regulations which would need to be met to make them suitable for such a use. A comparison with agreed assessments on six telephone exchanges in neighbouring towns supported the present assessment. The contractors' test in this case was so full of uncertainties that it could not carry sufficient weight to disturb the assessment of £10,000 gross value).

WEST OF OUSE INTERNAL DRAINAGE BOARD *v.* H. PRINS (1978) 247 E.G. 295 (unsuccessful appeal from Lands Tribunal decision LVC/541/1975 [1977] C.L.Y. 2452—when assessing the respondent's glasshouses for drainage rates, the value of the heating installations should be disregarded; these were not rateable under the Plant and Machinery (Rating) Orders. The local valuation court and Lands Tribunal had disregarded the value of the heating installations, and had assessed the annual value of the glass houses at £335, not £670 as the valuation officer had assessed. The local custom of applying Income Tax Sched. A valuations was wrong).

WOLVERHAMPTON ASSOCIATION OF RATEPAYERS *v.* STAMP (LVC/861/1977) (1977) 246 E.G. 751. (A ratepayers association appealed to the Lands Tribunal against a reduction in gross value by the LVC in respect of the appeal hereditament, in consequence of its change from multiple to single occupation. The association sought to quash the decision and order a rehearing because of alleged contravention of s. 76 (3) of the 1967 Act in that a further proposal was heard before the earlier proposal for the same hereditament was settled. *Held*, dismissing the appeal, s. 77 of the Act gives the tribunal no power to quash an LVC decision, or order a rehearing; such matters must be dealt with by the Divisional Court (*Hulme* v. *Bucklow Area Assessment Committee* [1940] 2 K.B. 255 followed). *Quaere* whether a ratepayers' association has *locus standi* to appeal to LVC).

F. W. WOOLWORTH & CO. *v.* MOORE, LVC/297, 198/1976 (the tribunal *held* that the actual rent of large shop premises in a new shopping centre was the best starting point when valuing the premises for rating purposes, rents of other large shops in the centre being used as a check, and that it would need some glaring inconsistency to arise before the evidence of rents and assessments of very much smaller shops in the centre could be taken to outweigh the evidence of the actual rents for the large shops. The tribunal did not accept the valuation officer's contention that the shop had been let substantially below its true value).

YELLAND *v.* ARDLEY (LVC/710–715/1976) (1978) 248 E.G. 509 (property was a shop with living accommodation above it, in Ipswich. The shop walls inside were bare brick to frieze level. A held it on a seven-year lease with onerous repairing covenants, and a covenant restricting user to a numismatist's shop. The rent was slightly low because of the repairing covenants. *Held*, the effect of the user covenant on the rent was only marginal. No deduction for bare brick walls, which were a decorative feature of the shop. Assessed: gross value £1,200; rateable value £972).

2230. Liability for rates—husband separated from wife—no interest in rateable property

A husband who is separated from his wife, and who has no legal or beneficial interest in the matrimonial home occupied exclusively by the wife, is not the rateable occupier thereof.

A husband and wife lived together until 1973 in a house bought by the wife in her sole name. In 1973 the husband left and in 1976 the wife obtained a decree of judicial separation, the husband in the meantime having been ordered to pay maintenance to the wife and children who lived with her. The husband claimed no interest in the house, but he was listed as the rateable occupier and a distress warrant was issued upon his failure to pay the rates for the year ended March 1977, the justices holding that he was deemed to be in beneficial occupation by reason of his obligation to maintain his wife and children. *Held*, allowing the husband's appeal and quashing the warrant, that since he had no interest in the house, the husband could not be the rateable occupier. (*Bromley London Borough Council* v. *Brooks* [1973] C.L.Y. 2779 distinguished.)

BROWN *v.* OXFORD CITY COUNCIL [1978] 3 All E.R. 1113, D.C.

2231. Natural gas terminals

NATURAL GAS TERMINALS (RATEABLE VALUES) (AMENDMENT) ORDER 1979 (No. 1373) [10p], made under the General Rate Act 1967 (c. 9), s. 33 (5), Sched. 6, para. 13; operative on November 27, 1979; amends S.I. 1976 No. 391 by substituting certain new formulae and by adding certain premises to column 2 of Sched. 1 to that order.

2232. Northern Ireland. See NORTHERN IRELAND.

2233. Rate rebates

RATE REBATE (AMENDMENT) REGULATIONS 1979 (No. 417) [10p], made under the Local Government Act 1974 (c. 7), s. 11 (1); operative on April 26, 1979; amend S.I. 1978 No. 1504 to enable the grant of a rate rebate to a residential occupier who is in receipt of supplementary benefit if he will have received less payment in supplementary benefit than he would otherwise have received in rate rebate.

RATE REBATE (AMENDMENT) (No. 2) REGULATIONS 1979 (No. 1303) [20p], made under the Local Government Act 1974, s. 11 (1); operative on November 12, 1979; amend the rate rebate scheme provided for in S.I. 1978 No. 1504 by increasing the needs allowance and the amount to be deducted for a non-dependent.

2234. Rate support grants

RATE SUPPORT GRANTS (ADJUSTMENT OF NEEDS ELEMENT) (AMENDMENT) REGULATIONS 1979 (No. 337) [10p], made under the Local Government Act 1974 (c. 7), s. 10 (3) (5), Sched. 2, para. 3; operative on April 1, 1979; amend S.I. 1976 No. 1939 and, in respect of each establishment of further education increase the amounts of capital expenditure from revenue in a financial year to which those regulations apply.

RATE SUPPORT GRANT REGULATIONS 1979 (No. 1514) [80p], made under the Local Government Act 1974, ss. 2 (4), 10 (3), Sched. 2, paras. 2, 6, 9, 11, and the General Rate Act 1967 (c. 9), s. 48 (4); operative on April 1, 1980; provide for carrying into effect the provisions of the 1974 Act with respect to the payment of rate support grants to local authorities for the year 1980–81.

2235. Rateable occupation—storage of furniture in house

The appellant authority appealed on a case stated against a magistrates' finding of non-occupation on the ground that such a decision could not reasonably have been reached. During the relevant period the respondent kept a freezer, cooker, fridge and gas fire in the premises; there were some carpets and curtains; he kept the heating on and visited the house to repair it; no one slept there. *Held*, dismissing the appeal, the decision, though surprising, could not be held to be unreasonable. Other chattels had been put into store and the magistrates were entitled to rely on the maxim *de minimis non curat lex*: WIRRAL BOROUGH COUNCIL *v.* LANE (1979) 251 E.G. 61, D.C.

2236. Rates—company in liquidation—when rate " due and payable "

[Companies Act 1948 (c. 38), s. 319 (1) (*a*); General Rate Act 1967 (c. 9), s. 79.]

A direction retrospectively bringing a property into rating has the effect that the rate is deemed to have been due and payable at the commencement of the rating period.

The company owned a site which was removed from the valuation list upon the hereditaments being demolished with a view to redevelopment. In March 1973 the council resolved to levy a general rate for the year ended March 1974 for the area including the site, but the site was not included in the valuation list introduced on April 1, 1973. The site was brought into the list by a direction made on February 13, 1974, and a demand for rates for the year ended March 1974 was dispatched. On April 1, 1974, the company went into voluntary liquidation. The liquidators disputed the council's claim for rates for the period April 1 to December 3, 1973, contending that no priority should be given to the same by virtue of s. 319 of the 1948 Act since the rate had been due and payable more than 12 months prior to the liquidation, namely on March 8, 1973. *Held*, that by virtue of s. 79 of the 1967 Act, the direction of February 13, 1974, took effect from April 1, 1973, upon which date the rate was deemed to have been due and payable. (*Thomson* v. *Beckenham Rating Authority* (1947) C.L.C. 8276 distinguished; *Re Airedale Garage* [1933] Ch. 64, applied.)

Re PICCADILLY ESTATE HOTELS (1978) 77 L.G.R. 79, Slade J.

2237. Rating surcharge—priority over legal mortgage. See WESTMINSTER CITY COUNCIL *v.* HAYMARKET PUBLISHING, § 1830.

2238. Unoccupied property—date of commencement of liability for rating— moratorium

[General Rate Act 1967 (c. 9), s. 17 and Sched. 1 as amended by Local Government Act 1974 (c. 7).] B, as the Rating Authority, claimed from L, the tenants of two floors in an office block, £7,013 in respect of rates alleged to be due during a period when those floors were let though unoccupied. B claimed rates from the date when the tenancy began. L claimed that the rating should begin on the expiry of a three months' moratorium. or the date of actual occupation. They also raised numerous technical objections, all of which were rejected. *Held*, L became liable for rates from the date when tenancy began (*Camden London Borough Council* v. *Post Office* [1977] C.L.Y. 2449 applied; *B. Kettle* v. *Newcastle-under-Lyme Borough Council* [1979] C.L.Y. 2245 applied and extended): BRENT LONDON BOROUGH COUNCIL v. LADBROKE RENTALS (1979) 252 E.G. 702, Kilner-Brown J.

2239. —— **effect of resolution—distress warrant for penal rates**
[General Rate Act 1967 (c. 9), s. 17, Sched. 1.] The appellant owner of nine newly built warehouses at Bar Hill, Cambridgeshire, appealed by case stated from a magistrates' decision authorising the issue of a distress warrant in respect of non-payment of penal rates. The warehouses were unoccupied at all material times and the respondent council had made a proper resolution in accordance with the section. The appellant took various technical points as to the specification of the proportion of the rate to be levied, the alleged late posting of the letter of notice of levy, the lack of specific authorisation of that letter and of the distress proceedings and the validity of levying penal rates on property which was not in the valuation list. *Held*, on all points that the appellant failed. The resolution and all subsequent proceedings were valid within the meaning of the Act. Appeal dismissed: BAR HILL DEVELOPMENTS v. SOUTH CAMBRIDGESHIRE DISTRICT COUNCIL (1979) 252 E.G. 915, D.C.

2240. —— **resolution of authority—validity**
[General Rate Act 1967 (c. 9), s. 17 and Sched. 1.] The appellant, faced with an order of magistrates that a distress warrant should issue for £173,000 unpaid rates on an unoccupied office block, argued on a case stated that the resolution of the respondent authority to levy rates on unoccupied property was void. The resolution purported to apply s. 17 of the Act without reference to Sched. 1: a rate of 100 per cent. was resolved thereby. *Held*, dismissing the appeal, the resolution was sufficiently clear and had not misled the appellant. Resolutions or recommendations of this kind are not to be construed formally (*Sheffield City Council* v. *Grainger Wines* [1977] C.L.Y. 2472 followed): GRAYLAW INVESTMENTS v. HARLOW DISTRICT COUNCIL (1979) 251 E.G. 573, D.C.

2241. —— **substantial completion—completion notice served—whether time for doing " customary work " runs from date of completion or date of notice**
In assessing when a building became subject to rates, time runs from the date of substantial completion of the building and not from the date of service of the completion notice. There is no jurisdiction to extend such a period once it has expired.
An office building was substantially completed in 1975 and the local authority notified. The remaining work was that customarily done after completion of the structural work such as the erection of internal partitions. On March 7, 1977, a completion notice was served to take effect from April 30, whereupon the building would be subject to rates. The owners appealed and on July 12, 1977, were granted a six month extension from the date of the completion notice. The local authority appealed. *Held*, allowing the appeal, that the time allowed for the completion of the customary work ran from the date of substantial completion not the date of service of the completion notice. There was no jurisdiction to extend such a period once it had expired.
GRAYLAW INVESTMENTS v. IPSWICH BOROUGH COUNCIL (1978) 77 L.G.R. 297, C.A.

2242. —— **surcharge—previously used for industrial purposes—whether a " factory "**
[General Rate Act 1967 (c. 9), s. 17A; Rating Surcharge (Exemption) Regulations 1974 (S.I. 1974 No. 1563), reg. 3 (*a*).]
Where premises are used largely for the sale and preparation of new and used cars they can properly be regarded as a factory or as premises of a

"similar character used mainly for industrial purposes" for the purpose of a rating surcharge exemption.

The Post Office owned premises, of which 72·5 per cent. of the area had been used for over 40 years as a garage workshop. The premises were registered under the Factories Act 1961. They became vacant and the Post Office were assessed in respect of a rating surcharge. The justices decided the premises were commercial and not exempt from surcharge. On appeal, *held*, allowing the appeal, that as 72·5 per cent. of the premises were used for workshop and ancillary purposes they came within the scope of reg. 3 (*a*) of the 1974 Regulations.

POST OFFICE *v.* OXFORD CITY COUNCIL (1979) 77 L.G.R. 534, D.C.

2243. —— —— principles governing relief—hardship
[General Rate Act 1967 (c. 9), ss. 17, 17A, Sched. 1, para. 3A.]
Where a rating authority is considering an application for remission of rates on the grounds of hardship, it is not unreasonable for it to refuse the application in a case where it has received only limited information from the applicant as to his financial position.

In 1973 W Ltd. entered negotiations to buy an office building in which many tenants remained, with the intention of gaining vacant possession, demolishing and redeveloping the site. By 1975 W Ltd. had still been unable to gain vacant possession of the property and were assessed on the unoccupied rate and to a rating surcharge. W Ltd. applied for remission on grounds of hardship but failed to comply with a request to provide the rating authority with accounts for the previous three years. The application was refused. On appeal to the Court of Appeal, *held*, dismissing the appeal, that if the company refused to supply the authority with proper information on the one pertinent point, namely "hardship to the person liable" for the rates, it was not unreasonable for the authority to reject the application without reasons. (*Associated Provincial Picture Theatres* v. *Wednesbury Corporation* (1947) C.L.C. 8107, and *Padfield* v. *Minister of Agriculture, Fisheries and Food* [1968] C.L.Y. 1667 considered.)

WINDSOR SECURITIES *v.* LIVERPOOL CITY COUNCIL (1978) 77 L.G.R. 502, C.A.

2244. Valuation—agricultural land—capital gains tax purposes. See HALLEY *v.* WEIGHTMAN, § 1455.

2245. —— amendment of list—demand of rates pending valuation court decision—whether valid
[General Rate Act 1967 (c. 9), ss. 2 (4), 6 (1) (2).] A local valuation officer proposed to alter the valuation list to include a rateable value of £13,000 for a hitherto unrated coal tip occupied by the appellant company. The company lodged an objection at the valuation court as to the figure. Meanwhile the respondent authority demanded rates in the appropriate sum on the original assessment and the Divisional Court, upon a case stated by magistrates, found the authority to be entitled thereto. *Held*, dismissing the appeal, ss. 2 and 6 of the Act empowered the authority to amend the list without referring each amendment to the full council. The purported alteration to include the tip came under the umbrella of the annual general resolution of the council of the respondent authority to levy rates upon chargeable hereditaments at a particular rate in the pound. Accordingly the rates were payable when the proposal was made, before the matter had gone to the court and had entered the list. Any overpayment upon reduction of the assessment by the valuation court would be refundable under the Act: B. KETTLE *v.* NEWCASTLE-UNDER-LYME BOROUGH COUNCIL (1979) 251 E.G. 59, C.A.

2246. —— local valuation court—contempt—whether a "court" protected by High Court jurisdiction. See ATT.-GEN. *v.* BRITISH BROADCASTING CORP., § 2121.

2247. Valuers—valuation for mortgage—principles to be applied
P lent A £60,000, secured by a second mortgage on a hotel valued by D at £275,000. D's valuation was made during the property boom of 1973, and took no account of a possible slump, or the effect on the value of the property of the owner's having to comply with the fire regulations. A went

into liquidation, and the hotel was sold, realising only £100,000, all of which went to the first mortgagee. P sued D. *Held*, a valuation for mortgage purposes must take account of possible lower prices realised by a forced sale, and a discount should be made of any amount attributable to the " speculative content " of the valuation. A mortgage valuation must look for a certain period into the future: in the present case there were definite signs at the date of the valuation that the property boom was coming to an end. D could reasonably have been expected to consider, not only the value at the date of valuation, but also the value of the property in six or 12 months' time. An allowance should also have been made for the cost of complying with the fire certificate works. The valuation of the property should have been £220,000, less £8,000 for the fire certificate works, on which P would have lent £16,300. P's loss was accordingly £43,700, for which sum judgment was given: CORISAND INVESTMENTS *v.* DRUCE & CO. (1978) 248 E.G. 315, Gibson J.

BOOKS AND ARTICLES. See *post*, pp. [10], [29].

REAL PROPERTY AND CONVEYANCING

2248. Adverse possession—animus possidendi

A person who enters upon land as a trespasser and later seeks to show that he has dispossessed the owner must produce compelling evidence of the *animus possidendi* and that he has made it clear to the world.

D owned a field which was used as agricultural land by an area of landscape value. Nearby P later acquired a small farm with which his family has been associated for many years. The field was planted with Christmas trees. D bought a neighbouring plot for a house. In 1955 D, who was a civil servant, was posted overseas where he remained for 11 years. P, who was then 14, used the land to graze his cow, Kushla, having first writen to D for permission and having received no reply. He cut hay there, to feed the cow and later, made the fence stockproof so that he could leave the cow there. In 1968, the cow died. Between 1956 and 1973 P also used the land occasionally for shooting, and for a friend to tether a goat. P put up a sign advertising his business, which was visible from the road, D's wife had visited the field and noticed nothing untoward, but when D visited in August 1972, he found that the trees were gone, the fence was in disrepair, and the land overgrown. D then made a grazing agreement with X, the second defendant. P sought a declaration that he had been in adverse possession for more than 12 years. *Held*, refusing the declaration, that a person claiming adverse possession must show factual possession which was simple and conclusive and also that he had been dealing with the land in the manner in which the owner might have been to do so; he must also adduce compelling evidence an *animus possidendi* which had been made clear to the world. The activities of P when a 14 year old boy who owned no land in the neighbourhood was not necessarily referable to an intention on his part to dispossess D. (*Wallis's Cayton Bay Holiday Camp* v. *Shell-Mex and B.P.* [1974] C.L.Y. 3148, *Treloar* v. *Nute* [1976] C.L.Y. 811 and *Gray* v. *Wykeham-Martin* [1977] C.L.Y. (Unreported Cases § 537).)
POWELL *v.* McFARLANE (1979) 38 P. & C.R. 452, Slade J.

2249. Conveyance—rectification—mistake by solicitor. See WEEDS *v.* BLANEY, § 747.

2250. Covenants—restrictive covenants—Lands Tribunal decisions

NEW IDEAL HOMES' APPLICATION (Ref. L.P./16/1977) (1978) 36 P. & C.R. 476 (in 1973 land was conveyed by the U.D.C. to the applicants subject to a restrictive covenant that they would build only 75 houses on the 9·66 acres. Planning permission was later granted for four additional houses. In 1976 permission was granted for another 156 houses. The applicants sought to have the restriction modified. The objectors were the borough council, the covenantee. The benefit of the covenant was annexed to, *inter alia*, 13 acres adjoining the applicants' land. They argued it would deprive them of the option of selling part of the site to private developers at a high price for low density development. *Held*, (1) there was no real shortage of land which had the benefit of planning permission; (2) the objectors' land would not be developed at less than 16 houses per acre and hence the restriction did not secure any practical benefits to the objectors that could not be adequately compensated in money).

Re OSBORN'S AND EASTON'S APPLICATION (1978) 38 P. & C.R. 251 (an estate was laid out in plots in 1913, and there were restrictive covenants restraining development. A and B, who owned large plots, obtained planning permission to build blocks of flats. They sought modification of the restrictive covenants to permit the development under ss. 84 (*aa*) and 84 (1A) of the Law of Property Act 1925 as amended by the Law of Property Act 1969. They contended that repeal would be against the public interest in view of the Government's policy towards higher density development. *Held*, it did not follow that any but high density development would be contrary to public interest within subs. (1A) of s. 84, and the applications would be refused).

2251. —— —— not disclosed by vendor—whether purchaser deemed to have notice. See FARUQI *v.* ENGLISH REAL ESTATES, § 2771.

2252. Exchange of contracts—exchange by telephone. See DOMB *v.* ISOZ, § 2766.

2253. Land charges. See LAND CHARGES.

2254. Land registration. See LAND REGISTRATION.

2255. Mortgages. See MORTGAGES.

2256. Northern Ireland. See NORTHERN IRELAND.

2257. Registered land. See LAND REGISTRATION.

2258. Sale of land. See VENDOR AND PURCHASER.

2259. Stamp duties. See STAMP DUTIES.

2260. Town and country planning. See TOWN AND COUNTRY PLANNING.

2261. Trusts. See SETTLEMENTS AND TRUSTS.

BOOKS AND ARTICLES. See *post,* pp. [10], [29].

REGISTRATION OF BIRTHS, DEATHS AND MARRIAGES

2262. Registration—consular officers
REGISTRATION OF BIRTHS AND DEATHS (CONSULAR OFFICERS) (AMENDMENT) REGULATIONS 1979 (No. 1072) [10p], made under the British Nationality Act 1948 (c. 56), s. 29 (1) (*f*) (*g*); operative on September 24, 1979; provide for the registration of births and deaths of U.K. citizens in the New Hebrides; amend S.I. 1974 No. 2136.

ARTICLES. See *post,* p. [30].

REVENUE AND FINANCE

2263. Appropriation Act 1979 (c. 24)
This Act provides for the appropriation of the supplies granted in this Session of Parliament.
S. 1 appropriates sums voted for supply services; s. 2 gives the short title.
The Act received the Royal Assent on April 4, 1979, and came into force on that date.

2264. Appropriation (No. 2) Act 1979 (c. 51)
This Act applies a sum out of the Consolidated Fund to the service of the year ending March 31, 1980; it also appropriates supplies granted in this session of Parliament, and repeals certain Consolidated Fund and Appropriation Acts.
S. 1 provides for the issue out of the Consolidated Fund for the year ending March 31, 1980; s. 2 appropriates sums voted for supply services; s. 3 contains repeals; s. 4 gives the short title.
The Act received the Royal Assent on July 27, 1979, and came into force on that date.

2265. Borrowing control
CONTROL OF BORROWING (AMENDMENT) ORDER 1979 (No. 794) [10p], made under the Borrowing (Control and Guarantees) Act 1946 (c. 58), ss. 1, 3 (4);

operative on August 3, 1979; amends S.I. 1958 No. 1208 and exempts from borrowing control under Pt. I of that Order, issues of sterling securities by or on behalf of an open ended investment trust company which is resident in the scheduled territories but outside the U.K.

2266. Capital transfer tax. See CAPITAL TAXATION.

2267. Consolidated Fund Act 1979 (c. 20)

This Act authorises the issue of certain moneys out of the Consolidated Fund.

The Act received the Royal Assent on March 22, 1979, and came into force on that date.

2268. Consolidated Fund (No. 2) Act 1979 (c. 56)

This Act authorises the issue of certain moneys out of the consolidated Fund.

The Act received the Royal Assent on December 20, 1979, and came into force on that date.

2269. Counter-inflation

PRICES AND CHARGES (NOTIFICATION OF INCREASES) (AMENDMENT) ORDER 1979 (No. 60) [10p], made under the Counter-Inflation Act 1973 (c. 9), ss. 5, 15, Sched. 3, para. 1 (1) (2) (6); operative on January 25, 1979; provides that an intended increase in the price of specified animal foodstuff need not be notified to the Price Commission but particulars of such an increase must be furnished to the Commission not later than 14 days after it is implemented.

PRICES AND CHARGES (NOTIFICATION OF INCREASES) (AMENDMENT No. 2) ORDER 1979 (No. 178) [10p], made under the Counter-Inflation Act 1973, ss. 5, 15, Sched. 3, para. 1 (4) (6); operative on March 26, 1979; varies S.I. 1978 No. 1083 by the omission of provisions inserted by S.I. 1979 No. 60 which is revoked.

PRICES AND CHARGES (NOTIFICATION OF INCREASES) (REVOCATION) ORDER 1979 (No. 568) [10p], made under the Counter-Inflation Act 1973, ss. 5, 15, Sched. 3, para. 1 (6); operative on May 24, 1979; revokes S.I. 1978 No. 1083. It removes the obligation to give notice of intended increases in prices or charges to the Price Commission.

2270. Customs and excise. See CUSTOMS AND EXCISE.

2271. Death duties. See DEATH DUTIES.

2272. Double taxation. See INCOME TAX.

2273. Exchange control

EXCHANGE CONTROL (AUTHORISED DEALERS AND DEPOSITARIES) (AMENDMENT) ORDER 1979 (No. 321) [10p], made under the Exchange Control Act 1947 (c. 14), ss. 36 (5), 42 (1); operative on April 2, 1979; amends the lists of: (a) banks and other persons authorised under the 1947 Act to deal in gold and foreign currencies; and (b) those who are entitled to act as authorised depositaries for the purpose of the deposit of securities as required by the Act.

EXCHANGE CONTROL (IMPORT AND EXPORT) (AMENDMENT) ORDER 1979 (No. 647) [10p], made under the Exchange Control Act 1947, ss. 31, 36 (5); operative on June 13, 1979; amends S.I. 1966 No. 1351 and permits travellers to destinations outside the U.K., the Channel Islands and the Republic of Ireland to take with them £1,000 worth of foreign currency notes.

EXCHANGE CONTROL (GOLD COINS EXEMPTION) ORDER 1979 (No. 648) [10p], made under the Exchange Control Act 1947, ss. 31, 36 (5); operative on June 13, 1979; revokes S.I. 1975 No. 609 and allows gold coin to be bought, sold, borrowed and lent without permission under s. 1 (1) of the 1947 Act and to be held without permission under s. 2 (1) of that Act.

EXCHANGE CONTROL (AUTHORISED DEALERS AND DEPOSITARIES) (AMENDMENT) (No. 2) ORDER 1979 (No. 740) [10p], made under the Exchange Control Act 1947, ss. 36 (5), 41 (1); operative on July 13, 1979; amends the list of banks and other persons authorised to deal in gold and foreign currencies, and those who are authorised to act as depositaries for the purpose of the deposit of securities as required by the 1947 Act.

EXCHANGE CONTROL (AUTHORISED DEALERS AND DEPOSITARIES) (AMENDMENT) (No. 3) ORDER 1979 (No. 1194) [20p], made under the Exchange Control

Act 1947, ss. 36 (5), 42 (1); operative on October 2, 1979; amends the list of Banks and other persons authorised under the 1947 Act to deal in gold and foreign currencies and amends the list of those entitled to act as authorised depositaries for the purposes of the deposit of securities.

EXCHANGE CONTROL (GOLD AND FOREIGN CURRENCY) (EXEMPTION) ORDER 1979 (No. 1331) [20p], made under the Exchange Control Act 1947, ss. 1 (2), 2 (1), 31 and 36 (5); operative on October 24, 1979; exempts from the provisions of s. 1 (1) of the 1947 Act the buying, borrowing, selling or lending of gold and foreign currency other than Southern Rhodesian currency.

EXCHANGE CONTROL (PAYMENTS ETC.) (EXEMPTION) ORDER 1979 (No. 1332) [20p], made under the Exchange Control Act 1947, ss. 31 and 36 (5); operative on October 24, 1979; exempts from the prohibitions imposed by ss. 5–7 of the 1947 Act every payment except a payment made to a person resident in Southern Rhodesia, and exempts from the provisions of s. 5 (c) the placing of any sum to the credit of any person except a resident in Southern Rhodesia.

EXCHANGE CONTROL (SECURITIES ETC.) (EXEMPTION) ORDER 1979 (No. 1333) [20p], made under the Exchange Control Act 1947, ss. 15 (1) (b), 31 and 36 (5); operative on October 24, 1979; grants conditional exemptions, except in relation to transactions involving persons resident in Southern Rhodesia, from ss. 8–14 and 28 of the 1947 Act. It also completely abolishes the obligation to place certain securities in the custody of an Authorised Depositary, the restrictions on Authorised Depositaries parting with securities already in their custody, and the restrictions on dealing in securities etc. imposed by ss. 15 and 16 of the 1947 Act.

EXCHANGE CONTROL (IMPORT AND EXPORT) (EXEMPTION) ORDER 1979 (No. 1334) [20p], made under the Exchange Control Act 1947, ss. 31 and 36 (5); operative on October 24, 1979; completely exempts all the things referred to in s. 21 of the 1947 Act from the prohibition on imports imposed by that section, completely exempts from the prohibtion on exports imposed by s. 22 all currency notes, postal orders and travellers' cheques, letters of credit etc., and exempts from that prohibition on export securities etc. and documents relating thereto unless owned by a person resident in Southern Rhodesia.

EXCHANGE CONTROL (EXPORTS) (SOUTHERN RHODESIA) ORDER 1979 (No. 1335) [10p], made under the Exchange Control Act 1947 s. 23; operative on October 24, 1979; s. 23 of the 1947 Act henceforth applies only to exports to destinations in Southern Rhodesia.

EXCHANGE CONTROL (SETTLEMENTS) (EXEMPTION) ORDER 1979 (No. 1336) [10p], made under the Exchange Control Act 1947, s. 31; operative on October 24, 1979; provides that henceforth s. 29 of the 1947 Act only applies to a settlement made (otherwise than by will) so as to confer an interest in property on a person resident in Southern Rhodesia; and to the exercise of a power of appointment in favour of any such person.

EXCHANGE CONTROL (BODIES CORPORATE) (EXEMPTION) ORDER 1979 (No. 1337) [10p], made under the Exchange Control Act 1947, s. 31; operative on October 24, 1979; gives partial exemption from s. 30 (2) of the Act and complete exemption from s. 30 (3) and (3A).

EXCHANGE CONTROL (AUTHORISED DEALERS AND DEPOSITARIES) (AMENDMENT) (No. 4) ORDER 1979 (No. 1338) [10p], made under the Exchange Control Act 1947, ss. 36 (5) and 42 (1); operative on October 24, 1979; provides that all existing Authorised Depositaries continue to have that status, although they no longer have special functions under ss. 15 and 16 of the 1947 Act. The continuation of the status enables them to go on fulfilling their functions in relation to the reduced rate of stamp duty on transactions by persons resident outside the scheduled territories by virtue of the Finance Act 1974, s. 49.

EXCHANGE CONTROL (REVOCATION) DIRECTIONS 1979 (No. 1339) [10p], made under the Exchange Control Act 1947, s. 37 (2) (b); operative on October 24, 1979; revoke all the directions at present in force under ss. 26, 34 (2) and 40 of the 1947 Act.

EXCHANGE CONTROL (GENERAL EXEMPTION) ORDER 1979 (No. 1660) [10p], made under the Exchange Control Act 1947, ss. 31, 36 (5) and 37 (1);

operative on December 13, 1979; all exchange controls relating to Southern Rhodesia are now removed.

CONTROL OF GOLD AND TREASURY BILLS (SOUTHERN RHODESIA) (REVOCATION) DIRECTIONS 1979 (No. 1661) [10p], made under the Emergency Laws (Re-enactments and Repeals) Act 1964 (c. 60), ss. 2, 7 (2); operative on December 13, 1979; following the lifting of sanctions imposed in relation to Southern Rhodesia, these Directions revoke S.I. 1965 No. 1939.

EXCHANGE CONTROL (REVOCATION) (No. 2) DIRECTIONS 1979 (No. 1662) [10p], made under the Exchange Control Act 1947, s. 37 (2) (b); operative on December 13, 1979; extends the relaxation of Exchange Control contained in S.I. 1979 No. 1660 to Southern Rhodesia.

2274. —— breach—power of Treasury to require information—person charged
[Exchange Control Act 1947 (c. 14), Sched. 5, Pt. I, para. 1 (1).]
The Treasury has power under para. 1 (1) of Pt. I of Sched. 3 to the Exchange Control Act 1947 to direct a person to furnish information which may incriminate himself, but that power ceases once the person has been charged and cautioned.

Customs officers who were investigating breaches of the Exchange Control Act 1947 seized documents of companies of which A and B were directors. B declined to answer a questionnaire, was arrested, charged with contravention of s. 23, and conspiracy at common law, and cautioned. The Treasury required him to answer another questionnaire under para. 1 (1) of Pt. I of Sched. 5 to the Act. The questionnaire was to obtain information which would incriminate B on the charges against him. The Treasury also required A to answer a similar questionnaire. A and B took out originating summonses to find out if they were bound in law to comply. *Held*, as B had been charged and cautioned, he was not bound to comply, because he had the right to remain silent; A, however, had not been charged, and was bound to comply, whether or not in doing so he incriminated himself. (*D.P.P.* v. *Ellis* [1973] C.L.Y. 2858 distinguished.)

A. v. H.M. TREASURY; B. v. H.M. TREASURY [1979] 2 All E.R. 586, T. P. Russell Q.C.

2275. —— practice. See § 2132.

2276. Exchange Equalisation Account Act 1979 (c. 30)
This Act consolidates enactments relating to the Exchange Equalisation Account.

S. 1 continues the Exchange Equalisation Account and states for what purposes it is to be used; s. 2 relates to the funding of the Account; s. 3 provides for investment of the Account's funds; s. 4 provides for the annual examination and certification of the Account; s. 5 contains the short title and repeals.

The Act received the Royal Assent on April 4, 1979, and came into force on May 4, 1979.

2277. Finance Act 1979 (c. 25)
This Act continues income tax and corporation tax at the existing rates, increases the main personal reliefs, and withdraws child allowances.

S. 1 states the rate of income tax for 1979–80, and increases certain personal allowances; s. 2 charges corporation tax for 1979–80; s. 3 gives the short title.

The Act received the Royal Assent on April 4, 1979, and came into force on that date.

2278. Finance (No. 2) Act 1979 (c. 47)
This Act grants certain duties, alters other duties, amends the law relating to the National Debt and the Public Revenue, and makes further provision in connection with finance.

Pt. I (ss. 1–4) relates to value added tax and excise duties: s. 1 increases the rate of value added tax; s. 2 amends ss. 6 (1), 11 (1) (b) and 14 (1) of the Hydrocarbon Oil Duties Act 1979; s. 3 increases the duty on cigarettes under the Tobacco Products Duty Act 1979; s. 4 continues the regulatory powers under the Excise Duties (Surcharges or Rebates) Act 1979.

Pt. II (ss. 5–17) relates to income tax, corporation tax and capital gains tax: s. 5 states the income tax rates for the year 1979–80; s. 6 outlines the rate of advance corporation tax for the financial year 1979; s. 7 deals with marginal relief for small companies; s. 8 makes alterations in the personal and age allowances; s. 9 exempts pensions in respect of death due to war service etc.; s. 10 extends the transitional relief for interest; s. 11 makes consequential provisions upon the withdrawal of child tax allowances; s. 12 makes consequential provisions relating to the Social Security Pensions Act; s. 13 grants relief for increase in stock values; s. 14 amends the law relating to capital allowances for motor vehicles; s. 15 specifies the deduction rate for sub-contractors in the construction industry; s. 16 relates to the United States Double Taxation Convention; s. 17 states that any compensation paid for delay in national savings payments shall be disregarded for all purposes of tax.

Pt. III (ss. 18–22) relates to petroleum revenue tax; s. 18 increases the rate of petroleum revenue tax; s. 19 reduces the uplift for allowable expenditure under the Oil Taxation Act 1975; s. 20 provides for extension of allowable expenditure; s. 21 deals with the reduction of oil allowances and metrication of measurements; s. 22 ends the exemption from tax of the British National Oil Corporation.

Pt. IV (ss. 23–25) contains miscellaneous and supplementary provisions: s. 23 extends transitional relief for capital transfer tax; s. 24 makes provision as to development land tax; s. 25 deals with short title, interpretation, construction and repeals.

The Act received the Royal Assent on July 26, 1979, and came into force on that date, except for s. 2 which came into force on June 12, 1979, and s. 3 which came into force on August 13, 1979.

2279. Inland Revenue officers—powers of search and seizure—suspected tax fraud
[Taxes Management Act 1970 (c. 9), s. 20C.] On July 13, 1979, officers of the Inland Revenue entered and searched the offices of Rossminster Ltd. and A.J.R. Financial Services Ltd. and the homes of Mr. Roy Tucker and Mr. Ronald Plummer. They seized and removed large quantities of documents. They were acting under warrants issued the previous day under Taxes Management Act 1970, s. 20C, by the Common Serjeant. It was claimed that (1) the warrants were invalid because they did not sufficiently particularise the alleged offences, and (2) the action taken was unlawful since the officers had not had, or could not have had, reasonable cause to believe that the documents seized might be required as evidence in proceedings for "tax fraud." *Held* (Lord Salmon dissenting), reversing the decision of the Court of Appeal, that (1) the warrants were issued in accordance with, and in the form prescribed by Taxes Management Act 1970, s. 20C, and were valid, (2) the evidence fell very far short of showing that the action actually taken by the officers of the Inland Revenue was in excess of their powers: I.R.C. *v.* ROSS-MINSTER, *The Times*, December 14, 1979, H.L.

2280. International Monetary Fund Act 1979 (c. 29)
This Act consolidates the enactments relating to the International Monetary Fund, and repeals the European Monetary Agreement Act 1959.

S. 1 provides that payments by the U.K. Government to the International Monetary Fund shall be paid out of the National Loans Fund; s. 2 relates to loans to the International Monetary Fund; s. 3 states that receipts from the International Monetary Fund shall be paid into the National Loans Fund; s. 4 empowers the Treasury to create and issue notes and other obligations to the fund; s. 5 authorises provision to be made by Her Majesty in Council relating to the status, immunities and privileges of the fund; s. 6 contains repeals; s. 7 gives the short title.

The Act received the Royal Assent on April 4, 1979, and came into force on May 4, 1979.

2281. Local government finance. See LOCAL GOVERNMENT.

2282. National debt.
NATIONAL SAVINGS STOCK REGISTER (AMENDMENT) REGULATIONS 1979 (No. 1677) [10p], made under the National Debt Act 1972 (c. 65), s. 3; operative on January 4, 1980; amend S.I. 1976 No. 2012 and exempt the Accountant

General of the Supreme Court from the £5,000 limit on the amount of stock of any one description which may be purchased by any one person on any one day.

EXCHANGE OF SECURITIES (GENERAL) RULES 1979 (No. 1678) [40p], made under the National Loans Act 1968 (c. 13), s. 14 (3); operative on January 1, 1980; provide for the exchange and conversion of Government securities except National Savings Certificates, and consolidate (with amendments) earlier rules relating to the exchange of securities.

2283. Northern Ireland. See NORTHERN IRELAND.

2284. Price Commission (Amendment) Act 1979 (c. 1)

This Act limits the application of s. 9 of the Price Commission Act 1977.

S. 1 makes various amendments to the Price Commission Act 1977, and in particular it removes the obligation on the Secretary of State under s. 9 relating to minimum levels of profit safeguarded during a price investigation; s. 2 relates to the duration of the Act; s. 3 gives the short title.

The Act received the Royal Assent on February 12, 1979, and came into force on that day.

2285. Prices

PRICE MARKING (FOOD AND DRINK ON PREMISES) ORDER 1979 (No. 361) [25p], made under the Prices Act 1974 (c. 24), s. 4; operative on July 30, 1979; revokes S.I. 1975 No. 1737 and requires prices to be displayed on any premises where an indication is given that food or drink is or may be for sale for consumption there.

2286. Purchase tax. See PURCHASE TAX.

2287. Savings certificates

SAVINGS CERTIFICATES (AMENDMENT) REGULATIONS 1979 (No. 1388) [20p], made under the National Debt Act 1972 (c. 65), s. 11; operative on December 2, 1979; amend S.I. 1972 No. 641 and consolidate the list of maximum permitted holdings of certificates and distinguish between the two types of certificate listed as being on sale at a price of £10 per unit certificate namely index-linked certificates of the Retirement Issue and certificates of the 18th Issue.

SAVINGS CERTIFICATES (AMENDMENT) (NO. 2) REGULATIONS 1979 (No. 1533) [10p], made under the National Debt Act 1972, s. 11; operative on December 3, 1979; amend S.I. 1972 No. 641 and increase the maximum permitted holding of the index-linked Retirement Issue of National Savings Certificates from 70 to 120.

2288. Stamp duties. See STAMP DUTIES.

BOOKS AND ARTICLES. See *post*, pp. [10], [30].

ROAD TRAFFIC

2289. Accident—duty to stop and report—length of stop

[Road Traffic Act 1972 (c. 20), s. 25 (1) (2) (4); Road Traffic Act 1974 (c. 50), s. 24 (2), Sched. 6, para. 12.]

The obligation to stop after an accident includes an obligation to remain near the vehicle for a sufficient period to enable requests for particulars to be made.

R drove into a fence, damaged it and his car. He inspected the damage, locked his car and left, across a field. He did not exchange particulars with the agent of the owner of the fence who had seen the collision and who reported the matter to the police. *Held*, allowing P's appeal from R's acquittal on the charge of failing to stop and failing to report an accident, that R should have, but had not, stayed for a sufficient period to enable any person having reasonable cause to do so to exchange particulars with him; he had not fulfilled the duty to stop.

WARD v. RAWSON [1978] R.T.R. 498, D.C.

2290. —— officer making inquiries—whether caution necessary

A police officer ariving at the scene of an accident is not bound to administer a caution prior to enquiring what had happened.

The defendant was involved in an accident when his car collided with another which had in turn collided with another vehicle. A police officer arrived at the scene pursuant to a radio message and upon his arrival he asked the defendant what had happened. Justices trying an allegation of careless driving ruled inadmissible the defendant's answer upon the grounds that the officer had failed to caution the defendant; they further dismissed the summons. *Held,* allowing the prosecutor's appeal and ordering a re-hearing, that, since the officer was at the " gathering of information " stage it was not incumbent upon him to administer a caution (*R.* v. *Osbourne* [1973] C.L.Y. 559, applied.)

DILKS *v.* TILLEY [1979] R.T.R. 459, D.C.

2291. Construction and use

MOTOR VEHICLES (CONSTRUCTION AND USE) (AMENDMENT) (NO. 2) REGU-LATIONS 1979 (No. 843) [20p], made under the Road Traffic Act 1972 (c. 20), ss. 40 (1) (3), 199 (2); operative on August 16, 1979; amend S.I. 1978 No. 1017 so as to make provision for agricultural or forestry tractors that have been issued with an approval certificate or a certificate of conformity under S.I. 1979 No. 221.

MOTOR VEHICLES (CONSTRUCTION AND USE) (AMENDMENT) (NO. 3) REGU-LATIONS 1979 (No. 1062) [50p], made under the Road Traffic Act 1972, s. 40 (1) (3); operative on September 20, 1979; amend S.I. 1978 No. 1017 so as to consolidate with amendments regs. 17 and 17A relating to seat belts and anchorage points.

2292. —— articulated vehicle of excessive length—whether container an " indivisible load "

[Motor Vehicle (Construction and Use) Regulations 1973 (S.I. 1973 No. 24), regs. 3 (1), 9 (1).]

A container constructed for the purpose of being lifted on and off a vehicle together with its contents is not itself the " load " when considering whether the load is indivisible.

An information was laid against the defendant alleging a breach of reg. 9 (1) of the 1973 Regulations. The justices dismissed the information on finding, *inter alia,* that the container itself was an indivisible load of exceptional length. On appeal by case stated, *held,* allowing the appeal, that the container itself did not constitute the load or part of the load when considering whether the load was indivisible.

PATTERSON *v.* REDPATH BROTHERS [1979] 2 All E.R. 108, D.C.

2293. —— defective tyre—informations—amendment

[Magistrates' Courts Act 1952 (c. 55), ss. 100, 104; Road Traffic Act 1972 (c. 20), s. 40 (1) (5); Motor Vehicles (Construction and Use) Regulations 1973 (S.I. 1973 No. 24), reg. 99 (1) (c) (d) (e).]

An amendment of an information from alleging one defective tyre to another defective tyre does not create a new offence to which the time limitation of s. 104 of the Magistrates' Courts Act 1952 applies.

D's bus was used on a road with the rear offside tyre defective in three places. Three informations, which were heard a year later, alleged that the defects were on the rear nearside tyre. When the police office gave evidence of the correct tyre, the justices allowed the informations to be amended accordingly. D had brought the correct tyre to court. D sought an order prohibiting the justices from hearing the amended informations, contending that they were fresh informations, laid out of time under s. 104 of the Magistrates' Courts Act 1952. *Held,* refusing the order that the amendments were improper, that, since the tyre had been brought to court, and there was only one tyre involved in the case, the justices might well have dispensed with an amendment altogether. (*Garfield* v. *Maddocks* [1973] C.L.Y. 470 and *R.* v. *Newcastle-upon-*

Tyne Justices, ex p. John Bryce (Contractors) [1976] C.L.Y. 1686 applied; *Saines* v. *Woodhouse* [1970] C.L.Y. 2501 distinguished.)

R. *v.* SANDWELL JUSTICES, *ex p.* WEST MIDLANDS PASSENGER TRANSPORT EXECUTIVE [1979] R.T.R. 17, D.C.

2294. —— " using " by partner in firm—vehicle driven by employee

[Road Traffic Act 1972 (c. 20), s. 40 (5) (*b*); Motor Vehicles (Construction and Use) Regulations 1973 (S.I. 1973 No. 24), reg. 99 (1) (*f*).]

An employer " uses " a vehicle when it is driven by an employee, whether or not he takes an active part in the running of the business.

X, an employee of a taxi firm, drove the firm's Cortina with two bald tyres and was involved in an accident. D, a silent partner in the firm, was prosecuted for offences under reg. 99 (1) (*f*) of the Motor Vehicles (Construction and Use) Regulations 1973. The justices upheld a submission of no case on the ground that D was not " using " the vehicle. On appeal by the prosecution, *held*, allowing the appeal, that D was an employer, the vehicle was driven by an employee, therefore D was guilty of " using " the vehicle.

PASSMOOR *v.* GIBBONS [1979] R.T.R. 53, D.C.

2295. Cycle racing

CYCLE RACING ON HIGHWAYS (SPECIAL AUTHORISATION) (ENGLAND AND WALES) REGULATIONS 1979 (No. 233) [25p], made under the Road Traffic Act 1972 (c. 20), s. 20 (2) and (3); operative on April 1, 1979; vary a condition in S.I. 1960 No. 250, which authorises certain races or trials of speed between bicycles or tricycles, not being motor vehicles, to be held on public highways. The maximum number of competitors is increased to 84 in the case of the " Tour of Britain (Milk Race) " and " Sealink International," and to 60 in the case of other specified events.

2296. Dangerous driving—careless driving charge preferred on appeal—jurisdiction of Crown Court

[Road Traffic Act 1972 (c. 20), ss. 2, 3, Sched. 4, Pt. IV, para. 4; Courts Act 1971 (c. 23), s. 9 (2) (*c*).] Having allowed D's appeal against conviction of dangerous driving contrary to s. 2 of the 1972 Act the judge directed that a charge of careless driving contrary to s. 3 be put to D. D was convicted of the s. 3 offence. *Held*, that as the justices would have had power to take this course by virtue of Sched. 4, Pt. IV, para. 4, of the 1972 Act, the Crown Court could do so by virtue of the Courts Act 1971, s. 9 (2) (*c*): KILLINGTON *v.* BUTCHER [1979] Crim.L.R. 458, D.C.

2297. —— charge preferred of careless driving—whether valid procedure more than six months after offence

[Magistrates' Courts Act 1952 (c. 55), s. 104; Road Traffic Act 1972 (c. 20), Sched. 4, Pt. IV, para. 4.]

Proceedings for an offence under s. 3 of the Road Traffic Act 1972 which are substituted for proceedings under s. 2 by virtue of para. 4 of Pt. IV of Sched. 4 to the Act are not " the trial of an information " under s. 104 of the Magistrates' Courts Act 1952, and accordingly the six-month limitation does not apply.

D was charged with dangerous driving contrary to s. 2 of the Road Traffic Act 1972. The case was heard over six months after the alleged offence. The magistrates acquitted him of the charge but caused to be preferred a charge of driving without due care and attention contrary to s. 3, exercising their powers under para. 4 of Pt. IV of Sched. 4 to the Act. They convicted him. D applied for an order of certiorari to quash the conviction, on the grounds that the proceedings were outside the six-month limitation imposed by s. 104 of the Magistrates' Courts Act 1952. *Held*, refusing the application, that the limitation period did not apply.

R. *v.* COVENTRY JUSTICES, *ex p.* SAYERS [1979] R.T.R. 22, D.C.

2298. —— potential danger only—requirement to take test

[Road Traffic Act 1972 (c. 20), ss. 2, 93 (1) (3) (5) (7).]

The requirement to take a driving test should be imposed only in cases of age, infirmity, or where the circumstances suggest incompetence.

D was fined £400 and ordered to take a driving test, as well as being dis-

qualified from driving for six months, for driving up the M23 at 120 m.p.h.
It was his third motoring offence within three years. *Held,* allowing his appeal,
reducing the fine to £200 and removing the requirement to take a driving test,
that (1) the fine of £400 was excessive because only potential and not actual
danger had been caused; and (2) the requirement to take a driving test should
not be imposed as a punishment but only in cases of age, infirmity or other
appropriate circumstances.

    R. *v.* BANKS [1978] R.T.R. 535, C.A.

**2299. Death by dangerous driving—drinking and driving—sentence—three years'
imprisonment**

    [Road Traffic Act 1972 (c. 20), ss. 1 (1), 5 (1).]

    A sentence of three years' imprisonment for a bad case of drinking and
causing death by dangerous driving, even though the defendant may have been
ostracised for a long time between the offence and trial, is not too severe.

    D lived in a small township where everyone was known to each other.
After going out drinking, he drove his car down a street where there were
many people at 50 m.p.h., and into four people who were in their sixties, on
a zebra crossing. He killed two and injured a third. Between that time and
his trial for causing death by dangerous driving and driving whilst unfit through
drink, nine months elapsed during which D was ostracised by the rest of the
community. He was sentenced to three years' imprisonment on the first offence
and one year on the second, concurrent. On appeal against sentence, *held,*
dismissing the appeal, that the sentence adequately had regard to the unpleasant
time D had had before his trial, and could not possibly be said to be too
heavy.

    R. *v.* WRIGHT [1979] R.T.R. 15, C.A.

2300. —— **sentence**

    [Road Traffic Act 1972 (c. 20), ss. 1 (1), 93 (1), Sched. 4, para. 1.]

    To impose detention centre and an extended period of disqualification may be
excessive for a first offence of causing death by dangerous driving where no
recklessness is involved.

    Y drove his motor bike too fast and killed a pedestrian. A young man of 20
with no previous convictions, he had been driving at some 40/50 m.p.h. and
overtaking a line of traffic. He was sentenced to 15 months' disqualification
and detention centre. *Held,* allowing his appeal, that as there had been no
recklessness in the speed of the driving, the sentence would be reduced to 12
months' disqualification and a fine of £25, Y having already spent 12 days in
custody.

    R. *v.* YARNOLD [1978] R.T.R. 526, C.A.

2301. —— —— **whether imprisonment appropriate.** See R. *v.* BRUIN, § 559.

2302. Death by reckless driving—definition of " recklessness "

    [Road Traffic Act 1972 (c. 20), s. 1 (as amended by Criminal Law Act 1977
(c. 45), s. 50 (1)).]

    The court approved a direction as to the meaning of " recklessness," including
knowingly taking the risk of a vehicle getting out of control.

    The appellant drove a large pantechnicon too fast around a bend, mounting
the verge and swerving out of control into the path of an oncoming vehicle,
killing its driver. He was convicted of causing death by reckless driving,
following a direction in which the judge had told the jury that recklessness
involved more than carelessness, but was deliberately doing something knowing
it to involve the risk of losing control: " once you get out of control in a
vehicle of this size, anything might happen." *Held,* dismissing the appeal, that
such direction (if a subjective approach was appropriate, which question the
court did not decide) was easily understood and accurate.

    R. *v.* DAVIS [1979] R.T.R. 316, C.A.

2303. —— —— **subjective or objective approach**

    [Road Traffic Act 1972 (c. 20), s. 1 (as amended by Criminal Law Act 1977
(c. 45), s. 50 (1)).]

    The Court of Appeal considering a jury direction as to the meaning of recklessly has refrained from indicating whether an objective or subjective approach is required.

The appellant was convicted of causing death by reckless driving. In summing up the recorder initially directed the jury that it was for them to set the standard as to what amounted to reckless driving. Subsequently at counsel's invitation the recorder directed that the prosecution had to prove that (1) the appellant knew that by the manner of his driving there was a risk of such an accident as in fact happened; (2) with that knowledge he drove in the manner described; and (3) he could have avoided the risk had he so chosen. The appellant appealed on the grounds, _inter alia_, that the jury might have been confused by the conflicting directions. _Held_, dismissing the appeal, that the court was satisfied that upon their retirement the jury had in mind the second direction given by the recorder, which direction was conceded by the appellant to be favourable to him.

R. _v._ CLANCY [1979] R.T.R. 312, C.A.

2304. —— test of recklessness
[Road Traffic Act 1972 (c. 20), s. 1, as amended by Criminal Law Act 1977 (c. 45), s. 50.] The test to be applied is that to be reckless a person must be driving knowing that there is a risk that a serious accident may result if he drives in a certain way but drives in that way all the same. " Knowing " means that there must pass through his mind the realisation that there may be a serious accident: R. _v._ WHEELER, January 25, 1979; Judge ap Robert, Newport Crown Ct. (_Ex rel. Tom Crowther, Esq., Barrister._)

2305. Disqualification—driving whilst disqualified—committal proceedings—when proceedings " commenced." See R. _v._ BRENTWOOD JUSTICES, _ex p._ JONES, § 1717.

2306. Drink or drugs—blood or urine specimen—evidence unlawfully obtained
[Road Traffic Act 1972 (c. 20), s. 7 (1).] The defendant appealed on the ground that a sample of his blood, which contained an excess concentration of alcohol, was unlawfully obtained and should not have been admitted as evidence at his trial. _Held_, dismissing the appeal, that as there had been no deliberate misconduct by the police officer, it was not a case where the court should seek to discipline the police even if there might be cases where the exclusion of evidence for disciplinary reasons might be justified. If the judge had a discretion, he had clearly exercised it properly: R. _v._ TRUMP, _The Times_, December 29, 1979, C.A.

2307. —— —— failure to provide—conditional refusal
[Road Traffic Act 1972 (c. 20), ss. 9, 12.]
The fact that police may in their discretion allow a motorist to attempt to contact a solicitor for advice prior to agreeing to supply a specimen of blood or urine does not mean that the police must indefinitely postpone the request until such advice is actually received.

The defendant motorist, having been arrested on suspicion of driving with excess alcohol, was allowed to attempt to contact his solicitor by telephone to seek advice when asked to provide a specimen of blood or urine. He was unsuccessful. Thereafter further requests were made which were declined by the defendant until he had received advice. He was charged with and convicted of failing to provide a specimen. _Held_, dismissing his appeal, that there was reason to suppose that the defendant was simply trying to delay providing the specimen lawfully requested and that his conditional agreement to its provision clearly amounted to a refusal. (_Pettigrew_ v. _Northumbria Police Authority_ [1976] C.L.Y. 2391 applied.)

BROWN _v._ RIDGE [1979] R.T.R. 138, D.C.

2308. —— —— —— reasonable excuse—inability to understand reasons for requirement
[Road Traffic Act 1972 (c. 20), s. 9 (1) (3) (7).]
A driver's failure to understand what was being required of him or the possible penal consequences flowing from failure to comply with a request is sufficient to amount to a reasonable excuse for failing to provide a specimen.

The defendant, a Libyan, on failing a breath test was taken to a police station. He was requested to provide a blood or urine sample and was warned as to penalties for refusal. He failed to understand the questions or the meaning of " fine," " disqualification " or " urine " and did not provide the specimen. The justices dismissed the information that the defendant's failure to understand was a reasonable excuse. On appeal by the prosecutor, *held*, dismissing the appeal, that (1) the clear purpose of the mandatory warning was to ensure that nobody should be found guilty of failing to provide a specimen unless he had appreciated the possible consequences flowing from the failure; (2) where a driver did not understand what was required of him or the possible penalties for failure, he had not undergone the mental process intended by the statute, and in the present case there was evidence for the conclusion that the defendant's failure of understanding was sufficient to amount to a reasonable excuse.

BECK *v.* SAGER [1979] R.T.R. 475, D.C.

2309. —— —— —— —— **invincible repugnance to giving blood**
[Road Traffic Act 1972 (c. 20), s. 9 (3).] D was lawfully required to provide a specimen of blood or urine. He provided a urine specimen but was unable to provide a second within the time limit. He refused to provide a blood specimen as he had an invincible repugnance to giving blood. He was charged with failing, without reasonable excuse, to provide a specimen of blood or urine, contrary to s. 9 (3) of the 1972 Act. *Held,* dismissing the prosecutor's appeal against D's acquittal, that a genuine invincible repugnance to the giving of blood could be a reasonable excuse for refusing to provide a blood specimen. (*R. v. Harding* [1974] C.L.Y. 3282 applied): ALCOCK *v.* READ [1979] Crim.L.R. 534, D.C.

2310. —— —— —— **request to speak to solicitor first**
[Road Traffic Act 1972 (c. 20), s. 9 (3).] D refused to provide a laboratory specimen and asked to speak to his solicitor. After speaking to his solicitor he offered to provide a specimen but his offer was declined. *Held*, dismissing D's appeal against conviction of failing to provide a specimen of blood or urine contrary to s. 9 (3) of the 1972 Act, that his request to see a solicitor did not make his refusal to provide a specimen conditional upon receipt of advice. The refusal thus constituted a failure within s. 9 (3): PAYNE *v.* DICCOX [1979] Crim.L.R. 670, D.C.

2311. —— —— —— **whether " accident " had occurred**
[Road Traffic Act 1972 (c. 20), s. 8 (2).]
The word " accident " in s. 8 (2) of the Road Traffic Act 1972 is to be given its popular meaning, *i.e.* it is still an " accident " even if it is deliberate.
D was accused of deliberately taking a police car and damaging it. He refused to take a breath test when police who were making inquiries asked him to. He was charged with failing to take a breath test without reasonable excuse when required to do so after an accident. The justices held that if a motor-vehicle was set in motion on a slope and left to its own devices, the resulting damage could not be said to be an " accident " because it was deliberate. They therefore upheld a submission of no case. On appeal by the prosecutor, *held*, allowing the appeal, that if an ordinary man would say there was an accident, then there was an accident, and this case would be remitted to the justices for further consideration. (Dicta of Viscount Haldane L.C. in *Trim Joint District School Board of Management* v. *Kelly* [1914] A.C. at 674–675 and of Lord Widgery C.J. in *R.* v. *Morris* [1972] C.L.Y. 3015 applied.)
CHIEF CONSTABLE OF WEST MIDLANDS POLICE *v.* BILLINGHAM [1979] 2 All E.R. 182, D.C.

2312. —— —— **first sample spilt—whether second requirement valid**
[Road Traffic Act, 1972 (c. 20), s. 6 (1).] D was charged with driving with excess alcohol contrary to s. 6 (1) of the 1972 Act. At the police station he had provided a blood specimen in accordance with a requirement to provide a specimen. The doctor who took the specimen spilt it and asked D to give a further sample. *Held,* dismissing the prosecutor's appeal against dismissal of the information, that a blood specimen taken from the defendant did not cease

to be sufficient because the doctor spilt it. Nothing further could be required of D. Accordingly, the analyst's certificate relating to the second specimen was inadmissible as evidence against D: BECK *v.* WATSON [1979] Crim.L.R. 533, D.C.

2313. —— —— **information referring to wrong section of Act—validity of conviction**

[Magistrates' Courts Act 1952 (c. 55), s. 100 (1); Road Traffic Act 1972 (c. 20), ss. 8 (1) (2), 9 (1) (3).]

Where the defect in an information is merely technical and cannot mislead, a conviction under it is good.

L had been charged with contravening s. 9 (3) of the 1972 Act but the particulars of the offence referred to s. 8 of the 1972 Act whereas the statutory requirement was under s. 9. The justices convicted him and he appealed to the Crown Court where his conviction was quashed. On appeal by the prosecutor, *held,* allowing the appeal, the question was whether the defect misled the defendant and whether it would create injustice unless amended. However, where the defect was merely technical and could not mislead, a conviction under it was good (*Garfield* v. *Maddocks* [1973] C.L.Y. 470 applied; *Hickmott* v. *Curd* [1971] C.L.Y. 2829 explained; *Meek* v. *Powell* [1952] C.L.Y. 2102 distinguished.)

LEE *v.* WILTSHIRE CHIEF CONSTABLE [1979] R.T.R. 349, D.C.

2314. —— —— **requirement for specimen for laboratory test made outside police station—whether made " at a police station "**

[Scot.] It has been *held* that there was no reason to confine the meaning of the words " at a police station " where they appear in ss. 8 (7) and 9 (1) of the Road Traffic Act 1972 to the interior of the police station. The expression is wide enough to cover the precincts of a police station: BLYTH *v.* MACPHAIL, 1977 J.C. 74, Ct. of Justiciary.

2315. —— —— **requirement in hospital—whether reasonable cause to suspect alcohol**

[Road Traffic Act 1972 (c. 20), s. 9 (2) (*b*).]

If no evidence is adduced that a constable had reasonable cause to suspect that a motorist in hospital as a patient had alcohol in his body, such grounds for suspicion will not be inferred so as to justify the requirement of a test, even after a valid requirement and failure to provide a breath test.

D was at a hospital as a patient after an accident. A constable properly required a specimen of breath which D failed to provide. He subsequently provided a laboratory test specimen which revealed an excessive blood-alcohol concentration. He was convicted of an offence under s. 6 (1) of the Road Traffic Act 1972. No evidence was adduced that the constable had reasonable excuse to suspect D of having alcohol in his body before requiring the laboratory test specimen under s. 9 (2) (*b*). On appeal by D, *held,* allowing the appeal, that reasonable cause for suspicion could not be inferred so as to fill the gap in the evidence.

GRIFFITHS *v.* WILLETT [1979] R.T.R. 195, D.C.

2316. —— **breath test—" driving or attempting to drive "—not restricted to driving which supports requirement of breath test**

[Road Traffic Act 1972 (c. 20), ss. 6 (1), 8 (2), 9 (3), Sched. 4, Pt. I, Pt. V, para. 1 (*b*).]

Nothing in s. 6 (1) of the Road Traffic Act 1972 restricts the words " driving or attempting to drive " to the piece of driving which justifies a breath test under s. 8 (2).

D went home after an accident. He was given a breath test, arrested and subsequently found to have alcohol in his blood which exceeded the prescribed limit. He was convicted on agreed facts that the constable had reasonable cause to believe he had been driving at the time of the accident. He appealed on the basis that, on the agreed facts, there was no evidence that he actually was so driving. *Held,* dismissing his appeal, that he had driven a vehicle on a road when the alcohol in his blood exceeded the prescribed limit and there was nothing in s. 6 (1) of the Road Traffic Act 1972 which restricted the words

" driving or attempting to drive " to that piece of driving which justifies the administering of a breath test under s. 8 (1).
R. *v.* WEDLAKE [1978] R.T.R. 529, C.A.

2317. —— —— failure to provide—reasonable excuse
[Road Traffic Act 1972 (c. 20), ss. 8 (3), 9 (3).] D failed to inflate a breatha-lyser bag properly after a proper requirement for him to do so. He made a second attempt at the police station, the result being positive, but refused to provide a blood or urine specimen. *Held*, allowing appeals against acquittals of failure to provide breath, blood or urine specimens contrary to ss. 8 (3) and 9 (3) of the 1972 Act, that the justices had erred in finding that (1) there was reasonable excuse for failing to inflate the bag in that the failure was not deliberate since D had not relied on any excuse but had claimed that he had inflated the bag; and (2) the refusal of the police to allow D to see the breath test result was a reasonable excuse for not providing a blood or urine specimen. For an excuse in law to be reasonable it must relate to the capacity of the person concerned to provide a specimen: MALLOWS *v.* HARRIS [1979] Crim. L.R. 320, D.C.

2318. —— —— —— validity of arrest
[Road Traffic Act 1972 (c. 20), s. 8 (5).]
The mere fact that a constable has required the provision of a breath specimen does not of itself evince a suspicion of the presence of alcohol.
Learning that the defendant had been involved in a traffic accident, a police-man called at his home and, having ascertained that the defendant had not had a drink since the accident, required him to take a breath test. The defendant refused and was arrested: the officer did not say that he had reasonable cause to suspect the defendant of having alcohol in his body. There was no other direct evidence as to this requirement. The defendant was convicted of refusing to provide a specimen at the police station, notwithstanding his contention that this arrest was invalid. *Held,* allowing the defendant's appeal, that there was no evidence unequivocally establishing that the officer had a suspicion of alcohol and that the arrest was accordingly invalid. (*R.* v. *Banks* [1916] 2 K.B. 621 applied.)
SIDDIQUI *v.* SWAIN [1979] R.T.R. 454, D.C.

2319. —— —— —— wife's interference
[Road Traffic Act 1972 (c. 20), s. 8 (5).]
A defendant will be held to have failed to provide a breath test specimen where no specimen is provided and no fault can be attributed to the police to explain the failure.
The police stopped the applicant and required him to provide a breath test specimen. He agreed to do so, but because of his wife's interference with the proceedings, did not provide a specimen. He was arrested for failing to provide a specimen. A subsequent test specimen revealed a blood alcohol concentration above the prescribed limit. He admitted driving with the excess blood alcohol concentration but contended that his arrest was unlawful because he had not failed to provide a specimen since the factual circumstances prevented him from doing so and he could be responsible for the failure. The trial judge held, as a matter of law, he had failed to provide the specimen. On application for leave to appeal against conviction, *held,* refusing the application, that (1) since no fault could be attributed to the police for the failure, it was impossible to say he had not failed to provide a specimen; (2) on the admissions and evidence, there was no issue to leave to the jury on the failure to provide a specimen, therefore, the trial judge was entitled, as a matter of law, to decide the case. (Dictum of Lawton L.J. in *R.* v. *Kelly* [1973] C.L.Y. 2900 and *R.* v. *Ferguson* [1971] C.L.Y. 2542 applied.)
R. *v.* MILES [1979] R.T.R. 509, C.A.

2320. —— —— initial suspicion without reasonable cause
[Road Traffic Act 1972 (c. 20), s. 6.] Police officers heard the squeal of D's brakes at a junction. They approached D's van and D wound down the window. An officer smelt alcohol on his breath and D admitted having drunk two pints of alcoholic drink. He was required to provide a breath test and was later

charged with an offence under s. 6 of the 1972 Act of driving with excess alcohol. *Held*, allowing the prosecutor's appeal against a finding of no case to answer, that although the initial suspicion was not aroused by circumstances which could amount to reasonable cause, it was sustained by subsequent events sufficiently proximate in time to be whilst D was still driving. The requirement to provide a specimen was therefore lawful: MULCASTER *v.* WHEATSTONE [1979] Crim.L.R. 728, D.C.

2321. —— —— **mouthpiece not correctly attached to tube—whether same equipment may be used again**
[Road Traffic Act 1972 (c. 20), ss. 8 (2) (3) (5), 9 (3), 12 (1); Alcotest Instructions Book, para. 3.]
If a first breath test fails to inflate the bag and the mouthpiece is incorrectly attached to the tube, the same equipment may be used for a second attempt.
Per curiam: In the same circumstances, a motorist should be offered a new device if he objects to using the same one again.
D was involved in an accident. A constable required a specimen of breath. He assembled an Alcotest (R) 80 A device. D failed to inflate it, and the constable noticed that the mouthpiece was incorrectly attached to the tube. He reassembled it and D again failed to inflate it. D was arrested. There was no suggestion of *mala fides* on the part of the officer. D subsequently refused to give a laboratory specimen, and she was charged with offences against ss. 8 (3) and 9 (3) of the Road Traffic Act 1972. The justices held that the arrest was invalid on the ground that a new device should have been offered to D for the second attempt. On appeal by the prosecutor, *held,* allowing the appeal, that there was no risk of prejudice to D, the justices had come to the wrong conclusion, and the case would be remitted with a direction to convict.
PRICE *v.* DAVIES [1979] R.T.R. 204, D.C.

2322. —— —— **police trespassing in defendant's home—admissibility of evidence**
[Road Traffic Act 1972 (c. 20), s. 8 (2).]
If the conditions of s. 8 (2) of the Road Traffic Act 1972 have been strictly complied with, an arrest for failing to provide a specimen of breath is lawful notwithstanding that a constable has in other respects acted unlawfully.
Per curiam: If in the pursuit of a suspected person the police do infringe the strict rights of privacy of the subject, such infringement is not necessarily to be regarded as oppressive.
Police officers in uniform went to B's house shortly after B had been involved in a motor accident. They were invited in by B's son. B refused to see them and passed on a message to them that they were trespassing. The officers went into the bedroom where B was and asked him to supply a specimen of breath. He refused and was arrested. The justices dismissed charges under s. 8 of the 1972 Act holding that the arrest had been invalid by virtue of the trespass. On appeal, *held*, allowing the appeal, that (1) if the conditions of s. 8 had been strictly complied with, the request for a specimen was lawful and the arrest for refusal was lawful notwithstanding that the constable may have been a trespasser. (*Spicer* v. *Holt* [1977] C.L.Y. 2583 applied); (2) since the arrest was lawful, the evidence on subsequent matters was admissible subject to the justices' discretion to exclude evidence obtained in an oppressive manner.
MORRIS *v.* BEARDMORE [1979] 3 W.L.R. 93, D.C.

2323. —— —— **refusal to provide specimen—reasonable excuse—consuming alcohol after ceasing to drive**
[Road Traffic Act 1972 (c. 20), ss. 8 (3), 9 (3).]
The fact that a driver has consumed alcohol after ceasing to drive and before the requirement of a specimen of breath or of blood or urine is not a reasonable excuse for failure to supply a specimen.
D, whilst driving his car, collided with a bridge and fell into a river. The lorry driver who pulled him out gave him some brandy for shock. Later, at home, D drank a quantity of sherry. The police then arrived and required him to take a breath test. He refused. At the police station he refused further requests for a specimen of breath, and of blood or urine. He was convicted by justices of failing to supply specimens of breath, and blood or urine with-

out reasonable excuse contrary to ss. 8 (3) and 9 (3) of the Road Traffic Act 1972. On appeal, *held,* dismissing the appeal, that D had no reasonable excuse for refusal, since he was physically and mentally able to provide specimens. (*R.* v. *Lennard* [1973] C.L.Y. 2896 applied; *Glendinning* v. *Bell* [1973] C.L.Y. 2907 disapproved.)

WILLIAMS *v.* CRITCHLEY [1979] R.T.R. 47, D.C.

2324. —— —— **requirement by one officer—arrest by another officer**
[Road Traffic Act 1972 (c. 20), s. 8.]
Where two constables are jointly engaged in requiring a motorist to provide a specimen of breath, each has the right of arrest in the event of refusal.

Two constables stopped the appellant motorist. One noticed the smell of alcohol and required the motorist to supply a specimen of breath while the second assembed the test equipment and instructed the appellant as to its use. The appellant, having failed properly to inflate the bag, ran off, being chased and subsequently arrested by the second constable. He appealed against his later convictions for refusing specimens of breath and blood or urine on the grounds that his arrest was invalid in that it had not been effected by the officer who had suspected him to have consumed alcohol. *Held*, dismissing the appeal, that the constables were clearly acting jointly in requiring the provision of a breath specimen and in those circumstances each had the power of arrest.

KNIGHT *v.* TAYLOR [1979] R.T.R. 304, D.C.

2325. [Scot.] [Road Traffic Act 1972 (c. 20), s. 8.]
Where two constables acting " as a team " are present when a motorist is breathalysed, one may require the provision of a specimen of breath and the other may validly arrest the motorist if he sees the test to be positive.

Two constables stopped a motorist : one required the motorist to provide a specimen of breath and handed him the equipment. Upon the test proving positive the second constable arrested him. *Held*, that the arrest was valid as the two constables were working as a team.

STEWART *v.* FEKKES (NOTE) [1979] R.T.R. 306, High Ct. of Justiciary.

2326. —— —— **requirement to provide breath test specimen while driver in an ambulance—whether test made " at a hospital "**
[Scot.] It has been *held,* that the protection provided by s. 8 (2) of the Road Traffic Act 1972 was given only to persons who were at hospitals as patients, and no protection was given for persons in any other place. The words " at a hospital " were unambiguous and meant being within the precincts of the hospital itself; they did not include being in an ambulance en route for a hospital : MANZ *v.* MILN, 1977 J.C. 78, Ct. of Justiciary.

2327. —— —— **sample one hour after driving—failure to stop after collision**
[Scot.] A driver, A, drove past another who had stopped. In order to do so he mounted the verge and heard a bump which he thought was his exhaust hitting a stone, and which his passenger thought was a scraping noise underneath the car. It was found as a fact that there had been a collision between the vehicles. An hour later the police requested A to give a sample of breath for a breath test, which was positive. He was arrested and taken to the police station where he gave a sample of blood which was later analysed and found to contain 166 mg of alcohol in 100 ml. of blood. At the trial there was no evidence A had taken alcohol before he began to drive, but there was evidence he had drunk on three occasions after he ceased driving and before he provided a sample of blood. *Held,* (1) as A only established that some alcohol had been taken after the driving ceased, the evidential value of the analyst's certificate had not been displaced, and he had been properly convicted; (2) regarding the collision, since some noise was heard by A it was his duty in the circumstances to stop and see if he had been involved in an accident : SUTHERLAND *v.* AITCHISON, 1975 J.C. 1, Ct. of Justiciary.

2328. —— —— **suspicion of offence—defendant still driving**
[Road Traffic Act 1972 (c. 20), ss. 6, 8.]
A constable, suspecting upon a driver getting out of his car that the driver has consumed alcohol, is entitled to demand that a breath test be supplied.

The defendant was stopped by a constable whilst driving; the constable did

not suspect a moving traffic offence. Upon the defendant getting out of the car, the constable suspected the presence of alcohol. The breath test and subsequent procedure revealed an excess of alcohol and the defendant was charged with driving with excess alcohol. At the hearing, justices accepted the defendants' contention that in the absence of the commission of a traffic offence the constable had no right to require a specimen of breath, on the prosecutor's appeal, the defendant sought that a new trial be ordered. *Held,* allowing the appeal and directing the justices to convict, that the constable was clearly entitled to require the specimen; and that since the justices had been misled by the defendant (they not having their clerk's advice) and would otherwise have been bound to convict, there was no merit in the request for a retrial.
SHERSBY v. KLIPPEL [1979] R.T.R. 116, D.C.

2329. —— —— **validity—last drink taken " short while ago "**
[Road Traffic Act 1972 (c. 20), s. 8 (1).]
A breath test may be validly required by a constable acting reasonably and in good faith, notwithstanding the suspect's assertion to having last drunk alcohol " a short while ago."
The appellant was stopped by a constable whilst driving his motor car after midnight; he told the constable that he had been drinking " a short time ago " in a public house known to the constable to be about 10 minutes' drive away. Without further delay a breath test was required and upon it proving positive the appellant was arrested. Subsequent analysis of a blood specimen showed it to contain alcohol in excess of the prescribed limit and the appellant was charged accordingly. At his trial he unsuccessfully disputed the validity of the breath test on the grounds that the constable had reason to believe that the appellant had taken drink within 20 minutes of the test and that the test should therefore have been delayed in accordance with the manufacturers' instructions. He appealed against his conviction, contending that the jury should have been directed to acquit if they found that the constable had reasonable grounds for so believing. *Held*, dismissing the appeal, that a constable was not bound to accept and/or act upon everything said by a suspect driver, the jury had been correctly directed to consider the constable's good faith and reasonableness at the time of requiring the test. (*R.* v. *Aspden* [1975] C.L.Y. 2956 applied.)
R. v. MOORE [1979] R.T.R. 98, C.A.

2330. —— —— **whether defendant arrested for road traffic offences**
[Road Traffic Act 1972 (c. 20), ss. 6 (1), 8 (1); Police Act 1964 (c. 48), s. 51 (1).] D was asked by a police officer to provide a specimen of breath pursuant to s. 8 (1) of the 1972 Act but refused to do so and attacked the officer. He was arrested for assaulting a police officer in the execution of his duty under s. 51 (1) of the 1964 Act. At the police station he complied with a second request to provide a specimen, which proved positive. *Held*, dismissing D's appeal against conviction of driving with excess alcohol contrary to s. 6 (1) of the 1972 Act, that as D must have known when he was detained at the police station and found to have excess alcohol in his blood that he was being arrested for an offence under the 1972 Act as well as under the 1964 Act, although he was not so informed, the original arrest remained lawful and the subsequent proceedings were valid: GRANT v. GORMAN [1979] Crim.L.R. 669, D.C.

2331. —— **disqualification—special reasons—emergency**
[Road Traffic Act 1972 (c. 20), s. 93 (1), Sched. 4, Pt. I.]
The onus is on the defendant who seeks to establish " special reasons " to adduce cogent and substantial evidence of facts or of a medical condition which supports his contention; nebulous medical evidence is not sufficient.
The defendant pleaded guilty to driving with excess alcohol, his urine reading being 188. He sought to establish a " special reason " to avoid disqualification. His evidence was that his wife had suffered brain damage and had been advised not to get excited; he and his wife were at a party whence they anticipated being driven home by their host; an incident occurred at 3.00 a.m. which the defendant considered gave him no alternative but to drive his wife home for her own safety. No other evidence was given about the wife's medical con-

dition. The justices found special reasons. On the prosecutor's appeal, *held*, allowing the appeal, that the onus was on the defendant to set up the facts from which special reasons could be inferred, and that far more substantial medical evidence was necessary before such an inference could be drawn. (*Jacobs* v. *Reed* [1974] C.L.Y. 3267 applied.)

PARK *v.* HICKS [1979] R.T.R. 259, D.C.

2332. —— —— —— foreseeable " crisis "
[Road Traffic Act 1972 (c. 20), s. 93 (1), Sched. 4, Pt. I.]
A motorist seeking to rely upon a " crisis " as having justified driving with excess alcohol will not succeed where the advent thereof was foreseeable and no alternative solution was sought or considered.

The defendant motorist was convicted of driving with excess alcohol but succeeded before justices in contending that there were special reasons for not disqualifying her, she gave evidence that she and her husband had gone to a party some 30 miles from her home, intending to stay the night; her husband was a paraplesic who could only use a specially-fitted lavatory. There being no such lavatory at the party venue, when her husband at about midnight wished to use a lavatory, she decided to drive him home for that purpose; *en route* the offence was committed. *Held*, allowing the prosecutor's appeal, that the crisis was partly of the defendant's own making, she having made no plans for the possibility of her husband needing to use a lavatory, nor having contacted local emergency services prior to deciding to drive home; and that accordingly the reasons advanced were not so compelling as to justify non-disqualification.

POWELL *v.* GLIHA [1979] R.T.R. 126, D.C.

2333. —— unfit to drive—arrest—no roadside breath test—subsequent excess alcohol charge
[Road Traffic Act 1972 (c. 20), ss. 5 (2) (5), 6 (1), 8 (1) (7), 9 (1).]
Where an arrest is made under s. 5 (5) of the 1972 Road Traffic Act a road-side breath test is not a necessary precondition for the subsequent laboratory specimen procedure at the police station.

The defendant was arrested by a constable attempting to start his car, he was unsteady and his breath smelt of alcohol. The arrest was under s. 5 (5) for a s. 5 (2) offence and no roadside breath test was administered. At the station he provided a breath specimen (s. 8 (7)) which was analysed and gave a blood reading of 254. He was charged with offences under ss. 5 (2) and 6 (1) of the Act. The magistrates upheld a submission of no case on the s. 6 (1) offence but convicted on s. 5 (2). On the prosecutor's appeal, *held*, allowing the appeal, that where the arrest was under s. 5 (5) there was no question of the need for a roadside breath test, and since s. 9 (1) empowered the requirement of a laboratory specimen after arrest under s. 5 (5), the charge under s. 6 (1) was properly available to the prosecution.

SHARPE *v.* PERRY [1979] R.T.R. 235, D.C.

2334. Driver—duty of care—passenger tripping over loose seat belt. See McCREADY *v.* MILLER, § 1863.

2335. Driver's hours—excessive—circumstances not reasonably foreseeable—puncture
[Transport Act 1968 (c. 73), ss. 86 (3) (11) (i), 103 (1); Driver's Hours (Passenger and Goods Vehicles) (Modifications) Order 1971 art. 4 (3).]
A delay on the outward part of a journey, not related to the return part of the journey, is not a delay " in the completion of the journey."

The defendant, a minibus driver, was delayed on the outward part of the journey by a puncture. On the return journey several hours were spent at a cafe and leisure centre, thereby causing the round trip to exceed 16 hours. When charged with exceeding the 16 hours permitted as a " working day," the justices decided that the puncture had caused an unavoidable delay within the defence provided by s. 96 (11) (i) of the 1968 Act, and dismissed the case. *Held,* allowing the prosecution's appeal, that the defence in s. 96 (11) (i) did not apply since the circumstances which caused the delay on the outward part of the journey had nothing to do with the return part of the journey, and therefore, there was not a delay " in the completion of the journey."

GREEN *v.* HARRISON [1979] R.T.R. 483, D.C.

2336. Driving licences

MOTOR VEHICLES (DRIVING LICENCES) (AMENDMENT) REGULATIONS 1979 (No. 1412) [10p], made under the Road Traffic Act 1972 (c. 20), ss. 84 (5), 107, 199 (2); operative on December 5, 1979; amend reg. 23 of S.I. 1976 No. 1076 by extending to one year the period during which a person who becomes resident in Great Britain, may be treated as the holder of a driving licence for any motor car.

2337. Driving whilst disqualified—alibi—whether alibi notice necessary

CY was charged with driving whilst disqualified and MY with aiding and abetting. The defence was that MY was driving and CY was the passenger. *Held,* that an alibi notice was not appropriate: R. *v.* YOUNG [1979] Crim.L.R. 651, Inner London Crown Ct.

2338. Driving without due care and attention—unexplained accident—inference

[Road Traffic Act 1972 (c. 20), s. 3.]

The justices have a duty to determine what inferences should be drawn from the primary facts found (in the absence of any explanation) and such inference is not a matter of speculation.

Immediately after a sharp bend in the road, the defendant's car rolled over more than once and was pushed off the road. No other vehicle was involved and the accident was not attributable to any defect in the car or to the road surface or the weather. The defendant gave no evidence or explanation for the accident when charged with careless driving. The justices decided that they were not to speculate on the cause of the accident where no satisfactory or full explanation was given, and dismissed the case. *Held,* allowing the prosecution's appeal and remitting the case, that the justices had a duty to determine the inference to be drawn from the primary facts which they found in the absence of any explanation and infer, for example, that the defendant either drove too fast or paid insufficient attention. Such inference was not speculation but presented an overwhelming inference of driving without due care and attention.

JARVIS *v.* WILLIAMS [1979] R.T.R. 497, D.C.

2339. Goods vehicles

GOODS VEHICLES (AUTHORISATION OF INTERNATIONAL JOURNEYS) (FEES) (AMENDMENT) REGULATIONS 1979 (No. 42) [10p], made under the Finance Act 1973 (c. 51), s. 56 (1), (2); operative on February 15, 1979; substitute in S.I. 1976 No. 2199, as amended, a new definition of "community authorisation" which takes account of the adoption on December 19, 1978, by the E.C. Council of a regulation on the Community quota for the carriage of goods by road between Member States which amends EEC Reg. No. 3164/76 of December 16, 1976.

GOODS VEHICLES (OPERATORS' LICENCES) (FEES) REGULATIONS 1979 (No. 1732) [20p], made under the Transport Act 1968 (c. 73), ss. 89 (1), 91 (1); operative on February 1, 1980; consolidate, with amendments, S.I. 1974 No. 2060 and S.I. 1976 No. 460.

2340. —— licensing—transitional provisions

[Road Traffic Act 1972 (c. 20), s. 114 (1); Road Traffic (Drivers' Ages and Hours of Work) Act 1976 (c. 3), s. 1 (2) (4), Sched. 1 para. 8, Sched. 2, para. 3 (3) (*a*).]

An application for the grant of a licence to drive a heavy goods vehicle is "made" or effective only when received by the licensing authority and not when posted.

The complainant was required to apply for a heavy goods vehicle licence when his lorry was classified as such by virtue of the 1976 Act. In accordance with the 1976 Act, he posted his application on December 22, 1976, but the licensing authority received it on January 5, 1977, postmarked January 4, 1977. The authority declined to grant the licence on the sole ground that the application was not made during 1976. The justices decided that the application was made before January 1, 1977, and ordered the authority to grant the licence. The authority appealed, *held,* allowing the appeal, that an application for the grant of a licence to drive a heavy goods vehicle was not "made" within the 1976 Act until the application was received by the authority.

NORTH WEST TRAFFIC AREA LICENSING AUTHORITY *v.* BRADY [1979] R.T.R. 500, D.C.

2341. —— overloaded lorry—proceeding to "nearest" weighbridge—defences available

[Road Traffic Act 1972 (c. 20), s. 40 (5) (6) (*a*); Motor Vehicles (Construction and Use) Regulations 1973, reg. 142 (1) (*a*).] D drove a lorry from docks to premises where he delivered the load and where the lorry was weighed on a weighbridge to ascertain the amount delivered. The weighbridge was the nearest to the dock by a straight line on a map but not by road. *Held*, dismissing D's appeal against conviction of using on a road a goods vehicle which exceeded the maximum permitted gross weight contrary to reg. 142 (1) (*a*) of the 1973 regulations and s. 40 (6) (*a*) of the 1972 Act, that the vehicle was not proceeding to the "nearest" weighbridge for the purpose of being weighed, within the defence under s. 40 (6) (*a*). It was not the "nearest"; nor was the defence available to a driver going to a weighbridge solely to weigh the load in connection with delivering it. (*Hayes* v. *Kingsworthy Foundry Co.* [1971] C.L.Y. 10162 applied): LOVETT *v.* PAYNE [1979] Crim.L.R. 729, D.C.

2342. —— —— two offences arising from one incident

Both the axle weights and the gross weight of a lorry were found to exceed the permitted weight. The owner and driver pleaded guilty to using a vehicle when the gross weight was exceeded, contrary to the Motor Vehicles (Construction and Use) Regulations 1973, reg. 89 (4) (*a*), and were convicted of using a goods vehicle when the axle weight exceeded the maximum, contrary to reg. 89 (4) (*b*). *Held*, dismissing appeals against the convictions, that the facts required to support a conviction under reg. 89 (4) (*a*) were different from those required under reg. 89 (4) (*b*). Accordingly, separate offences were proved. It was not oppressive for more than one penalty to be imposed even though the lorry was overloaded on only one occasion. No principle analogous to *autrefois convict* was applicable: J. THEOBOLD (HOUNSLOW) *v.* STACY [1979] Crim.L.R. 595, D.C.

2343. Highways. See HIGHWAYS AND BRIDGES.

2344. Insurance—contract—implied term

[Scot.] P's car was insured with D under a policy which provided, *inter alia,* that "the company may at its own option repair the vehicle"; and that "the company shall not be liable for loss of use." The car was damaged by fire, and D opted to repair it. P brought an action against D alleging that, since the car was off the road for 40 weeks and a reasonable time for completion of the repairs was eight weeks, D were in breach of an implied term of the policy that if they exercised their option to repair they would exercise reasonable care to ensure that the repairs were executed within a reasonable time, and were thus liable in damages for loss of the use of the car. D contended that there was no such implied term, and that in any event they were not liable to P for any loss of use arising from accidental damage to a vehicle insured by them. *Held*, on appeal, that (1) the policy was framed and printed by D and any ambiguity had to be construed *contra proferentem*; (2) normal loss of use during repair of the car would be excepted because the exceptions clause limited the indemnity in the risk, but loss of use due to breach of contract was not covered by the exceptions clause and the policy did not deal with breach of contract; (3) the breach on which P sued was caused by the manner in which D attempted to carry out their contractual obligation of repair under the policy, but the policy was otherwise irrelevant to P's claim; (4) in any event D could not succeed since "loss of use" could be based on some other ground than breach of contract or negligence, namely loss of use while the vehicle was being repaired and arising directly from the risk insured (*Canada S.S. Lines* v. *The King* [1952] C.L.Y. 610 considered and applied): DAVIDSON *v.* GUARDIAN ROYAL EXCHANGE ASSURANCE [1979] 1 Lloyd's Rep. 406, Ct. of Session.

2345. —— **indemnity—personal injury—whether plaintiff entitled to be indemnified**

P's car was insured with D under a policy which provided, *inter alia*, " If [D] shall disclaim liability to [P] for any claim hereunder and if within 12 months from the date of such disclaimer legal proceedings have not been instituted in respect thereof by [P] then the claim shall for all purposes be deemed to have been abandoned and shall not thereafter be recoverable hereunder." In August 1970, W, a passenger in P's car, was injured in a collision. In November W notified P of a potential claim, and in December P notified D that he would expect to be indemnified. In March 1971 D disclaimed liability on the ground that as there were eight adults in the car at the time, the car was unroadworthy and P was in breach of the policy conditions. In October 1972 W issued a writ, and in November 1976 damages were assessed at and judgment entered for £6,065·22. On P's action for a declaration that he was entitled to be indemnified by D, *held,* that (1) D by their disclaimer in March 1971 did not repudiate the contract; they acknowledged it, but said that on the facts they were not liable to indemnify P; (2) P could not contend that no claim was made in 1971 because it was necessary to have an amount claimed before there was a claim; the writ was issued before the amount of W's damage was assessed, and D could be put in the position of not being free of all obligations until 12 months after every possible claim arising out of an accident had been finalised; (3) the contract provided for the manner in which the validity of D's view that they could disclaim liability could be tested and did not give rise to a right to damages for wrongful repudiation. Judgment for D: WALKER *v.* PENNINE INSURANCE Co. [1979] 2 Lloyd's Rep. 139, Sheen J.

2346. —— **Motor Insurers' Bureau—unable to trace driver**

[M.I.B. Agreement 1972 (Uninsured Drivers), cll. 1, 2; M.I.B. Agreement 1972 (Untraced Drivers), cll. 1 (1), 3; R.S.C., Ord. 65, r. 4 (1) (3).]

Where a person is injured by an identified but uninsured driver, he can proceed by action and the liability of the Motor Insurers' Bureau under cll. 1 and 2 of the M.I.B. Agreement 1972 (Uninsured Drivers) depends on the result; but where the driver is untraced, the victim cannot proceed by action, he can only apply to the M.I.B. for an award under cll. 1 (1) and 3 of the M.I.B. Agreement 1972.

P was run down by a motor-cyclist who gave a false name and address. The motor-cycle was stolen and the motor-cyclist was therefore untraced. P commenced proceedings against the motor-cyclist in the false name and obtained an order for substituted service at the address of the Motor Insurers' Bureau. The M.I.B applied to be joined as defendants and appealed successfully against the order for substituted service. On appeal by P, *held,* dismissing the appeal, that since the motor-cyclist could not be traced, P's only remedy was by way of application to the M.I.B. under the M.I.B. Agreement 1972 (Untraced Drivers). (*Porter* v. *Freudenberg* [1915] 1 K.B. 857, applied; *Murfin* v. *Ashbridge* [1941] 1 All E.R. 231 and *Gurtner* v. *Circuit* [1968] C.L.Y. 3160 considered.)

CLARKE *v.* VEDEL [1979] R.T.R. 26, C.A.

2347. —— **uninsured driver—knowledge or belief of plaintiff**

[Motor Insurers Bureau Agreement 1972 (Uninsured Drivers) U2, 6 (1) (c) (iii).]

A person does not " have reason to believe that no . . . contract (of insurance is) in force " where she assumes a driver to be insured.

P had no insurance to drive a car. She asked a friend, A, who drove a car at work, to drive it for her. She assumed him to be an insured driver. He was not. An accident occurred. On the question of the liability of the MIB to pay out P's claim, *held*, that P was entitled to rely on her assumption that A was an insured driver so that she did not have " reason to believe that no . . . contract . . . (of insurance was) in force " and that MIB should pay accordingly.

PORTER *v.* ADDO; PORTER *v.* MOTOR INSURERS BUREAU [1978] R.T.R. 503, Forbes J.

2348. Lighting

ROAD VEHICLES LIGHTING (AMENDMENT) REGULATIONS 1979 (No. 803) [10p], made under the Road Traffic Act 1972 (c. 20), ss. 40 (1) (2A), 75 (3), 78 (2), 199 (2); operative on August 9, 1979; amend S.I. 1971 No. 694 by providing that s. 7 (1) of the 1972 Act shall not apply to reflectors (regardless of colour) which are attached to or incorporated in or form part of any wheel, or of any tyre attached to any wheel, of a pedal cycle having four or more wheels, a pedal tricycle, a pedal bicycle, a bicycle propelled by mechanical power, a side-car attached to any such vehicle, or an invalid carriage.

2349. London traffic. See LONDON.

2350. Motor racing—agreement to drive competitively—no breach of law—whether offence

[Road Traffic Act 1972 (c. 20), s. 14.] A police officer on motor patrol duty saw H driving a Rover vehicle along a dual carriageway towards a roundabout. The Rover was alongside a Hillman vehicle being driven in the same direction. Both vehicles entered the roundabout together. Part way round the roundabout a minor collision occurred between the two vehicles. H was summonsed for taking " part in a race or trial of speed between motor vehicles on a public highway," contrary to s. 14 of the Road Traffic Act 1972, and was convicted by justices. On his appeal to the Crown Court on January 2, 1979, he gave evidence that he had entered into a bet with the driver of the Hillman vehicle as to which was the quickest of two different routes from the roundabout to a given point in a city some miles distant. It had been agreed that the relevant speed limits and all relevant road traffic regulations were to be observed and in each vehicle was a passenger acting to ensure that the driver did not cheat. *Held*, dismissing the appeal, that, although according to common understanding, s. 14 was aimed at the dangers created by two drivers racing along the same stretch of road, its terms were sufficiently wide to cover the present situation where two drivers had agreed to drive competitively, though without offending any road traffic regulation, so as to test which driver arrived first at the given finishing point from a common starting point, although by different routes: HAY *v.* POLICE, January 2, 1979; Judge Bennett, Q.C., Wakefield Crown Court. (*Ex rel. Patrick E. Robertshaw, Esq., Barrister.*)

2351. Motor vehicles

MOTOR VEHICLES (DESIGNATION OF APPROVAL MARKS) REGULATIONS 1979 (No. 1088) [£1·50], made under the Road Traffic Act 1972 (c. 20), s. 63 (1); operative on October 1, 1979; provide for a marking which includes the common features and numbers of two or more Community Instruments at least one of which provides for the application of a common mark where the U.K. has approved the use of such mark; and add specified markings to the markings which are designated as approval marks.

MOTOR VEHICLES (TYPE APPROVAL) (AMENDMENT) REGULATIONS 1979 (No. 1089) [20p]; made under the European Communities Act 1972 (c. 68), s. 2 (2); operative on October 1, 1979; amend the 1973 (No. 1199) Regs. so as to comply with EEC Directives.

MOTOR VEHICLES (TYPE APPROVAL) (GREAT BRITAIN) REGULATIONS 1979 (No. 1092) [£1·25], made under the Road Traffic Act 1972, ss. 47 (1), 49, 50 (1), 51 (1) and 52 (2); operative on October 1, 1979; consolidate specified Regulations, and provide for a scheme of type approval of motor vehicles and motor vehicle parts, in relation to certain classes of motor vehicle, in Great Britain on a national basis.

MOTOR VEHICLES (AUTHORISATION OF SPECIAL TYPES) GENERAL ORDER 1979 (No. 1198) [£1·25], made under the Road Traffic Act 1972, s. 42; operative on November 1, 1979; authorises the use on roads, subject to certain conditions specified in the Order, of certain vehicles notwithstanding that they do not comply with all or some of the construction and use regulations.

2352. Northern Ireland. See NORTHERN IRELAND.

2353. Offence—notice of intended prosecutions—whether warned at the time offence was committed

[Road Traffic Act 1972 (c. 20), s. 179 (1) (2) (*a*), Sched. 4, Pt. I, col. 7.]

Whether a person is "warned at the time the offence was committed" is a question of fact and degree depending on the circumstances of each case.

D, when stopped by police, was seen to climb from the driving seat to the back of his car when he was arrested. Some two-and-a-half hours later after inquiries had been made as to who might have been the driver he was warned that he might be prosecuted for dangerous driving. On appeal against conviction on the ground that he was not given that warning "at . . . time . . . offence . . . committed," *held,* dismissing the appeal, that that question depended on the facts of each case and since there were adequate reasons for the delay there was no reason for concluding that it was unreasonable or unjustifiable.

R. *v.* OKIKE [1978] R.T.R. 489, C.A.

2354. —— —— wrong road named—oral warning
[Road Traffic Act 1972 (c. 20), s. 179 (2).]
Where an oral notice of intended prosecution gives the correct road as being the site of an accident, it is not invalidated by the subsequent service of a written notice naming a different road.

A constable warned D that he might be prosecuted for a driving offence on road X, where the offence was in fact committed. He then handed D a written notice which specified road Y, some 80 yards away, as being the place where the offence was committed. *Held*, allowing P's appeal, that D had not been misled and that by his oral warning the constable had complied with the requirements of s. 179 (2) of the Road Traffic Act 1972.

SHIELD *v.* CRIGHTON (NOTE) [1978] R.T.R. 494, D.C.

2355. Parking
CONTROL OF OFF-STREET PARKING (SCOTLAND) ORDER 1979 (No. 119) [40p], made under the Transport Act 1978 (c. 55), s. 11; operative on April 1, 1979; applies with appropriate modifications, the provisions of s. 36 of, and Sched. 5 to, the Transport (London) Act 1969 to Scotland. These provisions deal with the control of public off-street parking.

CONTROL OF OFF-STREET PARKING OUTSIDE GREATER LONDON (APPEALS PROCEDURE) (ENGLAND AND WALES) REGULATIONS 1979 (No. 236) [30p], made under S.I. 1978 No. 1535; operative on April 3, 1979; prescribe the procedure for appeals to the Secretary of State against decisions of local authorities in England and Wales in connection with licences for the operation of public off-street parking places in those areas where such operation is controlled under the provisions of S.I. 1978 No. 1535.

2356. —— validity of order—excess charge of £10—power of authority to allow discount
[Road Traffic Regulation Act 1967 (c. 76), ss. 28 (1), 31 (1) (3), 84D (1).]
A single excess parking charge of £10 for any period of excess is not so excessive as to make the council's order unreasonable and bad on its face.

The Solihull Borough Council, by an order made under the 1967 Act, imposed excess parking charges of £3 for a period over one hour. They were losing money and amended the order to one excess charge of £10 for any period. The council made a voluntary concession to accept only £1·50 if paid within seven days. The applicant sought to quash the order on the grounds that the order was so excessive as to be unreasonable, and was a penalty payment for not paying within a specified period. *Held*, refusing the application, that the £10 excess charge was not so unreasonable as to make the order bad, nor did the council's concession make the imposition of the charge invalid.

STARTIN *v.* SOLIHULL METROPOLITAN BOROUGH COUNCIL [1979] R.T.R. 228, O'Connor J.

2357. Passenger services
ROAD TRANSPORT (INTERNATIONAL PASSENGER SERVICES) AMENDMENT REGULATIONS 1979 (No. 654) [25p], made under the European Communities Act 1972 (c. 68), s. 2 (2), and the Road Traffic Act 1960 (c. 16), s. 160 (1) (*k*); operative on July 12, 1979; amend S.I. 1973 No. 806.

2358. Passenger vehicles

PASSENGER VEHICLES (EXPERIMENTAL AREAS) DESIGNATION ORDER 1977 (VARIATION AND EXTENSION OF DURATION) ORDER 1979 (No. 1167) [10p], made under the Passenger Vehicles (Experimental Areas) Act 1977 (c. 21), s. 1 (4) and (6); operative on October 17, 1979; varies S.I. 1977 No. 1554.

2359. Pedestrian crossings

' PELICAN ' PEDESTRIAN CROSSINGS (AMENDMENT) REGULATIONS AND GENERAL DIRECTIONS 1979 (No. 401) [20p], made under the Road Traffic Regulation Act 1967 (c. 76), ss. 23, 54, 55 (1), 107 (2); operative on June 1, 1979; amend S.I. 1969 No. 888.

2360. Public service vehicles—licence—whether vehicle used as contract carriage

[Road Traffic Act 1960 (c. 16), ss. 117 (1) (*b*) (4), 118 (3) (*a*), 127 (1), 129 (4).]

If a vehicle is being used without a public service vehicle licence, it must be determined whether it is being used as a contract carriage.

D was the driver of a 52-seater coach conveying children to school under contract to a local authority. The vehicle's certificate of fitness under the 1960 Act had expired which automatically determined his public service vehicle licence. He was charged with causing the coach to be used on a contract carriage contrary to the 1960 Act. The justices found no evidence of any payment and dismissed the charges. On appeal, *held*, allowing the appeal, since D's public service licence had determined and the children were obviously carried at a contract fare, not at separate fares, the preconditions of a contract carriage were established and the case would be remitted to the justices with a direction to continue the hearing.

MIDDLEMAS *v.* MCALEER [1979] R.T.R. 245, D.C.

2361. Rear markings

ROAD VEHICLES (REAR FOG LAMPS) (AMENDMENT) REGULATIONS 1979 (No. 1145 [10p], made under the Road Traffic Act 1972 (c. 20), s. 40 (1), (2A) and (3); operative on October 1, 1979; provide that the approval mark with which certain rear fog lamps are required to be marked shall be either the marking specified in Council Directive 77/538/EEC, or the one specified in Reg. 38 annexed to the Agreement concerning the adoption of uniform conditions of approval for Motor Vehicle Equipment and Parts and reciprocal recognition thereof concluded at Geneva on March 20, 1958, to which the U.K. is a party.

2362. Reckless driving—appeal against sentence—all sentences automatically appealed against

[Criminal Appeal Act 1968 (c. 19), s. 11 (2) (as amended); Courts Act 1971 (c. 23), s. 56, Sched. 4; Road Traffic Act 1972 (c. 20) (as substituted), ss. 1, 6 (1); Criminal Law Act 1977 (c. 45), s. 50 (1).]

An appeal against a sentence of imprisonment for a motoring offence is an appeal against the whole sentence, including any disqualification imposed: by virtue of s. 11 (2) of the Criminal Appeal Act 1968 as amended.

D, a respectable man, aged 29, went out drinking with his friends, and whilst driving them home, hit a traffic sign, and overturned the car, killing the front seat passenger. He pleaded guilty to driving with 157 mg. of alcohol in 100 ml. of blood contrary to s. 6 (1) of the Road Traffic Act 1972, and causing death by reckless driving contrary to s. 1. He was sentenced to 15 months' imprisonment and seven years disqualification for causing death by reckless driving, and six months' imprisonment concurrent and seven years' disqualification for the drink-driving charge. He appealed against the length of the sentence accepting that an immediate sentence of imprisonment was inevitable, and putting forward no argument against the length of disqualification. *Held*, allowing the appeal, that the sentence of imprisonment would be reduced to six months; and since the appeal against the sentence of imprisonment was also an appeal against the disqualification by virtue of s. 11 (2) of the Criminal Appeal Act 1968 (as amended by s. 56 of, and Sched. 8 to, the Courts Act 1971), despite the fact that the matter had not been argued, the period would be reduced from seven years to four.

R. *v.* MIDGLEY [1979] R.T.R. 1, C.A.

2363. Recording equipment
PASSENGER AND GOODS VEHICLES (RECORDING EQUIPMENT) REGULATIONS 1979 (No. 1746) [50p], made under the Transport Act 1968 (c. 73), ss. 95 (1) (1A), 101 (1) (2) (5), 157; operative on January 14, 1980; make certain amendments to Pt. VI (Drivers' Hours) of the Transport Act 1968.

2364. Road—" to which public has access "—unadopted road used by dustmen, milkmen and postmen
[Road Traffic Act 1972 (c. 20), s. 196 (1).]
The fact that an unadopted road is used by dustmen, milkmen and postmen does not make it a road to which the public has access, within s. 196 (1) of the Road Traffic Act 1972.
D was charged with using a motor vehicle on a road in contravention of various statutory regulations and provisions of the Road Traffic Act 1972. The road was concrete, on a housing estate, and was unadopted by the local authority. The prosecution adduced evidence that it was used by dustmen, milkmen and postmen. The justices ruled that there was no prima facie case that the road was a " road " within the meaning of the Act. On appeal by the prosecutor, *held,* dismissing the appeal, that it was impossible to say that the justices should have concluded that the road was a road to which the public had access.
LOCK *v.* LEATHERDALE [1979] R.T.R. 201, D.C.

2365. Road haulage permit—forgery
[Road Traffic Act 1972 (c. 20), s. 169 (1) (*a*) (*b*); International Road Haulage Permits Act 1975 (c. 46), s. 3 (2).]
The offence of using an international road haulage permit with intent to deceive is not the same as that of using a document forged to resemble such a permit.
D possessed a document forged to resemble an international road haulage permit. He used it with intent to deceive and was convicted of using an international road haulage permit with intent to deceive. *Held,* allowing his appeal, that the document used was not an international road haulage permit.
HOLLOWAY *v.* BROWN [1978] R.T.R. 537, D.C.

2366. Sale of vehicle. See SALE OF GOODS.

2367. Seat belts—failure to wear—contributory negligence—no statutory obligation to fit belts
[Road Traffic Act 1972 (c. 20), s. 37 (5); Motor Vehicles (Construction and Use) Regulations 1973 (S.I. 1973 No. 24), reg. 17 (1) (2) (4); Highway Code (1968 ed.), r. 23.]
Where there is no statutory obligation to fit a vehicle with safety belts it is a question of fact not of law whether a person has failed to take proper care for his own safety.
P's 1963 van was exempted from the requirement of being fitted with a safety belt. D attempted but failed to pass P's van on a steep hill and caused P's van to crash and P to be injured. The judge held D wholly liable and because P was under no legal obligation to fit a safety belt that P's failure to wear a safety belt did not constitute contributory negligence. On appeal that the judge had erred in law, *held,* dismissing the appeal, that where a vehicle was not obliged by statute to be fitted with a safety belt, it was a question of fact not of law whether a person was regarded as having failed to take proper care for his own safety by not having had safety belts fitted. Since the judge had found in P's favour on this question of fact the award should not be reduced. (*Pickett* v. *British Rail Engineering* [1979] C.L.Y. 656 applied; *Froom* v. *Butcher* [1975] C.L.Y. 2295 distinguished.)
HOADLEY *v.* DARTFORD DISTRICT COUNCIL [1979] R.T.R. 359, C.A.

2368. —— —— learner driver—failure of instructor to advise
A reasonably competent supervising driver may justifiably permit a learner driver to drive without dual controls; failure to advise the learner on the advantages and disadvantages of seat-belts may be negligent but it is not the cause of the accident, and is relevant only on the question of contributory negligence.
P, a learner driver, had made reasonably good progress with her driving

lessons and was a reasonably intelligent person. D, the instructor, told her she could use the seat-belts at her discretion. He was not enthusiastic about their use because they got in the way of certain manoeuvres. D tried P out in her husband's car which had no dual controls. Neither wore seat-belts. P drove satisfactorily for 40 minutes. Then she panicked and drove into a tree. Her injuries would have been less if she had been wearing a seat-belt. She sued D and the driving school for letting her drive without dual controls and seat-belts. *Held*, giving judgment for D, that driving without dual controls was a reasonable and natural progression in P's driving training, and failure to advise her about seat-belts was not a cause of the collision. It would only have been relevant if D had been liable and had alleged contributory negligence against P.

GIBBONS *v.* PRIESTLEY [1979] R.T.R. 4, Judge Lymbery, Q.C.

2369. Testing of vehicles
MOTOR VEHICLES (TESTS) (AMENDMENT) REGULATIONS 1979 (No. 439) [10p], made under the Road Traffic Act 1972 (c. 20), ss. 43 (6), 199 (2); operative on July 1, 1979; amend S.I. 1976 No. 1977, Sched. 3, Pt. II, para. 10, so as to make obligatory at a vehicle-testing station the use of beam-setting equipment for testing the direction of the headlamp beams of vehicles in Classes III, IV and V.
MOTOR VEHICLES (TESTS) (AMENDMENT) (No. 2) REGULATIONS 1979 (No. 1215) [10p], made under the Road Traffic Act 1972, ss. 43 (6), 199 (2); operative on November 1, 1979; amend S.I. 1976 No. 571 by increasing fees for M.O.T.s, specifically the fee for motorcycles is increased to £3·36 and that for cars is increased to £5·60.

2370. Traffic warden—refusal to obey signal—whether in execution of duty—whether indorsable offence
[Road Traffic Act 1972 (c. 20), s. 22; Functions of Traffic Wardens Order 1970 (S.I. 1970 No. 1958).] D disobeyed a signal of a traffic warden directing him away from the road in which there was a busy car park to which D wished to go. By joining the queue to the car park D caused no obstruction but the warden had been giving precedence to traffic from another road to join the queue in order to relieve congestion in that other road. *Held,* that (1) even if it were right that a warden controlling traffic was only acting in the execution of his duty if acting with a view to protecting life or property, by assisting to relieve congestion the warden made his overall conduct to protect property; (2) accordingly S's appeal against conviction of failing to conform to the signal of a traffic warden acting in the execution of his duty, contrary to s. 22 of the 1972 Act and the 1970 Order, should be dismissed; (3) the offence was not an indorsable offence. (*Hoffman* v. *Thomas* [1974] C.L.Y. 3396 and *Johnson* v. *Phillips* [1975] C.L.Y. 2566 considered): R. *v.* SAUNDERS [1978] Crim.L.R. 98, Nottingham Crown Ct.

BOOKS AND ARTICLES. See *post*, pp. [11], [30].

SALE OF GOODS

2371. Agency—seller's agent—motor car—authority to demonstrate car controls
An agent appointed for the purposes of handing over a car to the purchaser thereof has authority to demonstrate the car controls.
The defendant agreed to buy a car from the plaintiff who appointed F as the person authorised to hand over the car to the defendant in exchange for payment of the price. When the defendant called to collect the car he asked F to demonstrate the automatic transmission. F attempted unsuccessfully to do so: eventually the car sped forward and was written off in a collision. The defendant stopped his cheque tendered in payment for the car, but the plaintiff obtained judgment in an action upon the cheque. *Held,* allowing the defendant's appeal, that the plaintiff was responsible for the negligence of F, his agent, in demonstrating the car; and that the plaintiff was liable to the defendant, the former having failed to prove that he, by his agent, had exercised all due care in respect of the car.

NELSON *v.* RAPHAEL [1979] R.T.R. 437, C.A.

2372. C.i.f. contract—non-acceptance—whether insurance certificate tendered complied with contract

V sold cotton seed expellers c.i.f. as per bills of lading to P by a contract incorporating the terms of G.A.F.T.A. 15. Cl. 17 provided that the insurance to be effected by V was to include *inter alia*, " the risks of war " and the " usual warehouse to warehouse clause." A subsequent variation to the contract was made to the effect that payment would be made against certain documents, including an insurance certificate, and that V would provide P with free warehouse rent and insurance for a period of 45 days from the date of presentation of the documents. R, from whom V had agreed to purchase their goods, instructed S, their brokers, to arrange the necessary cover, and S obtained the insurers' confirmation that the policy would cover the storage of the goods in the warehouse. The certificates were made out in the name of R and required to be indorsed, and the insurers undertook to issue policies in their standard form of marine policy, which, with the Institute Cargo Clauses attached, could only provide warehouse to warehouse cover, and so were inapplicable to insurance of goods in store. Upon presentation of the documents, P rejected them as not in accordance with the terms and conditions of an ex-store purchase. V's brokers effected insurance cover for the goods in store, and the cover note was delivered to P together with an indorsement in respect of the original certificate. P again rejected the documents. On a special case stated, *held*, that (1) no certificate which did not show free rent and insurance for the 45-day period was a proper certificate under the varied contract, and none of the documents presented provided insurance for that period; (2) the fact that cl. 17 did not apply to the insurance of goods in store did not mean that it had to be expunged from the contract as inconsistent, as then there would be no provision at all with regard to the risks to be covered; and cl. 17 would survive, save and in so far as there were provisions in it which could not apply to an in-store insurance; (3) the certificate originally provided did not indicate V's intent, or that the insurance applied to P; and the form of policy to which it referred made it quite plain that the insurance covered only warehouse to warehouse, and not goods in store; (4) P were further entitled to reject the document because it had not been indorsed and was inconsistent with the contract as to place of payment of claims, and excluded war; (5) the cover note was no more than a certificate that V had effected insurance on unspecified terms, and was not the same as a certificate, to which P were entitled under the contract; and further failed in that it was not for the required period and did not cover war as required by cl. 17; (6) V could not rely on the indorsement since it did not cure the defects of period, of place of payment of claims, and of there being no indorsement on a certificate which on its face required indorsement; (7) P were entitled to reject the documents and were not in breach in purporting to reject them: PROMOS S.A. *v.* EUROPEAN GRAIN & SHIPPING [1979] 1 Lloyd's Rep. 375, Parker J.

2373. Consumer credit

CONSUMER CREDIT (NOTICE OF VARIATION OF AGREEMENTS) (AMENDMENT) REGULATIONS 1979 (No. 661) [10p], made under the Consumer Credit Act 1974 (c. 39), ss. 82 (1), 182 (2), 189 (1); operative on June 18, 1979; S.I. 1977 No. 328 prescribes the manner in which notice is given of a variation of a hire agreement. This Order makes special provision where the variation relates solely to changes in VAT.

CONSUMER CREDIT (NOTICE OF VARIATION OF AGREEMENTS) (AMENDMENT No. 2) REGULATIONS 1979 (No. 667) [10p], made under the Consumer Credit Act 1974, ss. 82 (1), 182 (2), 189 (1); operative on June 18, 1979; corrects an error in S.I. 1979 No. 661.

CONSUMER CREDIT (PERIOD OF STANDARD LICENCE) (AMENDMENT) REGULATIONS 1979 (No. 796) [10p], made under the Consumer Credit Act 1974, s. 22 (1) (*a*), 147 (1), 189 (1); operative on August 1, 1979; vary S.I. 1975 No. 2124 by extending the period during which a standard licence, as defined in s. 22 (1) (*a*) of the 1974 Act, is to have effect from three to 10 years.

CONSUMER CREDIT (EXEMPT AGREEMENTS) (AMENDMENT) ORDER 1979 (No.

1099) [10p], made under the Consumer Credit Act 1974, ss. 16 (1), (4) and 182 (2) and (4); operative on October 1, 1979; varies S.I. 1977 No. 326 by specifying further bodies to be included in the Schedule to that Order.

2374. Consumer Credit Act 1974—commencement

CONSUMER CREDIT ACT 1974 (COMMENCEMENT NO. 5) ORDER 1979 (No. 1685 (C. 42)) [10p], made under the Consumer Credit Act 1974 (c. 39), ss. 182 (2), 192 (4); operative on January 27, 1980; brings into effect the repeals set out in Sched. 5 of the Consumer Credit Act 1974, which relate to moneylenders and agreements which are not consumer credit agreements.

2375. Consumer protection

BALLOON-MAKING COMPOUNDS (SAFETY) ORDER 1979 (No. 44) [10p], made under the Consumer Safety Act 1978 (c. 38), s. 3 (1) (*a*) (2), Sched. 1, para. 5; operative on January 18, 1979; prohibits persons from supplying, offering to supply, agreeing to supply, exposing for supply or possessing for supply, any substance for making balloons which contains Benzene.

TEAR-GAS CAPSULES (SAFETY) ORDER 1979 (No. 887) [10p], made under the Consumer Safety Act 1978, s. 3 (1) (*a*), Sched. 1, paras. 1, 2; operative on August 20, 1979; prohibits persons from supplying, offering to supply, agreeing to supply, exposing for supply or possessing for supply any injurious tear-gas capsule.

OIL LAMPS (SAFETY) REGULATIONS 1979 (No. 1125) [40p], made under the Consumer Protection Act 1961 (c. 40), ss. 1, 2, Sched., para. 3; operative on March 1, 1980, save for those parts of the Order that are specified as being operative on December 31, 1980; imposes safety requirements for indoor oil lamps based on the provisions of British Standard BS 2049: 1976 as amended.

2376. Contract—breach—nomination of vessel—extension of time for loading—whether sellers repudiated contract

V sold soya beans to P by a contract dated July 1, 1974, incorporating the terms of the standard Anec f.o.b. contract 1974. This provided, by cl. 7, that P give V at least 15 days' notice of the earliest time of arrival of the vessel; by cl. 10 that P pay carrying charges in the event of any or all the goods not being on board by the last day of the period of delivery; and by cl. 14 that all terms and conditions not in contradiction with the Anec form be as per GAFTA 64. This provided, by cl. 7, that P could claim an extension of time for tendering suitable tonnage by notifying V not later than the last day of the specified period for the delivery. On July 19 P nominated two vessels, stating their respective estimated times of arrival to be July 27 and August 3. On July 22, V rejected both nominations as not in accordance with cl. 7 of the Anec form and considered the contract null and void. P rejected this and called for an extension of loading time under cl. 7 of GAFTA 64. On July 23, P nominated a third vessel, due to arrive on August 7, V again rejected nomination, and advised P that the contract was null and void. P again invoked cl. 7 of GAFTA 64, but on July 29 accepted the repudiation as an anticipatory breach of the contract. On a special case stated, *held*, allowing P's appeal that (1) there was no contradiction between cl. 7 of GAFTA 64 and cl. 7 of the Anec form; nor between the provisions of cll. 4 and 10 of the Anec form and cl. 7 of GAFTA 64. (*Société Co-operative Suisse des Céréales et Matières Fourragères* v. *La Plata Cereal Co. S.A.* (1947) C.L.C. 9226 applied); (2) P were entitled to damages from V for breach of contract; (3) when P accepted V's repudiation on July 29, it was sufficient for them to have shown that they could fulfil their obligations by a valid nomination in time for delivery on August 21, and that it was their intention to take delivery on board on the first day the vessel was available for that purpose; and P were entitled to damages as at August 21: BREMER HANDELSGESELLSCHAFT MBH v. J. H. RAYNER & CO. [1979] 2 Lloyd's Rep. 216, C.A.

2377. —— **credit terms—EEC.** See SOCIÉTÉ BERTRAND v. PAUL OTT KG, § 〵 ⸗ ⸗⸗

2378. —— **sale of chattels and land—contract referring to land only.** ⸗ NARAYAN S/O SHANKAR v. RISHAD HUSSAIN S/O TASADUQ HUSS⸗ § 182.

2379. Letter of credit—amendment of contract—appointment of arbitrator

In November 1974, V sold to P U.S. wheat c. & f. free out Alexandria or Port Said, knowing that P had purchased the wheat to fulfil a contract with Egyptian buyers whose identity was known to V: The contract incorporated G.A.F.T.A. 30, which provided, *inter alia,* " Quality and condition final at loading as per official Inspection Certificate. Certificates issued by independent laboratories indicating equivalence natural weight in kg/Hl of the test weight in lbs/bushel acceptable." The contract also incorporated the arbitration rules of G.A.F.T.A. 125, which provided, *inter alia,* " 1 (c) An appointment shall be valid if the claim has been dispatched to the other party within the time limit laid down in these rules. 3. General Notice of the intention to proceed to arbitration shall be dispatched and an arbitrator appointed . . . (b) (i) within 90 days of the date of completion of final discharge of the ship; (G) (ii) in respect of final invoices within 24 days of the dispute having arisen (f) In the event of non-compliance with any of the preceding provisions of this Rule, claims shall be deemed to be waived and absolutely barred unless the Board of Appeal shall in their absolute discretion otherwise determine." The last shipment was discharged at Alexandria on September 22, 1975, and V sent to the bank which had confirmed a letter of credit agreed between V and P, but which was not in accordance with the contract, the necessary documents. On these, the natural weights were expressed in kg/Hl, but these weights were not the mathematical equivalent from the weights in lbs/bushel stated in the official certificate, and were higher than such equivalent. P did not see any of the documents, and in January 1975, their Egyptian buyer claimed for the amount over paid under the contract based upon natural weights as specified in the official certificates. P claimed \$481,784.56 from V by issuing " final invoices " on December 18, 1975. On January 5, 1976, P rejected the claim, and on January 6, P claimed arbitration. On January 13, V responded that P's claim was unacceptable and time-barred. On a special case stated, *held,* that (1) it was clear from the " quality " clause in the original contract that there should be an official certificate stating the natural weight in lbs/bushel and an independent certificate indicating the equivalence of natural weight in kg/Hl and the test weight in lbs/bushel; (2) since the function of the natural weight certificate under the letter of credit was materially different from that of the certificate under the original contract, the contract would be taken to have been amended in so far as the agreement between V and P resulted in a letter of credit materially different from the contract (*W. J. Alan & Co.* v. *El Nasr Export & Import Co.* [1972] C.L.Y. 3138 applied); (3) on the facts, P had not waived their rights to claim damages in respect of V's breach of the sale contract; (4) the question whether V had admitted that the damages payable amounted to \$481,784.56 would be remitted to the board; (5) on the question of the time bar, the case did not fall within r. 3 (b) (ii), since this presupposed a " final invoice " issued by V, and the documents issued by P on December 18 were not " final invoices "; (6) P's claim was, however, time-barred unless the board had power to extend their time under the concluding sentence of r. 3; and the words " this Rule " in that sentence referred to the whole of r. 3 and not just r. 3 (f) (*Bunge S.A.* v. *Kruse* [1979] 4 C.L. 184b distinguished); (7) the words " these rules " in r. 1 (c) referred to all the rules, and the board had power to extend the time for the appointment of P's arbitrator under r. 3, and had validly exercised that power; (8) even if the board did not have such power, since P did not know until the time bar had expired that the documents were not in order and that they had a claim for damages, their application for extension of time under s. 27 of the Arbitration Act 1950 would have been granted: ETS SOULES & CIE *v.* INTERNATIONAL TRADE DEVELOPMENT CO. [1979] 2 Lloyd's Rep. 122, Goff J.

2380. Non-acceptance—c.i.f.—whether " payment against documents " clause a condition

V bought from U 1,000 tonnes of rapeseed, of which he resold 750 tonnes ⌐. The resale contract contained a special clause, which provided " Payment: ⌐ash against documents and/or delivery order on arrival of the vessel at ⌐ discharge but not later than 20 days after date of Bill of Lading. . . ."

The rapeseed was shipped, and bills of lading issued dated December 11, 1974. The shippers gave notice of appropriation on December 17, and this was passed on by V to P in accordance with the contract. The time for payment of the goods was related to the arrival of the ship and the expiration of 20 days after the bill of lading date, *i.e.* December 31. However, on December 20 the ship grounded, the damage caused requiring such lengthy repairs that in March 1975 the cargo was transhipped, arriving at destination in April. V received the bills of lading in January 1975, and delivery orders were tendered to P in February, but rejected as being out of time. On March 4, V declared P to be in default, and claimed arbitration. On a special case stated, *held*, that (1) the payment clause imposed mutual obligations, and defined neither the latest nor the earliest date for payment, but *the* date; and the time-table substituted by the parties for that which would have been provided by the mercantile law was intended to bind both parties; (2) there was no reason to distinguish provisions as to time for the presentation of documents from those as to the time of shipment and the time of appropriation, which it was clear law that in commodity contracts were conditions, and the fact that this was a commodity contract with an elaborate time-table indicated that the provisions as to the time of presentation of documents were of the essence, and breach would entitle P to rescind, despite the fact that once the ship had suffered the casualty, the time of presentation of the documents ceased to be of any importance: TOEPFER *v.* LENERSAN-POORTMAN N.V.; TOEPFER *v.* VERHEIJDENS VEERVOEDER COMMISSIEHANDEL [1978] 2 Lloyd's Rep. 555, Donaldson J.

2381. —— defective goods—whether delay unreasonable
During March and April 1974, V, Italian manufacturer, delivered a quantity of textiles to P1, English buyers. P1 were first put on notice that the goods might not be of contract quality by a complaint in writing from P2, a sub-buyer on May 14. During May and June a number of telexes passed between V and P1, there was a meeting, and an expert's report was obtained. By July 3, P1 were unable, despite their efforts, to ascertain the quantity of defective goods, and how much if any P2 were willing to accept, and on July 8 P1 notified V of rejection of all the goods which had not been accepted by P2. V contended that the notice was not given within a reasonable time. *Held*, dismissing V's appeal, that (1) P1 were reasonably entitled as a matter of commerce to make sure which goods were defective, and whether P2 would reject any of the goods delivered to them, especially when threatened that V would regard rejection as a breach of contract; (2) P1 had therefore not lost their right of rejection under ss. 34, 35 and 56 of the Sale of Goods Act 1893: MANIFATTURE TESSILE LANIERA WOOLTEX *v.* J. B. ASHLEY [1979] 2 Lloyd's REP. 28, C.A.

2382. Non-delivery—frustration—force majeure
V sold coffee c.i.f. Piraeas to P by a contract which provided, *inter alia*, by art. 30, " the responsibility in connection with the authority . . . to import into the country of destination shall be that of [P] "; and by art. 37 " *Force majeure*: . . . non-performance . . . of the contract can only be justified by a case of *force majeure*." P followed the normal procedure for applying for an import licence, but the application was finally refused, whereupon V resold the coffee and claimed damages. On a special case stated, *held*, that (1) the only term which could be implied into art. 30 was not an absolute warranty, but the more limited obligation for P to use their best endeavour to obtain the licence, since " responsibility " did not constitute the clear words required to impose an absolute warranty in a commercial contract, and the limited obligation was more consistent with the presence of the *force majeure* clause in the same contract; (2) the reference to P's *final* failure to obtain a licence (which indicated that they did not give up at the first attempt) and the fact that they applied in good time was sufficient to show that they had taken all steps reasonably open to them; (3) accordingly, P could justify their inability to complete the contract. Judgment for P. (*Anglo-Russian Traders* v. *John Batt & Co.* (*London*) [1917] 2 K.B. 679 applied): COLONIALE IMPORT-EXPORT *v.* LOUMIDIS SONS [1978] 2 Lloyd's Rep. 560, Lloyd J.

2383.   In August 1972 V sold to P 800 tonnes of groundnut expellers c.i.f. Rouen, shipment March 1973, on the conditions of GAFTA 100, cl. 22 of which provided, *inter alia*, " *Force majeure*, strikes, etc.—[V] shall not be responsible for delay in shipment of the goods or any part thereof occasioned by any breakdown of machinery or any cause comprehended in the term ' *force majeure.'* If delay in shipment is likely to occur for any of the above reasons, shipper shall give notice to [P]. . . . The notice shall state the reason(s) for the anticipated delay. If after giving such notice an extension to the shipping period is required, then shipper shall give further notice not later than two business days after the last day of the contract period of shipment stating the port or ports of loading from which the goods were intended to be shipped. . . . If shipment be delayed for more than one calendar month, [P] shall have the option of cancelling the delayed portion of the contract. . . ." V intended to fulfil the contracts by appropriations under an f.o.b. contract for 1,000 tonnes of groundnut expellers between themselves and S, the sole producers. On February 6, 1973, S notified V of a machinery breakdown at their manufacturing plant, whereupon V notified P of the breakdown and invoked *force majeure* under cl. 22. On March 27, S advised V that loading would be about May 15. On March 28, V telexed P requesting an extension of the shipment date and declaring Dakar and/or Abidjan as ports of shipment. P did not exercise any option to cancel the contracts. In consequence of the breakdown and due to delays in the supply by rail of raw materials to the factory, S were only able to deliver 511 tonnes to V for shipment and V appropriated this to another contract with P dated February 6, 1973. On May 23, P informed V that unles they were told within 24 hours the date on which V intended to ship the goods they would consider V in default and claim arbitration. V rejected the notice as uncontractual, maintaining that the position was one of *force majeure*. On a special case stated, *held*, on appeal, (1) the events which had occurred were commonplace in the world of affairs and accordingly the contracts had not been frustrated; (2) if breakdown of machinery was of itself sufficient to prevent shipment by the end of May, V were protected by cl. 22; but if shortage of raw materials was also effective, there were two causes, and to be protected V should have given another notice stating the additional reason; (3) accordingly the matter would be remitted to the GAFTA Board of Appeal for a further finding; (4) should V be found liable on the remission, the measure of damages would be the difference between the contract price and the value of the goods if the documents had been tendered on the last date for appropriation under the extended shipment period, *i.e.* June 14, 1973: INTERTRADEX S.A. *v.* LESIEUR-TORTEAUX S.A.R.L. [1978] 2 Lloyd's Rep. 509, C.A.

2384. —— **prohibition of export—force majeure**
     By a contract dated October 30, 1972, V sold to P 1,200 tonnes of U.S. soya bean meal c.i.f. Rotterdam, shipment to be made at the rate of 200 tonnes in each of the months April to September 1973, at U.S. $135.25 per tonne. The contract incorporated GAFTA 100 which contained cl. 10 (an appropriation clause providing for, *inter alia,* the dispatch of notices of appropriation by sellers in a string of sales within certain stipulated times), cl. 21 (a prohibition clause providing for cancellation of the contract or of any unfulfilled portion affected by the prohibition, in case, *inter alia,* of prohibition of export), and cl. 22 (a *force majeure* clause providing that V would not be responsible for delay in shipment occasioned by *force majeure*). A partial embargo on the export of soya bean meal was imposed by the U.S. authorities in the summer of 1973. A dispute arose between the parties as to the June shipment insofar as 159.5 tonnes were concerned. Bills of lading dated July 18 showed that 40 tonnes had been shipped on the vessel. P contended that there was a default by V as regards the full 159.5 tonnes. V maintained that P had waived his right to have performance under June bills of lading, or, if there was no waiver in respect of the full 159.5 tonnes, there was waiver at least in respect of the 40 tonnes. On a special case stated, *held*, on appeal, that (1) it was not enough for V to prove the general embargo, since it permitted the export of goods for which loading on board an exporting vessel had actually commenced; V

had to show that the shippers had no goods available within the permitted loopholes, but had failed to discharge the burden of proof and so could not rely on cl. 21; (2) although it was open to V to rely on cl. 22 as a reason for not shipping in June 1973, the burden on them was the same as when relying on cl. 21, and they had not discharged that burden; (3) on the facts, the nature of P's telexes coupled with his delay in rejecting the documents in respect of the June shipment indicated strongly that he had waived his right to treat V as being in default; (4) P could not rely on the telexes reserving his contractual rights, since such reservation was in respect of the 60 per cent. which was not delivered, and did not extend to the 40 per cent. which was tendered; (5) P could not recover damages in respect of the 40 per cent. of the June shipment which he ought to have taken up, in that their acceptance of the notice of appropriation without demur had led V to believe that the notice was good and to forward the shipping documents for acceptance; but he could recover damages in respect of the 60 per cent. which was never delivered; (6) damages would be assessed as at July 11, 1973. (*Bremer Handelsgesellschaft mbH* v. *Vanden Avenne-Izegem P.V.B.A.* [1978] C.L.Y. 2727 applied): BREMER HANDELSGESELLSCHAFT MBH v. C. MACKPRANG JR. [1979] 1 Lloyd's Rep. 221, C.A.

2385. By a contract dated August 1, 1972, V sold to P 1,320 tonnes of U.S. soya bean meal c.i.f. Rotterdam for shipment 220 tonnes each month April to September 1973. The contract incorporated the terms of GAFTA 100 which provided, by cl. 22, *inter alia*, " [V] shall not be responsible for delay in shipment of the goods or any part thereof occasioned by *force majeure*. If the delay in shipment is likely to occur, [V] shall give notice to [P] within seven consecutive days of the occurrence, or not less than 21 consecutive days before the commencement of the contract period whichever is later. The notice shall state the reason(s) for the anticipated delay. If after giving such notice an extension to the shipping period is required then [V] shall give further notice not later than two business days after the last day of the contract period of shipment stating the port of loading. If shipment be delayed for more than one month [P] shall have the option of cancelling the delayed portion of the contract. If [P] do not exercise this option such delayed portion shall automatically be extended for a further period of one month. If shipment under this clause be prevented during the further one month's extension, the contract shall be considered void." Owing to severe flooding in the Mississippi River, delays to shipping occurred, and on April 27, 1973, V telexed to P: " Declare extension shipment for the contracts and reserve the right to apply B/L April." On May 8, 1973, V received a telex from their sellers advising them that loading was curtailed, invoking the *force majeure* clause in GAFTA 100, and nominating Mississippi River ports. V passed this message on to P in telexes dated May 16 and 17. As a result of the flooding, the U.S. authorities on June 27 placed an embargo on soya bean meal except that already on lighter or in the process of being loaded, and on July 2 introduced a system permitting 40 per cent. of unfulfilled contracts. V failed to appropriate goods of the contractual description for the April instalment, and on July 5 telexed to P: "Since you did not cancel contract on May 31, there has been an automatic extension to June 30. Unfortunately there has been a total embargo from June 27 to June 30 and according to cl. 22 we consider the contract as void." P disputed this, and claimed damages. On a special case stated, *held*, that (1) although the flooding constituted *force majeure*, V were unable to establish a chain of contracts back to an affected shipper, and so were unable to rely on the *force majeure* notices to P; (2) even if V could rely on the notices, they were not passed on without delay as required by cl. 23, and since this deficiency did not appear on the face of the notices, P had not waived it; (3) if V could rely on the notices and P had waived the deficiency, V would have been able to extend the shipment date by two months to June 30; but since V could not prove that the goods they intended to appropriate to the contract did not escape the embargo by being on lighter or in the course of loading, they could not prove that shipment was prevented during June; (4) since the *force majeure* notices of May 16 and 17 were bad, P were entitled to treat V in default on May 11: Avimex S.A. *v.* Dewulf & Cie [1979] 2 Lloyd's Rep. 57, Goff J.

2386. —— —— —— **extension of shipment period—invalid notice**

By a contract dated December 19, 1972, V sold to P 1,000 tonnes of soya bean meal c.i.f. Rotterdam for shipment 500 tonnes each April and May 1973. The contract incorporated the terms of GAFTA 100, which provided, *inter alia,* that provided the shipper gave proper notice, the shipment period could be extended by eight days, under cl. 9, and by cl. 22, for two months in case of *force majeure.* On April 25, 1973, V telexed P invoking cl. 22 owing to flooding conditions on the Mississippi River. On May 3, 1973, V telexed P declaring extensions under both cl. 9 and cl. 22. On July 13, P telexed V to the effect that despite the *force majeure* extension the first shipment had taken place under a bill of lading dated May 31, which indicated normalisation of the river, and calling for the April shipment with a bill of lading dated not later than June 30. V never tendered the April shipment. On a special case stated, *held,* on appeal, that the judgment of the court below, and the reasons on which it was founded, were right in holding that the cl. 22 extension was valid and the cl. 9 extension invalid ([1978] C.L.Y. 2637); save that as a result of the subsequent decision of the House of Lords in *Bremer Handels-gesellschaft mbH* v. *Vanden Avenne-Izegem P.V.B.A.* [1978] C.L.Y. 2727, the relevant date of default from which damages were to be calculated was not July 10, as held below, but July 11: Bunge GmbH *v.* Alfred C. Toepfer [1979] 1 Lloyd's Rep. 554, C.A.

2387. —— —— —— **time of appointment of arbitrator**

In August 1972, V contracted to sell to P, *inter alia,* 700 tonnes of U.S. soya bean meal c.i.f. Bremen, to be shipped in each of the months April to September 1973. The contract incorporated GAFTA 100, which provided, by cl. 21, " Prohibition—In case of prohibition of export done by the Government of the country of origin where the ports of shipment are situate, preventing fulfilment, this contract or any unfulfilled portion thereof so affected shall be cancelled ". There was also provision for the application of the then existing GAFTA arbitration rules (the old rules) which provided, *inter alia,* that notice of intention to proceed to arbitration and the appointment of the arbitrator should be within three calendar months of the expiry of the contract time. In October, 1972 the rules were amended by changing the time limit to 90 days (the amended rules). On July 2, 1973, the U.S. authorities issued a bulletin permitting the export of 40 per cent. only of the unfulfilled balance of contracts of sale of soya bean meal. Disputes arose concerning the non-delivery of 60 per cent. (420 tonnes) of the July, August and September shipments, P claiming for the non-delivery, and V contending that cl. 21 relieved them of liability. P appointed their arbitrator, H, in respect of the July shipment, on October 31, 1973, *i.e.* in time under the old rules, but two days out of time under the amended rules. In respect of the August and September shipments, H was appointed in time under both rules. On a special case stated, *held,* that (1) since they were procedural and not substantive, the rules to be applied were those in force at the time of invoking them, and accordingly P were out of time in respect of the July shipment; (2) on the facts found, P had not agreed to abandon their claim in respect of 700 tonnes by concluding an accord and satisfaction with V; (3) the consequences to P of V's breach of their obligation to give notice of cancellation to P without delay were not such as to turn it into a breach of condition rather than of warranty, and did not prevent V from relying on cl. 21 as a defence in respect of the August and September shipments; and V did not have to show that they could not have bought goods on lighters destined for an exporting vessel in order to rely on cl. 21; (4) in respect of the July shipment, the court would exercise its discretion under s. 27 of the Arbitration Act 1950 and retrospectively extend P's time for the appointment of H on the grounds that the delay was very short, the mistake was understandable and not culpable, and caused no prejudice to V (*Offshore International S.A.* v. *Banco Central S.A.* [1977] C.L.Y. 343; *Hongkong Fir Shipping Co.* v. *Kawasaki Kisen Kaisha* [1962] C.L.Y. 2838; *Bremer Handels-*

gesellschaft mbH v. *Vanden Avenne-Izegem P.V.B.A.* [1978] C.L.Y. 2727
applied): BUNGE S.A. v. KRUSE [1979] 1 Lloyd's Rep. 279, Brandon J.

2388. —— strike extension clause

V agreed to sell beans to P for shipment October 5 to 25, 1971, c. & f.
one port Lisbon/Bilbao range. The contract provided, *inter alia,* " should
shipment of the goods . . . be prevented at any time during guaranteed
contract period by reason of strikes at port or ports of loading then shipper
shall be entitled at the termination of such strikes to an extension of time
for shipment. Shipper shall give notice naming the port or ports not later
than two days after the last day of guaranteed shipment, if he intends to
claim an extension of time for shipment." It was further provided that V
would declare the quantity to be shipped at chartering, but no vessel was
chartered, and on October 25 V telexed to P invoking the strike extension
clause, and naming eight loading ports. P claimed arbitration on October 27.
On a special case stated, *held,* that (1) it was for V to explain why they
had not shipped during the contract period and to make good their claim to be
entitled to an extension against a commercial background in which the words
" should shipment of the goods be prevented by reason of strikes at port or
ports of loading " were to be construed as referring to the ports through
which V intended to ship before the strike, or would have shipped but for
the strike; (2) the finding that V would have been able to ship from any of
the eight named ports meant that but for the strikes they would in fact have
shipped from one or more of those ports, and were therefore entitled to an
extension of the shipment period and were not in default; (3) V's failure to
make a chartering declaration did not entitle P to treat the contract as
repudiated as at October 25; P could not regard the contract as repudiated
until after the last day for appropriation, *i.e.* 35 days after October 25.
Judgment for V: SOCIEDAD IBERICA DE MOLTURACION S.A. v. TRADAX EXPORT
S.A. [1978] 2 Lloyd's Rep. 545, Donaldson J.

2389. Passing of property—" Romalpa " clause—whether registrable

[Companies Act 1948, (c. 38), s. 95 (1) (2) (*f*).]

A retention of title clause, where property passes to the buyer on payment
which refers to " equitable and beneficial ownership " does not create a bare
trust for the benefit of the sellers, but a floating equitable charge granted by
the buyers which as such is registrable, and void for non-registration.

The buyers, a carpet manufacturing company, purchased man-made fibre
from the sellers which they used in the manufacture of carpets. The conditions
of sale included a " retention of title " clause. The buyers went into receivership when a large sum of money was owing to the sellers under various contracts containing the " title " clause. The sellers notified the receiver of their
claim. On the joint receivers' summons for determination of the claim, *held,*
that (1) the clause though referring to " equitable and beneficial ownership "
did not create a bare trust for the benefit of the sellers, but a floating equitable
charge in favour of the sellers (*Coburn* v. *Collins* (1887) 35 Ch.D. 373 and
Re Yorkshire Woolcombers Association [1903] 2 Ch. 284 applied; *Aluminium
Industrie Vaassen B.V.* v. *Romalpa Aluminium* [1976] C.L.Y. 2474 distinguished); (2) such a floating charge was created by the buyer company and
therefore registerable; it was void if not registered.

Re BOND WORTH [1979] 3 W.L.R. 629, Slade J.

2390. —— title to manufactured goods—tracing

[Companies Act 1948 (c. 38), s. 95.]

Where a product, such as resin, is used in a manufacturing process pursuant
to the intention of the parties, and on such use becomes irreversibly part of
a new product, it ceases to exist as such and so does the owners' title to it;
in consequence the initial product is no longer identifiable and an interest in
it cannot be traced into the new product.

The plaintiffs supplied the defendants with resin to be used in the manufacture of chipboard pursuant to a contract in which property in the resin
was to pass when all goods supplied to the defendants had been paid for.
The manufacturing process was such that the resin could no longer be recovered.

The plaintiffs claimed against the defendants' receiver a sum in respect of un-paid-for resin contending that any chipboard made with the resin was charged with the outstanding sum, and that charge was not void by reason of s. 95 of the Companies Act. On appeal by the defendants, *held,* that once pursuant to the intention of the parties the resin was used, the plaintiff's title thereto ceased, and it could not be traced into the chipboard; and if a charge had arisen it would have been void as aginst the liquidator and creditors of the defendants. (*Aluminium Industrie Vaassen B.V.* v. *Romalpa Aluminium* [1976] C.L.Y. 2474 and *Re Hallett's Estate* (1880) 13 Ch.D. 696 distinguished.)

BORDEN (U.K.) v. SCOTTISH TIMBER PRODUCTS [1979] 3 W.L.R. 672, C.A.

2391. Performance—letter of credit—whether contract illegal or impossible of performance—date of default

By a contract dated November 1, 1974, V sold to Turkish buyers, P, 350,000 tonnes of wheat, 10 per cent. more or less, c. & f. named Turkish ports. The contract provided, *inter alia,* " Payment : by letter of credit to be opened in [V's] favour with and confirmed by a first class U.S. or West European Bank. Letter of credit shall be opened by March 31, 1975, the latest." Payment was to be in Swiss francs. The contract further incorporated G.A.F.T.A. 27, which by cl. 28, provided, *inter alia,* " In default of fulfilment of contract the damages payable by the party in default in the absence of special circumstances shall not exceed the difference between the contract price and the market price on the day of default." In January 1975, V exercised their option to deliver 10 per cent. more than the contract quantity, *i.e.* 385,000 tonnes, and entered into a charterparty with C for the carriage of the wheat. In March 1975, P applied to the Ministry of Finance for a foreign currency allocation, which was not granted. On April 25, C cabled the first two nominations under the charter, but since no letter of credit was opened, on April 30 V telexed P, treating them in default, holding them responsible for damages and loss, and invoking arbitration. On March 1, V cancelled the charter by payment to C of a cancellation fee and compensation for cancellation. On a special case stated, *held,* dismissing P's appeal, that (1) the place of performance was not Turkey and illegality by the law of Turkey was no answer to this claim; the letter of credit had to be confirmed by a first class U.S. or West European bank, and V were not concerned with how P achieved this (*Kleinwort Sons & Co.* v. *Ungarische Baumwolle Industrie Aktiengesellschaft* [1939] 2 K.B. 678 applied); (2) there was ample ground to infer from P's conduct that there was an extension of time until such time as V determined the contract; and the date of default was April 30, 1975 (*Richards* v. *Oppenheim* (1950) C.L.C. 1806 applied); (3) on the facts, the inference was that both V and P would have taken advantage of the 10 per cent. more, and the damages should be assessed at 358,000 tonnes (*Hadley* v. *Baxendale* (1854) 9 Ex. 341 applied); (4) V were not entitled to damages with regard to the cancellation of the charter in that on the true interpretation of cl. 28 the difference between the market price on April 30 and the contract price applied: TOPRAK MAHSULLERI OFISI v. FINAGRAIN COMPAGNIE COMMERCIALE AGRICOLE ET FINANCIERE S.A. [1979] 2 Lloyd's Rep. 98, C.A.

2392. Price Commission

DISTRIBUTION OF FOOTWEAR (PRICES) (AMENDMENT) ORDER 1979 (No. 129) [10p], made under the Price Commission Act 1977 (c. 33), s. 12 (3) (5); operative on February 12, 1979; amends S.I. 1978 No. 1307 by adding to the list of distributors of footwear exempt from that order having offered undertakings relating to their profit margins.

PRICES AND CHARGES (SAFEGUARD FOR BASIC PROFITS) REGULATIONS 1979 (No. 229) [30p], made under the Price Commission Act 1977, ss. 9 (1) and 22 (3); operative on March 28, 1979; provide safeguards for the profits of enterprises which are subject to restriction under s. 13 of the 1977 Act following a report on an examination carried out by the Price Commission under a direction by the Secretary of State.

PRICE COMMISSION (NUMBER OF MEMBERS) ORDER 1979 (No. 795) [10p], made under the Counter-Inflation Act 1973 (c. 9), s. 1 (5); operative on July 31, 1979; reduces the minimum number of members of the Price Commission from five to three.

2393. Price marking

PRICE MARKING (BARGAIN OFFERS) ORDER 1979 (No. 364) [25p], made under the Prices Act 1974 (c. 24), s. 4 (3); operative on July 2, 1979; prohibits the indication of a price for the retail sale of goods or a charge for the provision of services to non-businesss users which includes an express or implied statement that the price or charge in question is lower than another price or charge for goods or services of the same description.

PRICE MARKING (BARGAIN OFFERS) (AMENDMENT) ORDER 1979 (No. 633) [10p], made under the Prices Act 1974, s. 4 (3); operative on July 2, 1979; amends S.I. 1979 No. 364 and substitutes fresh provisions for those relating to the comparison of an indicated price with a recommended or suggested price which would otherwise be prohibited.

PRICE MARKING (BARGAIN OFFERS) (AMENDMENT No. 2) ORDER 1979 (No. 1124) [10p], made under the Prices Act 1974, s. 4 (3); operative on December 10, 1979; further amends S.I. 1979 No. 364 by extending the prohibition imposed by art. 5 on comparisons with recommended or suggested sale prices to four additional sectors: domestic electrical appliances and similar appliances powered by other fuels, consumer electronic goods, carpets and furniture.

2394. Repudiation—non-acceptance of one instalment—whether whole contract repudiated

In March 1973, V agreed to sell to P 2,000 tonnes of rapeseed oil of good wholesome merchantable quality, f.o.b. Genoa, 1,000 tonnes to be shipped in each of the months September and October, 1973. On October 5, 1973, P rejected the first shipment as being of an unacceptable colour, asked V to replace it and requested arbitration. On October 9, the parties agreed loading dates for the October shipment and P nominated a vessel. Meanwhile, the vessel carrying the September shipment returned to Genoa. On October 19, P confirmed their refusal to take up the documents for the September oil and claimed arbitration. V informed P that they could only provide oil for the October shipment which was similar in quality to that of the September shipment, and advised P that if the October shipment were refused, V would consider P in breach of contract. On October 22, P replied by telex "We call your attention to the fact that the parcel must be wholesome and merchantable. Any other oil will be refused and we shall take you to arbitration." On October 23, V, by telex, accepted P's refusal to take up the documents and pay for the September oil as a repudiation of the whole contract, and claimed arbitration. On a special case stated, *held*, allowing V's appeal, that (1) V's telex of October 23 constituted a prompt acceptance of P's repudiation of the whole contract, and V did nothing to affirm the contract; (2) the inference that P were in default by refusing to take up and pay for the documents meant that no plea of *res judicata* or issue estoppel could succeed; (3) P's letter of October 19 and telex of October 22 in their context amounted to repudiation of the whole contract by them: WARINCO A.G. *v.* SAMOR S.P.A. [1979] 1 Lloyd's Rep. 450, C.A.

2395. Sale by description—f.o.b.—buyers' duty to mitigate damage

V sold to P 2,400 tonnes of fine-ground meal f.o.b. Hamburg by a contract incorporating the terms of GAFTA 119. P chartered a ship and appointed C as loading superintendents to attend the loading as their representatives and to supervise it on their behalf. After 1,900 tonnes had been loaded, it was realised that the meal was only coarse-ground and not fine-ground. The size of the grinding was altered to fine-ground, and the remaining 500 tonnes loaded. C did not mention in their report to P that part of the meal was coarse-ground and part fine-ground, and this was not discovered by P until the meal arrived at destination in Greece. There was no market for coarse-ground meal in Greece, and P incurred loss in separating the coarse-ground from the fine-ground meal, and in settling claims for allowances to sub-buyers amounting to U.S.$12,512.07. P claimed damages for breach of contract from V, who in turn denied liability on the ground that C had accepted the goods loaded f.o.b. Hamburg without protest. On a special case stated, *held*, that (1) this was a contract for the sale of goods by description, and therefore it was a condition of the contract that the meal to be delivered by V was to be fine-ground; (2) by reason of C's not protesting and thus making an unequivocal representation to V that they had no objection. V had delivered 1,900 tonnes of coarse-ground meal instead of delivering only fine-ground meal; (3) however, in the absence of a finding that C had actual or apparent authority from P to vary or waive the terms of the contract, especially so far as a condition of correspondence with the description was concerned, such representation did not have this result, and V's defence of waiver was therefore not established; (4) despite such absence of authority, it was within C's authority to protest as soon as it was, or should have been apparent to them that the wrong kind of meal was being delivered; (5) accordingly P, through C, had failed to act reasonably to mitigate the damage resulting from V's breach, which, if they had acted reasonably, would have been virtually nothing, and P were entitled to nominal damages only: TOEPFER *v.* WARINCO A.G. [1978] 2 Lloyd's Rep. 569, Brandon J.

2396. Sale of Goods Act 1979 (c. 54)

This Act provides for the consolidation of the law relating to the sale of goods.

Pt. I (s. 1) specifies the contracts dealt with by the Act: s. 1 sets out the contracts to which the Act applies.

Pt. II (ss. 2–15) deals with the formation of the contract: s. 2 defines a contract of sale of goods; s. 3 deals with capacity to buy and sell; s. 4 stipulates how a contract of sale is made; s. 5 defines the subject matter of the contract; s. 6 relates to goods which have perished; s. 7 concerns goods perishing before sale but after agreement to sell; s. 8 ascertains how the price in a contract may be fixed; s. 9 provides for agreements to sell at valuation; s. 10 deals with stipulations about time; s. 11 relates to conditions and warranties; s. 12 sets out the implied terms as to title; s. 13 applies to sale by description; s. 14 implies terms as to quality or fitness for purposes of goods supplied under a contract of sale; s. 15 concerns sale by sample.

Pt. III (ss. 16–26) deals with the effects of the contract: s. 16 lays down when property passes in unascertained goods; s. 17 concerns the passing of property in specific or ascertained goods; s. 18 provides rules for ascertaining the intention of the parties as to the passing of property; s. 19 reserves the right for the disposal of goods until certain conditions are fulfilled, where the contract of sale stipulates conditions; s. 20 relates to the passing of risk; s. 21 deals with a sale by a person who is not owner; s. 22 relates to goods sold in market overt; s. 23 provides for sale under a voidable title; s. 24 passes a good title to a purchaser in good faith who buys from a seller in possession; s. 25 concerns sales by a buyer in possession; s. 26 defines " mercantile agent ".

Pt. IV (ss. 27–37) concerns performance of the contract: s. 27 sets out the duties of seller and buyer; s. 28 makes payment and delivery concurrent conditions, unless otherwise agreed; s. 29 gives rules relating to delivery; s. 30 concerns delivery of the wrong quantity of goods; s. 31 relates to instalment deliveries; s. 32 provides for delivery to carrier; s. 33 deals with risk where goods are delivered at a place other than the place of sale; s. 34 allows for the buyer to examine goods; s. 35 governs acceptance of goods by the buyer; s. 36 states that a buyer is not bound to return rejected goods, unless otherwise agreed; s. 37 concerns a buyer's liability for not taking delivery of goods.

Pt. V (ss. 38–48) concerns the rights of unpaid sellers against goods: s. 38 defines an unpaid seller; s. 39 sets out an unpaid seller's rights; s. 40 concerns the right of attachment by a seller in Scotland; s. 41 stipulates the grounds upon which the seller may exercise his right of lien; s. 42 deals with the unpaid seller's right of lien where there has been part delivery; s. 43 sets out when the right of lien is terminated; s. 44 details the right of stoppage in transit; s. 45 specifies the duration of transit; s. 46 states how stoppage in transit is to be effected; s. 47 gives the effect upon the unpaid seller's rights of a sale by the buyer; s. 48 provides that the contract is not generally rescinded by the unpaid seller's exercising the above rights and sets out the seller's right of resale.

Pt. VI (ss. 49–54) deals with actions for breach of contract: s. 49 permits a seller to bring an action for the price in certain circumstances; s. 50 deals with the seller's action for damages for non-acceptance; s. 51 sets out the buyer's action for non-delivery; s. 52 provides for the court to order specific performance in certain circumstances; s. 53 specifies the remedy for breach of warranty; s. 54 concerns the right of a litigant to interest.

Pt. VII (ss. 55–64) contains supplementary provisions: s. 55 relates to the exclusion of implied terms; s. 56 deals with conflict of laws: s. 57 concerns auction sales; s. 58 provides for payment into court in Scotland; s. 59 specifies that where reference is made to a " reasonable time " the question what is a reasonable time is a question of fact; s. 60 states that a right, duty or liability declared by the Act may, unless otherwise provided, be enforced by action; s. 61 contains the interpretation clause; s. 62 consists of miscellaneous provisions relating to, *inter alia,* the rules in bankruptcy and of common law; s. 63 details consequential amendments repeals and savings; s. 64 sets out the short title and commencement date.

The Act received the Royal Assent on December 6, 1979, and came into force on January 1, 1980.

2397. Street trading. See HAWKERS AND PEDLARS.

2398. Trade descriptions
TEXTILE PRODUCTS (DETERMINATION OF COMPOSITION) (AMENDMENT) REGULATIONS 1979 (No. 749) [10p], made under the European Communities Act 1972 (c. 68), s. 2 (2); operative on July 30, 1979; amend S.I. 1976 No. 202 which specified the test methods to be used to determine the composition of certain textile products.

2399. —— false description of model—no case to answer
[Trade Descriptions Act 1968 (c. 29), ss. 1, 2 (1) (*h*), 3 (3).] A vehicle manufactured as a van in 1972 was converted to a caravanette and was first registered in 1975. Later it was sold as a " used 1975 Ford." The vendors were accused of applying a false trade description contrary to s. 1 of the Trade Descriptions Act 1968. *Held,* that under ss. 2 (1) (*h*) and 3 (3) of the Act the question for the justices was whether the description was likely to be taken to indicate the year of manufacture, and the justices should not have upheld a submission of no case to answer: ROUTLEDGE *v.* ANSA MOTORS (CHESTER LE STREET) (1979) 123 S.J. 735, D.C.

2400. —— false description of weight—weight loss due to facts beyond defendant's control
[Trade Descriptions Act 1968 (c. 29), s. 1 (1) (*a*).] D, a self-employed coal merchant, loaded his lorry with sacks marked " 1 cwt." D knew the weight of the fuel would fall as moisture from recent heavy rain evaporated. He paid according to the weight recorded on the sacks. When the sacks were reweighed later by an officer of the Avon Consumer Protection Department they were deficient. The total deficiency was 1 cwt. 26 lbs. in a one-and-a-half ton load. *Held,* allowing the prosecutor's appeal against an acquittal of applying a false trade description, contrary to s. 1 (1) (*a*) of the 1968 Act, that the justices were wrong in deciding that D could only compensate for moisture loss by grossly overweighing and that this was an unreasonable requirement. D should have attempted to achieve the proper weight. Doing nothing could not amount to taking all necessary precautions: KINCHIN *v.* HAINES [1979] Crim.L.R. 329, D.C.

2401. —— odometer reading—previous seller
[Trade Descriptions Act 1968 (c. 29), ss. 1 and 23.]
The seller of a motor car who has " zeroed " the odometer reading with full disclaimers is not liable for a subsequent sale of the car in which the reading is represented to be accurate.

The defendants followed the practice of winding-back the odometer readings upon second-hand cars sold by them to zero; they exhibited full disclaimers relating thereto. They sold a car, which had formerly shown some 59,000 miles on the odometer, to S who in turn sold it to J. J sold the car when the odometer reading was some 5,000 miles. The defendants were charged under s. 27 of the Act in relation to the sale by J, it being contended that the application of the false trade description was due to their act or default. They appealed against their conviction. *Held,* allowing the appeal, that the defendants had no responsibility for the sale by J and in any event had not been guilty of any wrongful act or default.

K. LILL HOLDINGS (TRADING AS STRATFORD MOTOR CO.) *v.* WHITE [1979] R.T.R. 120, D.C.

2402. Transport tribunal decisions. See TRANSPORT.

2403. Value added tax. See VALUE ADDED TAX.

BOOKS AND ARTICLES. See *post,* p. [11], [31].

SAVINGS BANKS

2404. Registrar's fees

SAVINGS BANKS (REGISTRAR'S FEES) (AMENDMENT) WARRANT 1979 (No. 1761) [20p], made under the Trustee Savings Banks Act 1969 (c. 50), s. 88; operative on January 1, 1980; increases the fees to be paid for certificates given by the Registrar of Friendly Societies.

2405. Trustee Savings Banks

SAVINGS BANKS (REGISTRAR'S FEES) (AMENDMENT) WARRANT 1979 (No. 258) [10p], made under the Trustee Savings Banks Act 1969 (c. 50), s. 88; operative on March 16, 1979; amends S.I. 1976 No. 738 by increasing fees to be paid for certificates given by the Registrar of Friendly Societies as to the rules of trustee savings banks.

TRUSTEE SAVINGS BANKS (AMENDMENT) REGULATIONS 1979 (No. 259) [10p], made under the Trustee Savings Banks Act 1969, ss. 28, 86; operative on March 16, 1979; amend S.I. 1972 No. 583. A depositor is no longer required to make a declaration about other accounts held by him in a TSB and a new definition of a current account deposit is provided. Also remove the restrictions in the repayment of deposits on death without the necessity of proof from the Inland Revenue that any death duties or capital transfer tax, chargeable on the death of the depositor have been paid.

TRUSTEE SAVINGS BANKS (FUND FOR THE BANKS FOR SAVINGS) ORDER 1979 (No. 551) [10p], made under the Trustee Savings Banks Act 1976 (c. 4), s. 16 (4); operative on May 21 1979; specifies the limits of the sums which a trustee savings bank may withdraw from the amounts standing to its credit in the Fund for the Banks for Savings during the half-year ending on November 20, 1979.

TRUSTEE SAVINGS BANKS LIFE ANNUITY (AMENDMENT) REGULATIONS 1979 (No. 552) [10p], made under the Government Annuities Act 1929 (c. 29), ss. 43 and 52; operative on May 21, 1979; amend S.I. 1930 No. 106.

POST OFFICE REGISTER (TRUSTEE SAVINGS BANKS) (AMENDMENT) REGULA-TIONS 1979 (No. 553) [10p], made under the National Debt Act 1972 (c. 65), s. 3; operative on May 21, 1979; amend S.I. 1930 No. 41, which provide for the trustee savings banks to invest in government stock through the National Debt Commissioners.

TRUSTEE SAVINGS BANKS (FUND FOR THE BANKS FOR SAVINGS) (NO. 2) ORDER 1979 (No. 1183) [40p], made under the Trustee Savings Banks Act 1976 (c. 4), s. 16 (4); operative on September 25, 1979; revokes S.I. 1979 No. 551 and specified revised limits on the sums which a trustee savings bank may withdraw from amounts standing to its credit in the Fund for the Banks for Savings during the half year ending on November 20, 1979. The Order also specifies the limit on the sums which a trustee savings bank may withdraw from the Fund during the half years falling within the period from November 20, 1979 and ending on May 20, 1986.

2406. Trustee Savings Banks Act 1976—commencement

TRUSTEE SAVINGS BANKS ACT 1976 (COMMENCEMENT NO. 7) ORDER 1979 (No. 1475 (C. 34)) [20p], made under the Trustee Savings Bank Act 1976 (c. 4), s. 38 (3); operative on November 21, 1979; in part brings into operation s. 36 (1) (2) and Scheds. 5, paras 8 (1) (*a*) 15 (*a*), 6.

SEA AND SEASHORE

2407. Continental shelf

CONTINENTAL SHELF (PROTECTION OF INSTALLATIONS) ORDER 1979 (No. 641) [10p], made under the Continental Shelf Act 1964 (c. 29), s. 2 (1); operative on June 12, 1979; specifies as a safety zone a sea area (being an area within a radius of 500 metres of a certain offshore installation) and prohibits ships from entering the zone except with the permission of the Secretary of State or in the circumstances provided for in art. 2 (2).

CONTINENTAL SHELF (PROTECTION OF INSTALLATIONS) (No. 2) ORDER 1979 (No. 1058) [10p], made under the Continental Shelf Act 1964, s. 21; operative on August 23, 1979; specifies as a safety zone a sea area and prohibits ships from entering the zone except with the permission of the Secretary of State.

CONTINENTAL SHELF (PROTECTION OF INSTALLATIONS) (No. 3) ORDER 1979 (No. 1083) [10p], made under the Continental Shelf Act 1964, s. 2 (1); operative on August 29, 1979; specifies a certain sea area as a safety zone.

CONTINENTAL SHELF (PROTECTION OF INSTALLATIONS) (No. 4) ORDER 1979 (No. 1136) [10p], made under the Continental Shelf Act 1964, s. 2 (1); operative on September 11, 1979; specifies as a safety zone an area surrounding a specified installation and prohibits ships from entering the zone except with permission.

CONTINENTAL SHELF (DESIGNATION OF ADDITIONAL AREAS) ORDER 1979 (No. 1447) [10p], made under the Continental Shelf Act 1964, s. 1 (7); operative on November 14, 1979; designates further areas of the Continental Shelf in the northern North Sea as areas in which the rights of the U.K. with respect to the sea bed and subsoil and their natural resources may be exercised.

2408. Fisheries. See FISH AND FISHERIES.

2409. Offshore installations

OFFSHORE INSTALLATIONS (LIFE-SAVING APPLIANCES AND FIRE-FIGHTING EQUIPMENT) (AMENDMENT) REGULATIONS 1979 (No. 1023) [10p], made under the Mineral Workings (Offshore Installations) Act 1971 (c. 61), s. 6; operative on September 1, 1979; substitute a new table for calculating the fees chargeable for life-safety examiners of appliances on offshore installations.

CONTINENTAL SHELF (PROTECTION OF INSTALLATIONS) (VARIATION) ORDER 1979 (No. 1273) [10p], made under the Continental Shelf Act 1964 (c. 29), s. 2 (1) (3); operative on November 2, 1979; varies S.I. 1979 Nos. 641 and 1136 by deleting from the Scheds. incorrect designations of installations and inserting the correct designations.

2410. —— safety standards for stand-by vessels

The Department of Trade has issued new " Instructions for the guidance of surveyors " which set down minimum performance and equipment requirements for stand-by vessels. The major function of such vessels is to save the lives of those on oil rigs and similar offshore installations in the event of an emergency. The new safety standards came into effect on January 1, 1979. Copies are available from Offshore Safety Section, Marine Division, Department of Trade, Room 723, Chancery House, Chancery Lane, London W.C.2 [£1·30].

2411. Shipping. See SHIPPING AND MARINE INSURANCE.

ARTICLES. See *post*, p. [31].

SETTLEMENTS AND TRUSTS

2412. Breach of trust—liability of solicitor's partner

Assets were dissipated in breach of trust. The various transactions which amounted to the breach were known to and assisted in by H, a partner in a firm of solicitors. On the question of the liability of H's partner, *held*, H had acted as agent of express trustees and no liability could be imposed upon his partner (*Mara* v. *Browne* [1896] 1 Ch. 199 applied): *Re* BELL'S INDENTURE; BELL *v.* HICKLEY (1979) 123 S.J. 322, Vinelott J.

2413. ——— solicitor retained by trustees—beneficiary's claim against solicitors

The plaintiff beneficiary claimed the trustees had committed breaches of trust and that the solicitors retained by the trustees, in failing to advise, contributed to the breaches whereby the trust had suffered loss and damage. The solicitors sought to strike out part of the statement of claim. *Held,* the benefit of the trustees' contract with the solicitors was not a trust asset. It was solely for the benefit of the trustees. In this case, he pleadings could be clarified, no order made: WILLS *v.* COOKE (1979) 123 S.J. 405, Slade J.

2414. Constructive trust—purchase of house as joint tenants—down-payment by woman—whether man's share held on constructive trust for woman

[Can.] A and R purchased a town-house as joint tenants. They had lived together for some time and shared living expenses. In 1975 they purchased the town-house, the major portion of the funds for the down-payment being borrowed from R, the woman's father. Both parties executed the agreement of purchase and sale, and both parties signed a mortgage. A few days after the transaction had been completed and before the first payment on the mortgage fell due the parties separated and A, the man, left the town-house. On appeal, *held,* that (1) the common intention of the parties was that they would both have an equal beneficial interest in the house. The evidence of a common intention at the time of purchase was an incontrovertible rebuttal of any presumption of resulting trust in favour of R; (2) any unjust enrichment in favour of A was only with respect to the legal fees and down-payment and other incidentals paid by R. That amount was easily ascertainable and could be offset against A's share of moneys received by R from her subsequent rental of the house and from its subsequent increase in value. It would be wrong to class as unjust enrichment the potential return the parties might receive on the sale of the house as a result of its increase in value. (*Shephard v. Cartwright* [1954] C.L.Y. 1600, *Gissing* v. *Gissing* [1970] C.L.Y. 1243 referred to): RUFF *v.* STROBEZ (1978) 86 D.L.R. (3d) 284, Alta.Sup.Ct.

2415. Conveyancing. See REAL PROPERTY AND CONVEYANCING.

2416. Discretionary trust—power to accumulate—accumulation during lives of settlor's children

[Scot.] [Trusts (Scotland) Act 1961 (c. 57), s. 5 (2).]

The power to accumulate trust income during the lives of the settlor's children, even where discretionary, infringes s. 5 (2) of the Trusts (Scotland) Act 1961 and therefore determines on the death of the settlor.

Under a settlement made in Scotland a settlor directed trustees to apply the income of the trust estate for the benefit of his children and their issue, to accumulate such income at their discretion and to pay the trust estate among the issue when the trust period expired. On a claim for estate duty the question arose as to whether the power to accumulate determined with the settlor's death. At first instance the answer was yes. On appeal, *held,* dismissing the appeal, that the power to accumulate infringed the Act and determined on the settlor's death.

BAIRD *v.* LORD ADVOCATE [1979] 2 W.L.R. 369, H.L.

2417. Northern Ireland. See NORTHERN IRELAND.

2418. Powers of appointment. See POWERS.

2419. Public Trustee

PUBLIC TRUSTEE (FEES) (AMENDMENT) ORDER 1979 (No. 189) [10p], made under the Public Trustee Act 1906 (c. 55), s. 9, as amended by the Public Trustee (Fees) Act 1957 (c. 12), s. 1, and the Administration of Justice Act 1965 (c. 2), s. 2 (1); operative on April 1, 1979; amends S.I. 1977 No. 508 by increasing the standard rate of the administration fee for estates and trusts accepted before April 1, 1979, to 1¼ per cent. and by increasing the rate of the income collection fee to 2 per cent.

2420. Resulting trust—presumption—joint tenancy—whether severed

[Can.] M purchased a house in her name for herself and her daughter (D) on the understanding that D would assist in paying off the mortgages. When D reached her majority, the title was transferred to M and D as joint tenants.

Subsequently D executed a quitclaim in M's favour at M's insistence because M feared D, who was seeing a man of whom M disapproved, would liquidate her interest. During the whole time D paid a substantial sum to pay off the mortgages. After M's death D brought an action for a declaration that M held the property on a resulting trust for herself and D in joint tenancy. *Held,* she was entitled to the declaration on the grounds: (1) where a person transfers his property to another gratuitously, a presumption of a resulting trust is raised in favour of the transfer. That presumption may be supported or rebutted by evidence of the parties' intentions at the time of the transaction, and their subsequent acts and declarations; (2) a joint tenancy may be severed by destroying one of the four unities of time, possession, title and interest, or by interfering with the right of survivorship in one of three ways: (a) by an act of one tenant such as a sale or a mortgage of their interest, (b) by mutual agreement, (c) by a course of dealing indicating that the parties treated the joint tenancy as a tenancy in common. A joint tenancy is not severed when one of the joint tenants is constituted a trustee for the other and the property is conveyed to the first. Thus the joint tenancy was not severed under the first method by the execution of the quitclaim deal in favour of M since the right of survivorship was not interfered with, and there was no evidence that it was severed under either the second or third method. (*Burgess* v. *Rawnsley* [1975] C.L.Y. 3115 referred to): GROVES v. CHRISTIANSEN (1978) 86 D.L.R. (3d) 296, Brit.Col.Sup.Ct.

2421. Secret trusts—standard of proof—whether secret trust or moral obligation

In order to establish a secret trust where there is no question of fraud the standard of proof is the ordinary civil standard of proof required to establish an ordinary trust.

The testatrix, widowed and childless, gave the residue of her estate to her executors to hold for her brother absolutely. The brother died six days after the testatrix, having made his son his executor and sole residuary beneficiary. There was some evidence that she had told S, her executor, that she wanted to be " fair to everyone " and wanted her brother to " look after the division for her." On a summons the question arose as to whether the gift of the residue to the brother was subject to a secret trust. *Held,* that (1) the ordinary civil standard of proof was required to establish a secret trust; (2) the brother had only a moral obligation to distribute the residue, and he took it therefore free from any secret trust. (Dictum of Christian L.J. in *M'Cormick* v. *Grogan* (1867) I.R.Eq. 313 applied.)

Re SNOWDEN (DECD.) [1979] 2 W.L.R. 654, Megarry V.C.

2422. Trust—existence—travel agent—advance payment by customers

[Can.] A .travel agent received advance payments from travellers. He deposited them in a " trust account." *Held,* he did not thereby become a trustee of the moneys. The mere fact that the travel agent keeps moneys in a segregated account does not make them trust moneys, and on the travel agent's insolvency, the moneys are available to its general creditors. (*Henry* v. *Hammond* [1913] 2 K.B. 515 applied): *Re* H. B. HAINA AND ASSOCIATES INC. (1978) 86 D.L.R. (3d) 262, Brit.Col. Sup.Ct.

2423. Trustees—power to compromise litigation

[Trustee Act 1925 (c. 19), s. 15 (*f*).]

The surrender of a limited interest under a settlement merely eliminates a pre-existing interest while leaving the trust intact, and a trustee therefore has power to compromise a claim to trust property in consideration of the surrender by adverse claimants of their life interests under the trust.

By his will the testator settled lands and bequeathed all his chattels on trusts under which life interests were given to various beneficiaries. A dispute arose between the trustee and the beneficiaries as to the allocation of various chattels. A compromise was reached which, *inter alia,* involved the surrender by some of the beneficiaries of their life interests in the chattels. The compromise was opposed. Megarry V.-C. held that the proposed compromise was within the trustees' powers. On appeal, *held,* dismissing the appeal, that s. 15 conferred on a trustee wide and flexible powers of compromising disputes, and since the surrender of the limited interests did not amount to a variation of the trust, the trustee had power to implement the compromise. (*Chapman* v. *Chapman* [1954] C.L.Y. 3043 distinguished.)

Re EARL OF STRAFFORD (DECD.); ROYAL BANK OF SCOTLAND *v.* BYNG [1979] 1 All E.R. 513, C.A.

BOOKS AND ARTICLES. See *post*, pp. [12], [31].

SHERIFFS

2424. Fees

SHERIFFS' FEES (AMENDMENT) ORDER 1979 (No. 1442 (L. 20)) [10p], made under the Sheriffs Act 1887 (c. 55), s. 20 (2); operative on December 17, 1979; increases the mileage fee payable to sheriffs on execution of writs of *fieri facias*, possession or delivery to 16·4 pence per mile.

SHIPPING AND MARINE INSURANCE

2425. Admiralty—costs—limitation fund—expenses

[Scot.] In an action arising out of a collision between P's vessel and D's vessel, P and D were found equally to blame, and D were further found to be entitled to limit their liability, under the Merchant Shipping Act, s. 503, to £2,513·46 (see § 239). D had tendered the limitation fund " in full of the conclusion of the summons," and P contended that since this made no provision for interest they were entitled to the expenses of the actions. *Held,* that (1) what D had offered " in full of the conclusion of the summons " was the limitation fund alone; and had P accepted the tender, the absence of reference to interest would have defended a claim by P for interest (*Carmichael* v. *Caledonian Railway Co.* (1868) 6 M. 671; *Riddell* v. *Lanarkshire and Ayrshire Railway Co.* (1904) 6 F. 432 applied); (2) accordingly the award in favour of P exceeded the amount tendered, and D's counterclaim for expenses failed; and the question of expenses could be considered without reference to the tender; (3) P had established that D were 50 per cent. liable for the collision, whilst D had successfully established the right to limit their liability; and the fair solution was that each side would bear its own expenses, and no order would be made: THE DEVOTION II (No. 2) [1979] 1 Lloyd's Rep. 515, Ct. of Session.

2426. —— limitation of liability—only one claim made

[Merchant Shipping Act 1894 (c. 60), ss. 503, 504; Merchant Shipping (Liability of Shipowners and Others) Act 1958 (c. 62).] Defendant cargo receivers obtained an award in respect of damage to goods on plaintiffs' vessel. Plaintiffs, who had not claimed to limit their liability in the arbitration, brought an action under s. 503 of the Merchant Shipping Act 1894 claiming limitation. The defendants' claim was the only one made. *Held,* that s. 504 of the Act was procedural only, the defendants were not entitled to invoke the principle of *res judicata*, and the plaintiffs were entitled to the relief sought. *Per* Brandon L.J. dissenting in part: The plaintiffs should only be entitled to bring an action for a declaration of their rights under s. 6 of the Merchant Shipping (Liability of Shipowners and Others) Act 1958: THE PENELOPE II, *The Times,* November 21, 1979, C.A.

2427. —— practice—form of writs

The following Practice Direction was issued by the Admiralty Registry on March 6, 1979.

(1) The practice of allowing a writ in an action *in rem* and a writ in an action *in personam* to be combined in one document and issued as a single writ will no longer be followed.

(2) The appropriate prescribed forms must be used and if it is desired to commence proceedings both *in rem* and *in personam* separate writs must be issued.

(3) This Practice Direction came into operation on April 2, 1979.

[1979] 1 W.L.R. 426; [1979] 2 All E.R. 155.

2428. ── ── **release of security—stay of action**

In July 1976, the S and her cargo, which was owned by P, an English company, were lost as a result of a collision with the M which was owned by D, a Polish company. In May 1977, P began an action against, and arrested, the W, a sister ship of the M. D brought a limitation action in Poland, and on June 1, 1977, paid their limitation fund into the Polish court; and on June 2 gave security for P's claim in the form of a guarantee by their P. & I. Club, as a result of which the W was released. Upon D's application under s. 5 of the Merchant Shipping (Liability of Shipowners and Others) Act 1958 for the release of the security given by their Club, *held,* that (1) P's claim did not appear to be founded on a liability to which a limit was set by s. 503 of the Merchant Shipping Act 1894 as amended, since D had not discharged the burden of proof regarding the issue of absence of actual fault or priority; (2) the court's power to release security extended to a guarantee provided by a third party outside the court; (3) D's payment into the Polish court was not security which had " previously been given " within the meaning of s. 5 (2) (*a*) of the 1958 Act, since it was made after the arrest of the W; but was satisfactory security, such part of which corresponding to P's claim, if established, would be actually available to P; (4) the further security offered by D together with that given earlier in Poland was for an amount not less than D's limit under s. 503 of the 1894 Act as amended. Application refused. (*The Lady Gwendolen* [1965] C.L.Y. 3625 considered; *The Putbus* [1969] C.L.Y. 3340 considered and applied.) Upon D's further application for a stay of action, *held,* that (1) it was open to doubt whether justice could be done at substantially less inconvenience and expense in Poland than in England; (2) P would be deprived of the personal advantage of suing in the courts of their own country, and the judicial advantages of having security for the full amount of their claim, and of having their claim adjudicated upon by a specialist court with long experience of dealing with this sort of action. Application refused. (*MacShannon* v. *Rockware Glass* [1978] C.L.Y. 2390 applied): THE WLADYSLAW LOKIETEK [1978] 2 Lloyd's Rep. 520, Brandon J.

2429. Agency—freight—claim for account of money due

D were appointed P's U.K. agents for the purpose of establishing a regular liner service by a contract of agency which provided, *inter alia*, that D were to be responsible for the collection of freight. D contended that P had contracted to provide a ship every month, and that by not doing so P had repudiated the contract, and D had accepted the repudiation. However, D had collected a considerable quantity of freight amounting to £122,000 which they had not remitted to P, but had paid to other persons. P, by R.S.C. Ord. 14 proceedings, brought a claim for a declaration and for an account and payment of money found due on the account. D, alleging loss of a considerable amount of profit due to P's failure to provide a ship every month, counterclaimed damages for breach of the contract of agency. *Held,* dismissing D's appeal, that (1) although arising out of an agency agreement, the subject matter of P's claim was " freights " since the moneys were received by D as agents for P's use in respect of freight; (2) the fact that the claim for freight was against D as P's agents, and not one of two parties to an ordinary shipping contract, was not a rational ground for distinguishing this case from *The Brede* [1973] C.L.Y. 3103 and *The Aries* [1977] C.L.Y. 2741; (3) accordingly, the counterclaim should be the subject of a cross-action, and could not be pleaded as a defence or set-off; (4) the trial judge was perfectly entitled in the exercise of his discretion to order the whole of the £122,000 to be brought into court as a condition of staying the execution on judgment: JAMES & CO., SCHEEPVAART EN HANDELMIJ B.V. v. CHINECREST [1979] 1 Lloyd's Rep. 126, C.A.

2430. Arbitration—stay of action—inconsistent clauses in contract of insurance

[U.S.] P claimed against D under a contract of marine insurance. D rejected the claim, but impleaded T on the ground that if D were held liable to P in the principal action, then they were entitled to a partial indemnity from T under the provisions of a treaty of reinsurance. The treaty provided, *inter alia*, by art. XII, " If any dispute shall arise between [D] and [T] with reference to the rights of either party with respect to any transaction under their contract, the dispute shall be referred to three arbitrators "; and by art. XV, " in the event of the failure of [T] to pay any amount claimed to be due hereunder, [T], at the request of [D], will submit to the jurisdiction of any court of competent jurisdiction within the United States." Upon T's application for a stay of action under art. XII, *held*, that (1) the issue between D and T as within the scope of art. XII, and, in accordance with 9 U.S.C., s. 3, a stay would be granted unless it could be shown that there were unusual circumstances giving rise to a waiver of T's art. XII arbitration right; (2) arts. XII and XV were not inconsistent in that T had not yet failed to pay an amount claimed to be due, but had merely denied an obligation to indemnify D; and art. XV was not a *pro tanto* waiver of art. XII; (3) T's failure to plead a defence of arbitration and delay in filing the motion for a stay did not constitute a waiver of T's arbitration rights, and D had suffered no prejudice; (4) T was therefore entitled to a stay of proceedings pending arbitration pursuant to art. XII: CHINA UNION LINES v. AMERICAN MARINE UNDERWRITERS INC., CALVERT FIRE INSURANCE CO., CANADIAN MARINE UNDERWRITERS AND C.N.A. ASSURANCE CO. INC.; AMERICAN MARINE UNDERWRITERS INC. AND CALVERT FIRE INSURANCE CO. v. POSGATE [1979] 1 Lloyd's Rep. 439, U.S. Dist.Ct.

2431. Bills of lading—documents clause—whether documents defective—validity of tender—liability for demurrage

Between 1967 and 1973 V sold grain to P by contracts in the GAFTA form which in each case incorporated the Tradax document clause. This provided " If any document whatsoever required to be furnished by V is missing or in apparent contradiction with the clauses and conditions of the sale contract and/or if such document contains errors or omissions of any kind, P must nevertheless perform and take up the documents if V gives . . . notice to P that V guarantees performance in accordance with the clauses and conditions of the contract." In July 1973 V sold nearly 5,000 tonnes of meal c.i.f. Venice to P by contract in the GAFTA 100 form, of which cl. 11 provided, *inter alia*, " in the event of the shipping documents not being available when called for by P or on arrival of vessel at destination V may provide other documents or an indemnity entitling P to obtain delivery of the goods and payment shall be made by P in exchange for same, but such payment shall not prejudice P's rights under the contract when shipping documents are eventually available." P received, but failed to sign and return, the Tradax documents clause. Three of the four groups of documents, which were accompanied by letters of guarantee, were presented to different banks, but rejected as being stale and defective. The meal arrived in Venice on September 11, and on the same day V telexed P that V both offered to hold P harmless from any responsibility and/or consequence arising from the fact that the bills of lading provided that the destination should be as per charterparty and assured P that the destination was Venice as per sales contract. On September 25 the master of the vessel substituted the word " Venezia " as the destination on the bills of lading for the words " Ancona/Ravenna " in the case of one group and the words " as per charterparty " on the other two. The documents were then re-presented and again rejected. On October 4, 1974, P agreed to take the meal at U.S. $ 240 per tonne on a without prejudice basis pending arbitration, and claimed a laytime allowance from that date. On a special case stated, *held*, that (1) the Tradax documents clause formed part of the contract since P had always signed and returned it in the past and V were entitled to assume that P had accepted it in this case; (2) the bills of lading marked " Ancona/Ravenna " were defective as being inconsistent with the contract of sale c.i.f. Venice; (3) the other bills were also defective as not showing whether they complied with a contract of carriage to Venice or in the absence of a charterparty, with the other terms of the contract of sale; (4) P were entitled to reject the altered bills since an altered bill of lading was not " reasonably and readily fit to pass current in commerce"; (5) cl. 11 absolved V from forwarding the documents within a particular time, but not from producing contractual documents when eventually tendered; (6) the Tradax documents clause altered the whole documentary basis of the contract and had to be strictly construed; it seemed to intend that the price paid by V for failure to produce the contractual documents was that failure to ensure physical performance of the contract became a breach of condition; (7) the guarantee letters read by themselves or with the telex of September 11 merely expanded the printed indemnity and gave P an assurance that the destination of the grain was Venice; they did not amount to a notice guaranteeing performance of the contract and P were under no obligation to accept or pay for the documents; (8) the finding that the value of the meal was U.S. $ 240 per tonne meant that this was its value with its inherent liability for demurrage and P were liable to reimburse V for all demurrage payments made by them. (*McCutcheon* v. *David MacBrayne* [1964] C.L.Y. 568; *Hardwick Game Farm* v. *S.A.P.P.A.* [1968] C.L.Y. 3526; *British Crane Hire Corp.* v. *Ipswich Plant Hire* [1974] C.L.Y. 442 distinguished): S.I.A.T. DI DEL FERRO *v.* TRADAX OVERSEAS S.A. [1978] 2 Lloyd's Rep. 470, Donaldson J.

2432. Carriage by sea—bill of lading—allegation of fraud—amendment

P contracted to manufacture fibre glass making equipment for T1 who instructed T2 to open a letter of credit in favour of P. An irrevocable letter of credit was opened through D, requiring shipment to be from London to Callas on or before October 15, 1976, while the credit was to remain open until October 30 for negotiation of the shipping documents, and providing that the credit could "neither be amended nor cancelled without the agreement of all parties thereto." On August 26, D advised P that the credit had been amended by the addition of a requirement that invoices be signed by an executive of T1. P did not confirm their agreement to this. On November 9 D notified P that the credit had been further amended by the extension of the shipment date to December 15, and the date for presentation of documents to December 31. The goods were put on board the A at Felixstowe on December 16. B, as loading broker for the carriers, issued shipped on board bills of lading, describing London as the port of loading, and dated December 15. On December 22, the documents were presented, and D rejected them, contending that the invoices had not been signed as per the amendment of August 26, and that B had made out the bills of lading fraudulently on P's behalf with the intention that D would act on them. *Held,* that (1) applying the tests in *Derry* v. *Peek* (1889) 14 App.Cas. 374, B had made a fraudulent misrepresentation as to the date of shipment, knowing that the correct date was a matter of importance in relation to a letter of credit; (2) before December 22, D, T1 and T2 knew that shipment had been at Felixstowe; (3) although B had acted fraudulently, he was not acting on behalf of P, but of the carriers, and fraud had not been established against P; (4) presentation of the documents in December was sufficient acceptance of the extensions of the original letter of credit; but D were not entitled to require signed invoices, as the amendment of August 26 had never been accepted; (5) since B was not P's agent, there was no fraud on the part of P in presenting the bills of lading; there was nothing on the face of them to indicate that they did not comply with the letter of credit as extended by the amendment; there was no implied warranty that the presenter of documents under a letter of credit warranted their accuracy, and P were entitled to succeed: UNITED CITY MERCHANTS (INVESTMENTS) AND GLASS FIBRES AND EQUIPMENTS *v.* ROYAL BANK OF CANADA, VITROREFUERZOS S.A. AND BANCO CONTINENTAL S.A.; THE AMERICAN ACCORD [1979] 1 Lloyd's Rep. 267, Mocatta J.

2433. —— —— exemption clause—whether stevedores entitled to benefit—liability of stevedores

[Aust.] P were the consignees of 37 cartons of razor blades shipped on the N. Cl. 2 of the U.S. bills of lading contained an exemption clause which was expressed to operate in favour, *inter alia,* of every independent contractor from time to time employed by the carrier while acting in the course of or in connexion with his employment," the carrier's immunities being extended to such independent contractors "acting as aforesaid." Cl. 8 provided that "Delivery of the goods shall be taken by the consignee from the vessel's rail immediately the vessel is ready to discharge"; and cl. 17 provided that "the carrier shall be discharged from all liability in respect of loss or damage unless suit is brought within one year after the date when the goods should have been delivered." D, stevedores, were engaged by the shipowners' agents to discharge the N and to hand over the consignment to P. After discharge, but before delivery to P, 33 of the cartons were stolen. After one year from the date when the goods should have been delivered had elapsed, P claimed damages from, *inter alia*, D. The question arose whether D were entitled to the benefit of the relevant clauses in the bills of lading. *Held,* that (1) the words in cl. 2 constituted a contract then and there concluded, and in relation to D necessarily fell foul of the doctrine of consideration; (2) under cl. 2 the carrier's immunities extended to D only so long as they were carrying out the carrier's obligations under the bills of lading; (3) under cl. 8 the carriers' obligations determined once and for all when by discharge ex ship's rail they effected due delivery of the goods; (4) the relevant employment of D referred to in cl. 2 and immunities conferred by that clause would also determine at that time, and would have no operation when the goods were lying in D's custody (*York Products Pty.* v. *Gilchrist Watt & Sanderson Pty.* [1971] C.L.Y. 11071; *Keith Bray Pty.* v. *Hamburg Amerikanische* (unreported) applied); (5) D did not misdeliver the goods as agents for the carrier, but rather failed to take reasonable care of them as bailees; this act of negligence was not within cl. 2, and D were not entitled to rely upon the limitation provisions in cl. 17: SALMOND AND SPRAGGON (AUSTRALIA) PTY. *v.* PORT JACKSON STEVEDORING PTY.; THE NEW YORK STAR [1979] 1 Lloyd's Rep. 298, Aust. High Ct.

2434. —— —— **limitation of liability—Hague Rules**
    [Can.] In June 1976, D contracted to carry five lift vans belonging to P from Madras to Vancouver. It was an oral term of the contract that the goods would be carried below deck and freight was paid accordingly. P was advised that the goods would be transhipped at some point in the voyage. In November 1976, the goods were loaded on board, and a bill of lading incorporating the Hague Rules was issued. On November 14 the goods were discharged at Singapore and put into a transit storage. D knew that the lift vans were not waterproof and should have been kept in covered storage, but they were not moved into covered storage until December 3. On December 22 the goods were loaded on to another vessel belonging to D, and a bill of lading issued the same day. Upon discharge at Vancouver, it was discovered that the goods inside the vans had suffered fresh water damage amounting to $32,262.48, and it was agreed that the damage could only have been sustained at Singapore. D contended, *inter alia*, that they were entitled to limit their liability. *Held,* that (1) the Hague Rules were incorporated into the contract between the parties, but the part of the contract relating to holding the goods on the dock awaiting the transhipment was not within the rules because it did not relate to "the carriage of goods by water" (*Anticosti Shipping Co.* v. *Viateur St.-Amand* [1959] C.L.Y. 3031; *A. R. Kitson Trucking and Wolridge* v. *Rivtow Straits and Renner* [1975] 4 W.W.R. 1, and *Pyrene Co.* v. *Scindia Navigation Co.* [1954] C.L.Y. 3080, 3197 applied; *The Ardennes* (1950) C.L.C. 9468 and *Falconbridge Nickel Mines* v. *Chimo Shipping* [1974] C.L.Y. 3545 distinguished); (2) although D had carried the goods from Madras to Vancouver, which was the principal thing for which they had contracted, the oral term that the goods would be carried below deck went to the root of the contract, and equally obliged D to protect the goods in covered storage at Singapore; their failure to do so constituted a fundamental breach, and accordingly P was entitled to damages of $32,268.48 (*Suisse Atlantique Société d'Armement Maritime S.A.* v. *N.V. Rotterdamsche Kolen Centrale* [1966] C.L.Y. 1797 and *Levison* v. *Patent Steam Carpet Cleaning Co.* [1977] C.L.Y. 377 considered): CAPTAIN *v.* FAR EASTERN STEAMSHIP CO. [1979] 1 Lloyd's Rep. 595, Can.Sup.Ct.

2435.   [U.S.] P contracted with D for the carriage of four component parts of a power plant from the U.S. to Saudi Arabia. The parts were stored on the deck of the L, and during the voyage the vessel encountered bad weather which resulted in the loss overboard of one of the parts, and damage to two of the remaining parts. The bill of lading provided that the Hague Rules as enacted in the country of shipment would apply; that deck cargo would be carried subject to the Rules; and that D's liability for cargo was governed by the Rules even if it was carried on deck. By s. 4 (5) of the U.S. Carriage of Goods by Sea Act, D's liability for loss or damage to cargo was limited to $500 unless a higher valuation of the goods was declared by P and inserted in the bill of lading. The bill of lading contained no reference to s. 4 (5), there was no clause limiting D's liability, and no designated spot for a shipper to insert the declared value of the cargo, or reference to P's option to insert the greater value. On D's motion for partial summary judgment in the sum of $500 instead of the $517,000 claimed by P, *held*, that the motion would be denied as P had never been afforded a fair opportunity to comply with s. 4 (5) by declaring the actual value of the goods and inserting it in the bill of lading (*Pan American World Airways Inc.* v. *California Stevedore and Ballast Co.* (1977) 559 F. 2d 1173, *Wientex Trading Co.* v. *Flota Mercante Gran Centro Americana S.A.* (1977) 75 Civ. 1458 applied): GENERAL ELECTRIC CO. *v.* M.V. LADY SOPHIE; THE LADY SOPHIE [1979] 2 Lloyd's Rep. 173, U.S.Dist.Ct.

2436. —— —— payment against " clean " bill of lading—post-shipment damage noted on bill

A bill of lading is " clean " if it states without qualification that the goods were in good order at the time of shipment and that the shipowner has no claim against them, except for freight.

The plaintiffs contracted to sell a quantity of sugar c. and f. Bandarshapur subject to the rules of the Refined Sugar Association which provided (*a*) for payment against a signed set of clean " on board " bills of lading and (*b*) for insurance to be effected by the buyer, such insurance to be for the seller's protection until payment was made. After loading on board part of the sugar was damaged in a fire and was discharged. The plaintiffs tendered a separate bill in respect of the damaged sugar, which bill acknowledged shipment in apparent good order and condition, and contained a note to the effect that the sugar had been discharged due to fire damage; the bill was stamped " freight pre-paid." The defendants rejected the bill on the basis that it was not " clean." In arbitration the plaintiffs claimed payment of the bill or damages for the defendants' failure to insure the sugar. The arbitrators found that the bill was not clean and that since the plaintiffs could not show that the fire was not caused by inherent vice (the packing used) the loss on a balance of probabilities would have fallen with the exception to normal marine insurance. *Held*, that (1) the bill was " clean " in all essential respects and the plaintiffs were entitled to payment thereon; and (2) in any event the plaintiffs would have been entitled to damages for the failure to insure, since they only had to prove the loss by fire, it being incumbent upon the insurers to prove that the loss fell within an exception to the policy. (*Hansson* v. *Hamel & Horley* [1922] A.C. 36 considered; *Munro-Brice* v. *War Risks Association* [1918] 2 K.B. 78 applied.)

M. GOLODETZ & CO. INC. *v.* CZARNIKOW-RIONDA CO. INC.; THE GALATIA [1979] 2 All E.R. 726, Donaldson J.

2437. —— —— short delivery—recovery of duty on goods not delivered

[Can.] P, importers, and D, carriers, were the parties to a contract represented by a bill of lading for the carriage of 50 bales of merchandise to Montreal and P brought an action against D for the recovery of an amount equal to the customs duty paid on 34 of the bales which were never delivered. *Held*, dismissing D's appeal, that (1) as the undelivered goods were included by D in the manifest delivered to customs, in the absence of proof to the contrary they were deemed to have been landed in Canada by virtue of the Customs Act; (2) D had in effect advised P that the goods were on board the vessel; (3) D at no time advised P that the goods were not imported, nor supplied them with proof to that effect; (4) accordingly, it could not be said that P should have prosecuted a refund claim for the customs duty; (5) P were entitled to an indemnity from D for the loss caused by having paid the duty: THE CITY OF COLOMBO [1978] 2 Lloyd's Rep. 587, Federal C.A.

2438. —— —— **signed on behalf of carrier—goods damaged in transit—whether owner entitled to benefit of clause in bill**

[Aust.] A cargo of tinplate was carried from New South Wales to Western Australia in a ship owned by A.C.S.C. and chartered to B. The ship suffered damage causing rust in transit. The bills of lading were issued by and signed on behalf of the charterer. They were not signed on behalf of the ship, or the shipowners A.C.S.C. The opening words of each bill provided that it was to have effect subject to the provisions of the Hague Rules set out in the Schedule to the relevant Australian statute. The consignees sued A.C.S.C. in bailment and tort and obtained judgment at first instance after two defences raised by the shipowners had been rejected, namely defences based upon r. 6 of art. III of the Rules, which provided that the carrier and the ship should be discharged from all liability in respect of loss or damage unless the suit was brought within one year after delivery of the goods. It was conceded that proceedings were commenced more than three years after the goods were delivered. On appeal, *held,* (1) the shipowner, not being a party to the bill of lading, was not entitled to the benefit of r. 6 of art. III of the Hague Rules, as being a term thereof (*Elder Dempster* v. *Paterson, Zochonis* [1929] A.C. 552 distinguished); (2) the shipowner was not entitled to the benefit of r. 6 as being a statutory exemption to the benefit of which the ship (*i.e.* including the shipowner) was entitled; (3) this was because the Hague Rules, by art. II, relate only to contracts "of carriage of goods by sea" and, by art. I (*b*) only to such contracts as are "covered by a bill of lading," etc.; (4) because a party has the option to sue the carrier *in personam* or the ship *in rem,* r. 6 is framed to provide a discharge for both carrier and ship. Thus, the discharge given by r. 6 to the ship does not extend to the owner when the owner is not the carrier (*Aries Tanker Corp.* v. *Total Transport* [1977] C.L.Y. 2741 distinguished): J. GADSEN v. AUSTRALIAN COASTAL SHIPPING COMMISSION (1977) 31 F.L.R. 157, N.S.W.Sup.Ct.

2439. —— **charterparty—bunker costs—freight in accordance with worldscale**

O let their vessel M to C for as many consecutive voyages as the M could perform within 18 months of first tendering her notice of readiness by a charter on the Exxonvoy form dated October 12, 1973, which provided, *inter alia,* "F. Freight Rate. In accordance with 250 per cent. of the rate stipulated in the Worldwide Tanker Nominal Freight Scale 'WORLDSCALE' Schedule as applicable at the date of each loading . . . M.(3) Worldscale terms and conditions as applicable at the date of each loading are to apply to this charterparty." As a result of the sharp increase in bunker prices at the end of 1973, on January 15, 1974, the publishers of Worldscale published a document which provided "it has now been decided to put in operation a system whereby changes in bunker prices can be reflected by the provision of a monthly bunker index [which] is in no way to be construed as an amendment to the basic Worldscale Schedule [and whose] use must be a matter of specific agreement between the parties to a contract." The M began her first voyage out of 28 under the charter in January 1974, and C paid the freight during 1974 in accordance with the Worldscale document issued at the end of 1973 and applicable to 1974, but with no increment in relation to the bunker indices. O contended that the increments of freight resulting from the bunker indices were recoverable by virtue of cll. F. and M.(3), and claimed a declaration accordingly. On a special case stated, *held,* that (1) the charter was entered into on October 12, 1973, and the first Worldscale amendment was in January 1974, and in the absence of express agreement between the parties, cl. F. could not be construed so as to incorporate the monthly bunker indices into the contract; (2) if, which was open to doubt, cl. M.(3) applied to the monthly bunker indices, there by themselves without reference to the document of January 15, 1974, were meaningless; (3) on the facts, there was no basis for awarding O something in view of the changed circumstances, and O's claim failed: POLE STAR COMPANIA NAVIERA S.A. v. KOCH MARINE INC.; THE MARITSA [1979] 1 Lloyd's Rep. 581, Mocatta J.

2440. —— —— **contaminated cargo—right to freight**

Freight payable " on delivery of the cargo " remains payable notwithstanding some contamination of the cargo, provided that the description of the cargo remains the same as when it was shipped.

Under a charterparty of a vessel for the carriage of crude oil, freight was payable on delivery of the cargo. The vessel carried a cargo of Bachaquero Crude, a particularly high quality and paraffin free oil, but on its discharge the charterers refused to pay freight, alleging that the oil had been contaminated by paraffin left over from a previous cargo. On a reference by the arbitrators, *held*, that if on delivery the cargo would commercially still be described as " Bachaquero Crude," the freight was payable; if it was so contaminated as to render that description inappropriate, the charterers were entitled to withold payment. (Dictum of Lord Esher M.R. in *Asfar and Co.* v. *Bundell* [1896] 1 Q.B. at p. 127 applied.)

MONTEDISON S.P.A. *v.* ICROMA S.P.A.; THE CASPIAN SEA [1979] 3 All E.R. 378, Donaldson J.

2441. —— —— contract of affreightment—bunker escalation clause—principles to be applied

By a contract of affreightment in the Essovoy 1969 form dated September 1, 1971, O agreed to provide C with tanker vessels to be nominated by O over a period of three years. Cl. M(14), the escalation clause, provided " [C] shall reimburse [O] for any extra cost of bunkers over and above the cost of bunkers in effect October 14, 1971." In November 1973, as a result of heavy increases in bunker prices which could lead to considerable bunker escalation claims, O and C orally entered into the Clarkson's agreement whereby in the case of vessels chartered rather than owned by O, O would prepare bunker escalation invoices on the basis of speed and consumption figures taken from Clarkson's Tank Register and applied to BP's Mileage Tables. On completion of the contract in 1974, O claimed $810,518.20 in respect of three vessels for which C had not paid, and C counterclaimed $1,276,807.77, being the escalated bunker costs which they had paid to O in respect of nine vessels, contending that the money had been paid under a mistake in that C had not appreciated that the vessels in question had not been owned by O or demise or time-chartered to O, in each of which cases O would have had to buy and pay for the necessary bunker. On a special case stated, *held*, that (1) although in certain circumstances " reimburse " could mean no more than " pay," here, in cl. M(14), it meant that C would have to compensate O only for expense or liability incurred by O of paying for bunker at prices in excess of those in effect on October 14, 1971; (2) O were not entitled to bunker escalation costs in respect of two of the vessels, but were in respect of the third, which was under demise charter to them; (3) the Clarkson agreement was not a course of dealing altering the true construction of cl. M(14), but an express oral variation of the basis to which the figures of cl. M(14) should be applied when that clause was otherwise relevant; (4) C had not waived their right to rely on the true construction of cl. M(14) save as and when affected by the Clarkson agreement, since the bunker escalation invoices did not indicate the facts of the case, which C did not know and about which O did not enlighten them; (5) the nine payments were made, not under a mistake of law, but of fact in that C did not know that O had not incurred any extra costs due to the price of bunkers having escalated; (6) C's claim was not estopped, and there was nothing against conscience in C's recovering money which they were only asked to pay because of a wrong construction of cl. M(14), or, more likely, a mis-understanding of the Clarkson's agreement; (7) accordingly, C were entitled to recover the sums paid in respect of the bunker escalation invoices for all nine vessels. (*The Alexandra I* [1972] C.L.Y. 3200, and *Hardwick Game Farm* v. *S.A.P.P.A.* [1966] C.L.Y. 10837 considered): SARONIC SHIPPING CO. *v.* HURON LIBERIAN CO. [1979] 1 Lloyd's Rep. 341, Mocatta J.

2442. —— —— guarantee—off hire

O time-chartered the A to C by a contract containing the usual off-hire clause and incorporating the Hague Rules, delivery being on February 24, 1977. In March 1977, in attempting to berth at Reydharfjordhur in Iceland, the A heavily struck the quayside, causing serious damage to herself, for which temporary repairs were done in Iceland, and permanent repairs upon her subsequent arrival at Antwerp. Owing to the delay so caused, the A lost her cargo and had to wait 39 days for a new one. The A was redelivered on July 14, 1977, and C paid $120,000 on account of the total hire due, $400,000. O brought an action for the balance against G, guarantors of C's obligations under the charter, and sought judgment under R.S.C., Ord. 14. *Held,* on appeal, that (1) if the damage to the A was caused by the negligence of her master, O were not liable under the Hague Rules; (2) there was no suggestion that the master was incompetent, but it was clear that the damage was caused by giving the astern order too late and not by any defect in the engines; accordingly the defence of unseaworthiness failed; (3) there were legitimate grounds of set-off with regard to the off-hire clause and the periods during which the A was off-hire; (4) G's cross-claim for the damage sustained by the 39 days wait was not a ground for equitable set-off, since that relief was only available where C was deprived of the vessel by the fault of O, whereas here C had the use of the A but could not get a cargo; further, the cross-claim arose out of the alleged negligence of the master, and so was inadmissible as excluded by the Hague Rules. Judgment for O: Aliakmon Maritime Corp. *v.* Trans Ocean Continental Shipping and Frank Truman Export; The Aliakmon Progress [1978] 2 Lloyd's Rep. 499, C.A.

2443. —— —— **hire—charterer's notices suspending payment of hire—validity**

By three charterparties dated March 28, 1973, C timechartered the H, the K and the G from O for a period expiring on December 31, 1995, for the carriage of liquefied natural gas from the plant in Das Island, Abu Dhabi, which was operated by A, to Tokyo Bay. The charter provided, *inter alia,* by cl. 59, " (a) If through any cause beyond the reasonable control of [C] the production of LNG by [A] or its delivery to Japan is interrupted or terminated, [C] may at their option suspend the operation of this charter, including the payment of hire for a maximum of six months in any five-year period paying interest at 8 per cent. per annum on such loss of hire incurred. In this event the period of such suspension shall be added as an additional period at the end of this charter; (b) In the event of [C] exercising their option to suspend the operation of this charter, then they shall give notice in writing to [O] of the date from which it is intended that such suspension and cessation of hire shall take effect. Thereupon [O] and [C] shall consult together over a maximum period of 30 days from the date of the notice in an endeavour to find alternative employment for the vessel acceptable to [C]. If after the expiry of the said period [O] have failed in their endeavours or have failed to reach agreement with [C], then the provision of sub-clause (a) shall apply from the date of the notice, although [O] and [C] will continue in their endeavours to find alternative employment." The LNG plant consisted of two production trains, each producing half the required output independently of the other. Production from train 2 commenced on January 10, 1977, but subsequently ceased when the flash drum was declared unfit for service. The flash drum from train 1 was transferred to train 2, and production on train 2 resumed on March 13. Production from train 1 commenced on August 14. On September 12, both trains were shut down due to a failure in the utility power plant. Power was restored on September 24 and train 2 resumed production, but cracks in the pipe welds in train 1 were discovered, and train 1 remained out of action. On March 11, due to the flash drum incident in train 2, C gave their first notice, suspending payment of hire in respect of the charter of the G. On October 21, due to train 1 being unable to resume production on September 24, C gave their second notice, suspending payment of hire in respect of the charter of the H and the K. Disputes arose regarding, *inter alia,* C's entitlement to give notices suspending hire, the date at which the notices took effect, and the meaning of the words " production " being " interrupted " in cl. 59 (a). *Held,* that (1) although on September 12 the plant was not working at full production, train 1 had been producing for about one month and train 2 for about eight months, and it could not be said that there had not been any production within the meaning of cl. 59; such a conclusion would require the clearest possible words, and those words were not there; (2) there was an interruption in production within the meaning of cl. 59 after September 24, even though only one train producing half the total output remained shut down; (3) when C gave their second notice on October 21, there was an interruption in production beyond the reasonable control of C, and the notice was valid; the fact that cl. 59 was in the nature of a *force majeure* clause rather than an ordinary off-hire clause made no difference; (4) when C gave their first notice on March 11, there was no interruption in production, since production on train 1 did not start until August 14, and the flash drum incident did not interrupt production; but only delayed it; the only interruption was on train 2 and that had ended by March 13, and therefore the first notice was invalid; accordingly, C succeeded in relation to the H and the K, but failed in relation to the G; (5) a notice under cl. 59 could not take effect immediately, but from a date not earlier than 30 days from the date of the notice; therefore the second notice was only valid from November 22; (6) the period over which interest was payable was year by year until the period of suspension was added at the end of the charter: THE HILLI, KHANNUR AND GIMI [1979] 1 Lloyd's Rep. 153, Lloyd J.

2444. —— —— **owners' withdrawal of vessel—hire paid in advance—whether right to withdraw waived.**

An owner's acceptance of an underpayment of hire paid in advance does not necessarily deprive him of the right to withdraw the vessel.

By a charterparty on the Baltine form a vessel was chartered for " 8/10 months at the charterer's option," hire to be payable monthly in advance save for the last month's hire in respect of which disbursements made on the owners' behalf could be deducted up to the expected delivery time. When the nine months' hire was due the charterers estimated that the vessel would be redelivered within the ninth month (an estimate later found by the arbitrator to be unreasonable) whereas the owners contended that the charterparty period would extend into the tenth month. After some dispute the charterers paid the ninth months' hire on time but deducted from it some $31,000 allegedly representing owner's disbursements. The owners accepted such sum but queried the details of the deductions. Six days after receipt of the reduced hire, the owners withdrew the vessel in purported exercise of their right to do so " in default of payment " of hire in full. The arbitrator ruled, *inter alia*, that by accepting the reduced hire the owners had waived their right to withdraw, such decision being upheld by the Court of Appeal. *Held*, allowing the owners' appeal, that the underpayment entitled the owners to withdraw and that there had been no unequivocal election to waive that right. (Decision of C.A. [1978] C.L.Y. 2719, reversed.)

CHINA NATIONAL FOREIGN TRADE TRANSPORTATION CORP. *v.* EVLOGIA SHIPPING CO. S.A. OF PANAMA; THE MIHALIOS XILAS [1979] 1 W.L.R. 1018, H.L.

2445. —— —— **safe berth—damage to vessel—whether charterers liable**

I, the owners of the K, time-chartered the vessel to C on the New York Produce Exchange form for a round voyage via safe ports including Valparaiso. In May 1973, the K was ordered to Baron Wharf in Valparaiso, which was outside the shelter of the breakwater. In the event of bad weather, vessels sometimes had to leave the berth to avoid hull damage and to do so required a pilot, a tug and unencumbered water in the immediate vicinity for manoeuvring. During the night of May 18/19, 1973, the weather deteriorated, and at 04.00 the bad weather warning light was displayed. The master prepared to move the K from the berth, and by 05.00 the pilot was on board. By 05.45 the tug was alongside. The K was prevented from leaving as two other vessels were anchored close by and remained so until 08.50. The K suffered ranging damage by contact with the pier, and I claimed damages from C. On a special case stated, *held*, dismissing C's appeal, that (1) a port or berth was not necessarily unsafe because a vessel might have to leave it in the event, and onset, of bad weather (*The Stork* [1955] C.L.Y. 2559, *The Eastern City* [1958] C.L.Y. 3144 and *The Dagmar* [1969] C.L.Y. 3301 affirmed); (2) for a berth to be safe when a vessel had to leave it, there had to be (a) an adequate weather forecasting system; (b) an adequate availability of pilots and tugs; (c) adequate searoom to manoeuvre; (d) an adequate system for ensuring that such searoom was always available; and here, requirements (c) and (d) had not been satisfied: THE KHIAN SEA [1979] 1 Lloyd's Rep. 545, C.A.

2446. —— contract—short delivery—recovery of money paid for shortfall

V sold to P tapioca pellets c. & f. Rotterdam by a contract incorporating GAFTA 100, cl. 16 of which provided, *inter alia*, " final settlement shall be made on the basis of gross delivered weights and the goods shall be weighed at time and place of discharge at port of destination herein named." P subsequently agreed with the shippers, but not with V, that discharge could be at Bremen instead of Rotterdam. Upon discharge at Bremen, a shortage was discovered, and P invoiced V for the shortfall, claiming DM.92,135.18. On a special case stated, *held,* on appeal, that a party seeking an adjustment of the figures in the bill of lading in his favour had to proceed in accordance with cl. 16 and could not substitute a port of which the other party had no knowledge. Judgment for V: KROHN & CO. *v.* MITSUI AND CO. EUROPE GMBH [1978] 2 Lloyd's Rep. 419, C.A.

2447. —— damage to cargo—inherent defect—presumed knowledge of expert—Hague Rules

[Can.] P contracted for the carriage of a cargo of apples from Buenos Aires to Vancouver aboard D's vessel, the H. Before loading, the apples were inspected by A, independent fruit inspection specialists engaged by D's underwriters, to determine whether the shipment should be inspected. A clean bill of lading was issued, but the cargo arrived in a damaged condition. P claimed that the damage was due to bad circulation of cool air in the refrigeration holds and, further, if the fruit was overripe on loading, then D's expert should have discovered this, and, as D's agent, his knowledge would be deemed knowledge of D, so preventing D from relying on the defence of inherent vice, condition or defect. *Held*, that (1) D had established that the cargo was properly stowed and refrigerated throughout the voyage, and it was therefore open to them to establish that the damage was due to inherent defect, quality or vice under art. IV, r. 2 (*m*), of the Hague Rules, and this was established since the damage was caused by overripeness prior to loading which was not evident to the ordinary non-expert observer; (2) D, by employing A, had not contented themselves with an ordinary inspection, and it would be wrong to fix them with a liability based on the lack of knowledge or expertise of an expert whom D was not by law nor by duty to the consignee bound to engage (*Silver* v. *Ocean Steam Ship Co.* [1930] 1 K.B. 416; *Wm. Fergus Harris & Son* v. *China Mutual Steam Navigation Co.* [1960] C.L.Y. 2937 applied); (3) D as carrier was responsible for the proper stowage, carriage and care of the cargo, but it was the shipper and consignee who were presumed to know the hidden weaknesses and defects of the cargo. Judgment for D: THE HOYANGER [1979] 2 Lloyd's Rep. 79, Can.Fed.Ct.

2448. —— —— sea water in hatch—Hague Rules

On February 12, 1972, D's vessel the B was on a voyage from Northfleet to the U.S.A. laden with 19,034 tons of cement belonging to P when she encountered a south-westerly gale. The lid of an access hatch on the forecastle deck opened and was forcibly thrown back into a fully open position, as a result of which sea water entered into No. 1 hold, causing damage to 2801·1 tons of cement. On P's claim for damages, D relied on the Hague Rules, art. IV, r. 2, which provided, *inter alia*, " neither the carrier nor the ship shall be responsible for loss or damage arising from (a) act neglect or default of the master mariner pilot or the servants of the carrier in the navigation or in the management of the ship . . . (p) latent defects not discoverable by due diligence." *Held*, that (1) there was sufficient evidence of a breach by D of their obligation under art. III, r. 2, to " properly and carefully load, handle, stow, carry, keep, care for and discharge the goods carried," and the burden of bringing the cause of the damage specifically within art. IV was on D; (2) there was no evidence of any latent defect which would bring D within exception (p); (3) no question of navigation arose with regard to exception (a); it would be a misuse of language to suggest that the surreptitious opening of a hatch by a member of the crew was an act or default in the management of the ship;

and D were not protected by art. IV, r. 2, and were liable to P: THE BULKNES [1979] 2 Lloyd's Rep. 39, Sheen J.

2449. —— **delay—whether port " safe " at time**

In accordance with a charterparty dated May 17, 1973, the owners, O, nominated the vessel H and the charterers, C, nominated as a safe port for loading D, on the Mississippi river. To sail from D to the open sea involved passing through a dredged channel, the depth of which varied. After completing loading, the H was delayed for several weeks by (a) congestion due to fog in the channel; (b) the subsequent grounding of the T blocking the channel; (c) the subsequent reduction of the controlling draught in the channel to less than the sailing draught of the H; (d) the subsequent grounding of the M at the entrance to the channel. O claimed damages for detention in respect of (c) and (d). On a special case stated, *held*, allowing C's appeal, that (1) it was clear law that before O could treat C's conduct as a repudiation of C's obligation to load, the delay had to be such as would frustrate the adventure, and not merely as to constitute a commercially unacceptable delay (*Universal Cargo Carriers Corp.* v. *Citati* [1957] C.L.Y. 130 and *S.S. Knutsford* v. *Tillmans & Co.* [1908] A.C. 406 applied); (2) an obstruction which merely caused delay did not render a port unsafe unless the delay was sufficient to frustrate the adventure; (3) accordingly, since here it was conceded that the commercial adventure had not been frustrated, D was not an unsafe port: THE HERMINE [1979] 2 Lloyd's Rep. 212, C.A.

2450. —— **demurrage—" used laytime "**

O voyage-chartered their tanker T to C under a charter in the Exxonvoy 1969 form, of which cl. 6 provided, *inter alia*, that laytime would commence six hours after receipt of notice of readiness at the port of loading or discharge; cl. 7 set out periods which were not to count as laytime; and cl. 8 provided " Demurrage: [C] shall pay demurrage for all time that loading and discharging and used laytime exceeds the allowed laytime." The T wholly used up her 72 hours' permitted laytime at the port of loading, and a dispute arose as to whether certain periods were to be charged for as time on demurrage after the T's arrival at the port of discharge. On a special case stated, *held*, that (1) nothing in either cl. 6 or 7 indicated that the provisions as to time not counting as laytime applied once the T was on demurrage; (2) inconsistencies in the charter over use of the phrase " used laytime " suggested that there was no technical distinction between that and " allowed laytime "; and " used laytime " was not a term of art; (3) cl. 8 not only applied to the time actually used in discharging together with used laytime, but also to any time which exceeded the 72 permitted hours before the completion of the discharging operation excluding the time taken to travel from the loading port to the discharging port; and on the true construction of the charter, demurrage ran continuously (*Union of India* v. *Compania Naviera Aeolus S.A.* [1962] C.L.Y. 2832; *Dias Compania Naviera S.A.* v. *Louis Dreyfus Corp.* [1978] C.L.Y. 2707 applied); (4) it was for C to protect themselves against the misfortune of demurrage accruing by mere passage of time by inserting in the charter exception clauses applicable to the period on demurrage as well as to the period when laytime was running but had not been consumed; and there was no such clause in the charter: NIPPON YUSEN KAISHA v. SOCIÉTÉ ANONYME MAROCAINE DE L'INDUSTRIE DU RAFFINAGE; THE TSUKUBA MARU [1979] 1 Lloyd's Rep. 459, Mocatta J.

2451. —— **general average—Jason clause—engine failure—crew negligence**

D issued bills of lading in respect of P's cargoes, which were loaded on to D's vessel, the H, in various U.S. ports. The bills of lading incorporated the new Jason clause, which provided, *inter alia*, that in case of damage after commencement of the voyage resulting from any cause whatsoever, whether due to negligence or not, for the consequences of which D were not responsible by statute, P would contribute with D in general average to the payment of any losses or expenses of a general average nature that may be made or incurred, and would make any deposit to cover the estimated contribution as may be required by D before delivery of the goods. Shortly after leaving her last U.S. loading port, the H sustained an engine failure which interrupted the voyage for 48 days. D declared general average and collected the appropriate deposits from P. The general average statement stated that the engine failure of the H was caused by crew negligence. P claimed for the return of their deposit, contending that D were not entitled to general average contribution for the losses suffered because of engine failure. *Held*, that (1) since the cargoes were loaded at U.S. ports for foreign commerce, the Carriage of Goods by Sea Act was incorporated into each bill of lading and was the statute referred to in the Jason clause; (2) although by s. 1304 (2) (*a*) of the Carriage of Goods by Sea Act D were not liable for damages resulting from the negligence of the crew in not replacing a split pin in a bearing bolt inside the engine, the engine failure occurred on a later voyage after the H had been in U.S. ports and subject to inspection by D, and it was for D to show that the absence of the pin was a latent defect not discoverable by due diligence; (3) to require D to check for the presence or absence of split pins did not impose a burden which rose to the level of "unreasonableness"; (4) D had failed to exercise due diligence to make the H seaworthy before the commencement of the voyage and were not therefore entitled to general average contributions; and P were entitled to recovery of the deposits paid to D: THE HELLENIC GLORY [1979] 1 Lloyd's Rep. 424, U.S. Dist.Ct.

2452. —— hire—direction not to sign freight pre-paid bills of lading—whether repudiatory breach

An instruction by owners to masters of vessels prohibiting the signing of freight pre-paid bills of lading may be a repudiatory breach of contract.

By time-charters, the owners let three ships to the charterers for periods of six years. Most of the cargoes were carried on c.i.f. terms in which freight pre-paid bills of lading were used. A dispute arose and the owners instructed the masters not to sign any pre-paid lading bills. The charterers accepted the owners' conduct as a repudiation and referred the matter to arbitration. After a series of appeals the matter was finally appealed by both parties to the House of Lords. *Held*, that since the signing of the pre-paid bills was essential to the charterers' trade, the owners' instruction constituted an anticipatory breach of contract which in the circumstances amounted to a repudiation of the contract. (*James Shaffer* v. *Findlay, Durham & Brodie* [1953] C.L.Y. 674 and *Sweet & Maxwell* v. *Universal News Service* [1964] C.L.Y. 2073 distinguished.)

FEDERAL COMMERCE AND NAVIGATION CO. *v.* MOLENA ALPHA INC. [1978] 3 W.L.R. 991, H.L.

2453. —— —— non-payment—ownership of vessel

[Sing.] D timechartered their vessel, the B, to C, who fell into arrears of hire amounting to U.S. $3,929,090.24. D issued a writ, and on September 20, 1976, the P was arrested. At that date, the P was owned by O, but under the full possession and control of C under a "Purchase Contract" between O and C, by which upon full payment of 72 instalments, of which five had been paid when the writ was issued, O had to transfer title to the P free from all encumbrances and maritime liens to C. O had the option to rescind the contract and withdraw or retake the P in the event of C's default. C applied for the writ and all subsequent proceedings to be set aside on the ground that on the true construction of the High Court (Admiralty Jurisdiction) Act, s. 4 (4), P was not "beneficially owned as respects all the shares therein" by C. *Held*, dismissing D's appeal, that (1) these words referred only to ownership vested in a person who had the right to sell, dispose of or alienate all the shares in a vessel, and clearly covered a person who, whether or not the legal owner, was the equitable owner of all the shares in a vessel; (2) it was such ownership which rendered a vessel "beneficially owned as respects all the shares therein," and not full possession and control with the beneficial use of the vessel, which did not relate to title; (3) since D claimed the right to arrest the P as security for unpaid hire on the B, in which O had no legal or equitable proprietary interest, and O owed nothing to D, equity would not regard O as holding the P on constructive trust for C; the "Purchase Contract" relied on was a conditional sale agreement in that O owed the P until payment of the full purchase price and had the right to retake possession of the P in case of default by C; (4) accordingly, C were not the equitable owners of the P with bare legal title in O; and O had some beneficial interest in the P which was sufficient to disentitle D from invoking the court's Admiralty jurisdiction under s. 4 (4). (*The Andrea Ursula* [1971] C.L.Y. 10859 distinguished): THE PERMINA 3001 [1979] 1 Lloyd's Rep. 327, Sing. C.A.

2454. —— —— —— withdrawal

O time-chartered their vessel to C by a charter on the New York Produce Exchange form, which provided, *inter alia,* by cl. 5. " Payment of hire to be made in [Genoa] in cash in United States Currency monthly in advance . . . otherwise failing the punctual and regular payment of the hire [O] shall be at liberty to withdraw the vessel from the service of [C]." The 81st instalment of hire of U.S. $68,863.86 fell due and payable by C to O on or before January 22, 1976, and on that date, by telex message, there was a credit transfer of the hire to O's bank " value 26," which under Italian banking law and practice became irrevocable and available for payment to O, although interest would not start to run until January 26. On January 22, O's bank credited O's account with U.S. $68,863.84, on which, although O had the immediate use of the money, if they had withdrawn it they would probably have incurred a liability to their bank to pay interest until January 26. On January 23, O instructed their bank to refuse payment of the hire, and on January 24 withdrew their vessel under cl. 5. On a special case stated, *held,* (1) a telex transfer was a payment in cash on the due date if it complied with the test that the transferee was given the unconditional and immediate use of the funds transferred, (2) the effect of the " value 26 " clause was that the transfer was conditional upon interest not accruing to the benefit of O until a date later than the specified due date; (3) accordingly, O did not have the unconditional use of the funds, and thus, as the transfer did not comply with the test, it was not equivalent to a payment in cash; (4) O were therefore entitled to withdraw the vessel on January 24 under cl. 5 (*The " Brimnes "* [1973] C.L.Y. 3111 applied): AWILCO A/S *v.* FULVIA S.P.A. DI NAVIGAZIONE; THE CHIKUMA [1979] 1 Lloyd's Rep. 367, Goff J.

2455. —— notice of shipment—rejection—validity of notice

By a contract incorporating FOSFA 24, V, who were about eighth in a string of sellers and buyers, sold to P soya beans c.i.f. Rotterdam for shipment in June 1977 from U.S. Gulf Ports. The contract provided by cl. 10, *inter alia,* that declaration of shipment was to be passed on with due despatch, and that a valid declaration could not be withdrawn except with P's consent. On June 10, 1977, P received a notice of shipment from V, which they rightly rejected as being out of time. On June 23, V passed a new notice relating to goods shipped on another vessel, which, although in time, was rejected by P on the ground that once V had given a valid declaration, albeit out of time, they could not give a further declaration without withdrawing the first one, and P did not consent to such withdrawal. On a special case stated, *held,* that (1) an attempt to apply a declaration of shipment to a contract by a stale notice was as ineffective as the tender of goods without the shipping documents, and such tender left V free to make a fresh tender of different goods with the shipping documents; (2) P could not maintain that the notice was a valid declaration of shipment which could not be withdrawn without their consent and an invalid one because it was sent to them out of time, and P were entitled to damages: GERTREIDE IMPORT GESELLSCHAFT M.B.H. *v.* ITOH & CO. (AMERICA) INC. [1979] 1 Lloyd's Rep. 592, Donaldson J.

2456. Collision

COLLISION REGULATIONS AND DISTRESS SIGNALS (AMENDMENT) ORDER 1979 (No. 462) [10p], made under the Merchant Shipping Act 1894 (c. 60), ss. 418, 424, 738; operative on May 14, 1979; amends S.I. 1977 No. 982 in consequence of Admiralty Notice No. 17 to Mariners 1979 which gives effect to traffic separation schemes adopted by IMCO in 1978.

SAFETY (COLLISION REGULATIONS AND DISTRESS SIGNALS) REGULATIONS 1979 (No. 1659) [20p], made under the Merchant Shipping Act 1979 (c. 39), ss.

21 (1), (3) (*k*) and 4 (*a*), 22 (1) (*d*) and (3) (*a*); operative on January 9, 1980; amend the Collisions Regulations and Distress Signals Order 1977 with references to traffic separation schemes, and by substituting an up-to-date list of foreign countries to whose vessels the Rules apply.

2457. —— crossing vessels—apportionment of blame

On October 28, 1970, P's ship the G came into collision with D's ship the E, the stem of the E striking the starboard side aft of the G at an angle of 50° leading forward on the G. The G had been on a course of 040° at 15 knots and first saw the E by radar distant 18 miles bearing 2–3° on the starboard bow. This bearing broadened to 8° at five miles, when she ceased to be visible because of rain. Those on board the G estimated that the ships would pass starboard to starboard at half a mile. The E first saw the G by radar at 20 miles bearing 6° on her port bow. The G disappeared at three miles range because of "clutter." Those on board the E estimated that the ships would pass port one and a half to two miles distant. The E altered 10° to starboard. When the lights of the G were seen, the E altered hard to starboard. Very shortly before the collision the G altered hard to port. *Held,* dismissing D's appeal, that (1) the evidence established that there was restricted visibility and that accordingly the crossing rules did not apply; (2) the trial judge's finding that the E's final manoeuvre preceded that of the G could not be impugned; (3) the Assessors and the Elder Brother were all agreed as to the faults of seamanship disclosed by the facts found by the judge ([1977] C.L.Y. 2776) and therefore the matter could not be interfered with by way of appeals and nor could the apportionment of blame decided by the judge of the G 40 per cent, and the E 60 per cent: THE ERCOLE [1979] 1 Lloyd's Rep. 539, C.A.

2458. —— liability—apportionment

After dark on March 23, 1971, D's vessel, the A, was proceeding out of Dakar Harbour with on board a pilot who, once outside the harbour, left the A and proceeded by launch to P's vessel, the B, which had been waiting outside the harbour for the pilot to take her in. While the pilot was on his way to the B, the two vessels collided, the bow of the A striking the starboard side of the B at a broad angle. Visibility was clear and the wind force 2–3. The issues arose as to whether the B was stationary and the A altered course to port, or whether the B was moving ahead and the A was maintaining a steady outward course. *Held,* that (1) the B's engine movement book showed that the B had moved ahead about one and a half cables during the period C–3 to 3½, and still had residual headway of about one knot at the time of collision; (2) the fact that the A would at a later stage have had to make a small alteration to port afforded no ground for inferring that she had made a much more substantial alteration to port at a much earlier stage; (3) accordingly the collision was caused by the B moving across the A and not by an alteration to port by A; (4) as to responsibility, the B was not at fault for waiting off the harbour entrance, since on a normal outward course the A could pass at least half a cable ahead of her; but the closer to the line of the entrance the B was, the greater the duty on her not to manoeuvre so as to cross the line; (5) the B was seriously at fault in working her engines so as to move across the line of the outcoming A; this was negligent, and the primary cause of the collision; (6) the master of the A had every reason to suppose that those on board the B, which was waiting for his pilot, knew that he was leaving on a normal outward course, and could see him doing so; the crossing rules did not apply and the A was not bound to keep her course and speed; and accordingly it was not negligent for the master of the A not to sound five short blasts; (7) the master of the A would have been prudent in taking earlier avoiding action, and he made an error of judgment in not doing so; but it could not be said in all the circumstances that he was negligent; (8) the B alone was to blame for the collision. Judgment for D: THE AVANCE [1979] 1 Lloyd's Rep. 143, Brandon J.

2459. —— narrow channel—liability for collision—apportionment

On March 11, 1972, in darkness and clear weather, P's vessel, the M, and D's vessel, the G, collided in the Irako channel, which connected the port of

Nagoya with the open sea. The axis of the channel was marked by two flashing white buoys about five miles apart, the course of the axis being 133–313°. Local rules required inward-bound vessels to pass to the east, and outward-bound vessels to the west of the buoys, *i.e.* each to the starboard side of the channel. The G, which was inward bound, kept to her side of the channel, but the M, which was outward bound, steered progressively onto her port side of it. At about 1½ minutes before collision, the G altered course hard to starboard, and the M hard to port, but the stern and port bow of the G struck the starboard side of the M at an angle of about 45° leading forward on the M, both vessels at the time of collision doing about 15–17 knots. P admitted to 60 per cent. liability for the failure of the M to keep to her own side of the channel; D contended that the M was alone to blame. *Held*, that (1) although the M was heading about 10° to port of her direct course along the channel, she was proceeding along the channel in a contrary direction to that of the G, and the narrow channel rather than the crossing rules applied, so that the G was free to alter her course or speed in accordance with the principles of good seamanship in order to avoid a collision rather than obliged to hold her course and speed; (2) the M was at fault in steering a course of 123° which took her to the wrong side of the channel; not appreciating, through bad lookout, that the G was showing her masthead lights a little open to starboard and her red side light; taking avoiding action much too late; and when finally taking such action, putting her wheel hard to port instead of hard to starboard; and all these faults were causative of the collision; (3) the G was at fault in not reducing speed not later than when the ships were two miles apart, despite the difficult position she was put in by the bad navigation of the M; (4) the fact that both ships were allowed to close at 36–37 knots before either took avoiding action contributed to the collision; (5) since the M created the situation of danger, whilst the G's only fault was her inadequate reaction to such situation, a fair decision of blame was the M 80 per cent. and the G 20 per cent.: THE GLENFALLOCH [1979] 2 Lloyd's Rep. 247, Brandon J.

2460. —— **negligence—whether stationary vessel a give way vessel**

[Scot.] On February 1, 1973, by day and in good visibility, P's vessel the M was lying some distance off the G on a northerly heading to stand-by while the G hauled in her nets. D's vessel the D was proceeding in a westerly direction at seven knots and, seeing the M dead ahead at a distance of one-half to three-quarter of a mile, the D's skipper assumed that the M was proceeding slowly northward to join up with the G. M first saw the D at a range of about one-quarter of a mile heading for her starboard beam and her shipper, being of the view that it was the duty of other vessels to keep clear of vessels which were drifting under way but not under command, assumed that the D would alter course. Both vessels failed to keep a proper look out and although they tried to take avoiding action at the last moment, the D struck and holed the starboard side of the M, as a result of which the M sank, and her crew was taken off by the D. *Held*, that (1) the M was not a give-way vessel, since the words "under way" in r. 19 of the Collision Regulations meant a vessel making way through the water, and did not cover a vessel lying stationary at sea, which was a very different situation and in conditions of good visibility, as here, required no special provisions, (2) the collision was caused by both skippers' failure to keep even a minimal lookout, and liability would be equally apportioned; (3) P's claim that the whaleback deck on the D restricted visibility from the wheelhouse and that a special lookout system should be instituted failed since there was no evidence that such precautions had ever been thought necessary or desirable; (4) even if such precautions were necessary, the D's skipper's losing sight of the M had nothing to do with the slight impairment of vision occasioned by the whaleback deck; (5) accordingly, the requirements of the Merchant Shipping Act 1894, s. 503, were satisfied, and the D's limitation fund agreed at £2,513·46: THE DEVOTION II [1979] 1 Lloyd's Rep. 509, Ct. of Session.

2461. —— **negligent navigation—liability for collision—apportionment**

After dark on October 11, 1972, P's vessel the K and D's vessel the R were both inward bound in the Thames Estuary when the K, which was in relation to the R an overtaking vessel, struck the starboard side of the R forward of amidships at considerable speed, with her stem leading forward at an angle of about 80°. The wind was north-easterly force 6–7 and the tide was flood, setting westerly at about one to one and a half knots. As a result of the collision, the R sank, with the loss of life of one of her crew. The Port of London Authority, acting under their powers conferred by the Port of London Act 1968, s. 120, marked the wreck of the R, and later raised, removed and sold such wreck. P claimed and D counterclaimed in negligence. The P.L.A. claimed the balance of the expenses incurred in marking, raising and removing the wreck after giving credit for the proceeds of sale, against D as a statutory debt, and against P and D as damages for negligence and nuisance. *Held,* that (1) the K was to blame for bad lookout leading to wholly erroneous estimates of the relative course and distance of the R by relying solely on visual observations instead of using the radar; although there was nothing improper in the K attempting to overtake the R in the place or at the speed or on the side of the R which she did, she had made the attempt much too close on a converging course, and so was in breach of r. 24 (*a*) of the Collision Regulations; and the bad lookout and breach of r. 24 (*a*) were the main causes of the collision; not sounding an overtaking signal as required by by-law 42 of the Port of London River By-laws 1967 and overtaking without prior agreement by signal under that by-law were causative of the collision; but the K's breach of by-law 27 in not carrying three all-round red lights was not causative; (2) the R was to blame for bad lookout in not appreciating that the K was shaping to overtake her; in altering course to starboard in breach of her obligation under r. 21 of the Collision Regulations to maintain her course and speed; in failing to indicate her intention to alter to starboard by one short blast in breach of r. 28 (*a*) of the Collision Regulations; failing to alter course to port to haul away from the side on which she was to be overtaken as required by by-law 17 of the Port of London River By-laws; and all these faults were causative of the collision; (3) since the main burden of effecting a safe overtaking was on the overtaking vessel, the blame would be apportioned as to 80 per cent. to the K and 20 per cent. to the R; (4) the P.L.A. would have judgment in liability in negligence (but not nuisance) against P and D, and in statutory debt against D: THE KYLIX AND RUSTRINGEN [1979] 1 Lloyd's Rep. 133, Brandon J.

2462. Conflict of laws—proper law—whether domestic policy superseded substantive law

[U.S.] In August 1975 P's vessel the S was proceeding through the Welland Canal of the St. Lawrence Seaway from the United States to Canada when she collided with Bridge 12, causing damage to herself and to the bridge. Claims were brought against P for losses due to the delay caused by the debris obstructing the waterway. It was determined in earlier proceedings that since the collision occurred in a Canadian waterway, the rights and liabilities of the parties were governed by the law of Canada. Actions against P in the Canadian court were dismissed on the grounds that there was no relationship of sufficient proximity that gave rise to a duty by P to the claimants. *Held,* that (1) Canadian law denied recovery for economic loss from vessel delay; and the court in accordance with its earlier finding that the *lex loci delicti commissi* controlled the issues of substantive law had to follow the ruling of the Canadian court as the law most directly in point (*Black Diamond S.S. Corp.* v. *Robert Stewart and Sons,* 336 U.S. 386 (1949) applied); (2) it did not follow that the established test of foreseeability in providing redress for the wrongful acts of negligent tortfeasors rose to the level of domestic policy sufficient in depth and weight to override the controlling law of a foreign nation; (3) the court was therefore compelled to adopt the findings of substantive law of the Canadian court and the claims for damages resulting from vessel delay would be dismissed under the law of Canada: THE STEELTON (No. 2) [1979] 1 Lloyd's Rep. 431, U.S.Dist.Ct.

2463. Crew accommodation

MERCHANT SHIPPING (CREW ACCOMMODATION) (AMENDMENT) REGULATIONS 1979 (No. 491) [10p], made under the Merchant Shipping Act 1970 (c. 36), ss. 20, 99 (2); operative on July 1, 1979; amend the provisions of S.I. 1978 No. 795 relating to the minimum floor area to be provided in sleeping rooms for officers and cadets so as to take account of the case where two cadets are accommodated in one sleeping room.

2464. Fees

MERCHANT SHIPPING (FEES) (AMENDMENT) REGULATIONS 1979 (No. 631) [25p], made under the Merchant Shipping (Mercantile Marine Fund) Act 1898 (c. 44), s. 3, the Fishing Vessels (Safety Provisions) Act 1970 (c. 27), s. 6 and the Merchant Shipping Act 1970 (c. 36), s. 84; operative on July 1, 1979; increases specified fees.

MERCHANT SHIPPING (FEES) REGULATIONS 1979 (No. 798) [£1·25], made under the Merchant Shipping Act 1948 (c. 44), ss. 1, 3, 5, (3), the Merchant Shipping (Safety Convention) Act 1949 (c. 43), s. 33 as extended by the Merchant Shipping Act 1964 (c. 47), s. 2 (4), the Merchant Shipping (Load Lines) Act 1967 (c. 27), s. 26, the Fishing Vessels (Safety Provisions) Act 1970, s. 6, the Merchant Shipping Act 1970, s. 84 and the Merchant Shipping Act 1974 (c. 43), s. 17, Sched. 5; operative on August 1, 1979 save for Reg. 3 (2) and Pt. XI of the Schedule which are operative on September 1, 1979; revoke S.I. 1978 No. 600 and S.I. 1979 No. 631 and re-enact the fees laid down in those regulations but prescribe increased fees in special circumstances.

2465. Fishing. See FISH AND FISHERIES.

2466. Harbours and docks

HARWICH HARBOUR REVISION ORDER 1979 (No. 1656) [20p], made under the Harbours Act 1964 (c. 40), s. 14; operative on December 4, 1979; extends the seaward limit of jurisdiction of the Harwich Harbour Conservancy Board, corrects an inconsistency in art. 3 of the Harwich Harbour Revision Order 1973 relating to the number of members of the Board, and amends s. 13 of the Harwich Harbour Act 1974 to insert reference to the fact that the exercise of dredging powers under that section is subject to Crown Rights.

2467. —— work performed by registered dockworkers—position of "listed weekly workers" under scheme

[Dock Workers Employment Scheme 1967.] The National Dock Labour Board sought to establish that work done by crane drivers on the dockside and by conveyor operators employed by E. Ltd. was dock work. The work had never been done by registered dockworkers, but had been done by "listed weekly workers," that is by workers whose names had been, amongst others, on a list lodged with the Board as available, subject to approval by the Board under claim 10 (3) (*b*) of the scheme, to carry out dock work, although approval had never in fact been sought by E. Ltd. in respect of the particular jobs of crane operating and conveyor driving. It was argued for the Board that because the work had been done by listed weekly workers and E. Ltd. had in fact paid a levy, (a) there had been a blanket approval under claim 10 (3) (*b*) of the scheme that the work should be done by "listed weekly workers" whose names might from time to time appear on the list, such that accordingly they were "10 (3) (*b*) workers"; (b) the work was consequently work "ordinarily performed by dockworkers of the classes or descriptions to which the scheme applied" (Lord Cross in the leading case of *National Dock Labour Board* v. *B.S.C.* [1973] C.L.Y. 3131 (H.L.) not having expressly considered the position of "listed weekly workers"). *Held*, upholding the submissions of E. Ltd., that (1) even if they were 10 (3) (*b*) workers they were not "dockworkers of the classes or descriptions to which the scheme applies," such that work is only dock work if performed by registered dockworkers; (2) in any event no blanket approval had been given; and *semble* (3) even if given would not have been approved within the meaning of cl. 10 (3) (*b*) (*National Dock Labour Board* v. *B.S.C.* [1973] C.L.Y. 3131 applied): E.C.C. PORTS *v.* NATIONAL DOCK LABOUR BOARD, January 26, 1979, Industrial Tribunal Exeter. (*Ex rel. Michael Burston, Esq., Barrister.*)

2468. Hovercraft

HOVERCRAFT (CIVIL LIABILITY) ORDER 1979 (No. 305) [60p], made under the Hovercraft Act 1968 (c. 59), s. 1 (1) (*h*) and (*i*), as amended by the

Carriage of Goods by Sea Act 1971 (c. 19), s. 6 (3), and s. 1 (3) (*f*) and (*g*) of the 1968 Act; operative on April 1, 1979; revokes and re-enacts S.I. 1971 No. 720, and takes account of the 1971 Act, and the Merchant Shipping (Liability of Shipowners and Others) Act 1958 as modified in respect of hovercraft.

2469. Load lines

MERCHANT SHIPPING (LOAD LINES) (AMENDMENT) RULES 1979 (No. 1267) [80p], made under the Merchant Shipping (Load Lines) Act 1967 (c. 27), s. 2; operative on January 1, 1980; further amend S.I. 1968 No. 1053 by deleting references to the Surveyor's report which formerly formed part of the record of particulars relating to conditions of assignment of freeboards issued to ships complying with the load line agreements. The form of the record has been revised in accordance with the recommendation of the Intergovernmental Maritime Consultative Organisation.

2470. Marine insurance—exclusion clause—war risks—sunken dredger

In August 1974 P's dredger the N was was engaged in dredging around the island of Mauritius under a contract with the Government of that island when she sucked up a number of 20mm. Oerlikon shells. There was an explosion which removed a sizeable portion of the casing of the discharge pump. The discharge pump pumped the N full of water and she sank. P collected the insurance money in respect of the N, and D, H.M. Inspector of Taxes, claimed a balancing charge pursuant to the Capital Allowances Act 1968. P resisted liability on the ground that the loss of the N was due to a war risk, and so exempt from the charge by virtue of s. 33 (7) of the 1968 Act. " War risk " was defined as meaning " the risks of war which would be excluded from an ordinary English policy of marine insurance by the following or similar but not more extensive clause: Warranted free from the consequences of hostilities of war-like operations but this warranty shall not exclude collision, contact with any fixed or floating object unless caused directly by a hostile act by or against a belligerent power." *Held*, dismissing P's appeal against the decision of the Special Commissioners, that (1) it was reasonable to deduce that the shells were dumped by the British Forces after the end of the war; (2) the word " consequences " referred only to the effect of the hostilities or war-like operations and did not enlarge the excepted perils; it did not deal with the consequences of the hostilities; (3) the ammunition was dumped as being of no more practical use, and although it was the consequence of a war-like operation, it itself was the very reverse of a war-like operation; (4) the categories of " fixed and floating " were exhaustive of the various things with which a ship might come into contact at sea; and there was no reason to limit the width of the word " contact," and here a contact did in fact take place. (*The Priam* (1948) C.L.C. 9641 applied): COSTAIN-BLANKEVOORT (U.K.) DREDGING CO. *v.* DAVENPORT; THE NASSAU BAY [1979] 1 Lloyd's Rep. 395, Walton J.

2471. —— scuttling—total loss of vessel—claim for loss by perils of sea—claim for loss by barratry

P insured their vessel, the M, with D under a standard marine policy which included, *inter alia*, loss by barratry. Whilst the M was on a voyage in January 1973, her engines broke down in heavy weather. Shortly afterwards, it was noticed that the M was sinking. The crew abandoned ship and were taken on board a tug which was standing by, without loss of life. The M sank, becoming a total loss, and P claimed for loss by barratry, it being common ground that the M had been scuttled by K, an engineer, who had been taken on in December 1972, by flooding the engine room. D contended that K had scuttled the M with the knowledge and consent of P, and that P's initial claim for loss by perils of the sea was fraudulent or reckless in that P then knew or strongly suspected that the M had been scuttled by K. P denied all knowledge. *Held*, dismissing D's appeal, that (1) it was for P to prove the absence of complicity upon " a clear balance of probabilities," and there were no grounds for disturbing the trial judge's conclusion that P had successfully and satisfactorily discharged that burden; (2) there was nothing to suggest that until October 1973 the perils of the sea claim had not been honestly believed in, and D had failed to discharge the burden on them of showing that a fraudulent claim had been made or maintained by P: PIERMAY SHIPPING CO. S.A. AND BRANDT'S v. CHESTER; THE MICHAEL [1979] 2 Lloyd's Rep. 1, C.A.

2472. —— subrogation—whether insurers of cargo could bring action against ship-owners—whether cargo-owners entitled to damages

O chartered their vessel to C for the carriage of C's cargo from the U.K. to India. In accordance with cl. 41 of the charter, by which O were to provide over-age insurance in respect of vessels of 15 years of age or more, O took out a policy of insurance in the Lloyd's S.G. form covering the charterer/ receiver against, *inter alia*, total loss of the cargo. A bill of lading was issued incorporating the terms of the charter and also the Hague Rules. The vessel became a total loss, the receivers were paid under the policy of insurance, and the preliminary issue arose whether the insurers could bring an action under the bill of lading against O in the name of C, alleging that the vessel was unseaworthy at the commencement of the voyage. *Held*, that (1) it was settled law that the proceeds of insurance were to be disregarded when assessing damages: there was no distinction between C paying the premium or its being paid on C's behalf, and here O had paid the premium in the first instance as part of the overall bargain (*Bradburn* v. *Great Western Railway Co.* (1874) L.R. 10 Ex. 1, *Parry* v. *Cleaver* [1969] C.L.Y. 906 applied); (2) it made no difference that the benefit under the policy came from the same source as the loss to C in that they both arose out of or were provided for in the same contract, since the insurance proceeds, which were payable on an event, were different in kind from the loss suffered by C, which required proof of a breach by O (*Parry* v. *Cleaver* [1969] C.L.Y. 906 applied); (3) O were named in the policy as agents for C only, and not also to insure their own interest in the cargo as bailees; this was not inconsistent with O being liable as between themselves and C for the premium, which was the consideration for the right to perform the charter with a 15-year-old vessel; (4) there was no injustice in allowing the insurers' right of subrogation, since cl. 41 specifically preserved O's obligation to furnish the vessel in accordance with the charter, and it made no difference to the insurers whether the premiums were paid by C or by O. Preliminary issue decided in favour of C: THE YASIN [1979] 2 Lloyd's Rep. 45, Lloyd J.

2473. —— third party rights—exercise of discretion of P and I club

In June 1969, I entered their vessel V in class 5 of D, a P. and I. club, whose rules provided, *inter alia*, by r. 7 (*h*) that forwarding charges would only be paid at the sole discretion of the Committee; by r. 8 (*h*) that the Committee had discretion to decide whether and by how much a deduction should be made where a member had not taken such steps to protect his interests as he would have done if the vessel had not been entered in that class; and by r. 13, that if notice of a claim was given to the Club more than 12 months after receipt of it by a member or if a claim or liability was contested, compromised or settled without the authority of the Club, the Committee would have power to reject or reduce the sum payable by the Club. In September 1969, P chartered the V for the carriage of goods from the U.S.A. to Venezuela. During the voyage the V became immobilised and was towed into Curaçao. In January 1970 I advised P that the voyage was frustrated, and in July P transhipped the goods for carriage to Venezuela. By March 1975, P had obtained a default judgment against I in the U.S.A., and in order to proceed directly against D under the Third Party (Rights against Insurers) Act 1930, petitioned the English Companies Court for a winding-up order. I held an affidavit opposing the petition, and on July 11 asked D's advice, and whether they would enter on appearance, which D declined to do. On July 21, I were wound up by the Companies Court. In October 1975, P issued a writ claiming a total $280,635.77 against D. *Held*, that (1) on the facts, notice under r. 13 was not given to D until July 11, 1975, whereas the claim against I was made on November 12, 1970, and D had power to reject I's claim, and accordingly P's claim (*Farrell* v. *Federated Employers' Insurance Association* [1970] C.L.Y. 1378 applied); (2) under the circumstances, D had acted fairly and in good faith in reaching their decision; whether by rejecting the claim of P standing in the shoes of I under r. 13, or by making a reduction of 100 per cent. under r. 8 (*h*); (3) the inaction of I and those standing in their shoes, *i.e.* P, denied them any right there might otherwise have been against forfeiture; (4) part of P's claim related to forwarding charges and fell to be recovered if D favourably excercised their discretion under r. 7 (*h*); but in the absence of such discretion, there was no enforceable right to such recovery; (5) although under s. 1 of the 1930 Act I's rights against D under the contract in respect of the liabilities were transferred to and vested in P, since I were not insured in respect of forwarding expenses, no rights relating thereto were transferred to P under the Act; and in any event, there was no improper, unjustified or misguided refusal by D to exercise the discretion under r. 7 (*h*). Judgment for D: C.V.G. SIDERURGICIA DÉL ORINOCO S.A. *v.* LONDON STEAMSHIP OWNERS' MUTUAL INSURANCE ASSOCIATION; THE VAINQUEUR JOSÉ [1979] 1 Lloyd's Rep. 557, Mocatta J.

2474. Master and servant—injury to seaman—negligence—damages

P, the boatswain aboard D's vessel, the Y, was in charge of cleaning the no. 2 hold, in the forward port corner of which was a stringer forming a small platform, which was divided by an upright diaphragm plate. Positioned against the stringer, which was 13 ft. above the bottom of the hold, was a 22 ft. ladder, which was secured by one line over the forward hatch coaming, and another over the port hatch coaming. It had long been the practice that as one man mounted the ladder to clean the top surface of the stringer, another would foot the ladder for him. M, who had been drinking, climbed the ladder while P footed it, and P, when he looked up, saw M with his arm through the lightening hole in the diaphragm, shouting. There was nobody else in the hold to foot the ladder, but P went up to give M such assistance as he could to prevent him from falling. The ladder slewed when P was at the top, and P fell, suffering, *inter alia*, a fracture dislocation of the right elbow and of the right wrist. On P's claim for damages for personal injuries, *held*, that (1) P had reasonably concluded that M was in very real peril of falling if P hesitated or waited for somebody else to foot the ladder while he went up; (2) a reasonable employer would have provided a ladder of 18 ft., not 22 ft., a different method of lashing the ladder, a system whereby the ladder was always footed when somebody went up, and safety harnesses; and P could not be reproached for following a system which was approved of, or at least not objected to, by the ship's officers; (3) P was not at fault in taking a risk which was far outweighed by the danger to M; (4) the accident was wholly due to D's failure to act as reasonably careful employers, and P was not guilty of any failure to exercise reasonable care for his own safety; (5) damages for pain and suffering and loss of amenity would be £7,500; agreed special damages would be £5,952; and damages for future loss of earnings, applying a multiplier of seven (P being aged 45 at the date of judgment) would be £29,561. Judgment for P for £43,013: O'KEEFE *v.* JOHN STEWART & CO. SHIPPING; THE YEWKYLE [1939] 1 Lloyd's Rep. 182, Kenneth-Jones J.

2475. Merchant shipping

MERCHANT SHIPPING (REPATRIATION) REGULATIONS 1979 (No. 97) [30p], made under the Merchant Shipping Act 1970 (c. 36), ss. 9 (*d*), 62, 68 (2) (5), 99 (2); operative on March 1, 1979; revoke and re-enact with modifications S.I. 1972 No. 1805. The changes relate to the return and relief of seamen left behind or shipwrecked and to the wages and accounts of such seamen.

MERCHANT SHIPPING (CONFIRMATION OF LEGISLATION) (SOUTH AUSTRALIA) ORDER 1979 (No. 110) [10p], made under the Merchant Shipping Act 1894 (c. 60), s. 735; operative on March 7, 1979; confirms an Act passed by the Legislature of South Australia to amend certain provisions of the South Australia Boating Act 1974–1975.

MERCHANT SHIPPING (FOREIGN DESERTERS) (DISAPPLICATION) ORDER 1979 (No. 120) [10p], made under the Merchant Shipping Act 1970, s. 89 (5); operative on March 7, 1979; provides that s. 89 of the 1970 Act, which prescribes the procedure for dealing in the U.K. with deserters from ships of certain foreign countries, shall cease to apply to Estonia, Japan, Latvia and Roumania.

MERCHANT SHIPPING (FOREIGN DESERTERS) (REVOCATION) ORDER 1979 (No. 293) [10p], made under the Merchant Shipping Act 1894, ss. 238, 738; operative on April 12, 1979; revokes specified orders to the extent to which they had provided for the apprehension and return to their ship of deserters from Romanian, Japanese, Estonian and Latvian merchant ships in the Channel Islands, the Isle of Man or any Colony.

MERCHANT SHIPPING (SHIPS' NAMES) REGULATIONS 1979 (No. 341) [20p], made under the Merchant Shipping Act 1906 (c. 48), s. 50; operative on April 18, 1979; revoke S.R. & O. 1907 No. 740, S.R. & O. 1922 No. 729 and S.R. & O. 1936 No. 390, and re-enact those provisions with the exception of the regulations prescribing conditions for the registry of a ship by a name which is already the name of a British ship, and a regulation referring to ships appearing in the Mercantile Navy List and which has been deleted following the withdrawal of that List. The notice of proposed names of ships to be registered at various ports is provided for.

MERCHANT SHIPPING (CERTIFICATION OF MARINE ENGINEER OFFICERS) (AMENDMENT) REGULATIONS 1979 (No. 599) [20p], made under the Merchant Shipping Act 1970, ss. 43, 99 (2); operative on September 1, 1981; amend S.I. 1977 No. 2072 so as to change the requirements for specified certificates for engineering officers to be regarded as equivalent to certificates of competence and to change the standards and conditions applicable with respect to the issue of certificates of service.

MANCHESTER PILOTAGE (AMENDMENT) ORDER 1979 (No. 712) [10p], made under the Pilotage Act 1913 (c. 31), s. 7; operative on September 1, 1979; extends the limits of the Manchester Pilotage District.

MERCHANT SHIPPING (STERLING EQUIVALENTS) (VARIOUS ENACTMENTS) ORDER 1979 (No. 790) [20p], made under the Merchant Shipping (Liability of Shipowners and others) Act 1958 (c. 62), s. 1 (3), the Carriage of Goods by Sea Act 1971 (c. 19), s. 1 (5), the Merchant Shipping (Oil Pollution) Act 1971 (c. 59), s. 4 (4) as amended by the Merchant Shipping Act 1974 (c. 43), s. 9, by the latter Act, s. 1 (7), and the Unfair Contract Terms Act 1977 (c. 50), s. 28 (4); operative on August 1, 1979; specifies the sterling amounts which are to be taken as equivalent to the amounts expressed in gold francs in the above enactments.

MERCHANT SHIPPING (DANGEROUS GOODS) (AMENDMENT) RULES 1979 (No. 976) [10p], made under the Merchant Shipping (Safety Convention) Act 1949 (c. 43), s. 23; operative on September 1, 1979; amend the 1978 (No. 1543) Rules by substituting the definitions of " The Blue Book " and " The IMDG Code."

MERCHANT SHIPPING (CONFIRMATION OF LEGISLATION) (BERMUDA) ORDER 1979 (No. 1448) [10p], made under the Merchant Shipping Act 1894 s. 735; operative on December 17, 1979; confirms an Act of the Legislature of Bermuda which repeals certain provisions of specified enactments so far as they relate to ships registered in Bermuda.

MERCHANT SHIPPING (COLONIES) (AMENDMENT) ORDER 1979 (No. 1449) [10p], made under the Merchant Shipping (International Labour Conventions) Act 1925 (c. 42), s. 6; operative on December 17, 1979; amends S.R. & O. 1927 No. 715 by deleting Bermuda from the Schedule to the Order.

MERCHANT SHIPPING (INCREASED PENALTIES) REGULATIONS 1979 (No. 1519) [40p], made under the Merchant Shipping Act 1965 (c. 47), s. 1 (2) (*d*), the Merchant Shipping Act 1970, ss. 2 (2), 3 (4), 62 (6), 65 (3), 68 (5), 69 (5), 70 (2), 71 (2), 99 (2), the Merchant Shipping Act 1974, Sched. 5, para. 3 (2) and the Merchant Shipping Act 1979 (c. 39), s. 43 (3), Sched. 6, Pt. VI, paras. 4, 6, 8, 20; operative on January 1, 1980; increase the maximum penalties which may be imposed on summary conviction for breach of specified Regulations.

MERCHANT SHIPPING (RETURNS OF BIRTHS AND DEATHS) REGULATIONS 1979 (No. 1577) [40p], made under the Merchant Shipping Act 1970, ss. 72, 92, and the Merchant Shipping Act 1979, ss. 30 (2) and 43 (3), Sched. 6, Pt. VI, para. 4; operative on January 1, 1980; provide that where a master is unable to perform the duty imposed on him by reg. 3 because he has himself died or missing or incapacitated, and the death in question has been established as mentioned in reg. 7, the Registrar-General of Shipping and Seamen is required to record the information specified in Sched. 2 about the death.

MERCHANT SHIPPING (METRICATION) (HONG KONG) ORDER 1979 (No. 1706) [10p], made under the Merchant Shipping Act 1970, s. 94; operative on January 24, 1980; extends the provisions relating to the metrication of the marking on ships' sides to Hong Kong.

MERCHANT SHIPPING (SAFETY CONVENTION) (HONG KONG) (AMENDMENT) ORDER 1979 (No. 1707) [20p], made under the Merchant Shipping (Safety and Load Line Conventions) Act 1932 (c. 9), s. 36 (as amended by the Merchant Shipping (Safety Conventions) Act 1949, s. 30, the Merchant Shipping Act 1964 (c. 47), s. 1 and the Merchant Shipping (Safety Convention) Act 1977 (c. 24), s. 1); operative on May 25, 1980; amends previous orders relating to Hong Kong Safety Conventions.

2476. Merchant Shipping Act 1970—commencement

MERCHANT SHIPPING ACT 1970 (COMMENCEMENT No. 6) ORDER 1979 (No. 809 (C. 21)) [10p], made under the Merchant Shipping Act 1970 (c. 36), s. 101 (4); operative on August 1, 1979; brings into force ss. 15, 19, 95 (2) and 100 (3) (part) of, and Sched. 5 (part) to the 1970 Act.

2477. Merchant Shipping Act 1974—commencement

MERCHANT SHIPPING ACT 1974 (COMMENCEMENT No. 4) ORDER 1979 (No. 808 (C. 20)) [10p], made under the Merchant Shipping Act 1974 (c. 43), s. 24 (2); operative on August 1, 1979; brings into force ss. 14 and 15 of, and Sched. 4 to the 1974 Act.

2478. Merchant Shipping Act 1979 (c. 39)

This Act amends the law relating to pilotage, carriage by sea, liability of shipowners and salvors, pollution from ships, and seamen.

S. 1 outlines the constitution of the Pilotage Commission; s. 2 concerns payment by pilotage authorities to the Commission; s. 3 makes other financial provisions relating to the Commission; s. 4 sets out the functions of the Commission; s. 5 deals with the annual report of the Commission; s. 6 provides for a review of pilotage services and non-compulsory pilotage areas; s. 7 sets out the procedure connected with the making and coming into force of pilotage orders; s. 8 amends s. 11 of the Pilotage Act 1913 relating to compulsory pilotage; s. 9 deals with pilotage charges; s. 10 concerns refusal and cancellation of pilotage certificates; s. 11 allows for employment of pilots by pilotage authorities; s. 12 relates to pilots' pension and compensation schemes; s. 13 makes miscellaneous amendments to the Pilotage Act 1913; s. 14 states that the Convention relating to the Carriage of Passengers and their Luggage by Sea as set out in Pt. I of Sched. 3 to this Act is to have the force of law; s. 15 contains provisions supplementary to s. 14; s. 16 deals with the application of Sched. 3 to international carriage before the coming into force of s. 14 (1) and (2) and to domestic carriage; s. 17 concerns limitations on liability; s. 18 deals with the exclusion of liability; s. 19 contains provisions supplementary to ss. 17 and 18; s. 20 provides for the prevention of pollution from ships; s. 21 concerns safety and health on ships; s. 22 makes provisions supplementary to s. 21; s. 23 relates to breaches by seamen of codes of conduct and local industrial agreements; s. 24 makes regulations determining the amount of deductions from seamen's wages; s. 25 specifies the offence of unauthorised liquor on fishing vessels; s. 26 extends the power to appoint Department of Trade inspectors; s. 27 outlines the powers of Department of Trade inspectors; s. 28 contains provisions supplementary to s. 27; s. 29 amends s. 61 of the Merchant Shipping Act 1970 with respect to inquiries as to whether a person has died on a U.K. ship; s. 30 amends s. 72 of the Merchant Shipping Act 1970 relating to the record of certain deaths on ships; s. 31 amends s. 85 of the Merchant Shipping Act 1894 dealing with dues for space occupied by deck cargo; s. 32 amends s. 464 of the Merchant Shipping Act 1894 relating to shipping casualties; s. 33 concerns Commissioncrs of Northern Lighthouses and Irish Lights; s. 34 provides for repeal of spent provisions and amendment of Pt. XI of the Merchant Shipping Act 1894; s. 35 amends s. 503 of the 1894 Act; s. 36 makes certain amendments to the Merchant Shipping (Mercantile Marine Fund) Act 1898; s. 37 amends ss. 15, 43, 52, 54, 76 (1), 92 and 101 (4) of the Merchant Shipping Act 1970 and s. 23 of the Prevention of Oil Pollution Act 1971; s. 38 deals with the replacement of gold francs by special drawing rights for certain purposes of the Merchant Shipping (Oil Pollution) Act 1971 and the Merchant Shipping Act 1974; s. 39 relates to attachment of earnings; s. 40 amends s. 14 of the Merchant Shipping Act 1974 dealing with foreign action affecting shipping; s. 41 applies the Merchant Shipping Acts to certain structures, etc.; s. 42 makes an alteration to the time for certain summary prosecutions; s. 43 makes provisions for alteration of penalties; s. 44 concerns an offence in respect of a dangerously unsafe ship; s. 45 amends certain offences provisions of the Merchant Shipping Act 1970; s. 46 specifies offences by officers of bodies corporate; s. 47 grants power to extend the Act to certain countries; s. 48 applies the Act to hovercraft; s. 49 deals with orders and regulations under the Act; s. 50 contains interpretation and repeal provisions; s. 51 provides for the payment of expenses; s. 52 deals with citation and commencement.

The Act received the Royal Assent on April 4, 1979, and comes into force on a day to be appointed.

2479. —— commencement

MERCHANT SHIPPING ACT 1979 (COMMENCEMENT NO. 1) ORDER 1979 (NO. 807 (C. 19)) [40p.], made under the Merchant Shipping Act 1979 (c. 39), s. 52 (2); operative on August 1, 1979; brings into force on August 1, 1979, ss. 1–6, 12, 13 (1) (part), 16, 20–22, 26, 32 (1), 33, 34, 35 (1), 36 (1) (3), 37 (1)–(3) (5) (7) (8), 39–41, 47 (1) (2) (part) (3), 48, 49, 50 (1) (2) (4) (part), 51 (1) (3) and 52 of, and Scheds. 1, 2 (part) and 7 (part) to the 1979 Act; brings into force on October 1, 1979, ss. 27, 28, 46 (part), 47 (2) (part), and 50 (4) (part) of, and Sched. 7 (part) to the 1979 Act; brings into force on January 1, 1980, ss. 13 (1) (part) (2)–(4), 29, 30, 42–45, 47 (2) (part), 50 (4) (part) of, and Scheds. 2 (part), 6 and 7 (part) to the 1979 Act.

MERCHANT SHIPPING ACT 1979 (COMMENCEMENT NO. 2) ORDER 1979 (NO. 1578 (C. 37)) [10p], made under the Merchant Shipping Act 1979, s. 52 (2); operative on December 17, 1979; brings into force ss. 15 (1) (2), 19 (2) (3), 38 (5) and 47 (1) (2).

2480. Northern Ireland. See NORTHERN IRELAND.

2481. Offshore installations. See SEA AND SEASHORE.

2482. Oil pollution

PREVENTION OF OIL POLLUTION (CONVENTION COUNTRIES) (ADDITIONAL COUNTRIES) ORDER 1979 (NO. 721) [10p], made under the Prevention of Oil Pollution Act 1971 (c. 60), s. 21 (3); operative on July 25, 1979; specifies additional countries that have accepted the International Convention for the Prevention of Pollution of the Sea by Oil 1954.

MERCHANT SHIPPING (OIL POLLUTION) (PARTIES TO CONVENTIONS) (AMENDMENT) ORDER 1979 (NO. 1450) [40p], made under the Merchant Shipping (Oil Pollution) Act 1971 (c. 59), ss. 8A (3), 19 (2) as amended by the Merchant Shipping Act 1974 (c. 43), s. 9; operative on December 17, 1979; amends the list of countries that are parties to the International Convention on Civil Liability for Oil Pollution Damage signed in Brussels on November 29, 1969, which is contained in S.I. 1975 No. 1036.

PREVENTION OF OIL POLLUTION ACT 1971 (HONG KONG) ORDER 1979 (NO. 1452) [40p], made under the Prevention of Oil Pollution Act 1971, s. 25 (1); operative on December 17, 1979; extends to Hong Hong those provisions of the 1971 Act that enable measures to be taken to prevent, mitigate or eliminate grave and imminent danger to the coastline or related interests from oil pollution, following a maritime casualty.

PREVENTION OF OIL POLLUTION ACT 1971 (HONG KONG) (NO. 2) ORDER 1979 (NO. 1453) [10p], made under the Prevention of Oil Pollution Act 1971

s. 16 (1) as extended by S.I. 1979 No. 1452; operative on December 17, 1979; applies ss. 12–15 of the 1971 Act as extended to Hong Hong to ships not registered in Hong Hong and which are outside the territorial waters of Hong Kong.

OIL POLLUTION (COMPULSORY INSURANCE) (AMENDMENT) REGULATIONS 1979 (No. 1593) [10p], made under the Merchant Shipping (Oil Pollution) Act 1971, s. 11 (3) (*a*); operative on January 2, 1980; amend S.I. 1977 No. 85 by increasing the fee to be paid on application for a certificate of compulsory insurance from £12 to £19.

2483. —— report

The Department of Trade has published a report of an inter-departmental group on " Liability and Compensation for Marine Oil Pollution Damage." The report examines the question of liability for pollution damage and recommends an increase of the compensation ceiling for such damage. The report is available from the Marine Library, Sunley House, 90/93 High Holborn, London W.C.1.

2484. —— White Paper

The Government has published a White Paper entitled " Eleni V: The Government's Reply to the Fourth Report from the Select Committee on Science and Technology." The White Paper deals with the Eleni V incident and on the contingency arrangements for dealing with oil spills from ships at sea. It is available from HMSO, Cmnd. 7429 [40p].

2485. Pilotage

FOWEY PILOTAGE (AMENDMENT) ORDER 1979 (No. 1340) [10p], made under the Pilotage Act 1913 (c. 31), s. 7; operative on December 17, 1979; amends the Fowey Pilotage Order 1921 and provides for the reconstitution of the Pilotage Committee of the Fowey Pilotage District set up under the 1921 Order.

2486. Protection of wrecks

PROTECTION OF WRECKS (DESIGNATION No. 1) ORDER 1979 (No. 31) [10p], made under the Protection of Wrecks Act 1973 (c. 33), s. 1 (1) (2) (4); operative on February 9, 1979; designates as a restricted area an area in Cardigan Bay which is thought to be the site of the wreck of a vessel of historical and archaeological importance.

PROTECTION OF WRECKS (DESIGNATION No. 1 AND No. 4 ORDERS 1978) (AMENDMENT) ORDER 1979 (No. 56) [10p], made under the Protection of Wrecks Act 1973, ss. 1 (1) (2) (4), 3 (2); operative on February 16, 1979; amends S.I. 1978 Nos. 199 and 764 by respectively redefining the centre of the site and increasing the restricted area around the site.

2487. —— report

The Department of Trade has recently published a report on action taken under the Protection of Wrecks Act 1973. The report " Historic Wrecks: the role of the Department of Trade " is the first account to be produced of action taken in this field since the Act came into force. Copies are available from Marine Library, Sunley House, 90–93 High Holborn, London W.C.1.

2488. Sale of ship—Mareva injunction. See NEGOCIOS DEL MAR S.A. *v.* DORIC SHIPPING CORP. S.A.; THE ASSIOS, § 2144.

2489. Salvage—action in personam—proper amount to be awarded—interest on award

[Scot.] At about 18.00 hours on February 21, 1975, D's trawler, the B, was immobilised whilst fishing off the Faroe Islands when her engines were stopped because of rising water in the engine room due to a bilge pump failure. The S, a smaller trawler belonging to P, was asked to stand by, and at 18.45 was asked to tow the B into Klaksvik. The tow continued uneventfully up to a position north of the port, when at about 23.15 the S came alongside the port side of the B and the two trawlers were lashed together. Just past the harbour entrance, a combination of the south-east wind on the superstructure of the larger B and the strong northerly tide caused the lashings to part, and the B was driven aground on the shallows of the west side of the harbour. She was later pulled off by the S, which received some damage to her propeller when she hit the bottom. The B was tied alongside the star-board side of the S, which eventually put the B alongside the main pier at about 03.30 on February 22, the B using her engine at the very last moment to get her berthed. On P's action *in personam* to determine the proper amount of the salvage to be awarded, *held*, that (1) on the evidence, while the tow was being connected between 20.00 and 20.30, the wind was south-south-west force 6 to 7; and although the B was drifting broadside to the wind in a northerly direction with her engines stopped, she was not in a position of immediate danger; (2) the B's engines were only used for about two minutes at the time of berthing during the whole period of the tow; (3) during the whole period between 23.15 and 03.30 the crew of the S exercised reasonable care and considerable skill in towing the much larger B against a strong tide and wind within the harbour entrance; (4) on the evidence, the B's engine damage occurred before she berthed; and her salved value was £80,000 less £24,619·02, *i.e.* £55,380·98; (5) the award for salvage to the S would be £5,400 including loss of fishing, to be apportioned two thirds, *i.e.* £3,600 to the owners, and one third, *i.e.* £1,800 to the crew, which would in turn be apportioned £650 to the skipper, £250 to the mate, and and £100 each to the remaining nine members of the crew; (6) interest on the £5,400 would be at the rate of 11 per cent. from the date of termination of the services (*The Aldora* [1975] C.L.Y. 3236 applied); (7) interest of the award of £3,463·63 for actual damage and loss of gear would be at the rate of 11 per cent. from the date when the accounts were actually paid; but, in the absence of agreement as to that date, would run from the date of the interlocutor: BRUCE'S STORES (ABERDEEN) *v.* RICHARD IRVIN AND SONS; THE BEN GAIRN [1979] 1 Lloyd's Rep. 410, Ct. of Session.

2490. —— **arbitration award—rights of superseded salvors**
On February 6, 1977, P's vessel, the U, grounded 13 miles south-west of Singapore. After unsuccessfully attempting to refloat her, at 14.12 on February 8 the master cabled to the ship's managers, T, for assistance who at 15.03 replied that a suitable tug would be dispatched from Singapore. At 16.40, the captain of D's tug, the S, offered to salve the U, and the master, mistakenly believing the S to be the tug sent by T, signed Lloyd's Standard Form of Salvage Agreement No Cure No Pay. At 18.05 the master received a cable from T that the tug A would reach him by noon on February 9, whereupon he told the captain that he was to do no more with regard to the salvage of the U. On February 9 the A arrived and successfully refloated the U on February 10, whereupon the S left the scene and returned to her previous activities. D claimed damages for breach of contract and for salvage remuneration under Lloyd's Form. On a special case stated, *held*, that (1) salvors who were engaged without any express salvage agreement and who were later dismissed and superseded by other salvors were entitled to remuneration in the nature of salvage both for services actually rendered and by way of compensation for loss of opportunity to complete the services, but not to full compensation assessed on the basis of *restitutio in integrum*; and the right to compensation for supersession was not dependent on any benefit having been conferred; (2) the owners of property to be salved were under no obligation to allow such salvors to complete their services, but were entitled to dismiss and supersede them; (3) the rights and obligations of parties to Lloyd's Form were governed by the terms of that contract, and the general maritime law of salvage only applied in so far as it was expressly or impliedly incorporated into such contract; (4) an implied term of such contract was that so long as salvors were willing and able to perform the services undertaken, the owners of the property to be salved would not act so as to prevent them doing so; and this included an obligation not to dismiss or supersede; (5) since the S was ready and able to perform the services, the act of the master of the U in superseding her with the A was a breach of the contract between P and D which amounted to a repudiation of the contract by P and accepted by D; (6) accordingly, D were not entitled to remuneration for services actually rendered, but to damages for breach of contract to be assessed on the usual principles of *restitutio in integrum*; (7) the fact that P had to pay the owners

of the A and the amount of such payment were both irrelevant to the assessment of D's damages; but the fact that the S stood by until February 10, the dangers to which the U would have been exposed, the act that the A was on hand and her comparative status were factors whose relevance would depend upon the findings of fact of the arbitrator. (*The Maude* (1876) 3 Asp.Mar. Law Cas. 338; *The Maasdam* (1893) 7 Asp.Mar. Law Cas. 400; *The Loch Tulla* (1950) C.L.C. 9699; *The Hassel* [1959] C.L.Y. 3109 considered): THE UNIQUE MARINER (No. 2) [1979] 1 Lloyd's Rep. 37, Brandon J.

2491. —— bailment—salvage services to cargo—whether salvors entitled to remuneration

A Lloyd's salvage agreement gives salvors an implied authority to look after cargo and to charge reasonable expenses to the cargo owners.

The vessel chartered by D to carry wheat from the United States to India ran aground off Manila. On behalf of D the ship's master engaged P under Lloyd's standard form of salvage agreement. The salvage services resulted in saving a substantial amount of cargo, stored partly in another chartered vessel and partly in a bonded warehouse. The shipowners abandoned the voyage. P claimed D were liable for the whole cost of salvage since the cargo had undoubtedly benefited from the salvaging services rendered. D maintained that it was the shipowners and not D who were liable for the period prior to the abandonment of the voyage. *Held*, a direct contractual relationship arose between P and D when the master signed the Lloyd's agreement on D's behalf, and thereafter P were bailees of the cargo and D bailors. The evidence showed that the services performed by P were on D's behalf and that there was no express or implied agreement between P and the shipowners. P had implied authority, by virtue of the Lloyd's agreement, to look after the cargo and to charge D reasonable expenses for doing so. In any event P would be entitled in quasi-contract because it would be unjust for D to retain the benefit of the services without paying compensation. (*Gaudet* v. *Brown*; *Cargo ex Argos* (1873) L.R. 5 P.C. 134; *Great Northern Railway Co.* v. *Swaffield* [1874–80] All E.R.Rep. 1065 and *Société Franco-Tunisienne d'Armement* v. *Sidermar S.p.A.* [1960] C.L.Y. 536 applied.)

CHINA-PACIFIC S.A. v. FOOD CORP. OF INDIA; THE WINSON [1979] 2 All E.R. 35, Lloyd J.

2492. —— practice—costs

In October 1976 the S, a 30ft yacht, was in difficulties in a position off Chichester Harbour. She was abandoned by her owner and she continued sailing eastwards along a lee shore in high winds and in a considerable sea. P, a foreman bricklayer, swam to the casualty from the beach and succeeded in making her fast between two groynes. Thereafter P enlisted the aid of F, a local marine surveyor and others, and hired a crane and other equipment with which the casualty was winched up the cliff and eventually transported to a place of safety. P began proceedings *in rem* in the High Court to which the owner of S entered an appearance. Subsequently the *res* was sold by the Admiralty Marshal *pendente lite* for £1,320 and the proceedings were transferred to the Mayor's and City of London Court. At the hearing, which was undefended, it was found that the salved value of the *res* was £8,000, that the *res* was in considerable danger of grounding and total loss and that P had incurred "out-of-pocket" expenses of £1,197. *Held*, that P should be awarded £4,000 together with interest to run at 10 per cent. per annum from a date six months after the termination of the services. Judgment was given *in rem* and *in personam*. The defendant was ordered to pay High Court costs until the date of the transfer to the county court and thereafter on new scale 4 together with a direction (under Ord. 47, r. 21 (2) of the County Court Rules) to the registrar on taxation that he should not be bound by the amounts appearing in the scale in respect of items specified in Ord. 47, r. 21 (3) of the County Court Rules and to allow such larger sums as the registrar should think reasonable (*The Dupleix* [1912] P. 8; *The Lyrma* (No. 2) [1978] C.L.Y. 2688; *The Rena K* [1978] C.L.Y. 91 referred to in argument): THE SNOW-GOOSE, March 18, 1979, Mayor's and City of London Court. (*Ex rel. Jervis Kay, Barrister.*)

2493. —— remuneration—assessment of reward—interest

On January 28, 1976, D's tug the R and her tow were proceeding on a southerly course in the Irish sea, when a southerly gale was encountered, with a forecast of worse weather to come, and it was decided to seek shelter in Rosslare. However, in the early morning of January 29. The R grounded on the Dogger Bank off Wexford, as a result of which her rudder was torn off, so that when she refloated she could not be steered. P's trawler, the N, which was sheltering from the gale in Rosslare, set out, and with the aid of the Rosslare lifeboat was able to make a towage connection, although in doing so she suffered some damage. The flotilla steamed to Rosslare in daylight, the N being occupied for about six hours. The owners, master and crew of the N claimed for a salvage reward, it being agreed that the salved value of the R and her tow was £200,000. That the cost of repairs to the N was £500, and that the N had lost time in which £800 worth of fish could have been caught. *Held,* that (1) on the evidence, when the services of the N began the R was in a position of grave danger, between half and three-quarters of a mile from the shore, with two anchors down, but probably dragging; (2) there was no possibility of alternative assistance; (3) in assessing the reward, the facts for consideration were the state of the weather, the degree of damage and danger to the casualty, the risk and peril of the salvors, the time employed and the value of the property, and a fair and proper reward was £21,000 (*The Industry* (1835) 3 Hag.Adm. 203 applied); (4) the court had power to award interest on a salvage reward (*The Aldora* [1975] C.L.Y. 3236 applied); but it would be absurd and unreal to think that salvors could be paid at the moment when the services were successfully terminated, since it could take weeks or months to assess the value of the property salved; and D would pay interest at the rate of 10 per cent. from July 29, 1976: THE RILLAND [1979] 1 Lloyd's Rep. 455. Sheen J.

2494. Ship-broker. See AGENCY.

2495. Shipbuilding

SHIPBUILDING (REDUNDANCY PAYMENTS SCHEME) (NORTHERN IRELAND) (AMENDMENT) ORDER 1979 (No. 881) [20p], made under the Shipbuilding (Redundancy Payments) Act 1978 (c. 11), ss. 1, 2; operative on July 24, 1979; amends the scheme established by S.I. 1978 No. 1127 for the payment of benefits to the employees of any company engaged in shipbuilding the whole of whose equity share capital is owned by the Crown who are made redundant or transferred to less well-paid employment. The principal amendments extend the scope of the scheme.

SHIPBUILDING (REDUNDANCY PAYMENTS SCHEME) (GREAT BRITAIN) (AMENDMENT) ORDER 1979 (No. 898) [20p], made under the Shipbuilding (Redundancy Payments) Act 1978, ss. 1, 2; operative on July 24, 1979; amends the Scheme established by S.I. 1978 No. 1191 for the payment of benefits to employees of British Shipbuilders who are made redundant.

BRITISH SHIPBUILDERS BORROWING POWERS (INCREASE OF LIMIT) ORDER 1979 (No. 961) [10p], made under the Aircraft and Shipbuilding Industries Act 1977 (c. 3), s. 11 (7) (10); operative on July 28, increases the borrowing limit of British Shipbuilders to £300 million.

2496. —— guarantee—default in payment—R.S.C., Ord. 14

In October 1975, P entered into four contracts for the construction of four ships, these contracts replacing two earlier contracts for which a payment of U.S.$1¼ million had been made on account, such payment to be applied to the first of five instalments which were to be paid under each of the four contracts. The contracts were guaranteed by D, the letters of guarantee providing, *inter alia,* " In consideration of your entering into the shipbuilding contract [D] hereby irrevocably and unconditionally guarantees the payment in accordance with the terms of the contract of all sums due or to become due by the buyer to you under the contract and in case the buyer is in default of any such payment [D] will forthwith make the payment in default on behalf of the buyer." The buyers defaulted in that the payment on account was insufficient to discharge the whole of the first instalments payable under each of the four

contracts, no further sums were paid, and the second instalment was not paid
in one of the four cases. In October 1976, P treated the contracts as repudiated,
brought actions against D under the letters of guarantee, and applied for
judgment under R.S.C., Ord. 14. *Held*, dismissing D's appeal, that (1) the true
meaning of the guarantee was to bind the guarantor to pay if the buyer did
not pay in time, and not to bind the guarantor to ensure performance by the
buyer of the buyer's obligations; (2) the fact of the contracts coming to an
end in October 1976 did not free the buyers from their obligations to pay the
various instalments which had accrued before then, and D's liabilities for those
instalments under the guarantees remained unaffected; (3) the object of the
guarantees was to enable P to recover from D the amount due, and D were
not entitled to the benefit of any set-off to which the buyers might be entitled,
being the difference between the amount of the instalments and the sum
representing the loss or damages suffered by P; (4) there was nothing unconscionable in making D pay over large sums of money to P in circumstances
in which there might be little hope of getting it back, *i.e.* in holding D to their
contracts; (5) D had no arguable defence, and summary judgment would be
given for P: HYUNDAI SHIPBUILDING & HEAVY INDUSTRIES CO. *v*. POURNARAS;
SAME *v*. BOUBOULINA SHIPPING S.A. [1978] 2 Lloyd's Rep. 502, C.A.

2497. ———— ———— ———— rescission—right to unpaid instalments

P agreed to construct a ship by a contract which was guaranteed by D, the
letter of guarantee providing, *inter alia*, " [D] hereby jointly and severally
irrevocably guarantee the payment in accordance with the terms of the contract of all sums due or to become due by the buyer under the contract and
in case the buyer is in default of any such payment [D] will forthwith make
the payment in default on behalf of the buyer." Cl. 11 gave P the right to
rescind, and provided that the rights thereby accorded were to be " in addition
to such other rights powers and remedies as [P] may have elsewhere in this
contract and/or at law, at equity or otherwise." The buyers defaulted in payment and P rescinded the contract and claimed under the guarantee. D contended that the rescission was based upon the contractual right to rescind given
by cl. 11, and that since the contract had been rescinded before the date of
issue of the writ there was, on that date, no accrued right to the unpaid instalments which had become due before the date of the rescission. *Held*, dismissing
D's appeal, that (1) there was no distinction between the earlier decision in
Hyundai Shipbuilding and Heavy Industries Co. v. *Pournaras* and this case;
and given that that decision was right, there was no arguable defence here;
(2) the words " in addition to " in cl. 11 could not be read as meaning " in
derogation or in subtraction of " and the fact of the contract coming to an end
did not free the buyers from their obligation to pay the various instalments
which had accrued before then, and D's liability for those instalments under
the guarantee remained unaffected; (3) the accrued right to the unpaid instalments should not be affected by whether the rescission or the writ came first,
since in either event there was an accrued right to the instalment in question
when the writ was issued; (4) D were liable forthwith to make the payments
in respect of which the buyers had defaulted. Judgment for P. (*Hyundai Shipbuilding and Heavy Industries Co.* v. *Pournaras; Same* v. *Bouboulina Shipping
S.A.* [1979] C.L.Y. 2496 applied): HYUNDAI HEAVY INDUSTRIES CO. *v*. PAPA-
DOPOULOS [1979] 1 Lloyd's Rep. 130, C.A.

2498. Shipbuilding Act 1979 (c. 59)

This Act increases the financial limits of British Shipbuilders.

S. 1 increases the limits on borrowing as imposed by s. 11 (7) of the Aircraft
and Shipbuilding Industries Act 1977; s. 2 authorises the Secretary of State to
guarantee payment for alterations, as well as constructions which were already
covered by s. 10 of the Industry Act 1972; s. 3 gives the short title and extent.

The Act received the Royal Assent on December 20, 1979, and came into
force on that day.

2499. Tonnage

MONEGASQUE TONNAGE ORDER 1979 (No. 306) [10p], made under the
Merchant Shipping Act 1894 (c. 60), s. 84 (1) and the Merchant Shipping Act

1965 (c. 47), s. 1; operative on April 12, 1979; provides that the tonnage shown in the certificates of registry or other national papers of Monegasque ships shall be recognised in the same way as the tonnage is shown in the certificate of registry of a British ship.

2500. Wrecks

PROTECTION OF WRECKS (REVOCATION) ORDER 1979 (No. 6) [10p], made under the Protection of Wrecks Act 1973 (c. 33) s. 3 (2) (*a*); operative on January 31, 1979; revokes S.I. 1974 No. 458 which related to an area in the Sound of Mull around the vessel H.M.S. Dartmouth.

BOOKS AND ARTICLES. See *post*, p. [11], [31].

SHOPS

2501. Sale of goods. See SALE OF GOODS.

2502. Sunday trading

SHOPS REGULATIONS 1979 (No. 1294) [20p], made under the Shops Act 1950 (c. 28), s. 69; operative on December 1, 1979; amend S.R. & O. 1937 No. 271 in relation to the opening of premises owned by a person of the Jewish religion on Sundays. The amendments require any person making a declaration to state that he has not been employed or engaged on the Jewish Sabbath in any trade or business and that the application shall be supported by a certificate by a panel appointed by the Board of Deputies of British Jews that the applicant conscientiously objects to carrying on trade or business on the Jewish Sabbath.

2503. —— movable market—whether a stall a " place " where retail trade is carried on
[Shops Act 1950 (c. 28), ss. 47, 58.]
For the purposes of the restriction on Sunday trading a market stall may be treated as if it were a shop.

Sunday markets were organised at different times on three different sites owned by the second defendant within the jurisdiction of the plaintiff council. A stall holder on one site was convicted for selling goods other than those authorised under Sched. 5 to the 1950 Act; the organisers, the first defendant, and the second defendant were convicted as aiders and abettors. The plaintiffs sought injunctions restraining the defendants from organising or holding markets on any land within the council's area for the purpose of Sunday trading in contravention of the Act. Interlocutory injunctions were granted at first instance. *Held*, dismissing the defendants' appeals, that where a trader regularly attends a market the pitch occupied by him thereat may be treated as a " place " within the meaning of s. 58 of the Act; the fact that the market was held in different places did not exempt the defendants from the legislation. (*Maby* v. *Warwick Corporation* [1972] C.L.Y. 3264, applied.)

NEWARK DISTRICT COUNCIL *v.* E. & A. MARKET PROMOTIONS (1978) 77 L.G.R. 6, C.A.

ARTICLES. See *post*, p. [31].

SOCIAL SECURITY

2504. Attendance allowance

SOCIAL SECURITY (ATTENDANCE ALLOWANCE) AMENDMENT REGULATIONS 1979 (No. 375) [20p], made under the Social Security Act 1975 (c. 14), ss. 35 (2) (*b*), (2A) (5A), 139 (1) (2), Sched. 15, para. 16; operative on April 2, 1979; provide that in certain circumstances persons who suffer from renal failure satisfy one of the two conditions relating to entitlement to attendance allowance contained in s. 35 (1) of the 1975 Act.

SOCIAL SECURITY (ATTENDANCE ALLOWANCE) AMENDMENT (No. 2) REGULATIONS 1979 (No. 1684) [20p], made under the Social Security Act 1975, ss. 35 (1), (6) and 106; operative on January 14, 1980; amend S.I. 1975 No. 598.

2505. —— child—ability to satisfy " night " conditions

A claim for attendance allowance was made by the mother of a child suffering from spina bifida. The delegated medical practitioner decided that the child satisfied one of the day conditions (frequent attention) but neither of the night conditions. On appeal, *held*, that (1) " night " began when all normal activities of the household ceased and not necessarily when the child was put to bed; (2) accordingly, the practitioner's decision was not erroneous and the appeal was disallowed: DECISION NO. R(A) 1/78.

2506. —— decision of Board—question of natural justice

A claimant requiring haemodialysis had two sessions a week on a dialysis machine and had been awarded attendance allowance previously. Her claim for a further period was disallowed as the Attendance Allowance Board had decided that a person should require at least three sessions a week on a machine in order to qualify for the allowance. *Held*, that the Board's decision was not erroneous in law, as it had been guided by the delegated medical practitioner for the claimant and there had been no affront to the rules of natural justice: DECISION NO. R(A) 4/78.

2507. —— mentally handicapped child with epilepsy—night conditions

The parents of a severely disabled boy, who suffered several epileptic fits most nights of the week, claimed attendance allowance. The delegated medical practitioner found that the child did not require prolonged or repeated attention at night in connection with his bodily functions because there were no health risks involved in the fits as such, and any harm arising from incontinence could be avoided. *Held*, that the approach taken by the practitioner was erroneous in law because it is not sufficient to focus attention exclusively on the limited question of possible harm attached to the disabling condition itself. All the circumstances in which such a condition may manifest itself must be taken into account: DECISION NO. R(A) 3/78.

2508. —— overpayment—repayment

Attendance allowance was paid to the claimant from July 26, 1971, to July 18, 1976, in respect of N, a minor. In May or June 1972 N was admitted to hospital and was subsequently transferred to a semi-residential unit. The transfer, a relevant change in circumstances, was not notified to the insurance officer. Had this been known, the allowance would have been reduced. There was no question about the good faith of the claimant: the sole question was whether she and anyone acting for her used such care and diligence to avoid the overpayment that she ought to be relieved of the obligation to repay the amount overpaid. *Held*, that the claimant and her husband, a solicitor, who acted for her, had not used due care and diligence to avoid the overpayment, and that there should be repayment. Inquiries had been made of medical staff, and the husband had consulted a summary of the relevant law in a book which he had, but the local office was not asked, in spite of the fact that the notes in the order book for the weekly payments clearly stated that the office should be notified if N went into hospital: DECISION No. R(A) 1/79.

2509. Benefits

SOCIAL SECURITY (HOSPITAL IN-PATIENTS) AMENDMENT REGULATIONS 1979 (No. 223) [10p], made under the Social Security Act 1975 (c. 14), ss. 81 (4) (*d*), 82 (6) (*b*) and 85 (1); operative on April 6, 1979; amend S.I. 1975 No. 555.

SOCIAL SECURITY (BENEFIT) (TRANSITIONAL) REGULATIONS 1979 (No. 345) [25p], made under the Social Security Pensions Act 1975 (c. 60), ss. 61 (1) (*f*), 63 and the Social Security Act 1975, s. 139 (1); operative on April 6, 1979, save for Reg. 7 which is operative on March 24, 1979; make provision for transitional matters connected with the coming into force of the Social Security Pensions Act 1975.

SOCIAL SECURITY (OVERLAPPING BENEFITS AND MISCELLANEOUS AMENDMENTS) REGULATIONS 1979 (No. 359) [20p], made under the Social Security Act 1975, ss. 3 (2), 66 (3), 85; operative on April 6, 1979; amend S.I. 1975 No. 554 and S.I. 1978 No. 1698.

SOCIAL SECURITY BENEFIT (PERSONS ABROAD) AMENDMENT REGULATIONS 1979 (No. 463) [20p], made under the Social Security Act 1975, s. 131;

operative on April 17, 1979; further amend S.I. 1975 No. 563 so as to modify the restrictions relating to entitlement to industrial injuries benefit under the 1975 Act in the case of employed earners who have suffered accidents or contracted prescribed diseases in the territory of a Member State of the EEC.

SOCIAL SECURITY (OVERLAPPING BENEFITS) REGULATIONS 1979 (No. 597) [40p], made under the Social Security Act 1975, ss. 83 (1), 85, 139 (1), Sched. 15, para. 20; operative on June 29, 1979; contain provisions relating to adjustment of benefit under the 1975 Act by reference to other benefits payable for the same period.

SOCIAL SECURITY (WIDOW'S BENEFIT AND RETIREMENT PENSIONS) REGULATIONS 1979 (No. 642) [40p], made under the Social Security Act 1975, ss. 29 (5), 30 (3), 33, 39 (1) (4), 40 (2), 85 (1), 139 (1), 162, Scheds. 15, para. 20, 20 and the Social Security Pensions Act 1975, s. 20, Sched. 1, paras. 2 (2) (*a*), 3; operative on July 10, 1979; consolidate specified regulations and certain provisions relating to widows' benefits, retirement pensions and age addition under the 1975 Acts.

SOCIAL SECURITY (WIDOW'S BENEFIT, RETIREMENT PENSIONS AND OTHER BENEFITS) (TRANSITIONAL) REGULATIONS 1979 (No. 643) [40p], made under the Social Security (Consequential Provisions) Act 1975 (c. 18), s. 2, Sched. 3, paras. 3–5, 7 and 9, and the Social Security Pensions Act 1975, s. 63; operative on July 10, 1979; provide for transitional matters connected with the Social Security Act 1975 and the Social Security Pensions Act 1975.

SOCIAL SECURITY (UNEMPLOYMENT, SICKNESS AND INVALIDITY BENEFIT) AMENDMENT REGULATIONS 1979 (No. 934) [20p], made under the Social Security Act 1975, s. 20 (3); operative on July 27, 1979; further amend S.I. 1975 No. 564 so as to impose an additional condition with respect to the receipt of unemployment benefit by persons following a course of full-time education at a university, college or school.

SOCIAL SECURITY (UNEMPLOYMENT, SICKNESS AND INVALIDITY BENEFIT) AMENDMENT (No. 2) REGULATIONS 1979 (No. 940) [20p], made under the Social Security (Consequential Provisions) Act 1975, s. 2 (1), Sched. 3, paras. 3, 9 and the Social Security Act 1975, s. 20 (3); operative on July 27, 1979; further amend S.I. 1975 No. 564 by revoking Reg. 19 and substituting a new Reg. 19 imposing additional conditions with respect to the receipt of unemployment benefit by seasonal workers in their off-season.

SOCIAL SECURITY BENEFITS UP-RATING ORDER 1979 (No. 993) [50p], made under the Social Security Act 1975, ss. 124, 126A, and the Social Security Pensions Act 1975, s. 23 (1); operative on November 12, 1979; alters the rates and amounts of benefits specified in Pts. I, III, IV and V of Sched. 4 to the 1975 Act, the rates and amounts of certain benefits under Pt. II of the 1975 Pensions Act and the rate of graduated retirement benefit under the National Insurance Act 1965.

SOCIAL SECURITY (GENERAL BENEFIT) AMENDMENT REGULATIONS 1979 (No. 1067) [10p], made under the Social Security Act 1975, s. 119 (3); operative on October 15, 1979; amend reg. 13 of the 1974 (No. 2079) Regs. so as to include decisions requiring payment of overpaid benefit made under s. 119 (2A) of the 1975 Act.

SOCIAL SECURITY BENEFITS UP-RATING REGULATIONS 1979 (No. 1278) [20p], made under the Social Security Act 1975, ss. 17 (2) (*a*), 36 (9) (*b*), 58 (3), 131, 139 (1) (2), Scheds. 14, para. 2 (1), 15, para. 17; operative on November 12, 1979; made in consequence of S.I. 1979 No. 993 these Regs. specify circumstances in which the rate of benefit which is awarded before the date from which altered rates become payable is not automatically altered by virtue of Sched. 14, para. 2 to the 1975 Act.

SOCIAL SECURITY (UNEMPLOYMENT, SICKNESS AND INVALIDITY BENEFIT) AMENDMENT (No. 3) REGULATIONS 1979 (No. 1299) [10p], made under Social Security Act 1975, ss. 17 (1) (*a*) (2), 20 (2); operative on October 19, 1979; amend S.I. 1975 No. 564 by revoking reg. 7 (1) (*g*) and by inserting a new reg. 3 (3), which provides that in certain circumstances a person who is found to be not incapable of work by reason only of the fact that he has done some work may be deemed to be incapable of work if the work done satisfies specified conditions.

SOCIAL SECURITY BENEFITS UP-RATING (AMENDMENT) ORDER 1979 (No. 1429) [10p], made under the Social Security Act 1975, s. 124; operative on November 10, 1979; substitutes a new art. 8 in S.I. 1979 No. 993.

SOCIAL SECURITY (EARNINGS-RELATED ADDITION TO WIDOW'S ALLOWANCE) (SPECIAL PROVISIONS) REGULATIONS 1979 (No. 1431) [10p], made under the Social Security Act 1975, s. 130; operative on January 6, 1980; modify Sched. 6, Pt. I to the 1975 Act in cases where the late husband had attained pensionable age and during the whole or part of the relevant year would have had liability for Class I contributions but for s. 4 (1) of the Social Security Pensions Act 1975. The earnings-related addition will be calculated in these cases by reference to the late husband's earnings and not to an earnings factor which is based on Class I contributions.

2510. —— entitlement—Irish prisoner—EEC. See KENNY *v.* INSURANCE OFFICER, § 1241.

2511. Capacity for work—exercise of discretion
[Social Security (Unemployment, Sickness and Invalidity Benefit) Regulations 1975 (S.I. 1975 No. 564), reg. 3 (1) (*a*).] When considering the exercise of the discretion given under reg. 3 (1) (*a*) of the Social Security (Unemployment, Sickness and Invalidity Benefit) Regulations 1975, all the circumstances of the case must be taken into account. A claimant should only be deemed incapable of work if it appears from the evidence as a whole that there is some medical reason why he should abstain from work. A certifying doctor need not use formal presentation or language as long as reasons for deeming a claimant incapable for work could be found: DECISION NO. R (S) 2/79.

2512. Charges for accommodation
NATIONAL ASSISTANCE (CHARGES FOR ACCOMMODATION) REGULATIONS 1979 (No. 823) [20p], made under the National Assistance Act 1948 (c. 29), s. 22; operative on November 12, 1979; supersede S.I. 1978 No. 1073 and increase the minimum amount that a person is required to pay for accommodation managed by a local authority under Pt. III of the 1948 Act.

2513. Child benefit. See FAMILY ALLOWANCES.

2514. Claims
SOCIAL SECURITY (CLAIMS AND PAYMENTS) REGULATIONS 1979 (No. 628) [70p], made under the Social Security Act 1975 (c. 14), ss. 45 (3), 79–81, 88–90, 115 (1), 139 (1) (2), 141 (1) (2), Scheds. 13; 15, para. 20; 16, para. 12 and the Social Security (Consequential Provisions) Act 1975 (c. 18), Sched. 3, para. 9 (1) (*a*) (*c*); operative on July 9, 1979; consolidate S.I. 1975 No. 560 with subsequent amending regs. They provide for the manner in which claims for and payments of benefits under the Social Security Act 1975 are to be made.

SOCIAL SECURITY (CLAIMS AND PAYMENTS) AMENDMENT REGULATIONS 1979 (No. 781) [30p], made under the Social Security Act 1975, ss. 79 (1) (3), 115, Sched. 13; operative on September 5, 1979; amend S.I. 1979 No. 628 so as to make provision to allow certain claims for unemployment benefit to be made for a period falling partly after the date on which the claim is made.

SOCIAL SECURITY (DETERMINATION OF CLAIMS AND QUESTIONS) AMENDMENT REGULATIONS 1979 (No. 1163) [20p], made under the Social Security Act 1975, s. 119 (3) and (4); operative on November 5, 1979; amend S.I. 1975 No. 558.

SOCIAL SECURITY (CLAIMS AND PAYMENTS) AMENDMENT (NO. 2) REGULATIONS 1979 (No. 1199) [10p], made under the Social Security Act 1975, s. 81; operative on October 25, 1979; amend S.I. 1979 No. 628 and enable the Secretary of State to arrange for weekly payments of guardian's allowance to be made on Mondays instead of Tuesdays.

2515. Contributions
SOCIAL SECURITY (CONTRIBUTIONS, RE-RATING) CONSEQUENTIAL AMENDMENT REGULATIONS 1979 (No. 9) [10p], made under the Social Security Act 1975

(c. 14), s. 129 (1) and S.I. 1978 No. 1840; operative on April 6, 1979; further amend S.I. 1975 No. 492 by increasing the special rate of Class 2 contributions payable by share fishermen.

SOCIAL SECURITY (CONTRIBUTIONS) AMENDMENT REGULATIONS 1979 (No. 358) [10p], made under the Social Security Act 1975, ss. 4 (7) and 134 (6), as amended by the Social Security Act 1979 (c. 18), s. 14; operative on April 6, 1979; further amend S.I. 1975 No. 492.

SOCIAL SECURITY (CONTRIBUTIONS) REGULATIONS 1979 (No. 591) [£2·00], made under the Social Security Act 1975, ss. 1 (6), 3, 4 (2) (*b*), (5)–(7), 7 (5) (6), 8 (1) (2), 9 (7)–(9), 10 (1) (2), 11, 13 (4), 128 (2) (3), 129 (1) (2), 130–132, 134 (6), 146 (5), Sched. 1, paras. 1, 2, 3, 4 (*a*) (*c*) (*d*), 5, 6, 8, the Social Security (Northern Ireland) Act 1975 (c. 15), s. 123, the Social Security (Consequential Provisions) Act 1975, Sched. 3, paras. 3, 6, 7, 9, and the Social Security Pensions Act 1975 (c. 60), ss. 1, 3 (2), 5, 27 (3), 63 (1); operative on July 6, 1979; consolidate the regulations hitherto in force relating to contributions under the 1975 Acts.

SOCIAL SECURITY (EARNINGS FACTOR) REGULATIONS 1979 (No. 676) [30p], made under the Social Security Act 1975, ss. 13 (5), 115 (1), Sched. 13, para. 2, the Social Security Pensions Act 1975, s. 35 (3) and the Social Security (Miscellaneous Provisions) Act 1977 (c. 5), s. 1 (5); operative on July 16, 1979; consolidate the Regulations revoked in Sched. 2.

SOCIAL SECURITY (CONTRIBUTIONS) (EARNINGS LIMITS) AMENDMENT REGULATIONS 1979 (No. 1483) [10p], made under the Social Security Pensions Act 1975, ss. 1, 61 (1) (*a*) and the Social Security Act 1975, s. 139; operative on April 6, 1980; amend S.I. 1979 No. 591 by substituting new lower and upper earnings limits for Class 1 contributions for the tax year beginning April 6, 1980.

SOCIAL SECURITY (CONTRIBUTIONS, RE-RATING) ORDER 1979 (No. 1694) [20p], made under the Social Security Act 1975, ss. 120 (5) and (6), 121 (2) and 122 (1) (*a*); operative on April 6, 1980; increases the rates of class 1, 2 and 3 contributions payable under the 1975 Act. It increases the amount of earnings below which an earner may be excepted from liability for class 2 contributions and the lower and upper limits of profits or gains between which class 4 contributions are payable.

SOCIAL SECURITY (CONTRIBUTIONS, RE-RATING) (No. 2) ORDER 1979 (No. 1736) [10p], made under the Social Security Act 1975, s. 123 (1); operative on April 6, 1980; substitutes a lower rate of secondary Class 1 contribution in s. 4 (6) (*b*) of the Social Security Act 1979 and amends s. 134 (4) of that Act.

2516. Earnings factors

SOCIAL SECURITY REVALUATION OF EARNINGS FACTORS ORDER 1979 (No. 832) [10p], made under the Social Security Pensions Act 1975 (c. 60), s. 21; operative on July 16, 1979; directs that the earnings factors relevant to calculating the additional component in the rate of any long-term benefit for the tax year 1978–79 are to be increased by 13·3 per cent.

2517. Family income supplements. See FAMILY ALLOWANCES.

2518. Forms—stateless person—EEC. See *Re* MEDICAL TREATMENT IN GERMANY, § 1252.

2519. Industrial disablement benefit—occupational deafness—time limits—tests for ceasing employment

[Social Security (Industrial Injuries) (Prescribed Diseases) Regulations 1975 (S.I. 1975 No. 1537), reg. 40 (2).] The claimant, a plater and press operator apprenticed in 1930, was employed at the Royal Ordnance Factory, Leeds from 1950. On March 24, 1975, he was off work due to sickness and never returned to work. On December 9, 1975, the factory medical officer examined the claimant and reported him permanently unfit for any type of work at the factory. The claimant was discharged on February 20, 1976, and made a claim for disablement benefit on February 17, 1977. The local tribunal disallowed the claim as being out of time under reg. 40 (2) of the Social Security (Industrial Injuries) (Prescribed Diseases) Regulations 1975. *Held*, that (1) reg. 40 (2) was not *ultra vires,* the time limit of 12 months after the claimant has ceased to be employed is absolute, and cannot be extended; (2) the regulations are directed to work done rather than to the contractual regulations to do it, therefore the tribunal adopted the "actual work" approach and rejected the argument that the claimant ceased to be employed on February 20, 1976, when his contract of service terminated. The reason for the cessation of work is irrelevant; (3) in calculating the 20 years in employment, normal breaks, which include weekends, holidays, short term absences for sickness or absenteeism and short term interruptions due to industrial troubles, should be disregarded. In deciding whether a break was normal or abnormal each case should be examined individually; there should not be an inflexible rule determining abnormal breaks. The claimant's break from March 24, 1975, to February 20, 1976, was abnormal. He ceased work on March 24, 1975, and at that date ceased to be employed within the meaning of reg. 40 (2): DECISION No. R(I) 2/79.

2520. —— prescribed disease—occupational deafness
[Social Security (Industrial Injuries) (Prescribed Diseases) Regulations 1975 (S.I. 1975 No. 1537), Sched. 1, para. 48 (*a*).] The claimant was employed as a welder in a chemical factory, inserting new linings in chemical vessels as well as repairing cracked and fractured linings. His work also included cutting and dressing the new cast metal and using high-speed grinding tools to smooth its surface. *Held,* (1) the words "cleaning, dressing and finishing" are used disjunctively in para. 48 (*a*) of Sched. 1 to the 1975 Regulations; (2) the claimant's occupation involved the use of high-speed grinding tools in the "dressing" of cast metal and he was therefore entitled to the benefit; DECISION No. R(I) 2/78.

2521. [Social Security (Industrial Injuries) (Prescribed Diseases) Regulations 1975 (S.I. 1975 No. 1537), reg. 2 (*d*) and Sched. 1 para. 48 (*c*).] The claimant had been continuously employed for 24 years by one firm when he claimed disablement benefit for industrial benefit on November 19, 1976. For just under $13\frac{1}{2}$ years certain functions had taken the claimant within the vicinity of the prescribed plant. *Held,* the employment lacked the features which would have classified it as comprising separate and distinct occupations, therefore the claimant was engaged upon a single occupation within reg. (2) (*d*) and para. 48 (*c*) of Sched. 1 to the Social Security (Industrial Injuries) (Prescribed Diseases) Regulations 1975: DECISION No. R (1) 3/78.

2522. Industrial injuries benefits
SOCIAL SECURITY (INDUSTRIAL INJURIES) (PRESCRIBED DISEASES) AMENDMENT REGULATIONS 1979 (No. 264) [10p], made under the Social Security Act 1975 (c. 14), s. 113 (1) (2); operative on April 6, 1979; amend reg. 49 of S.I. 1975 No. 1537 with regard to the right of appeal to a medical appeal tribunal against a decision of a pneumoconiosis medical board on any diagnosis question relating to pneumoconiosis or byssinosis.
SOCIAL SECURITY (INDUSTRIAL INJURIES) (PRESCRIBED DISEASES) AMENDMENT (NO. 2) REGULATIONS 1979 (No. 265) [10p], made under the Social Security Act 1975, s. 76; operative on April 6, 1979; amend reg. 2 of S.I. 1975 No. 1537 so that, for the purpose of deciding whether byssinosis is a prescribed disease in relation to a person, it is no longer necessary that he should have been employed for a specific minimum period in an occupation prescribed in relation to byssinosis.
SOCIAL SECURITY (INDUSTRIAL INJURIES) (PRESCRIBED DISEASES) AMENDMENT (NO. 3) REGULATONS 1979 (No. 632) [10p], made under the Social Security Act 1975, ss. 76, 77; operative on August 8, 1979; add nasal carcinoma to Sched. 1 of S.I. 1975 No. 1537.
SOCIAL SECURITY (INDUSTRIAL INJURIES) (PRESCRIBED DISEASES) AMENDMENT (NO. 4) REGULATIONS 1979 (No. 992) [30p], made under the Social Security Act 1975, ss. 76, 77; operative on September 3, 1979; amend the 1975 (No. 1537) Regulations relating to benefits in respect of occupational deafness.
WORKMEN'S COMPENSATION (SUPPLEMENTATION) (AMENDMENT) SCHEME 1979 (No. 1190) [20p], made under the Industrial Injuries and Diseases (Old Cases)

Act 1975 (c. 16), ss. 2, 4 (2); operative on November 14, 1979; amends S.I. 1966 No. 165 by making adjustments to the intermediate rates of lesser incapacity allowance consequential upon the increase of the maximum rate of incapacity allowance made by S.I. 1979 No. 993.

SOCIAL SECURITY (INDUSTRIAL INJURIES) (PRESCRIBED DISEASES) AMENDMENT (No. 5) REGULATIONS 1979 (No. 1569) [10p], made under the Social Security Act 1975, ss. 76 and 77; operative on January 7, 1980; extend cover under the industrial injuries provisions of the 1975 Act to infection by leptospira of all kinds in relation to persons working in places infested by rats, field mice or voles, or working with dogs or bovine animals or pigs.

2523. Invalidity benefit—EEC—overlapping benefits. See *Re* INDUSTRIAL DISABLE-MENT, § 1244.

2524. —— married woman—ability to perform " normal household duties "
The claimant, a married woman aged 44, residing with her husband, suffered from paralysis of the left arm, leaving it virtually useless. Her household duties were performed very slowly, often taking her all day. *Held*, that the claimant was not entitled to an invalidity pension as she was not incapable of performing normal household duties: DECISION No. R(S) 4/78.

2525. The claimant, a married woman residing with her husband, applied for a non-contributory invalidity pension on the basis that she was incapable of performing normal household duties. The claimant suffered from a foot deformity and a right hemiplegia with little or no function in her right arm and hand. *Held*, that (1) the claimant's incapacity for her own normal household duties was to be compared objectively with the performance of a capable housewife in the same circumstances; (2) she could perform some duties to a limited extent but as that amount was less than could properly be described as substantial, she was entitled to the benefit: DECISION No. R(S) 5/78.

2526. The claimant, aged 54, sustained an extensive coronary thrombosis and developed angina of effort. As a result she was incapable of sustained exertion and her ability to perform household duties was severely restricted. The insurance officer contended that the amount the claimant could do by way of household duties was substantial. *Held*, that the essential point is not what a woman is able to do but what, because of disease or disablement, she is unable to do. In this case what the claimant was unable to do was substantial and she was therefore entitled to the invalidity benefit: DECISION R(S) 7/78.

2527. —— review—conflicting medical opinions
Awards of invalidity benefit were made to the claimant on the basis of his doctor's certificate. Shortly afterwards, departmental medical officers examined the claimant and concluded he was not incapable of his usual occupation. After a review by the insurance officer the claimant appealed. *Held*, (1) the existence of a different medical opinion was not a change of circumstances for the purposes of review under s. 104 (1) (*b*) of the Social Security Act 1975; (2) medical opinions by themselves do not show that the requirements for payment have not been satisfied and the insurance officer was not entitled to review the decision: DECISION No. R(S) 6/78.

2528. Maternity allowance—earnings-related supplement—relevant income tax year
Maternity allowance was awarded to the claimant for the period January 12 to May 22, 1976. An earnings-related supplement to the allowance was also awarded for the same period, calculated by reference to the 1973–74 income tax year. *Held*, that the earnings-related supplement had been calculated with reference to the correct income tax year as the linking provision of s. 17 (1) (*d*) of the Social Security Act 1975 did apply to maternity allowances: DECISION No. R(G) 1/78.

2529. Mobility allowance
MOBILITY ALLOWANCE AMENDMENT REGULATIONS 1979 (No. 172) [20p], made under the Social Security Act 1975 (c. 14), s. 37A (2), (6), as amended by the Social Security Pensions Act 1975 (c. 60), s. 22; operative on March 21, 1979; prescribe more precisely the circumstances in which a person is to be

treated as suffering from physical disablement such that he is virtually unable to walk, and also secure that mobility allowance may be payable to a person who has the use of a vehicle provided by the Secretary of State under s. 33 of the Health Services and Public Health Act 1968, where that vehicle is not a power driven road vehicle controlled by the occupant.

2530. —— inability to walk—child suffering from mongolism

A boy suffering from mongolism was awarded mobility allowance by a medical appeal tribunal, which found that his erratic behaviour seriously impaired his mobility and was directly due to his mongolism which could be classified as a physical disorder. On appeal by the Secretary of State, *held,* the tribunal was correct in finding that where a physical factor was present throughout in the causation of the boy's inability to walk, he was virtually unable to walk because of physical disablement: DECISION No. R(M) 2/78.

2531. —— —— spastic child

A mother was awarded by a medical appeal tribunal mobility allowance for her spastic child who was liable to epileptic seizures. Her doctor had advised that the child should not be allowed to walk unattended. On appeal by the Secretary of State, *held,* that the tribunal's decision was erroneous in point of law, as there was no evidence to support the finding that the child was unable or virtually unable to walk: DECISION No. R(M) 1/78.

2532. —— Medical Appeal Tribunal—appeal on question of law

A medical board decided that the claimant did not satisfy the conditions for an award of a mobility allowance. The Medical Appeal Tribunal refused the claimant's appeal. The claimant appealed to the National Insurance Commissioner by virtue of s. 112 of the Social Security Act 1975. *Held,* that (1) questions of medical fact are for the tribunal (*R.* v. *Medical Appeal Tribunal (North Midland Region), ex p. Hubble* [1959] C.L.Y. 2147 and *Global Plant* v. *Secretary of State for Social Security* [1971] C.L.Y. 3949 followed); (2) the word " walk " as used in reg. 3 of the Mobility Allowance Regulations 1975 means " to move by means of a person's legs or feet or combination of them." Only in exceptional circumstances should a test of seeing a person walk by the medical members require further investigation; (3) it is for the tribunal to decide the extent and nature of any tests in order to ascertain whether a claimant " is unable or virtually unable to walk." (*Brutus* v. *Cozens* [1972] C.L.Y. 706 applied); (4) " the exertion required to walk " is the sole condition governing reg. 3 (1) (*b*) and the expression does not extend to symptoms which might intervene during the course of walking: DECISION R (M) 3/78.

2533. Overlapping benefits—EEC law. See *Re* GERMAN RETIREMENT PENSION, § 1247.

2534. Pneumoconiosis

PNEUMOCONIOSIS ETC. (WORKERS' COMPENSATION) (DETERMINATION OF CLAIMS) REGULATIONS 1979 (No. 727) [20p], made under the Pneumoconiosis etc. (Worker's Compensation) Act 1979 (c. 41), ss. 4, 5 and 7; operative on July 4, 1979; prescribe the manner in which claims must be made under the Act.

PNEUMOCONIOSIS, BYSSINOSIS AND MISCELLANEOUS DISEASES BENEFIT (AMENDMENT) SCHEME 1979 (No. 996) [10p], made under the Industrial Injuries and Diseases (Old Cases) Act 1975 (c. 16), s. 5; operative on August 8, 1979; adds nasal carcinoma to the list of diseases in respect of which benefit is payable under the 1966 Scheme.

PNEUMOCONIOSIS ETC. (WORKERS' COMPENSATION) (PAYMENT OF CLAIMS) REGULATIONS 1979 (No. 1726) [50p], made under the Pneumoconiosis etc. (Workers' Compensation) Act 1979, ss. 1, 4 (1), 7; operative on January 1, 1980; prescribe the amount or level of payments to be made to persons or dependants who qualify under the Pneumoconiosis etc. (Workers' Compensation) Act 1979.

2535. Pneumoconiosis etc. (Workers' Compensation) Act 1979 (c. 41)

This Act makes provision for lump sum payments to certain persons who are disabled by pneumoconiosis, byssinosis or diffuse mesothelioma.

S. 1 provides for lump sum payments to certain persons suffering from pneumoconiosis, byssinosis and diffuse mesothelioma; s. 2 sets out the conditions of entitlement; s. 3 defines "dependant" in relation to a person who, immediately before he dies, was disabled by one of the specified diseases; s. 4 deals with determination of claims; s. 5 concerns reconsideration of determinations; s. 6 provides for payments for the benefit of minors; s. 7 empowers the Secretary of State to make regulations under the Act; s. 8 relates to fraudulent statements, etc.; s. 9 contains financial provisions; s. 10 deals with short title, construction, commencement and extent. The Act does not extend to Northern Ireland.

The Act received the Royal Assent on April 4, 1979, and came into force on July 4, 1979.

2536. Portugal

SOCIAL SECURITY (PORTUGAL) ORDER 1979 (No. 921) [80p], made under the Social Security Act 1975 (c. 14), s. 143 (1), and the Child Benefit Act 1975 (c. 61), s. 15 (1); operative on October 1, 1979; modifies the 1975 Acts so as to give effect to the Convention on Social Security between the United Kingdom and Portugal.

2537. Reciprocal agreements

SOCIAL SECURITY (RECIPROCAL AGREEMENTS) ORDER 1979 (No. 290) [20p], made under the Social Security Act 1975 (c. 14), s. 143 (1); operative on April 6, 1979; provides for the Scheduled Orders in Council (which give effect to agreements made between the U.K. government and other countries providing for reciprocity in certain social security matters) to have effect subject to modifications to take account of changes in social security law made by the Social Security Pensions Act 1975.

2538. Sickness benefit—EEC—Irish woman. See *Re* SICKNESS BENEFIT FOR AN ELDERLY IRISHWOMAN, § 1251.

2539. —— —— rest cure in Member State. See *Re* CONVALESCENCE IN GERMANY, § 1250.

2540. —— incapacity for work—work not done for remuneration

The claimant, a video consultant, became incapable of work by reason of vein thrombosis in his right leg and was paid sickness benefit for a period. During that time he was involved in a toy shop business in which he was in partnership with his wife. The question arose as to whether the amount of work done by the claimant in the toy shop business would disqualify him from payment of benefit. *Held,* that the work done by the claimant was not undertaken with the intention or hope of obtaining remuneration in return for his services and was therefore not "work" within s. 17 (1) (*a*) (ii) of the Social Security Act 1975. The claimant was therefore entitled to the benefit: DECISION No. R(S) 4/79.

2541. —— late claim

A claim for sickness benefit was received after the expiry of the time limit as it had first been sent to the claimant's employer. *Held,* that the claimant was disqualified from receiving sickness benefit because he had failed, without good cause, to claim within the time prescribed by regulations. *Per* the Commissioner: It is the responsibility of claimants to ensure that their claims get to the appropriate office of the D.H.S.S. or are posted, in time: DECISION No. R(S) 5/79.

2542. A claim for increased sickness benefit was received after the expiry of the time limit due to the claimant's ignorance as to his rights. *Held,* that the claimant had good cause for his failure to claim earlier; his claim had been submitted promptly once he became aware of his entitlement. A claimant may be excused for failing to attend to information concerning benefit if his state of health prevented him from doing so at the time of receipt: DECISION No. R (S) 3/79.

2543. Social Security Act 1979 (c. 18)

This Act amends the law relating to social security.

S. 1 is the interpretation section; s. 2 amends s. 35 of the Social Security

Act 1975 relating to attendance allowances; s. 3 makes amendments to s. 37A of the 1975 Act concerning mobility allowance; s. 4 amends ss. 30 and 167 of, and Sched. 15 to, the 1975 Act relating to earnings after retirement age; s. 5 makes miscellaneous amendments to the 1975 Act, the Social Security Pensions Act 1975 and the Social Security (Miscellaneous Provisions) Act 1977 relating to retirement and invalidity pensions; s. 6 relates to appeals from and to Supplementary Benefit Appeal Tribunals; s. 7 amends s. 86 of the Social Security Act 1975 relating to incompatible benefits; s. 8 amends s. 119 of the 1975 Act dealing with repayment of benefits; s. 9 concerns the qualification of National Insurance Commissioners in Great Britain and Northern Ireland; s. 10 amends s. 21 of the Social Security Pensions Act 1975 regarding revaluation of earnings factors; s. 11 deals with increase of official pensions; s. 12 provides for up-rating of increments in guaranteed minimum pensions; s. 13 relates to maternity grants and death grants; s. 14 amends the Social Security Act 1975 in relation to adjustments of secondary Class 1 contributions for exceptions to redundancy provisions; s. 15 amends the 1975 Act dealing with overlap with benefits under legislation of other Member States of the EEC; s. 16 concerns the meaning of "business" in criminal proceedings; s. 17 relates to the reference of regulations to the National Insurance Advisory Committee; s. 18 inserts a new s. 60A into the Social Security Pensions Act 1975 relating to the treatment of insignificant amounts; s. 19 provides for the enactment of the same provisions of this Act for Northern Ireland; s. 20 contains financial provisions; s. 21 deals with the short title and commencement. This Act does not extend to Northern Ireland except for ss. 9 (2) and 19 and Sched. 3, paras. 3 and 12.

The Act received the Royal Assent on March 22, 1979, and came into force on that date except for ss. 11 and 12 and Sched. 1, paras. 2–22 and Sched. 3, paras. 5–7, 11, 14–20, 22, 23, 29 (*a*) (*b*) which came into force on April 6, 1979.

2544. —— commencement

SOCIAL SECURITY ACT 1979 (COMMENCEMENT NO. 1) ORDER 1979 (No. 369 (C. 10)) [10p], made under the Social Security Act 1979 (c. 18), s. 21 (2); operative on March 29, 1979; brings into force provisions of the 1979 Act relating to mobility allowance.

SOCIAL SECURITY ACT 1979 (COMMENCEMENT NO. 2) ORDER 1979 (No. 1031 (C. 29)) [10p], made under the Social Security Act 1979, s. 21 (2); operative on September 5, 1979; brings into force s. 3 (3) of the 1979 Act in relation to women born after November 29, 1914, but before June 7, 1918, for purposes of mobility allowance and appoints November 28, 1979, for all other purposes.

2545. Social Security Pensions Act 1975—commencement

SOCIAL SECURITY PENSIONS ACT 1975 (COMMENCEMENT NO. 13) ORDER 1979 (No. 171 (C. 5)) [10p], made under the Social Security Pensions Act 1975 (c. 60), s. 67 (1) (2), in relation to men born between June 7, 1918, and December 21, 1919, brings into force ss. 22, 65 (1), Sched. 4, paras. 47, 49, 51– 53. For the purposes of making claims for mobility allowance they shall be operative on March 7, 1979, and for all other purposes shall be operative on June 6, 1979.

SOCIAL SECURITY PENSIONS ACT 1975 (COMMENCEMENT NO. 14) ORDER 1979 (No. 367 (C. 9)) [10p], made under the Social Security Pensions Act 1975, s. 67 (2); operative on March 29, 1979; brings into force provisions of the 1975 Act relating to mobility allowance which are brought into force on days to coincide with the provisions of the Social Security Act 1979 which is brought into force by S.I. 1979 No. 369.

SOCIAL SECURITY PENSIONS ACT 1975 (COMMENCEMENT NO. 15) ORDER 1979 (No. 394 (C. 11)) [10p], made under the Social Security Pensions Act 1975, s. 67 (2); operative on March 31, 1979; brings into force s. 65 (1) so far as it relates to Sched. 4, paras. 47, 49, 51–53, which for the purposes of making claims for determining claims and questions relating to mobility allowance are operative on March 31, 1979, and for all other purposes are operative on June 6, 1979. The commencement of these provisions only apply to women born between March 23, 1919, and December 21, 1919.

SOCIAL SECURITY PENSIONS ACT 1975 (COMMENCEMENT No. 16) ORDER 1979 (No. 1030 (C. 28)) [10p], made under the Social Security Pensions Act 1975, s. 67 (1) (2); operative on September 5, 1979; brings into force provisions of the 1975 Act relating to mobility allowance.

2546. Social services—report

The Department of Health and Social Services has published the report of the official Co-Ordinating Committee on Abuse for the period since September 1977. The report shows that social security fraud prosecutions for 1978 are expected to increase by about 16 per cent. but concludes that this is a measure of the increasing efforts staff are putting into anti-fraud work and of its growing effectiveness.

2547. Supplementary benefits

SUPPLEMENTARY BENEFITS (DETERMINATION OF REQUIREMENTS) REGULATIONS 1979 (No. 997) [20p], made under the Supplementary Benefits Act 1976 (c. 71), s. 2 (2) (3); operative on November 12, 1979; vary the provisions of Pt. II of Sched. 1 to the 1976 Act relating to weekly amounts allowed for requirements, the attendance requirements of severely disabled persons and the rent addition for non-householders.

2548. —— calculation—reduction of allowance—claim for unemployment benefit not determined—whether reduction validly made

[Supplementary Benefits Act 1976 (c. 71), Sched. 1, para. 9.]

However difficult it may be for a supplementary benefit appeal tribunal to form an opinion as to whether an applicant will be disqualified from receiving employment benefit, they are nonetheless required to do so before making a deduction under para. 9 of Sched. 1 to the Supplementary Benefits Act 1976.

The applicant left his job and applied for supplementary allowance and unemployment benefit. When his supplementary allowance application came to be considered his other application had been suspended pending inquiries. The Commission calculated his allowance and then purported to deduct 40 per cent. under para. 9 of Sched. 1 to the 1976 Act. R's appeal was dismissed by the appeal tribunal who in reply to R's solicitor's letter stated they had not been in a position to form an opinion as to the extent of R's contribution to his own dismissal. On application for certiorari, *held*, granting the order, that the appeal tribunal were required to form such an opinion before making the deduction, and their failure to do so appeared on the face of the record (the solicitor's letter).

R. *v.* GREATER BIRMINGHAM SUPPLEMENTARY BENEFIT APPEAL TRIBUNAL, *ex p.* KHAN [1979] 3 All E.R. 759, D.C.

2549. —— —— whether wages paid at termination of employment "resources"

[Supplementary Benefits Act 1976 (c. 71), s. 6; Supplementary Benefits (General) Regulations 1977 (S.I. 1977 No. 1141), reg. 3.]

In assessing "resources" on a claim for supplementary benefit, wages paid in arrears are nevertheless present income.

C, the claimant, who was a student, worked from July 26 until September 10. He received a full week's supplementary allowance for the first week because payment of wages did not fall due until August 4. When he finished working C made a further claim. The Supplementary Benefits Commission refused it on the ground that on September 15 C received a sum of £86·80, the last week's wages and holiday pay. The Supplementary Benefits Appeal Tribunal allowed C's appeal on the ground that the £86·80 was attributable to the week when it was earned. On application to the High Court, *held*, granting an order of certiorari quashing that decision, that the Commission had rightly regarded the £86·80 as income for the purpose of assessing C's resources in relation to the two weeks following September 15. (Dictum of Lord Denning M.R. in R. v. *Preston Supplementary Benefits Appeal Tribunal, ex p. Moore* [1975] C.L.Y. 3288 and R. v. *West London Supplementary Benefits Appeal Tribunal, ex p. Taylor* [1975] C.L.Y. 3255 applied.)

R. *v.* MANCHESTER SUPPLEMENTARY BENEFITS APPEAL TRIBUNAL, *ex p.* RILEY [1979] 1 W.L.R. 426, Sheen J.

2550. —— **full time education—claimant on pre-nursing course**
[Supplementary Benefits Act 1976 (c. 71), s. 7 (1).] The claimant, aged 17, attended a technical college on a pre-nursing course; she applied for a supplementary allowance, which was refused on the ground that she was receiving full-time instruction of a kind given in schools within s. 7 (1) of the Supplementary Benefits Act 1976. *Held*, that the commission had completely abdicated their responsibility to look at the facts by treating the words of the statute as meaning " non-advanced education," and the claimant's appeal would be allowed: SAMPSON *v.* SUPPLEMENTARY BENEFITS COMMISSION (1979) 123 S.J. 284, Watkins J.

2551. —— **youth " attending school "—illness**
[Supplementary Benefits Act 1976 (c. 71), s. 7 (1).] Whether a youth is " receiving full time education " and so is not entitled to claim supplementary benefit in his own right under s. 7 (1) of the Supplementary Benefits Act 1976 is a question of fact; he may be " attending school " even if he spends a whole term away from public school because of illness: BLOOMFIELD *v.* SUPPLEMENTARY BENEFITS COMMISSION (1978) 123 S.J. 33, Sheen J.

2552. Unemployment benefit—dismissal—misconduct—effect of industrial tribunal's decision
The claimant, a maintenance fitter, was summarily dismissed for allegedly threatening violence against the works maintenance engineer. The claimant applied to an industrial tribunal alleging unfair dismissal, but this decided he had been fairly dismissed. The national insurance tribunal disqualified the claimant from receiving unemployment benefit for six weeks and stated that it had followed the industrial tribunal's decision as to his misconduct. On appeal, *held,* that the claimant's conduct amounted to misconduct within the meaning of s. 20 (1) (*a*) of the Social Security Act 1975 and that the six weeks' disqualification was not inappropriate. The Commissioner commented that though there can be no question of the decisions of industrial tribunals being binding on national insurance tribunals, it may be proper for a national insurance tribunal to take full cognisance of any evidence given to an industrial tribunal which is relevant to the particular issue being considered: DECISION R(U) 4/78.

2553. —— **earnings-related supplement—withdrawal of claim**
Unemployment benefit was claimed by the applicant from December 8, 1975, to April 21, 1976, and also from May 1, 1976. The claim was disallowed because the applicant did not satisfy the necessary contribution conditions. He then applied to withdraw his claim for the period prior to January 5, 1976, so as to be entitled to earnings-related supplement as from May 3, 1976. *Held*, dismissing the appeal, that the applicant was not entitled to withdraw his claim once it had been adjudicated upon and accordingly the earnings-related supplement was not payable: DECISION No. R(U) 2/79.

2554. —— **EEC—absence abroad.** See *Re* UNEMPLOYMENT BENEFITS, § 1255.

2555. —— —— **absence in another Member State.** See COCCIOLI *v.* BUNDESANSTALT FÜR ARBEIT, § 1254.

2556. —— —— **seeking employment abroad.** See *Re* A FARM MANAGER, § 1256.

2557. —— **increase for children—written undertaking by father**
A father of two children applied for an increase in unemployment benefit in respect of the children. During the period in question the applicant had not lived with his family nor had he provided for their maintenance. About nine months later the applicant gave a written undertaking to contribute to the children's maintenance. *Held,* (1) the increase in benefit was not payable in respect of the children because no provision had been made for them by the applicant and they were not living with him; (2) the written undertaking had no retrospective effect in a case such as this where it was given some nine months after the period in question: DECISION R(U) 3/78.

2558. —— **special capital payment—redundant member of armed forces**
[Social Security (Unemployment, Sickness and Invalidity Benefit) Regulations 1975 (S.I. No. 564), reg. 7 (1) (*d*).]
A special capital payment made to a member of the armed forces on

redundancy is not a payment in lieu of remuneration within reg. 7 (1) (*d*) of the Social Security (Unemployment, Sickness and Invalidity) Benefit Regulations 1975.

A squadron leader with a permanent commission was made redundant. He received a special capital sum under a government scheme in lieu of a redundancy payment. Loss of remuneration was one, but only one, of the factors in its calculation. The Chief National Insurance Commissioner held that he was thereby disqualified from receiving unemployment benefit on the ground that the special capital payment contained an element of payment in lieu of remuneration within the meaning of reg. 7 (1) (*d*) of the Social Security (Unemployment, Sickness and Invalidity Benefit) Regulations 1975. The Divisional Court granted an order of certiorari to quash that decision. On appeal, *held*, dismissing the appeal, that the payment was a compensation for being made redundant not to cover day-to-day expenses whilst unemployed, and it was not in lieu of remuneration.

R. *v.* NATIONAL INSURANCE COMMISSIONER, *ex p.* STRATTON [1979] 2 W.L.R. 389, C.A.

2559. —— trade dispute—dispute over protective clothing

[Social Security Act 1975 (c. 14), s. 19 (2) (*b*).] The claimants were employed by a contractor responsible for the erection of boilers at a new power station. Their trade union claimed the provision of free protective clothing; the employer offered to supply the clothing on payment by the employees. On the breakdown of negotiations, the claimants stopped work. They contended that the dispute was not a trade dispute within the meaning of s. 19 (2) (*b*) of the 1975 Act and that they had stopped work because of the unhealthy atmosphere at work. *Held*, that (1) the dispute which gave rise to the loss of employment was a "trade dispute" and accordingly unemployment benefit was not payable; (2) there was no substance in the argument that the employer was failing his obligations under the Health and Safety at Work, etc., Act 1974 and that this was the real cause of the stoppage: R. *v.* NATIONAL INSURANCE COMMISSIONER, *ex p.* THOMPSON, Appendix to Social Security Decision No. R(U) 5/77, D.C.

2560. Welfare foods. See FOOD AND DRUGS.

2561. Widow's benefit—cohabitation—evidence of relationship

In 1975 the claimant's husband died and in 1976 she changed her name to that of the man with whom she was living in the same house and with whom she had had a business relationship since 1963. There was evidence from the electoral register that the claimant had been using the man's name since 1969. *Held*, dismissing the appeal, that it could be inferred from the facts that the claimant was living with the man as his wife and was accordingly not entitled to a widow's allowance: DECISION No. R(G) 1/79.

BOOKS AND ARTICLES. See *post*, p. [11], [31].

SOLICITORS

2562. Action by client against solicitor—contract or tort

[Can.] When a client brings an action against a solicitor in respect of an alleged breach of duty by the solicitor to ensure that the client got a good title to certain land, his claim can be equally founded in contract and in tort, and he can rely on whichever foundation gives him the more favourable position under a statute of limitations. (*Esso Petroleum* v. *Mardon* [1976] C.L.Y. 341 applied; *Bagot* v. *Stevens Scanlan* [1964] C.L.Y. 358 disapproved): POWER *v.* HALLEY (1978) 88 D.L.R. (3d) 381, Nfld.Sup.Ct.

2563. Beneficiary under trust—action against solicitor retained by trustees. See WILLS *v.* COOKE, § 2413.

2564. Costs—client's right to certificate

[Solicitors' Remuneration Order 1972 (S.I. 1972 No. 1139), art. 3 (2).] In order to comply with his duty under art. 3 (2) of the Solicitors' Remuneration Order 1972 a solicitor should tell his client of his right under para. (1)

to a certificate that the sum charged for costs is fair and reasonable and also that ss. 70, 71 and 72 of the Solicitors Act 1974 are the provisions which relate to taxation of costs, and that those provisions give the right to have the costs checked by an officer of the court. There is no need to send a copy of the provisions, nor should the solicitor risk attempting to summarise them: CLEMENT-DAVIS *v.* INTER GSA (1979) 123 S.J. 505, C.A.

2565. Disputed will—duty of solicitors—Law Society's recommendation

The plaintiffs were executors of the testatrix's will. The validity of the will was disputed by the defendants on the grounds of undue influence. Several requests were made by the defendant's solicitors to the first plaintiff, a solicitor, for a copy of the will but none was forthcoming. *Held*, the first plaintiff had not fully understood the implications of The Law Society's recommendation. In litigation over a will, the ruling principle was that every effort should be made by executors to avoid costly litigation and where there were suspicious circumstances surrounding a will it was right that full information should be given to those attacking the will. In this case the copy requested by the defendants ought reasonably to have been provided: LARKE *v.* NUGUS (1979) 123 S.J. 337, C.A.

2566. Fees—basis of taxation—telephone calls

On a taxation of a bill of costs in the Family Division, the appropriate rate for costing a solicitor's time spent on the telephone, instead of in personal interviews, is the hourly rate.

A firm of solicitors applied for a review of taxation of their bill of costs in a matrimonial matter. The solicitors had conducted various telephone calls in place of personal interviews with their clients and objected to these being taxed at the base rate. *Held*, that telephone calls made in place of personal attendances which achieve material progress in preparation for the trial are to be calculated on the hourly, and not flat rate, basis.

BWANAOGA *v.* BWANAOGA [1979] 2 All E.R. 105, Payne J.

2567. —— Law Society's publication—consideration by taxing master

The Law Society's publication *The Expense of Time* is a praiseworthy attempt to " establish the expense to the solicitor of doing his work " but it would be wrong to say that it had the seal of approval of the Royal Commission or the accountants' profession. The taxing master is not obliged to accede to the proposition that he should treat the publication as a guide in taxing solicitors' bills; nor, in a criminal legal aid case, is a solicitor entitled, in respect of his court attendance, to a mark-up for care and conduct in addition to his daily fee. Taxation of costs, together with market forces, provides an element of discipline which provides some resistance to uncontrolled increases in solicitors' expense rates; the publication, on the other hand, would provide for costs to " float on the actual expenses of the relevant firm, rather in the manner of an index-linked pension ": R. *v.* WILKINSON, *The Times*, November 29, 1979, Robert Goff J.

2568. —— unpaid—lien on client's documents. See GAMLEN CHEMICAL CO. (U.K.) *v.* ROCHEM, § 1661.

2569. Lay Observer

The Lay Observer has published, pursuant to s. 45 of the Solicitors Act 1974 (c. 47), his Fourth Annual Report for the year ending December 31, 1978. The report examines allegations made by or on behalf of members of the public concerning The Law Society's treatment of complaints about solicitors' conduct. The report is available from HMSO [40p].

2570. Negligence—duty of care—beneficiary's claim under will

[Wills Act 1837 (c. 26), s. 15.]

A solicitor may be liable in contractual negligence to his client; he may also be liable in tortious negligence not only to his client but to anyone towards whom a duty of care must be shown, such as a beneficiary under a will.

Solicitors who prepared a will and sent it for execution failed to warn T, the testator, that it should not be attested by a beneficiary's spouse. The will was attested by the residuary beneficiary's husband, and the gift of residue was therefore void. On the beneficiary's claim for damages, the solicitors admitted negligence but contended that a duty of care was owed only to the testator. *Held*, that the solicitors owed the beneficiaries a duty of care, there was a breach of that duty and the beneficiary had suffered loss. It was immaterial that the beneficiary had not relied upon the solicitor's skill since she was a person within the solicitors' direct contemplation as being likely to be injured by their failure to carry out the testator's instructions. The beneficiary therefore should recover by way of damages the benefits she would have been entitled to under the will. (*Ministry of Housing and Local Government* v. *Sharp* [1970] C.L.Y. 1493; *Dutton* v. *Bognor Regis Urban District Council* [1972] C.L.Y. 2352 and dictum of Lord Wilberforce in *Anns* v. *Merton London Borough Council* [1977] C.L.Y. 2030 applied; *Whittingham* v. *Crease* [1978] C.L.Y. 2825 and *Caltex Oil (Australia) Pty.* v. *The Dredge Willemstad* [1977] C.L.Y. 2009 considered.)

ROSS *v.* CAUNTERS [1979] 3 W.L.R. 605, Megarry V.-C.

2571. —— **expiry of time—whether client prejudiced.** See BROWES *v.* JONES & MIDDLETON (A FIRM), § 1666.

2572. —— **immunity—acceptance of any client.** See DEMARCO *v.* UNGARO, § 2110.

2573. **Practice.** See PRACTICE.

2574. **Undertaking to vendor—registration of title—claim by third party.** See DAMODARAN S/O RAMAN *v.* CHOE KUAN HIM, § 1567.

BOOKS AND ARTICLES. See *post*, pp. [11], [32].

STAMP DUTIES

BOOKS AND ARTICLES. See *post*, pp. [11], [32].

STATUTES AND ORDERS

2575. **Construction—statutory instrument—designation of priority schools—validity.** See LEWIS *v.* DYFED COUNTY COUNCIL, § 813.

2576. **Parliament.** See PARLIAMENT.

2576a. **Repeals**
STATUTE LAW (REPEALS) ACT 1976 (COLONIES) ORDER 1979 (No. 111) [10p], made under the Statute Law (Repeals) Act 1976 (c. 16), s. 3 (2); operative on February 27, 1979; extends the repeal of certain enactments that are no longer of practical utility to specified colonies.

2577. **Royal Assent**
The following Acts received the Royal Assent during 1979:
Administration of Justice (Emergency Provisions) (Scotland) Act 1979 (c. 19), March 22 [20p], § 2101.
Agricultural Statistics Act 1979 (c. 13), March 22 [30p], § 55.
Alcoholic Liquor Duties Act 1979 (c. 4), February 22 [£1.25], § 615.
Ancient Monuments and Archaeological Areas Act 1979 (c. 46), April 4 [£1.50], § 2605.
Appropriation Act 1979 (c. 24), April 4 [£1·25], § 2263.
Appropriation (No. 2) Act 1979 (c. 51), July 27 [£1·50], § 2264.
Arbitration Act 1979 (c. 42), April 4 [30p], § 95.
Banking Act 1979 (c. 37), April 4 [£1·50], § 149.
Capital Gains Tax Act 1979 (c. 14), March 22 [£2·75], § 1456.
Carriage by Air and Road Act 1979 (c. 28), April 4 [80p], § 234.
Charging Orders Act 1979 (c. 53), December 6 [50p], § 2115.
Confirmation to Small Estates (Scotland) Act 1979 (c. 22), March 29 [20p], § 1283.
Consolidated Fund Act 1979 (c. 20), March 22 [10p], § 2267.
Consolidated Fund (No. 2) Act 1979 (c. 56), December 20 [10p], § 2268.
Credit Unions Act 1979 (c. 34), April 4 [70p], § 1495.
Criminal Evidence Act 1979 (c. 16), March 22 [10p], § 429.
Crown Agents Act 1979 (c. 43), April 4 [90p], § 30.

Customs and Excise Duties (General Reliefs) Act 1979 (c. 3), February 22 [40p], § 618.

Customs and Excise Management Act 1979 (c. 2), February 22 [£2·50], § 619.

Education Act 1979 (c. 49), July 26 [10p], § 807.

Electricity (Scotland) Act 1979 (c. 11), March 22 [90p], § 829.

Estate Agents Act 1979 (c. 38), April 4 [90p], § 38.

European Assembly (Pay and Pensions) Act 1979 (c. 50), July 26 [40p], § 1151.

European Communities (Greek Accession) Act 1979 (c. 57), December 20 [10p], § 1152.

Exchange Equalisation Account Act 1979 (c. 30), April 4 [25p], § 2276.

Excise Duties (Surcharges or Rebates) Act 1979 (c. 8), February 22 [25p], § 625.

Films Act 1979 (c. 9), February 22 [10p], § 2203.

Finance Act 1979 (c. 25), April 4 [10p], § 2277.

Finance (No. 2) Act 1979 (c. 47), July 26 [90p], § 2278.

Forestry Act 1979 (c. 21), March 29 [20p], § 1342.

House of Commons (Redistribution of Seats) Act 1979 (c. 15), March 22 [10p], § 2014.

Hydrocarbon Oil Duties Act 1979 (c. 5), February 22 [70p], § 630.

Independent Broadcasting Authority Act 1979 (c. 35), April 4 [20p], § 2584.

Industry Act 1979 (c. 32), April 4 [25p], § 2668.

International Monetary Fund Act 1979 (c. 29), April 4 [25p], § 2280.

Isle of Man Act 1979 (c. 58), December 20 [80p], § 635.

Justices of the Peace Act 1979 (c. 55), December 6, 1979 [£1·75], § 1732.

Kiribati Act 1979 (c. 27), June 19 [25p], § 188.

Land Registration (Scotland) Act 1979 (c. 33), April 4 [70p], § 1564.

Leasehold Reform Act 1979 (c. 44), April 4 [10p], § 1611.

Legal Aid Act 1979 (c. 26), April 4 [40p], § 2161.

Matches and Mechanical Lighters Duties Act 1979 (c. 6), February 22 [30p], § 636.

Merchant Shipping Act 1979 (c. 39), April 4 [£2·00], § 2478.

Nurses, Midwives and Health Visitors Act 1979 (c. 36), April 4 [70p], § 1762.

Pensioners' Payments and Social Security Act 1979 (c. 48), July 26 [50p], § 2068.

Pneumoconiosis etc. (Workers' Compensation) Act 1979 (c. 41), April 4 [25p], § 2535.

Price Commission (Amendment) Act 1979 (c. 1), February 12 [20p], § 2284.

Prosecution of Offences Act 1979 (c. 31), April 4 [25p], § 539.

Public Health Laboratory Service Act 1979 (c. 23), March 29 [10p], § 2216.

Public Lending Right Act 1979 (c. 10), March 22 [30p], § 1673.

Representation of the People Act 1979 (c. 40), April 4 [20p], § 827.

Sale of Goods Act 1979 (c. 54), December 6 [£1·50], § 2396.

Shipbuilding Act 1979 (c. 59), December 20 [10p], § 2498.

Social Security Act 1979 (c. 18), March 22 [60p], § 2543.

Southern Rhodesia Act 1979 (c. 52), November 14 [20p], § 202.

Tobacco Products Duty Act 1979 (c. 7), February 22 [30p], § 645.

Vaccine Damage Payments Act 1979 (c. 17), March 22 [30p], § 2602.

Wages Councils Act 1979 (c. 12), March 22 [80p], § 1071.

Weights and Measures Act 1979 (c. 45), April 4 [£1·00], § 2802.

Zimbabwe Act 1979 (c. 60), December 20 [70p], § 209.

BOOKS AND ARTICLES. See *post*, pp. [11], [32].

STOCK EXCHANGE

2578. Designation of nominees

STOCK EXCHANGE (DESIGNATION OF NOMINEES) ORDER 1979 (No. 238) [10p], made under the Stock Exchange (Completion of Bargains) Act 1976 (c. 47), s. 7 (2); operative on March 19, 1979; the Secretary of State designates SEPON as a nominee of the Stock Exchange for the purposes of the 1976 Act.

STOCK EXCHANGE (DESIGNATION OF NOMINEES) (STAMP DUTY) ORDER 1979 (No. 370) [10p], made under the Finance Act 1976 (c. 40), s. 127 (5) (6); operative on March 30, 1979; designates Sepon Ltd. as a nominee of the Stock Exchange for the purposes of s. 127 of the 1976 Act.

2579. Stock Exchange (Completion of Bargains) Act 1976—commencement

STOCK EXCHANGE (COMPLETION OF BARGAINS) ACT 1976 (COMMENCEMENT) ORDER 1979 (No. 55 (C. 1)) [10p], made under the Stock Exchange (Completion of Bargains) Act 1976 (c. 47), s. 7 (4); operative on February 12, 1979; brings into force the 1976 Act.

2580. Stock transfer

STOCK TRANSFER (ADDITION OF FORMS) ORDER 1979 (No. 277) [25p], made under the Stock Transfer Act 1963 (c. 18), s. 3 (2); operative on April 4, 1979; amends Sched. 1 to the 1963 Act by adding forms for use, as alternatives to the stock transfer form prescribed therein, where securities are transferred to or from a nominee of the Stock Exchange.

TELECOMMUNICATIONS

2581. Broadcasting

WIRELESS TELEGRAPH (BROADCAST LICENCE CHARGES & EXEMPTION) (AMENDMENT) REGULATIONS 1979 (No. 841) [20p], made under the Wireless Telegraphy Act 1949 (c. 54), s. 2 (1) as extended by S.I. 1952 Nos. 1899, 1900; operative on July 31, 1979; amend S.I. 1970 No. 548 and substitute a new scale of fees for licences granted for the purpose of relaying sound or television programmes by cable from authorised broadcasting stations to the premises of users of the licensee's broadcast relay service. They also amend the definition of the licence.

2582. Independent Broadcasting Authority Act 1973—Channel Islands

INDEPENDENT BROADCASTING AUTHORITY ACT 1973 (CHANNEL ISLANDS) ORDER 1979 (No. 114) [20p], made under the Independent Broadcasting Authority Act 1973 (c. 19), ss. 39 (2) (3), 40 (3); operative on February 6, 1979; extends the 1973 Act with adaptations and modifications to the Channel Islands.

2583. Independent Broadcasting Authority Act 1978—Isle of Man

INDEPENDENT BROADCASTING AUTHORITY ACT 1978 (ISLE OF MAN) ORDER 1979 (No. 461) [10p], made under the Independent Broadcasting Authority Act 1978 (c. 43), s. 3 (3); operative on April 12, 1979; extends s. 1 of the 1978 Act to the Isle of Man thereby amending s. 2 (1) of the Independent Broadcasting Authority Act 1973 so as to extend the duration of the Authority's function until December 31, 1981.

2584. Independent Broadcasting Authority Act 1979 (c. 35)

This Act confers power on the Independent Broadcasting Authority to equip themselves to transmit an additional television broadcasting service.

S. 1 relates to the provision of transmitting equipment for a new television broadcasting service; s. 2 contains financial provisions; s. 3 deals with the short title and extent. The Act extends to Northern Ireland.

The Act received the Royal Assent on April 4, 1979, and came into force on that date.

2585. Post Office. See POST OFFICE.

2586. Telegraph

WIRELESS TELEGRAPHY ACT 1967 (PRESCRIBED FORMS, ETC.) REGULATIONS 1979 (No. 563) [25p], made under the Wireless Telegraphy Act 1967 (c. 72), ss. 1 (2), (5), 2 (3), (4) and (7), 13; operative on August 1, 1979; make new provision as to the information to be supplied by television dealers in place of the provisions contained in S.I. 1967 No. 1692.

2587. Television licences

WIRELESS TELEGRAPHY (BROADCAST LICENCE CHARGES AND EXEMPTION) (AMENDMENT) (NO. 2) REGULATIONS 1979 (No. 1490) [10p], made under the

Wireless Telegraphy Act 1949 (c. 54), s. 2 (1), as extended by S.I. 1952 Nos. 1899 and 1900; operative on November 24, 1979; raise the amount of the basic fee for television licences from £10 to £12 in the case of monochrome and from £25 to £34 in the case of colour.

2588. —— use of unlicensed television owned by defendant's spouse
[Wireless Telegraphy Act 1949 (c. 54), s. 1 (1).] D admitted to a television records officer that there was an unlicensed television in her home. She claimed that previous licences and the agreement with the television company were in her husband's name and she had no responsibility for the set. *Held*, allowing an appeal against acquittal, that a husband and wife both used a television within s. 1 (1) of the 1949 Act if they switched it on, even if it belonged only to one of them: MONKS v. PILGRIM [1979] Crim.L.R. 595, D.C.

ARTICLES. See *post*, p. [32].

TIME

2589. **Limitation of actions.** See LIMITATION OF ACTIONS.

TORT

2590. **Breach of statutory duty—local authority—inspection of foundations.** See MARSH v. BETSTYLE CONSTRUCTION CO. AND THE GREATER LONDON COUNCIL, § 1875.

2591. —— **statutory remedy available—closure of schools during strike.** See MEADE v. HARINGEY LONDON BOROUGH COUNCIL, § 816.

2592. **Building—defendant's actions causing damage—whether plaintiff entitled to meticulous repair.** See DODD PROPERTIES v. CANTERBURY CITY COUNCIL, § 657.

2593. **Crown proceedings.** See PRACTICE.

2594. **Damages.** See DAMAGES.

2595. **Deceit—false representation—parties entering form of marriage—measure of damages**
[Can.] In 1965 D, a male, married B. In 1970, while still married he went through a form of marriage with P, representing he was a bachelor. In 1971 P became pregnant, but lost the child and required an operation for hysterectomy. In 1976 P was served on behalf of D with decree nisi of the marriage of B to D: D then admitted to P he was married when he went through the marriage ceremony with P in 1970. Thereafter P suffered depression but continued to live with D until she asked D to leave in 1977, which he did. During most of their life together, P was in employment. However, while she still believed the marriage to be valid, she cancelled two insurance policies she held to give D $650 to make a down payment on a motor car. P claimed both special and general damages. *Held*, the deceit of D seriously prejudiced any hope of P for a proper marriage. She was entitled to special damages of $650, and also to general damages in the sum of $10,000 (*Wilkinson* v. *Downton* [1897] 2 Q.B. 57, *Janvier* v. *Sweeney* [1919] 2 K.B. 316 referred to): BEAULNE v. RICKETTS (1979) 96 D.L.R. (3d) 550, Alta.Sup.Ct.

2596. **Defamation.** See LIBEL AND SLANDER.

2597. **Interference with goods—obscene articles—whether unlawful.** See ROANDALE v. METROPOLITAN POLICE COMMISSIONER, § 518.

2598. **Negligence.** See NEGLIGENCE.

2599. **Nuisance.** See NUISANCE.

2600. **Passing off.** See TRADE MARKS AND TRADE NAMES.

2601. **Vaccine damage payments**
VACCINE DAMAGE PAYMENTS REGULATIONS 1979 (No. 432) [25p], made under the Vaccine Damage Payments Act 1979 (c. 17), ss. 2 (5), 3 (1) (b), 4 (1), 5 (2), 7 (5), 8 (3); operative on April 6, 1979; contain provisions relating to claims for payment made under s. 1 (1) of the 1979 Act, the information to

be given when claiming and for treating claims made prior to the passing of the Act as claims falling within s. 3 (1) of that Act.

VACCINE DAMAGE PAYMENTS (AMENDMENT) REGULATIONS 1979 (No. 1441) [10p], made under the Vaccine Damage Payments Act 1979, s. 1 (3); operative on December 13, 1979; amend S.I. 1979 No. 432 by adding a new regulation dealing with the situation where a person is disabled as a result of contracting a disease from a third party who was vaccinated against it.

2602. Vaccine Damage Payments Act 1979 (c. 17)

This Act provides for payments to be made in cases where severe disablement occurs as a result of vaccination against certain diseases.

S. 1 provides for payments to persons severely disabled by vaccination; s. 2 sets out the conditions of entitlement; s. 3 concerns the determination of claims; s. 4 deals with review of extent of disablement and causation by independent tribunals; s. 5 relates to reconsideration of determinations and recovery of payments in certain cases; s. 6 authorises payments to or for the benefit of disabled persons; s. 7 deals with payment, claims, etc., made prior to the Act; s. 8 empowers the Secretary of State to make regulations; s. 9 imposes a penalty for fraudulent statements; s. 10 relates to Scotland; s. 11 relates to Wales; s. 12 contains financial provisions; s. 13 deals with short title and extent. The Act extends to Northern Ireland and the Isle of Man.

The Act received the Royal Assent on March 22, 1979, and came into force on that date.

2603. Volenti non fit injuria. See NEGLIGENCE.

BOOKS AND ARTICLES. See *post*, pp. [11], [32].

TOWN AND COUNTRY PLANNING

2604. Advertisements—unauthorised—continuing offence

[Town and Country Planning (Control of Advertisements) Regulations 1969 (S.I. 1969 No. 1532); Town and Country Planning Act 1971 (c. 78), s. 109 (2).] E was convicted of displaying an advertisement board without planning consent. They took the advertisement down, but a week after their appeal against conviction failed, they replaced it. The magistrates dismissed a further complaint of continuing offence. The borough appealed. *Held*, dismissing the appeal, that it would be an abuse of language to regard the replacement as being a continuing offence; it was a fresh offence for which a new information could have been issued: ROYAL BOROUGH OF KENSINGTON AND CHELSEA v. ELMTON (1978) 246 E.G. 1011, D.C.

2605. Ancient Monuments and Archaelogical Areas Act 1979 (c. 46)

This Act consolidates and amends the law relating to ancient monuments and makes provision for the investigation, preservation and recording of matters of archaeological or historical interest.

Pt. I (ss. 1–32) relates to ancient monuments: s. 1 makes provision for a schedule of monuments; s. 2 deals with the control of works affecting scheduled monuments; s. 3 provides for the grant of scheduled monument consent by order of the Secretary of State; s. 4 sets out the duration, modification and revocation provisions of scheduled monument consent; s. 5 allows for the execution of works for preservation of a scheduled monument by the Secretary of State in cases of urgency; s. 6 grants powers of entry for inspection of scheduled monuments; s. 7 provides for compensation for refusal of scheduled monument consent; s. 8 allows for recovery of compensation under s. 7 where consent is subsequently given; s. 9 grants compensation where works affecting a scheduled monument cease to be authorised; s. 10 provides for compulsory acquisition of ancient monuments by the Secretary of State; s. 11 deals with acquisition by agreement or gift of ancient monuments; s. 12 grants power to place ancient monuments under guardianship; s. 13 sets out the effect of guardianship; s. 14 states the methods for terminating guardianship; s. 15 provides for the acquisition and guardianship of land in the vicinity of an ancient monument; s. 16 relates to the acquisition of easements and other similar rights over land in the vicinity of an ancient monument; s. 17

deals with agreements concerning ancient monuments and land in their vicinity; s. 18 outlines the powers of limited owners for the purposes of ss. 12, 16 and 17; s. 19 allows the public access to monuments under public control; s. 20 makes provision for public facilities in connection with ancient monuments; s. 21 provides for the transfer of ancient monuments between local authorities and the Secretary of State; s. 22 allows for the continued existence of Ancient Monuments Boards; s. 23 relates to the annual reports of the Ancient Monuments Boards; s. 24 concerns expenditure by the Secretary of State or local authorities on acquisition and preservation of ancient monuments; s. 25 allows for advice and superintendence by the Secretary of State; s. 26 empowers the Secretary of State to authorise entry on land believed to contain an ancient monument; s. 27 contains general provisions as to compensation for depreciation under Pt. I; s. 28 states the offence of damaging certain ancient monuments; s. 29 provides for compensation orders for damage to monuments under guardianship in England and Wales; s. 30 concerns disposal of land acquired under Pt. I; s. 31 deals with voluntary contributions towards expenditure under Pt. I; s. 32 contains interpretation provisions relating to Pt. I.

Pt. II (ss. 33–41) relates to archaeological areas: s. 33 deals with designation of areas of archaeological importance; s. 34 concerns the appointment of investigating authorities for areas of archaeological importance; s. 35 states the notice required of operations in areas of archaeological importance; s. 36 provides for the certificate to accompany operations notice under s. 35; s. 37 exempts certain operations from s. 35; s. 38 outlines the powers of investigating authorities to enter and excavate site of operations covered by an operations notice; s. 39 grants power to the investigating authority to investigate in advance of operations notice any site which may be acquired compulsorily; s. 40 sets out other powers of entry on site of operations covered by an operations notice; s. 41 concerns the interpretation of Pt. II.

Pt. III (ss. 42–65) contains miscellaneous and supplemental provisions: s. 42 places restrictions on the use of metal detectors; s. 43 grants power of entry for survey and valuation; s. 44 contains supplementary provisions with respect to powers of entry; s. 45 provides for expenditure on archaeological investigation; s. 46 allows for compensation for damage caused by the exercise of certain powers under this Act; s. 47 contains general provisions with respect to claims for compensation under the Act; s. 48 provides for recovery of grants for expenditure in conservation areas and on historic buildings; s. 49 enables the Secretary of State to make grants to the Architectural Heritage Fund; s. 50 applies the Act, with certain exceptions, to Crown land; s. 51 relates to ecclesiastical property; s. 52 relates to the application of the Act to the Isles of Scilly; s. 53 concerns monuments in territorial waters; s. 54 relates to the treatment and preservation of finds; s. 55 provides for proceedings for questioning validity of certain orders, etc.; s. 56 deals with the service of documents; s. 57 grants power to require information as to interests in land; s. 58 outlines offences by corporations; s. 59 concerns prosecution of offences in Scotland; s. 60 deals with regulations and orders under the Act; s. 61 is the general interpretation section; s. 62 makes special provision for Scotland; s. 63 makes special provision for Wales; s. 64 contains transitional provisions, consequential amendments and repeals; s. 65 contains the short title, commencement and extent. The Act does not extend to Northern Ireland.

The Act received the Royal Assent on April 4, 1979, and comes into force on days to be appointed.

2606. —— **commencement**

ANCIENT MONUMENTS AND ARCHAEOLOGICAL AREAS ACT 1979 (COMMENCE-MENT No. 1) ORDER 1979 (No. 786 (C. 18)) [10p], made under the Ancient Monuments and Archaeological Areas Act 1979 (c. 46), s. 65 (2); operative on July 16, 1979; brings into force ss. 48 and 49 of the Act.

2607. Appeal—procedure—time

[R.S.C., Ord. 55, r. 4 (3).] The decision letter of March 6, 1979, from the Secretary of State was received on March 7, 1979. The notice of appeal to the Divisional Court was lodged on April 4, 1979. The rules required appeal to be entered within 28 days from the decision. The question arose whether time ran from the date of the letter or the date it was received. *Held*, time ran from the date of the letter. Accordingly the appeal was invalid.

RINGROAD INVESTMENTS AND COURTBURN *v.* SECRETARY OF STATE FOR THE ENVIRONMENT [1979] J.P.L. 770, D.C.

2608. Change of use—division of single planning unit—conversion to flats—detrimental to character of house

[Town and Country Planning Act 1971 (c. 78), ss. 22 (1) (3) (*a*).]

The division of one house and grounds which form one planning unit constitutes a material change of use within s. 22 of the Town and Country Planning Act 1971.

A house was set in two acres of ground and formed part of a residential area of large houses. In 1965 the owner was granted planning permission to build a lodge and garages in the grounds on condition that it should not be occupied by anyone other than a close relative or member of the staff. In 1972 planning permission was granted to new owners to convert the lodge into two self-contained flats and garages. The flats were used as guest suites. In 1975 a new purchaser sought planning permission for separate and unrelated occupancy of the lodge. The planning authority refused permission, and the Secretary of State dismissed an appeal. The purchaser's appeal was allowed by the High Court judge. On appeal by the Secretary of State, held, allowing the appeal, that if the house and grounds were turned into separate dwellings for two or three families, even without alteration of the buildings, there was a material change of use, and the planning authority's decision should stand. (*Burdle* v. *Secretary of State for the Environment* [1972] C.L.Y. 3335 and *Ashbridge Investments* v. *Minister of Housing and Local Government* [1965] C.L.Y. 522 considered.)

WAKELIN *v.* SECRETARY OF STATE FOR THE ENVIRONMENT (1978) 77 L.G.R. 101, C.A.

2609. —— established use certificate—whether certificate conclusive

[Town and Country Planning Act 1971 (c. 78), s. 94 (7).]

An established use certificate is conclusive as to the use of a site from the date of its issue.

Per curiam: Great care should be exercised concerning the terms of an established use certificate otherwise an authority may be precluded from preventing a use for which planning permission would not have been granted.

In 1972 an established use certificate was issued specifying that the use of the site was for storing, sawing, resawing and disposing of timber in the round and for the storing, maintenance, repair and overhaul of vehicles and plant incidental to that use. The site was sold and in 1975 its character changed from rural to industrial use. Timber planks were stored in high stacks, concrete roads constructed and two buildings erected. Enforcement notices were served and at the inquiry the inspector reported that there had been a material change of use compared with the actual use prior to 1975. The Secretary of State quashed the notices on the basis that there had not been a material change of use from that specified in the certificate. The local authority appealed on the basis that the Secretary of State should have considered the actual use prior to 1975, not the use specified in the certificate. *Held*, the function of the certificate was to preclude the necessity of investigating the actual use of the land in determining whether there had been a material change in use. The certificate was conclusive as to the use of the site from the date of issue of the certificate.

BROXBOURNE BOROUGH COUNCIL *v.* SECRETARY OF STATE FOR THE ENVIRONMENT [1979] 2 All E.R. 13, D.C.

2610. —— permission for mineral excavations—disposal of waste materials on site —necessity for further planning permission

[Control of Pollution Act 1974 (c. 40), s. 5 (2).]

Where a licence to deposit wastes involves a use of land but is primarily concerned with the manner in which the waste should be deposited, no further planning permission is required.

In 1969 J Co. was granted a planning permission for opencast mineral excavations. Condition 4 of the permission required the site to be backfilled and condition 8 required the site to be worked in successive phases, each phase being restored to agricultural use when the next phase began. Condition 8 was never observed but some backfilling took place leaving 21 acres unfilled when excavations ceased. In 1978 C company purchased the land and was granted a disposal licence by the County Council to deposit various waste products including sewage sludge on the 21 acres. Condition 3 of the licence required an access road to be constructed, and conditions 7 and 8 required that walls and a base of impervious materials be built. The District Council applied for an order of certiorari to quash the disposal licence on the ground that no planning permission existed in relation to the intended use of the land as required by s. 5 (2) of the 1974 Act. The County Planning Officer deposed in an affidavit that the purpose of the restoration was to return the site to agricultural use and any material consistent with that use was acceptable. *Held,* dismissing the application, that (1) condition 8 of the planning permission had been irremediably breached but that the present occupiers could voluntarily comply with condition 4 (*Alexandra Transport Co.* v. *Secretary of State for Scotland* [1974] C.L.Y. 3714 distinguished); (2) the deposit of wastes involved a use of land, but the licence was concerned with the manner in which the waste should be deposited and further planning permission was not required; (3) the land to which the licence related was confined to the land where the waste was to be deposited and did not extend to the land where the access road was to be built; and (4) the word " fill " in condition 4 to the licence included materials which permitted the restored site to be used for agriculture.

R. v. Derbyshire County Council, *ex p.* North East Derbyshire District Council (1979) 77 L.G.R. 389, D.C.

2611. —— permission to convert to showroom—sale of different goods

New planning units cannot be created simply by dividing an existing planning unit and conveying one part to an owner or occupier different and separate from the owner or occupier of the remaining part.

On part of the area occupied, a petrol station and garage, stood a large building used as a workshop. Planning permission was granted to convert this workshop into a retail showroom, but no restriction was placed on the character or nature of the goods that could be sold in the retail showroom. Subsequently the appellants acquired an interest in the workshop (though not the remainder of the garage) and began to use it as a retail supermarket. The local authority served an enforcement notice. The Secretary of State upheld the notice against the appellants' appeal. The appellants appealed again on the grounds that a new planning unit had been created when they acquired the workshop and as its use was not expressly restricted, they could use it as a supermarket. *Held,* dismissing the appeal, that new planning units could not be created simply by dividing an existing planning unit and conveying one part of an owner or occupier different and separate from the owner-occupier of the remaining part. There was an implied restriction in the planning permission granted that the sales would be restricted to automobile products.

Kwik Save Discount Group v. Secretary of State for Wales (1979) 37 P. & C.R. 170, D.C.

2612. Compulsory purchase. See Compulsory Purchase.

2613. Conservation area—demolition of building—relevant considerations

[Town and Country Planning Act 1971 (c. 78) (as amended by Town and Country Amenities Act 1974 (c. 32), s. 1 (1)), ss. 55, 277 (5), 277A.]

The Secretary of State is entitled to take into consideration the merits of a proposed development in considering whether to give consent for the demolition of buildings.

The applicant local planning authority granted planning permission to itself for the redevelopment of a site. This included the demolition of buildings in a conservation area. The Secretary of State, following an inquiry, refused permission on the ground that the new buildings proposed would intrude to an unacceptable degree in the conservation area. The authority sought an order quashing this decision on the grounds that the Secretary of State was not entitled to consider the merits of the proposed development, that he had failed to consider properly the cost of preserving the buildings and that he had not considered the utility of a repaired building. *Held,* dismissing the application, that the Minister was entitled to consider the merits of the proposed development. The question of the cost of preserving the buildings had been taken into account, as had the utility of the repaired building. (*Kent Messenger* v. *Secretary of State for the Environment* [1976] C.L.Y. 2708 considered.)

RICHMOND-UPON-THAMES LONDON BOROUGH COUNCIL *v.* SECRETARY OF STATE FOR THE ENVIRONMENT (1979) 37 P. & C.R. 151, Sir Douglas Frank, Q.C.

2614. Control of office and industrial development

TOWN AND COUNTRY PLANNING (INDUSTRIAL DEVELOPMENT CERTIFICATES) REGULATIONS 1979 (No. 838) [30p], made under the Town and Country Planning Act 1971 (c. 78), ss. 67, 68 (2) and the Town and Country Planning (Scotland) Act 1972 (c. 52), ss. 65, 66 (2); operative on August 7, 1979; supersede S.I. 1972 No. 904, S.I. 1973 No. 149, S.I. 1977 Nos. 682 and 705 and broaden the scope of those Regulations to include employment office areas located in intermediate areas.

TOWN AND COUNTRY PLANNING (INDUSTRIAL DEVELOPMENT CERTIFICATES: EXEMPTION) ORDER 1979 (No. 839) [10p], made under the Town and Country Planning Act 1971 ss. 69, 287 and the Town and Country Planning (Scotland) Act 1972, ss. 67, 273; operative on August 7, 1979; provides that industrial development in England, Wales and Scotland will now require an industrial development certificate only: the industrial floor space created together with any related development does not exceed 50,000 square feet.

CONTROL OF OFFICE DEVELOPMENT (CESSATION) ORDER 1979 (No. 908) [10p], made under the Town and Country Planning Act 1971, s. 86 (1) as amended by the Town and Country Planning (Amendment) Act 1972 (c. 42), s. 5 (1) and the Control of Office Development Act 1977 (c. 40), s. 1; operative on August 6, 1979; provides for the cessation of the provisions of the 1971 Act relating to the control of office development in England and Wales.

2615. Development plans

TOWN AND COUNTRY PLANNING (REPEAL OF PROVISIONS No. 17) (HUMBERSIDE) ORDER 1979 (No. 328) [10p], made under the Town and Country Planning Act 1971 (c. 78), ss. 21 (2), 287; operative on April 16, 1979; repeals for the area of the County of Humberside the provisions of the 1971 Act relating to development plans which are contained in Pt. I of Sched. 5 and Sched. 6 to that Act.

2616. Enforcement notice—appeal—grounds of appeal not indicated

[Town and Country Planning Act 1971 (c. 78), ss. 28, 246.] The local authority served enforcement notices on the plaintiffs who wrote purportedly to appeal but giving no grounds of appeal or facts in their letter. The Department of the Environment replied that the appeal could not be entertained because the letter of appeal did not indicate the grounds of appeal. The Department refused to reopen the appeal and the plaintiffs applied to the High Court for a declaration that the letter of June was a good and valid notice of appeal. *Held,* the refusal to accept the appeal was a decision of the Minister and stood unless reversed by an appeal. By taking no action, the plaintiffs had abandoned their appeal and the matter could not now be reopened: WAIN AND L.D.R.S. *v.* SECRETARY OF STATE FOR THE ENVIRONMENT AND WALTHAM FOREST LONDON BOROUGH [1979] J.P.L. 231, Stocker J.

2617. —— change of use—intensification of existing use

The Secretary of State is not entitled to reach a conclusion where there is no sufficient evidence and where the inspector has made no such finding.

H owned a farm and was granted planning permission to erect a building to be used only for the storage of agricultural produce and farm implements in conjunction with the use of that farm. The local authority later took the view that there had been an intensification of H's activities and it served an enforcement notice on H alleging, *inter alia,* that H was using the building for the wholesale distribution of produce not grown on his farm. H appealed against the notice. In upholding the notice the Secretary of State said " [the activities] localised within the appeal building have constituted an intensification of this particular use which has so affected the character of the land as a whole as to amount to a material change of use." The Divisional Court dismissed an appeal by H. On appeal, *held,* the planning unit was the whole farm, but the evidence at the inquiry had been directed to the excessive use of the building, and there was no sufficient evidence on which a finding of intensification of the use of the farm as a whole could properly have been made. The inspector made no such finding and the Secretary of State had not been entitled to reach such a conclusion.

HILLIARD *v.* SECRETARY OF STATE FOR THE ENVIRONMENT (1979) 37 P. & C.R. 129, C.A.

2618. —— —— within use class—not development by material change of use
[Town and Country Planning (Use Classes) Order 1972 (S.I. 1972 No. 1385), art. 3.] An hotel, consisting of three adjoining houses, contained a small non-residents' bar by virtue of planning permission in 1974. In 1976 the appellant company widened the area of the bar open to non-residents. The Secretary of State deemed this to be a material change of use and served an enforcement notice. *Held,* allowing the appeal therefrom, that art. 3, which provides that the use of the subject property for any other purpose of the same class shall not be deemed to involve " development," applied. The enlargement of the non-residents' bar, whatever effect it might have on the locality, did not bring the hotel outside Class XI use "as a boarding or guest house, or an hotel providing sleeping accommodation ": EMMA HOTELS *v.* SECRETARY OF STATE FOR THE ENVIRONMENT (1979) 250 E.G. 157, D.C.

2619. —— inquiry—disagreement—finding of fact
[Town and Country Planning (Inquiries Procedure) Rules 1974 (S.I. 1974 No. 419).] The local authority served an enforcement notice alleging a material change of use from the storage of vans to the repair of motor vehicles. An appeal was lodged on the ground that the breach had occurred before the beginning of 1964. The inspector concluded that the activities which had been taking place prior to 1964 justified such a conclusion. The Secretary of State disagreed on the ground that the vehicle repair use which had taken place was ancillary and not a primary use. The question arose whether this was a finding of fact and so within r. 12 of the 1974 Rules or only a disagreement on a conclusion of fact. *Held,* whether or not such a distinction existed this disagreement came within r. 12. The matter would go back to the Secretary of State with an indication that he should give notice to the interested parties in accordance with r. 12 and reconsider his decision when he had had their representations: POLLOCK *v.* SECRETARY OF STATE FOR THE ENVIRONMENT AND GREENWICH LONDON BOROUGH [1979] J.P.L. 680, D.C.

2620. —— no safeguard of lawful use
[Town and Country Planning Act 1971 (c. 78), ss. 23 (9) and 246.] The appellant D was served with an enforcement notice requiring him to remedy a breach of control whereby he had changed a car repairing garage into a bus depot. The notice did not specify any safeguards to allow for any activities which might lawfully remain within the light industrial use for which the premises were zoned. *Held,* allowing the appeal from the respondent's decision to uphold the notice, the matter would be sent back to the respondent for consideration of the requirements of s. 23 (9): DAY *v.* SECRETARY OF STATE FOR THE ENVIRONMENT (1979) 251 E.G. 163, D.C.

2621. —— non-service—prejudice
[Town and Country Planning Act 1971 (c. 78), s. 88 (1) (*e*), (4) (*b*).] S was the freeholder of a site which included four buildings which he let to four different tenants, and which were used for industrial purposes. The local authority served an enforcement notice on S in respect of the whole site, and individual notices on each of the four tenants; no copy of any individual notice was served on S, who claimed that he had been substantially prejudiced; the Secretary of State found that there was no such prejudice. *Held,* dismissing S's appeal, that even accepting everything in S's favour up to the s. 88 (4) (*b*) point, the Secretary of State had expressed his findings, and the burden was on S to show that there was no evidence on which he could have reached his

conclusion, or that he had adopted an erroneous principle, the court could not interfere with his finding. In any event, however, the court was satisfied that there had been no prejudice to S: SKINNER *v.* SECRETARY OF STATE FOR THE ENVIRONMENT (1978) 247 E.G. 1179, D.C.

2622. —— planning unit—material change of use

Part of a ground floor of a mews house was used as a sauna prior to 1964. Later the use spread to the rest of the floor. An enforcement notice was served requiring the total discontinuance of the sauna use, but this was amended so that a use prior to 1964 was excluded from the terms of the notice. The question arose whether the Secretary of State had addressed himself to the correct planning unit and whether he had the power of amendment. The borough applied for the decision to be quashed on the ground that he had failed to consider whether there had been a material change of use in the whole ground floor, which was the correct planning unit. *Held*, the Secretary of State had looked at the whole of the ground floor at the date of the enforcement notice. He had properly exercised his discretion. The decision was not open to review: CAMDEN LONDON BOROUGH *v.* SECRETARY OF STATE FOR THE ENVIRONMENT AND ALLEN MARSTON [1979] J.P.L. 311, C.A.

2623. —— scrap-yard—immunity

[Town and Country Planning Act 1971 (c. 78), s. 88 (1) (*d*).] In about 1958 S started a firewood business on land rented by his grandfather. He also began to collect scrap metal there and sell it. In 1965 the grandfather died, and in 1967 S bought the freehold. In 1968 he sought planning permission to use the land as a scrap-yard; this was refused, as was his application for an Established User Certificate in 1975. In August 1975 an enforcement notice was served, requiring S to stop using the land for scrap metal, and S appealed to the Secretary of State on the ground that the breach of planning control occurred before the beginning of 1964. The Secretary of State rejected S's arguments, saying that (1) S had not discharged the onus of proof that the alleged use was carried on before 1964; and (2) it was unlikely to have commenced on a commercial scale before 1965. He also accepted the inspector's conclusion that the steps required by the enforcement notice did not exceed what was necessary to remedy the breach of planning control. S appealed, saying that the steps went beyond what was necessary, and that the Secretary had misdirected himself in not taking account of the extent to which the activities forbidden by the notice had taken place before December 31, 1963. *Held*, dismissing the appeal, the Secretary had found that S had utterly failed to discharge the onus of proof on him, and whatever might have been the circumstances prior to the end of 1963, nothing of significance in relation to scrap metal was going on then which prevented his conclusion that he could ignore it. He had considered all the circumstances, and had not erred in law: STANTON *v.* SECRETARY OF STATE FOR THE ENVIRONMENT (1978) 248 E.G. 227, D.C.

2624. —— Secretary of State's decision

The local authority served an enforcement notice on the appellants alleging a breach of planning control by use of the land for office purposes, instead of residential purposes. The Secretary of State proposed to extend the period for compliance to one year. The owners applied for the decision to be quashed. *Held*, that it was entirely a matter for the Secretary of State having taken into account all the relevant matters to decide which was the proper course to adopt. All the issues in this case were matters of fact or expert opinion not law: MOLDDENE *v.* SECRETARY OF STATE FOR THE ENVIRONMENT [1979] J.P.L. 177, D.C.

2625. —— stop notice—incorporation of enforcement notice

[Town and Country Planning Act 1971 (c. 78), ss. 87 (6), 90 (1).] BS managed a stadium in Bristol, which was used for football matches and greyhound racing. A substantial project to adapt the stadium for use as a motor-cycle racing circuit was in hand when on April 7, 1977, B served an enforcement notice and a stop notice on BS. B successfully prosecuted BS for contravening the stop notice, and BS appealed on the grounds that (1) the enforcement notice only referred specifically to some of the particular operations complained of and was therefore ineffective; (2) unless the enforcement notice was effective, the stop notice would also be ineffective; (3) the stop notice failed to specify the operations objected to. *Held,* dismissing the appeal, the general activity complained of is the only requisite of an enforcement notice under s. 87 (6), and where (as here) the stop notice incorporates the terms of the enforcement notice a deficiency of particularity in the stop notice can be validated and cured by the fact that the language of the enforcement notice can be relied upon (*Miller-Mead* v. *Minister of Housing and Local Government* [1963] C.L.Y. 3406 considered): BRISTOL STADIUM v. BROWN (1979) 252 E.G. 803, D.C.

2626. ——— **use as a tip—unauthorised tipping prior to 1964**

Planning permission was granted in 1950 to use land as a tip. A condition was imposed that materials to be deposited would be approved by the local authority. Unauthorised tipping occurred prior to 1964 and without enforcement and in 1976 the local authority informed the owners what materials could be deposited. An enforcement notice was served in 1975. which the appellants applied to have quashed. *Held,* that the Secretary of State was not bound to adopt the view that there must have been some formal consent at some stage by the local authority to the then owner; (2) the council could take enforcement notices in respect of the unauthorised deposits after 1964 despite the deposits before that date. The enforcement notices should be upheld: J. F. BILBOE v. SECRETARY OF STATE FOR THE ENVIRONMENT AND WEST LANCASHIRE DISTRICT COUNCIL [1979] J.P.L. 100, D.C.

2627. Gypsy encampments—acquisition—suitability—Minister's decision contrary to inspector's report

[Caravan Sites Act 1968 (c. 52).] A compulsory purchase order was made under the Caravan Sites Act 1968 to acquire the site for the accommodation of gypsies. The council had investigated and compared five other sites. An inquiry was held and the inspector considered the proposed site the worst. He recommended that the order should not be confirmed. The Secretary of State approved the order. The owners applied for the decision to be quashed. *Held,* the Minister had wrongly regarded the suitability of the other sites as irrelevant, and if he had considered them he had not set out adequately his reasons for disagreeing. Decision quashed: BROWN AND GILSTON ESTATES v. SECRETARY OF STATE FOR THE ENVIRONMENT [1979] J.P.L. 454, Forbes J.

2628. Inquiry—natural justice—inquiry procedure

[Town and Country Planning Appeals (Determination by Appointed Persons (Inquiries and Procedure)) Rules 1974 (S.I. 1974 No. 420), r. 14.] The applicant respondent applied for permission to build a new house on land for which previous permission had lapsed in 1963. The subject land already contained a house which he found too small for his purposes. The appellant authority refused permission as being contrary to the development plan. On appeal the inspector gave permission as an exceptional case, taking the view that the present house on the site was of such quality that it should not be enlarged and that the applicant should be allowed to build a new and larger house separately on the site. The appellant was discouraged from calling expert architectural evidence in rebuttal; it appealed on the grounds that (1) new expert evidence should have been allowed; and (2) under the rules, it had not been notified of the new evidence upon which the inspector relied after a view of the site. *Held,* dismissing the appeal, matters of aesthetic taste or common sense do not require expert evidence. The view was not " new evidence " within the meaning of the rule. Procedure at inquiries should not become too technical. There had been no breach of natural justice and the inspector came to a reasonable and just conclusion: WINCHESTER CITY COUNCIL v. SECRETARY OF STATE FOR THE ENVIRONMENT (1979) 251 E.G. 259, C.A.

2629. Lands Tribunal decision

LOROMAH ESTATES v. HARINGEY LONDON BOROUGH (1978) 38 P. & C.R. 234 (in 1971 the authority made a revocation order under s. 45 of the Town and

Country Planning Act 1971 revoking a grant of planning permission to the plaintiff company. Six months later the revocation order was confirmed by the Minister. The plaintiff company sought compensation under s. 164 for depreciation and, *inter alia*, for bank interest payable through non-payment of compensation between 1971 and 1978, when the case was heard. *Held*, that (1) the claim for depreciation was acceptable; (2) the claim for interest was totally inadmissible: the alleged loss of the use of compensation could not be said to be attributable to the revocation order).

2630. New towns

NEW TOWNS (LIMIT ON BORROWING) ORDER 1979 (No. 204) [10p], made under the New Towns Act 1965 (c. 59), ss. 43 and 53, as amended by the New Towns Act 1975 (c. 42), s. 1, and the New Towns Act 1977 (c. 23), s. 1; operative on March 2, 1979; specifies a new limit for the total of the sums outstanding at any one time in respect of the principal of sums advanced by the Secretary of State, out of public funds, to development corporations in England, Scotland and Wales, and to the Commission for the New Towns, and of sums borrowed by those bodies under statutory powers.

2631. Northern Ireland. See NORTHERN IRELAND.

2632. Planning permission—appeal—sewerage

[Water Act 1973 (c. 37), s. 16.] W applied for planning permission to develop residentially a site adjacent to land which they were already developing. The land was white land on the development plan but shown as a growth area on the strategic plan for the South East. The Secretary of State accepted the inspector's recommendation for refusal. The applicants applied to the High Court for the decision to be quashed. *Held*, (1) the Secretary of State had given adequate reasons; (2) the contention failed that the Secretary of State had taken into account alleged inadequacies of the present sewerage system but had failed to take into account the duty of the Water Authority under the Water Act 1973, s. 16. The duty to provide sewers did not arise until planning permission was granted: GEORGE WIMPEY AND CO. *v.* SECRETARY OF STATE FOR THE ENVIRONMENT AND MAIDSTONE DISTRICT COUNCIL [1978] J.P.L. 773, Forbes J.

2633. —— —— whether adequate consideration and reasons given

[Town and Country Planning Act 1971 (c. 78), s. 245.] After the third refusal in five years by the appellant authority of planning permission for extension of offices in a designated residential area, the respondent company appealed successfully to the Secretary of State. The latter did not, in his written decision, refer expressly to a draft district plan which had formed the basis for the authority's refusal of planning permission. The authority appealed on the grounds that (1) the Secretary of State failed to consider the plan; and (2) he failed to give adequate reasons for his decision. *Held*, dismissing the appeal, in the circumstances it was clear that the Secretary of State had given due consideration to all relevant matters and had given adequate reasons, despite the "unhappy error" by which he failed to mention the plan: SHEFFIELD CITY COUNCIL *v.* SECRETARY OF STATE FOR THE ENVIRONMENT (1979) 251 E.G. 165, Drake J.

2634. —— conditions—no reasons given—reasons ascertained by court

[Control of Office and Industrial Development Act 1965 (c. 33) (as amended by Town and Country Planning Act 1968 (c. 72), s. 106, Sched. 9, para. 62), ss. 6 (4), 8 (3).]

Where by omission no reasons are given for a condition attached to planning permission, the court may ascertain them by looking at all the surrounding circumstances in which the permission was granted.

P Co. were leasehold owners of a building built in 1966 for warehouses but never used as such. In 1971 they were let for occupation as offices to the Inner London Executive Council of the National Health Service ("the Executive Council"). In March 1971 the Secretary of State for the Environment issued to the Executive Council an office development permit subject to a condition that the development should be used by the Executive Council only. In April 1971, the defendant council issued a planning permission subject to the same conditions without any limitation as to duration. They certified that the condition was one they could and would have imposed apart from the provisions of Pt. I of the Control of Office and Industrial Development Act 1965 and ss. 85 and 86 of the Town and Country Planning Act 1968. No reasons were given. The information in the planning permission was to the effect that should a scheme for residential development of other premises owned by P Co. and used as offices be carried out, that modification of the conditions would be considered. P Co. sought a declaration that the certificate was *ultra vires* and void, on the ground that one consideration in imposing it was the desire to induce P Co. to give up their existing office use rights in other premises. *Held*, looking at all the surrounding circumstances, that the certification would have been *ultra vires* if that had been its purpose. However, on the facts, office use was contrary to the development plan for the area, and had only been granted because of the special needs of the Executive Council, whose staff mostly lived in the area. Accordingly, the imposition of the condition was valid. (Dictum of Lord Denning in *Pyx Granite Co.* v. *Ministry of Housing and Local Government* [1958] C.L.Y. 3343; dictum of Megaw J. in *Hanks* v. *Minister of Housing and Local Government* [1963] C.L.Y. 397 and *Poppetts' (Caterers)* v. *Maidenhead Corp.* [1970] C.L.Y. 1531 applied; *Slough Estates* v. *Slough Borough Council (No. 2)* [1970] C.L.Y. 2775 distinguished.)

R.K.T. INVESTMENTS *v.* HACKNEY LONDON BOROUGH COUNCIL (1978) 36 P. & C.R. 442, Sir Douglas Frank, Q.C.

2635. —— —— **power to secure compliance—promissory estoppel**

Where an applicant for planning permission gives an undertaking to fulfil a condition, and planning permission is granted conditionally upon that undertaking, the applicant is estopped from denying that there is power to require compliance with it.

H Co. applied for planning permission to extract sand and gravel from their land. Permission was refused and H Co. appealed to the Secretary of State. The primary objection was in relation to the traffic effects. H Co. undertook to provide visibility splays to give satisfactory sight lines for traffic; although they did not own the necessary land, they claimed that the owner was prepared to dispose of it. The Secretary of State granted planning permission subject to the condition that the visibility splays would be provided. A preservation association applied to quash the decision on the ground that the Secretary of State could not have been satisfied that the condition would be observed. *Held*, dismissing the application, that the undertaking was not one which no reasonable body would have accepted; where planning permission was granted in reliance on, and in terms broad enough to embrace an undertaking, the applicant would be estopped by promissory estoppel from later saying that there was no power to secure compliance with it. (*Hughes* v. *Metropolitan Railway* (1877) 2 App.Cas. 439, H.L., *Central London Property Trust* v. *High Trees House* (1947) C.L.C. 5601, *H. Clark (Doncaster)* v. *Williamson* [1965] C.L.Y. 3073, *Durham Fancy Goods* v. *Michael Jackson (Fancy Goods)* [1968] C.L.Y. 203, and *Crabb* v. *Arun District Council* [1975] C.L.Y. 1191 applied.)

AUGIER *v.* SECRETARY OF STATE FOR THE ENVIRONMENT (1979) 38 P. & C.R. 219, D.C.

2636. —— —— **void—Secretary of State's obligation to grant permission**

Planning permission for residential development was refused because of lack of sewage and highway facilities. The Secretary of State rejected an inspector's recommendation that the appeal be allowed subject to a condition that the houses should not be occupied in advance of the provision of infrastructure. The decision was quashed on the ground that there was no evidence to support the Secretary of State's assertion that the proposed condition was impractical. The owners subsequently applied to the High Court for a declaration that the Secretary of State was obliged to grant planning permission since the reason for refusal had disappeared. *Held*, it was open to the Secretary of State to rewrite his decision. There was no obligation to grant planning permission:

PRICE BROTHERS (RODE HEATH) v. SECRETARY OF STATE FOR THE ENVIRONMENT [1979] J.P.L. 387, Forbes J.

2637. —— —— **whether land " under control " of applicant**
[Town and Country Planning Act 1971 (c. 78), s. 30 (1) (a).] The applicant company appealed from the Secretary of State's refusal of permission for development where access was required for construction traffic across land over which the applicant had a revocable licence of a way from the dominant owner. *Held,* allowing the appeal, the Secretary of State was correct in holding that the character of the applicant's control over the access land was not expedient for the purpose of implementing the condition as to access to be imposed upon permission and the test for " control " under s. 30 (1) (a) was a question of fact and degree. But the possibility of imposing a negative condition preventing the use of particular roads for access under s. 29 should have been considered. Appeal allowed on that ground: GEORGE WIMPEY & CO. v. NEW FOREST DISTRICT COUNCIL (1979) 250 E.G. 249, Sir Douglas Frank, Q.C.

2638. —— **considerations—natural justice**
L had received outline planning permission to develop a site by building 23 houses on it and later applied for approval of certain matters which had been reserved by the original permission. In November 1976 L had a meeting with the Council's planning officers, to discuss, and, if possible, agree on, the reserved matter which were to be submitted for approval. Approval was refused because the Council said that it had not been given enough detail, and that the proposed rerouting of a bridleway was unsatisfactory. Both parties accepted, however, that the bridleway would have to be rerouted. The inspector, on the parties' written representations because the siting of the proposed roads was unsatisfactory and if the bridleway were rerouted the " delightful rural character " of the area would suffer. L appealed. *Held,* allowing the appeal, (1) the parties had been *ad idem* on the siting of the roads, and had therefore advanced no arguments on the details: it was contrary to natural justice that the application should fail on a ground that was quite outside any issue appearing on the documents without giving L a chance to be heard; and (2) as to urbanisation, the Council had recognised that this was inevitable when they granted outline planning permission, and they could not resile from this: LEWIS THIRKELL v. SECRETARY OF STATE FOR THE ENVIRONMENT (1978) 248 E.G. 685, Willis J.

2639. —— —— **supply sources**
BH applied for planning permission to extract sedge peat from his land, which was grade one agricultural land. The inspector produced a report in which he said that a large area of peat deposit in Yorkshire was nearer BH's main customer than the appeal site and provided a reasonable alternative source of peat. The Secretary of State, acting on the report, refused permission. *Held,* allowing BH's appeal, further evidence showed that the peat available in Yorkshire was of the wrong type and that the inspector had failed to consider other important factors such as availability, suitability and cost. Accordingly there was no evidence on which the inspector could have reached his conclusion: BANKS HORTICULTURAL PRODUCTS v. SECRETARY OF STATE FOR THE ENVIRONMENT (1979) 252 E.G. 811, Phillips J.

2640. —— **economic viability—inspector's decision**
Where an inspector, in refusing an appeal against the refusal of outline planning permission, states in his decision that he has considered road safety limits, economic factors and market demand, these may be relevant considerations in the sense that because of severe design constraints it is possible that an acceptable scheme cannot be devised.
An inspector was appointed to determine an appeal against the refusal of outline planning permission for the erection of five houses. The inspector, dismissing the appeal, stated that he was uncertain that a scheme could be designed so as to take into account road safety requirements, economic factors and market demand. In addition he failed to mention access plans which had been adduced in evidence. On application to quash the decision, *held,* refusing

the application, that these matters were relevant in the sense that because of severe design constraints there was a possibility that a suitable scheme could not be devised; the inspector need make no mention in his decision of the evidence he had heard. (*Brighton Borough Council* v. *Secretary of State for the Environment* [1979] C.L.Y. 2642, *Niarchos (London)* v. *Secretary of State for the Environment* [1978] C.L.Y. 2902, and *Sovmots Investments* v. *Secretary of State for the Environment* [1976] C.L.Y. 307 considered.)

WALTERS *v.* SECRETARY OF STATE FOR WALES (1978) 77 L.G.R. 529, Sir Douglas Frank, Q.C.

2641. —— **extension of duration—principles**

Outline planning permission was granted. An application was made for extension of the life of the planning permission. Permission was refused. On appeal the inspector granted permission on the ground that the onus was on the planning authority to show that since the initial grant there had been some material change in the planning policy. The Peak Park Joint Planning Board applied to the High Court on the grounds that the inspector had erred in debarring himself from looking at the matter afresh. *Held*, Circular 17/69 advised that planning permissions should be renewed unless, *inter alia*, there had been a change in planning circumstances. This was *ultra vires*. In this case however the inspector had properly considered the matter on the information before him. He had to decide whether the case alleged by the local planning authority was properly made out. The Board had themselves stated that the issue was whether there had been a material change of circumstances and they could not now change their ground. The question was whether he had dealt sufficiently with the change of circumstances alleged. The inspector had dealt adequately with this question. Appeal dismissed: PEAK PARK JOINT PLANNING BOARD *v.* SECRETARY OF STATE FOR THE ENVIRONMENT AND KAY [1979] J.P.L. 618, Sir Douglas Frank Q.C.

2642. —— **financial considerations—listed building to benefit from development**

The trustees of a private school applied for planning permission to develop an unused area of its playing fields for building houses and flats. The main building of the school, elsewhere and in a conservation area, was listed grade II. On appeal against the refusal of permission by the borough council the inspector granted permission, *inter alia*, on the ground of the special financial factor that the school building would very probably benefit from the development profit by way of urgently needed repairs estimated to cost £100,000. The council applied to the High Court to quash the inspector's decision. *Held*, dismissing the application, that the restoration and maintenance of the listed school building was a planning consideration, albeit a financial one, properly taken into account: BRIGHTON BOROUGH COUNCIL *v.* SECRETARY OF STATE FOR THE ENVIRONMENT (1979) 249 E.G. 747, Sir Douglas Frank, Q.C.

2643. —— **flooding problems—effects of proposed improvements**

The owners of two adjoining sites, A and B, applied for planning permission which was refused because of flooding problems. An inquiry was held. The Secretary of State dismissed the appeals. *Held*, (1) the Minister had not considered whether the proposed balancing lagoon would have been acceptable as a permanent solution to the problem of surface drainage; (2) once one considered site A, independently of site B, it was necessary to consider the lagoon as a permanent solution. The decision must be quashed: GEORGE WIMPEY AND CO. *v.* SECRETARY OF STATE FOR THE ENVIRONMENT [1978] J.P.L. 776, Sir Douglas Frank, Q.C.

2644. —— **green belt—inspector's decision**

Application was to erect eight dwelling-houses. Permission was refused although permission for three houses had already been granted. The principal reason for refusal was the green belt consideration. The appellants attacked the decision on the ground that the inspector had failed to deal with the point that the site had ceased to be green belt. *Held*, that the inspector's reasons were reasonably intelligible to the recipient of the letter and he had clearly dealt with the points raised: SHEPPERTON BUILDERS *v.* THE SECRETARY OF STATE FOR THE ENVIRONMENT [1979] J.P.L. 102, Sir Douglas Frank, Q.C.

2645. —— —— whether inspector took account of improper matters

[Town and Country Planning Act 1971 (c. 78), s. 245.] On appeal under the section against the inspector's refusal of permission, the applicant argued that the inspector had taken account of the prematurity of the application before approval of the local structure plan. *Held*, confirming the refusal, the inspector had founded his decision on the fact that the subject land was green belt and had not been swayed by the possibility of changes in a proposed structure plan: CHARLES CHURCH *v.* SECRETARY OF STATE FOR THE ENVIRONMENT (1979) 251 E.G. 674, Sir Douglas Frank Q.C.

2646. —— gypsies—formal consultations

[Caravan Sites Act 1968 (c. 52), ss. 6 (1), 8 (1); Town and Country Planning Act 1971 (c. 78), s. 29 (1).]

There is no obligation upon a planning authority to hold formal consultations with any interested body prior to granting planning permission.

In 1968 the council consulted many interested bodies, including representatives of the gypsy community, prior to selecting a site for a gypsy encampment; but in due course planning permission for the selected site was set aside. Thereafter the council continued its search for a site and held informal discussions, *inter alia*, with gypsy representatives. Eventually in 1976 it granted itself planning permission for another site. A nearby resident sought an order of certiorari quashing the grant on the grounds that the council had failed to have regard to a material consideration, namely that the gypsies opposed the site selected, and that it was incumbent upon the council to hold formal discussions with the gypsies prior to granting planning permission. *Held*, dismissing the application, that no such obligation existed and that by holding informal discussions the council had paid regard to the material considerations. (*R.* v. *Hereford Corporation, ex p. Harrower* [1970] C.L.Y. 1608 and *R.* v. *Hendon Rural District Council, ex p. Chorley* [1933] 2 K.B. 696 applied.)
R. *v.* SHEFFIELD CITY COUNCIL, *ex p.* MANSFIELD (1978) 37 P. & C.R. 1, D.C.

2647. —— inquiry—natural justice

Application for planning permission to erect a bungalow was refused. The site was in an area of outstanding natural beauty. At an inquiry into the refusal it was argued that the bungalow would enhance the appearance of the site. This argument was rejected by the inspector who upheld the refusal. B applied to the High Court for the decision to be quashed on the ground that it was unreasonable and also that there had been a breach of the rules of natural justice, in that he had been unable to comment on the photographs submitted by representatives of the local planning authority. *Held*, whether or not it was better to leave ugly buildings on land than permit the erection of a dwelling-house, was a purely planning question and the inspector's decision was not to be interfered with. The planning authority swore that the photographs had been submitted in chief without objection from the plaintiff. No breach of the rules of natural justice had taken place: BEHRMAN *v.* SECRETARY OF STATE FOR THE ENVIRONMENT AND EAST DEVON DISTRICT COUNCIL [1979] J.P.L. 677, Forbes J.

2648. —— mistake of fact—adequate reasons

Planning permission to build a single dwelling-house was refused. An inquiry was held and the inspector made a mistake of fact as to the location of the site. The Secretary of State refused the appeal following the inspector's recommendation. On application to quash the decision, *held*, that the inspector had concentrated his mind on the crucial issues and had given adequate reasons to comply with the rules: HOPE *v.* SECRETARY OF STATE FOR THE ENVIRONMENT [1979] J.P.L. 104, Sir Douglas Frank, Q.C.

2649. —— refusal—valid planning considerations

The appellant sought planning permission to use part of their warehouse for direct retail trade. The inspector recommended refusal, and the Secretary of State accepted the recommendation and noted that permission had been granted in relation to a similar application on a site two miles away. He feared that a substantial number of " cash and carry " warehouses might have a damaging effect on the established shopping centres nearby. *Held*, on application to set aside the Secretary of State's decision, (1) the possible consequence on other sites was a material consideration; (2) the Secretary of State could rely on grounds not relied upon by his inspector provided that he had evidence; (3) there was no burden of proof issue in a planning appeal. Application dismissed. (*Collis Radio* v. *Secretary of State for the Environment* [1975] C.L.Y. 3352 followed): TEMPO DISCOUNT WAREHOUSE v. ENFIELD LONDON BOROUGH AND THE SECRETARY OF STATE FOR THE ENVIRONMENT [1979] J.P.L. 98, Sir Douglas Frank, Q.C.

2650. —— regional planning policies—natural justice

Two companies owned a site for which they sought planning permissions for residential development. The inspector recommended that the main application be allowed subject to conditions, but the Secretary of State rejected the recommendation. The applicants applied to the High Court for the decision to be quashed on 12 different grounds. *Held,* (1) the " Strategic Plan for the North West " and the Government response were ambiguous and the Minister could resolve it as he chose; (2) the Secretary's reasons for not following the inspector's recommendation were not sufficient in relation to a number of matters. The decision should be quashed, whether or not substantial prejudice had occurred: SEDDON PROPERTIES v. SECRETARY OF STATE FOR THE ENVIRON-MENT AND MACCLESFIELD BOROUGH COUNCIL [1978] J.P.L. 835, Forbes J.

2651. —— representations by council—existing use rights—estoppel

[Town and Country Planning Act 1971 (c. 78), ss. 53, 94; Town and Country Planning (Use Classes) Order 1972 (S.I. 1972 No. 1385), Sched., Class IX.]

The equitable principle of " proprietary estoppel " is confined, with some exceptions, to rights and interests created in and over the land of another and is inapplicable to a landowner spending money to take advantage of existing (or supposedly existing) rights over his own land.

The plaintiffs bought a site with the buildings of a disused factory on it, which had been used for the production of fish fertiliser and other products. The plaintiffs intended to carry on there the business of manufacturing fish products, which involved some substantial rebuilding. A representative of the chief planning officer appeared satisfied that the plaintiffs had an " established user right." The plaintiffs then began their rebuilding to the knowledge of the council, but were asked to submit an application under the 1971 Act as a " pure formality." The applications were refused, and the plaintiffs challenged the council's right to do so. On appeal by the plaintiffs, *held,* dismissing the appeal, that, *inter alia,* (1) the principle of " proprietary estoppel " was confined to rights and interests created in and over the land of another; (2) in general an estoppel could not be raised to prevent the exercise of a statutory discretion or performance of a statutory duty, and this case did not fall within one of the exceptions. (*Ramsden* v. *Dyson* (1866) L.R. 1 H.L. 129 and *Crabb* v. *Arun District Council* [1975] C.L.Y. 1191 applied; *Evenden* v. *Guildford City Association Football Club* [1975] C.L.Y. 1143 distinguished; dictum of Lord Widgery C.J. in *Brooks and Burton* v. *Secretary of State for the Environment* [1976] C.L.Y. 2699 affirmed.)

WESTERN FISH PRODUCTS v. PENWITH DISTRICT COUNCIL (1978) 77 L.G.R. 185, C.A.

2652. —— unauthorised grant—ratification—ultra vires—district and county council

[Local Government Act 1972 (c. 70), Sched. 16; Town and Country Planning General Development Order 1973 (S.I. 1973 No. 31).] Tesco and the Co-op were vying for a hypermarket site in South Wales. It was unclear whether it fell to the district or county council to determine the issue of planning permission. The district council resolved to put the matter before the county council. Then the district clerk purported to grant permission to Tesco; this action was ratified by the district but not by the county council. The Co-op failed before Sir Douglas Frank, Q.C., to get a declaration of invalidity of the grant. *Held,* allowing the appeal, the purported grant of planning permission was *ultra vires* and void. The legislation dividing the district and county jurisdiction was complex, but it was clear in this case that no grant should have been made without county council consultation. The grant was void even in the hands of the bona fide holders, Tesco. It could not be ratified. *Per* Lord Denning M.R.: planning law exists to protect the public interest and cannot be pre-empted without authority (*Slough Estates* v. *Slough Borough Council* [1970] C.L.Y. 2775 distinguished; *Ashbury Railway Carriage and Iron Co.* v. *Richie* (1875) L.R. 7 H.L. 653 followed): ATT.-GEN., *ex rel.* CO-OPERATIVE RETAIL SERVICES v. TAFF-ELY BOROUGH COUNCIL (1979) 250 E.G. 757, C.A.

2653. Public inquiry—inspector's report deficient—admissibility of further evidence

Planning permission to build 226 units of residential property on 17 acres was refused. The local authority stated at an inquiry that, *inter alia*, having regard to the amount of land already released for development, it was considered that the need for housing development on this site was insufficient to outweigh the objections. The inspector recommended that the appeal should be allowed and the Minister accepted the inspector's recommendation. The local authority applied for the decision to be quashed on the grounds that the inspector had not adequately dealt with the question of housing need. The trial judge quashed the decision. The developer appealed. *Held,* there had been a material omission and error in that the inspector had not put in his report the evidence of the principal planning officer which might well have influenced the Minister's decision: EAST HAMPSHIRE DISTRICT COUNCIL v. SECRETARY OF STATE FOR THE ENVIRONMENT AND C. H. JOSEPHI [1979] J.P.L. 533, C.A.

2654. Stop notice—temporary use—activity carried on for more than 12 months

[Town and Country Planning Act 1971 (c. 78), s. 90 as amended by Town and Country Planning (Amendment) Act 1977 (c. 29), s. 1 (1).]

A stop notice may not be served where the activity sought to be stopped has been carried on on the land for more than 12 months previously, whether with or without planning consent.

The plaintiffs had conditional planning permission for the use of land as an open-air market from 1975 until June 30, 1978. Prior to expiry thereof they unsuccessfully applied for an extension. After June 1978 the plaintiff continued to use the land as before and in August 1978 the defendant council threatened to serve enforcement and stop notices. The plaintiffs sought to restrain the issue of a stop notice on the grounds that under s. 90 (2) of the Act such a notice would be invalid as they had been carrying on the activity sought to be stopped for more than 12 months. Mars-Jones J. held that the limitation period applied only to a period of unlawful activity. *Held*, allowing the plaintiffs' appeal (Brandon L.J. dissenting) that on a proper construction of s. 90 (2) of the Act it mattered not whether the activity was lawfully or unlawfully carried on.

SCOTT MARKETS v. WALTHAM FOREST LONDON BOROUGH COUNCIL (1979) 77 L.G.R. 565, C.A.

2655. Structure and local plans

TOWN AND COUNTRY PLANNING (STRUCTURE AND LOCAL PLANS) (AMENDMENT) REGULATIONS 1979 (No. 1738) [10p], made under the Town and Country Planning Act 1971 (c. 78), ss. 7 (3), 9 (3) (*a*), 18 (1) (2), 287; operative on January 31, 1980; make certain amendments to S.I. 1974 No. 1486.

2656. Town and Country Planning Act 1971—commencement

TOWN AND COUNTRY PLANNING ACT 1971 (COMMENCEMENT NO. 43) (WEST BERKSHIRE) ORDER 1979 (No. 200 (C. 6)) [20p], made under the Town and Country Planning Act 1971 (c. 78), ss. 21 and 287; brings into force on April 2, 1979, for those parts of Berkshire described in Sched. 1, s. 20 of and part of Sched. 23, Pt. I to the 1971 Act.

TOWN AND COUNTRY PLANNING ACT 1971 (COMMENCEMENT NO. 44) (OXFORDSHIRE) ORDER 1979 (No. 201 (C. 7)) [10p], made under the Town and Country Planning Act 1971, ss. 21 and 287; brings into force on April 2, 1979, for the county of Oxfordshire, s. 20 of, and certain provisions of Sched. 23, Pt. I to the 1971 Act.

TOWN AND COUNTRY PLANNING ACT 1971 (COMMENCEMENT NO. 45) (HUMBERSIDE) ORDER 1979 (No. 329 (C. 8)) [10p], made under the Town and Country Planning Act 1971, ss. 21, 287; operative on April 16, 1979; brings into force for the County of Humberside s. 20 and certain provisions of Pt. I of Sched. 23 to the 1971 Act.

TOWN AND COUNTRY PLANNING ACT 1971 (COMMENCEMENT No. 46) (CHESHIRE) ORDER 1979 (No. 891 (C. 23)) [20p], made under the Town and Country Planning Act 1971, ss. 21, 287; operative on August 13, 1979; brings into force for specified parts of the County of Cheshire s. 20 of and Sched. 23, Pt. I to the 1971 Act.

TOWN AND COUNTRY PLANNING ACT 1971 (COMMENCEMENT No. 47) (SUFFOLK) ORDER 1979 (No. 1043 (C. 30)) [10p], made under the Town and Country Planning Act 1971, ss. 21, 287; operative on September 10, 1979; brings into force s. 20 and Sched. 3, Pt. I, in relation to Suffolk.

TOWN AND COUNTRY PLANNING ACT 1971 (COMMENCEMENT No. 48) (HERTFORDSHIRE) ORDER 1979 (No. 1187 (C. 31)) [10p], made under the Town and Country Planning Act 1971, ss. 21, 287; operative on October 15, 1979; brings into force for Hertfordshire s. 20 of and certain of the provisions of Sched. 23, Pt. I to the 1971 Act.

TOWN AND COUNTRY PLANNING ACT 1971 (COMMENCEMENT No. 49) (NORTH EAST LANCASHIRE) ORDER 1979 (No. 1485 (C. 35)) [10p], made under the Town and Country Planning Act 1971, ss. 21, 287; operative on December 10, 1979; brings into force s. 20 of and certain provisions of Sched. 23, Pt. I, to the 1971 Act in relation to north east Lancashire.

2657. —— repeals

TOWN AND COUNTRY PLANNING (REPEAL OF PROVISIONS No. 15) (WEST BERKSHIRE) ORDER 1979 (No. 202) [10p], made under the Town and Country Planning Act 1971 (c. 78), ss. 21 (2) and 287; operative on April 2, 1979; repeals for the area covered by the structure plan the provisions of the 1971 Act relating to development plans contained in Sched. 5, Pt. I, and Sched. 6 to that Act.

TOWN AND COUNTRY PLANNING (REPEAL OF PROVISIONS No. 16) (OXFORDSHIRE) ORDER 1979 (No. 203) [10p], made under the Town and Country Planning Act 1971, ss. 21 (2) and 287; operative on April 2, 1979; repeals for the area covered by the structure plan for Oxfordshire the provisions of the 1971 Act relating to development plans contained in Sched. 5, Pt. I, and Sched. 6 to the Act.

TOWN AND COUNTRY PLANNING (REPEAL OF PROVISIONS No.18) (CHESHIRE) ORDER 1979 (No. 890) [20p], made under the Town and Country Planning Act 1971, ss. 21 (2), 287; operative on August 13, 1979; repeals for a specified part of Cheshire the provisions relating to development plans which are contained in Scheds. 5, Pt. I, and 6 to the 1971 Act.

TOWN AND COUNTRY PLANNING (REPEAL OF PROVISIONS No. 19) (SUFFOLK) ORDER 1979 (No. 1042) [10p], made under the Town and Country Planning Act 1971, ss. 21 (2), 287; operative on September 10, 1979; repeals for scheduled areas the 1971 Act provisions relating to development plans which are contained in Scheds. 5 and 6 to that Act.

TOWN AND COUNTRY PLANNING (REPEAL OF PROVISIONS No. 20) (HERTFORDSHIRE) ORDER 1979 (No. 1189) [10p], made under the Town and Country Planning Act 1971, ss. 21 (2), 287; operative on October 15, 1979; repeals for Hertfordshire provisions relating to development plans which are contained in Scheds. 5, Pt I and 6 to the 1971 Act.

TOWN AND COUNTRY PLANNING (REPEAL OF PROVISIONS No. 21) (NORTH EAST LANCASHIRE) ORDER 1979 (No. 1486) [10p], made under the Town and Country Planning Act 1971, ss. 21 (2), 287; operative on December 10, 1979; repeals for scheduled areas provisions contained in Scheds. 5, 6 to the 1971 Act which relate to development plans.

2658. Vendor and purchaser. See VENDOR AND PURCHASER.

BOOKS AND ARTICLES. See *post*, pp. [11], [32].

TRADE AND INDUSTRY

2659. Building industry. See BUILDING AND ENGINEERING.

2660. Coal industry. See MINING LAW.

2661. Counter-inflation. See REVENUE AND FINANCE.

2662. Employment. See EMPLOYMENT.

2663. Export guarantees

EXPORT GUARANTEES (EXTENSION OF PERIOD) ORDER 1979 (No. 180) [10p], made under the Export Guarantees and Overseas Investment Act 1978 (c. 18), s. 13; operative on February 23, 1979; extends for a further year the period of time during which arrangements may be made by the Secretary of State under s. 5 of the 1978 Act for making payments to persons carrying on business in the U.K. who have entered into export contracts.

2664. False trade description. See SALE OF GOODS.

2665. Industrial development

IRON CASTING INDUSTRY (SCIENTIFIC RESEARCH LEVY) (AMENDMENT) ORDER 1979 (No. 748) [10p], made under the Industrial Organisation and Development Act 1947 (c. 40), s. 9; operative on July 1, 1979; provides that the amount of that part of the levy on the iron castings industry to finance scientific research which is determined by the amount of iron castings produced will be determined by reference to a 1975-based index instead of a 1970-based index as has been the rule in the past.

ASSISTED AREAS ORDER 1979 (No. 837) [70p], made under the Local Employment Act 1972 (c. 5), ss. 1 (1) (4), 18 (1), and the Industry Act 1972 (c. 63), ss. 1 (4), 5 (3), Sched. 2, para. 2; operative on July 18, 1979; varies the designations of specified development areas.

REGIONAL DEVELOPMENT GRANTS (VARIATION OF PRESCRIBED PERCENTAGES) ORDER 1979 (No. 975) [10p], made under the Industry Act 1972, ss. 3 (1), 5 (4), Sched. 2, para. 2; operative on July 31, 1979; varies the rate of regional development grant payable under Part I of the 1972 Act on capital expenditure incurred in providing assets on qualifying premises in development areas. The amount of grant is reduced to 15 per cent. of the expenditure incurred.

2666. Industrial relations. See EMPLOYMENT; TRADE UNIONS.

2667. Industrial training

INDUSTRIAL TRAINING (TRANSFER OF THE ACTIVITIES OF ESTABLISHMENTS) ORDER 1979 (No. 793) [30p], made under the Industrial Training Act 1964 (c. 16), s. 9A (2); operative on August 3, 1979; transfers the activities of specified establishments from the industry of the industrial training board concerned with paper and paper products to the industry of the industrial training board concerned with the production of man-made fibres.

INDUSTRIAL TRAINING (RUBBER AND PLASTICS PROCESSING BOARD) ORDER 1967 (AMENDMENT) ORDER 1979 (No. 1595) [40p], made under the Industrial Training Act 1964, s. 9; operative on January 18, 1980; amends S.I. 1967 No. 1062 which specifies the activities in relation to which the Rubber and Plastics Processing Industry Training Board exercises its functions.

HOSIERY AND KNITWEAR INDUSTRY (SCIENTIFIC RESEARCH LEVY) (AMENDMENT) ORDER 1979 (No. 1740) [10p], made under the Industrial Organisation and Development Act 1947 (c. 40), s. 9; operative on January 1, 1980; provides that scientific research levies shall cease to be payable in the hosiery and knitwear industry and extends the exemption from liability to pay the levy in certain cases.

S.I. 1979 Nos. 184 (knitting, lace and net–levy) [25p]; 185 (petroleum–levy) [25p]; 251 (levy–wool, jute and flax) [25p]; 313 (levy–iron and steel) [25p]; 386 (levy–air transport and travel) [25p]; 387 (levy–food, drink and tobacco) [25p]; 544 (levy–clothing and allied products) [25p]; 545 (levy–distributive board) [25p]; 546 (levy–shipbuilding) [25p]; 558 (levy–paper and paper products) [25p]; 623 (levy–chemical and allied products) [25p]; 778 (levy–engineering) [40p]; 845 (levy–hotel and catering) [50p]; 902 (levy–ceramics, glass and mineral products) [50p]; 903 (levy–furniture and timber) [30p]; 1024 (levy–road transport) [40p]; 1049 (levy–cotton and allied textiles) [40p]; 1207 (levy–construction) [50p]; 1271 (levy–footwear, leather and furskin) [40p]; 1492 (levy–printing and publishing) [40p]; 1548 (levy–carpet) [40p].

2668. Industry Act 1979 (c. 32)

This Act provides for the limits on sums borrowed by, or paid by Ministers of the Crown to the National Enterprise Board, the Scottish Development Agency and the Welsh Development Agency.

S. 1 increases the limit on loans made and capital made available to the National Enterprise Board and other agencies, s. 2 gives the short title.

The Act received the Royal Assent on April 4, 1979, and came into force on that date.

2669. Northern Ireland. See NORTHERN IRELAND.

2670. Prices

SECRETARY OF STATE FOR TRADE ORDER 1979 (No. 578) [10p], made under the Ministers of the Crown Act 1975 (c. 26), ss. 1, 2; operative on June 1, 1979; transfers to the Secretary of State for Trade the remaining statutory function of the Secretary of State for Prices and Consumer Protection.

FOOD (PROHIBITION OF REPRICING) (AMENDMENT) ORDER 1979 (No. 660) [10p], made under the Prices Act 1974 (c. 24), s. 2 (6); operative on June 18, 1979; excludes from the provisions of S.I. 1978 No. 1014 any increase in price which is solely attributable to a change in the VAT chargeable.

2671. Private security industry

The Home Office have published a discussion paper on the private security industry, which gives background information on the industry and sets out some arguments for and against control. The paper is available from HMSO [80p].

2672. Shipping. See SHIPPING AND MARINE INSURANCE.

2673. Smell. See NUISANCE.

2674. Special development area

SPECIAL DEVELOPMENT AREA (FALMOUTH) ORDER 1979 (No. 269) [10p], made under the Industry Act 1972 (c. 63), s. 1 (4); upgrades the employment office area of Falmouth to a special development area. Also contains transitional financial provisions.

2675. Statistics

CENSUS OF PRODUCTION (1980) (RETURNS AND EXEMPTED PERSONS) ORDER 1979 (No. 1484) [10p], made under the Statistics of Trade Act 1947 (c. 39), ss. 2 and 11; operative on December 31, 1979; prescribes the matters about which a person carrying on an undertaking may be required to furnish returns for the purposes of the Census of Production being taken in 1980, and exempts from that obligation a person carrying on an undertaking in the exploration for and extraction of petroleum on land and offshore.

2676. Trade unions. See TRADE UNIONS.

2677. Transport. See TRANSPORT.

BOOKS AND ARTICLES. See *post*, pp. [12], [33].

TRADE MARKS AND TRADE NAMES

2678. Application—consolidation of actions—practice

[H.K.] The defendants denied infringement and pleaded honest concurrent use since the date of registration. The defence alleged that the defendant was entitled to have the mark registered in its own name. The defendant sought to consolidate an application for registration of the mark with the trade mark infringement action. *Held*, the court had no jurisdiction. The applicant was not able to by-pass the procedure laid down for application for registration: CHUNG FAI TRADING CO.'S TRADE MARK APPLICATION [1979] F.S.R. 169, Sup.Ct. of Hong Kong.

2679. —— descriptive mark—deception

[Trade Marks Act 1938 (c. 22), ss. 9, 10, 11.] Application was to register the mark "THE CHEF" and device in Part A. The applicant's goods were stationery, periodicals and photographs. The Registrar refused registration on the grounds that the mark directly referred to goods concerning cookery. Registration in Part B was refused as the mark did not have inherent capacity to distinguish. Any limitation of the specification of goods covered by the registration would emphasise the descriptive significance of the mark. The applicants appealed. *Held,* dismissing the appeal, that the mark, if applied to the applicants' goods, would be deceptive and the mark was too descriptive of goods within the specification relating to cookery: THE CHEF TRADE MARK [1979] R.P.C. 143, Board of Trade.

2680. —— **opposition—classification of marks**
[Trade Marks Act 1938 (c. 22), s. 3, 11, 12; Trade Marks Rules 1938 (S.I. 1938 No. 661), r. 5.] Application was to register TORNADO in Part A for metal dowels and wall plugs in class 6 and apparatus for inserting staples, etc. in class 8. The application was opposed by the proprietors of the mark TORNA, which was registered in Part B, class 9, for electrically operated hand-held tools. Their use of the mark was largely in relation to percussion drills, and it had been used on goods within their registered specification and on goods identical to the applicants'. They contended that their electric hand-held tools were within the applicants class 8 specification. *Held,* (1) there was no likelihood of confusion between the two marks; (2) the Registrar can have regard to the English edition of the French text of the Nice International Classification of Goods; (3) cartridge hammers in class 8 are goods of the same description as percussion drills in class 7; (4) metal dowels and expanding metal wall plugs are goods of the same description as electrically, operated hand-held rotary hammer drilling machines in class 7: TORNADO TRADE MARK [1979] R.P.C. 155, Trade Mark Registry.

2681. —— —— **disclaimer**
[Trade Marks Act 1938 (c. 22), ss. 12, 14, 18.] Application was to register the mark GRANADA in Pt. B for motor cars and fittings and parts. The opponent's mark was registered for hand vehicles and parts and fittings therefor included in Class 12. The word GRANADA had earlier been disclaimed. It was agreed that because of the disclaimer the opponents were not entitled to oppose under the Trade Marks Act, s. 12 (1). *Held,* allowing the application to proceed, that (1) the criteria for objection under s. 12 (1) are the whole of the opponent's mark including the disclaimer matter, and use in a fair way should be assumed; (2) confusion was likely in this case and the opposition under s. 12 (1) succeeded; (3) the Registrar should exercise his discretion under s. 12 (2) in favour of the applicants bearing in mind the extent of use in time and quantity, the honesty of the user and likelihood of confusion: GRANADA TRADE MARK [1979] R.P.C. 303, Trade Marks Registry.

2682. —— —— **objection**
[Trade Marks Act 1938 (c. 22), ss. 9, 10, 11, 12.] Application was to register a device mark containing a three-pointed star for use on clothing. The opponents used a similar device on cars, and other goods. They adduced evidence that since 1962 they had aimed for the mark and words "Three-pointed star" to symbolise their products alone. *Held,* since the applicants had not filed any evidence they had not discharged the onus of showing that confusion was likely. The opposition therefore succeeded: GOLDEN JET TRADE MARK [1979] R.P.C. 19, Trade Marks Registry.

2683. —— —— **prefix—confusion**
[Trade Marks Act 1938 (c. 22), ss. 11, 12.] Application was to register the word SEMIGRES in Pt. B for tiles in Class 19. The opponents alleged that SEM, used as a prefix and registered for 23 marks in connection with flooring tiles had come to indicate their products. *Held,* refusing the application, (1) SEM would be regarded by some people as a prefix; (2) the objection under s. 12 (1) did not succeed because there was no risk of oral or visual confusion: SEMIGRES TRADE MARK [1979] R.P.C. 330, Trade Marks Registry.

2684. —— —— **similarity**
[Trade Marks Act 1938 (c. 22), ss. 11, 12, 23.] Application was to register the mark FIF for soft drinks. The opponents were proprietors of the mark JIF for various products which included soft drinks. They produced evidence

of confusion in the form of questionnaires from traders. The Registrar allowed the application to proceed. *Held*, that (1) the evidence of similarity was not strong; (2) the marks were neither so similar visually or phonetically that confusion was likely: FIF TRADE MARK [1979] R.P.C. 355, Whitford J.

2685. —— —— **similarity with American name**

[N.Z.] [Trade Marks Act 1938 (c. 22), s. 16.] An Australian company applied for registration in New Zealand of the mark HY-LINE for live chickens and poultry. The mark was registered in 1959 in New South Wales and was similar to a mark registered in the United States in 1941. The Supreme Court of New Zealand disallowed registration on application by the American company. *Held*, dismissing the appeal, s. 16 was to protect the public and not the proprietory interests of traders. The criteria was whether the applicants' mark was likely to deceive or cause confusion in the New Zealand market: PIONEER HI-BRED CORN CO. *v.* HY-LINE CHICKS PTY. [1979] R.P.C. 410, N.Z.C.A.

2686. —— **user as trade mark—invented word**

[Trade Marks Act 1938 (c. 22), ss. 9, 10, 17, 26, 28.] The application was to register the mark UPDATE for printed matter and other articles in class 16. The journal had previously been published and freely distributed under the mark. The applicants drew their income from advertisers. The hearing officer held the mark was not invented and was descriptive, and that user was not established. *Held*, on appeal, that (1) free distribution was not trading. The mark was new and unused and not qualified for registration under s. 9; (2) the mark was being used as a service mark, and was therefore outside the scope of the Act. (*Hospital World Trade Mark* [1967] C.L.Y. 3931 followed): UPDATE TRADE MARK [1979] R.P.C. 165, Board of Trade.

2687. Confusion—goodwill—counterclaim

The plaintiffs since 1974 had marketed DANOL, a drug available only on prescription, in capsule form. The defendants since 1947 had marketed a liquid preparation DE-NOL available over the counter for the treatment of ulcers. The defendants wished to make DE-NOL in solid form. The plaintiffs sought a *quia timet* injunction. The defendants counter-claimed for similar relief. Both parties by the date of the trial had goodwill in their marks. *Held*, (1) there had been no confusion in the past and real likelihood of confusion would only arise if the defendants produced and marketed a solid formulation of their product; (2) when the plaintiffs introduced DANOL their choice of mark was reasonable. The plaintiffs were entitled to judgment but no injunction because there was no immediate market threat: STERWIN A.G. *v.* BROCADES (GREAT BRITAIN) [1979] R.P.C. 4812, Whitford J.

2688. Distinctiveness—registered user

[Can.] [Trade Marks Act 1952–53 (Canada), ss. 2, 6, 7, 18, 20, 49.] The first plaintiff was the Canadian subsidiary of the second plaintiff, a U.S. company which had registered the mark OFF! for insect repellent manufactured and sold in Canada by the second plaintiff. In 1975 the defendant marketed in Canada an insect repellent towel called BUGG OFF. *Held*, on appeal by the defendant, (1) that there was not sufficient evidence for a finding of causing confusion; (2) the mark was not distinctive; (3) the registered user provisions merely permitted user by the licensee without contravening the owners' rights. The appeal would be allowed and the trade mark expunged: OFF! TRADE MARK [1979] F.S.R. 243, Fed.Ct. of Canada.

2689. European Communities. See EUROPEAN COMMUNITIES.

2690. Passing-off—beverage—whether goods distinctive—unfair trading

Where a product, such as " advocaat," has gained by reason of its character and ingredients a public reputation under its descriptive name, it should be protected from deceptive use of its name by competitors, even though its ingredients do not come from any particular locality.

The first plaintiffs had for years manufactured and exported to Britain a liquor known as " advocaat." In 1974 a drink known as " Keeling's Old English Advocaat " was made and marketed in England by the defendants.

Though it could not be shown to be mistaken for the Dutch product, the English "advocaat" captured a share of the plaintiffs' English market. The plaintiffs won at first instance, lost on appeal, and on appeal, *held,* allowing the appeal, that there was a misrepresentation made by a trader to prospective customers calculated to injure the business or goodwill of the plaintiffs, and the action should succeed. (*Bollinger* v. *Costa Brava Wine Co.* (*No.* 3) [1959] C.L.Y. 3337 approved; *Native Guano Co.* v. *Sewage Manure Co.* (1889) 8 R.P.C. 125 distinguished.)

ERVEN WARNINK BESLOTEN VENNOOTSCHAP v. J. TOWNEND & SONS (HULL) [1979] 3 W.L.R. 68, H.L.

2691. —— **copyright—interlocutory relief**
　　[Trade Marks Act 1938 (c. 22), s. 4.] The plaintiffs sought an order restraining the defendants from buying second-hand models and converting the bodywork so that the cars looked like the more expensive model, modified; these would be sold under the name Rolls-Royce Panache. The defendants stated that they intended only to offer the service of conversion to existing owners of Silver Shadows, the cheaper models. *Held,* granting the relief sought, that (1) damage to the plaintiffs was incalculable, if anything impinged on their reputation; (2) there was an arguable case in each cause of action and the balance of convenience favoured the plaintiffs: ROLLS-ROYCE MOTORS v. ZANELLI [1979] R.P.C. 148, Browne-Wilkinson J.

2692. —— **interlocutory relief**
　　[H.K.] The plaintiff carried on a large retail business in the United States and had buying offices and a subsidiary purchasing company in Hong Kong. From September 1971 the defendant carried out a retail business named Penneys Fashion written the way the plaintiff used the word. The plaintiffs sought an interlocutory injunction. *Held,* (1) the plaintiff had a substantial reputation and goodwill in Hong Kong, the defendant had deliberately deceived the public and the confusion would damage the plaintiff's reputation; (2) the eight months' delay was not fatal to the grant of an interlocutory injunction because the defendants had shown no damage: J. C. PENNEY CO. INC. v. PUNJABI NICK [1979] F.S.R. 26, Sup.Ct. of Hong Kong.

2693.　　[H.K.] The first plaintiff carried on extensive retail business in the U.S. The second plaintiff had purchased goods in Hong Kong since 1966 for sale to the first plaintiff. The first defendant carried on retail business in Ireland and the U.K. They announced the opening in Hong Kong of a buying office for the first defendant. The plaintiffs obtained an *ex parte* injunction restraining the defendants from using the name "Penneys." *Held,* (1) there was a serious question to be tried in view of the decision in *J. C. Penney Co.* v. *Punjabi Nick* [1979] C.L.Y. 2692; (2) damages would not be an adequate compensation to the plaintiffs. Injunction granted: J. C. PENNEY CO. INC. v. PENNEYS [1979] F.S.R. 29, Sup.Ct. of Hong Kong.

2694. —— —— **common field of activity**
　　The plaintiffs were well-known producers of tobacco products called " Dunhill." Their American subsidiary had sold sunglasses in the U.S.A. The first defendant proposed to sell sunglasses and spectacle frames "CD Christopher Dunhill-London." The great-grandson of the founder was bearer of the name and had entered into a consultation agreement with the first defendants in return for substantial royalties. The trial judge refused an injunction. The plaintiff appealed to the court of appeal. *Held,* (1) there were substantial disputes on the facts and the case could not be decided by considering the respective merits; (2) damages would be an inadequate remedy to the plaintiff if they were ultimately to succeed, whereas damage to the defendants if an interlocutory injunction were granted was less than they had asserted in evidence; (3) the injunction granted was restricted to the U.K. and Switzerland, that being the only country in respect of which there was any evidence of foreign law: ALFRED DUNHILL v. SUNOPTIC S.A. AND C. DUNHILL [1979] F.S.R. 337, C.A.

2695. —— —— **likelihood of confusion**
　　The plaintiffs were publishers of a weekly news magazine namely *Newsweek*

and in the U.S.A. produced certain television programmes. The defendants proposed transmitting a programme named *Newsweek*. The plaintiffs alleged that viewers would believe the television programme was connected with them. The trial judge dismissed the motion and the plaintiffs appealed. *Held* (1) a prima facie case of passing off had been made out; (2) the word " newsweek " was almost an ordinary word; (3) the average viewer would not associate the programme with the plaintiffs and confusion was unlikely in relation to sources of interviews: NEWSWEEK INC. *v.* BRITISH BROADCASTING CORP. [1979] R.P.C. 441, C.A.

2696. —— —— **newspaper title**
    The plaintiffs published the *Morning Star* newspaper. 21,000 copies were sold daily and it contained mostly news and communist views. It was of broadsheet size. The defendants proposed to publish a newspaper entitled the *Daily Star*, smaller in size, with large headlines and many pictures of near-naked girls. The plaintiffs sought an interlocutory injunction, alleging that the title would lead to passing off. *Held*, the two newspapers were so different that confusion was very unlikely. The word " star " was a descriptive word when applied to newspapers. The balance of convenience was also against the grant of an interlocutory injunction: MORNING STAR CO-OPERATIVE SOCIETY *v.* EXPRESS NEWSPAPERS [1979] F.S.R. 113, Foster J.

2697. —— —— **overseas reputation—Hong Kong**
    [H.K.] The plaintiff was a company incorporated in Switzerland owning and managing " Wienerwald " restaurants in Europe, the U.S., S. Africa and Japan. The plaintiffs desired to enter a franchise agreement in Hong Kong. The defendants had previously renewed the word Wienerwald for company names under Hong Kong law. The plaintiff alleged passing-off. *Held*, the plaintiffs had failed to establish as a triable issue that it had acquired a reputation among a significant segment of the Hong Kong population. The court · could not protect goodwill outside the jurisdiction: WIENER-WALD HOLDING A.G. *v.* WONG, TAN AND FONG [1979] F.S.R. 381, High Ct. of Hong Kong.

2698. —— —— **principles**
    The plaintiffs were well-known retailers of goods for young children and expectant mothers, called " Mothercare." The defendants proposed to publish *Mother Care*. The plaintiffs sought an interlocutory injunction. The defendants admitted the claim was not frivolous and vexatious, but argued that they had no real chance of succeeding at the trial. *Held* that (1) there was some likelihood of confusion, and a serious question to be tried; (2) an injunction would merely preserve the status quo. Observed: the words " frivolous and vexatious " should not be used in this context: MOTHERCARE *v.* ROBSON BOOKS [1979] F.S.R. 467, Megarry V.-C.

2699. —— **practice—contempt—Anton Piller order**
    On March 29, 1979, an Anton Piller order was made in a case alleging passing off of goods labelled " Chanel " or " No. 5 Chanel " as the goods of the plaintiff. The order contained a further provision that " the defendants should not disclose the subject-matter of the action or the plaintiff's interest herein." The managing director of the defendant's company gave instructions to the staff not to co-operate with the order. *Held*, the disobedience was wilful and a contempt of court. Committal and sequestration were too grave in this case. The respondents should pay the plaintiff's costs of the application on an indemnity basis: CHANEL *v.* 3 PEARS WHOLESALE CASH AND CARRY CO. [1979] F.S.R. 393, Walton J.

2700. —— **unfair competition—trade mark**
    [Dubai] The plaintiffs imported and marketed BRYLCREEM in Dubai, and enjoyed a high local reputation. The defendants' presentation of their product was very similar. The plaintiffs sought prohibition of the use of the mark BRYLCREEM and the plaintiffs' get-up, and the prohibition of importing any non-medicated cream called BRYLCREEM. *Held*, relief granted. Deception probable and damage would be presumed: BEECHAM PRODUCTS *v.* MOHAMMED AHMED ZAMIN PIMA AND CO. [1979] F.S.R. 121, Ct. of Emir of Dubai.

2701. Rectification—non-use

[Trade Marks Act 1938 (c. 22), ss. 12, 26, 32, 68.] Application was to remove the mark REVUE from the register on the ground of non-use. The proprietors showed that the mark had been used in the United Kingdom for binoculars and exposure meters. The applicants filed evidence that they too had used the mark on their goods. *Held,* that no prima facie case of non-use had been shown and the proprietors had in any event successfully established user of certain goods: REVUE TRADE MARK [1979] R.P.C. 27, Trade Marks Registry.

2702. Application was to expunge the mark HUGGARS from the register on the ground of non-use. It was contended further that the respondents had never proposed to use the mark in relation to goods, and HUGGARS was therefore not a trade mark within s. 68. The respondents had extensively used the mark HUGGERS. *Held,* allowing the application, that HUGGERS was immediately suggestive of the quality of the clothing, whereas HUGGARS was not. An alteration would substantially affect its identity: HUGGARS TRADE MARK [1979] F.S.R. 310, Goulding J.

2703. —— —— goods of same description

[Trade Marks Act 1938 (c. 22), ss. 12, 23, 26, 27, 30, 32.] Application was to rectify the register by expunging the mark ATLAS for three classes of electrical goods. Evidence showed that the mark had been used only in relation to various lighting goods but had been used in relation to goods of the same description as those in respect of which the marks were registered. *Held,* that where identical marks were concerned and association under s. 23 (2) occurred, there were insufficient grounds to invoke s. 30 (1) to prevent goods of a different description being expunged: ATLAS TRADE MARK [1979] R.P.C. 59, Trade Marks Registry.

2704. Registration—objection—surname

[Eire] [Trade Marks Act 1963, ss. 17, 18.] Application was sought for the word DENT for watches and clocks. Objection was taken to Pt. A registration because its ordinary signification was that of a surname. Objection was taken to Pt. B registration on the ground that the mark was incapable of distinguishing the applicant's goods. *Held,* on appeal, that (1) the non-surnominal use was not overwhelmingly more common than its meaning as a surname. The mark was therefore incapable of distinguishing; (2) a surname was in the absence of special circumstances capable of distinguishing only when the name was unusual to the eyes and ears of the Irish people who would deal in them: DENT TRADE MARK [1979] F.S.R. 205, High Ct. of Ireland.

2705. —— persons aggrieved—opponent non-trading body in United States

[Trade Marks Act 1938 (c. 23), ss. 11–13, 17, 26, 32; Copyright Act 1956 (c. 74), s. 3.] E applied to register the word OSCAR and a silhouetted statue for audio-visual apparatus. The opponents conferred " Oscar " awards on outstanding films. The opponents also sought removal of two OSCAR marks registered for records and radio apparatus. They contended that it was not necessary for persons aggrieved to be engaged in the same trade as E or any trade at all. *Held,* on the first application, that (1) in the absence of simultaneous publication in the U.S. and U.K., the opponents' claim to copyright had not been sufficiently made out; (2) the opponents had not shown likelihood of confusion and deception. On the second application, rectification was refused as (1) the opponents were not a person aggrieved, there being no evidence that they had suffered damage; (2) the opponents could not claim proprietorship of the word OSCAR nor could they claim literary copyright; they had no *locus standi*: OSCAR TRADE MARK [1979] R.P.C. 197, Trade Marks Registry.

ARTICLES. See *post,* p. [33].

TRADE UNIONS

2706. Breach of union rules—validity of order to withdraw labour

The N.U.J.'s r. 20 (*b*) provided that the union's National Executive Council should not sanction a withdrawal from employment affecting a majority of the members unless a ballot of the whole of the members showed a two-thirds majority of those voting in favour of such action. In December 1978 the N.E.C. instructed all members employed in the Newspaper Society offices and in the Press Association to withdraw their labour. Also, over half the membership were instructed to black Newspaper Society houses and the Press Association or to impose sanctions. *Held,* allowing appeals from the refusal of an interim injunction restraining the N.U.J. from taking disciplinary proceedings against members who had not obeyed the union's instructions and an order that they be restored to membership pending trial of the action, that (1) " withdrawal from employment " included partial withdrawal by not doing work properly or inflicting sanctions or deliberately causing disruption; (2) those " affected " by the withdrawal included all those who received instructions to black or impose sanctions; (3) accordingly a majority of members were " affected " and the instruction to strike was *ultra vires;* (4) under r. 20 (*a*), which empowered only the N.E.C. to order a withdrawal from employment, however, the N.E.C. could order a withdrawal which was unlawful in that it required members to break the contracts of employment. Nor would the strike have been invalid if in breach of the national collective agreement with the employers, though that fact would provide a member with a defence for disobeying the instructions: PORTER *v.* NATIONAL UNION OF JOURNALISTS [1979] I.R.L.R. 404, C.A.

2707. Certification of independence—risk of interference by employers—certification officer's decision

[Trade Union and Labour Relations Act 1974 (c. 52), s. 30 (1); Employment Protection Act 1975 (c. 71), s. 88 (3).]

The words " liable to interference " when considering certification of a staff association as an independent trade union, mean exposed to risk or reasonable possibility, rather than likelihood, of interference by the employer.

A number of employees combined together to form a staff association to negotiate with their employers over pay and conditions. The employers provided them with facilities including rooms, telephone and stationery. The association applied for certification as an independent trade union. The certification officer refused the application on the grounds that the association was liable to interference. The E.A.T. allowed the association's appeal. On appeal, *held*, allowing the appeal, that " liable to interference " meant the risk or possibility of interference as contrasted with the likelihood of such interference.

SQUIBB UNITED KINGDOM STAFF ASSOCIATION *v.* CERTIFICATION OFFICER [1979] I.C.R. 235, C.A.

2708. Certification officer

CERTIFICATION OFFICER (AMENDMENT OF FEES) REGULATIONS 1979 (No. 1385) [10p], made under the Trade Union (Amalgamations etc.) Act 1964 (c. 24), s. 7; the Trade Union and Labour Relations Act 1974 (c. 52), s. 8 (4) and the Employment Protection Act 1975 (c. 71), s. 8 (2); operative on December 1, 1979; increase certain specified fees that are payable to the Certification Officer.

2709. Membership—Industrial Tribunal decision

CHEALL *v.* VAUXHALL MOTORS [1979] I.R.L.R. 253. (C transferred his membership of A.C.T.S.S. to APEX. Subsequently C was taken off shifts owing to illness and his wife's death. At a meeting held to consider extension of C's shift allowance, V.M. Co. refused to allow C's APEX representative to put C's case, on the ground that the T.U.C. Disputes Committee had issued an award in favour of A.C.T.S.S. requiring APEX to exclude C from membership. *Held*, that V.M. Co. had deterred C from and penalised him for being a member of APEX contrary to s. 53 (1) (*a*) of the Employment Protection Act 1975).

2710. Recognition—ACAS—duties in considering recognition issue

[Employment Protection Act 1975 (c. 71), ss. 12 (1), 14 (1) (2).]

In considering the form of questionnaire sent by ACAS to employees, the court can only intervene if the decision to use that form of questionnaire is a decision that no reasonable body could have come to, and that must be considered in the light of the facts and the expertise available at the relevant time.

A.S.T.M.S., which claimed to have 105 members amongst the employer's 500-odd employees, referred a recognition issue to ACAS. An attempt by certain of the staff to organise a staff association had failed, and another union, N.U.B.E., was unwilling to be involved. ACAS sent out a questionnaire to the employees in which their views on the staff association and N.U.B.E. were not sought. ACAS recommended A.S.T.M.S. The plaintiffs sought a declaration that ACAS had acted in breach of duty, that the questionnaire was biased, and that they had failed to ascertain the " opinion of the workers." *Held,* that (1) s. 14 (1) of the 1975 Act did not require ACAS to canvas opinions on matters it reasonably considered irrelevant; and (2) the court could only intervene if the decision to use that form of questionnaire was a decision which no reasonable body could have come to. (*Powley* v. *Advisory, Conciliation and Arbitration Service* [1978] C.L.Y. 3001 distinguished; *Associated Provincial Picture Houses* v. *Wednesbury Corporation* (1947) C.L.C. 8107 applied.)

NATIONAL EMPLOYERS LIFE ASSURANCE CO. *v.* ADVISORY, CONCILIATION AND ARBITRATION SERVICE [1979] I.C.R. 620, Browne-Wilkinson J.

2711. —— —— **duty to proceed with inquiries—Court of Appeal to rehear case as at date of appeal**
[Employment Protection Act 1975 (c. 71), ss. 12 (1), 14 (1).]

The duties imposed on ACAS by the Employment Protection Act 1975 are mandatory, and though ACAS has a discretion as to the method of inquiry, its discretion must be exercised reasonably and the statutory requirements fulfilled within a reasonable time; ACAS is not entitled to adjourn its inquiries indefinitely.

A complicated inter-union dispute arose between three unions as to recognition at a factory. An award was made against one union by the T.U.C. disputes committee. The unions concerned applied to ACAS for the reference of a recognition issue. ACAS started inquiries, but then a writ was issued concerning the disputes committee's award and ACAS resolved not to proceed with the recognition references. A writ was then issued against ACAS seeking declarations that it was in breach of statutory duty in refusing to investigate the recognition issue. Oliver J. found that ACAS had a discretion to defer consideration of the issue. On appeal, *held*, allowing the appeal, that the discretion of ACAS had to be exercised reasonably and its duties fulfilled within a reasonable time; ACAS was not entitled to adjourn its inquiries indefinitely. (Dictum in *Att.-Gen.* v. *Birmingham Tame and Rea District Drainage Board* [1912] A.C. 788 at 801, *Curwen* v. *James* [1963] C.L.Y. 954 and *Murphy* v. *Stone-Wallwork* (*Charlton*) [1969] C.L.Y. 901 applied.)

ENGINEERS' AND MANAGERS' ASSOCIATION *v.* ADVISORY, CONCILIATION AND ARBITRATION SERVICE [1979] I.C.R. 637, C.A.

2712. —— **bargaining rights—duty of ACAS**
[Employment Protection Act 1975 (c. 71), ss. 1, 12 (4).]

In reporting upon a recognition dispute it does not suffice for ACAS to set out the conflicting views expressed to it; its own objective conclusions must be included.

The respondent union recruited professional engineers. The majority of its members employed by a particular engineering company wished the respondent to represent them in collective bargaining. The company refused recognition; it relied upon existing collective bargaining arrangements between an employers' federation and a number of large trade unions. The issue was referred to ACAS. The opponents to recognition claimed that it was unnecessary and the opposing unions threatened industrial action in the event of recognition of the respondent. In its report ACAS declined to recommend recognition on the grounds that recognition would be inconsistent with present arrangements, would lead to fragmentation thereof, and would present the risk of industrial action being taken. No conclusions were expressed as to, *inter alia*, the viability of the respondent union as a bargaining unit or the adequacy of the existing arrangements. May J. declared the report to be a nullity. *Held*, dismissing the appeal by ACAS, that ACAS had failed in its duty to give its objective findings upon questions of fact before it and by failing fully to consider the case for an extension of collective bargaining, the attainment or encouragement of which was its statutory duty. *Per* Lord Denning M.R.: that ACAS should not have been influenced by threats of industrial action made by the big unions: so to do made ACAS the lackey of powerful trade unions.

UNITED KINGDOM ASSOCIATION OF PROFESSIONAL ENGINEERS *v.* ADVISORY, CONCILIATION AND ARBITRATION SERVICE [1979] I.C.R. 303, C.A.

2713. —— consultation—redundancy

[Employment Protection Act 1975 (c. 71), ss. 11 (2), 99, 101 (7).]

Before an employer is held to have recognised a trade union for the purposes of collective bargaining, clear and unequivocal evidence of an agreement, and/ or conduct from which recognition must be inferred, is required.

The employers belonged to a trade association which had entered various collective agreements with the applicant union as to conditions of employment within the trade. Although their employees were not members of the union, the employers treated such agreements as guidelines. In early May 1976 the union recruited eight of the 55 employees as members and thereafter met with the employers to discuss certain rates of pay which the union claimed fell below agreed standards; the employers indicated that they did not intend to change such rates. At the end of May three employees were dismissed for redundancy. The union claimed that it had been " recognised " by the employers, who had wrongly failed to consult it prior to the redundancies. An industrial tribunal, upheld by the E.A.T. dismissed the union's application for a protective award upon the grounds that the union had not been recognised. *Held*, dismissing the union's appeal, that since the consequences of recognition were serious and far reaching, clear evidence of recognition was required; the evidence as to discussions in May fell short of the required standard; and that membership of the trade association which negotiated with the union did not imply recognition by the employers. (*National Union of Tailors and Garment Workers* v. *Charles Ingram & Co.* [1977] C.L.Y. 3083 and *Joshua Wilson and Bros.* v. *Union of Shop, Distributive and Allied Workers* [1978] C.L.Y. 997 approved; decision of E.A.T. affirmed.)

NATIONAL UNION OF GOLD, SILVER & ALLIED TRADES *v.* ALBURY BROTHERS [1979] I.C.R. 84, C.A.

2714. Rules—interpretation—relief from contributions to political fund—jurisdiction of Certification Officer

[Trade Union Act 1913 (c. 30), s. 3.] M told APEX he wished to contract out of paying the political contribution and to pay his union dues at branch meetings. APEX told him he had to pay dues through the check-off system and that one penny per week would be deducted from the amount taken from his wages. The political levy was later found to amount to $1^5/_{13}$p per week. Thus M was forced by this system to claim a refund of five pence at the end of each quarter. *Held*, by the certification officer, that (1) by enforcing this system the union was in breach of its r. 81 which relieved exempt members from contributing to the political fund; (2) the fact that the five pence per quarter overpayment was kept in the general fund did not affect the position as r. 81 provided that 18p per quarter from the contribution was a contribution to the political fund and exempt members must be required to pay the " remainder " only; (3) r. 81 had to be interpreted as relating to the time when the political contributions are made and did not permit the requirement of overpayments subject to adjustments within the quarter; (4) the system was also in breach of the requirement in r. 83 that exempt members should not be directly or indirectly under any disability or disadvantage compared with other members by reason of their being exempt; (5) the union would be ordered to make arrangements for M to be able to pay his contributions less the political levy at branch meetings; (6) r. 81 requires that at least one method of collecting contributions should allow for exempt members to be relieved from the political levy and that that method should not be materially less convenient than the other methods; (7) payment at branch meetings would normally involve inconvenience in requiring the member to attend but not in M's case whilst he remained branch chairman; (8) the certification officer only had jurisdiction to deal with complaints about breach of rules made in pursuance of the Trade Union Act 1913, s. 3, and extension or procedural additions to the Act's provisions contained in the Rules, provided such rules are ancillary to the Act's provisions; (9) nor did the certification officer have jurisdiction to deal with complaints affecting members other than the complainant: McCARTHY v. ASSOCIATION OF PROFESSIONAL EXECUTIVE, CLERICAL AND COMPUTER STAFF [1979] I.R.L.R. 255, Certification Officer.

2715. —— political contribution—exempt members

[Trade Union Act 1913 (c. 30), s. 3 (2).] R. 24.7 of the T.G.W.U.'s rules provides that members who are exempt from paying the political contribution would be relieved from paying it. A part of the first week's union contribution each quarter was allocated for political purposes. The employer's payroll computer could not cope with irregular deductions in order that the political levy could be deducted in the first week of each quarter. Therefore the union refunded the political contribution to exempt members, sometimes in advance and sometimes after some arrears had accumulated. R complained to the Certification Officer under s. 3 (2) of the 1913 Act. *Held*, that in deducting the political contribution from the first week's union payment each quarter made by an exempt member and repaying him the appropriate amount in arrears the union was in breach of its r. 24.7. However, there was no breach where the refund was made in advance provided that no part of the member's contribution went into the political fund: REEVES v. TRANSPORT AND GENERAL WORKERS' UNION [1979] I.R.L.R. 290, Certification Officer.

2716. Trade dispute—federation of trade unions—whether immune from action in tort

[Trade Union and Labour Relations Act 1974 (c. 52), ss. 13 (1), 17 (2), 28 (1), 29 (1) (4) (as amended by Trade Union and Labour Relations (Amendment) Act 1976 (c. 7), s. 3 (2), and Employment Protection Act 1975 (c. 71), s. 125 (1), Sched. 16, Pt. III, para. 6).]

Where a dispute concerns terms and conditions of employment it falls within the ambit of s. 29 (1) of the Trade Union and Labour Relations Act 1974, as amended, and is a trade dispute even though it is being pursued for other motives which are predominant and extraneous.

The *Nawala* was a large bulk carrier built for Scandinavian shipowners and manned by a highly paid Norwegian crew. There was a slump in the freight market and her trading under the Norwegian flag was losing money. She was sold to Swedish buyers who formed a Hong Kong company so as to transfer her to Hong Kong registry. A crew was engaged in Hong Kong and flown to Hamburg, where they joined the vessel. The Hong Kong crew was paid a great deal less than European crews. The International Transport Workers Federation took exception to ships sailing under flags of convenience, and in order to secure higher wages and better conditions for the seamen took to blacking such vessels. In June 1979 when the *Nawala* was off Redcar, the owners were notified that the ship would be blacked unless they complied with I.T.F. conditions of employment. Donaldson J. granted injunctions preventing the blacking which were discharged by the Court of Appeal. The owners, fearing further blackings, obtained affidavit evidence that the crew were perfectly content with their pay and conditions and would not sign the I.T.F. agreement, since doing so would mean losing their jobs. They sought further injunctions against blacking, which Donaldson J. refused. The Court of Appeal upheld that refusal. On appeal to the House of Lords, *held,* dismissing both appeals that although the I.T.F.'s ultimate object was to prevent shipowners using flags of convenience, the dispute was neverthless connected with terms and conditions of employment in the shipping industry and was a trade dispute within s. 29 (1) of the Trade Union and Labour Relations Act 1974 (as amended). Decisions of C.A. affirmed; *Conway* v. *Wade* [1909] A.C. 506 and *American Cyanamid Co.* v. *Ethicon* [1975] C.L.Y. 2640, considered; *Star Sea Transport Corp. of Monrovia* v. *Slater*; *The Camilla M* [1978] 1 C.L.Y. 3005 overruled.)

N.W.L. v. WOODS; N.W.L. v. NELSON [1979] 1 W.L.R. 1294, H.L.

2717. —— furtherance—blacking advertisements—interim injunction

[Trade Union and Labour Relations Act 1974 (c. 52), ss. 2 (5), 13 (1), 17 (2) (as amended by Trade Union and Labour Relations (Amendment) Act 1976 (c. 7), s. 3 (2), and Employment Protection Act 1975 (c. 71), Sched. 16, Pt. III, para. 6).]

Where the losses of employers by virtue of " blacking " will be great, and the alternative is the interruption of a union's campaign costing practically nothing in money or effort, the balance of convenience in continuing or discharging an interim injunction to stop the blacking is likely to favour the employers.

The T.B.F. group of local newspapers around Nottingham did not recognise the National Graphical Association. In March 1978 the N.G.A. applied under s. 11 of the Employment Protection Act 1975 to A.C.A.S. for recognition, but later withdrew the application. Subsequently the N.G.A. and the Society of Lithographic Artists, Designers and Engravers instructed all their members on any newspapers and periodicals not to handle any advertising submitted by 16 organisations which had continued to advertise in T.B.F. Co.'s *Nottingham Evening Post* after an instruction by the N.G.A. to cease such advertising. The plaintiff, various newspapers, magazines, periodicals, advertisers and public authorities sought injunctions restraining the blacking. An interlocutory injunction was granted. On appeal by the union, *held, inter alia,* (1) it was arguable that the blacking was unlawful at common law as a deliberate interference with trade and business and an inducement to breach of contract by employees with their employers and by advertisers with their publishers; (2) the interference with trade and business was not rendered lawful by s. 2 (5) of the 1974 Act, which section validated only rules which would otherwise be unlawful only because they were in " restraint of trade." " Restraint of trade " was not the same as " interference with business "; (3) it was arguable that there was no " trade dispute " between the N.G.A. and T.B.F. Co. and that the dispute was now really one in which the union's motives were to punish T.B.F. Co. for anti-union activities rather than one about recognition, in order to secure removal of the managing director; (4) it was arguable that if there was a trade dispute, the blacking was " in furtherance " thereof, and therefore protected by s. 13 of the 1974 Act; but (5) the losses which the plaintiffs had suffered and would suffer by the blacking were very great. The union's campaign was costing practically nothing in money or effort. The former so greatly outweighed the latter that the balance of convenience plainly favoured the plaintiffs and the injunction would be continued. *Per* Lord Denning M.R.: interference with the freedom of the Press is so contrary to public interest that no trade union has the right to do it.

ASSOCIATED NEWSPAPERS GROUP *v.* WADE [1979] 1 W.L.R. 697, C.A.

2718. —— —— immunity

[Trade Union and Labour Relations Act 1974 (c. 52), s. 13 (1).] The immunity conferred by s. 13 (1) of the Trade Union and Labour Relations Act 1974 on actions in furtherance of a trade dispute is a wide one; the question whether the act in question is " in furtherance " of the dispute is subjective, to be decided by the person doing the act, not the courts (decision of C.A. reversed): EXPRESS NEWSPAPERS *v.* McSHANE, *The Times,* December 13, 1979, H.L.

2719. —— —— interlocutory relief

[Trade Union and Labour Relations Act 1974 (c. 52), s. 13 (1).] When P.B.D.S. were taken over by N.C. a meeting between the S.O.G.A.T. and N.U.R. Executive Councils was held at which it was agreed that the N.U.R. would have exclusive negotiating and membership rights but employees of P.B.D.S.(N.C.) would be entitled to dual membership in S.O.G.A.T. When P.B.D.S. began operations some former employees of P.B.D.S. began picketing and erected a placard calling the dispute " official " and bearing the signature of F, the paid secretary of the London Central Branch of S.O.G.A.T. The action was contrary to S.O.G.A.T.'s rules as the dispute was entered into without National Executive Council sanction. Members of the branch employed by publishers also refused to handle books dispatched by P.B.D.S.(N.C.) on F's instructions. *Held*, dismissing F's appeal against an interlocutory injunction restraining the picketing and blacking, that (1) the action was not genuinely in furtherance of a trade dispute but was in anger with the S.O.G.A.T. National Executive Council for overruling them by reaching the settlement with the N.U.R.; (2) furthermore, the defendants were outside the protection of s. 13 (1) of the 1974 Act because they were making demands which could not possibly be fulfilled. (*Star Sea Transport Corp. of Monrovia* v. *Slater*; *The Camilla M* [1978] C.L.Y. 3005 applied: P.B.D.S. (NATIONAL CARRIERS) v. FILKINS [1979] I.R.L.R. 356, C.A.

2720. —— —— secondary picketing

[Trade Union and Labour Relations Act 1974 (c. 52), s. 13.] UB Co. obtained raw materials from L and N Co. In January 1979, during a dispute between the T.G.W.U. and Roal Haulage Association member companies, F caused a picket line at L and N Co.'s premises to interfere with UB Co.'s collection by their own vehicles of raw materials. There was no dispute between UB Co. and the drivers or the T.G.W.U. or between L and N Co. and their employees. *Held*, that L's conduct was not " in contemplation or furtherance of a trade dispute " and was unlawful. Accordingly an interlocutory injunction should be granted. (*Beaverbrook Newspapers* v. *Keys* [1978] C.L.Y. 3004 and *Express Newspapers* v. *McShane* [1979] 1 W.L.R. 390, C.A. applied): UNITED BISCUITS (U.K.) v. FALL [1979] I.R.L.R. 110, Ackner J.

2721. —— picketing—whether union able to picket second company

[Can.] Members of D, a union, picketed a retail outlet owned by P. The union was on lawful strike against another company, two of whose principal shareholders were also shareholders of P. P asked for an injunction restraining the picketing. *Held*, the injunction was granted. The two companies were clearly distinguishable and shareholders of P, who had no connection with the company against whom D were on lawful strike, were being adversely affected: SECURITY BUILDING SUPPLIES v. MASSEY [1978] 6 W.W.R. 755, Sask.Q.B.

2722. —— vessel " blacked "—whether dispute with managers dispute with owners

In 1973, because of the slump in shipping, O decided to change the flag of their vessel, the M from German to Panamanian flag in order to be able to employ a cheaper crew. A Yugoslav crew was employed, not by O, but by S as agents for an independent Liberian company. O only had to pay S a lump sum to cover everything. In July 1979, the M arrived at Hull, where her crew complained to the I.T.F. about their wages, which were much lower than the I.T.F. terms. The I.T.F. instructed the N.U.R., which operated the lock gates at Hull, to " black " the M, which was accordingly unable to leave on a voyage for Rotterdam. The I.T.F. demanded that O and the crew sign an agreement in I.T.F. terms and that O pay the crew back pay from the time of their engagement. O brought over a German crew and terminated the agreement with S, but refused to pay the back pay, and applied for an injunction restraining the I.T.F. from " blacking " the M contending that the dispute was with S, and not with O, who were separate from S; and that O could not influence S, who were the employers, rather than O. *Held*, dismissing O's appeal, (1) it was plain that this was a trade dispute within the meaning of s. 29 (1) of the Trade Union and Labour Relations Act 1974, and that the acts done in regard to lock gates were done in furtherance of a trade dispute, so that s. 13 of the 1974 Act applied; (2) the relationhip between O and S was so close that a dispute with S was a dispute with O, and the " blacking " would bring pressure to bear, in the first instance, on S and then indirectly on O; (3) since this was a case where there was likely to be statutory immunity, it was not a case where the court would exercise its discretion and grant an injunction under the 1974 Act. PORR v. SHAW, JOHNSON AND HOLDEN; THE MARABU PORR [1979] 2 Lloyd's Rep. 331, C.A.

BOOKS AND ARTICLES. See *post*, pp. [12], [33].

TRANSPORT

2723. Hovercraft

HOVERCRAFT (FEES) (AMENDMENT) REGULATIONS 1979 (No. 1280) [10p], made under S.I. 1972 No. 674, art. 35; operative on December 1, 1979; amend S.I. 1978 No. 483 by prescribing increased fees payable for the issue of an Operating Permit.

HOVERCRAFT (APPLICATION OF ENACTMENTS) (AMENDMENT) ORDER 1979 (No. 1309) [10p], made under the Hovercraft Act 1968 (c. 59), s. 1 (1) (h) (3) (g) (4); operative on November 2, 1979; amends S.I. 1972 No. 971 by adding to Sched. 1 a reference to the Transport Act 1962, s. 67 (2) and to the Transport Act 1968, Sched. 16, para. 4 (5) thus extending to hovercraft operated by British Rail the power of the Board to make by-laws relating to ships operated by them.

2724. Ministers, transfer of functions

MINISTER OF TRANSPORT ORDER 1979 (No. 571) [10p], made under the Ministers of the Crown Act 1975 (c. 26), s. 1; operative on May 24, 1979; transfers to the Minister of Transport the functions previously exercised by the Secretary of State for Transport.

2725. Northern Ireland. See NORTHERN IRELAND.

2726. Railways. See RAILWAYS.

2727. Road Traffic. See ROAD TRAFFIC.

2728. Salaries—compulsory transfer—compensation—" worsening of position "

[Transport Act 1968 (c. 73), s. 135 (1); British Transport (Compensation to Employees) Regulations 1970 (S.I. 1970 No. 187), regs. 5 (1), 13 (1).]

It is not expressly stated, and is not to be implied from s. 135 of the Transport Act 1968, that the test of a " worsening of position " relates to a comparison between an employee's position after transfer, with what it would have been if he had remained with the original company.

British Transport Regulations allowed for the paying of compensation to employees compulsorily transferred to subsidiary companies if they had suffered a worsening of position due to the transfer. Several employees who had been thus transferred, applied for compensation on the grounds that they were receiving less with the subsidiary company than they would have been if they had remained with the parent company. An industrial tribunal found against the applicants, Donaldson J. allowed their appeal, the Court of Appeal affirmed his decision, and on the employer's appeal to the House of Lords, *Held,* allowing the appeal (Lord Wilberforce and Viscount Dilhorne dissenting), that the comparison for " worsening " was to be judged between the past and present position of the men within the subsidiary company only.

TUCK *v.* NATIONAL FREIGHT CORP. [1978] 1 W.L.R. 37, H.L.

2729. Shipping. See SHIPPING AND MARINE INSURANCE.

2730. Taxicabs

LONDON CAB ORDER 1979 (No. 706) [20p], made under the Metropolitan Public Carriage Act 1869 (c. 115), s. 9, the London Cab and Stage Carriage Act 1907 (c. 55), s. 1; and the London Cab Act 1968 (c. 7), s. 1; operative on July 22, 1979; increases the fares payable for the hiring of a cab in the Metropolitan Police District and the City in respect of all journeys beginning and ending there. It also increases the extra charges payable for hirings at night, at weekends and on public holidays.

HACKNEY CARRIAGE FARES (AMENDMENT OF BYELAWS) ORDER 1979 (No. 722) [10p], made under the Finance Act 1974 (c. 30), s. 55; operative on July 4, 1979; empowers a local authority to increase taxi fares which are fixed by by-law, with a view to off-setting higher operating costs attributable to the increases in VAT and the rates of excise duty on petrol and diesel oil.

TAXIMETERS (EEC REQUIREMENTS) REGULATIONS 1979 (No. 1379) [40p], made under the European Communities Act 1972 (c. 68), s. 2 (2); operative on December 1, 1979; implement Council Directive No. 77/95/EEC relating to taximeters.

2731. Transport company—contract with local authority—reorganisation of local government—whether implied term for termination—whether contract frustrated. See KIRKLEES METROPOLITAN BOROUGH COUNCIL *v.* YORKSHIRE WOOLLEN DISTRICT TRANSPORT, CO., § 345.

ARTICLES. See *post*, p. [33].

TRESPASS

2732. Residential property—possession—damages. See SWORDHEATH PROPERTIES *v.* TABET, § 1626.

2733. Right to sue—matrimonial home—desertion of husband—whether landlord going into occupation trespassing

D1 granted to H a tenancy of a dwelling-house from month to month. It was established that H acquired the tenancy for the purposes of a residence for himself, W his wife and their son, and that the house was so used. During the currency of the contractual tenancy H left for New Zealand with the intention of returning, but later decided not to do so. After H's departure and during the currency of the contractual tenancy, D2, the husband of D1, entered the house in the absence of W and the son, and took possession, refusing access to W and the son. D1 later went into occupation with him, having failed to persuade D2 to withdraw, and they remained in occupation for 15 days, until ordered to vacate by an interlocutory order in an action brought by W alone against D1 and D2 claiming damages for trespass. On the question whether W could maintain an action for trespass. *Held*, that in the special circumstances that H was virtually inaccessible, being in New Zealand, W was entitled to maintain the action although her right to occupy the house was not exclusive as against H unless she sought an injunction against him. Dictum of Lord Upjohn in *National Provincial Bank* v. *Ainsworth* [1965] C.L.Y. 1850 applied. On the question of damages, taking into account the character of W, and the fact that D1 was provoked by the attitude of W towards the protection of the Rent Acts, and the necessity to pay rent, £350 was an appropriate award, which included £40 special damages and an element of exemplary damages: TAYLOR *v.* REES, December 15, 1978, Judge Chope, Plymouth County Ct. (*Ex rel. Richard de Lacy, Esq., Barrister.*)

2734. Scaffolding—erected on adjoining property—remedy—interim injunction

In order to repair their premises the defendants needed to erect scaffolding on the plaintiff's adjoining land. Despite an offer of full indemnity, the plaintiff refused permission. When the scaffolding was erected the plaintiff secured an *ex parte* injunction. *Held*, the defendants had trespassed and the plaintiff could not be compensated in damages. The defendant's argument for the suspension of the injunction failed (*Woolerton and Wilson* v. *Richard Costain* [1970] C.L.Y. 2882 not approved). The injunction would be continued even though on an interlocutory motion: JOHN TRENBERTH *v.* NATIONAL WESTMINSTER BANK (1979) 123 S.J. 388, Walton J.

ARTICLES. See *post*, p. [34].

TROVER AND DETINUE

ARTICLES. See *post*, p. [34].

UNIVERSITIES

2735. Education. See EDUCATION.

2736. Membership—visitor—dispute—whether exclusive jurisdiction

If the constitution of a university provides for the appointment of a visitor, the court has no jurisdiction to hear any matter within the jurisdiction of the visitor.

P was a member of Bradford University reading computer science. He failed his first-year examinations and the university required him to withdraw.

P applied to re-enter. The university refused his application without improved " A " levels. P brought an action against the university seeking a declaration that he had unlawfully been refused re-admission, and an injunction and exemplary damages. The university contended that its visitor had exclusive jurisdiction, even though no appointment had in fact been made. Megarry V.-C. found in favour of the university. On appeal by P, *held*, dismissing the appeal, that the courts would not interfere on a matter within the visitor's jurisdiction. (Decision of Sir Robert Megarry V.-C. [1978] C.L.Y. 3026 affirmed.)

PATEL *v.* UNIVERSITY OF BRADFORD SENATE [1979] 2 All E.R. 582, C.A.

VAGRANCY

2737. Suspected person—loitering with intent—whether two distinct acts

P was seen to obscure his hand with a bag and to put his hand in a woman's bag when about to board a bus. He withdrew his hand when the woman jostled backwards as persons were leaving the bus. P followed the woman onto the platform of the bus and repeated his act. He was arrested. The whole incident lasted a matter of seconds. *Held*, allowing P's appeal against conviction of loitering with intent to commit an arrestable offence, that the evidence suggested that P was doing one continuous act disturbed by the woman moving back. Accordingly, there were not the necessary two distinct acts leading first to suspicion and then amounting to loitering: R. *v.* PRYCE [1979] Crim.L.R. 737, Knightsbridge Crown Ct.

VALUE ADDED TAX

2738. Appeal—failure to make returns and pay tax

[Finance Act 1972 (c. 41), ss. 31, 40; Value Added Tax Tribunals Rules 1972 (S.I. 1972 No. 1344), r. 31.] The taxpayer sought to bring an appeal before the tribunal, although the return for the relevant period had not been made and the disputed tax had not been paid or deposited. The taxpayer sought exemption from the requirement to pay or deposit the tax on the ground of severe financial hardship and applied for an adjournment to prepare the returns on the ground that he had not had access to his books which had been in the possession of the Customs and Excise. The tribunal found that the Commissioners had offered access to the books, and also found that the taxpayer had not shown that he would suffer financial hardship. The application was dismissed. *Held*, dismissing the appeal, that there were no grounds for interfering with the tribunal's decision: ABEDIN *v.* CUSTOMS AND EXCISE COMMISSIONERS [1979] S.T.C. 426, Neill J.

2739. —— failure to render outstanding returns

[Finance Act 1972 (c. 41), s. 40; Value Added Tax Tribunals Rules 1972, rr. 16 and 31.] The taxpayer was assessed to value added tax. He appealed against the assessment, but did not pay the outstanding tax assessed or submit returns for the relevant period. In these circumstances the Commissioners of Customs and Excise contended that the appeal could not be entertained. The tribunal refused to adjourn the hearing of the application by the Commissioners and dismissed the appeal. *Held*, that the tribunal had not acted wrongly in refusing to grant an adjournment: SHAHBAG RESTAURANT *v.* CUSTOMS AND EXCISE COMMISSIONERS [1978] T.R. 467, Neill J.

2740. Assessment—period covered—validity

[Finance Act 1972 (c. 41), s. 31.]

S. 31 of the Finance Act 1972 does not require an assessment to value added tax to be made for a specific prescribed accounting period.

G Ltd.'s value added tax returns having been found to be incorrect, the Commissioners made an assessment for a 21 month period and not for several successive three-month accounting periods, it not being possible to attribute the irregularities to any particular prescribed accounting period. G Ltd. contended that the assessment was invalid. *Held*, that where it was not possible to make an assessment related to a specific prescribed accounting period, an assessment for a longer period was in order; but the limitation period for the making of assessments prescribed by F.A. 1972, s. 31, would run from the end of the first prescribed accounting period included in the assessment.

S. J. GRANGE v. CUSTOMS AND EXCISE COMMISSIONERS [1979] 1 W.L.R. 239, C.A.

2741. Building works—" repair or maintenance " appeal from tribunal—whether a point of law

[Finance Act 1972 (c. 41), Sched. 4, Group 8, item 2.]

An appeal against the decision of a VAT tribunal based upon its interpretation of an ordinary English word for the purpose of applying a statute is an appeal upon a point of law.

The appellant builders worked upon buildings damaged by subsidence, the foundations of which buildings did not comply with building regulations. Since the problem could not be cured by replacing the original foundations, additional foundations were added to them. The appellants were assessed to VAT on the work as work of "maintenance," which assessment was upheld by a tribunal on the grounds that " maintenance " included improvements by substitution. *Held,* allowing the appeal, that (1) the purported interpretation of " maintenance," being incomplete and unsatisfactory, afforded the appellant the right of appeal on a point of law; and (2) the work was not work of " repair " or " maintenance "; work resulting in the building being significantly altered in character did not fall within that category; neither " repair " nor " maintenance " included replacing the existing building with something different; material considerations were whether any significant change in the building's life or market value had been effected or whether defects contravening building regulations had been remedied. (*Sotheby* v. *Grundy* (1947) C.L.C. 5413 and *Brew Bros.* v. *Snax (Ross)* [1969] C.L.Y. 2024 applied.)

A.C.T. CONSTRUCTION CO. v. CUSTOMS AND EXCISE COMMISSIONERS [1979] 2 All E.R. 691, Drake J.

2742. Cars

VALUE ADDED TAX (CARS) (AMENDMENT) ORDER 1979 (No. 819) [10p], made under the Finance Act 1972 (c. 41), ss. 3 (9), 43 (1); operative on July 16, 1979; varies S.I. 1977 No. 1795 by allowing input tax to be deducted on the purchase of new cars by certain organisations for the sole purpose of ultimately leading to disabled persons in receipt of mobility allowance.

2743. Church—business—propogation of religion

[Finance Act 1972 (c. 41), s. 2 (2).] The Church of Scientology of California occupied premises at East Grinstead. From there it ran training courses for persons interested in Scientology and sold books and other items of merchandise. *Held,* that for the purposes of value added tax the church carried on the business of the propogation of Scientology. Moneys which it received were for the supply of goods or services in the course of that business (*Customs and Excise Commissioners* v. *Morrison's Academy Boarding Houses Association* [1977] C.L.Y. 3128, applied): CHURCH OF SCIENTOLOGY OF CALIFORNIA v. CUSTOMS AND EXCISE COMMISSIONERS [1979] S.T.C. 297, Neill J.

2744. Club—entertainment—entrance charge

[Finance Act 1972 (c. 41), ss. 13, 31, 40, and Sched. 5, Group 4, item 1.] A working men's club, which was registered for VAT purposes, held regular bingo sessions. On certain evenings it also provided entertainment; on such evenings members had to pay a charge (between 10p and 65p) for entrance to the club. The Customs and Excise Commissioners assessed the club to VAT in respect of the entrance charges. A VAT tribunal dismissed the club's appeal. *Held,* that the case should be remitted to a new tribunal for determination of what part (if any) of the entrance charge was for the provision of bingo (an exempt supply) and what part was attributable to the provision of entertainment and admission fee (taxable supplies). (*British Railways Board* v. *Customs and Excise Commissioners* [1977] C.L.Y. 3133 applied): TYNEWYDD LABOUR WORKING MEN'S CLUB AND INSTITUTE v. CUSTOMS AND EXCISE COMMISSIONERS [1979] S.T.C. 570, Forbes J.

2745. —— **subscription—exempt supply**
[Finance Act 1972 (c. 41), s. 13 (1), Sched. 5, Group 1, item 1.] To enable a club to purchase the head lease of a parcel of land which was used by club members for recreational and holiday facilities, it was agreed that the annual membership subscription should be increased by £25. This brought the total subscription to £104, of which it was admitted that £79 was taxable at the standard rate as being the consideration for the supply of holiday and recreational facilities. It was contended that the excess of £25 was to be treated as an exempt supply on the ground that it was paid for the grant of an interest or right over land or a licence to occupy land. *Held,* that the £25 was not paid for any interest in or right over land, but was part of the subscription consideration for the supply of the club's facilities: CUSTOMS AND EXCISE COMMISSIONERS *v.* THE LITTLE SPAIN CLUB [1979] S.T.C. 170, Neill J.

2746. Construction industry—alteration works—remission to Tribunal
[Finance Act 1972 (c. 41), Sched. 4, Group 8.] Mecca Ltd. purchased a cinema and spent some £150,000 on converting it into a bingo hall. The account rendered by the contractor sought to distinguish between zero-rated and standard-rated supplies. The Customs and Excise Commisisoners agreed to zero-rate some items but not others. On appeal to the tribunals, it was held that nine out of 19 items were zero-rated supplies. Appeals and cross-appeals were brought. *Held,* that as the tribunal may have erred in their construction of Group 8 and failed to apply the correct treatment to refurbishments, the case should be remitted to the tribunal for further consideration: CUSTOMS AND EXCISE COMMISSIONERS *v.* MORRISON DUNBAR AND MECCA [1978] T.R. 267, Neill J.

2747. Exemptions
VALUE ADDED TAX (FINANCE) ORDER 1979 (No. 243) [10p], made under the Finance Act 1972 (c. 41), ss. 13 (2) and 43 (1); operative on April 2, 1979; extends the exemption under item 2 of Group 5 of the Exemption Schedule to the 1972 Act to include certain additional supplies associated with instalment credit finance, the total charges for which do not exceed £10.

2748. Gifts to employees—course of business
[Finance Act 1972 (c. 41), s. 2.] R.H.M. Bakeries (Northern) Ltd. made gifts of clocks and other articles to employees who had completed 25 years of service. The Customs and Excise claimed that VAT was exigible on the value of the gifts. *Held,* that VAT was chargeable, the articles being supplied (or deemed to be supplied) in the course of the company's business, and the fact that the gift might constitute emoluments of employment not excluding them from the scope of value added tax: R.H.M. BAKERIES (NORTHERN) *v.* CUSTOMS AND EXCISE COMMISSIONERS [1979] S.T.C. 72, Neill J.

2749. Group supplies—retrospective treatment
[Finance Act 1972 (c. 41), s. 21.] Following a re-organisation within the Save and Prosper Group, a particular subsidiary company, which was not registered or included in a group registration, commenced business. Consequently, inter-company supplies became chargeable to VAT. Save and Prosper applied for retrospective group treatment. *Held,* that the Commissioners of Customs and Excise had power to entertain an application for retrospective group treatment, and that the matter should be sent back to them so that they might re-consider the application: CUSTOMS AND EXCISE COMMISSIONERS *v.* SAVE AND PROSPER GROUP [1979] S.T.C. 205, Neill J.

2750. Higher rate—goods " suitable " for use
[Finance (No. 2) Act 1975 (c. 45), s. 17, Sched. 7, Group 3.]
" Suitable " in Sched. 7, Group 3, to the 1975 Act means " designed " or " adapted for."
The taxpayer company, which supplied sailing and other recreational equipment, sold couplings and winches which were standard fittings for linking a trailer to a towing vehicle. The question was whether the couplings and winches attracted value added tax at the higher rate as being goods of a kind suitable for use as parts of trailers and trolleys when used as accessories to boats. *Held,* allowing the taxpayer company's appeal from the decision

of the Divisional Court, that "goods of a kind suitable for use as parts of" meant a kind or genus of goods specially designed or intended for purposes ancillary to boats.

CUSTOMS AND EXCISE COMMISSIONERS *v.* MECHANICAL SERVICES (TRAILER ENGINEERS) [1979] 1 All E.R. 501, C.A.

2751. International services

VALUE ADDED TAX (INTERNATIONAL SERVICES) (NO. 2) ORDER 1979 (No. 1554) [10p], made under the Finance Act 1972 (c. 41), ss. 12 (4), 43 (1); operative on January 1, 1980; removes from eligibility to zero-rating under item 6 (*a*) of group 9 of Sched. 4 to the 1972 Act the supply of any certificate of deposit which is exempt, whether made to a person in the U.K. or to a person overseas.

2752. Management services—consideration—group relief payments

[Finance Act 1972 (c. 41), ss. 5 and 10.] From May 1973 the taxpayer company provided management services for group companies without making any charge. In consequence the taxpayer company sustained losses which it proposed to utilise under the group relief provisions in return for payments. In 1974 the auditors of the taxpayer company recommended that an agreement should be entered into formulating the group relief arrangements. Accordingly, an agreement was entered into which referred to the management services and provided that the parent company of the group would procure group relief payments to be made to the taxpayer company. *Held*, that VAT was chargeable on the group relief payments, such payments being consideration for the services supplied by the taxpayer company: CUSTOMS AND EXCISE COMMISSIONERS *v.* TILLING MANAGEMENT SERVICES [1979] S.T.C. 365, Neill J.

2753. Margin scheme—records—jurisdiction of tribunal

[Finance Act 1972 (c. 41), ss. 30, 40; Value Added Tax (Works of Art, Antiques and Scientific Collections) Order 1972 (S.I. 1972 No. 1971), art. 3 (5).]

The VAT Tribunal has jurisdiction to review the decision of the Commissioners as to the sufficiency of a taxpayer's books and records for the purposes of the "margin scheme."

The taxpayer company dealt in antique coins and medals; it sought to account for VAT under the "margin scheme" authorised by the Value Added Tax (Works of Art, Antiques and Scientific Collections) Order 1972. The scheme applied where the taxpayer's records and accounts complied with requirements specified by the Customs and Excise Commissioners, or were such as the Commissioners recognised as sufficient. The Commissioners determined that the taxpayer's records were not sufficient for the purposes of the scheme. The taxpayer appealed. The point in issue was whether the tribunal had jurisdiction to review the determination of the Commissioners. *Held* (Eveleigh L.J. dissenting), reversing the decision of Neill J., that it was open to the tribunal to review the Commissioners' decision as to the sufficiency of the taxpayer's records.

CUSTOMS AND EXCISE COMMISSIONERS *v.* J. H. CORBITT (NUMISMATISTS) [1979] 3 W.L.R. 300, C.A.

2754. Practice—debts due to Crown—set off—bankruptcy. See *Re* CUSHLA, § 160.

2755. Purchase tax—relief—tribunal—jurisdiction

[Finance Act 1972 (c. 41), s. 4 (1).] The taxpayers claimed relief under F.A. 1972, s. 4, on the ground that purchase tax had been charged on goods held in stock by them on March 31, 1973. The Customs and Excise investigated the claim, but was not satisfied that purchase tax had in fact been charged on the goods. Accordingly, relief was refused. The taxpayers' appeal to the tribunal was opposed by the Commissioners on the ground that the tribunal had no jurisdiction to review the Commissioners' decision as to relief for purchase tax and, in any event, relief was available only where the purchase tax was intended to be accounted for and paid by the supplier. The tribunal held that it had jurisdiction to entertain the appeal and that relief was available where the goods had been bought in circumstances which rendered the supplier liable to pay purchase tax. *Held,* that the tribunal had jurisdiction and that the decision as to the availability of relief was correct: CUSTOMS AND EXCISE COMMISSIONERS *v.* C. & A. MODES [1979] S.T.C. 433, Drake J.

2756. Receiver—tax received—accountability—discretion
[Law of Property Act 1925 (c. 20), s. 109 (8).]
Even though he is not personally liable, a receiver must pay VAT which is due to the Commissioners of Customs and Excise in preference to payment to a debenture holder.

X Co. issued a debenture in favour of the bank in the form of a floating charge over the whole of the company's undertaking. The bank appointed R as receiver and manager of X Co.'s property under the debenture. X Co. continued to trade and to charge VAT to its customers. X Co. had insufficient funds to pay the bank and the Commissioners of Customs and Excise. R issued an originating summons to determine whether he was bound to account for the money to the Commissioners or whether he had a discretion to apply it towards payment under the debenture. *Held,* although the tax was not recoverable from R personally or as receiver, nor from the bank, to fail to pay it was a criminal offence by the company, and therefore R had no discretion.
Re JOHN WILLMENT (ASHFORD) [1979] 2 All E.R. 615, Brightman J.

2756a. Regulations
VALUE ADDED TAX (GENERAL) (AMENDMENT) REGULATIONS 1979 (No. 1614) [10p], made under the Finance Act 1972 (c. 41), s. 16; operative on January 1, 1980; converts the weight limit applied to determine whether a motor car shall be entitled to relief given in Regulation 40 of the Value Added Tax (General) Regulations 1977 to a convenient metric measure.

2757. Returns—failure to furnish—date for calculation of penalty
[Finance Act 1972 (c. 41), s. 38 (7); Value Added Tax (General) Regulations (S.I. 1975 No. 2204) reg. 51.]
The period of calculation for the penalty aspect of a failure to make a VAT return does not terminate with the laying of the information, but continues to the date of hearing.

On March 9, 1977, an information was laid by Customs and Excise alleging failure to furnish a return for the period June–August 1976 by January 31, 1977. The justices, in addition to a fine, imposed a penalty of £3 per day from January 1 to March 9, 1977, the date the information was laid. On appeal by the commissioners, *held,* allowing the appeal, that the calculation period for the penalty did not stop with the laying of the information but continued to the date of hearing.
GRICE *v.* NEEDS [1979] 3 All E.R. 501, D.C.

2758. Sale of stolen cars—supply
[Finance Act 1972 (c. 41), s. 5.] A second-hand car dealer, who was a taxable person for the purposes of value added tax, stole and sold 17 motor-cars. *Held,* that the sale of the cars was a taxable supply made in the course of the car dealer's business: CUSTOMS AND EXCISE COMMISSIONERS *v.* OLIVER, *The Times,* December 8, 1979, Griffiths J.

2759. Supplies
VALUE ADDED TAX (SUPPLIES BY RETAILERS) (AMENDMENT) REGULATIONS 1979 (No. 224) [10p], made under the Finance Act 1972 (c. 41); s. 30; operative on April 2, 1979; amends S.I. 1972 No. 1148 to make clear that a notice includes a leaflet and that the Commissioners of Customs and Excise may vary the terms of any method described in a notice published by them without republishing the whole of any notice previously issued.

2760. Tribunal decisions
Appeal—extension of time
TRIPPETT *v.* THE COMMISSIONERS (1978) V.A.T.T.R. 260 (in 1973 and 1974 assessments to VAT were made on a partnership of which the Commissioners considered the applicant to be a member. No appeal was made, and High Court proceedings were taken to recover the tax assessed. In April 1976 the Commissioners notified the applicant that they considered him to be a member of the partnership. In April 1978 the applicant gave notice disputing that decision and applied for extension of time to appeal. *Held,* that where, as in this case, there was no prejudice to any party which could not be compensated

by the imposition of conditions (*e.g.*, as to costs), extension of time should be granted).

Assessment—appeal—mistake of law

KYFFIN *v.* THE COMMISSIONERS (1978) V.A.T.T.R. 175 (The applicant was assessed to VAT on the ground that certain input tax relating to the training of racehorses had been incorrectly deducted by him. The applicant paid the tax. Subsequently, a tribunal decision indicated that deduction of such input tax might have been proper. The applicant applied for extension of time to allow him to appeal. *Held,* that there was no jurisdiction to grant extension of time where tax had been paid voluntarily under a mistake of law).

Association—building used by Masonic Lodges—payments/donations by Lodges

SWINDON MASONIC ASSOCIATION *v.* THE COMMISSIONERS (1978) V.A.T.T.R. 200 (the Association, which was resistered for VAT purposes, owned and maintained a building which it made available for use by Masonic Lodges. In respect of each occasion of use a Lodge paid to the Association a pre-determined amount (" expenses reclaimed "). In addition, Lodges collected donations from members for the Association ("donations "), and entertainment committees of Lodges organised fund rising events for the Association (" Swindon receipts "). The Commissioners sought to treat the Association as a club and to treat all three classes of payments as consideration for supplies by the Association. *Held*, that (1) the " donations " were not payments for any supply; (2) the " Swindon receipts " were donations by the Lodges and were not payments for any supply; and (3) the " expenses reclaimed " were for a licence to occupy land, and such supply was exempt under F.A. 1972, Sched. 5, Group 1, item 1).

Buildings—construction

HULME EDUCATIONAL FOUNDATION *v.* THE COMMISSIONERS (1978) V.A.T.T.R. 179 (the appellants, estate managers of a charitable foundation, entered into an agreement with trustees of a pension fund for a long lease of property. The property was to be redeveloped, and to this end an agreement was made with a development company. The development company entered into a contract with a builder for the demolition and construction work. The Commissioners of Customs and Excise determined that the appellants did not make taxable supplies and so should not be registered for the purposes of VAT. *Held,* that the appellants were not a person constructing a building, since they neither did the actual construction works nor entered into the building contract. Since they made exempt, and not taxable supplies, they were not qualified for registration).

MONSELL YOUELL DEVELOPMENTS *v.* THE COMMISSIONERS [1978] V.A.T.T.R. 1 (D Ltd. bought land for development, laid out roads and sewers, and sold plots to individual purchasers. Y Ltd., an associated company, entered into contracts with the purchasers to build houses. D Ltd. claimed that the sales of plots by it were zero-rated under F.A. 1972, Sched. 4, Group 8, item 1. *Held*, that D Ltd. was not a person constructing a building, so that the supply was not zero-rated, but was an exempt supply under F.A. 1972, Sched. 5, Group 1, item 1).

Charity—business—building

ROYAL EXCHANGE TRUST *v.* THE COMMISSIONERS (1978) V.A.T.T.R. 139 (a charitable trust was created to advance public education by the erection and endowment of a threatre in Manchester. The trust obtained a long lease of part of the Royal Exchange building and, with finance raised by it, caused a free-standing theatre to be erected within the hall thereof. The lease was then voluntarily assigned by the trust to a company incorporated by it. The trust, which was registered for VAT, claimed deduction of certain input tax. *Held,* that the input tax was deductible, as (1) the activities of the trust constituted a business, and (2) the theatre was a " building," notwithstanding that it was in essential respects dependent on exterior sources, so that the assignment of the lease was a taxable supply).

Club—members required to subscribe for bonds—composite supply
DYRHAM PARK COUNTRY CLUB *v.* THE COMMISSIONERS (1978) V.A.T.T.R.
244 (the rules of a golf and country club provided for different categories of
members. Members were required to pay annual subscriptions (which varied
with membership categories) and also to subscribe for bonds (the amount of
which varied with membership categories). The Commissioners contended that
the moneys subscribed for bonds was consideration for the rights and facilities
made available by the club. *Held*, that (1) the transaction was a composite
supply of (a) the bond, and (b) the right to membership; and (2) that the
amount attributable to the bond was exempt from VAT (F.A. 1972, Sched. 5,
Group 5), but the amount attributable to membership attracted VAT at the
standard rate).

Gifts—incentive schemes—estoppel
G.U.S. MERCHANDISE CORP. *v.* THE COMMISSIONERS [1978] V.A.T.T.R. 28
(the appellant carried on a mail order business. It operated a number of " gift "
and incentive schemes to recruit agents and to induce agents to become
more active. It had been advised by officers of the Customs and Excise in
August 1972 that VAT would not be chargeable on supplies made
under such schemes. Subsequently, the appellant's books were examined and
no point was made as to the omission to account for tax on such supplies.
The amounts were later assessed. *Held*, (1) where gifts of negligible value were
supplied, no tax was chargeable (F.A. 1972, Sched. 3, para. 6); (2) tax was
chargeable on goods supplied under other incentive schemes; (3) no estoppel
lay against the Commissioners in relation to the mandatory provisions of the
Finance Act 1972 imposing the tax; and (4) the assessments were not made
out of time, as they were made within one year of the Commissioners discovering all the information enabling them to make the assessments).

Goods obtained by deception—supply
HARRY B. LITHERLAND & CO. *v.* THE COMMISSIONERS (1978) V.A.T.T.R. 226
(the appellant, a dealer in electrical goods, was fraudulently induced by G to
supply to him 150 colour television sets. The invoiced price was £25,000 plus
VAT of £3,187·50. G failed to make any payments; the appellant notified the
police; G was subsequently convicted of dishonestly obtaining the television
sets, which were not recovered by the appellant. The Commissioners claimed
payment of £3,187·50 VAT. *Held*, that (1) as the appellant had avoided the
contract by notifying the police, there had been no supply by him for VAT;
and (2) as the television sets had been lost or destroyed so as to be unavailable
for supply by the appellant, the assessment should be reduced accordingly).

Input tax—estoppel
NORMAL MOTOR FACTORS *v.* THE COMMISSIONERS [1978] V.A.T.T.R. 20 (the
appellant company supplied motor products, and as part of the service
guaranteed to reimburse to owners repairs costs which might subsequently be
incurred by them. An officer of the Customs and Excise informed the company
that it would be entitled to deduct as input tax the VAT in any amount
reimbursed. Subsequently, the Commissioners decided that such amounts were
not deductible as input tax. *Held*, that the amounts were not deductible input
tax of the appellant company, and that the Commissioners were not estopped
from obtaining payment, the officer's representation being of law and not of
fact).

—— *racehorses—business entertainment*
BRITISH CAR AUCTIONS *v.* THE COMMISSIONERS [1978] V.A.T.T.R. 56 (the
appellant company bought and trained racehorses and raced them in its name.
It claimed to do this for the purposes of advertising and as a public relations
exercise. It sought to deduct as input tax value added tax charged. *Held*, that
deduction of the tax as input tax was prohibited by art. 3 of the Input Tax
(Exceptions) (No. 3) Order 1972, because the racehorses and their training had
been used for the purposes of business entertainment).

Jersey company—place of supply
INTERBET TRADING *v.* THE COMMISSIONERS (No. 2) (1978) V.A.T.T.R. 235

(the appellant company carried on business of a racing tipster from Jersey. It made an arrangement with a company in York for transmission of information to the appellant's clients. The company in York also collected and accounted to the appellant for moneys due from clients, and carried out certain other administrative services for the appellant. The agreement between the appellant and the York company expressly precluded the latter from negotiating or concluding contracts for the appellant and provided that the York company should not be a branch or fixed place of business of the appellant. *Held*, that the appellant was rendering services for reward through the agency of the York company and such services were supplied in the U.K. The appellant was, therefore, liable to be registered as a taxable person).

Meals and accommodation—entertainment

SHAKLEE INTERNATIONAL *v.* THE COMMISSIONERS; SHAKLEE U.K. SERVICE CORP. *v.* THE COMMISSIONERS (1978) V.A.T.T.R. 267 (from time to time throughout the year the appellant companies held meetings for their distribution agents; the purpose of the meetings was the training and instruction of the agents. The spouses of the agents attended; meals and accommodation were provided. The Commissioners held that the meals and accommodation were " business entertainment " and that VAT attributable thereto was not deductible as input tax. *Held*, that the provision of the meals and accommodation in the course of training sessions was not " business entertainment ").

Society—registration—exemption

ROYAL PHOTOGRAPHIC SOCIETY *v.* THE COMMISSIONERS (1978) V.A.T.T.R. 191 (the Society's object was the advancement of photographic science. It had some 7,000 members, consisting mainly, but not exclusively, of persons who used photography in the course of their professions. The Society held examinations. The Society claimed that it was not required to register for VAT as it was a professional association (item 1 (*b*) of Group 9), or an association the primary purpose of which was the advancement of a branch of knowledge connected with the past or present professions or employments of its members. *Held*, that the membership of the Society was such that it was not exempt under either item 1 (*b*) or (*c*)).

Supply—goods—passing of property

VERNITRON *v.* THE COMMISSIONERS (1978) V.A.T.T.R. 157 (the appellant company sold goods on terms that property should not pass until the purchase price had been paid in full. The purchaser of certain goods went into receivership before making payment in respect of certain goods delivered to it by the appellant. The appellant claimed that the goods delivered but not paid for had not been supplied for VAT purposes. *Held*, that as goods were not " on approval " or " on sale or return " they had been supplied by the appellant when removed by it for delivery).

Voluntary body—self-build project—extra-statutory concession

CANDO 70 *v.* THE COMMISSIONERS (1978) V.A.T.T.R. 211 (the appellant was a " project organisation " of a Baptist Church, established for the purposes of carrying out works of conversion of a church into a social, educational and recreational centre. The appellant sought registration for VAT purposes in accordance with Public Notice " SHP 1 " entitled " Value Added Tax: Voluntary Bodies engaged in Self-Build or Self-Help Construction Projects." The Commissioners refused registration on the ground that the works were alteration and enlargement of an existing building. *Held*, that (1) the Church made gratuitous supplies of facilities and not taxable supplies, and so was not entitled to be registered; and (2) where registration was available only on a concessionary basis the tribunal had no jurisdiction to interfere with the Commissioners' decision).

Works of art—consideration—margin scheme

JOCELYN FIELDING FINE ARTS *v.* THE COMMISSIONERS (1975) V.A.T.T.R. 164 (the appellant, an art dealer, accounted for VAT on the basis that the consideration for goods supplied was the excess of the consideration given for the goods over their cost of acquisition to it. It sold goods at Sotheby's and Christie's on terms whereby it paid a commission on the " hammer price " and the purchaser paid a buyer's premium to the auctioneers. *Held,* that the buyer's premium was not part of the consideration for the supply by the appellant).

Works of restoration—repair
P.C.C. OF ST. LUKES, GREAT CROSBY *v.* THE COMMISSIONERS (1978) V.A.T.T.R. 218 (a church was badly damaged by fire. Extensive works of restoration were carried out, the church effectively being completely redesigned. The P.C.C. claimed that all the supplies made to it by the contractor were zero-rated supplies. *Held,* that in the question whether works are in the nature of repair, the criterion is restoration of efficiency in function and not repetition of form or material. On this basis, the works were repairs chargeable to VAT at the standard rate).

2761. Zero-rating
VALUE ADDED TAX (DONATED MEDICAL EQUIPMENT) ORDER 1979 (No. 242) [10p], made under the Finance Act 1972 (c. 41), ss. 12 (4) and 43 (1); operative on April 2, 1979; extends the zero-rate relief to supplies of medical or scientific equipment for donation to designated Regional and Area Health Authorities in England and Wales, Health Boards in Scotland and Health and Social Services Boards in Northern Ireland.
VALUE ADDED TAX (INTERNATIONAL SERVICES) ORDER 1979 (No. 244) [10p], made under the Finance Act 1972, ss. 12 (4) and 43 (1); operative on April 2, 1979; varies Sched. 4, Group 9 to the 1972 Act. It zero-rates the supply of taxable insurance and re-insurance services, and revokes note (7), thus allowing zero-rating under item 5 or 6 for the services of valuing, carrying out work on goods and those services described in item 3 (*a*) or (*b*) of the Group.
VALUE ADDED TAX (AIDS FOR THE DISABLED) ORDER 1979 (No. 245) [10p], made under the Finance Act 1972, ss. 12 (4) and 43 (1); operative on April 2, 1979; zero-rates the supply to the RNIB, the National Listening Library and similar charities of apparatus designed for the reproduction, for the blind or severely handicapped, of speech recorded on magnetic tape.
VALUE ADDED TAX (MEDICAL GOODS AND SERVICES) ORDER 1979 (No. 246) [20p], made under the Finance Act 1972, ss. 12 (4), 13 (2) and 43 (1); operative on April 2, 1979; takes account of changes in the registers of qualified medical practitioners introduced by the Medical Act 1978.
VALUE ADDED TAX (GENERAL) ORDER 1979 (No. 657) [10p], made under the Finance Act 1972, ss. 12 (4), 43 (1); operative on June 18, 1979; continues the exclusion from the zero-rate provisions of the supply of marine, aviation and transport insurance in respect of certain types of boats, aircraft and hovercraft.

2762. —— management course—foreign participants
[Finance Act 1972 (c. 41), Sched. 4, Group 9, item 6.] The company, which was registered for VAT, provided management services for commerce and industry. It held an intensive management course in Birmingham for foreign executives. The price charged for the course included travel, accommodation and board, and tuition. A number of executives from Nigeria attended, and payment for the course was made in foreign currency in Nigeria. The company claimed that the supply was of services to an overseas resident and was not used by a person present in the U.K., and so fell to be zero-rated. *Held,* allowing the Crown's appeal, (1) the executives " used " the services supplied when they attended the courses, so that the supply was not a zero-rated supply; and (2) there was a single composite supply, so that it was not appropriate to remit the case to the tribunal for an apportionment. (*Customs and Excise Commissioners* v. *Scott* [1978] C.L.Y. 3044 applied): CUSTOMS AND EXCISE COMMISSIONERS *v.* G. & B. PRACTICAL MANAGEMENT DEVELOPMENT [1979] S.T.C. 280, D.C.

2763. —— single service or separate service
[Finance Act 1972 (c. 41), s. 12 (2), Sched. 4, Group 1, general item 2.] The

taxpayers operated a stud farm; animals brought to stud were also kept and fed. Separate charges were made for the stud services and the keep and feed. The taxpayers claimed that the latter items were zero-rated for the purposes of VAT. *Held,* that the services supplied by the taxpayers constituted a single supply (stud services), the whole of which supply was a taxable supply under the Finance Act 1972 (*Customs and Excise Commissioners* v. *Scott* [1978] C.L.Y. 3044 applied): CUSTOMS AND EXCISE COMMISSIONERS *v.* BUSHBY [1979] S.T.C. 8, Neill J.

BOOKS AND ARTICLES. See *post,* pp. [12], [34].

VENDOR AND PURCHASER

2764. Conveyancing. See REAL PROPERTY AND CONVEYANCING.

2765. Covenants. See REAL PROPERTY AND CONVEYANCING.

2766. Exchange of contracts—exchange by telephone
Where a solicitor, acting for a vendor or purchaser, holds his client's signed part of the contract, exchange of contracts may be effected in any way recognised by the law as amounting to an exchange. A telephone conversation was such an exchange and therefore a binding contract was created by exchange of contracts by a telephone conversation. Any uncertainties about terms or effects could perhaps be solved as a question of practice by both solicitors recording an identical attendance note: DOMB *v.* ISOZ, *The Times*, December 5, 1979, C.A.

2767. Failure of purchaser to complete—Law Society's General Conditions of Sale—damages—rate of interest
[The Law Society's General Conditions of Sale (1973 rev.), conds. 16 (1), 19.]
Under condition 19 (4) (*b*) of the Law Society's General Conditions of Sale, a vendor may choose between either rescinding the contract and suing for restitution or affirming the contract and suing for damages for breach, either reselling or not reselling, or suing for specific performance; but if he chooses to exercise his rights under condition 19 (4) (*c*) he may only recover the liquidated damages defined by it.
V contracted to sell a house to P for £55,000. P paid a deposit of £5,500. The property was to be sold subject to the Law Society's General Conditions of Sale (1973 rev.). The rate of interest payable under condition 16 was 15 per cent., and completion was to take place on July 28. V served a notice to complete on August 2. Then on September 4 V forfeited the deposit; V resold the house for £51,000, on December 4 V claimed (i) the difference in price, £4,000; (ii) costs of resale £1,153; (iii) interest at 15 per cent. on the purchase price from the original date of completion until completion on resale under condition 16, alternatively at such rate as might be found just. P was admittedly in breach and did not dispute (i) and (ii). Under (iii) the judge awarded interest on the £5,500 prior to its forfeiture and on the £49,500 from original completion date until completion on resale, at 11.2 per cent. P appealed on the ground that the liquidated damages were agreed damages and no further damages were payable. V contended that the condition merely provided a means of quantification of one element in the damages to which they were entitled at common law. *Held,* that V had chosen to exercise his rights and remedies under condition 19 (4) (*c*). He could only do so within the limits of the provisions of the condition and could only recover the liquidated damages defined by it.
TALLEY *v.* WOLSEY-NEECH (1979) 38 P. & C.R. 45, C.A.

2768. Memorandum—in writing—whether letter sufficient memorandum
[Eire.] [Statute of Frauds (Ireland) 1695 (c. 12).] The plaintiff orally agreed with an estate agent, who had acted for the defendants in a previous sale of land to the plaintiff, to purchase adjoining land from the defendants. The agent wrote to the defendants' property adviser stating that he and the plaintiff had agreed terms subject to contract and setting out the terms. The defendants' solicitors sent a contract to the plaintiff's solicitors requesting its return within

seven days. When the plaintiff for various reasons was unable to comply the defendants refused to complete and the plaintiff sued for specific performance. *Held*, that the agent's letter to the defendants' adviser contained all the necessary terms and was a sufficient memorandum in writing for the purposes of the Statute of Frauds. The seven-day period for the return of the contract was an arbitrarily imposed and unreasonably short period and it would be inequitable to allow the vendors by that device to defeat an otherwise valid agreement: KELLY *v.* PARK HALL SCHOOL (1978) 111 I.L.T.R. 9, Eire Sup.Ct.

2769. Northern Ireland. See NORTHERN IRELAND.

2270. Sale of land—contract—damages for breach—rule in Bain v. Fothergill

[Can.] R accepted an offer from J to purchase a building. Mistakenly thinking J had not fulfilled its part of the contract, R accepted an offer from A. J succeeded in an action for specific performance and A sued for damages. The trial judge held the agreement with J, although unregistered, was effective against R and hence operated as a defect in their title. By the rule in *Bain* v. *Fothergill* (" the rule "), A was denied recovery for the loss of its bargain and its damages were limited to its out-of-pocket expenses. On appeal, the questions were whether (1) the rule was properly applied, and (2) the rule should no longer be followed in common law Canada if it had been properly applied. *Held*, the reason for the rule lay in the uncertainty of English titles. Because the English system lacked a reliable registration system it was felt unfair to penalise a vendor who, due to a mistake as to the validity of his title, was unable to give good title to a purchaser. The exceptions to the rule were (1) fraud on the vendor's part; (2) bad faith on the vendor's part; (3) defects arising out of matters of conveyancing; (4) breach of covenants in an executed conveyance. Although there was not a fraud or want of good faith here, the rule could not be applied as R had either voluntarily disabled himself from being able to convey or had risked and lost his ability to do so by having concurrent dealings with two different purchasers. On the second question, if it had been necessary to decide the case on this point, the rule should no longer be followed where a Torrens system of title registration, or a near similar system, applies. (*Bain* v. *Fothergill* (1874) L.R. 7 H.L. not followed; *Day* v. *Singleton* [1899] 2 Ch. 320, *Wroth* v. *Tyler* [1973] C.L.Y. 3466 considered): A.V.G. MANAGEMENT SCIENCE *v.* BARWELL DEVELOPMENTS [1979] 1 W.W.R. 330, Can.Sup.Ct.

2771. —— defect in title—duty to disclose

In equity, the vendors of land are obliged to make a full and frank disclosure of known defects in the title in language which would show to the ordinary purchaser that such defects exist.

By a contract subject to the National Conditions of Sale (19th ed.) The plaintiffs agreed to purchase registered land from the defendants and paid a deposit to a stakeholder. By a special condition the sale was " subject to entries on the registers of title "; by the general conditions the property was sold subject to any covenants, a copy of which could be inspected at the vendor's solicitors offices, the purchaser being deemed to purchase with notice thereof whether or not he had made an inspection. Inspection of the register revealed that title in the land was subject to restrictive covenants under an 1883 deed which had not been produced on first registration. In response to a requisition, the vendor's solicitors said that a copy of the deed could not be supplied. *Held*, that notwithstanding the strict terms of the contract, the vendor was in equity obliged to disclose such a defect and that since the vendor had not done so, specific performance of the contract would not be ordered; that accordingly the plaintiff was entitled to a declaration that only he could give a good receipt and discharge for the deposit to the stakeholder. (*Williams* v. *Wood* (1868) 16 W.R. 1005 and *Nottingham Patent Brick & Tile Co.* v. *Butler* (1885) 15 Q.B.D. 261, applied.)

FARUQI *v.* ENGLISH REAL ESTATES [1979] 1 W.L.R. 963, Walton J.

2772. —— delay in completion—damages

[Law of Property Act 1925 (c. 20), s. 41; Law Society's Conditions of Sale (1973 revision) condition 19.]

A term in a contract providing for completion on a named day cannot, except in clear context, be construed as providing for completion on some later date; the effect of s. 41 of the Law of Property Act 1925 is not to negative the existence of a breach, but merely to bar, in certain circumstances, the assertion that the breach amounts to a repudiation.

By a contract (incorporating the Law Society's Conditions) the third party agreed to sell a house to the defendants, with completion on July 12, 1977. The defendants agreed to sell a house to the plaintiffs with the same completion date. The third party could not complete in time, the plaintiffs had already moved out, and the defendants were unable to give the plaintiffs' vacant possession. The defendants served a notice to complete on the third party, and the contract was completed by the specified day. The plaintiff had incurred accommodation expenses for which he recovered damages. The defendants served a notice claiming indemnity on the third party. The judge dismissed the proceedings. On appeal, *held*, allowing the appeal, that (1) a term providing for completion on a named day could not, in the absence of a clear context, be construed as meaning it was to be completed on a later date; (2) the service of a notice to complete under condition 19 did not affect or discharge any accrued rights or cause of action. (Dicta in *Howe* v. *Smith* (1884) 27 Ch.D. 89 and *Stickney* v. *Keeble* [1915] A.C. 386 applied; *Babacomp* v. *Rightside Properties* [1974] C.L.Y. 3931 distinguished; *Smith* v. *Hamilton* (1950) C.L.C. 10579 disapproved.)

RAINERI *v.* MILES; WIEJSKI (THIRD PARTY) [1979] 3 All E.R. 763, C.A.

2773. —— evidence of earlier contract for sale—presumption of advancement
[Land Registration Act 1925 (c. 21), s. 13 (*c*).]
The court should declare a good title shown where in the opinion of the court, the facts and circumstances of the case are so compelling as to show beyond reasonable doubt that no risk of a successful assertion of the incumbrance exists.

Per curiam, it was inconceivable that where the court had found a good marketable title, the Chief Land Registrar should find something less.

The vendors sold land as trustees. Subsequent examination of the title showed a pre-existing contract for sale made in 1912, the details of which were not available and which was described as " suspended " on terms which were not known. Goulding J. held that the trustees had failed to show good title. The Court of Appeal allowed the trustees' appeal and held that the court should presume facts where a jury would formally have been directed so as to presume them. On the purchasers' appeal to the House of Lords, *held*, dismissing the appeal, that where the facts and circumstances of a case were so compelling to the mind of the court that it concludes beyond reasonable doubt that the purchaser would not be at risk of a successful assertion against him of the incumbrance, a good title should be declared. (Dictum of Lord Cozens-Hardy M.R. in *Smith* v. *Colbourne* [1914] 2 Ch. 533 and *Johnson* v. *Clarke* [1928] Ch. 847 applied.)

M.E.P.C. *v.* CHRISTIAN-EDWARDS [1979] 3 W.L.R. 713, H.L.

2774. —— private caveat—application to remove—burden upon caveator. See ENG MEE YONG *v.* LETCHUMANAN S/O VELAYUTHAM, § 2201.

2775. —— purchaser unable to complete—forfeiture—discretion to order return of deposit
[Law of Property Act 1925 (c. 20), s. 49 (2).]
The court has an unqualified discretion under s. 49 (2) of the 1925 Act to order the repayment of a deposit where the justice of the case so requires.

The plaintiffs agreed to buy a substantial property in London and paid a 10 per cent. deposit. The purchasers, who were financing the transaction from moneys deposited in Nigeria, were unable to complete on time and were served with a 28 day completion notice. Unforeseen delays caused by Nigerian exchange regulations prevented the purchasers complying with the notice, although the money duly arrived within a few days of the expiry of the notice. The vendors forfeited the deposit. The purchasers brought an action seeking to recover the deposit, which action was struck out at first instance. On appeal,

held, allowing the appeal, that the court had an unqualified discretion to order
the return of the deposit subject only to the discretion being exercised judicially
and with regard to all the relevant considerations (*Schindler* v. *Pigault* [1976]
C.L.Y. 2682 approved).

UNIVERSAL CORP. *v.* FIVE WAYS PROPERTIES [1979] 1 All E.R. 552, C.A.

2776. —— repudiation—date damages calculated

[Can.] It has been *held,* that where a purchaser repudiates a contract for
the sale of land, and the land subsequently decreases in value, the appropriate
time for calculating damages is at the date of the breach, not the date of trial
(*Wroth* v. *Tyler* [1973] C.L.Y. 3466 and *Grant* v. *Dawkins* [1973] C.L.Y.
3469 distinguished; *Livingston* v. *Rawyards Coal* (1880) 5 App.Cas. 25 applied):
WOODFORD ESTATES *v.* POLLACK (1978) 93 D.L.R. (3d) 350, Ont. H.C.J.

2777. —— time of the essence—postponement of completion—rescission ab initio

Time, once of the essence, does not cease to be so merely because one
party gives the other an extension of time to a fixed date to complete.

On September 19, 1973, P agreed to buy a property from V, completion
to be not later than October 31. P could not complete due to lack of funds.
On November 2 V served a notice to complete within 28 days, *i.e.* by December
1. V introduced P to X, a possible substitute purchaser but negotiations failed.
P was given extensions of time to December 6, then to January 28, 1974.
He failed to complete, and on February 7 P wrote to D, V's solicitors, formally
rescinding the contract, stating interest payable, and indicating a sum in settlement in default of which proceedings would be taken for V's full losses. In
July V and P, with D's encouragement, tried to revive the contract, but P
was still unable to complete. V obtained summary judgment against P who
then sued his solicitors D for negligence in failing to advise P that (1) by
February 7 time was no longer of the essence due to the extensions of time,
and (2), the letter rescinded the contract *ab initio,* so that if the contract had
not been revived. V would have had no remedy in damages against P. The
judge held against P. On appeal by P, *held,* dismissing the appeal, that (1)
time did not cease to be of the essence merely because of extensions of time
to fixed dates; (2) having regard to the terms of the letter, the contract
was rescinded only in the sense accepting P's breach as a repudiation discharging
the contract leaving V's rights under it intact, not annulling it *ab initio.*
Per Goff L.J.: where there is breach of a fundamental term of a contract
for the sale of land, and time is of the essence, the aggrieved party cannot
rescind *ab initio.* (Dicta of Viscount Sumner in *Hirji Mulji* v. *Cheong Yue
Steamship Co.* [1926] A.C. 497, of Lord Porter in *Heyman* v. *Darwins* [1942]
1 All E.R. 356 and of Farwell J. in *Mussen* v. *Van Diemen's Land Co.* [1938]
Ch. 253 applied; *Webb* v. *Hughes* (1870) L.R. 10 Eq. 281 and *Luck* v. *White*
[1973] C.L.Y. 3446 distinguished; *Horsler* v. *Zorro* [1975] C.L.Y. 3547
doubted.)

BUCKLAND *v.* FARMAR & MOODY (A FIRM) [1978] 3 All E.R. 929, C.A.

2778. —— vendor's notice to complete—ineffective—return of deposit

[Law Society's Conditions of Sale, 1970 ed., Condition 19.]

A vendor is not "ready to complete" when his solicitor has not obtained
confirmation that entries in the search certificate relate to charges of which
he is aware, and consequently cannot undertake their discharge on completion.

The purchaser agreed to buy the vendor's house subject to the Law Society's
conditions of sale, and paid a substantial deposit on the property. The house
was subject to three charges but the vendor undertook only the discharge of
two on completion. The purchaser subsequently discovered the third charge
of which the vendor was aware but awaiting confirmation before giving an
undertaking. The vendors then served a notice to complete, but the purchaser
failed to complete within 28 days. The vendors subsequently found a purchaser at a higher price and purported to rescind the contract and forfeit the
deposit. *Held,* the notice to complete was ineffective because the vendors were
not in fact ready to complete at that time, so that they could not rely on
condition 19 *re* forfeiture; further it was not the purchaser's unreasonable
delay that had caused the vendors to rescind but the advent of another buyer.

COLE *v.* ROSE [1978] 3 All E.R. 1121, Mervyn-Davies Q.C.

2779. —— whether lender of purchase money entitled to be subrogated to rights of vendor

[Eire] The plaintiff bank agreed to lend money to the defendant company to enable it to purchase certain lands the defendant promising to deposit the title deeds of the lands with the plaintiff as security for the loan. The lands were conveyed by the vendor to the defendant company but it failed to repay the loan to the plaintiff or deposit the title deeds. The plaintiff claimed a lien on the lands. *Held,* that the plaintiff was entitled to an unpaid vendor's lien by subrogation up to the completion of the sale to the defendant company and thereafter to an equitable charge. The right of subrogation after completion of the sale was not excluded by the agreement to deposit the title deeds: BANK OF IRELAND FINANCE *v.* DALY [1978] I.R. 79, McMahon J.

2780. Specific performance—contract to sell council house—whether enforceable—correspondence and conduct of parties

A contract alleged to have been made by an exchange of correspondence in which successive communications other than the first are in reply to one another, is not an exception to the normal analysis of a contract as being constituted by offer and acceptance.

G was the tenant and occupier of a council house owned M Corp., by whom he had been employed for 16 years. In November 1970, M Corp. sent G a form and a brochure giving details of how he could buy the house. G completed the form and returned it, requesting information as to its price. In February 1971, M Corp. wrote informing G of the price, and saying that if he wished to purchase the house, he should return the enclosed application. G completed the form, leaving the price blank, and returned it with a covering letter asking for consideration to be given to defects in the path to the house. M Corp. replied that the price had been fixed according to the condition of the property. G wrote back asking the corporation to " carry on with the purchase as per my application." M Corp. took the house off the list of tenant-occupied houses and G did some work on the house. Then Labour gained control of the M Corp. and passed a resolution not to sell council houses except where legally binding contracts had been previously concluded. G was notified that the sale would not proceed. The County Court judge and the Court of Appeal held that in the light of the correspondence as a whole and the conduct of the parties, there was a concluded contract, and ordered specific performances. On appeal to the House of Lords, *held,* allowing the appeal, that there never was an offer capable of acceptance, merely negotiations which never reached fruition. (*Storer* v. *Manchester City Council* [1974] C.L.Y. 3952 distinguished.)

GIBSON *v.* MANCHESTER CITY COUNCIL [1979] 1 W.L.R. 294, H.L.

2781. —— failure to complete—whether also entitled to rescind

[Aust.] It has been *held*, that a vendor who is entitled to rescind a contract for the sale of land because of the purchaser's failure to complete on time, but who elects to sue for specific performance, is not thereby precluded from later rescinding the contract and claiming damages for the continued refusal by the purchaser to complete if the purchaser's conduct evinces an intention no longer to be bound by the contract. (*Mayson* v. *Clouet* [1924] A.C. 980 referred to): OGLE *v.* COMBOYURO INVESTMENTS (1976) 136 C.L.R. 444, Aust. High Ct.

2782. —— innocent misrepresentation—unjust to grant decree. See SMELTER CORP. *v.* O'DRISCOLL, § 1344.

2783. —— jurisdiction to award damages—damages in lieu

[Chancery Amendment Act 1858 (c. 27), s. 2.]

Although a vendor has, at trial, to elect whether to go for damages or specific performance, if he chooses the latter and the order is not complied with, he can still apply to the court to terminate the contract and is then entitled to damages for its breach.

The plaintiff vendors, being in arrears with mortgage repayments, entered into a written agreement for the sale of the properties. The purchasers failed to complete whereon the vendors obtained an order for specific performance. The purchasers failed to carry out the order, and the mortgagees duly enforced

their securities by selling the properties. The proceeds of the sale were insufficient to discharge the mortgage in full, and the vendors moved for an order
that the purchasers should pay the balance of the purchase price to the
vendors. The judge made no order, and the Court of Appeal allowed
the vendor's appeal. On appeal by the purchaser, *held*, dismissing the appeal
that where specific performance was ordered but not complied with, damages
was still available as an alternative remedy, and damages would be assessed
on a common law basis as at the date when the remedy of specific performance
was aborted.

JOHNSON *v.* AGNEW [1979] 2 W.L.R. 487, H.L.

**2784. Vacant possession—tenancy on one floor—occupation limited to one
household—purchaser's entitlement to abatement**

" Vacant possession " means more than empty and unoccupied; the property
conveyed must be capable of occupation by a purchaser.

A house was advertised for sale as having a first-floor tenant but with
vacant possession of the ground floor. At two auctions it was withdrawn, and
P purchased it by private treaty with the auctioneer. P had not made searches
but had made a personal inspection and had telephoned the local authority.
Unknown to P, a notice under s. 19 of the Housing Act 1961 directing that the
house should only be occupied by one household had been served. P sought an
abatement of the purchase price and specific performance since D refused to
complete unless the full price was paid. *Held*, " vacant possession " constituted more than that the ground floor was unoccupied and the vendors were
bound to hand over the ground floor in a state which would enable the
purchaser to occupy it. Specific performance and abatement of the purchase
price ordered.

TOPFELL *v.* GALLEY PROPERTIES [1979] 1 W.L.R. 446, Templeman J.

ARTICLES. See *post*, p. [34].

WATER AND WATERWORKS

2785. Discharge

WELSH WATER AUTHORITY (CWMYSTRADLLYN RESERVOIR DISCHARGE) ORDER
1979 (No. 1767) [20p], made under Water Resources Act 1971 (c. 34), s. 1;
operative on February 5, 1980; authorises the Welsh Water Authority to
discharge water from the Cwmystradllyn Reservoir into the Cwmystradllyn
River.

2786. Drainage. See LAND DRAINAGE.

2787. Northern Ireland. See NORTHERN IRELAND.

2788. Sewerage. See PUBLIC HEALTH.

2789. Water authorities

WATER AUTHORITIES (COLLECTION OF CHARGES) ORDER 1979 (No. 228) [40p],
made under the Local Government Act 1972 (c. 70), s. 254 (1) (*a*) and (2) (*c*),
as applied by the Water Act 1973 (c. 37), s. 34 (1) and Sched. 6; operative on
March 31, 1979; provides for the collection and recovery on behalf of water
authorities, by local authorities who are rating authorities, of charges made by
water authorities for the supply of water and for sewerage and environmental
services during the year beginning on April 1, 1979.

SOUTHERN WATER AUTHORITY (TRANSFER OF LOWER MEDWAY NAVIGATION
FUNCTIONS) ORDER 1979 (No. 1196) [40p], made under the Water Resources
Act 1963 (c. 38), s. 82; operative on October 1, 1979; transfers the functions of
the Medway Ports Authority to the Southern Water Authority.

WELSH WATER AUTHORITY (CWMYSTRADLLYN RESERVOIR) ORDER 1979 (No.
1499) [20p], made under the Water Resources Act 1963, s. 67 and
the Compulsory Purchase Act 1965 (c. 56), s. 36; operative on November 2,
1979; makes provision for the construction of the Cwmystradllyn Reservoir
by the Welsh Water Authority.

Orders made under the Water Act 1973, ss. 2 (4), 3 (1), (9), and 36 (2):
S.I. 1979 Nos. 466 (Anglian Water Authority) [10p]; 467 (Northumbrian
Water Authority) [10p]; 468 (North West Water Authority) [20p]; 469

(Severn–Trent Water Authority) [20p]; 470 (Southern Water Authority) [10p]; 471 (South West Water Authority) [10p]; 472 (Thames Water Authority) [20p]; 473 (Wessex Water Authority) [20p]; 474 (Yorkshire Water Authority) [20p].

2790. —— **provision of new main—whether " necessary "—deposit**

[Water Act 1945 (c. 42), s. 37 (1), as amended by Housing Act 1949 (c. 60), and Water Act 1973 (c. 37).]

For the purposes of s. 37 (1) of the Water Act 1945 (as amended) a "necessary main" is one which is reasonably required to carry water from an existing water main to the point of distribution by service pipes.

The appellant owners, and proposed developers, of a site to be used for residential development required the respondent water authority to provide a domestic water supply, which the respondents considered would need a new main 3·5 kilometres long from an existing main. The respondents required the appellants under s. 37 (1) of the Act to enter into an undertaking and to deposit £115,000 as security for the annual sums due pursuant thereto. The appellants deposited £16,000 under protest and sought a declaration that the respondents were not entitled to demand a deposit; they contended, *inter alia*, that they were liable save in respect of a distribution main from the nearest existing main. Forbes J. dismissed the action. *Held*, dismissing the appeal, that there was no evidence that the distribution main could start from a point nearer to the appellant's site and that accordingly the undertaking and deposit were properly demanded. (Decision of Forbes J. affirmed; *Cherwell District Council* v. *Thames Water Authority* [1975] C.L.Y. 3557 distinguished.)

ROYCO HOMES v. SOUTHERN WATER AUTHORITY [1979] 1 W.L.R. 1366, H.L.

2791. Water charges

WATER CHARGES EQUALISATION ORDER 1979 (No. 1754) [20p], made under the Water Charges Equalisation Act 1977 (c. 41), ss. 1 (1) (2) (7) (8), 2, 3 (1) (3) (5); operative on December 28, 1979; details the equalisation levies and equalisation payments to be made during the calendar year 1980.

2792. Water orders

Orders made under the Water Act 1945 (c. 42):

S. 19 (6) proviso: S.I. 1979 Nos. 7 (Northumbrian Water) [10p]; 8 (Severn–Trent Water) [10p]; 28 (East Anglia) [10p]; 39 (Thames Water Authority) [10p]; 48 (Anglian Water) [10p]; 57 (Newcastle and Gateshead Water) [10p]; 101 (Severn–Trent) [10p]; 128 (Severn–Trent) [10p]; 147 (Eastbourne Waterworks) [10p]; 161 (Anglian Water) [10p]; 199 (Tees Valley and Cleveland) [10p]; 248 (Rickmansworth and Uxbridge Valley) [10p]; 335 (South West Water) [10p]; 343 (Lee Valley) [10p]; 344 (Thames Water) [10p]; 479 (Folkestone and District) [10p]; 502 (Anglian Water) [10p]; 505 (York Waterworks) [10p]; 536 (Anglian Water) [10p]; 537 (South Staffordshire Waterworks) [10p]; 557 (Essex Water) [10p]; 561 (Severn–Trent) [10p]; 593 (Thames) [10p]; 596 (South West Water) [20p]; 684 (Portsmouth Water) [10p]; 1329 (Southern Water) [10p]; 1330 (Thames Water) [10p].

S. 23: S.I. 1979. Nos. 175 (South West Water) [10p]; 176 (North West Water) [20p]; 500 (East Worcestershire Water) [20p]; 512 (Eastbourne Water) [20p]; 513 (Yorkshire Water) [10p]; 562 (Anglian Water) [10p]; 679 (Southern Water) [10p]; 801 (Wrexham and East Denbighshire) [20p]; 831 (Southern Water) [10p]; 901 (Wessex Water) [20p]; 1065 (Thames) [10p]; 1078 (Cambridge) [10p]; 1168 (Bristol) [40p]; 1361 (Portsmouth) [40p]; 1369 (South Staffordshire Water) [20p]; 1457 (Sunderland and South Shields) [40p]; 1498 (Welsh Water) [40p]; 1527 (York Water) [10p]; 1560 (Wessex Water) [20p].

S. 32: S.I. 1979. Nos. 801 (Wrexham and East Denbighshire) [20p]; 1079 (West Kent) [10p]; 1528 (Portsmouth Water) [10p].

S. 33: S.I. 1979 No. 1079 (West Kent) [10p]; 1527 (York Water) [10p].

S. 50: S.I. 1979 No. 48 (Anglian Water) [10p]; 801 (Wrexham and East Denbighshire) [20p]; 1079 (West Kent) [10p]; 1168 (Bristol) [40p]; 1369 (South Staffordshire Water) [20p]; 1528 (Portsmouth Water) [10p].

Orders made under the Water Resources Act 1971 (c. 34), s. 1:
S.I. 1979 Nos. 994 (Severn–Trent) [10p]; 995 (Severn–Trent) [10p];
1020 (Severn–Trent) [60p].

BOOKS AND ARTICLES. See *post*, pp. [12], [34].

WEIGHTS AND MEASURES

2793. Alcohol tables

ALCOHOL TABLES REGULATIONS 1979 (No. 132) [10p], made under the European Communities Act 1972 (c. 68), s. 2 (2); operative on April 1, 1979; implement Council Directive No. 76/766/EEC relating to alcohol tables. They provide definitions of "alcoholic strength by volume" and "alcoholic strength by mass," and symbols to be used for both.

2794. Egg-grading machines

WEIGHTS AND MEASURES (EGG-GRADING MACHINES) (REVOCATION) (REGULATIONS 1979 (Nos. 729) [10p], made under the Weights and Measures Act 1963 (c. 31), ss. 11 (1) and (3), 14 (1) and 58; operative on August 1, 1979; revoke S.I. 1964 No. 39, which Regulations prescribe those machines grading eggs into one or more of the categories large, standard, medium or small. That grading into those categories is now unlawful, as the grades have been replaced by those provided for in Council Reg. EEC. No. 2772/75.

2795. Equipment

WORKING STANDARDS AND TESTING EQUIPMENT (TESTING AND ADJUSTMENT) (AMENDMENT) REGULATIONS 1979 (No. 1719) [20p], made under the Weights and Measures Act 1963 (c. 31), s. 5 (4); operative on February 1, 1980; amend regulations relating to the methods of testing and adjusting, and the limits of error for, the working standards and testing equipment used by inspectors of weights and measures.

2796. Fees

MEASURING INSTRUMENTS (EEC REQUIREMENTS) (FEES) REGULATIONS 1979 (No. 1342) [20p], made under the Finance Act 1973 (c. 51), s. 56 (1) and (2); operative on November 26, 1979; increase certain fees payable in connection with services provided by the Department of Trade in respect of EEC pattern approval of specified measuring instruments.

WEIGHTS AND MEASURES (TESTING AND ADJUSTMENT FEES) REGULATIONS 1979 (No. 1359) [20p], made under the Weights and Measures Act 1963 (c. 31), ss. 11 (3), 43, 48; operative on January 1, 1980; prescribe the fee to be paid for the testing of weighing or measuring equipment and for adjusting such equipment.

2797. Local standards

WEIGHTS AND MEASURES (LOCAL STANDARDS: PERIODS OF VALIDITY) REGULATIONS 1979 (No. 1436) [10p], made under the Weights and Measures Act 1963 (c. 31), ss. 4 (5), 58; operative on December 10, 1979; prescribe the periods of validity of certificates of fitness of local standards of weights and measures maintained by the authorities in accordance with s. 4 of the 1963 Act. The periods replace those in s. 4 (5) which ceased to have effect by virtue of amendments in the Weights and Measures Act 1979, s. 24 (3) (*c*), Sched. 5, para. 1.

2798. Measuring instruments

MEASURING INSTRUMENTS (INTOXICATING LIQUOR) (AMENDMENT) REGULATIONS 1979 (No. 41) [20p], made under the Weights and Measures Act 1963 (c. 31), ss. 11 (3), 14 (1), 54 (1), 58; operative on February 12, 1979; amend S.I. 1965 No. 1815 and prohibit measuring instruments used for measuring beer or cider being fitted with sight glasses to show the chamber is properly charged as an alternative to devices which prevent liquid being discharged until the chamber is full.

MEASURING INSTRUMENTS (EEC REQUIREMENTS) (AMENDMENT) REGULATIONS 1979 (No. 80) [10p], made under the European Communities Act 1972 (c. 68), s. 2 (2); operative on February 21, 1979; apply Council Directive No. 75/33/EEC to cold-water meters and amend S.I. 1975 No. 1173.

MEASURING INSTRUMENTS (EEC REQUIREMENTS) (AMENDMENT No. 2) REGULATIONS 1979 (No. 847) [30p], made under the European Communities Act 1972, s. 2 (2); operative on August 20, 1979; apply S.I. 1975 No. 1173 to measuring systems for liquids other than water and components of such systems, to which Council Directive No. 77/313/EEC applies.

MEASURING INSTRUMENTS (EEC REQUIREMENTS) (GAS VOLUME METERS) (FEES) (AMENDMENT) REGULATIONS 1979 (No. 1257) [10p], made under the Finance Act 1973 (c. 51), s. 56 (1) (2); operative on October 30, 1979; amend S.I. 1975 No. 1874 which prescribed the fees payable in connection with the services provided by the Department of Energy in respect of the EEC pattern approval and EEC initial verification of gas volume meters in consequence of Commission Directive 78/365/EEC.

MEASURING INSTRUMENTS (EEC REQUIREMENTS) (AMENDMENT No. 3) REGULATIONS 1979 (No. 1459) [20p], made under the European Communities Act 1972, s. 2 (2); operative on January 2, 1980; apply S.I. 1975 No. 1173 to non-automatic weighing machines to which Council Directive 73/360 applies.

MEASURING INSTRUMENTS (LIQUID FUEL AND LUBRICANTS) REGULATIONS 1979 (No. 1605) [50p], made under the Weights and Measures Act 1963, ss. 11 (1) and (3), 12 (4), 14 (1), 54 (1) and 58; operative on January 1, 1980 (reg. 3 (2)) and March 1, 1980 (remainder); replace the Measuring Instruments (Liquid Fuel and Lubricants) Regulations 1963, making provision for principles of construction, making, inspection etc. of equipment and prescribed limits of error in relation to measurement of certain fuels.

WEIGHTS AND MEASURES (AMENDMENT) REGULATIONS 1979 (No. 1612) [10p], made under the Weights and Measures Act 1963, ss. 11 (1) and 54 (1); operative on January 1, 1980; amend the Weights and Measures Regulations 1963 by excluding certain weighing and measuring equipment from those regulations.

MEASURING EQUIPMENT (LIQUID FUEL DELIVERED FROM ROAD TANKERS) REGULATIONS 1979 (No. 1720) [£1·25], made under the Weights and Measures Act 1963, ss. 11 (1) (3), 12 (4), 14 (1) and 58; operative on July 1, 1980 (except for regs. 4 and 8 (1), and July 1, 1983 (regs. 4 and 8 (1)); prescribe measuring equipment used for trade for measuring bulk supplies of liquid fuel dispensed from road tankers and set out certain exceptions.

2799. Milk products

WEIGHTS AND MEASURES ACT 1963 (MILK) ORDER 1979 (No. 1752) [20p], made under the Weights and Measures Act 1963, ss. 21 (2) (3) (5), 54 (1) (4); operative on January 1, 1980; deals with the requirements imposed by the EEC in relation to pre-packed liquid cows' milk.

2800. Packaged goods

WEIGHTS AND MEASURES (PACKAGED GOODS) REGULATIONS 1979 (No. 1613) [£1·75], made under the Weights and Measures Act 1979 (c. 45), ss. 1, 3, 5, 13, 14, 15, Sched. 1 para. 1, 2; operative on January 1, 1980; provide for implementing the system of quantity control (commonly known as "the average system") applicable to the packaging of goods sold by weight or volume for which the main provision is made by Pt. I of the 1979 Act.

2801. Solid fuel

WEIGHTS AND MEASURES (SOLID FUEL) (CARRIAGE BY RAIL) (AMENDMENT) ORDER 1979 (No. 955) [10p], made under the Weights and Measures Act 1963 (c. 31), s. 54 (2); operative on September 1, 1979; amends S.I. 1966 No. 238 and brings rail vehicles in the specified circumstances within that Order, not only, as previously, steel rail vehicles of a capacity of not less than 24 tons.

WEIGHTS AND MEASURES ACT 1963 (SOLID FUEL) ORDER 1979 (No. 1753) [10p], made under the Weights and Measures Act 1963, s. 21 (2) (3); operative on January 1, 1980; adds to the quantities in which solid fuel may be made in a container for sale or for delivery after sale.

2802. Weights and Measures Act 1979 (c. 45)

This Act makes further provision with respect to weights and measures. Pt. I (ss. 1–15) relates to packaged goods: s. 1 sets out the duties of packers and importers of packages; s. 2 contains enforcement provisions; s. 3 specifies offences under the Act; s. 4 deals with local administration of Pt. I; s. 5 makes special provision for certain packages; s. 6 establishes the Metrological Co-ordinating Units; s. 7 outlines the functions of the Unit; s. 8 provides for supervision by the Unit of certain functions of inspectors; s. 9 concerns annual reports by the Unit; s. 10 imposes on the Unit a duty to keep proper accounts and provide for an annual audit; s. 11 gives the Secretary of State power to extend or transfer the Unit's functions and to abolish the Unit; s. 12 deals with disclosure of information; s. 13 allows for modifications of Pt. I by regulations; s. 14 is the interpretation section for Pt. I; s. 15 contains supplemental provisions.

Pt. II (ss. 16–20) amends the Weights and Measures Act 1963: s. 16 amends ss. 11 and 14 of the 1963 Act relating to weighing or measuring equipment for use for trade; s. 17 amends s. 12 of the 1963 Act with respect to approved patterns of equipment for use for trade; s. 18 alters certain penalties set out in the 1963 Act; s. 19 relates to the measurement of beer and cider; s. 20 makes other amendments to the 1963 Act.

Pt. III (ss. 21–24) contains general provisions: s. 21 provides for application of the Act to Northern Ireland; s. 22 sets out provisions relating to expenses, etc.; s. 23 concerns repeals; s. 24 deals with citation, interpretation and commencement.

The Act received the Royal Assent on April 4, 1979, and came into force on that date except for ss. 1–5, 8–13, 15, 20 (part), 23 (part) and Scheds. 1 and 2, Sched. 5, para. 16, and Sched. 7 which come into force on January 1, 1980; s. 20 (part) and Sched. 5, para. 1 which come into force on October 4, 1979; and ss. 6, 7 and 19 and Sched. 3 which come into force on a day to be appointed.

2803. —— commencement
WEIGHTS AND MEASURES ACT 1979 (COMMENCEMENT No. 1) ORDER 1979 (No. 1228 (C. 33)) [10p], made under the Weights and Measures Act 1979 (c. 45), s. 24 (3) (*b*); operative on October 2, 1979; brings into force ss. 6, 7 of and Sched. 3 to the 1979 Act.

BOOKS. See *post*, p. [12].

WILLS

2804. Construction—residuary gift—purpose of gift
The rule that the court regards as absolute a gift made for a purpose of a whole sum or income, and the purpose as merely the motive of the gift, applies where the gift is to more than one person.

T, the testator, by a clause of his will bequeathed to his wife all rents from certain properties " for her maintenance and for the training of my daughter up to university age and for the maintenance of my aged mother." By cl. 5 he bequeathed and devised the resident to his wife upon the same trusts. *Held*, T was by those bequests merely stating his motives for creating the trust; the gift of residue was not limited to a specific use or uses, but was a gift of the whole fund to the wife, the mother and the daughter absolutely, in equal shares. (*Barlow* v. *Grant* (1684) 1 Vern. 255, *Re Sanderson's Trust* (1857) 3 K. & J. 497 and *Presant* v. *Goodwin* (1860) 1 Sw. & Tr. 544 applied; *Re Andrew's Trust* [1905] 2 Ch. 48, *Re Foord* [1922] 2 Ch. 519 and *Re Dunn* [1916] 1 Ch. 97 distinguished.)

Re OSOBA, DECD.; OSOBA v. OSOBA [1979] 1 W.L.R. 247, C.A.

2805. Death duties. See DEATH DUTIES.

2806. Family provision—dependant—maintenance immediately before testator's death
[Inheritance (Provision for Family and Dependants) Act 1975 (c. 63), ss. 1 (1) (3) and 3 (4).]

An applicant for reasonable financial provision from the estate of a deceased person must establish, *inter alia*, that the deceased was making " a substantial contribution " towards his needs.

From 1940 until 1976 the male plaintiff and the deceased lived together as man and wife. After their retirement each was in receipt of a separate pension. They lived in a bungalow owned by the deceased, the plaintiff paying a regular fixed amount in respect of the accommodation and also contributing towards the weekly shopping bill. The deceased paid all outgoings in respect of the bungalow and on occasion paid the plaintiff for decorating work performed by him. Following the deceased's death in 1976 the plaintiff made application for reasonable financial provision, none having been made in the deceased's will. On application by the executors, *held*, striking out the plaintiff's claim as disclosing no reasonable cause of action, that (1) in order to show that he was " maintained " by the deceased (within the meaning of s. 1 (1) (*e*) of the Act) the plaintiff had to show that he was the recipient of " a substantial contribution " from the deceased towards his needs; (2) contributions made for full consideration, whether by agreement or otherwise, were to be disregarded; (3) regard should be had to the general arrangements existing between the parties immediately before the deceased's death; (4) by virtue of s. 3 (4) of the Act the plaintiff needed to establish that the deceased had assumed responsibility for his maintenance and that the plaintiff had failed to establish more than that the parties shared their lives.

Re BEAUMONT (DECD.); MARTIN *v.* MIDLAND BANK TRUST Co. [1979] 3 W.L.R. 818, Sir Robert Megarry V.-C.

2807. —— intestacy—whether son a dependant
[Inheritance (Provision for Family and Dependants) Act 1975 (c. 63), ss. 1, 2 (1), 3.]

Where a son seeks financial provision out of his father's estate, he must establish that, looked at objectively, the absence of provision for him was unreasonable.

The plaintiff, born in 1931, continued living with his father after his mother's departure in 1957 and looked after the father thereafter. He married in 1961 and his wife ran the household until she left in 1975, whereupon the plaintiff continued to live with his father until the latter's death, intestate, in 1976. The mother was entitled to the deceased's estate by virtue of his intestacy, the net value of the estate being some £7,000. The mother's sole means of support consisted of a state pension and associated benefits; she was entitled in any event to a one third share in the value of the house (worth some £12,000), she having contributed towards its purchase. The plaintiff was in employment earning some £52 net per week and was liable to pay £12 per week maintenance to his wife. Upon his claim for financial provision, the plaintiff was awarded £2,000 by the master, but Oliver J., upon the summons being adjourned to him, dismissed the summons. *Held*, dismissing the plaintiff's appeal, that the circumstances found by the judge warranted dismissal of the summons. (Decision of Oliver J. affirmed; *Re E., E.* v. *E.* [1966] C.L.Y. 12596, *Millward* v. *Shenton* [1972] C.L.Y. 3566 and *Re Christie (decd.)* [1979] C.L.Y. 2810 considered.)

Re COVENTRY (DECD.); COVENTRY *v.* COVENTRY [1979] 3 W.L.R. 802, C.A.

2808. —— mistress—reasonable financial provision
[Inheritance (Provision for Family and Dependants) Act 1975 (c. 63), ss. 1 (2) (*b*), 3.]

A mistress wholly supported for 12 years is entitled to reasonable financial provision following the death of her lover.

In 1965 the plaintiff, then aged 23, met the deceased, a wealthy businessman, who persuaded her to give up her job (as a telephonist) and travel abroad with him. The deceased had separated in 1939 from his wife, whom he continued to support thereafter, and from 1958 until his death in 1977 cohabited with and supported one CM and her son. From 1965 the deceased paid the plaintiff's living expenses, took her frequently to Malta where he bought a flat in their joint names and provided her with a flat in England, also in joint names. He objected to her working but provided her with a nominal position in one of his companies from which she received some £60 per month. During the deceased's lifetime the plaintiff received approximately £4,000 per annum from him, together with shares valued at £15,000. The flat in Malta was worth some

£10,000. By his will the deceased made provision for CM and her son and for his wife and brother, but not the plaintiff. Upon her application for financial provision, *held*, that she was entitled to provision the deceased having made himself responsible for her maintenance; that provision would be made by way of lump sum award; and that the same would be calculated by assuming the plaintiff's loss of income to be £2,000 per annum (her earning capacity being assessed at £2,000 per annum) and applying a multiplier of 11 (making £22,000); in addition a capital sum of £20,000 would be added; from the total of £42,000 would be deducted £13,000 representing her current free capital and the value of the flat in Malta.

MALONE *v.* HARRISON [1979] 1 W.L.R. 1353, Hollings J.

2809. —— **persons entitled to apply**

[Inheritance (Provision for Family and Dependants) Act 1975 (c. 63), ss. 1, 2.] In 1971 McC, a divorcee, made a will leaving his estate to his infant son A in trust with whom he lived. Subsequently in 1972 McC befriended a Miss A and her six-month-old illegitimate son. In May 1974 a planned child was born to McC and Miss A and marriage was seriously considered. Early in 1976 McC discussed changing his will with his solicitors and showed an intention to act as a fair and reasonable father of two children and a *de facto* wife. In July 1976 McC died. The elder child was returned to his own mother and Miss A continued to look after the younger child on social security. She then made application under the 1975 Act for herself and her son for an order under s. 2 claiming that they came within s. 1 (1) (c) (e). The estate was worth £20,000–£35,000. *Held,* that all the evidence pointed to a family unit in this case and it was incumbent upon the estate to provide for Miss A and her child. Equity was equality and the child would take equally with the elder boy A in trust upon certain terms. Miss A needed a roof over her head and it would be some time before she could look after herself. The size of estate, age of parties, and years together were factors to be taken into consideration. The child's trustee would also have power to co-operate in financing habitation. £5,000 regarded as being appropriate figure. Order accordingly: *Re* McC. (1979) 9 Fam. Law 26, Sir George Baker P.

2810. —— **" reasonable "—son applying for maintenance—not in financial need**

[Inheritance (Provision for Family and Dependants) Act 1975 (c. 63), ss. 1 (2) (b), 3.]

Reasonable financial provision out of an estate for an applicant's " maintenance " under s. 1 (2) (b) of the Inheritance (Provision for Family and Dependants) Act 1975 does not require the applicant to be in financial difficulty; " maintenance " refers to the way of life, health, financial security and well-being of the applicant and his family.

M, the mother, devised house " A " to the son, her interest in house " B " to her daughter, and the residue to be divided between them. Before her death she gave her interest in house " B " to her daughter, she sold house " A " and bought another one instead. She expressed her intention of leaving the new house to the son but died before she could make a new will. M's residuary estate therefore consisted of the new house and £4,500. The son applied for provision from the estate under the Inheritance (Provision for Family and Dependants) Act 1975. *Held,* granting the application, that he did not need to prove that he was destitute or in financial difficulty. " Maintenance " referred to the way of life, health, financial security and well-being of the applicant and his family. Accordingly the new house would be transferred to the son.

Re CHRISTIE (DECD.); CHRISTIE *v.* KEEBLE [1979] 2 W.L.R. 105, Vivian Price Q.C.

2811. Probate. See EXECUTORS AND ADMINISTRATORS.

2812. Trusts. See SETTLEMENTS AND TRUSTS.

2813. Validity—gift to family and friends

A testamentary direction giving an option to purchase parts of the estate to " members of my family and friends of mine " is not invalid for uncertainty.

At the time of her death the unmarried testatrix's closest family were various nephews and nieces and great and great-great nephews and nieces.

After specific bequests of various paintings, she directed that the remaining paintings be sold subject to " any members of my family and friends of mine " wishing to purchase the same at a price well below their true value. Her executor sought directions from the court. *Held,* that (1) since the uncertainty as to the persons who might be " friends " did not affect the quantum of the gift, the direction was valid since it would be possible to determine by reference to the length and nature of the acquaintance whether a particular person could be said to be a " friend "; (2) the reference to " family " would include all those related by blood to the testatrix and not solely the next of kin; the court was encouraged in that connection by the bequest to a particular great niece described as such in the will and clearly regarded by the testatrix as " family." (*Re Allen; Faith* v. *Allen* [1953] C.L.Y. 3824, applied; *Re Gulbenkian's Settlement Trusts, Whishaw* v. *Stevens* [1968] C.L.Y. 3031, distinguished.)

Re BARLOW'S WILL TRUSTS [1979] 1 All E.R. 296, Browne-Wilkinson J.

BOOKS AND ARTICLES. See *post*, pp. [12], [34].

WORDS AND PHRASES

2814. Cumulative table

Accident, 2311.
Activity, 2654.
Associated employers, 1011.
Child, 178.
Company, 920.
Country, 248.
Damage, 140.
Driving or attempting to drive, 2316.
Exceptional hardship, 783.
Failure to discharge obligations, 1808.
Family, 2813.
Fishing, 1319.
Fixed term contract, 1019.
Friends, 2813.
Frivolous, 390.
Goods, 632.
Grasskeep, 47.
House or other building, 295.
In public, 365.
Liable to interference, 2707.
Livestock, 2229.
Living with, 1306.
Maintenance (of building), 2741.
Nearest, 2341.
Occupier, 436.

Officer (of a company), 272
Opportunity to take part, 771.
Other proceedings, 772.
Part of a building, 415.
Payment, 1440.
Permit, 1597.
Possession (of drugs), 502.
Property, 595.
Provisions in relation to retirement, 939.
Public place, 543.
Reckless disregard, 497.
Recklessness, 2302; 2303; 2304.
Relevant employees, 1025.
Repair, 2741.
Road to which public has access, 2364.
Room (Rent Acts), 1620.
Sentence, 498.
Settlement, 1487.
Special occasion, 1545.
Suitable, 2750.
Supplying, 506.
Trade dispute, 2716.
Vacant possession, 2784.
Withdrawal from employment, 2706.

BOOKS AND ARTICLES

BOOKS

[*The books published in 1979 are grouped under their appropriate "Current Law" headings. Books relating to countries outside the jurisdiction are placed under the headings* BRITISH COMMONWEALTH *and* INTERNATIONAL LAW, *except that books relating to Scotland will be found under the heading* SCOTLAND *and tax books have been grouped under the collective heading* REVENUE LAW.]

ACCOUNTANCY
    Willott, Robert—Current Accounting Law and Practice 1979. [Paperback, £12·50.]

ADMINISTRATIVE LAW
    Dunsire, Andrew—Implementation in a Bureaucracy; Control in a Bureaucracy. The Execution Process, Vols. I and II. (Government and Administration Series.) [Cloth, £15 each.]
    Garner, J. F.—Administrative Law. 5th ed. [Cased, £19·50. Paperback, £14·75.]

AGENCY
    Kay, Maurice—Agency in Commerce. (Essential Business Law Series.) [Paperback, £1·25.]
    Markesinis, B. S. and Munday, R. J. C.—An Outline of the Law of Agency. [Paperback, £3·95.]

AGRICULTURE
    Scammell and Densham's Law of Agricultural Holdings. 6th ed. by H. A. C. Densham. [Cased, £33.]

ANIMALS
    Weatherill, John—Horses and the Law. (Pelham Horsemaster Series.) [Cloth, £4·95.]

ARBITRATION
    Russell on the Law of Arbitration. 19th ed. by Anthony Walton. [Cased, £30.]

BAILMENT
    Palmer, N. E.—Bailment. [Cloth, £44.]

BANKING
    Gutteridge, H. C. and Megrah, Maurice—The Law of Bankers' Commercial Credits. 6th ed. [Cased, £9.]
    Ryder, F. R.—The Banking Act 1979. (Current Law Statutes Reprints.) [Paperback, £5·50.]

BANKRUPTCY
    Farrar, John—Company Insolvency. (Essential Business Law Series.) [Paperback, £1·25.]
    Hooper's Voluntary Liquidation. 5th ed. by George Anger. [Cased, £12·50.]
    Williams and Muir Hunter on Bankruptcy. 19th ed. by Muir Hunter and David Graham. [Cased, £45.]

BILLS OF EXCHANGE
    Byles on Bills of Exchange. 24th ed. by Maurice Megrah and Frank R. Ryder. [Cased, £35.]

BRITISH COMMONWEALTH
Australia
    Dorter, John B. and Widmer, Gary K.—Arbitration (Commercial) in Australia. [Cased.]
    Pannam, C. L. and Hooker, P. J.—Cases and Materials on Contract. [Cased and Paperback.]
    Stein, Leslie A.—Locus Standi. [Cased and Paperback.]
    Sykes, E. I. and Pryles, M.C.—Australian Private International Law. [Cloth and Paperback.]

BOOKS AND ARTICLES

BRITISH COMMONWEALTH—*continued*

Canada
> Castel, Jean Gabriel—Conflict of Laws: Cases, Notes and Materials. 4th ed. [Cloth, £29.]
> Picard, Ellen I.—Legal Liability of Doctors and Hospitals in Canada. [Cased.]
> Schiffer, M. E.—Mental Disorder and the Criminal Trial Process. [Cloth, £18·60.]

Lesotho
> Poulter, Sebastian—Legal Dualism in Lesotho. [Paperback, £2·50.]

Nigeria
> Obilade, A. O.—The Nigerian Legal System. [Cased, £9. Paperback, £7.]
> Orojo, J. Ola—Company Tax Law in Nigeria. [Cased, £14.]
> Orojo, J. Ola—Conduct and Etiquette for Legal Practitioners. [Cloth, £7.]

BUILDING AND ENGINEERING, ARCHITECTS AND SURVEYORS
> Abrahamson, Max W.—Engineering Law and the I.C.E. Contracts. 4th ed. [Cased, £32.]
> Baum, Andrew and Mackmin, David—The Income Approach to Property Valuation. [Paperback, £3·95.]
> Card, Richard—The Estate Agents Act 1979. (Butterworths Annotated Legislation.) [Cased, £12·80.]
> Douglas, C. M. and Lee, R. G.—The Estate Agents Act 1979. (Current Law Statutes Reprints.) [Paperback, £2·25.]
> Elder, A. J.—Guide to the Building Regulations 1976. 6th ed. with 1978 Amendments. [Cased, £8·95.]
> Hudson's Building and Engineering Contracts. 10th ed. First Supplement by I. N. Duncan Wallace. [Cloth, £9·50.]
> Murdoch, J. R.—The Estate Agents Act 1979. [Limp, £2·50.]
> Wallace, I. N. Duncan—The I.C.E. Conditions of Contract. 5th ed. A Commentary [Cloth, £25.]

BUILDING SOCIETIES
> Tunnard, Jo and Whately, Clare—Rights Guide for Home Owners. 3rd ed. [Paperback, 70p.]

CAPITAL TAXATION
> Butterworths Editorial Staff—Handbook on the Capital Gains Tax Act 1979. [Paperback, £7·50.]
> Dymond's Capital Transfer Tax. 2nd Cumulative Supplement by Reginald K. Johns and Roy R. Greenfield. [Paperback, £10·50.]
> Dymond's Capital Transfer Tax. 3rd Cumulative Supplement by Reginald K. Johns and Roy R. Greenfield. [Paperback, £15.]
> Hardman, J. Philip, Stanfield, Russ and Wignall, Geoffrey A.—Capital Transfer Tax. [Limp, £3·25.]
> Tolley's Capital Gains Tax 1978–79 by David G. Young and David R. Harris. [Paperback, £5.]
> Wheatcroft and Whiteman on Capital Gains Tax. 3rd Cumulative Supplement. [Paperback, £2·50.]

CHARITIES
> Chesterman, Michael—Charities, Trusts and Social Welfare. (Law in Context Series.) [Cased, £17·50. Paperback, £10.]
> Family Welfare Association—Charities Digest 1978. 85th ed. [Paperback, £3·85.]
> Longley, A. R., Dockray, Martin and Sallon, Jaqueline—Charity Trustees' Guide. [Paperback, £1·25.]

CLUBS AND ASSOCIATIONS
> Daly's Club Law. 7th ed. by J. M. Martin. [Cased, £11·95.]
> Field, David—Practical Club Law. [Cased, £9·50. Paperback, £5·60.]

COMPANY LAW
> Albery, S. G.—A Business of Your Own. [Cased, £2·50.]
> Gower, L. C. B., Cronin, J. B., Easson, A. J. and Charlton, Lord Wedderburn of—Gower's Principles of Modern Company Law. 4th ed. [Cased, £17·50. Paperback, £12.]
> Jordans' Company Law Materials I—Private Limited Companies. 3rd ed. [Spiral bound, £3.]
> Morse, Geoffrey—Company Finance, Takeovers and Mergers. (Essential Business Law Series.) [Paperback, £1·25.]

BOOKS

COMPANY LAW—*continued*

Morse, Geoffrey—Company Structure. (Essential Business Law Series.) [Paperback, £1·25.]

Morse, Geoffrey and Williams, David—Profit Sharing. [Paperback, £7·50.]

Oliver, M. C.—Company Law. 7th ed. (M & E Handbooks.) [Paperback, £2·25.]

Pennington's Company Law. 4th ed. by Robert R. Pennington. [Cloth, £27·50. Paperback, £16.]

Tolley's Profit Sharing by Francis G. Sandison. [Paperback, £8·95.]

Weinberg and Blank on Take-overs and Mergers. 4th ed. by M. A. Weinberg, M. V. Blank and A. L. Greystoke. [Cased, £45.]

CONFLICT OF LAWS

Cheshire and North's Private International Law. 10th ed. by P. M. North. [Cased, £22·75. Paperback, £14·95.]

Dicey and Morris: The Conflict of Laws. 6th Cumulative Supplement to the 9th ed. [Paperback, £5.]

CONSTITUTIONAL LAW

Bogdanor, Vernon—Devolution. [Paperback, £2·95.]

Henkin, Louis—The Rights of Man Today. [Cloth, £9.]

Keir, D. L. and Lawson, I. H.—Cases in Constitutional Law. 6th ed. by F. H. Lawson and D. J. Bentley. [Cased, £15. Paperback, £6·95.]

Michael, James—The Politics of Secrecy. [Paperback, 90p.]

Phillips, O. Hood—Leading Cases in Constitutional and Administrative Law. 5th ed. [Cased, £13·75. Paperback, £10·85.]

Randall, F.—British Government and Politics. (M & E Handbooks.) [Paperback, £2·25.]

Scott, D. M. M. and Kobrin, D. L.—" O " Level British Constitution. 3rd ed. [Paperback, £3·95.]

Stevens, Robert—Law and Politics: The House of Lords as a Judicial Body 1800–1976. (Law in Context Series.) [Cloth, £18·50.]

CONTRACT

Atiyah, P. S.—The Rise and Fall of Freedom of Contract. [Cased, £30.]

Brazier, Rodney—Cases and Statutes on Contract. (Concise College Casenotes.) [Paperback, £3·75.]

Chitty on Contracts. First Supplement to 24th ed. by Gen. Ed. A. G. Guest. (Common Law Library.) [Paperback, £3·75.]

Duncanson, Ian—Contract. (New Nutshells.) [Paperback, £1·25.]

Hearn, Patrick—Successful Negotiation of Commercial Contracts. [Cloth, £7·50.]

Keenan, Denis—Contract. (Law Unit.) [Paperback, £2·50.]

Keenan, Denis—The Law of Contract. 2nd ed. [Paperback, £1·75.]

Knipe, Joan Clara—Law of Contract. [Paperback, £2·25.]

Lawson, Richard—Exclusion Clauses after the Unfair Contract Terms Act. [Paperback, £6·75.]

Morgan, Richard—Computer Contracts. [Cased, £10.]

Treitel, G. H.—An Outline of the Law of Contract. 2nd ed. [Paperback, £6·95.]

Treitel, G. H.—The Law of Contract. 5th ed. [Cased, £16. Paperback, £13.]

COPYRIGHT

Flint, Michael F.—A User's Guide to Copyright. [Paperback, £8·50.]

Munro, Colin R.—Television Censorship and the Law. [Cased, £9·75.]

CORPORATION TAX

Bramwell, Richard and Dick, John—Taxation of Companies. 2nd ed. [Cased, £17.]

Tolley's Corporation Tax 1979–80 by David R. Harris and John W. Sutcliffe. [Paperback, £4·25.]

Topple, B. S.—Corporation Tax. (M & E Handbooks.) 4th ed. [Paperback, £2·75.]

COUNTY COURT PRACTICE

Collins, Hugh C.—Notes on County Court Practice and Procedure. 5th ed. (Oyez Practitioner Series.) [Paperback, £6·50.]

County Court Costs and Fees. (Lawyers Costs and Fees Series 1.) [Paperback, £1·10.]

County Court Costs and Fees. 2nd ed. (Lawyers Costs and Fees Series.) [Paperback £1·10.]

The County Court Practice 1979. Edited by Judge Ruttle, R. C. L. Gregory *et al.* [Cased, £33.]

BOOKS AND ARTICLES

CRIMINAL LAW

Archbold Pleading, Evidence and Practice in Criminal Cases. 40th ed. by Stephen Mitchell. [Leather bound, £62·50. Cased, £40.]

Brandon, Steve—Criminal Law. (New Nutshells.) [Paperback, £1·25.]

Fallon, Peter and Bursell, Rupert—Crown Court Practice: Trial. Supplement. [Paperback, £5·95.]

Greaves, Alan and Pickover, David—The Criminal Law Book 1. Offences Against Property. [Paperback, £2·50.] 2. Offences Against the Person. [Paperback, £3·60.]

Gloss, Hyman—A Theory of Criminal Justice. [Cased, £9·50. Paperback, £3·95.]

Hodgkin, E. C. and N. I.—The Involvement of the Community in Criminal Justice and the Treatment of Offenders. [Paperback, £1·70.]

Robertson, Geoffrey—Obscenity. (Law in Context Series.) [Cased, £16. Paperback, £8·50.]

Smith J. C.—The Law of Theft. 4th ed. [Cased, £12·50. Paperback, £7·95.]

Teasdale, Jonathan P.—A Guide to Costs and Legal Aid in Criminal Cases. [Paperback, £5·95.]

Thomas, D. A.—Principles of Sentencing. 2nd ed. (Cambridge Studies in Criminology.) [Cased, £15. Paperback, £7·50.]

Thompson, Master D. R., Morrish, Peter and McLean, Ian—Proceedings in the Criminal Division of the Court of Appeal: An Index of Practice and Procedure. [Cased, £17·40.]

Williams, Glanville—Textbook of Criminal Law. Supplement to 1st ed. [Paperback, £1.]

CRIMINOLOGY

Bottomley, A. Keith—Criminology in Focus—Past Trends and Future Prospects. [Paperback, £3·50.]

Downes, David and Rock, Paul (Editors)—Deviant Interpretations. (Law in Society Series.) [Cloth, £7·95. Paperback, £2·95.]

DIVORCE AND MATRIMONIAL CAUSES

Berkin, Martyn and Young, Maurice—Matrimonial Suits and Property Proceedings. [Cased, £14.]

Costs in Matrimonial Causes. (Lawyers Costs and Fees Series 2.) [Paperback, £1·10.]

Harper, W. M.—Divorce and Your Money. [Cased, £4·95.]

Humphrey's Matrimonial Causes. 14th ed. by Hugh C. Collins. (Oyez Practitioner Series.) [Paperback, £7·95.]

Passingham, Bernard—Domestic Proceedings and Magistrates' Courts Act 1978. [Cased, £11·50.]

Passingham, Bernard—Law and Practice in Matrimonial Causes. 3rd ed. [Cased, £19·50. Paperback, £14·50.]

Rakusen, Michael L. and Hunt, D. Peter—Distribution of Matrimonial Assets on Divorce. [Cased, £9.]

Rayden's Law and Practice in Divorce and Family Matters in All Courts. 13th ed. Editor in Chief: Joseph Jackson. Two Volumes. [Cloth, £78.]

Thornes, Barbara and Collard, Jean—Who Divorces? (Routledge Direct Editions.) [Paperback, £4·95.]

Williams, Donald B. and Newman, Joel—Tax on Maintenance Payments 1979–80. 3rd ed. [Paperback, £3·95.]

EDUCATION

Barrell, G. R.—Teachers and the Law. 5th ed. [Cased, £10·50. Paperback, £6·95.]

EMPLOYMENT

Employment Protection Practice Guide. [Paperback in folder, £6·95.]

Bercusson, Brian—The Employment Protection (Consolidation) Act 1978. (Current Law Statutes Reprints.) [Paperback, £3·50.]

Butterworths Employment Law Handbook. Edited by Peter Wallington. [Limp, £9·25.]

Creighton, W. B.—Working Women and the Law. (Studies in Labour and Social Law Volume 3.) [Cased, £15.]

Davies, Paul and Freedland, Mark—Labour Law Texts and Materials. (Law in Context Series.) [Cased, £20. Paperback, £12.]

Goodman, Michael J.—Industrial Tribunals Procedure. 2nd ed. [Paperback, £6·95.]

Hepple and O'Higgins Employment Law. 3rd ed. by B. A. Hepple. [Paperback, £11.]

Hunt, Dennis D.—Employment and Dismissal Without Fear. [Cased, £4·95.]

Janner's Compendium of Employment Law by Greville Janner. [Cased, £18·50.]

Keenan, Denis—Contract of Employment. (Law Unit.) [Paperback, £1·75.]

McGlyne, John E.—Unfair Dismissal Cases. 2nd ed. [Paperback, £11.]

Mills, Michael—The New Manager. [Paperback, £5·50.]

Munkman, John—Employer's Liability at Common Law. 9th ed. [Cased, £24.]

BOOKS

EMPLOYMENT—*continued*

Rideout, Roger—Principles of Labour Law. 3rd ed. [Cased, £20. Paperback, £11·25.]

Slade, Elizabeth A.—Tolley's Employment Handbook. 2nd ed. [Paperback, £7·95.]

Sweet and Maxwell's Labour Relations Statutes and Materials. Advisory Editors: B. A. Hepple, Paul O'Higgins, Lord Wedderburn of Charlton. [Cloth, £18. Paperback, £11·95.]

Upex, Robert—Employment Protection Legislation. [Cased, £14.]

Whincup, Michael—Modern Employment Law. 2nd ed. [Paperback, £4·50.]

Wright, M.—Labour Law. (M & E Handbooks.) 2nd ed. [Paperback, £2·50.]

EQUITY

Pettit, Philip H.—Equity and the Law of Trusts. 4th ed. [Cased, £18. Paperback, £12·50.]

EUROPEAN COMMUNITIES

A Common Man's Guide to the Common Market. Edited by Hugh Arbuthnott and Geoffrey Edwards. [Cased, £8·95. Paperback, £3·95.]

Cook, Chris and Francis, Mary—The First European Elections. A Handbook and Guide. [Cased, £7·95. Paperback, £2·95.]

Drew, John—Doing Business in the European Community. [Cased, £9·95.]

Hand, Geoffrey, Georgel, Jacques and Sasse, Christoph—European Electoral Systems Handbook. [Cased, £10.]

Korah, Valentine—An Introductory Guide to EEC Competition Law and Practice. [Cased, £6·75.]

EVIDENCE

Phipson on Evidence. 2nd Supplement to the 12th edition. (Common Law Library.) [Paperback, £2·75.]

Walker, Martin and Brittain, Bernadette—Identification Evidence: Practices and Malpractices. [Paperback, £1.]

EXECUTORS AND ADMINISTRATORS

Taylor, J..N. R.—Executorship Law and Accounts. (M & E Handbooks.) [Paperback, £1·95.]

FIREARMS

Sandys-Wilson, Godfrey—Gun Law. 3rd ed. [Paperback, £3·50.]

FORENSIC MEDICINE

Pearce, Gerald H.—The Medical Report and Testimony. [Cased, £6·50.]

Simpson, Keith—Forensic Medicine. 8th ed. [Cased, £13·50.]

FRAUD, MISREPRESENTATION AND UNDUE INFLUENCE

Campbell, D.—The Investigation of Fraud. 2nd ed. [Limp, £3·90.]

GAMING AND WAGERING

National Council of Social Service—Lotteries and Gaming—Voluntary Organisations and the Law. 2nd ed. [Paperback, 95p.]

HEALTH AND SAFETY

Broadhurst, Alison—The Health and Safety at Work Act in Practice. [Limp, £5·95.]

Davis, Keith P.—Health and Safety. [Cased, £5. Limp, £2·25.]

Redgrave's Health and Safety in Factories. Supplement by Judge Ian Fife and Anthony Machin. [Paperback, £2·50.]

HIGHWAYS AND BRIDGES

Parrish, Harold—The Law relating to Private Street Works. [Limp, £6·50.]

HOUSING

Cutting, Marion—A Housing Rights Handbook. [Paperback, £1·50.]

Hadden, Tom—Housing: Repairs and Improvements. (Social Work and Law.) [Paperback, £4·50.]

West's Law of Housing. 4th ed. by Keith Davies. [Cased, £11·25.]

HUSBAND AND WIFE

Cretney, S. M.—Principles of Family Law. 3rd ed. [Cased, £19. Paperback, £14.]

Pinder, J. S. and Pace, P. J.—Cases and Statutes on Family Law. (Concise College Casenotes.) [Cloth, £6. Paperback, £3·50.]

BOOKS AND ARTICLES

INNKEEPERS

Bull, Frank J. and Hooper, John D. G.—Hotel and Catering Law. 7th ed. [Cloth, £5·95.]

Field, David—Cases and Statutes on Hotel and Catering Law. 2nd ed. (Concise College Casenotes.) [Paperback, £3·35.]

INSURANCE

Birds, John—Insurance. (Essential Business Law.) [Paperback, £1·25.]

Carter, R. L.—Reinsurance. [Cloth, £36·50.]

Colinvaux, Raoul—The Law of Insurance. 4th ed. [Cased, £22.]

Ivamy, E. R. Hardy—General Principles of Insurance Law. 4th ed. (Butterworths Insurance Library.) [Cased, £35.]

INTERNATIONAL LAW

Abi-Saab, Georges—The United Nations Operations in the Congo 1960–64 (International Crises and the Role of Law.) [Limp, £2·75.]

Crawford, James—The Creation of States in International Law. [Limp, £18.]

Dowrick, F. E. (Ed.)—Human Rights: Problems, Perspectives and Texts. [Cased, £8·50.]

Fisher, Roger—Points of Choice. (International Crises and the Role of Law.) [Limp, £1·95.]

Harris, D. J.—Cases and Materials on International Law. 2nd ed. [Cloth, £17. Paperback, £13·50.]

Merrills, J. G.—A Current Bibliography of International Law. [Cased: £18·50.]

Schneider, Jan—World public order of the environment: towards an international ecological law and organization. [Cased, £10·15.]

The Year Book of World Affairs 1979. Edited by G. W. Keeton and G. Schwarzenberger. [Cased, £11.]

France

Kahn-Freund, Sir Otto, Levy, Claudine and Rudden, Bernard—A Source-book on French Law. 2nd ed. [Paperback, £9.]

Republic of Ireland

Harvey, Eric and Lambert, Nigel—Tolley's Taxation in the Republic of Ireland, 1978–79. [Paperback, £5.]

The Netherlands

Campbell, D. L. (Ed.)—Comparative Law Yearbook Volume II, 1978. [Cased, US$52.50.]

Oda, S.—The International Law of Ocean Development. Supplement. [Paperback, US$36.]

South Africa

Hobstein and Van Winsen—The Civil Practice of the Superior Courts in South Africa. 3rd ed. by Van Winsen *et al.* [Cased.]

Sweden

Bruzelius, Anders and Thelin, Krister—The Swedish Code of Judicial Procedure Revised Edition. (The American Series of Foreign Penal Codes No. 24.) [Cased, £15.]

United States of America

Bennett-Sadlett, G. *et al.*—Law Enforcement and Criminal Justice—An Introduction. [Cased, £9·50.]

Cary, Eve and Peratis, Kathleen—Woman and the Law. (To Protect these Rights.) [Paperback, £4.]

Gora, Joel M.—Due Process of Law. (To Protect these Rights.) [Paperback, £4.]

Haiman, Franklyn S.—Freedom of Speech. (To Protect these Rights.) [Paperback, £4.]

Kintner, Earl W.—A Primer on the Law of Deceptive Practices. 2nd ed. [Cased, £14·95.]

MacNamara, Doual E. J. and Sagarin, Edward—Sex, Crime and the Law. [Paperback, £3·75.]

McDonald, Laughlin—Raical Equality. (To Protect these Rights.) [Paperback, £4.]

Pfeffer, Leo—Religious Freedom. (To Protect these Rights.) [Paperback, £4.]

Sage Research Progress Series in Criminology. Vols. 6, 7 and 8. [Paperback, £3·75 each.]

Shattuck, John H. F.—Rights of Privacy. (To Protect these Rights.) [Paperback, £4.]

Tiger, Edith (Ed.)—In Re Alger Hiss. [Paperback, £6·95.]

Wice, Paul B.—Criminal Lawyers. An Endangered Species. (Sage Library of Social Research.) [Paperback, £4·25.]

BOOKS

INTERNATIONAL LAW—*continued*
U.S.S.R.
Leuitsky, Serge L.—Copyright, Defamation and Privacy in Soviet Civil Law, Vol. 1. (Law in Eastern Europe No. 22 (1).) [Cloth, US$42.50.]

INTOXICATING LIQUORS
Paterson's Licensing Acts. 87th ed. by J. N. Martin. [Cased, £23.]
Underhill, Michael—The New Licensing Guide. 7th ed. (Oyez Practice Notes.) [Paperback, £5·50.]

JUDGES
Devlin, Patrick—The Judge. [Cased, £7·50.]
Griffith, J. A. G.—Administrative Law and the Judges. [Paperback, 50p.]
Terrell, Richard—The Chief Justice—A Portrait from the Raj. [Cased, £5·95.]

JURIES
Baldwin, John and McConville, Michael—Jury Trials. [Cloth, £4·95.]
Harman, Harriet and Griffith, John—Justice Deserted—The Subversion of the Jury. [Paperback, 50p.]

JURISPRUDENCE
Atkinson, J. Maxwell and Drew, Paul—Order in Court. (Oxford Socio-Legal Studies.) [Cased, £15.]
Benditt, Theodore M.—Law as Rule and Principle. (Problems of Legal Philosophy.) [Cased, £10·50.]
Brooke, Rosalind—Law, Justice and Social Policy. [Cased, £7·95. Paperback, £3·95.]
Cain, Maureen and Hunt, Alan—Marx and Engels on Law. (Law, State and Society Series.) [Paperback, £4·75.]
Current Legal Problems 1978 (Volume 31). Edited by Lord Lloyd of Hampstead and Roger W. Rideout. [Cloth, £9·75.]
Current Legal Problems 1979 (Volume 32). Edited by Lord Lloyd of Hampstead and Roger W. Rideout. [Cased, £13·75.]
Lord Denning—The Discipline of Law. [Cased, £8. Paperback, £4·50.]
Dias, R. W. M.—A Bibliography of Jurisprudence. 3rd ed. [Cloth, £10.]
Farringdon, David *et al.* (Editors)—Psychology, Law and Legal Processes. (Oxford Socio-Legal Studies.) [Cased, £12.]
Fehrenbacher, Don E.—The Dred Scott Case. Its significance in American Law and Politics. [Cloth, £13·25.]
Finch, John D.—Introduction to Legal Theory. [Cased, £10·80. Paperback, £5·35.]
Harris, J. W.—Law and Legal Science. [Cased, £7·50.]
Hayek, F. A.—Law, Legislation and Liberty. Volume 3: The Political Order of a Free People. [Cased, £5·95.]
Jackson, Paul—Natural Justice. 2nd ed. (Modern Legal Studies.) [Cased, £9·50. Paperback, £5·85.]
Lord Lloyd of Hampstead—Introduction to Jurisprudence. 4th ed. [Cased, £18·75. Paperback, £13·50.]
MacCormick, Neil—Legal Reasoning and Legal Theory. (Clarendon Law Series.) [Cased, £5·75.]
Raz, Joseph—The Authority of Law. [Cased, £10.]
Roberts, Simon—Order and Dispute. (Law in Society Series.) [Cased, £7·95.]
Sumner, Colin—Reading Ideologies. (Law, State and Society Series.) [Paperback, £4·95.]
Woozley, A. D.—Law and Obedience. The Arguments of Plato's Clito. [Cased, £9·80.]

Australia
Maher, F. K. H., Waller, Louis and Derham, Sir David—Cases and Materials on the Legal Process. 3rd ed. by Kevin S. Pose and Malcolm D. H. Smith. [Cased, £18·50. Paperback, £13·50.]

LAND REGISTRATION
Simpson, S.—Land Law and Registration. Book 1. [Paperback, £7·50.]

LANDLORD AND TENANT
Dawson, I. J. and Pearce, Robert A.—Licences relating to the occupation or use of land. [Cased, £20.]
Fox-Andrews, James—Business Tenancies. 3rd ed. [Cased, £10.]
Hill and Redman's Law of Landlord and Tenant. 2nd Cumulative Supplement to the 16th ed. by Michael Barnes, David Hands and Christopher Lockhart-Mummery. [Cased, £15.]

[7]

LANDLORD AND TENANT—*continued*
    Prophet, John—Fair Rents. 2nd ed. [Paperback, £6·50.]
    West, W. A.—The Law of Dilapidations. 8th ed. by P. F. Smith. [Paperback, £11.]
    Yates, David—Leases of Business Premises. (Essential Business Law.) [Paperback, £1·25.]

LEGAL AID
    Zemans, Frederick H. (Ed.)—Perspectives on Legal Aid. An International Survey. [Cased, £12·50.]

LEGAL HISTORY
    Baker, J. H.—An Introduction to English Legal History. 2nd ed. [Cased, £12·50. Paperback, £7·50.]
    Allason, Julian *et al.*—The English Legal Heritage. [Cased, £15.]
    Keeton, George W.—Harvey to Hasty—A Medieval Chief Justice. [Cased, £14·50.]

LIBEL AND SLANDER
    Gatley on Libel and Slander. 1st Supplement to the 7th ed. by Sir Robert McEwen and Philip Lewis. (Common Law Library.) [Paperback, £1·60.]

LOCAL GOVERNMENT
    Prophet, John—The Law of Local Councils. 2nd ed. [Paperback, £2·75.]
    Schofield's Local Government Elections. 8th ed. by A. J. Little. [Cloth, £17·50.]

MAGISTERIAL LAW
    Anthony and Berryman's Magistrates' Court Guide 1979. Edited by C. J. Acred. [Limp, £5·75.]
    Berkin, Martyn and Young, Maurice—Domestic Proceedings and Magistrates' Courts Act 1978. [Paperback, £2·75.]
    Brooke-Taylor, John C. and Booth, David (Eds.)—A Magistrates' Court Handbook. 5th ed. [Limp, £2·50.]
    Burney, Elizabeth—J.P.: Magistrate, Court and Community. [Cased, £6·95.]
    Harris, Brian—The Criminal Jurisdiction of Magistrates. 7th ed. [Cased, £17. Paperback, £15.]
    Oke's Magisterial Forms List. 19th ed. by C. J. Acred. [Cased, £47·50.]
    Raymond, Brian—Bail. A Practical Guide. [Paperback, £3·50.]
    Shannon, Frank—A Handbook of Cautions, Oaths and Recognizances, etc. 9th ed. [Spiral bound, £1·75.]
    Skyrme, Sir Thomas—The Changing Image of the Magistracy. [Cased, £8·95.]
    Stone's Justices Manual 1979. 111th ed. by John Rickmann and A. T. Draycott. [Cased in 3 volumes, £39·50.]

MEETINGS
    Moore, Matthew—The Law and Procedure of Meetings. (Concise College Texts.) [Cased, £7·75. Paperback, £4·85.]
    Shaw, S. Sebag and Smith, Judge Dennis—The Law of Meetings. 5th ed. [Cased, £6·50.]

MINORS
    Allison, C. E.—Care Proceedings. [Paperback £2.]
    Clarke Hall and Morrison Law relating to Children and Young Persons. Supplement to 9th ed. by Joseph Jackson, Dame Margaret Booth and Brian Harris. [Paperback, £14.]
    Lowe, N. V. and White, R. A. H.—Wards of Court. [Cased, £26.]
    Moore, V. W.—Digest of Law relating to Juveniles and the Courts. [Limp, £1·75.]
    Phillips, Brian—Patterns of Juvenile Crime. [Paperback, £4·50.]
    Smith, Roger—Children and the Courts. (Social Work and Law.) [Paperback, £3·95.]
    Terry, Jennifer—A Guide to the Children Act 1975 (as amended). 2nd ed. (Social Work and Law.) [Paperback, £3·35.]

MISCELLANEOUS
    Abbott, Keith—Foundation and " A " Level Law. [Paperback, £4·95.]
    The Bar List of the United Kingdom 1979. [Limp, £13·50.]
    Brandon, Steve, Duncanson, Ian, Samuel, Geoffrey—English Legal System. (New Nutshells.) [Paperback, £1·25.]
    Cooper, Ian—The Individual and the Law. [Paperback, £2·50.]
    Current Law Year Book 1978 and Current Law Citator 1978. General Editor: Peter Allsop. [Cased, £25.]
    Curzon, L. B.—A Dictionary of Law. [Paperback, £3·50.]

BOOKS

MISCELLANEOUS—*continued*

Cusworth, G. R. N.—The Lawyer's Remembrancer 1980. [Cased, £6·84.]

Dane, Jean and Thomas, Philip—How to Use a Law Library. [Cased, £5·50. Paperback, £2·50.]

Dunbar-Brunton, James—The Law and the Individual. Revised edition. (Macmillan Text for Business Studies.) [Paperback, £3·30.]

Halil, Kiamtan—Cocktails-at-Law. [Paperback, £2·95.]

Hazell, Robert (Ed.)—The Bar on Trial. [Paperback, £1·95.]

James, Philip S.—Introduction to English Law. 10th ed. [Paperback, £6·50.]

McColl, Miles—Court Teasers. [Limp, £3.]

Price, J. P.—The English Legal System. (M & E Handbooks.) [Paperback, £1·50.]

Raistrick, D. and Rees, J.—Lawyer's Law Books. 1st Supplement. [Paperback, £3·50.]

Redmond, P. W. D., Price, J. P. and Stevens, I. N.—General Principles of English Law. (M & E Handbooks.) 5th ed. [Paperback, £2·50.]

Shaw's Directory of Courts in England and Wales. 1979 ed. [Paperback, £4·20.]

Smith, Peter—Law and the Legal System. (Essential Business Law.) [Paperback, £1·25.]

Stroud's Judicial Dictionary. 1st Supplement to the 4th ed. by John S. James. [Cloth, £6.]

Zander, Michael (Ed.)—Pears Guide to the Law. [Cased, £7·25.]

MUSLIM LAW

Pearl, David—A Textbook on Muslim Law. [Cased, £14·95. Paperback, £6·95.]

NATIONAL HEALTH

Farndale, W. A. J.—Law on Hospital Consent Forms. (Studies in Law and Practice for Health Service Management.) [Cased, £10.]

Martin, C. R. A.—Law Relating to Medical Practice. 2nd ed. [Cased, £35.]

NEGLIGENCE

Charlesworth on Negligence. 1st Supplement to the 6th ed. by R. A. Percy. [Paperback, £1·50.]

Tye, James and Egan, Bowes—The Management Guide to Product Liability. (NCPC New Law Guidance Series No. 3.) [Paperback, £8.]

Whincup, Michael—Defective Goods. (Essential Business Law.) [Paperback, £1·25.]

PARTNERSHIP

Scamell, Ernest H. and Banks, R. C. I.—Lindley on the Law of Partnership. 14th ed. [Cased, £40.]

PATENTS AND DESIGNS

Chartered Institute of Patent Agents—Patent Law of the United Kingdom. 5th Cumulative Supplement. [Paperback, £4·25.]

Costner, Thomas E. (Ed.)—Intellectual Property Law Review 1978. Vol. 10. [Cased, £32.]

Melville, L. W.—Forms and Agreements on Intellectual Property and International Licensing. 3rd ed. [Looseleaf, £30.]

Whittman, Alfred, Schiffels, Rudolf and Hill, Michael—Patent Documentation. [Paperback, £19·50.]

PENSIONS AND SUPERANNUATION

Ellison, Robin—Private Occupational Pension Schemes. 2 Vols. [Cloth, £60.]

Pilch, Michael and Wood, Victor—Pension Schemes. [Cased, £12·50.]

POLICE

Baker and Wilkie's Police Promotion Handbook 2. Criminal Evidence and Procedure. 6th ed. by E. R. Baker and F. B. Dodge. [Paperback, £3·50.]

Bunyard, R. S.—Police: Organisation and Command. (Police Studies Series.) [Cased, £5·50.]

Campbell, Don—Police: The Exercise of Power. (Police Studies Series.) [Cased, £3·50.]

Fearnley, James—The Police. What they'll do for you. [Paperback, 25p.]

Fowler, Norman—After the Riots. [Cased, £7.]

Hain, Peter (Ed.), Humphry, Derek and Rose-Smith, Brian—Policing the Police, Volume 1. [Cloth, £6·95. Paperback, £2·95.]

Institute of Race Relations—Police against Black People. (Race and Class Pamphlet No. 6.) [Paperback, 95p.]

Trouble with the Law. The Release Bust Book. [Paperback, £1·25.]

Walsh, D. P.—Shoplifting—controlling a major crime. [Cloth, £6·95. Paperback, £2·95.]

BOOKS AND ARTICLES

PRACTICE

Bean, David—Injunctions. (Oyez Practice Notes.) [Paperback, £7·50.]
Black, Alistair—Execution of a Judgment. 6th ed. (Oyez Practice Notes.) [Paperback, £5·50.]
Hanbury, H. G. and Yardley, D. C. M.—English Courts of Law. 5th ed. by D. C. M. Yardley. [Paperback, £2·25.]
Heyward, Edmund—Guide to Chancery Practice. 5th ed. [Cloth, £6·50.]
Simmons, Frank—High Court Practice Manual. (Oyez Practice Series.) [Paperback, £9·50.]
Supreme Court Costs and Fees. (Lawyers Cost and Fees Series.) [Paperback, £1·10.]
Witchell, Roland G.—Practice and Procedure Vol. 1. County Courts and Magistrates' Courts. 7th ed. [Paperback, £5·50.]
Witchell, Roland G.—Practice and Procedure Vol. 3. High Court. 7th ed. [Paperback, £4·95.]

PRESS

McNae, L. C. J.—Essential Law for Journalists. Vol. 1. Revised by Walter Greenwood and Tom Welsh. [Paperback, £4·95.]

PRISONS

Fitzgerald, Mike and Sim, Joe—British Prisons. [Cased, £7·50. Paperback, £2·50.]

PUBLIC HEALTH

Penn, Christopher N.—Noise Control. [Paperback, £6·50.]
Walker, Andrew—Law of Industrial Pollution Control. [Cased, £10.]
Wisdom, A. S.—Freshwater Pollution. [Limp, £2·50.]

RATING AND VALUATION

Ryde on Rating. Supplement to the 13th ed. by G. R. G. Ross. [Paperback, £5·95.]

REAL PROPERTY AND CONVEYANCING

Aldridge, Trevor M.—A Guide to the National Conditions of Sale. 19th ed. [Paperback, £1·75.]
Curzon, L. B.—Land Law. 3rd ed. (M & E Handbooks.) [Paperback, £2·95.]
Farrand, J. T.—Contract and Conveyance. 3rd ed. [Paperback, £11·50.]
Maudsley, Ronald H.—The Modern Law of Perpetuities. [Cased, £20.]
Oyez Conveyancing Fees and Charges. 4th ed. [Paperback, £2·50.]
Riddall, J. G.—Introduction to Land Law. 2nd ed. [Cased, £11·50. Paperback, £7·95.]
Ruoff, Theodore B. F. and Roper, Robert B.—Ruoff and Roper on the Law and Practice of Registered Conveyancing. 4th ed. (Property and Conveyancing Library No. 5.) [Cased, £50.]
Stratton, Ian G. C.—Building Land and Estates. (Oyez Practice Notes.) [Paperback, £7·50.]
Wontner's Guide to Land Registry Practice. 13th ed. by F. Quickfall. (Oyez Practitioner Series.) [Paperback, £9·50.]

REVENUE LAW

Butterworths 1979 Budget Tax Tables. Edited by Leslie Livens and Gary Hart. [Paperback, £1·50.]
Butterworths Orange Tax Handbook 1979–80. Edited by Moiz Sadikali. 4th ed. [Limp, £9·50.]
Butterworths Yellow Tax Handbook 1979–80. Edited by David Roberts and Moiz Sadikali. 8th ed. [Limp, £11·50.]
Deloitte Haskins and Sells—Finance Bill 1979. [Paperback, £1·25.]
Deloitte Haskins and Sells—Taxation in Europe. [Paperback, £7·50.]
Lawton and Sumption's Tax and Tax Planning. 8th ed. by Philip Lawton and Anthony Sumption. [Paperback, £9·50.]
Lewis, Mervyn—British Tax Law. Supplement. (Legal Topics Series.) [Paperback, £3.]
Newman, John—United Kingdom Double Tax Treaties. [Paperback, £7·50.]
Pinson on Revenue Law. 12th ed. by Barry Pinson. [Cased, £18. Paperback, £10·50.]
Pinson, Barry—Pinson on Revenue Law. Supplement to 12th ed. [Paperback, £1.]
Pritchard, W. E.—Income Tax. 8th ed. [Paperback, £3·60.]
Rowland's Tax Guide 1978–79. 2nd ed. by Nigel Eastway and David Trill. [Paperback, £12·75.]
Sumption, Anthony—Taxation of Overseas Income and Gains. 3rd ed. [Paperback, £7·80.]
Tax Planning Review 1979 by Leslie Livens and Neil Thomas. [Paperback, £4·50.]
The Tax Practitioner's Diary 1979–80. [Paperback, £4·89.]
Tolley's Development Land Tax. 2nd ed. by Robert W. Maar. [Paperback, £6·75.]

BOOKS

REVENUE LAW—*continued*
Tolley's Income Tax 1979–80 by Eric L. Harvey. [Paperback, £7.]
Tolley's Tax Cases. 3rd ed. by Victor Grout. [Paperback, £7.]
Tolley's Tax Tables 1979–80. Budget ed. [Paperback, £1·20.]
Whillans' Tax Tables 1979–80. 32nd ed. by Leslie Livens. [Paperback, £1·75.]

ROAD TRAFFIC
Janner, Greville—The Motorists' Lawyer. [Paperback, £1·25.]
Kitchin's Road Transport Law. 20th ed. by James Duckworth. [Limp, £7·50.]
Latham, David and Halnan, Patrick—Drink/Driving Offences. (Oyez Practice Notes.) [Paperback, £6·75.]
McLean, Ian and Morrish, Peter—The Trial of Breathalyser Offences. 1st Supplement. [Paperback, £2.]
Moiser, C. H.—Endorsements and Disqualifications Under the Road Traffic Acts. [Limp, £1·50.]
Wilkinson's Road Traffic Offences. Supplement to the 9th ed. by Patrick Halnan. [Limp, £7·50.]

SALE OF GOODS
Smith, T. B.—Property Problems in Sale. [Cloth, £7.]

SCOTLAND
Scots Mercantile Law Statutes. [Paperback, £5.]

SHIPPING AND MARINE INSURANCE
Brown, R. H. and Novitt, J. J.—Marine Insurance Vol. 2: Cargo Insurance. 3rd ed. [Cased, £8.]
Payne and Ivamy's Carriage of Goods by Sea. 11th ed. by E. R. Hardy Ivamy. [Cased, £11·50. Paperback, £7·95.]
Summerskill, Michael—Oil Rigs: Law and Insurance. [Cloth, £38.]
Tiberg, Hugo—The Law of Demurrage. 3rd ed. [Cloth, £30.]

SOCIAL SECURITY
Calvert, Harry—Cases and Materials on Social Security Law. [Paperback, £12·50.]
Partington, Martin and Jowell, Jeffrey—Welfare Law and Policy. [Cased, £15.]
Social Work and the Courts. Edited by Howard Parker. [Paperback, £4·50.]

SOLICITORS
Alston, Richard and Phillips, Jim—Partnership Administration—a practical guide for professional firms. [Cased, £8·50.]
Halberstadt, Richard—Basic Book-Keeping for Solicitors. [Paperback, £2·85.]
Kelly's Draftsman. 14th ed. by R. W. Ramage. [Cased, £30.]
Lawton, Philip, Goldberg, David and Fraser, Ross—The Law of Partnership Taxation. 2nd ed. [Cased, £18.]

STAMP DUTIES
Serjeant and Sims on Stamp Duties. Supplement to the 7th ed. by B. J. Sims. [Paperback, £2·75.]

STATUTES AND ORDERS
Statute Law Society—Renton and the Need for Reform. [Paperback, £3·50.]
Thornton, G. C.—Legislative Drafting. 2nd ed. [Cased, £25.]

TORT
Allen, D. K. *et al.* (Eds.)—Accident Compensation after Pearson. [Limp, £9·75.]
Clerk and Lindsell on Torts. 3rd Cumulative Supplement to the 14th ed. [Paperback, £5·25.]
Pritchard, John—Personal Injury Litigation. 2nd ed. (Oyez Practitioner Series.) [Paperback, £8·50.]
Samuel, Geoffrey—Tort. (New Nutshells.) [Paperback, £1·25.]
Weir, Tony—A Casebook on Tort. 4th ed. [Cased, £18. Paperback, £11·25.]
Winfield and Jolowicz on Tort. 11th ed. by W. V. H. Rogers. [Cased, £17·75. Paperback, £13.]

TOWN AND COUNTRY PLANNING
Alder, John—Development Control. (Modern Legal Studies.) [Cased, £9·65. Paperback, £4·85.]
Hart, G. R. R. (Ed.)—Development Control—Thirty Years On. (J.P.E.L. Occasional Papers.) [Paperback, £4.]

BOOKS AND ARTICLES

TRADE AND INDUSTRY

Ball, Brian and Rose, Frank—Principles of Business Law. [Cased: £18. Paperback, £9·85.]

Burnett, D. *et al.*—The Organisation. (The Organisation 1.) [Cased, £5·75. Paperback, £2·85.]

Burnett, D. *et al.*—The Organisation and its Resources. (The Organisation 2.) [Cased, £8·30. Paperback, £4·25.]

Burnett, D. *et al.*—The Organisation. Its Markets, Customers and Clients. (The Organisation 3.) [Cased, £7·50. Paperback, £3·95.]

Burnett, D., Newell, M. J., Rutherford, L. A., Todd, I. A.—The Organisation, The State and The Community. (The Organisation 4.) [Cased, £7·50. Paperback, £3·85.]

Clark, T. M.—Leasing. [Cased, £12.]

Clayton, Patricia—Law for the Small Businessman. [Paperback, £7·95.]

Cranston, Ross—Regulating Business Law. (Oxford Socio-Legal Studies.) [Cased, £12.]

Dobson, Paul—Consumer Credit. (Essential Business Law.) [Paperback, £1·25.]

Goode, R. M.—The Consumer Credit Act. [Paperback, £9.]

Ivamy, E. R. Hardy and Latimer, Paul—Casebook on Commercial Law. 3rd ed. [Limp, £6·50.]

Ison, Terence G.—Credit Marketing and Consumer Protection. [Cased, £29·50.]

Mickelburgh, John—Consumer Protection. [Cased, £15. Limp, £9·50.]

Oliver, J. M.—Law and Economics. An Introduction. (Economics and Society Series.) [Cased, £7·95. Paperback, £3·50.]

Peters, M. A.—Basic Business Management, 2nd ed. [Paperback, £3.]

Redmond, P. W. D.—Mercantile Law. 5th ed. by R. G. Lawson. (M & E Handbooks.) [Paperback, £1·95.]

Rose, Francis—International Trade. (Essential Business Law.) [Paperback, £1·25.]

Samuel, G. H.—Cases in Consumer Law. (M & E Handbooks.) [Paperback, £3·75.]

Sweet and Maxwell's Commercial Law Statutes. Advisory Editor: R. M. Goode. [Cased, £14. Paperback, £10·50.]

Wainman, David and Brown, Howard—Leasing. The Accounting and Taxation Implications. [Paperback, £10.]

United States of America

Starr, R. and Donin, R.—Doing Business in the United States—an Executive's Guide. [Cloth, £15.]

TRADE UNIONS

Crouch, Colin—The Politics of Industrial Relations. (Political Issues of Modern Britain.) [Paperback, £1·50.]

Kidner, Richard—Trade Union Law. [Paperback, £10·75.]

TRUSTS AND TRUSTEES

Parker, David and Mellows, Anthony—The Modern Law of Trusts. 4th ed. [Cased, £11·25. Paperback, £8.]

Soares, Patrick—Trusts and Tax Planning. [Cased, £10.]

Underhill's Law relating to Trusts and Trustees. 13th ed. by David J. Hayton. [Cased, £37·50.]

VALUE ADDED TAX

Price, A.—VAT Made Easy. [Paperback, £2·25.]

WATER AND WATERWORKS

Wisdom, A. S.—Law of Rivers and Watercourses. 4th ed. [Cased, £12·50.]

WEIGHTS AND MEASURES

Mills, Michael—Product Labelling. A Special Report. [Cased, £18·50.]

WILLS

Hallett, V. G. H. and Warren, Nicholas—Settlements, Wills and Capital Transfer Tax. [Paperback, £11·95.]

Maurice, Spencer G.—Family Provision Practice. 4th ed. (Oyez Practice Notes.) [Paperback, £7·95.]

Probate. (Lawyers' Costs and Fees Series 3.) [Paperback, £1·10.]

Tristram and Coote's Probate Practice. Supplement to the 25th ed. by R. B. Rowe, Edmund Heyward *et al*. [Paperback, £2·50.]

INDEX OF ARTICLES

BOOKS AND ARTICLES

BILLS OF EXCHANGE

A new hazard in stopping a cheque (*J. Brooke-Taylor*): 76 L.S.Gaz. 264

Securitibank's collapse and the commercial bills market in New Zealand (*E. Ellinger*): 20 Mal.L.R. 84

The legal nature of travellers' cheques (*J. C. Stassen*): 95 S.A.L.J. 180

BOUNDARIES AND FENCES

Hedgerows—preserving the testimony? (*M. Dockray*): [1979] Conv. 53

BRITISH COMMONWEALTH

Adaptation of western law in Papua New Guinea (*B. Nasokobi*): 5 Mel.L.J. 52

Asia-Pacific regional meeting on the recognition and enforcement of judgments and orders, the service of process and the resealing of grants of administration within the Commonwealth: 5 C.L.B. 916

Boardman in the Commonwealth (*F. Bates*): 129 New L.J. 534

Consumer door-to-door hire and instalment sale: law reform in Singapore and Malaysia (*T. Feng*): [1979] 2 M.L.J. xix.

Current legal research in Singapore (*K. Koh*): 21 Mal.L.R. 69.

Kiribati achieves independence: 5 C.L.B. 911

Legal education in Singapore (*S. Tan*): 21 Mal.L.R. 58.

Legal research in Singapore: a conspectus and development proposal (*P. Pillai*): 21 Mal.L.R. 88.

Liberty and law in Singapore (*R. Hickling*): 21 Mal.L.R. 1

Private caveats: entry, extension and removal (*W. Fatt*): [1979] 1 M.L.J. lxxxv, 2 M.L.J. iii.

Problems of pollution in Malaysia (*Z. Yatim*): [1979] 2 M.L.J. xlvi

Recent enactments on the administration of Islamic law (*Prof. A. Ibrahim*): [1979] 2 M.L.J. xiii.

Recent legislation and reform proposals for customary and area courts in Nigeria (*A. Collett*): 22 J.A.L. 161

Safeguards for the judiciary—Malaysia (*Dr. M. Suffian*): [1979] 1 M.L.J. xcv

The effect of registration of title upon customary land rights in Kenya (*S. Coldham*): 22 J.A.L. 91

The need for a single all-Australian court system (*The Hon. R. Ellicott*): 52 A.L.J. 431

The question of accountability in the customary law of pledge (*C. Olawoye*): 22 J.A.L. 125

The Territories Representation case—*stare decisis* in constitutional cases (*Sir A. Bennett*): 52 A.L.J. 664

BUILDING AND ENGINEERING, ARCHITECTS AND SURVEYORS

Defective premises: negligence liability of builders (*N. P. Gravells*): [1979] Conv. 97

BUILDING AND ENGINEERING, ARCHITECTS AND SURVEYORS—*cont.*

The contractor's programme (*J. Uff*): [1979] L.G.C. 604

CAPITAL TAXATION

A gift horse's mouth (*B. McCutcheon*): [1979] B.T.R. 161

CTT: annuities under trusts (*B. McCutcheon*): 129 New L.J. 616

C.T.T.—business property relief (*K. Tingley*): 102 Tax. 94, 113, 147

Capital transfer tax and stamp duty (*P. Nellist*): 123 S.J. 135

Capital transfer tax and the extinguishment of rights (*H. Baxter*): [1978] Conv. 291

Capital transfer tax appeals (*J. Morcom*): 128 New L.J. 1161

C.T.T. business property relief (*K. Tingley*): 102 Tax. 130

Capital taxation and the small business—the case of agriculture (*J. Abecassis*): [1978] B.T.R. 343

Capital transfer tax in Scotland (*A. Sutherland and J. MacLeod*): [1978] B.T.R. 271

Development Land Tax—recent changes (*K. R. Tingley*): 103 Tax. 445

Expenditure on tourist structures (*H. Macnair*): 180 Acct. 131

Finance Act 1978 (*B. Harvey and J. Kerr*): 122 S.J. 632

Interest in possession and capital transfer tax (*A. Shipwright*): 123 S.J. 87

Relief from capital gains tax for gifts of business assets—practical aspects and anomalies (*J. Hardman*): [1978] B.T.R. 344

Settlements and capital transfer tax (*H. Macnair*): [1979] Acct. 765

The capital gains tax expenditure rules (*R. Burgess*): [1978] B.T.R. 291

The captive child: 103 Tax. 297

The executive pension plan—planning for capital transfer tax (*S. Jackson*): 76 L.S.Gaz. 124

The revised retirement relief (*K. Tingley*): 103 Tax. 109

CARRIERS

Gold values in carriage of goods conventions—an up-to-date review (*A. M. Costabel*): [1979] Lloyd's M.C.L.Q. 326

The Himalaya clause (*D. A. Powles*): [1979] Lloyd's M.C.L.Q. 331

Waybills and short form documents: a lawyer's view (*R. Williams*): [1979] Lloyd's M.C.L.Q. 297

CHARITIES

Charity law on the football field (*M. Bryan*): 129 New L.J. 86

Charity: the purport of "purpose" (*T. G. Watkin*): [1978] Conv. 277

Recreational charities—a change of tactics required? (*A. Hutchinson*): [1978] Conv. 355

ARTICLES

BOOKS AND ARTICLES

COMPANY LAW—*cont.*

Winding-up by the court: effect of the Companies (Winding Up) (Amendment) Rules 1979 on petitions brought after April 1, 1979 (*A. Samuels*): 129 New L.J. 953

Winding up: " just and equitable " again (*H. Markson*): 129 New L.J. 577

COMPULSORY PURCHASE

Challenging a compulsory purchase order (*A. Samuels*): [1979] J.P.L. 72

Compensation—lifting the corporate veil: 19 R.V.R. 147

Law and fact in the assessment of compensation (*P. Clarke*): [1979] J.P.L. 277

Rule (3) and *Dicconson Holdings* (*W. A. Leach*): 250 E.G. 437

CONFLICT OF LAWS

A new distinction in conflict of laws (*J. Fawcett*): 7 Anglo-Am. 230

Choice of law in delict: rules or approach? (*A. Edwards*): 96 S.A.L.J. 48

Foreign divorces and financial provision (*J. Miller*): 123 S.J. 4

Formation of international contracts (*D. Libling*): 42 M.L.R. 169

Maritime liens in the conflict of laws (*T. Beazley*): 20 Mal.L.R. 111

The EEC Judgments Convention—a personal view (*Kerr J.*): 75 L.S.Gaz. 1190

CONSTITUTIONAL LAW

An Englishperson's castle on low walls (*A. N. Khan*): 123 S.J. 24

Balloonists, bills of rights and dinosaurs (*I. Duncanson*): [1978] P.L. 391

Britain's Bill of Rights (*F. A. Mann*): 94 L.Q.R. 512

Can the House of Lords lawfully be abolished? (*P. Mirfield*): 95 L.Q.R. 36

Government defeats in the House of Commons: myth and reality (*P. Norton*): [1978] P.L. 360

Habeas corpus (*T. Gifford and P. O'Connor*): [1979] L.A.G.Bul. 182

Human rights: the road ahead (*M. M. Corbett*): 96 S.A.L.J. 192

Ombudsman revisited (*G. Drewry*): 129 New L.J. 604

Protest and public order (*V. T. Bevan*): [1979] P.L. 163

Restrictive sovereign immunity: the state as international trader (*G. Triggs*): 53 A.L.J. 244

Should Parliament enact a Religious Discrimination Act? (*St. John Robilliard*): [1978] P.L. 379

The consequences of a dual system of state and federal courts (*The Hon. Sir L. Street*): 52 A.L.J. 434

The courts and parliament: who whom? (*P. Allott*): 38 C.L.J. 79

CONSTITUTIONAL LAW—*cont.*

The Crown and the people (*J. Sweetman*): 122 S.J. 738

The *Gouriet* case: public interest litigation in Britain and Canada (*P. P. Mercer*): [1979] P.L. 214

The reform of British nationality law (*T. Bates*): 1979 S.L.T. 33

CONTRACT

Assignments without the consent of the debtor (*D. Kloss*): [1979] Conv. 133

Commercial contracts: damages for distress (*H. Markson*): 129 New L.J. 359

Consideration and the joint promisee (*B. Coote*): 37 C.L.J. 301

Contract remedies and the consumer surplus (*D. Harris, A. Ogus and J. Phillips*): 95 L.Q.R. 581

Damages in lieu of rescission (*F. G. Glover*): 129 New L.J. 841

Frustrated holidaymakers and frustrated contracts (*A. Tettenborn*): 129 New L.J. 62

Legislative and administrative controls over standard forms of contract in England (*G. Borrie*): [1978] J.B.L. 317

Liability for defective products (*C. J. Miller*): 122 S.J. 631

Long live the fundamental breach (*A. Khan*): 123 S.J. 106

Misstatement and the Unfair Contract Terms Act 1977 (*J. Murdoch*): 129 New L.J. 4

Occupiers, trespassers and the Unfair Contract Terms Act 1977 (*J. Mesher*): [1979] Conv. 59

Offer and acceptance in the supermarket (*B. Jackson*): 129 New L.J. 775

Plant hire: liability (*M. Lazarides*): 122 S.J. 767, 787

Professional negligence (*A. Churchward*): 75 L.S.Gaz. 1145

Recent development in the law of contract (*W. McBryde*): 1979 S.L.T. 25

Remoteness of damage—contract and tort reconciled? (*C. Manchester*): 128 New L.J. 1113

Remoteness of damage and judicial discretion (*Sir R. Cooke*): 37 C.L.J. 288

Reservation of title—the lessons of *Bond Worth* (*M. Burke*): 129 New L.J. 651

Romalpa clauses: recent cases (*H. Pearson*): 123 S.J. 207

The effect of illegality in South African Law (*L. E. Teakman*): 94 S.A.L.J. 327

The great gamble (*G. Benson*): 122 S.J. 853

The new German law on standard contract terms (*W. F. von Marschall*): [1979] Lloyd's M.C.L.Q. 279

The Unfair Contract Terms Act 1977 (*A. Forte*): 1979 S.L.T. 41

The Unidroit initiation for the progressive codification of international trade law (*M. J. Bonell*): 27 I.C.L.Q. 413

Viewpoint: small print (*C. Rivers*): 123 S.J. 399

ARTICLES

BOOKS AND ARTICLES

CRIMINAL LAW—*cont.*

Delinquency causation: a typological comparison of path models (*M. G. Aultman*): [1979] J.C.L. & Crim. 153

Determining criminal liability for robbery —no putting of new wine into old bottles (*J. Bentil*): 142 J.P.N. 251

Developments in criminal law and penal systems, 1979: Holland (*Dr. D. W. Sreenhuis*): [1979] Crim.L.R. 645

Developments in criminal law and penal systems: Norway 1977–78 (*Prof. J. Andenaes*): [1979] Crim.L.R. 447

Developments in criminal law and penal systems 1978: West Germany (*Prof. Dr. G. Kaiser*): [1979] Crim.L.R. 719

Developments in the law of blackmail in England and Australia (*L. G. Tooher*): 27 I.C.L.Q. 337

Doubtful convictions by jury (*J. Baldwin and M. McConville*): [1979] Crim.L.R. 230

Duress and international killing (*J. M. Burchell*): 94 S.A.L.J. 282

Entrapment buried: 143 J.P.N. 229

Exculpatory statements by accused persons (*D. Elliot and J. Wakefield*): [1979] Crim.L.R. 428

Film censorship—the effects of the Criminal Law Act 1977 (*C. P. Walker*): 75 L.S.Gaz. 992

Firearms law (*W. West*): 122 S.J. 753

Forcible eviction and the Criminal Law Act 1977 (*J. Ottaway*): 129 New L.J. 792

Forms of complicity in crime (*J. Beaumont*): 142 J.P.N. 658

From sentences to paragraphs: 1979 S.L.T. 1

Going equipped for cheating—need for determining the limits of the offence (*J. Bentil*): 143 J.P.N. 47

Identification parades—the new Home Office circular 109/1978 (*J. Dundon*): [1978] L.A.G.Bul. 256

Incest: legislation paternalism below expectation (*J. K. Bentil*): 122 S.J. 687

Inciting the impossible (*M. Cohen*): [1979] Crim.L.R. 239

Incomplete attempts of crimes (*G. Maddison and A. Khan*): 123 S.J. 465, 482

Inferior courts—the developing law of contempt: 143 J.P.N. 529

Informers (*D. K. Bryant*): 143 J.P.N. 378

Interim care orders in care proceedings (*C. Derbyshire*): 143 J.P.N. 215

Intermediate treatment: 143 J.P.N. 431

Interrogation and the test of fairness: 1979 S.L.T. 189

Intoxication and crime: a comparative approach (*F. Daly*): 27 I.C.L.Q. 378

Juvenile offenders in the Magistrates' Court (*R. R. Hopkins*): 142 J.P.N. 620

Liability for defective products (*C. J. Miller*): 122 S.J. 631

Manslaughter and omissions to act (*L. E. Squire and R. Rainter*): 128 New L.J. 994

CRIMINAL LAW—*cont.*

Marital coercion—anachronism or modernism? (*P. Pace*): [1979] Crim.L.R. 82

Matters that need not be proved (*B. Parsons*): 3 Court 3

Maximum penalties under the Criminal Law Act 1977 (*J. Spencer*): 143 J.P.N. 314

Mental illness and crimes of dishonesty— a review (*R. Davis*): 142 J.P.N. 735

Mentally disordered offenders in an interim regional medium secure unit (*M. Faulk*): [1979] Crim.L.R. 686

Migration of companies: tax and the criminal law (*R. Burrow and A. Shipwright*): 123 S.J. 173

Misleading advertising and the publishers' defence—a critique of *Universal Telecasters (Qld)* v. *Guthrie* (*A. Duggan*): 6 A.B.L.R. 309

Misleading prices (*G. Stephenson*): 143 J.P.N. 113

Murder under duress (*Sir R. Cross*): xxviii U.T.L.J. 369

Natural justice in the criminal context (*J. Fisher*): 143 J.P.N. 189

New developments in the law of provocation (*P. English*): 123 S.J. 119, 139

Official secrets and jury vetting (*A. Nicol*): [1979] Crim.L.R. 284

Pandora's box: the general verdict and the principles of proof (*M. McConville*): 143 J.P.N. 285

Passing sentence on facts (*P. J. Davies*): 129 New L.J. 824

Pleading guilty under mistake of law: 122 S.J. 820

Pleas in mitigation (*J. Morton*): 129 New L.J. 348

Police interrogation and the right to see a solicitor (*J. Baldwin and M. McConville*): [1979] Crim.L.R. 145

Police powers of arrest without warrant— not a *carte blanche* (*J. Bentil*): 143 J.P.N. 246

Possession and section 28 of the Misuse of Drugs Act 1971 (*R. Ribeiro and J. Perry*): [1979] Crim.L.R. 90

" Possession " as a concept applicable in relation to drug offences (*J. K. Bentil*): 143 J.P.N. 155, 173

Pressure groups beware (*W. Hofler*): 123 S.J. 223

Prosecution barred by acquittal: 142 J.P.N. 249

Prosecutions: procedural errors or errors of substance (*B. Strachan*): 122 S.J. 783

Prostitution and the law (*R. Jerrard*): 143 J.P.N. 531

Provocation (*F. G. Glover*): 142 J.P.N. 580

Psychology and the law (*Prof. H. Eysenck*): 123 S.J. 3

Public order (*A. Samuels*): 123 S.J. 239

R. v. *Lemon* (*C. Manchester*): 143 J.P.N. 300

Rape by a husband (*M. Freeman*): 129 New L.J. 332

ARTICLES

BOOKS AND ARTICLES

ARTICLES

BOOKS AND ARTICLES

ARTICLES

BOOKS AND ARTICLES

ARTICLES

BOOKS AND ARTICLES

ARTICLES

BOOKS AND ARTICLES

ARTICLES

BOOKS AND ARTICLES

ARTICLES

BOOKS AND ARTICLES

ARTICLES

BOOKS AND ARTICLES

TRESPASS
Occupiers, trespassers and the Unfair Contract Terms Act 1977 (*J. Mesher*): [1979] Conv. 58

TROVER AND DETINUE
The law of treasure and treasure hunters (*M. Nash*): 128 New L.J. 1163

VALUE ADDED TAX
The European value added tax system (*M. Loftus*): 7 A.T.R. 223
VAT in perspective (*P. Landon*): 180 Acct. 369
When sauce for the goose is not sauce for the gander (*H. Mainprice*): 180 Acct. 702

VENDOR AND PURCHASER
Contract subject to specific performance (*F. Graham Glover*): 128 New L.J. 692
Options open in enforcing contracts for sale of land (*A. Tettenborn*): 123 S.J. 427
The sale of council houses (*I. R. Storey*): 129 New L.J. 663
Time of the essence—waiver (*H. Wilkinson*): 129 New L.J. 185

WATER AND WATERWORKS
The implications of the constitution and functions of regional water authorities (*H. Purdue*): [1979] P.L. 119

WILLS
A reappraisal of the rule in favour of *per stirpes* division (*G. Robertson*): 1979 S.L.T. 133
Barred and bypassed beneficiaries (*H. Markson*): 123 S.J. 792
Gift by will to friends (*F. Glover*): 129 New L.J. 742
Inheritance (Provision for Family and Dependants) Act 1975—subjective or objective test? (*J. L. Davies*): 75 L.S. Gaz. 1005
Probate problem (*H. E. Markson*): 128 New L.J. 1077
Revocation of wills by marriage (*P. K. Virdi*): 9 Fam. Law 99
Revocation of wills on divorce (*G. Bates*): 129 New L.J. 556
Revocation of wills on marriage (*G. Bates*): 129 New L.J. 547
Section 3 of the Inheritance Act 1833 and *Shelley's Case*, a forgotten piece of learning (*J. D. A. Brooke-Taylor*): [1979] Conv. 164
Succession 1978: 1979 S.L.T. 176
The notarially executed will (*A. Duncan*): 1979 S.L.T. 173
Varying a will after death (*A. Tunkel*): 123 S.J. 153

INDEX 1972–79

Criminal Law—*cont.*
sentence—*cont.*
insurance fraud, 78/618
international drug smuggling, 77/651
judge indicating likely sentence, 75/717
judge's powers, 78/619
kidnapping, 74/739; 76/567
liaison officer's report, 73/619
life, 73/620; 74/740
magisterial law. *See* MAGISTERIAL LAW.
manslaughter, 79/570
maximum, 75/718
review of, 78/1826
mental treatment, 75/719
mistake as to defendant's age, 73/621
mitigation, 74/570
motorist impersonating another, 76/587
murder, 78/620
offence committed for financial gain, 74/742
perjury, 75/720
persistent shoplifter, 73/622
plea bargaining, 76/539, 541, 589; 77/652; 78/621–5
possession of controlled drug, 77/653
Post Office employee, 73/623
power to postpone, 76/575
powers of Court of Appeal, 78/1932
printing and distributing obscene literature, 78/627
probation, 74/743–745; 79/571
procedure, 78/628
rape, 73/624
recommendation for deportation, 73/625; 78/629
remission to High Court (Scotland), 75/724
repeated previous offences, 75/725
resumed hearing, 73/626
retributive and deterrent elements, 78/630
robbery and burglary, 73/627
shoplifting, 74/746; 77/654
smuggling animals, 77/655
social inquiry report, 76/590
social nuisances, 76/591
soliciting, 77/661
suspended sentence, 72/732–5; 73/628, 629; 77/656; 79/572, 573
tax evasion, 76/592
tax fraud, 77/657
threats of damage to property of potential witness, 73/630
trial by jury, 75/727
unlawful sexual intercourse, 77/658
uttering forged banknote, 73/631
variation, 78/632
variation because of muddle in court, 76/593
whether jurisdiction to bring suspended sentence into effect, 73/632
whether sentence passed when probation order made, 75/728
young offender, 72/736; 73/633–634; 76/588, 594–6; 78/633
sexual offences, 72/737, 738; 73/524, 635, 637; 74/736, 740, 751–4; 75/691, 1934; 76/591, 597, 1586; 77/659; 79/574–6

Criminal Law—*cont.*
Sexual Offences Act, 1956 (c. 69)...56/2137
Sexual Offences (Amendment) Act 1976 (c. 82)...76/600; 78/634
Sexual Offences (Scotland) Act 1976 (c. 67)...76/601
shops, 77/2825
smuggling. *See* CUSTOMS AND EXCISE.
soliciting, 76/602; 78/635
statistics, 72/739; 73/638
stolen goods, 72/740–3; 73/639–46
suicide, 77/662; 78/636
Suicide Act, 1961 (c. 60)...61/2127
summary jurisdiction. *See* MAGISTERIAL LAW.
suppression of terrorism, 78/1456
taking a conveyance, 73/647–50; 74/757; 76/63–5; 78/638; 79/577, 578
taking vehicle without authority, 77/663
taxis, 77/2613
theft, 72/744–55; 74/161, 534, 758–760; 75/731–5, 3006; 76/167, 411, 607–10; 77/199, 665, 667–74; 78/638a–42; 79/579–97
Theft Act 1978 (c. 31)...78/642
trade descriptions, 79/598
transfer of proceedings, 72/756
treatment of accused, 73/657
trial, 72/757–68; 73/659–62, 1855; 74/688, 765–9; 75/595, 623, 687, 737, 740–2; 76/611–9, 2207; 77/591, 675–85; 78/643–55; 79/599–606
undischarged bankrupt, 77/1365
unlawful assembly, 72/769
unlawful eviction and harassment, 73/1932
unlawful sexual intercourse, 78/656
unlicensed collection, 74/302; 76/239
unreasonable force, 76/1917
vagrancy, 73/664; 74/3901
vandalism, 78/657
vehicle used in crime, 77/687
verdict, 72/771, 772; 73/665; 74/774; 78/658, 659
vicarious liability, 78/660; 79/608
warrant for committal, 72/773
witnesses, 72/1498; 73/668, 1420, 2076; 74/587, 699, 777, 778; 75/647; 78/661–3
wounding, 75/745
youthful offender, 72/775; 74/779, 780; 76/588; 78/633; 79/609
Criminal Law Act, 1967 (c. 58)...67/728
Criminal Law Act 1977 (c. 45)...77/498, 499; 78/450
Criminal Law Amendment Act, 1951 (c. 36)...2047
Criminal Procedure (Attendance of Witnesses) Act, 1965 (c. 69)...65/884
Criminal Procedure (Insanity) Act, 1964 (c. 84)...64/692
Criminal Procedure (Right of Reply) Act, 1964 (c. 34)...64/693
Criminal Procedure (Scotland) Act (c. 21)...75/540
Crofting Reform (Scotland) Act 1976 (c. 21)...76/50, 3475

Factories—*cont.*
 hoists, 72/1526
 industrial diseases, 73/1455. *See also* WORKMEN'S COMPENSATION.
 inflammable liquids, 72/1527; 74/1618
 lighting, 78/1461
 machinery, 77/1399
 master and servant. *See* EMPLOYMENT.
 medical examination, 73/1041
 Northern Ireland. *See* NORTHERN IRELAND.
 pottery works, 73/1459
 power presses, 72/1528
 Royal ordnance factories, 74/3214
 safe system of work, 73/1460, 2321; 75/1431
 safety, 72/1531; 77/1402; 1403
 shops. *See* SHOPS.
 thermal insulation, 72/1532
 women and young persons, 76/1236
 woodworking machinery, 74/1623
Factories Act, 1948 (c. 55)...3932
Factories Act, 1959 (c. 67)...59/1282, 1283; 60/1266
Factories Act, 1961 (c. 34)...61/3491
Faculty, 73/959–61; 75/1026–8; 76/821–3; 78/848, 849; 79/798
Faculty Jurisdiction Measure, 1964 (No. 5)... 64/1221
Fair comment, 76/1602; 77/1783
Fair Employment (Northern Ireland) Act 1976 (c. 25)...76/1933
Fair rent, 77/2517–20; 78/2507
Fair trading. *See* SALE OF GOODS.
Fair Trading Act, 1973 (c. 41)...73/3276
Falkland Islands, 72/249–51; 75/203, 3218a; 76/174; 77/205
False imprisonment. *See* MALICIOUS PROSE-CUTION AND FALSE IMPRISONMENT.
False trade description, 72/3125–33; 74/3440–52; 75/3062, 3064, 3067; 76/467–8, 2470–2
Families from abroad, 72/1537
Family Allowances, 72/1533–40; 73/1463–8; 74/1624–8; 75/1433–43; 76/1241–7; 77/1405–8; 78/1464–6; 79/1305–9
 Child Benefit Act 1975 (c. 61)...75/1433, 1434; 76/1242
 child benefits, 75/1435; 76/1241; 77/1405; 78/1464; 79/1305–7
 children, 72/1533; 74/3649; 75/3261; 76/1243
 claims and payments, 72/1534; 73/1463; 75/1437, 1440; 76/1244
 decisions of Commissioner, 73/1464–6
 determination of claims and questions, 72/1535, 1536
 entitlement, 77/1352
 families from abroad, 72/1537
 Family Allowances and National Insur-ance Acts, 56/3512, 3513; 61/3543, 3544; 62/1276–7, 1975–7; 64/1552, 1552a; 65/1663; 67/1658; 68/1610, 1611
 family income supplements, 74/1625; 75/1439; 76/1245; 77/1407; 78/1465; 79/1308
 Family Income Supplements Act 1970 (c. 55)...70/1765
 Finance Act...71/4867

Family Allowances—*cont.*
 Gibraltar, 74/2497
 guides, 72/1538
 illegitimate child, 74/1627; 76/1246
 increase, 75/1440
 international arrangements, 72/2282
 Jersey, 73/1467
 national assistance. *See* NATIONAL ASSIS-TANCE.
 Northern Ireland. *See* NORTHERN IRELAND.
 polygamous marriages, 72/2296; 75/1442
 social security. *See* SOCIAL SECURITY.
 Spain, 75/1443
Family Allowances Act, 1965 (c. 53)...65/1663
Family Allowances and National Insurance Act, 1952 (c. 29)...52/2297, 2298
Family Allowances and National Insurance Act, 1956 (c. 50)...56/5726, 5727
Family Allowances and National Insurance Act, 1959 (c. 18)...59/2138, 2139
Family Allowances and National Insurance Act, 1961 (10 & 11 Eliz. 2, c. 6)...61/5703; 62/1276–7, 1975–7
Family Allowances and National Insurance Act, 1964 (c. 10)...64/1552, 1552a
Family Allowances and National Insurance Act, 1967 (c. 90)...67/1658
Family Allowances and National Insurance Act, 1968 (c. 40)...68/1610, 1611
Family arrangements. *See* COMPROMISES AND FAMILY ARRANGEMENTS.
Family Division, 77/880, 2331, 2333; 78/1602, 2368
Family income supplements, 77/1407; 78/1465; 79/1308
Family Income Supplements Act, 1970 (c. 55)...70/1765
Family Law Reform Act, 1969 (c. 46)... 69/1773, 1774; 71/5886
Family Practitioner Committees, 79/1836
Family provision. *See* WILLS.
Family Provision Act, 1966 (c. 35)...66/12603, 12604
Farm and Garden Chemicals Act, 1967 (c. 50)...67/60
Farm vehicles, 72/3058
Farms. *See* AGRICULTURE.
Farnham Castle Measure, 1961 (No. 1)... 61/2998
Farriers (Registration) Act 1975 (c. 35)... 75/54; 78/83
Farriers (Registration) (Amendment) Act 1977 (c. 31)...77/71
Fatal accidents, 72/819; 74/830–6, 2575, 3581; 75/149, 772, 780, 782, 784, 785; 76/671–2, 2133; 77/732–4; 78/708, 709; 79/651
Fatal Accidents Act, 1959 (c. 65)...59/874
Fatal Accidents Act 1976 (c. 30)...76/674
Fatal Accidents and Sudden Deaths Inquiry (Scotland) Act 1976 (c. 14)...76/472, 3002, 3440
Fatstock, 73/62
Federation of Malaya Independence Act, 1957 (c. 60)...57/307

INDEX 1972–79

Purchase Tax—*cont.*
termination, 72/2873; 73/2757
VAT. *See* VALUE ADDED TAX.
yoghurt, 72/2874
Purchase Tax Act, 1963 (c. 9)...63/2932

Quatar, 72/1881
Quarries, 74/3098, 3113
Queen's Bench Division, 72/2789, 2790; 76/2188; 77/2389, 2390
Queen's speech, 72/2250; 73/2469; 75/2476

Rabies Act, 1974 (c. 17)...74/100
Race relations, 72/28; 73/18–20; 75/11, 24, 25; 76/28, 923; 77/25–28; 78/26, 29, 983, 2408
Race Relations Act, 1965 (c. 73)...65/888
Race Relations Act, 1968 (c. 71)...68/17
Race Relations Act, 1976 (c. 74)...76/29; 77/29
Racial discrimination, 73/18–20; 78/983, 2408; 79/913–7
Radioactive substances, 74/122, 1184; 75/134; 76/114
Radioactive Substances Act, 1948 (c. 37)...546
Radioactive Substances Act, 1960 (c. 34)...60/154
Radiological Protection Act, 1970 (c. 46)...70/107, 108
Rag Flock and Other Filling Materials Act, 1951 (c. 63)...8162
Railway and Canal Commission, 1513, 7839, 8249–51
Railway and Canal Commission (Abolition) Act, 1949 (c. 11)...8250, 8251
Railways, 72/2875–84; 73/2758–62; 74/3086–94; 75/2755a–61; 76/2252–4; 77/2440–5; 78/2458, 2459; 79/2221–3
administrative committee, 72/2875
British Railways, 73/2534; 75/2529a, 2548, 2756
British Railways Acts, 63/2934; 64/3077; 65/3317; 66/10176, 68/3292; 71/9794
British Railways Board, 74/2811; 75/2529a, 2548, 2756; 77/2440; 79/2221
carriage by rail, 73/2759; 74/3092; 75/2758
carriage conditions, 72/2877–9
fares, 77/2441; 78/2458
international arrangements, 72/2880, 2881; 73/2762
light railways, 72/2882; 73/2761; 74/3089; 75/2760; 76/2252; 77/2442; 78/2459; 79/2222
negligence, 72/2398; 74/2577, 3091; 75/2319; 76/1854; 79/1888
Northern Ireland. *See* NORTHERN IRELAND.
Offices, Shops and Railway Premises Act, 1963 (c. 41)...63/2939; 66/10194; 71/9814
passengers, 73/2762; 74/3092
pensions, 76/2254; 77/2443. *See also* PENSIONS AND SUPERANNUATIONS.
premises, 77/2444

Railways—*cont.*
Railways Act, 1974 (c. 48)...74/3093, 3094
rating, 72/1882–4
transport nationalisation and denationalisation. *See* TRANSPORT.
VAT, 77/3133
Railways Act, 1974 (c. 48)...74/3093
Rape, 73/604; 74/702, 703; 75/679–83, 685, 1934; 76/558–9; 77/635–7; 78/589
Rate Rebate Act, 1973 (c. 28)...73/2772
Ratification
Rating Act, 1966 (c. 9)...66/10291
Rating Act, 1971 (c. 39)...71/9873
Rating and Valuation, 72/2885–904; 73/2763–88; 74/3095–3120; 75/2762–88; 76/2255–87; 77/2446–73; 78/2460–77; 79/2224–47
agricultural land, 72/2885; 78/2460
angling rights, 76/2281
appeal, 78/2460a
assessment, 77/2446
assessment committee, 72/2886
charities, 74/3095, 3096; 75/2762, 2763; 78/2461; 79/244
club, 73/2763
commercial premises, 77/2447
completion notice, 77/2448, 2449
convent, 72/2887
derating, 78/2470
distress, 72/2888; 74/3097; 76/2255; 79/2225–7
distress for rates, 73/2764
docks and harbours, 73/2765; 75/2764; 76/2256; 78/2462
electricity boards, 72/2889; 76/2257
exchequer grants
exemption, 76/166; 77/2450
gas boards, 72/2890; 73/2769; 76/2259; 79/2228
General Rate Acts, 67/3347; 70/2405; 75/2765; 77/2451
hereditament, 78/2463
Lands Tribunal, 72/2891; 73/2766; 74/3098; 75/2766; 76/2260; 79/2229
lands tribunal decisions, 77/2452; 78/2464
liability for rates, 77/2453; 78/2465, 2465a; 79/2230
Local Government Acts, 8281, 8282; 56/7259, 7260
local government reorganisation, 73/2767–68; 74/2201
local valuation panels, 75/2767
mines and quarries, 72/2892
minor structural alterations, 74/3100
National Coal Board, 77/2454
natural gas terminals, 72/2893; 73/2769; 76/2261; 79/2231
negligent valuation, 77/2455
Northern Ireland. *See* NORTHERN IRELAND.
owners, 73/2771
payment by instalments, 74/3102
part of hereditament, 76/2263
person aggrieved, 77/2457
plant and machinery, 74/3103; 75/2769; 77/2458
post office, 72/2895; 76/2264
precepts, 72/2896; 74/3104; 75/2770

[142]